THE TIMES

REFERENCE
ATLAS
OF THE WORLD

TIMES BOOKS

LONDON

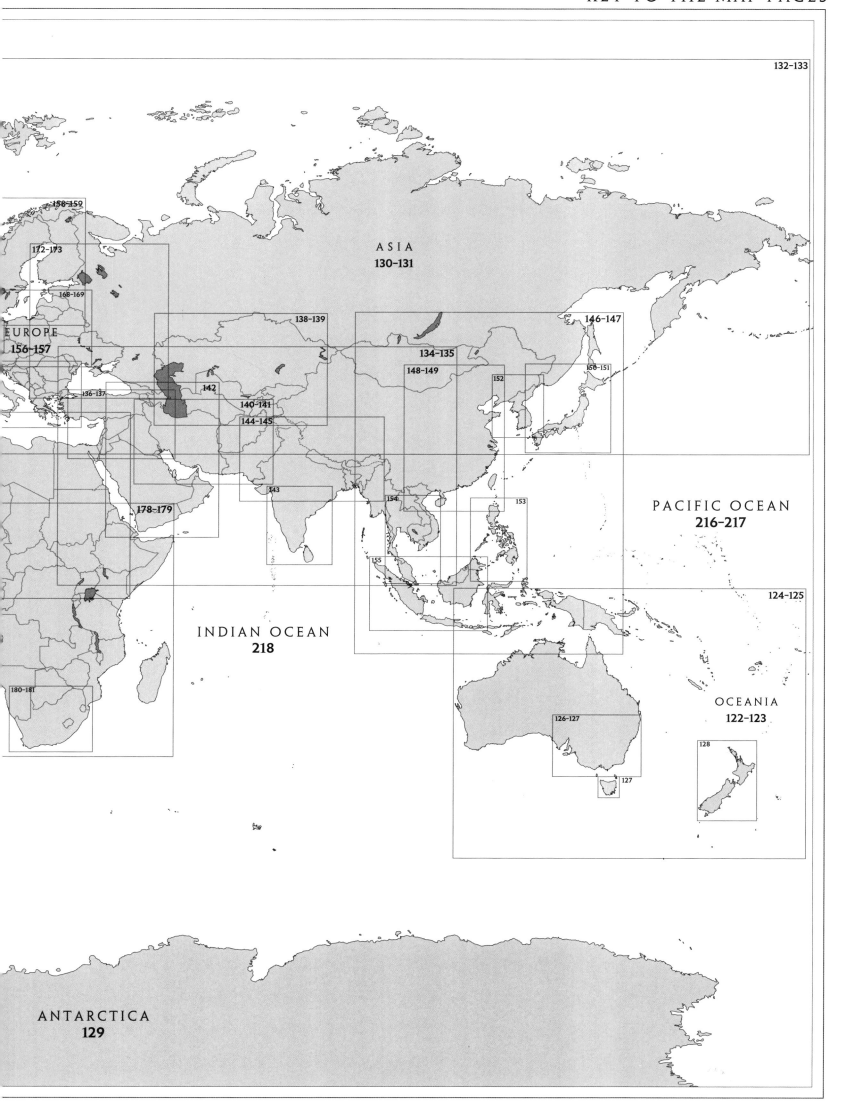

132-133

158-159

172-173

ASIA
130-131

168-169

146-147

EUROPE
156-157

138-139

134-135

148-149

150-151

152

136-137

142

140-141

144-145

PACIFIC OCEAN
216-217

178-179

143

154

153

155

124-125

INDIAN OCEAN
218

180-181

OCEANIA
122-123

126-127

128

127

ANTARCTICA
129

Published by Times Books
An imprint of HarperCollins Publishers
Westerhill Road, Bishopbriggs, Glasgow G64 2QT

First published 1995
Published as The Times Atlas of the World New Generation Edition 1997
Second Edition 2002
Third Edition 2005
Fourth Edition 2008
Fifth Edition 2010
Sixth Edition 2013

Seventh Edition 2015
Reprinted 2016

A catalogue record for this book is available from the British Library.

ISBN 978-0-00-814400-5
ISBN 978-0-00-794996-0

10 9 8 7 6 5 4 3 2

Printed and bound in Hong Kong

All mapping in this atlas is generated from Collins Bartholomew digital databases.
Collins Bartholomew, the UK's leading independent geographical information supplier,
can provide a digital, custom, and premium mapping service to a variety of markets.
For further information:
Tel: +44 (0) 208 307 4515
e-mail: collinsbartholomew@harpercollins.co.uk
or visit our website at: www.collinsbartholomew.com

If you would like to comment on any aspect of this atlas,
please contact us at the above address or online.

www.timesatlas.com
e-mail: timesatlas@harpercollins.co.uk

 @timesatlas
 Facebook.com/thetimesatlas

CONTENTS

6–7 OCEANIA

The continent of Oceania comprises Australia, New Guinea, New Zealand and the islands of the Pacific Ocean. The main Pacific island groups of Melanesia, Micronesia and Polynesia sit amongst the complex of ridges and troughs which make up the Pacific seafloor. Notable among these, and visible extending northwards from New Zealand, are the Kermadec and Tonga trenches – the latter reaching a depth of 10 800 m (35 424 ft) at Horizon Deep. Australia itself appears largely dry and barren, its vast interior consisting of several deserts, with brighter salt lakes in the low artesian basin of the east central area. The east coast of Australia, separated from the interior by the Great Dividing Range – the source of the continent's longest rivers the Murray and the Darling – is more densely vegetated. New Guinea is covered by dense tropical forest, while New Zealand displays a great variety of land cover types, most prominent being the snow-capped Southern Alps on South Island.

8–9 ASIA

This vast continent – the world's largest – covers an enormous area and contains a great variety of landscapes, evident on this image. It stretches from the Mediterranean Sea in the west to the far east of Russia and Japan, and from arctic Siberia in the north to the tropical islands of Indonesia. The Caspian Sea – the world's largest lake – is prominent in the west. The snow-capped Caucasus mountains stretching

from the Caspian Sea to the Black Sea clearly mark the divide between Asia and Europe. Just east of the Caspian Sea lies the complex shape of the Aral Sea. This was once the world's fourth largest lake, but is now drastically reduced in size because of climate change and the extraction of water for irrigation. In the centre of the image, the long arc of the mountain ranges of the Himalaya, Karakoram, Hindu Kush and Tien Shan circle the featureless Tarim Pendi basin and the lake-riddled Plateau of Tibet.

10–11 EUROPE

The generally densely vegetated continent of Europe contains some dramatic geographical features. Its northern and western limits are marked by the complex coastlines of Iceland, Scandinavia and north-western Russian Federation, while the British Isles sit on the flat, wide continental shelf. Europe's mountain ranges divide the continent – in the southwest, the Pyrenees separate France from the drier Iberian Peninsula, the wide arc of the Alps separates Italy from the rest of western Europe, the Carpathian Mountains, appearing as a dark curve between the Alps and the Black Sea, mark the edge of the vast European plains, and the Caucasus, stretching between the Black Sea and the Caspian Sea, create a prominent barrier between Europe and Asia. Two of Europe's greatest rivers are also clearly visible on this image – the Volga, Europe's longest river, flowing south from the Ural Mountains into the Caspian Sea and the Dnieper flowing across the plains into the northern Black Sea.

12–13 AFRICA

This image of Africa clearly shows the change in vegetation through the equatorial regions from the vast, dry Sahara desert covering much of the north of the continent, through the rich forests of the Congo basin – the second largest drainage basin in the world – to the high plateau of southern Africa. Lake Victoria dominates central east Africa and the Nile and its delta create a distinctive feature in the desert in the northeast. The path of the Great Rift Valley can be traced by the pattern of linear lakes in east Africa, to Ethiopia, and along the Red Sea. The dark fan-shaped feature in central southern Africa is the Okavango Delta in Botswana – one of the world's most ecologically sensitive areas. To the east of the continent lies Madagascar, and in the Indian Ocean northeast of this is the Mascarene Ridge sea feature stretching from the Seychelles in the north to Mauritius and Réunion in the south.

14–15 NORTH AMERICA

Many well-known geographical features are identifiable on this image of North America, which also illustrates the contrasts in landscapes across the continent. Greenland, the world's largest island, sits off the northeast coast while the dramatic chain of the Aleutian Islands in the northwest stretches from Alaska across the Bering Sea to the Kamchatka Peninsula in the Russian Federation. Further south in the Pacific Ocean, at the far left of the image, lie the Hawai'ian Islands and their very distinctive ocean ridge. There is a strong west-east contrast across the continent. The west is

dominated by the Rocky Mountains, which give way to the Great Plains. In the east, the Great Lakes, largest of which, Lake Superior, is second in size only to the Caspian Sea, the valley of the Mississippi and the Coastal Plain are prominent.

16–17 SOUTH AMERICA

The Andes mountains stretch along the whole length of the west coast of South America, widening into the high plains of the Altiplano in Bolivia and Peru in the centre of the continent. Lake Titicaca, the world's highest large navigable lake, lies on the Altiplano, straddling the Bolivia–Peru border. Running parallel to the Andes, just off the west coast, is the Peru–Chile Trench which marks the active boundary between the Nazca and South American tectonic plates. Movement between these plates gives rise to numerous volcanoes in the Andes. The Amazon river runs across almost the whole width of the continent in the north, meeting the Atlantic Ocean in its wide delta on the northeast coast. The vast Amazon basin is one of the most ecologically diverse areas of the Earth. In the south, the wide continental shelf stretches eastward from the tip of the continent to the Falkland Islands and South Georgia on the bottom edge of the image.

18–19 ANTARCTICA

Protected by the Antarctic Treaty, implemented in 1959, from commercial exploitation and from the realization of territorial claims, Antarctica is perhaps the world's greatest unspoilt, and relatively unexplored, wilderness. This image combines bathymetric data (incomplete in some black areas) with a mosaic of over a thousand Landsat ETM+ scenes to show the extent of the continental ice sheet in an austral summer. Floating sea ice is not shown. The Antarctic Peninsula – home to numerous scientific research stations – in the top left of the image reaching towards South America, the huge Ronne and Ross ice shelves, and the Transantarctic Mountains – dividing the continent into West and East Antarctica – are the dominant physical features.

20–21 TROPICAL CYCLONES, AUSTRALIA

This image mosaic from 11 March 2015 shows three tropical cyclones across Australia. In the west is category 3 cyclone Olwyn, which caused power losses in Western Australia on 13 March. Centrally is cyclone Nathan, which was executing a cyclonic loop, and then in the east is Pam. Cyclone Pam crossed Vanuatu on 13 March 2015 as a category 5 storm. Winds speeds of 270 km per hour (165 mph) were reached as it approached Vanuatu and it hit the eastern side of the island of Éfaté hardest. The capital city Port Vila on the same island was also hit hard. The island nation was crippled with an early estimate suggesting that around 90 per cent of buildings in the country were affected in some way. Other south Pacific nations were also affected by cyclone Pam including Tuvalu and the Solomon Islands.

22–23 BADAIN JARAN DESERT, CHINA

This desert in Inner Mongolia is a section of the Gobi Desert and is unusual as a part of the desert area is made up of mega dunes that are between 200 m and 400 m in height. The tallest measured so far is around 460 m (1500 feet) high making it about as high as the Willis (Sears) Tower in Chicago, once the world's tallest building. The high dunes seem to be the result of a complex process and scientists have suggested that the dune height is not just due to the wind characteristics and sand type, but is also affected by the shape of the bedrock under the sand. These dunes also produce the rare phenomenon known as "singing dunes" or "whistling sands" which start off sand avalanches. The lakes in this desert are intriguing as there are over 100 of them and the water source is not obvious. Scientific research suggests it may be a combination of factors including groundwater, precipitation and snowmelt from local mountains and also paleowater.

24–25 LIGHTS AT NIGHT, EUROPE

The bright lights of Europe shine at night and illuminate the coastline very clearly in this composite image. Light was detected in a range of wavelengths and filters were then used to create a usable image that is not too bright. This image is part of a global composite that was created from data acquired by the Suomi National Polar-orbiting Partnership in 2012 and made available in October 2014. Certain cities are very clear such as Moscow, Paris, Madrid and Athens. Others make up part of a much larger bright area as can be seen in Belgium and the Netherlands and also in northern Italy. Transport barriers such as the Alps and the Pyrennees stand out as dark patches with slivers of light in the valleys. Many of the main transport routes are easily identified with the route between Moscow and St Petersburg showing up particularly well. However there are also areas of light in unexpected places. The North Sea oil platforms show clearly and some of the lights in the sea may be groups of fishing trawlers.

26–27 ARQUIPÉLAGO DOS BIJAGÓS, GUINEA-BISSAU

The coast of Guinea-Bissau is an area with many mangrove swamps. These are important feeding grounds for marine creatures such as oysters and birds like heron and flamingo, and the mammal the African manatee. However, the mangrove swamps are threatened as trees are cut down for timber or to clear land for agriculture. The main river in this image is the Geba, which has a wide estuary. The ancient delta of the Geba formed the Arquipélago dos Bijagós or Bissagos Islands some of which can also be seen. The Orango Islands, which are also a National Park, are at the very bottom of the image and look a little like a tree in shape and are the home to the rare saltwater hippopotamus. The archipelago has been a UNESCO Biosphere Reserve since 1996 due to the diversity of mammals, birds, reptiles and fish found there. The area is recognized as the most important African site for Green sea turtles to lay their eggs and it is estimated that there are around ten thousand adult females here. Other protected and rare species can also be found here including the Nile crocodile, the dwarf crocodile and the bottlenose dolphin.

28–29 MISSISSIPPI DELTA, USA

The United States longest river, the Mississippi, is constantly changing course and the evidence for this can be seen in the meanders and ox-bow lakes. At the moment the river is flowing far to the east, this benefits New Orleans and Baton Rouge as they are port cities, but from the 1950s it became clear that the river was starting to change course to head west again. This would have meant that much of the flow of the Mississippi would have gone into the Atchafalaya river which distributes the waters of the Mississippi. This makes it a distributary of the Mississippi rather than a tributary. Controlling the river to prevent this change has meant that many structures have been put in place, some of which can been seen in this image. For example the Bonnet Carre Spillway is visible in the southwest corner of Lake Pontchartrain. This image shows very clearly not only how low-lying the land is here, but also how the river affects settlement and agriculture. The Bayou Lafourche runs from the Mississippi to the Gulf of Mexico, right between two main roads and it has been referred to as 'the longest main street in the world'. At 171 km (106 miles) long it has been cut off from the river since 1905, however there is a plan to reconnect it to the river with a control in place that will regulate the water discharge. This will help with the problems of land loss and improve water quality.

30–31 TORRES DEL PAINE NATIONAL PARK, CHILE

This summer view of part of the Torres del Paine National Park, is oriented with east at the top of the image and north to the left. It shows the Grey Glacier at the bottom centre, with Lago Nordenskjöld the lighter lake top right. This lake is named after the Swedish geologist, geographer and polar explorer, Otto Nordenskjöld, who discovered it. The waterfall Salto Grande can be seen where the lake flows into the darker blue coloured Lago Pehoé. In the area between the Grey Lake and the Lago Nordenskjöld is the Cordillera del Paine. This is a small group of mountains that includes the well-known Torres del Paine, three granite monoliths that have been shaped by glacial ice. This is a popular area for trekking and camping. The park has been a UNESCO Biosphere Reserve since 1978 and some of the wildlife that can been seen include the guanaco, a close relative of the llama, as well as puma, condor, and the endangered South Andean deer or huemul. It is estimated that there are only about 2000 huemul left. Both the condor and the huemul appear on Chile's National Coat of Arms.

32–33 SOLAR ECLIPSE, ARCTIC OCEAN

A total solar eclipse occurs when the Moon completely covers the Sun from the view of observers on Earth. This casts the shadow of the Moon on the Earth's surface. The phenomenon occurs on a regular basis around the world but very infrequently in the same location. A total solar eclipse occurred on 20 March 2015, but very little of the penumbra (shadow) crossed land so most of the totality was over water. NASA's Terra satellite was passing over the Arctic Ocean at the time of the total eclipse and caught this image of the shadow. The islands of Svalbard and Jan Mayen are in the top left of the image with Ostrov Severny in the bottom right, under the penumbra that shows in a golden colour. This image also shows the phenomenon known as cloud streets where clouds can be seen lined up in close parallel rows. Air blowing over cold, snow-covered land and then over ice becomes both cold and dry. When the air then moves over water that is relatively warmer and much moister it leads to the development of parallel cylinders of spinning air. On the top edge of these cylinders where the air is rising, small clouds form. Where air is descending, the skies are clear. This pattern of alternating clear and cloudy, formed in parallel rows, gives an impression of streets.

34–35 MOUNT SIDLEY, ANTARCTICA

While Mount Vinson is well documented as the highest mountain in Antarctica, the highest volcano is less well known due to its remote location. The peak with the shadow over the caldera is Mount Sidley. This volcano is part of a chain of eighteen major volcanoes on the Pacific coast of Antarctica, and makes up one of five peaks in the Executive Committee Range, so named because the range was discovered by a flight from the United States Antarctic Service in December 1940 and is named after the service's Executive Committee. Mount Sidley is not named after an Executive committee member as it was discovered in 1934, but the others in this image are. Below it is Mount Waesche, and to the left are Mount Hartigan and Mount Cumming, with Mount Hampton just out of the frame. The volcano has a summit elevation over 4000 m and the first recorded ascent was not until 1990. The caldera is over 5km wide but the volcano is dormant although this is the youngest volcano in the range. Recent work by seismologists in Antarctica has suggested that a new volcano may be forming under the ice about 30 miles away.

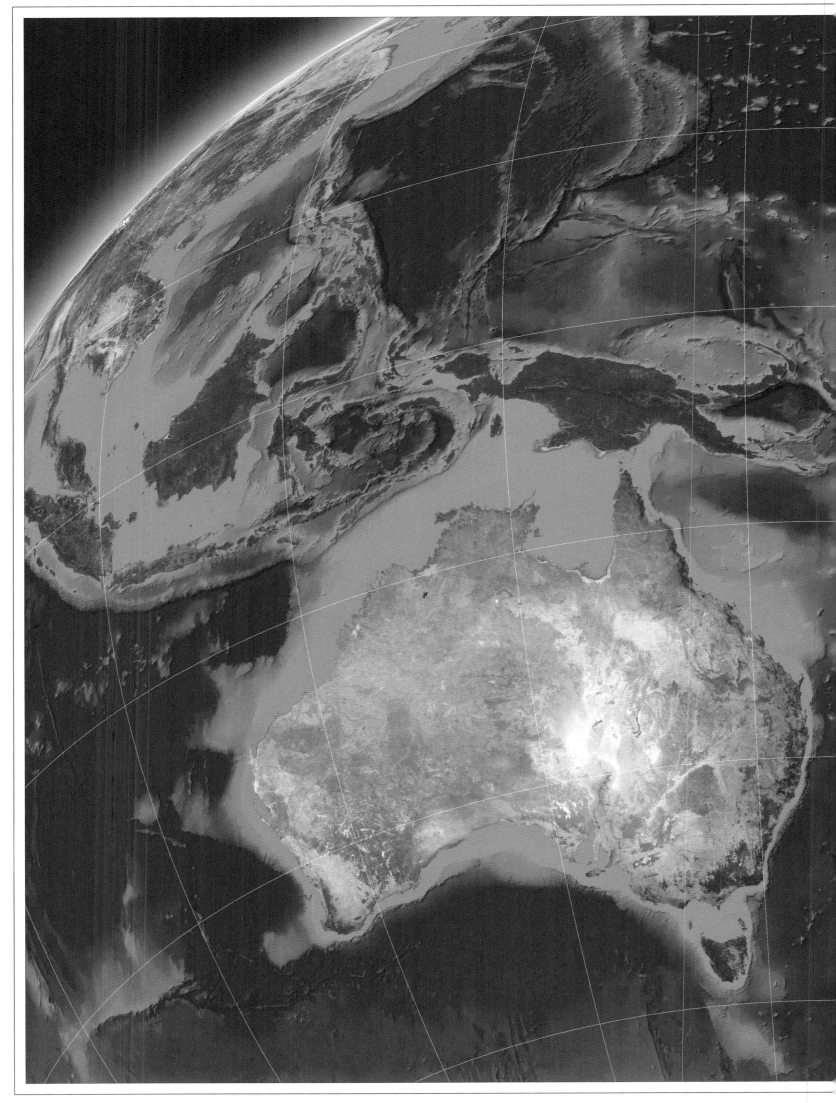

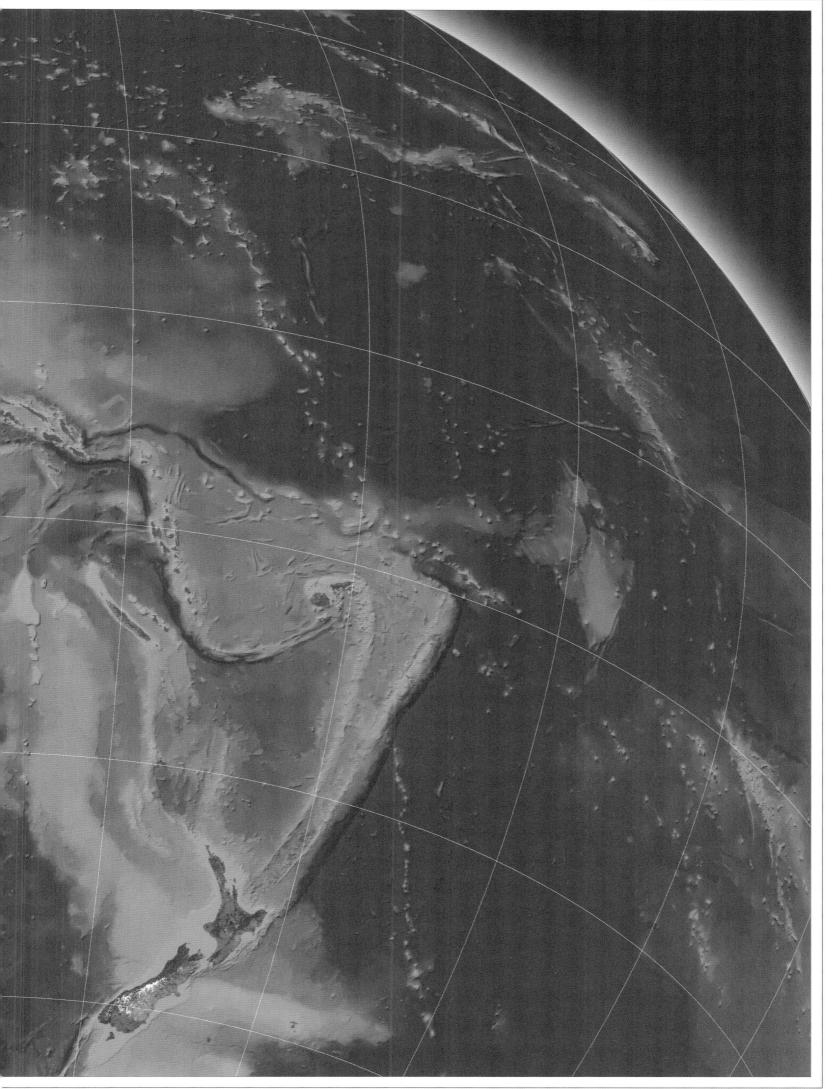

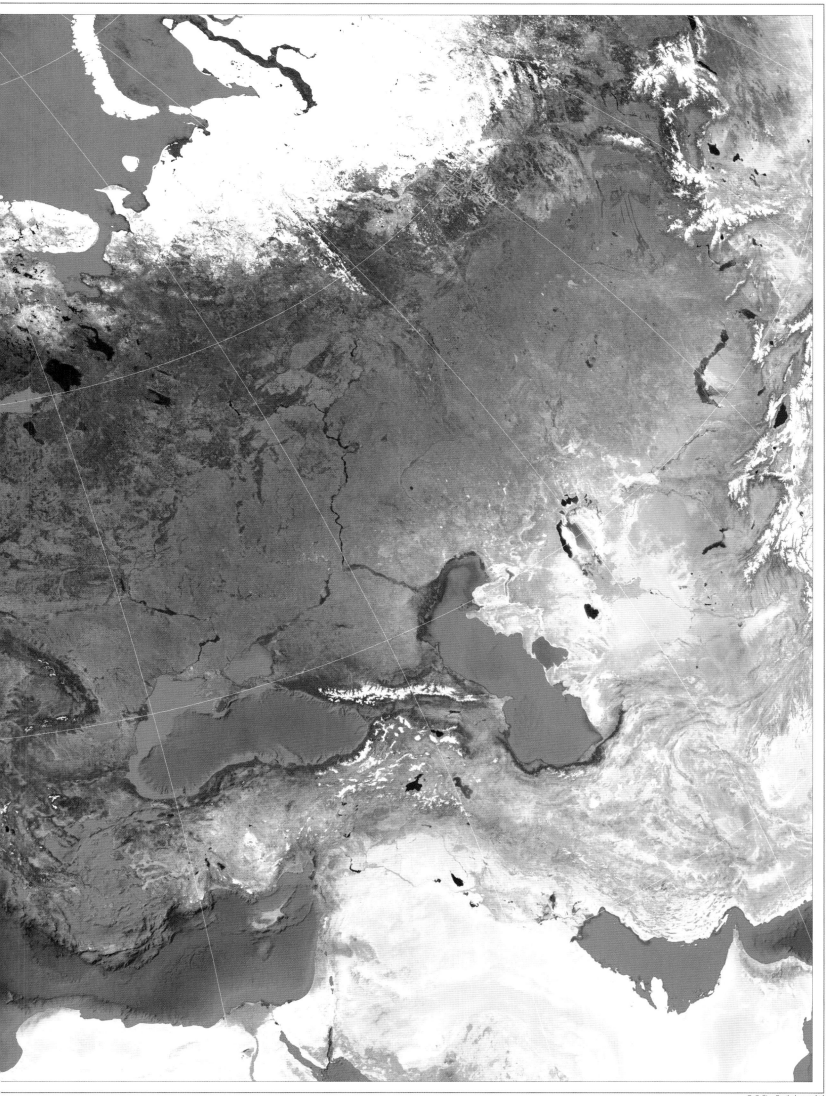

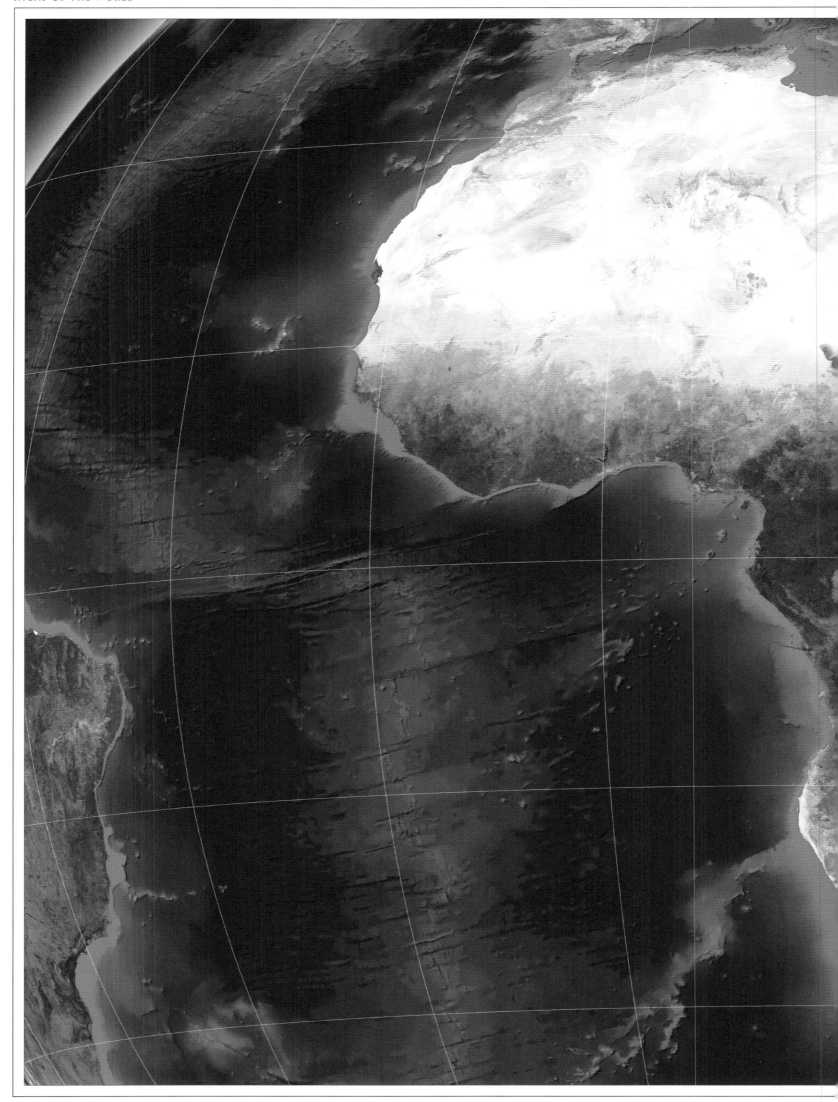

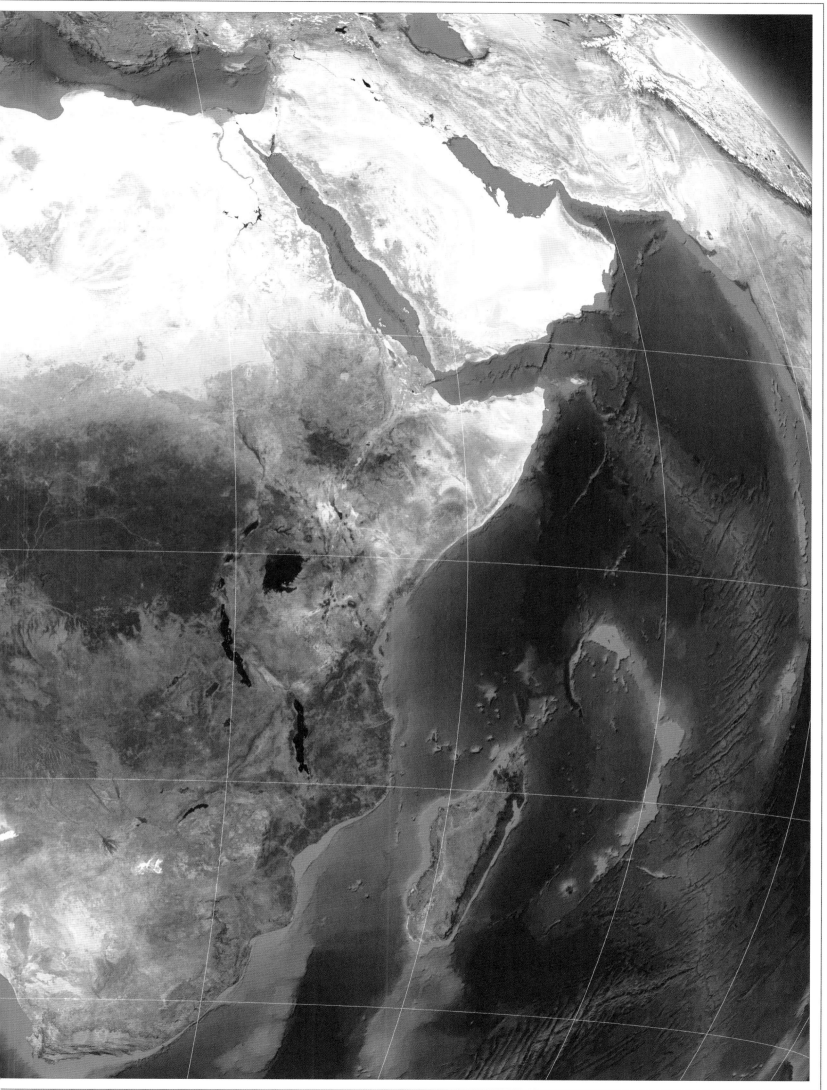

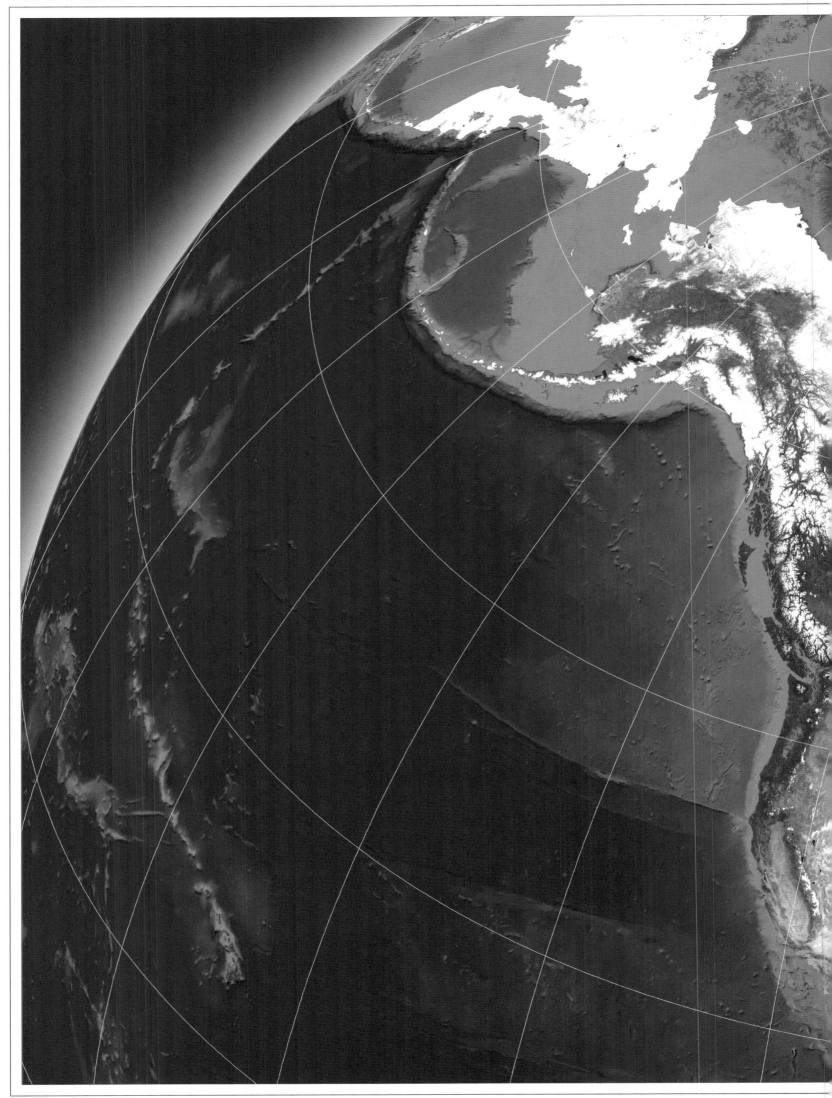

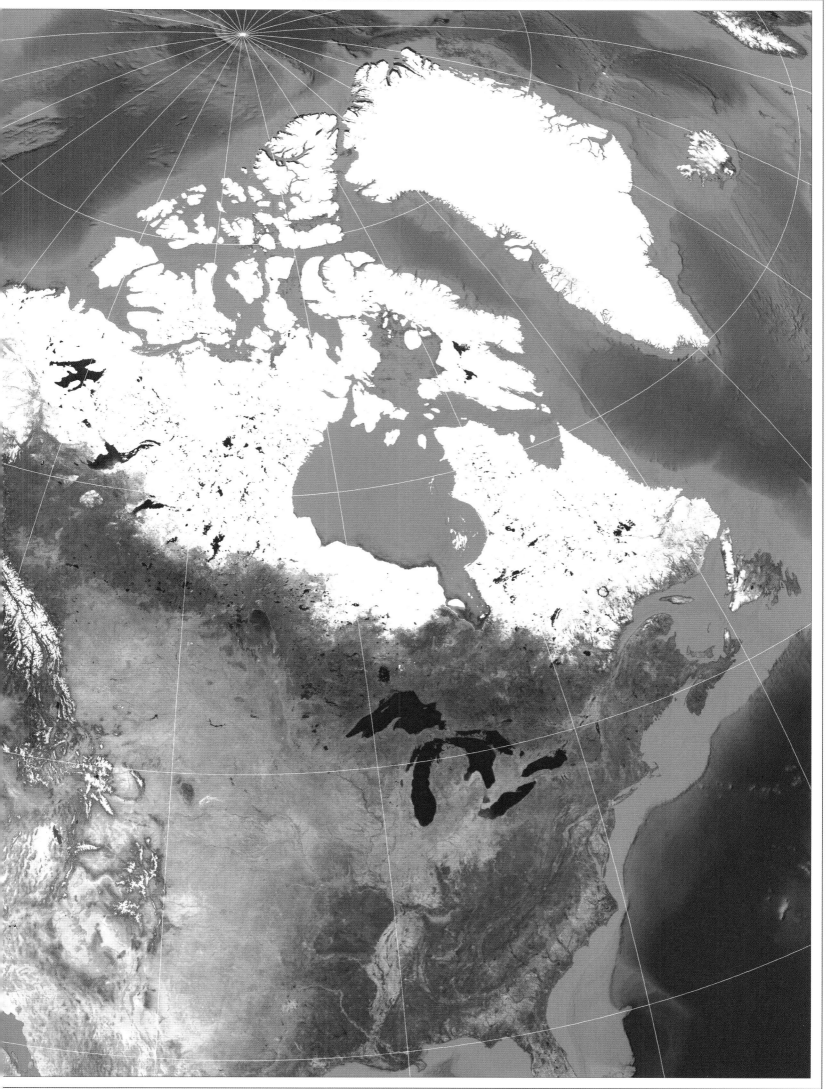

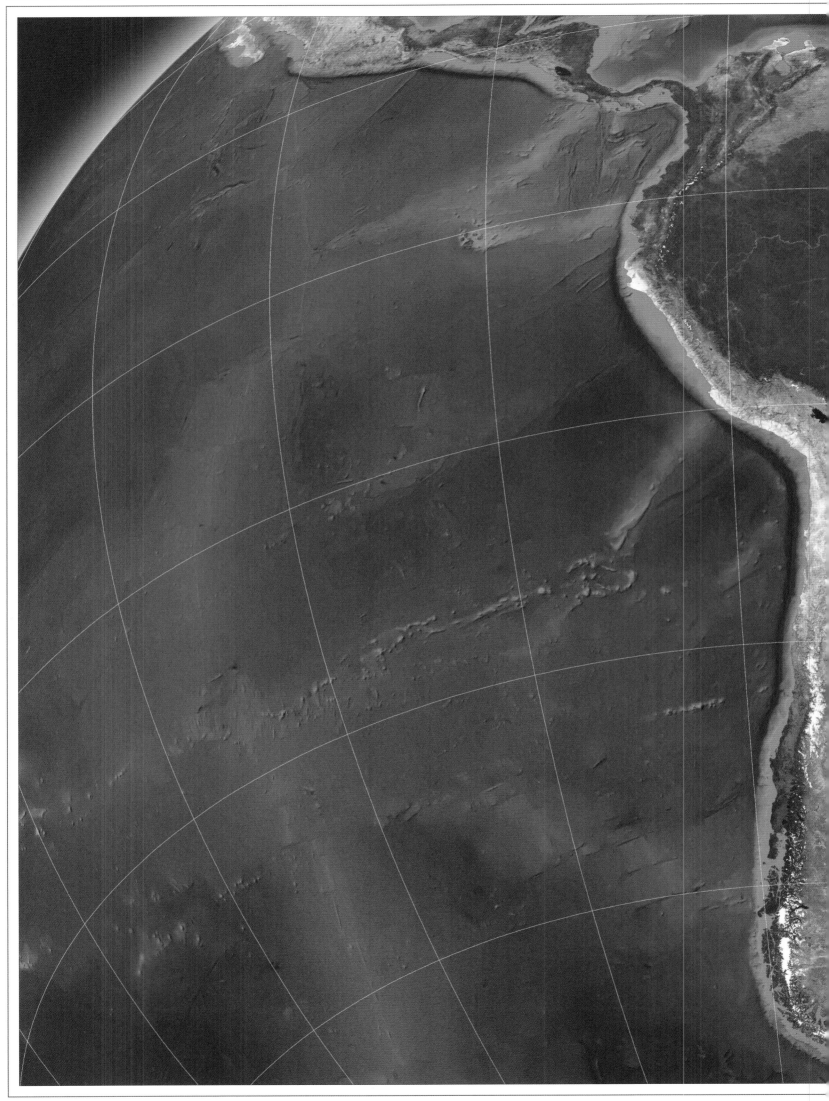

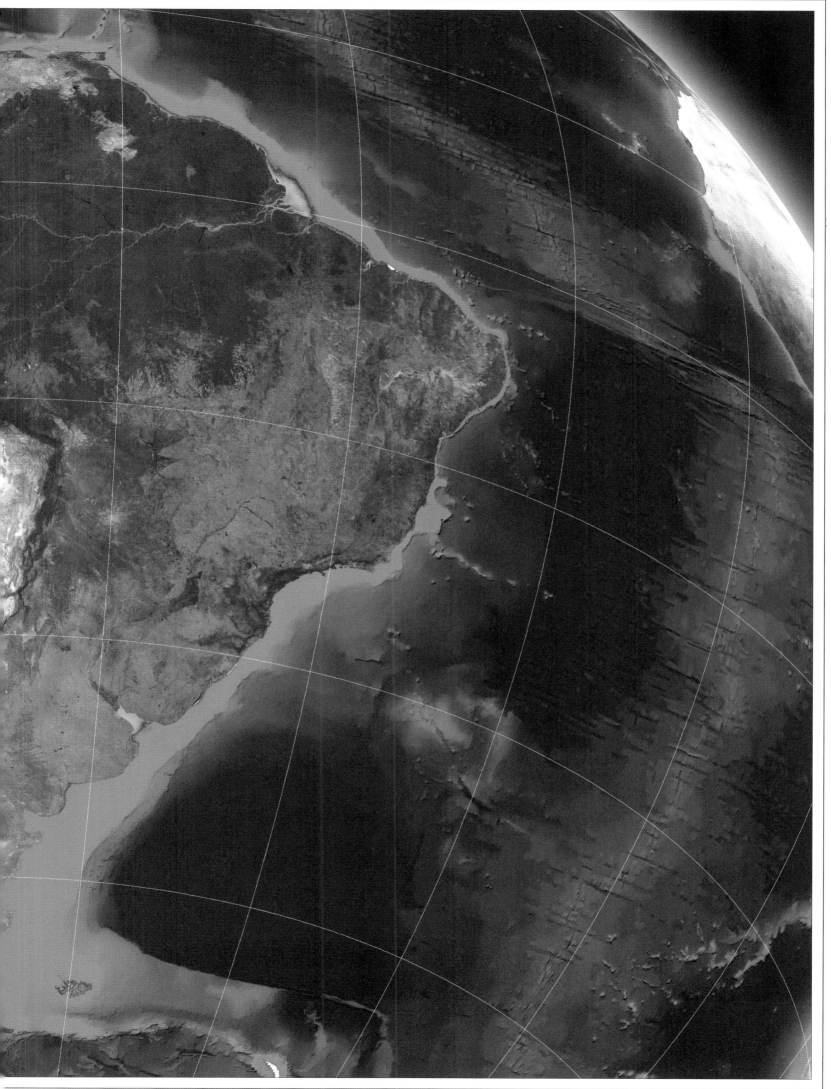

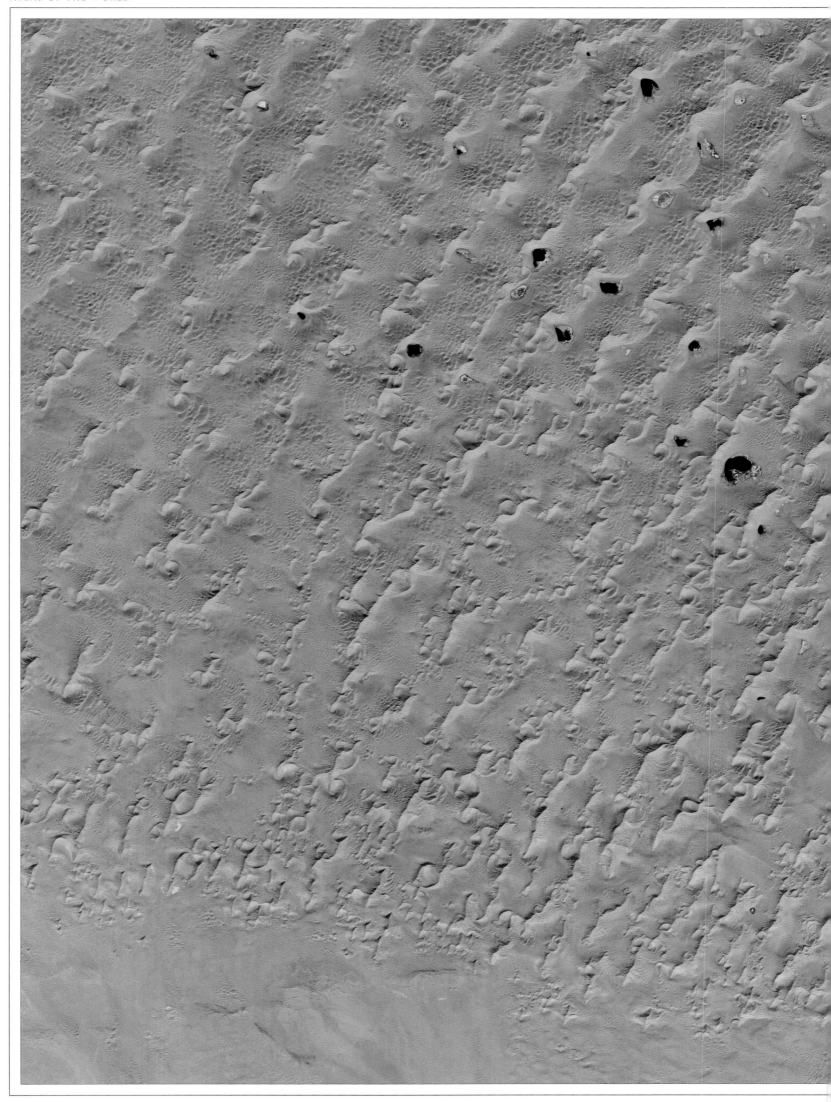

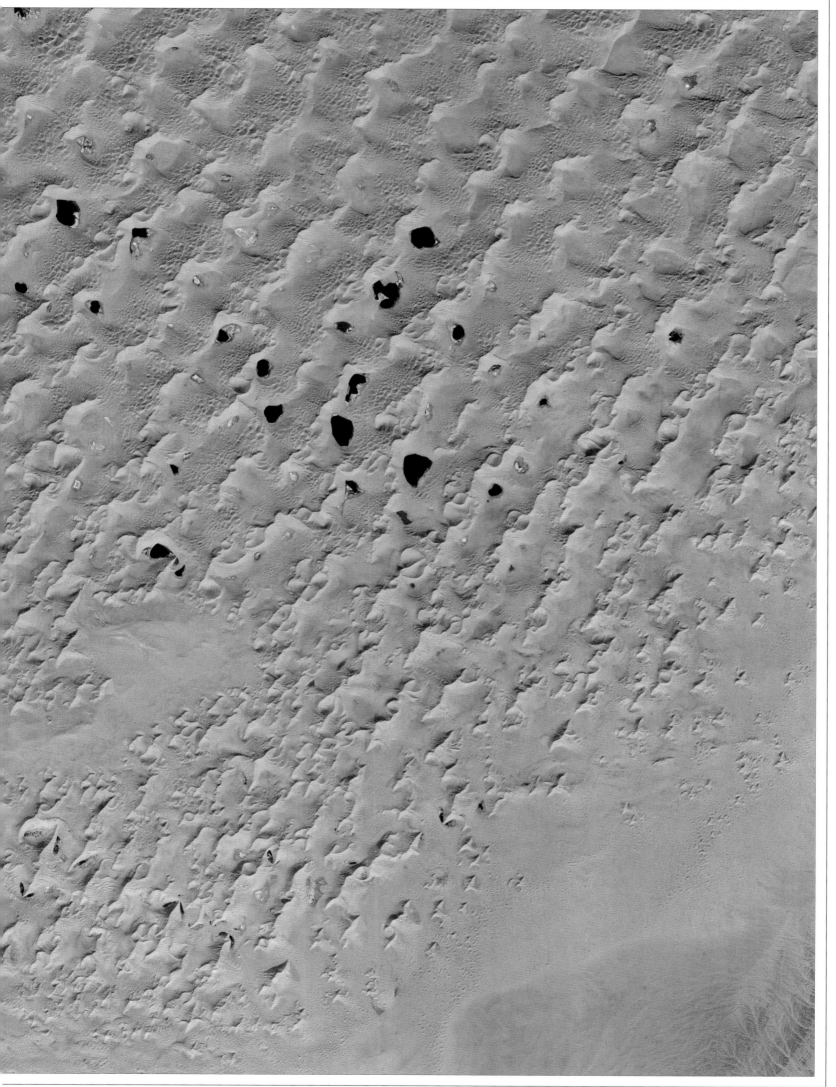

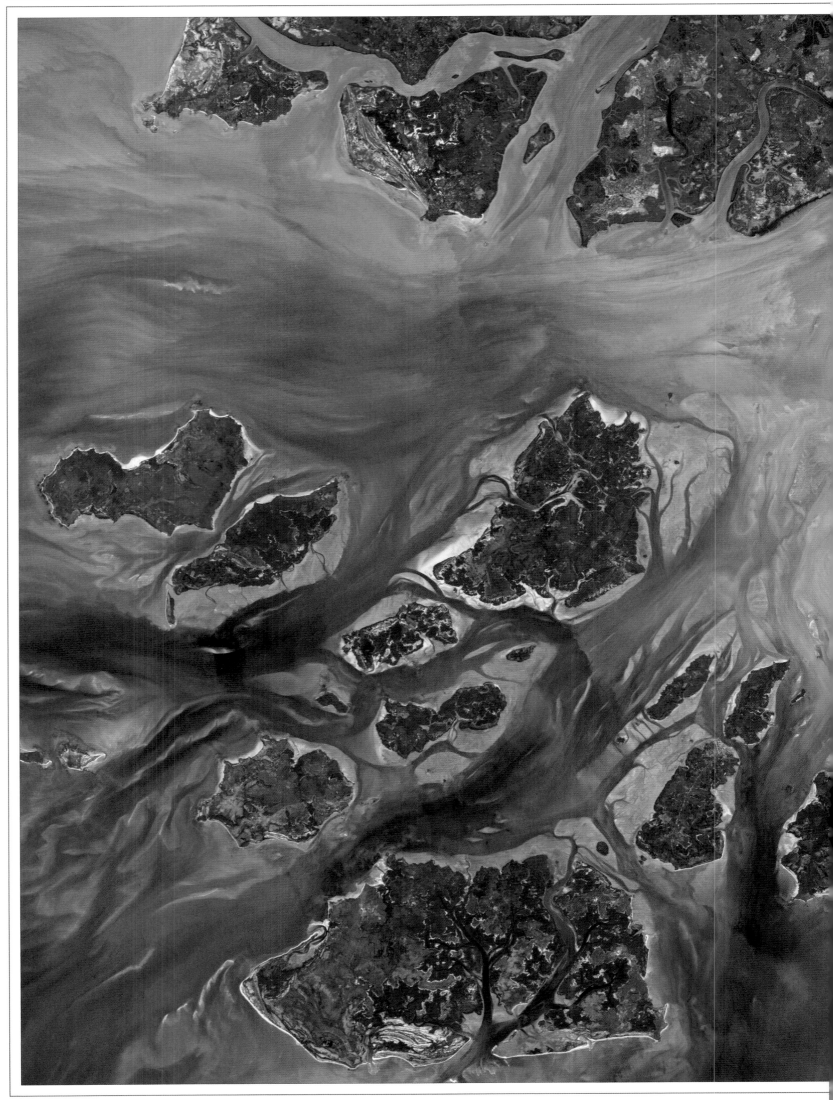

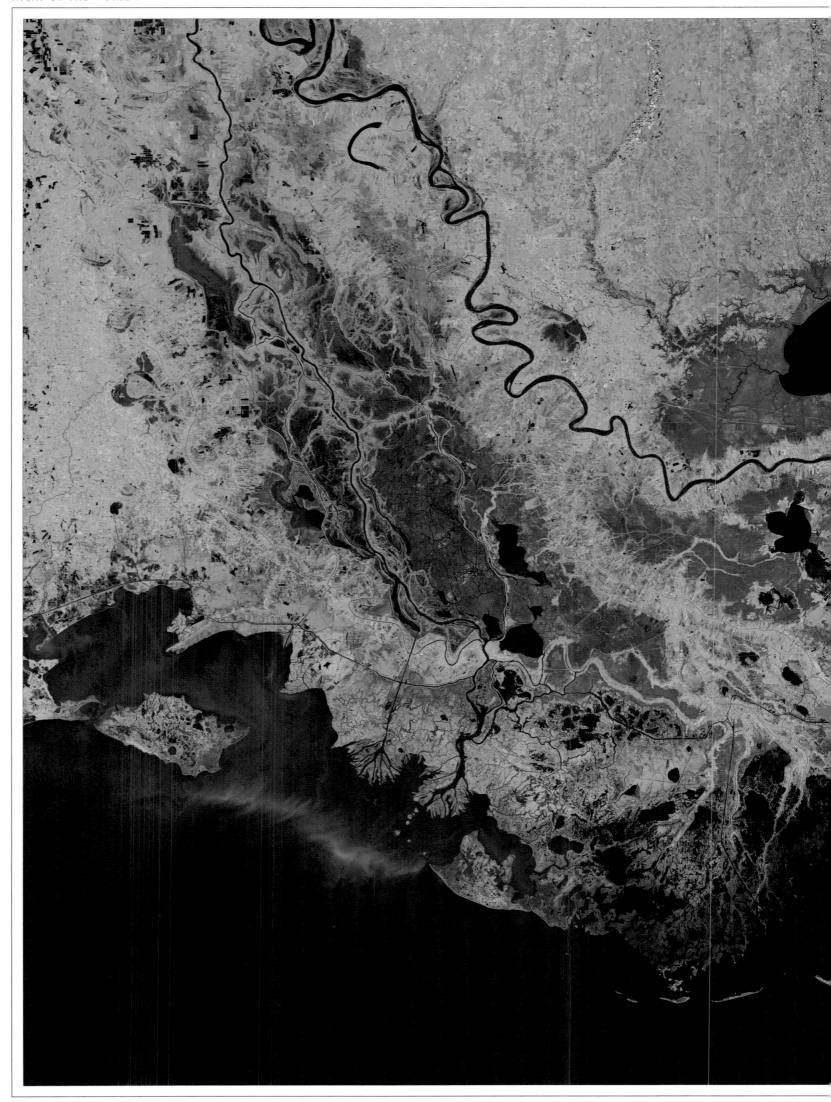

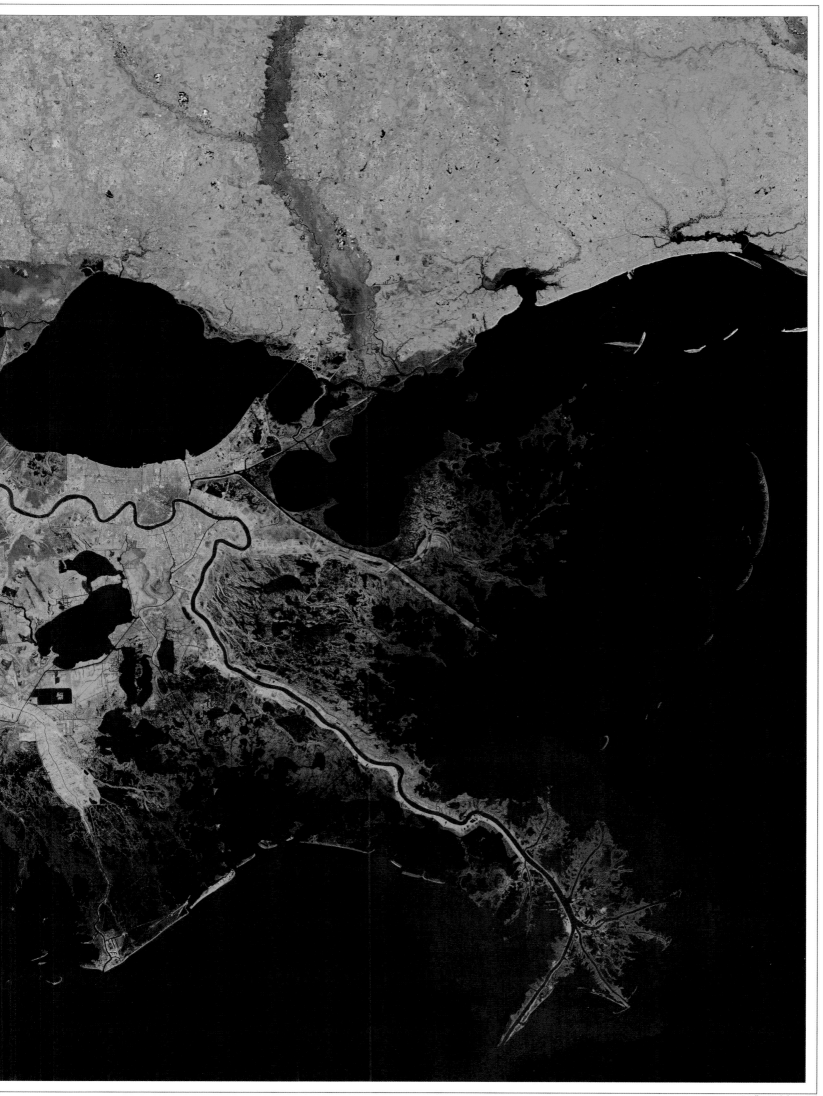

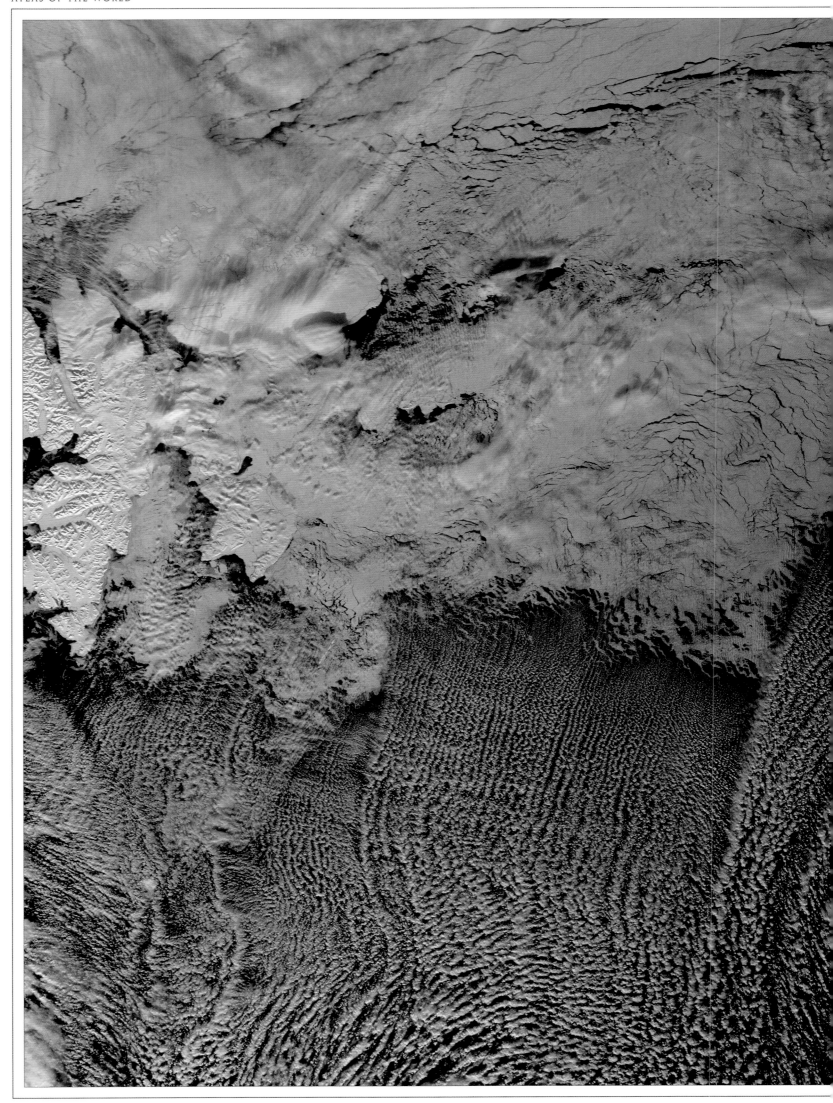

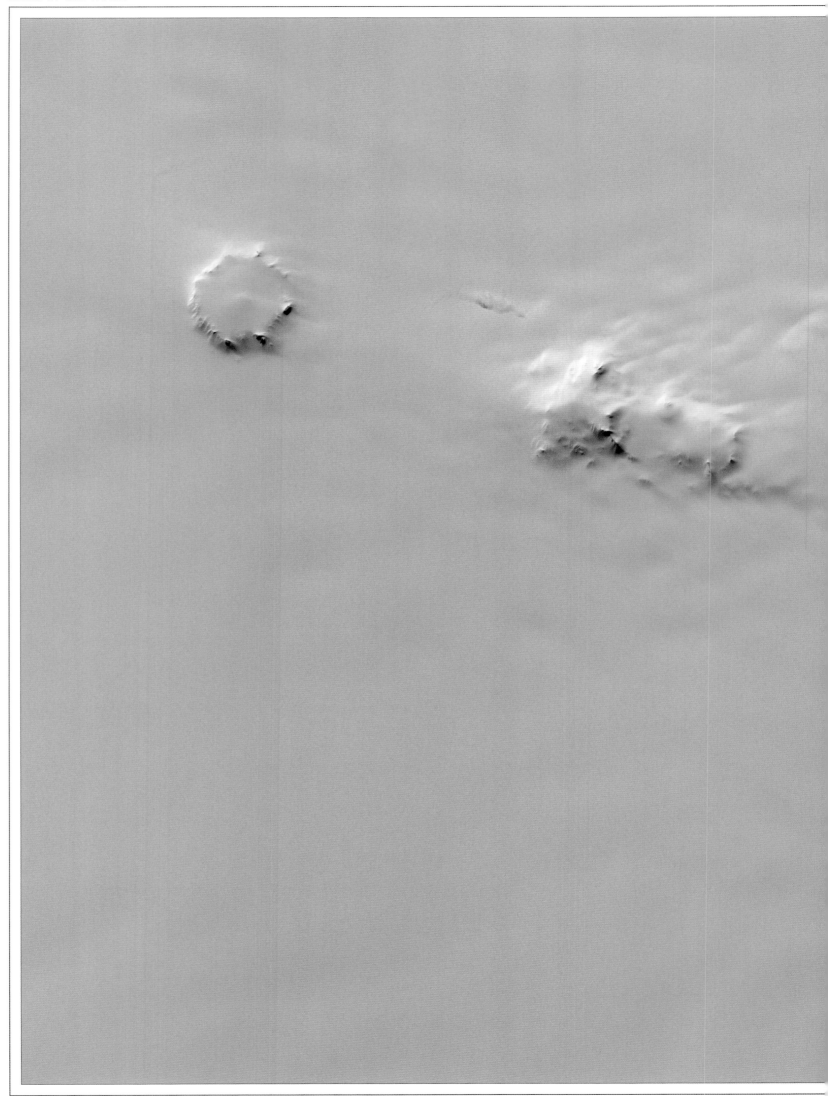

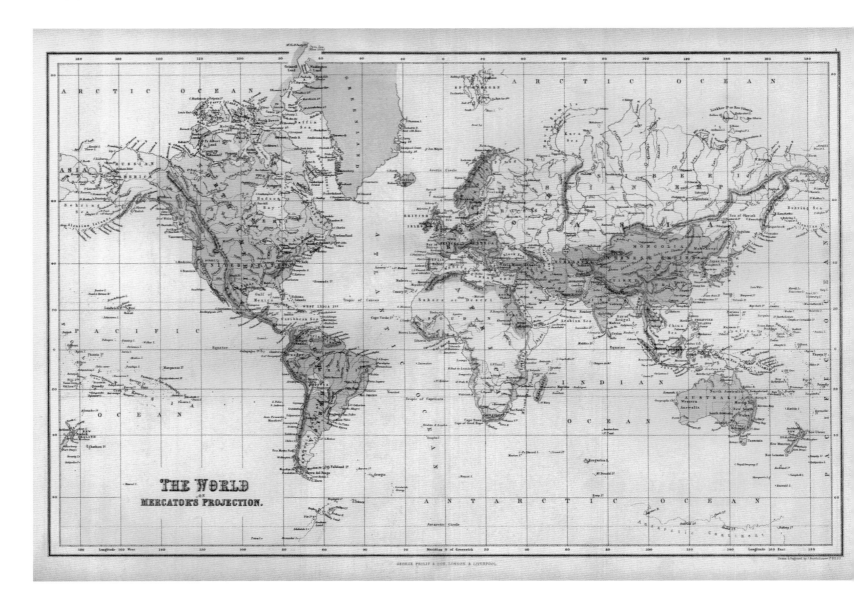

38–39 THE WORLD ON MERCATOR'S PROJECTION 1858

From the *Family Atlas of Physical, General and Classical Geography*. Drawn and engraved by J. Bartholomew Jr, F.R.G.S.

The nineteenth century was known as the 'Age of Empire', when all the major European powers harboured imperial ambitions and used their commercial and military might to extend their influence. In the first half of the century, the process had been gradual. Britain had emerged as the pre-eminent overseas power, extending the boundaries of her established colonial possessions in North America, India and Australia. In the second half of the century, the pace of imperial expansion increased markedly and the world depicted here was on the cusp of a dramatic change.

40–41 POLITICAL MAP OF THE WORLD 1914

From the *International Reference Atlas of the World*. Cartography by J. G. Bartholomew, LL.D., F.R.G.S., Cartographer to the King.

This map shows the imperial divisions of the world at the onset of the First World War in 1914. European colonial empires had grown rapidly over the past century and by now the Great Powers of Europe had engrossed nine-tenths of Africa and much of Asia. Prior to 1914, Europe had been run on balance-of-power politics, where a status quo was maintained between the major powers, often with unofficial agreements and alliances.

42–43 WORLD POLITICAL DIVISIONS 1936

From the *Advanced Atlas, Fifth Edition*. Cartography by John Bartholomew, M.C., M.A., F.R.S.E., F.R.G.S., Cartographer to the King.

The political situation of the world three years before the outbreak of the Second World War can be seen from this map. The power of empires had waned significantly after the First World War, and a number of treaties and pacts were signed between countries to safeguard against military attacks. Growing political and social conflict was leading to nationalist uprisings, while both communism and fascism were on the rise in Europe.

44–45 WORLD ROUTES OF COMMERCE 1950

From the *Advanced Atlas of Modern Geography*. Cartography by John Bartholomew, M.C., Director, the Geographical Institute, Edinburgh.

Just as the First World War had acted as a catalyst for massive change to the existing world order, so too the fallout from the Second World War brought significant political, territorial and economic upheaval across the globe. The most significant development in world politics post-1945 was the emergence of the USA and USSR as hostile superpowers, and the ideological alignment of other nations with each respective camp. The armed stand-off which emerged between the two power blocs became known as the Cold War and lasted until the fall of Soviet communism in the early 1990s.

46–47 WORLD POLITICAL CHART 1963

From the *Edinburgh World Atlas, Fifth Edition*. Cartography by John Bartholomew, C.B.E., M.C., LL.D., F.R.S.E., F.R.G.S.

Almost twenty years on from the end of the Second World War, the 'Age of Empire' was close to its end. International politics had instead become dominated by two superpowers – the United States and the Union of Soviet Socialist Republics (USSR) – who were opposed to each other during the lengthy Cold War. Significant changes affected French and British possessions worldwide at this time. After the war, European powers no longer had the military strength to defend against nationalist movements, nor the economic strength to enforce their rule. Decolonisation in Africa increased.

48–49 STATES OF THE WORLD 1982

From the *Bartholomew World Atlas, Twelfth Edition*. Cartography by John Bartholomew, M.A., F.R.S.E., Director, the Geographical Institute, Edinburgh.

This map represents a transition between one extensive series of changes and another – beforehand, the decolonisation which had gone on, especially in Africa; and afterwards, the collapse of communist regimes in the 1990s. One of the inset maps plots the many changes of sovereignty that had occurred since 1939. Britain sought to maintain association with its former colonies through the Commonwealth. The changes that came after this map was published mostly resulted from political changes in the Soviet Union and its Warsaw Pact allies.

50–51 UNITED STATES OF AMERICA 1879

From the *Handy General Atlas of America*, Philip's. Cartography by J. G. Bartholomew, F.R.G.S.

This 1879 map of the United States of America depicts the country at a particularly interesting time in its history. Following the Union victory in the civil war in 1865 the southern states were very slow to re-build. The northern states by comparison, driven by an unprecedented influx of immigrants from Europe, forged ahead with rapid urbanization, infrastructure development and economic growth.

One of the main barriers to westward expansion into California was the Sierra Nevada mountain range. Emigrants attempting to cross the range by wagon faced a long and dangerous journey that many did not survive. In 1844 a party travelling westward into the mountains followed the Truckee River. This led them to what is now called the Donner Pass at 2 160 m (7 085 ft). This low narrow pass became the gateway west into California for thousands of emigrants. A direct rail connection came in 1869 with the completion of the First Transcontinental Railroad through the Donner Pass. While the pass is not named on the map, the railroad can be seen crossing the Nevada/ California state boundary and then the Sierra Nevada mountains to the northwest of Carson City.

52–53 WEST AFRICA, COLONIAL MAP 1895

From *The Times Atlas, First Edition*.

This composite map of colonial West Africa from the end of the nineteenth century centres on the coast around Equatorial Africa – the Gulf of Guinea to the north and the mouth of the Congo. Holding the coastal land was key to gaining and maintaining territory in Africa: from the coast, materials and supplies could be shipped in and out, especially along navigable rivers, allowing further annexation. All the major European powers are represented in these maps of coastal areas.

France was the largest power in West Africa. Dahomey was only a small part of their massive swathe of territory that ran from the Mediterranean to the equator. In 1895, the year the map was drawn, the French amalgamated all their holdings into the Federation of French West Africa, a colony that would prove successful for France. The small coastal wedge marked as Belgian territory belied the massive interior lands of the Congo Free State. Belgian King Leopold II privately controlled the rich area through a corporation but at a heavy price to the local people because of the harsh treatment they received.

54–55 SOUTH AMERICA 1895

From *The Times Atlas, First Edition*.

The South America map of 1895 depicts a continent whose borders are mostly recognisable today. The political forces that shaped national boundaries throughout the nineteenth century were virtually spent. The Spanish and Portuguese empires had been driven off the continental mainland and in their former colonies local establishment alliances ran the new republics. Greater political stability allowed increased economic development and South America became a major exporter of minerals and commodities including beef, coffee, wheat, rubber and sugar to the industrialised world.

Border changes after 1895 were largely contained to disputed territories between neighbours. The exception was Panama, which appears on the 1895 map as a region of Colombia. Panama declared independence in 1903 with the backing of the USA; in return, the USA agreed to build and maintain a canal within a predesignated zone across the isthmus. The Panama Canal was completed in 1914.

56–57 AFRICA POLITICAL 1895

From *The Times Atlas, First Edition*.

The African continent was parcelled up between competing European powers in the late nineteenth century and this map illustrates those divisions. Before then, little of Africa was ruled directly by Europeans, with the exceptions of the British Cape Colony, French Algeria and some smaller coastal footholds. But the work of explorers such as Livingstone, Stanley, Burton and Speke revealed the vast resources that lay in what was then the unknown 'Dark Continent'.

The imperial 'Scramble for Africa' began in the 1880s, fuelled by strategic rivalries, national ambitions and a commercial imperative to find new markets and new materials. Britain was the chief beneficiary, spurred on by the desire to secure communication channels with India, keystone of the empire. For this reason, Egypt was effectively annexed in 1882 to protect the strategically vital Suez Canal; and neighbouring Sudan would be annexed in 1898. But Britain would shortly face its sternest African military test from the Dutch Boers who from 1899–1902 would fight to re-establish the autonomy of their southern African republics.

58–59 NORTH POLAR REGIONS AND SOUTH POLAR REGIONS 1898

From the *Citizen's Atlas*. Cartography by J. G. Bartholomew, F.R.G.S.

These maps of the polar regions allow a variety of interesting comparisons to be drawn about these extremes of the Earth and how they were being explored. Far from being homogeneous ice masses, the northern and southern polar regions are physically very different. The North Pole is at the centre of the Arctic Ocean and is an almost landlocked body of water largely composed of drifting pack ice; the South Pole, by contrast, lies on a continental land mass.

The motivations of those who ventured into these unexplored regions were different. For many northern polar explorers, the intention was to find a navigable passage through the ice to open up a trade route to link the Atlantic and Pacific Oceans – the so-called Northwest Passage. Unlike the northern polar region, the physical boundaries of the southern polar region were poorly understood. It was not until the 1820s that Antarctica was first actually sighted, probably by the Russian explorer, Bellingshausen. From the 1830s a series of national expeditions embarked for Antarctica.

60–61 AUSTRALIA 1898

From the *Citizen's Atlas*. Cartography by J. G. Bartholomew, F.R.G.S.

This map records the geopolitical make-up of Australia immediately prior to the ending of British colonial rule. Three years after it was drawn, the federal Commonwealth of Australia came into being, holding Dominion status under the British Crown. The political boundaries depicted here had been established during the course of the nineteenth century, and with minor exceptions have remained unchanged to the present day. A particularly striking feature of the map is the pattern of settlement. The temperate and subtropical climates of the southwestern and eastern coastal areas attracted the original European settlers and 60 per cent of the Australian population still lives there. The drive inland was accelerated by a series of goldrushes beginning in the 1850s.

62–63 THE FAR EAST 1907

From *The Atlas of the World's Commerce*, George Newnes. Edited by J. G. Bartholomew, F.R.G.S.

One of the most striking features of this map of the Far East from 1907 is the web of activity around the coasts and inland. Shipping lines, railways and, to a lesser extent, canals and navigable rivers all form a network of

connections designed to facilitate movement. Lines of communication, notably undersea cables and consular offices, back up the mass of transport links, all together painting a picture of a mercantile system whose very density portrays a vibrant energy.

By the early twentieth century, trade and economic activity spanned the globe, connecting people on opposite sides of the world. A nation's trade was not just with its neighbours a packhorse ride away, but was across seas and international boundaries. The industrialized nations opened up new markets in the Far East, buying raw materials and foods for manufacture, driving new industries and inventions and benefitting buyers and sellers alike.

64–65 TURKEY IN ASIA, PERSIA, ARABIA, &c. 1914

From the *International Reference Atlas of the World*. Cartography by J. G. Bartholomew, LL.D., F.R.G.S., Cartographer to the King.

The late nineteenth and early twentieth centuries had seen a dramatic contraction of the Ottoman Empire, particularly in the Balkans but also in North Africa, where Algeria and Tunisia had been ceded to France, and Libya to Italy. Although never formally invaded, Persia was economically dependent on Europe, and as a result, Britain and Russia effectively divided the country between them from 1907 into two spheres of economic interest in which each power could exert its influence.

In October 1914, Turkey entered the First World War on Germany's side, starting the train of events that would bring about the dissolution of the Ottoman Empire and the creation of the modern Turkish republic.

66–67 EUROPE POLITICAL 1922

From *The Times Survey Atlas of the World*, Prepared at "The Edinburgh Geographical Institute" under the direction of J. G. Bartholomew, LL.D., F.R.S.E., F.R.G.S., Cartographer to the King.

The aftermath of the First World War and the Treaty of Versailles in 1919 redrew the world map and brought an end to the centuries of dynastic power in central and eastern Europe. The new separate states of Austria, Hungary, Czechoslovakia and Yugoslavia emerged after the demise of the Habsburg dynasty. At this time, ethnic nationalism was threatening European colonial empires with ideas of democracy and social reform.

Following the Russian Revolution in 1917, the Russian Empire lost much of its western frontier – the new Baltic states of Estonia, Latvia and Lithuania successfully fought independence and were recognised as independent countries in 1920. The map, however, shows these states during only a brief spell of independence.

68–69 WORLD POWERS 1957

From *The Times Atlas of the World*, Mid-Century Edition 1958. Cartography by John Bartholomew, M.C., LL.D.

The most striking feature of this map is its unusual viewpoint (or projection). Devised in 1948 by John Bartholomew, the Atlantis Projection abandons the common atlas convention of showing the Arctic at the top and the Antarctic at the bottom. Here the projection is tilted to focus on the Atlantic Ocean. In this instance it is particularly effective in conveying the combative nature of relations between the United States and the Soviet Union, the two 'superpowers' which emerged to dominate the new world order following the Second World War.

Within a few short years of this particular map being drawn, significant colour changes would be required for a number of countries: Alaska would become a full member state of the USA (1959); Fidel Castro would establish a Marxist government in Cuba (1959), and the process by which many African nations would shake off the remnants of European colonialism would begin in earnest.

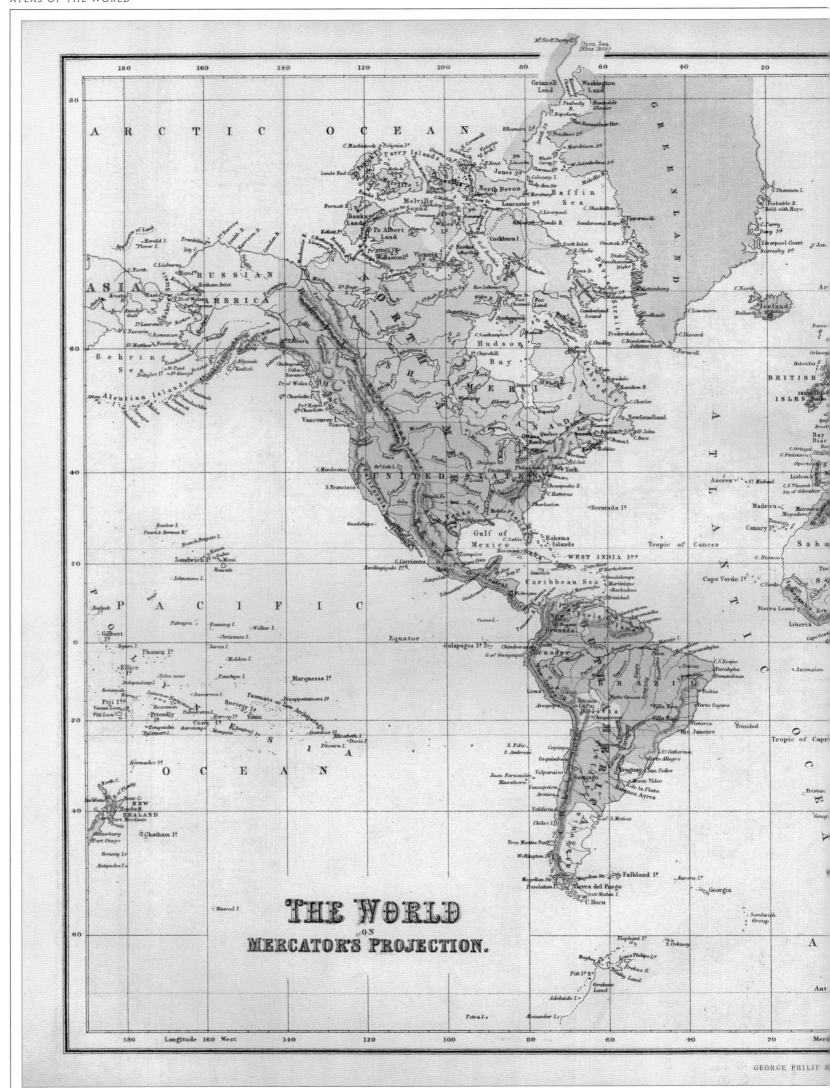

THE WORLD
ON
MERCATOR'S PROJECTION.

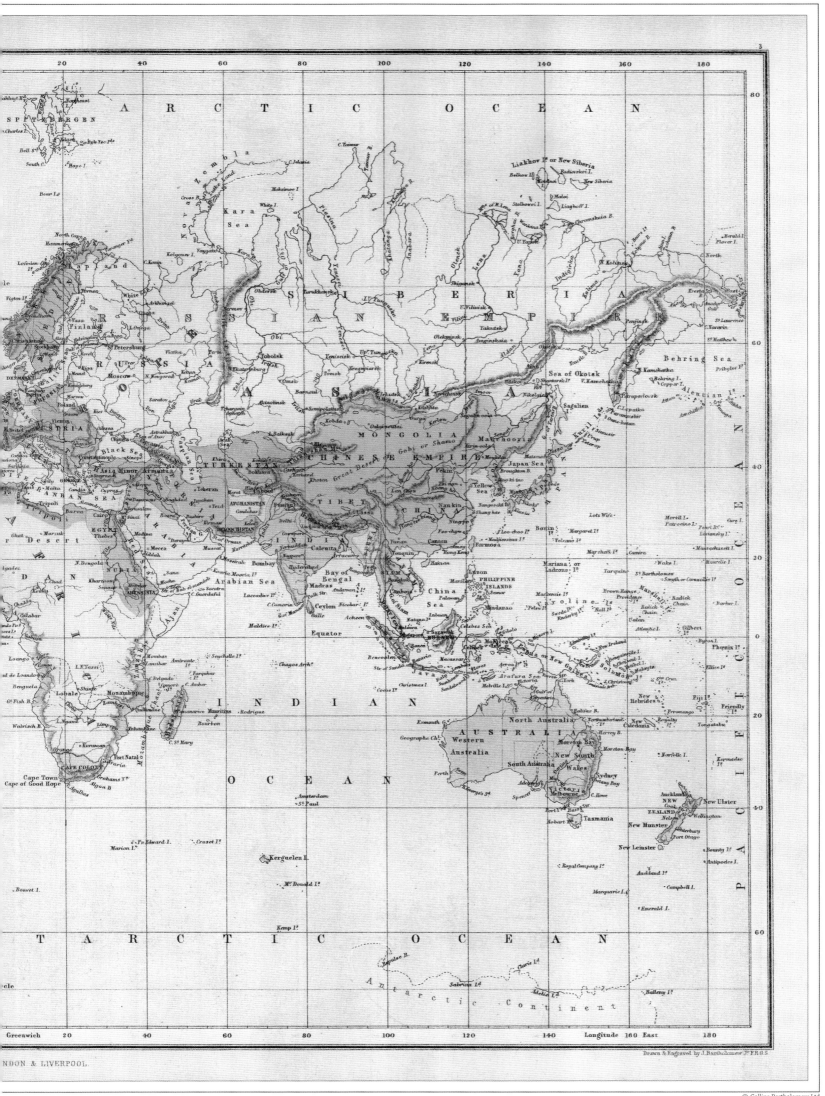

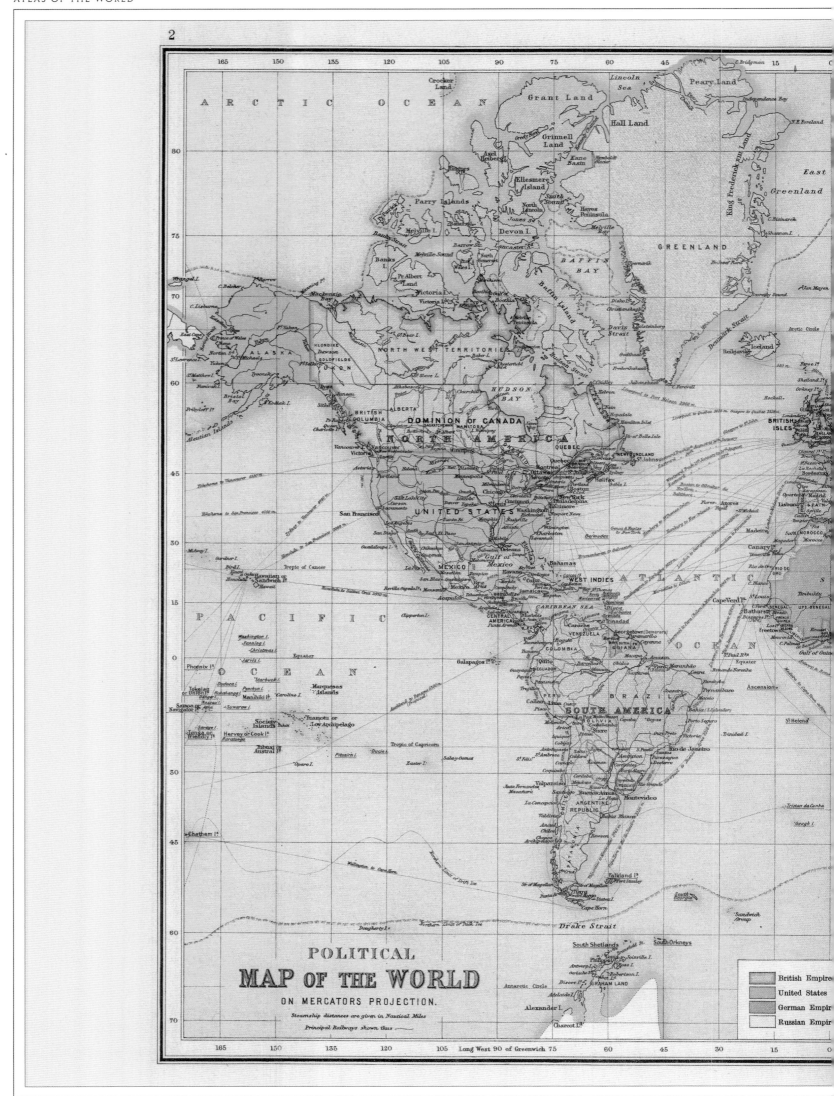

POLITICAL
MAP OF THE WORLD
ON MERCATORS PROJECTION.

Steamship distances are given in Nautical Miles

Principal Railways shown thus ———

	British Empire
	United States
	German Empire
	Russian Empire

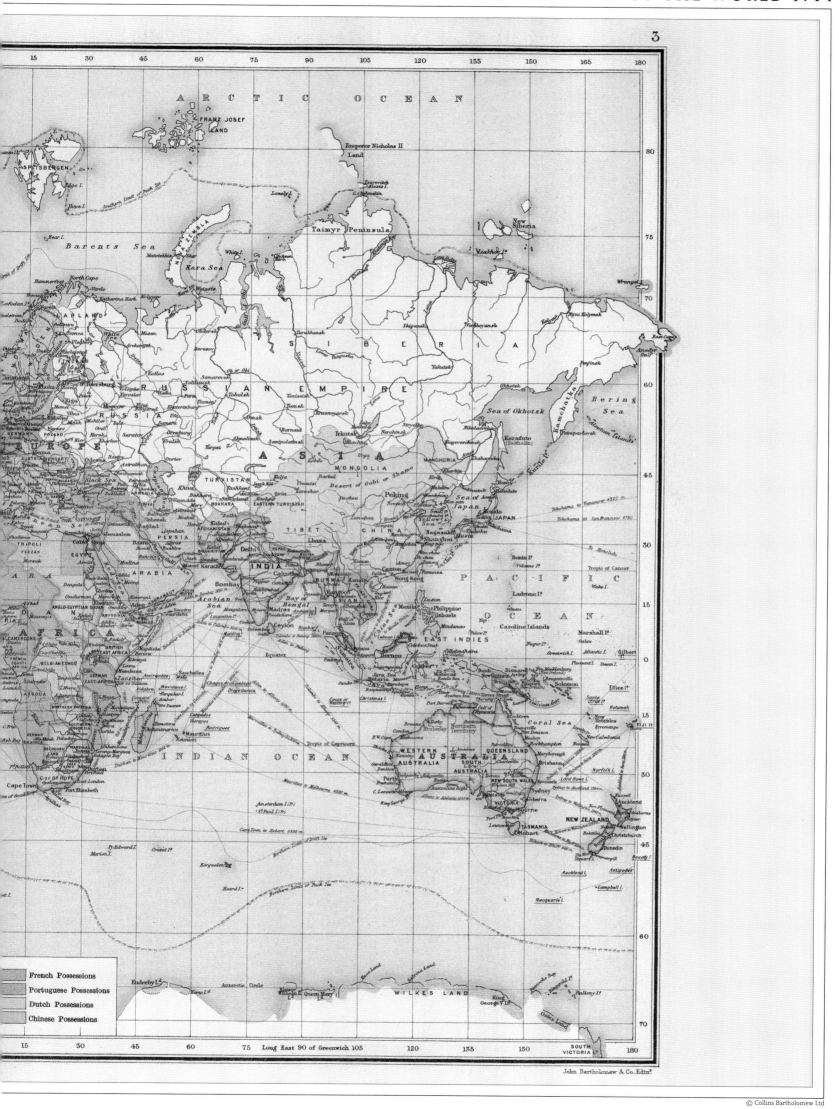

French Possessions
Portuguese Possessions
Dutch Possessions
Chinese Possessions

John Bartholomew & Co., Edin.

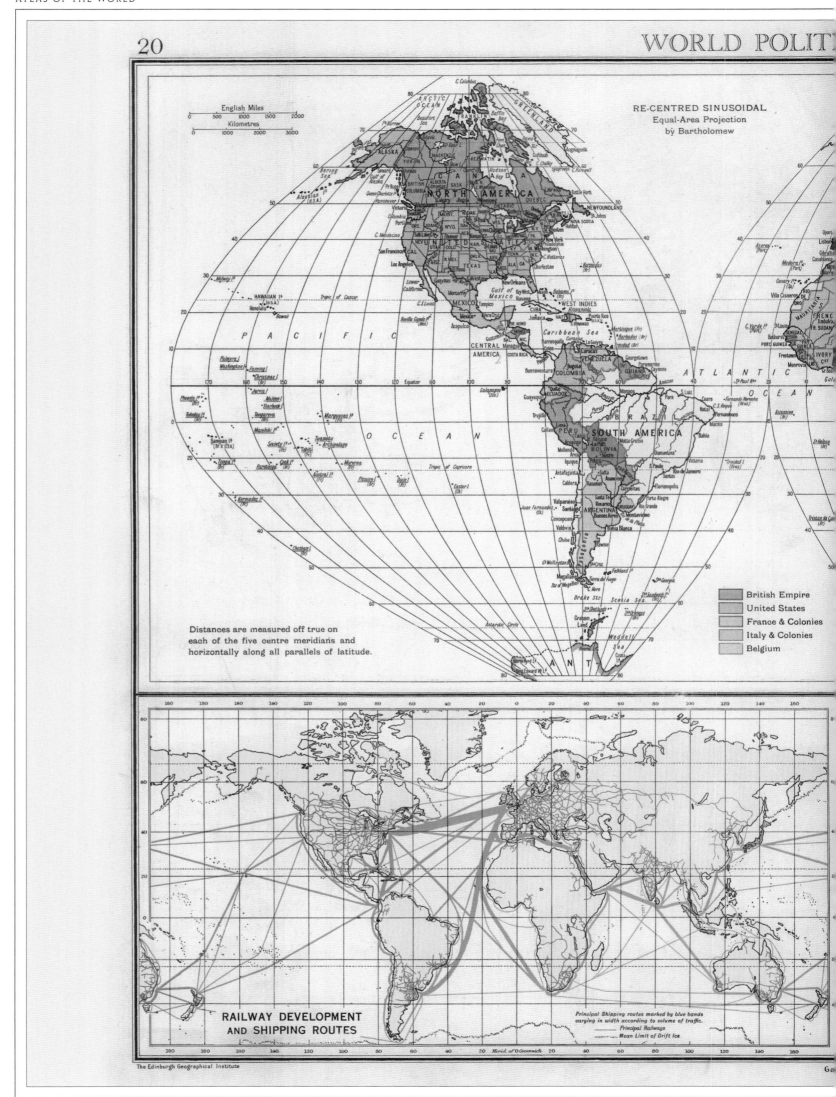

WORLD POLIT

RE-CENTRED SINUSOIDAL
Equal-Area Projection
by Bartholomew

English Miles

Kilometres

Distances are measured off true on
each of the five centre meridians and
horizontally along all parallels of latitude.

British Empire
United States
France & Colonies
Italy & Colonies
Belgium

RAILWAY DEVELOPMENT
AND SHIPPING ROUTES

Principal Shipping routes marked by blue bands
varying in width according to volume of traffic.
Principal Railways
Mean Limit of Drift Ice.

Merid. of O Greenwich

The Edinburgh Geographical Institute

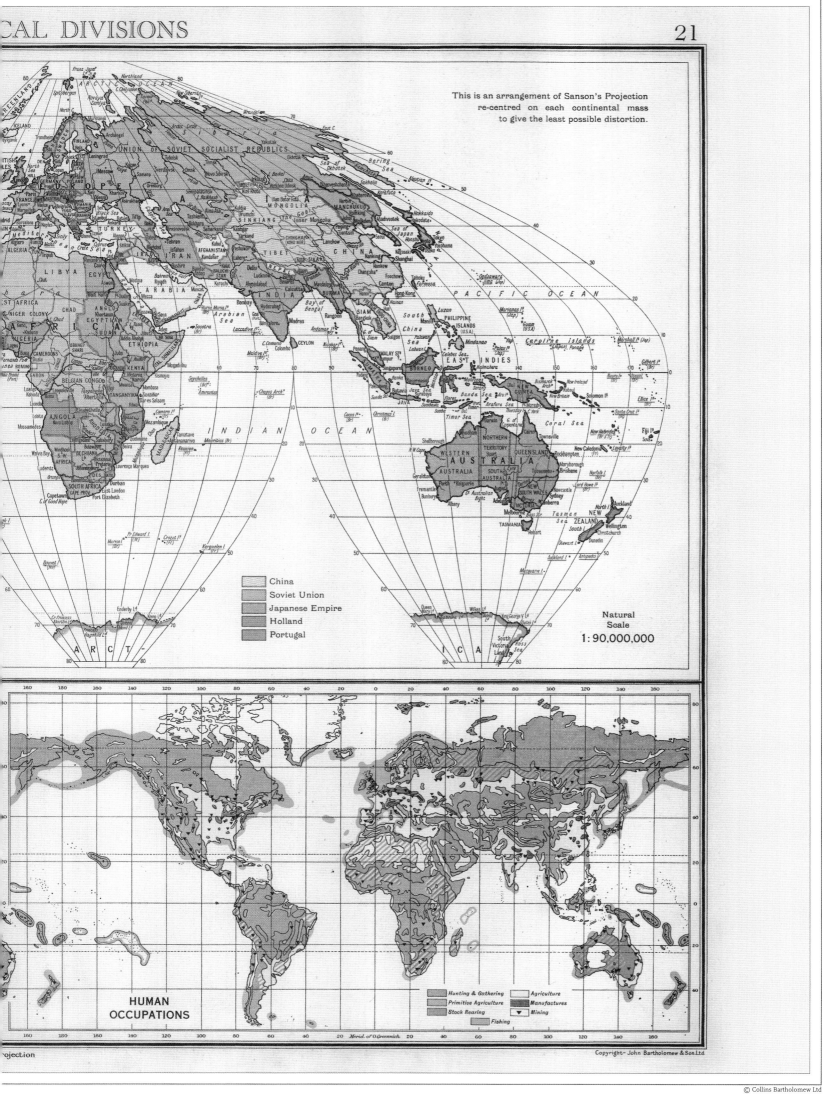

This is an arrangement of Sanson's Projection
re-centred on each continental mass
to give the least possible distortion.

China
Soviet Union
Japanese Empire
Holland
Portugal

Natural
Scale
1 : 90,000,000

**HUMAN
OCCUPATIONS**

Hunting & Gathering
Primitive Agriculture
Stock Rearing
Fishing
Agriculture
Manufactures
Mining

Copyright- John Bartholomew & Son.Ltd

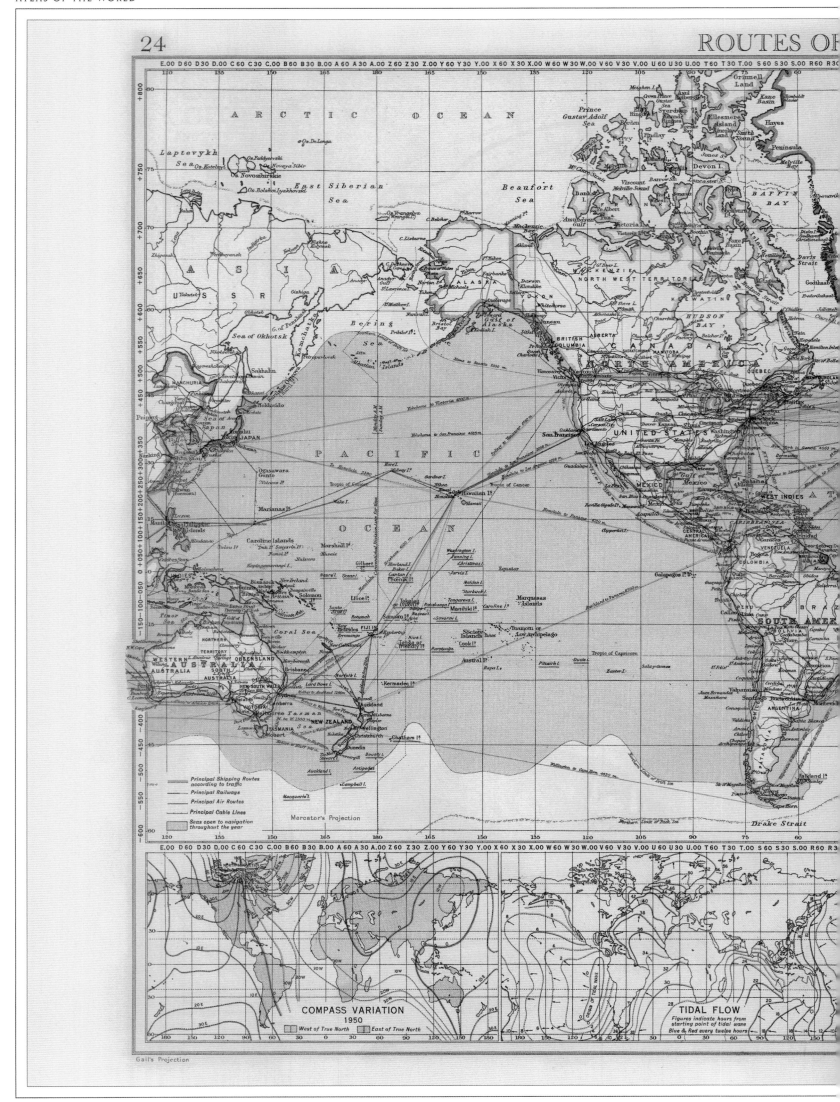

Principal Shipping Routes according to traffic
Principal Railways
Principal Air Routes
Principal Cable Lines
Seas open to navigation throughout the year

Mercator's Projection

COMPASS VARIATION
1950
☐ West of True North   ☐ East of True North

TIDAL FLOW
Figures indicate hours from starting point of tidal wave
Blue & Red every twelve hours

Gall's Projection

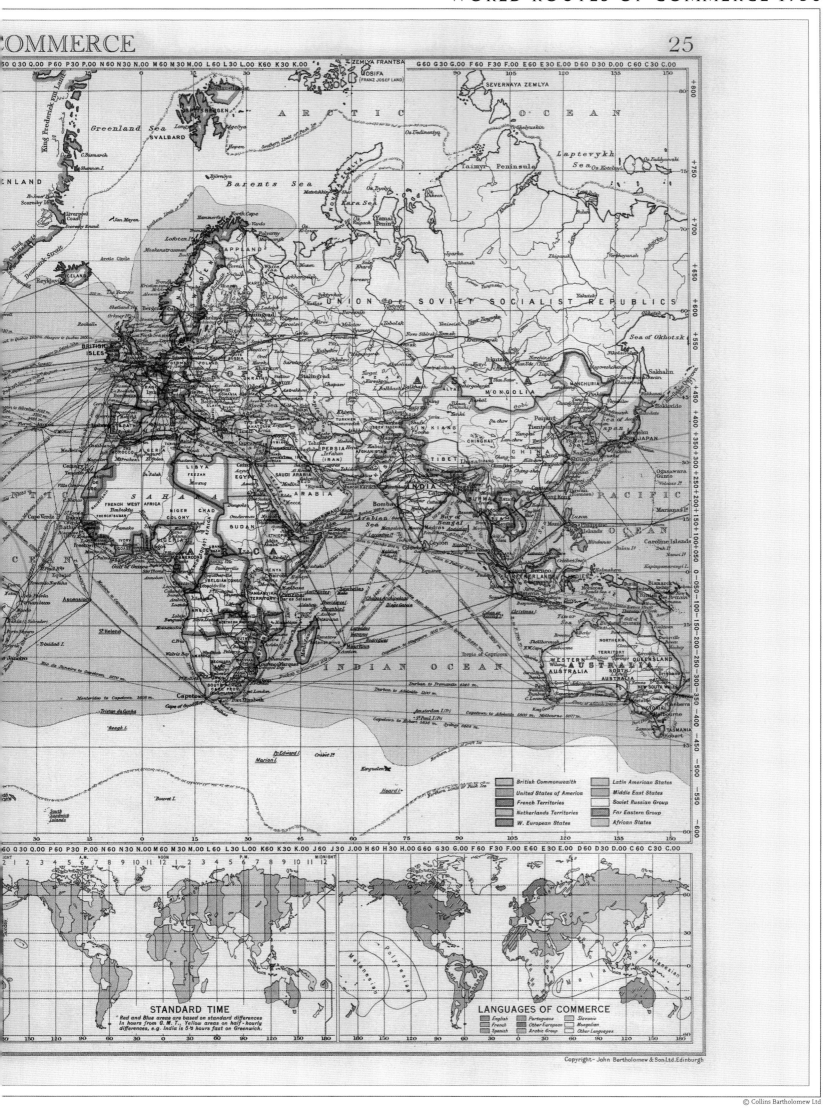

STANDARD TIME

*Red and Blue areas are based on standard differences
in hours from G.M.T. Yellow areas on half-hourly
differences, e.g. India is 5½ hours fast on Greenwich.*

LANGUAGES OF COMMERCE

English	Portuguese
French	Other European
Spanish	Arabic Group

Slavonic
Mongolian
Other Languages

British Commonwealth	Latin American States
United States of America	Middle East States
French Territories	Soviet Russian Group
Netherlands Territories	Far Eastern Group
W. European States	African States

Copyright- John Bartholomew & Son.Ltd.Edinburgh

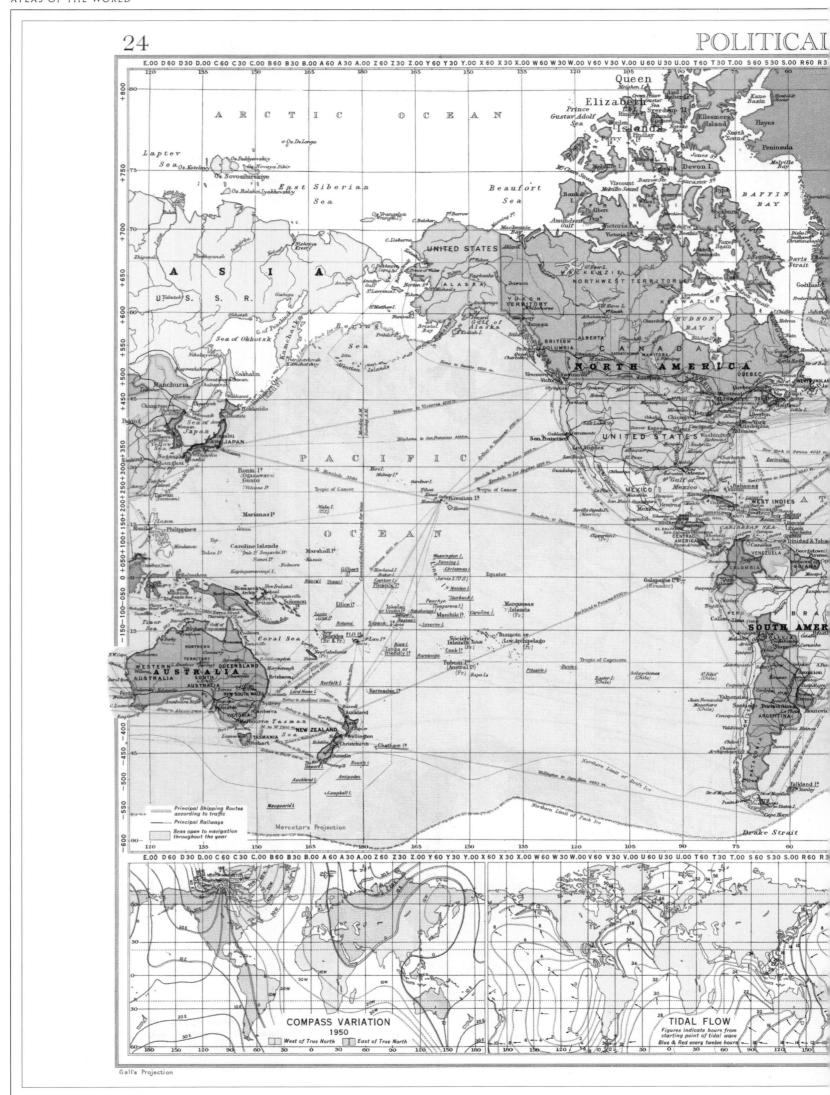

POLITICAL

COMPASS VARIATION
1950
West of True North   East of True North

TIDAL FLOW
Figures indicate hours from
starting point of tidal wave
Blue & Red every twelve hours

Principal Shipping Routes
according to traffic
Principal Railways
Seas open to navigation
throughout the year

Mercator's Projection

Gall's Projection

STANDARD TIME

Red and Blue areas are based on standard differences
in hours from G.M.T., Yellow areas on half-hourly
differences, e.g. India is 5½ hours fast on Greenwich.

LANGUAGES OF COMMERCE

English	Portuguese	Slavonic
French	Other European	Mongolian
Spanish	Arabic Group	Other Languages

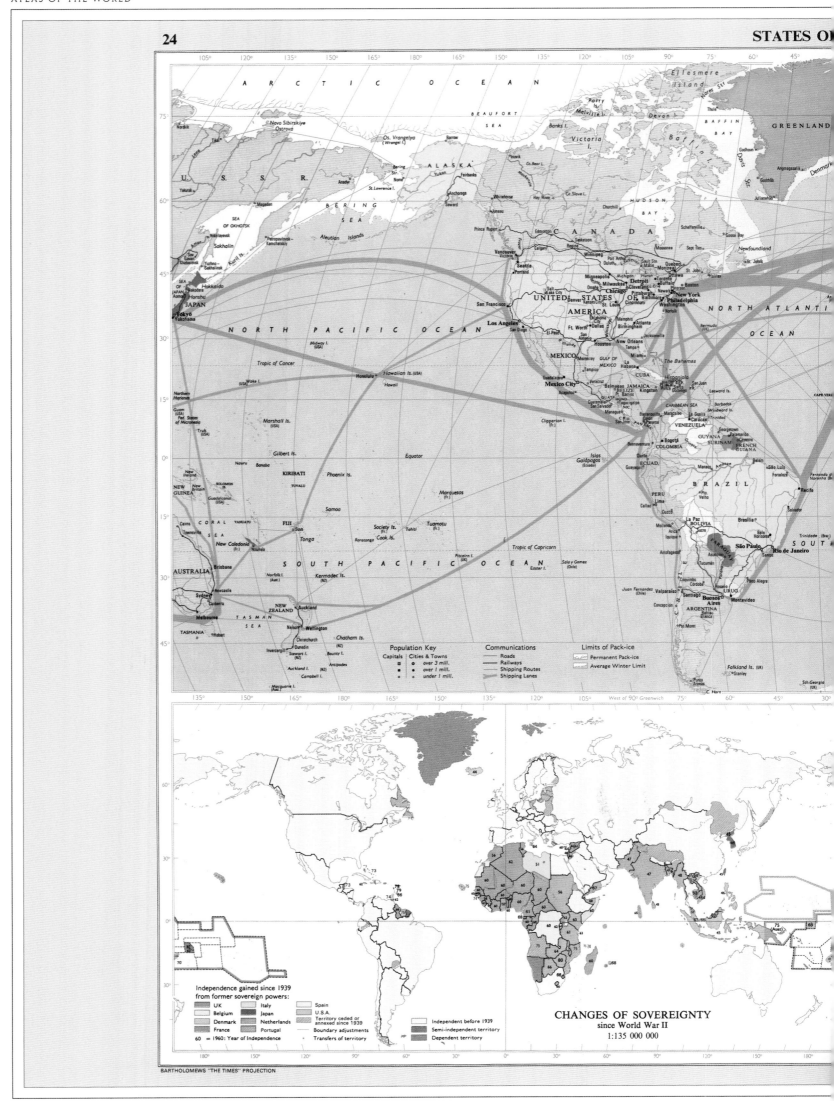

STATES O|

ARCTIC OCEAN

BEAUFORT SEA

GREENLAND

U.S.S.R.

ALASKA

BERING SEA

SEA OF OKHOTSK

CANADA

HUDSON BAY

JAPAN

Tokyo
Yokohama

NORTH PACIFIC OCEAN

UNITED STATES OF AMERICA

San Francisco

Los Angeles
San Diego

NORTH ATLANTI

OCEAN

New York
Philadelphia
Washington

Tropic of Cancer

Midway I.
(USA)

Wake I.
(USA)

Hawaiian Is. (USA)

Honolulu
Hawaii

MEXICO

GULF OF MEXICO

CUBA

The Bahamas

Hispaniola

Mexico City
Acapulco

JAMAICA
BELIZE

Guatemala

Marshall Is.
(USA)

CARIBBEAN SEA

VENEZUELA

GUYANA
SURINAM
FRENCH GUIANA

Gilbert Is.

Equator

Galápagos
(Ecuador)

COLOMBIA

ECUAD.

KIRIBATI

Phoenix Is.

TUVALU

BRAZIL

PERU
Lima

Marquesas
(Fr.)

Samoa

NEW GUINEA

SOLOMON

FIJI

Society Is.
(Fr.)

Tahiti

Tuamotu

BOLIVIA

Brasília

La Paz

New Caledonia
(Fr.)

Nouméa

Tonga

Rarotonga

Cook Is.

SOUTH

São Paulo
Rio de Janeiro

AUSTRALIA

Brisbane

CORAL SEA

VANUATU

Tropic of Capricorn

Pitcairn I.
(UK)

Easter I.
(Chile)

Sala y Gomez
(Chile)

Sydney

Newcastle

Canberra

SOUTH PACIFIC OCEAN

ARGENTINA

Melbourne

TASMAN SEA

NEW ZEALAND

Auckland

Norfolk I.
(Aust.)

Kermadec Is.
(NZ)

Valparaíso
(Chile)

Santiago

Buenos Aires

URUG.

Montevideo

TASMANIA

Hobart

Christchurch

Dunedin

Wellington

Chatham Is.
(NZ)

Falkland Is. (UK)

Stanley

Population Key

Capitals | **Cities & Towns**
over 3 mill.
over 1 mill.
under 1 mill.

Communications

Roads
Railways
Shipping Routes
Shipping Lanes

Limits of Pack-ice

Permanent Pack-ice
Average Winter Limit

West of 90° Greenwich

CHANGES OF SOVEREIGNTY
since World War II
1:135 000 000

Independence gained since 1939
from former sovereign powers:

UK
Belgium
Denmark
France

Italy
Japan
Netherlands
Portugal

Spain
U.S.A.
Territory ceded or
annexed since 1939
Boundary adjustments
Transfers of territory

60 = 1960: Year of Independence

Independent before 1939
Semi-independent territory
Dependent territory

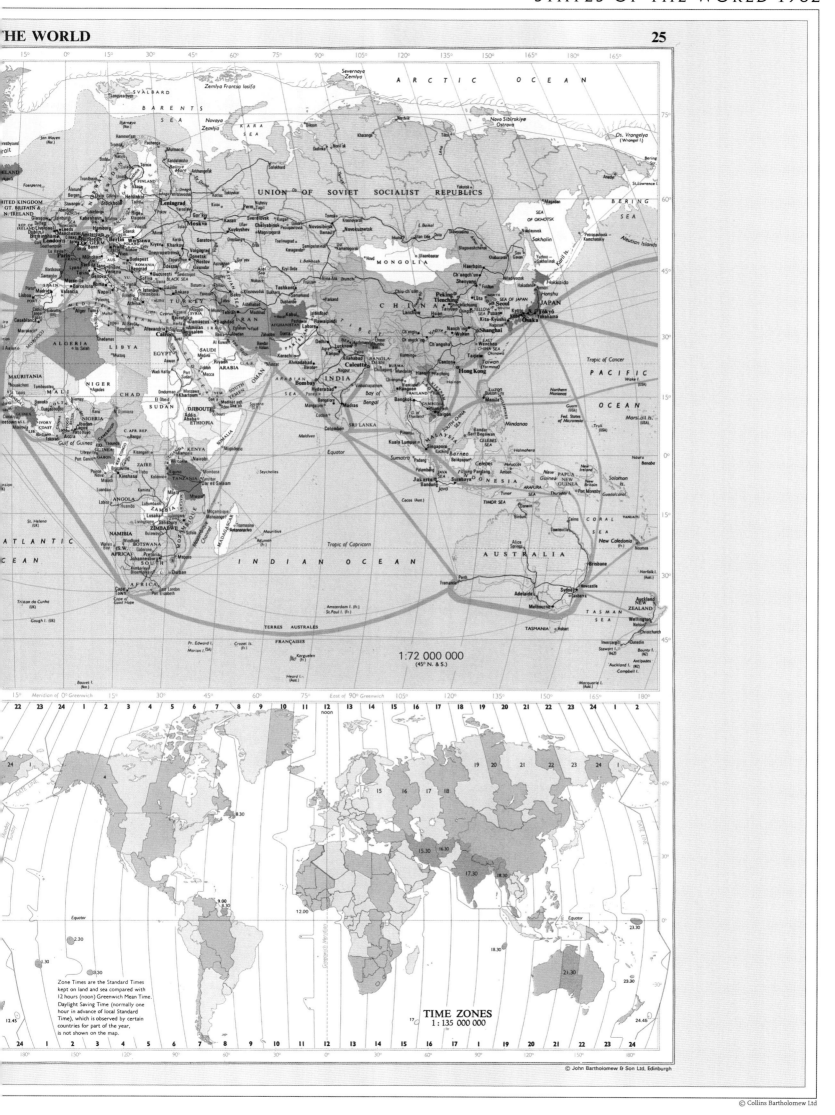

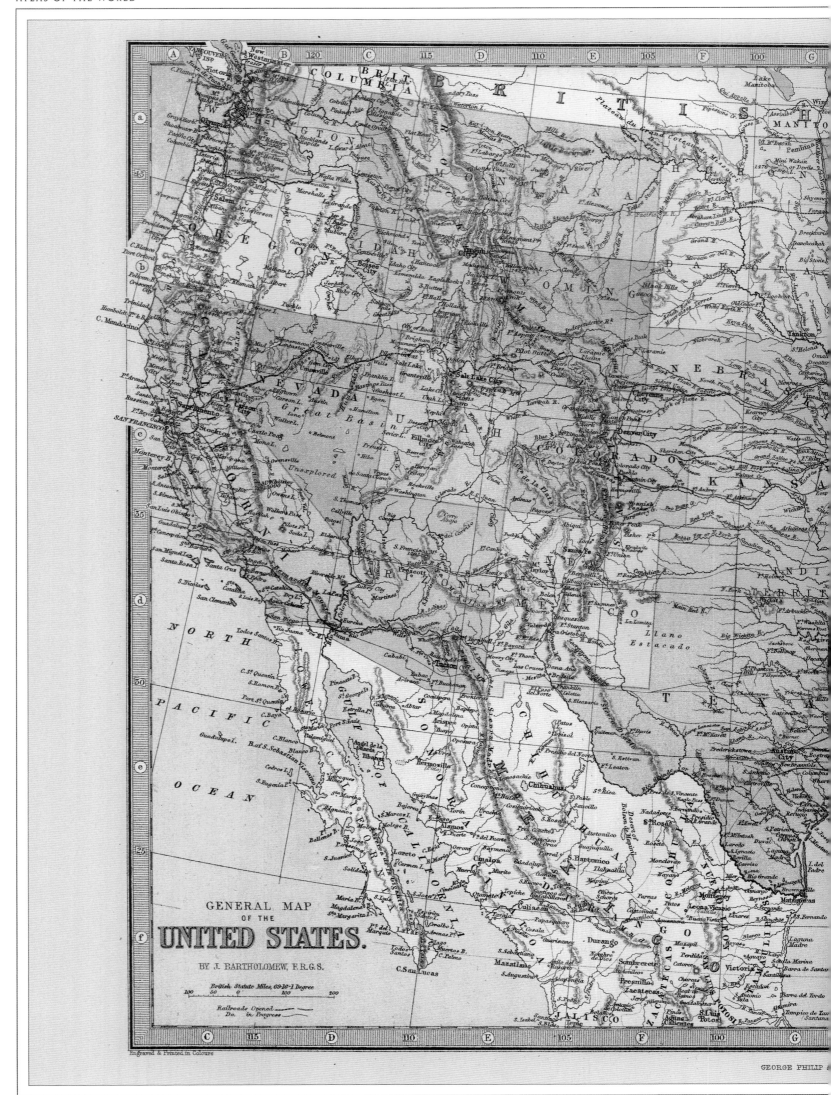

GENERAL MAP
OF THE
UNITED STATES.

BY J. BARTHOLOMEW, F.R.G.S.

British Statute Miles, 69·16·1 Degree
100   50   0   100   200

Railroads Opened
Do.   in Progress

Engraved & Printed in Colours

GEORGE PHILIP &

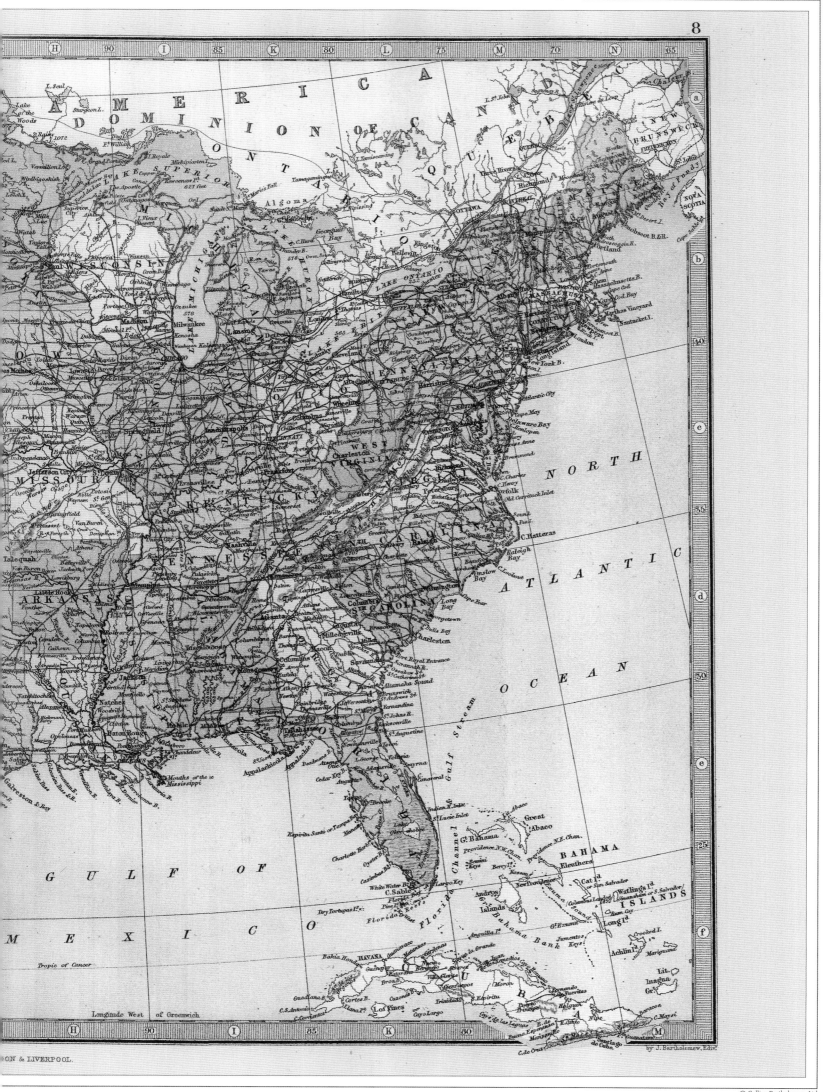

WEST AFRICA

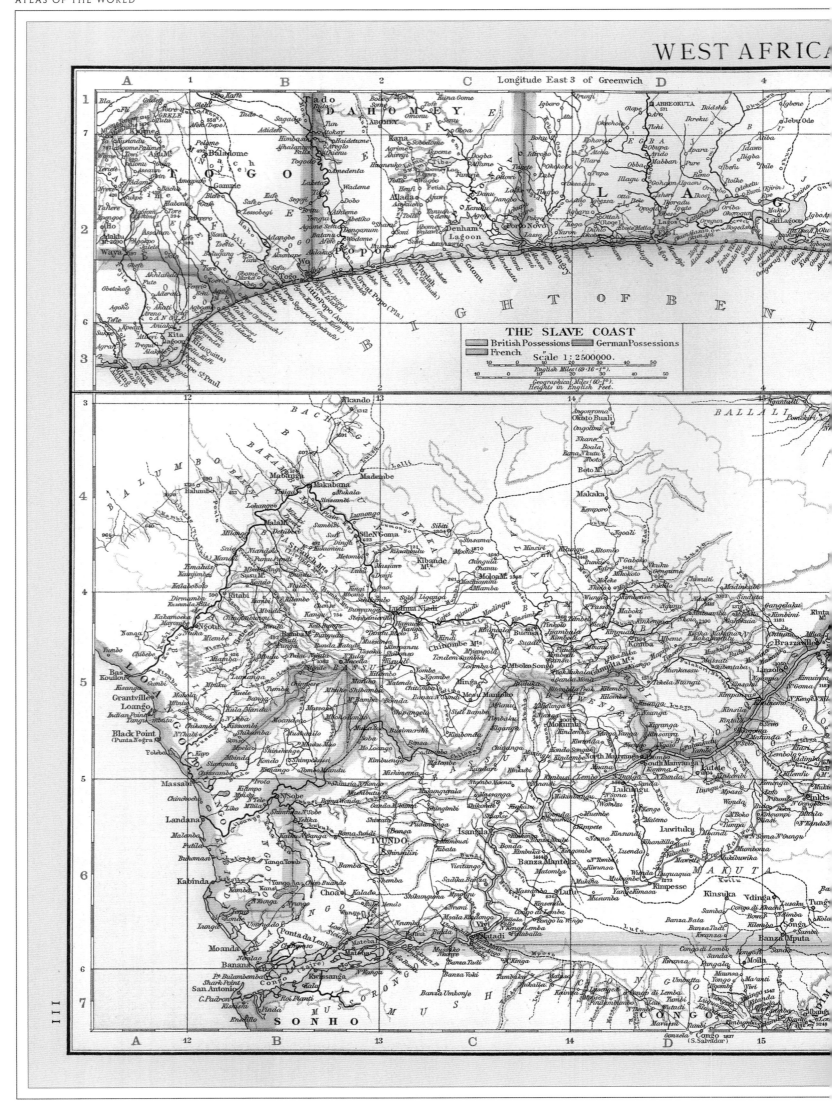

Longitude East 3 of Greenwich

THE SLAVE COAST
British Possessions   German Possessions
French   Scale 1 : 2500000.

English Miles (69·16 = 1°).
Geographical Miles (60 = 1°).
Heights in English Feet.

COLONIAL MAP

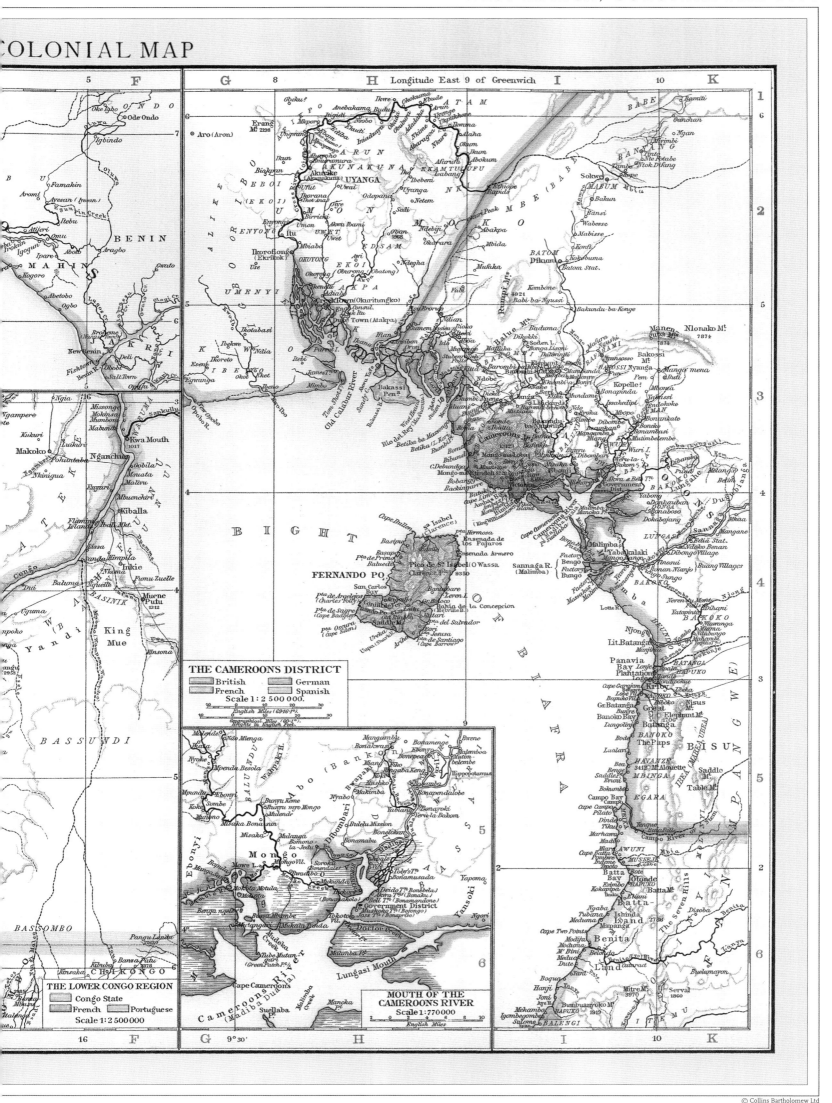

THE CAMEROONS DISTRICT
British
French
German
Spanish
Scale 1 : 2 500 000

MOUTH OF THE
CAMEROONS RIVER
Scale 1 : 770 000

THE LOWER CONGO REGION
Congo State
French
Portuguese
Scale 1 : 2 500 000

© Collins Bartholomew Ltd

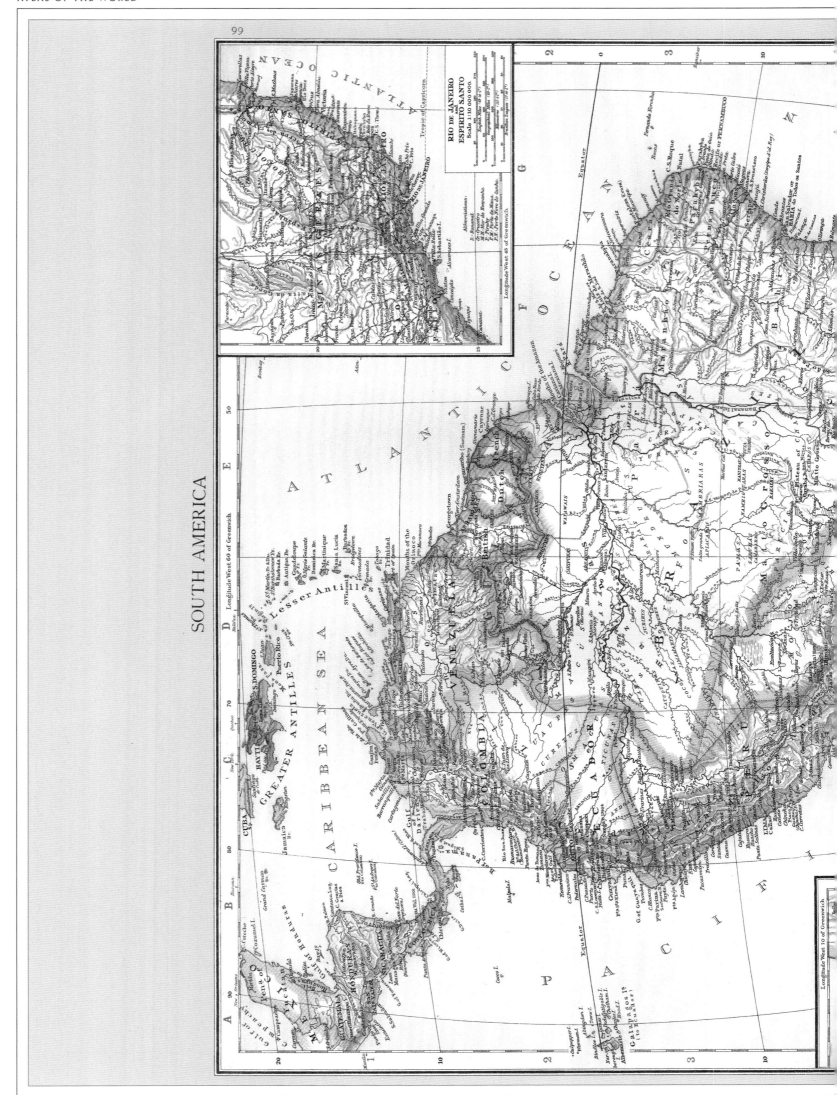

SOUTH AMERICA

RIO DE JANEIRO
ESPIRITO SANTO
Scale 1:10 000 000.

ATLANTIC OCEAN

CARIBBEAN SEA

GREATER ANTILLES

Lesser Antilles

ATLANTIC OCEAN

VENEZUELA

COLOMBIA

PACIFIC

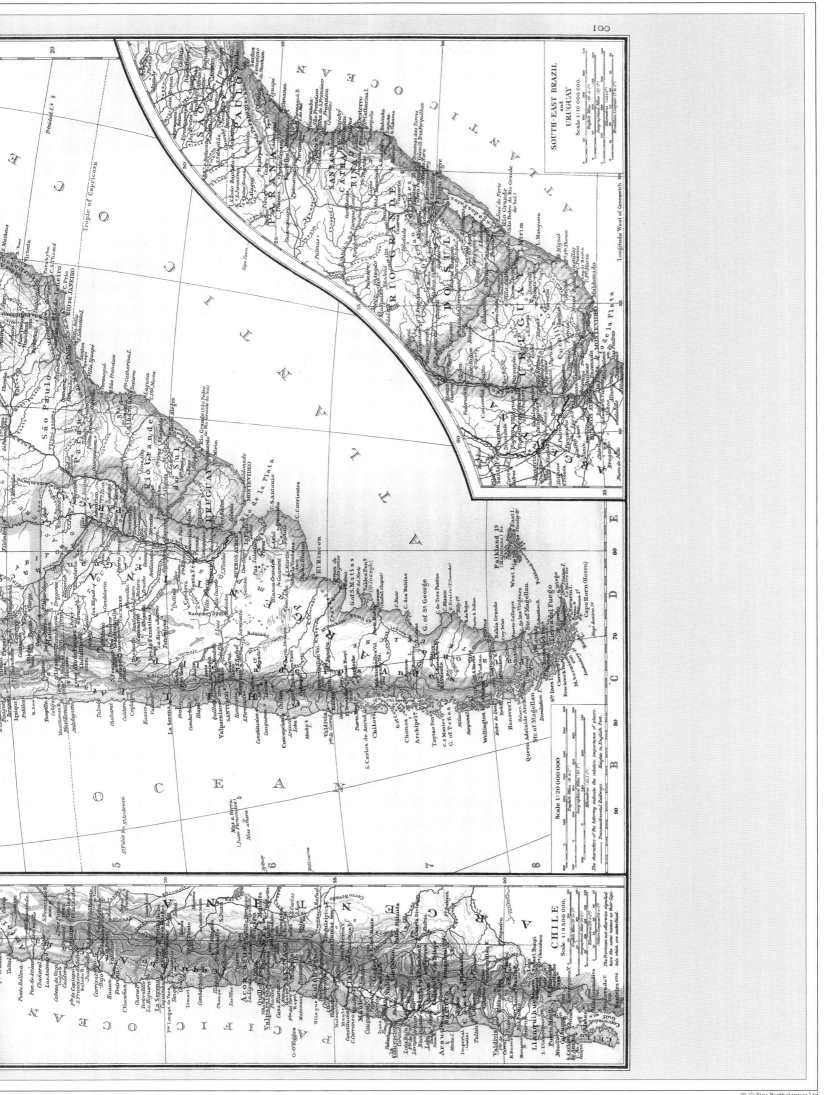

SOUTH-EAST BRAZIL
and
URUGUAY
Scale 1:10 000 000

Scale 1:20 000 000

CHILE
Scale 1:9 500 000

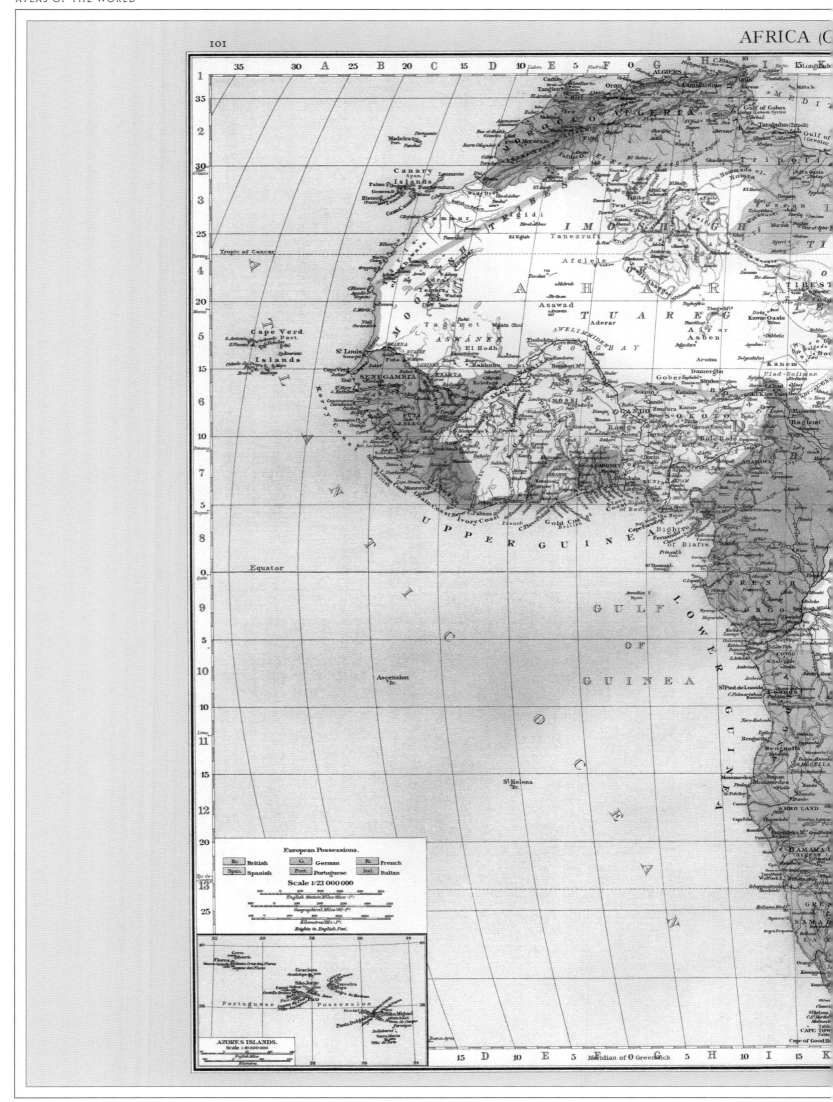

ERAL MAP)

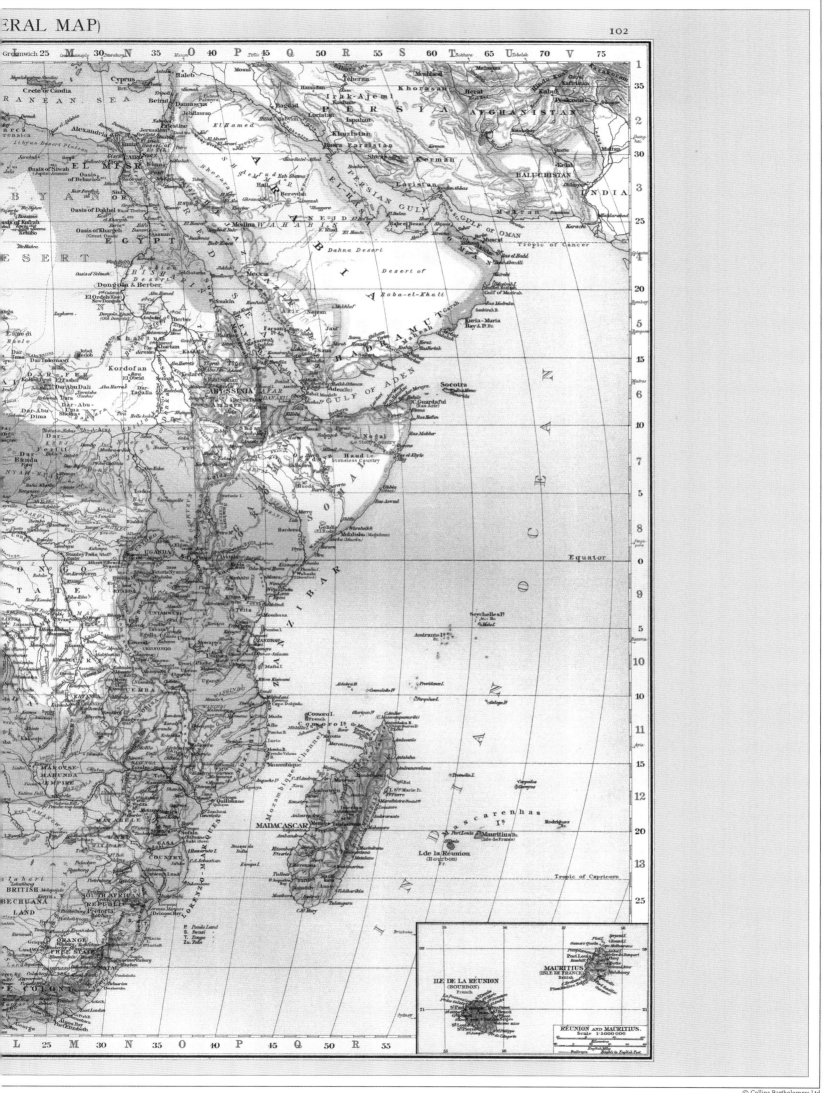

REUNION AND MAURITIUS.
Scale 1:5 000 000

ILE DE LA RÉUNION
(BOURBON)
French

MAURITIUS
(ISLE DE FRANCE)
British

NORTH POLAR REGIONS

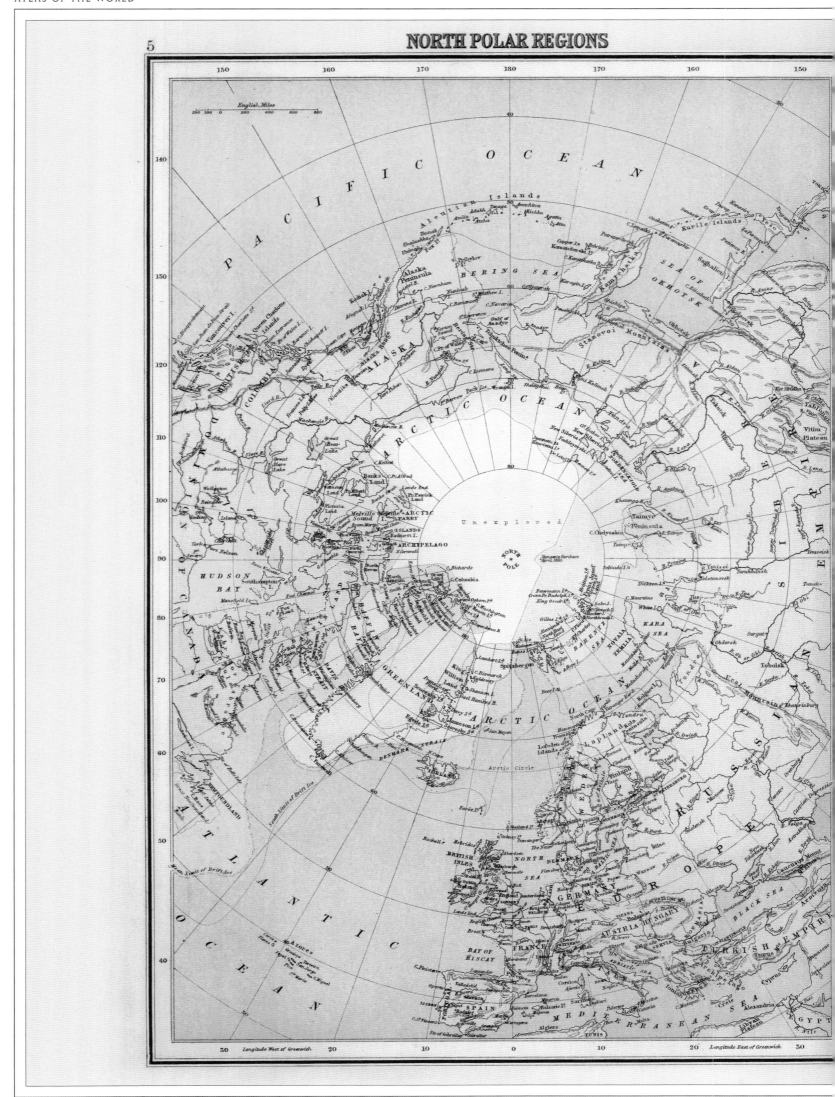

SOUTH POLAR REGIONS

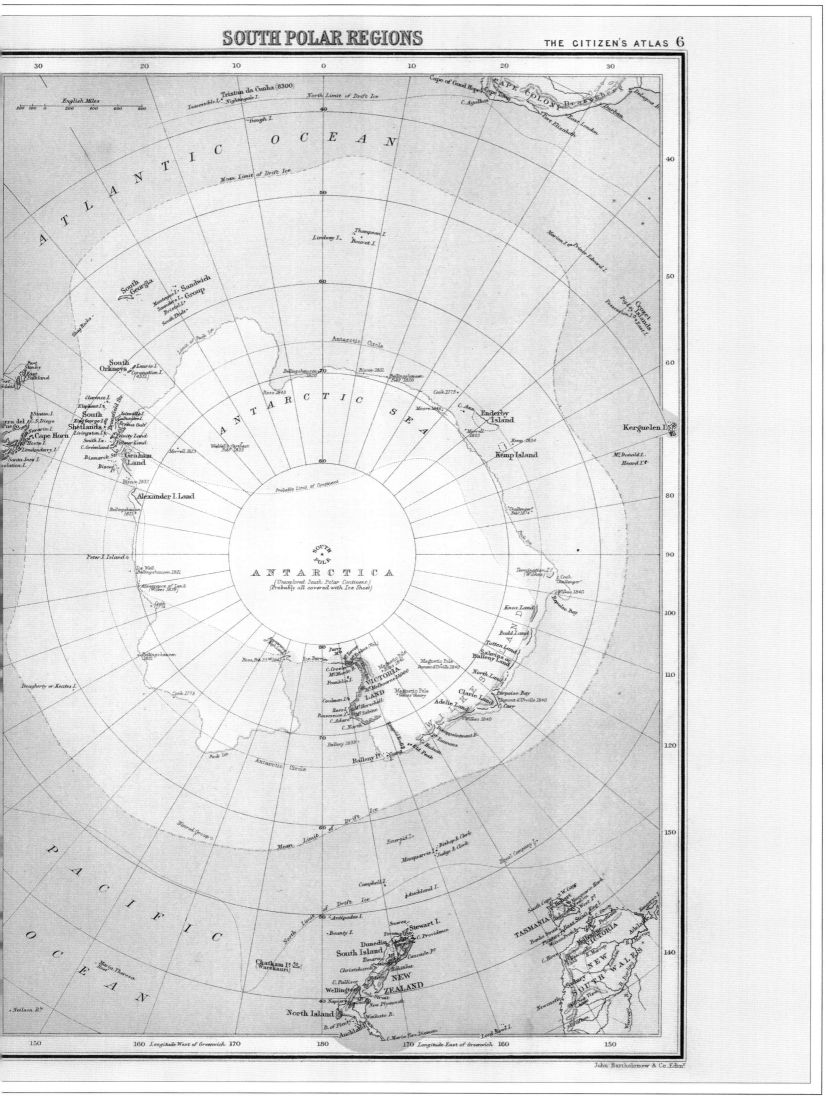

ATLANTIC OCEAN

ANTARCTIC SEA

ANTARCTICA
(Unexplored South Polar Continent)
(Probably all covered with Ice Sheet)

SOUTH POLE

VICTORIA LAND

PACIFIC OCEAN

NEW ZEALAND

TASMANIA

ALIA

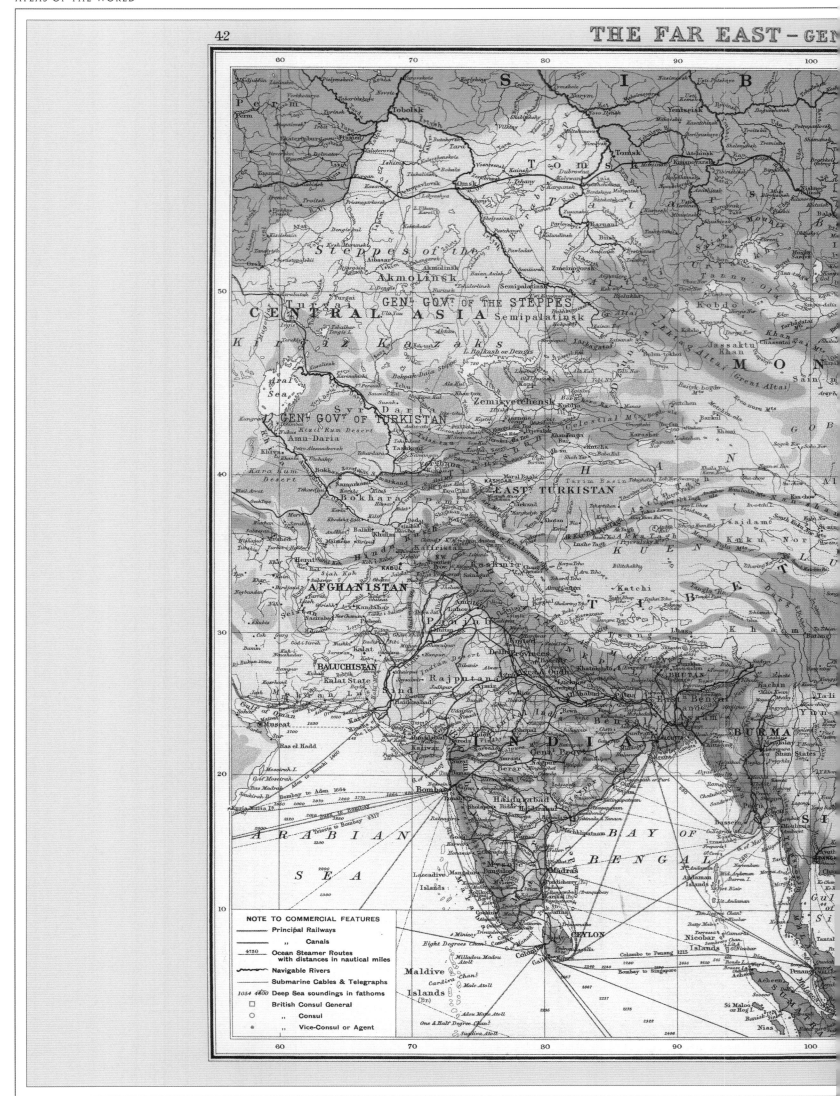

NOTE TO COMMERCIAL FEATURES

——————	Principal Railways
„	Canals
4750	Ocean Steamer Routes with distances in nautical miles
	Navigable Rivers
------------	Submarine Cables & Telegraphs
1054 4600	Deep Sea soundings in fathoms
□	British Consul General
○	„ Consul
•	„ Vice-Consul or Agent

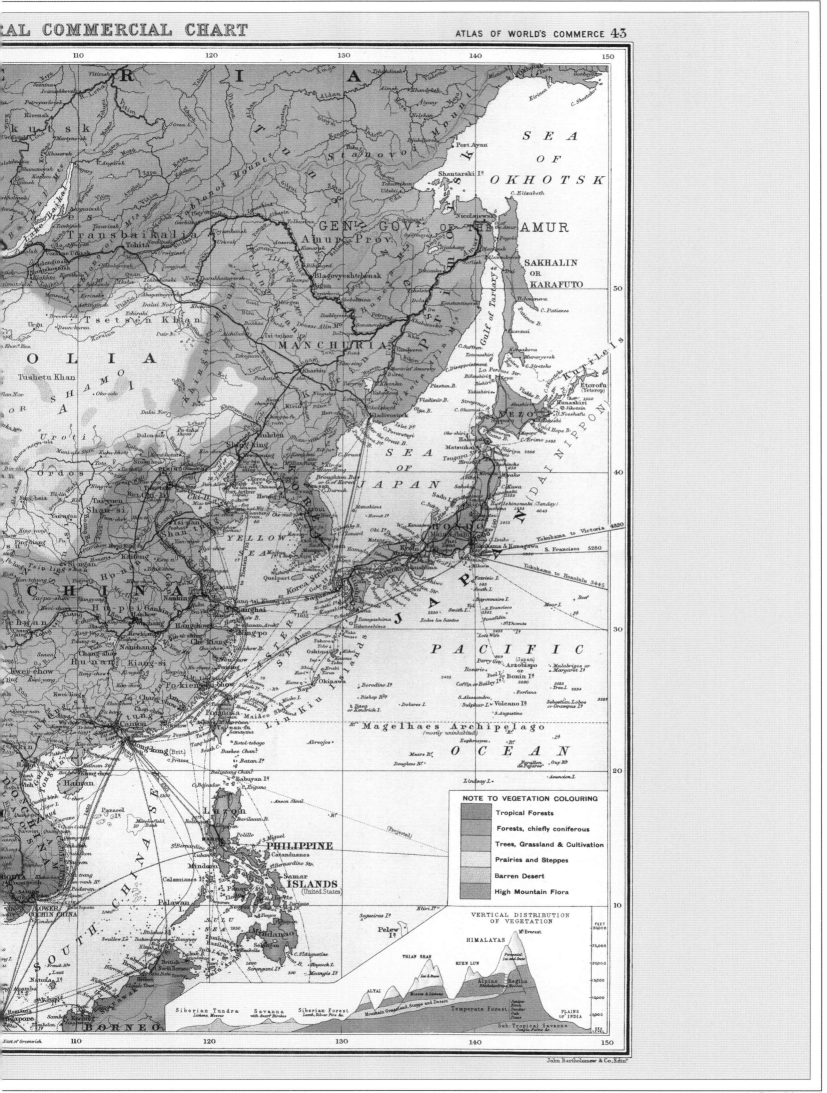

NOTE TO VEGETATION COLOURING

Tropical Forests

Forests, chiefly coniferous

Trees, Grassland & Cultivation

Prairies and Steppes

Barren Desert

High Mountain Flora

VERTICAL DISTRIBUTION
OF VEGETATION

John Bartholomew & Co. Edinr

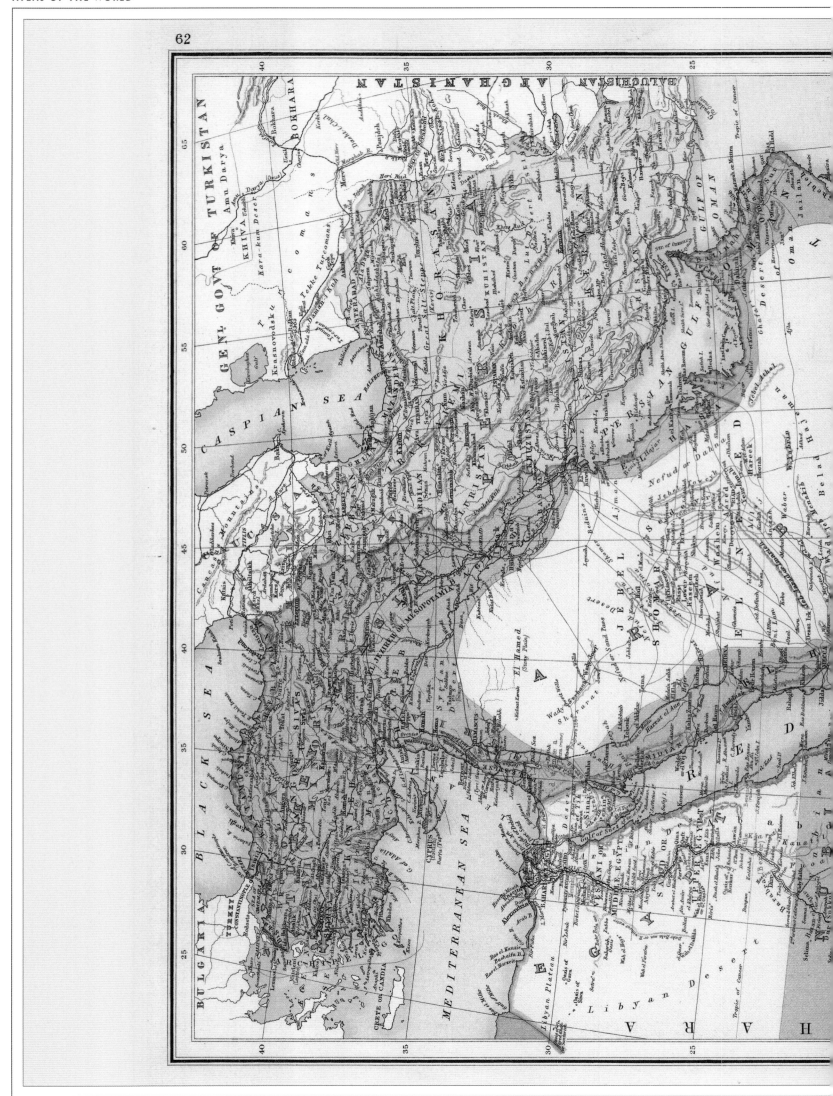

62

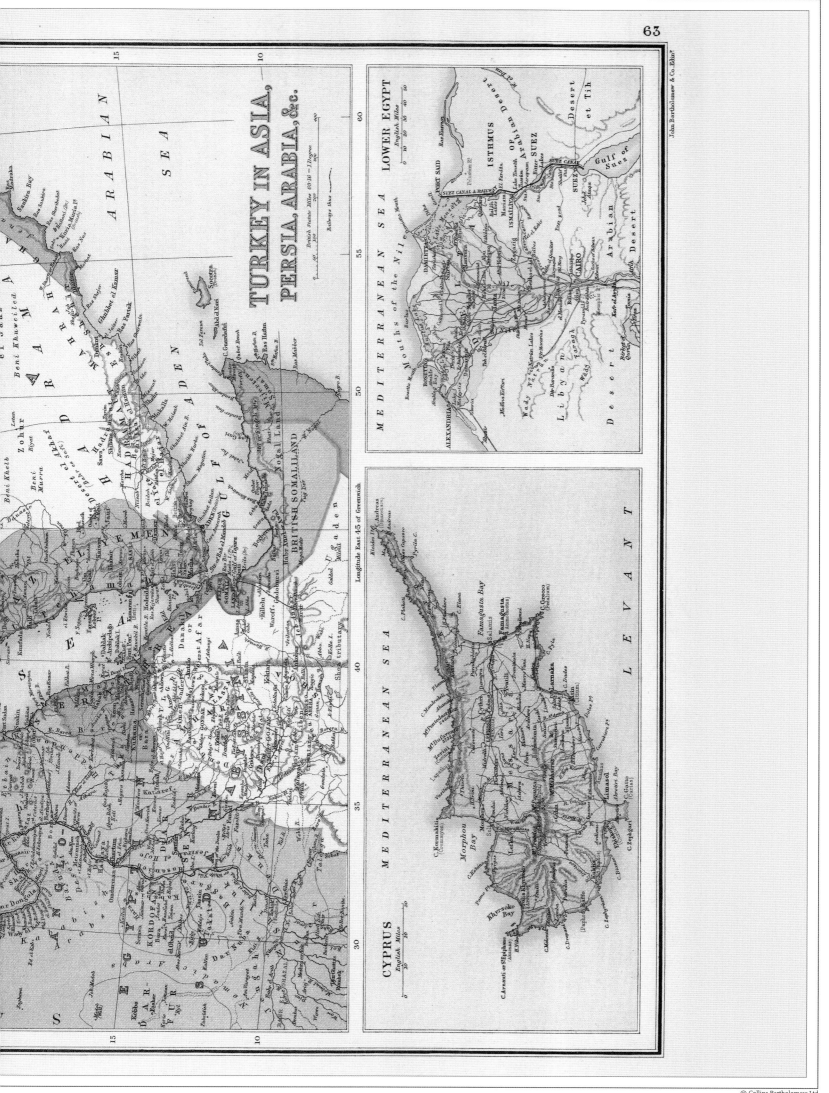

TURKEY IN ASIA, PERSIA, ARABIA, &c.

British Statute Miles 69·16 = 1 Degree

Railways thus

LOWER EGYPT

MEDITERRANEAN SEA

English Miles

CYPRUS

MEDITERRANEAN SEA

English Miles

LEVANT

John Bartholomew & Co. Edin.r

POLITICAL

PLATE 10

JOHN BARTHOLOMEW & SON, LTD.

WORLD POWERS 1957

THE TIMES ATLAS

Frontispiece Vol. I

THE "ATLANTIS" PROJECTION
*A Transverse Oblique Homolographic
Equal-Area Arrangement*
By John Bartholomew, M.C., LL.D.

1:90,000,000

UNITED NATIONS ORGANISATION

	U.N.O. Member States	Non-Member States
WESTERN ALLIANCES		
COMMUNIST STATES		
ARAB-MUSLIM LANDS		
OTHER LANDS		

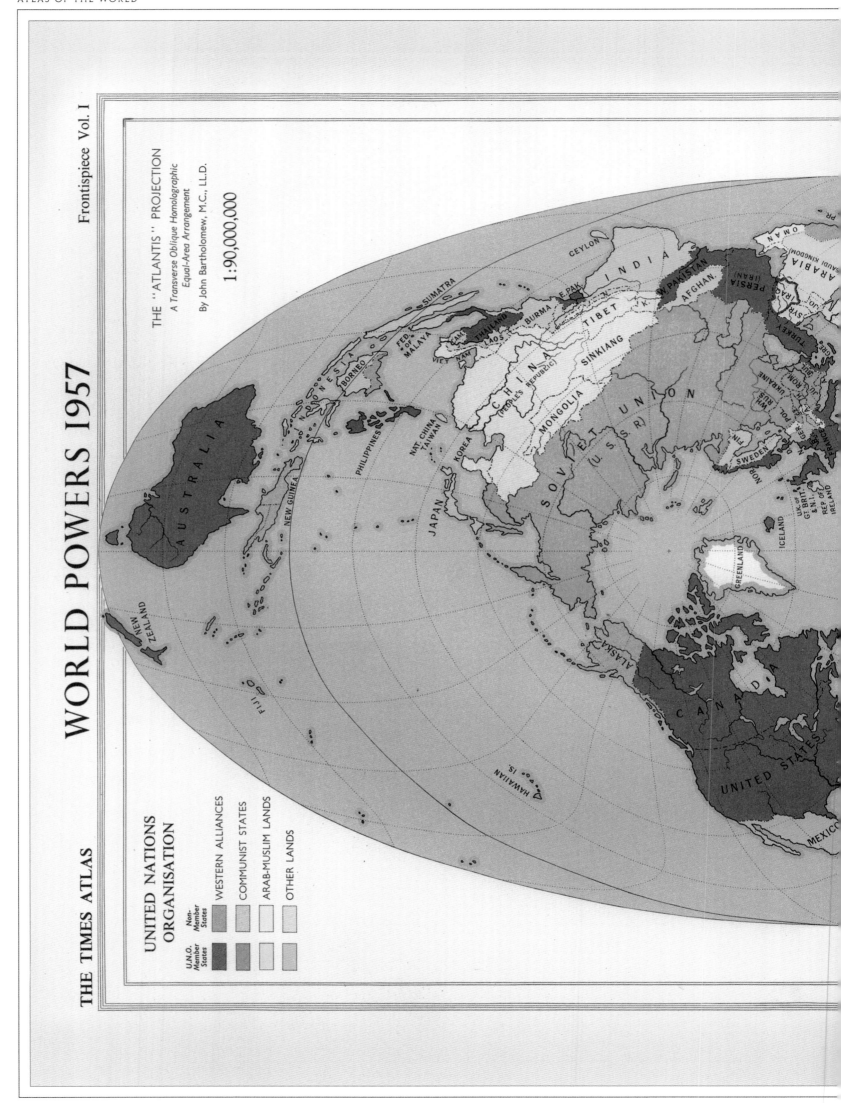

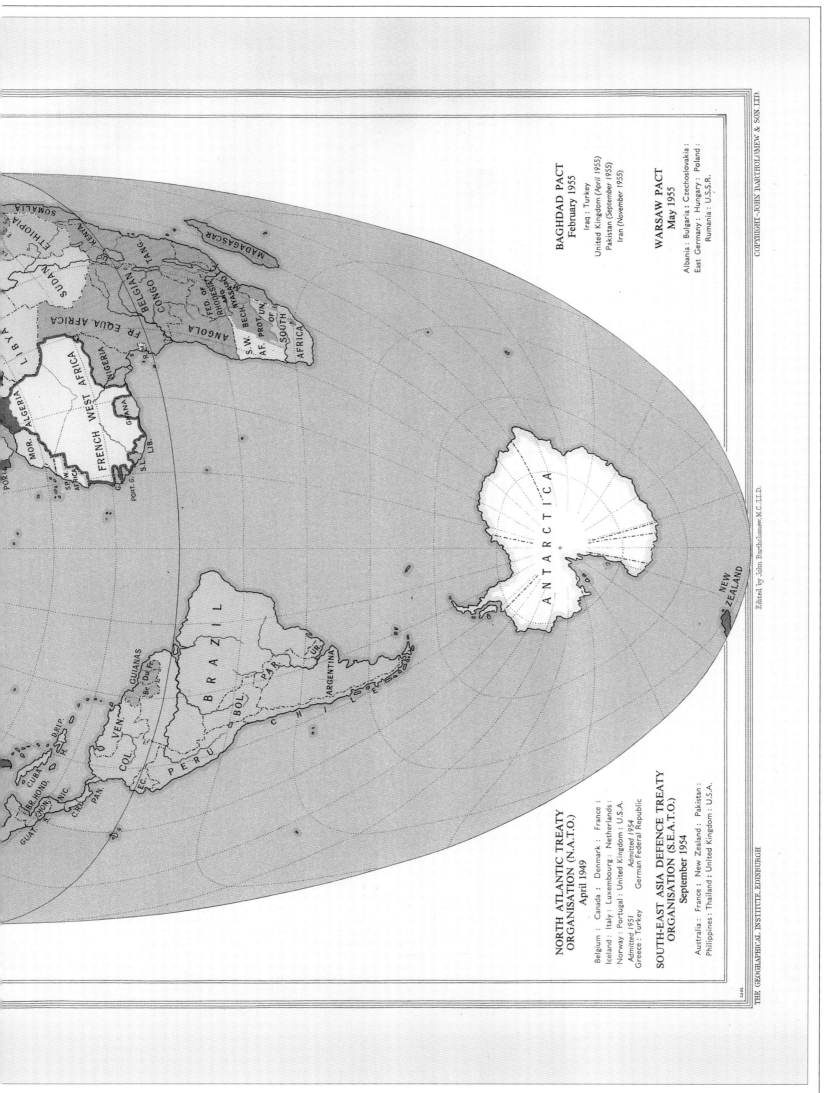

BAGHDAD PACT
February 1955

Iraq : Turkey
United Kingdom (April 1955)
Pakistan (September 1955)
Iran (November 1955)

WARSAW PACT
May 1955

Albania : Bulgaria : Czechoslovakia :
East Germany : Hungary : Poland :
Rumania : U.S.S.R.

NORTH ATLANTIC TREATY
ORGANISATION (N.A.T.O.)
April 1949

Belgium : Canada : Denmark : France :
Iceland : Italy : Luxembourg : Netherlands :
Norway : Portugal : United Kingdom : U.S.A.
Admitted 1951   Admitted 1954
Greece : Turkey   German Federal Republic

SOUTH-EAST ASIA DEFENCE TREATY
ORGANISATION (S.E.A.T.O.)
September 1954

Australia : France : New Zealand : Pakistan :
Philippines : Thailand : United Kingdom : U.S.A.

THE GEOGRAPHICAL INSTITUTE, EDINBURGH

Edited by John Bartholomew, M.C, LL.D.

COPYRIGHT.-JOHN BARTHOLOMEW & SON, LTD.

STATES AND TERRITORIES

All 196 independent countries and all populated dependent and disputed territories are included in this list of the states and territories of the world; the list is arranged in alphabetical order by the conventional name form. For independent states, the full name is given below the conventional name, if this is different; for territories, the status is given. The capital city name is given in conventional English form with selected alternative, usually local, form in brackets.

Area and population statistics are the latest available and include estimates. The information on languages and religions is based on the latest information on 'de facto' speakers of the language or 'de facto' adherents of the religion. This varies greatly from country to country because some countries include questions in censuses while others do not, in which case best estimates are used. The order of the languages and religions reflects their relative importance within the country; generally, languages or religions are included when more than one per cent of the population are estimated to be speakers or adherents.

ABBREVIATIONS

CURRENCIES

CFA	Communauté Financière Africaine
CFP	Comptoirs Français du Pacifique

Membership of selected international organizations is shown by the abbreviations below; dependent territories do not normally have separate memberships of these organizations.

ORGANIZATIONS

APEC	Asia-Pacific Economic Cooperation
ASEAN	Association of Southeast Asian Nations
CARICOM	Caribbean Community
CIS	Commonwealth of Independent States
Comm.	The Commonwealth
EU	European Union
GCC	Gulf Cooperation Council
NATO	North Atlantic Treaty Organization
OECD	Organisation for Economic Co-operation and Development
OPEC	Organization of the Petroleum Exporting Countries
SADC	Southern African Development Community
UN	United Nations

Abkhazia
Disputed territory

Area Sq Km	8 700	**Languages**	Abkhaz, Russian, Georgian
Area Sq Miles	3 359	**Religions**	Abkhaz Orthodox Christianity, Sunni Muslim
Population	180 000		
Capital	Sokhumi (Aq"a)	**Currency**	Russian rouble, Abkhaz apsar

Map page 173 An autonomous republic within Georgia, Abkhazia has an active separatist movement seeking independence from Georgia. Although it is de jure part of Georgia, it effectively currently functions as an independent state with backing from Russia. This dispute has led to intermittent, but serious, armed conflict over the last twenty years. Abkhazia voted to separate from Georgia in 1992, a move rejected by Georgia and prompting a Georgian invasion. Abkhazian and Russian forces ousted Georgia and a cease-fire was established in 1994.

AFGHANISTAN
Islamic Republic of Afghanistan

Area Sq Km	652 225	**Languages**	Dari, Pashtu (Pushtu), Uzbek, Turkmen
Area Sq Miles	251 825		
Population	30 552 000	**Religions**	Sunni Muslim, Shi'a Muslim
Capital	Kābul	**Currency**	Afghani
		Organizations	UN

Map page 141

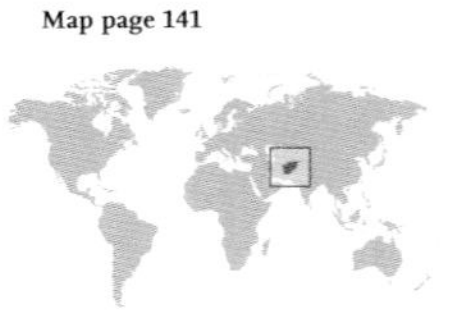

A landlocked country in central Asia with central highlands bordered by plains in the north and southwest, and by the mountains of the Hindu Kush in the northeast. The climate is dry continental. Over the last thirty years war has disrupted the economy, which is highly dependent on farming and livestock rearing. Most trade is with the former USSR, Pakistan and Iran.

ALBANIA
Republic of Albania

Area Sq Km	28 748	**Languages**	Albanian, Greek
Area Sq Miles	11 100	**Religions**	Sunni Muslim, Albanian Orthodox, Roman Catholic
Population	3 173 000		
Capital	Tirana (Tiranë)	**Currency**	Lek
		Organizations	NATO, UN

Map page 171

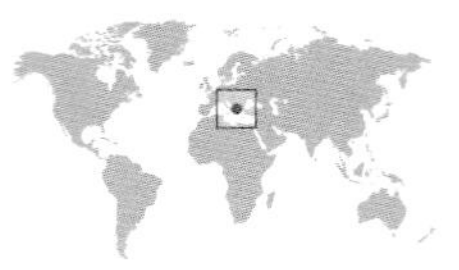

Albania lies in the western Balkan Mountains in southeastern Europe, bordering the Adriatic Sea. It is mountainous, with coastal plains where half the population lives. The economy is based on agriculture and mining. Albania is one of the poorest countries in Europe and relies heavily on foreign aid.

ALGERIA
People's Democratic Republic of Algeria

Area Sq Km	2 381 741	**Languages**	Arabic, French, Berber
Area Sq Miles	919 595	**Religions**	Sunni Muslim
Population	39 208 000	**Currency**	Algerian dinar
Capital	Algiers (Alger)	**Organizations**	OPEC, UN

Map page 176

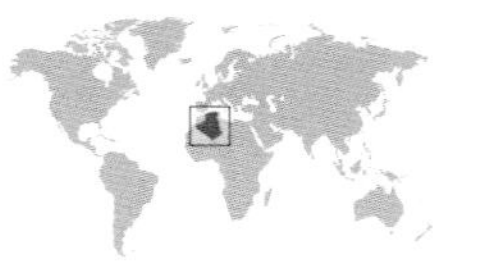

Algeria, the largest country in Africa, lies on the Mediterranean coast of northwest Africa and extends southwards to the Atlas Mountains and the dry sandstone plateau and desert of the Sahara. The climate ranges from Mediterranean on the coast to semi-arid and arid inland. The most populated areas are the coastal plains and the fertile northern slopes of the Atlas Mountains. Oil, natural gas and related products account for over ninety per cent of export earnings. Agriculture employs about a fifth of the workforce, producing mainly food crops. Algeria's main trading partners are Italy, France and the USA.

American Samoa
United States Unincorporated Territory

Area Sq Km	197	**Languages**	Samoan, English
Area Sq Miles	76	**Religions**	Protestant, Roman Catholic
Population	55 000	**Currency**	United States dollar
Capital	Fagatogo		

Map page 123

Lying in the south Pacific Ocean, American Samoa consists of five main islands and two coral atolls. The largest island is Tutuila. Tuna and tuna products are the main exports, and the main trading partner is the USA.

ANDORRA
Principality of Andorra

Area Sq Km	465	**Languages**	Catalan, Spanish, French
Area Sq Miles	180	**Religions**	Roman Catholic
Population	79 000	**Currency**	Euro
Capital	Andorra la Vella	**Organizations**	UN

Map page 167

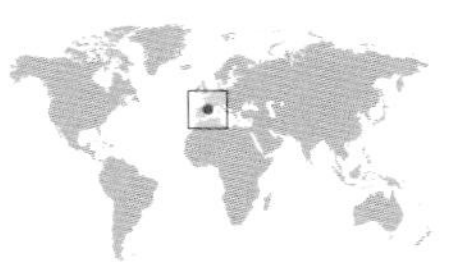

A landlocked state in southwest Europe, Andorra lies in the Pyrenees mountain range between France and Spain. It consists of deep valleys and gorges, surrounded by mountains. Tourism, encouraged by the development of ski resorts, is the mainstay of the economy. Banking is also an important economic activity.

ANGOLA
Republic of Angola

Area Sq Km	1 246 700	**Languages**	Portuguese, Bantu, other local languages
Area Sq Miles	481 354		
Population	21 472 000	**Religions**	Roman Catholic, Protestant, traditional beliefs
Capital	Luanda		
		Currency	Kwanza
		Organizations	OPEC, SADC, UN

Map page 178–179

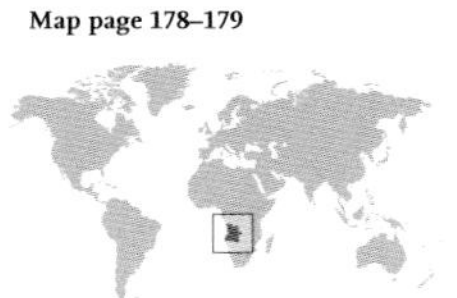

Angola lies on the Atlantic coast of south central Africa. Its small northern province, Cabinda, is separated from the rest of the country by part of the Democratic Republic of the Congo. Much of Angola is high plateau. In the west is a narrow coastal plain and in the southwest is desert. The climate is equatorial in the north but desert in the south. Around seventy per cent of the population relies on subsistence agriculture. Angola is rich in minerals (particularly diamonds), and oil accounts for approximately ninety per cent of export earnings. The USA, South Korea and Portugal are its main trading partners.

Anguilla
United Kingdom Overseas Territory

Area Sq Km	155	**Languages**	English
Area Sq Miles	60	**Religions**	Protestant, Roman Catholic
Population	14 000	**Currency**	East Caribbean dollar
Capital	The Valley		

Map page 205 Anguilla lies at the northern end of the Leeward Islands in the eastern Caribbean. Tourism and fishing form the basis of the economy.

ANTIGUA AND BARBUDA

Area Sq Km	442	**Languages**	English, Creole
Area Sq Miles	171	**Religions**	Protestant, Roman Catholic
Population	90 000	**Currency**	East Caribbean dollar
Capital	St John's	**Organizations**	CARICOM, Comm., UN

Map page 205

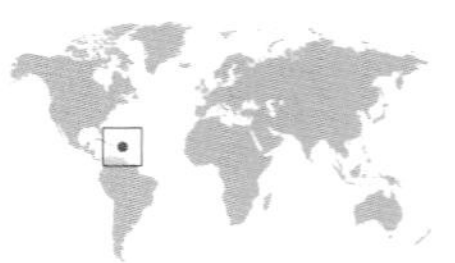

The state comprises the islands of Antigua, Barbuda and the tiny rocky outcrop of Redonda, in the Leeward Islands in the eastern Caribbean. Antigua, the largest and most populous island, is mainly hilly scrubland, with many beaches. The climate is tropical, and the economy relies heavily on tourism. Most trade is with other eastern Caribbean states and the USA.

ARGENTINA
Argentine Republic

Area Sq Km	2 766 889	**Languages**	Spanish, Italian, Amerindian languages
Area Sq Miles	1 068 302		
Population	41 446 000	**Religions**	Roman Catholic, Protestant
Capital	Buenos Aires	**Currency**	Argentinian peso
		Organizations	UN

Map page 212

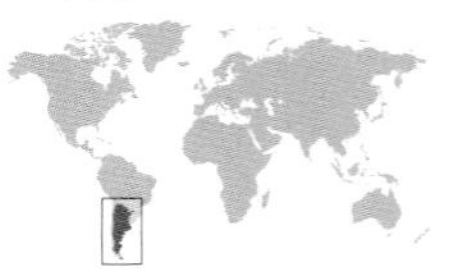

Argentina, the second largest state in South America, extends from Bolivia to Cape Horn and from the Andes mountains to the Atlantic Ocean. It has four geographical regions: subtropical forests and swampland in the northeast; temperate fertile plains or Pampas in the centre; the wooded foothills and valleys of the Andes in the west; and the cold, semi-arid plateaus of Patagonia in the south. The highest mountain in South America, Cerro Aconcagua, is in Argentina. Over ninety per cent of the population lives in towns and cities. The country is rich in natural resources including petroleum, natural gas, ores and precious metals. Agricultural products dominate exports, which also include motor vehicles and crude oil. Most trade is with Brazil and the USA.

ARMENIA
Republic of Armenia

Area Sq Km	29 800	**Languages**	Armenian, Kurdish
Area Sq Miles	11 506	**Religions**	Armenian Orthodox
Population	2 977 000	**Currency**	Dram
Capital	Yerevan (Erevan)	**Organizations**	CIS, UN

Map page 137

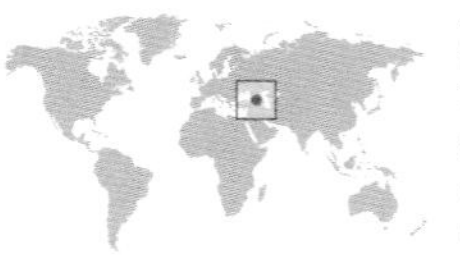

A landlocked state in southwest Asia, Armenia lies in the south of the Lesser Caucasus mountains. It is a mountainous country with a continental climate. One-third of the population lives in the capital, Yerevan. Exports include diamonds, scrap metal and machinery. Many Armenians depend on remittances from abroad.

Aruba
Self-governing Netherlands Territory

Area Sq Km	193	**Languages**	Papiamento, Dutch, English
Area Sq Miles	75	**Religions**	Roman Catholic, Protestant
Population	103 000	**Currency**	Aruban florin
Capital	Oranjestad		

Map page 213 The most southwesterly of the islands in the Lesser Antilles in the Caribbean, Aruba lies just off the coast of Venezuela. Tourism, offshore finance and oil refining are the most important sectors of the economy. The USA is the main trading partner.

AUSTRALIA
Commonwealth of Australia

Area Sq Km	7 692 024	**Languages**	English, Italian, Greek
Area Sq Miles	2 969 907	**Religions**	Protestant, Roman Catholic, Orthodox
Population	23 343 000		
Capital	Canberra	**Currency**	Australian dollar
		Organizations	APEC, Comm., OECD, UN

Map page 124

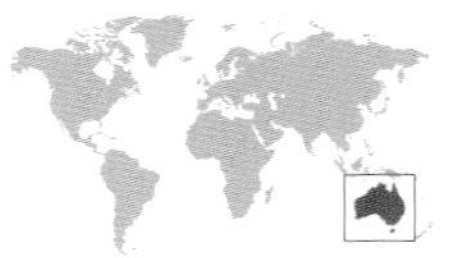

Australia, the world's sixth largest country, occupies the smallest, flattest and driest continent. The western half of the continent is mostly arid plateaus, ridges and vast deserts. The central eastern area comprises the lowlands of river systems draining into

Lake Eyre, while to the east is the Great Dividing Range, a belt of ridges and plateaus running from Queensland to Tasmania. Climatically, more than two-thirds of the country is arid or semi-arid. The north is tropical monsoon, the east subtropical, and the southwest and southeast temperate. The majority of Australia's highly urbanized population lives along the east, southeast and southwest coasts. Australia has vast mineral deposits and various sources of energy. It is among the world's leading producers of iron ore, bauxite, nickel, copper and uranium. It is a major producer of coal, and oil and natural gas are also being exploited. Although accounting for under four per cent of the workforce, agriculture continues to be an important sector of the economy, with food and agricultural raw materials making up most of Australia's export earnings. Fuel, ores and metals, and manufactured goods, account for the remainder of exports. China, Japan and the USA are Australia's main trading partners.

Australian Capital Territory (Federal Territory)
Area Sq Km (Sq Miles) 2 358 (910)   Population 379 600   Capital Canberra

Jervis Bay Territory (Territory)
Area Sq Km (Sq Miles) 73 (28)   Population 378

New South Wales (State)
Area Sq Km (Sq Miles) 800 642 (309 130)   Population 7 348 900   Capital Sydney

Northern Territory (Territory)
Area Sq Km (Sq Miles) 1 349 129 (520 902)   Population 236 900   Capital Darwin

Queensland (State)
Area Sq Km (Sq Miles) 1 730 648 (668 207)   Population 4 610 900 Capital Brisbane

South Australia (State)
Area Sq Km (Sq Miles) 983 482 (379 725)   Population 1 662 200 Capital Adelaide

Tasmania (State)
Area Sq Km (Sq Miles) 68 401 (26 410)   Population 512 400   Capital Hobart

Victoria (State)
Area Sq Km (Sq Miles) 227 416 (87 806)   Population 5 679 600 Capital Melbourne

Western Australia (State)
Area Sq Km (Sq Miles) 2 529 875 (976 790)   Population 2 472 700 Capital Perth

AUSTRIA
Republic of Austria

Area Sq Km	83 855	Languages	German, Croatian, Turkish
Area Sq Miles	32 377	Religions	Roman Catholic, Protestant
Population	8 495 000	Currency	Euro
Capital	Vienna (Wien)	Organizations	EU, OECD, UN

Map page 168

Two-thirds of Austria, a landlocked state in central Europe, lies within the Alps, with lower mountains to the north. The only lowlands are in the east. The Danube river valley in the northeast contains almost all the agricultural land and most of the population. Although the climate varies with altitude, in general summers are warm and winters cold with heavy snowfalls. Manufacturing industry and tourism are the most important sectors of the economy. Exports are dominated by manufactured goods. Germany is Austria's main trading partner.

AZERBAIJAN
Republic of Azerbaijan

Area Sq Km	86 600	Languages	Azeri, Armenian, Russian, Lezgian
Area Sq Miles	33 436	Religions	Shi'a Muslim, Sunni Muslim, Russian and Armenian Orthodox
Population	9 413 000		
Capital	Baku	Currency	Azerbaijani manat
		Organizations	CIS, UN

Map page 137

Azerbaijan lies to the southeast of the Caucasus mountains, on the Caspian Sea. Its region of Naxçıvan is separated from the rest of the country by part of Armenia. It has mountains in the northeast and west, valleys in the centre, and a low coastal plain. The climate is continental. It is rich in energy and mineral resources. Oil production, onshore and offshore, is the main industry and the basis of heavy industries. Agriculture is important, with cotton and tobacco the main cash crops.

THE BAHAMAS
Commonwealth of The Bahamas

Area Sq Km	13 939	Languages	English, Creole
Area Sq Miles	5 382	Religions	Protestant, Roman Catholic
Population	377 000	Currency	Bahamian dollar
Capital	Nassau	Organizations	CARICOM, Comm., UN

Map page 205

The Bahamas, an archipelago made up of approximately seven hundred islands and over two thousand cays, lies to the northeast of Cuba and east of the Florida coast of the USA. Twenty-two islands are inhabited, and seventy per cent of the population lives on the main island of New Providence. The climate is warm for much of the year, with heavy rainfall in the summer. Tourism is the islands' main industry. Offshore banking, insurance and ship registration are also major foreign exchange earners.

BAHRAIN
Kingdom of Bahrain

Area Sq Km	691	Languages	Arabic, English
Area Sq Miles	267	Religions	Shi'a Muslim, Sunni Muslim, Christian
Population	1 332 000		
Capital	Manama (Al Manāmah)	Currency	Bahraini dinar
		Organizations	GCC, UN

Map page 140

Bahrain consists of more than thirty islands lying in a bay in The Gulf, off the coasts of Saudi Arabia and Qatar. Bahrain Island, the largest island, is connected to other islands and to the mainland of Arabia by causeways. Oil production and processing are the main sectors of the economy.

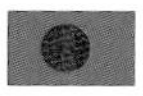

BANGLADESH
People's Republic of Bangladesh

Area Sq Km	143 998	Languages	Bengali, English
Area Sq Miles	55 598	Religions	Sunni Muslim, Hindu
Population	156 595 000	Currency	Taka
Capital	Dhaka (Dacca)	Organizations	Comm., UN

Map page 145

The south Asian state of Bangladesh is in the northeast of the Indian subcontinent, on the Bay of Bengal. It consists almost entirely of the low-lying alluvial plains and deltas of the Ganges and Brahmaputra rivers. The southwest is swampy, with mangrove forests in the delta area. The north, northeast and southeast have low forested hills. Bangladesh is one of the world's most densely populated and least developed countries. The economy is based on agriculture, though the garment industry is the main export sector. Storms during the summer monsoon season often cause devastating flooding and crop destruction. The country relies on large-scale foreign aid and remittances from workers abroad.

BARBADOS

Area Sq Km	430	Languages	English, Creole
Area Sq Miles	166	Religions	Protestant, Roman Catholic
Population	285 000	Currency	Barbadian dollar
Capital	Bridgetown	Organizations	CARICOM, Comm., UN

Map page 205

The most easterly of the Caribbean islands, Barbados is small and densely populated. It has a tropical climate and is subject to hurricanes. The economy is based on tourism, financial services, light industries and sugar production.

BELARUS
Republic of Belarus

Area Sq Km	207 600	Languages	Belarusian, Russian
Area Sq Miles	80 155	Religions	Belarusian Orthodox, Roman Catholic
Population	9 357 000		
Capital	Minsk	Currency	Belarusian rouble
		Organizations	CIS, UN

Map page 169

Belarus, a landlocked state in eastern Europe, consists of low hills and plains, with many lakes, rivers and, in the south, extensive marshes. Forests cover approximately one-third of the country. It has a continental climate. Agriculture contributes one-third of national income, with beef cattle and grains as the major products. Manufacturing industries produce a range of items, from construction equipment to textiles. Russia and Ukraine are the main trading partners.

BELGIUM
Kingdom of Belgium

Area Sq Km	30 520	Languages	Dutch (Flemish), French (Walloon), German
Area Sq Miles	11 784		
Population	11 104 000	Religions	Roman Catholic, Protestant
Capital	Brussels (Brussel/Bruxelles)	Currency	Euro
		Organizations	EU, NATO, OECD, UN

Map page 164

Belgium lies on the North Sea coast of western Europe. Beyond low sand dunes and a narrow belt of reclaimed land, fertile plains extend to the Sambre-Meuse river valley. The land rises to the forested Ardennes plateau in the southeast. Belgium has mild winters and cool summers. It is densely populated and has a highly urbanized population. With few mineral resources, Belgium imports raw materials for processing and manufacture. The agricultural sector is small, but provides for most food needs. A large services sector reflects Belgium's position as the home base for over eight hundred international institutions. The headquarters of the European Union are in the capital, Brussels.

BELIZE

Area Sq Km	22 965	Languages	English, Spanish, Mayan, Creole
Area Sq Miles	8 867	Religions	Roman Catholic, Protestant
Population	332 000	Currency	Belizean dollar
Capital	Belmopan	Organizations	CARICOM, Comm., UN

Map page 207

Belize lies on the Caribbean coast of central America and includes numerous cays and a large barrier reef offshore. The coastal areas are flat and swampy. To the southwest are the Maya Mountains. Tropical jungle covers much of the country and the climate is humid tropical, but tempered by sea breezes. A fifth of the population lives in the former capital Belize City. The economy is based primarily on agriculture, forestry and fishing, and exports include raw sugar, orange concentrate and bananas.

BENIN
Republic of Benin

Area Sq Km	112 620	Languages	French, Fon, Yoruba, Adja, other local languages
Area Sq Miles	43 483		
Population	10 323 000	Religions	Traditional beliefs, Roman Catholic, Sunni Muslim
Capital	Porto-Novo		
		Currency	CFA franc
		Organizations	UN

Map page 176

Benin is in west Africa, on the Gulf of Guinea. The climate is tropical in the north, equatorial in the south. The economy is based mainly on agriculture and transit trade. Agricultural products account for two-thirds of export earnings. Oil, produced offshore, is also a major export.

Bermuda
United Kingdom Overseas Territory

Area Sq Km	54	Languages	English
Area Sq Miles	21	Religions	Protestant, Roman Catholic
Population	65 000	Currency	Bermuda dollar
Capital	Hamilton		

Map page 205   In the Atlantic Ocean to the east of the USA, Bermuda comprises a group of small islands with a warm and humid climate. The economy is based on international business and tourism.

BHUTAN
Kingdom of Bhutan

Area Sq Km	46 620	Languages	Dzongkha, Nepali, Assamese
Area Sq Miles	18 000	Religions	Buddhist, Hindu
Population	754 000	Currency	Ngultrum, Indian rupee
Capital	Thimphu	Organizations	UN

Map page 145

Bhutan lies in the eastern Himalaya mountains, between China and India. It is mountainous in the north, with fertile valleys. The climate ranges between permanently cold in the far north and subtropical in the south. Most of the population is involved in livestock rearing and subsistence farming. Bhutan is a producer of cardamom. Tourism is an increasingly important foreign currency earner, and hydroelectric power is also sold to India from the Tala site in the southwest.

BOLIVIA
Plurinational State of Bolivia

Area Sq Km	1 098 581	Languages	Spanish, Quechua, Aymara
Area Sq Miles	424 164	Religions	Roman Catholic, Protestant, Baha'i
Population	10 671 000	Currency	Boliviano
Capital	La Paz/Sucre	Organizations	UN

Map page 210

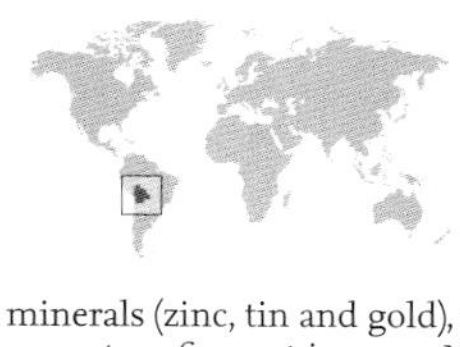

Bolivia is a landlocked state in central South America. Most Bolivians live on the high plateau within the Andes mountains. The lowlands range between dense rainforest in the northeast and semi-arid grasslands in the southeast. Bolivia is rich in minerals (zinc, tin and gold), and sales generate approximately a quarter of export income. Natural gas, timber and soya beans are also exported. Brazil is the main trading partner.

BOSNIA AND HERZEGOVINA

Area Sq Km	51 130	**Languages**	Bosnian, Serbian, Croatian
Area Sq Miles	19 741	**Religions**	Sunni Muslim, Serbian Orthodox, Roman Catholic, Protestant
Population	3 829 000	**Currency**	Convertible mark
Capital	Sarajevo	**Organizations**	UN

Map page 170–171

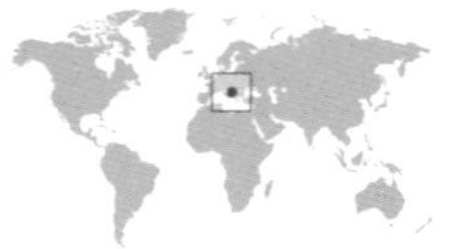

Bosnia and Herzegovina lies in the western Balkan Mountains of southern Europe, on the Adriatic Sea. It is mountainous, with ridges running northwest-southeast. The main lowlands are around the Sava valley in the north. Summers are warm, but winters can be very cold. The economy relies heavily on overseas aid.

BOTSWANA
Republic of Botswana

Area Sq Km	581 370	**Languages**	English, Setswana, Shona, other local languages
Area Sq Miles	224 468	**Religions**	Traditional beliefs, Protestant, Roman Catholic
Population	2 021 000	**Currency**	Pula
Capital	Gaborone	**Organizations**	Comm., SADC, UN

Map page 179

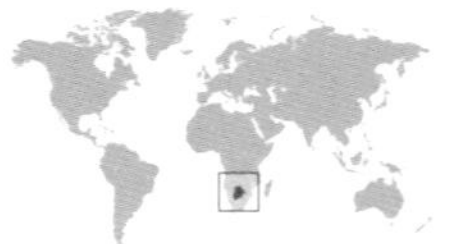

Botswana is a landlocked state in southern Africa. Over half of the country lies within the Kalahari Desert, with swamps to the north and salt-pans to the northeast. Most of the population lives near the eastern border. The climate is subtropical, but drought-prone. The economy was founded on cattle rearing, and although beef remains an important export, the economy is now based on mining. Diamonds account for seventy per cent of export earnings. Copper-nickel matte is also exported. The main trading partners are the UK and South Africa.

BRAZIL
Federative Republic of Brazil

Area Sq Km	8 514 879	**Languages**	Portuguese
Area Sq Miles	3 287 613	**Religions**	Roman Catholic, Protestant
Population	200 362 000	**Currency**	Real
Capital	Brasília	**Organizations**	UN

Map page 210–211

Brazil, in eastern South America, covers almost half of the continent, and is the world's fifth largest country. The northwest contains the vast basin of the Amazon, while the centre-west is largely a vast plateau of savanna and rock escarpments. The northeast is mostly semi-arid plateaus, while to the east and south are rugged mountains, fertile valleys and narrow, fertile coastal plains. The Amazon basin is hot, humid and wet; the rest of the country is cooler and drier, with seasonal variations. The northeast is drought-prone. Most Brazilians live in urban areas along the coast and on the central plateau. Brazil has well-developed agricultural, mining and service sectors, and the economy is larger than that of all other South American countries combined. Brazil is the world's biggest producer of coffee, and other agricultural crops include grains and sugar cane. Mineral production includes iron, aluminium and gold. Manufactured goods include food products, transport equipment, machinery and industrial chemicals. The main trading partners are the USA, China and Argentina. Economic reforms in Brazil have turned it into one of the fastest growing economies.

BRUNEI
Brunei Darussalam

Area Sq Km	5 765	**Languages**	Malay, English, Chinese
Area Sq Miles	2 226	**Religions**	Sunni Muslim, Buddhist, Christian
Population	418 000	**Currency**	Bruneian dollar
Capital	Bandar Seri Begawan	**Organizations**	APEC, ASEAN, Comm., UN

Map page 155

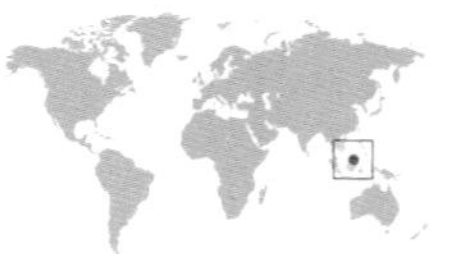

The southeast Asian oil-rich state of Brunei lies on the northwest coast of the island of Borneo, on the South China Sea. Its two enclaves are surrounded by the Malaysian state of Sarawak. Tropical rainforest covers over two-thirds of the country. The economy is dominated by the oil and gas industries.

BULGARIA
Republic of Bulgaria

Area Sq Km	110 994	**Languages**	Bulgarian, Turkish, Romany, Macedonian
Area Sq Miles	42 855	**Religions**	Bulgarian Orthodox, Sunni Muslim
Population	7 223 000	**Currency**	Lev
Capital	Sofia	**Organizations**	EU, NATO, UN

Map page 171

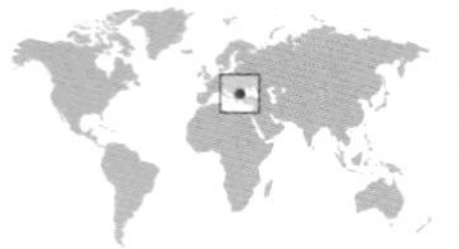

Bulgaria, in southern Europe, borders the western shore of the Black Sea. The Balkan Mountains separate the Danube plains in the north from the Rhodope Mountains and the lowlands in the south. The economy has a strong agricultural base. Manufacturing industries include machinery, consumer goods, chemicals and metals. Most trade is with Russia, Italy and Germany.

BURKINA FASO

Area Sq Km	274 200	**Languages**	French, Moore (Mossi), Fulani, other local languages
Area Sq Miles	105 869	**Religions**	Sunni Muslim, traditional beliefs, Roman Catholic
Population	16 935 000	**Currency**	CFA franc
Capital	Ouagadougou	**Organizations**	UN

Map page 176

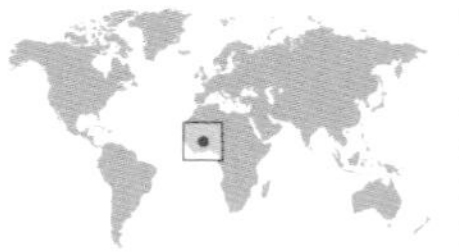

Burkina Faso, a landlocked country in west Africa, lies within the Sahara desert to the north and semi-arid savanna to the south. Rainfall is erratic, and droughts are common. Livestock rearing and farming are the main activities, and cotton, livestock, groundnuts and some minerals are exported. Burkina Faso relies heavily on foreign aid, and is one of the poorest and least developed countries in the world.

BURUNDI
Republic of Burundi

Area Sq Km	27 835	**Languages**	Kirundi (Hutu, Tutsi), French
Area Sq Miles	10 747	**Religions**	Roman Catholic, traditional beliefs, Protestant
Population	10 163 000	**Currency**	Burundian franc
Capital	Bujumbura	**Organizations**	UN

Map page 178

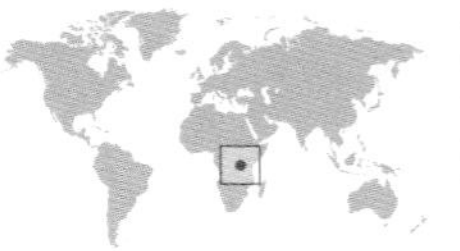

The densely populated east African state of Burundi consists of high plateaus rising from the shores of Lake Tanganyika in the southwest. It has a tropical climate and depends on subsistence farming. Coffee is its main export, and its main trading partners are Germany and Belgium. The country has been badly affected by internal conflict since the early 1990s.

CAMBODIA
Kingdom of Cambodia

Area Sq Km	181 035	**Languages**	Khmer
Area Sq Miles	69 884	**Religions**	Buddhist, Roman Catholic, Sunni Muslim
Population	15 135 000	**Currency**	Riel
Capital	Phnom Penh (Phnom Pénh)	**Organizations**	ASEAN, UN

Map page 154

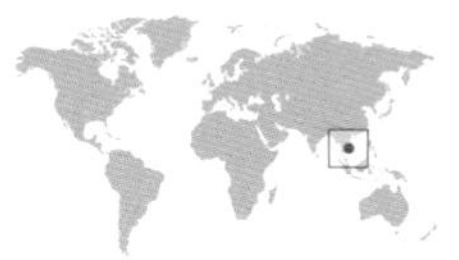

Cambodia lies in southeast Asia on the Gulf of Thailand, and occupies the Mekong river basin, with the Tônlé Sap (Great Lake) at its centre. The climate is tropical monsoon. Forests cover half the country. Most of the population lives on the plains and is engaged in farming (chiefly rice growing), fishing and forestry. The economy is recovering following the devastation of civil war in the 1970s, with rapid progress since 2000. Mineral resources are starting to be identified for development.

CAMEROON
Republic of Cameroon

Area Sq Km	475 442	**Languages**	French, English, Fang, Bamileke, other local languages
Area Sq Miles	183 569	**Religions**	Roman Catholic, traditional beliefs, Sunni Muslim, Protestant
Population	22 254 000	**Currency**	CFA franc
Capital	Yaoundé	**Organizations**	Comm., UN

Map page 176–177

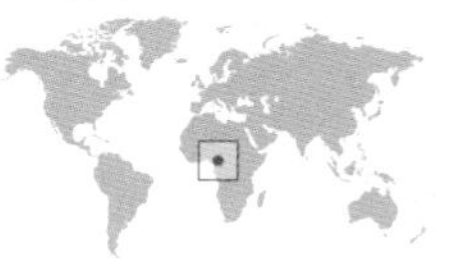

Cameroon is in west Africa, on the Gulf of Guinea. The coastal plains and southern and central plateaus are covered with tropical forest. Despite oil resources and favourable agricultural conditions Cameroon still faces problems of underdevelopment. Oil, timber and cocoa are the main exports. France is the main trading partner.

CANADA

Area Sq Km	9 984 670	**Languages**	English, French
Area Sq Miles	3 855 103	**Religions**	Roman Catholic, Protestant, Eastern Orthodox, Jewish
Population	35 182 000	**Currency**	Canadian dollar
Capital	Ottawa	**Organizations**	APEC, Comm., NATO, OECD, UN

Map page 184–185

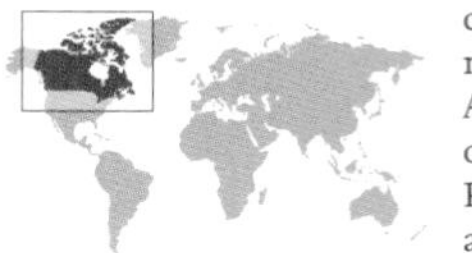

The world's second largest country, Canada covers the northern two-fifths of North America and has coastlines on the Atlantic, Arctic and Pacific Oceans. In the west are the Coast Mountains, the Rocky Mountains and interior plateaus. In the centre lie the fertile Prairies. Further east, covering about half the total land area, is the Canadian Shield, a relatively flat area of infertile lowlands around Hudson Bay, extending to Labrador on the east coast. The Shield is bordered to the south by the fertile Great Lakes-St Lawrence lowlands. In the far north climatic conditions are polar, while the rest has a continental climate. Most Canadians live in the urban areas of the Great Lakes-St Lawrence basin. Canada is rich in mineral and energy resources. Only five per cent of land is arable. Canada is among the world's leading producers of wheat, of wood from its vast coniferous forests, and of fish and seafood from its Atlantic and Pacific fishing grounds. It is a major producer of nickel, uranium, copper, iron ore, zinc and other minerals, as well as oil and natural gas. Its abundant raw materials are the basis for many manufacturing industries. Main exports are machinery, motor vehicles, oil, timber, newsprint and paper, wood pulp and wheat. Since the 1989 free trade agreement with the USA and the 1994 North America Free Trade Agreement, trade with the USA has grown and now accounts for around fifty per cent of imports and around seventy-five per cent of exports.

Alberta (Province)
Area Sq Km (Sq Miles) 661 848 (255 541) **Population** 3 965 339 **Capital** Edmonton

British Columbia (Province)
Area Sq Km (Sq Miles) 944 735 (364 764) **Population** 4 650 004 **Capital** Victoria

Manitoba (Province)
Area Sq Km (Sq Miles) 647 797 (250 116) **Population** 1 277 339 **Capital** Winnipeg

New Brunswick (Province)
Area Sq Km (Sq Miles) 72 908 (28 150) **Population** 754 039 **Capital** Fredericton

Newfoundland and Labrador (Province)
Area Sq Km (Sq Miles) 405 212 (156 453) **Population** 513 568 **Capital** St John's

Northwest Territories (Territory)
Area Sq Km (Sq Miles) 1 346 106 (519 734) **Population** 43 349 **Capital** Yellowknife

Nova Scotia (Province)
Area Sq Km (Sq Miles) 55 284 (21 345) **Population** 945 015 **Capital** Halifax

Nunavut (Territory)
Area Sq Km (Sq Miles) 2 093 190 (808 185) **Population** 34 023 **Capital** Iqaluit (Frobisher Bay)

Ontario (Province)
Area Sq Km (Sq Miles) 1 076 395 (415 598) **Population** 13 583 710 **Capital** Toronto

Prince Edward Island (Province)
Area Sq Km (Sq Miles) 5 660 (2 185) **Population** 145 763 **Capital** Charlottetown

Québec (Province)
Area Sq Km (Sq Miles) 1 542 056 (595 391) **Population** 8 099 095 **Capital** Québec

Saskatchewan (Province)
Area Sq Km (Sq Miles) 651 036 (251 366) **Population** 1 093 880 **Capital** Regina

Yukon (Territory)
Area Sq Km (Sq Miles) 482 443 (186 272) **Population** 36 418 **Capital** Whitehorse

CAPE VERDE (Cabo Verde)
Republic of Cabo Verde

Area Sq Km	4 033	**Languages**	Portuguese, Creole
Area Sq Miles	1 557	**Religions**	Roman Catholic, Protestant
Population	499 000	**Currency**	Cape Verdean escudo
Capital	Praia	**Organizations**	UN

Map page 176

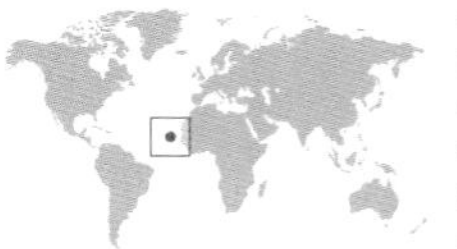

Cape Verde is a group of semi-arid volcanic islands lying off the coast of west Africa. The economy is based on fishing, subsistence farming and service industries. Windfarms on four islands supply around a quarter of all electricity.

Cayman Islands
United Kingdom Overseas Territory

Area Sq Km	259	**Languages**	English
Area Sq Miles	100	**Religions**	Protestant, Roman Catholic
Population	58 000	**Currency**	Cayman Islands dollar
Capital	George Town		

Map page 205 A group of islands in the Caribbean, northwest of Jamaica. There are three main islands: Grand Cayman, Little Cayman and Cayman Brac. The Cayman Islands are one of the world's major offshore financial centres. Tourism is also important to the economy.

CENTRAL AFRICAN REPUBLIC

Area Sq Km	622 436	Languages	French, Sango, Banda, Baya, other local languages
Area Sq Miles	240 324	Religions	Protestant, Roman Catholic, traditional beliefs, Sunni Muslim
Population	4 616 000	Currency	CFA franc
Capital	Bangui	Organizations	UN

Map page 177

A landlocked country in central Africa, the Central African Republic is mainly savanna plateau, drained by the Ubangi and Chari river systems, with mountains to the east and west. The climate is tropical, with high rainfall. Most of the population lives in the south and west, and a majority of the workforce is involved in subsistence farming. Some cotton, coffee, tobacco and timber are exported, but diamonds account for over sixty per cent of export earnings.

CHAD
Republic of Chad

Area Sq Km	1 284 000	Languages	Arabic, French, Sara, other local languages
Area Sq Miles	495 755	Religions	Sunni Muslim, Roman Catholic, Protestant, traditional beliefs
Population	12 825 000	Currency	CFA franc
Capital	Ndjamena	Organizations	UN

Map page 177

Chad is a landlocked state of north-central Africa. It consists of plateaus, the Tibesti mountains in the north and the Lake Chad basin in the west. Climatic conditions range between desert in the north and tropical forest in the southwest. With few natural resources, Chad relies on subsistence farming, exports of raw cotton, and foreign aid. The main trading partners are France, Portugal and Cameroon.

CHILE
Republic of Chile

Area Sq Km	756 945	Languages	Spanish, Amerindian languages
Area Sq Miles	292 258	Religions	Roman Catholic, Protestant
Population	17 620 000	Currency	Chilean peso
Capital	Santiago	Organizations	APEC, OECD, UN

Map page 212

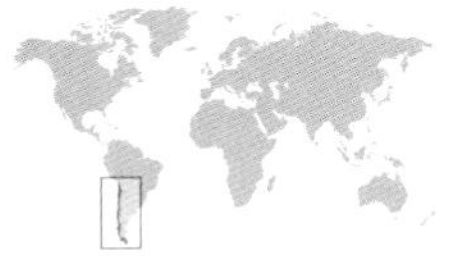

Chile lies along the Pacific coast of the southern half of South America. Between the Andes in the east and the lower coastal ranges is a central valley, with a mild climate, where most Chileans live. To the north is the arid Atacama Desert and to the south is cold, wet forested grassland. Chile has considerable mineral resources and is a major exporter of copper. Nitrates, molybdenum, gold and iron ore are also mined. Agriculture (particularly viticulture), forestry and fishing are also important to the economy.

CHINA
People's Republic of China

Area Sq Km	9 606 802	Languages	Mandarin (Putonghua), Wu, Cantonese, Hsiang, regional languages
Area Sq Miles	3 709 186	Religions	Confucian, Taoist, Buddhist, Christian, Sunni Muslim
Population	1 369 993 000	Currency	Yuan, Hong Kong dollar, Macao pataca
Capital	Beijing (Peking)	Organizations	APEC, UN

Map page 146

China, the world's most populous and fourth largest country, occupies a large part of east Asia, borders fourteen states and has coastlines on the Yellow, East China and South China Seas. It has a huge variety of landscapes. The southwest contains the high Plateau of Tibet, flanked by the Himalaya and Kunlun Shan mountains. The north is mountainous with arid basins and extends from the Tien Shan and Altai Mountains and the vast Taklimakan Desert in the west to the plateau and Gobi Desert in the centre-east. Eastern China is predominantly lowland and is divided broadly into the basins of the Yellow River (Huang He) in the north, the Yangtze (Chang Jiang) in the centre and the Pearl River (Xi Jiang) in the southeast. Climatic conditions and vegetation are as diverse as the topography: much of the country experiences temperate conditions, while the southwest has an extreme mountain climate and the southeast enjoys a moist, warm subtropical climate. Just under fifty per cent of China's huge population lives in rural areas, and agriculture employs over thirty-five per cent of the working population. The main crops are rice, wheat, soya beans, peanuts, cotton, tobacco and hemp. China is rich in coal, oil and natural gas and has the world's largest potential in hydroelectric power. It is a major world producer of iron ore, molybdenum, copper, asbestos and gold. Economic reforms from the early 1980s led to an explosion in manufacturing development concentrated on the 'coastal economic open region'. The main exports are machinery, textiles, footwear, toys and sports goods. Japan and the USA are China's main trading partners.

Anhui (Province)
Area Sq Km (Sq Miles) 139 000 (53 900) Population 59 680 000 Capital Hefei

Beijing (Municipality)
Area Sq Km (Sq Miles) 16 411 (6 336) Population 20 186 000 Capital Beijing (Peking)

Chongqing (Municipality)
Area Sq Km (Sq Miles) 82 400 (31 815) Population 29 190 000 Capital Chongqing

Fujian (Province)
Area Sq Km (Sq Miles) 124 000 (47 876) Population 37 200 000 Capital Fuzhou

Gansu (Province)
Area Sq Km (Sq Miles) 425 800 (164 401) Population 25 642 000 Capital Lanzhou

Guangdong (Province)
Area Sq Km (Sq Miles) 179 800 (69 421) Population 105 048 000 Capital Guangzhou (Canton)

Guangxi Zhuangzu Zizhiqu (Autonomous Region)
Area Sq Km (Sq Miles) 237 600 (91 737) Population 46 450 000 Capital Nanning

Guizhou (Province)
Area Sq Km (Sq Miles) 176 000 (67 954) Population 34 687 000 Capital Guiyang

Hainan (Province)
Area Sq Km (Sq Miles) 35 000 (13 514) Population 8 773 000 Capital Haikou

Hebei (Province)
Area Sq Km (Sq Miles) 188 000 (72 587) Population 72 405 000 Capital Shijiazhuang

Heilongjiang (Province)
Area Sq Km (Sq Miles) 473 000 (182 625) Population 38 340 000 Capital Harbin

Henan (Province)
Area Sq Km (Sq Miles) 167 000 (64 479) Population 93 880 000 Capital Zhengzhou

Hong Kong (Xianggang) (Special Administrative Region)
Area Sq Km (Sq Miles) 1 104 (426) Population 7 112 000 Capital Hong Kong (Xianggang)

Hubei (Province)
Area Sq Km (Sq Miles) 185 900 (71 776) Population 57 575 000 Capital Wuhan

Hunan (Province)
Area Sq Km (Sq Miles) 211 800 (81 776) Population 65 956 000 Capital Changsha

Jiangsu (Province)
Area Sq Km (Sq Miles) 102 600 (39 614) Population 78 988 000 Capital Nanjing

Jiangxi (Province)
Area Sq Km (Sq Miles) 166 900 (64 440) Population 44 884 000 Capital Nanchang

Jilin (Province)
Area Sq Km (Sq Miles) 187 400 (72 355) Population 27 494 000 Capital Changchun

Liaoning (Province)
Area Sq Km (Sq Miles) 148 000 (57 143) Population 43 830 000 Capital Shenyang

Macao (Special Administrative Region)
Area Sq Km (Sq Miles) 30 (12) Population 557 000 Capital Macao

Nei Mongol Zizhiqu Inner Mongolia **(Autonomous Region)**
Area Sq Km (Sq Miles) 1 183 000 (456 756) Population 24 817 000 Capital Hohhot

Ningxia Huizu Zizhiqu (Autonomous Region)
Area Sq Km (Sq Miles) 66 400 (25 637) Population 6 395 000 Capital Yinchuan

Qinghai (Province)
Area Sq Km (Sq Miles) 722 300 (278 880) Population 5 682 000 Capital Xining

Shaanxi (Province)
Area Sq Km (Sq Miles) 205 800 (79 459) Population 37 426 000 Capital Xi'an

Shandong (Province)
Area Sq Km (Sq Miles) 157 100 (60 656) Population 96 370 000 Capital Jinan

Shanghai (Municipality)
Area Sq Km (Sq Miles) 6 340 (2 448) Population 23 475 000 Capital Shanghai

Shanxi (Province)
Area Sq Km (Sq Miles) 156 700 (60 502) Population 35 930 000 Capital Taiyuan

Sichuan (Province)
Area Sq Km (Sq Miles) 486 000 (187 645) Population 80 500 000 Capital Chengdu

Tianjin (Municipality)
Area Sq Km (Sq Miles) 11 917 (4 601) Population 13 550 000 Capital Tianjin

Xinjiang Uygur Zizhiqu Sinkiang **(Autonomous Region)**
Area Sq Km (Sq Miles) 1 664 900 (642 818) Population 22 087 000 Capital Ürümqi

Xizang Zizhiqu Tibet **(Autonomous Region)**
Area Sq Km (Sq Miles) 1 202 200 (464 169) Population 3 033 000 Capital Lhasa

Yunnan (Province)
Area Sq Km (Sq Miles) 394 000 (152 123) Population 46 308 000 Capital Kunming

Zhejiang (Province)
Area Sq Km (Sq Miles) 101 800 (39 305) Population 54 630 000 Capital Hangzhou

Taiwan: The People's Republic of China claims Taiwan as its 23rd Province

Christmas Island
Australian External Territory

Area Sq Km	135	Languages	English
Area Sq Miles	52	Religions	Buddhist, Sunni Muslim, Protestant, Roman Catholic
Population	2 072	Currency	Australian dollar
Capital	The Settlement (Flying Fish Cove)		

Map page 147 The island is situated in the east of the Indian Ocean, to the south of Indonesia. The economy was formerly based on phosphate extraction, although the mine is now closed. Tourism is developing and is a major employer.

Cocos (Keeling) Islands
Australian External Territory

Area Sq Km	14	Languages	English
Area Sq Miles	5	Religions	Sunni Muslim, Christian
Population	550	Currency	Australian dollar
Capital	West Island		

Map page 147 The Cocos Islands consist of numerous islands on two coral atolls in the eastern Indian Ocean between Sri Lanka and Australia. Most of the population lives on West Island or Home Island. Coconuts are the only cash crop, and the main export.

COLOMBIA
Republic of Colombia

Area Sq Km	1 141 748	Languages	Spanish, Amerindian languages
Area Sq Miles	440 831	Religions	Roman Catholic, Protestant
Population	48 321 000	Currency	Colombian peso
Capital	Bogotá	Organizations	UN

Map page 213

A state in northwest South America, Colombia has coastlines on the Pacific Ocean and the Caribbean Sea. Behind coastal plains lie three ranges of the Andes mountains, separated by high valleys and plateaus where most Colombians live. To the southeast are grasslands and the forests of the Amazon. The climate is tropical, although temperatures vary with altitude. Only five per cent of land is cultivable. Coffee (Colombia is the world's third largest producer), sugar, bananas, cotton and flowers are exported. Coal, nickel, gold, silver, platinum and high-quality emeralds are mined. Oil and its products are the main export. Industries include the processing of minerals and crops. The main trade partner is the USA. Internal violence – both politically motivated and relating to Colombia's leading role in the international trade in illegal drugs – continues to hinder development.

COMOROS
Union of the Comoros

Area Sq Km	1 862	Languages	Shikomor (Comorian), French, Arabic
Area Sq Miles	719	Religions	Sunni Muslim, Roman Catholic
Population	735 000	Currency	Comorian franc
Capital	Moroni	Organizations	UN

Map page 179

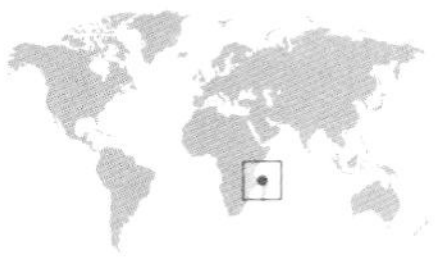

This state, in the Indian Ocean off the east African coast, comprises three volcanic islands of Ngazidja (Grande Comore), Nzwani (Anjouan) and Mwali (Mohéli), and some coral atolls. These tropical islands are mountainous, with poor soil and few natural resources. Subsistence farming predominates. Vanilla, cloves and ylang-ylang (an essential oil) are exported, and the economy relies heavily on workers' remittances from abroad.

CONGO
Republic of the Congo

Area Sq Km	342 000	Languages	French, Kongo, Monokutuba, other local languages
Area Sq Miles	132 047	Religions	Roman Catholic, Protestant, traditional beliefs, Sunni Muslim
Population	4 448 000	Currency	CFA franc
Capital	Brazzaville	Organizations	UN

Map page 178

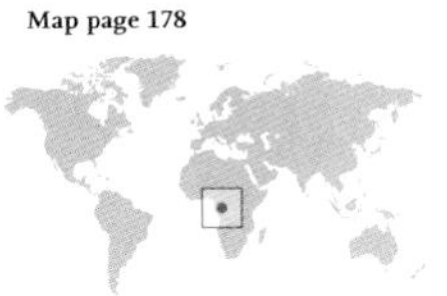

Congo, in central Africa, is mostly a forest or savanna-covered plateau drained by the Ubangi-Congo river systems. Sand dunes and lagoons line the short Atlantic coast. The climate is hot and tropical. Most

Congolese live in the southern third of the country. Half of the workforce are farmers, growing food and cash crops including sugar, coffee, cocoa and oil palms. Oil and timber are the mainstays of the economy, and oil generates over two-thirds of the country's export revenues.

CONGO, DEMOCRATIC REPUBLIC OF THE

Area Sq Km	2 345 410	Languages	French, Lingala, Swahili, Kongo, other local languages
Area Sq Miles	905 568	Religions	Christian, Sunni Muslim
Population	67 514 000	Currency	Congolese franc
Capital	Kinshasa	Organizations	SADC, UN

Map page 178–179

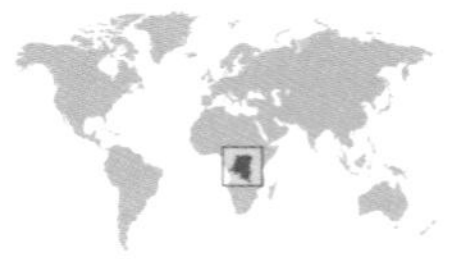

This central African state, formerly Zaire, consists of the basin of the Congo river flanked by plateaus, with high mountain ranges to the east and a short Atlantic coastline to the west. The climate is tropical, with rainforest close to the Equator and savanna to the north and south. Fertile land allows a range of food and cash crops to be grown, chiefly coffee. The country has vast mineral resources, with copper, cobalt and diamonds being the most important.

Cook Islands

Self governing New Zealand Overseas Territory

Area Sq Km	293	Languages	English, Maori
Area Sq Miles	113	Religions	Protestant, Roman Catholic
Population	21 000	Currency	New Zealand dollar
Capital	Avarua		

Map page 123 These consist of groups of coral atolls and volcanic islands in the southwest Pacific Ocean. The main island is Rarotonga. Distance from foreign markets and restricted natural resources hinder development.

COSTA RICA

Republic of Costa Rica

Area Sq Km	51 100	Languages	Spanish
Area Sq Miles	19 730	Religions	Roman Catholic, Protestant
Population	4 872 000	Currency	Costa Rican colón
Capital	San José	Organizations	UN

Map page 206

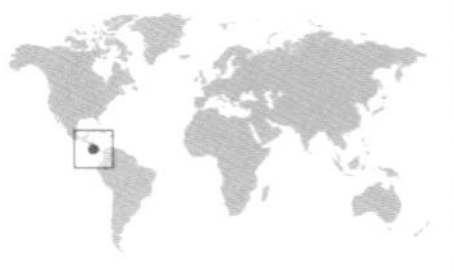

Costa Rica, in central America, has coastlines on the Caribbean Sea and Pacific Ocean. From tropical coastal plains, the land rises to mountains and a temperate central plateau, where most of the population lives. The economy depends on agriculture and tourism, with ecotourism becoming increasingly important. Main exports are textiles, coffee and bananas, and the USA is the main trading partner.

CÔTE D'IVOIRE (Ivory Coast)

Republic of Côte d'Ivoire

Area Sq Km	322 463	Languages	French, Creole, Akan, other local languages
Area Sq Miles	124 504	Religions	Sunni Muslim, Roman Catholic, traditional beliefs, Protestant
Population	20 316 000	Currency	CFA franc
Capital	Yamoussoukro	Organizations	UN

Map page 176

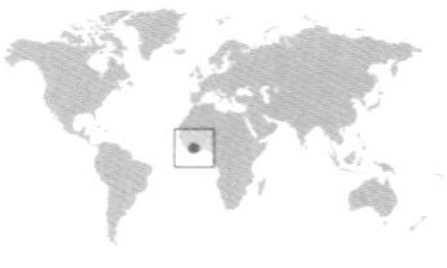

Côte d'Ivoire (Ivory Coast) is in west Africa, on the Gulf of Guinea. In the north are plateaus and savanna; in the south are low undulating plains and rainforest, with sand-bars and lagoons on the coast. Temperatures are warm, and rainfall is heavier in the south. Most of the workforce is engaged in farming. Côte d'Ivoire is a major producer of cocoa and coffee, and agricultural products (also including cotton and timber) are the main exports. Oil and gas have begun to be exploited.

Crimea

Disputed territory

Area Sq Km	27 000	Languages	Ukrainian, Russian
Area Sq Miles	10 400	Religions	Russian Orthodox, Sunni Muslim
Population	2 348 600	Currency	Russian Rouble
Capital	Simferopol'		

Map page 173 Following internal unrest in Ukraine in 2014, Russian-supported separatists in Crimea in southern Ukraine seized power in that region and a quickly arranged referendum resulted in the two administrative divisions in Crimea – the Autonomous Republic of Crimea (Respublika Krym) and the municipality of Sevastopol' – declaring independence from Ukraine as the Republic of Crimea. The referendum and its outcome were not recognized by the majority of the international community.Russia then passed a law in March 2014 annexing the Republic of Crimea, declaring it to be part of Russia – a move similarly not recognized, and strongly condemned by the majority of the international community. Ukrainian forces withdrew from Crimea soon after this annexation.

CROATIA

Republic of Croatia

Area Sq Km	56 538	Languages	Croatian, Serbian
Area Sq Miles	21 829	Religions	Roman Catholic, Serbian Orthodox, Sunni Muslim
Population	4 290 000	Currency	Kuna
Capital	Zagreb	Organizations	EU, NATO, UN

Map page 170

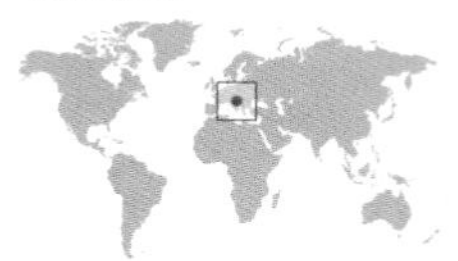

The southern European state of Croatia has a long coastline on the Adriatic Sea, with many offshore islands. Coastal areas have a Mediterranean climate; inland is cooler and wetter. Croatia was once strong agriculturally and industrially, but conflict in the early 1990s, and associated loss of markets and a fall in tourist revenue, caused economic difficulties from which recovery has been slow.

CUBA

Republic of Cuba

Area Sq Km	110 860	Languages	Spanish
Area Sq Miles	42 803	Religions	Roman Catholic, Protestant
Population	11 266 000	Currency	Cuban peso
Capital	Havana (La Habana)	Organizations	UN

Map page 205

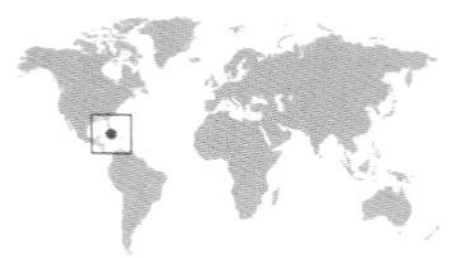

The country comprises the island of Cuba (the largest island in the Caribbean), and many islets and cays. A fifth of Cubans live in and around Havana. Cuba is slowly recovering from the withdrawal of aid and subsidies from the former USSR. Sugar remains the basis of the economy, although tourism is developing and is, together with remittances from workers abroad, an important source of revenue.

Curaçao

Self-governing Netherlands territory

Area Sq Km	444	Languages	Dutch, Papiamento
Area Sq Miles	171	Religions	Roman Catholic, Protestant
Population	159 000	Currency	Caribbean guilder
Capital	Willemstad		

Map page 213 Situated in the Caribbean Sea off the north coast of Venezuela, Curaçao was previously part of the Netherlands Antilles until they were dissolved in October 2010. It consists of the main island and the smaller uninhabited Klein Curaçao and is the largest and most populous of the Lesser Antilles. Oil refining and tourism form the basis of the economy.

CYPRUS

Republic of Cyprus

Area Sq Km	9 251	Languages	Greek, Turkish, English
Area Sq Miles	3 572	Religions	Greek Orthodox, Sunni Muslim
Population	1 141 000	Currency	Euro
Capital	Nicosia (Lefkosia)	Organizations	Comm., EU, UN

Map page 136

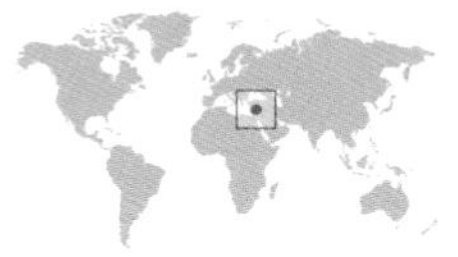

The eastern Mediterranean island of Cyprus has effectively been divided into two since 1974. The economy of the Greek-speaking south is based mainly on specialist agriculture and tourism, with shipping and offshore banking. The ethnically Turkish north depends on agriculture, tourism and aid from Turkey. The island has hot dry summers and mild winters. Cyprus joined the European Union in May 2004.

CZECH REPUBLIC

Area Sq Km	78 864	Languages	Czech, Moravian, Slovakian
Area Sq Miles	30 450	Religions	Roman Catholic, Protestant
Population	10 702 000	Currency	Koruna
Capital	Prague (Praha)	Organizations	EU, NATO, OECD, UN

Map page 168

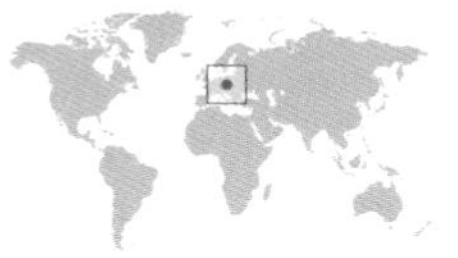

The landlocked Czech Republic in central Europe consists of rolling countryside, wooded hills and fertile valleys. The climate is continental. The country has substantial reserves of coal and lignite, timber and some minerals, chiefly iron ore. It is highly industrialized, and major manufactured goods include industrial machinery, consumer goods, cars, iron and steel, chemicals and glass. Germany is the main trading partner. The Czech Republic joined the European Union in May 2004.

DENMARK

Kingdom of Denmark

Area Sq Km	43 075	Languages	Danish
Area Sq Miles	16 631	Religions	Protestant
Population	5 619 000	Currency	Danish krone
Capital	Copenhagen (København)	Organizations	EU, NATO, OECD, UN

Map page 159

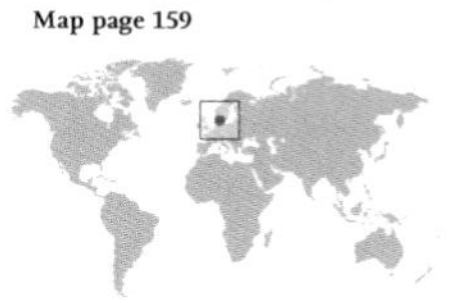

In northern Europe, Denmark occupies the Jutland (Jylland) peninsula and nearly five hundre islands in and between the North and Baltic Seas. The country is low-lying, with long, indented coastlines. The climate is cool and temperate, with rainfall throughout the year. A fifth of the population lives in and aroun the capital, Copenhagen (København), on the largest of the islands, Zealand (Sjælland). The country's main natural resource is its agricultural potential: two-thirds of the total area is fertile farmland or pasture. Agriculture is high-tech, and with forestry and fishing employs only around six per cent of the workforce. Denmark is self-sufficient in oil and natural gas, produced from fields in the North Sea. Manufacturing, largely based on imported raw materials, accounts for over half of all exports, which include machinery, food, furniture and pharmaceuticals. The main trading partners are Germany and Sweden.

DJIBOUTI

Republic of Djibouti

Area Sq Km	23 200	Languages	Somali, Afar, French, Arabic
Area Sq Miles	8 958	Religions	Sunni Muslim, Christian
Population	873 000	Currency	Djiboutian franc
Capital	Djibouti	Organizations	UN

Map page 178

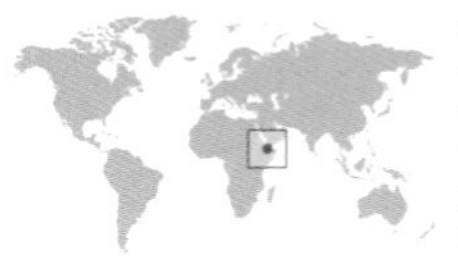

Djibouti lies in northeast Africa, on the Gulf of Aden at the entrance to the Red Sea. Most of the country is semi-arid desert with high temperatures and low rainfall. More than two-thirds of the population live in the capital. There is some camel, sheep and goat herding, but with few natural resources the economy is based on services and trade. Djibouti serves as a free trade zone for northern Africa, and the capital's port is a major transhipment and refuelling destination. It is linked by rail to Addis Ababa in Ethiopia.

DOMINICA

Commonwealth of Dominica

Area Sq Km	750	Languages	English, Creole
Area Sq Miles	290	Religions	Roman Catholic, Protestant
Population	72 000	Currency	East Caribbean dollar
Capital	Roseau	Organizations	CARICOM, Comm., UN

Map page 205

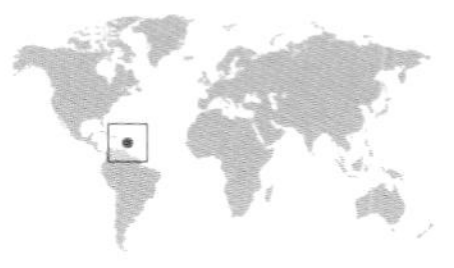

Dominica is the most northerly of the Windward Islands, in the eastern Caribbean It is very mountainous and forested, with a coastline of steep cliffs. The climate is tropical and rainfall is abundant. Approximately a quarter of Dominicans live in the capital. The economy is based on agriculture, with bananas, coconuts and citrus fruits the most important crops. Tourism is a developing industry.

DOMINICAN REPUBLIC

Area Sq Km	48 442	Languages	Spanish, Creole
Area Sq Miles	18 704	Religions	Roman Catholic, Protestant
Population	10 404 000	Currency	Dominican peso
Capital	Santo Domingo	Organizations	UN

Map page 205

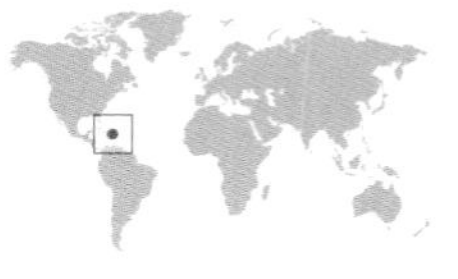

The state occupies the eastern two-thirds of the Caribbean island of Hispaniola (the western third is Haiti). It has a series of mountain ranges, fertile valleys and a large coastal plain in the east. The climate is hot tropical, with heavy rainfall. Sugar, coffee and cocoa are the main cash crops. Nickel (the main export), and gold are mined, and there is some light industry. The USA is the main trading partner. Tourism is the main foreign exchange earner.

EAST TIMOR (Timor-Leste)

Democratic Republic of Timor-Leste

Area Sq Km	14 874	Languages	Portuguese, Tetun, English
Area Sq Miles	5 743	Religions	Roman Catholic
Population	1 133 000	Currency	United States dollar
Capital	Dili	Organizations	UN

Map page 147

The island of Timor is part of the Indonesian archipelago, to the north of western Australia. East Timor occupies the eastern section of the island, and a small coastal enclave (Ocussi) to the west. A referendum in 1999 ended Indonesia's occupation, after which the country was under UN transitional administration until full independence was achieved in 2002. The economy is in a poor state and East Timor is heavily dependent on foreign aid.

ECUADOR
Republic of Ecuador

Area Sq Km	272 045	**Languages**	Spanish, Quechua, and other Amerindian languages
Area Sq Miles	105 037	**Religions**	Roman Catholic
Population	15 738 000	**Currency**	United States dollar
Capital	Quito	**Organizations**	OPEC, UN

Map page 210

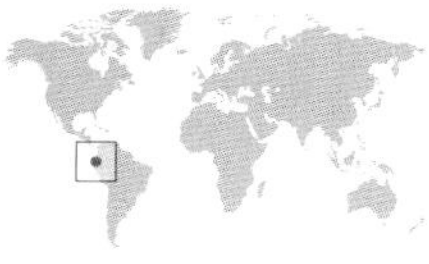

Ecuador is in northwest South America, on the Pacific coast. It consists of a broad coastal plain, high mountain ranges in the Andes, and part of the forested upper Amazon basin to the east. The climate is tropical, moderated by altitude. Most people live on the coast or in the mountain valleys. Ecuador is one of South America's main oil producers, and mineral reserves include gold. Most of the workforce depends on agriculture. Petroleum, bananas, shrimps, coffee and cocoa are exported. The USA is the main trading partner.

EGYPT
Arab Republic of Egypt

Area Sq Km	1 001 450	**Languages**	Arabic
Area Sq Miles	386 660	**Religions**	Sunni Muslim, Coptic Christian
Population	82 056 000	**Currency**	Egyptian pound
Capital	Cairo (Al Qāhirah)	**Organizations**	UN

Map page 177

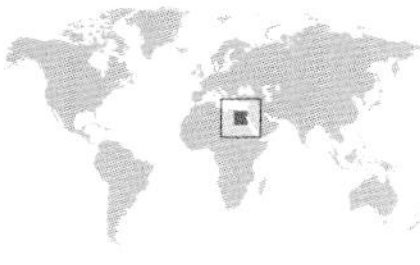

Egypt, on the eastern Mediterranean coast of north Africa, is low-lying, with areas below sea level in the Qattara depression. It is a land of desert and semi-desert, except for the Nile valley, where ninety-nine per cent of Egyptians live. The Sinai peninsula in the northeast of the country forms the only land bridge between Africa and Asia. The summers are hot, the winters mild and rainfall is negligible. Less than four per cent of land (chiefly around the Nile floodplain and delta) is cultivated. Farming employs about one-third of the workforce; cotton is the main cash crop. Egypt imports over half its food needs. There are oil and natural gas reserves, although nearly a quarter of electricity comes from hydroelectric power. Main exports are oil and oil products, cotton, textiles and clothing.

EL SALVADOR
Republic of El Salvador

Area Sq Km	21 041	**Languages**	Spanish
Area Sq Miles	8 124	**Religions**	Roman Catholic, Protestant
Population	6 340 000	**Currency**	United States dollar
Capital	San Salvador	**Organizations**	UN

Map page 207

Located on the Pacific coast of central America, El Salvador consists of a coastal plain and volcanic mountain ranges which enclose a densely populated plateau area. The coast is hot, with heavy summer rainfall; the highlands are cooler. Coffee (the chief export), sugar and cotton are the main cash crops. The main trading partners are the USA and Guatemala.

EQUATORIAL GUINEA
Republic of Equatorial Guinea

Area Sq Km	28 051	**Languages**	Spanish, French, Fang
Area Sq Miles	10 831	**Religions**	Roman Catholic, traditional beliefs
Population	757 000	**Currency**	CFA franc
Capital	Malabo	**Organizations**	UN

Map page 176

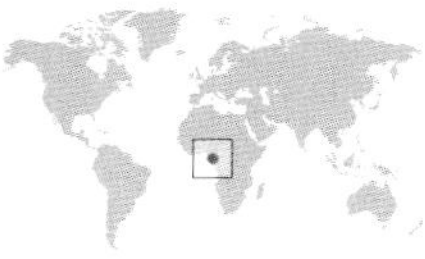

The state consists of Rio Muni, an enclave on the Atlantic coast of central Africa, and the islands of Bioko, Annobón and the Corisco group. Most of the population lives on the coastal plain and upland plateau of Rio Muni. The capital city, Malabo, is on the fertile volcanic island of Bioco. The climate is hot, humid and wet. Oil production started in 1992, and oil is now the main export, along with timber. The economy depends heavily on foreign aid.

ERITREA
State of Eritrea

Area Sq Km	117 400	**Languages**	Tigrinya, Tigre
Area Sq Miles	45 328	**Religions**	Sunni Muslim, Coptic Christian
Population	6 333 000	**Currency**	Nakfa
Capital	Asmara	**Organizations**	UN

Map page 178

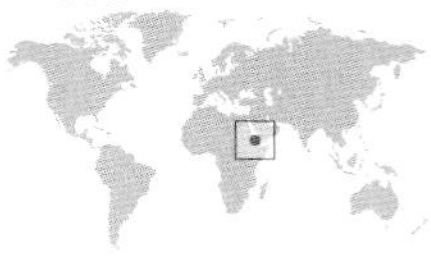

Eritrea, on the Red Sea coast of northeast Africa, consists of a high plateau in the north with a coastal plain which widens to the south. The coast is hot; inland is cooler. Rainfall is unreliable. The agriculture-based economy has suffered from over thirty years of war and occasional poor rains. Eritrea is one of the least developed countries in the world.

ESTONIA
Republic of Estonia

Area Sq Km	45 200	**Languages**	Estonian, Russian
Area Sq Miles	17 452	**Religions**	Protestant, Estonian and Russian Orthodox
Population	1 287 000	**Currency**	Euro
Capital	Tallinn	**Organizations**	EU, NATO, OECD, UN

Map page 159

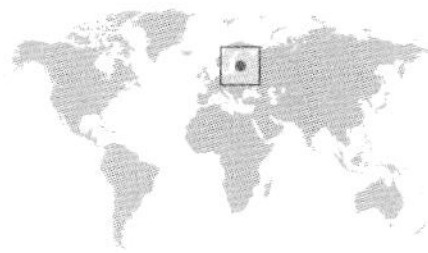

Estonia is in northern Europe, on the Gulf of Finland and the Baltic Sea. The land, over one-third of which is forested, is generally low-lying with many lakes. Approximately one-third of Estonians live in the capital, Tallinn. Exported goods include machinery, wood products, textiles and food products. The main trading partners are Russia, Finland and Sweden. Estonia joined the European Union in May 2004.

ETHIOPIA
Federal Democratic Republic of Ethiopia

Area Sq Km	1 133 880	**Languages**	Oromo, Amharic, Tigrinya, other local languages
Area Sq Miles	437 794	**Religions**	Ethiopian Orthodox, Sunni Muslim, traditional beliefs
Population	94 101 000	**Currency**	Birr
Capital	Addis Ababa (Ādīs Ābeba)	**Organizations**	UN

Map page 178

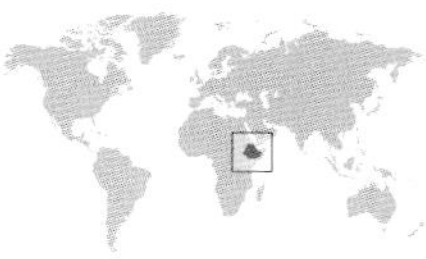

A landlocked country in northeast Africa, Ethiopia comprises a mountainous region in the west which is traversed by the Great Rift Valley. The east is mostly arid plateau land. The highlands are warm with summer rainfall. Most people live in the central–northern area. In recent years civil war, conflict with Eritrea and poor infrastructure have hampered economic development. Subsistence farming is the main activity, although droughts have led to frequent famines. Coffee is the main export and there is some light industry. Ethiopia is one of the least developed countries in the world.

Falkland Islands (Islas Malvinas)
United Kingdom Overseas Territory

Area Sq Km	12 170	**Languages**	English
Area Sq Miles	4 699	**Religions**	Protestant, Roman Catholic
Population	2 931	**Currency**	Falkland Islands pound
Capital	Stanley		

Map page 212 Lying in the southwest Atlantic Ocean, northeast of Cape Horn, two main islands, West Falkland and East Falkland and many smaller islands, form the territory of the Falkland Islands. The economy is based on sheep farming and the sale of fishing licences.

Faroe Islands
Self-governing Danish Territory

Area Sq Km	1 399	**Languages**	Faroese, Danish
Area Sq Miles	540	**Religions**	Protestant
Population	49 000	**Currency**	Danish krone
Capital	Thorshavn (Tórshavn)		

Map page 158 A self-governing territory, the Faroe Islands lie in the north Atlantic Ocean between the UK and Iceland. The islands benefit from the North Atlantic Drift ocean current, which has a moderating effect on the climate. The economy is based on deep-sea fishing.

FIJI
Republic of Fiji

Area Sq Km	18 330	**Languages**	English, Fijian, Hindi
Area Sq Miles	7 077	**Religions**	Christian, Hindu, Sunni Muslim
Population	881 000	**Currency**	Fijian dollar
Capital	Suva	**Organizations**	UN

Map page 125

The southwest Pacific republic of Fiji comprises two mountainous and volcanic islands, Vanua Levu and Viti Levu, and over three hundred smaller islands. The climate is tropical and the economy is based on agriculture (chiefly sugar, the main export), fishing, forestry, gold mining and tourism.

FINLAND
Republic of Finland

Area Sq Km	338 145	**Languages**	Finnish, Swedish, Sami languages
Area Sq Miles	130 559	**Religions**	Protestant, Greek Orthodox
Population	5 426 000	**Currency**	Euro
Capital	Helsinki (Helsingfors)	**Organizations**	EU, OECD, UN

Map page 158–159

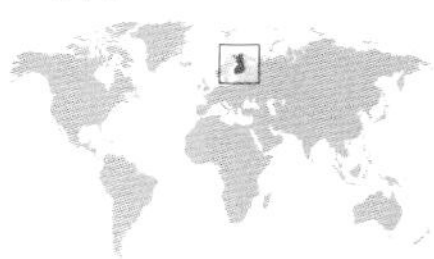

Finland is in northern Europe, and nearly one-third of the country lies north of the Arctic Circle. Forests cover over seventy per cent of the land area, and ten per cent is covered by lakes. Summers are short and warm, and winters are long and severe, particularly in the north. Most of the population lives in the southern third of the country, along the coast or near the lakes. Timber is a major resource and there are important minerals, chiefly chromium. Main industries include metal working, electronics, paper and paper products, and chemicals. The main trading partners are Germany, Sweden and the UK.

FRANCE
French Republic

Area Sq Km	543 965	**Languages**	French, German dialects, Italian, Arabic, Breton
Area Sq Miles	210 026	**Religions**	Roman Catholic, Protestant, Sunni Muslim
Population	64 291 000	**Currency**	Euro
Capital	Paris	**Organizations**	EU, NATO, OECD, UN

Map page 166

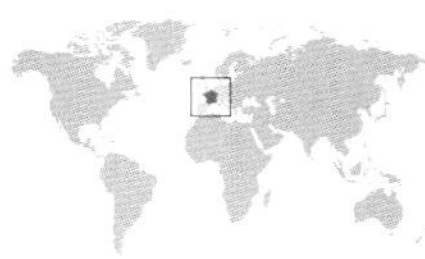

France lies in western Europe and has coastlines on the Atlantic Ocean and the Mediterranean Sea. It includes the Mediterranean island of Corsica. Northern and western regions consist mostly of flat or rolling countryside, and include the major lowlands of the Paris basin, the Loire valley and the Aquitaine basin, drained by the Seine, Loire and Garonne river systems respectively. The centre-south is dominated by the hill region of the Massif Central. To the east are the Vosges and Jura mountains and the Alps. In the southwest, the Pyrenees form a natural border with Spain. The climate is temperate with warm summers and cool winters, although the Mediterranean coast has hot, dry summers and mild winters. Over eighty per cent of the population lives in towns, with almost a sixth of the population living in the Paris area. The French economy has a substantial and varied agricultural base. It is a major producer of both fresh and processed food. There are relatively few mineral resources; it has coal reserves, and some oil and natural gas, but it relies heavily on nuclear and hydroelectric power and imported fuels. France is one of the world's major industrial countries. Main industries include food processing, iron, steel and aluminium production, chemicals, cars, electronics and oil refining. The main exports are transport equipment, plastics and chemicals. Tourism is a major source of revenue and employment. Trade is predominantly with other European Union countries.

French Guiana
French Overseas Department

Area Sq Km	90 000	**Languages**	French, Creole
Area Sq Miles	34 749	**Religions**	Roman Catholic
Population	249 000	**Currency**	Euro
Capital	Cayenne		

Map page 211 French Guiana, on the north coast of South America, is densely forested. The climate is tropical, with high rainfall. Most people live in the coastal strip, and agriculture is mostly subsistence farming. Forestry and fishing are important, but mineral resources are largely unexploited and industry is limited. French Guiana depends on French aid. The main trading partners are France and the USA.

French Polynesia
French Overseas Collectivity

Area Sq Km	3 265	**Languages**	French, Tahitian, other Polynesian languages
Area Sq Miles	1 261	**Religions**	Protestant, Roman Catholic
Population	277 000	**Currency**	CFP franc
Capital	Papeete		

Map page 123 Extending over a vast area of the southeast Pacific Ocean, French Polynesia comprises more than one hundred and thirty islands and coral atolls. The main island groups are the Marquesas Islands, the Tuamotu Archipelago and the Society Islands. The capital, Papeete, is on Tahiti in the Society Islands. The climate is subtropical, and the economy is based on tourism. The main export is cultured pearls.

GABON
Gabonese Republic

Area Sq Km	267 667	**Languages**	French, Fang, other local languages
Area Sq Miles	103 347	**Religions**	Roman Catholic, Protestant, traditional beliefs
Population	1 672 000	**Currency**	CFA franc
Capital	Libreville	**Organizations**	UN

Map page 178

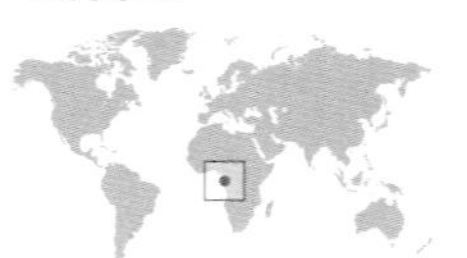

Gabon, on the Atlantic coast of central Africa, consists of low plateaus and a coastal plain lined by lagoons and mangrove swamps. The climate is tropical and rainforests cover over three-quarters of the land area. Nearly ninety per cent of the population lives in towns. The economy is heavily dependent on oil, which accounts for over eighty per cent of exports; manganese, uranium and timber are the other main exports. Agriculture is mainly at subsistence level.

THE GAMBIA
Republic of The Gambia

Area Sq Km	11 295	**Languages**	English, Malinke, Fulani, Wolof
Area Sq Miles	4 361	**Religions**	Sunni Muslim, Protestant
Population	1 849 000	**Currency**	Dalasi
Capital	Banjul	**Organizations**	UN

Map page 176

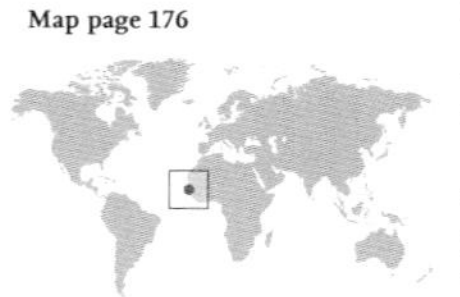

The Gambia, on the coast of west Africa, occupies a strip of land along the lower Gambia river. Sandy beaches are backed by mangrove swamps, beyond which is savanna. The climate is tropical, with most rainfall in the summer. Over seventy per cent of Gambians are farmers, growing chiefly groundnuts (the main export), cotton, oil palms and food crops. Livestock rearing and fishing are important, while manufacturing is limited. Re-exports, mainly from Senegal, and tourism are major sources of income.

Gaza
Disputed territory

Area Sq Km	363	**Languages**	Arabic
Area Sq Miles	140	**Religions**	Sunni Muslim, Shi'a Muslim
Population	1 701 437	**Currency**	Israeli shekel
Capital	Gaza		

Map page 136 Gaza is a narrow strip of land on the southeast corner of the Mediterranean Sea, between Egypt and Israel. This Palestinian territory has limited autonomy from Israel, but hostilities between Israel and the indigenous Arab population continue to restrict its economic development.

GEORGIA

Area Sq Km	69 700	**Languages**	Georgian, Russian, Armenian, Azeri, Ossetian, Abkhaz
Area Sq Miles	26 911	**Religions**	Georgian Orthodox, Russian Orthodox, Sunni Muslim
Population	4 341 000	**Currency**	Lari
Capital	Tbilisi	**Organizations**	UN

Map page 173

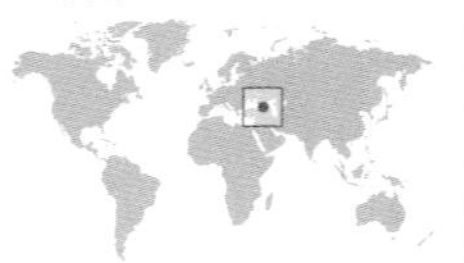

Georgia is in the northwest Caucasus area of southwest Asia, on the eastern coast of the Black Sea. Mountain ranges in the north and south flank the Kura and Rioni valleys. The climate is generally mild, and along the coast it is subtropical. Agriculture is important, with tea, grapes, and citrus fruits the main crops. Mineral resources include manganese ore and oil, and the main industries are steel, oil refining and machine building. The main trading partners are Turkey, Ukraine and Azerbaijan.

GERMANY
Federal Republic of Germany

Area Sq Km	357 022	**Languages**	German, Turkish
Area Sq Miles	137 849	**Religions**	Protestant, Roman Catholic
Population	82 727 000	**Currency**	Euro
Capital	Berlin	**Organizations**	EU, NATO, OECD, UN

Map page 168

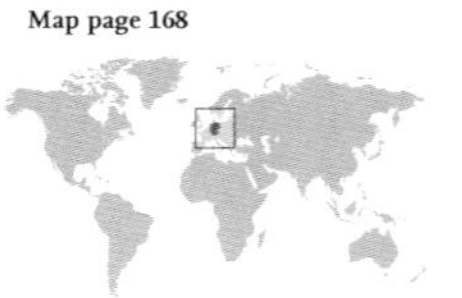

The central European state of Germany borders nine countries and has coastlines on the North and Baltic Seas. Behind the indented coastline, and covering about one-third of the country, is the north German plain, a region of fertile farmland and sandy heaths drained by the country's major rivers. The central highlands are a belt of forested hills and plateaus which stretch from the Eifel region in the west to the Erzgebirge mountains along the border with the Czech Republic. Farther south the land rises to the Swabian Alps (Schwäbische Alb), with the high rugged and forested Black Forest (Schwarzwald) in the southwest. In the far south the Bavarian Alps form the border with Austria. The climate is temperate, with continental conditions in eastern areas. The population is highly urbanized, with nearly seventy-five per cent living in cities and towns. With the exception of coal, lignite, potash and baryte, Germany lacks minerals and other industrial raw materials. It has a small agricultural base, although a few products (chiefly wines and beers) enjoy an international reputation. Germany is the world's fourth ranking economy after the USA, China and Japan. Its industries are amongst the world's most technologically advanced. Exports include machinery, vehicles and chemicals. The majority of trade is with other countries in the European Union, the USA and Japan.

Baden-Württemberg (State)
Area Sq Km (Sq Miles) 35 752 (13 804) **Population** 10 842 000 **Capital** Stuttgart

Bayern (State)
Area Sq Km (Sq Miles) 70 550 (27 240) **Population** 12 670 000 **Capital** Munich (München)

Berlin (State)
Area Sq Km (Sq Miles) 892 (344) **Population** 3 544 000 **Capital** Berlin

Brandenburg (State)
Area Sq Km (Sq Miles) 29 476 (11 381) **Population** 2 492 000 **Capital** Potsdan

Bremen
Area Sq Km (Sq Miles) 404 (156) **Population** 663 000 **Capital** Bremen

Hamburg (State)
Area Sq Km (Sq Miles) 755 (292) **Population** 1 814 000 **Capital** Hamburg

Hessen (State)
Area Sq Km (Sq Miles) 21 114 (8 152) **Population** 6 116 000 **Capital** Wiesbaden

Mecklenburg-Vorpommern (State)
Area Sq Km (Sq Miles) 23 173 (8 947) **Population** 1 629 000 **Capital** Schwerin

Niedersachsen (State)
Area Sq Km (Sq Miles) 47 616 (18 385) **Population** 7 919 000 **Capital** Hannover

Nordrhein-Westfalen (State)
Area Sq Km (Sq Miles) 34 082 (13 159) **Population** 17 853 000 **Capital** Düsseldorf

Rheinland-Pfalz (State)
Area Sq Km (Sq Miles) 19 847 (7 663) **Population** 4 000 000 **Capital** Mainz

Saarland (State)
Area Sq Km (Sq Miles) 2 568 (992) **Population** 1 010 000 **Capital** Saarbrücken

Sachsen (State)
Area Sq Km (Sq Miles) 18 413 (7 109) **Population** 4 134 000 **Capital** Dresden

Sachsen-Anhalt (State)
Area Sq Km (Sq Miles) 20 447 (7 895) **Population** 2 297 000 **Capital** Magdeburg

Schleswig-Holstein (State)
Area Sq Km (Sq Miles) 15 761 (6 085) **Population** 2 842 000 **Capital** Kiel

Thüringen (State)
Area Sq Km (Sq Miles) 16 172 (6 244) **Population** 2 211 000 **Capital** Erfurt

GHANA
Republic of Ghana

Area Sq Km	238 537	**Languages**	English, Hausa, Akan, other local languages
Area Sq Miles	92 100	**Religions**	Christian, Sunni Muslim, traditional beliefs
Population	25 905 000	**Currency**	Cedi
Capital	Accra	**Organizations**	Comm., UN

Map page 176

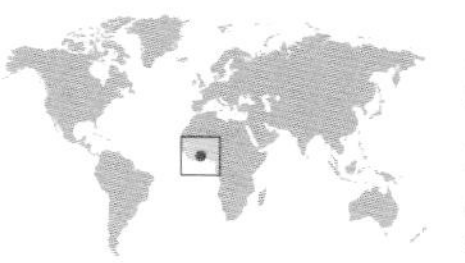

A west African state on the Gulf of Guinea, Ghana is a land of plains and low plateaus covered with savanna and rainforest. In the east is the Volta basin and Lake Volta. The climate is tropical, with the highest rainfall in the south, where most of the population lives. Agriculture employs over fifty per cent of the workforce. Main exports are gold, timber, cocoa, bauxite and manganese ore.

Gibraltar
United Kingdom Overseas Territory

Area Sq Km	7	**Languages**	English, Spanish
Area Sq Miles	3	**Religions**	Roman Catholic, Protestant, Sunni Muslim
Population	29 000	**Currency**	Gibraltar pound
Capital	Gibraltar		

Map page 167 Gibraltar lies on the south coast of Spain at the western entrance to the Mediterranean Sea. The economy depends on tourism, offshore banking and shipping services.

GREECE
Hellenic Republic

Area Sq Km	131 957	**Languages**	Greek
Area Sq Miles	50 949	**Religions**	Greek Orthodox, Sunni Muslim
Population	11 128 000	**Currency**	Euro
Capital	Athens (Athína)	**Organizations**	EU, NATO, OECD, UN

Map page 171

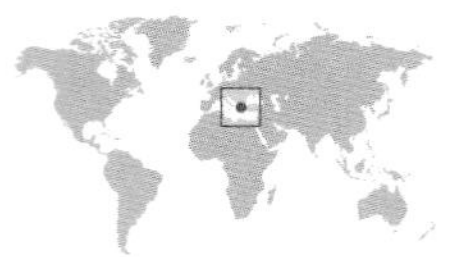

Greece comprises a mountainous peninsula in the Balkan region of southeastern Europe and many islands in the Ionian, Aegean and Mediterranean Seas. The islands make up over one-fifth of its area. Mountains and hills cover much of the country. The main lowland areas are the plains of Thessaly in the centre and around Thessaloniki in the northeast. Summers are hot and dry while winters are mild and wet, but colder in the north with heavy snowfalls in the mountains. One-third of Greeks live in the Athens area. Employment in agriculture accounts for approximately twenty per cent of the workforce, and exports include citrus fruits, raisins, wine, olives and olive oil. Aluminium and nickel are mined and a wide range of manufactures are produced, including food products and tobacco, textiles, clothing, and chemicals. Tourism is an important industry and there is a large services sector. Most trade is with other European Union countries.

Greenland
Self-governing Danish Territory

Area Sq Km	2 175 600	**Languages**	Greenlandic, Danish
Area Sq Miles	840 004	**Religions**	Protestant
Population	57 000	**Currency**	Danish krone
Capital	Nuuk (Godthåb)		

Map page 185

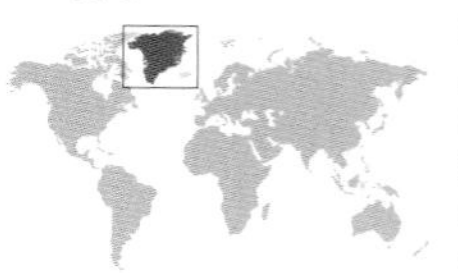

Situated to the northeast of North America between the Atlantic and Arctic Oceans, Greenland is the largest island in the world. It has a polar climate and over eighty per cent of the land area is covered by permanent ice cap. The economy is based on fishing and fish processing.

GRENADA

Area Sq Km	378	**Languages**	English, Creole
Area Sq Miles	146	**Religions**	Roman Catholic, Protestant
Population	106 000	**Currency**	East Caribbean dollar
Capital	St George's	**Organizations**	CARICOM, Comm., UN

Map page 213

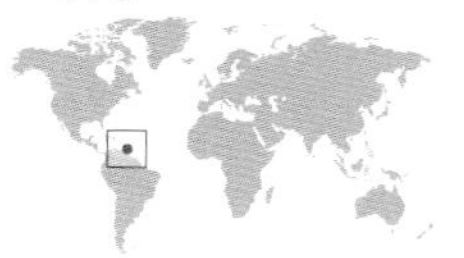

The Caribbean state comprises Grenada, the most southerly of the Windward Islands, and the southern islands of the Grenadines. Grenada has wooded hills, with beaches in the southwest. The climate is warm and wet. Agriculture is the main activity, with bananas, nutmeg and cocoa the main exports. Tourism is the main foreign exchange earner.

Guadeloupe
French Overseas Department

Area Sq Km	1 780	**Languages**	French, Creole
Area Sq Miles	687	**Religions**	Roman Catholic
Population	466 000	**Currency**	Euro
Capital	Basse-Terre		

Map page 205 Guadeloupe, in the Leeward Islands in the Caribbean, consists of two main islands (Basse-Terre and Grande-Terre, connected by a bridge), Marie-Galante, and a few outer islands. The climate is tropical, but moderated by trade winds. Bananas, sugar and rum are the main exports and tourism is a major source of income.

Guam
United States Unincorporated Territory

Area Sq Km	541	**Languages**	Chamorro, English, Tagalog
Area Sq Miles	209	**Religions**	Roman Catholic
Population	165 000	**Currency**	United States dollar
Capital	Hagåtña		

Map page 147 Lying at the south end of the Northern Mariana Islands in the western Pacific Ocean, Guam has a humid tropical climate. The island has a large US military base and the economy relies on that and on tourism.

GUATEMALA
Republic of Guatemala

Area Sq Km	108 890	**Languages**	Spanish, Mayan languages
Area Sq Miles	42 043	**Religions**	Roman Catholic, Protestant
Population	15 468 000	**Currency**	Quetzal
Capital	Guatemala City	**Organizations**	UN

Map page 207

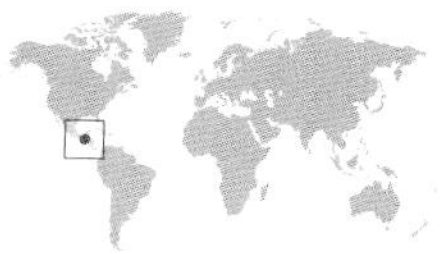

The most populous country in Central America after Mexico, Guatemala has long Pacific and short Caribbean coasts separated by a mountain chain which includes several active volcanoes. The climate is hot tropical in the lowlands and cooler in the highlands, where most of the population lives. Farming is the main activity and coffee, sugar and bananas are the main exports. There is some manufacturing of clothing and textiles. The main trading partner is the USA.

Guernsey
United Kingdom Crown Dependency

Area Sq Km	78	**Languages**	English, French
Area Sq Miles	30	**Religions**	Protestant, Roman Catholic
Population	65 578	**Currency**	Pound sterling
Capital	St Peter Port		

Map page 166 Guernsey is one of the Channel Islands, lying off northern France. The dependency also includes the nearby islands of Alderney, Sark and Herm. Financial services are an important part of the island's economy.

GUINEA
Republic of Guinea

Area Sq Km	245 857	**Languages**	French, Fulani, Malinke, other local languages
Area Sq Miles	94 926	**Religions**	Sunni Muslim, traditional beliefs, Christian
Population	11 745 000	**Currency**	Guinean franc
Capital	Conakry	**Organizations**	UN

Map page 176

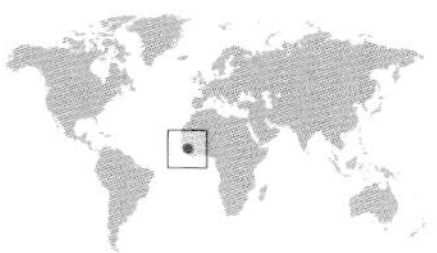

Guinea is in west Africa, on the Atlantic Ocean. There are mangrove swamps along the coast, while inland are lowlands and the Fouta Djallon mountains and plateaus. To the east are savanna plains drained by the upper Niger river system. The southeast is hilly. The climate is tropical, with high coastal rainfall. Agriculture is the main activity, employing nearly eighty per cent of the workforce, with coffee, bananas and pineapples the chief cash crops. There are huge reserves of bauxite, which accounts for more than seventy per cent of exports. Other exports include aluminium oxide, gold, coffee and diamonds.

GUINEA-BISSAU
Republic of Guinea-Bissau

Area Sq Km	36 125	**Languages**	Portuguese, Crioulo, other local languages
Area Sq Miles	13 948	**Religions**	Traditional beliefs, Sunni Muslim, Christian
Population	1 704 000	**Currency**	CFA franc
Capital	Bissau	**Organizations**	UN

Map page 176

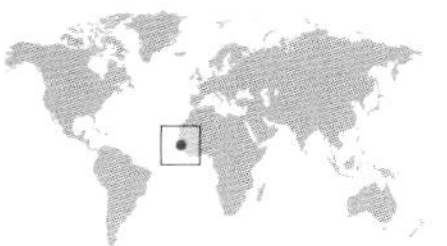

Guinea-Bissau is on the Atlantic coast of west Africa. The mainland coast is swampy and contains many estuaries. Inland are forested plains, and to the east are savanna plateaus. The climate is tropical. The economy is based mainly on subsistence farming. There is little industry, and timber and mineral resources are largely unexploited. Cashews account for seventy per cent of exports. Guinea-Bissau is one of the least developed countries in the world.

GUYANA
Co-operative Republic of Guyana

Area Sq Km	214 969	**Languages**	English, Creole, Amerindian languages
Area Sq Miles	83 000	**Religions**	Protestant, Hindu, Roman Catholic, Sunni Muslim
Population	800 000	**Currency**	Guyanese dollar
Capital	Georgetown	**Organizations**	CARICOM, Comm., UN

Map page 210–211

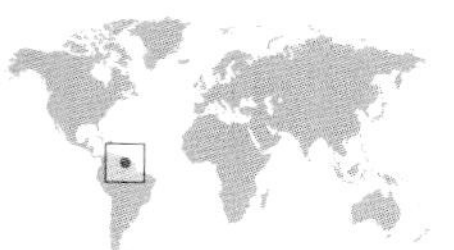

Guyana, on the northeast coast of South America, consists of highlands in the west and savanna uplands in the southwest. Most of the country is densely forested. A lowland coastal belt supports crops and most of the population. The generally hot, humid and wet conditions are modified along the coast by sea breezes. The economy is based on agriculture, bauxite, and forestry. Sugar, bauxite, gold, rice and timber are the main exports.

HAITI
Republic of Haiti

Area Sq Km	27 750	**Languages**	French, Creole
Area Sq Miles	10 714	**Religions**	Roman Catholic, Protestant, Voodoo
Population	10 317 000	**Currency**	Gourde
Capital	Port-au-Prince	**Organizations**	CARICOM, UN

Map page 205

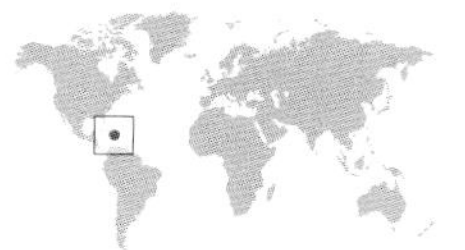

Haiti, occupying the western third of the Caribbean island of Hispaniola, is a mountainous state with small coastal plains and a central valley. The Dominican Republic occupies the rest of the island. The climate is tropical, and is hottest in coastal areas. Haiti has few natural resources, is densely populated and relies on exports of local crafts and coffee, and remittances from workers abroad. The country has not yet recovered from the 2010 earthquake.

HONDURAS
Republic of Honduras

Area Sq Km	112 088	**Languages**	Spanish, Amerindian languages
Area Sq Miles	43 277	**Religions**	Roman Catholic, Protestant
Population	8 098 000	**Currency**	Lempira
Capital	Tegucigalpa	**Organizations**	UN

Map page 206

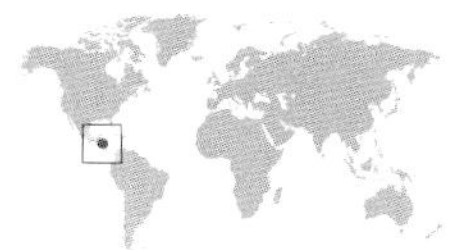

Honduras, in central America, is a mountainous and forested country with lowland areas along its long Caribbean and short Pacific coasts. Coastal areas are hot and humid with heavy summer rainfall; inland is cooler and drier. Most of the population lives in the central valleys. Coffee and bananas are the main exports, along with shellfish and zinc. Industry involves mainly agricultural processing.

HUNGARY

Area Sq Km	93 030	**Languages**	Hungarian
Area Sq Miles	35 919	**Religions**	Roman Catholic, Protestant
Population	9 955 000	**Currency**	Forint
Capital	Budapest	**Organizations**	EU, NATO, OECD, UN

Map page 168–169

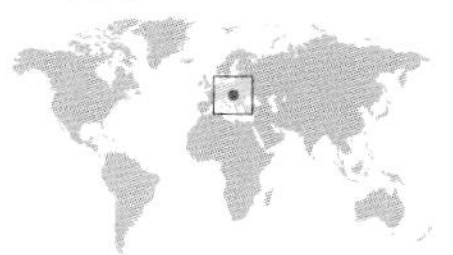

The Danube river flows north-south through central Hungary, a landlocked country in eastern Europe. In the east lies a great plain, flanked by highlands in the north. In the west low mountains and Lake Balaton separate a smaller plain and southern uplands. The climate is continental. Seventy per cent of the population lives in urban areas, and one-sixth lives in the capital, Budapest. Some minerals and energy resources are exploited, chiefly bauxite, coal and natural gas. Hungary has an industrial economy based on metals, machinery, transport equipment, chemicals and food products. The main trading partners are Germany and Austria. Hungary joined the European Union in May 2004.

ICELAND
Republic of Iceland

Area Sq Km	102 820	**Languages**	Icelandic
Area Sq Miles	39 699	**Religions**	Protestant
Population	330 000	**Currency**	Icelandic króna
Capital	Reykjavík	**Organizations**	NATO, OECD, UN

Map page 158

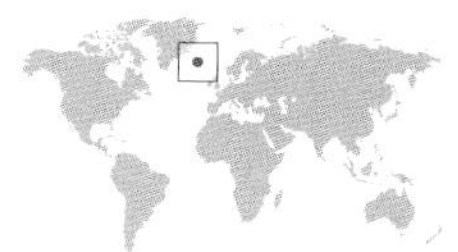

Iceland lies in the north Atlantic Ocean near the Arctic Circle, to the northwest of Scandinavia. The landscape is volcanic, with numerous hot springs, geysers, and approximately two hundred volcanoes. One-tenth of the country is covered by ice caps. Only coastal lowlands are cultivated and settled, and over half the population lives in the Reykjavik area. The climate is mild, moderated by the North Atlantic Drift ocean current and by southwesterly winds. The mainstays of the economy are fishing and fish processing, which account for a third of export earnings. Agriculture involves mainly sheep and dairy farming. Hydroelectric and geothermal energy resources are considerable. The main industries produce aluminium, ferro-silicon and fertilizers. Tourism, including ecotourism, is growing in importance.

INDIA
Republic of India

Area Sq Km	3 166 620	**Languages**	Hindi, English, many regional languages
Area Sq Miles	1 222 632	**Religions**	Hindu, Sunni Muslim, Shi'a Muslim, Sikh, Christian
Population	1 252 140 000	**Currency**	Indian rupee
Capital	New Delhi	**Organizations**	Comm., UN

Map page 134–135

The south Asian country of India occupies a peninsula that juts out into the Indian Ocean between the Arabian Sea and Bay of Bengal. The heart of the peninsula is the Deccan plateau, bordered on either side by ranges of hills, the western Ghats and the lower eastern Ghats, which fall away to narrow coastal plains. To the north is a broad plain, drained by the Indus, Ganges and Brahmaputra rivers and their tributaries. The plain is intensively farmed and is the most populous region. In the west is the Thar Desert. The mountains of the Himalaya form India's northern border, together with parts of the Karakoram and Hindu Kush ranges in the northwest. The climate shows marked seasonal variation: a hot season from March to June; a monsoon season from June to October; and a cold season from November to February. Rainfall ranges between very high in the northeast Assam region to negligible in the Thar Desert. Temperatures range from very cold in the Himalaya to tropical heat over much of the south. Over sixty-seven per cent of the huge population – the second largest in the world – is rural, although Delhi, Mumbai (Bombay) and Kolkata (Calcutta) all rank among the ten largest cities in the world. Agriculture, forestry and fishing account for a quarter of national output and two-thirds of employment. Much of the farming is on a subsistence basis and involves mainly rice and wheat. India is a major world producer of tea, sugar, jute, cotton and tobacco. Livestock is reared mainly for dairy products and hides. There are major reserves of coal, reserves of oil and natural gas, and many minerals, including iron, manganese, bauxite, diamonds and gold. The manufacturing sector is large and diverse – mainly chemicals and chemical products, textiles, iron and steel, food products, electrical goods and transport equipment; software and pharmaceuticals are also important. All the main manufactured products are exported, together with diamonds and jewellery. The USA, Germany, Japan and the UK are the main trading partners.

INDONESIA
Republic of Indonesia

Area Sq Km	1 919 445	**Languages**	Indonesian, other local languages
Area Sq Miles	741 102	**Religions**	Sunni Muslim, Protestant, Roman Catholic, Hindu, Buddhist
Population	249 866 000	**Currency**	Rupiah
Capital	Jakarta	**Organizations**	APEC, ASEAN, UN

Map page 147

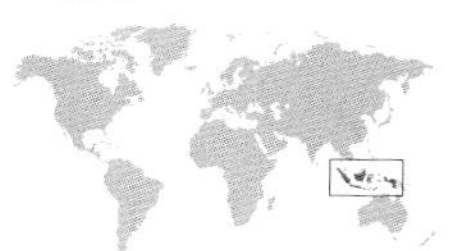

Indonesia, the largest and most populous country in southeast Asia, consists of over thirteen thousand islands extending between the Pacific and Indian Oceans. Sumatra, Java, Sulawesi (Celebes), Kalimantan (two-thirds of Borneo) and Papua (formerly Irian Jaya, western New Guinea) make up ninety per cent of the land area. Most of Indonesia is mountainous and covered with rainforest or mangrove swamps, and there are over three hundred volcanoes, many active. Two-thirds of the population lives in the lowland areas of the islands of Java and Madura. The climate is tropical monsoon. Agriculture is the largest sector of the economy and Indonesia is among the world's top producers of rice, palm oil, tea, coffee, rubber and tobacco. Many goods are produced, including textiles, clothing, cement, tin, fertilizers and vehicles. Main exports are oil, natural gas, timber products and clothing. Main trading partners are Japan, the USA and Singapore.

IRAN
Islamic Republic of Iran

Area Sq Km	1 648 000	**Languages**	Farsi, Azeri, Kurdish, regional languages
Area Sq Miles	636 296	**Religions**	Shi'a Muslim, Sunni Muslim
Population	77 447 000	**Currency**	Iranian rial
Capital	Tehrān	**Organizations**	OPEC, UN

Map page 140–141

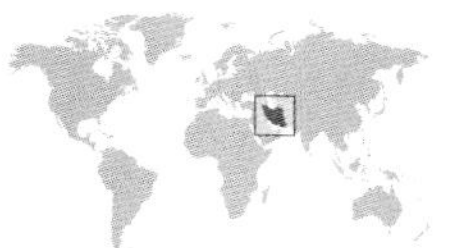

Iran is in southwest Asia, and has coasts on The Gulf, the Caspian Sea and the Gulf of Oman. In the east is a high plateau, with large salt pans and a vast sand desert. In the west the Zagros Mountains form a series of ridges, and to the north lie the Elburz Mountains. Most farming and settlement is on the narrow plain along the Caspian Sea and in the foothills of the north and west. The climate is one of extremes, with hot summers and very cold winters. Most of the light rainfall is in the winter months. Agriculture involves approximately one-fifth of the workforce. Wheat is the main crop, but fruit (especially dates) and pistachio nuts are grown for export. Petroleum (the main export) and natural gas are Iran's leading natural resources. Manufactured goods include carpets, clothing, food products and construction materials.

IRAQ
Republic of Iraq

Area Sq Km	438 317	**Languages**	Arabic, Kurdish, Turkmen
Area Sq Miles	169 235	**Religions**	Shi'a Muslim, Sunni Muslim, Christian
Population	33 765 000	**Currency**	Iraqi dinar
Capital	Baghdād	**Organizations**	OPEC, UN

Map page 137

Iraq, in southwest Asia, has at its heart the lowland valley of the Tigris and Euphrates rivers. In the southeast, where the two rivers join, are the Mesopotamian marshes and the Shaṭṭ al 'Arab waterway leading to The Gulf. The north is hilly, while the west is mostly desert. Summers are hot and dry, and winters are mild with light, unreliable rainfall. The Tigris-Euphrates valley contains most of the country's arable land. One in five of the population lives in the capital, Baghdad. The economy has suffered following the 1991 Gulf War and the invasion of US-led coalition forces in 2005. The latter resulted in the overthrow of the dictator Saddam Hussein, but there is continuing internal instability. Oil is normally the main export.

IRELAND

Area Sq Km	70 282	**Languages**	English, Irish
Area Sq Miles	27 136	**Religions**	Roman Catholic, Protestant
Population	4 627 000	**Currency**	Euro
Capital	Dublin (Baile Átha Cliath)	**Organizations**	EU, OECD, UN

Map page 163

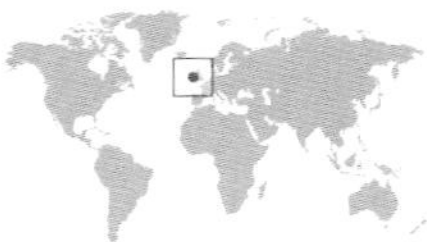

The Irish Republic occupies some eighty per cent of the island of Ireland, in northwest Europe. It is a lowland country of wide valleys, lakes and peat bogs, with isolated mountain ranges around the coast. The west coast is rugged and indented with many bays. The climate is mild due to the modifying effect of the North Atlantic Drift ocean current and rainfall is plentiful, although highest in the west. Over sixty per cent of the population lives in urban areas, Dublin and Cork being the main cities. Resources include natural gas, peat, lead and zinc. Agriculture, the traditional mainstay, now employs less than six per cent of the workforce, while industry employs nearly thirty per cent. The main industries are electronics, pharmaceuticals and engineering as well as food processing, brewing and textiles. Service industries are expanding, with tourism a major earner. The UK and USA are the main trading partners.

Isle of Man
United Kingdom Crown Dependency

Area Sq Km	572	**Languages**	English
Area Sq Miles	221	**Religions**	Protestant, Roman Catholic
Population	86 000	**Currency**	Pound sterling
Capital	Douglas		

Map page 160

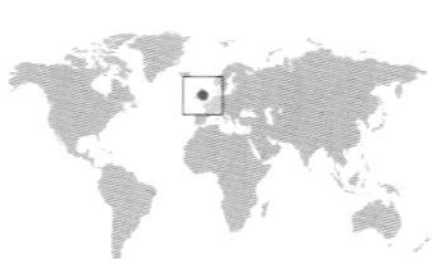

The Isle of Man lies in the Irish Sea between England and Northern Ireland. The island is self-governing, although the UK is responsible for its defence and foreign affairs. It is not part of the European Union, but has a special relationship with the EU which allows for free trade. Eighty per cent of the economy is based on the service sector, particularly financial services.

ISRAEL
State of Israel

Area Sq Km	22 072	**Languages**	Hebrew, Arabic
Area Sq Miles	8 522	**Religions**	Jewish, Sunni Muslim, Christian, Druze
Population	7 733 000	**Currency**	Shekel
Capital	Jerusalem (Yerushalayim) (El Quds) De facto capital. Disputed.	**Organizations**	OECD, UN

Map page 136

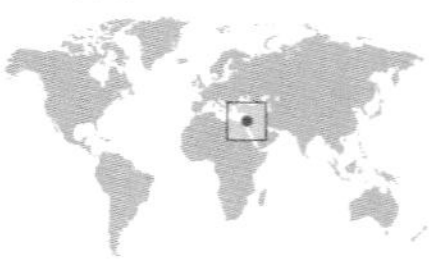

Israel lies on the Mediterranean coast of southwest Asia. Beyond the coastal Plain of Sharon are the hills and valleys of Samaria, with the Galilee highlands to the north. In the east is a rift valley, which extends from Lake Tiberias (Sea of Galilee) to the Gulf of Aqaba and contains the Jordan river and the Dead Sea. In the south is the Negev, a triangular semi-desert plateau. Most of the population lives on the coastal plain or in northern and central areas. Much of Israel has warm summers and mild, wet winters. The south is hot and dry. Agricultural production was boosted by the occupation of the West Bank in 1967. Manufacturing makes the largest contribution to the economy, and tourism is also important. Israel's main exports are machinery and transport equipment, software, diamonds, clothing, fruit and vegetables. The country relies heavily on foreign aid. Security issues relating to territorial disputes over the West Bank and Gaza have still to be resolved.

ITALY
Italian Republic

Area Sq Km	301 245	**Languages**	Italian
Area Sq Miles	116 311	**Religions**	Roman Catholic
Population	60 990 000	**Currency**	Euro
Capital	Rome (Roma)	**Organizations**	EU, NATO, OECD, UN

Map page 170–171

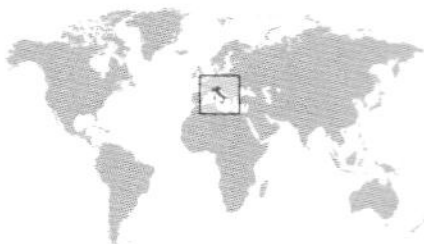

Most of the southern European state of Italy occupies a peninsula that juts out into the Mediterranean Sea. It includes the islands of Sicily and Sardinia and approximately seventy much smaller islands in the surrounding seas. Italy is mountainous, dominated by the Alps, which form its northern border, and the various ranges of the Apennines, which run almost the full length of the peninsula. Many of Italy's mountains are of volcanic origin, and its active volcanoes are Vesuvius, near Naples, Etna and Stromboli. The main lowland area, the Po river valley in the northeast, is the main agricultural and industrial area and is the most populous region. Italy has a Mediterranean climate, although the north experiences colder, wetter winters, with heavy snow in the Alps. The economy is fairly diversified. Some oil, natural gas and coal are produced, but most fuels and minerals used by industry are imported. Agriculture is important, with about a third of the land under cultivation and cereals, vines, fruit and vegetables are the main crops. Italy is the world's second largest wine producer. The north is the centre of Italian industry, especially around Turin, Milan and Genoa. Leading manufactures include industrial and office equipment, domestic appliances, cars, textiles, clothing, leather goods, chemicals and metal products. There is a strong service sector, and with over forty-six million visitors a year, tourism is a major employer and accounts for ten per cent of the national income. Finance and banking are also important. Most trade is with other European Union countries.

JAMAICA

Area Sq Km	10 991	**Languages**	English, Creole
Area Sq Miles	4 244	**Religions**	Protestant, Roman Catholic
Population	2 784 000	**Currency**	Jamaican dollar
Capital	Kingston	**Organizations**	CARICOM, Comm., UN

Map page 205

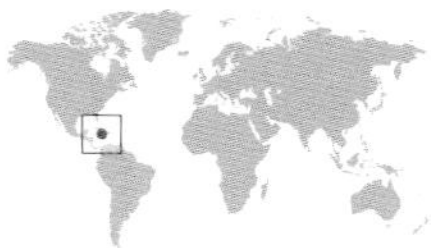

Jamaica, the third largest Caribbean island, has beaches and densely populated coastal plains traversed by hills and plateaus rising to the forested Blue Mountains in the east. The climate is tropical, but cooler and wetter on high ground. The economy is based on tourism, agriculture, mining and light manufacturing. Bauxite, aluminium oxide, sugar and bananas are the main exports. The USA is the main trading partner. Foreign aid is also significant.

JAPAN

Area Sq Km	377 727	**Languages**	Japanese
Area Sq Miles	145 841	**Religions**	Shintoist, Buddhist, Christian
Population	127 144 000	**Currency**	Yen
Capital	Tōkyō	**Organizations**	APEC, OECD, UN

Map page 150–151

Japan lies in the Pacific Ocean off the coast of eastern Asia and consists of four main islands – Hokkaidō, Honshū, Shikoku and Kyūshū – and more than three thousand smaller islands in the surrounding Sea of Japan, East China Sea and Pacific Ocean. The central island of Honshū accounts for sixty per cent of the total land area and contains eighty per cent of the population. Behind the long and deeply indented coastline, nearly three-quarters of the country is mountainous and heavily forested. Japan has over sixty active volcanoes, and is subject to frequent earthquakes and typhoons. The climate is generally temperate maritime, with warm summers and mild winters, except in western Hokkaidō and northwest Honshū, where the winters are very cold with heavy snow. Only fourteen per cent of the land area is suitable for cultivation, and its few raw materials (coal, oil, natural gas, lead, zinc and copper) are insufficient for its industry. Most materials must be imported, including about ninety per cent of energy requirements. Yet Japan has the world's second largest industrial economy, with a range of modern heavy and light industries centred mainly around the major ports of Yokohama, Ōsaka and Tōkyō. It is the world's largest manufacturer of cars, motorcycles and merchant ships, and a major producer of steel, textiles, chemicals and cement. It is also a leading producer of many consumer durables, such as washing machines, and electronic equipment, chiefly office equipment and computers. Japan has a strong service sector, banking and finance being particularly important, and Tōkyō has one of the world's major stock exchanges. Owing to intensive agricultural production, Japan is seventy per cent self-sufficient in food. The main food crops are rice, barley, fruit, wheat and soya beans. Livestock rearing (chiefly cattle, pigs and chickens) and fishing are also important, and Japan has one of the largest fishing fleets in the world. A major trading nation, Japan has trade links with many countries in southeast Asia and in Europe, although its main trading partner is the USA.

Jersey
United Kingdom Crown Dependency

Area Sq Km	116	**Languages**	English, French
Area Sq Miles	45	**Religions**	Protestant, Roman Catholic
Population	99 000	**Currency**	Pound sterling
Capital	St Helier		

Map page 166 One of the Channel Islands lying off the west coast of the Cherbourg peninsula in northern France. Financial services are the most important part of the economy.

JORDAN
Hashemite Kingdom of Jordan

Area Sq Km	89 206	**Languages**	Arabic
Area Sq Miles	34 443	**Religions**	Sunni Muslim, Christian
Population	7 274 000	**Currency**	Jordanian dinar
Capital	'Ammān	**Organizations**	UN

Map page 136–137

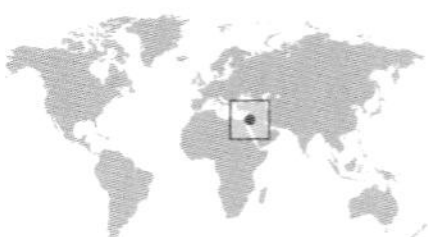

Jordan, in southwest Asia, is landlocked apart from a short coastline on the Gulf of Aqaba. Much of the country is rocky desert plateau. To the west of the mountains, the land falls below sea level to the Dead Sea and the Jordan river. The climate is hot and dry. Most people live in the northwest. Phosphates, potash, pharmaceuticals, fruit and vegetables are the main exports. The tourist industry is important, and the economy relies on workers' remittances from abroad and foreign aid.

KAZAKHSTAN
Republic of Kazakhstan

Area Sq Km	2 717 300	**Languages**	Kazakh, Russian, Ukrainian, German, Uzbek, Tatar
Area Sq Miles	1 049 155	**Religions**	Sunni Muslim, Russian Orthodox, Protestant
Population	16 441 000	**Currency**	Tenge
Capital	Astana (Akmola)	**Organizations**	CIS, UN

Map page 138–139

Stretching across central Asia, Kazakhstan covers a vast area of steppe land and semi-desert. The land is flat in the west, with large lowlands around the Caspian Sea, rising to mountains in the southeast. The climate is continental. Agriculture and livestock rearing are important, and cotton and tobacco are the main cash crops. Kazakhstan is very rich in minerals, including coal, chromium, gold, molybdenum, lead and zinc, and has substantial reserves of oil and gas. Mining, metallurgy, machine building and food processing are major industries. Oil, gas and minerals are the main exports, and Russia is the dominant trading partner.

KENYA
Republic of Kenya

Area Sq Km	582 646	**Languages**	Swahili, English, other local languages
Area Sq Miles	224 961	**Religions**	Christian, traditional beliefs
Population	44 354 000	**Currency**	Kenyan shilling
Capital	Nairobi	**Organizations**	Comm., UN

Map page 178

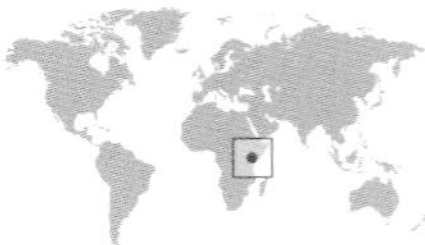

Kenya is in east Africa, on the Indian Ocean. Inland beyond the coastal plains the land rises to plateaus interrupted by volcanic mountains. The Great Rift Valley runs north-south to the west of the capital, Nairobi. Most of the population lives in the central area. Conditions are tropical on the coast, semi-desert in the north and savanna in the south. Hydroelectric power from the Upper Tana river provides most of the country's electricity. Agricultural products, mainly tea, coffee, fruit and vegetables, are the main exports. Light industry is important, and tourism, oil refining and re-exports for landlocked neighbours are major foreign exchange earners.

KIRIBATI
Republic of Kiribati

Area Sq Km	717	**Languages**	Gilbertese, English
Area Sq Miles	277	**Religions**	Roman Catholic, Protestant
Population	102 000	**Currency**	Australian dollar
Capital	Bairiki	**Organizations**	Comm., UN

Map page 123

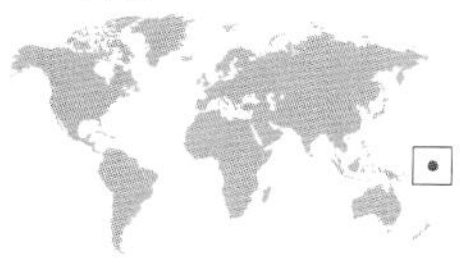

Kiribati, in the Pacific Ocean, straddles the Equator and comprises coral islands in the Gilbert, Phoenix and Line Island groups and the volcanic island of Banaba. Most people live on the Gilbert Islands, and the capital, Bairiki, is on Tarawa island in this group. The climate is hot, and wetter in the north. Copra and fish are exported. Kiribati relies on remittances from workers abroad and foreign aid.

KOSOVO
Republic of Kosovo

Area Sq Km	10 908	**Languages**	Albanian, Serbian
Area Sq Miles	4 212	**Religions**	Sunni Muslim, Serbian Orthodox
Population	1 815 606	**Currency**	Euro
Capital	Prishtinë (Priština)		

Map page 171

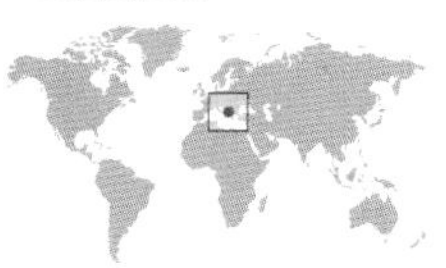

Kosovo, traditionally an autonomous southern province of Serbia, was the focus of ethnic conflict between Serbs and the majority ethnic Albanians in the 1990s until international intervention in 1999, after which it was administered by the UN. Kosovo declared its independence from Serbia in February 2008. The landscape is largely hilly or mountainous, especially along the southern and western borders.

KUWAIT
State of Kuwait

Area Sq Km	17 818	**Languages**	Arabic
Area Sq Miles	6 880	**Religions**	Sunni Muslim, Shi'a Muslim, Christian, Hindu
Population	3 369 000	**Currency**	Kuwaiti dinar
Capital	Kuwait (Al Kuwayt)	**Organizations**	GCC, OPEC, UN

Map page 137

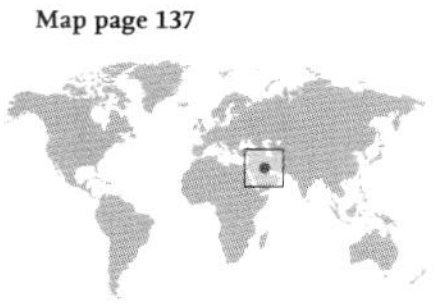

Kuwait lies on the northwest shores of The Gulf in southwest Asia. It is mainly low-lying desert, with irrigated areas along the bay, Kuwait Jun, where most people live. Summers are hot and dry, and winters are cool with some rainfall. The oil industry, which accounts for over ninety per cent of exports, has recovered from the damage caused by the Gulf War in 1991. Income is also derived from extensive overseas investments. Japan and the USA are the main trading partners.

KYRGYZSTAN
Kyrgyz Republic

Area Sq Km	198 500	**Languages**	Kyrgyz, Russian, Uzbek
Area Sq Miles	76 641	**Religions**	Sunni Muslim, Russian Orthodox
Population	5 548 000	**Currency**	Kyrgyz som
Capital	Bishkek (Frunze)	**Organizations**	CIS, UN

Map page 139

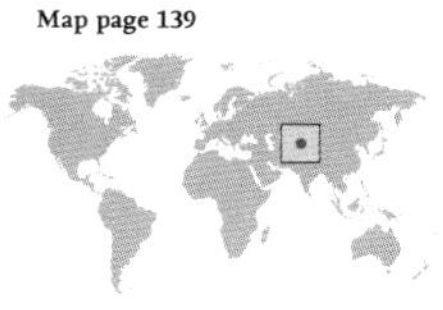

A landlocked central Asian state, Kyrgyzstan is rugged and mountainous, lying to the west of the Tien Shan mountain range. Most of the population lives in the valleys of the north and west. Summers are hot and winters cold. Agriculture (chiefly livestock farming) is the main activity. Some oil and gas, coal, gold, antimony and mercury are produced. Manufactured goods include machinery, metals and metal products, which are the main exports. Most trade is with Germany, Russia, Kazakhstan and Uzbekistan.

LAOS
Lao People's Democratic Republic

Area Sq Km	236 800	**Languages**	Lao, other other local languages
Area Sq Miles	91 429	**Religions**	Buddhist, traditional beliefs
Population	6 770 000	**Currency**	Kip
Capital	Vientiane (Viangchan)	**Organizations**	ASEAN, UN

Map page 147

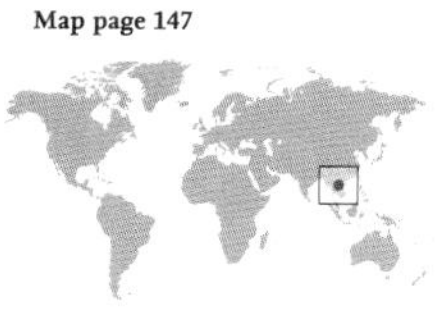

A landlocked country in southeast Asia, Laos is a land of mostly forested mountains and plateaus. The climate is tropical monsoon. Most of the population lives in the Mekong valley and the low plateau in the south, where food crops, chiefly rice, are grown. Hydroelectricity from a plant on the Mekong river, timber, coffee and tin are exported. Laos relies heavily on foreign aid.

LATVIA
Republic of Latvia

Area Sq Km	64 589	**Languages**	Latvian, Russian
Area Sq Miles	24 938	**Religions**	Protestant, Roman Catholic, Russian Orthodox
Population	2 050 000	**Currency**	Euro
Capital	Rīga	**Organizations**	EU, NATO, UN

Map page 159

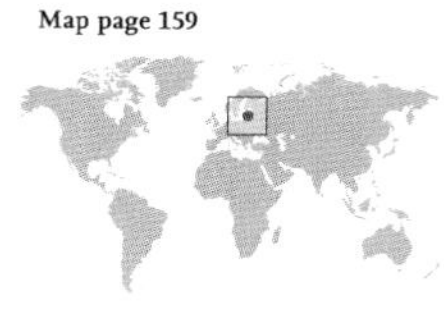

Latvia is in northern Europe, on the Baltic Sea and the Gulf of Riga. The land is flat near the coast but hilly with woods and lakes inland. The country has a modified continental climate. Over a quarter of the people live in the capital, Rīga. Crop and livestock farming are important. There are few natural resources. Industries and main exports include food products, transport equipment, wood and wood products and textiles. The main trading partners are Russia and Germany. Latvia joined the European Union in May 2004.

LEBANON
Lebanese Republic

Area Sq Km	10 452	**Languages**	Arabic, Armenian, French
Area Sq Miles	4 036	**Religions**	Shi'a Muslim, Sunni Muslim, Christian
Population	4 822 000	**Currency**	Lebanese pound
Capital	Beirut (Beyrouth)	**Organizations**	UN

Map page 136

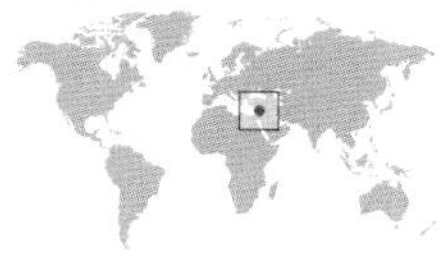

Lebanon lies on the Mediterranean coast of southwest Asia. Beyond the coastal strip, where most of the population lives, are two parallel mountain ranges, separated by the Bekaa Valley (El Beq'a). The economy and infrastructure have been recovering since the 1975–1991 civil war crippled the traditional sectors of financial services and tourism. Switzerland, the USA, France and the UAE are the main trading partners.

LESOTHO
Kingdom of Lesotho

Area Sq Km	30 355	**Languages**	Sesotho, English, Zulu
Area Sq Miles	11 720	**Religions**	Christian, traditional beliefs
Population	2 074 000	**Currency**	Loti, South African rand
Capital	Maseru	**Organizations**	Comm., SADC, UN

Map page 181

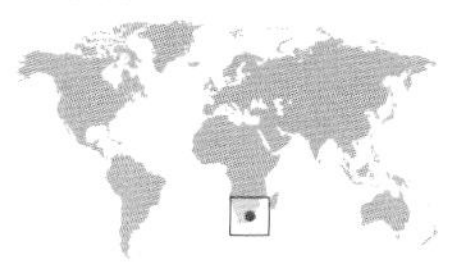

Lesotho is a landlocked state surrounded by South Africa. It is a mountainous country lying within the Drakensberg mountain range. Farming and herding are the main activities. The economy depends heavily on South Africa for transport links and employment. A major hydroelectric plant completed in 1998 allows the sale of water to South Africa. Exports include manufactured goods (mainly clothing and road vehicles), food, live animals, wool and mohair.

LIBERIA
Republic of Liberia

Area Sq Km	111 369	**Languages**	English, Creole, other local languages
Area Sq Miles	43 000	**Religions**	Traditional beliefs, Christian, Sunni Muslim
Population	4 294 000	**Currency**	Liberian dollar
Capital	Monrovia	**Organizations**	UN

Map page 176

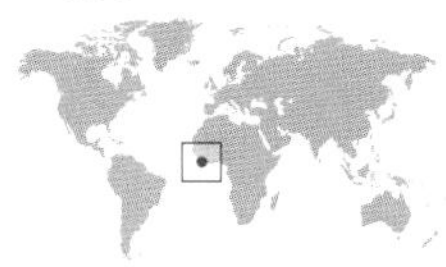

Liberia is on the Atlantic coast of west Africa. Beyond the coastal belt of sandy beaches and mangrove swamps the land rises to a forested plateau and highlands along the Guinea border. A quarter of the population lives along the coast. The climate is hot with heavy rainfall. Liberia is rich in mineral resources and forests. The economy is based on the production and export of basic products. Exports include diamonds, iron ore, rubber and timber. Liberia has a huge international debt and relies heavily on foreign aid.

LIBYA
State of Libya

Area Sq Km	1 759 540	**Languages**	Arabic, Berber
Area Sq Miles	679 362	**Religions**	Sunni Muslim
Population	6 202 000	**Currency**	Libyan dinar
Capital	Tripoli (Ṭarābulus)	**Organizations**	OPEC, UN

Map page 176–177

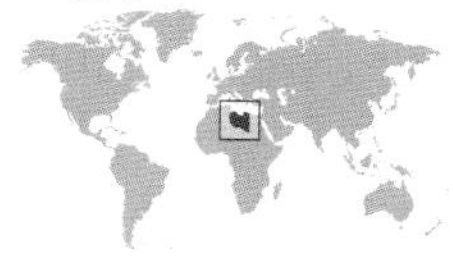

Libya lies on the Mediterranean coast of north Africa. The desert plains and hills of the Sahara dominate the landscape and the climate is hot and dry. Most of the population lives in cities near the coast, where the climate is cooler with moderate rainfall. Farming and herding, chiefly in the northwest, are important but the main industry is oil. Libya is a major producer, and oil accounts for most of its export earnings. Italy and Germany are the main trading partners. As a result of the civil war in 2011 oil exports were disrupted and there was severe damage to the infrastructure of the country.

LIECHTENSTEIN
Principality of Liechtenstein

Area Sq Km	160	**Languages**	German
Area Sq Miles	62	**Religions**	Roman Catholic, Protestant
Population	37 000	**Currency**	Swiss franc
Capital	Vaduz	**Organizations**	UN

Map page 166

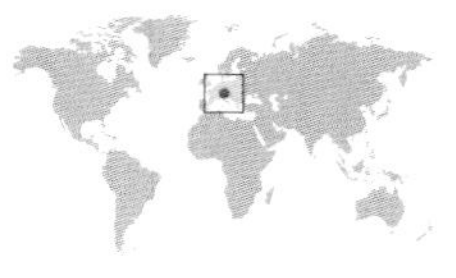

A landlocked state between Switzerland and Austria, Liechtenstein has an industrialized, free-enterprise economy. Low business taxes have attracted companies to establish offices which provide approximately one-third of state revenues. Banking is also important. Major products include precision instruments, ceramics and textiles.

LITHUANIA
Republic of Lithuania

Area Sq Km	65 200	**Languages**	Lithuanian, Russian, Polish
Area Sq Miles	25 174	**Religions**	Roman Catholic, Protestant, Russian Orthodox
Population	3 017 000	**Currency**	Euro
Capital	Vilnius	**Organizations**	EU, NATO, UN

Map page 159

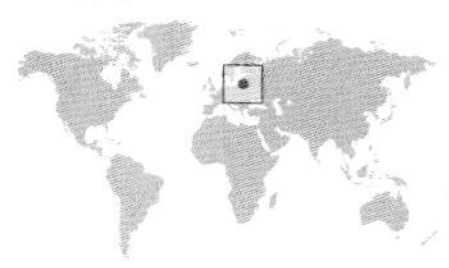

Lithuania is in northern Europe on the eastern shores of the Baltic Sea. It is mainly lowland with many lakes, rivers and marshes. Agriculture, fishing and forestry are important, but manufacturing dominates the economy. The main exports are machinery, mineral products and chemicals. Russia and Germany are the main trading partners. Lithuania joined the European Union in May 2004.

LUXEMBOURG
Grand Duchy of Luxembourg

Area Sq Km	2 586	**Languages**	Letzeburgish, German, French
Area Sq Miles	998	**Religions**	Roman Catholic
Population	530 000	**Currency**	Euro
Capital	Luxembourg	**Organizations**	EU, NATO, OECD, UN

Map page 164

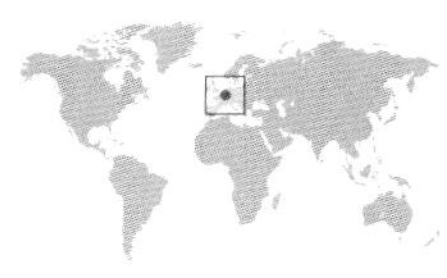

Luxembourg, a small landlocked country in western Europe, borders Belgium, France and Germany. The hills and forests of the Ardennes dominate the north, with rolling pasture to the south, where the main towns, farms and industries are found. The iron and steel industry is still important, but light industries (including textiles, chemicals and food products) are growing. Luxembourg is a major banking centre. Main trading partners are Belgium, Germany and France.

MACEDONIA (F.Y.R.O.M.)
Republic of Macedonia

Area Sq Km	25 713	**Languages**	Macedonian, Albanian, Turkish
Area Sq Miles	9 928	**Religions**	Macedonian Orthodox, Sunni Muslim
Population	2 107 000	**Currency**	Macedonian denar
Capital	Skopje	**Organizations**	NATO, UN

Map page 171

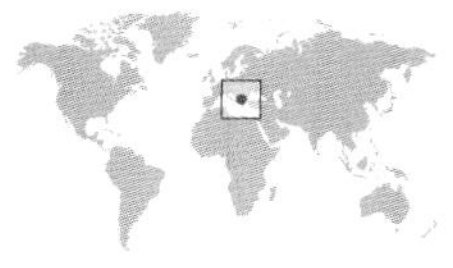

The Former Yugoslav Republic of Macedonia is a landlocked state in southern Europe. Lying within the southern Balkan Mountains, it is traversed northwest-southeast by the Vardar valley. The climate is continental. The economy is based on industry, mining and agriculture, but conflicts in the region have reduced trade and caused economic difficulties. Foreign aid and loans are now assisting in modernization and development of the country.

MADAGASCAR
Republic of Madagascar

Area Sq Km	587 041	**Languages**	Malagasy, French
Area Sq Miles	226 656	**Religions**	Traditional beliefs, Christian, Sunni Muslim
Population	22 925 000	**Currency**	Ariary
Capital	Antananarivo	**Organizations**	SADC, UN

Map page 179

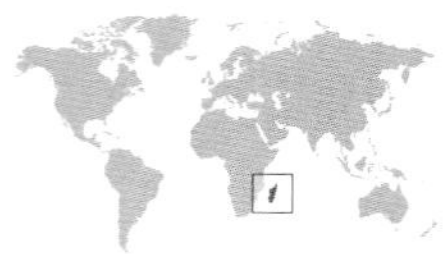

Madagascar lies off the east coast of southern Africa. The world's fourth largest island, it is mainly a high plateau, with a coastal strip to the east and scrubby plain to the west. The climate is tropical, with heavy rainfall in the north and east. Most of the population lives on the plateau. Although the amount of arable land is limited, the economy is based on agriculture. The main industries are agricultural processing, textile manufacturing and oil refining. Foreign aid is important. Exports include coffee, vanilla, cotton cloth, sugar and shrimps. France is the main trading partner.

MALAWI
Republic of Malawi

Area Sq Km	118 484	**Languages**	Chichewa, English, other local languages
Area Sq Miles	45 747	**Religions**	Christian, traditional beliefs, Sunni Muslim
Population	16 363 000	**Currency**	Malawian kwacha
Capital	Lilongwe	**Organizations**	Comm., SADC, UN

Map page 179

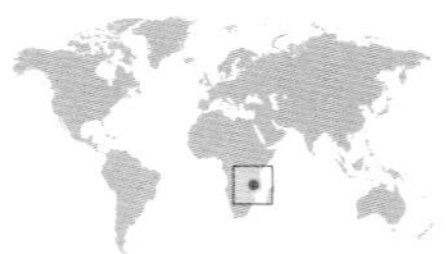

Landlocked Malawi in central Africa is a narrow hilly country at the southern end of the Great Rift Valley. One-fifth is covered by Lake Nyasa. Most of the population lives in rural areas in the southern regions. The climate is mainly subtropical, with varying rainfall. The economy is predominantly agricultural, with tobacco, tea and sugar the main exports. Malawi is one of the world's least developed countries and relies heavily on foreign aid. South Africa is the main trading partner.

MALAYSIA

Area Sq Km	332 965	**Languages**	Malay, English, Chinese, Tamil, other local languages
Area Sq Miles	128 559	**Religions**	Sunni Muslim, Buddhist, Hindu, Christian, traditional beliefs
Population	29 717 000	**Currency**	Ringgit
Capital	Kuala Lumpur/ Putrajaya	**Organizations**	APEC, ASEAN, Comm., UN

Map page 155

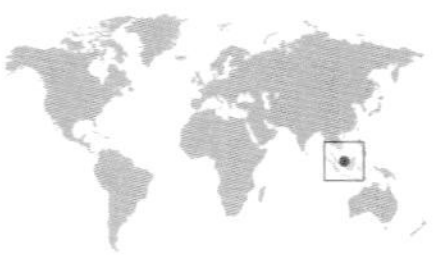

Malaysia, in southeast Asia, comprises two regions, separated by the South China Sea. The western region occupies the southern Malay Peninsula, which has a chain of mountains dividing the eastern coastal strip from wider plains to the west. East Malaysia, consisting of the states of Sabah and Sarawak in the north of the island of Borneo, is mainly rainforest-covered hills and mountains with mangrove swamps along the coast. Both regions have a tropical climate with heavy rainfall. About eighty per cent of the population lives in Peninsular Malaysia. The country is rich in natural resources and has reserves of minerals and fuels. It is an important producer of tin, oil, natural gas, rubber and tropical hardwoods. Agriculture remains a substantial part of the economy, but industry is the most important sector. The main exports are transport and electronic equipment, oil, chemicals, palm oil, wood and rubber. The main trading partners are Japan, China, the USA and Singapore.

MALDIVES
Republic of the Maldives

Area Sq Km	298	**Languages**	Divehi (Maldivian)
Area Sq Miles	115	**Religions**	Sunni Muslim
Population	345 000	**Currency**	Rufiyaa
Capital	Male	**Organizations**	Comm., UN

Map page 130

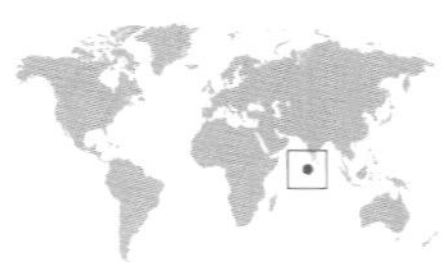

The Maldive archipelago comprises over a thousand coral atolls (around two hundred of which are inhabited), in the Indian Ocean, southwest of India. Over eighty per cent of the land area is less than one metre above sea level. The main atolls are North and South Male and Addu. The climate is hot, humid and monsoonal. There is little cultivation and almost all food is imported. Tourism has expanded rapidly and is the most important sector of the economy.

MALI
Republic of Mali

Area Sq Km	1 240 140	**Languages**	French, Bambara, other local languages
Area Sq Miles	478 821	**Religions**	Sunni Muslim, traditional beliefs, Christian
Population	15 302 000	**Currency**	CFA franc
Capital	Bamako	**Organizations**	UN

Map page 176

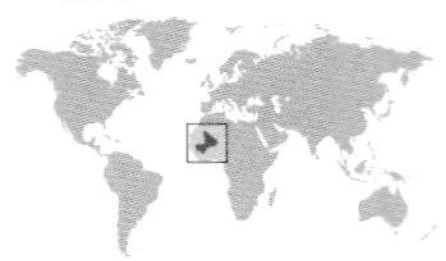

A landlocked state in west Africa, Mali is low-lying, with a few rugged hills in the northeast. Northern regions lie within the Sahara desert. To the south, around the Niger river, are marshes and savanna grassland. Rainfall is unreliable. Most of the population lives along the Niger and Falémé rivers. Exports include cotton, livestock and gold. Mali is one of the least developed countries in the world and relies heavily on foreign aid.

MALTA
Republic of Malta

Area Sq Km	316	**Languages**	Maltese, English
Area Sq Miles	122	**Religions**	Roman Catholic
Population	429 000	**Currency**	Euro
Capital	Valletta	**Organizations**	Comm., EU, UN

Map page 170

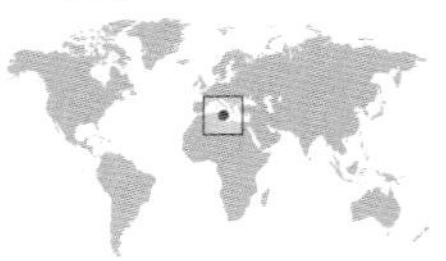

The islands of Malta and Gozo lie in the Mediterranean Sea, off the coast of southern Italy. The islands have hot, dry summers and mild winters. The economy depends on foreign trade, tourism and the manufacture of electronics and textiles. Main trading partners are the USA, France and Italy. Malta joined the European Union in May 2004.

MARSHALL ISLANDS
Republic of the Marshall Islands

Area Sq Km	181	**Languages**	English, Marshallese
Area Sq Miles	70	**Religions**	Protestant, Roman Catholic
Population	53 000	**Currency**	United States dollar
Capital	Delap-Uliga-Djarrit	**Organizations**	UN

Map page 123

The Marshall Islands consist of over a thousand atolls, islands and islets, within two chains in the north Pacific Ocean. The main atolls are Majuro (home to half the population), Kwajalein, Jaluit, Enewetak and Bikini. The climate is tropical, with heavy autumn rainfall. About half the workforce is employed in farming or fishing. Tourism is a small source of foreign exchange and the islands depend heavily on aid from the USA.

Martinique
French Overseas Department

Area Sq Km	1 079	**Languages**	French, Creole
Area Sq Miles	417	**Religions**	Roman Catholic, traditional beliefs
Population	404 000	**Currency**	Euro
Capital	Fort-de-France		

Map page 205 Martinique, one of the Caribbean Windward Islands, has volcanic peaks in the north, a populous central plain, and hills and beaches in the south. Tourism is a major source of foreign exchange, and substantial aid is received from France. The main trading partners are France and Guadeloupe.

MAURITANIA
Islamic Republic of Mauritania

Area Sq Km	1 030 700	**Languages**	Arabic, French, other local languages
Area Sq Miles	397 955	**Religions**	Sunni Muslim
Population	3 890 000	**Currency**	Ouguiya
Capital	Nouakchott	**Organizations**	UN

Map page 176

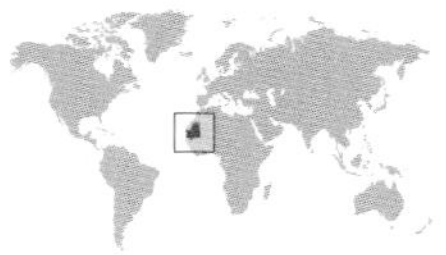

Mauritania is on the Atlantic coast of northwest Africa and lies almost entirely within the Sahara desert. Oases and a fertile strip along the Senegal river to the south are the only areas suitable for cultivation. The climate is generally hot and dry. About a quarter of Mauritanians live in the capital, Nouakchott. Most of the workforce depends on livestock rearing and subsistence farming. There are large deposits of iron ore which account for more than half of total exports. Mauritania's coastal waters are among the richest fishing grounds in the world. The main trading partners are France, Japan, China and Italy.

MAURITIUS
Republic of Mauritius

Area Sq Km	2 040	**Languages**	English, Creole, Hindi, Bhojpurī, French
Area Sq Miles	788	**Religions**	Hindu, Roman Catholic, Sunni Muslim
Population	1 244 000	**Currency**	Mauritian rupee
Capital	Port Louis	**Organizations**	Comm., SADC, UN

Map page 175

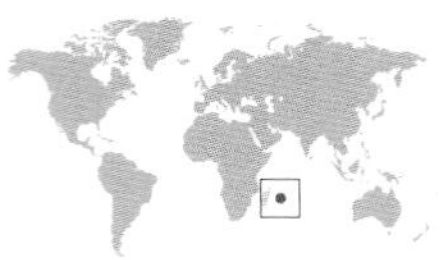

The state comprises Mauritius, Rodrigues and some twenty small islands in the Indian Ocean, east of Madagascar. The main island of Mauritius is volcanic in origin and has a coral coast, rising to a central plateau. Most of the population lives on the north and west sides of the island. The climate is warm and humid. The economy is based on sugar production, light manufacturing (chiefly clothing) and tourism.

Mayotte
French Overseas Department

Area Sq Km	373	**Languages**	French, Mahorian (Shimaore), Kibu
Area Sq Miles	144	**Religions**	Sunni Muslim, Christian
Population	222 000	**Currency**	Euro
Capital	Dzaoudzi		

Map page 179

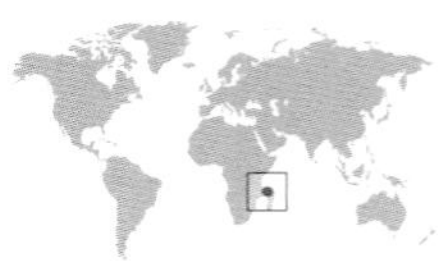

Lying in the Indian Ocean off the east coast of central Africa, Mayotte is geographically part of the Comoro archipelago. The economy is based on agriculture, but Mayotte depends heavily on aid from France.

MEXICO
United Mexican States

Area Sq Km	1 972 545	**Languages**	Spanish, Amerindian languages
Area Sq Miles	761 604	**Religions**	Roman Catholic, Protestant
Population	122 332 000	**Currency**	Mexican peso
Capital	Mexico City (México)	**Organizations**	APEC, OECD, UN

Map page 206–207

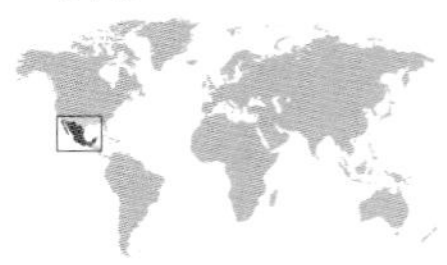

The largest country in Central America, Mexico extends south from the USA to Guatemala and Belize, and from the Pacific Ocean to the Gulf of Mexico. The greater part of the country is high plateau flanked by the western and eastern ranges of the Sierra Madre mountains. The principal lowland is the Yucatán peninsula in the southeast. The climate varies with latitude and altitude: hot and humid in the lowlands, warm on the plateau and cool with cold winters in the mountains. The north is arid, while the far south has heavy rainfall. Mexico City is the fourth largest conurbation in the world and the country's centre of trade and industry. Agriculture involves a sixth of the workforce; crops include grains, coffee, cotton and vegetables. Mexico is rich in minerals, including copper, zinc, lead, tin, sulphur, and silver. It is one of the world's largest producers of oil, from vast reserves in the Gulf of Mexico. The oil and petrochemical industries still dominate the economy, but a variety of manufactured goods are produced, including iron and steel, motor vehicles, textiles, chemicals and food and tobacco products. Tourism is growing in importance. Over three-quarters of all trade is with the USA.

MICRONESIA, FEDERATED STATES OF

Area Sq Km	701	**Languages**	English, Chuukese, Pohnpeian, other local languages
Area Sq Miles	271	**Religions**	Roman Catholic, Protestant
Population	104 000	**Currency**	United States dollar
Capital	Palikir	**Organizations**	UN

Map page 122–123

Micronesia comprises over six hundred atolls and islands of the Caroline Islands in the north Pacific Ocean. A third of the population lives on Pohnpei. The climate is tropical, with heavy rainfall. Fishing and subsistence farming are the main activities. Fish, garments and bananas are the main exports. Income is also derived from tourism and the licensing of foreign fishing fleets. The islands depend heavily on aid from the USA.

MOLDOVA
Republic of Moldova

Area Sq Km	33 700	**Languages**	Romanian, Ukrainian, Gagauz, Russian
Area Sq Miles	13 012	**Religions**	Romanian Orthodox, Russian Orthodox
Population	3 487 000		
Capital	Chişinău (Kishinev)	**Currency**	Moldovan leu
		Organizations	CIS, UN

Map page 173

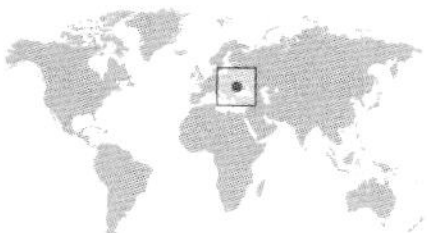

Moldova lies between Romania and Ukraine in eastern Europe. It consists of hilly steppe land, drained by the Prut and Dniester rivers. Moldova has no mineral resources, and the economy is mainly agricultural, with sugar beet, tobacco, wine and fruit the chief products. Food processing, machinery and textiles are the main industries. Russia is the main trading partner.

MONACO
Principality of Monaco

Area Sq Km	2	**Languages**	French, Monégasque, Italian
Area Sq Miles	1	**Religions**	Roman Catholic
Population	38 000	**Currency**	Euro
Capital	Monaco-Ville	**Organizations**	UN

Map page 166

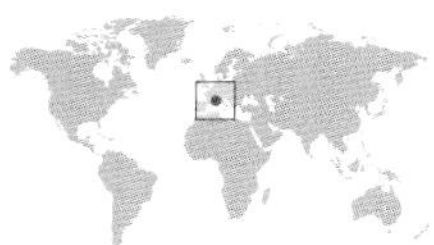

The principality occupies a rocky peninsula and a strip of land on France's Mediterranean coast. Monaco's economy depends on service industries (chiefly tourism, banking and finance) and light industry.

MONGOLIA

Area Sq Km	1 565 000	**Languages**	Khalka (Mongolian), Kazakh, other local languages
Area Sq Miles	604 250		
Population	2 839 000	**Religions**	Buddhist, Sunni Muslim
Capital	Ulan Bator (Ulaanbaatar)	**Currency**	Tugrik (tögrög)
		Organizations	UN

Map page 146

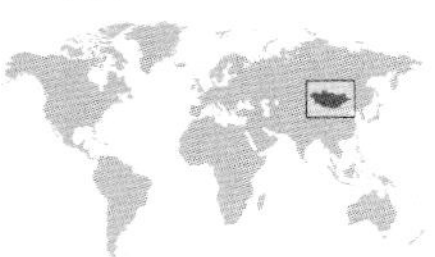

Mongolia is a landlocked country in eastern Asia between Russia and China. Much of it is high steppe land, with mountains and lakes in the west and north. In the south is the Gobi Desert. Mongolia has long, cold winters and short, mild summers. A quarter of the population lives in the capital, Ulaanbaatar. Livestock breeding and agricultural processing are important. There are substantial mineral resources. Copper and textiles are the main exports. China and Russia are the main trading partners.

MONTENEGRO

Area Sq Km	13 812	**Languages**	Serbian (Montenegrin), Albanian
Area Sq Miles	5 333	**Religions**	Montenegrin Orthodox, Sunni Muslim
Population	621 000		
Capital	Podgorica	**Currency**	Euro
		Organizations	UN

Map page 171

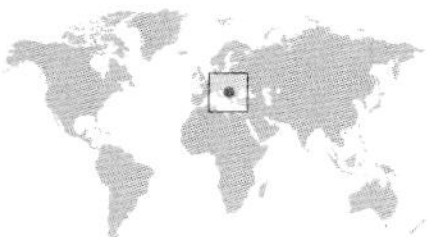

Montenegro was the last constituent republic of the former Yugoslavia to become an independent nation, in June 2006. At that time it opted to split from the state union of Serbia and Montenegro. Montenegro separates the much larger Serbia from the Adriatic coast. The landscape is rugged and mountainous, and the climate Mediterranean.

Montserrat
United Kingdom Overseas Territory

Area Sq Km	100	**Languages**	English
Area Sq Miles	39	**Religions**	Protestant, Roman Catholic
Population	4 922	**Currency**	East Caribbean dollar
Capital	Brades (temporary capital)	**Organizations**	CARICOM

Map page 205

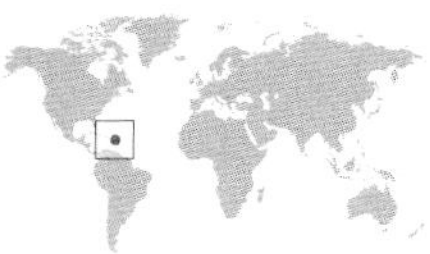

An island in the Leeward Islands group in the Lesser Antilles, in the Caribbean. From 1995 to 1997 the volcanoes in the Soufrière Hills erupted for the first time since 1630. Over sixty per cent of the island was covered in volcanic ash and Plymouth, the capital was, virtually destroyed. Many people migrated, and the remaining population moved to the north of the island. Brades has replaced Plymouth as the temporary capital. Reconstruction is being funded by aid from the UK.

MOROCCO
Kingdom of Morocco

Area Sq Km	446 550	**Languages**	Arabic, Berber, French
Area Sq Miles	172 414	**Religions**	Sunni Muslim
Population	33 008 000	**Currency**	Moroccan dirham
Capital	Rabat	**Organizations**	UN

Map page 176

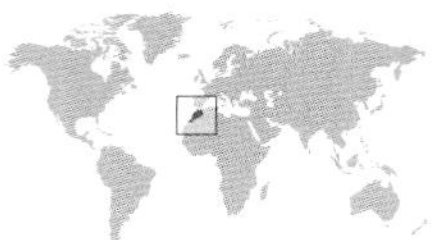

Lying in the northwest of Africa, Morocco has both Atlantic and Mediterranean coasts. The Atlas Mountains separate the arid south and disputed region of western Sahara from the fertile west and north, which have a milder climate. Most Moroccans live on the Atlantic coastal plain. The economy is based on agriculture, phosphate mining and tourism; the most important industries are food processing, textiles and chemicals.

MOZAMBIQUE
Republic of Mozambique

Area Sq Km	799 380	**Languages**	Portuguese, Makua, Tsonga, other local languages
Area Sq Miles	308 642		
Population	25 834 000	**Religions**	Traditional beliefs, Roman Catholic, Sunni Muslim
Capital	Maputo		
		Currency	Metical
		Organizations	Comm., SADC, UN

Map page 179

Mozambique lies on the east coast of southern Africa. The land is mainly a savanna plateau drained by the Zambezi and Limpopo rivers, with highlands to the north. Most of the population lives on the coast or in the river valleys. In general the climate is tropical with winter rainfall, but droughts occur. The economy is based on subsistence agriculture. Exports include shrimps, cashews, cotton and sugar, but Mozambique relies heavily on aid, and remains one of the least developed countries in the world.

MYANMAR (Burma)
Republic of the Union of Myanmar

Area Sq Km	676 577	**Languages**	Burmese, Shan, Karen, other local languages
Area Sq Miles	261 228		
Population	53 259 000	**Religions**	Buddhist, Christian, Sunni Muslim
Capital	Nay Pyi Taw		
		Currency	Kyat
		Organizations	ASEAN, UN

Map page 147

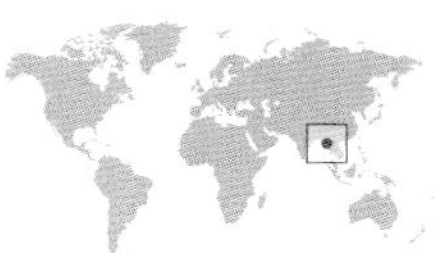

Myanmar (Burma) is in southeast Asia, bordering the Bay of Bengal and the Andaman Sea. Most of the population lives in the valley and delta of the Irrawaddy river, which is flanked by mountains and high plateaus. The climate is hot and monsoonal, and rainforest covers much of the land. Most of the workforce is employed in agriculture. Myanmar is rich in minerals, including zinc, lead, copper and silver. Political and social unrest and lack of foreign investment have affected economic development.

Nagorno-Karabakh
Disputed territory

Area Sq Km	6 000	**Languages**	Armenian
Area Sq Miles	2 317	**Religions**	Armenian Orthodox
Population	146 600	**Currency**	Armenian dram
Capital	Xankändi (Stepanakert)		

Map page 137 Established as an Autonomous Region within Azerbaijan in 1923, Nagorno-Karabakh is a disputed enclave of Azerbaijan. It is legally part of Azerbaijan, but is populated largely by ethnic Armenians who have established what amounts to a separatist de facto republic operating with support from Armenia. In 1991, the local Armenian population declared independence and Azerbaijan abolished the area's autonomous status. As a result of conflict, Nagorno-Karabakh/Armenia occupies approximately twenty per cent of Azerbaijan. A Russian-brokered cease-fire has been in place since 1994, with the cease-fire line enclosing the territory of Nagorno-Karabakh and the additional parts of Azerbaijan, up to the Armenian border, seized by Karabakh Armenians during the fighting. The area between the cease-fire line and the boundary of Nagorno-Karabakh is effectively a 'no-go' area.

NAMIBIA
Republic of Namibia

Area Sq Km	824 292	**Languages**	English, Afrikaans, German, Ovambo, other local languages
Area Sq Miles	318 261		
Population	2 303 000	**Religions**	Protestant, Roman Catholic
Capital	Windhoek	**Currency**	Namibian dollar
		Organizations	Comm., SADC, UN

Map page 179

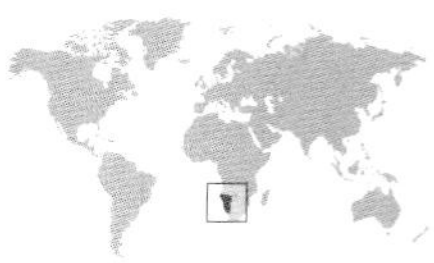

Namibia lies on the southern Atlantic coast of Africa. Mountain ranges separate the coastal Namib Desert from the interior plateau, bordered to the south and east by the Kalahari Desert. The country is hot and dry, but some summer rain in the north supports crops and livestock. Employment is in agriculture and fishing, although the economy is based on mineral extraction – diamonds, uranium, lead, zinc and silver. The economy is closely linked to South Africa.

NAURU
Republic of Nauru

Area Sq Km	21	**Languages**	Nauruan, English
Area Sq Miles	8	**Religions**	Protestant, Roman Catholic
Population	10 000	**Currency**	Australian dollar
Capital	Yaren	**Organizations**	Comm., UN

Map page 125

Nauru is a coral island near the Equator in the Pacific Ocean. It has a fertile coastal strip and a barren central plateau. The climate is tropical. The economy is based on phosphate mining, but reserves are near exhaustion and replacement of this income is a serious long-term problem.

NEPAL
Federal Democratic Republic of Nepal

Area Sq Km	147 181	**Languages**	Nepali, Maithili, Bhojpuri, English, other local languages
Area Sq Miles	56 827		
Population	27 797 000	**Religions**	Hindu, Buddhist, Sunni Muslim
Capital	Kathmandu	**Currency**	Nepalese rupee
		Organizations	UN

Map page 144–145

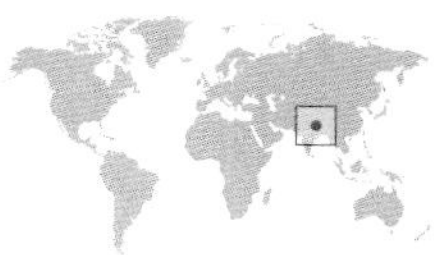

Nepal lies in the eastern Himalaya mountains between India and China. High mountains (including Everest) dominate the north. Most people live in the temperate central valleys and subtropical southern plains. The economy is based largely on agriculture and forestry. There is some manufacturing, chiefly of textiles and carpets, and tourism is important. Nepal relies heavily on foreign aid.

NETHERLANDS
Kingdom of the Netherlands

Area Sq Km	41 526	**Languages**	Dutch, Frisian
Area Sq Miles	16 033	**Religions**	Roman Catholic, Protestant, Sunni Muslim
Population	16 759 000		
Capital	Amsterdam/ The Hague	**Currency**	Euro
		Organizations	EU, NATO, OECD, UN

Map page 164

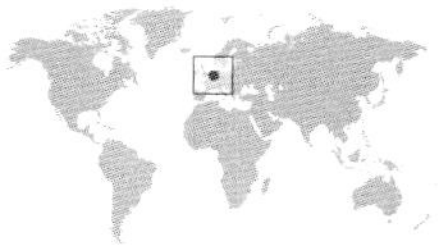

The Netherlands lies on the North Sea coast of western Europe. Apart from low hills in the far southeast, the land is flat and low-lying, much of it below sea level. The coastal region includes the delta of five rivers and polders (reclaimed land), protected by sand dunes, dykes and canals. The climate is temperate, with cool summers and mild winters. Rainfall is spread evenly throughout the year. The Netherlands is a densely populated and highly urbanized country, with the majority of the population living in the cities of Amsterdam, Rotterdam and The Hague. Horticulture and dairy farming are important activities, although they employ less than three per cent of the workforce. The Netherlands ranks as the world's third agricultural exporter, and is a leading producer and exporter of natural gas from reserves in the North Sea. The economy is based mainly on international trade and manufacturing industry. The main industries produce food products, chemicals, machinery, electrical and electronic goods and transport equipment. Germany is the main trading partner, followed by other European Union countries.

New Caledonia
French Overseas Collectivity

Area Sq Km	19 058	**Languages**	French, other local languages
Area Sq Miles	7 358	**Religions**	Roman Catholic, Protestant, Sunni Muslim
Population	256 000		
Capital	Nouméa	**Currency**	CFP franc

Map page 125

An island group lying in the southwest Pacific, with a sub-tropical climate. New Caledonia has over one-fifth of the world's nickel reserves, and the main economic activity is metal mining. Tourism is also important. New Caledonia relies on aid from France.

NEW ZEALAND

Area Sq Km	270 534	Languages	English, Maori
Area Sq Miles	104 454	Religions	Protestant, Roman Catholic
Population	4 506 000	Currency	New Zealand dollar
Capital	Wellington	Organizations	APEC, Comm., OECD, UN

Map page 128

New Zealand comprises two main islands separated by the narrow Cook Strait, and a number of smaller islands. North Island, where three-quarters of the population lives, has mountain ranges, broad fertile valleys and a central plateau with hot springs and active volcanoes. South Island is also mountainous, with the Southern Alps running its entire length. The only major lowland area is the Canterbury Plains in the centre-east. The climate is generally temperate, although South Island has colder winters. Farming is the mainstay of the economy. New Zealand is one of the world's leading producers of meat (beef, lamb and mutton), wool and dairy products; fruit and fish are also important. Hydroelectric and geothermal power provide much of the country's energy needs. Other industries produce timber, wood pulp, iron, aluminium, machinery and chemicals. Tourism is the fastest growing sector of the economy. The main trading partners are Australia, the USA, China, the UK and Japan.

NICARAGUA
Republic of Nicaragua

Area Sq Km	130 000	Languages	Spanish, Amerindian languages
Area Sq Miles	50 193	Religions	Roman Catholic, Protestant
Population	6 080 000	Currency	Córdoba
Capital	Managua	Organizations	UN

Map page 206

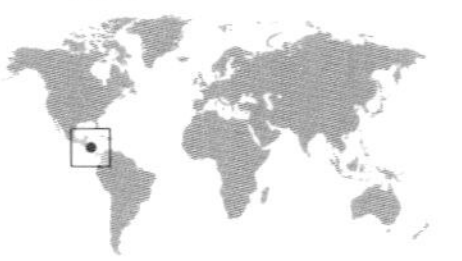

Nicaragua lies at the heart of Central America, with both Pacific and Caribbean coasts. Mountain ranges separate the east, which is largely rainforest, from the more developed western regions, which include Lake Nicaragua and some active volcanoes. The highest land is in the north. The climate is tropical. Nicaragua is one of the western hemisphere's poorest countries, and the economy is largely agricultural. Exports include coffee, seafood, cotton and bananas. The USA is the main trading partner. Nicaragua has a huge national debt, and relies heavily on foreign aid.

NIGER
Republic of Niger

Area Sq Km	1 267 000	Languages	French, Hausa, Fulani, other local languages
Area Sq Miles	489 191	Religions	Sunni Muslim, traditional beliefs
Population	17 831 000	Currency	CFA franc
Capital	Niamey	Organizations	UN

Map page 176–177

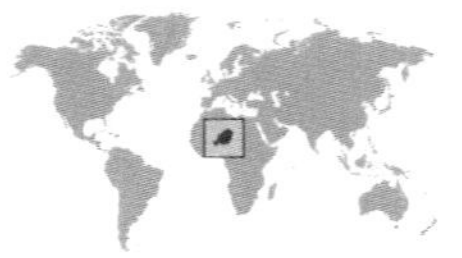

A landlocked state of west Africa, Niger lies mostly within the Sahara desert, but with savanna in the south and in the Niger valley area. The mountains of the Massif de l'Aïr dominate central regions. Much of the country is hot and dry. The south has some summer rainfall, although droughts occur. The economy depends on subsistence farming and herding, and uranium exports, but Niger is one of the world's least developed countries and relies heavily on foreign aid. France is the main trading partner.

NIGERIA
Federal Republic of Nigeria

Area Sq Km	923 768	Languages	English, Hausa, Yoruba, Ibo, Fulani, other local languages
Area Sq Miles	356 669	Religions	Sunni Muslim, Christian, traditional beliefs
Population	173 615 000	Currency	Naira
Capital	Abuja	Organizations	Comm., OPEC, UN

Map page 176–177

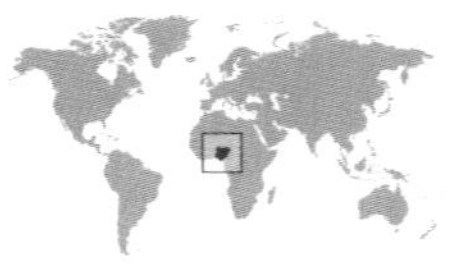

Nigeria is in west Africa, on the Gulf of Guinea, and is the most populous country in Africa. The Niger delta dominates coastal areas, fringed with sandy beaches, mangrove swamps and lagoons. Inland is a belt of rainforest which gives way to woodland or savanna on high plateaus. The far north is the semi-desert edge of the Sahara. The climate is tropical, with heavy summer rainfall in the south but low rainfall in the north. Most of the population lives in the coastal lowlands or in the west. About half the workforce is involved in agriculture, mainly growing subsistence crops. Agricultural production, however, has failed to keep up with demand, and Nigeria is now a net importer of food. Cocoa and rubber are the only significant export crops. The economy is heavily dependent on vast oil resources in the Niger delta and in shallow offshore waters, and oil accounts for over ninety per cent of export earnings. Nigeria also has natural gas reserves and some mineral deposits, but these are largely undeveloped. Industry involves mainly oil refining, chemicals (chiefly fertilizers), agricultural processing, textiles, steel manufacture and vehicle assembly. Political instability in the past has left Nigeria with heavy debts, poverty and unemployment but it is now the largest economy in Africa.

Niue
Self-governing New Zealand Territory

Area Sq Km	258	Languages	English, Nivean
Area Sq Miles	100	Religions	Christian
Population	1 460	Currency	New Zealand dollar
Capital	Alofi		

Map page 125

Niue, one of the largest coral islands in the world, lies in the south Pacific Ocean about 500 kilometres (300 miles) east of Tonga. The economy depends on aid and remittances from New Zealand. The population is declining because of migration to New Zealand.

Norfolk Island
Australian External Territory

Area Sq Km	35	Languages	English
Area Sq Miles	14	Religions	Protestant, Roman Catholic
Population	2 302	Currency	Australian dollar
Capital	Kingston		

Map page 125

In the south Pacific Ocean, Norfolk Island lies between Vanuatu and New Zealand. Tourism has increased steadily and is the mainstay of the economy and provides revenues for agricultural development.

Northern Mariana Islands
United States Commonwealth

Area Sq Km	477	Languages	English, Chamorro, other local languages
Area Sq Miles	184	Religions	Roman Catholic
Population	54 000	Currency	United States dollar
Capital	Capitol Hill		

Map page 147

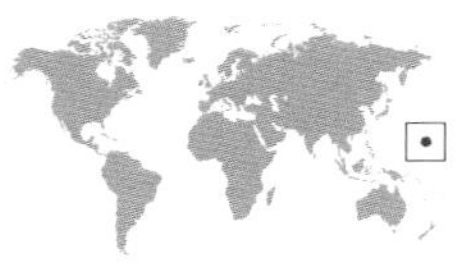

A chain of islands in the northwest Pacific Ocean, extending over 550 kilometres (350 miles) north to south. The main island is Saipan. Tourism is a major industry, employing approximately half the workforce.

NORTH KOREA
Democratic People's Republic of Korea

Area Sq Km	120 538	Languages	Korean
Area Sq Miles	46 540	Religions	Traditional beliefs, Chondoist, Buddhist
Population	24 895 000	Currency	North Korean won
Capital	P'yŏngyang	Organizations	UN

Map page 152

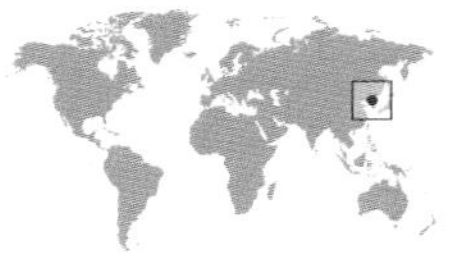

Occupying the northern half of the Korean peninsula in eastern Asia, North Korea is a rugged and mountainous country. The principal lowlands and the main agricultural areas are the plains in the southwest. Over sixty per cent the population lives in urban areas, mainly on the coastal plains. North Korea has a continental climate, with cold, dry winters and hot, wet summers. Approximately one-third of the workforce is involved in agriculture, mainly growing food crops on cooperative farms. Various minerals, notably iron ore, are mined and are the basis of the country's heavy industries. Exports include minerals (lead, magnesite and zinc) and metal products (chiefly iron and steel). The economy declined after 1991, when ties to the former USSR and eastern bloc collapsed, and there have been serious food shortages.

NORWAY
Kingdom of Norway

Area Sq Km	323 878	Languages	Norwegian, Sami languages
Area Sq Miles	125 050	Religions	Protestant, Roman Catholic
Population	5 043 000	Currency	Norwegian krone
Capital	Oslo	Organizations	NATO, OECD, UN

Map page 158–159

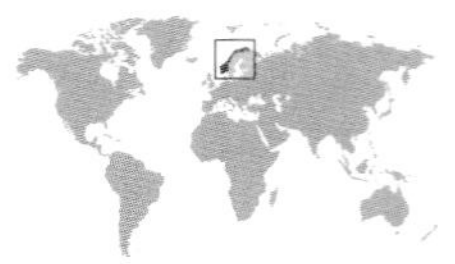

Norway stretches along the north and west coasts of Scandinavia, from the Arctic Ocean to the North Sea. Its extensive coastline is indented with fjords and fringed with many islands. Inland, the terrai is mountainous, with coniferou forests and lakes in the south. The only major lowland areas are along the southern North Sea and Skagerrak coasts, where most of the population lives. The climate is modified by the effect of the North Atlantic Drift ocean current. Norway has vast petroleum and natural gas resources in the North Sea. It is one of western Europe's leading producers of oil and gas, and exports of oil account for approximately half of total export earnings. Related industries include engineering (oil and gas platforms) and petrochemicals. More traditional industries process local raw materials, particularly fish, timber and minerals. Agriculture is limited, but fishing and fish farming are important. Norway is the world's leading exporter of farmed salmon. Merchant shipping and tourism are major sources of foreign exchange.

OMAN
Sultanate of Oman

Area Sq Km	309 500	Languages	Arabic, Baluchi, Indian languages
Area Sq Miles	119 499	Religions	Ibadhi Muslim, Sunni Muslim
Population	3 632 000	Currency	Omani rial
Capital	Muscat (Masqaṭ)	Organizations	GCC, UN

Map page 142

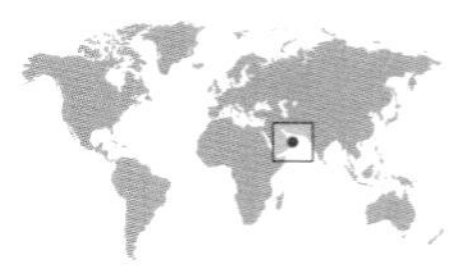

In southwest Asia, Oman occupies the east and southeast coasts of the Arabian Peninsula and an enclave north of the United Arab Emirates. Most of the land is desert, with mountains in the north and south. The climate is hot and mainly dry. Most of the population lives on the coastal strip on the Gulf of Oman. The majority depend on farming and fishing, but the oil and gas industries dominate the economy with around eighty per cent of export revenues coming from oil.

PAKISTAN
Islamic Republic of Pakistan

Area Sq Km	881 888	Languages	Urdu, Punjabi, Sindhi, Pashtu (Pasht English, Balochi
Area Sq Miles	340 497	Religions	Sunni Muslim, Shi'a Muslim, Christian, Hindu
Population	182 143 000	Currency	Pakistani rupee
Capital	Islamabad	Organizations	Comm., UN

Map page 141

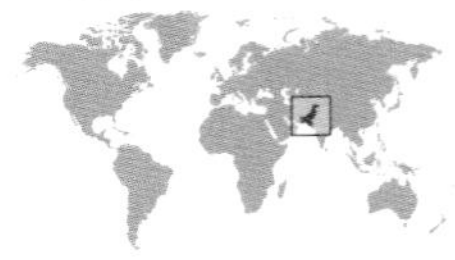

Pakistan is in the northwest part of the Indian subcontinent in south Asia, on the Arabian Sea. The east and south are dominated by the great basin of the Indus river system. This is the main agricultural area and contains most of the predominantly rural population. To the north the land rises to the mountains of the Karakoram, Hindu Kush and Himalaya mountains. The west is semi-desert plateaus and mountain ranges. The climate ranges between dry desert, and arctic tundra on the mountain tops. Temperatures are generally warm and rainfall is monsoonal. Agriculture is the main sector of the economy, employing over a third of the workforce, and is based on extensive irrigation schemes. Pakistan is one of the world's leading producers of cotton and a major exporter of rice. Pakistan produces natural gas and has a variety of mineral deposits including coal and gold, but they are little developed. The main industries are textiles and clothing manufacture and food processing, with fabrics and ready-made clothing the leading exports. Pakistan also produces leather goods, fertilizers, chemicals, paper and precision instruments. The country depends heavily on foreign aid and remittances from workers abroad.

PALAU
Republic of Palau

Area Sq Km	497	Languages	Palauan, English
Area Sq Miles	192	Religions	Roman Catholic, Protestant, traditional beliefs
Population	21 000	Currency	United States dollar
Capital	Melekeok	Organizations	UN

Map page 147

Palau comprises over three hundred islands in the western Caroline Islands, in the west Pacific Ocean. The climate is tropical. The economy is based on farming, fishing and tourism but Palau is heavily dependent on aid from the USA.

PANAMA
Republic of Panama

Area Sq Km	77 082	**Languages**	Spanish, English, Amerindian languages
Area Sq Miles	29 762	**Religions**	Roman Catholic, Protestant, Sunni Muslim
Population	3 864 000	**Currency**	Balboa
Capital	Panama City (Panamá)	**Organizations**	UN

Map page 206

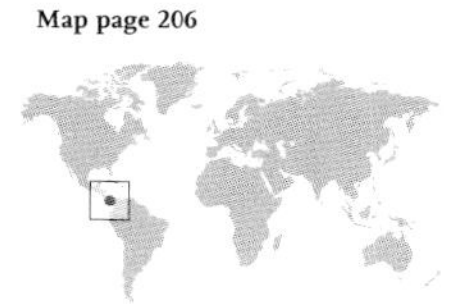

Panama is the most southerly state in central America and has Pacific and Caribbean coasts. It is hilly, with mountains in the west and jungle near the Colombian border. The climate is tropical. Most of the population lives on the drier Pacific side. The economy is based mainly on services related to the Panama Canal: shipping, banking and tourism. Exports include bananas, shrimps, coffee, clothing and fish products. The USA is the main trading partner.

PAPUA NEW GUINEA
Independent State of Papua New Guinea

Area Sq Km	462 840	**Languages**	English, Tok Pisin (Creole), other local languages
Area Sq Miles	178 704	**Religions**	Protestant, Roman Catholic, traditional beliefs
Population	7 321 000	**Currency**	Kina
Capital	Port Moresby	**Organizations**	APEC, Comm., UN

Map page 124

Papua New Guinea occupies the eastern half of the island of New Guinea and includes many island groups. It has a forested and mountainous interior, bordered by swampy plains, and a tropical monsoon climate. Most of the workforce are farmers. Timber, copra, coffee and cocoa are important, but exports are dominated by minerals, chiefly gold and copper. The country depends on foreign aid. Australia, the USA and Singapore are the main trading partners.

PARAGUAY
Republic of Paraguay

Area Sq Km	406 752	**Languages**	Spanish, Guaraní
Area Sq Miles	157 048	**Religions**	Roman Catholic, Protestant
Population	6 802 000	**Currency**	Guaraní
Capital	Asunción	**Organizations**	UN

Map page 212

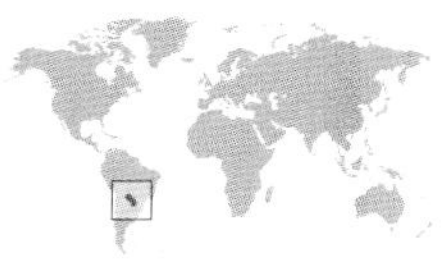

Paraguay is a landlocked country in central South America, bordering Bolivia, Brazil and Argentina. The Paraguay river separates a sparsely populated western zone of marsh and flat alluvial plains from a more developed, hilly and forested region to the east and south. The climate is subtropical. Virtually all electricity is produced by hydroelectric plants, and surplus power is exported to Brazil and Argentina. The hydroelectric dam at Itaipú is one of the largest in the world. The mainstay of the economy is agriculture and related industries. Exports include cotton, soya bean and edible oil products, timber and meat. Brazil and Argentina are the main trading partners.

PERU
Republic of Peru

Area Sq Km	1 285 216	**Languages**	Spanish, Quechua, Aymara
Area Sq Miles	496 225	**Religions**	Roman Catholic, Protestant
Population	30 376 000	**Currency**	Sol
Capital	Lima	**Organizations**	APEC, UN

Map page 210

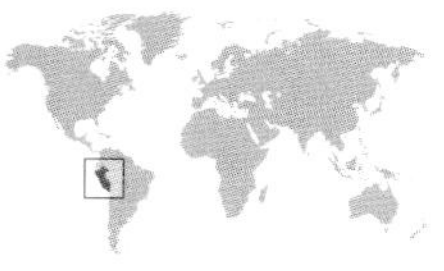

Peru lies on the Pacific coast of South America. Most Peruvians live on the coastal strip and on the plateaus of the high Andes mountains. East of the Andes is the Amazon rainforest. The coast is temperate with low rainfall while the east is hot, humid and wet. Agriculture involves one-third of the workforce and fishing is also important. Agriculture and fishing have both been disrupted by the El Niño climatic effect in recent years. Sugar, cotton, coffee and, illegally, coca are the main cash crops. Copper and copper products, fishmeal, zinc products, coffee, petroleum and its products, and textiles are the main exports. The USA and China are the main trading partners.

PHILIPPINES
Republic of the Philippines

Area Sq Km	300 000	**Languages**	English, Filipino, Tagalog, Cebuano, other local languages
Area Sq Miles	115 831	**Religions**	Roman Catholic, Protestant, Sunni Muslim, Aglipayan
Population	98 394 000	**Currency**	Philippine peso
Capital	Manila	**Organizations**	APEC, ASEAN, UN

Map page 153

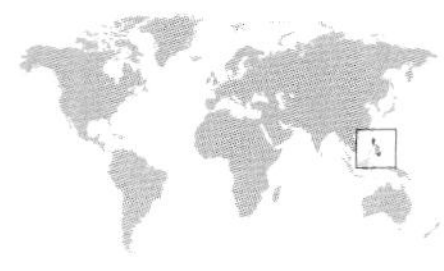

The Philippines, in southeast Asia, consists of over seven thousand islands lying between the South China Sea and the Pacific Ocean. The main islands are mountainous and forested. Volcanoes are active, and earthquakes and tropical storms are common. Most of the population lives on the plains or the coastal strips. The climate is hot and humid with monsoonal rainfall. Rice, coconuts, sugar cane, pineapples and bananas are the main crops, and fishing is important. Exports include electronic and transport equipment and machinery, clothing, and coconuts. Foreign aid and remittances from workers abroad are important to the economy. The USA and Japan are the main trading partners.

Pitcairn Islands
United Kingdom Overseas Territory

Area Sq Km	45	**Languages**	English
Area Sq Miles	17	**Religions**	Protestant
Population	50	**Currency**	New Zealand dollar
Capital	Adamstown		

Map page 123

An island group in the southeast Pacific Ocean consisting of Pitcairn Island and three uninhabited islands, Henderson, Ducie and Oeno Islands. It was originally settled by mutineers from HMS *Bounty* in 1790.

POLAND
Republic of Poland

Area Sq Km	312 683	**Languages**	Polish, German
Area Sq Miles	120 728	**Religions**	Roman Catholic, Polish Orthodox
Population	38 217 000	**Currency**	Złoty
Capital	Warsaw (Warszawa)	**Organizations**	EU, NATO, OECD, UN

Map page 168–169

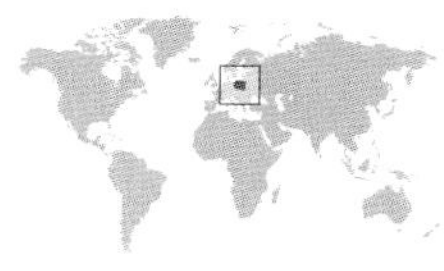

Poland lies on the Baltic coast of eastern Europe. The Oder (Odra) and Vistula (Wisła) river deltas dominate the coast. Inland, much of the country is low-lying, with woods and lakes. In the south the land rises to the Sudeten Mountains and the western part of the Carpathian Mountains, which form the borders with the Czech Republic and Slovakia respectively. The climate is continental. Around a sixth of the workforce is involved in agriculture, and exports include livestock products and sugar. The economy is heavily industrialized, with mining and manufacturing accounting for over thirty per cent of national income. Poland is one of the world's major producers of coal, and also produces copper, zinc, lead, sulphur and natural gas. The main industries are machinery and transport equipment, shipbuilding, and metal and chemical production. Exports include machinery and transport equipment, manufactured goods, food and live animals. Germany is the main trading partner. Poland joined the European Union in May 2004.

PORTUGAL
Portuguese Republic

Area Sq Km	88 940	**Languages**	Portuguese
Area Sq Miles	34 340	**Religions**	Roman Catholic, Protestant
Population	10 608 000	**Currency**	Euro
Capital	Lisbon (Lisboa)	**Organizations**	EU, NATO, OECD, UN

Map page 167

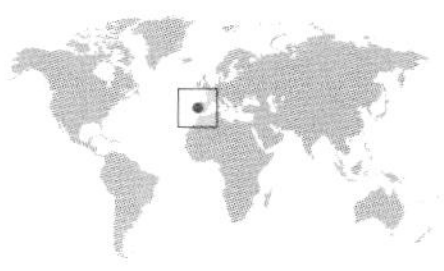

Portugal lies in the western part of the Iberian peninsula in southwest Europe, has an Atlantic coastline and is bordered by Spain to the north and east. The island groups of the Azores and Madeira are parts of Portugal. On the mainland, the land north of the river Tagus (Tejo) is mostly highland, with extensive forests of pine and cork. South of the river is undulating lowland. The climate in the north is cool and moist; the south is warmer, with dry, mild winters. Most Portuguese live near the coast, and more than one-third of the total population lives around the capital, Lisbon (Lisboa). Agriculture, fishing and forestry involve approximately ten per cent of the workforce. Mining and manufacturing are the main sectors of the economy. Portugal produces kaolin, copper, tin, zinc, tungsten and salt. Exports include textiles, clothing and footwear, electrical machinery and transport equipment, cork and wood products, and chemicals. Service industries, chiefly tourism and banking, are important to the economy, as are remittances from workers abroad. Most trade is with other European Union countries.

Puerto Rico
United States Commonwealth

Area Sq Km	9 104	**Languages**	Spanish, English
Area Sq Miles	3 515	**Religions**	Roman Catholic, Protestant
Population	3 688 000	**Currency**	United States dollar
Capital	San Juan		

Map page 205

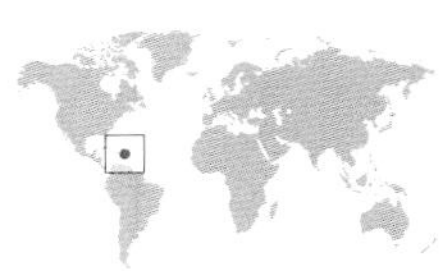

The Caribbean island of Puerto Rico has a forested, hilly interior, coastal plains and a tropical climate. Half of the population lives in the San Juan area. The economy is based on manufacturing (chiefly chemicals, electronics and food), tourism and agriculture. The USA is the main trading partner.

QATAR
State of Qatar

Area Sq Km	11 437	**Languages**	Arabic
Area Sq Miles	4 416	**Religions**	Sunni Muslim
Population	2 169 000	**Currency**	Qatari riyal
Capital	Doha (Ad Dawḩah)	**Organizations**	GCC, OPEC, UN

Map page 140

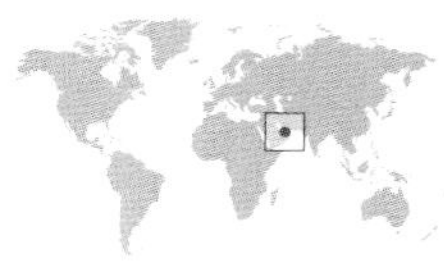

Qatar occupies a peninsula in southwest Asia that extends northwards from east-central Saudi Arabia into The Gulf. The land is flat and barren with sand dunes and salt pans. The climate is hot and mainly dry. Most people live in the area of the capital, Doha. The economy is heavily dependent on oil and natural gas production and the oil-refining industry. Income also comes from overseas investment. Japan is the largest trading partner.

Réunion
French Overseas Department

Area Sq Km	2 551	**Languages**	French, Creole
Area Sq Miles	985	**Religions**	Roman Catholic
Population	875 000	**Currency**	Euro
Capital	St-Denis		

Map page 175

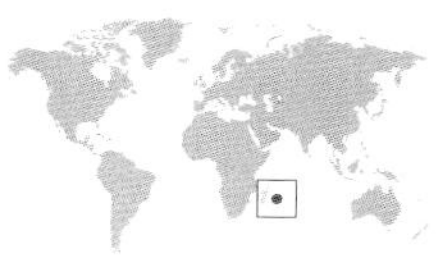

The Indian Ocean island of Réunion is mountainous, with coastal lowlands and a warm climate. The economy depends on tourism, French aid, and exports of sugar. In 2005 France transferred the administration of various small uninhabited islands in the seas around Madagascar from Réunion to the French Southern and Antarctic Lands.

ROMANIA

Area Sq Km	237 500	**Languages**	Romanian, Hungarian
Area Sq Miles	91 699	**Religions**	Romanian Orthodox, Protestant, Roman Catholic
Population	21 699 000	**Currency**	Romanian leu
Capital	Bucharest (București)	**Organizations**	EU, NATO, UN

Map page 171

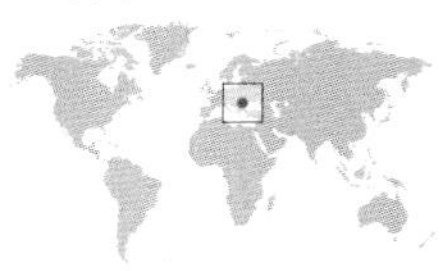

Romania lies in eastern Europe, on the northwest coast of the Black Sea. Mountains separate the Transylvanian Basin in the centre of the country from the populous plains of the east and south and from the Danube delta. The climate is continental. Romania has mineral resources (zinc, lead, silver and gold) and oil and natural gas reserves. Economic development has been slow and sporadic, but measures to accelerate change were introduced in 1999. Agricultural employment has since declined. The main exports are textiles, mineral products, chemicals, machinery and footwear. The main trading partners are Germany and Italy.

RUSSIA

Area Sq Km	17 075 400	**Languages**	Russian, Tatar, Ukrainian, other local languages
Area Sq Miles	6 592 849	**Religions**	Russian Orthodox, Sunni Muslim, Protestant
Population	142 834 000	**Currency**	Russian rouble
Capital	Moscow (Moskva)	**Organizations**	APEC, CIS, UN

Map page 132–133

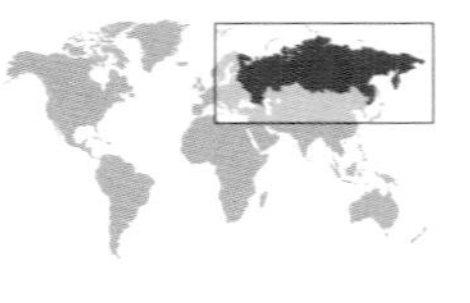

Russia occupies much of eastern Europe and all of northern Asia, and is the world's largest country. It borders fourteen countries to the west and south and has long coastlines on the Arctic and Pacific Oceans to the north and east. European Russia lies west of the Ural Mountains. To the south the land rises to uplands and the Caucasus mountains on the border with Georgia and Azerbaijan. East of the Urals lies the flat West Siberian Plain and the Central Siberian Plateau. In the south-east is Lake Baikal, the world's deepest lake, and the Sayan ranges on the border with Kazakhstan and Mongolia. Eastern Siberia is rugged and mountainous, with many active volcanoes in the Kamchatka Peninsula. The country's major rivers are the Volga in the west and the Ob', Irtysh, Yenisey, Lena and Amur in Siberia. The climate and vegetation range between arctic tundra in the north and semi-arid steppe towards the Black and Caspian Sea coasts in the south. In general, the climate is continental with extreme temperatures. The majority of the population (the tenth largest in the world), and industry and agriculture are concentrated in European Russia. The economy is dependent on exploitation of raw materials and on heavy industry. Russia has a wealth of mineral resources, although they are often difficult to exploit because of climate and remote locations. It is one of the world's leading producers of petroleum, natural gas and coal as well as iron ore, nickel, copper, bauxite, and many precious and rare metals. Forests cover over forty per cent of the land area and supply an important timber, paper and pulp industry. Approximately eight per cent of the land is suitable for cultivation. Agriculture has shown steady growth since 1999, with grain now exported. Fishing is important and Russia has a large fleet operating around the world. The transition to a market economy has been slow and difficult, with considerable underemployment. As well as mining and extractive industries there is a wide range of manufacturing industry, from steel mills to aircraft and space vehicles, shipbuilding, synthetic fabrics, plastics, cotton fabrics, consumer durables, chemicals and fertilizers. Exports include fuels, metals, machinery, chemicals and forest products. The most important trading partners include Germany, the USA and Belarus.

RWANDA
Republic of Rwanda

Area Sq Km	26 338	**Languages**	Kinyarwanda, French, English
Area Sq Miles	10 169	**Religions**	Roman Catholic, traditional beliefs, Protestant
Population	11 777 000	**Currency**	Rwandan franc
Capital	Kigali	**Organizations**	Comm., UN

Map page 178

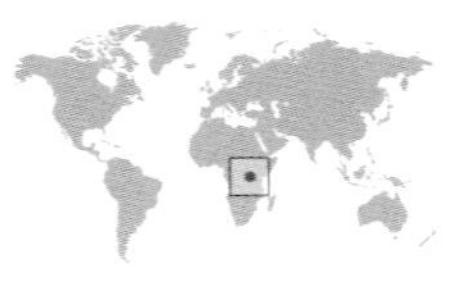

Rwanda, the most densely populated country in Africa, is situated in the mountains and plateaus to the east of the western branch of the Great Rift Valley in east Africa. The climate is warm with a summer dry season. Rwanda depends on subsistence farming, coffee and tea exports, light industry and foreign aid. The country is slowly recovering from serious internal conflict which caused devastation in the early 1990s.

St-Barthélemy
French Overseas Collectivity

Area Sq Km	21	**Languages**	French
Area Sq Miles	8	**Religions**	Roman Catholic
Population	9 072	**Currency**	Euro
Capital	Gustavia		

Map page 205

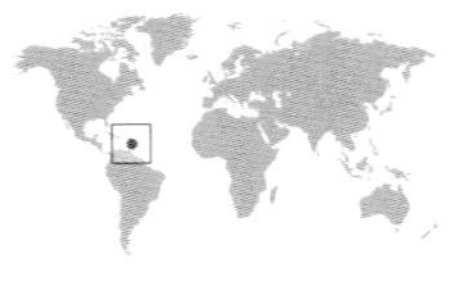

An island in the Leeward Islands in the Lesser Antilles, in the Caribbean south of St-Martin. It was separated from Guadeloupe politically in 2007. Tourism is the main economic activity.

St Helena, Ascension and Tristan da Cunha
United Kingdom Overseas Territory

Area Sq Km	410	**Languages**	English
Area Sq Miles	158	**Religions**	Protestant, Roman Catholic
Population	5 366	**Currency**	St Helena pound, Pound sterling
Capital	Jamestown		

Map page 174 Known until 2009 as St Helena and Dependencies, this UK territory lies in the south Atlantic Ocean. The islands, all of volcanic origin, are very remote from each other and from Africa and South America. The economy varies from island to island, but depends also on UK aid. Main trading partners are the UK and South Africa.

ST KITTS AND NEVIS
Federation of St Kitts and Nevis

Area Sq Km	261	**Languages**	English, Creole
Area Sq Miles	101	**Religions**	Protestant, Roman Catholic
Population	54 000	**Currency**	East Caribbean dollar
Capital	Basseterre	**Organizations**	CARICOM, Comm., UN

Map page 205

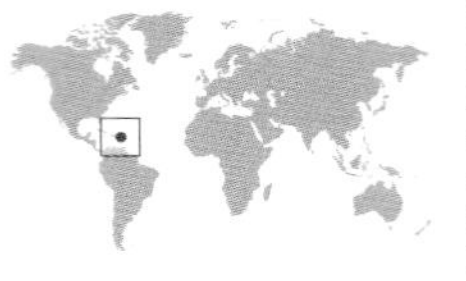

St Kitts and Nevis are in the Leeward Islands, in the Caribbean. Both volcanic islands are mountainous and forested, with sandy beaches and a warm, wet climate. About three-quarters of the population lives on St Kitts. Agriculture is the main activity, with sugar the main product. Tourism and manufacturing (chiefly garments and electronic components) and offshore banking are important activities.

ST LUCIA

Area Sq Km	616	**Languages**	English, Creole
Area Sq Miles	238	**Religions**	Roman Catholic, Protestant
Population	182 000	**Currency**	East Caribbean dollar
Capital	Castries	**Organizations**	CARICOM, Comm., UN

Map page 205

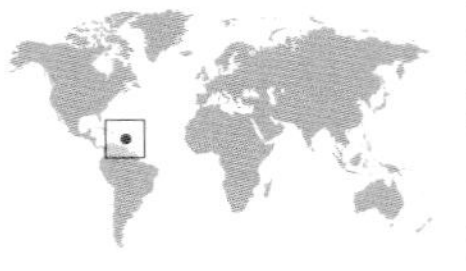

St Lucia, one of the Windward Islands in the Caribbean Sea, is a volcanic island with forested mountains, hot springs, sandy beaches and a wet tropical climate. Agriculture is the main activity, with bananas accounting for approximately forty per cent of export earnings. Tourism, agricultural processing and light manufacturing are increasingly important.

St-Martin
French Overseas Collectivity

Area Sq Km	54	**Languages**	French
Area Sq Miles	21	**Religions**	Roman Catholic
Population	37 630	**Currency**	Euro
Capital	Marigot		

Map page 205

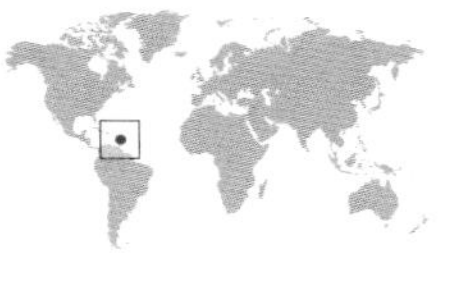

The northern part of St-Martin, one of the Leeward Islands, in the Caribbean. The other part of the island is a self-governing Netherlands territory (Sint Maarten). It was separated from Guadeloupe politically in 2007. Tourism is the main source of income.

St Pierre and Miquelon
French Territorial Collectivity

Area Sq Km	242	**Languages**	French
Area Sq Miles	93	**Religions**	Roman Catholic
Population	6 312	**Currency**	Euro
Capital	St-Pierre		

Map page 185

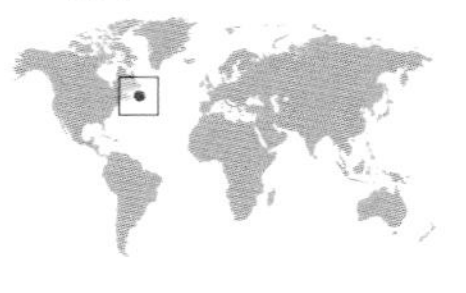

A group of islands off the south coast of Newfoundland in eastern Canada. The islands are largely unsuitable for agriculture, and fishing and fish processing are the most important activities. The islands rely heavily on financial assistance from France.

ST VINCENT AND THE GRENADINES

Area Sq Km	389	**Languages**	English, Creole
Area Sq Miles	150	**Religions**	Protestant, Roman Catholic
Population	109 000	**Currency**	East Caribbean dollar
Capital	Kingstown	**Organizations**	CARICOM, Comm., UN

Map page 205

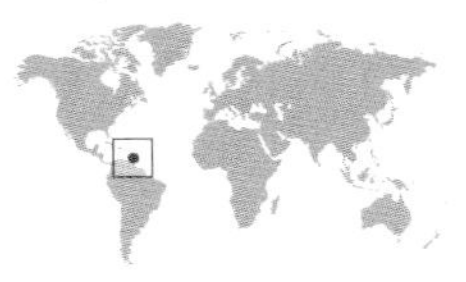

St Vincent, whose territory includes islets and cays in the Grenadines, is in the Windward Islands, in the Caribbean. St Vincent itself is forested and mountainous, with an active volcano, Soufrière. The climate is tropical and wet. The economy is based mainly on agriculture and tourism. Bananas account for approximately one-third of export earnings and arrowroot is also important. Most trade is with the USA and other CARICOM countries.

SAMOA
Independent State of Samoa

Area Sq Km	2 831	**Languages**	Samoan, English
Area Sq Miles	1 093	**Religions**	Protestant, Roman Catholic
Population	190 000	**Currency**	Tala
Capital	Apia	**Organizations**	Comm., UN

Map page 125

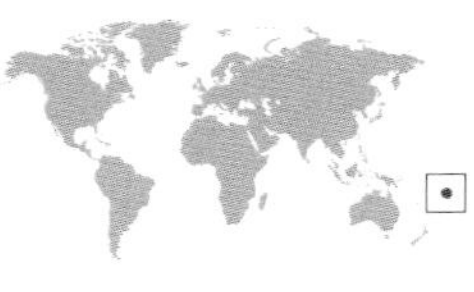

Samoa consists of two larger mountainous and forested islands, Savai'i and Upolu, and seven smaller islands, in the south Pacific Ocean. Over half the population lives on Upolu. The climate is tropical. The economy is based on agriculture, with some fishing and light manufacturing. Traditional exports are coconut products, fish and beer. Tourism is increasing, but the islands depend on workers' remittances and foreign aid.

SAN MARINO
Republic of San Marino

Area Sq Km	61	**Languages**	Italian
Area Sq Miles	24	**Religions**	Roman Catholic
Population	31 000	**Currency**	Euro
Capital	San Marino	**Organizations**	UN

Map page 170

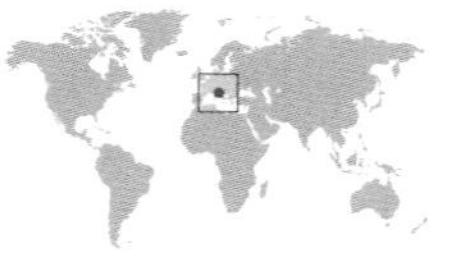

Landlocked San Marino lies in northeast Italy. A third of the people live in the capital. There is some agriculture and light industry, but most income comes from tourism. Italy is the main trading partner.

SÃO TOMÉ AND PRÍNCIPE
Democratic Republic of São Tomé and Príncipe

Area Sq Km	964	**Languages**	Portuguese, Creole
Area Sq Miles	372	**Religions**	Roman Catholic, Protestant
Population	193 000	**Currency**	Dobra
Capital	São Tomé	**Organizations**	UN

Map page 176

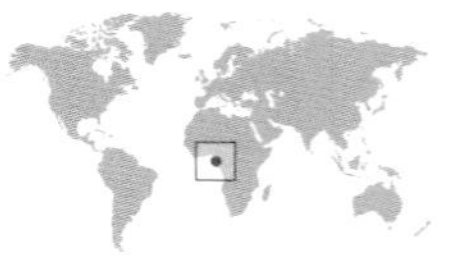

The two main islands and adjacent islets lie off the coast of west Africa in the Gulf of Guinea. São Tomé is the larger island, with over ninety per cent of the population. Both São Tomé and Príncipe are mountainous and tree-covered, and have a hot and humid climate. The economy is heavily dependent on cocoa, which accounts for around ninety per cent of export earnings.

SAUDI ARABIA
Kingdom of Saudi Arabia

Area Sq Km	2 200 000	**Languages**	Arabic
Area Sq Miles	849 425	**Religions**	Sunni Muslim, Shi'a Muslim
Population	28 829 000	**Currency**	Saudi Arabian riyal
Capital	Riyadh (Ar Riyāḍ)	**Organizations**	GCC, OPEC, UN

Map page 142

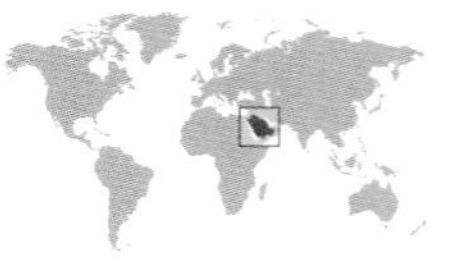

Saudi Arabia occupies most of the Arabian Peninsula in southwest Asia. The terrain is desert or semi-desert plateaus, which rise to mountains running parallel to the Red Sea in the west and slope down to plains in the southeast and along The Gulf in the east. Over eighty per cent of the population lives in urban areas. There are over five million foreign workers in Saudi Arabia, employed mainly in the oil and service industries. Summers are hot, winters are warm and rainfall is low. Saudi Arabia has the world's largest reserves of oil and significant natural gas reserves, both onshore and in The Gulf. Crude oil and refined products account for over eighty per cent of export earnings. Other industries and irrigated agriculture are being encouraged, but most food and raw materials are imported. Saudi Arabia has important banking and commercial interests. China and the USA are the main trading partners.

SENEGAL
Republic of Senegal

Area Sq Km	196 720	**Languages**	French, Wolof, Fulani, other local languages
Area Sq Miles	75 954	**Religions**	Sunni Muslim, Roman Catholic, traditional beliefs
Population	14 133 000	**Currency**	CFA franc
Capital	Dakar	**Organizations**	UN

Map page 176

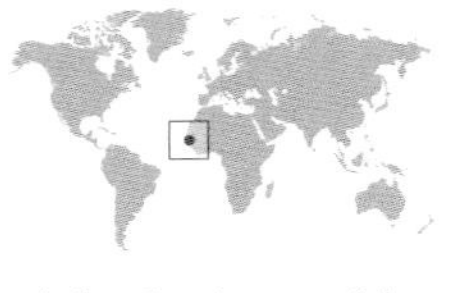

Senegal lies on the Atlantic coast of west Africa. The north is arid semi-desert, while the south is mainly fertile savanna bushland. The climate is tropical with summer rains, although droughts occur. One-fifth of the population lives in and around Dakar, the capital and main port. Fish, groundnuts and phosphates are important exports. France is the main trading partner.

SERBIA
Republic of Serbia

Area Sq Km	77 453	**Languages**	Serbian, Hungarian
Area Sq Miles	29 904	**Religions**	Serbian Orthodox, Roman Catholic, Sunni Muslim
Population	7 181 505	**Currency**	Serbian dinar
Capital	Beograd (Belgrade)	**Organizations**	UN

Map page 171

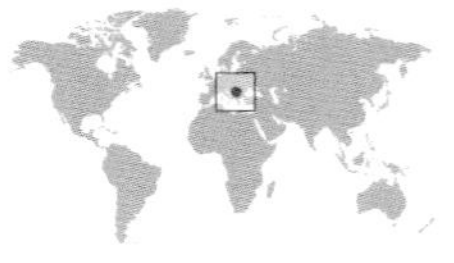

Following ethnic conflict and the break-up of Yugoslavia through the 1990s, the state union of Serbia and Montenegro retained the name Yugoslavia until 2003. The two then became separate

independent countries in 2006. The southern Serbian province of Kosovo declared its independence from Serbia in February 2008. The landscape is rugged, mountainous and forested in the south, while the north is low-lying and drained by the Danube river system.

SEYCHELLES
Republic of Seychelles

Area Sq Km	455	**Languages**	English, French, Creole
Area Sq Miles	176	**Religions**	Roman Catholic, Protestant
Population	93 000	**Currency**	Seychelles rupee
Capital	Victoria	**Organizations**	Comm., SADC, UN

Map page 175

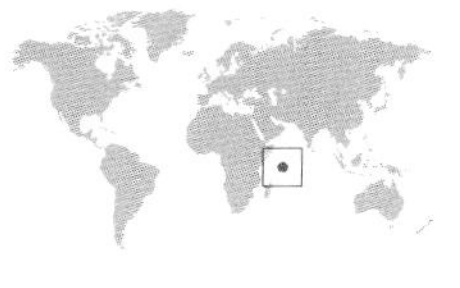

The Seychelles comprises an archipelago of over one hundred granitic and coral islands in the western Indian Ocean. Over ninety per cent of the population lives on the main island, Mahé. The climate is hot and humid with heavy rainfall. The economy is based mainly on tourism, fishing and light manufacturing.

SIERRA LEONE
Republic of Sierra Leone

Area Sq Km	71 740	**Languages**	English, Creole, Mende, Temne, other local languages
Area Sq Miles	27 699	**Religions**	Sunni Muslim, traditional beliefs
Population	6 092 000	**Currency**	Leone
Capital	Freetown	**Organizations**	Comm., UN

Map page 176

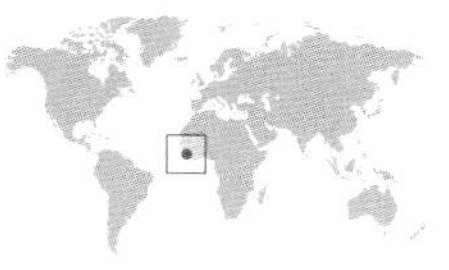

Sierra Leone lies on the Atlantic coast of west Africa. Its coastline is heavily indented and is lined with mangrove swamps. Inland is a forested area rising to savanna plateaus, with mountains to the northeast. The climate is tropical and rainfall is heavy. Most of the workforce is involved in subsistence farming. Cocoa and coffee are the main cash crops. Diamonds and rutile (titanium ore) are the main exports. Sierra Leone is one of the world's poorest countries, and the economy relies on substantial foreign aid.

SINGAPORE
Republic of Singapore

Area Sq Km	639	**Languages**	Chinese, English, Malay, Tamil
Area Sq Miles	247	**Religions**	Buddhist, Taoist, Sunni Muslim, Christian, Hindu
Population	5 412 000	**Currency**	Singapore dollar
Capital	Singapore	**Organizations**	APEC, ASEAN, Comm., UN

Map page 150

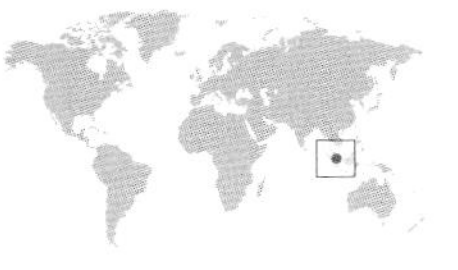

The state comprises the island of Singapore and over fifty others, at the tip of the Malay Peninsula in southeast Asia. Singapore is generally low-lying and includes areas of reclaimed land. The climate is hot and humid, with heavy rainfall all year. Most food has to be imported. Singapore lacks natural resources; industries and services have fuelled the nation's economic growth during recent decades. Main industries include electronics, oil refining, chemicals, pharmaceuticals, ship repair, food processing and textiles. Singapore is also a major financial centre. Its port is one of the world's largest and busiest. Tourism is also important. Japan, the USA and Malaysia are the main trading partners.

Sint Maarten
Self-governing Netherlands territory

Area Sq Km	34	**Languages**	Dutch, English
Area Sq Miles	13	**Religions**	Roman Catholic, Protestant
Population	45 000	**Currency**	Caribbean guilder
Capital	Philipsburg		

Map page 205 The southern part of one of the Leeward Islands, in the Caribbean; the other part of the island is a dependency of France. Sint Maarten was previously part of the Netherlands Antilles until they were dissolved in October 2010. Tourism and fishing are the most important industries.

SLOVAKIA
Slovak Republic

Area Sq Km	49 035	**Languages**	Slovak, Hungarian, Czech
Area Sq Miles	18 933	**Religions**	Roman Catholic, Protestant, Orthodox
Population	5 450 000	**Currency**	Euro
Capital	Bratislava	**Organizations**	EU, NATO, OECD, UN

Map page 168–169

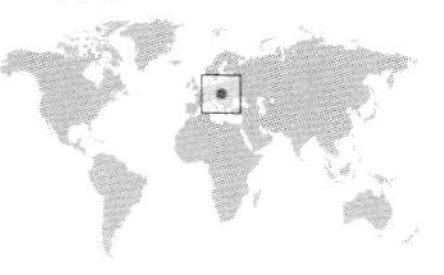

A landlocked country in central Europe, Slovakia is mountainous in the north, but low-lying in the southwest. The climate is continental. There is a range of manufacturing industries, and the main exports are machinery and transport equipment, but in recent years there have been economic difficulties and growth has been slow. Slovakia joined the European Union in May 2004. Most trade is with other EU countries, especially the Czech Republic and Germany.

SLOVENIA
Republic of Slovenia

Area Sq Km	20 251	**Languages**	Slovene, Croatian, Serbian
Area Sq Miles	7 819	**Religions**	Roman Catholic, Protestant
Population	2 072 000	**Currency**	Euro
Capital	Ljubljana	**Organizations**	EU, NATO, OECD, UN

Map page 170

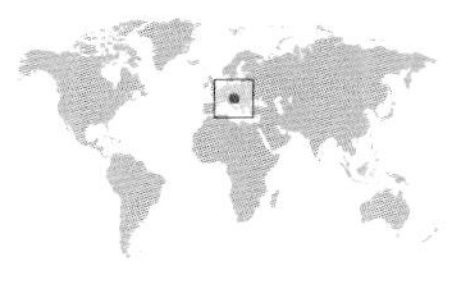

Slovenia lies in the northwest Balkan Mountains of southern Europe and has a short coastline on the Adriatic Sea. It is mountainous and hilly, with lowlands on the coast and in the Sava and Drava river valleys. The climate is generally continental inland and Mediterranean nearer the coast. The main agricultural products are potatoes, grain and sugar beet; the main industries include metal processing, electronics and consumer goods. Trade has been re-orientated towards western markets and the main trading partners are Germany and Italy. Slovenia joined the European Union in May 2004.

SOLOMON ISLANDS

Area Sq Km	28 370	**Languages**	English, Creole, other local languages
Area Sq Miles	10 954	**Religions**	Protestant, Roman Catholic
Population	561 000	**Currency**	Solomon Islands dollar
Capital	Honiara	**Organizations**	Comm., UN

Map page 125

The state consists of the Solomon, Santa Cruz and Shortland Islands in the southwest Pacific Ocean. The six main islands are volcanic, mountainous and forested, although Guadalcanal, the most populous, has a large lowland area. The climate is generally hot and humid. Subsistence farming, forestry and fishing predominate. Exports include timber products, fish, copra and palm oil. The islands depend on foreign aid.

SOMALIA
Federal Republic of Somalia

Area Sq Km	637 657	**Languages**	Somali, Arabic
Area Sq Miles	246 201	**Religions**	Sunni Muslim
Population	10 496 000	**Currency**	Somali shilling
Capital	Mogadishu (Muqdisho)	**Organizations**	UN

Map page 178

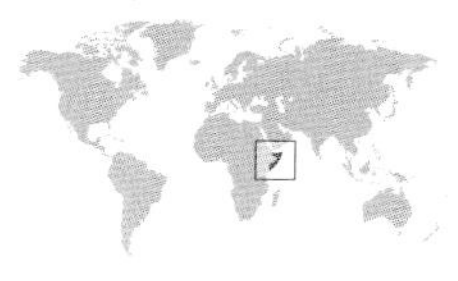

Somalia is in northeast Africa, on the Gulf of Aden and Indian Ocean. It consists of a dry scrubby plateau, rising to highlands in the north. The climate is hot and dry, but coastal areas and the Jubba and Wabē Shebelē Wenz river valleys support crops and most of the population. Subsistence farming and livestock rearing are the main activities. Exports include livestock and bananas. Frequent drought and civil war have prevented economic development. Somalia is one of the poorest, most unstable and least developed countries in the world.

Somaliland
Disputed territory

Area Sq Km	140 000	**Languages**	Somali, Arabic, English
Area Sq Miles	54 054	**Religions**	Sunni Muslim
Population	3 500 000	**Currency**	Somaliland shilling
Capital	Hargeysa		

Map page 178 After the collapse of the central Somali government in 1991 and at the start of the civil war, Somaliland, in the northwest of the country, covering the area of the former British Protectorate of Somaliland, declared its independence from Somalia as the Republic of Somaliland. A referendum in 2001 saw a majority vote for secession, and Somaliland currently operates as a de facto independent country, with fairly close relations with Ethiopia. The Transitional Federal Government of Somalia does not recognize its independence and conflicts still arise between Somaliland and the neighbouring region of Puntland over ownership of the administrative regions of Sanaag and Sool.

SOUTH AFRICA

Area Sq Km	1 219 090	**Languages**	Afrikaans, English, nine other official languages
Area Sq Miles	470 693	**Religions**	Protestant, Roman Catholic, Sunni Muslim, Hindu
Population	52 776 000	**Currency**	Rand
Capital	Bloemfontein/ Cape Town/ Pretoria (Tshwane)	**Organizations**	Comm., SADC, UN

Map page 180–181

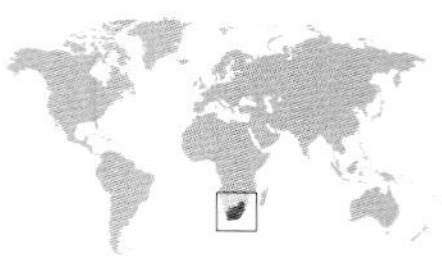

South Africa occupies most of the southern part of Africa. It surrounds Lesotho and has a long coastline on the Atlantic and Indian Oceans. Much of the land is a vast plateau, covered with grassland or bush and drained by the Orange and Limpopo river systems. A fertile coastal plain rises to mountain ridges in the south and east, including Table Mountain near Cape Town and the Drakensberg range in the east. South Africa has warm summers and mild winters. Most of the country has the majority of its rainfall in summer, but the coast around Cape Town has winter rains. South Africa has the largest economy in Africa, although wealth is unevenly distributed and unemployment is very high. Agriculture employs about six per cent of the workforce, and produce includes fruit, wine, wool and maize. The country is the world's leading producer of gold and chromium and an important producer of diamonds. Many other minerals are also mined. The main industries are mineral and food processing, chemicals, electrical equipment, textiles and motor vehicles. Financial services are also important.

SOUTH KOREA
Republic of Korea

Area Sq Km	99 274	**Languages**	Korean
Area Sq Miles	38 330	**Religions**	Buddhist, Protestant, Roman Catholic
Population	49 263 000	**Currency**	South Korean won
Capital	Seoul (Sŏul)	**Organizations**	APEC, OECD, UN

Map page 152

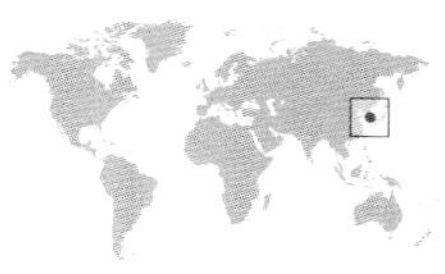

The state consists of the southern half of the Korean Peninsula in eastern Asia and many islands lying off the western and southern coasts in the Yellow Sea. The terrain is mountainous, although less rugged than that of North Korea. Population density is high and the country is highly urbanized; most of the population lives on the western coastal plains and in the river basins of the Han-gang in the northwest and the Naktong-gang in the southeast. The climate is continental, with hot, wet summers and dry, cold winters. Arable land is limited by the mountainous terrain, but because of intensive farming South Korea is nearly self-sufficient in food. Sericulture (silk) is important, as is fishing, which contributes to exports. South Korea has few mineral resources, except for coal and tungsten. It has achieved high economic growth based mainly on export manufacturing. The main manufactured goods are cars, electronic and electrical goods, ships, steel, chemicals and toys, as well as textiles, clothing, footwear and food products. The USA, China and Japan are the main trading partners.

South Ossetia
Disputed territory

Area Sq Km	4 000	**Languages**	Ossetian, Russian, Georgian
Area Sq Miles	1 544	**Religions**	Eastern Orthodox
Population	70 000	**Currency**	Russian rouble
Capital	Tskhinvali		

Map page 173 The formerly autonomous region of South Ossetia seeks independence from Georgia and looks to Russia, which recognizes its independence, as its principal ally. South Ossetia's autonomous status was removed in 1990. Violent conflicts followed between Georgia and the separatists, supported by Russia, who wished to unite with Russian North Ossetia. A cease-fire was agreed in 1992. Elections in 1996 were not recognized by Georgia, nor were elections and an independence referendum, voting in favour of independence, in 2006. Russian interference and interest in the area has continued to cause tensions with the Georgian government, the most recent conflict was in 2008 when Georgian troops attacked separatists. Russia responded and a week of fighting was ended by a cease-fire and resulted in Russia recognising South Ossetia's independence.

SOUTH SUDAN
Republic of South Sudan

Area Sq Km	644 329	**Languages**	English, Arabic, Dinka, Nuer, other local languages
Area Sq Miles	248 775	**Religions**	Traditional beliefs, Christian
Population	11 296 000	**Currency**	South Sudanese pound
Capital	Juba	**Organizations**	UN

Map page 177

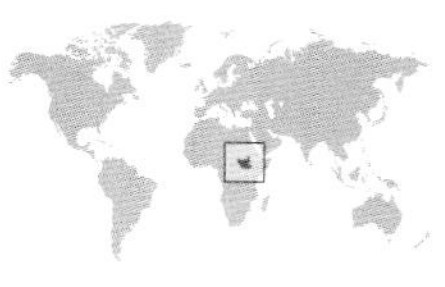

South Sudan in northeast Africa has grasslands, tropical forests and swamps in the north with higher lands in the south. The equatorial climate has moderate temperatures, high humidity and heavy rainfall. Independence from Sudan was gained in July 2011 as a result of a referendum held as part of the agreement which ended decades of civil war between north and south. The government plan to move the capital from Juba to Ramciel in the centre of the country. The economy is mostly agricultural, but the vast natural resources, including huge oil-reserves, are now being exploited.

SPAIN
Kingdom of Spain

Area Sq Km	504 782	Languages	Spanish (Castilian), Catalan, Galician, Basque
Area Sq Miles	194 897	Religions	Roman Catholic
Population	46 927 000	Currency	Euro
Capital	Madrid	Organizations	EU, NATO, OECD, UN

Map page 167

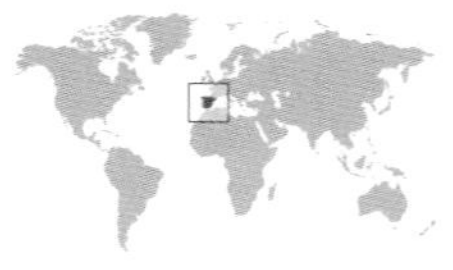

Spain occupies most of the Iberian peninsula in southwest Europe. It includes the Canary Islands, and two enclaves in north Africa. Much of the mainland is a high plateau, and the Pyrenees form the border with France. Summers are hot and winters cool, especially in the north. Most of the population is urban, and agriculture involves only a tenth of the workforce. Fruit, vegetables and wine are exported. Mineral resources include lead, copper, mercury and fluorspar. Some oil is produced, but Spain has to import energy. Manufacturing industries include machinery, transport equipment, vehicles and food products. Fishing, tourism and financial services are also important. Most trade is with other EU countries.

SRI LANKA
Democratic Socialist Republic of Sri Lanka

Area Sq Km	65 610	Languages	Sinhalese, Tamil, English
Area Sq Miles	25 332	Religions	Buddhist, Hindu, Sunni Muslim, Roman Catholic
Population	21 273 000	Currency	Sri Lankan rupee
Capital	Sri Jayewardenepura Kotte	Organizations	Comm., UN

Map page 143

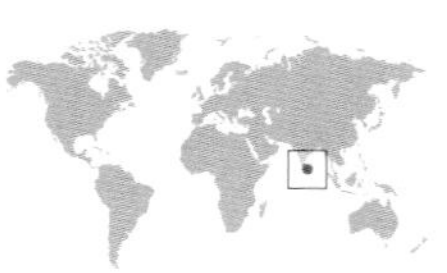

Sri Lanka lies in the Indian Ocean off the southeast coast of India in south Asia. It has rolling coastal plains, with mountains in the centre-south. The climate is hot and monsoonal. Most people live on the west coast. Manufactures (chiefly textiles and clothing), tea, rubber, copra and gems are exported. The economy relies on foreign aid and workers' remittances. The USA and the UK are the main trading partners.

SUDAN
Republic of the Sudan

Area Sq Km	1 861 484	Languages	Arabic, English, Nubian, Beja, Fur, other local languages
Area Sq Miles	718 725	Religions	Sunni Muslim, traditional beliefs, Christian
Population	37 964 000	Currency	Sudanese pound (Sudani)
Capital	Khartoum	Organizations	UN

Map page 177

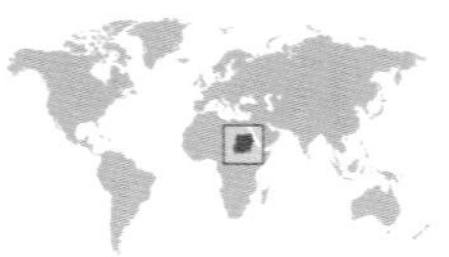

The Sudan is in the northeast of the continent of Africa, on the Red Sea. It lies within the upper Nile basin, much of which is arid plain but with swamps to the south. Mountains lie to the northeast, west and south. The climate is hot and arid with light summer rainfall, and droughts occur. Most people live along the Nile and are farmers and herders. Cotton, gum arabic, livestock and other agricultural products are exported. The government is working with foreign investors to develop oil resources, but the independence of South Sudan in July 2011 after civil war, and ethnic cleansing in Darfur continue to restrict the economy. Main trading partners are Saudi Arabia, China and UAE.

SURINAME
Republic of Suriname

Area Sq Km	163 820	Languages	Dutch, Surinamese, English, Hindi
Area Sq Miles	63 251	Religions	Hindu, Roman Catholic, Protestant, Sunni Muslim
Population	539 000	Currency	Surinamese dollar
Capital	Paramaribo	Organizations	CARICOM, UN

Map page 211

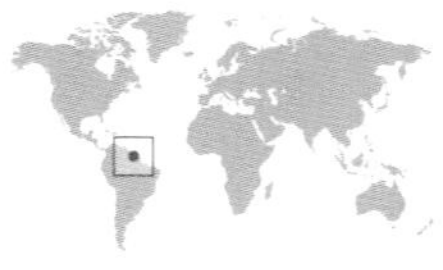

Suriname, on the Atlantic coast of northern South America, consists of a swampy coastal plain (where most of the population lives), central plateaus, and highlands in the south. The climate is tropical, and rainforest covers much of the land. Bauxite mining is the main industry, and alumina and aluminium are the chief exports, with shrimps, rice, bananas and timber also exported. The main trading partners are the Netherlands, Canada and the USA.

SWAZILAND
Kingdom of Swaziland

Area Sq Km	17 364	Languages	Swazi, English
Area Sq Miles	6 704	Religions	Christian, traditional beliefs
Population	1 250 000	Currency	Lilangeni, South African rand
Capital	Mbabane	Organizations	Comm., SADC, UN

Map page 181

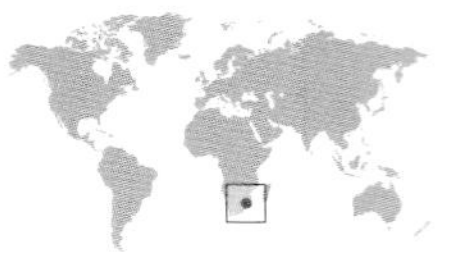

Landlocked Swaziland in southern Africa lies between Mozambique and South Africa. Savanna plateaus descend from mountains in the west towards hill country in the east. The climate is subtropical, but temperate in the mountains. Subsistence farming predominates. Asbestos and diamonds are mined. Exports include sugar, fruit and wood pulp. Tourism and workers' remittances are important to the economy. Most trade is with South Africa.

SWEDEN
Kingdom of Sweden

Area Sq Km	449 964	Languages	Swedish, Sami languages
Area Sq Miles	173 732	Religions	Protestant, Roman Catholic
Population	9 571 000	Currency	Swedish krona
Capital	Stockholm	Organizations	EU, OECD, UN

Map page 158–159

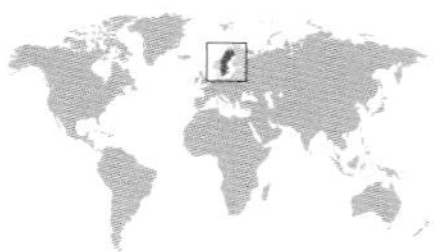

Sweden occupies the eastern part of the Scandinavian peninsula in northern Europe and borders the Baltic Sea, the Gulf of Bothnia, and the Kattegat and Skagerrak. Forested uplands cover the northern half, which extends beyond the Arctic Circle. The south is a lowland lake region where most of the population lives. Sweden has warm summers and cold winters, severe in the north. Natural resources include forests, minerals and water. Dairy products, meat, cereals and vegetables are produced. Iron and copper are mined, and also zinc, lead, silver and gold. Exports include machinery and transport equipment, chemicals, forest products, furniture and telecommunications equipment. Most trade is with other EU countries.

SWITZERLAND
Swiss Confederation

Area Sq Km	41 293	Languages	German, French, Italian, Romansch
Area Sq Miles	15 943	Religions	Roman Catholic, Protestant
Population	8 078 000	Currency	Swiss franc
Capital	Bern	Organizations	OECD, UN

Map page 166

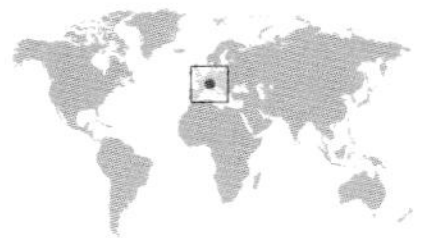

Switzerland is a mountainous, landlocked country in west-central Europe. The southern half lies within the Alps, and the Jura mountains are in the northwest. The rest is a high plateau, where most of the population lives. Climate varies depending on altitude, but in general summers are mild and winters are cold. Switzerland has a very high living standard, yet it has few mineral resources, and most food and raw materials are imported. Manufacturing (especially precision instruments and heavy machinery, chemicals and pharmaceuticals) and financial services are the mainstay of the economy. Tourism, and international organizations based in Switzerland, are also major foreign currency earners. Germany is the main trading partner.

SYRIA
Syrian Arab Republic

Area Sq Km	184 026	Languages	Arabic, Kurdish, Armenian
Area Sq Miles	71 052	Religions	Sunni Muslim, Shi'a Muslim, Christian
Population	21 898 000	Currency	Syrian pound
Capital	Damascus (Dimashq)	Organizations	UN

Map page 136–137

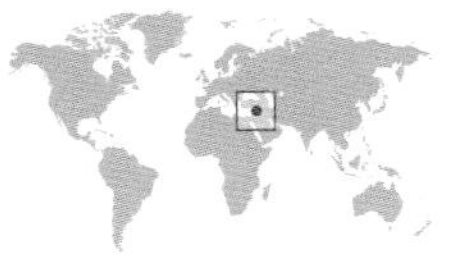

Syria is in southwest Asia, has a short coastline on the Mediterranean Sea, and stretches inland to a plateau traversed northwest-southeast by the Euphrates river. Mountains flank the southwest borders with Lebanon and Israel. The climate is Mediterranean in coastal regions, hotter and drier inland. Most Syrians live on the coast or in the river valleys. Syria's economy has been struggling since the start of the civil unrest in 2011 and the oil and gas industry has collapsed.

TAIWAN
Republic of China

Area Sq Km	36 179	Languages	Mandarin (Putonghua), Min, Hakka, other local languages
Area Sq Miles	13 969	Religions	Buddhist, Taoist, Confucian, Christian
Population	23 344 000	Currency	New Taiwan dollar
Capital	Taibei (T'aipei)	Organizations	APEC

Map page 149

The east Asian state consists of the island of Taiwan, separated from mainland China by the Taiwan Strait, and several much smaller islands. Much of Taiwan is mountainous and forested. Densely populated coastal plains in the west contain the bulk of the population and most economic activity. Taiwan has a tropical monsoon climate, with warm, wet summers and mild winters. Agriculture is highly productive. The country is virtually self-sufficient in food and exports some products. Coal, oil and natural gas are produced and a few minerals are mined, but none of them are of great significance to the economy. Taiwan depends heavily on imports of raw materials and exports of manufactured goods. The main manufactures are electrical and electronic goods, including television sets, personal computers and calculators, textiles, fertilizers, clothing, footwear and toys. The main trading partners are the USA, Japan and Germany. The People's Republic of China claims Taiwan as its 23rd Province.

TAJIKISTAN
Republic of Tajikistan

Area Sq Km	143 100	Languages	Tajik, Uzbek, Russian
Area Sq Miles	55 251	Religions	Sunni Muslim
Population	8 208 000	Currency	Somoni
Capital	Dushanbe	Organizations	CIS, UN

Map page 139

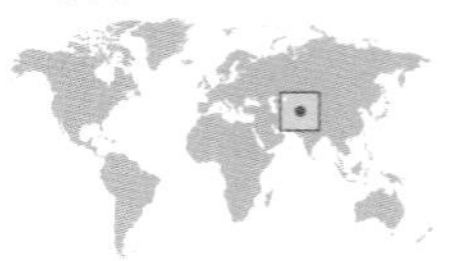

Landlocked Tajikistan in central Asia is a mountainous country, dominated by the mountains of the Alai Range and the Pamir. In the less mountainous western areas summers are warm, although winters are cold. Agriculture is the main sector of the economy, chiefly cotton growing and cattle breeding. Mineral deposits include lead, zinc, and uranium. Processed metals, textiles and clothing are the main manufactured goods; the main exports are aluminium and cotton. Uzbekistan, Kazakhstan and Russia are the main trading partners.

TANZANIA
United Republic of Tanzania

Area Sq Km	945 087	Languages	Swahili, English, Nyamwezi, other local languages
Area Sq Miles	364 900	Religions	Shi'a Muslim, Sunni Muslim, traditional beliefs, Christian
Population	49 253 000	Currency	Tanzanian shilling
Capital	Dodoma	Organizations	Comm., SADC, UN

Map page 178–179

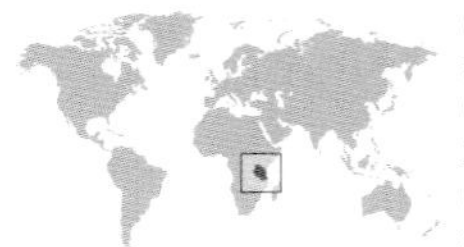

Tanzania lies on the coast of east Africa and includes the island of Zanzibar in the Indian Ocean. Most of the mainland is a savanna plateau lying east of the Great Rift Valley. In the north, near the border with Kenya, is Kilimanjaro, the highest mountain in Africa. The climate is tropical. The economy is predominantly based on agriculture, which employs about three-quarters of the workforce. Agricultural processing and gold and diamond mining are the main industries, although tourism is growing. Coffee, cotton, cashew nuts and tobacco are the main exports, with cloves from Zanzibar. Most export trade is with India, China and Switzerland. Tanzania depends heavily on foreign aid.

THAILAND
Kingdom of Thailand

Area Sq Km	513 115	Languages	Thai, Lao, Chinese, Malay, Mon-Khmer languages
Area Sq Miles	198 115	Religions	Buddhist, Sunni Muslim
Population	67 011 000	Currency	Baht
Capital	Bangkok (Krung Thep)	Organizations	APEC, ASEAN, UN

Map page 154

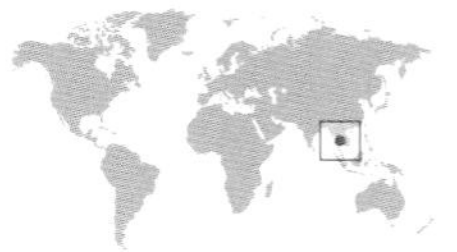

Thailand lies between the Gulf of Thailand and the Andaman Sea and includes the northern Malay Peninsula and many islands lining the coast. To the east of the extensive Chao Phraya basin is a plateau drained by the Mekong, while much of the rest is forested upland. The climate is hot, humid and monsoonal. Half the workforce is involved in agriculture, and fishing is also important, but tourism is the major earner. Minerals include gas, oil, lignite, tin, tungsten and baryte, and gemstones, and manufacturing includes electronics, clothing and food processing. Thailand is a leading exporter of rice, rubber, palm oil and cassava. Japan, China and the USA are the main trading partners.

TOGO
Togolese Republic

Area Sq Km	56 785	**Languages**	French, Ewe, Kabre, other local languages
Area Sq Miles	21 925	**Religions**	Traditional beliefs, Christian, Sunni Muslim
Population	6 817 000	**Currency**	CFA franc
Capital	Lomé	**Organizations**	UN

Map page 176

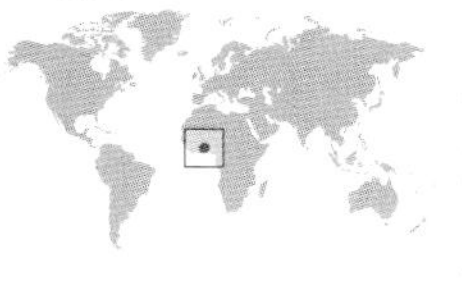

Togo is a long narrow country in west Africa with a short coastline on the Gulf of Guinea. The interior consists of plateaus rising to mountainous areas. The climate is tropical, and is drier inland. Agriculture is the mainstay of the economy. Phosphate mining and food processing are the main industries. Cotton, phosphates, coffee and cocoa are the main exports. Lomé, the capital, is an entrepôt trade centre.

Tokelau
New Zealand Overseas Territory

Area Sq Km	10	**Languages**	English, Tokelauan
Area Sq Miles	4	**Religions**	Christian
Population	1 411	**Currency**	New Zealand dollar

Map page 125 Tokelau consists of three atolls, Atafu, Nukunonu and Fakaofa, lying in the Pacific Ocean north of Samoa. Subsistence agriculture is the main activity, and the islands rely on aid from New Zealand and remittances from workers overseas.

TONGA
Kingdom of Tonga

Area Sq Km	748	**Languages**	Tongan, English
Area Sq Miles	289	**Religions**	Protestant, Roman Catholic
Population	105 000	**Currency**	Pa'anga
Capital	Nuku'alofa	**Organizations**	Comm., UN

Map page 125

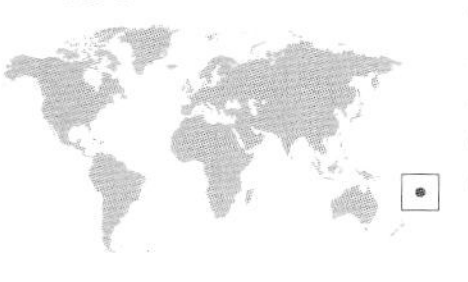

Tonga comprises some one hundred and seventy islands in the south Pacific Ocean, northeast of New Zealand. The three main groups are Tongatapu (where sixty per cent of Tongans live), Ha'apai and Vava'u. The climate is warm and wet, and the economy relies heavily on agriculture. Tourism and light industry are also important to the economy. Exports include squash, fish, vanilla beans and root crops. Most trade is with New Zealand, Japan and Australia.

Transnistria
Disputed territory

Area Sq Km	4 200	**Languages**	Russian, Ukrainian, Moldovan
Area Sq Miles	1 622	**Religions**	Eastern Orthodox, Roman Catholic
Population	520 000	**Currency**	Transnistrian rouble, Moldovan leu
Capital	Tiraspol		

Map page 173 Transnistria, the area of Moldova mainly between the Dniester river and the Ukrainian border, is a predominantly ethnic Russian, and Russian-speaking region. Campaigns for Transnistrian autonomy and independence led to civil war between Moldovan forces and separatists who had proclaimed the self-styled 'Dniester Republic', aligned to Russia, in 1990. A peace agreement with Russia in 1992 ended this war, granted Transnistria special status and established a security zone along its border with Moldova, controlled by Russian, Moldovan and Transnistrian troops. An agreement between Moldova and Transnistria in 1996 stated that Transnistria would remain a part of Moldova, but the campaign for independence continues and the status of the region remains to be resolved. It currently functions as a (predominantly Russian) de facto autonomous republic, separate from Moldova – the Pridnestrovian Moldavian Republic.

TRINIDAD AND TOBAGO
Republic of Trinidad and Tobago

Area Sq Km	5 130	**Languages**	English, Creole, Hindi
Area Sq Miles	1 981	**Religions**	Roman Catholic, Hindu, Protestant, Sunni Muslim
Population	1 341 000	**Currency**	Trinidad and Tobago dollar
Capital	Port of Spain	**Organizations**	CARICOM, Comm., UN

Map page 213

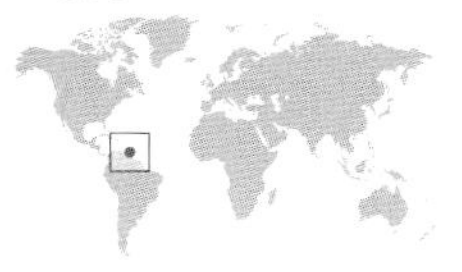

Trinidad, the most southerly Caribbean island, lies off the Venezuelan coast. It is hilly in the north, with a central plain. Tobago, to the northeast, is smaller, more mountainous and less developed. The climate is tropical. The main crops are cocoa, sugar cane, coffee, fruit and vegetables. Oil and petrochemical industries dominate the economy. Tourism is also important. The USA is the main trading partner.

TUNISIA
Republic of Tunisia

Area Sq Km	164 150	**Languages**	Arabic, French
Area Sq Miles	63 379	**Religions**	Sunni Muslim
Population	10 997 000	**Currency**	Tunisian dinar
Capital	Tunis	**Organizations**	UN

Map page 176

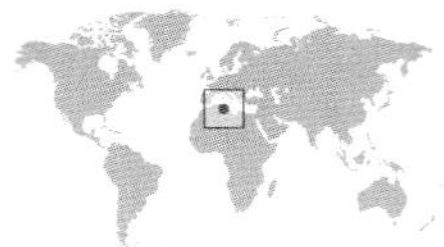

Tunisia is on the Mediterranean coast of north Africa. The north is mountainous with valleys and coastal plains, has a Mediterranean climate and is the most populous area. The south is hot and arid. Oil and phosphates are the main resources, and the main crops are olives and citrus fruit. Tourism is an important industry. Exports include petroleum products, textiles, fruit and phosphorus. Most trade is with European Union countries.

TURKEY
Republic of Turkey

Area Sq Km	779 452	**Languages**	Turkish, Kurdish
Area Sq Miles	300 948	**Religions**	Sunni Muslim, Shi'a Muslim
Population	74 933 000	**Currency**	Lira
Capital	Ankara	**Organizations**	NATO, OECD, UN

Map page 136–137

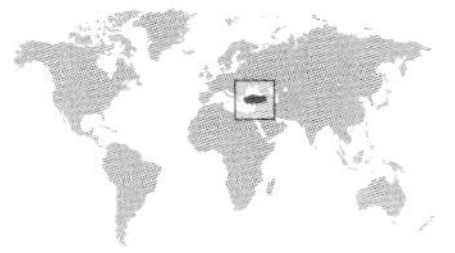

Turkey occupies a large peninsula in southwest Asia. It includes eastern Thrace, in southeastern Europe. The Asian mainland consists of the semi-arid Anatolian plateau, flanked to the north, south and east by mountains. The coast has a Mediterranean climate, but inland conditions are more extreme, with hot, dry summers and cold, snowy winters. Cotton, grains, tobacco, fruit, nuts and livestock are produced, and minerals include chromium, iron ore, lead, tin, borate, baryte, and some coal. Manufacturing includes clothing, textiles, food products, steel and vehicles. Tourism is a major industry, around forty milion visitors a year. Germany and the Russian Federation are the main trading partners. Remittances from workers abroad are important to the economy.

TURKMENISTAN

Area Sq Km	488 100	**Languages**	Turkmen, Uzbek, Russian
Area Sq Miles	188 456	**Religions**	Sunni Muslim, Russian Orthodox
Population	5 240 000	**Currency**	Turkmen manat
Capital	Aşgabat (Ashkhabad)	**Organizations**	UN

Map page 138

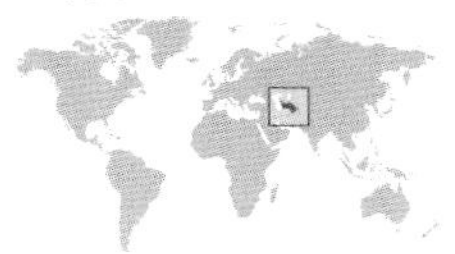

Turkmenistan, in central Asia, comprises the plains of the Karakum Desert, the foothills of the Kopet Dag mountains in the south, the Amudar'ya valley in the north and the Caspian Sea plains in the west. The climate is dry, with extreme temperatures. The economy is based mainly on irrigated agriculture (chiefly cotton growing), and natural gas and oil. Main exports are natural gas, oil and cotton fibre. Ukraine, Iran, Turkey and Russia are the main trading partners.

Turks and Caicos Islands
United Kingdom Overseas Territory

Area Sq Km	430	**Languages**	English
Area Sq Miles	166	**Religions**	Protestant
Population	33 000	**Currency**	United States dollar
Capital	Grand Turk (Cockburn Town)		

Map page 205 The state consists of over forty low-lying islands and cays in the northern Caribbean. Only eight islands are inhabited, and two-fifths of the people live on Grand Turk and Salt Cay. The climate is tropical, and the economy is based on tourism, fishing and offshore banking.

TUVALU

Area Sq Km	25	**Languages**	Tuvaluan, English
Area Sq Miles	10	**Religions**	Protestant
Population	10 000	**Currency**	Australian dollar
Capital	Vaiaku	**Organizations**	Comm., UN

Map page 125

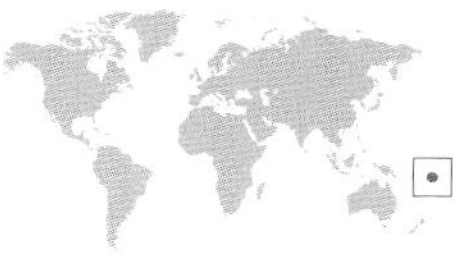

Tuvalu comprises nine low-lying coral atolls in the south Pacific Ocean. One-third of the population lives on Funafuti, and most people depend on subsistence farming and fishing. The islands export copra, stamps and clothing, but rely heavily on foreign aid. Most trade is with Fiji, Australia and New Zealand.

UGANDA
Republic of Uganda

Area Sq Km	241 038	**Languages**	English, Swahili, Luganda, other local languages
Area Sq Miles	93 065	**Religions**	Roman Catholic, Protestant, Sunni Muslim, traditional beliefs
Population	37 579 000	**Currency**	Ugandan shilling
Capital	Kampala	**Organizations**	Comm., UN

Map page 178

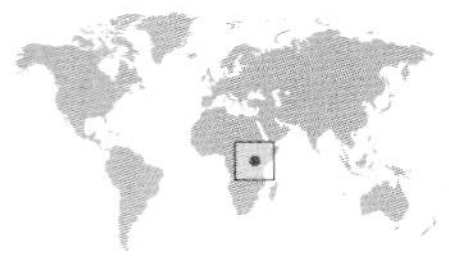

A landlocked country in east Africa, Uganda consists of a savanna plateau with mountains and lakes. The climate is warm and wet. Most people live in the southern half of the country. Agriculture employs over two-thirds of the workforce and dominates the economy. Coffee, tea, fish and fish products are the main exports. Uganda relies heavily on aid.

UKRAINE

Area Sq Km	603 700	**Languages**	Ukrainian, Russian
Area Sq Miles	233 090	**Religions**	Ukrainian Orthodox, Ukrainian Catholic, Roman Catholic
Population	45 239 000	**Currency**	Hryvnia
Capital	Kiev (Kyiv)	**Organizations**	UN

Map page 173

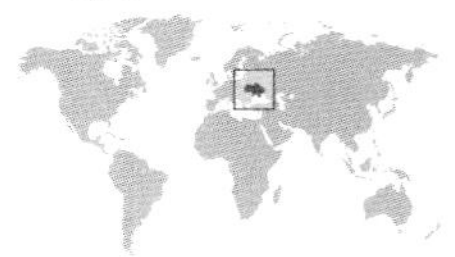

The country lies on the Black Sea coast of eastern Europe. Much of the land is steppe, generally flat and treeless, but with rich black soil, and it is drained by the river Dnieper. Along the border with Belarus are forested, marshy plains. The only uplands are the Carpathian Mountains in the west and smaller ranges on the Crimean peninsula. Summers are warm and winters are cold, with milder conditions in the Crimea. About a quarter of the population lives in the mainly industrial areas around Donets'k, Kiev and Dnipropetrovs'k. The Ukraine is rich in natural resources: fertile soil, substantial mineral and natural gas deposits, and forests. Agriculture and livestock rearing are important, but mining and manufacturing are the dominant sectors of the economy. Coal, iron and manganese mining, steel and metal production, machinery, chemicals and food processing are the main industries. The EU and Russia are the main trading partners but the economy is struggling.

UNITED ARAB EMIRATES
Federation of Emirates

Area Sq Km	77 700	**Languages**	Arabic, English
Area Sq Miles	30 000	**Religions**	Sunni Muslim, Shi'a Muslim
Population	9 346 000	**Currency**	United Arab Emirates dirham
Capital	Abu Dhabi (Abū Ẓaby)	**Organizations**	GCC, OPEC, UN

Map page 140

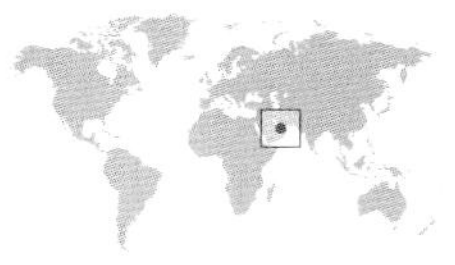

The UAE lies on the Gulf coast of the Arabian Peninsula. Six emirates are on The Gulf, while the seventh, Fujairah, is on the Gulf of Oman. Most of the land is flat desert with sand dunes and salt pans. The only hilly area is in the northeast. Over eighty per cent of the population lives in three of the emirates - Abu Dhabi, Dubai and Sharjah. Summers are hot and winters are mild, with occasional rainfall in coastal areas. Fruit and vegetables are grown in oases and irrigated areas, but the Emirates' wealth is based on hydrocarbons found in Abu Dhabi, Dubai, Sharjah and Ras al Khaimah. The UAE is one of the major oil producers in the Middle East. Dubai is an important entrepôt trade centre The main trading partners are India, Iran, Iraq and China.

Abu Dhabi (Abū Ẓaby) (Emirate)
Area Sq Km (Sq Miles) 67 340 (26 000) **Population** 1 628 000 **Capital** Abu Dhabi (Abū Ẓaby)

Ajman (Emirate)
Area Sq Km (Sq Miles) 259 (100) **Population** 250 000 **Capital** 'Ajman

Dubai (Emirate)
Area Sq Km (Sq Miles) 3 885 (1 500) **Population** 1 722 000 **Capital** Dubai (Dubayy)

Fujairah (Emirate)
Area Sq Km (Sq Miles) 1 165 (450) **Population** 152 000 **Capital** Fujairah

Ra's al Khaymah (Emirate)
Area Sq Km (Sq Miles) 1 684 (650) **Population** 241 000 **Capital** Ra's al Khaymah

Sharjah (Emirate)
Area Sq Km (Sq Miles) 2 590 (1 000) **Population** 1 017 000 **Capital** Sharjah (Ash Shāriqan)

Umm al Qaywayn (Emirate)
Area Sq Km (Sq Miles) 777 (300) **Population** 56 000 **Capital** Umm al Qaywayn

UNITED KINGDOM

United Kingdom of Great Britain and Northern Ireland

Area Sq Km	243 609	**Languages**	English, Welsh, Gaelic
Area Sq Miles	94 058	**Religions**	Protestant, Roman Catholic, Muslim
Population	63 136 000	**Currency**	Pound sterling
Capital	London	**Organizations**	Comm., EU, NATO, OECD, UN

Map page 160–163

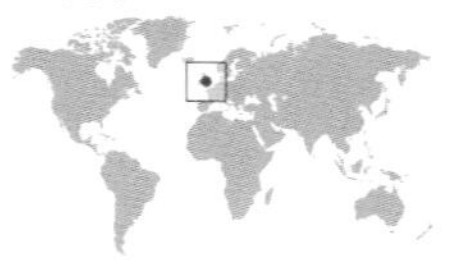

The United Kingdom, in northwest Europe, occupies the island of Great Britain, part of Ireland, and many small adjacent islands. Great Britain comprises England, Scotland and Wales. England covers over half the land area and supports over four-fifths of the population, at its densest in the southeast. The English landscape is flat or rolling with some uplands, notably the Cheviot Hills on the Scottish border, the Pennines in the centre-north, and the hills of the Lake District in the northwest. Scotland consists of southern uplands, central lowlands, the Highlands (which include the UK's highest peak) and many islands. Wales is a land of hills, mountains and river valleys. Northern Ireland contains uplands, plains and the UK's largest lake, Lough Neagh. The climate of the UK is mild, wet and variable. There are few mineral deposits, but important energy resources. Agricultural activities involve sheep and cattle rearing, dairy farming, and crop and fruit growing in the east and southeast. Productivity is high, but approximately one-third of food is imported. The UK produces petroleum and natural gas from reserves in the North Sea and is self-sufficient in energy in net terms. Major manufactures are food and drinks, motor vehicles and parts, aerospace equipment, machinery, electronic and electrical equipment, and chemicals and chemical products. However, the economy is dominated by service industries, including banking, insurance, finance and business services. London, the capital, is one of the world's major financial centres. Tourism is also a major industry, with approximately thirty-two million visitors a year. International trade is also important, equivalent to one-third of national income. Main trading partners are the USA and other European Union countries.

Name	Area Sq Km (Sq Miles)	Population	Capital
England (Constituent country)	130 433 (50 360)	53 493 700	London
Northern Ireland (Province)	13 576 (5 242)	1 823 600	Belfast
Scotland (Constituent country)	78 822 (30 433)	5 313 600	Edinburgh
Wales (Principality)	20 778 (8 022)	3 074 100	Cardiff

UNITED STATES OF AMERICA

Federal Republic

Area Sq Km	9 826 635	**Languages**	English, Spanish
Area Sq Miles	3 794 085	**Religions**	Protestant, Roman Catholic, Sunni Muslim, Jewish
Population	320 051 000	**Currency**	United States dollar
Capital	Washington D.C.	**Organizations**	APEC, NATO, OECD, UN

Map page 192–193

The USA comprises forty-eight contiguous states in North America, bounded by Canada and Mexico, plus the states of Alaska, to the northwest of Canada, and Hawaii, in the north Pacific Ocean. The populous eastern states cover the Atlantic coastal plain (which includes the Florida peninsula and the Gulf of Mexico coast) and the Appalachian Mountains. The central states occupy a vast interior plain drained by the Mississippi-Missouri river system. To the west lie the Rocky Mountains, separated from the Pacific coastal ranges by intermontane plateaus. The Pacific coastal zone is also mountainous, and prone to earthquakes. Hawaii is a group of some twenty volcanic islands. Climatic conditions range between arctic in Alaska to desert in the intermontane plateaus. Most of the USA has a temperate climate, although the interior has continental conditions. There are abundant natural resources, including major reserves of minerals and energy resources. The USA has the largest and most technologically advanced economy in the world, based on manufacturing and services. Although agriculture accounts for approximately two per cent of national income, productivity is high and the USA is a net exporter of food, chiefly grains and fruit. Cotton is the major industrial crop. The USA produces iron ore, copper, lead, zinc, and many other minerals. It is a major producer of coal, petroleum and natural gas, although being the world's biggest energy user it imports significant quantities of petroleum and its products. Manufacturing is diverse. The main industries are petroleum, steel, motor vehicles, aerospace, telecommunications, electronics, food processing, chemicals and consumer goods. Tourism is a major foreign currency earner, with approximately seventy-four million visitors a year. Other important service industries are banking and finance, Wall Street in New York being one of the world's major stock exchanges. Canada and Mexico are the main trading partners.

Name	Area Sq Km (Sq Miles)	Population	Capital
Alabama (State)	135 765 (52 419)	4 822 023	Montgomery
Alaska (State)	1 717 854 (663 267)	731 449	Juneau
Arizona (State)	295 253 (113 998)	6 553 255	Phoenix
Arkansas (State)	137 733 (53 179)	2 949 131	Little Rock
California (State)	423 971 (163 696)	38 041 430	Sacramento
Colorado (State)	269 602 (104 094)	5 187 582	Denver
Connecticut (State)	14 356 (5 543)	3 590 347	Hartford
Delaware (State)	6 446 (2 489)	917 092	Dover
District of Columbia (District)	176 (68)	632 323	Washington
Florida (State)	170 305 (65 755)	19 317 568	Tallahassee
Georgia (State)	153 910 (59 425)	9 919 945	Atlanta
Hawaii (State)	28 311 (10 931)	1 392 313	Honolulu
Idaho (State)	216 445 (83 570)	1 595 728	Boise
Illinois (State)	149 997 (57 914)	12 875 255	Springfield
Indiana (State)	94 322 (36 418)	6 537 334	Indianapolis
Iowa (State)	145 744 (56 272)	3 074 186	Des Moines
Kansas (State)	213 096 (82 277)	2 885 905	Topeka
Kentucky (State)	104 659 (40 409)	4 380 415	Frankfort
Louisiana (State)	134 265 (51 840)	4 601 893	Baton Rouge
Maine (State)	91 647 (35 385)	1 329 192	Augusta
Maryland (State)	32 134 (12 407)	5 884 563	Annapolis
Massachusetts (State)	27 337 (10 555)	6 646 144	Boston
Michigan (State)	250 493 (96 716)	9 883 360	Lansing
Minnesota (State)	225 171 (86 939)	5 379 139	St Paul
Mississippi (State)	125 433 (48 430)	2 984 926	Jackson
Missouri (State)	180 533 (69 704)	6 021 988	Jefferson City
Montana (State)	380 837 (147 042)	1 005 141	Helena
Nebraska (State)	200 346 (77 354)	1 855 525	Lincoln
Nevada (State)	286 352 (110 561)	2 758 931	Carson City
New Hampshire (State)	24 216 (9 350)	1 320 718	Concord
New Jersey (State)	22 587 (8 721)	8 864 590	Trenton
New Mexico (State)	314 914 (121 589)	2 085 538	Santa Fe
New York (State)	141 299 (54 556)	19 570 261	Albany
North Carolina (State)	139 391 (53 819)	9 752 073	Raleigh
North Dakota (State)	183 112 (70 700)	699 628	Bismarck
Ohio (State)	116 096 (44 825)	11 544 225	Columbus
Oklahoma (State)	181 035 (69 898)	3 814 820	Oklahoma City
Oregon (State)	254 806 (98 381)	3 899 353	Salem
Pennsylvania (State)	119 282 (46 055)	12 763 536	Harrisburg
Rhode Island (State)	4 002 (1 545)	1 050 292	Providence
South Carolina (State)	82 931 (32 020)	4 723 723	Columbia
South Dakota (State)	199 730 (77 116)	833 354	Pierre
Tennessee (State)	109 150 (42 143)	6 456 243	Nashville
Texas (State)	695 622 (268 581)	26 059 203	Austin
Utah (State)	219 887 (84 899)	2 855 287	Salt Lake City
Vermont (State)	24 900 (9 614)	626 011	Montpelier
Virginia (State)	110 784 (42 774)	8 185 867	Richmond
Washington (State)	184 666 (71 300)	6 897 012	Olympia
West Virginia (State)	62 755 (24 230)	1 855 413	Charleston
Wisconsin (State)	169 639 (65 498)	5 726 398	Madison
Wyoming (State)	253 337 (97 814)	576 412	Cheyenne

URUGUAY

Oriental Republic of Uruguay

Area Sq Km	176 215	**Languages**	Spanish
Area Sq Miles	68 037	**Religions**	Roman Catholic, Protestant, Jewish
Population	3 407 000	**Currency**	Uruguayan peso
Capital	Montevideo	**Organizations**	UN

Map page 215

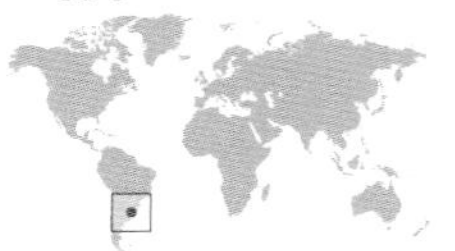

Uruguay, on the Atlantic coast of central South America, is a low-lying land of prairies. The coast and the River Plate estuary in the south are fringed with lagoons and sand dunes. Almost half the population lives in the capital, Montevideo. Uruguay has warm summers and mild winters. The economy is based on cattle and sheep ranching, and the main industries produce food products, textiles, and petroleum products. Meat, wool, hides, textiles and agricultural products are the main exports. Brazil and Argentina are the main trading partners.

UZBEKISTAN

Republic of Uzbekistan

Area Sq Km	447 400	**Languages**	Uzbek, Russian, Tajik, Kazakh
Area Sq Miles	172 742	**Religions**	Sunni Muslim, Russian Orthodox
Population	28 934 000	**Currency**	Uzbek som
Capital	Toshkent (Tashkent)	**Organizations**	CIS, UN

Map page 138–139

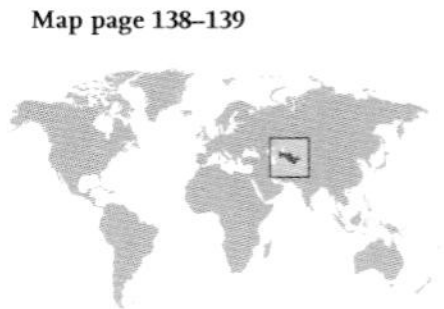

A landlocked country of central Asia, Uzbekistan consists mainly of the flat Kyzylkum Desert. High mountains and valleys are found towards the southeast borders with Kyrgyzstan and Tajikistan. Most settlement is in the Fergana basin. The climate is hot and dry. The economy is based mainly on irrigated agriculture, chiefly cotton production. Uzbekistan is rich in minerals, including gold, copper, lead, zinc and uranium, and it has one of the largest gold mines in the world. Industry specializes in fertilizers and machinery for cotton harvesting and textile manufacture. Russia is the main trading partner.

VANUATU
Republic of Vanuatu

Area Sq Km	12 190	Languages	English, Bislama (Creole), French
Area Sq Miles	4 707	Religions	Protestant, Roman Catholic, traditional beliefs
Population	253 000		
Capital	Port Vila	Currency	Vatu
		Organizations	Comm., UN

Map page 125

Vanuatu occupies an archipelago of approximately eighty islands in the southwest Pacific. Many of the islands are mountainous, of volcanic origin and densely forested. The climate is tropical, with heavy rainfall. Half of the population lives on the main islands of Éfaté and Espíritu Santo, and the majority of people are employed in agriculture. Copra, beef, timber, vegetables, and cocoa are the main exports. In March 2015 Cyclone Pam caused catastrophic damage to the islands.

VATICAN CITY
Vatican City State or Holy See

Area Sq Km	0.5	Languages	Italian
Area Sq Miles	0.2	Religions	Roman Catholic
Population	800	Currency	Euro
Capital	Vatican City (Città del Vaticano)		

Map page 170

The world's smallest sovereign state, the Vatican City occupies a hill to the west of the river Tiber within the Italian capital, Rome. It is the headquarters of the Roman Catholic church, and income comes from investments, voluntary contributions and tourism.

VENEZUELA
Bolivarian Republic of Venezuela

Area Sq Km	912 050	Languages	Spanish, Amerindian languages
Area Sq Miles	352 144	Religions	Roman Catholic, Protestant
Population	30 405 000	Currency	Bolívar
Capital	Caracas	Organizations	OPEC, UN

Map page 213

Venezuela is in northern South America, on the Caribbean. Its coast is much indented, with the oil-rich area of Lake Maracaibo at the western end, and the swampy Orinoco Delta to the east. Mountain ranges run parallel to the coast, and turn southwestwards to form a northern extension of the Andes. Central Venezuela is an area of lowland grasslands drained by the Orinoco river system. To the south are the Guiana Highlands, which contain the Angel Falls, the world's highest waterfall. Almost ninety per cent of the population lives in towns, mostly in the coastal mountain areas. The climate is tropical, with most rainfall in summer. Farming is important, particularly cattle ranching and dairy farming; coffee, maize, rice and sugar cane are the main crops. Venezuela is a major oil producer, and oil accounts for about seventy-five per cent of export earnings. Aluminium, iron ore, copper and gold are also mined, and manufactures include petrochemicals, aluminium, steel, textiles and food products. The USA, China and Brazil are the main trading partners.

VIETNAM
Socialist Republic of Vietnam

Area Sq Km	329 565	Languages	Vietnamese, Thai, Khmer, Chinese, other local languages
Area Sq Miles	127 246		
Population	91 680 000	Religions	Buddhist, Taoist, Roman Catholic, Cao Dai, Hoa Hao
Capital	Ha Nôi (Hanoi)		
		Currency	Dong
		Organizations	APEC, ASEAN, UN

Map page 147

Vietnam lies in southeast Asia on the west coast of the South China Sea. The Red River delta lowlands in the north are separated from the huge Mekong delta in the south by long, narrow coastal plains backed by the mountainous and forested terrain of the Annam Highlands. Most of the population lives in the river deltas. The climate is tropical, with summer monsoon rains. Over three-quarters of the workforce is involved in agriculture, forestry and fishing. Coffee, tea and rubber are important cash crops, but Vietnam is the world's second largest rice exporter. Oil, coal and copper are produced, and other main industries are food processing, clothing and footwear, cement and fertilizers. Exports include oil, coffee, rice, clothing, fish and fish products. Japan and Singapore are the main trading partners.

Virgin Islands (U.K.)
United Kingdom Overseas Territory

Area Sq Km	153	Languages	English
Area Sq Miles	59	Religions	Protestant, Roman Catholic
Population	28 000	Currency	United States dollar
Capital	Road Town		

Map page 205   The Caribbean territory comprises four main islands and over thirty islets at the eastern end of the Virgin Islands group. Apart from the flat coral atoll of Anegada, the islands are volcanic in origin and hilly. The climate is subtropical, and tourism is the main industry.

Virgin Islands (U.S.A.)
United States Unincorporated Territory

Area Sq Km	352	Languages	English, Spanish
Area Sq Miles	136	Religions	Protestant, Roman Catholic
Population	107 000	Currency	United States dollar
Capital	Charlotte Amalie		

Map page 205

The territory consists of three main islands and over fifty islets in the Caribbean's western Virgin Islands. The islands are hilly, of volcanic origin, and the climate is subtropical. The economy is based on tourism, with some manufacturing, including a major oil refinery on St Croix.

Wallis and Futuna Islands
French Overseas Collectivity

Area Sq Km	274	Languages	French, Wallisian, Futunian
Area Sq Miles	106	Religions	Roman Catholic
Population	13 000	Currency	CFP franc
Capital	Matä'utu		

Map page 125

The south Pacific territory comprises the volcanic islands of the Wallis archipelago and the Hoorn Islands. The climate is tropical. The islands depend on subsistence farming, the sale of licences to foreign fishing fleets, workers' remittances from abroad and French aid.

West Bank
Disputed territory

Area Sq Km	5 860	Languages	Arabic, Hebrew
Area Sq Miles	2 263	Religions	Sunni Muslim, Jewish, Shi'a Muslim, Christian
Population	2 719 112		
		Currency	Jordanian dinar, Israeli shekel

Map page 136

The territory consists of the west bank of the river Jordan and parts of Judea and Samaria. The land was annexed by Israel in 1967, but some areas have been granted autonomy under agreements between Israel and the Palestinian Authority. Conflict between the Israelis and the Palestinians continues to restrict economic development.

Western Sahara
Disputed territory

Area Sq Km	266 000	Languages	Arabic
Area Sq Miles	102 703	Religions	Sunni Muslim
Population	567 000	Currency	Moroccan dirham
Capital	Laâyoune		

Map page 176

Situated on the northwest coast of Africa, the territory of the Western Sahara is now effectively controlled by Morocco. The land is low, flat desert with higher land in the northeast. There is little cultivation and only about twenty per cent of the land is pasture. Livestock herding, fishing and phosphate mining are the main activities. All trade is controlled by Morocco.

YEMEN
Republic of Yemen

Area Sq Km	527 968	Languages	Arabic
Area Sq Miles	203 850	Religions	Sunni Muslim, Shi'a Muslim
Population	24 407 000	Currency	Yemeni riyal
Capital	Şan'a'	Organizations	UN

Map page 142

Yemen occupies the southwestern part of the Arabian Peninsula, on the Red Sea and the Gulf of Aden. Beyond the Red Sea coastal plain the land rises to a mountain range and then descends to desert plateaus. Much of the country is hot and arid, but there is more rainfall in the west, where most of the population lives. Farming and fishing are the main activities, with cotton the main cash crop. The main exports are crude oil, fish, coffee and dried fruit. Despite some oil resources Yemen is one of the poorest countries in the Arab world. Main trading partners are Thailand, China, South Korea and Saudi Arabia.

ZAMBIA
Republic of Zambia

Area Sq Km	752 614	Languages	English, Bemba, Nyanja, Tonga, other local languages
Area Sq Miles	290 586		
Population	14 539 000	Religions	Christian, traditional beliefs
Capital	Lusaka	Currency	Zambian kwacha
		Organizations	Comm., SADC, UN

Map page 179

A landlocked state in south central Africa, Zambia consists principally of high savanna plateaus and is bordered by the Zambezi river in the south. Most people live in the Copperbelt area in the centre-north. The climate is tropical, with a rainy season from November to May. Agriculture employs over sixty per cent of the workforce, but is mainly at subsistence level. Copper mining is the mainstay of the economy, although reserves are declining. Copper and cobalt are the main exports. Most trade is with South Africa.

ZIMBABWE
Republic of Zimbabwe

Area Sq Km	390 759	Languages	English, Shona, Ndebele
Area Sq Miles	150 873	Religions	Christian, traditional beliefs
Population	14 150 000	Currency	US dollar and other currencies
Capital	Harare	Organizations	SADC, UN

Map page 179

Zimbabwe, a landlocked state in south-central Africa, consists of high plateaus flanked by the Zambezi river valley and Lake Kariba in the north and the Limpopo river in the south. Most of the population lives in the centre of the country. There are significant mineral resources, including gold, nickel, copper, asbestos, platinum and chromium. Agriculture is a major sector of the economy, with crops including tobacco, maize, sugar cane and cotton. Beef cattle are also important. Exports include tobacco, gold, ferroalloys, nickel and cotton. South Africa is the main trading partner. The economy has suffered recently through significant political unrest and instability.

EARTHQUAKES AND VOLCANOES

DISTRIBUTION OF EARTHQUAKES AND VOLCANOES

- ● Deadliest earthquake
- ● Earthquake of magnitude >=7.5
- ○ Earthquake of magnitude 5.5 – 7.5
- ▲ Major volcano
- ▲ Other volcano

DEADLIEST EARTHQUAKES 1900–2015

Year	Location	Deaths
1905	**Kangra**, India	19 000
1907	west of **Dushanbe**, Tajikistan	12 000
1908	**Messina**, Italy	110 000
1915	**Abruzzo**, Italy	35 000
1917	**Bali**, Indonesia	15 000
1920	**Ningxia Province**, China	200 000
1923	**Tōkyō**, Japan	142 807
1927	**Qinghai Province**, China	200 000
1932	**Gansu Province**, China	70 000
1933	**Sichuan Province**, China	10 000
1934	**Nepal/India**	10 700
1935	**Quetta**, Pakistan	30 000
1939	**Chillán**, Chile	28 000
1939	**Erzincan**, Turkey	32 700
1948	**Aşgabat**, Turkmenistan	19 800
1962	northwest **Iran**	12 225
1970	**Huánuco Province**, Peru	66 794
1974	**Yunnan** and **Sichuan Provinces**, China	20 000
1976	central **Guatemala**	22 778
1976	**Tangshan**, Hebei Province, China	255 000
1978	**Khorāsān Province**, Iran	20 000
1980	**Ech Chélif**, Algeria	11 000
1988	**Spitak**, Armenia	25 000
1990	**Manjil**, Iran	50 000
1999	**İzmit (Kocaeli)**, Turkey	17 000
2001	**Gujarat**, India	20 000
2003	**Bam**, Iran	26 271
2004	**Sumatra**, Indonesia/Indian Ocean	>225 000
2005	northwest **Pakistan**	74 648
2008	**Sichuan Province**, China	>60 000
2010	**Léogâne**, Haiti	222 570
2011	**Tōhoku**, Japan	14 500
2015	**Gorkha**, Nepal	>8 000

Winkel Tripel Projection
scale approximately 1:95 000 000

On 25 April 2015, Nepal suffered an eathquake of magnitude 7.8 killing over 8 000 people and injuring many thousands more. In Bhaktapur, near Kathmandu, this image was taken on 9 May, as local residents clear some of the rubble and look for belongings they can salvage.

RICHTER SCALE

The scale measures the energy released by an earthquake. The scale is logarithmic – a quake measuring 4 is 30 times more powerful than one measuring 3, and a quake measuring 6 is 27 000 times more powerful than one measuring 3.

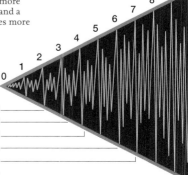

Not recorded
Recorded, tremor felt
Quake easily felt, local damage caused
Destructive earthquake
Major earthquake
Most powerful earthquake recorded – 9.5

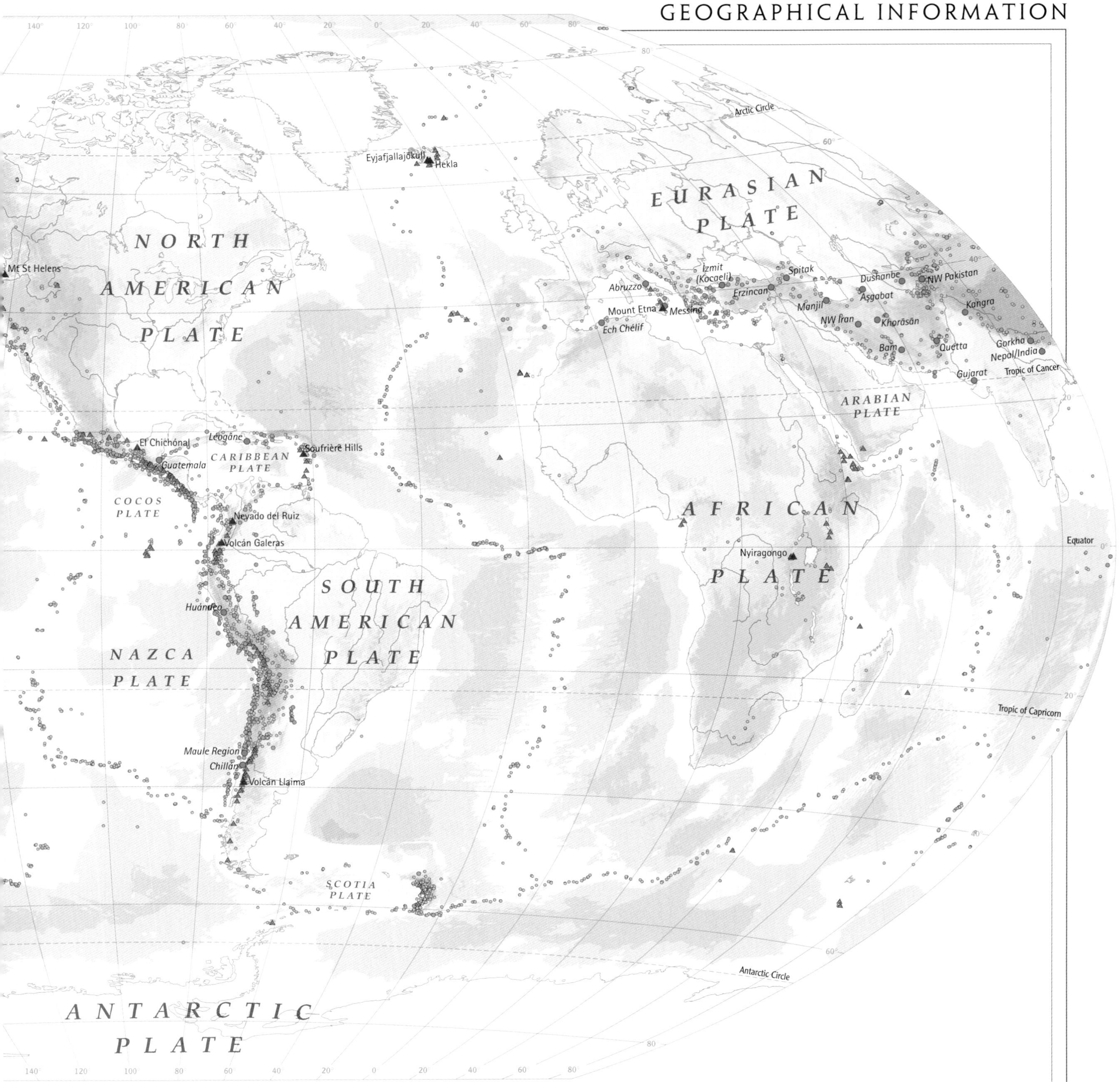

EURASIAN PLATE

NORTH AMERICAN PLATE

Arctic Circle

Eyjafjallajökull
Hekla

Mt St Helens

Izmit (Kocaeli)
Spitak
Abruzzo
Erzincan
Dushanbe
NW Pakistan
Mount Etna
Messina
Manjil
Asgabat
Kangra
Ech Chélif
NW Iran
Khorāsān
Quetta
Bam
Gorkha
Nepal/India
Gujarat
Tropic of Cancer

ARABIAN PLATE

El Chichónal
Léogâne
CARIBBEAN PLATE
Soufrière Hills
Guatemala
COCOS PLATE
Nevado del Ruiz
Volcán Galeras

AFRICAN PLATE

Nyiragongo

Equator

SOUTH AMERICAN PLATE

Huánuco

NAZCA PLATE

Tropic of Capricorn

Maule Region
Chillán
Volcán Llaima

SCOTIA PLATE

Antarctic Circle

ANTARCTIC PLATE

MAJOR VOLCANIC ERUPTIONS 1980–2014

Year	Volcano	Country
1980	Mt St Helens	USA
1982	El Chichónal	Mexico
1982	Gunung Galunggung	Indonesia
1983	Kilauea	Hawai'i, USA
1983	Ō-yama	Japan
1985	Nevado del Ruiz	Colombia
1991	Mt Pinatubo	Philippines
1991	Unzen-dake	Japan
1993	Mayon	Philippines
1993	Volcán Galeras	Colombia
1994	Volcán Llaima	Chile
1994	Rabaul	Papua New Guinea
1997	Soufrière Hills	Montserrat
2000	Hekla	Iceland
2001	Monte Etna	Italy
2002	Nyiragongo	Democratic Republic of the Congo
2010	Eyjafjallajökull	Iceland

Bárðarbunga is a subglacial stratovolcano under the Vatnajökull Glacier on Iceland. Local seismic activity had been gradually increasing from 2007, and this fissure opened in the Holuhraun lava field north east of the caldera in 2014.

CLIMATE I

MAJOR CLIMATIC REGIONS AND SUB-TYPES

Köppen classification system
Winkel Tripel Projection
scale 1:110 000 000

• Climate graph location   ○ Weather extreme location

Polar		Cooler humid		Warmer humid		Dry		Tropical humid	
EF	Ice cap	Dc Dd	Subarctic	Cb Cc	Temperate	BS	Steppe	Aw As	Savanna
ET	Tundra	Db	Continental cool summer	Ca	Humid subtropical	BW	Desert	Af Am	Rain forest
		Da	Continental warm summer	Cs	Mediterranean				

A Rainy climate with no winter: coolest month above 18°C (64.4°F).

B Dry climates; limits are defined by formulae based on rainfall effectiveness:
   BS Steppe or semi-arid climate.
   BW Desert or arid climate.

*C Rainy climates with mild winters: coolest month above 0°C (32°F), but below 18°C (64.4°F); warmest month above 10°C (50°F).

*D Rainy climates with severe winters: coldest month below 0°C (32°F); warmest month above 10°C (50°F).

E Polar climates with no warm season: warmest month below 10°C (50°F).
   ET Tundra climate: warmest month below 10°C (50°F) but above 0°C (32°F).
   EF Perpetual frost: all months below 0°C (32°F).

a Warmest month above 22°C (71.6°F).

b Warmest month below 22°C (71.6°F).

c Less than four months over 10°C (50°F).

d As 'c', but with severe cold: coldest month below -38°C (-36.4°F).

f Constantly moist rainfall throughout the year.

*h Warmer dry: all months above 0°C (32°F).

*k Cooler dry: at least one month below 0°C (32°F).

m Monsoon rain: short dry season, but is compensated by heavy rains during rest of the year.

n Frequent fog.

s Dry season in summer.

w Dry season in winter.

* Modification of Köppen definition

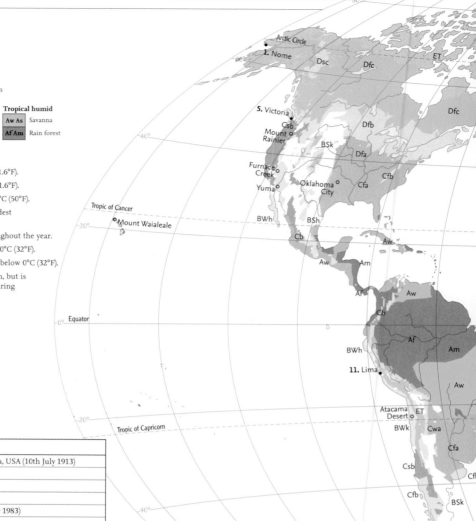

WORLD WEATHER EXTREMES

	Location
Highest shade temperature	56.7°C / 134°F Furnace Creek, Death Valley, California, USA (10th July 1913)
Hottest place – Annual mean	34.4°C / 93.9°F Dalol, Ethiopia
Driest place – Annual mean	0.1 mm / 0.004 inches Atacama Desert, Chile
Most sunshine – Annual mean	90% Yuma, Arizona, USA (over 4 000 hours)
Lowest screen temperature	-89.2°C / -128.6°F Vostok Station, Antarctica (21st July 1983)
Coldest place – Annual mean	-56.6°C / -69.9°F Plateau Station, Antarctica
Wettest place – Annual mean	11 873 mm / 467.4 inches Meghalaya, India
Most rainy days	Up to 350 per year Mount Waialeale, Hawai'i, USA
Windiest place	322 km per hour / 200 miles per hour in gales, Commonwealth Bay, Antarctica
Highest surface wind speed	512 km per hour / 318 miles per hour in a tornado, Oklahoma City, Oklahoma, USA (3rd May 1999)
Greatest snowfall	31 102 mm / 1 224.5 inches Mount Rainier, Washington, USA (19th February 1971 – 18th February 1972)
Highest barometric pressure	1 083.8 mb Agata, Siberia, Russia (31st December 1968)
Lowest barometric pressure	870 mb 483 km / 300 miles west of Guam, Pacific Ocean (12th October 1979)

Tropical Cyclone Pam, seen here in a close view crossing Vanuatu on 13 March 2015, was a Category 5 severe tropical cyclone which reached wind speeds of 155 mph (250 km). Shortly after this image was taken by the NASA Aqua satellite, the cyclone hit the island of Éfaté. For a wider view of cyclone activity at this time, see pages 20–21.

TRACKS OF TROPICAL STORMS

(wind speeds often over 160 km per hour)
scale 1:247 000 000

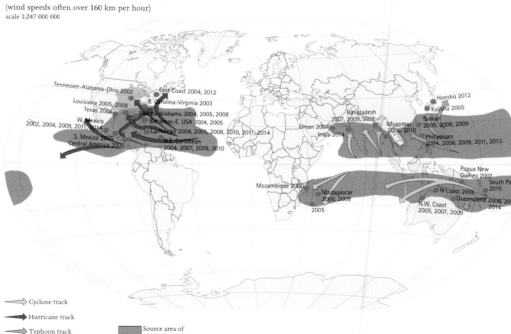

Cyclone track
Hurricane track
Typhoon track
● Major tropical storm (2000–2015)

Source area of tropical storms
Tornado high risk areas

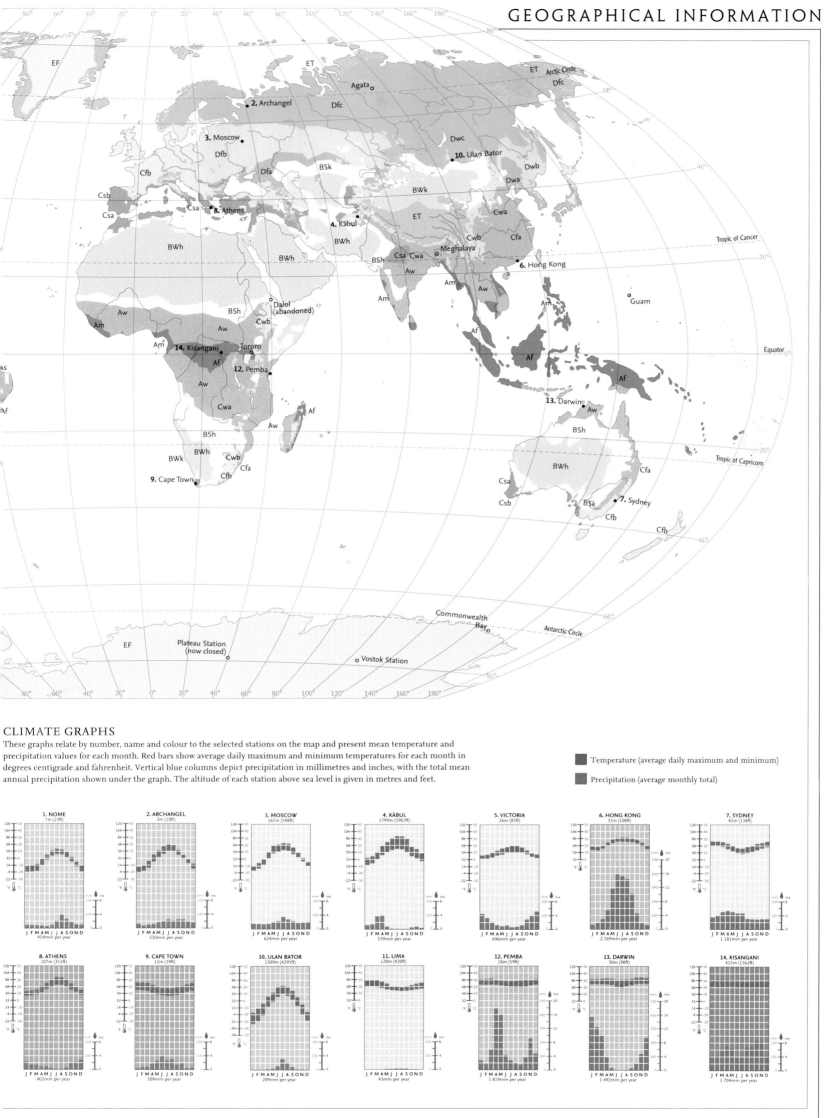

CLIMATE GRAPHS

These graphs relate by number, name and colour to the selected stations on the map and present mean temperature and precipitation values for each month. Red bars show average daily maximum and minimum temperatures for each month in degrees centigrade and fahrenheit. Vertical blue columns depict precipitation in millimetres and inches, with the total mean annual precipitation shown under the graph. The altitude of each station above sea level is given in metres and feet.

Temperature (average daily maximum and minimum)

Precipitation (average monthly total)

1. NOME
7m (23ft)
J F M A M J J A S O N D
454mm per year

2. ARCHANGEL
3m (10ft)
J F M A M J J A S O N D
530mm per year

3. MOSCOW
167m (548ft)
J F M A M J J A S O N D
624mm per year

4. KĀBUL
1799m (5902ft)
J F M A M J J A S O N D
339mm per year

5. VICTORIA
26m (85ft)
J F M A M J J A S O N D
696mm per year

6. HONG KONG
33m (108ft)
J F M A M J J A S O N D
2 169mm per year

7. SYDNEY
42m (138ft)
J F M A M J J A S O N D
1 181mm per year

8. ATHENS
107m (351ft)
J F M A M J J A S O N D
402mm per year

9. CAPE TOWN
12m (39ft)
J F M A M J J A S O N D
509mm per year

10. ULAN BATOR
1309m (4295ft)
J F M A M J J A S O N D
209mm per year

11. LIMA
128m (420ft)
J F M A M J J A S O N D
43mm per year

12. PEMBA
18m (59ft)
J F M A M J J A S O N D
1 819mm per year

13. DARWIN
30m (98ft)
J F M A M J J A S O N D
1 492mm per year

14. KISANGANI
415m (1362ft)
J F M A M J J A S O N D
1 704mm per year

© Collins Bartholomew Ltd

CLIMATE II

CLIMATE CHANGE

Climate records show that the global average temperature has risen by approximately 0.7°C since the end of the nineteenth century. Most of this warming is caused by human activities which result in a build-up of greenhouse gases, mainly carbon dioxide, allowing heat to be trapped within the atmosphere. Carbon dioxide emissions have increased since the beginning of the industrial revolution due to burning of fossil fuels, increased urbanization, population growth, deforestation and industrial pollution.

Annual climate indicators such as number of frost-free days, length of growing season, heat wave frequency, number of wet days, length of dry spells and frequency of weather extremes are used to monitor climate change. The map below shows how future changes in temperature will not be spread evenly around the world. Some regions will warm faster than the global average, while others will warm more slowly.

THREAT OF RISING SEA LEVEL

It has been suggested that further global warming of between 1.0 and 6.4 C° may occur by the end of the 21st century. Sea level is projected to rise by between 28 cm and 58 cm, threatening a number of coastal cities, low-lying deltas and small islands. Larger rises are predicted in some locations than others.

AREAS AT RISK OF SUBMERSION

○ Major cities

◻ Coastal areas at greatest risk

◼ Islands and archipelagos

▨ Areas of low-lying islands

The Pedersen Glacier in the Kenai Mountains, Alaska. The terminus has retreated by more than 2 km between 1917 (top) and 2005 (bottom).

LOWEST PACIFIC ISLANDS

Location	Maximum height above sea level	Land area sq km	Land area sq miles	Population
Kingman Reef	1 m (3 ft)	1	0.4	0
Palmyra Atoll	2 m (7 ft)	12	5	0
Ashmore and Cartier Islands	3 m (10 ft)	5	2	0
Howland Island	3 m (10 ft)	2	1	0
Johnston Atoll	5 m (16 ft)	3	1	0
Tokelau	5 m (16 ft)	10	4	1 466
Tuvalu	5 m (16 ft)	25	10	10 000
Coral Sea Islands Territory	6 m (20 ft)	22	8	0
Wake Island	6 m (20 ft)	7	3	0
Jarvis Island	7 m (23 ft)	5	2	0

PROJECTION OF GLOBAL TEMPERATURE CHANGE 2081–2100

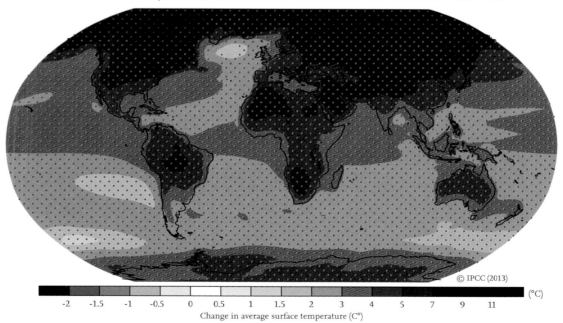

© IPCC (2013)

-2 -1.5 -1 -0.5 0 0.5 1 1.5 2 3 4 5 7 9 11 (°C)

Change in average surface temperature (C°)

Faster warming is expected near the poles, as the melting snow and sea ice exposes the darker underlying land and ocean surfaces which then absorb more of the sun's radiation instead of reflecting it back to space in the way that brighter ice and snow do.

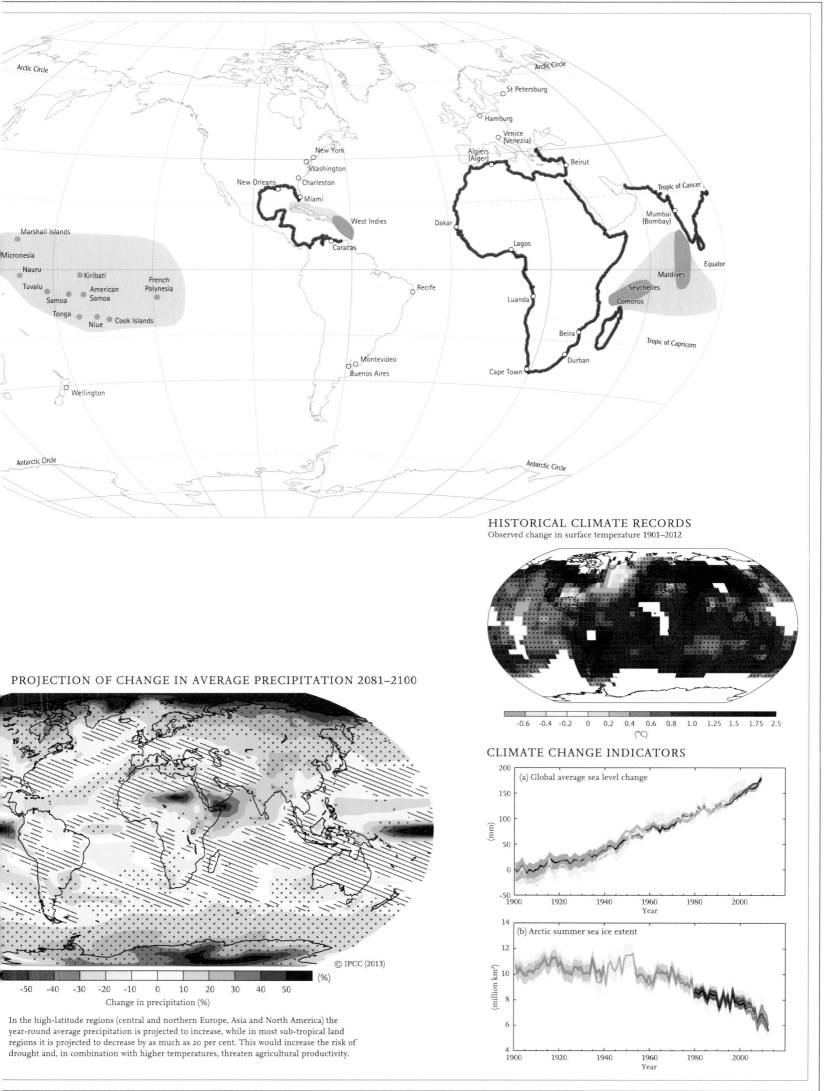

HISTORICAL CLIMATE RECORDS
Observed change in surface temperature 1901–2012

-0.6 -0.4 -0.2 0 0.2 0.4 0.6 0.8 1.0 1.25 1.5 1.75 2.5
(°C)

PROJECTION OF CHANGE IN AVERAGE PRECIPITATION 2081–2100

© IPCC (2013)

-50 -40 -30 -20 -10 0 10 20 30 40 50 (%)

Change in precipitation (%)

In the high-latitude regions (central and northern Europe, Asia and North America) the year-round average precipitation is projected to increase, while in most sub-tropical land regions it is projected to decrease by as much as 20 per cent. This would increase the risk of drought and, in combination with higher temperatures, threaten agricultural productivity.

CLIMATE CHANGE INDICATORS

(a) Global average sea level change

(mm)

1900 1920 1940 1960 1980 2000
Year

(b) Arctic summer sea ice extent

(million km²)

1900 1920 1940 1960 1980 2000
Year

POPULATION
TOP TWENTY COUNTRIES BY POPULATION AND POPULATION DENSITY 2013

Total population	Country	Rank	Country*	Inhabitants per sq mile	Inhabitants per sq km
1 369 993 000	China	1	Bangladesh	2 817	1 087
1 252 140 000	India	2	Taiwan	1 671	645
320 051 000	United States of America	3	South Korea	1 285	496
249 866 000	Indonesia	4	Rwanda	1 158	447
200 362 000	Brazil	5	Netherlands	1 045	404
182 143 000	Pakistan	6	India	1 024	395
173 615 000	Nigeria	7	Haiti	963	372
156 595 000	Bangladesh	8	Burundi	946	365
142 834 000	Russia	9	Belgium	942	364
127 144 000	Japan	10	Japan	872	337
122 332 000	Mexico	11	Philippines	849	328
98 394 000	Philippines	12	Sri Lanka	840	324
94 101 000	Ethiopia	13	Vietnam	720	278
91 680 000	Vietnam	14	United Kingdom	671	259
82 727 000	Germany	15	Germany	600	232
82 056 000	Egypt	16	Dominican Republic	556	215
77 447 000	Iran	17	Pakistan	535	207
74 933 000	Turkey	18	North Korea	535	207
67 514 000	Democratic Republic of the Congo	19	Italy	524	202
67 011 000	Thailand	20	Nepal	489	189

*Only countries with a population of over 10 million are considered.

AGE PYRAMIDS
World population by five-year age group and sex.

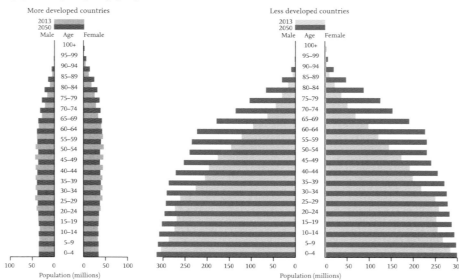

KEY POPULATION STATISTICS FOR MAJOR REGIONS

	Population 2013 (millions)	Growth (per cent)	Infant mortality rate	Total fertility rate	Life expectancy (years)	% aged 60 and over 2010	% aged 60 and over 2050
World	7 162	1.1	37	2.5	70	11	22
More developed regions[1]	1 253	0.3	6	1.7	78	22	32
Less developed regions[2]	5 909	1.3	40	2.6	67	9	19
Africa	1 111	2.5	64	4.7	58	5	9
Asia	4 299	1.0	31	2.2	71	10	24
Europe[3]	742	0.1	6	1.6	76	22	34
Latin America and the Caribbean[4]	617	1.1	18	2.2	75	10	25
North America	355	0.9	6	1.9	79	19	27
Oceania	38	1.4	20	2.4	78	15	23

Except for population and % aged 60 and over figures, the data are annual averages projected for the period 2010–2015.

1. Europe, North America, Australia, New Zealand and Japan.
2. Africa, Asia (excluding Japan), Latin America and the Caribbean, and Oceania (excluding Australia and New Zealand).
3. Includes Russia.
4. South America, Central America (including Mexico) and all Caribbean Islands.

WORLD POPULATION DISTRIBUTION
Winkel Tripel Projection
scale approximately 1:112 000 000

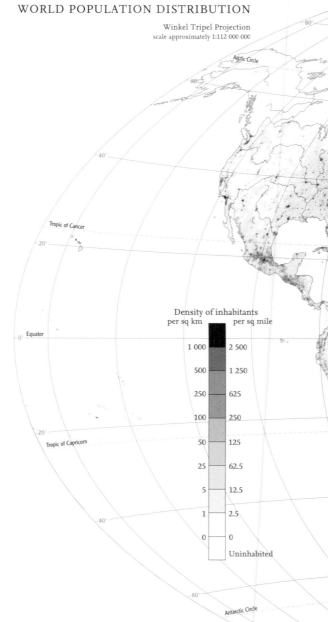

Density of inhabitants
per sq km / per sq mile

per sq km	per sq mile
1 000	2 500
500	1 250
250	625
100	250
50	125
25	62.5
5	12.5
1	2.5
0	0
Uninhabited	

Population growth in the 20th century was rapid and continued growth carried the world's population past seven billion in 2011.

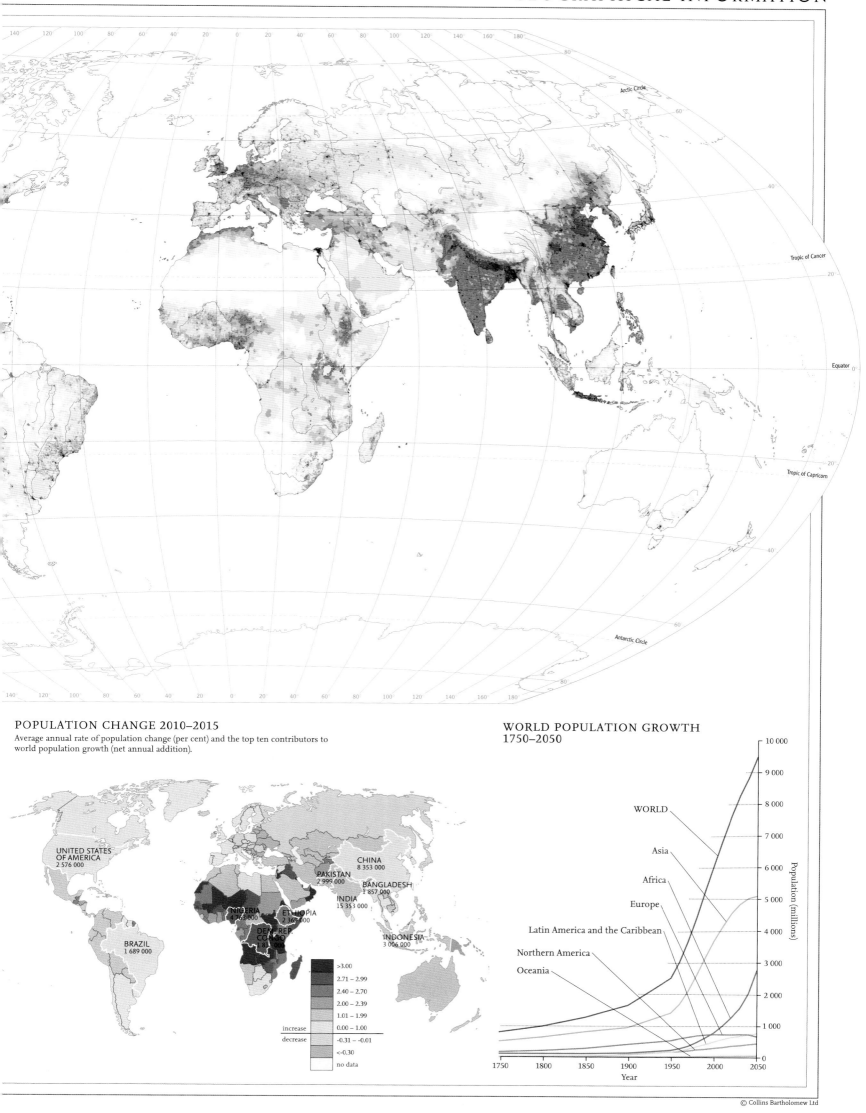

POPULATION CHANGE 2010–2015

Average annual rate of population change (per cent) and the top ten contributors to world population growth (net annual addition).

UNITED STATES OF AMERICA
2 576 000

CHINA
8 353 000

PAKISTAN
2 999 000

BANGLADESH
1 857 000

INDIA
15 353 000

NIGERIA
4 563 000

ETHIOPIA
2 365 000

DEM. REP. CONGO
1 8   000

BRAZIL
1 689 000

INDONESIA
3 006 000

	>3.00
	2.71 – 2.99
	2.40 – 2.70
	2.00 – 2.39
	1.01 – 1.99
increase	0.00 – 1.00
decrease	-0.31 – -0.01
	<-0.30
	no data

WORLD POPULATION GROWTH 1750–2050

WORLD

Asia

Africa

Europe

Latin America and the Caribbean

Northern America

Oceania

Population (millions)

10 000
9 000
8 000
7 000
6 000
5 000
4 000
3 000
2 000
1 000
0

1750   1800   1850   1900   1950   2000   2050

Year

COMMUNICATIONS

WORLD COMMUNICATIONS EQUIPMENT 1996–2014

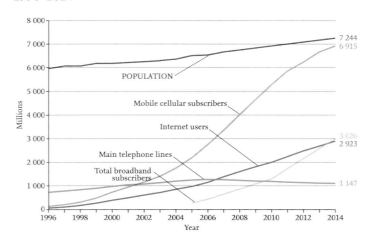

TOP BROADBAND ECONOMIES 2013

Countries with the highest broadband penetration rate – subscribers per 100 inhabitants

Top Economies	Fixed Broadband rate		Top Economies	Mobile Broadband rate
Monaco	44.7	1	Singapore	135.1
Switzerland	43.0	2	Finland	123.5
Denmark	40.2	3	Japan	120.5
Netherlands	40.1	4	Australia	110.5
France	38.8	5	Bahrain	109.7
South Korea	38.0	6	Sweden	108.7
Norway	36.4	7	Denmark	107.3
United Kingdom	35.7	8	South Korea	105.3
Iceland	35.1	9	Hong Kong, China	95.4
Germany	34.6	10	United States	92.8

INTERNATIONAL TELECOMMUNICATIONS INDICATORS BY REGION 2014

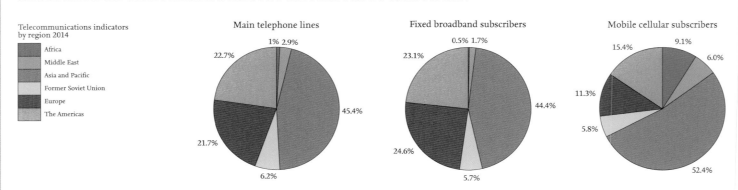

FIXED TELEPHONE SUBSCRIBERS 2013

Winkel Tripel Projection

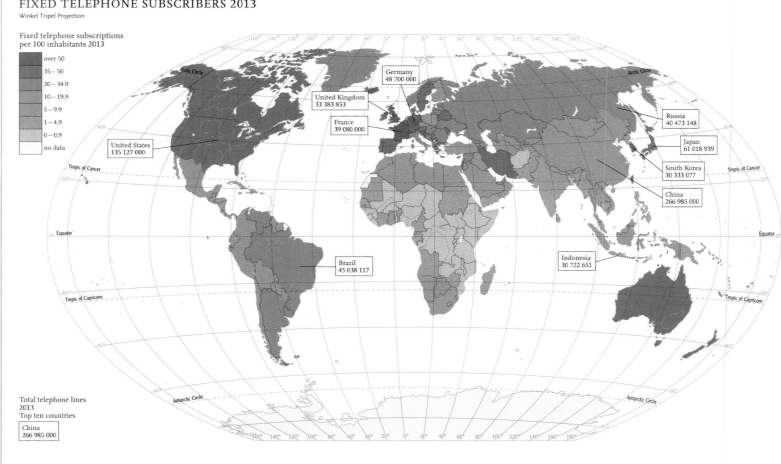

FIXED BROADBAND SUBSCRIBERS 2013
Winkel Tripel Projection

Fixed broadband subscribers
per 100 inhabitants 2013

- over 30
- 20–30
- 10–19.9
- 2–9.9
- 0–1.9
- no data

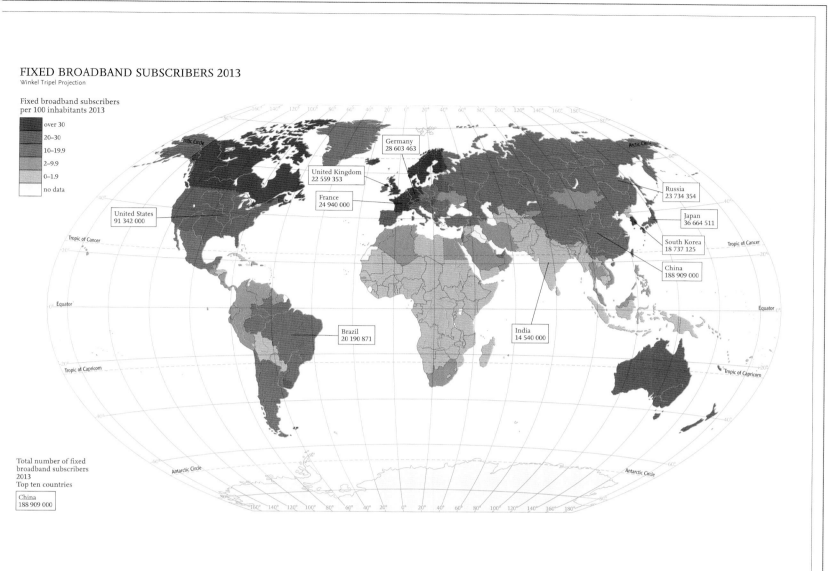

Germany
28 603 463

United Kingdom
22 559 353

France
24 940 000

Russia
23 734 354

Japan
36 664 511

South Korea
18 737 125

China
188 909 000

United States
91 342 000

Brazil
20 190 871

India
14 540 000

Total number of fixed
broadband subscribers
2013
Top ten countries

China
188 909 000

MOBILE CELLULAR SUBSCRIBERS 2013
Winkel Tripel Projection

Cellular mobile subscribers
per 100 inhabitants 2013

- over 150
- 120–150
- 90–119.9
- 60–89.9
- 30–59.9
- 0–29.9
- no data

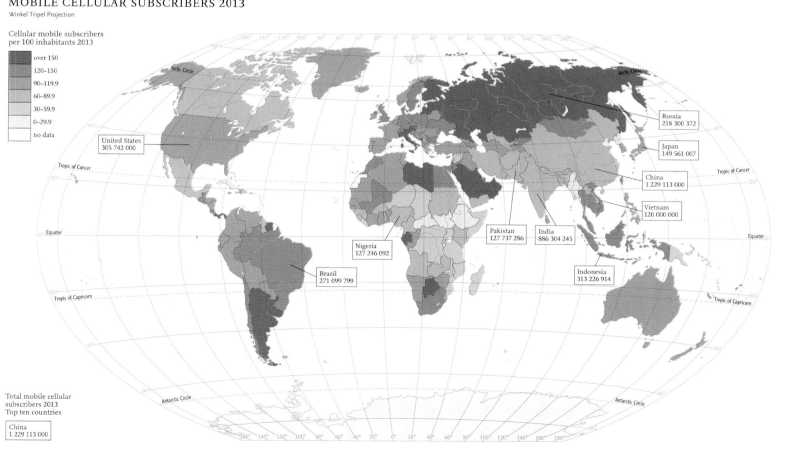

Russia
218 300 372

Japan
149 561 007

China
1 229 113 000

Vietnam
120 000 000

United States
305 742 000

Pakistan
127 737 286

India
886 304 245

Nigeria
127 246 092

Indonesia
313 226 914

Brazil
271 099 799

Total mobile cellular
subscribers 2013
Top ten countries

China
1 229 113 000

PHYSICAL FEATURES

The images below illustrate some of the major physical features of the world.

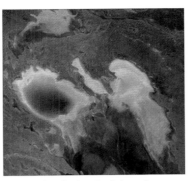

Kati Thanda-Lake Eyre, South Australia

Mississippi-Missouri, United States of America

The Caspian Sea

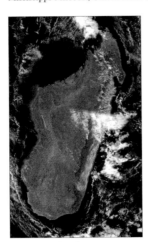

The island of Madagasgar

OCEANIA Total Land Area 8 844 516 sq km / 3 414 868 sq miles

HIGHEST MOUNTAINS	metres	feet
Puncak Jaya, Indonesia	4 884	16 023
Puncak Trikora, Indonesia	4 730	15 518
Puncak Mandala, Indonesia	4 700	15 420
Puncak Yamin, Indonesia	4 595	15 075
Mt Wilhelm, Papua New Guinea	4 509	14 793
Mt Kubor, Papua New Guinea	4 359	14 301

LONGEST RIVERS	km	miles
Murray-Darling	3 672	2 282
Darling	2 844	1 767
Murray	2 375	1 476
Murrumbidgee	1 485	923
Lachlan	1 339	832
Cooper Creek	1 113	692

LARGEST ISLANDS	sq km	sq miles
New Guinea	808 510	312 166
South Island (Te Waipounamu), New Zealand	151 215	58 384
North Island (Te Ika-a Māui), New Zealand	15 777	44 701
Tasmania	67 800	26 178

LARGEST LAKES	sq km	sq miles
Kati Thanda-Lake Eyre	0–8 900	0–3 436
Lake Torrens	0–5 780	0–2 232

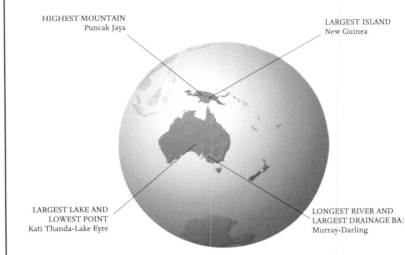

HIGHEST MOUNTAIN
Puncak Jaya

LARGEST ISLAND
New Guinea

LARGEST LAKE AND LOWEST POINT
Kati Thanda-Lake Eyre

LONGEST RIVER AND LARGEST DRAINAGE BA...
Murray-Darling

ANTARCTICA Total Land Area 12 093 000 sq km / 4 669 107 sq miles (excluding ice shelves)

HIGHEST MOUNTAINS	metres	feet
Mt Vinson	4 897	16 066
Mt Tyree	4 852	15 918
Mt Kirkpatrick	4 528	14 855
Mt Markham	4 351	14 275
Mt Sidley	4 285	14 058
Mt Minto	4 165	13 665

LARGEST KNOWN SUBGLACIAL LAKES	metres	feet
Lake Vostok	15 690	6 058
90°East Lake	2 000	772
Sovetskaya Lake	1 600	618

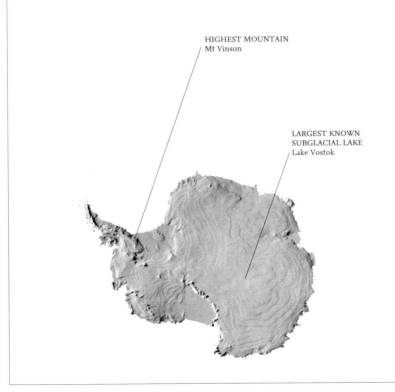

HIGHEST MOUNTAIN
Mt Vinson

LARGEST KNOWN SUBGLACIAL LAKE
Lake Vostok

ASIA Total Land Area 45 036 492 sq km / 17 388 590 sq miles

HIGHEST MOUNTAINS	metres	feet
Mt Everest (Sagarmatha/ Qomolangma Feng), China/Nepal	8 848	29 028
K2 (Chogori Feng), China/Pakistan	8 611	28 251
Kangchenjunga, India/Nepal	8 586	28 169
Lhotse, China/Nepal	8 516	27 939
Makalu, China/Nepal	8 463	27 765
Cho Oyu, China/Nepal	8 201	26 906

LONGEST RIVERS	km	miles
Yangtze (Chang Jiang)	6 380	3 965
Ob'-Irtysh	5 568	3 460
Yenisey-Angara-Selenga	5 550	3 449
Yellow (Huang He)	5 464	3 395
Irtysh (Yertis)	4 440	2 759
Mekong	4 425	2 750

LARGEST ISLANDS	sq km	sq miles
Borneo	745 561	287 861
Sumatra (Sumatera)	473 606	182 859
Honshū	227 414	87 805
Celebes (Sulawesi)	189 216	73 056
Java (Jawa)	132 188	51 038
Luzon	104 690	40 421

LARGEST LAKES	sq km	sq miles
Caspian Sea	371 000	143 243
Lake Baikal (Ozero Baykal)	30 500	11 776
Lake Balkhash (Ozero Balkash)	17 400	6 718
Aral Sea (Aral'skoye More)	17 158	6 625
Ysyk-Köl	6 200	2 394

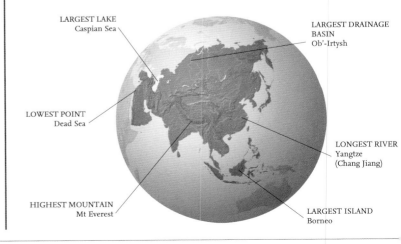

LARGEST LAKE
Caspian Sea

LARGEST DRAINAGE BASIN
Ob'-Irtysh

LOWEST POINT
Dead Sea

LONGEST RIVER
Yangtze (Chang Jiang)

HIGHEST MOUNTAIN
Mt Everest

LARGEST ISLAND
Borneo

EUROPE Total Land Area 9 908 599 sq km / 3 825 710 sq miles

HIGHEST MOUNTAINS	metres	feet
El'brus, Russia	5 642	18 510
Gora Dykh-Tau, Russia	5 204	17 073
Shkhara, Georgia/Russia	5 201	17 063
Kazbek, Georgia/Russia	5 047	16 558
Mont Blanc, France/Italy	4 810	15 781
Dufourspitze, Italy/Switzerland	4 634	15 203

LONGEST RIVERS	km	miles
Volga	3 688	2 292
Danube	2 850	1 771
Dnieper	2 285	1 420
Kama	2 028	1 260
Don	1 931	1 200
Pechora	1 802	1 120

LARGEST ISLANDS	sq km	sq miles
Great Britain	218 476	84 354
Iceland	102 820	39 699
Ireland	83 045	32 064
Ostrov Severnyy	47 079	18 177
Spitsbergen	37 814	14 600
Ostrov Yuzhnyy	33 246	12 836
Sicily (Sicilia)	25 426	9 817

LARGEST LAKES	sq km	sq miles
Caspian Sea	371 000	143 243
Lake Ladoga (Ladozhskoye Ozero)	18 390	7 100
Lake Onega (Onezhskoye Ozero)	9 600	3 707
Vänern	5 585	2 156
Rybinskoye Vodokhranilishche	5 180	2 000

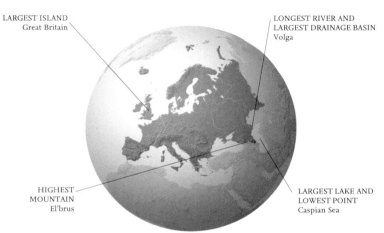

LARGEST ISLAND
Great Britain

LONGEST RIVER AND
LARGEST DRAINAGE BASIN
Volga

HIGHEST MOUNTAIN
El'brus

LARGEST LAKE AND
LOWEST POINT
Caspian Sea

NORTH AMERICA Total Land Area 24 680 331 sq km / 9 529 076 sq miles

HIGHEST MOUNTAINS	metres	feet
Mt McKinley, USA	6 194	20 321
Mt Logan, Canada	5 959	19 550
Pico de Orizaba, Mexico	5 610	18 405
Mt St Elias, USA	5 489	18 008
Volcán Popocatépetl, Mexico	5 452	17 887
Mt Foraker, USA	5 303	17 398

LONGEST RIVERS	km	miles
Mississippi-Missouri	5 969	3 709
Mackenzie-Peace-Finlay	4 241	2 635
Missouri	4 086	2 539
Mississippi	3 765	2 340
Yukon	3 185	1 979
St Lawrence	3 058	1 900

LARGEST ISLANDS	sq km	sq miles
Greenland	2 175 600	839 999
Baffin Island	507 451	195 927
Victoria Island	217 291	83 896
Ellesmere Island	196 236	75 767
Cuba	110 860	42 803
Newfoundland	108 860	42 031
Hispaniola	76 192	29 418

LARGEST LAKES	sq km	sq miles
Lake Superior	82 100	31 699
Lake Huron	59 600	23 012
Lake Michigan	57 800	22 317
Great Bear Lake	31 328	12 096
Great Slave Lake	28 568	11 030
Lake Erie	25 700	9 923
Lake Winnipeg	24 387	9 416
Lake Ontario	18 960	7 320

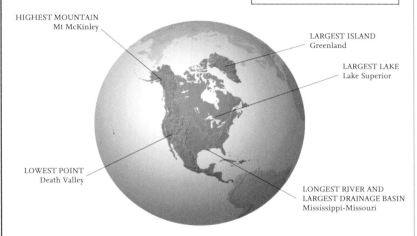

HIGHEST MOUNTAIN
Mt McKinley

LARGEST ISLAND
Greenland

LARGEST LAKE
Lake Superior

LOWEST POINT
Death Valley

LONGEST RIVER AND
LARGEST DRAINAGE BASIN
Mississippi-Missouri

AFRICA Total Land Area 30 343 578 sq km / 11 715 655 sq miles

HIGHEST MOUNTAINS	metres	feet
Kilimanjaro, Tanzania	5 892	19 330
Mt Kenya (Kirinyaga), Kenya	5 199	17 057
Margherita Peak, Democratic Republic of the Congo/Uganda	5 110	16 765
Meru, Tanzania	4 565	14 977
Ras Dejen, Ethiopia	4 533	14 872
Mt Karisimbi, Rwanda	4 510	14 796

LONGEST RIVERS	km	miles
Nile	6 695	4 160
Congo	4 667	2 900
Niger	4 184	2 600
Zambezi	2 736	1 700
Wabē Shebelē Wenz	2 490	1 547
Ubangi	2 250	1 398

LARGEST LAKES	sq km	sq miles
Lake Victoria	68 870	26 591
Lake Tanganyika	32 600	12 587
Lake Nyasa (Lake Malawi)	29 500	11 390
Lake Volta	8 482	3 275
Lake Turkana	6 500	2 510
Lake Albert	5 600	2 162

LARGEST ISLANDS	sq km	sq miles
Madagascar	587 040	226 656

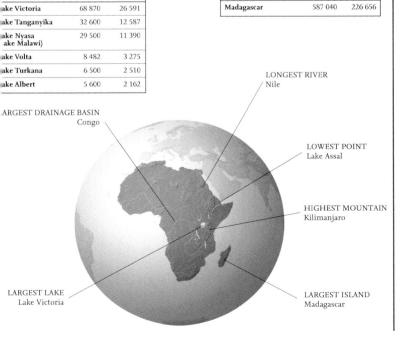

LARGEST DRAINAGE BASIN
Congo

LONGEST RIVER
Nile

LOWEST POINT
Lake Assal

HIGHEST MOUNTAIN
Kilimanjaro

LARGEST LAKE
Lake Victoria

LARGEST ISLAND
Madagascar

SOUTH AMERICA Total Land Area 17 815 420 sq km / 6 878 534 sq miles

HIGHEST MOUNTAINS	metres	feet
Cerro Aconcagua, Argentina	6 959	22 831
Nevado Ojos del Salado, Argentina/Chile	6 908	22 664
Cerro Bonete, Argentina	6 872	22 546
Cerro Pissis, Argentina	6 858	22 500
Cerro Tupungato, Argentina/Chile	6 800	22 309
Cerro Mercedario, Argentina	6 770	22 211

LONGEST RIVERS	km	miles
Amazon (Amazonas)	6 516	4 049
Río de la Plata-Paraná	4 500	2 796
Purus	3 218	2 000
Madeira	3 200	1 988
São Francisco	2 900	1 802
Tocantins	2 750	1 709

LARGEST ISLANDS	sq km	sq miles
Isla Grande de Tierra del Fuego	47 000	18 147
Isla de Chiloé	8 394	3 241
East Falkland	6 760	2 610
West Falkland	5 413	2 090

LARGEST LAKES	sq km	sq miles
Lake Titicaca	8 340	3 220

LONGEST RIVER AND
LARGEST DRAINAGE BASIN
Amazon (Amazonas)

LARGEST LAKE
Lake Titicaca

LOWEST POINT
Laguna del Carbón

HIGHEST MOUNTAIN
Cerro Aconcagua

LARGEST ISLAND
Isla Grande de Tierra del Fuego

WORLD CITIES

KEY TO CITY PLANS

Built-up area	Cemetery	Marsh
Park/Open space	Water	River/Canal

Road	Administrative boundary
Railway	Airport

General place of interest	Academic/Municipal building
Place of worship	Transport location

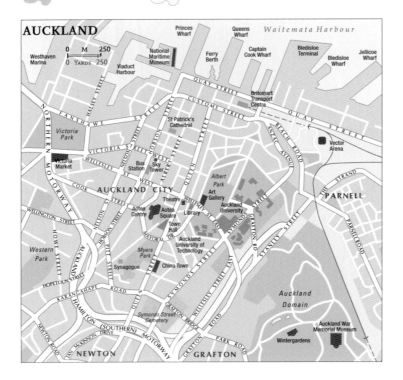

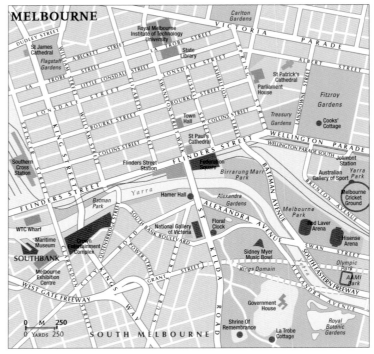

SINGAPORE

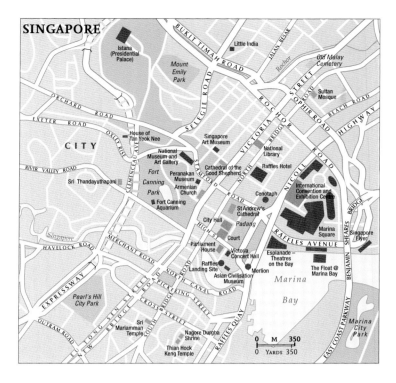

BANGKOK

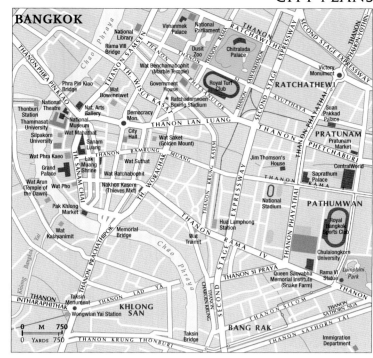

HONG KONG

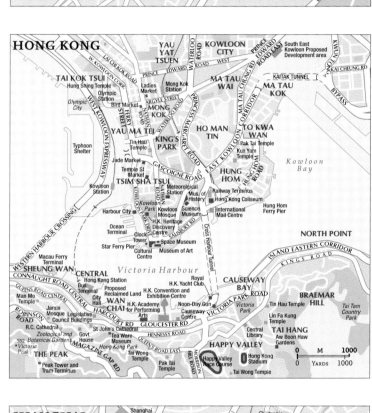

BEIJING

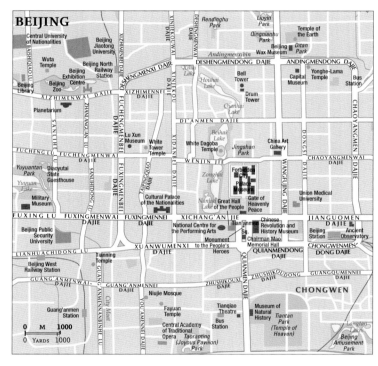

SHANGHAI

SEOUL

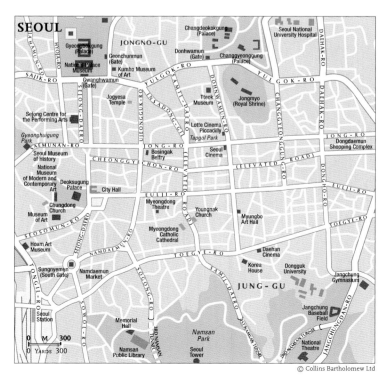

© Collins Bartholomew Ltd

TŌKYŌ

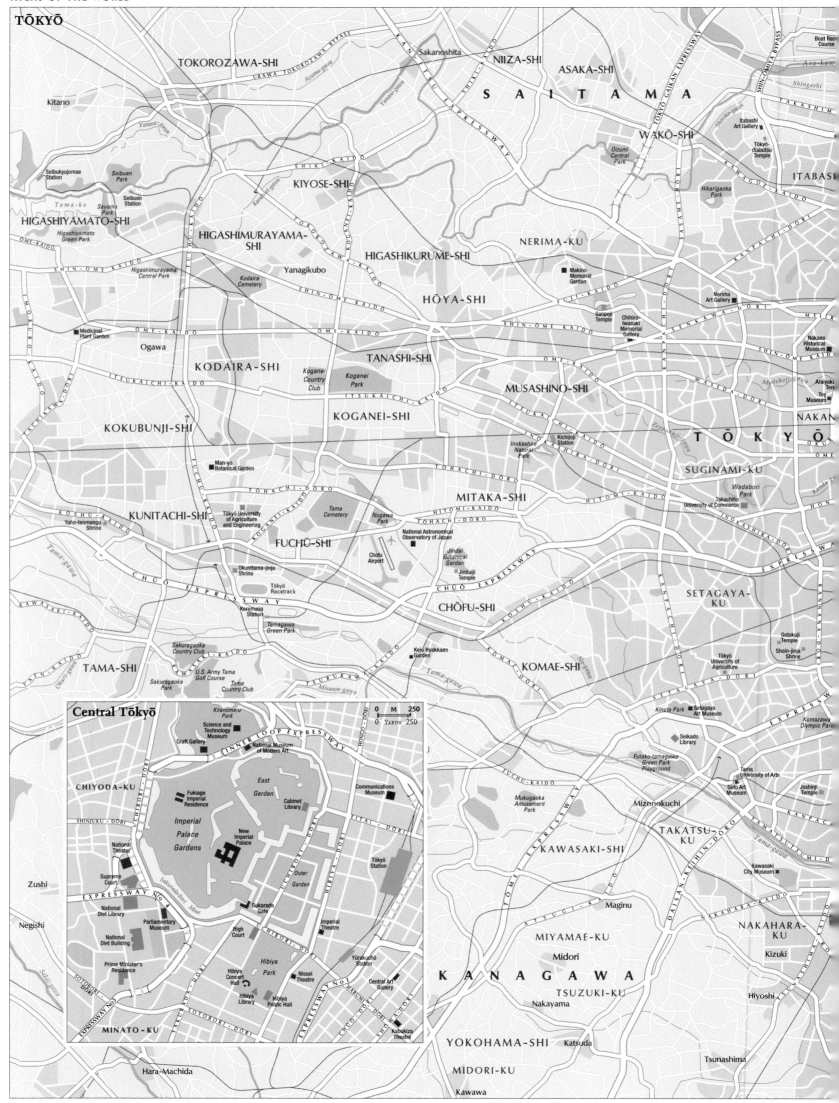

TOKOROZAWA-SHI

Sakanoshita

NIIZA-SHI

ASAKA-SHI

S A I T A M A

WAKŌ-SHI

Kitano

Boat Race Course

Ara-kaw

Shingashi

Itabashi Art Gallery

Tōkyō-daibutsu Temple

ITABASHI

Seibukyujomae Station

Seibuen Park

Oizumi Central Park

Hikarigaoka Park

HIGASHIYAMATO-SHI

Tama-ko

Sayama Park

Seibuen Station

KIYOSE-SHI

NERIMA-KU

Higashiyamato Green Park

Higashiyamayama Central Park

HIGASHIMURAYAMA-SHI

Yanagikubo

HIGASHIKURUME-SHI

Makino Memorial Garden

Nerima Art Gallery

Kodaira Cemetery

HŌYA-SHI

Sanpoji Temple

Chihiro-Iwasaki Memorial Gallery

Nakano Historical Museum

Medicinal Plant Garden

Ogawa

Araiyaku Ten

Toy Museum

KODAIRA-SHI

TANASHI-SHI

MUSASHINO-SHI

NAKAN

Koganei Country Club

Koganei Park

Inokashira Park

Kichijoji Station

TŌKYŌ

KOKUBUNJI-SHI

KOGANEI-SHI

SUGINAMI-KU

Man-yo Botanical Garden

Wadabori Park

Takachiho University of Commerce

KUNITACHI-SHI

Tama Cemetery

Nogawa Park

MITAKA-SHI

Yaho-tenmangu Shrine

Tōkyō University of Agriculture and Engineering

National Astronomical Observatory of Japan

Jindai Botanical Garden

Okunitama-jinja Shrine

Chofu Airport

Jindaiji Temple

FUCHŪ-SHI

SETAGAYA-KU

Tōkyō Racetrack

CHŪŌ EXPRESSWAY

Kosemasa Station

Tamagawa Green Park

CHŌFU-SHI

Gotokuji Temple

Shoin-jinja Shrine

Sakuragaoka Country Club

Keio Hyakkaen Garden

Tōkyō University of Agriculture

TAMA-SHI

U.S. Army Tama Golf Course

Tama-gawa

KOMAE-SHI

Sakuragaoka Park

Tama Country Club

Misawa-gawa

Kinuta Park

Setagaya Art Museum

Komazawa Olympic Par

Seikado Library

Futako-tamagawa Green Park Playground

Tama University of Arts

Mukogaoka Amusement Park

Goto Art Museum

Joshinji Temple

Mizonokuchi

KAWASAKI-SHI

TAKATSU-KU

Kawasaki City Museum

Maginu

K A N A G A W A

NAKAHARA-KU

MIYAMAE-KU

Midori

Kizuki

TSUZUKI-KU

Nakayama

YOKOHAMA-SHI

Katsuda

Hiyoshi

Hara-Machida

MIDORI-KU

Kawawa

Tsunashima

Central Tōkyō

Kitanomaru Park

Science and Technology Museum

Craft Gallery

National Museum of Modern Art

0 M 250

0 YARDS 250

CHIYODA-KU

INNER LOOP EXPRESSWAY

Fukiage Imperial Residence

East Garden

Communications Museum

Cabinet Library

Imperial Palace Gardens

New Imperial Palace

SHINJUKU-DORI

National Theatre

Tōkyō Station

Supreme Court

Outer Garden

Sukurada Gate

EXPRESSWAY NO 4

National Diet Library

Imperial Theatre

Parliamentary Museum

High Court

National Diet Building

Hibiya Park

Yūrakuchō Station

Prime Minister's Residence

Nissei Theatre

Central Art Gallery

Hibiya Concert Hall

MINATO-KU

Hibiya Library

Hibiya Public Hall

Kabukiza Theatre

Zushi

Negishi

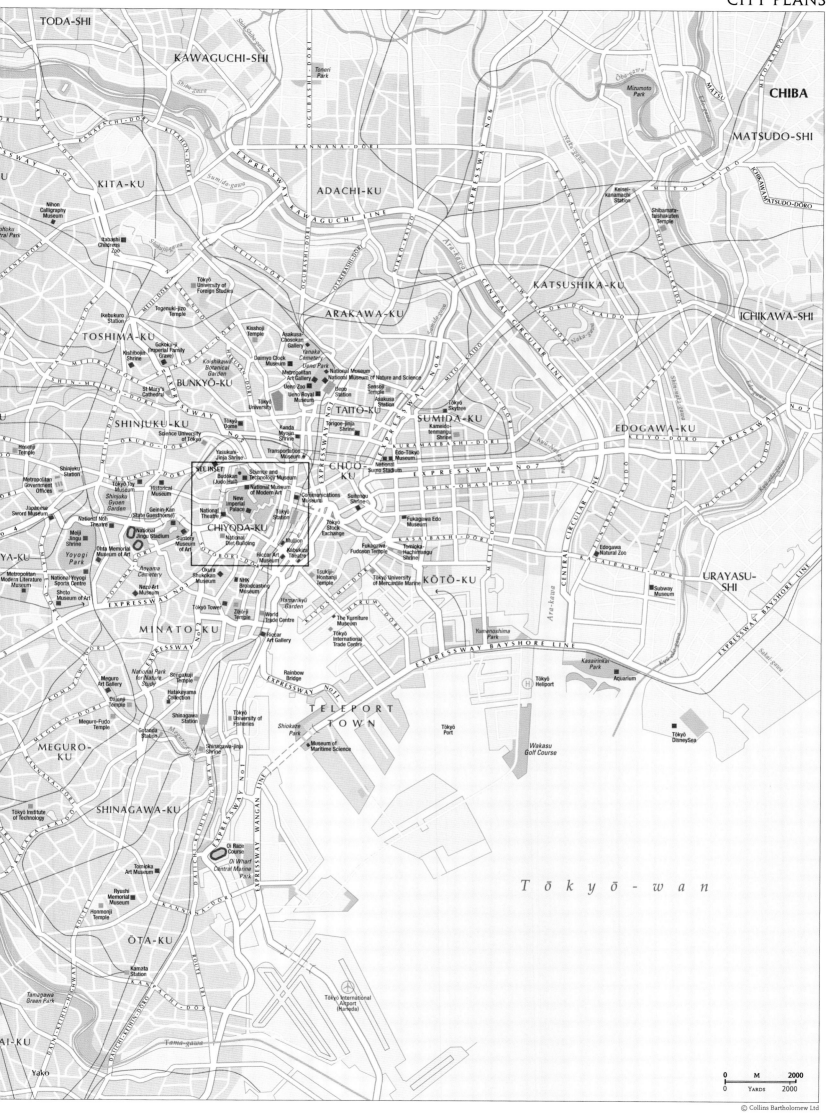

TODA-SHI

KAWAGUCHI-SHI

Toneri Park

CHIBA

MATSUDO-SHI

KITA-KU

ADACHI-KU

Mizumoto Park

Nihon Calligraphy Museum

Itabashi Childrens Zoo

KATSUSHIKA-KU

Keisei-kanamachi Station

Shibamata-taishakuten Temple

Tōkyō University of Foreign Studies

ARAKAWA-KU

ICHIKAWA-SHI

TOSHIMA-KU

Ikebukuro Station

Togenuki-jizo Temple

Kisshoji Temple

Asakusa-Chosokan Gallery

Yanaka Cemetery

Daimyo Clock Museum

Kishibojin Shrine

Gokoku-ji (Imperial Family Grave)

Koishikawa Botanical Garden

Ueno Park

National Museum

EDOGAWA-KU

BUNKYŌ-KU

St Mary's Cathedral

Metropolitan Art Gallery

National Museum of Nature and Science

Ueno Zoo

Tōkyō University

Ueno Royal Museum

Uepo Station

Sensōji Temple

Asakusa Station

Tōkyō Skytree

SHINJUKU-KU

Hosenji Temple

Tōkyō Dome

Kanda Myojin Shrine

Torigoe-jinja Shrine

SUMIDA-KU

Kameido-tenmangu Shrine

Science University of Tōkyō

TAITŌ-KU

Shinjuku Station

Yasukuni-Jinja Shrine

Transportation Museum

Edo-Tōkyō Museum

Metropolitan Government Offices

SEE INSET

Budōkan (Judo Hall)

Science and Technology Museum

National Museum of Modern Art

CHŪŌ-KU

National Sumo Stadium

Tōkyō Toy Museum

Historical Museum

New Imperial Palace

Suitengu Shrine

Fukagawa Edo Museum

Japanese Sword Museum

Geinin-Kan (State Guesthouse)

National Theatre

Tōkyō Station

Communications Museum

National Noh Theatre

Meiji Jingu Shrine

National Jingu Stadium

Suntory Museum of Art

National Diet Building

Tōkyō Stock Exchange

Mullion

Kabukiza Theatre

Fukagawa-Fudoson Temple

Tomioka-Hachimangu Shrine

KASAIBASHI-DORI

Edogawa Natural Zoo

URAYASU-SHI

Ohta Memorial Museum of Art

Yoyogi Park

Metropolitan Modern Literature Museum

National Yoyogi Sports Centre

Aoyama Cemetery

Nezu Art Museum

Ōkura Shukokan Museum

Riccar Art Museum

NHK Broadcasting Museum

Tsukiji-Honhanji Temple

Tōkyō University of Mercantile Marine

KŌTŌ-KU

Subway Museum

Shoto Museum of Art

Tōkyō Tower

Zōjō-ji Temple

Hamarikyū Garden

The Furniture Museum

World Trade Centre

MINATO-KU

Riccar Art Gallery

Tōkyō International Trade Centre

Yumenoshima Park

Meguro Art Gallery

National Park for Nature Study

Sengakuji Temple

Rainbow Bridge

Kasairinkai Park

Tōkyō Heliport

Daienji Temple

Hatakeyama Collection

EXPRESSWAY NO.11

Aquarium

Meguro-Fudo Temple

Shinagawa Station

Tōkyō University of Fisheries

TELEPORT TOWN

Tōkyō Port

Wakasu Golf Course

MEGURO-KU

Gotanda Station

Shinagawa-jinja Shrine

Shiokaze Park

Tōkyō DisneySea

SHINAGAWA-KU

Tōkyō Institute of Technology

Museum of Maritime Science

Tomioka Art Museum

Oi Race Course

Oi Wharf Central Marine Park

T ō k y ō - w a n

Ryushi Memorial Museum

Honmonji Temple

ŌTA-KU

Kamata Station

Tamagawa Green Park

Tōkyō International Airport (Haneda)

Yako

Tama-gawa

© Collins Bartholomew Ltd

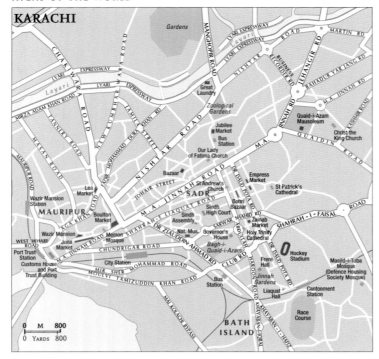

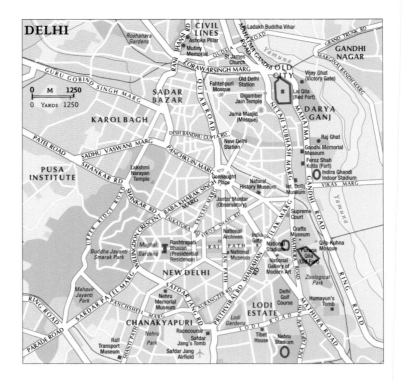

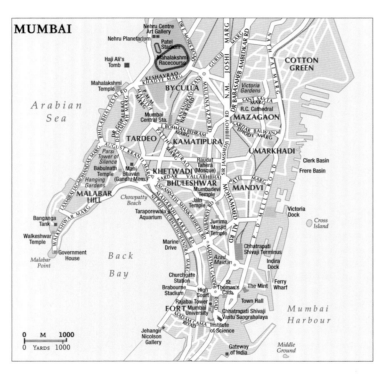

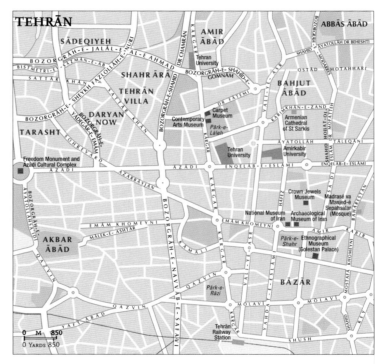

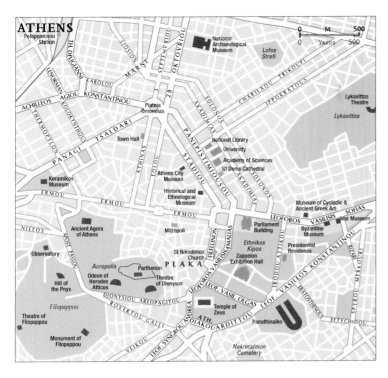

ATHENS

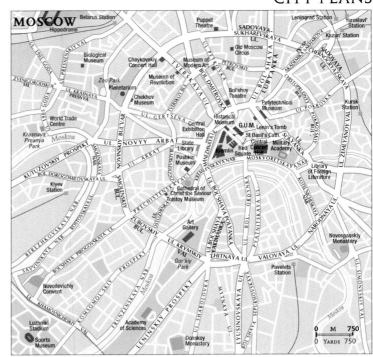

MOSCOW

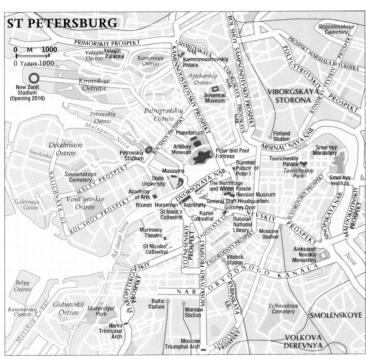

ST PETERSBURG

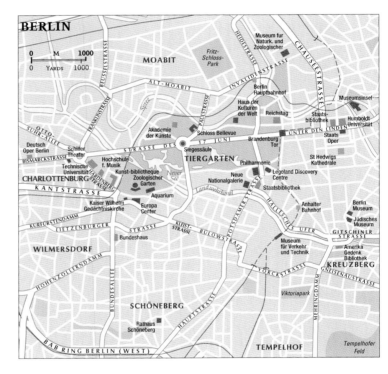

BERLIN

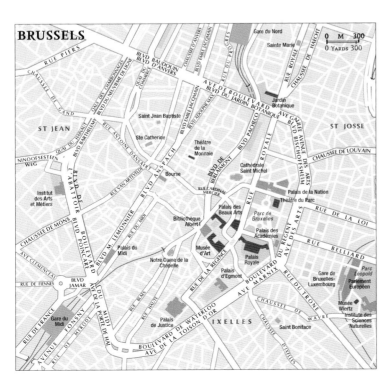

BRUSSELS

AMSTERDAM

© Collins Bartholomew Ltd

LONDON

Central London

The Wigmore Hall
OXFORD STREET
Palladium
REGENT STREET
New Bond Street
Soho
Dominion Theatre
British Museum
HIGH HOLBORN
HOLBORN
Holborn
Lincoln's Inn Fields
KINGSWAY
Lincoln's Inn
Royal Courts of Justice
Theatre Royal
STRAND
ALDWYCH
Royal Opera House
CHARING CROSS ROAD
SHAFTESBURY AVE
King's College
London Transport Museum
Royal Academy of Arts
PICCADILLY CIRCUS
HAYMARKET
National Gallery
STRAND
Somerset House
Mayfair
PICCADILLY
St James's
REGENT ST
TRAFALGAR SQUARE
Charing Cross Station
VICTORIA EMBANKMENT
Royal National Theatre
Admiralty Arch
WHITEHALL
WATERLOO BRIDGE
Queen Elizabeth Hall
Royal Festival Hall
WATERLOO RD
Green Park
PALL MALL
THE MALL
St James's Palace
Marlborough House
Government Buildings
HUNGERFORD BRIDGE
London Eye
Waterloo Station
ST JAMES'S ST
Thames
GROSVENOR PLACE
Buckingham Palace
CONSTITUTION HILL
St James's Park
BIRDCAGE WALK
DOWNING ST
PARLIAMENT STREET
Treasury
London Aquarium
County Hall
LAMBETH
WESTMINSTER
PARLIAMENT SQUARE
VICTORIA STREET
Westminster Abbey
Elizabeth Tower (Big Ben)
Houses of Parliament
WESTMINSTER BR
WESTMINSTER BRIDGE ROAD
Lambeth Palace Gardens
Victoria Station
Westminster Cathedral
Lambeth Palace
0 M 500
0 YARDS 500

Ickenham
North Hillingdon
Hillingdon
Hatch End
Pinner Park
Bayhurst Wood Country Park
Belmont
Queensbury
Kingsbury
Hendon
Burnt Oak
RAF Museums
GREAT N WAY
A1
Holders Hill
EDGWARE ROAD
Golders Green
HENDON
M1
A41
Cricklewood
Northwick Park
Fryent Country Park
Wembley Park
Brent Reservoir
NORTH CIRCULAR ROAD
Dollis Hill
Gladstone Park
A406
BRENT
Wembley Arena
Wembley Stadium
Wembley
Willesden
Willesden Green
Kilburn
Hayes End
Hayes
Sunbury Golf Course
EALING
Alperton
A406
Park Royal
Grand Union Canal
Harlesden
Yiewsley
Southall
Perivale
FOXO
EALING ROAD
North Acton
HARROW ROAD
West Drayton
Grand Union Canal
Norwood Green
Ealing Golf Course
Ealing
WESTERN
Acton
HANGER LANE
AVENUE
East Acton
Wormwood Scrubs
WESTWAY
A40
North Kensington
Notting Hill
A219
Pad
M4
Hanwell
M4
North Hyde
Gunnersbury
THE VALE
Shepherd's Bush
A402
HAMMERSMITH
Olympia
Holland Park
Harlington
BATH ROAD
A4
Heston
Osterley
GREAT WEST ROAD
Osterley Park
Brentford
A4
CHISWICK HIGH ROAD
Gunnersbury Park
Chiswick
AND FULHAM
Earls Court Exhibition Centre
Earls Court
Cranford
Syon House
Syon Park
Royal Botanic Gardens Kew
KEW ROAD
Chiswick House
Hammersmith Bridge
Castelnau
WWT London Wetland Centre
Football Stadium
FULHAM ROAD
KING'S
Hounslow West
Isleworth
Barnes
Putney Bridge
Parse
Stanwell
Heathrow Airport (London)
GREAT SOUTH WEST ROAD
A30
Hounslow
Mortlake
SOUTH CIRCULAR ROAD
A205
Wa
Hounslow Heath
Richmond
ROEHAMPTON LANE
Putney
HOUNSLOW
Rugby Ground
A316
RICHMOND UPON
Richmond Park
Putney Heath
WAN
East Bedfont
Twickenham
Thames
THAMES
Southfie
Feltham
Crane
All England Lawn Tennis and Croquet Club
Ashford
Hanworth
Teddington
Wimbledon Common
Wimbledon Park
A316
A3
KINGSTON HILL
Wimbledon
A308
Kempton Park Racecourse
Bushy Park
Coombe Hill Golf Course
Queen Mary Reservoir
Hampton
COOMBE LANE
KINGSTON ROAD
A24
Sunbury
M3
Molesey Reservoirs
Hampton Court Palace
Hampton Court Park
Norbiton
KINGSTON VALE
New Malden
Bushy Mead
Shepperton
Queen Elizabeth II Reservoir
Island Barn Reservoir
Mole
West Molesey
East Molesey
A308
A309
KINGSTON UPON THAMES
Kingston Upon Thames
West Barnes
Motspur Park
Morden Park
Baitul Futi Mosqu
Walton-on-Thames
Thames Ditton
Long Ditton
Surbiton
Old Malden
A3
Mor
0 M 800
0 YARDS 800

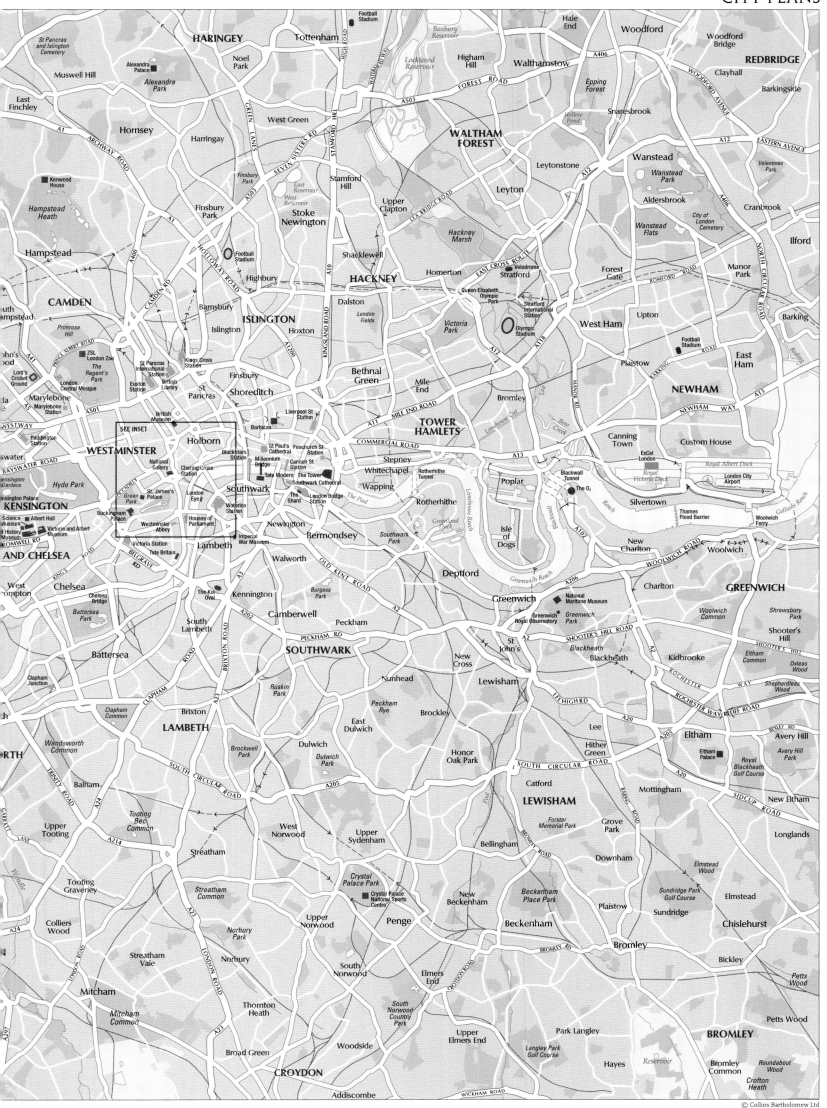

PARIS

Boisemont
Neuville-s.-Oise
Eragny
Pierrelaye
Beauchamp
St-Leu-la-Forêt
Montlignon
Andilly

le Champ Gaillard
la Plan-Chennevières
les Courlains
les Chabuts
Ste-Honorine
Bois de Poissy
Le Plessis-Bouchard
le Gros-Noyer
Margency
les Sources

Glatigny
la Croix Rouge
les Cailloux-Gris
AVENUE DE LA LIBERATION
JULES CESAR
les Hauts-de-St-Nicolas
Eaubonne
Soisy-Sous-Montmorency

Port-Maron
Conflans-Ste-Honorine
la Villa-du-Marais
l'Avenir
la Croix-de-Bois
Herblay
Montigny-lès-Cormeilles
St-Marc
la Mare-des-Noues
Franconville
Cernay
Ermont
Montmore

Maurecourt
les Charvaux
Conflans-Fin-d'Oise
le Plateau-du-Moulin
le Tarte-Mulet
Fort de Cormeilles
le Plan-St-Denis
Cormeilles-en-Parisis
Sannois
les Tartres
St-Gratien
Enghien-les-Bains

Verneuil-s.-Seine
Triel-s.-Seine
Chanteloup-les-Vignes
Andrésy-Fin-d'Oise
Ile de Devant
Ile d'Herblay
Parc urbain
Bois de St-Marc
Morifosse
les Raguenets
les Econdeaux

Cité du Parc
Butte des Gatriaux
la Daurade
Achères
Champs-Druets
Cité du Combattant
Mazagran
Vaucelle
Truet
Epinay-sur-Seine
les Béatus de St-Denis

Vernouillet
la Croix-d'Achères
Forêt
le Parc
Hippodrome
Parc de Maisons-Laffitte
Gdes-Fontaines
Argenteuil
Val-Notre-Dame
les Indes
Port de Gennevilliers
Villeneuve-la-Garen

Médan
Breteuil
Carrières-sous-Poissy
Ile de la Dérivation
Maisons-Laffitte
Sartrouville
les Aulnettes
Bezons
Colombes
Gennevilliers
les Fossés-de-l'Aumône

la Clémenterie
les Grésillons
le Mesnil-le-Roi
la Vaudoire
Houilles
Parc de l'Ile-Marante
les Mourinoux
les Agnettes
les Grésillons

Villennes-s.-Seine
la Reine Blanche
Poissy-Forêt
St-Germain
les Loges
Carrières-sous-Bois
la Borde
le Réveil-Matin
les Grèves
Bois-Colombes
les Vallées
Asnières-s.-Seine

Orgeval
Migneaux-la-Coudraie
Beauregard
Mare aux Canes
Montesson
Carrières-s.-Seine
le Petit-Nanterre
le Petit-Colombes
la Garenne-Colombes
Clichy

Béthemont
Parc de Béthemont
la Maladrerie
Chambourcy la Bretonnière
les Flageaux
les Rabaux
les Cormiers
le Vésinet
le Moulin Noir
Grand-Bray
Chatou
Ensemble Marcelin-Berthelot
Courbevoie
la Défense
Bécon-les-Bruyères
la Jatte

Aigremont
les Tailles d'Herbelay
Montaigu
le Mexique
le Pecq
Croissy-s.-Seine
les Martinets
NANTERRE
Puteaux
Levallois-Perret
Neuilly-s.-Seine

Bois de Dames
St-Germain-en-Laye
Fourqueux
le Buisson-Guérin
le Port-Marly
les Gabillons
Vieux-la Grenouillère
Rueil-Malmaison
Cimetière militaire américain
Mont-Valérien
Ile de Puteaux

Feucherolles
Le Val Martin
Joyenval Château
le Moulin-à-Vent
Mareil-Marly
Montval
Marly-Soleil
les Lotissements
Château de Malmaison
HAUTS-
Suresnes
Hippodrome de St-Cloud
Cité Jardin de Suresnes
Buzenval

St-Nom-la-Bretèche
la Bretèche
L'Étang-la-Ville
Marly-le-Roi
les Soudannes
Bougival
DE-
Forêt de la Malmaison
Garches
St-Cloud

le Vallon-Chavenay
le Clos-Salibert
Louveciennes
les Gressets
SEINE
Vaucresson
Parc de St-Cloud

Chavenay
Domaine des Trois-Côtes
la Tuilerie-Bignon
Parc de Marly
La Celle-St-Cloud

Aerodrome de Chavenay-Villepreux
Mézu
Domaine de la Tuilerie
Noisy-le-Roi
Réservoir
Fort du Trou-d'Enfer
Parc forestier de Beauregard
la Châtaigneraie

Villepreux
Rennemoulin
Bailly
Beauregard
Rocquencourt
Le Grand Chesnay
Parly II
BLVD DE LA RÉPUBLIQUE
Domaine de la Marche
Parc de Marnes
Jardin du Trocadéro

Château de Grand Maisons
Le Chesnay
Glatigny
Marnes-la-Coquette
le Bourg
Ville-d'Avray
Sèvres
Boulogne-Billancourt

les Clayes-sous-Bois
Fontenay-le-Fleury
Parc Montaigne
Aerodrome de St-Cyr-l'École
Trianons
Clagny
Étang de Ville-d'Avray
Chaville
Vanves
Issy-les-Moulineaux
Malakoff

YVELINES
Forêt de Bois-d'Arcy
Grand Canal
VERSAILLES
Notre Dame
Bois de Fausse Repose
Meudon
Montrouge

Bois d'Arcy
Parc St-Cyr
la Fontaine-St-Martin
la Chapelle
St-Cyr-l'École
Château de Versailles
Place d'Armes
BLVD DE LA REINE
AVE DE PARIS
Montreuil
Viroflay
Chaville Forêt
Châtillon
Cimetière parisien de Bagneux

la Croix-Blanche
la Tremblaye
l'Epi-d'Or
Camp des Matelots
Camp des Mortemets
Pièce d'Eau des Suisses
St-Louis
les Chantiers
Porchefontaine
Bois du Pont-Colbert
Meudon
Clamart
Arcueil

Étang de St-Quentin
Bois de Satory
Camp de Satory
Vélizy-Villacoublay
le Clos
Meudon-la-Forêt
le Petit-Clamart
Le Plessis-Robinson
Bagneux

Étang du Moulin-Renard
Étang du Val
les Prés
Bouviers
Troux
la Minière
Bois des Gonards
Robinson
Sceaux

Trappes
Montigny-le-Bretonneux
la Noël
les Metz
Bois de l'Homme-Mort
Aérodrome de Villacoublay
Carrefour du Petit-Clamart
Parc de Sceaux

St-Quentin-en-Yvelines
Buc
Jouy-en-Josas
A 86
Châtenay-Malabry

Bois de Trappes
Voisins-le-Bretonneux
Guyancourt
Vallée de la Bièvre
la Butte Rouge
Forêt de Verrières

Champfleury
Mérantais
Aérodrome de Toussus-le-Noble
Les Loges-en-Josas
le Petit-Jouy
ROUTE ILE JOUY
Bois du Loup-Pendu
Verrières-le-Buisson
les Bas-Graviers
Antony

Le Mesnil-St-Denis
Buloyer
Brouessy
le Petit-Vilain
le Val d'Albian
Centre d'Essais
Bièvres
Vaupéreux
les Gros-Chênes

Ancienne Abbaye de Port-Royal des Champs
Magny-les-Hameaux
le Grand-Vilain
Centre nucléaire de Saclay
Bois Communaux
le Salvert
les Coeurs
la Gravelle

St-Lambert
Romainville
Châteaufort
Orsigny
Villefavreuse
Igny

la Prieuré
Bois de St-Lambert
Milon-la-Chapelle
Toussus-le-Noble
le Christ-de-Saclay
Saclay
Abbaye de St-Louis du Temple
Gommonvilliers
Massy

la Brosse
Beauregard
Parc naturel régional
Cressely
Villiers-le-Bâcle
Centre d'Horticulture de la Ville de Paris
le Pileu
les Champarts

Bois de Chevreuse
Hauvilliers
Plateau de Beauplan
le Mesnil-Blondel
Vauhallan
les Champ
Wis

les Hauts de-Chevreuse
Rhodon
Chevincourt
St-Aubin
Palaiseau
Champlan
les Quatre-Fourchettes

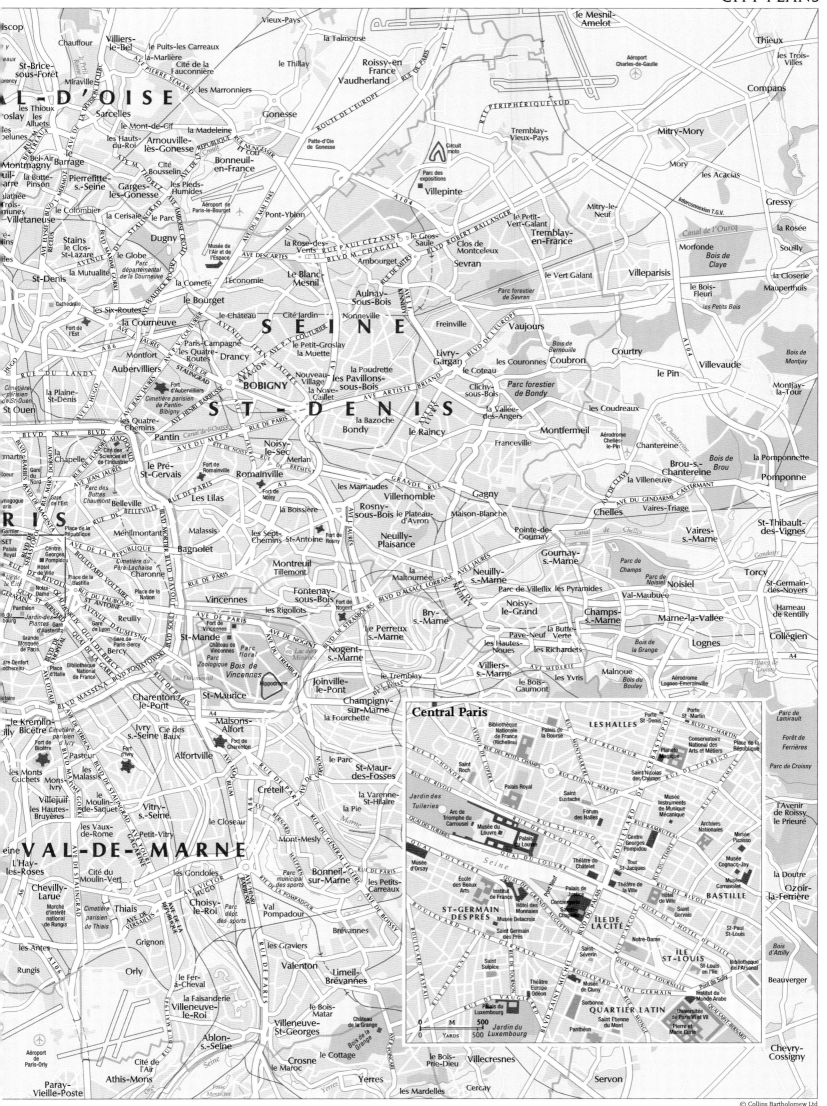

Central Paris

© Collins Bartholomew Ltd

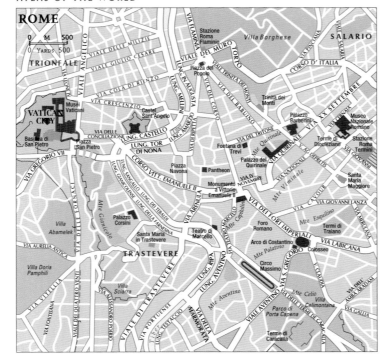

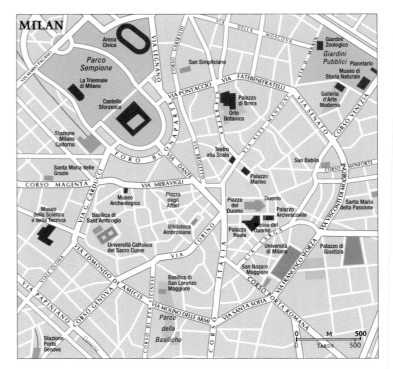

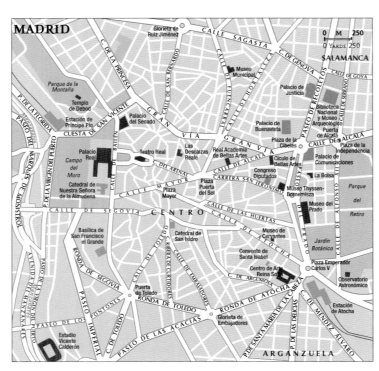

MONTRÉAL

TORONTO

CHICAGO

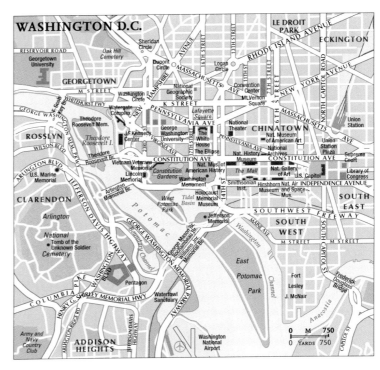

WASHINGTON D.C.

LOS ANGELES

SAN FRANCISCO

© Collins Bartholomew Ltd

NEW YORK

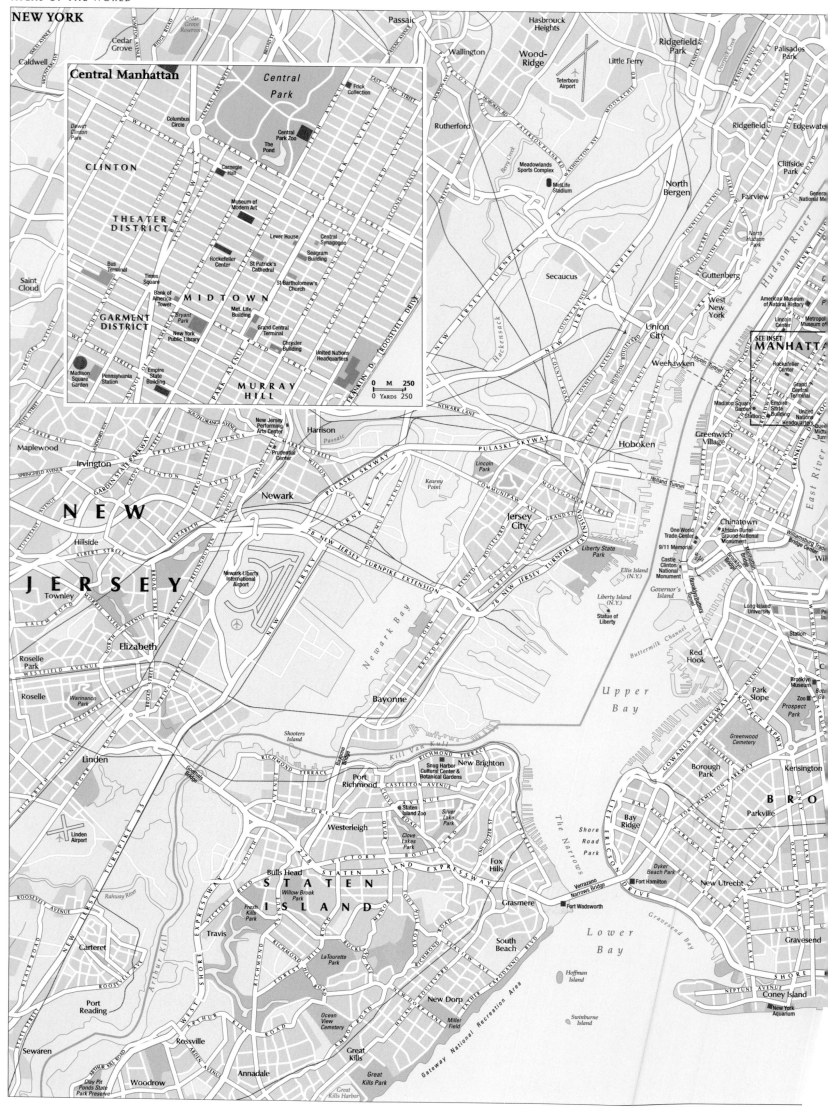

Central Manhattan

Central Park

Frick Collection

Columbus Circle

Central Park Zoo

DeWitt Clinton Park

The Pond

CLINTON

Carnegie Hall

Museum of Modern Art

THEATER DISTRICT

Lever House

Central Synagogue

Rockefeller Center

Seagram Building

Bus Terminal

St Patrick's Cathedral

St Bartholomew's Church

Times Square

MIDTOWN

Bank of America Tower

GARMENT DISTRICT

Bryant Park

Met. Life Building

New York Public Library

Grand Central Terminal

Chrysler Building

Madison Square Garden

Pennsylvania Station

Empire State Building

United Nations Headquarters

MURRAY HILL

0 M 250
0 Yards 250

Passaic

Hasbrouck Heights

Ridgefield Park

Palisades Park

Caldwell

Cedar Grove

Cedar Grove Reservoir

Wallington

Wood-Ridge

Little Ferry

Teterboro Airport

Ridgefield

Edgewater

Rutherford

Cliffside Park

Meadowlands Sports Complex

North Bergen

Fairview

MetLife Stadium

North Hudson Park

Saint Cloud

Secaucus

Guttenberg

Hudson River

West New York

American Museum of Natural History

Union City

Lincoln Center

Metropolitan

SEE INSET MANHATTAN

Hackensack

Weehawken

Rockefeller Center

Maplewood

New Jersey Performing Arts Center

Harrison

Passaic

Hoboken

Greenwich Village

Grand Central Terminal

Irvington

Prudential Center

Lincoln Tunnel

Empire State Building

Madison Square Garden Station

United Nations Headquarters

Newark

Pulaski Skyway

Lincoln Park

Holland Tunnel

East River

NEW

Kearny Point

Jersey City

One World Trade Center

Chinatown

African Burial Ground National Monument

Williamsburg Bridge

Hillside

9/11 Memorial

Townley

JERSEY

Newark Liberty International Airport

Castle Clinton National Monument

Long Island University

Elizabeth

Ellis Island (N.Y.)

Liberty State Park

Governor's Island

Roselle Park

Liberty Island (N.Y.)

Brooklyn

Roselle

Warinanco Park

Statue of Liberty

Buttermilk Channel

Red Hook

Park Slope

Brooklyn Museum

Zoo

Prospect Park

Upper Bay

Greenwood Cemetery

Linden

Bayonne

Borough Park

Kensington

BRO

Shooters Island

Bayonne Bridge

Kill Van Kull

Snug Harbor Cultural Center & Botanical Gardens

New Brighton

Bay Ridge

Goethals Bridge

Port Richmond

The Narrows

Shore Road Park

Parkville

Linden Airport

Staten Island Zoo

Silver Lake Park

Clove Lakes Park

Westerleigh

Dyker Beach Park

Fort Hamilton

New Utrecht

Bulls Head

STATEN

Fox Hills

Verrazano Narrows Bridge

Rahway River

Willow Brook Park

Fresh Kills Park

ISLAND

Grasmere

Fort Wadsworth

Gravesend Bay

Travis

South Beach

Lower Bay

Gravesend

Port Reading

LaTourette Park

Hoffman Island

Gateway National Recreation Area

Coney Island

Sewaren

Rossville

Great Kills

New Dorp

Swinburne Island

New York Aquarium

Clay Pit Ponds State Park Preserve

Woodrow

Annadale

Great Kills Park

Ocean View Cemetery

Miller Field

Great Kills Harbor

114

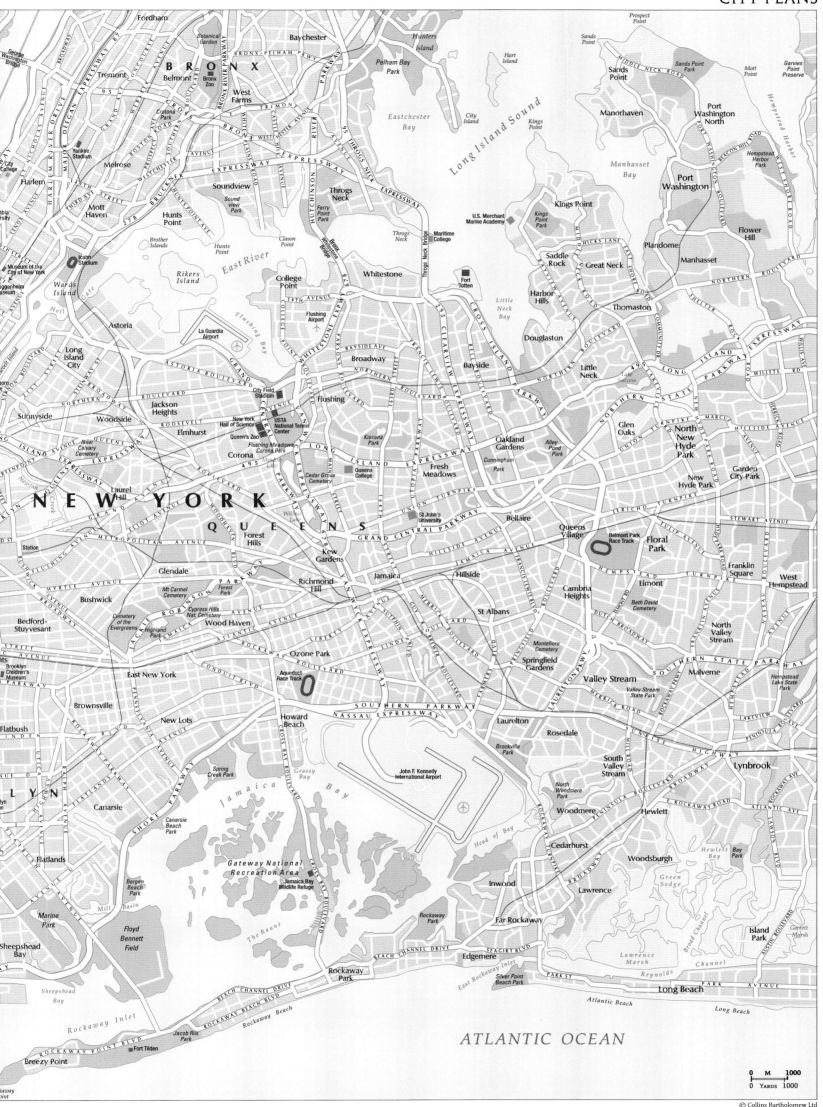

ATLANTIC OCEAN

© Collins Bartholomew Ltd

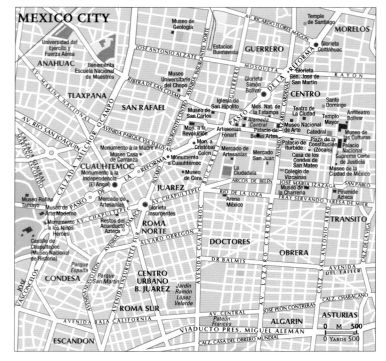

MEXICO CITY

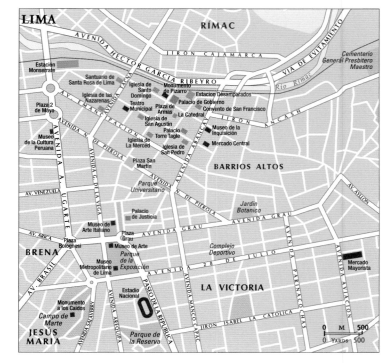

LIMA

RIO DE JANEIRO

SÃO PAULO

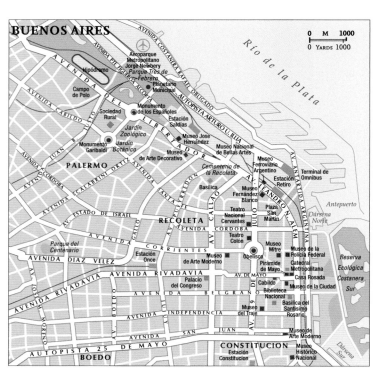

BUENOS AIRES

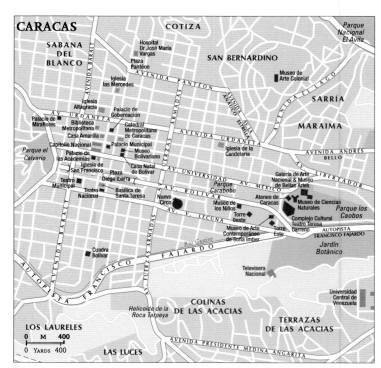

CARACAS

RELIEF

Contour intervals used in layer-colouring for land height and sea depth

Reference maps   Ocean maps

METRES
FEET

Reference maps	Ocean maps
6000 / 19686	4000 / 13124
5000 / 16404	3000 / 9843
4000 / 13124	2000 / 6562
3000 / 9843	1000 / 3281
2000 / 6562	500 / 1640
1000 / 3281	200 / 656
500 / 1640	0 / 0
200 / 656	200 / 656
0 / 0	2000 / 6562
LAND BELOW SEA LEVEL	3000 / 9843
	4000 / 13124
200 / 656	5000 / 16404
2000 / 6562	6000 / 19686
4000 / 13124	7000 / 22967
6000 / 19686	9000 / 29529
M / FT	M / FT

1234
△ Summit
Height in metres

123
‿ Ocean deep
Depth in metres

LAND AND WATER FEATURES

——— River

----- Impermanent river/Wadi

·-·-·- Canal

············ Flood dyke

Coral reef

·············· Escarpment

| Dam/Barrage

⇆ 123 Pass
Height in metres

1234
▲ Volcano
Height in metres

‖ Waterfall

‿ Oasis

Lake

Salt lake/Lagoon

Dry salt lake/Salt pan

Impermanent lake

Impermanent salt lake

Marsh

Sandy desert/Dunes

Rocky desert

Lava field

Ice cap/Glacier

TRANSPORT

═══ Motorway
Shown on large-scale maps only

——— Main road

——— Other road

----- Track

⊢⊣⊢⊣ Road tunnel

——— Main railway

——— Other railway

⊢·⊣·⊢ Railway tunnel

✈ Main airport

✈ Regional airport

CITIES AND TOWNS

Population	National Capital	Administrative Capital (Shown for selected countries only)	Other City or Town
over 10 million	**Tōkyō** ▣	**Karachi** ⊙	**New York** ⊙
5 million to 10 million	**Santiago** ▣	**Tianjin** ⊙	**Philadelphia** ⊙
1 million to 5 million	**Damascus** ▣	**Douala** ⊙	**Barranquilla** ⊙
500 000 to 1 million	**Bangui** ▣	**Bulawayo** ◎	**El Paso** ◎
100 000 to 500 000	Wellington ▢	Mansa ○	Mobile ○
50 000 to 100 000	Port of Spain ▢	Lubango ○	Zaraza ○
10 000 to 50 000	Malabo ▫	Chinhoyi ○	El Tigre ○
under 10 000	Roseau ▫	Ati ○	Soledad ○

STYLES OF LETTERING

Cities and towns are explained above

Country	**FRANCE**	Island	*Gran Canaria*
Overseas Territory/Dependency	**Guadeloupe**	Lake	*Lake Erie*
Disputed Territory	WESTERN SAHARA	Mountain	*Mont Blanc*
Administrative name Shown for selected countries only	SCOTLAND	River	*Thames*
Area name	PATAGONIA	Region	*LAPPLAND*

BOUNDARIES

⊷⊷⊷ International boundary

·-◆-·◆ Disputed international boundary/ alignment unconfirmed

***** Ceasefire line

///// UN buffer zone

▬▬▬ Administrative boundary

▬ ▬ ▬ Disputed territory boundary

MISCELLANEOUS SYMBOLS

-------- National park

·············· Reserve

∿∿∿∿ Ancient wall

∴ Site of specific interest

Built-up area

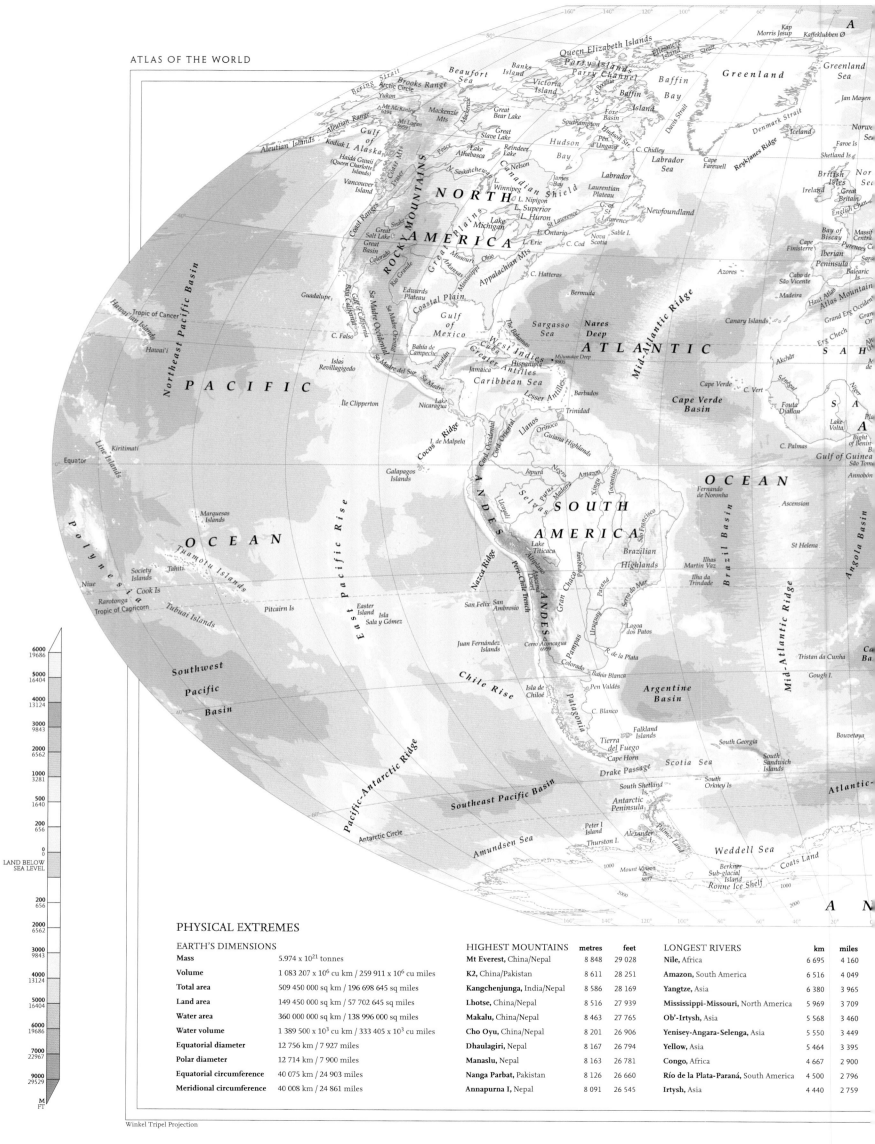

PHYSICAL EXTREMES

EARTH'S DIMENSIONS

Mass	5.974 x 10²¹ tonnes
Volume	1 083 207 x 10⁶ cu km / 259 911 x 10⁶ cu miles
Total area	509 450 000 sq km / 196 698 645 sq miles
Land area	149 450 000 sq km / 57 702 645 sq miles
Water area	360 000 000 sq km / 138 996 000 sq miles
Water volume	1 389 500 x 10³ cu km / 333 405 x 10³ cu miles
Equatorial diameter	12 756 km / 7 927 miles
Polar diameter	12 714 km / 7 900 miles
Equatorial circumference	40 075 km / 24 903 miles
Meridional circumference	40 008 km / 24 861 miles

HIGHEST MOUNTAINS	metres	feet
Mt Everest, China/Nepal	8 848	29 028
K2, China/Pakistan	8 611	28 251
Kangchenjunga, India/Nepal	8 586	28 169
Lhotse, China/Nepal	8 516	27 939
Makalu, China/Nepal	8 463	27 765
Cho Oyu, China/Nepal	8 201	26 906
Dhaulagiri, Nepal	8 167	26 794
Manaslu, Nepal	8 163	26 781
Nanga Parbat, Pakistan	8 126	26 660
Annapurna I, Nepal	8 091	26 545

LONGEST RIVERS	km	miles
Nile, Africa	6 695	4 160
Amazon, South America	6 516	4 049
Yangtze, Asia	6 380	3 965
Mississippi-Missouri, North America	5 969	3 709
Ob'-Irtysh, Asia	5 568	3 460
Yenisey-Angara-Selenga, Asia	5 550	3 449
Yellow, Asia	5 464	3 395
Congo, Africa	4 667	2 900
Río de la Plata-Paraná, South America	4 500	2 796
Irtysh, Asia	4 440	2 759

Winkel Tripel Projection

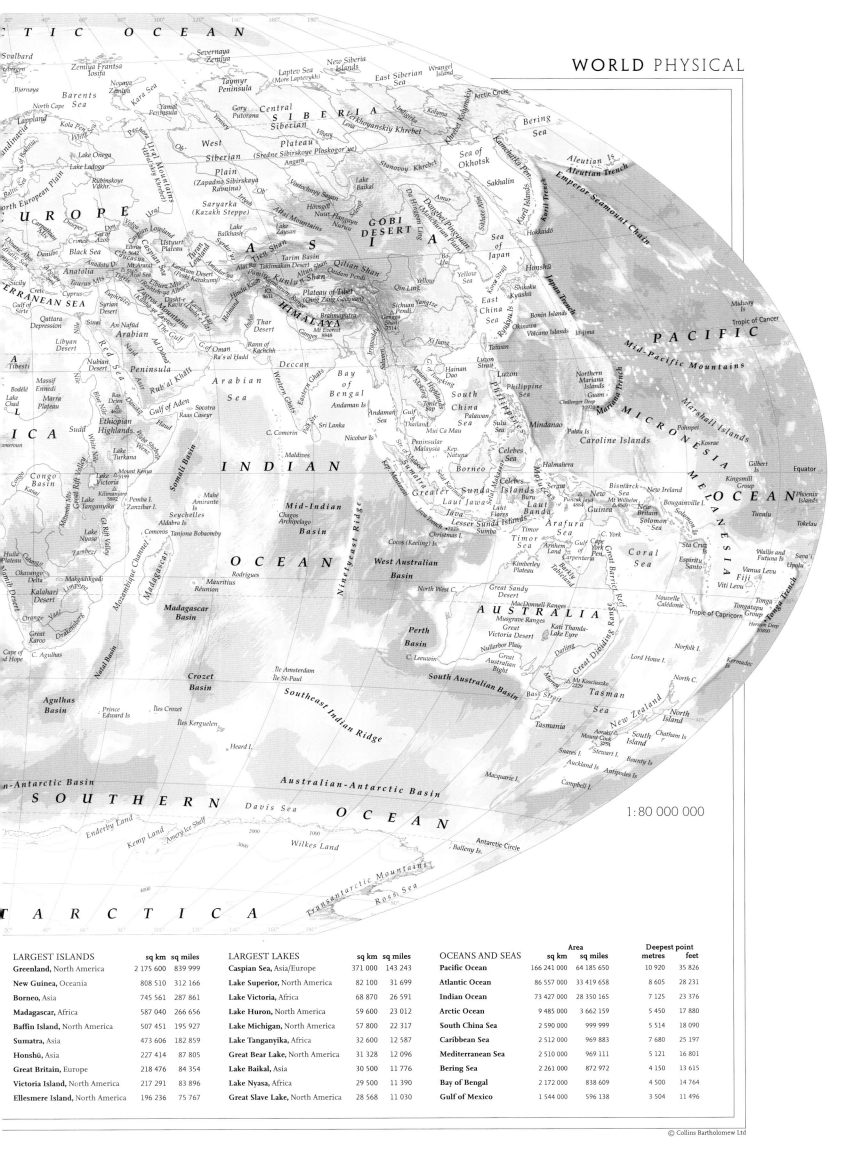

WORLD PHYSICAL

1:80 000 000

LARGEST ISLANDS	sq km	sq miles
Greenland, North America	2 175 600	839 999
New Guinea, Oceania	808 510	312 166
Borneo, Asia	745 561	287 861
Madagascar, Africa	587 040	266 656
Baffin Island, North America	507 451	195 927
Sumatra, Asia	473 606	182 859
Honshū, Asia	227 414	87 805
Great Britain, Europe	218 476	84 354
Victoria Island, North America	217 291	83 896
Ellesmere Island, North America	196 236	75 767

LARGEST LAKES	sq km	sq miles
Caspian Sea, Asia/Europe	371 000	143 243
Lake Superior, North America	82 100	31 699
Lake Victoria, Africa	68 870	26 591
Lake Huron, North America	59 600	23 012
Lake Michigan, North America	57 800	22 317
Lake Tanganyika, Africa	32 600	12 587
Great Bear Lake, North America	31 328	12 096
Lake Baikal, Asia	30 500	11 776
Lake Nyasa, Africa	29 500	11 390
Great Slave Lake, North America	28 568	11 030

OCEANS AND SEAS	Area sq km	sq miles	Deepest point metres	feet
Pacific Ocean	166 241 000	64 185 650	10 920	35 826
Atlantic Ocean	86 557 000	33 419 658	8 605	28 231
Indian Ocean	73 427 000	28 350 165	7 125	23 376
Arctic Ocean	9 485 000	3 662 159	5 450	17 880
South China Sea	2 590 000	999 999	5 514	18 090
Caribbean Sea	2 512 000	969 883	7 680	25 197
Mediterranean Sea	2 510 000	969 111	5 121	16 801
Bering Sea	2 261 000	872 972	4 150	13 615
Bay of Bengal	2 172 000	838 609	4 500	14 764
Gulf of Mexico	1 544 000	596 138	3 504	11 496

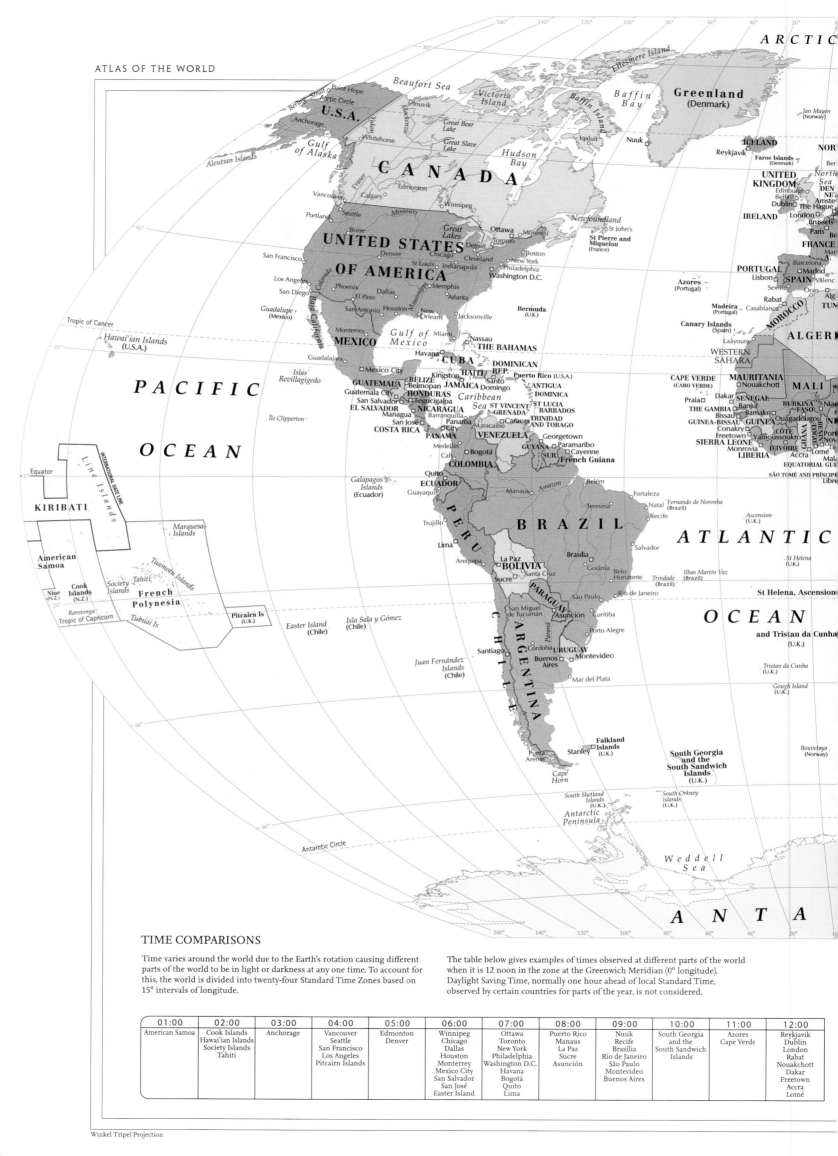

ARCTIC

Beaufort Sea

Greenland
(Denmark)

C A N A D A

UNITED STATES
OF AMERICA

P A C I F I C

O C E A N

KIRIBATI

American
Samoa

French
Polynesia

B R A Z I L

A T L A N T I C

O C E A N

A N T A

TIME COMPARISONS

Time varies around the world due to the Earth's rotation causing different parts of the world to be in light or darkness at any one time. To account for this, the world is divided into twenty-four Standard Time Zones based on 15° intervals of longitude.

The table below gives examples of times observed at different parts of the world when it is 12 noon in the zone at the Greenwich Meridian (0° longitude). Daylight Saving Time, normally one hour ahead of local Standard Time, observed by certain countries for parts of the year, is not considered.

01:00	02:00	03:00	04:00	05:00	06:00	07:00	08:00	09:00	10:00	11:00	12:00
American Samoa	Cook Islands Hawai'ian Islands Society Islands Tahiti	Anchorage	Vancouver Seattle San Francisco Los Angeles Pitcairn Islands	Edmonton Denver	Winnipeg Chicago Dallas Houston Monterrey Mexico City San Salvador San José Easter Island	Ottawa Toronto New York Philadelphia Washington D.C. Havana Bogotá Quito Lima	Puerto Rico Manaus La Paz Sucre Asunción	Nuuk Recife Brasília Rio de Janeiro São Paulo Montevideo Buenos Aires	South Georgia and the South Sandwich Islands	Azores Cape Verde	Reykjavik Dublin London Rabat Nouakchott Dakar Freetown Accra Lomé

Winkel Tripel Projection

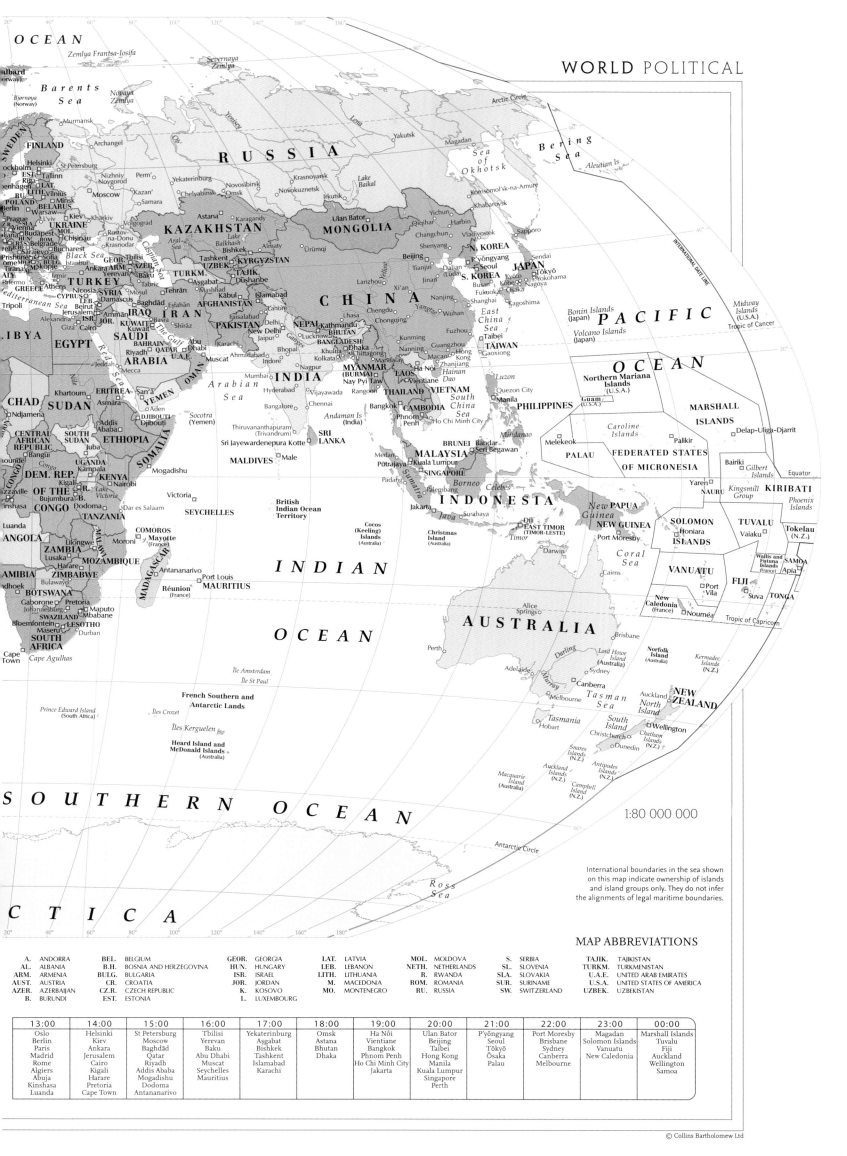

OCEAN
Zemlya Frantsa-Iosifa
albard
(orway)
Barents
Sea
Bjørnøya
(Norway)
Novaya
Zemlya
Severnaya
Zemlya

SWEDEN
FINLAND
Murmansk
Archangel
RUSSIA
Helsinki
ockholm St Petersburg
EST. Tallinn
Riga LAT.
enhagen Vilnius LITH.
RU. Minsk
Berlin Warsaw
POLAND BELARUS
Kiev Kharkiv
Prague
Vienna
Budapest UKRAINE MOL.
HUN.
iljana Belgrade Bucharest
ROM.
CR.
Pristina
me Sofia
Sarajevo
Skopje
Tiranã
ALY GREECE Athens
Mediterranean Sea
Tripoli

Nizhniy
Novgorod Perm'
Moscow Kazan'
Yekaterinburg
Samara Chelyabinsk Omsk Novosibirsk
Novokuznetsk

Astana
Karagandy
KAZAKHSTAN
Aral
Sea
Lake
Balkhash
Almaty
Bishkek
KYRGYZSTAN

Krasnoyarsk
Lake
Baikal
Irkutsk

Yakutsk

Komsomol'sk-na-Amure
Khabarovsk

Sea
of
Okhotsk

Bering
Sea
Aleutian Is

Arctic Circle

MONGOLIA
Ulan Bator
Ürümqi

Qiqihar Harbin
Changchun
Shenyang
Beijing
N. KOREA
P'yŏngyang
Seoul

Yichun

Vladivostok
Sapporo

Sendai

Midway
Islands
(U.S.A.)

PACIFIC

Volcano Islands
(Japan)

OCEAN

Tropic of Cancer

INTERNATIONAL DATE LINE

Bonin Islands
(Japan)

JAPAN
Kyōto Tōkyō
Yokohama
S. KOREA Busan Osaka Nagoya

Kagoshima

East
China
Sea

Fukuoka

TAIWAN
Taibei
Gaoxiong

Northern Mariana
Islands
(U.S.A.)

Guam
(U.S.A.)

MARSHALL
ISLANDS

Delap-Uliga-Djarrit

Caroline
Islands

Palikir

FEDERATED STATES
OF MICRONESIA

Bairiki
Gilbert
Islands

Equator

KIRIBATI

Phoenix
Islands

NAURU
Yaren
Kingsmill
Group

1:80 000 000

International boundaries in the sea shown
on this map indicate ownership of islands
and island groups only. They do not infer
the alignments of legal maritime boundaries.

SOUTHERN OCEAN

CTICA

Antarctic Circle

Ross
Sea

MAP ABBREVIATIONS

A.	ANDORRA	BEL.	BELGIUM	GEOR.	GEORGIA	LAT.	LATVIA	MOL.	MOLDOVA	S.	SERBIA	TAJIK.	TAJIKISTAN
AL.	ALBANIA	B.H.	BOSNIA AND HERZEGOVINA	HUN.	HUNGARY	LEB.	LEBANON	NETH.	NETHERLANDS	SL.	SLOVENIA	TURKM.	TURKMENISTAN
ARM.	ARMENIA	BULG.	BULGARIA	ISR.	ISRAEL	LITH.	LITHUANIA	R.	RWANDA	SLA.	SLOVAKIA	U.A.E.	UNITED ARAB EMIRATES
AUST.	AUSTRIA	CR.	CROATIA	JOR.	JORDAN	M.	MACEDONIA	ROM.	ROMANIA	SUR.	SURINAME	U.S.A.	UNITED STATES OF AMERICA
AZER.	AZERBAIJAN	CZ.R.	CZECH REPUBLIC	K.	KOSOVO	MO.	MONTENEGRO	RU.	RUSSIA	SW.	SWITZERLAND	UZBEK.	UZBEKISTAN
B.	BURUNDI	EST.	ESTONIA	L.	LUXEMBOURG								

13:00	14:00	15:00	16:00	17:00	18:00	19:00	20:00	21:00	22:00	23:00	00:00
Oslo	Helsinki	St Petersburg	Tbilisi	Yekaterinburg	Omsk	Ha Nôi	Ulan Bator	P'yŏngyang	Port Moresby	Magadan	Marshall Islands
Berlin	Kiev	Moscow	Yerevan	Asgabat	Astana	Vientiane	Beijing	Seoul	Brisbane	Solomon Islands	Tuvalu
Paris	Ankara	Baghdād	Baku	Bishkek	Bhutan	Bangkok	Taibei	Tōkyō	Sydney	Vanuatu	Fiji
Madrid	Jerusalem	Qatar	Abu Dhabi	Tashkent	Dhaka	Phnom Penh	Hong Kong	Ōsaka	Canberra	New Caledonia	Auckland
Rome	Cairo	Riyadh	Muscat	Islamabad		Ho Chi Minh City	Manila	Palau	Melbourne		Wellington
Algiers	Kigali	Addis Ababa	Seychelles	Karachi		Jakarta	Kuala Lumpur				Samoa
Abuja	Harare	Mogadishu	Mauritius				Singapore				
Kinshasa	Pretoria	Dodoma					Perth				
Luanda	Cape Town	Antananarivo									

	A	B	C	D	E

A S I A

Sea of Japan

East China Sea

Hokkaidō

Kuril Islands

Honshū

Shikoku

Kyūshū

Yangtze

Taiwan Strait

Ryukyu Islands

Bonin Islands

Volcano Islands

Pagan

Tinian Saipan
Rota

Northern Mariana Islands
(U.S.A.)

Luzon Strait

Luzon

Guam Hagåtña
(U.S.A.)

Hainan Dao

Tropic of Cancer

Mekong

Samar

Palau Islands

Ulithi Fais
Yap Faraulep Pikelot
Ngulu Sorol Chuuk
Eauripik

Caroline Islands

Hall Is

Palawan Negros
Panay

Mindanao

FEDERATED STAT

Mort
Island

Sulu Sea

Celebes Sea

Laut Maluku

Halmahera

Admiralty Islands

New Hanover

New Ireland

Bismarck Sea

Vanimo Wewak
Sepik Madang

Rabaul

New Britain

South China Sea

Bay of Bengal

Gulf of Thailand

Borneo

Selat Makassar

Celebes

Laut Banda

New Guinea

Mt Wilhelm
4509 Goroka
Lae
Balimo Kerema

PAPUA Solo
NEW GUINEA

Laut Flores

Laut Jawa

Daru Gulf of Papua

Port Moresby

Louisiade Archipelago

Timor

Arafura Sea

Torres Strait

Cape York

Coral Sea Islands Territory
(Australia)

Cora
Sea

Strait of Malacca

Sumatra

Kepulauan Mentawai

Laut Jawa

Sumbawa Flores

Bali Sumba

Timor Sea

Melville I.

Bathurst I. Darwin

Wessel Islands

Cape Arnhem

Cape York Peninsula

Great Barrier Reef

Java (Jawa)

Ashmore and Cartier Islands
(Australia)

Londonderry

Arnhem Land

Gulf of Carpentaria

Cooktown

Cairns

Christmas Island
(Australia)

Cape Lévêque

Broome

Wyndham

Halls Creek

NORTHERN TERRITORY

Normanton

Townsville

Mackay

Rockhampt
Gladsto

INDIAN OCEAN

Equator

Cocos Islands
(Australia)

Port Hedland

Karratha

Barrow Island

North West Cape

Paraburdoo

Newman

Great Sandy Desert

Mount Liebig
1524

Alice Springs

Mount Isa

Cloncurry

Longreach

QUEENSLAND

Charleville

Great Dividing Range

Maryboro

Bris

Gold Coast

AUSTRALIA

WESTERN AUSTRALIA

Great Victoria Desert

SOUTH AUSTRALIA

Oodnadatta

Toowoomba

Meekatharra

Mount Magnet

Leonora

Woomera

Broken Hill

NEW SOUTH WALES

Newcastle
Orange Lithgow

Darling

Tamwor

Geraldton

Kalgoorlie

Ceduna

Whyalla

Port Augusta
Port Pirie

Wagga Wagga

A.C.T. Canberra

Sydne
Wollongor

Perth
Fremantle

Bunbury

Esperance

Great Australian Bight

Port Lincoln

Adelaide

Kangaroo Island

Bendigo Albury

VICTORIA

Melbourne
Geelong

Albany

Cape Leeuwin

Mount Gambier

Bass Strait

Flinders Island

King Island

Devonport Launceston

TASMANIA

Hobart

South East Cape

	A	B	C	D	E

OCEANIA

MARSHALL ISLANDS

Wake Island
(U.S.A.)

Bikini

Ralik Chain

Ratak Chain

Kwajalein

Maloelap

Palikir

Pohnpei

Kosrae

Delap-Uliga-Djarrit

Mili

MICRONESIA

Gilbert
Islands

Tarawa **Bairiki**

Yaren

Aranuka

NAURU

Banaba

Nonouti
Tabiteuea

Beru Nikunau

Onotoa

Tamana

Arorae

Kingsmill Group

Nukumanu Islands

Ontong Java Atoll

Nanumea

Nanumanga

Niutao

Nui Vaitupu

**SOLOMON
ISLANDS**

Choiseul

Santa Isabel

Malaita

Guadalcanal

Honiara

Makira
(San Cristobal)

Rennell

Duff Islands

Santa Cruz
Islands

TUVALU

Nukufetau Funafuti

Vaiaku

Nukulaelae

Niulakita

Rotuma
(Fiji)

Banks
Islands

Espiritu Santo

Maéwo

VANUATU

Malakula

Ambrym

Epi

Port Vila

Éfaté

Erromango

Tanna

Anatom

Îles Chesterfield
(France)

Îles Loyauté
(France)

New Caledonia
(France)

Nouméa

Île des Pins

Hunter I.

Yasawa
Group

Viti Levu

Suva

Vanua Levu

Koro

FIJI

Kadavu

Totoya

Ceva-i-Ra

Ono-i-Lau

**Wallis and Futuna
Islands**
(France) **Matā'utu**

Îles Wallis

Îles de Horn

SAMOA

Savai'i

Apia

Upolu

**American
Samoa**

Tutuila Manu'a Is

Fagatogo

Niuafo'ou

Tafahi

Tofua

Vava'u
Group

TONGA

Nuku'alofa
*Tongatapu
Group*

Ata

Alafu

Nukunono

Tokelau
(New Zealand)

Swains Island

Fakaofo

Pukapuka

Nassau

Rakahanga

Manihiki

Penrhyn

Suwarrow

**Niue
Alofi**
(New Zealand)

Palmerston

Aitutaki

Cook Islands
(New Zealand)

Rarotonga

Mauke

Maria

Mangaia

*PACIFIC
OCEAN*

Hawaiian Islands

Kure
Atoll

**Midway
Islands**

Pearl and Hermes
Atoll

Lisianski
Island

Laysan
Island

Gardner
Pinnacles

Necker Island

Kaua'i

O'ahu

Maui

Hawai'i

Tropic of Cancer

Johnston Atoll
(U.S.A.)

Kingman Reef
(U.S.A.)

Palmyra Atoll
(U.S.A.)

Teraina

Tabuaeran

Kiritimati

Howland Island
(U.S.A.)

Baker Island
(U.S.A.)

Phoenix Islands

McKean

Nikumaroro Orona

Kanton

Rawaki

Manra

Jarvis Island
(U.S.A.)

KIRIBATI

Malden Island

Starbuck Island

Vostok Island

Flint Island

Caroline Island
(Millennium Island)

Nuku Hiva

*Îles du
Roi-Georges*

*Îles de
Désappointement*

Puka puka

Rangiroa

Fakarava

Tuamotu Islands

Hereheretue

Îles du Duc de Gloucester

Hao

Marutea

Anaa

Reao

Raroia

Marquesas Islands

Hiva Oa

Motu One

Papete

Tahiti

Society Islands

French

Rurutu

Tubuai

Raivavae

Tubuai Islands

Polynesia

Rapa

Marutiri

Groupe
Actéon

Îles Gambier

Adamstown

Pitcairn Islands
(U.K.)

Henderson
Island

Ducie I.

Pitcairn Island

Norfolk Island
(Australia)

Kingston

Lord Howe
Island
(Australia)

Raoul Island

Kermadec Islands
(New Zealand)

Cape Maria
van Diemen

Whangarei

Great Barrier
Island

North Island
(Te Ika-a-Māui)

Auckland

Manukau

Hamilton

New Plymouth

**NEW
ZEALAND**

Gisborne

Napier

Palmerston North

Nelson

Wellington

Greymouth

Blenheim

Aoraki/
Mount Cook

South Island
(Te Waipounamu)

Southern Alps

Christchurch

Cape
Providence

Timaru

Oamaru

Dunedin

Invercargill

Stewart Island

Snares Islands
(New Zealand)

Bounty Islands
(New Zealand)

Chatham Islands
(New Zealand)

Pitt Island

Antipodes Islands
(New Zealand)

Auckland Islands
(New Zealand)

Campbell Island
(New Zealand)

Macquarie Island
(Australia)

**TASMAN
SEA**

INTERNATIONAL DATE LINE

Equator

Tropic of Capricorn

Note: International boundaries in the sea
shown on this map indicate ownership
of islands and island groups only.
They do not infer the alignments of
legal maritime boundaries

MILES KM

1200 2000

1600

800 1200

800

400 400

0 0

1:32 000 000

Lambert Azimuthal Equal Area Projection

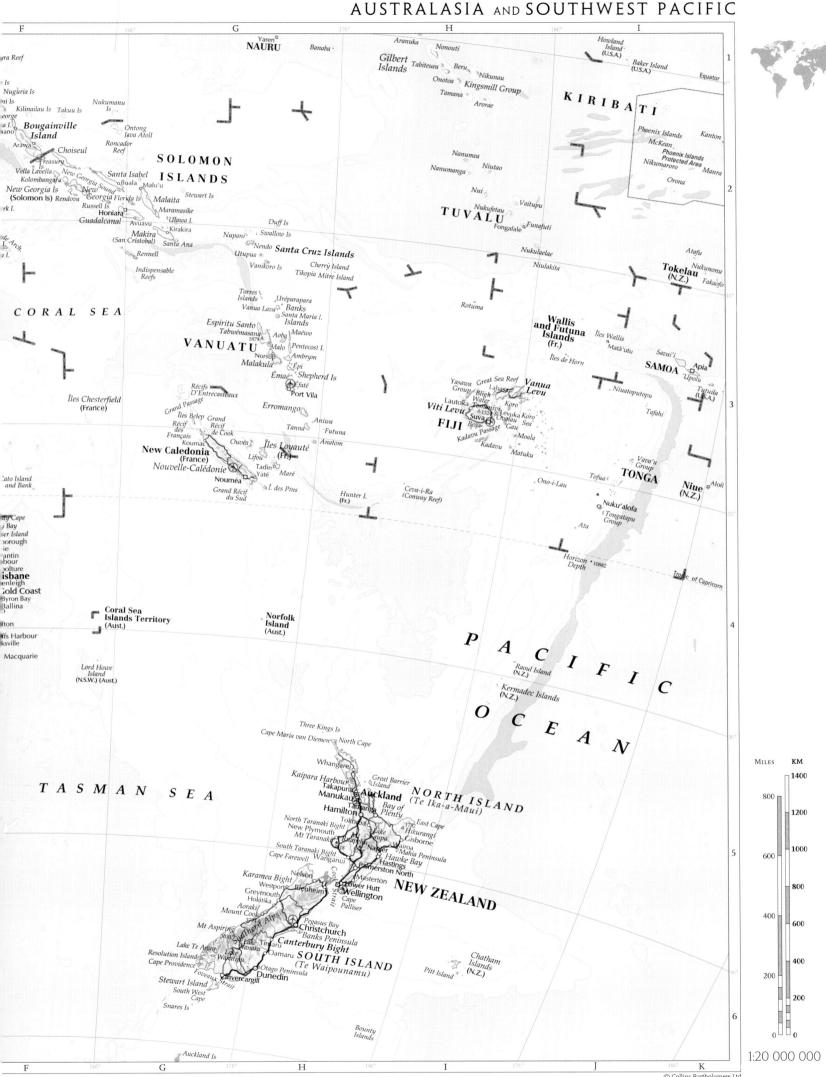

F · 160° · G · 170° · H · 180° · I

NAURU Yaren
Banaba

Aranuka Nonouti
Gilbert Tabiteuea Beru Nikunau
Islands Onotoa Kingsmill Group
Tamana Arorae

Howland
Island
(U.S.A.) Baker Island
(U.S.A.)
Equator

KIRIBATI

Phoenix Islands Kanton
McKean
Phoenix Islands
Protected Area Manra
Nikumaroro
Orona

Nuguria Is
Kilinailau Is Takuu Is
ni Is
George Ontong
Nukumanu Java Atoll
Is Roncador
Reef

**Bougainville
Island**
Arawa

Choiseul
Treasury
Is
Vella Lavella New Georgia Sound
Kolombangara Santa Isabel Buala
New Georgia Is New Georgia Florida Is Malaita
(Solomon Is) Rendova Russell Is Maramasike
rk I. Honiara Ulawa I.
Avuavu Kirakira
Guadalcanal Makira Santa Ana
(San Cristobal)
Rennell

**SOLOMON
ISLANDS**

Malu'u
Stewart Is

Duff Is
Swallow Is
Nupani
Santa Cruz Islands
Utupua Nendo
Vanikoro Is
Cherry Island
Tikopia Mitre Island

Nanumea
Nanumanga
Nui
Nukufetau
Vaitupu

Niutao

TUVALU Fongafale Funafuti

Nukulaelae

Atafu Nukunonu
Tokelau Fakaofo
(N.Z.)

Niulakita

Rotuma

Torres
Islands
Uréparapara
Vanua Lava Banks
Santa Maria I. Islands
Espiritu Santo Aoba
Tabwémasana Maéwo
1879 Malo Pentecost I.
VANUATU Norsup Ambrym
Malakula Épi
Émaé Shepherd Is
Récifs Efaté
D'Entrecasteaux Port Vila

Erromango

Aniwa
Tanna Futuna
Anatom

**Wallis
and Futuna
Islands
(Fr.)**
Îles Wallis
Matā'utu
Îles de Horn

Niuatoputopu

Great Sea Reef
Yasawa Bligh
Group Labasa **Vanua
Lautoka Water Levu**
Tomaniivi Koro
Viti Levu 1324 Levuka Koro
Suva Ovalau Sea
FIJI Beqa Gau
Kadavu Passage Moala
Kadavu Matuku

SAMOA Apia
Savai'i Upolu
Tutuila
(U.S.A.)

Tafahi

Vava'u
Group

Île Chesterfield
(France)

Grand Passage
Récifs Îles Belep
des Grand Récif
Français de Cook
Koumac Ouvéa
New Caledonia Lifou
(France) Tadin
Nouvelle-Calédonie Yaté
Nouméa Maré

Grand Récif
du Sud

Île des Pins

Îles Loyauté
(Fr.)

Ouvéa

Hunter I.
(Fr.)

Ceva-i-Ra
(Conway Reef)

Ono-i-Lau

Tofua

Ata

TONGA

Nuku'alofa Tongatapu
Group

Niue
(N.Z.) Alofi

Cato Island
and Bank

Horizon
Depth 10882

Tropic of Capricorn

ry Cape
i Bay
er Island
borough
rie
antin
bour
olture
isbane
enleigh
Gold Coast
Byron Bay
Ballina

**Coral Sea
Islands Territory
(Aust.)**

**Norfolk
Island
(Aust.)**

ton

s Harbour
cksville

Macquarie

Lord Howe
Island
(N.S.W.) (Aust.)

PACIFIC

Raoul Island
(N.Z.)

Kermadec Islands
(N.Z.)

TASMAN SEA

Three Kings Is
Cape Maria van Diemen North Cape

Whangarei
Kaipara Harbour Great Barrier
Takapuna Island
Auckland
Manukau
Hamilton Bay of
Tauranga Plenty
North Taranaki Bight Tokoroa
New Plymouth Lake Hikurangi East Cape
Mt Taranaki Taupo Gisborne
South Taranaki Bight Napier Wairoa
Wanganui Hastings Mahia Peninsula
Nelson Palmerston North Hawke Bay
Karamea Bight Blenheim Masterton
Westport Cook Wellington Cape
Greymouth Strait Lower Hutt Palliser
Hokitika **NEW ZEALAND**
Aoraki
Mount Cook Pegasus Bay
Mt Aspiring Christchurch
Lake Te Anau Southern Alps Banks Peninsula
Lake Tekapo Canterbury Bight
Resolution Island Wanaka Oamaru
Cape Providence **SOUTH ISLAND**
Foveaux Strait Invercargill (Te Waipounamu) Dunedin Otago Peninsula
Stewart Island
South West
Cape

**NORTH ISLAND
(Te Ika-a-Māui)**

Chatham
Islands
(N.Z.)
Pitt Island

OCEAN

Bounty
Islands

Auckland Is

CORAL SEA

F · 160° · G · 170° · H · 180° · I · 170° · J · 160° · K

MILES KM

1400

800 1200

1000

600 800

600

400 400

200 200

0 0

1:20 000 000

© Collins Bartholomew Ltd

Lambert Azimuthal Equal Area Projection

124

AUSTRALIA SOUTHEAST

QUEENSLAND

Moriarty's Ra.

DARLING DOWNS

Brisbane

Gold Coast

Tweed Heads

NEW ENGLAND RANGE

GREAT DIVIDING RANGE

SOUTH WALES

Liverpool Plains

Liverpool Range

Mount Range

Nandewar Range

Warrumbungle Range

Macquarie Marshes

Newcastle

Sydney

Botany Bay

Wollongong

TASMAN SEA

Canberra

AUSTRALIAN CAPITAL TERRITORY

Snowy Mts.

Gourock Range

GREAT DIVIDING RANGE

VICTORIA

Gippsland

Wilson's Promontory

Ninety Mile Beach

Cape Howe

Bass Strait

King Island

Flinders I.

Cape Barren I.

Hunter Is

Banks Strait

TASMANIA
1:5 000 000

Gt Western Tiers

Launceston

Great Lake

Lake Echo

Hobart

Bruny Island

South East Cape

MILES KM

1:5 000 000

127

© Collins Bartholomew Ltd

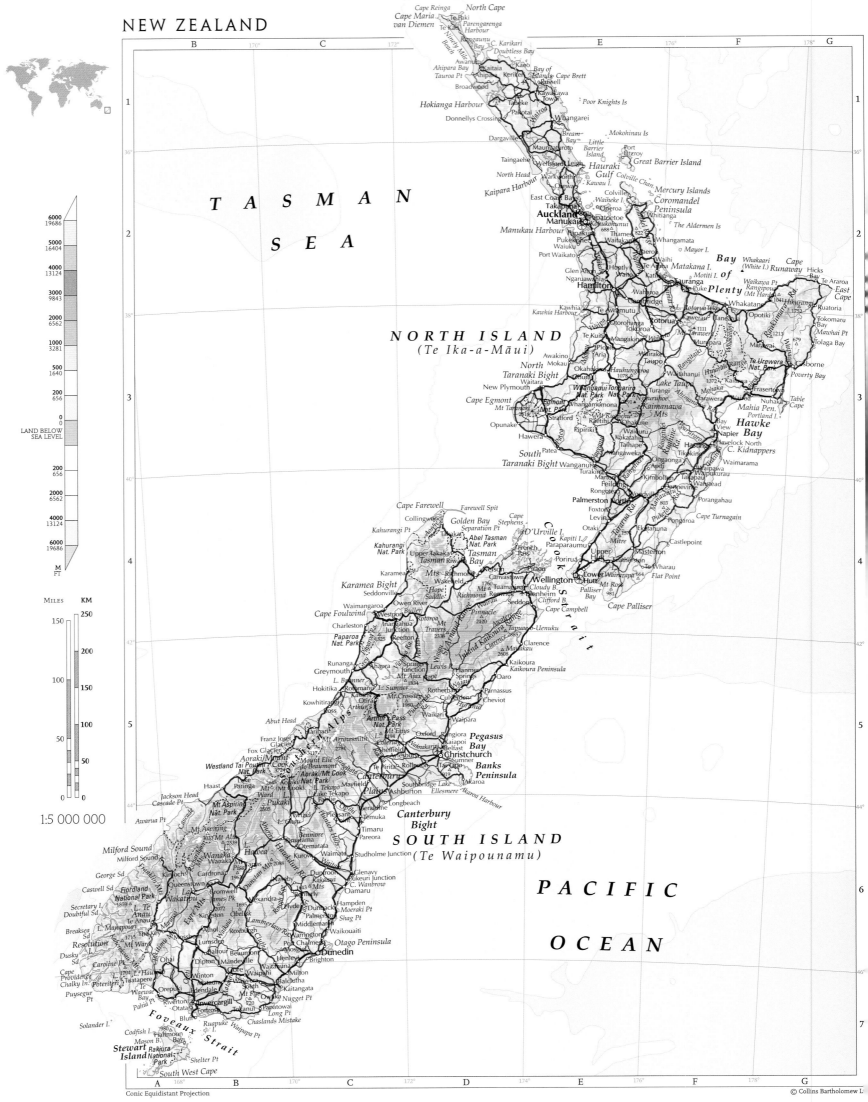

NEW ZEALAND

T A S M A N

S E A

NORTH ISLAND
(Te Ika-a-Māui)

SOUTH ISLAND
(Te Waipounamu)

P A C I F I C

O C E A N

1:5 000 000

Conic Equidistant Projection

© Collins Bartholomew Ltd

ANTARCTICA

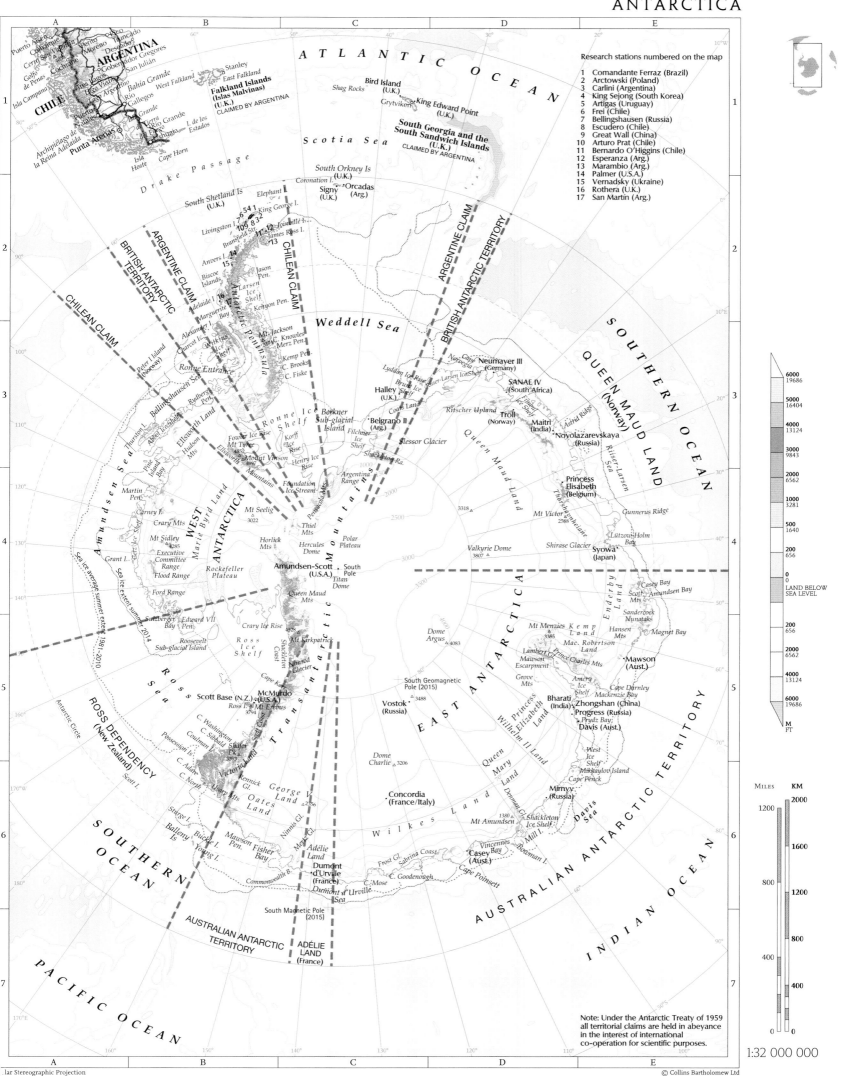

Note: Under the Antarctic Treaty of 1959 all territorial claims are held in abeyance in the interest of international co-operation for scientific purposes.

1:32 000 000

Polar Stereographic Projection

© Collins Bartholomew Ltd

OCEAN

Bering Strait

CENTRAL SIBERIAN
PLATEAU

Tiksi

Arctic Circle

A
S
I
A

Verkhoyanskiy Khrebet

Khrebet Kolymskiy

Ugolnye Kopi

BERING
SEA

Pribilof
Islands

1

Zhnaya Tunguska

Mirnyy

Lena

Vilyuy

Yakutsk

Aldan

Susuman

Magadan

*Sea
of Okhotsk*

Kamchatka Peninsula

Petropavlovsk-
Kamchatskiy

*Aleutian
Islands*

nsk

Bratsk

Ust'-Kut

Bodaybo

Stanovoy Khrebet

Tynda

Amur

Komsomol'sk-
na-Amure

Blagoveshchensk

Sakhalin

Amgun

Khabarovsk

Yuzhno-
Sakhalinsk

Korsakov

Kuril Islands

2

ara

Irkutsk

Lake
Baikal

Ulan-Ude

Chita

Argun

Heilong Jiang

Hulun
Buir

Qiqihar

Daqing

*Hulun
Nur*

Harbin

Lake Khanka

Wakkanai

Vladivostok

Sapporo

HOKKAIDO

Hakodate

llastay

Hövsgöl
Nuur

Darhan

■ Ulan Bator

MONGOLIA

Matad

*Buyr
Nuur*

Da Hinggan Ling

Changchun

Jilin

Ch'ŏngjin

NORTH
KOREA

*Sea
of Japan
(East Sea)*

Akita

Sendai

Niigata

JAPAN

HONSHŪ

GOBI DESERT

Dalandzadgad

INNER MONGOLIA

Hohhot

Baotou

Datong

Shenyang

Fushun

Anshan

P'yŏngyang

Kanazawa

Tōkyō ■

Yokohama

3

Laojunmiao

dian Shan

Wuhai

*Yellow
(Huang He)*

Beijing ■

Tianjin

Dalian

*Korea
Bay*

Seoul ●

SOUTH
KOREA

Daejeon

Kyōto

Kōbe

Ōsaka

Daegu

Yinchuan

Xining

*Qinghai
Hu*

Taiyuan

Shijiazhuang

Bo Hai

Yantai

Busan

Kita-Kyūshū

Hiroshima

Shikoku

ring

Handan

Jinan

Zibo

Qingdao

Gwangju

Fukuoka

Nagasaki

Kumamoto

Lanzhou

Zhengzhou

*Yellow
(Huang He)*

Jining

*Yellow
Sea*

Kagoshima

Kyūshū

Xi'an

Xuzhou

HINA

Chengdu

Nanchong

Yangtze (Chang Jiang)

Huaian

Nanjing

Wuxi

Suizhou

Hefei

Shanghai

Neijiang

Chongqing

Wuhan

Yueyang

Nanchang

Hangzhou

Ningbo

*East China
Sea*

Yibin

Changsha

Hengyang

Quzhou

*Bonin Islands
(Japan)*

PACIFIC

Tropic of Cancer

4

itkyina

Panzhihua

Guiyang

Wenzhou

Okinawa

Ryukyu Islands

*Volcano Islands
(Japan)*

Qujing

Liuzhou

Meizhou

Fuzhou

Taibei ●

OCEAN

Kunming

Nanning

Guangzhou

Xiamen

Shantou

Taiwan Strait

TAIWAN

Taidong

AR
A)

Ha Nôi ■

Hai Phong

Zhanjiang

Macao

Hong Kong

*Gulf
of
Tongking*

Haikou

*Hainan
Dao*

Batan Islands

Luzon Strait

Aparri

*Northern
Mariana
Islands*

Pagan

15°

5

Louangphabang

V
I
E
T
N
A
M

L
A
O
S

Chiang
Mai

Vientiane ■

Huê

Da Nang

Paracel Islands

SOUTH

CHINA

SEA

Luzon

PHILIPPINES

Quezon
City

Tinian

Saipan

Rota

Guam

amyaing

nu Zam

THAILAND

Nakhon
Ratchasima

Bangkok ■

*Tonle
Sap*

CAMBODIA

Phnom
Penh ■

Nha Trang

Ho Chi Minh City

Spratly Islands

Manila ●

Mindoro

Naga

Masbate

Panay

Iloilo

Samar

Cebu

Surigao

Palawan

Negros

Dapitan

Yap

Caroline Islands

Chuuk

Myeik

*Gulf
of
Thailand*

Sihanoukville

*Sulu
Sea*

Mindanao

Davao

PALAU

Melekeok ●

*Mortlock
Islands*

Nakhon Si
Thammarat

Zamboanga

6

George
Town

Malay Peninsula

Kota Bharu

Strait of Malacca

Ipoh

MALAYSIA

Kota Kinabalu

BRUNEI

Bandar Seri
Begawan

SABAH

Sandakan

*Sulu
Archipelago*

*Kepulauan
Talaud*

Manado

*Celebes
Sea*

Laut Maluku

Halmahera

Manokwari

Bismarck Archipelago

Equator

edan

Kuala
Lumpur ■

Putrajaya

SARAWAK

Kuching

Sibu

Sri Aman

*Kepulauan
Sangir*

Jayapura

*Bismarck
Sea*

New Britain

Singapore ■

Borneo

*Jazirah
Doberai*

Solomon
Sea

S
u
m
a
t
r
a

*Kepulauan
Lingga*

Pontianak

Balikpapan

Selat Makassar

Palu

*Kepulauan
Sula*

Maluku

Laut Seram

Seram

New
Guinea

Puncak Jaya
4884

Digul

Siberut

Padang

Bangka

Ketapang

Barito

Banjarmasin

Parepare

Celebes

Buru

Laut Banda

*Kepulauan
Aru*

Bengkulu

an Mentawai

Palembang

Bandar
Lampung

I
N
D
O
N
E
S
I
A

Makassar

Buton

*Gulf
of Papua*

7

Enggano

Selat Sunda

Jakarta ■

Java

Bandung

Semarang

Yogyakarta

*Laut
Jawa*

Surabaya

Madura

Laut Bali

Raba

Bali

Flores

Laut Flores

Wetar

Dili ■

EAST TIMOR
(TIMOR-LESTE)

Timor

EAST TIMOR
(TIMOR-LESTE)

Arafura Sea

Torres Strait

Cape
York
Peninsula

CORAL
SEA

Lombok

Sumbawa

Sumba

*Laut
Sawu*

Kupang

MILES		KM
1000		1500
750		1250
		1000
500		750
		500
250		250
0		0

1:28 000 000

© Collins Bartholomew Ltd

131

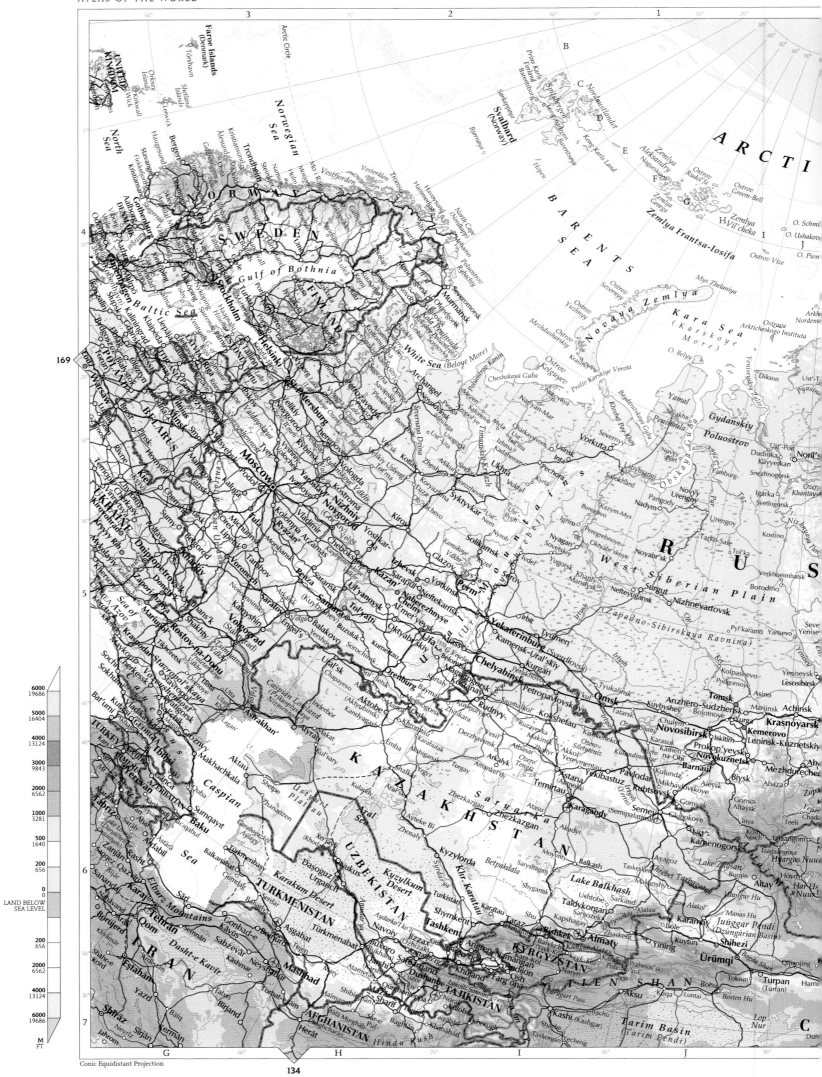

Conic Equidistant Projection

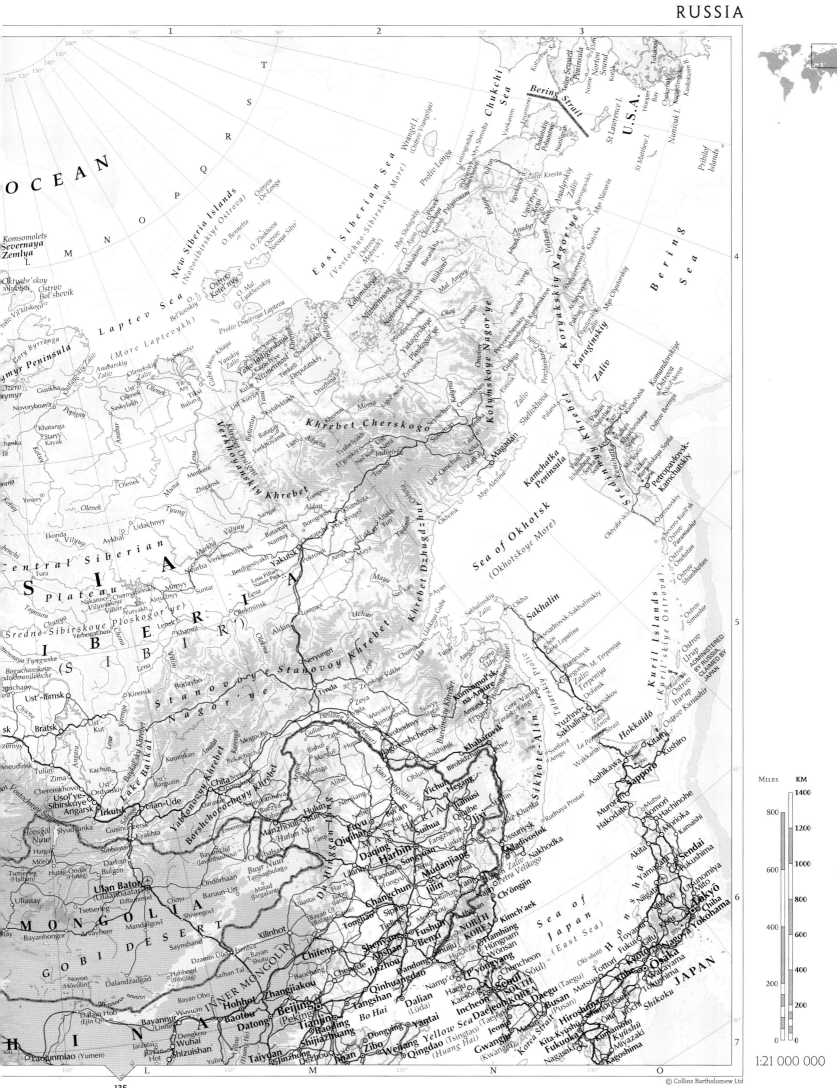

OCEAN

Komsomolets
Severnaya
Zemlya
Oktyabr'skoy
Revolyutsii
Ostrov
Bol'shevik

New Siberia Islands
(Novosibirskiye Ostrova)

Laptev Sea
(More Laptevykh)

East Siberian Sea
(Vostochno-Sibirskoye More)

Wrangel I.
(Ostrov Vrangelya)

Chukchi
Sea

Bering Strait

U.S.A.

Pribilof
Islands

Bering
Sea

Taymyr Peninsula
Gory Byrranga

Khrebet Cherskogo

Koryakskiy Nagor'ye

Karaginskiy
Zaliv

CENTRAL SIBERIAN
Plateau
Sredne-Sibirskoye Ploskogor'ye

SIBERIA
(S

Verkhoyanskiy Khrebet

Yakutsk

Khrebet Dzhugdzhur

Magadan

Kamchatka
Peninsula

Petropavlovsk-
Kamchatskiy

Sea of Okhotsk
(Okhotskoye More)

Stanovoye Nagor'ye

Stanovoy Khrebet

Sakhalin

Kuril Islands
(Kuril'skiye Ostrova)

ADMINISTERED
BY RUSSIA
CLAIMED BY
JAPAN

Ust'-Ilimsk
Bratsk

Lake Baikal

Chita

Komsomol'sk-
na-Amure

Yuzhno-
Sakhalinsk

Hokkaidō

Irkutsk
Ulan-Ude

Yablonovyy Khrebet

Borshchovochnyy Khrebet

Manzhouli

Hailar

Khabarovsk

Birobidzhan

Sikhote-Alin'

Asahikawa

Sapporo

Muroran
Hakodate

Sendai

Ulan Bator
(Ulaanbaatar)

MONGOLIA

GOBI DESERT

Buyr Nuur

Qiqihar

Daqing
Harbin

MANCHURIA

Suihua

Jixi

Vladivostok
Nakhodka

Ussuriysk

Sea of
Japan
(East Sea)

HONSHŪ

Tōkyō
Yokohama

JAPAN

Changchun

Mudanjiang

Jilin

NORTH
KOREA

P'yŏngyang

Hiroshima

Ōsaka

Nagoya

Shenyang
Anshan

Fushun
Benxi

Dandong

Seoul
(Sŏul)

SOUTH
KOREA

Busan
(Pusan)

Fukuoka

KYŪSHŪ

SHIKOKU

Hohhot
Zhangjiakou
Beijing
(Peking)

Datong
Baotou

Tianjin

Tangshan

Dalian
(Lüda)

Yantai

Bo Hai

Yellow Sea
(Huang Hai)

Qingdao
(Tsingtao)

INNER MONGOLIA

CHINA

Taiyuan

Shijiazhuang

Jinan

Zibo

© Collins Bartholomew Ltd

Miles   KM

1:21 000 000

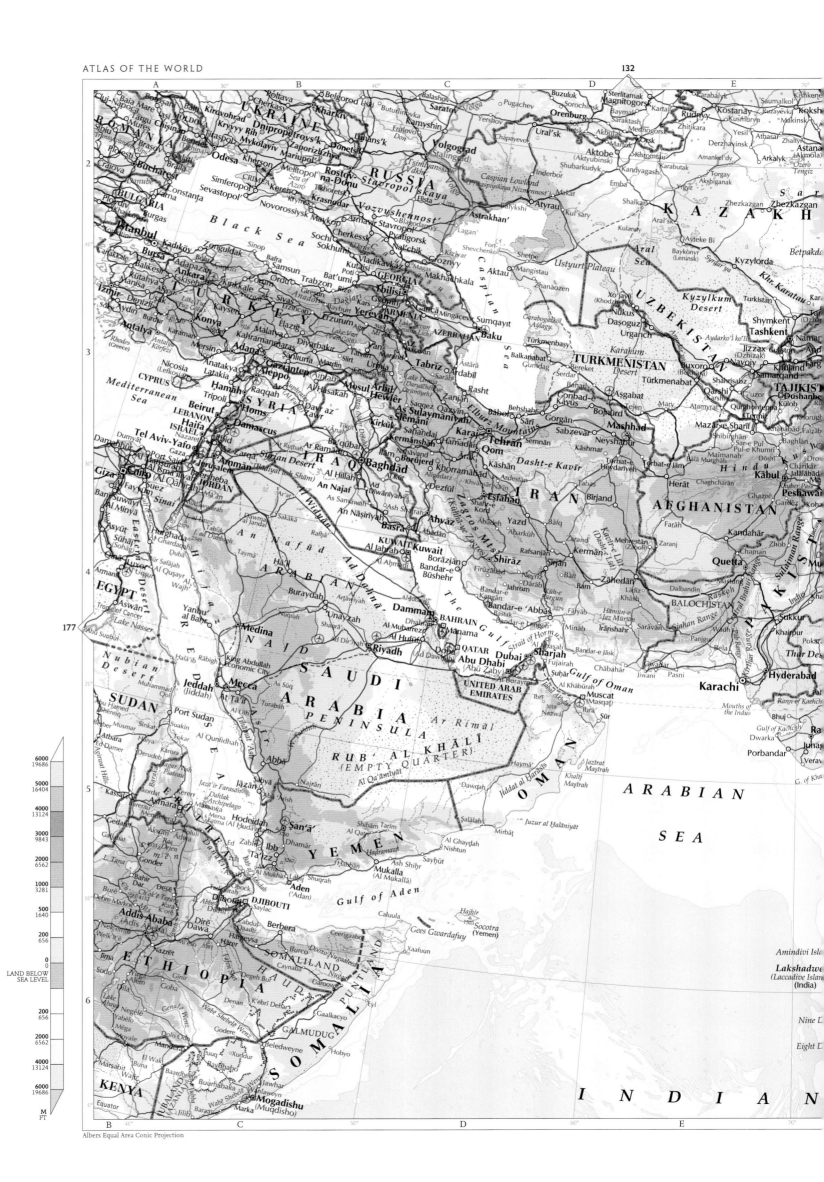

Albers Equal Area Conic Projection

146

147

155

1:20 000 000

MILES	KM
	1400
800	1200
600	1000
	800
400	600
200	400
	200
0	0

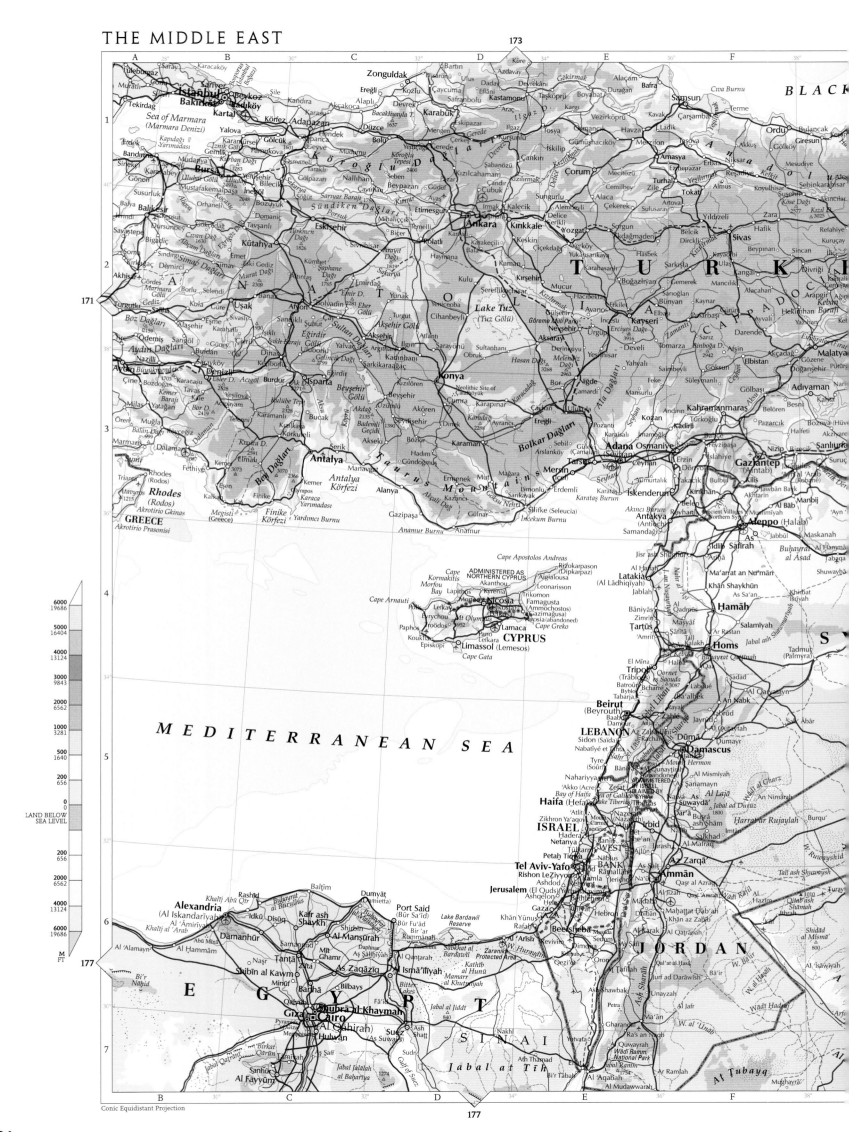

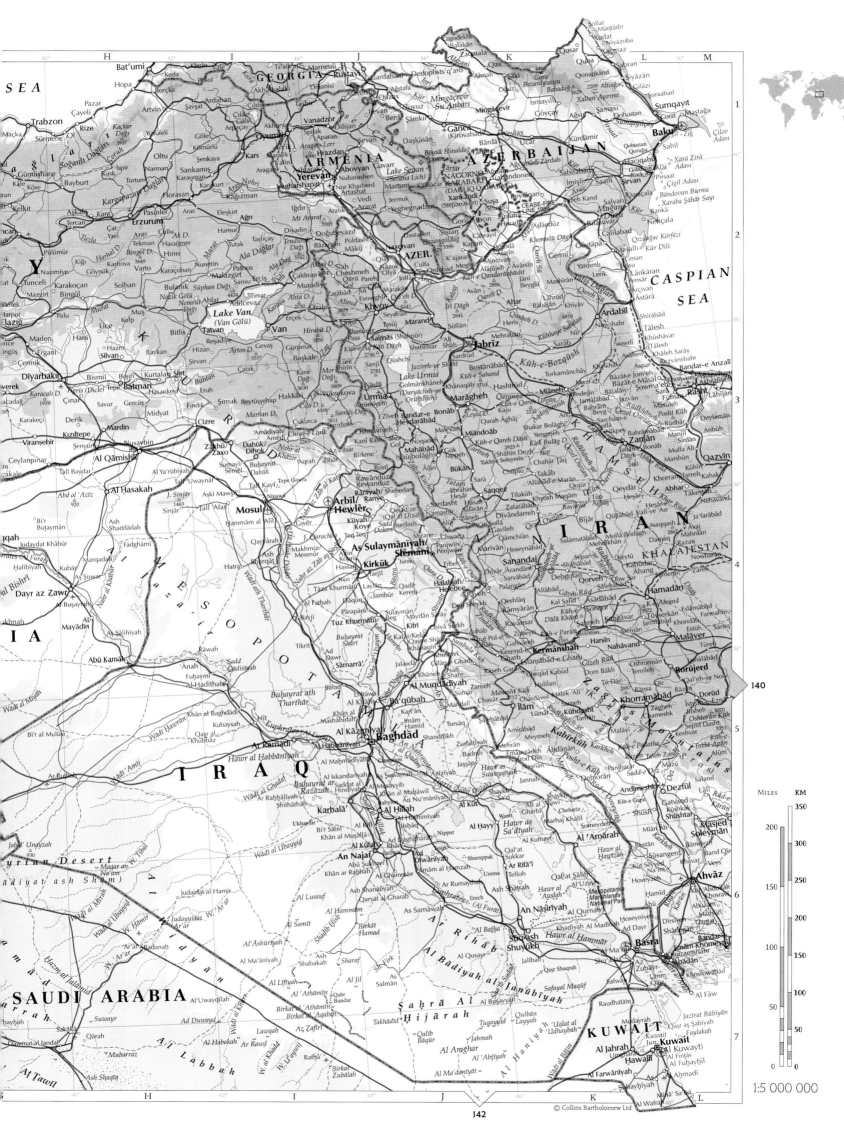

1:5 000 000

Conic Equidistant Projection

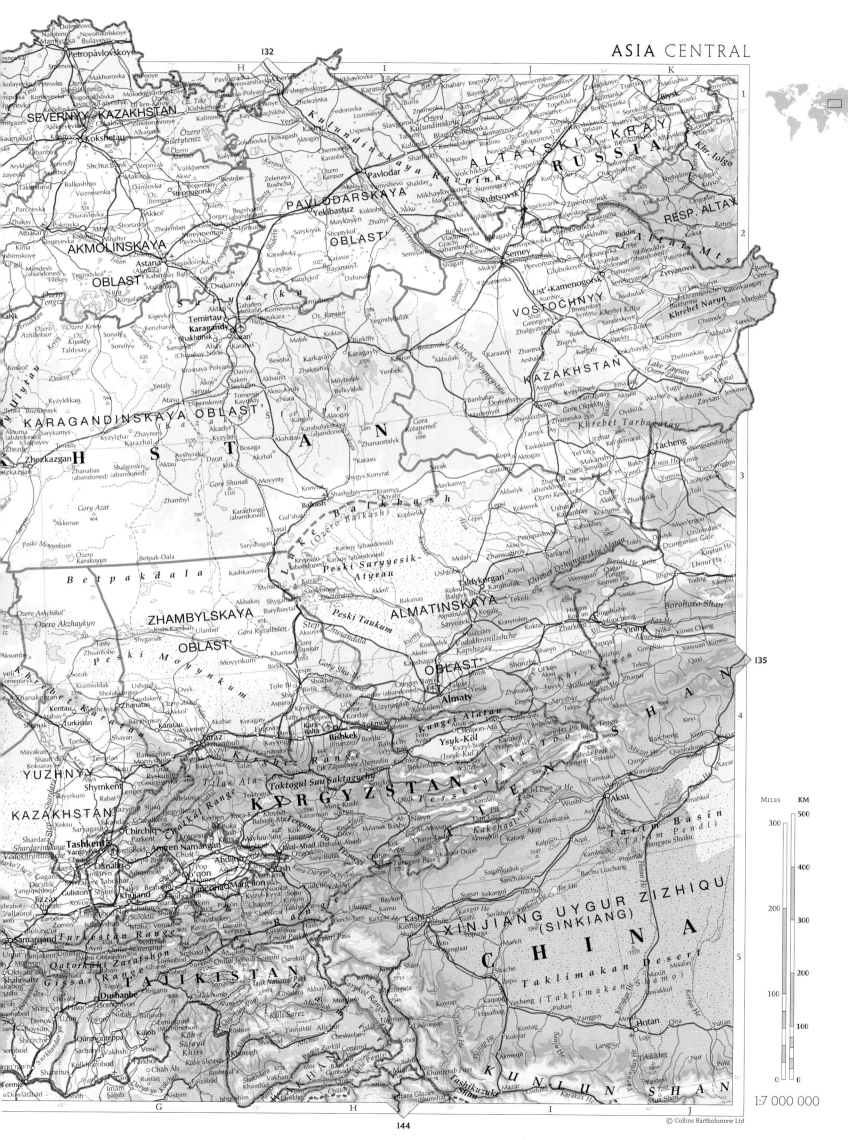

1:7 000 000

MILES   KM
300 —   — 500
          — 400
200 —   — 300
          — 200
100 —   — 100
0 —   — 0

© Collins Bartholomew Ltd

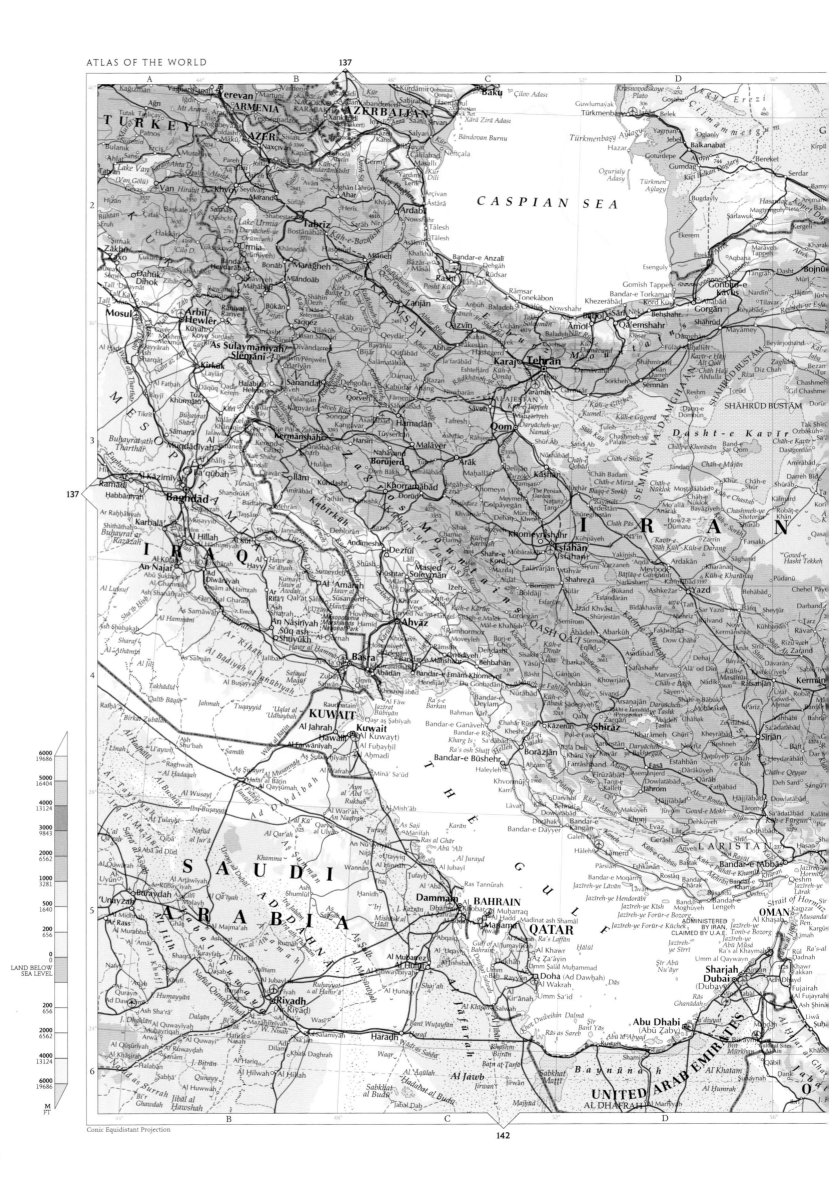

Conic Equidistant Projection

THE GULF, IRAN AND AFGHANISTAN

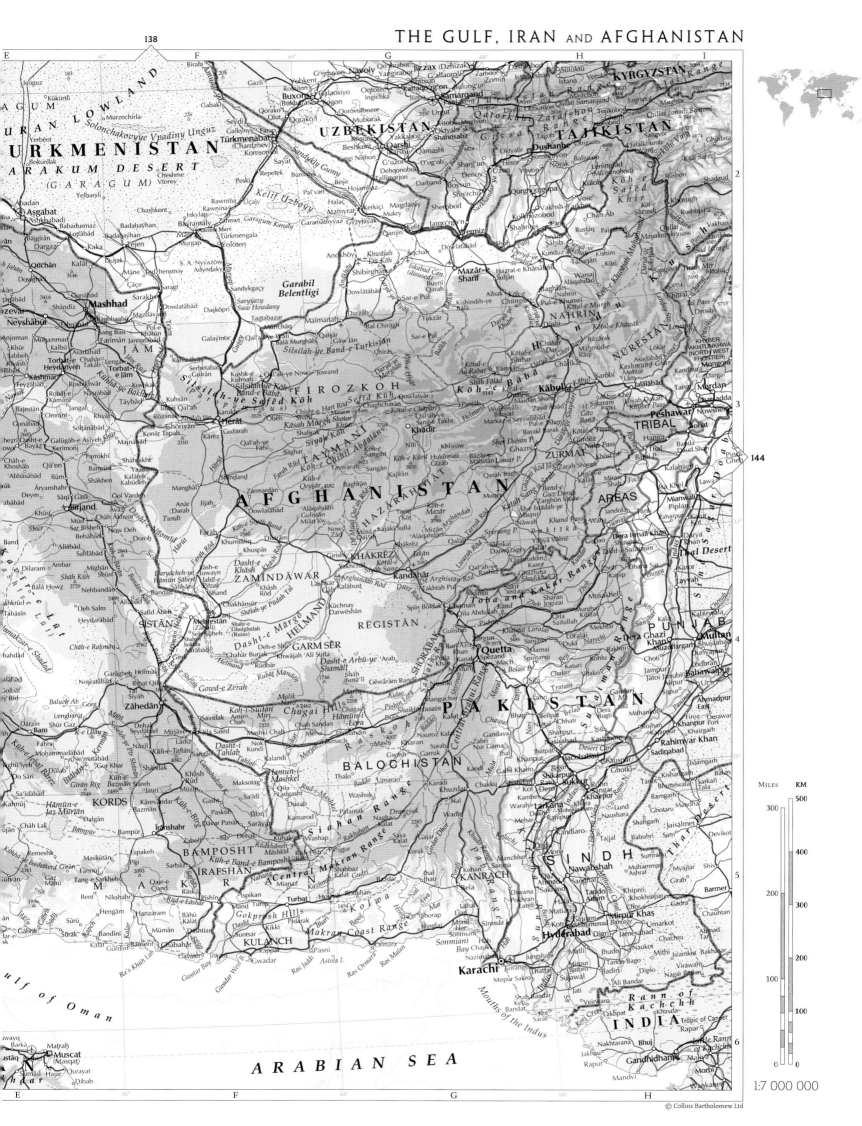

1:7 000 000

© Collins Bartholomew Ltd

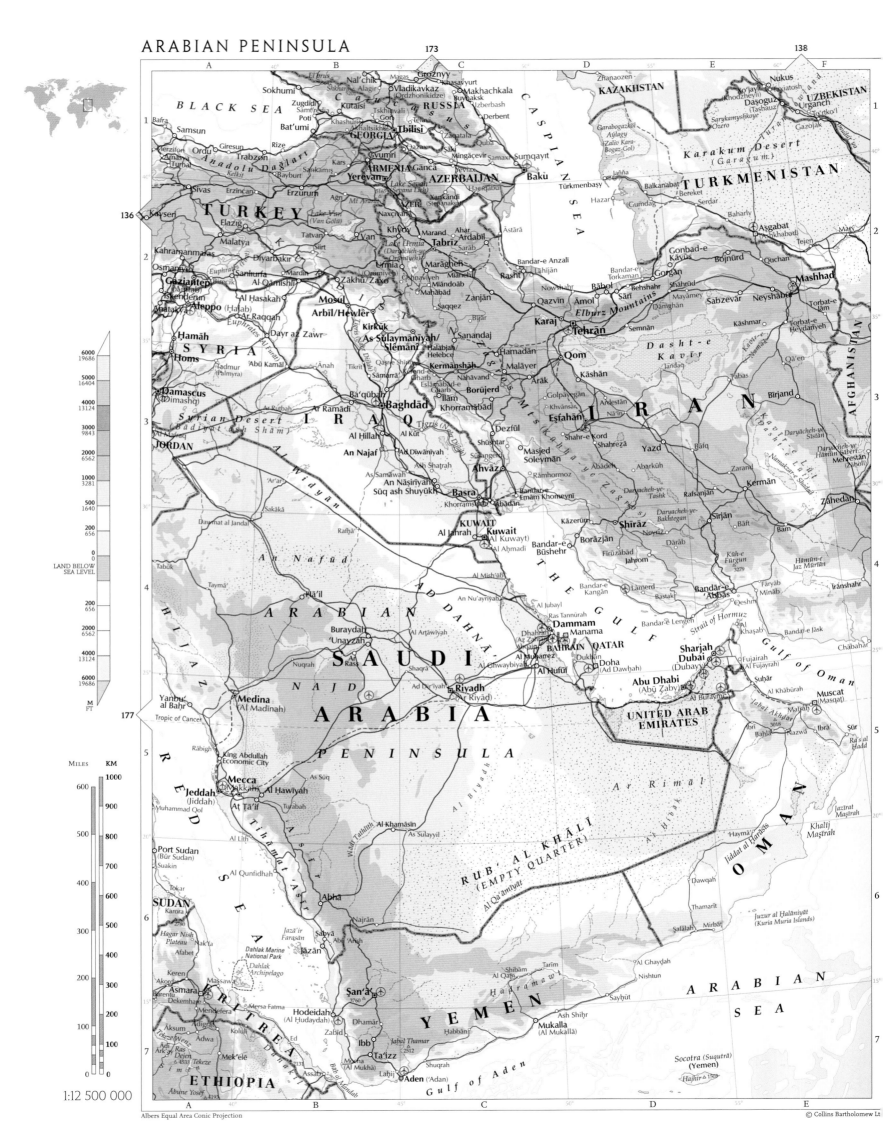

ARABIAN PENINSULA

173

138

136

177

1:12 500 000

Albers Equal Area Conic Projection

© Collins Bartholomew Lt

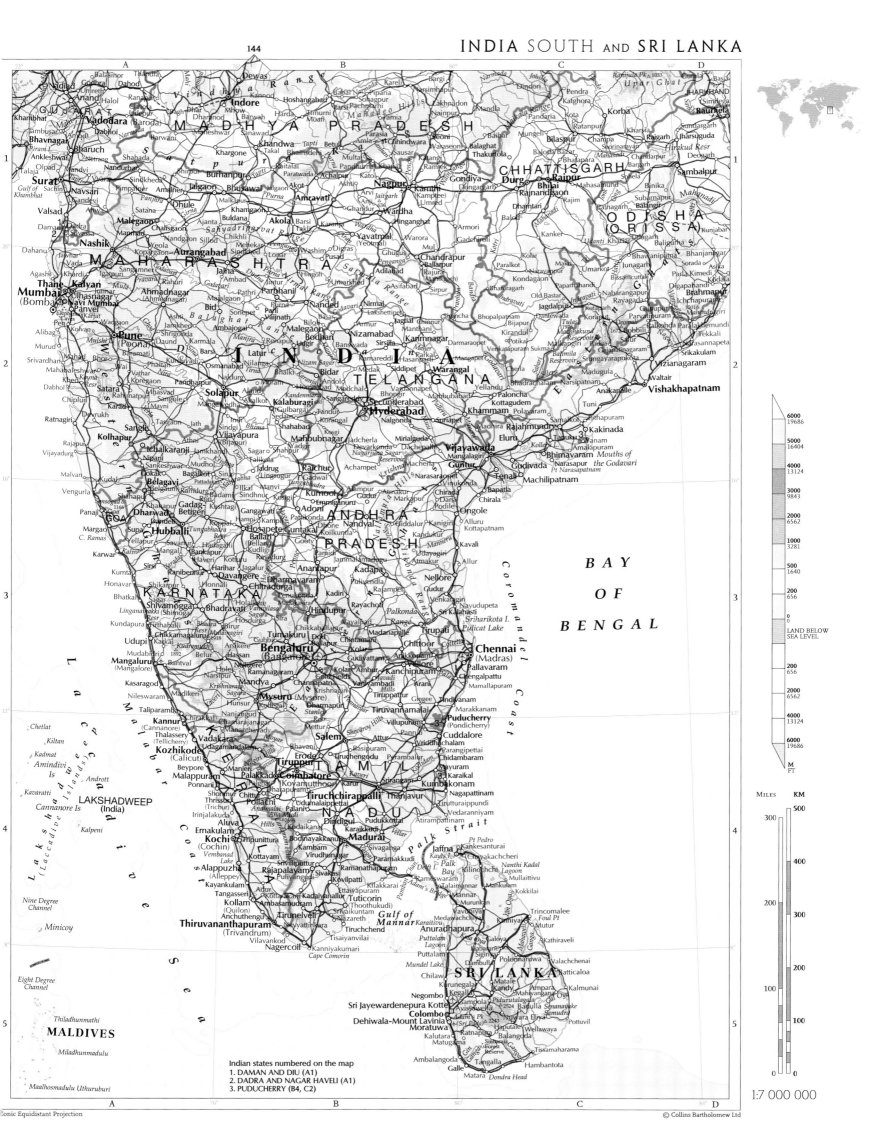

144

GUJARAT
Balasinor · Thandla · Dahod
Nadiad · Godhra · Dohad
Anand · Halol
Bhavnagar · Mhow · Indore · Dewas · Narmada · Johila · Upar Ghat · Gumla · Basia
Khambhat · Ankleshwar · Dhamnod · Hoshangabad · Harsud · Hatarsi · Mungeli · Bilaspur · Raigarh · Kharsia · Jharsuguda
Bhiram I · Opad · Sachin · Dabhoi · Khargone · Harda · Timurni · Mahadeo · Mandla · Korba · Champa · Serrinarayan · Bargarh
Surat · Navsari · Nandurbar · Burhanpur · Takal · Bhainsdehi · Chhindwara · Seoni · Balaghat · Balody Bazar · Chandrapur · Deogarh

MADHYA PRADESH

MAHARASHTRA

CHHATTISGARH

ODISHA (ORISSA)

INDIA

TELANGANA

ANDHRA PRADESH

KARNATAKA

GOA

TAMIL NADU

KERALA

BAY

OF

BENGAL

Arabian Sea

MALDIVES

LAKSHADWEEP (India)

SRI LANKA

Gulf of Mannar

Palk Strait

Indian states numbered on the map
1. DAMAN AND DIU (A1)
2. DADRA AND NAGAR HAVELI (A1)
3. PUDUCHERRY (B4, C2)

Conic Equidistant Projection

1:7 000 000

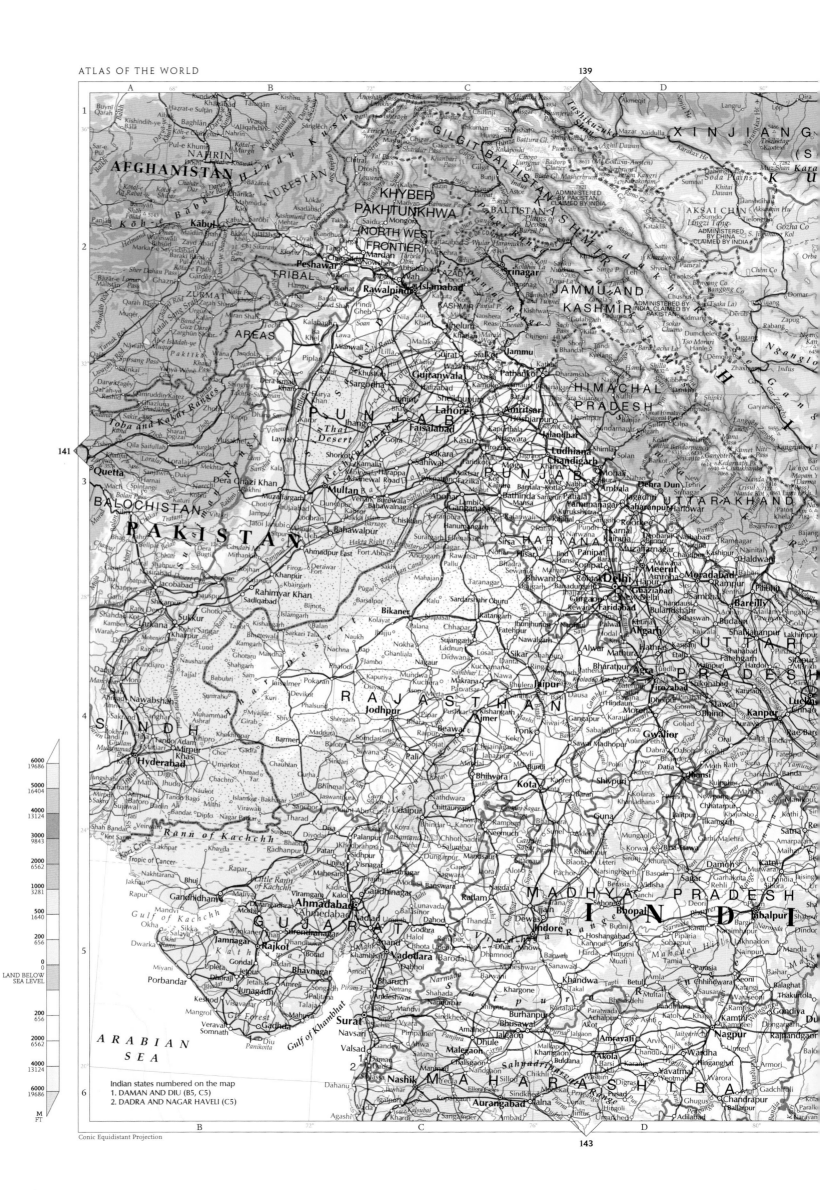

Indian states numbered on the map
1. DAMAN AND DIU (B5, C5)
2. DADRA AND NAGAR HAVELI (C5)

Conic Equidistant Projection

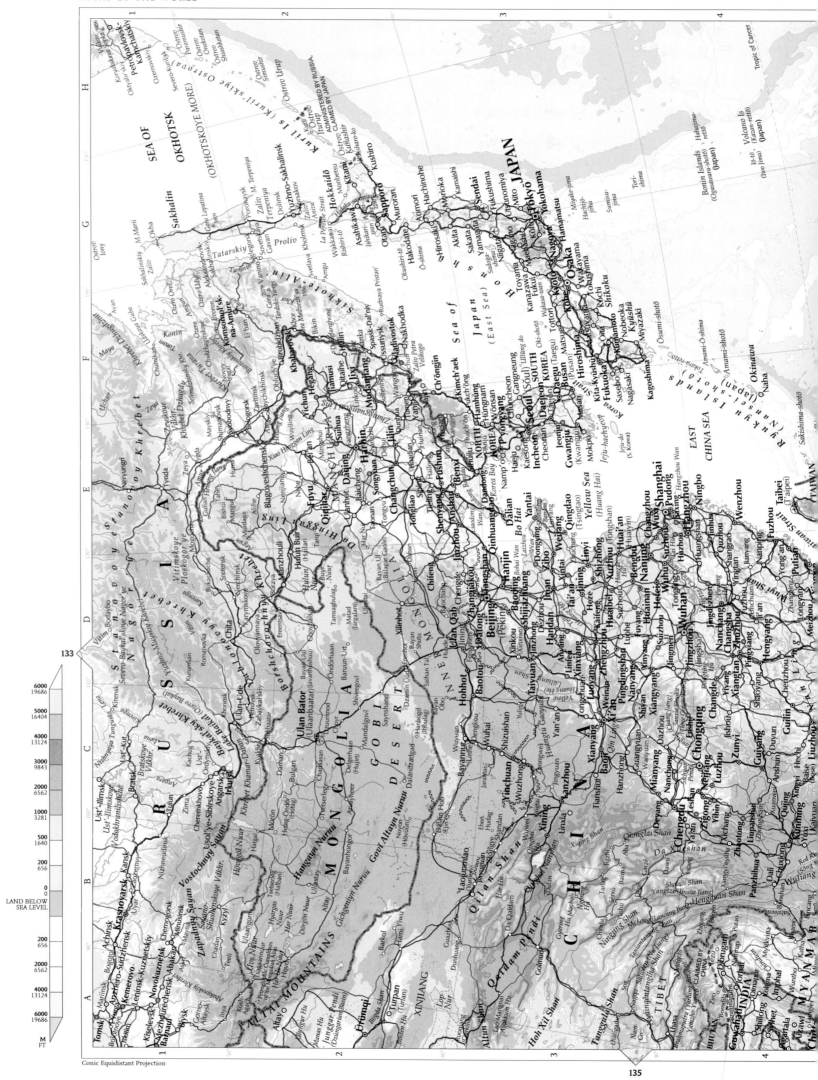

Conic Equidistant Projection

146

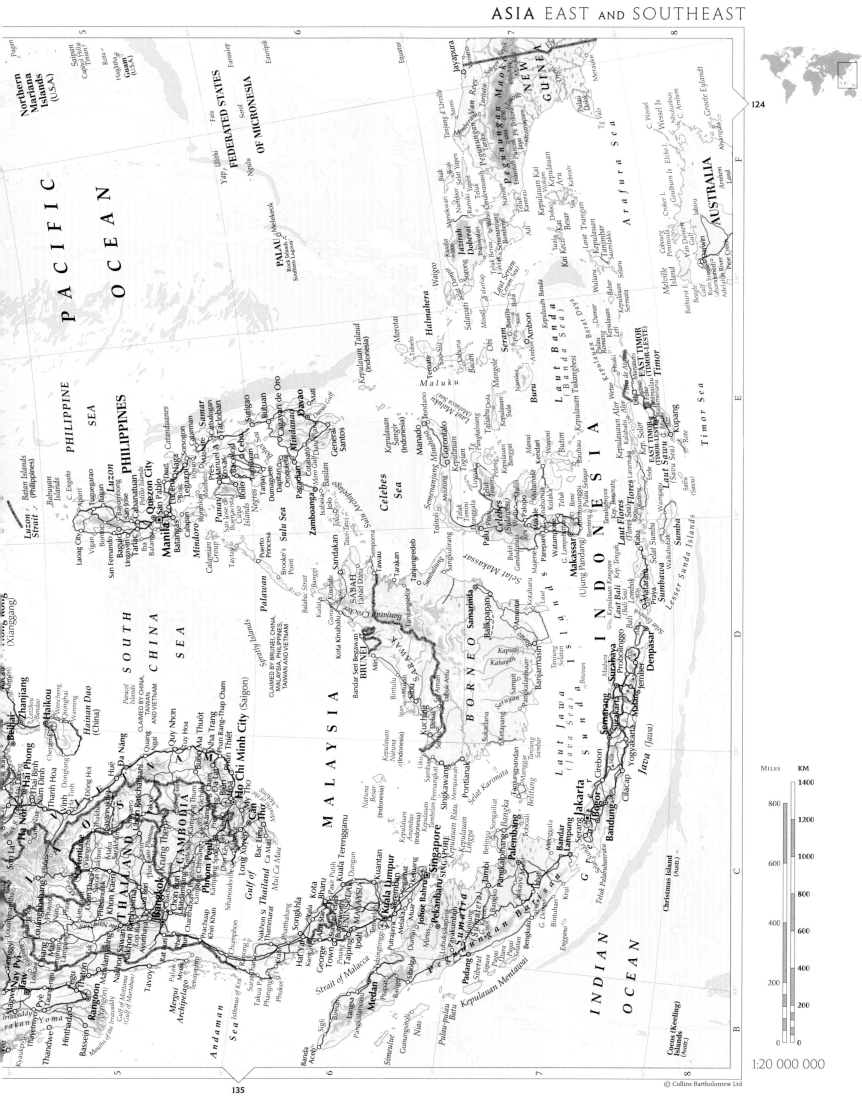

1:20 000 000

© Collins Bartholomew Ltd

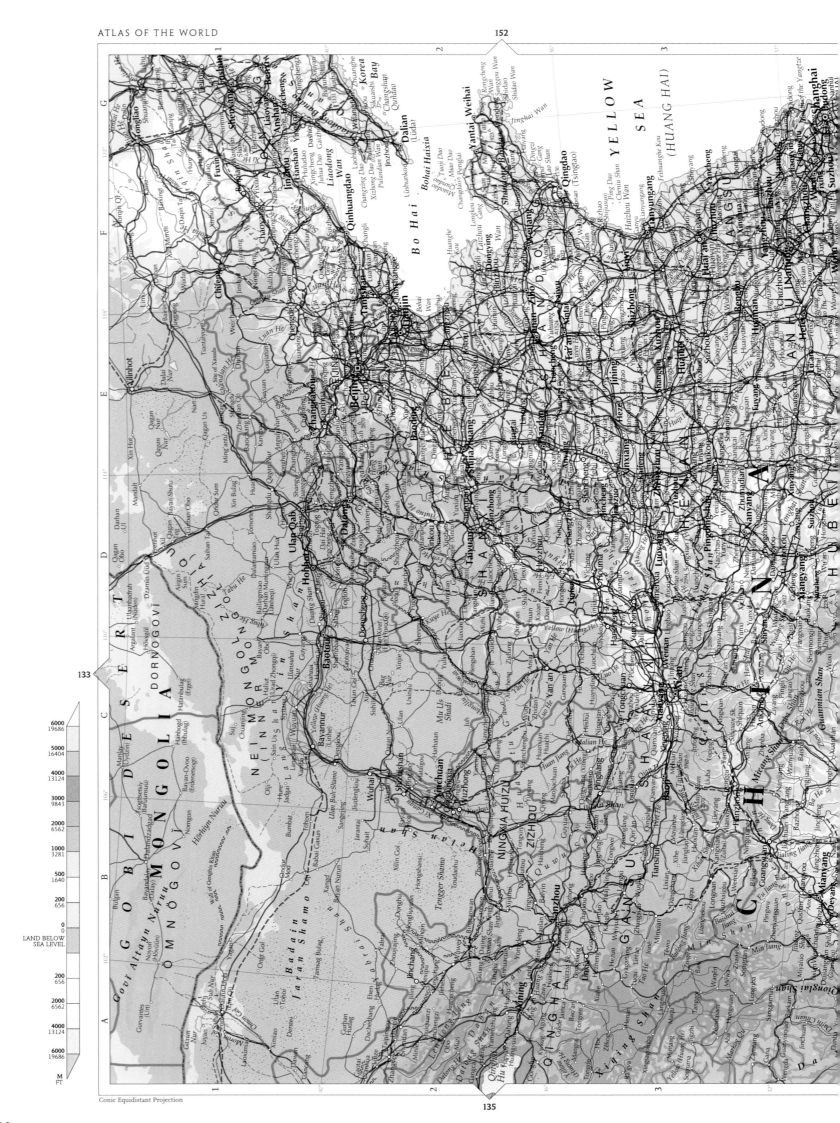

Conic Equidistant Projection

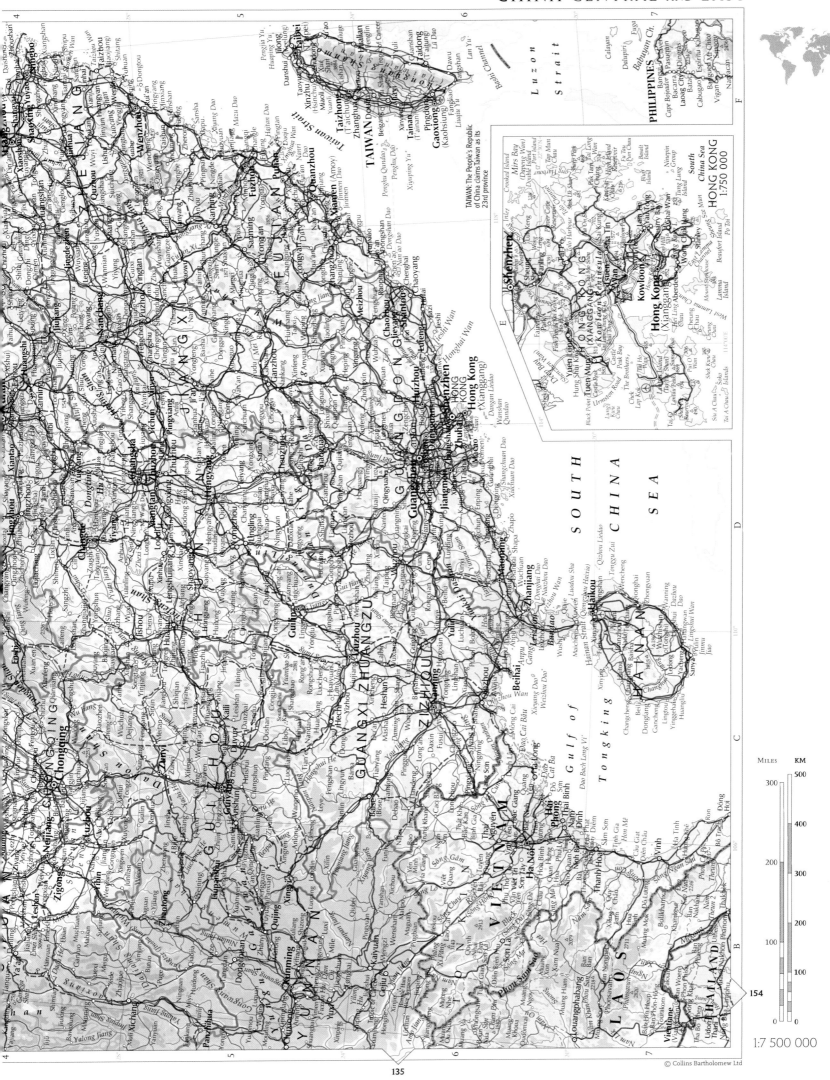

© Collins Bartholomew Ltd

1:7 500 000

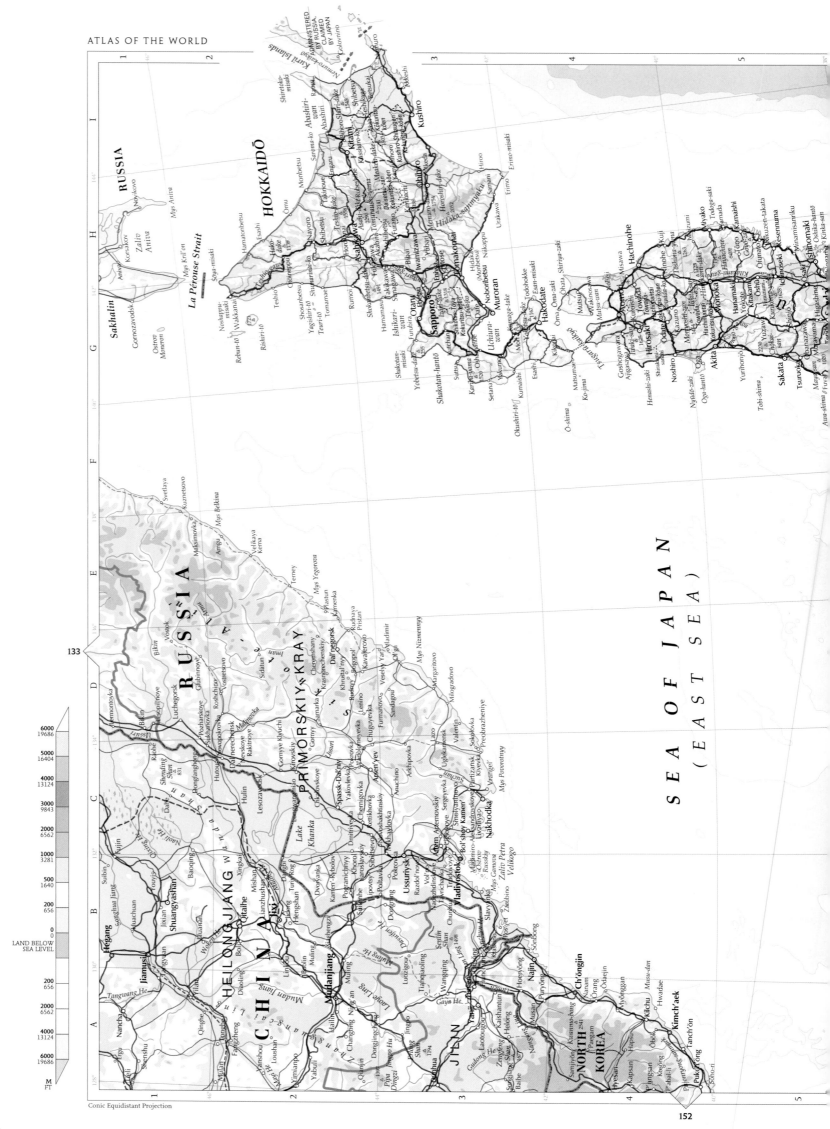

RUSSIA

Sakhalin

La Pérouse Strait

HOKKAIDŌ

SAPPORO

Hakodate

Muroran

Noboribetsu

Otaru

Kushiro

Kitami

Hachinohe

Hirosaki

Akita

Sakata

RUSSIA

PRIMORSKIY KRAY

S E A   O F   J A P A N
(E A S T   S E A)

133

HEILONGJIANG

CHINA

Hegang

Jiamusi

Shuangyashan

Qitaihe

Mudanjiang

Jilin

JILIN

Ussuriysk

Vladivostok

Nakhodka

Ch'ŏngjin

Najin

Kimch'aek

NORTH
KOREA

Conic Equidistant Projection

152

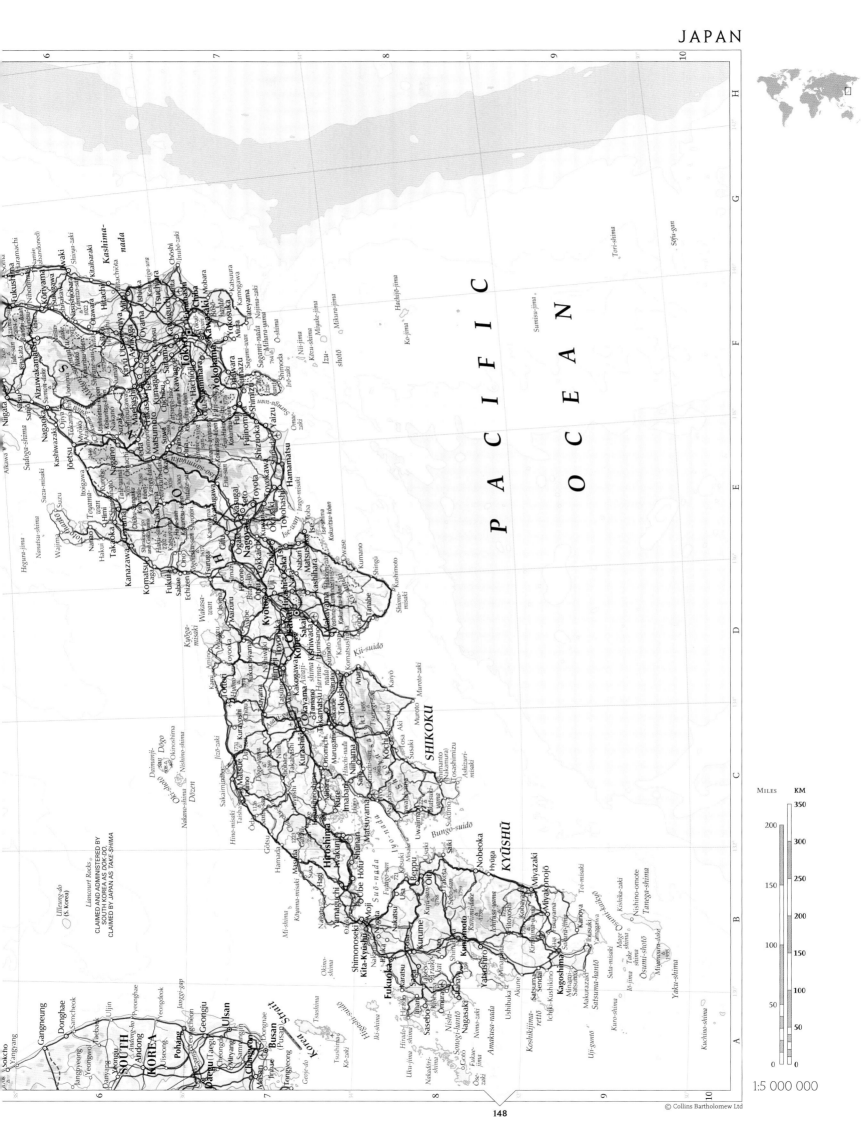

© Collins Bartholomew Ltd

1:5 000 000

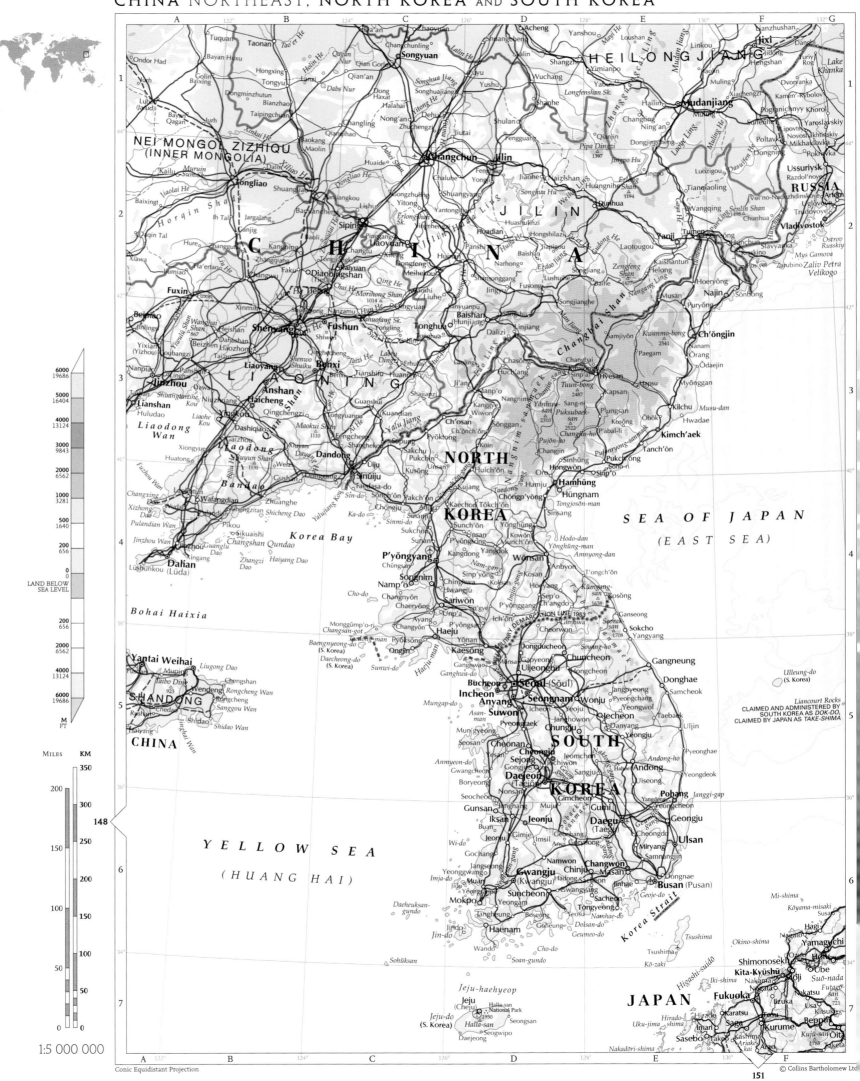

Conic Equidistant Projection

© Collins Bartholomew Ltd

1:5 000 000

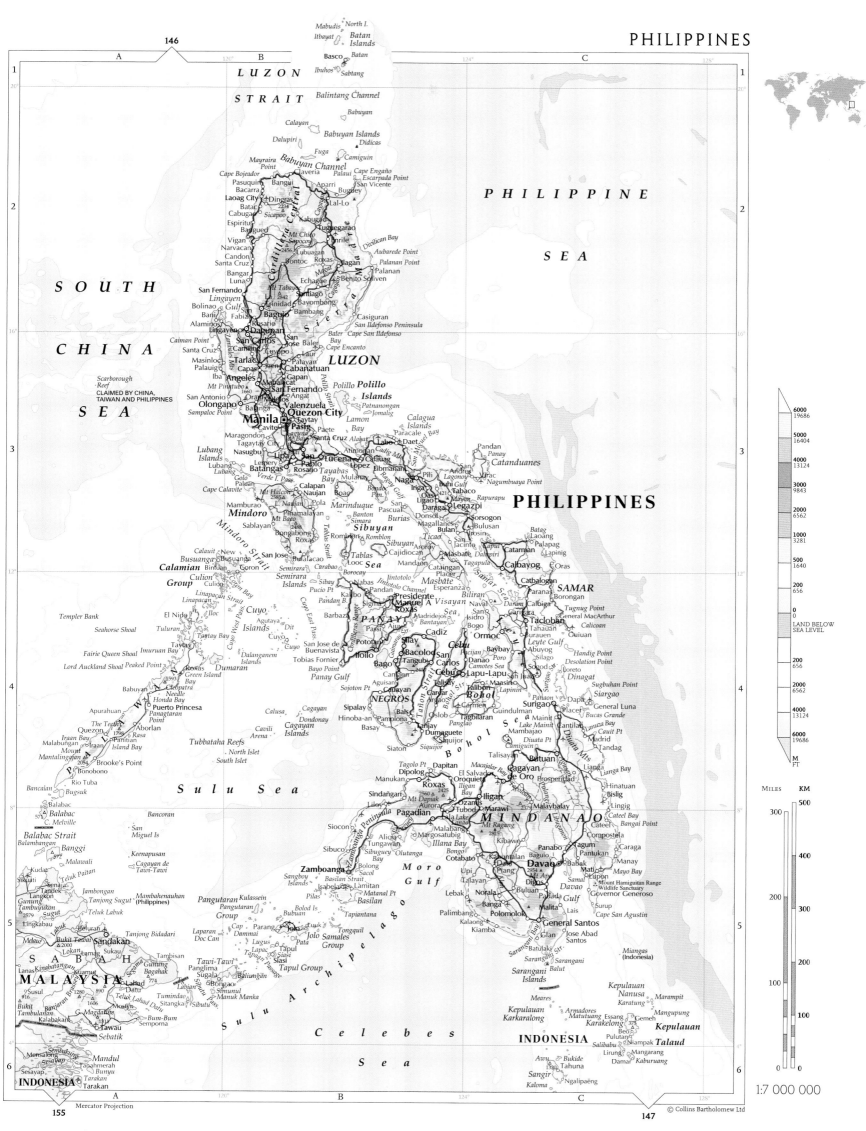

PHILIPPINES

1:7 000 000

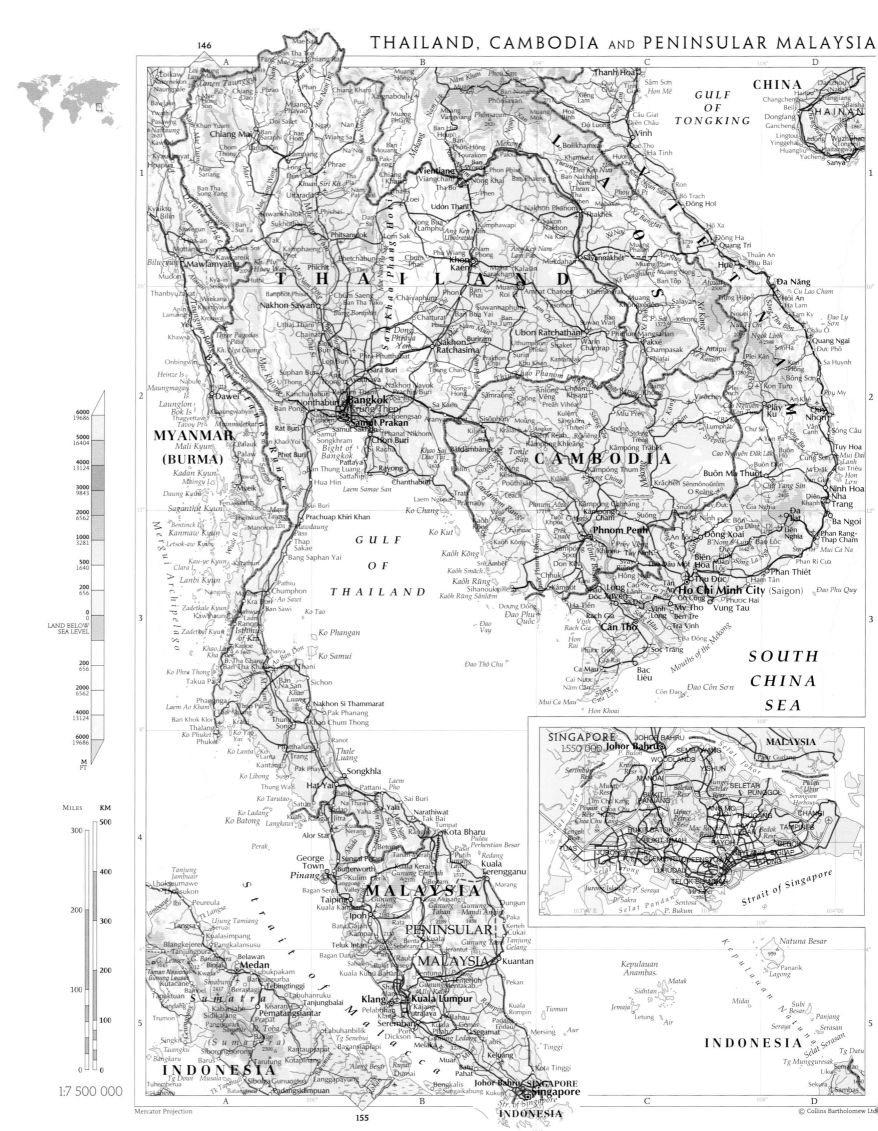

CHINA

GULF OF TONGKING

HAINAN

LAOS

THAILAND

MYANMAR (BURMA)

Chiang Mai

Vientiane

Bangkok
Krung Thep

Samut Prakan

GULF OF THAILAND

CAMBODIA

Phnom Penh

Ho Chi Minh City (Saigon)

Cân Thơ

VIETNAM

SOUTH CHINA SEA

MALAYSIA

PENINSULAR MALAYSIA

Kuala Lumpur

SINGAPORE
1:550 000

SINGAPORE
Singapore

JOHOR BAHRU

MALAYSIA

Strait of Singapore

INDONESIA

Medan

Sumatra

Natuna Besar

Kepulauan Anambas

1:7 500 000

LAND BELOW SEA LEVEL

MILES   KM

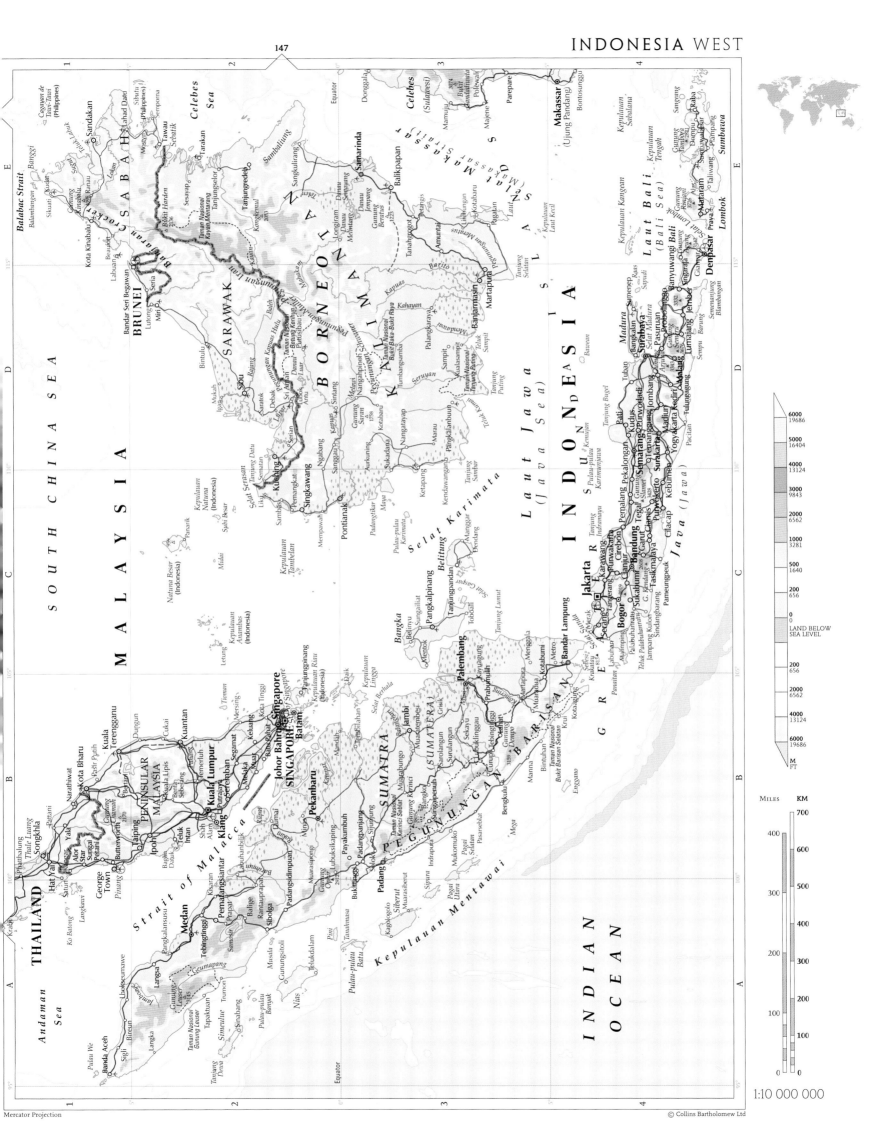

1 2 3 4

Balabac Strait

Cagayan de Tawi-Tawi (Philippines)

Balambangan Banggi

Sibutu (Philippines)

Sandakan
Lahad Datu
Mostyn (Philippines)
Semporna
Tawu
Sebatik

Celebes Sea

Celebes (Sulawesi)

Donggala
Equator
Parepare
Polewali
Bontosunggu

Makassar (Ujung Pandang)

E

Kota Kinabalu
S A B A H
Labuan

Gunung Kinabalu
Beaufort
Ranau
Tenom

Tarakan
Sangkulirang
Mamuju
Majene

Kepulauan Sabalana

Bukit Bandandiwata
3074
Kepulauan
Tengah

Laut Bali (Bali Sea)

Gunung Tambora
2851

Bima
Dompu
Raba
Plampang
Sumbawa

Bandar Seri Begawan
BRUNEI
Lutong
Miri
Seria
Longiram
Danau
Melintang
Danau
Jempang
Gunung
Beratus
1225

Samarinda
Balikpapan

Selat Makassar (Makassar Strait)

S U L
Laut Bali
Mataram
Ampenan
Gunung Rinjani
3726
Sandubaya
Selat Lombok
Lombok

D

Bukit Harden
2136

Taman Nasional
Kayan Mentarang

Tanjungselor
Tanjungredeb
Sesayap

Kotabaru
Pagatan

Denpasar
Bali
Gianyar
Ubung
Nusa Penida
Semarapura

SARAWAK
Bintulu
Sibu

B O R N E O
Kapuas

Muara Teweh
Barito

Tanjung
Selatan

Banyuwangi

Madiun
Malang
Lumajang
Jember

Mukah
Sarikei
Debak

Gunung
Saran
1758
Kotabaru

Banjarmasin
Martapura

Probolinggo
Pasuruan

D

Kuching
Serian

Ngabang

Pontianak

Mempawah

Singkawang

Sambas

Kepulauan Natuna (Indonesia)

Natuna Besar

Midai

Panarik

Kepulauan Anambas (Indonesia)

Kepulauan Tambelan

Kepulauan Karimata

Belitung

Pangkalpinang

Bangka

Laut Jawa (Java Sea)

I N D O N E S I A

Pulau-pulau Karimunjawa

Pemalang
Pekalongan
Tegal
Semarang
Purwokerto
Kendal
Cirebon
Indramayu

Tuban
Pati
Kudus
Bangkalan
Madura
Surabaya
Jombang
Kediri
Madiun

C

S O U T H   C H I N A   S E A

M A L A Y S I A

THAILAND

George Town
Pinang
Butterworth
Taiping
Ipoh

PENINSULAR
MALAYSIA

Kuala Lumpur
Klang

Johor Bahru
Singapore
SINGAPORE
Batam

Pekanbaru

S U M A T E R A
(SUMATRA)

Palembang

Jambi

Jakarta
Bogor
Bandung
Karawang
Purwakarta
Sukabumi
Cianjur
Tasikmalaya
Garut

J a w a (J a v a)

Yogyakarta
Surakarta

Bandar Lampung
Metro

B

P E G U N U N G A N   B A R I S A N

Padang
Bukittinggi

G R E A T

Medan
Pematangsiantar
Tebingtinggi

Strait of Malacca

Kisaran

Padangsidimpuan

Nias

Sibolga

Padang

Kepulauan Mentawai

Bengkulu

I N D I A N
O C E A N

A

*Andaman
Sea*

Banda Aceh

Taman Nasional
Gunung Leuser

Equator

Mercator Projection
© Collins Bartholomew Ltd

6000 19686
5000 16404
4000 13124
3000 9843
2000 6562
1000 3281
500 1640
200 656
0
LAND BELOW SEA LEVEL
200 656
2000 6562
4000 13124
6000 19686
M
FT

MILES   KM
400   700
600
300   500
400
200   300
200
100   100
0   0

1:10 000 000

155

F G H I J

Kara
Sea

Ostrov
Yuzhnyy

Novaya Zemlya

Ostrov
Kolguyev

Vorkuta

Arctic Circle

Yenisey

2

Murmansk

White Sea

Pechora

Ural Mountains

Ob'

Irtysh

RUSSIA

Altai Mountains

ASIA

Archangel

Severnaya Dvina

Syktyvkar

3

INLAND

Tampere

Petrozavodsk

Lake
Onega

Kirov   Perm'

Izhevsk   Naberezhnyye
Chelny

Ufa

Lake
Balkhash

Tien Shan

Turku   Helsinki

Lake
Ladoga

Vologda

Rubinskoye
Vodokhranilishche

Kazan'

Orenburg

Ysyk-Köl

St Petersburg

Yaroslavl'   Nizhniy Novgorod

Ulyanovsk

Samara

Aral Sea

ESTONIA

Tallinn

Lake
Peipus

Volga

Hindu Kush

Gotland   LATVIA   Riga

Moscow

Tula   Penza

Saratov

4

and   LITHUANIA   Vilnius

Vitsyebsk

Smolensk

Voronezh

Caspian Sea

Kaliningrad   RUSSIA

BELARUS   Minsk

Mahilyow

Don   Volgograd

Gdańsk   Białystok

Homyel'   Chernihiv   Belgorod

Astrakhan

Garabogazköl
Aylagy

POLAND   Brest

Sumy

Kharkiv

Volga

dgoszcz   Warsaw   UKRAINE

Kiev

Rostov-na-Donu

oznań   Łódź   Rivne

Dnipropetrovs'k

5

Odra   Wrocław   L'viv   Dniester   Kirovohrad   Donets'k   Stavropol'

Krasnodar   Elbrus   Groznyy   Caucasus

Katowice   Kraków   Carpathian Mountains   MOLDOVA   Iaşi   Chişinău

Prague   SLOVAKIA   Košice   Odessa   Sea
of Azov

CZECH   Brno   CRIMEA
EPUBLIC   Danube   Vienna   Bratislava   Debrecen   ROMANIA   Simferopol'   Novorossiysk

USTRIA   HUNGARY   Szeged   Braşov   Black Sea   TURKEY

Salzburg   Budapest

SLOVENIA   Zagreb   Timişoara   Bucharest

bljana   CROATIA   Craiova   Danube   Varna

Venice   Belgrade   Burgas

gna   BOSNIA AND   SERBIA   Niş   BULGARIA

SAN   HERZEGOVINA   Sofia

MARINO   Sarajevo   MONTENEGRO   Prishtinë   Edirne   Istanbul

ITALY   Split   Podgorica   KOSOVO   Skopje   Sea of
Marmara

ome   Adriatic Sea   Tirana   ALBANIA   MACEDONIA   Thessaloniki

Bari   Larisa   Aegean
Sea   GREECE

Naples   Ionian   Athens

Tyrrhenian   Sea   Dodecanese   Rhodes

Sea   Cosenza   Cyprus

Palermo   Messina

Sicily   Crete

Syracuse

R   Valletta   T   E   R
MALTA

A   N   E   A   N   S   E   A

Euphrates

Tigris   Zagros Mountains

The Gulf

ASIA

R   I   C   A

© Collins Bartholomew Ltd

MILES   KM

800   1200

1000

600   800

400   600

200   400

200

0   0

1:17 500 000

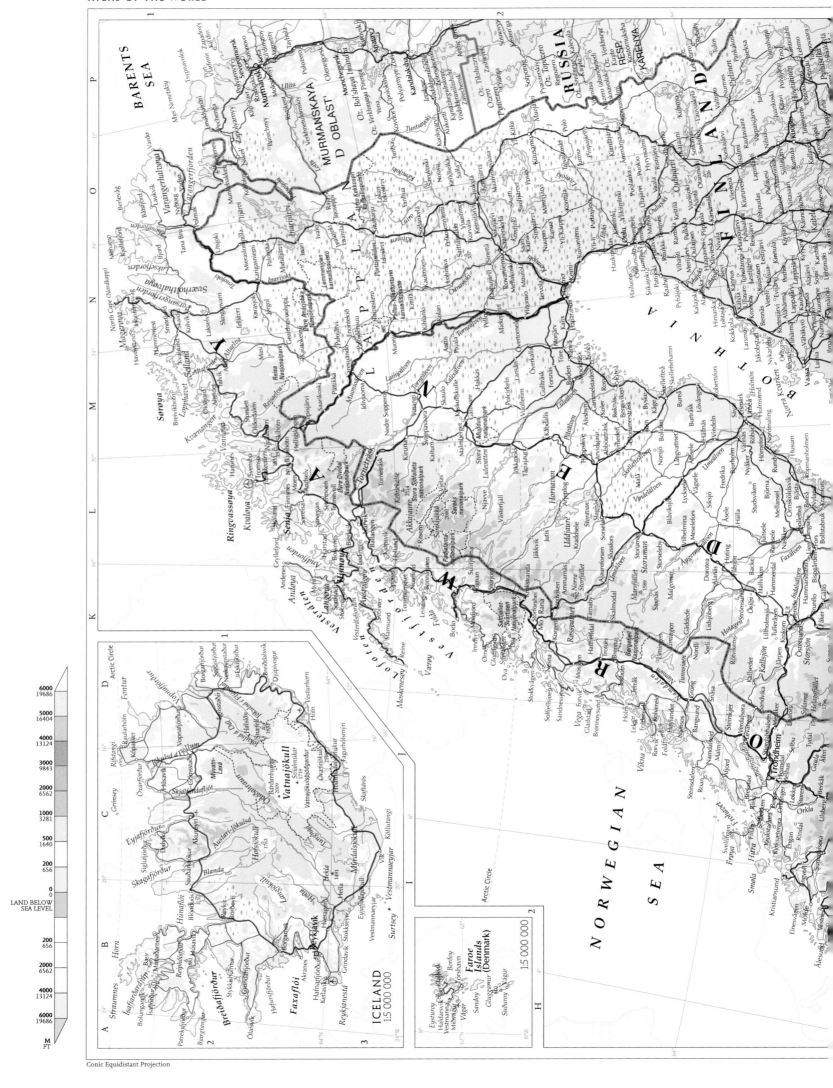

ICELAND
1:5 000 000

Faroe Islands (Denmark)
1:5 000 000

Conic Equidistant Projection

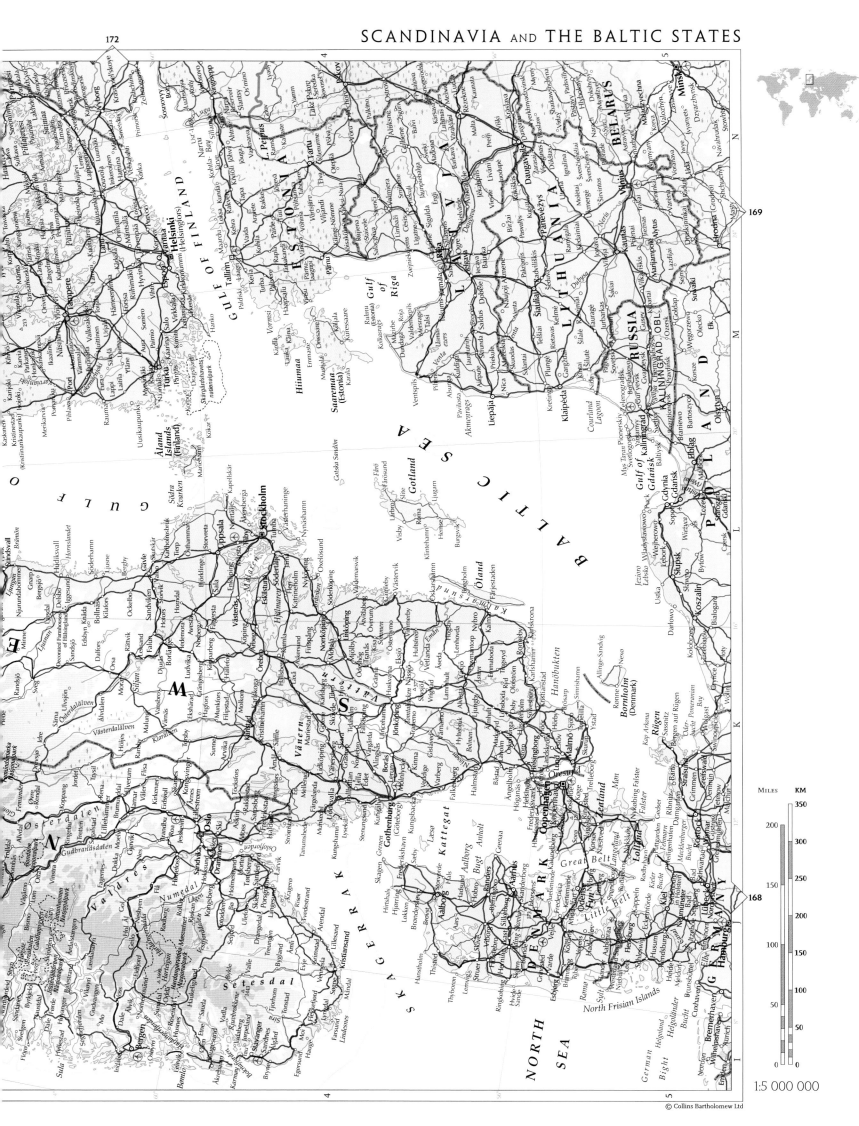

MILES   KM

1:5 000 000

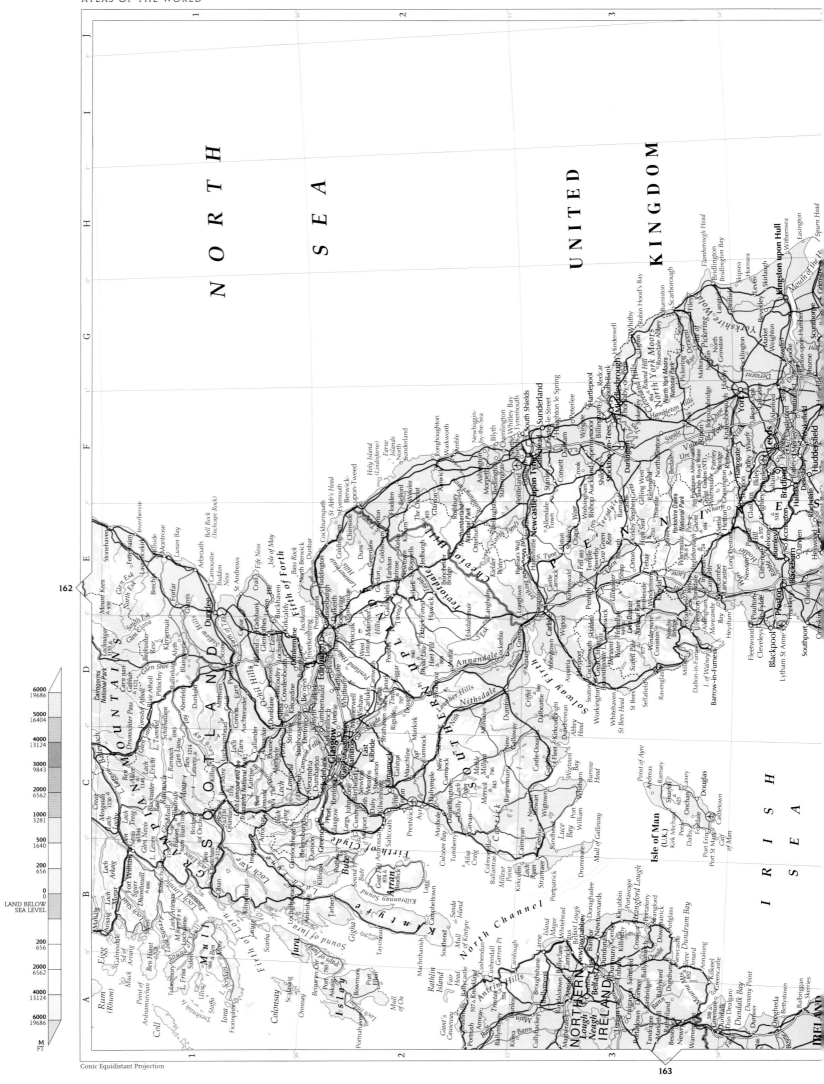

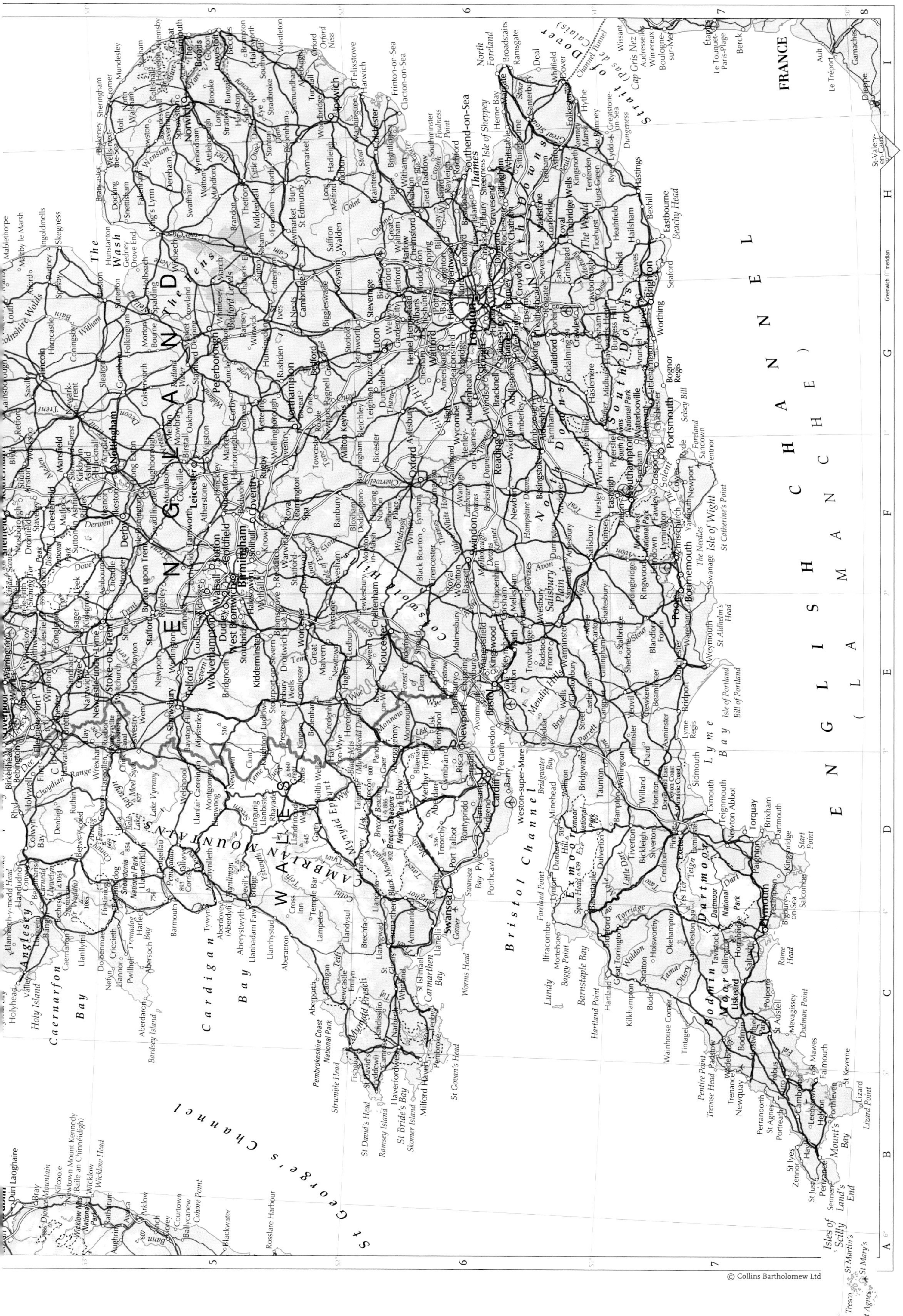

FRANCE

166

ENGLAND

WALES

CAMBRIAN MOUNTAINS

North Downs

South Downs

Chilterns

Cotswold Hills

The Fens

The Wash

Anglesey

Holy Island

Caernarfon Bay

Cardigan Bay

St George's Channel

Bristol Channel

ENGLISH CHANNEL (LA MANCHE)

Strait of Dover (Pas de Calais)

Isle of Wight

Isle of Portland

Lyme Bay

Bay of Biscay

Lundy

Isles of Scilly

Dartmoor

Exmoor

Bodmin Moor

Snowdonia National Park

Pembrokeshire Coast National Park

Brecon Beacons National Park

Thames

Severn

Trent

© Collins Bartholomew Ltd

MILES KM

1:2 000 000

SCOTLAND

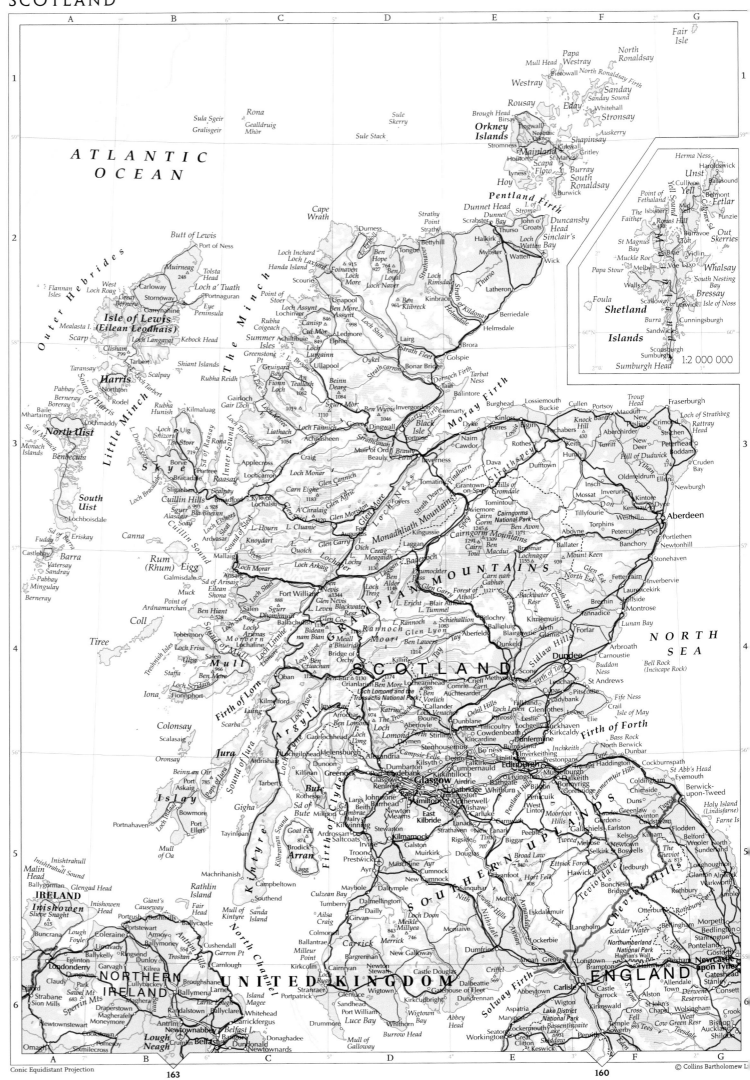

Conic Equidistant Projection

© Collins Bartholomew L...

163

160

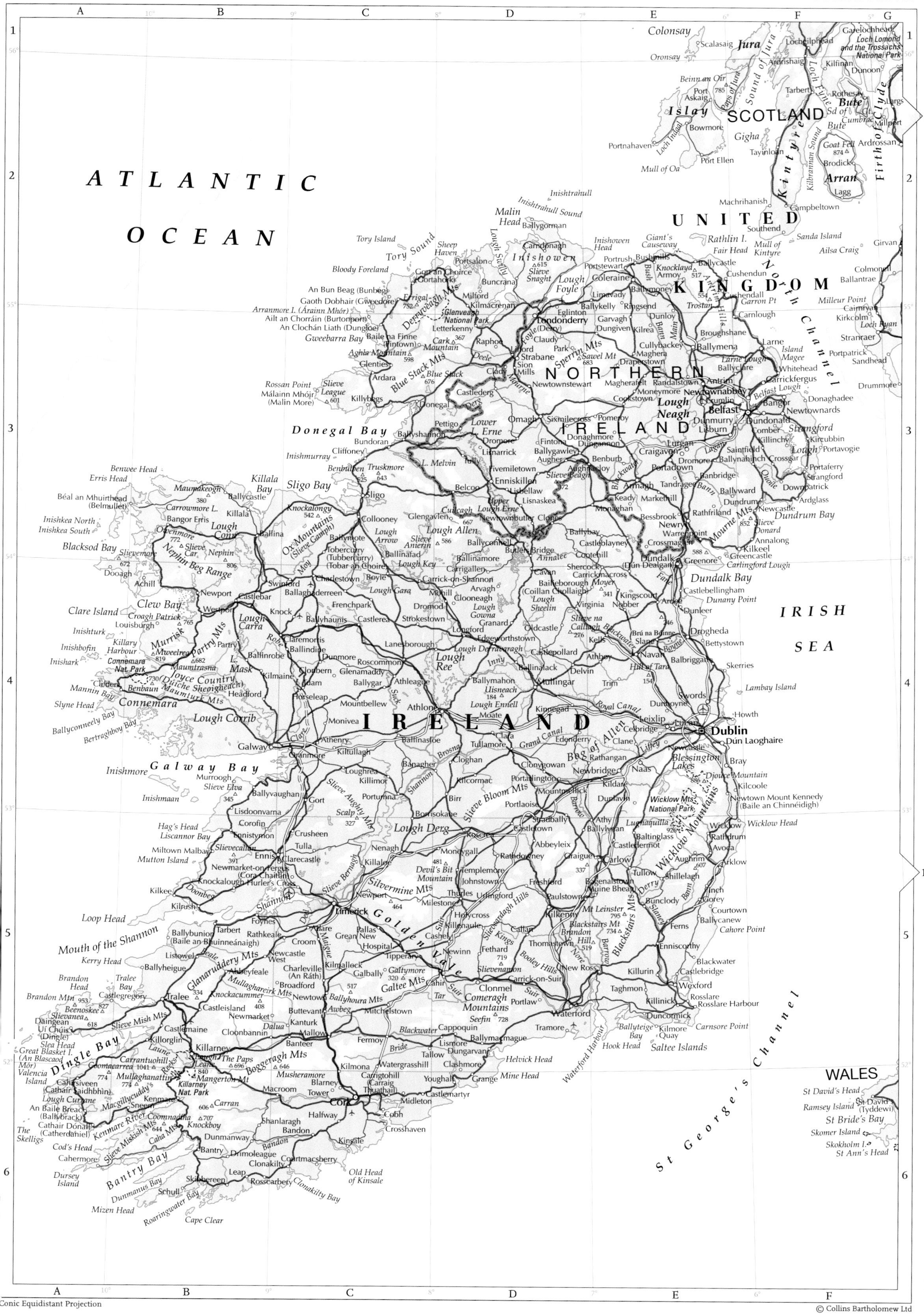

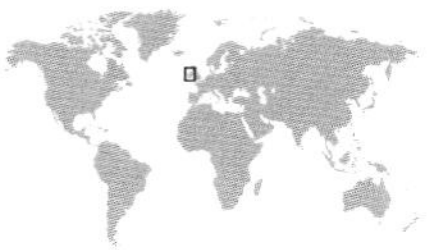

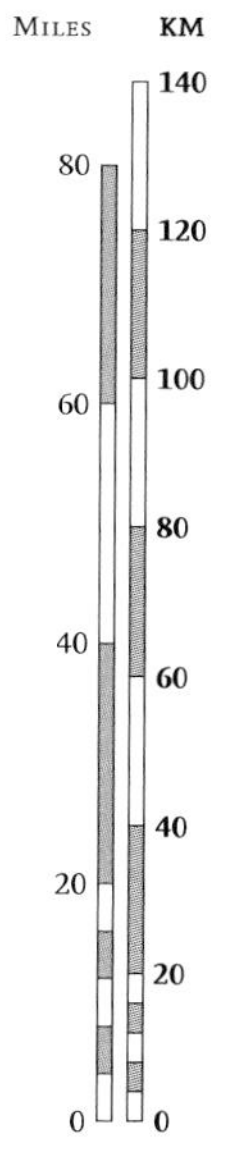

A B C D E F G

ATLANTIC

OCEAN

SCOTLAND

UNITED

KINGDOM

NORTHERN

IRELAND

IRELAND

IRISH

SEA

WALES

Colonsay
Jura
Islay
Arran
Bute

Malin Head
Inishowen
Lough Foyle
Londonderry (Derry)
Sperrin Mts
Lough Neagh
Belfast
Strangford Lough
Mourne Mts

Donegal Bay
Sligo Bay
Killala Bay

Clew Bay
Clare Island
Achill

Connemara
Galway Bay
Inishmore
Inishmaan

Lough Corrib
Lough Mask
Lough Derg
Lough Ree
Lough Allen
Shannon

Galway
Dublin
Dún Laoghaire
Wicklow Mountains
Wicklow Head

Mouth of the Shannon
Loop Head
Dingle Bay
Brandon Bay
Tralee Bay
Valencia Island

Bantry Bay
Mizen Head
Cape Clear
Dunmanus Bay
Roaringwater Bay

Cork
Youghal
Waterford
Wexford
Rosslare Harbour
Saltee Islands
Carnsore Point

St George's Channel

St David's Head
Ramsey Island
St Bride's Bay
Skomer Island

Conic Equidistant Projection

© Collins Bartholomew Ltd

MILES   KM

1:2 000 000

162
161

Conic Equidistant Projection

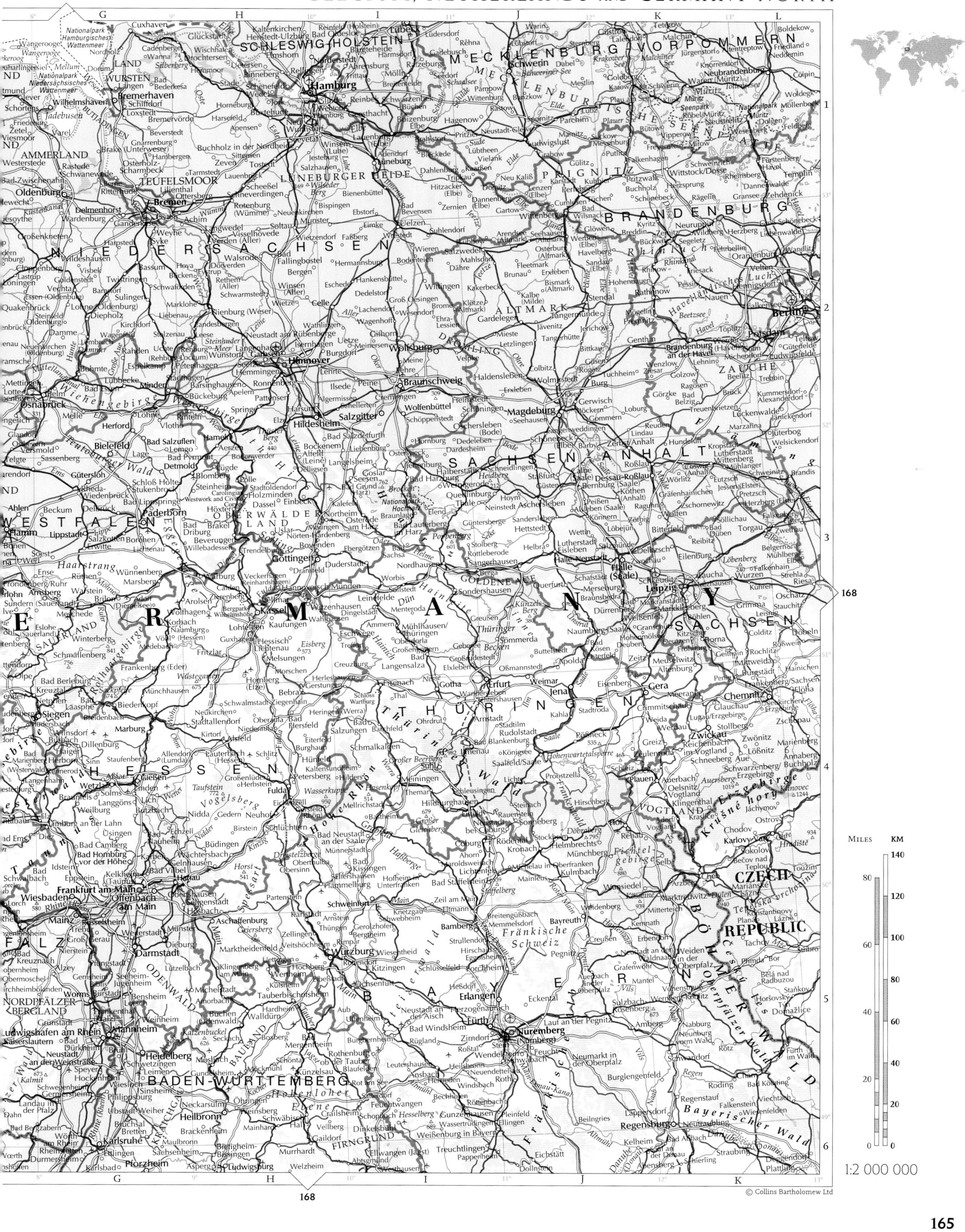

SCHLESWIG-HOLSTEIN

MECKLENBURG-VORPOMMERN

Hamburg

Bremerhaven

Bremen

LÜNEBURGER HEIDE

NIEDERSACHSEN

PRIGNITZ

BRANDENBURG

ALTMARK

Berlin

Potsdam

ZAUCHE

Hannover

Braunschweig

Wolfsburg

Magdeburg

Salzgitter

Hildesheim

SACHSEN-ANHALT

Bielefeld

WESTFALEN

Paderborn

Göttingen

Dessau

Leipzig

168

Halle (Saale)

SACHSEN

Kassel

GOLDENE AUE

GERMANY

Chemnitz

Gera

THÜRINGEN

Erfurt

Weimar

Jena

Marburg

HESSEN

Zwickau

Fulda

VOGTLAND

Frankfurt am Main

Wiesbaden

Offenbach am Main

Mainz

Aschaffenburg

Schweinfurt

Bamberg

Bayreuth

CZECH REPUBLIC

Darmstadt

ODENWALD

Würzburg

Mannheim

Ludwigshafen am Rhein

Heidelberg

Erlangen

Fürth

Nuremberg (Nürnberg)

BAYERN

Karlsruhe

BADEN-WÜRTTEMBERG

Heilbronn

Regensburg

Pforzheim

MILES   KM

140
120
100
80
60
40
20
0

1:2 000 000

© Collins Bartholomew Ltd

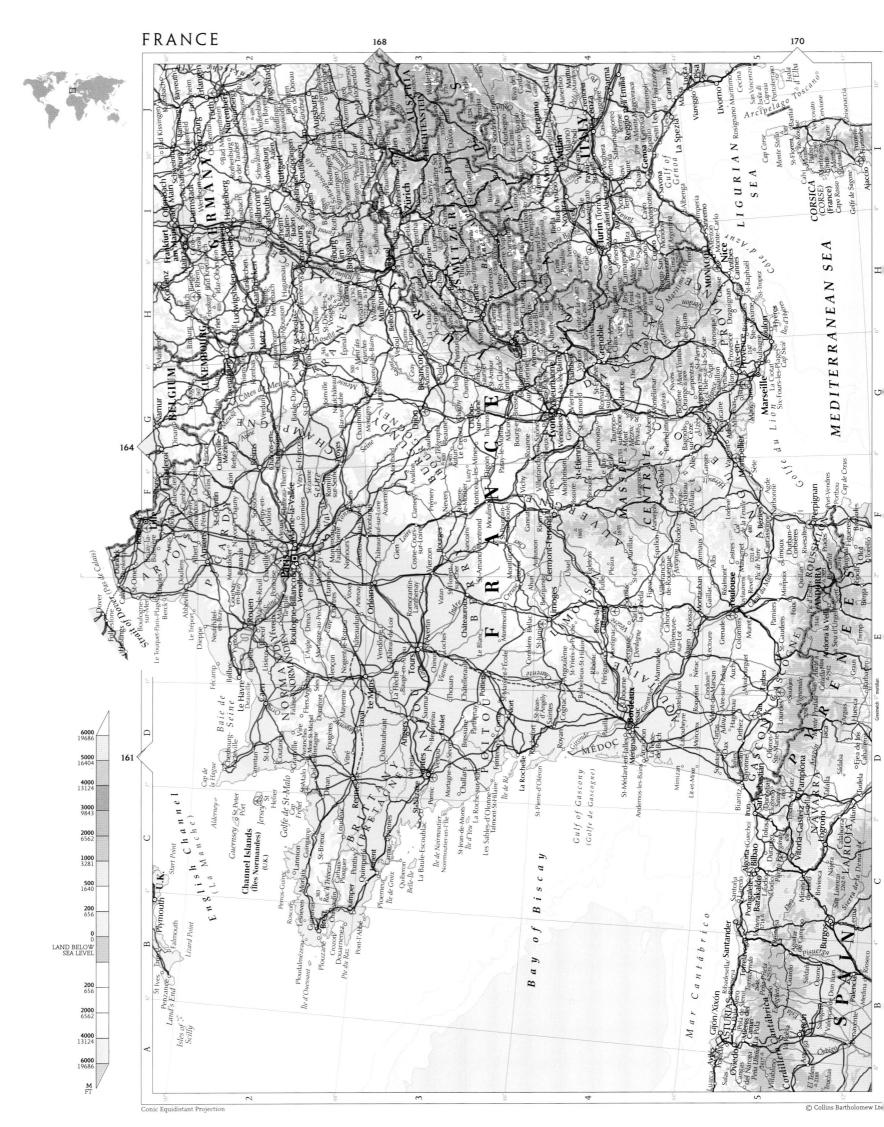

Conic Equidistant Projection

© Collins Bartholomew Ltd

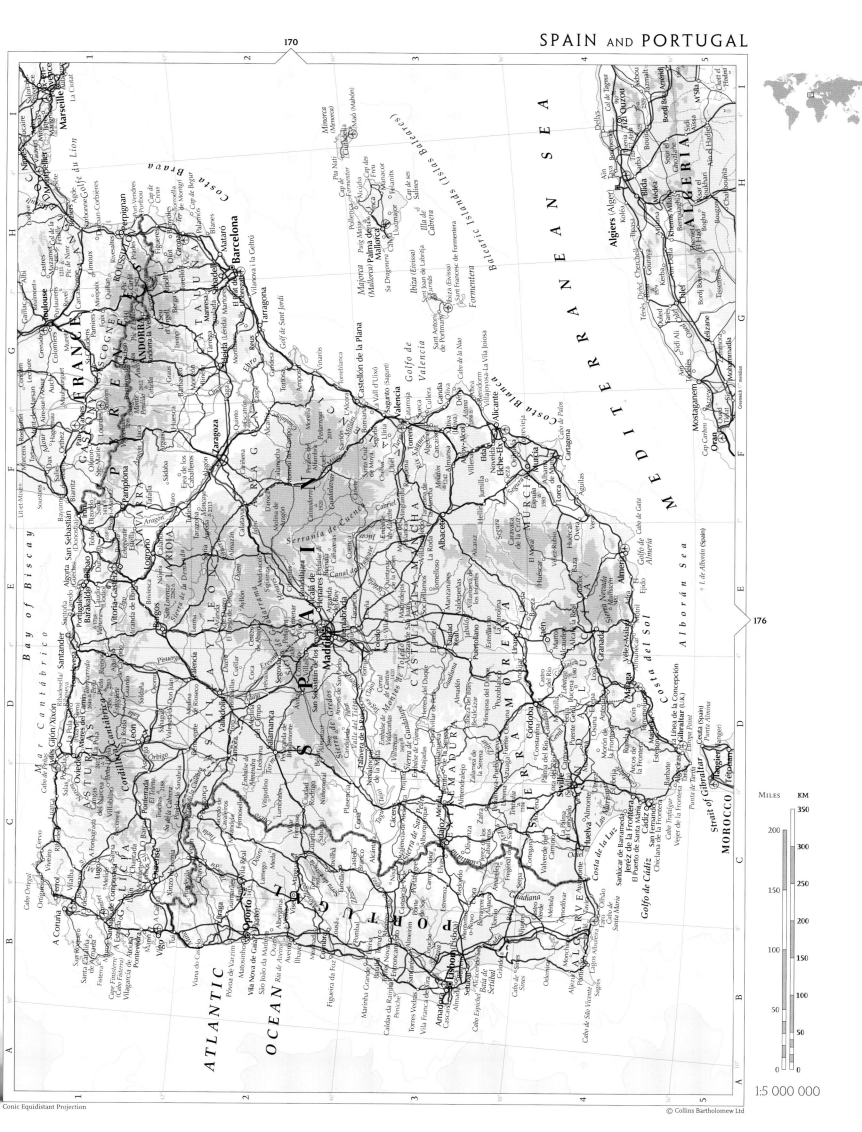

1:5 000 000

Conic Equidistant Projection

© Collins Bartholomew Ltd

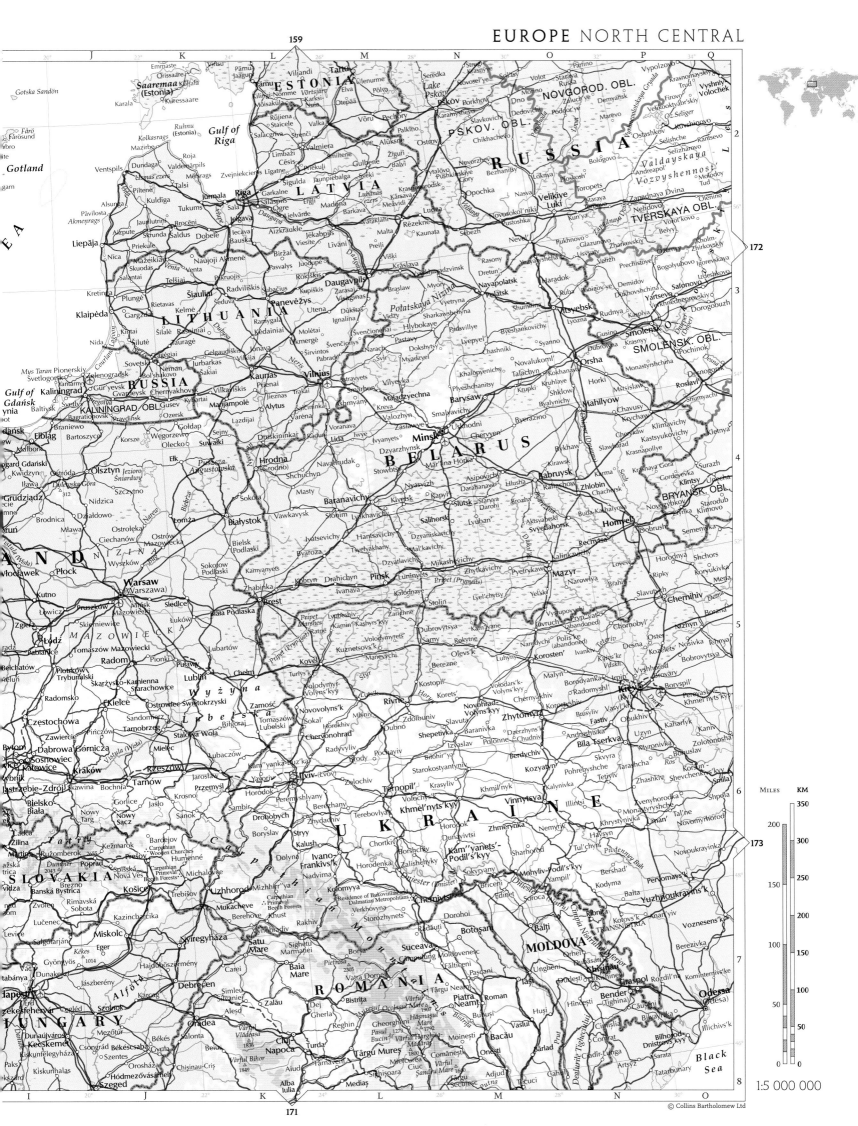

172

173

© Collins Bartholomew Ltd

MILES   KM

350

300

250

200

150

100

50

1:5 000 000

167

6000
19686
5000
16404
4000
13124
3000
9843
2000
6562
1000
3281
500
1640
200
656
0
0
LAND BELOW
SEA LEVEL
200
656
2000
6562
4000
13124
6000
19686
M
FT

Conic Equidistant Projection

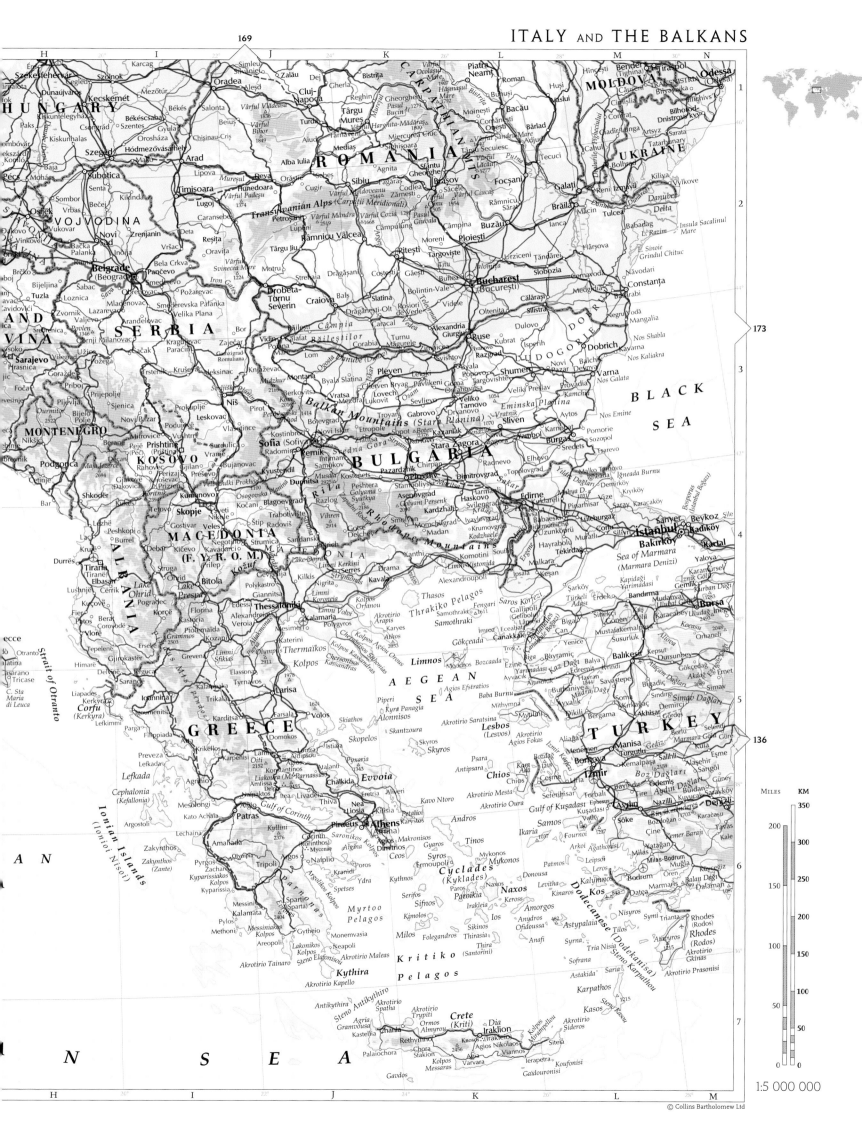

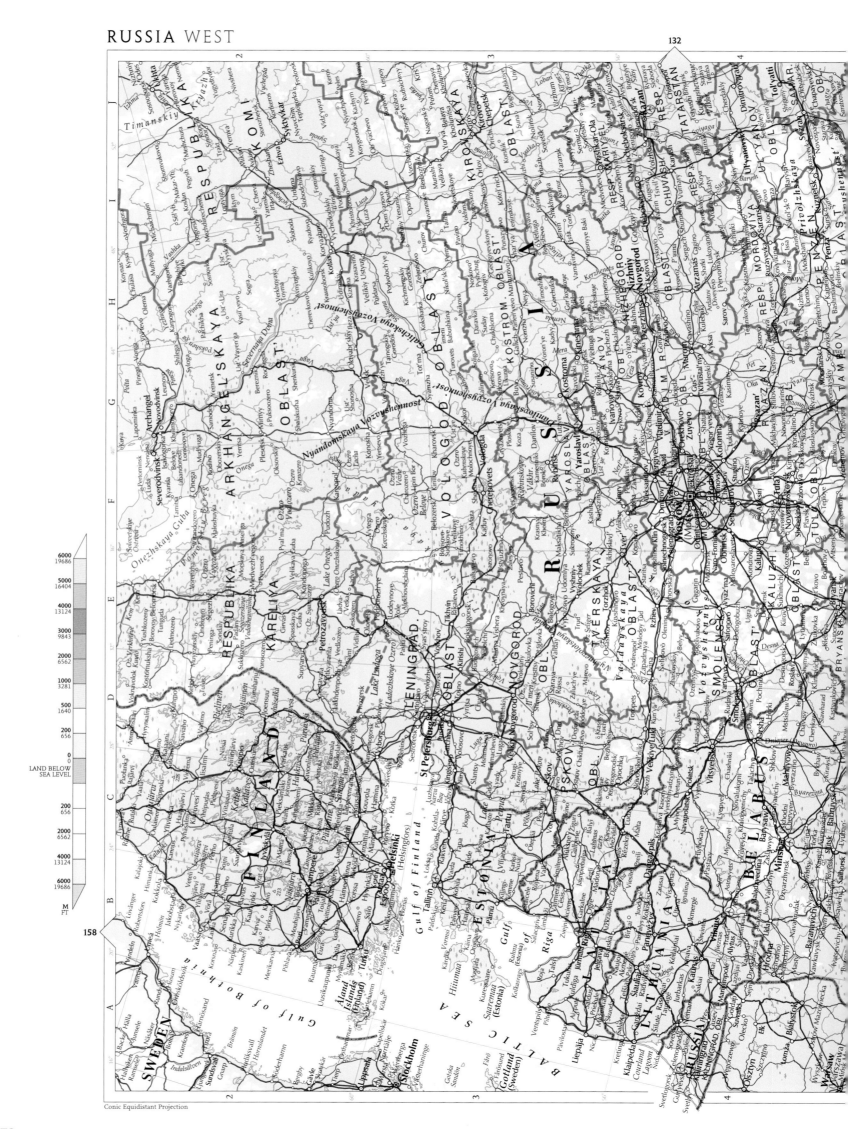

Conic Equidistant Projection

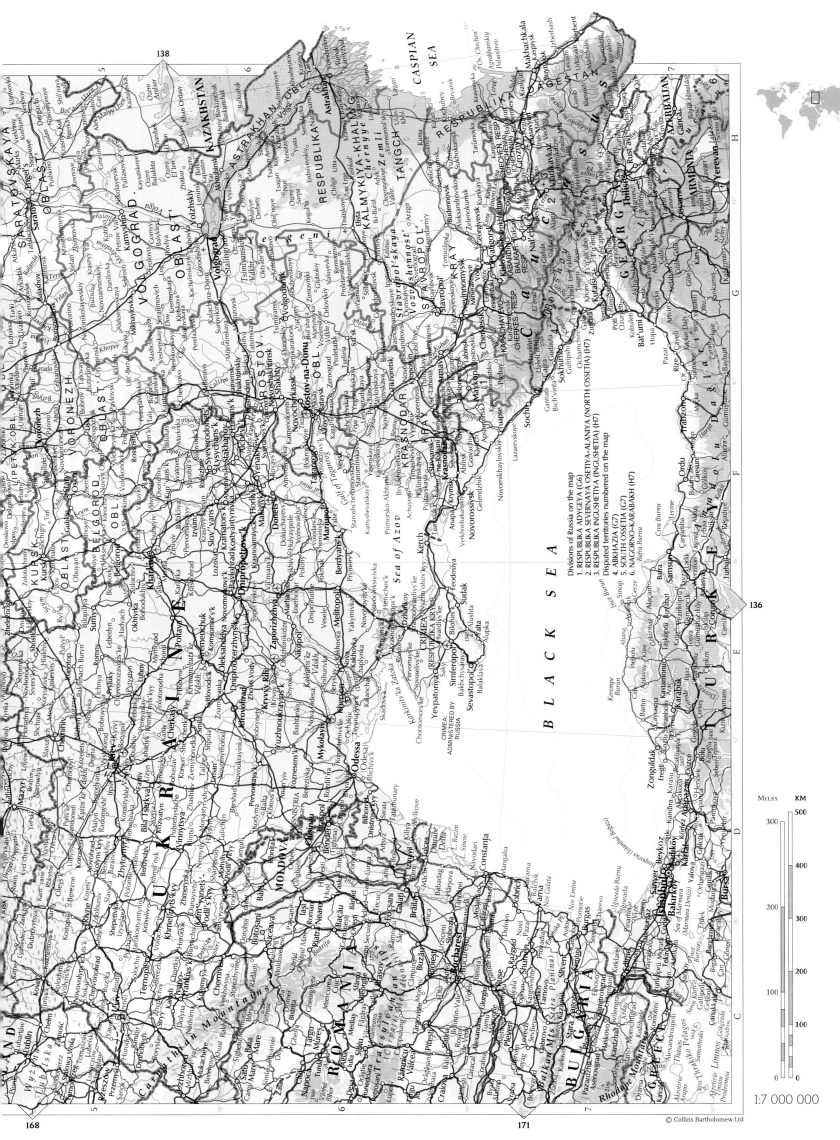

136

Divisions of Russia on the map
1. RESPUBLIKA ADYGEYA (G6)
2. RESPUBLIKA SEVERNAYA OSETIYA-ALANIYA (NORTH OSSETIA) (H7)
3. RESPUBLIKA INGUSHETIYA (INGUSHETIA) (H7)
Disputed territories numbered on the map
4. ABKHAZIA (G7)
5. SOUTH OSSETIA (G7)
6. NAGORNO-KARABAKH (H7)

CRIMEA:
ADMINISTERED BY
RUSSIA

MILES   KM

1:7 000 000

E U R O P E

Pyrenees
Corsica
Sardinia
Tyrrhe
Sea
Tagus
M E D I T
Bejaïa
Tangier ⊙ Str. of Gibraltar Oran **Algiers** ⊙ Annaba ⊙ **Tuni**
Rabat Fès ⊙ Sidi Bel Abbès Constantine ⊙ Gabes de G
Casablanca □ Laghouat **TUNISIA** Tr
MOROCCO Béchar
Marrakech ⊙ ATLAS MOUNTAINS
Canary Islands
(Spain) Lanzarote **A L G E R I A**
⊙ Tenerife **Las Palmas**
de Gran Canaria *Ahaggar*
Gran ⊙ Laâyoune Mt Tahat
Canaria ▲ 2918
WESTERN SAHARA S A H
Nouâdhibou Ténéré
du
Tafassâsset
M A U R I T A N I A M A L I N I G
Gao ⊙ Agadez
Nouakchott
Zinder ⊙
St-Louis ⊙ Niamey ⊙
CAPE Sénégal Ségou **BURKINA** Sokoto ⊙ Kano ⊙
VERDE Kayes ⊙ Niger Mopti ⊙ **FASO**
Santo Antão ⊙ Boa Vista ⊙ **Dakar** □ **SENEGAL** □ **Ouagadougou** Kaduna ⊙ Gombe ⊙
Santiago Kaolack ⊙ Bamako **Bobo-Dioulasso** Niger
Fogo **Praia** **Banjul** **BENIN** **N I G E R I**
THE GAMBIA Fouta **Parakou** ⊙
GUINEA- Djallon **Abuja** □
BISSAU White **CÔTE** Black Tamale ⊙ Ogbomoso ⊙ Benu
Bissau **GUINEA** **D'IVOIRE** Volta **TOGO**
Kankan ⊙ Lac **Porto-** Ibadan ⊙ Onitsha ⊙
Conakry **SIERRA** de Kossou **Bouaké** **GHANA** **Novo** Lagos CAM
LEONE (IVORY COAST) Lake Volta **Lomé** ⊙ Warri
Freetown **Yamoussoukro** Kumasi ⊙ **Accra** Port ⊙ Douala
Monrovia **LIBERIA** Abidjan ⊙ Cape Harcourt **Malabo** Yaoun
Coast Gulf **EQUATORIAL** Bioko
o f **GUINEA** Bata
SÃO TOMÉ AND PRÍNCIPE Príncipe Librevi
G u i n e a São Tomé ⊙ **São Tomé** GA
Port-Gentil ⊙

A T L A N T I C

Annobón
(Equatorial Guinea)

O C E A N

Ascension
(U.K.)
**St Helena, Ascension
and Tristan da Cunha**
(U.K.)

Nami

Jamestown □ St Helena
(U.K.)

Pointe-Noir
CABIN
(Ango

SOUTH

Ilha da Trindade Ilhas
Martin Vaz

AMERICA

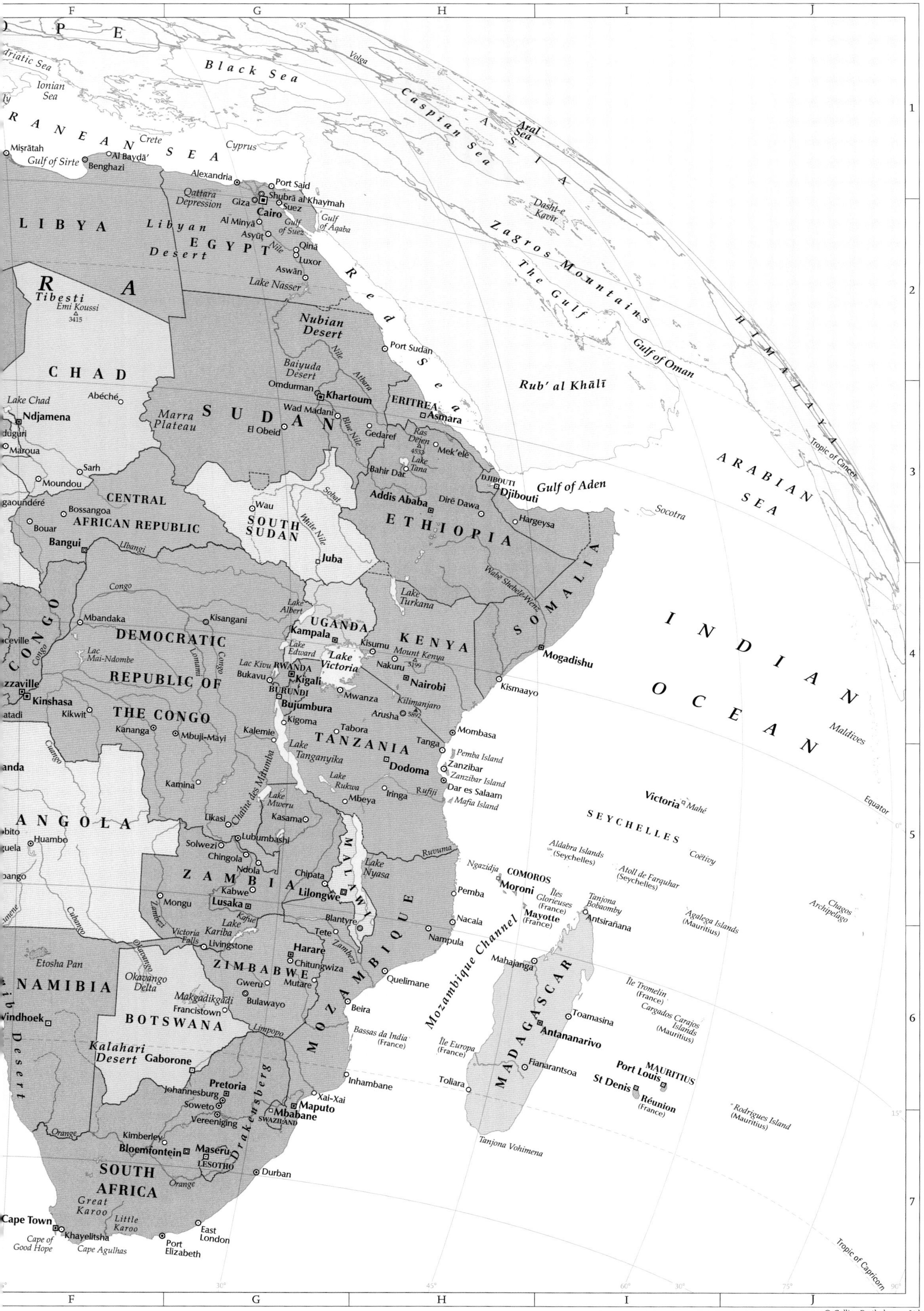

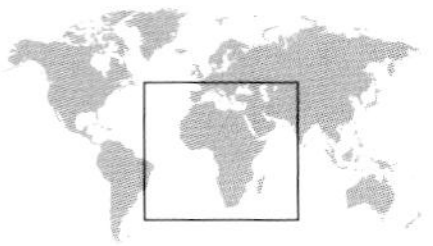

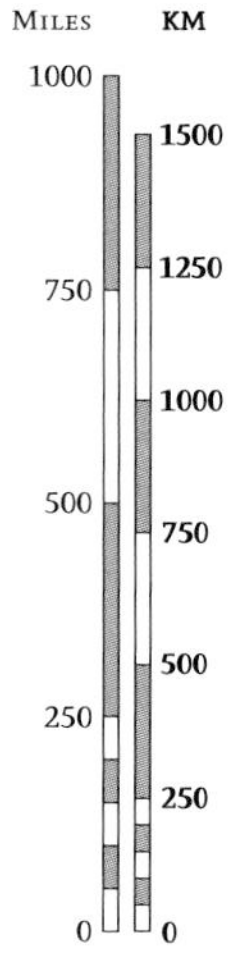

Misrātah
Al Baydā'
Gulf of Sirte
Benghazi

LIBYA

Black Sea

Crete
Cyprus

Ionian
Sea

RANEAN SEA

Alexandria
Port Said
Qattara
Depression
Giza
Shubrā al Khaymah
Cairo
Suez
Al Minyā
Gulf of Suez
Asyūt
Gulf of Aqaba
Qinā
Luxor
Aswān

Libyan
Desert
EGYPT

Nile

Lake Nasser

R A

Tibesti
Emi Koussi
3415

CHAD

Nubian
Desert

Baiyuda
Desert

Omdurman
Khartoum
Wad Madani
Atbara

Caspian Sea

Volga

Aral
Sea

Dasht-e
Kavir

Zagros Mountains

The Gulf
Gulf of Oman

Rub' al Khālī

A S I A

HIMALAYA

Tropic of Cancer

Lake Chad
Abéché
Ndjamena
duguri
Marqua
Sarh
Moundou

Marra
Plateau

SUDAN

El Obeid

Blue Nile

ERITREA
Asmara

Port Sudan

Red Sea

Gedaref
Ras
Dejen
4533
Mek'elē
Bahir Dar
Lake Tana

DJIBOUTI
Djibouti
Gulf of Aden

Hargeysa

Socotra

ARABIAN
SEA

**CENTRAL
AFRICAN REPUBLIC**
Bossangoa
Bouar
Bangui

Wau
**SOUTH
SUDAN**

White Nile

Sobat

Addis Ababa
Dirē Dawa

ETHIOPIA

gaoundéré

Ubangi

Juba

Congo

Lac
Mai-Ndombe

ceville

Congo

Mbandaka

DEMOCRATIC

Kisangani

Lomami

Lake
Albert

Lake
Turkana

Waha Shebele Wenz

SOMALIA

INDIAN

zzaville
Kinshasa
atadi

REPUBLIC OF

Lac Kivu RWANDA
Bukavu
Kigali

UGANDA
Kampala
Lake
Edward
**Lake
Victoria**
Kisumu

KENYA

Nakuru
Mount Kenya
5199
Nairobi

Mogadishu

OCEAN

Kikwit

THE CONGO

BURUNDI
Bujumbura
Kigoma

Mwanza

Kismaayo

Maldives

Kananga
Mbuji-Mayi

Kalemie

Arusha
Kilimanjaro
5892

Mombasa

Kamina

Chanal des Mitumba

Lake
Tanganyika

Tabora

TANZANIA

Tanga

Pemba Island

anda

Cuango

Likasi

Lake
Mweru

Lake
Rukwa

Dodoma

Iringa
Mbeya
Rufiji

Zanzibar
Zanzibar Island
Dar es Salaam
Mafia Island

SEYCHELLES

Victoria Mahé

Aldabra Islands
(Seychelles)

Atoll de Farquhar
(Seychelles)

Coëtivy

Equator

ANGOLA
bito
Huambo
guela
ango

Solwezi

Kasama

Ruvuma

Chingola
Ndola
Chipata

ZAMBIA

Kabwe

Lake
Nyasa

Lubumbashi

Mongu

Lusaka

Kafue
Lake
Kariba

MALAWI

Chipata
Lilongwe

Blantyre
Tete

Pemba

Nacala

Nampula

COMOROS
Ngazidja **Moroni**
Îles
Glorieuses
(France)

Tanjona
Bobaomby
Antsirañana

Agalega Islands
(Mauritius)

Chagos
Archipelago

Victoria
Falls
Livingstone

Harare
Chitungwiza

MOZAMBIQUE

Mayotte
(France)

Mahajanga

Quelimane

Île Tromelin
(France)

Cargados Carajos
Islands
(Mauritius)

Etosha Pan

Okavango
Delta

Makgadikgadi

Francistown

Zimbabwe
Gweru
Mutare
Bulawayo

Beira

Bassas da India
(France)

Île Europa
(France)

Toamasina

NAMIBIA
Windhoek

Kalahari
Desert

BOTSWANA

Gaborone

Limpopo

Zambezi

Mozambique Channel

MADAGASCAR

Antananarivo

MAURITIUS
Port Louis

Desert

Okavango

Johannesburg
Pretoria

Xai-Xai
Inhambane

Fianarantsoa
St Denis
Réunion
(France)

Rodrigues Island
(Mauritius)

Windhoek

Drakensberg

Makgadikgadi

Soweto
Vereeniging

Maputo
Mbabane
SWAZILAND

Toliara

Kimberley
Bloemfontein
Maseru
LESOTHO

Orange

**SOUTH
AFRICA**

Great
Karoo

Little
Karoo

Durban

East
London

Cape Town
Khayelitsha
Cape of
Good Hope
Cape Agulhas
Port
Elizabeth

Tanjona Vohimena

Tropic of Capricorn

MILES KM

1000

1500

750

1250

1000

500

750

250

500

250

0 0

1:28 000 000

175

© Collins Bartholomew Ltd

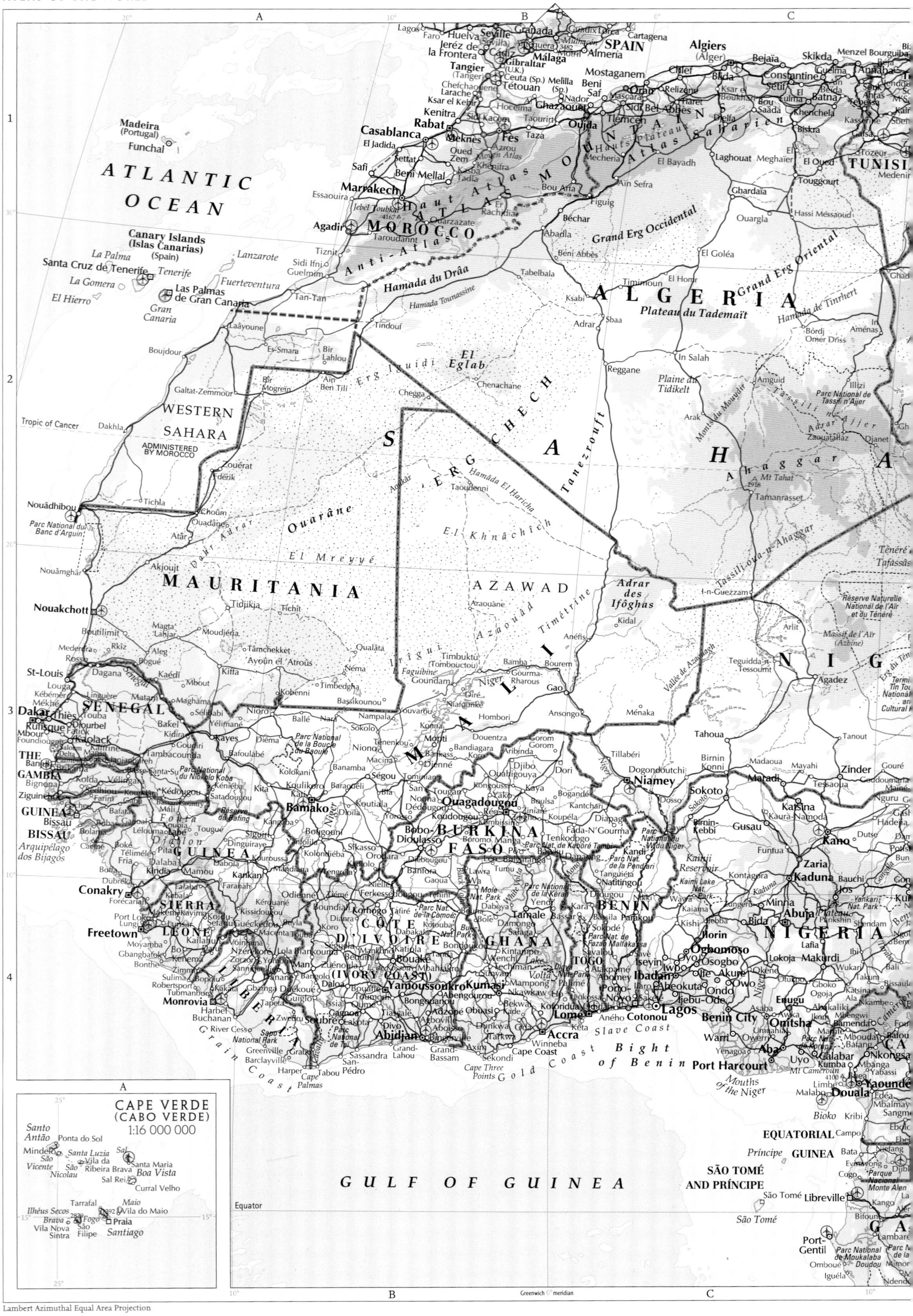

A B C

ATLANTIC OCEAN

SPAIN
Algiers (Alger)
TUNISI
Madeira (Portugal)
Funchal

Tangier (Tanger)
Ceuta (Sp.)
Melilla (Sp.)
Gibraltar (U.K.)
Tétouan
Casablanca
Rabat
Meknès
Fes
Oran
Constantine
Skikda
Bejaïa
Menzel Bourguiba

MOROCCO
Marrakech
Agadir
Canary Islands (Islas Canarias) (Spain)
Santa Cruz de Tenerife
Tenerife
La Palma
La Gomera
El Hierro
Gran Canaria
Las Palmas de Gran Canaria
Lanzarote
Fuerteventura

Haut Atlas MOUNTAINS
Jebel Toubkal
Anti-Atlas
Hamada du Drâa
Béchar

ALGERIA
Grand Erg Occidental
Grand Erg Oriental
Ouargla
El Goléa
In Salah
Plateau du Tademaït
Hamada de Tinrhert
Tassili-n-Ajjer

Tropic of Cancer
Dakhla
WESTERN SAHARA
ADMINISTERED BY MOROCCO

Laâyoune
Es-Smara
Bir Lahlou
Tindouf
El Eglab
ERG CHECH
Tanezrouft
AHAGGAR
Mt Tahat

Nouâdhibou
Parc National du Banc d'Arguin
Atâr
Choûm
Ouâdâne
Ouarâne
Taoudenni
El Khnâchîch
Adrar des Ifôghas
Timétrine

Nouakchott
MAURITANIA
AZAWAD
Kidal
NIGER
Agadez

St-Louis
Dagana
SENEGAL
Kaédi
Kiffa
Timbuktu (Tombouctou)
Gao
MALI
Ménaka
Tahoua
Tanout

Dakar
Thiès
Diourbel
THE GAMBIA
Banjul
Niono
Ségou
San
Mopti
Douentza
Niamey
Sokoto
Birnin Konni
Maradi
Zinder

GUINEA-BISSAU
Bissau
Arquipélago dos Bijagós

GUINEA
Bamako
Bobo-Dioulasso
BURKINA FASO
Ouagadougou
Kano
Zaria
Kaduna

Conakry
SIERRA LEONE
Freetown
CÔTE D'IVOIRE (IVORY COAST)
GHANA
TOGO
BENIN
NIGERIA
Abuja
Ilorin
Oyo
Ibadan
Ogbomoso

LIBERIA
Monrovia
Yamoussoukro
Kumasi
Lomé
Cotonou
Lagos
Benin City
Onitsha
Enugu

Abidjan
Accra
Cape Coast
Gold Coast
Slave Coast
Bight of Benin
Port Harcourt
Calabar
Mt Cameroun
Douala
Yaoundé

GULF OF GUINEA

EQUATORIAL GUINEA
Bioko
Príncipe
SÃO TOMÉ AND PRÍNCIPE
São Tomé
Libreville
GA

Cape Verde inset:
A
CAPE VERDE (CABO VERDE) 1:16 000 000
Santo Antão
Mindelo
São Vicente
Santa Luzia
São Nicolau
Sal
Boa Vista
Ponta do Sol
Vila da Ribeira Brava
Santa Maria
Sal Rei
Tarrafal
Ilhéus Secos
Brava
Vila Nova Sintra
Maio
Fogo
São Filipe
Praia
Santiago
Vila do Maio
Curral Velho

Equator
São Tomé
Port Gentil
Parc National de Moukalaba Doudou

B C
Greenwich 0° meridian

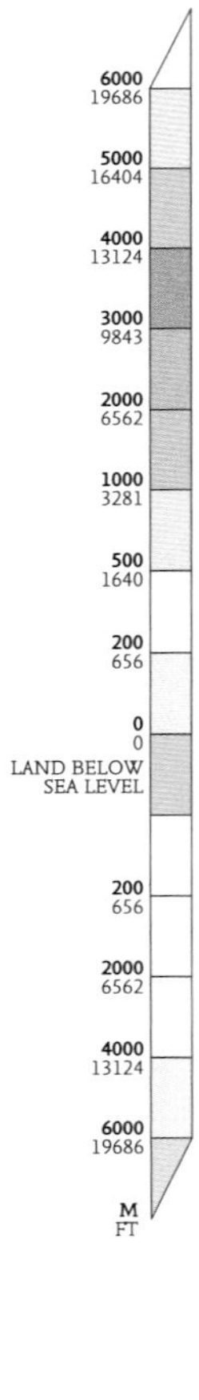

Lambert Azimuthal Equal Area Projection

Elevation scale:
6000 / 19686
5000 / 16404
4000 / 13124
3000 / 9843
2000 / 6562
1000 / 3281
500 / 1640
200 / 656
0
LAND BELOW SEA LEVEL
200 / 656
2000 / 6562
4000 / 13124
6000 / 19686
M FT

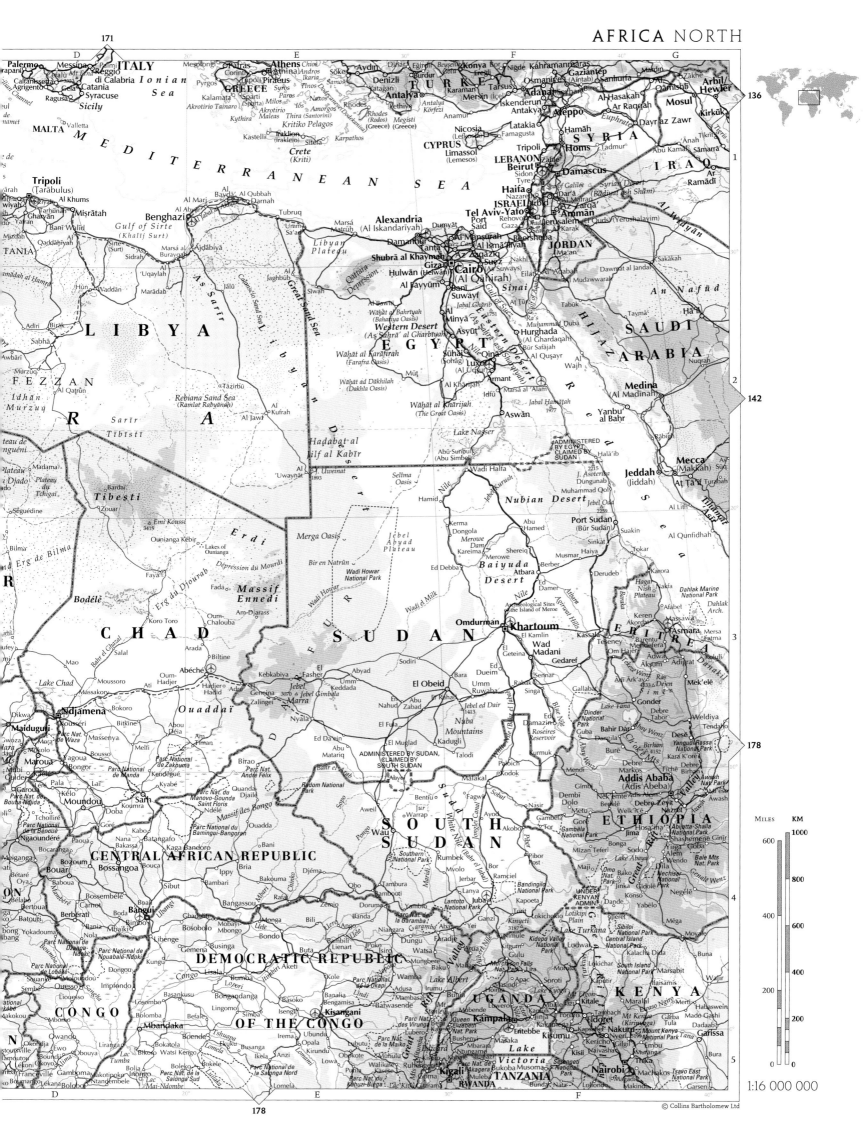

MILES   KM

600   1000

800

400   600

400

200

200

0   0

1:16 000 000

© Collins Bartholomew Ltd

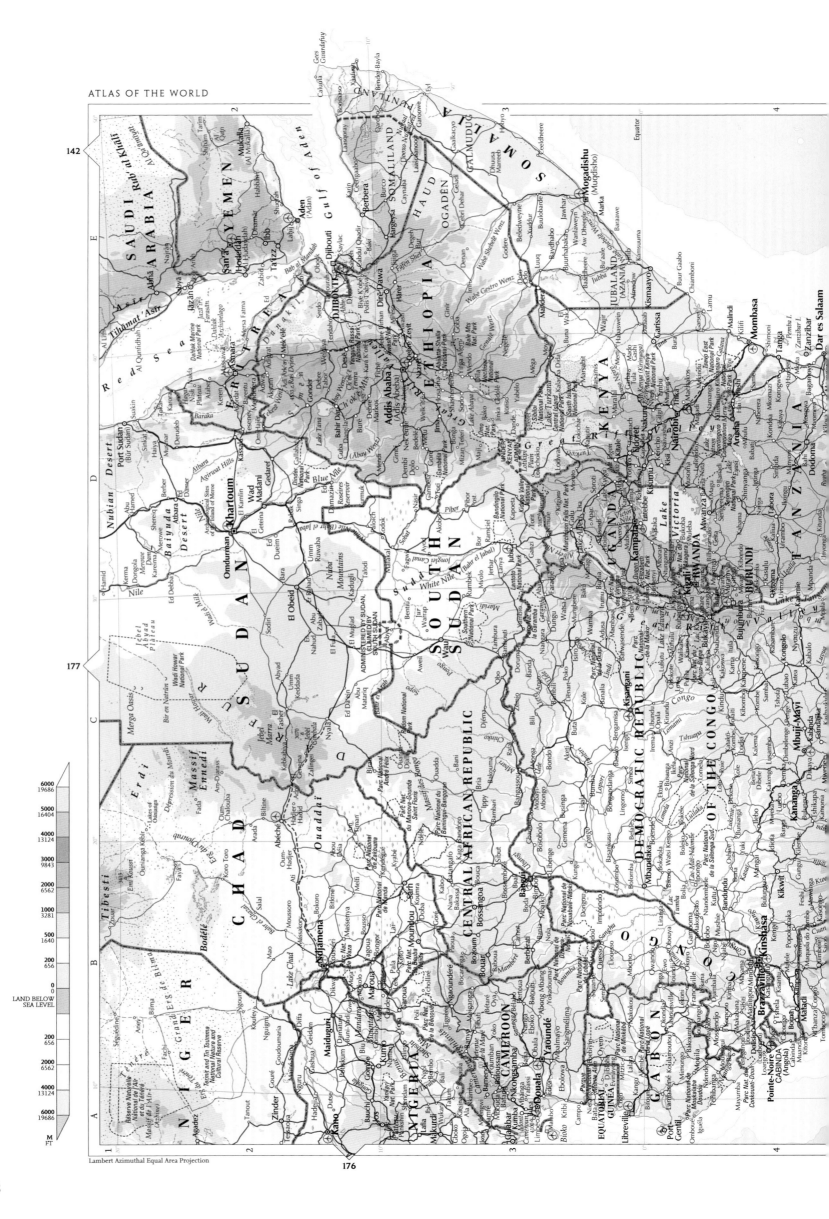

142

177

6000
19686
5000
16404
4000
13124
3000
9843
2000
6562
1000
3281
500
1640
200
656
0
LAND BELOW
SEA LEVEL
200
656
2000
6562
4000
13124
6000
19686
M
FT

Lambert Azimuthal Equal Area Projection

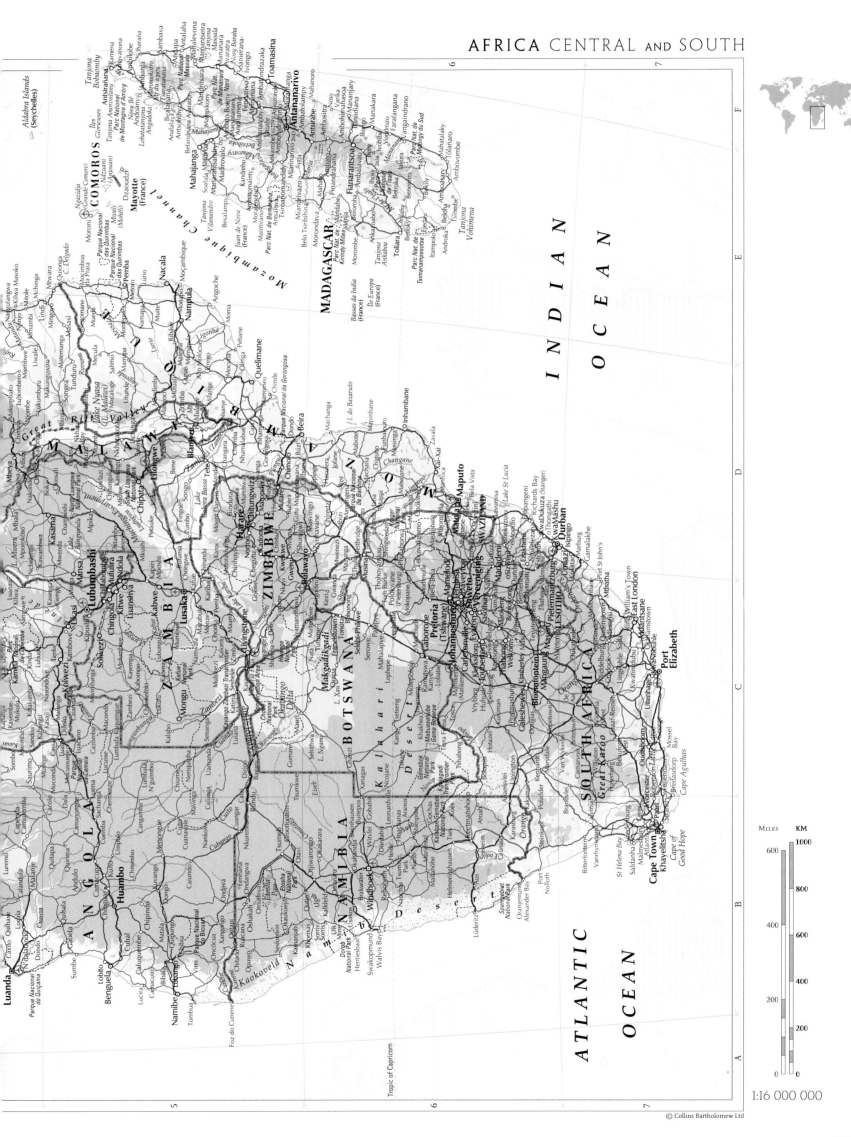

ATLANTIC

OCEAN

INDIAN

OCEAN

MILES   KM

600   1000

400   800

    600

200   400

    200

0   0

1:16 000 000

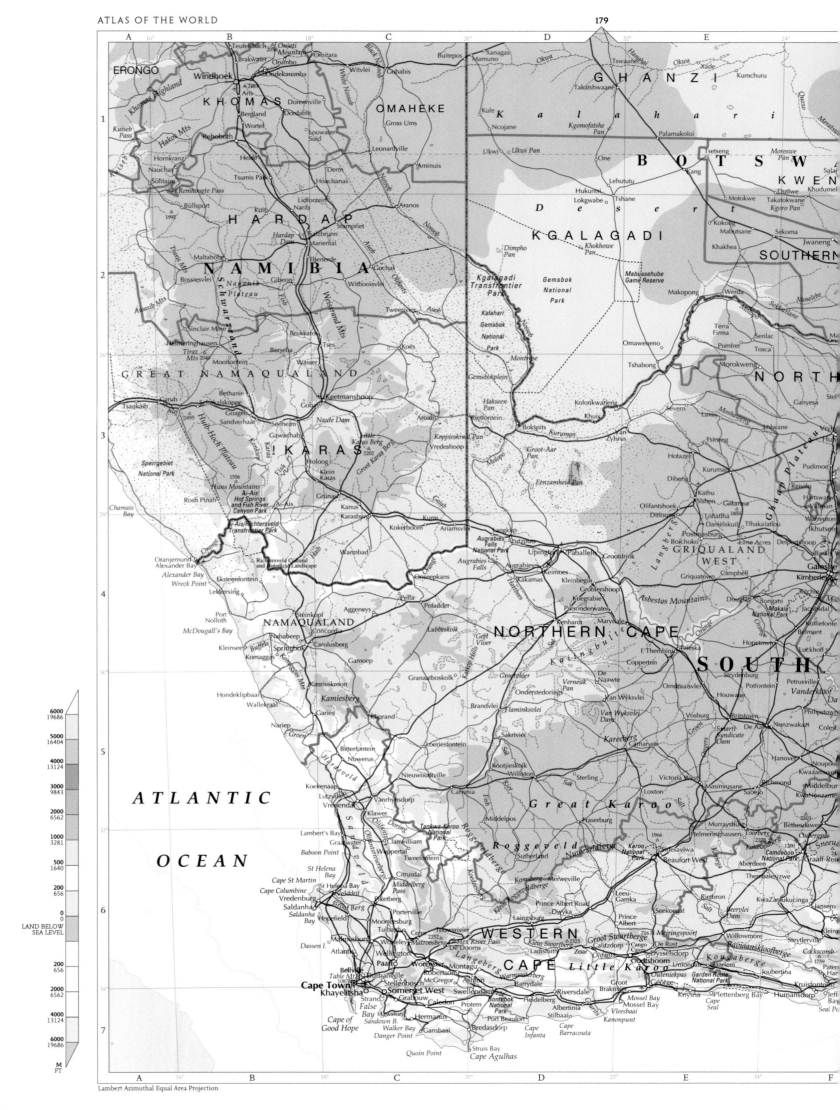

Lambert Azimuthal Equal Area Projection

MILES 200 150 100 50 0

KM 300 250 200 150 100 50 0

1:5 000 000

© Collins Bartholomew Ltd

Administrative divisions abbreviated on the map:

U.S.A.		CANADA	
CONN.	CONNECTICUT	P.E.I.	PRINCE EDWARD ISLAND
DEL.	DELAWARE		
MD	MARYLAND		
MASS.	MASSACHUSETTS		
N.H.	NEW HAMPSHIRE		
N.J.	NEW JERSEY		
R.I.	RHODE ISLAND		
VER.	VERMONT		

Orthographic Projection

F   G   H   I   J

1

2

3

4

5

6

7

EUROPE

AFRICA

ATLANTIC OCEAN

Greenland Sea

Greenland (Kalaallit Nunaat) (Denmark)

Arctic Circle

Station Nord
Daneborg
Kong Wilhelm Land
Kong Christian IX Land
Kong Frederik VI Kyst
Nuuk (Godthåb)
Tasiilaq
Ilulissat
Nuussuaq
Thule Air Base (U.S.A.)

Iceland

Denmark Strait

Davis Strait

Ellesmere Island
Knud Rasmussen Land
Nares Strait

Baffin Bay
Baffin Island
Clyde River
Cape Mercy
Cumberland Sd
Iqaluit
Resolution I.
Nanortalik
Labrador Sea

Somerset Island
Lancaster Sd
Devon Island
Prince of Wales I.
Melville Peninsula
Prince Charles I.
Foxe Basin
Repulse Bay
Gulf of Boothia
Boothia Pen
NUNAVUT

Southampton Island
Coral Harbour
Coats I.
Mansel I.
Cape Dorset
Arviat

HUDSON BAY
CANADA

Péninsule d'Ungava
Ungava Bay
Nain
NEWFOUNDLAND AND LABRADOR

MANITOBA
Thompson
Lake Winnipeg
ONTARIO
Belcher Islands
James Bay
Chisasibi
Caniapiscau
Smallwood Reservoir
Labrador
Gander
St John's
Cape Race
Newfoundland

Winnipeg
Lake Nipigon
Thunder Bay
Lake Superior
Sault Ste Marie
QUÉBEC
Moosonee
Timmins
Rouyn-Noranda
Chicoutimi
Sept-Îles
Île d'Anticosti
Gulf of St Lawrence
St Pierre and Miquelon (France)

Grand Forks
MINNESOTA
Duluth
MICHIGAN
North Bay
Québec
NEW BRUNSWICK
P.E.I.
Charlottetown
Fredericton
NOVA SCOTIA
Halifax
Cape Breton I.
Sable Island

Minneapolis
St Paul
WISCONSIN
Rochester
Milwaukee
Lansing
MICHIGAN
Ottawa
Toronto
Lake Ontario
Buffalo
NEW YORK
MAINE
VER.
N.H.
Augusta
Montpelier
Concord
Albany
MASS.
Boston
Providence
Cape Cod

Sioux Falls
IOWA
Chicago
L. Michigan
Detroit
Cleveland
L. Erie
Erie
PENNSYLVANIA
Pittsburgh
Hartford
New York
CONN.
R.I.
Trenton
Philadelphia
DEL.

Omaha
Des Moines
ILLINOIS
Indianapolis
INDIANA
OHIO
Columbus
Cincinnati
Baltimore
Washington D.C.

Lincoln
UNITED STATES OF AMERICA
St Louis
MISSOURI
KENTUCKY
WEST VIRGINIA
Charleston
Richmond
VIRGINIA
Raleigh

Kansas City
KANSAS
Springfield
TENNESSEE
Nashville
Knoxville
Charlotte
N. CAROLINA
Cape Hatteras

Oklahoma City
OKLAHOMA
ARKANSAS
Little Rock
Memphis
Atlanta
Columbia
S. CAROLINA

Fort Worth
Dallas
TEXAS
Shreveport
MISS.
Jackson
ALABAMA
Montgomery
GEORGIA
Savannah

Austin
Baton Rouge
LOUISIANA
New Orleans
Mobile
Tallahassee
Jacksonville
Cape Canaveral

San Antonio
Houston
Orlando
FLORIDA
Tampa
Miami

Corpus Christi
GULF OF MEXICO
Matamoros
Ciudad Victoria
Tampico
Yucatán Channel
Straits of Florida
THE BAHAMAS
Nassau
Turks and Caicos Is (U.K.)

Havana
CUBA
Santa Clara
Santiago
Holguín
Hispaniola
DOMINICAN REPUBLIC
HAITI
Port-au-Prince
Santo Domingo
San Juan
Puerto Rico (U.S.A.)
Virgin Is (U.K.)
Virgin Is (U.S.A.)
Anguilla (U.K.)
ANTIGUA AND BARBUDA
Montserrat (U.K.)
Guadeloupe (France)
ST KITTS AND NEVIS
DOMINICA

Mérida
Bahía de Campeche
Veracruz
Villahermosa
Yucatán
Cayman Is (U.K.)
Montego Bay
JAMAICA
Kingston
Greater Antilles
Lesser Antilles
CARIBBEAN SEA
Martinique (France)
ST LUCIA
BARBADOS
ST VINCENT AND THE GRENADINES

Mexico City
Puebla
Oaxaca
Acapulco
Gulf of Tehuantepec
BELIZE
Belmopan
San Pedro Sula
GUATEMALA
Guatemala City
HONDURAS
Tegucigalpa
NICARAGUA
Managua
Lake Nicaragua
GRENADA
Aruba (Neth.)
Curaçao (Neth.)
TRINIDAD AND TOBAGO
Port of Spain

San Salvador
EL SALVADOR
COSTA RICA
San José
Colón
PANAMA
Panama City
Gulf of Panama

SOUTH AMERICA
Amazon (Amazonas)

Bermuda (U.K.)

Azores
Madeira
Canary Islands
Tropic of Cancer
Cape Verde
Equator

MILES   KM

1200   2000

         1600

800   1200

         800

400   400

0   0

1:32 000 000

© Collins Bartholomew Ltd

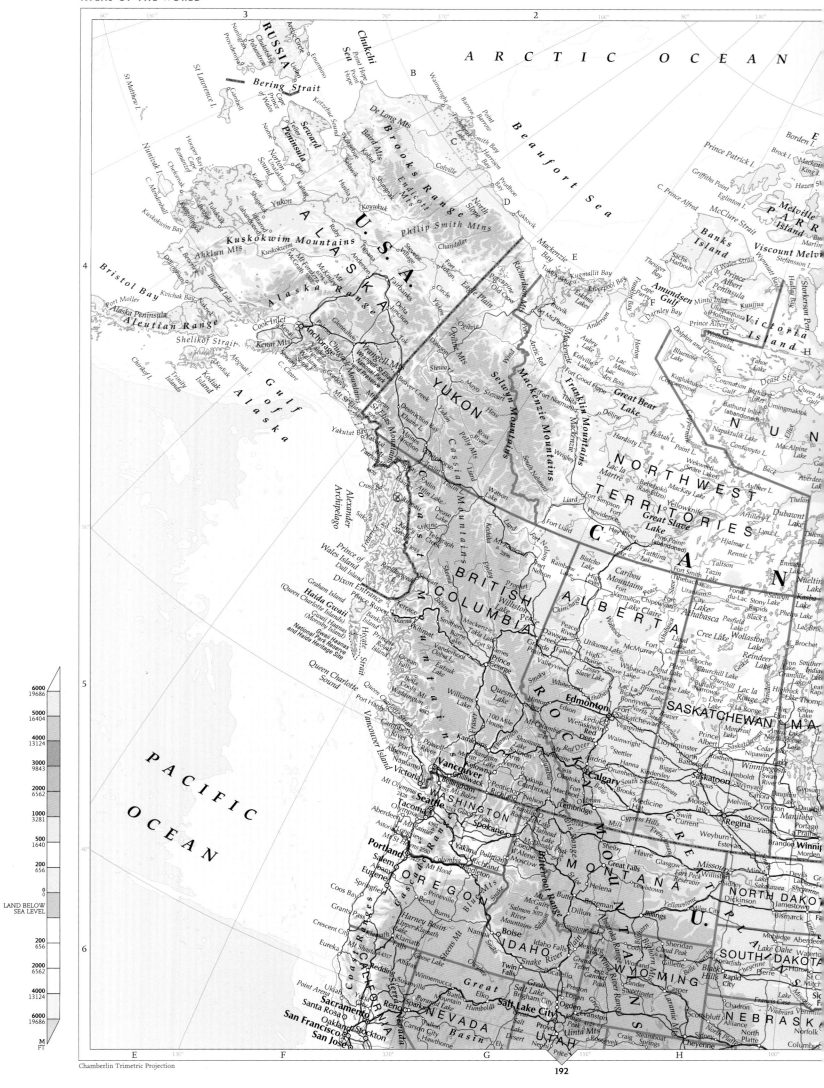

Chamberlin Trimetric Projection

192

ICELAND

Arctic Circle

Reykjavik

QUEEN
ELIZABETH
ISLANDS

North
Geomagnetic
Pole
2015

Ellesmere Island

Devon Island

Baffin
Bay

Greenland
(Kalaallit Nunaat)
(Denmark)

Denmark Strait

Nuuk
(Godthåb)

Cape Farewell
(Nunap Isua)

Baffin
Island

Davis
Strait

Cumberland
Peninsula

Cumberland
Sound

Labrador
Sea

NAVUT

Ukkusiksalik
National Park

Foxe
Basin

Foxe
Peninsula

Hall Pen.

Meta Incognita Pen.

Iqaluit

Hudson   Strait

Péninsule
d'Ungava

Ungava
Bay

NEWFOUNDLAND

A   D   A

Hudson

Bay

Churchill

Belcher
Islands

James
Bay

QUÉBEC

Smallwood
Reservoir

Labrador

NEWFOUNDLAND AND LABRADOR

Réservoir de
Caniapiscau

Réservoir
Robert-
Bourassa

Réservoir
La Grande 4

Réservoir
La Grande 3

Lac
Mistassini

Ashuanipi Lake

Newfoundland

St John's

Cape Race

Réservoir
Manicouagan

Gulf of
St Lawrence

Île d'Anticosti

PRINCE EDWARD
ISLAND

St Pierre
and
Miquelon
(France)

ONTARIO

MANITOBA

Lake Superior

NEW
BRUNSWICK

NOVA SCOTIA

Halifax

Sable Island

Thunder
Bay

MINNESOTA

St Paul

Minneapolis

WISCONSIN

Milwaukee

Lake Michigan

MICHIGAN

U.S.A.

Chicago

Lake Huron

Detroit

Cleveland

PENNSYLVANIA

Lake Erie

Buffalo

Toronto

Hamilton

Ottawa

Montréal

Québec

MAINE

VERMONT

NH

MASS.

Boston

New York

NEW YORK

Hartford

CONN.

ATLANTIC

OCEAN

MILES   KM

800

1200

600

1000

800

400

600

200

400

200

0   0

1:17 000 000

© Collins Bartholomew Ltd

185

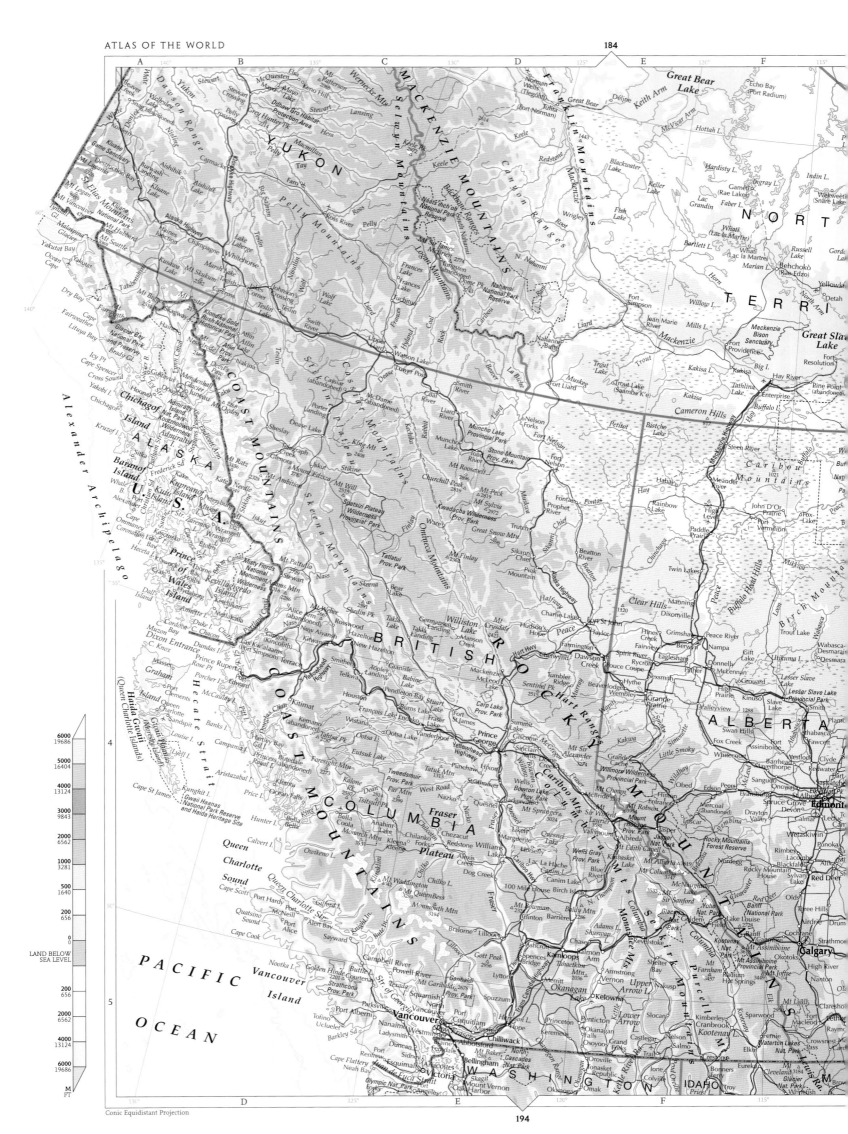

Conic Equidistant Projection

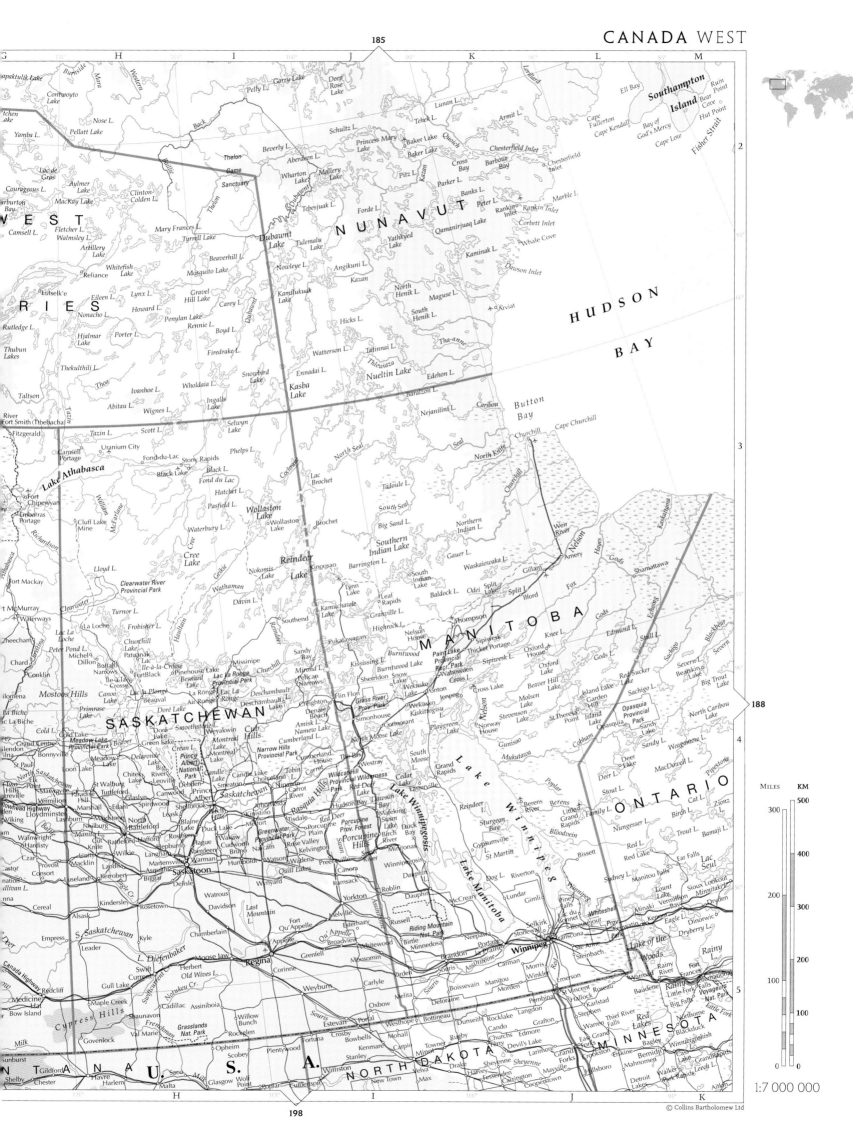

Southampton
Island

NUNAVUT

HUDSON

BAY

Button
Bay

MANITOBA

SASKATCHEWAN

Lake Athabasca

Lake Winnipeg

Lake Winnipegosis

Lake Manitoba

ONTARIO

CANADA
U.S.A.

NORTH DAKOTA

MINNESOTA

Winnipeg

Regina

Saskatoon

MILES   KM

300   500

          400

200   300

          200

100   100

0   0

1:7 000 000

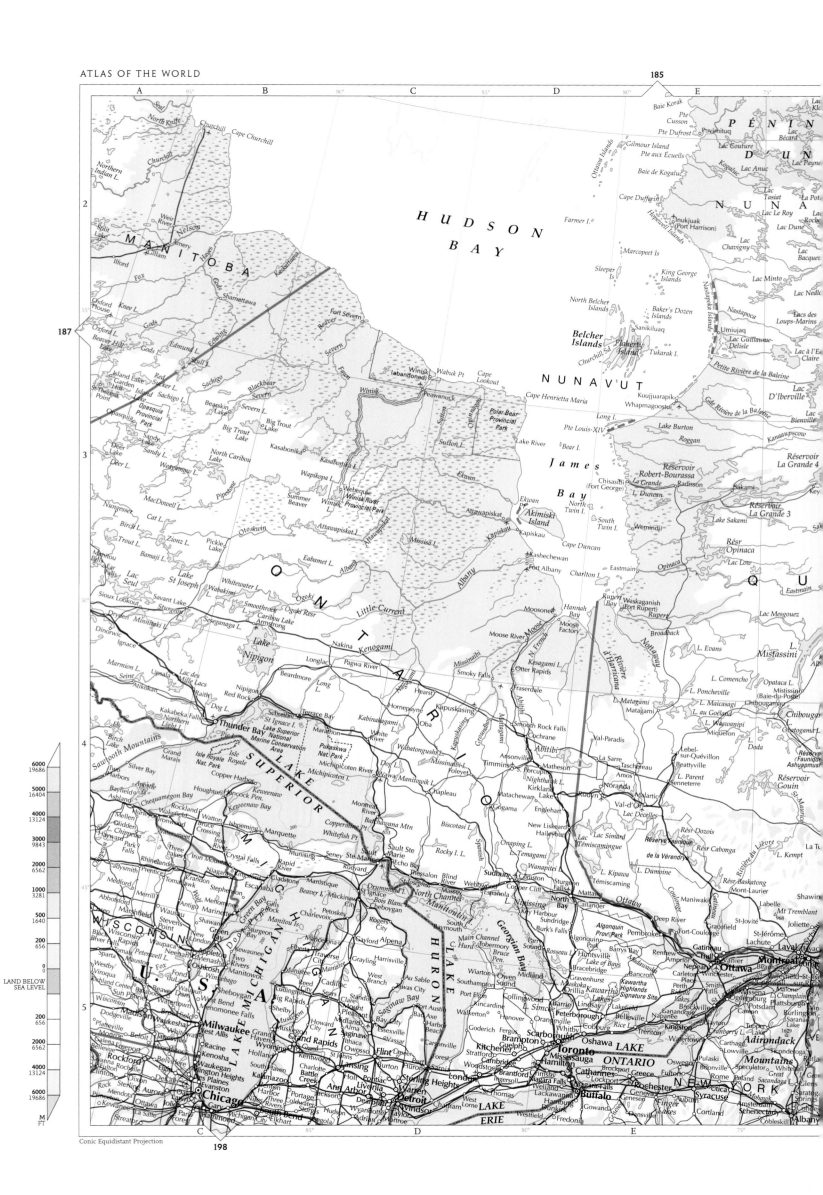

Conic Equidistant Projection

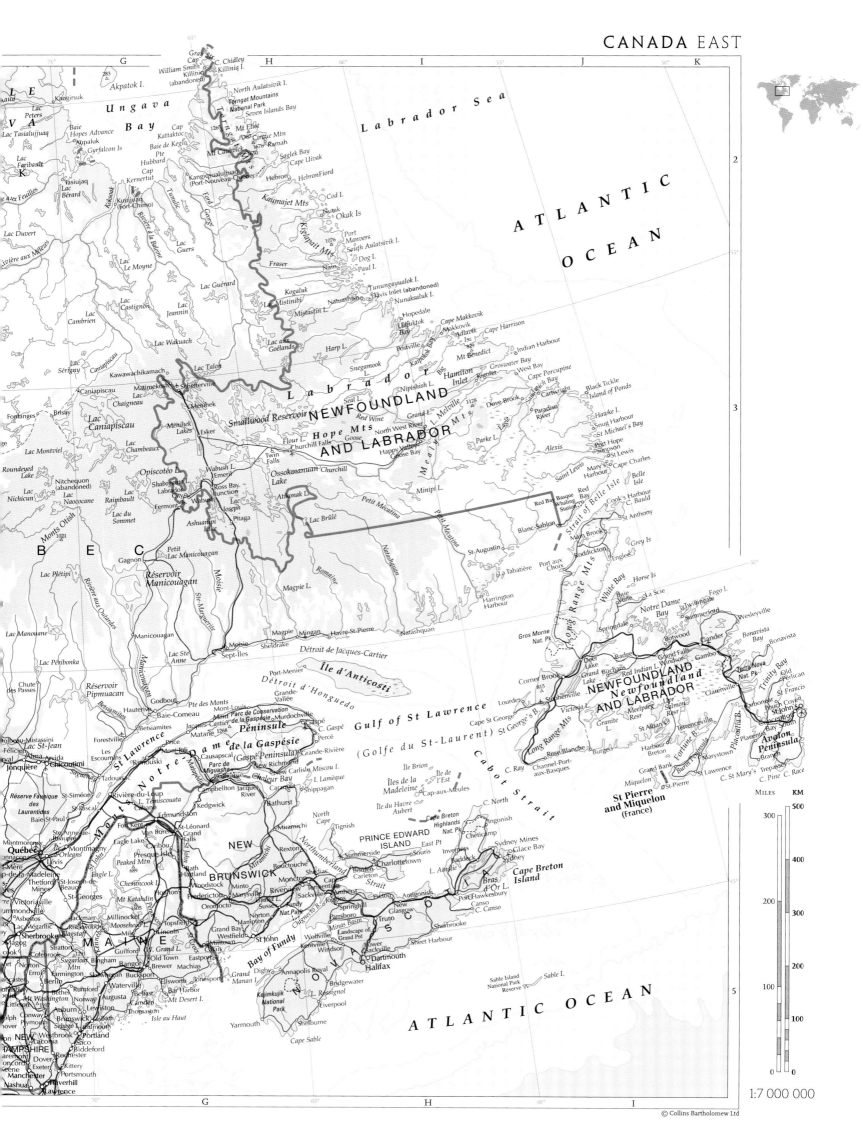

1:7 000 000

© Collins Bartholomew Ltd

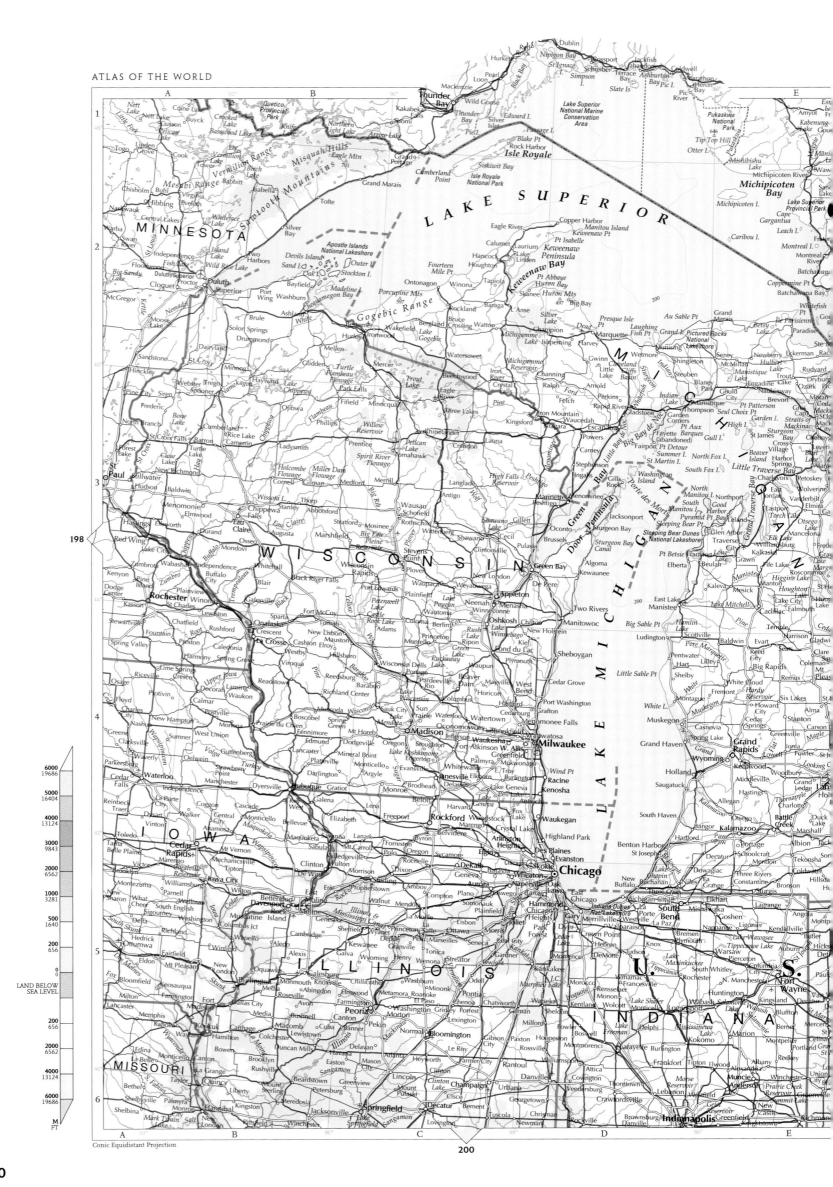

Conic Equidistant Projection

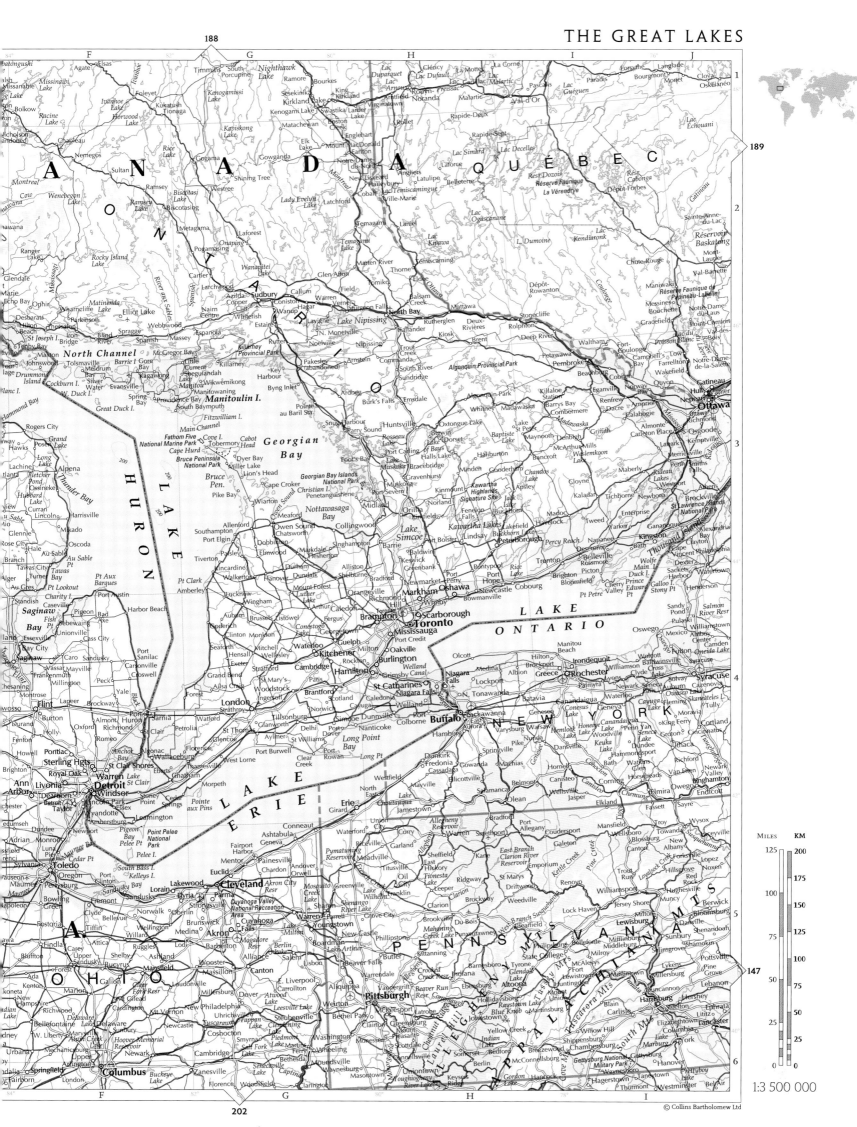

1:3 500 000

© Collins Bartholomew Ltd

Conic Equidistant Projection

6000
19686
5000
16404
4000
13124
3000
9843
2000
6562
1000
3281
500
1640
200
656
0
0
LAND BELOW
SEA LEVEL
200
656
2000
6562
4000
13124
6000
19686
M
FT

ATLANTIC
OCEAN

GULF OF MEXICO

THE BAHAMAS

1:12 000 000

© Collins Bartholomew Ltd

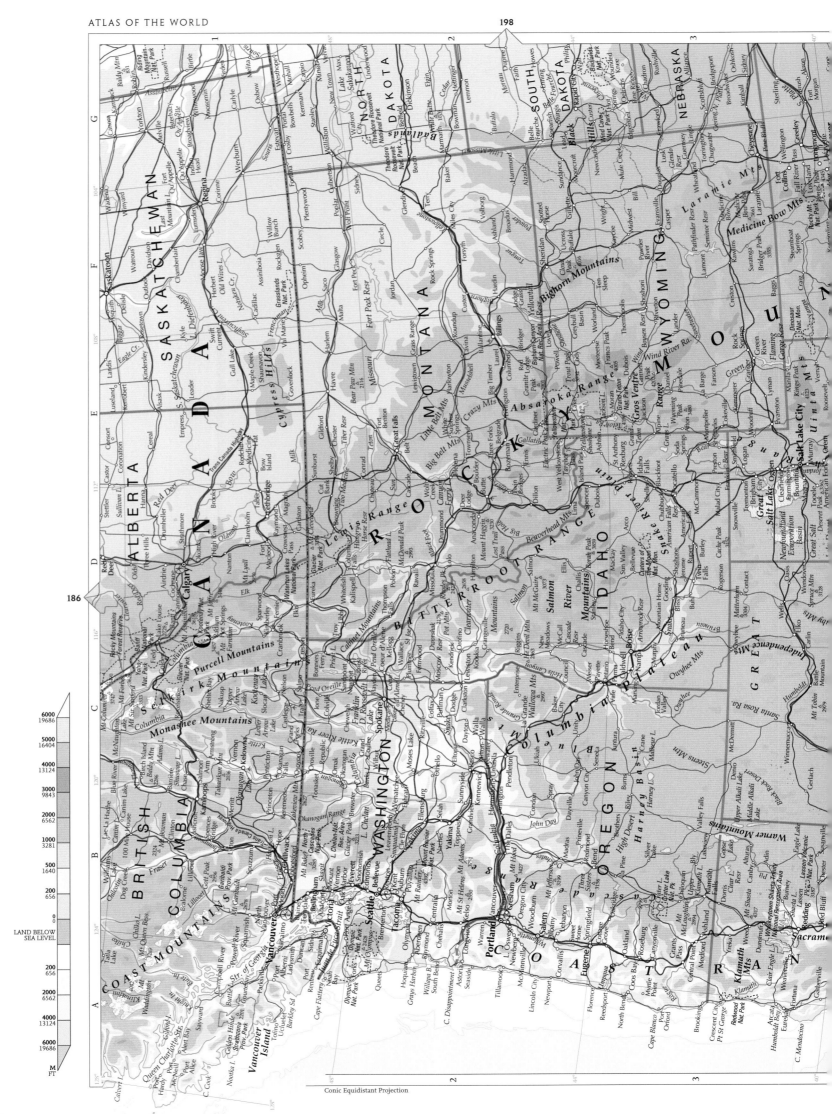

Conic Equidistant Projection

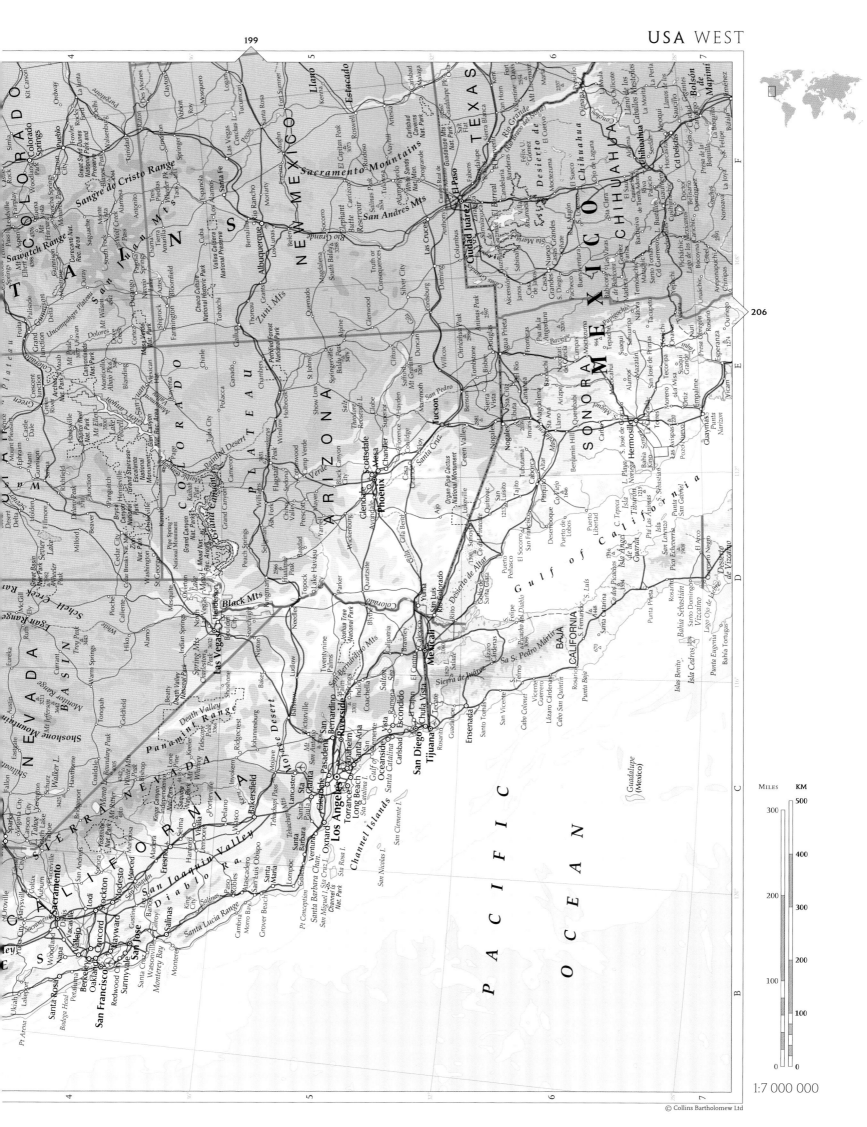

199

206

1:7 000 000

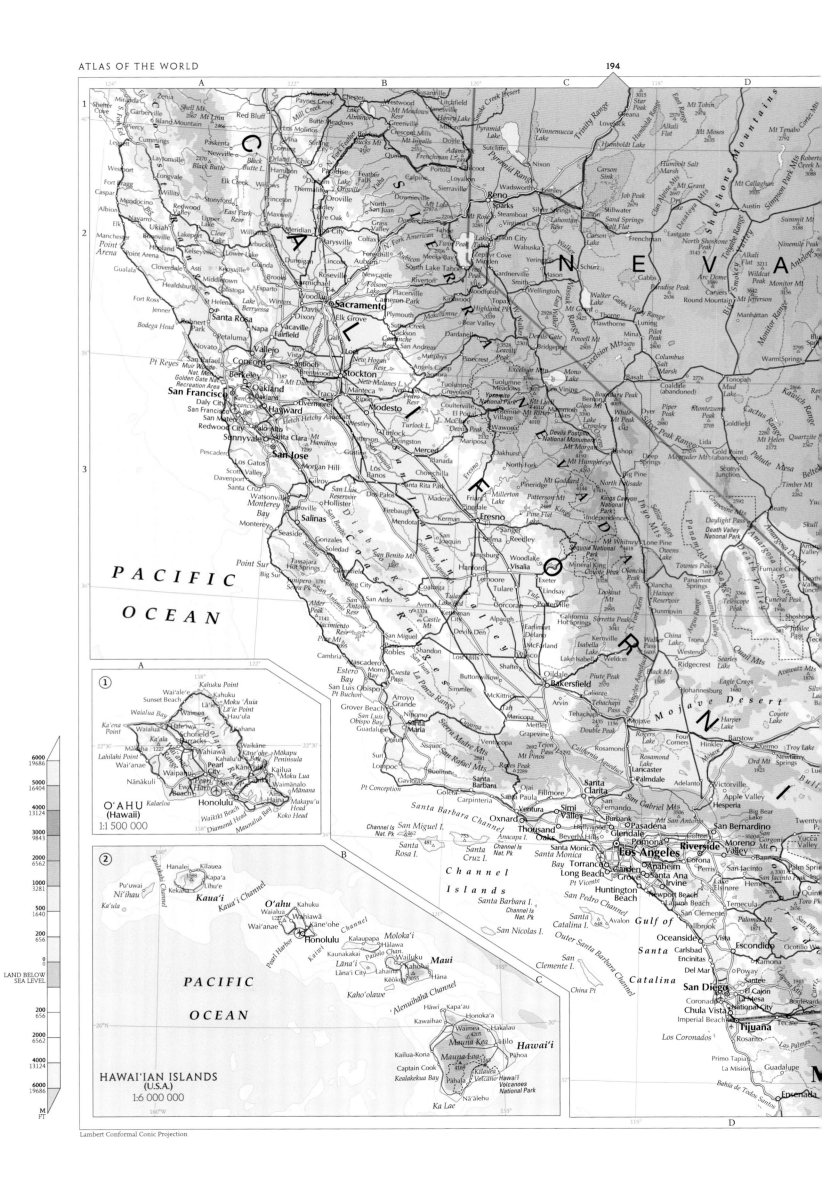

PACIFIC

OCEAN

① O'AHU
(Hawaii)
1:1 500 000

② HAWAI'IAN ISLANDS
(U.S.A.)
1:6 000 000

PACIFIC

OCEAN

6000
19686

5000
16404

4000
13124

3000
9843

2000
6562

1000
3281

500
1640

200
656

0
0

LAND BELOW
SEA LEVEL

200
656

2000
6562

4000
13124

6000
19686

M
FT

Lambert Conformal Conic Projection

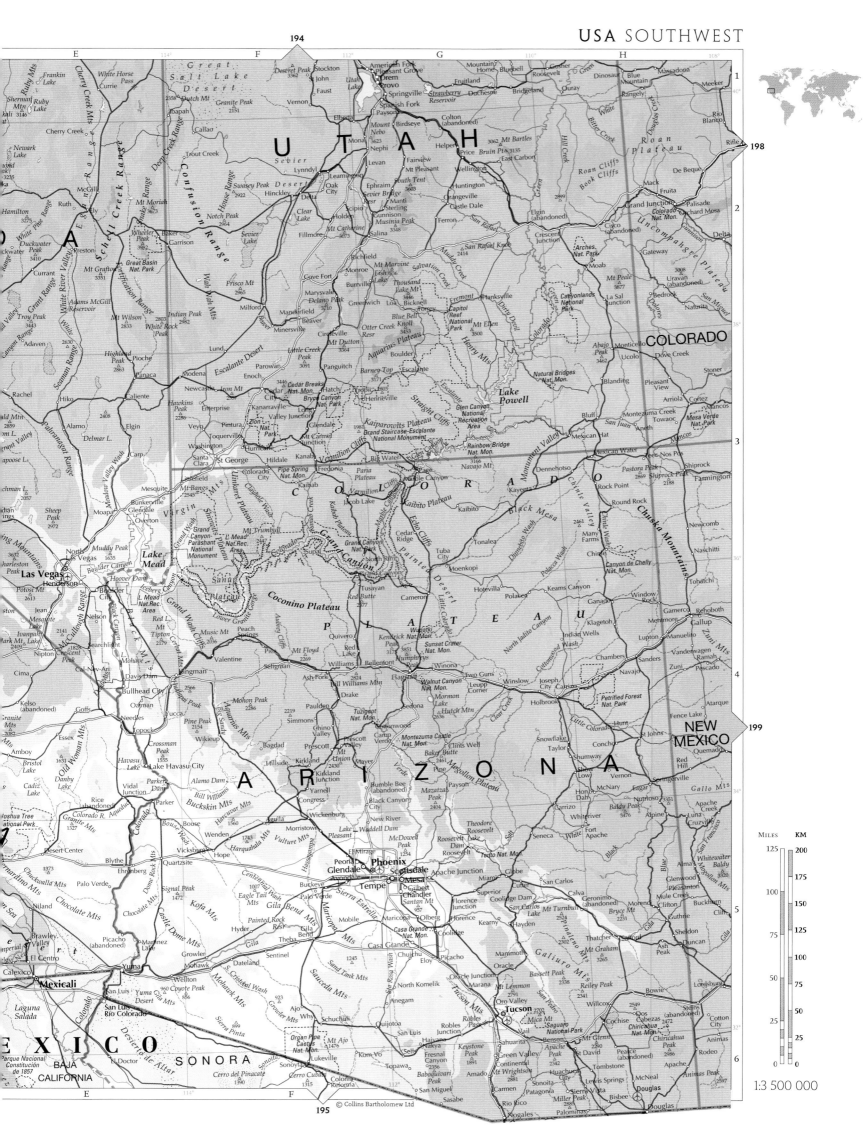

1

198

2

COLORADO

3

4

NEW
MEXICO

199

5

6

© Collins Bartholomew Ltd

E   F   G   H

UTAH

ARIZONA

MEXICO

SONORA

BAJA
CALIFORNIA

Las Vegas

Phoenix
Glendale   Scottsdale
Tempe   Mesa
Chandler
Gilbert

Tucson

Mexicali

Yuma

El Centro

Lake
Mead

Lake
Powell

Coconino Plateau

Grand Canyon

PLATEAU

MILES   KM
125 ——— 200
        — 175
100 ——— 150
        — 125
75 ——— 100
        — 75
50 ——— 50
        — 25
25 ———
0   ——— 0

1:3 500 000

197

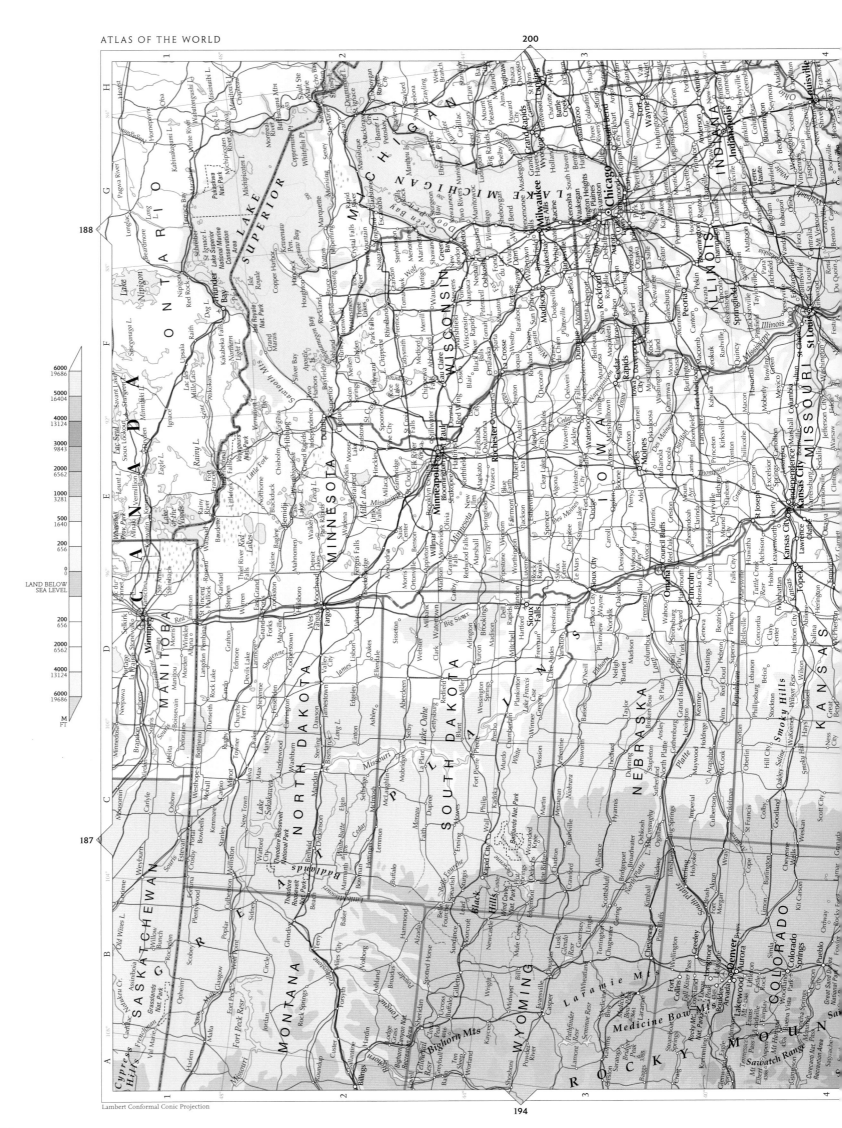

Lambert Conformal Conic Projection

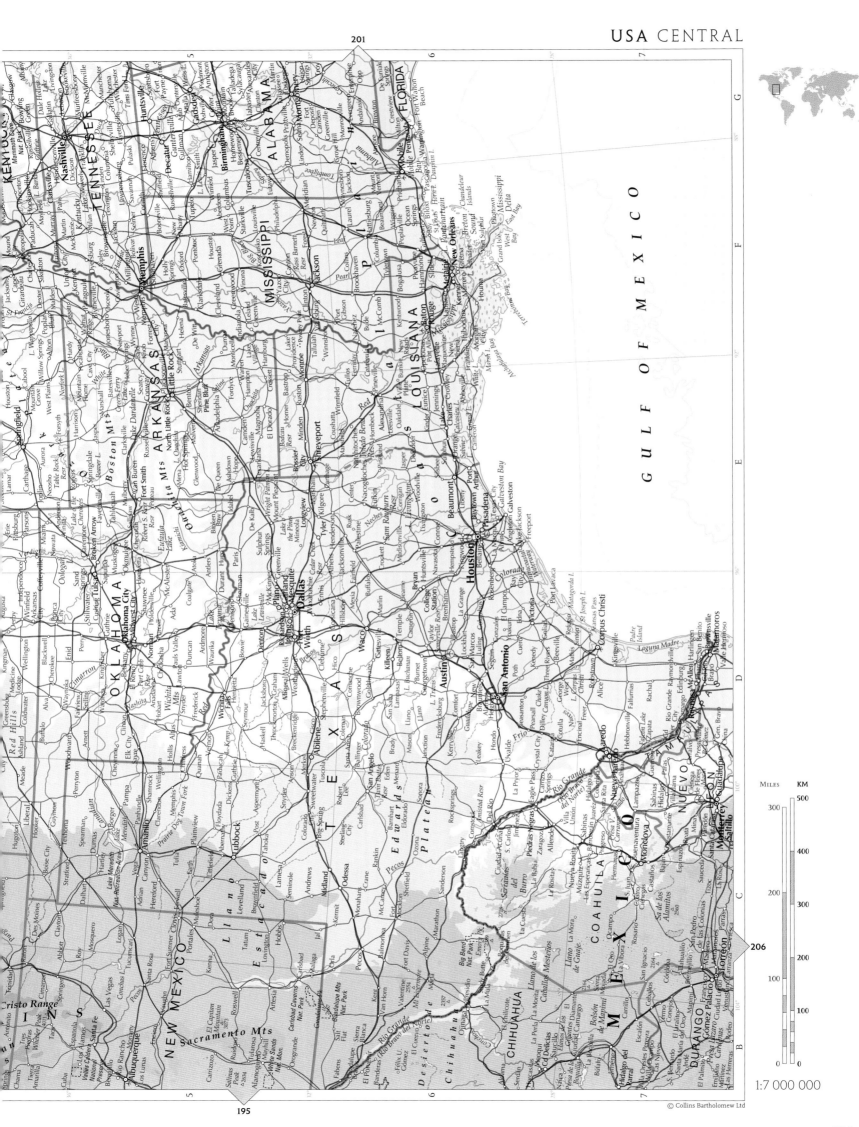

201

195

206

MILES KM

300

200

100

0

500

400

300

200

100

0

1:7 000 000

189

188

6000
19686

5000
16404

4000
13124

3000
9843

2000
6562

1000
3281

500
1640

200
656

0
0

LAND BELOW
SEA LEVEL

200
656

2000
6562

4000
13124

6000
19686

M
FT

Lambert Conformal Conic Projection

198

ATLANTIC

OCEAN

GULF

OF

MEXICO

THE

BAHAMAS

Grand Bahama

Great Abaco

Eleuthera

New Providence

Nassau

Andros

San Salvador

Long Island

Great Exuma

Cat Island

Rum Cay

Tropic of Cancer

Tongue of the Ocean

Northwest Providence Chan.

Northeast Providence Chan.

Exuma Sound

Straits of Florida

TENNESSEE

KENTUCKY

ARKANSAS

MISSISSIPPI

ALABAMA

GEORGIA

FLORIDA

SOUTH CAROLINA

NORTH CAROLINA

A P P A L A C H I A N   M O U N T A I N S

Nashville

Memphis

New Orleans

Mobile

Birmingham

Montgomery

Atlanta

Columbus

Tallahassee

Jacksonville

Orlando

Tampa

St Petersburg

Miami

Fort Lauderdale

Hollywood

Hialeah

Miami Beach

West Palm Beach

Boca Raton

Pompano Beach

Daytona Beach

Melbourne

Cape Canaveral

Savannah

Charleston

Columbia

Charlotte

Raleigh

Durham

Greensboro

Winston Salem

Knoxville

Chattanooga

Huntsville

Decatur

Cape Hatteras

Cape Fear

Cape Lookout

Cape Romain

Wilmington

Myrtle Beach

Long Bay

Dry Tortugas

Key West

Key Largo

Lake Okeechobee

Everglades

Apalachee Bay

Tampa Bay

Panama City

Pensacola

205

199

MILES   KM

300   500

400

200   300

200

100   100

0   0

1:7 000 000

© Collins Bartholomew Ltd

201

G

D

C

B

5   6   7

191

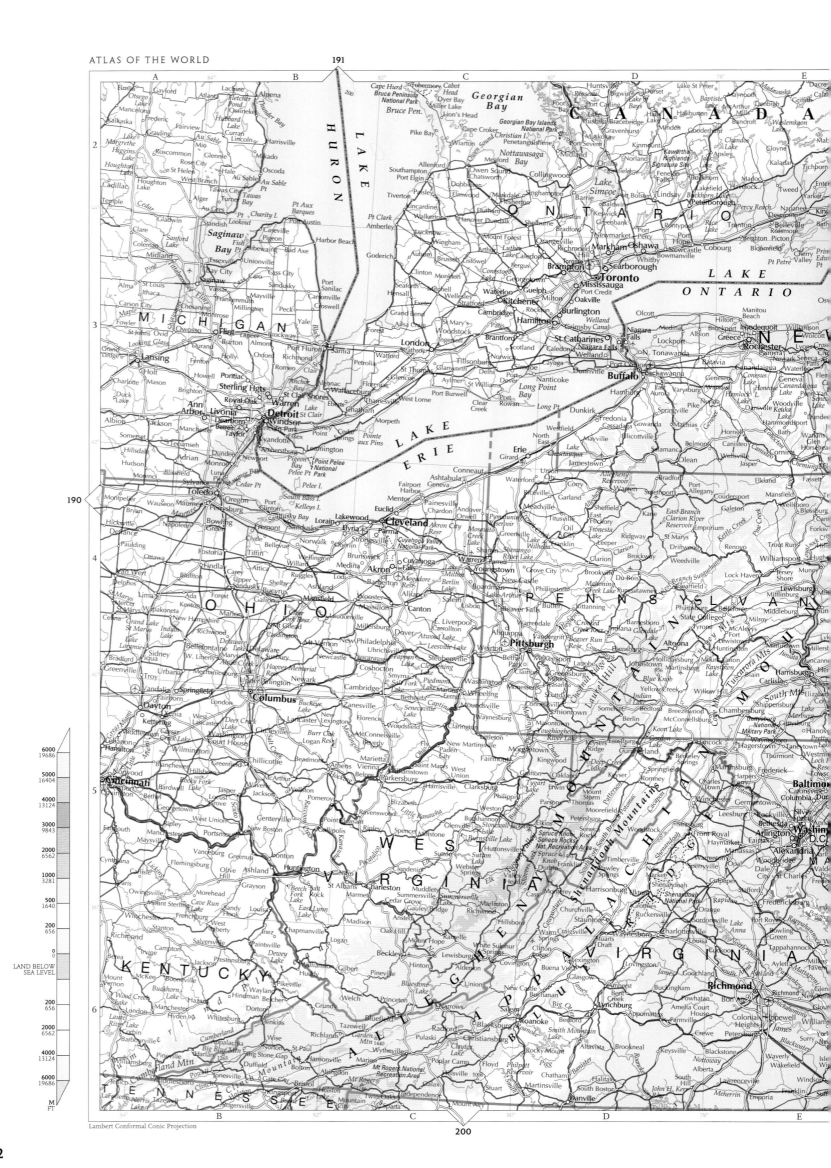

6000
19686
5000
16404
4000
13124
3000
9843
2000
6562
1000
3281
500
1640
200
656
0
0
LAND BELOW
SEA LEVEL
200
656
2000
6562
4000
13124
6000
19686

M
FT

190

200

Lambert Conformal Conic Projection

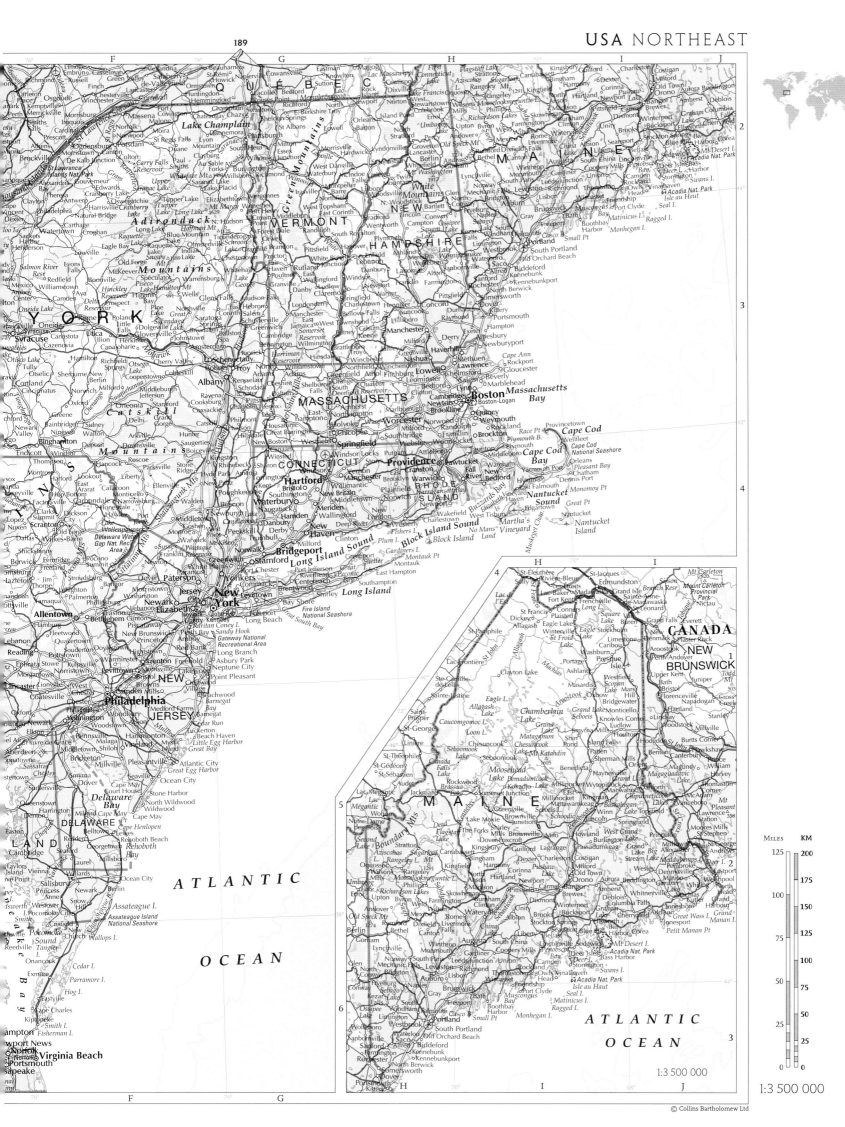

1:3 500 000

1:3 500 000

MILES   KM

125   200

      175

100   150

      125

75   100

50   75

      50

25   25

0   0

© Collins Bartholomew Ltd

PACIFIC

OCEAN

GULF OF MEXI

Lambert Azimuthal Equal Area Projection

ATLANTIC

OCEAN

Bermuda
(U.K.) Hamilton

Tropic of Cancer

THE BAHAMAS

Grand
Bahama

Little
Abaco

Great
Abaco

Freeport

Eleuthera

Governor's
Harbour

Nassau

Andros

Cat
Island

San Salvador

Exuma
Sound

Rum
Cay

Long
Island

Great
Exuma

Crooked
Island

Mayaguana

Turks and Caicos Islands
(U.K.)

Acklins
Island

Crooked I. Passage

Matthew
Town

Lake
Rosa

Great
Inagua

Caicos Is
Grand Turk
(Cockburn Town)

Turks Is

HISPANIOLA

LEEWARD ISLANDS

Anegada
(U.K.)

Virgin Is
(U.S.A.)

Virgin Is
(U.K.)

Anguilla
The (U.K.)
Valley

St-Martin (Fr.)
St Maarten (Neth.)
St-Barthélemy (Fr.)

ANTIGUA
AND
BARBUDA

Basseterre Barbuda

St John's

Antigua

ST KITTS AND NEVIS

Brades
Montserrat

Guadeloupe
(Fr.)

Basse-Terre
Marie-
Galante

Roseau

DOMINICA

Lesser Antilles

Martinique
(Fr.)

Fort-de-
France

Castries

ST LUCIA

Kingstown

ST VINCENT &
THE GRENADINES

Bridgetown

BARBADOS

CARIBBEAN SEA

GRENADA

St
George's

Tobago
Scarborough

TRINIDAD
AND
TOBAGO

Port of
Spain

Arima

WINDWARD ISLANDS

Lesser Antilles

Aruba
(Neth.)
Oranjestad

Curaçao
(Neth.)

Willemstad

Bonaire
(Neth.)

Islas Los Roques
(Ven.)

I. Orchila
(Ven.)

La Blanquilla
(Ven.)

Los Testigos
(Ven.)

I. de Margarita
(Ven.)
Porlamar

I. La Tortuga
(Ven.)

Los Roques

Carúpano

VENEZUELA

1:14 000 000

© Collins Bartholomew Ltd

MILES KM

500 800

400 600

400

300

200 200

100

0 0

211

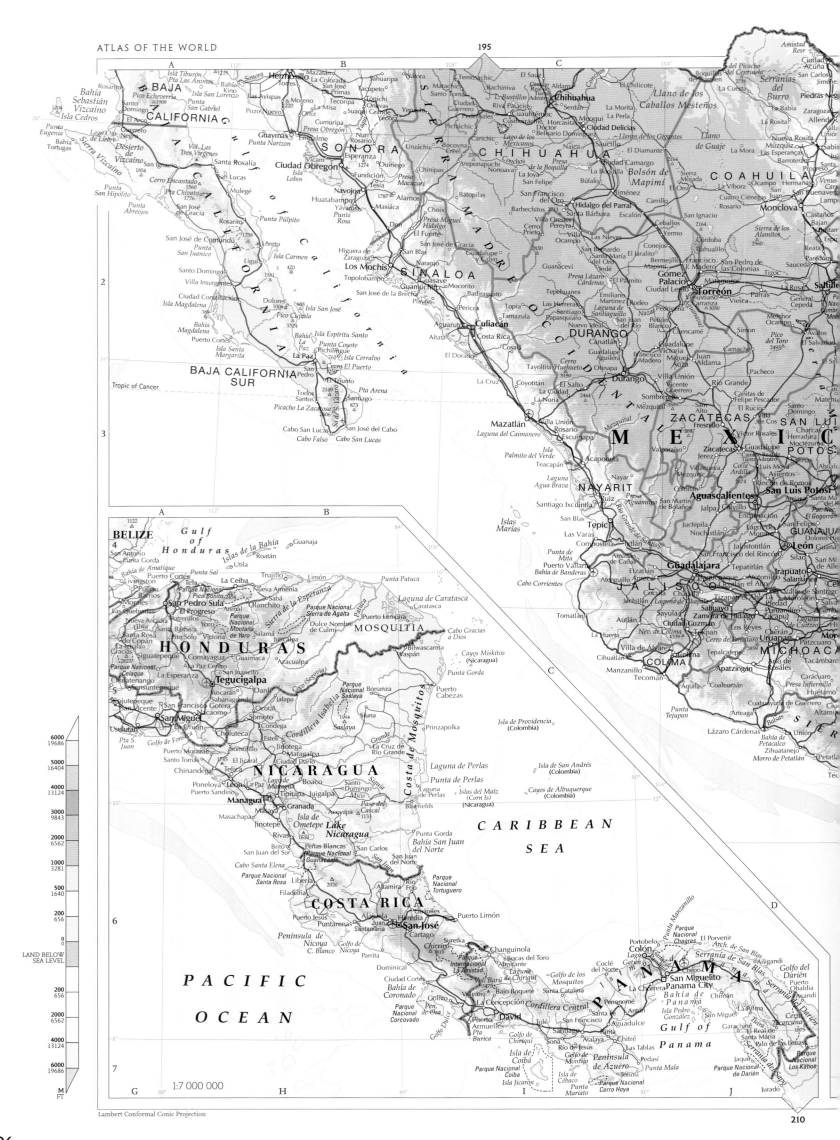

195

BAJA CALIFORNIA

Gulf of California

Isla Tiburón

Isla Cedros

Bahía Sebastián Vizcaíno

Desierto de Vizcaíno

Sierra Vizcaíno

HERMOSILLO

SONORA

CHIHUAHUA

Chihuahua

Ciudad Delicias

COAHUILA

Bolsón de Mapimí

Monclova

Ciudad Obregón

Navojoa

SINALOA

Los Mochis

Culiacán

DURANGO

Gómez Palacio

Torreón

Saltillo

La Paz

BAJA CALIFORNIA SUR

Tropic of Cancer

Cabo San Lucas

Mazatlán

MEXIC

ZACATECAS

SAN LUIS POTOSÍ

NAYARIT

Tepic

Aguascalientes

San Luis Potosí

GUANAJUATO

León

Guadalajara

JALISCO

COLIMA

MICHOACÁN

PACIFIC OCEAN

BELIZE

Gulf of Honduras

Islas de la Bahía

HONDURAS

San Pedro Sula

Tegucigalpa

MOSQUITIA

Puerto Cabezas

NICARAGUA

Managua

Lake Nicaragua

CARIBBEAN SEA

Isla de San Andrés (Colombia)

COSTA RICA

San José

Puerto Limón

PANAMA

Panama City

Colón

Gulf of Panama

1:7 000 000

Lambert Conformal Conic Projection

6000 / 19686
5000 / 16404
4000 / 13124
3000 / 9843
2000 / 6562
1000 / 3281
500 / 1640
200 / 656
0 / 0
LAND BELOW SEA LEVEL
200 / 656
2000 / 6562
4000 / 13124
6000 / 19686
M / FT

210

206

199

GULF OF MEXICO

Tropic of Cancer

Arrecife Alacrán

Bahía de
Campeche

PACIFIC

OCEAN

Gulf of
Tehuantepec

MILES	KM
300	500
	400
200	300
	200
100	100
0	0

1:7 000 000

© Collins Bartholomew Ltd

NORTH
AMERICA

Gulf of Mexico

Gulf of California

Bahía
de
Campeche

Yucatán

Cuba

Greater An

Hispani

Jamaica

CARIBBEA

Lake
Nicaragua

Gulf
of Panama

Barranquilla
Cartagena

Maraca

Montería

San Cristo

Medellín

Tunja

Isla de Coco

Ibagué

Bogotá

Isla de Malpelo
(Colombia)

COLOMB

Cali

Neiva

Pasto

Esmeraldas

Quito

Islas
Revillagigedo

Manta

ECUADOR

Tropic of Cancer

Guayaquil

Cuenca

Île Clipperton

Machala

Iquitos

Piura

Galapagos
Islands
(Ecuador)

Ucayali

Tarapoto

Chiclayo

Pucallpa

Cruz
do S

Trujillo

PERU

PACIFIC

Callao

Huancayo

Cu

Lima

Ica

Ju

Arequipa

Iq

OCEAN

Antofag

Islas
Desventurados
(Chile)

Cop

Marquesas Islands

La Sere

Hiva Oa

Îles
du Désappointement

Isla Sala y Gómez

Cerro Acon

Valparaíso

Easter Island
(Isla de Pascua)
(Rapa Nui)
(Chile)

Juan Fernández
Islands
(Chile)

Santia

Talca

Tuamotu Islands

Henderson Island

Chillán

Îles
du Roi Georges

Hao

Îles Gambier

Pitcairn Island

Concepción

Rangiroa

Valdivia

Tahiti

Society
Islands

Marutea

OCEANIA

Puerto Mont

Isla de Chiloé

Archipiélago
de los Chonos

Tubuai Islands

Golfo de Penas

Tropic of Capricorn

Puerto Natales

Punta Are

Equator

H · I · J · K · L · M · N

Puerto Rico
Anguilla
Antigua
Guadeloupe
Dominica
Martinique
St Lucia
Lesser Antilles
Barbados
St Vincent
and the Grenadines
Grenada
Tobago
Trinidad

E A
racay **Caracas**
encia
Cumaná
Ciudad Bolívar
Orinoco
VENEZUELA
Puerto Ayacucho
Georgetown
Paramaribo
Boa Vista
GUYANA
SURINAME
Cayenne
French
Guiana
Macapá

Negro
 purá
antins
Carauari
Manaus
Amazon
Santarém
Belém
São Luís
Parnaíba

Madeira
Branco
Tapajós
Maraba
Teresina
Fortaleza

Porto
Velho
B R A Z I L
Araguaína
Fernando
de Noronha
(Brazil)

Xingu
Palmas
Barragem
de Sobradinho
Floresta
Natal
João Pessoa
Recife

Trinidad
Represa
Serra da Mesa
Juàzeiro
Maceió
Aracaju

La Paz
BOLIVIA
Cochabamba
Santa Cruz
Cuiabá
Brasília
Goiânia
São Francisco
Salvador
Ilhéus

Potosí
Sucre
Tarija
Campo
Grande
Patos
de Minas
Teófilo
Otôni

PARAGUAY
Araçatuba
Uberaba
Ribeirão
Preto
Belo
Horizonte
Vitória

San Salvador
de Jujuy
Pedro Juan
Caballero
Paraná
Maringá
Campinas
São Paulo
Nevado
Ojos del Salado
Asunción
Coronel
Oviedo
Curitiba
Santos
Rio
de Janeiro

amarca
Formosa
Resistencia
Encarnación
Posadas
Joinville
Ilha da Trindade
(Brazil)
Ilhas
Martín Vaz
(Brazil)

La Rioja
Corrientes
Florianópolis

Córdoba
Santa Fé
Paraná
Santa María
Concordia
Lagoa
dos Patos
Porto Alegre

endoza
Rosario
URUGUAY
Rio Grande

San Luis
Buenos
Aires
Montevideo

ARGENTINA
La
Plata
Rio de la Plata

Santa Rosa
Mar del Plata

uén
Bahía Blanca

Viedma
Golfo San Matías

Trelew

Comodoro Rivadavia
Golfo de San Jorge

hía
ande
Gallegos
Falkland
Islands
(U.K.)
Stanley

a Grande
Tierra del Fuego
huaia

ape Horn
Isla de los Estados

ake Passage
Shag
Rocks
South Georgia

South Georgia
and the
South Sandwich
Islands
(U.K.)
Traversay Islands
Candlemas Islands
Saunders Island
Montagu Island

South Shetland
Islands
South
Sandwich
Islands
Southern Thule
Bristol Island

ntarctic Peninsula
South Orkney
Islands

Madeira

Canary
Islands
Gran
Canaria

Santo Antão
Cape Verde
Boa Vista
São Tiago
Tropic of Cancer
Senegal

Niger

A F

Gulf
of
Guinea

Ascension
Equator

A T L A N T I C

St Helena

O C E A N

R
I
C
A

Tristan
da Cunha
Tropic of Capricorn

Cape of Good Hope
Orange

MILES	KM
	2000
1200	1600
800	1200
	800
400	400
0	0

1:32 000 000

H · I · J · K · L · M · N

© Collins Bartholomew Ltd

209

6000	19686		
5000	16404		
4000	13124		
3000	9843		
2000	6562		
1000	3281		
500	1640		
200	656		
0	0		

LAND BELOW
SEA LEVEL

200	656
2000	6562
4000	13124
6000	19686

M
FT

CARIBBEAN

SEA

NICARAGUA

COSTA RICA

San José

PANAMA

Panama City

PACIFIC OCEAN

COLOMBIA

ECUADOR

Quito

VENEZUELA

Caracas

Bogotá

PERU

Lima

GALAPAGOS IS
(Ecuador)

Isla Darwin
Isla Wolf

I. Pinta
Pta Albemarle   I. Marchena
Parque Nacional
Galápagos   Vol. Wolf   Isla Santiago
I. Fernandina   Isla Santa Cruz   Equator
Isla Isabela   Puerto
Cabo Rosa   Baquerizo   I. San Cristóbal
Moreno
Isla Floreana
I. Española

1:15 000 000

Tropic of Capricorn

BOLIVIA

La Paz

ARGENTINA

Lambert Azimuthal Equal Area Projection

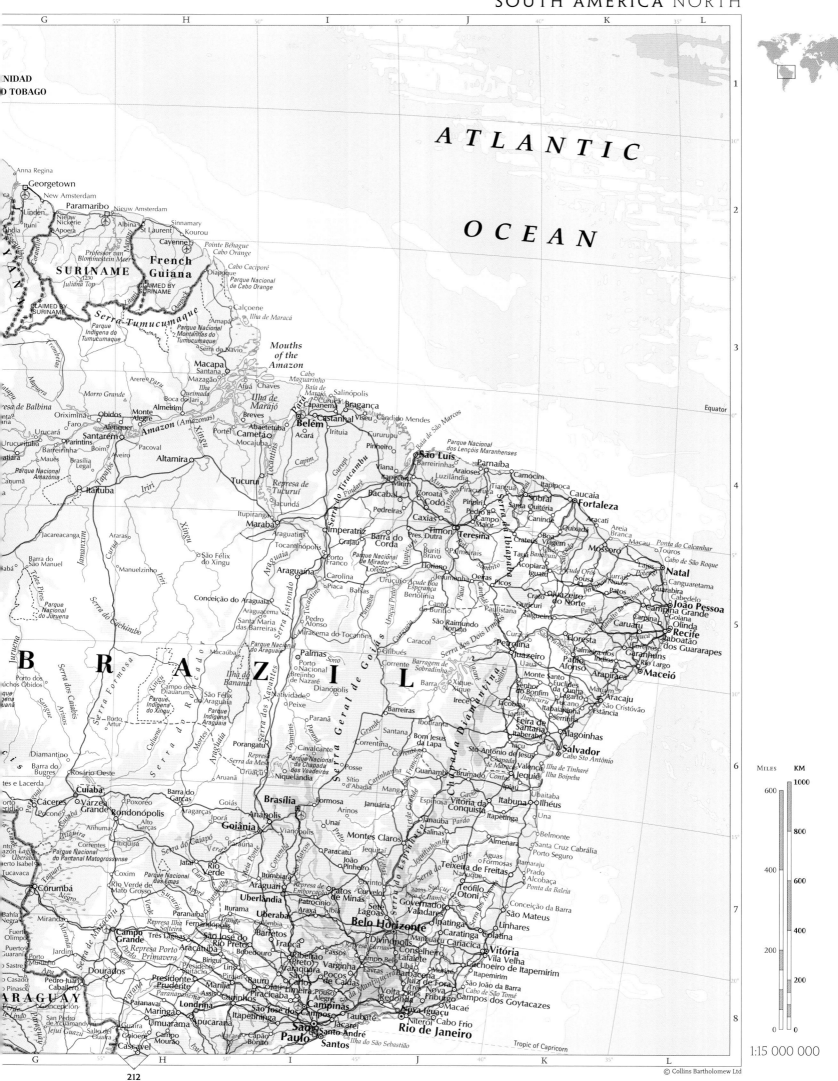

G 55° H 50° I 45° J 40° K 35° L

1

ATLANTIC

OCEAN

2

NIDAD
O TOBAGO

Anna Regina
Georgetown
New Amsterdam
Linden   Paramaribo   Nieuw Amsterdam
Ituni   Nieuw Nickerie   Albina   Sinnamary
Apoera   St Laurent   Kourou
Professor van   Cayenne
Blommestein Meer   Pointe Béhague
SURINAME   French   Cabo Orange
1230   Guiana   Parque Nacional
Juliana Top   de Cabo Orange
CLAIMED BY   Diappoque
SURINAME   Calçoene
CLAIMED BY
SURINAME   Serra Tumucumaque   Amapá   3
Parque   Parque Nacional   Ilha de Maracá
Indígena do   Montanhas do
Tumucumaque   Tumucumaque
Serra do Navio
Macapá   Mouths
Santana   of the
Mazagão   Amazon
Morro Grande   Ilha   Cabo   Equator
Queimada   Maguarinho
Afuá   Chaves   Baía de   Salinópolis
resa de Balbina   Óbidos   Almeirim   Marajó   Capanema   Bragança
Oriximiná   Monte   Ilha de   Breves   Curuçá   Viseu
Faro   Alegre   Marajó   Belém   Castanhal   Cândido Mendes
Urucará   Amazon (Amazonas)   Portel   Abaetetuba   Acará   Irituia   4
Parintins   Santarém   Cametá   Mocajuba   Cururupu   São Luís
Barreirinha   Boim   Pacoval   Pinheiro   Barreirinhas
Maués   Aveiro   Viana   Araioses
Brasília   Tucuruí   Itapecuru   Parnaíba
Legal   Altamira   Represa de   Bacabal   Mirim   Luzilândia   Camocim
Parque Nacional   Tucuruí   Coroatá   Tianguá   Itapipoca
Amazônia   Jacundá   Caxias   Piripiri   Sobral   Caucaia
Itaituba   Itupiranga   Maraba   Codó   Pedro   Santa Quitéria   Fortaleza
Tocantinópolis   Imperatriz   Barra do   Pres.   Timon   Teresina   Canindé   Aracati   5
Jacareacanga   Grajaú   Corda   Dutra   Palmeirais   Crateús   Quixadá   Macau
Porto   Buriti   Oeiras   Tauá   Curral   Mossoró   Natal
Araras   Franco   Bravo   Floriano   Picos   Novos   Natal
São Félix   Carolina   Piacã   Balsas   Jerumenha   Crato   Juazeiro   Patos   Canguaretama
do Xingu   Araguaína   Conceição do Araguaia   Açude Boa   Esperança   do Norte   Campina Grande   João Pessoa
Serra do Cachimbo   Santa Maria   Bertolínia   São Raimundo   Currais   Salgueiro   Caruaru   Olinda
das Barreiras   Miracema do Tocantins   Nonato   Pallistana   Floresta   Recife
B R A Z I L   Palmas   Petrolina   Jaboatão
Porto   Juazeiro   Garanhuns
Nacional   Barragem de   Maceió
Represa   Sobradinho   6
Ilha do   Barreiras   Xique-Xique   Monte Santo   Arapiraca
Bananal   Ibotirama   Feira de   Alagoinhas
Santana   Itaberaba   Salvador
Cuiabá   Barra do   Niquelândia   Bom Jesus   da Lapa   Valença   Ilha de Tinharé
Várzea   Garças   Brasília   Posse   Sto. António de Jesus   Jequié   Itabuna   Ilhéus
Grande   Rondonópolis   Anápolis   Formosa   Vitória da   7
Goiânia   Conquista   Belmonte
Goiás   Montes Claros   Itapetinga   Porto Seguro
Rio   Araguari   Teixeira de Freitas   8

Tropic of Capricorn

212

© Collins Bartholomew Ltd

1:15 000 000

MILES   KM
1000
600   800
600
400   600
400
200   400
200
200
0   0

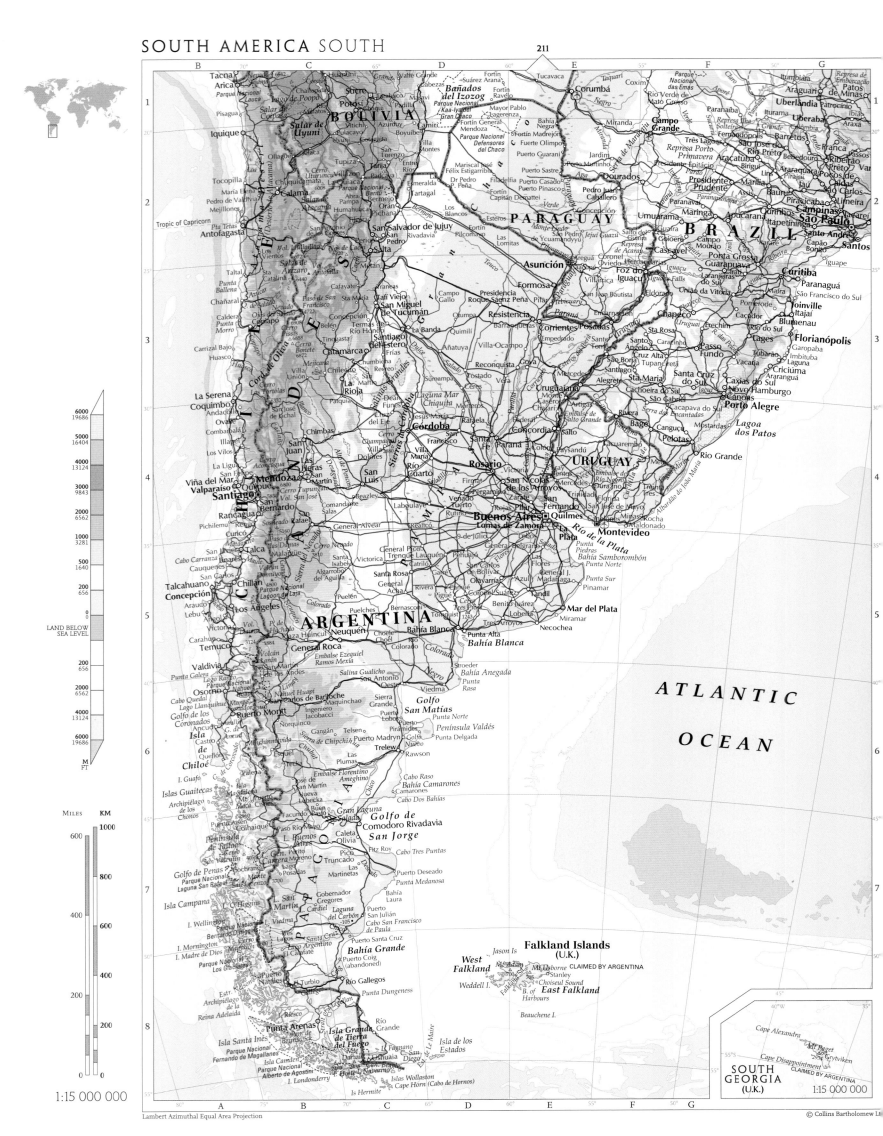

Lambert Azimuthal Equal Area Projection

© Collins Bartholomew Ltd

1:15 000 000

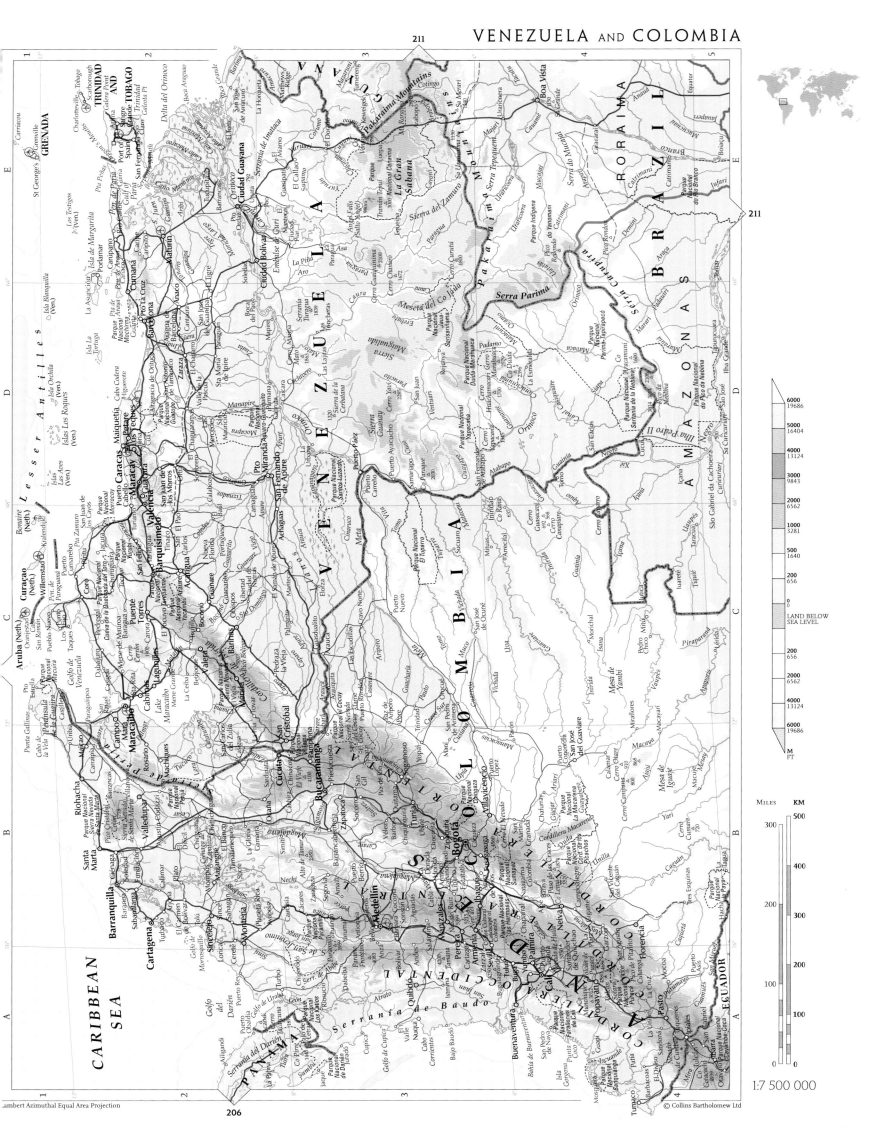

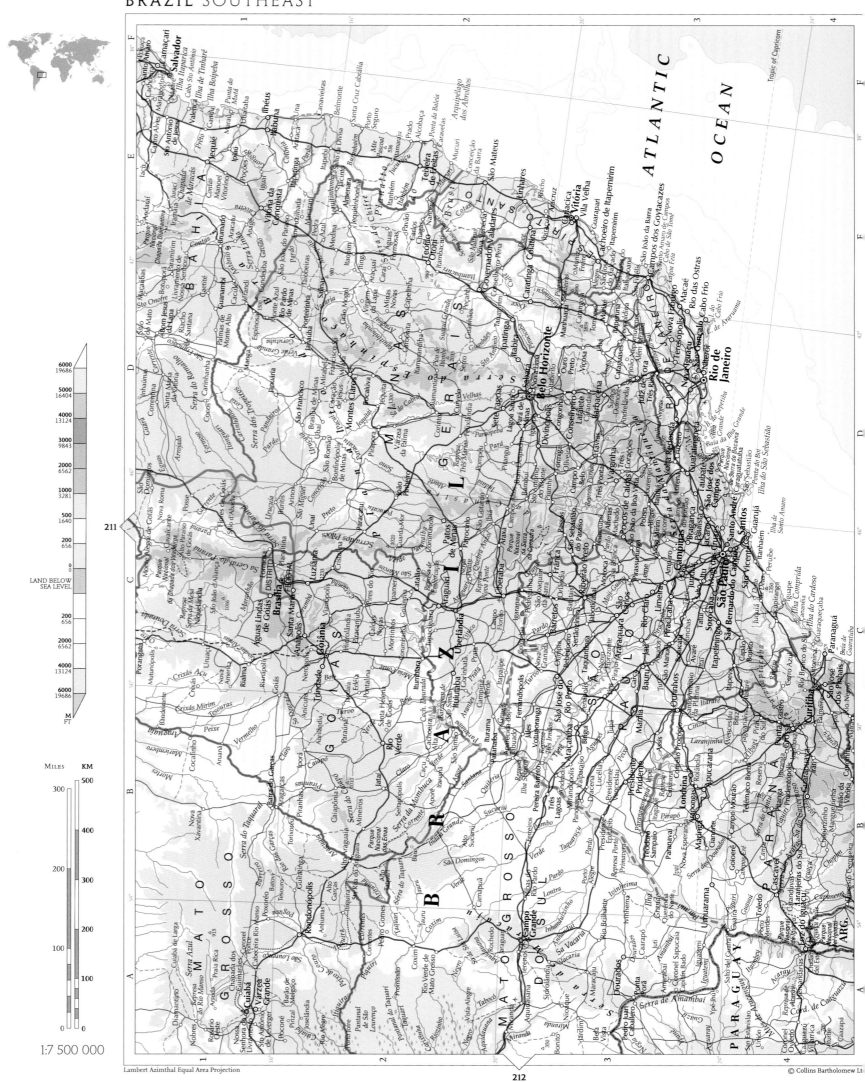

ATLANTIC

OCEAN

6000
19686
5000
16404
4000
13124
3000
9843
2000
6562
1000
3281
500
1640
200
656

LAND BELOW
SEA LEVEL

200
656
2000
6562
4000
13124
6000
19686

M
FT

211

MILES   KM

300   500

          400

200   300

          200

100   100

0   0

1:7 500 000

Lambert Azimthal Equal Area Projection

212

© Collins Bartholomew Lt

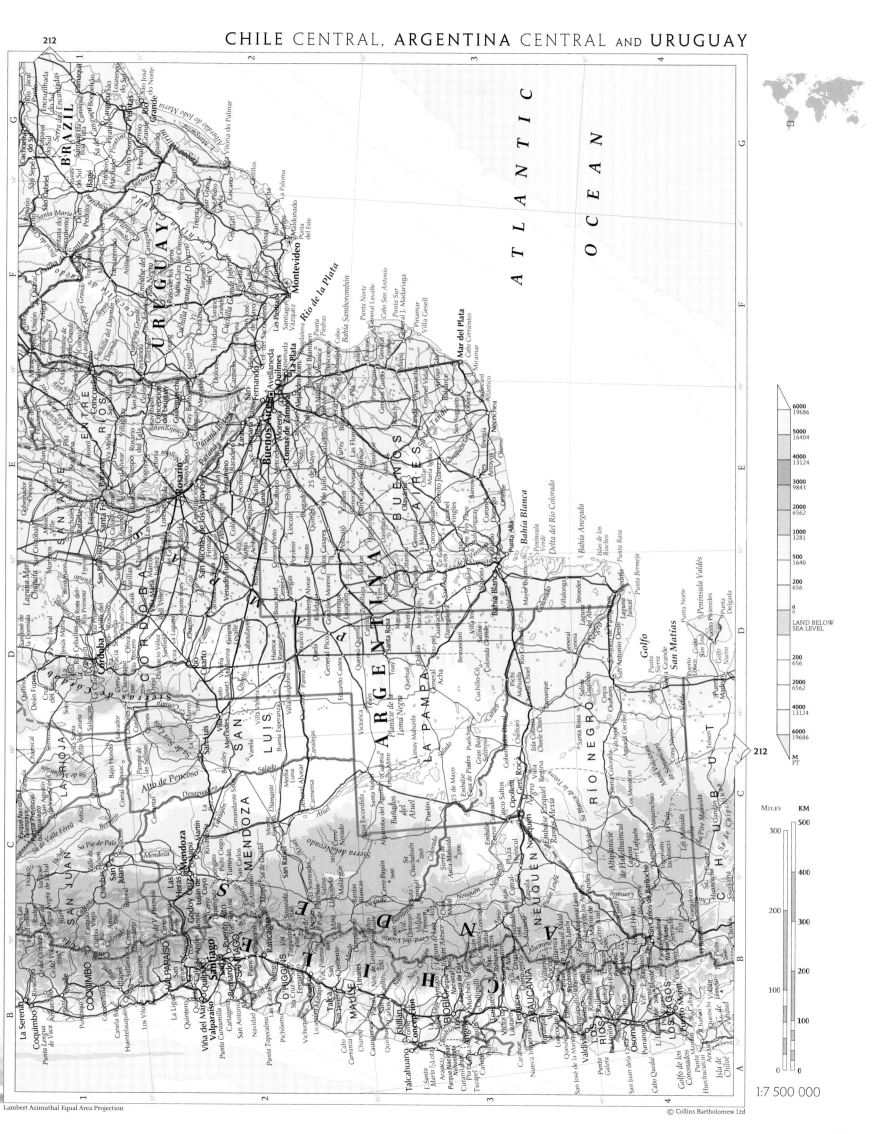

Lambert Azimuthal Equal Area Projection

© Collins Bartholomew Ltd

1:7 500 000

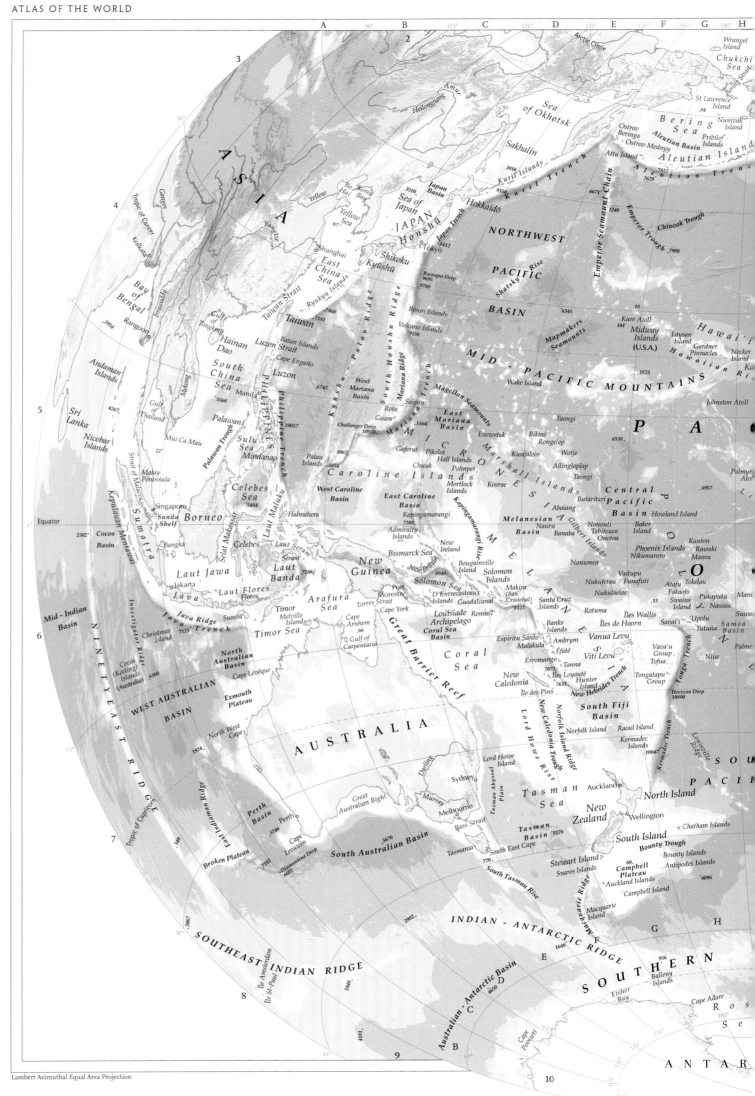

Lambert Azimuthal Equal Area Projection

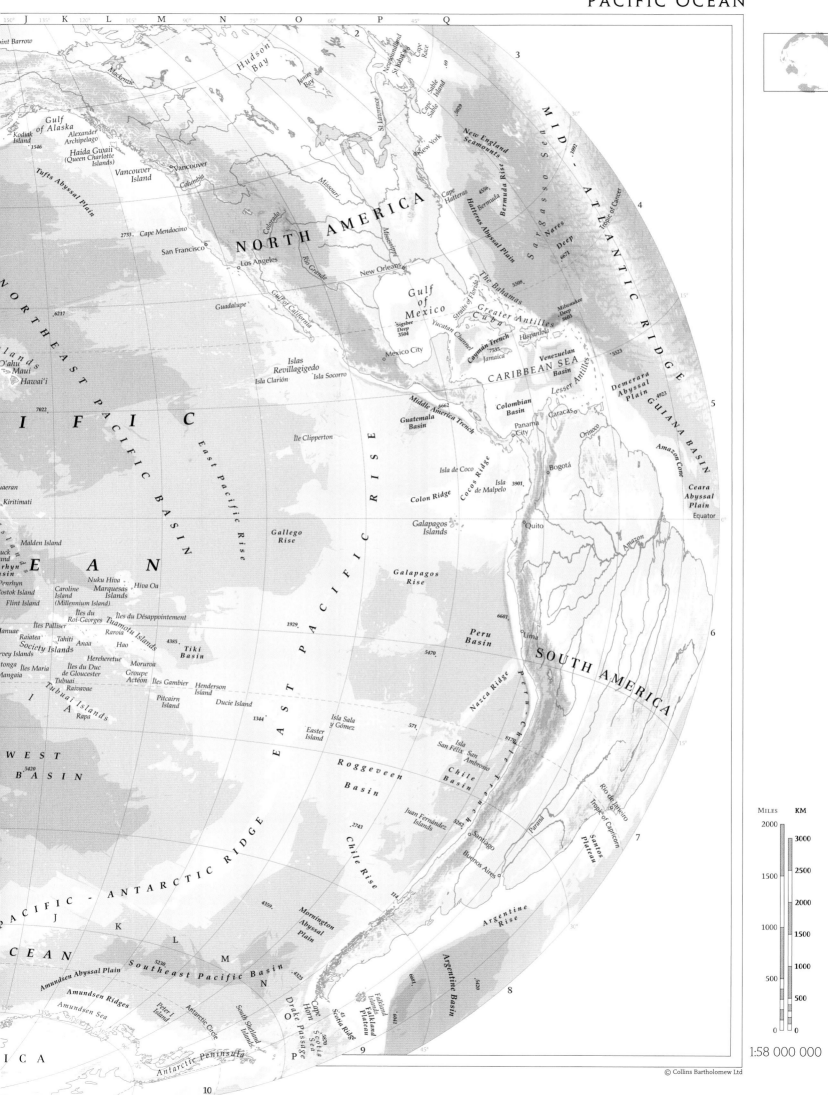

J 150° 135° K 120° L 105° M 90° N 75° O 60° P 45° Q

int Barrow

2

3

Gulf
of Alaska

Kodiak
Island *1546*

Alexander
Archipelago

Haida Gwaii
(Queen Charlotte
Islands)

Vancouver
Island

Vancouver

Columbia

Mackenzie

Hudson
Bay

James
Bay

St Lawrence

Newfoundland

St John's

Cape
Race

Cape
Sable

Sable
Island

New York

NORTH AMERICA

Missouri

Colorado

Rio Grande

New Orleans

Cape
Hatteras

New England
Seamounts

Hatteras Abyssal
Plain

Bermuda
Rise

Bermuda

4556

5092

Nares
Deep
6671

Tufts Abyssal Plain

2733. Cape Mendocino

San Francisco

Los Angeles

Guadalupe

Gulf of California

Gulf
of
Mexico

Sigsbee
Deep
3504

Mexico City

Yucatan Channel

Straits of Florida

The Bahamas

Cuba

Greater Antilles

5508

Milwaukee
Deep
8605

Hispaniola

Cayman Trench
7535

Jamaica

Tropic of Cancer

MID - ATLANTIC RIDGE

Sargasso

4

15°

ORTHEAST PACIFIC

6217

Islas
Revillagigedo

Isla Clarión

Isla Socorro

CARIBBEAN SEA

Colombian
Basin

Panama
City

Venezuelan
Basin

5523

Caracas

Lesser Antilles

Demerara
Abyssal
Plain

4923

GUIANA BASIN

5

lands
O'ahu
Maui
Hawai'i

7022

IFIC

Middle America Trench

Guatemala
Basin

6662

Colon Ridge

Cocos Ridge

Isla de Coco

Isla
de Malpelo

3901.

Bogotá

Orinoco

Amazon Cone

Ceara
Abyssal
Plain

Equator

aeran

Kiritimati

E A N

Île Clipperton

Galapagos
Islands

Quito

Amazon

lands
and
rhyn
sin

Malden Island

Gallego
Rise

Galapagos
Rise

East Pacific Rise

Penrhyn
ostok Island

Flint Island

Caroline
Island
(Millennium Island)

Nuku Hiva

Marquesas
Islands

Hiva Oa

1929.

Peru
Basin

6601

SOUTH AMERICA

6

anuae
Raiatea'
Tahiti
Society Islands
Anaa

Îles du
Roi-Georges

Îles du Désappointement

Tuamotu Islands

Raroia

Hao

4385.

Tiki
Basin

5470

Lima

East Pacific Rise

tonga
Îles Maria
angaia

Îles du Duc
de Gloucester

Hereheretue

Moruroa

Groupe
Actéon

Îles Gambier

Henderson
Island

Nazca Ridge

8170.

PERU-CHILE TRENCH

Tubuai Islands

Raivavae

Tubuai

Pitcairn
Island

Ducie Island

Isla Sala
y Gómez

571.

San Félix
Isla
San
Ambrosio

15°

I
A

Rapa

1344

Easter
Island

Chile
Basin

W E S T

BASIN

5420

Roggeveen

Basin

2743.

Juan Fernández
Islands

5282.

Santiago

Buenos Aires

Valparaíso

Paraná

Río de Janeiro

Tropic of Capricorn

Santos
Plateau

7

PACIFIC - ANTARCTIC RIDGE

Chile Rise

114.

Argentine
Rise

4359.

Mornington
Abyssal
Plain

Argentine Basin

5420.

8

OCEAN

Amundsen Abyssal Plain

5230.

Southeast Pacific Basin

N

4325.

Amundsen Ridges

Peter I
Island

Antarctic Circle

South Shetland
Islands

Cape
Horn

Scotia Sea

Drake Passage

Scotia Ridge

5870.

65

Falkland
Islands
Islas Malvinas

Falkland
Plateau

6641.

150° 135° J K L M N O P 45° 9

ICA

Amundsen Sea

Antarctic
Peninsula

10

MILES   KM

2000   3000

1500   2500

           2000

1000   1500

           1000

500   500

0   0

1:58 000 000

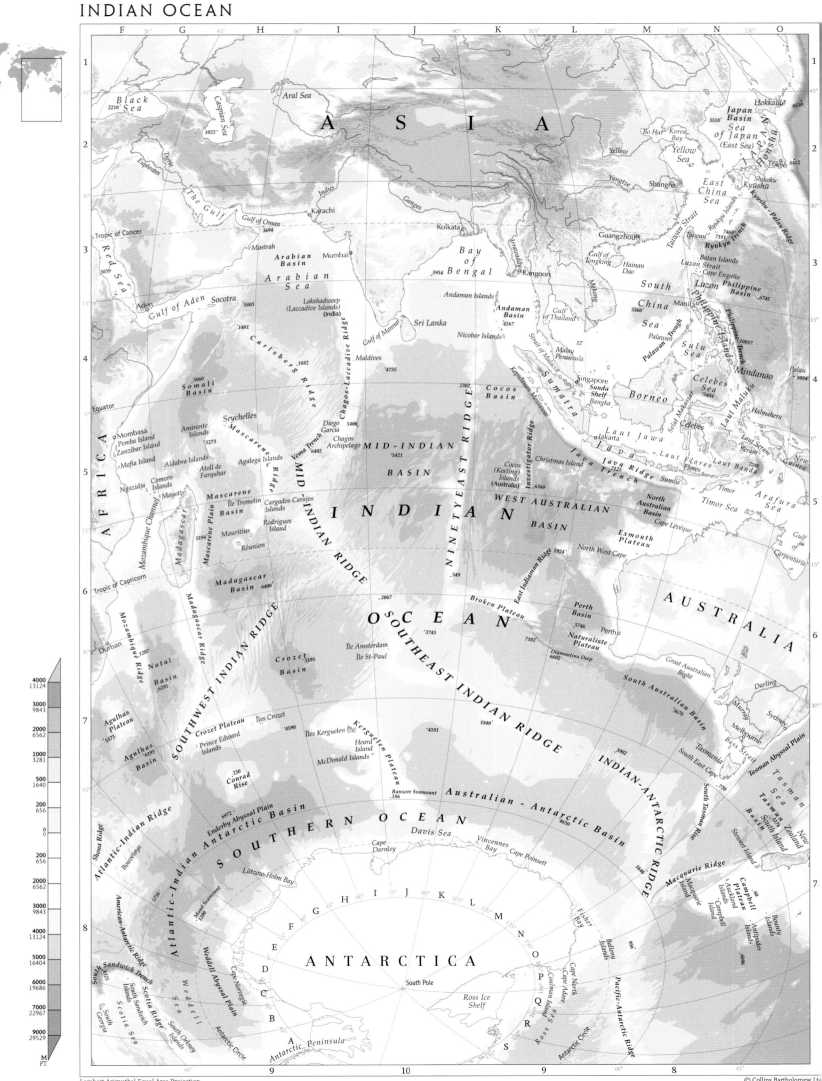

Lambert Azimuthal Equal Area Projection

© Collins Bartholomew Lt

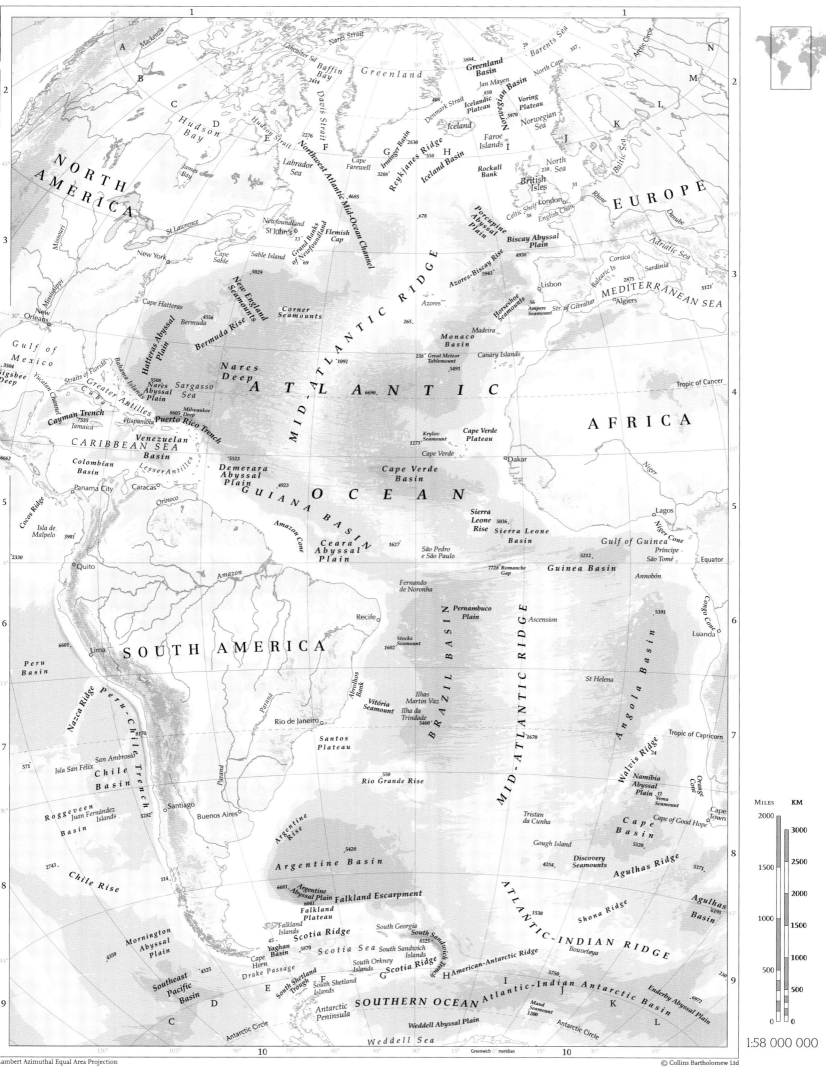

ATLANTIC OCEAN

North

North America

Greenland
Greenland Basin

Mackenzie
Lancaster Sd
Baffin Bay
Nares Strait
Barents Sea
357.
Arctic Circle
North Cape
N

3884.
Jan Mayen

A
B
C
D
E
F
G
H
I
J
K
L
M
N

Davis Strait
2276
2414
405.
Denmark Strait
810.
Icelandic Plateau
3970
Voring Plateau
Norwegian Basin

Hudson Bay
James Bay

Iceland
2830
Norwegian Sea

NORTH AMERICA

Labrador Sea
Cape Farewell
3206
550.
Irminger Basin
Reykjanes Ridge
Iceland Basin
Faroe Islands

Rockall Bank
North Sea
238.
Baltic Sea

St Lawrence
Missouri
4685.
Northwest Atlantic Mid-Ocean Channel

British Isles
31
London
EUROPE

Celtic Shelf
English Chan.
38
Rhine
Danube

New York
Newfoundland
St John's
13
Grand Banks of Newfoundland
69
Flemish Cap

678.
Porcupine Abyssal Plain
Biscay Abyssal Plain
4938.

Adriatic Sea

Cape Sable
Sable Island
5029.

Azores-Biscay Rise
5943.

Corsica
Sardinia
2875.
5121.

New England Seamounts

MID-ATLANTIC RIDGE

Azores
Lisbon
Algiers
MEDITERRANEAN SEA

Cape Hatteras
Corner Seamounts
265.
Horseshoe Seamounts
56
Ampere Seamount
Str. of Gibraltar

New Orleans
Bermuda
4556.
Bermuda Rise
Monaco Basin
Madeira
Canary Islands

Gulf of Mexico
Hatteras Abyssal Plain
1092.
Great Meteor Tablemount
5491.
Tropic of Cancer
238.

Sigsbee Deep
3504.
Nares Deep
6690.
ATLANTIC
AFRICA

Yucatan Channel
5508.
Nares Abyssal Plain
Sargasso Sea

Bahama Islands
Greater Antilles
8605.
Milwaukee Deep
Puerto Rico Trench

Cuba
Straits of Florida
Jamaica
7535.
Cayman Trench
Hispaniola
OCEAN

Krylov Seamount
1273.
Cape Verde Plateau

CARIBBEAN SEA
Venezuelan Basin
Lesser Antilles
5523.
Cape Verde

6662.
Colombian Basin
Demerara Abyssal Plain
4923.
Cape Verde Basin
Dakar
Niger

Panama City
Caracas
Orinoco
GUIANA BASIN

Cocos Ridge
Quito
2330.
Amazon Cone
Sierra Leone Rise
5036.
Sierra Leone Basin
Lagos
Niger Cone
Gulf of Guinea

Isla de Malpelo
3901.
Ceara Abyssal Plain
1627.
São Pedro e São Paulo
5212.
Príncipe
São Tomé
Equator

Amazon
7728.
Romanche Gap
Guinea Basin
Annobón

Lima
6601.
Fernando de Noronha
Ascension
5391.
Congo Cone

SOUTH AMERICA
Recife
Pernambuco Plain
Luanda

Peru Basin
Stocks Seamount
1602.
St Helena
Angola Basin

Nazca Ridge
Abrolhos Bank
Vitória Seamount
Ilhas Martin Vaz
Ilha da Trindade
5460.
BRAZIL BASIN
MID-ATLANTIC RIDGE

Rio de Janeiro
Santos Plateau
1670.
Tropic of Capricorn

Peru-Chile Trench
8170.
Paraná
Walvis Ridge
24.
Namibia Abyssal Plain
11
Vema Seamount
Orange Cone

San Ambrosio
571.
Isla San Félix
Chile Basin
550.
Rio Grande Rise
Cape Town

Roggeveen Basin
Juan Fernández Islands
3282.
Santiago
Argentine Rise
Tristan da Cunha
Cape of Good Hope
Cape Basin

Buenos Aires
5420.
Gough Island
5520.

Chile Rise
2743.
Argentine Basin
4254.
Discovery Seamounts
Agulhas Ridge
5371.

114.
6681.
Argentine Abyssal Plain
Falkland Escarpment
ATLANTIC-INDIAN RIDGE
Agulhas Basin
6195.

Mornington Abyssal Plain
6041.
Falkland Plateau
1530.
Shona Ridge

4359.
45.
Scotia Ridge
South Georgia
South Sandwich Islands

Cape Horn
Yaghan Basin
5870.
Scotia Sea
8325.
South Sandwich Trench
Bouvetøya

Drake Passage
4325.
South Shetland Trough
South Orkney Islands
G
Scotia Ridge
H
American-Antarctic Ridge
I
5750.
230.

Southeast Pacific Basin
South Shetland Islands
SOUTHERN OCEAN
Atlantic-Indian Antarctic Basin
Enderby Abyssal Plain
6972.

Antarctic Peninsula
Weddell Abyssal Plain
Maud Seamount
1200.
Antarctic Circle

Antarctic Circle
Weddell Sea
Greenwich meridian

Lambert Azimuthal Equal Area Projection
© Collins Bartholomew Ltd

MILES
KM
2000
3000
1500
2500
2000
1000
1500
1000
500
500
0
0

1:58 000 000

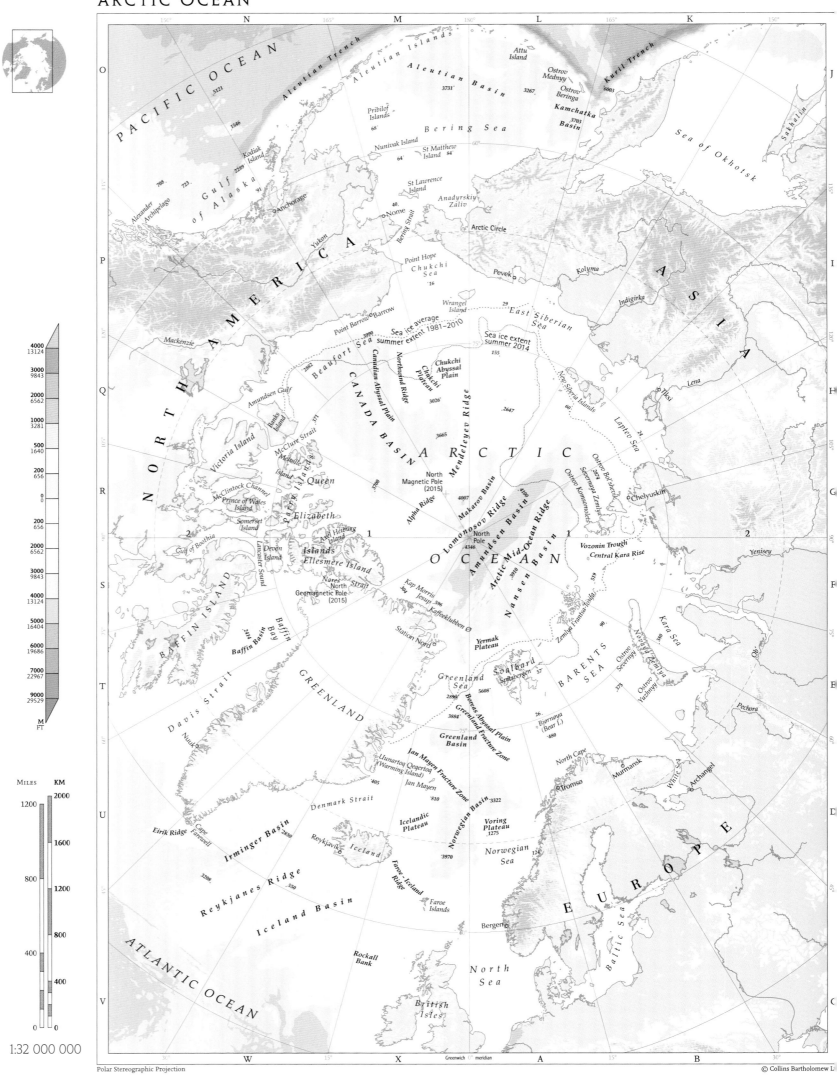

Polar Stereographic Projection

© Collins Bartholomew L

1:32 000 000

The index includes all names shown on the reference maps in the atlas. Each entry includes the country or geographical area in which the feature is located, a page number and an alphanumeric reference. Additional entry details and aspects of the index are explained below.

REFERENCING

Names are referenced by page number and by grid reference. The grid reference relates to the alphanumeric values which appear in the margin of each map. These reflect the graticule on the map – the letter relates to longitude divisions, the number to latitude divisions.

Names are generally referenced to the largest scale map page on which they appear. For large geographical features, including countries, the reference is to the largest scale map on which the feature appears in its entirety, or on which the majority of it appears.

Rivers are referenced to their lowest downstream point – either their mouth or their confluence with another river. The river name will generally be positioned as close to this point as possible.

Entries relating to names appearing on insets are indicated by a small box symbol: □ followed by a grid reference if the inset has its own alphanumeric values.

ALTERNATIVE NAMES

Alternative names appear as cross-references and refer the user to the index entry for the form of the name used on the map.

For rivers with multiple names – for example those which flow through several countries – all alternative name forms are included within the main index entries, with details of the countries in which each form applies.

ADMINISTRATIVE QUALIFIERS

Administrative divisions are included in an entry to differentiate duplicate names – entries of exactly the same name and feature type within the one country – where these division names are shown on the maps. In such cases, duplicate names are alphabetized in the order of the administrative division names. Additional qualifiers are included for names within selected geographical areas, to indicate more clearly their location.

DESCRIPTORS

Entries, other than those for towns and cities, include a descriptor indicating the type of geographical feature. Descriptors are not included where the type of feature is implicit in the name itself, unless there is a town or city of exactly the same name.

NAME FORMS AND ALPHABETICAL ORDER

Name forms are as they appear on the maps, with additional alternative forms included as cross-references. Names appear in full in the index, although they may appear in abbreviated form on the maps.

The German character ß is alphabetized as 'ss'. Names beginning with Mac or Mc are alphabetized exactly as they appear. The terms Saint, Sainte, etc, are abbreviated to St, Ste, etc, but alphabetized as if in the full form.

NUMERICAL ENTRIES

Entries beginning with numerals appear at the beginning of the index, in numerical order. Elsewhere, numerals are alphabetized before 'a'.

PERMUTED TERMS

Names beginning with generic, geographical terms are permuted – the descriptive term is placed after, and the index alphabetized by, the main part of the name. For example, Lake Superior is indexed as Superior, Lake; Mount Everest as Everest, Mount. This policy is applied to all languages. Permuting has not been applied to names of towns, cities or administrative divisions beginning with such geographical terms. These remain in their full form, for example, Lake Isabella, USA.

INDEX ABBREVIATIONS

admin. dist.	administrative district	IN	Indiana	Phil.	Philippines
admin. div.	administrative division	Indon.	Indonesia	plat.	plateau
admin. reg.	administrative region	is	islands	P.N.G.	Papua New Guinea
Afgh.	Afghanistan	isth.	isthmus	Port.	Portugal
AK	Alaska	Kazakh.	Kazakhstan	prov.	province
AL	Alabama	KS	Kansas	pt	point
Alg.	Algeria	KY	Kentucky	Qld	Queensland
Alta	Alberta	Kyrg.	Kyrgyzstan	Que.	Québec
AR	Arkansas	l.	lake	r.	river
Arg.	Argentina	LA	Louisiana	reg.	region
aut. comm.	autonomous community	lag.	lagoon	res.	reserve
aut. reg.	autonomous region	Lith.	Lithuania	resr	reservoir
aut. rep.	autonomous republic	Lux.	Luxembourg	RI	Rhode Island
AZ	Arizona	MA	Massachusetts	r. mouth	river mouth
Azer.	Azerbaijan	Madag.	Madagascar	S.	South
b.	bay	Man.	Manitoba	S.A.	South Australia
Bangl.	Bangladesh	MD	Maryland	salt l.	salt lake
B.C.	British Columbia	ME	Maine	Sask.	Saskatchewan
Bol.	Bolivia	Mex.	Mexico	SC	South Carolina
Bos. & Herz.	Bosnia and Herzegovina	MI	Michigan	SD	South Dakota
Bulg.	Bulgaria	MN	Minnesota	sea chan.	sea channel
c.	cape	MO	Missouri	Sing.	Singapore
CA	California	Moz.	Mozambique	stn	station
C.A.R	Central African Republic	MS	Mississippi	str.	strait
CO	Colorado	MT	Montana	Switz.	Switzerland
Col.	Colombia	mt.	mountain	Tajik.	Tajikistan
CT	Connecticut	mts	mountains	Tanz.	Tanzania
Czech Rep.	Czech Republic	mun.	municipality	Tas.	Tasmania
DC	District of Columbia	N.	North, Northern	terr.	territory
DE	Delaware	nat. park	national park	Thai.	Thailand
Dem. Rep. Congo	Democratic Republic of the Congo	N.B.	New Brunswick	TN	Tennessee
depr.	depression	NC	North Carolina	Trin. and Tob.	Trinidad and Tobago
des.	desert	ND	North Dakota	Turkm.	Turkmenistan
Dom. Rep.	Dominican Republic	NE	Nebraska	TX	Texas
Equat. Guinea	Equatorial Guinea	Neth.	Netherlands	U.A.E.	United Arab Emirates
esc.	escarpment	Nfld. and Lab.	Newfoundland and Labrador	U.K.	United Kingdom
est.	estuary	NH	New Hampshire	Ukr.	Ukraine
Eth.	Ethiopia	NJ	New Jersey	U.S.A.	United States of America
Fin.	Finland	NM	New Mexico	UT	Utah
FL	Florida	N.S.	Nova Scotia	Uzbek.	Uzbekistan
for.	forest	N.S.W.	New South Wales	VA	Virginia
Fr. Guiana	French Guiana	N.T.	Northern Territory	val.	valley
Fr. Polynesia	French Polynesia	N.W.T.	Northwest Territories	Venez.	Venezuela
g.	gulf	N.Z.	New Zealand	Vic.	Victoria
GA	Georgia	NV	Nevada	vol.	volcano
Guat.	Guatemala	NY	New York	vol. crater	volcanic crater
h.	hill	OH	Ohio	VT	Vermont
hd	headland	OK	Oklahoma	W.	West, Western
HI	Hawaii	Ont.	Ontario	WA	Washington
Hond.	Honduras	OR	Oregon	W.A.	Western Australia
i.	island	PA	Pennsylvania	WI	Wisconsin
IA	Iowa	Pak.	Pakistan	WV	West Virginia
ID	Idaho	Para.	Paraguay	WY	Wyoming
IL	Illinois	P.E.I.	Prince Edward Island	Y.T.	Yukon
imp. l.	impermanent lake	pen.	peninsula		

9 de Julio

1

215 E2 9 de Julio Arg.
215 E2 25 de Mayo Buenos Aires Arg.
215 C3 25 de Mayo La Pampa Arg.
186 E4 100 Mile House Canada

A

159 J5 Aabenraa Denmark
164 E4 Aachen Germany
159 J4 Aalborg Denmark
159 J4 Aalborg Bugt b. Denmark
168 E6 Aalen Germany
145 H3 Aalo India
164 C4 Aalst Belgium
159 J4 Aarhus Denmark
159 J4 Aars Denmark
164 C4 Aarschot Belgium
148 A3 Aba China
178 D3 Aba Dem. Rep. Congo
176 C4 Aba Nigeria
140 B5 Abā ad Dūd Saudi Arabia
140 C4 Ābādān Iran
138 D5 Abadan Turkm.
140 D4 Ābādeh Iran
140 D4 Ābādeh Ṭashk Iran
176 B1 Abadla Alg.
214 D2 Abaeté r. Brazil
211 I4 Abaetetuba Brazil
216 G6 Abaiang atoll Kiribati
195 E4 Abajo Peak U.S.A.
176 C4 Abakaliki Nigeria
146 B1 Abakan Russia
146 A1 Abakanskiy Khrebet mts Russia
173 E7 Abana Turkey
210 D6 Abancay Peru
140 D4 Abarkūh Iran
140 D4 Abarkūh, Kavīr-e des. Iran
150 I2 Abashiri Japan
150 I2 Abashiri-wan b. Japan
124 E3 Abau P.N.G.
139 H2 Abay Kazakh.
178 D3 Abaya, Lake Eth.
Ābaya Hāyk' l. Eth. see Abaya, Lake
Ābay Wenz r. Eth. see Blue Nile
132 K4 Abaza Russia
141 E3 'Abbāsābād Iran
170 C4 Abbasanta Sardinia Italy
190 C2 Abbaye, Point U.S.A.
178 E2 Abbe, Lake Eth.
166 E1 Abbeville France
199 E6 Abbeville LA U.S.A.
201 D5 Abbeville SC U.S.A.
163 B5 Abbeyfeale Ireland
162 E6 Abbey Head U.K.
163 D5 Abbeyleix Ireland
160 D3 Abbeytown U.K.
158 L2 Abborrträsk Sweden
129 B3 Abbot Ice Shelf ice feature Antarctica
186 E5 Abbotsford Canada
190 B3 Abbotsford U.S.A.
195 F4 Abbott U.S.A.
144 C2 Abbottabad Pak.
137 H3 'Abd al 'Azīz h. Syria
137 K5 Ābdānān Iran
138 C1 Abdulino Russia
177 E3 Abéché Chad
128 D4 Abel Tasman National Park N.Z.
176 B4 Abengourou Côte d'Ivoire
Åbenrå Denmark see Aabenraa
165 J6 Abensberg Germany
176 C4 Abeokuta Nigeria
161 C5 Aberaeron U.K.
162 F3 Aberchirder U.K.
127 H5 Abercrombie r. Australia
161 D6 Aberdare U.K.
161 C5 Aberdaron U.K.
127 I4 Aberdeen Australia
187 H4 Aberdeen Canada
149 □ Aberdeen Hong Kong China
180 F6 Aberdeen S. Africa
162 F3 Aberdeen U.K.
203 E5 Aberdeen MD U.S.A.
199 F5 Aberdeen MS U.S.A.
198 D2 Aberdeen SD U.S.A.
194 B2 Aberdeen WA U.S.A.
187 I2 Aberdeen Lake Canada
161 C5 Aberdovey U.K.
Aberdyfi U.K. see Aberdovey
162 E4 Aberfeldy U.K.
160 F4 Aberford U.K.
162 D4 Aberfoyle U.K.
161 D6 Abergavenny U.K.
199 C5 Abernathy U.S.A.
161 C5 Aberporth U.K.
161 C5 Abersoch U.K.
161 C5 Aberystwyth U.K.
142 B6 Abhā Saudi Arabia
140 C2 Abhar Iran
140 C2 Abhar Rūd r. Iran
Abiad, Bahr el r. Africa see White Nile
alt. Abiad, Bahr el,
alt. Jabal, Bahr el
213 A2 Abibe, Serranía de mts Col.
176 B4 Abidjan Côte d'Ivoire
178 D3 Abijatta-Shalla National Park Eth.
140 E3 Ab-i-Kavīr salt flat Iran
198 D4 Abilene KS U.S.A.
199 D5 Abilene TX U.S.A.
161 F6 Abingdon U.K.
190 B5 Abingdon IL U.S.A.
202 C6 Abingdon VA U.S.A.
173 F6 Abinsk Russia
Abiseo, Parque Nacional nat. park Peru see Río Abiseo, Parque Nacional
187 H2 Abitau Lake Canada
188 D4 Abitibi r. Canada
188 E4 Abitibi, Lake Canada
173 G7 Abkhazia disp. terr. Georgia
144 C3 Abohar India
176 B4 Aboisso Côte d'Ivoire
176 C4 Abomey Benin
177 D4 Abong Mbang Cameroon
153 A4 Aborlan Phil.
177 D3 Abou Déia Chad
137 J1 Abovyan Armenia
162 F3 Aboyne U.K.
142 C4 Abqaiq Saudi Arabia
Abra, Lago del l. Arg. see Abra, Laguna del
215 D4 Abra, Laguna del l. Arg.
167 B3 Abrantes Port.
212 C2 Abra Pampa Arg.
206 A2 Abreojos, Punta pt Mex.
214 E2 Abrolhos, Arquipélago dos is Brazil
219 G7 Abrolhos Bank sea feature S. Atlantic Ocean
194 E2 Absaroka Range mts U.S.A.
165 H6 Abtsgmünd Germany
140 D5 Abū al Abyaḍ i. U.A.E.
140 C5 Abū 'Alī i. Saudi Arabia
Abū al Jirāb i. U.A.E. see Abū al Abyaḍ
142 B6 Abū 'Arīsh Saudi Arabia
142 D5 Abu Dhabi U.A.E.
177 F3 Abu Hamed Sudan
176 C4 Abuja Nigeria
137 H4 Abū Kamāl Syria
177 E3 Abu Matariq Sudan
136 B6 Abū Mīnā tourist site Egypt
140 D5 Abū Mūsá, Jazīreh-ye i. U.A.E.
210 E6 Abunã r. Bol.
210 E5 Abunã Brazil
142 A7 Ābune Yosēf mt. Eth.
136 C6 Abū Qīr, Khalīj b. Egypt
135 F4 Abu Road India
Abu Simbel Egypt see Abū Sunbul
137 J6 Abū Şukhayr Iraq
177 F2 Abū Sunbul Egypt
128 C5 Abut Head N.Z.
153 C4 Abuyog Phil.
177 E3 Abu Zabad Sudan
Abū Ẓaby U.A.E. see Abu Dhabi
137 L6 Abūzam Iran
177 E3 Abyad Sudan
177 E4 Abyei Sudan
140 C2 Ābyek Iran
138 D1 Abzakovo Russia
138 D2 Abzanovo Russia
203 I2 Acadia National Park U.S.A.
206 D3 Acambaro Mex.
207 G3 Acancéh Mex.
213 A2 Acandí Col.
167 B1 A Cañiza Spain
206 C3 Acaponeta Mex.
207 E4 Acapulco Mex.
211 I4 Acará Brazil
211 J4 Acaraú r. Brazil
214 A4 Acaray r. Para.
212 E3 Acaray, Represa de resr Para.
213 C2 Acarigua Venez.
207 E4 Acatlán Mex.
207 E4 Acatzingo Mex.
207 F4 Acayucán Mex.
176 B4 Accra Ghana
160 E4 Accrington U.K.
213 C3 Achaguas Venez.
144 D5 Achalpur India
143 B2 Achampet India
133 S3 Achayvayam Russia
152 D1 Acheng China
164 A4 Achicourt France
163 B4 Achill Ireland
163 A4 Achill Island Ireland
162 C2 Achiltibuie U.K.
165 H1 Achim Germany
146 B1 Achinsk Russia
162 C3 Achnasheen U.K.
162 C3 A'Chralaig mt. U.K.
173 F6 Achuyevo Russia
136 B3 Acıgöl l. Turkey
136 B3 Acıpayam Turkey
170 F6 Acireale Sicily Italy
198 E3 Ackley U.S.A.
205 J4 Acklins Island Bahamas
161 I5 Acle U.K.
215 B2 Aconcagua r. Chile
215 B2 Aconcagua, Cerro mt. Arg.
211 K5 Acopiara Brazil
156 A6 Açores, Arquipélago dos is N. Atlantic Ocean
167 B1 A Coruña Spain
206 H6 Acoyapa Nicaragua
170 G4 Acquaviva delle Fonti Italy
170 C2 Acqui Terme Italy
126 A4 Acraman, Lake salt flat Australia
Acre Israel see 'Akko
170 G5 Acri Italy
168 I7 Ács Hungary
123 J6 Actéon, Groupe is Fr. Polynesia
202 B4 Ada OH U.S.A.
199 D5 Ada OK U.S.A.
167 D2 Adaja r. Spain
212 E8 Adam, Mount h. Falkland Is
138 D2 Adamovka Russia
203 G3 Adams MA U.S.A.
190 C4 Adams WI U.S.A.
194 B2 Adams, Mount U.S.A.
143 B4 Adam's Bridge sea feature India/Sri Lanka
186 F4 Adams Lake Canada
197 E2 Adams McGill Reservoir U.S.A.
186 C3 Adams Mountain U.S.A.
143 C5 Adam's Peak Sri Lanka
196 B2 Adams Peak U.S.A.
'Adan Yemen see Aden
136 E3 Adana Turkey
136 C1 Adapazarı Turkey
163 C5 Adare Ireland
129 B6 Adare, Cape c. Antarctica
197 E2 Adaven U.S.A.
137 J5 Ad Daghghārah Iraq
142 C5 Ad Dahnā' des. Saudi Arabia
Ad Dammām Saudi Arabia see Dammam
140 B5 Ad Dawādimī Saudi Arabia
Ad Dawḩah Qatar see Doha
137 I4 Ad Dawr Iraq
137 K6 Ad Dayr Iraq
140 B5 Ad Dibdibah plain Saudi Arabia
140 B6 Ad Dilam Saudi Arabia
142 C5 Ad Dir'īyah Saudi Arabia
178 D3 Addis Ababa Eth.
203 J2 Addison U.S.A.
137 J6 Ad Dīwānīyah Iraq
161 G6 Addlestone U.K.
181 F6 Addo Elephant National Park S. Africa
137 I6 Ad Duwayd well Saudi Arabia
201 D6 Adel GA U.S.A.
198 E3 Adel IA U.S.A.
126 C5 Adelaide Australia
201 E7 Adelaide Bahamas
181 G6 Adelaide S. Africa
129 B2 Adelaide Island i. Antarctica
124 D3 Adelaide River Australia
196 D4 Adelanto U.S.A.
129 C6 Adélie Land reg. Antarctica
127 H5 Adelong Australia
139 G4 Adelunga Uzbek.
142 C7 Aden Yemen
142 C7 Aden, Gulf of Somalia/Yemen
164 E4 Adenau Germany
165 I1 Adendorf Germany
140 D5 Adh Dhayd U.A.E.
147 F7 Adi i. Indon.
178 D2 Ādī Ārk'ay Eth.
178 D2 Ādīgrat Eth.
144 D6 Adilabad India
137 I2 Adilcevaz Turkey
194 B3 Adin U.S.A.
177 D2 Adīrī Libya
203 F2 Adirondack Mountains U.S.A.
Ādīs Ābeba Eth. see Addis Ababa
178 D3 Ādīs Alem Eth.
136 G3 Adıyaman Turkey
169 M7 Adjud Romania
207 E3 Adjuntas, Presa de las resr Mex.
189 I3 Adlavik Islands Canada
124 C3 Admiralty Gulf Australia
185 J2 Admiralty Inlet Canada
186 C3 Admiralty Island U.S.A.
186 C3 Admiralty Island National Monument-Kootznoowoo Wilderness nat. park U.S.A.
124 E2 Admiralty Islands P.N.G.
143 B3 Adoni India
165 G3 Adorf (Diemelsee) Germany
165 K4 Adorf/Vogtland Germany
166 D5 Adour r. France
167 E4 Adra Spain
170 F6 Adrano Sicily Italy
176 B2 Adrar Alg.
176 A2 Adrar mts Alg.
176 A2 Adrar, Ḍahr hills Mauritania
139 G4 Adrasmon Tajik.
177 E3 Adré Chad
191 E5 Adrian MI U.S.A.
199 C5 Adrian TX U.S.A.
170 E2 Adriatic Sea Europe
143 B4 Adur India
178 C3 Adusa Dem. Rep. Congo
178 D2 Ādwa Eth.
133 O3 Adycha r. Russia
173 F6 Adygeya, Respublika aut. rep. Russia
173 F6 Adygeysk Russia
173 H6 Adyk Russia
176 B4 Adzopé Côte d'Ivoire
171 K5 Aegean Sea Greece/Turkey
165 H2 Aerzen Germany
167 B1 A Estrada Spain
178 D2 Afabet Eritrea
137 J3 Āfān Iran
141 F3 Afghanistan country Asia
158 J3 Åfjord Norway
178 E3 Afmadow Somalia
184 C4 Afognak Island U.S.A.
167 C1 A Fonsagrada Spain
174 Africa
136 F3 'Afrīn, Nahr r. Syria/Turkey
136 F2 Afşin Turkey
164 D2 Afsluitdijk barrage Neth.
194 E3 Afton U.S.A.
211 H4 Afuá Brazil
136 E5 'Afula Israel
136 C2 Afyon Turkey
165 K4 Aga Germany
176 C3 Agadez Niger
176 B1 Agadir Morocco
175 I5 Agalega Islands Mauritius
138 D1 Agapovka Russia
145 G5 Agartala India
144 C6 Agashi India
191 F2 Agate Canada
171 L6 Agathonisi i. Greece
176 B4 Agboville Côte d'Ivoire
137 K1 Ağcabädi Azer.
137 K2 Ağdam (abandoned) Azer.
166 F5 Agde France
166 E4 Agen France
180 C4 Aggeneys S. Africa
164 F4 Agger r. Germany
144 D1 Aghil Dawan China
163 C3 Aghla Mountain h. Ireland
171 K7 Agia Varvara Greece
136 G2 Ağın Turkey
171 J6 Agios Dimitrios Greece
171 K5 Agios Efstratios i. Greece
171 L5 Agios Fokas, Akrotirio pt Greece
171 J5 Agios Konstantinos Greece
171 K7 Agios Nikolaos Greece
171 J4 Agiou Orous, Kolpos b. Greece
177 F3 Agirwat Hills Sudan
181 F3 Agisanang S. Africa
176 B4 Agnibilékrou Côte d'Ivoire
171 K2 Agnita Romania
148 A2 Agong China
144 D4 Agra India
173 H7 Agrakhanskiy Poluostrov pen. Russia
167 F2 Ágreda Spain
137 I2 Ağrı Turkey
171 J7 Agria Gramvousa i. Greece
170 E6 Agrigento Sicily Italy
171 I5 Agrinio Greece
215 B3 Agrio r. Arg.
170 F4 Agropoli Italy
137 J1 Ağstafa Azer.
137 L1 Ağsu Azer.
207 G5 Agua, Volcán de vol. Guat.
206 C3 Agua Brava, Laguna lag. Mex.
207 G4 Aguada Mex.
215 D4 Aguada Cecilio Arg.
213 B3 Aguadas Col.
213 B3 Agua de Dios Col.
205 K5 Aguadilla Puerto Rico
206 I6 Aguadulce Panama
215 C3 Agua Escondida Arg.
206 C3 Aguamilpa, Presa l. Mex.
204 D4 Aguanaval r. Mex.
215 C1 Agua Negra, Paso del pass Arg./Chile
214 B3 Aguapeí r. Brazil
204 C2 Agua Prieta Mex.
214 A3 Aguaray Guazú r. Para.
213 D2 Aguaro-Guariquito, Parque Nacional nat. park Venez.
206 C2 Aguaruto Mex.
206 D3 Aguascalientes Mex.
206 D3 Aguascalientes state Mex.
214 E2 Águas Formosas Brazil
214 C1 Águas Lindas de Goiás Brazil
214 C3 Agudos Brazil
197 F5 Aguila U.S.A.
167 D1 Aguilar de Campoo Spain
167 F4 Águilas Spain
153 B4 Aguisan Phil.
180 D7 Agulhas, Cape S. Africa
219 K9 Agulhas Basin sea feature Southern Ocean
214 D3 Agulhas Negras mt. Brazil
218 F7 Agulhas Plateau sea feature Southern Ocean
219 J8 Agulhas Ridge sea feature S. Atlantic Ocean
155 E4 Agung, Gunung vol. Indon.
153 C4 Agusan r. Phil.
213 B2 Agustín Codazzi Col.
153 B4 Agutaya Phil.
176 C2 Ahaggar plat. Alg.
176 C2 Ahaggar, Parc National de l' nat. park Alg.
176 C2 Ahaggar, Tassili oua-n- plat. Alg.
140 B2 Ahar Iran
128 C5 Ahaura N.Z.
164 F2 Ahaus Germany
128 F3 Ahimanawa Range mts N.Z.
128 D1 Ahipara N.Z.
128 D1 Ahipara Bay N.Z.
184 B4 Ahklun Mountains U.S.A.
137 I2 Ahlat Turkey
165 F3 Ahlen Germany
144 C5 Ahmadabad India
143 A2 Ahmadnagar India
144 B3 Ahmadpur East Pak.
144 B4 Ahmad Tar Pak.
Ahmedabad India see Ahmadabad
Ahmednagar India see Ahmadnagar
165 I4 Ahorn Germany
140 C4 Ahram Iran
165 I1 Ahrensburg Germany
137 I2 Ahta Dağı mt. Turkey
158 N3 Ähtäri Fin.
159 N4 Ahtme Estonia
137 L6 Āhū Iran
207 G5 Ahuachapán El Salvador
206 D3 Ahualulco Mex.
166 F3 Ahun France
128 B6 Ahuriri r. N.Z.
140 C4 Ahvāz Iran
144 C5 Ahwa India
180 B3 Ai-Ais Namibia
180 B3 Ai-Ais Hot Springs and Fish River Canyon Park Namibia
180 B4 Ai-Ais/Richtersveld Transfrontier Park Namibia/S. Africa
148 D1 Aibag He r. China
141 H2 Aībak Afgh.
Aidin Turkm. see Aýdyň
196 □1 'Aiea U.S.A.
136 E4 Aigialousa Cyprus
171 J6 Aigina i. Greece
171 J5 Aigio Greece
166 H4 Aigle de Chambeyron mt. France
215 F2 Aiguá Uruguay
152 C3 Ai He r. China
151 F5 Aikawa Japan
201 D5 Aiken U.S.A.
206 J6 Ailigandi Panama
216 G6 Ailinglaplap atoll Marshall Is
164 A5 Ailly-sur-Noye France
191 G4 Ailsa Craig Canada
162 C5 Ailsa Craig i. U.K.
163 C3 Ailt an Chorráin Ireland
214 E2 Aimorés, Serra dos hills Brazil
196 □1 'Āina Haina U.S.A.
176 C1 Aïn Beïda Alg.
176 B2 'Aïn Ben Tili Mauritania
167 H4 Aïn Defla Alg.
167 H5 Aïn el Hadjel Alg.
176 B1 Aïn Sefra Alg.
189 H4 Ainslie, Lake Canada
198 D3 Ainsworth U.S.A.
Aintab Turkey see Gaziantep
167 H4 Aïn Taya Alg.
167 G5 Aïn Tédélès Alg.
213 B4 Aipe Col.
154 C5 Air i. Indon.
176 C3 Aïr, Massif de l' mts Niger
186 G4 Airdrie Canada
162 E5 Airdrie U.K.
164 D6 Aire r. France
166 D5 Aire-sur-l'Adour France
176 C3 Aïr et du Ténéré, Réserve Naturelle Nationale de l' nature res. Niger
185 K3 Air Force Island Canada
148 D1 Airgin Sum China
187 H3 Air Ronge Canada
148 F2 Ai Shan h. China
186 B2 Aishihik Canada
186 B2 Aishihik Lake Canada
166 G2 Aisne r. France
167 F3 Aitana mt. Spain
124 E2 Aitape P.N.G.
198 E2 Aitkin U.S.A.
138 C1 Aitovo Russia
123 I5 Aitutaki i. Pacific Ocean
169 K7 Aiud Romania
166 G5 Aix-en-Provence France
166 G4 Aix-les-Bains France
145 F5 Aiyar Reservoir India
145 H5 Aizawl India
159 N4 Aizkraukle Latvia
159 M4 Aizpute Latvia
151 F6 Aizuwakamatsu Japan
170 C4 Ajaccio Corsica France
213 B4 Ajajú r. Col.
207 E4 Ajalpán Mex.
143 A1 Ajanta India
158 K2 Ajaureforsen Sweden
128 D5 Ajax, Mount N.Z.
177 E1 Ajdābiyā Libya
150 G4 Ajigasawa Japan
176 C2 Ajjer, Tassili n' plat. Alg.
136 E5 'Ajlūn Jordan
140 D5 'Ajman U.A.E.
144 C4 Ajmer India
197 F5 Ajo U.S.A.
197 F5 Ajo, Mount U.S.A.
153 B4 Ajuy Phil.
150 H3 Akabira Japan
139 H2 Akadyr Kazakh.
178 D4 Akagera, Parc National de l' Rwanda
143 B2 Akalkot India
150 I3 Akan Kokuritsu-kōen nat. park Japan
136 D4 Akanthou Cyprus
128 D5 Akaroa N.Z.
128 D5 Akaroa Harbour N.Z.
145 H4 Akas reg. India
139 H3 Akbakay Kazakh.
139 I3 Akbalyk Kazakh.
141 H3 Akbar Khēl Afgh.
145 E4 Akbarpur India
138 E3 Akbasty Kazakh.
139 H2 Akbaur Kazakh.
139 H5 Akbaytal Tajik.
139 G2 Akbeyit Kazakh.
167 I4 Akbou Alg.
139 I2 Akbulak Vostochnyy Kazakhstan Kazakh.
139 K2 Akbulak Vostochnyy Kazakhstan Kazakh.
138 B2 Akbulak Zapadnyy Kazakhstan Kazakh.
138 C2 Akbulak Russia
136 F2 Akçadağ Turkey
137 G3 Akçakale Turkey
136 C1 Akçakoca Turkey
136 D3 Akçali Dağ mt. Turkey
136 C3 Akdağ mt. Turkey
136 C3 Ak Dağı mt. Turkey
137 H2 Ak Dağı mts Turkey
136 E2 Akdağmadeni Turkey
138 D4 Akdepe Turkm.
159 L4 Åkersberga Sweden
164 C2 Akersloot Neth.
138 E3 Akespe Kazakh.
178 C3 Aketi Dem. Rep. Congo
138 C4 Akgyr Erezi hills Turkm.
137 I1 Akhalkalaki Georgia
173 G7 Akhaltsikhe Georgia
145 G5 Akhaura Bangl.
177 E1 Akhḑar, Al Jabal al mts Libya
142 E5 Akhḑar, Jabal mts Oman
136 A2 Akhisar Turkey
136 F3 Akhtarīn Syria
173 H5 Akhtubinsk Russia
138 D1 Akhunovo Russia
137 I1 Akhuryan Armenia
151 C8 Aki Japan
188 D3 Akimiski Island Canada
136 E3 Akıncı Burun pt Turkey
136 G1 Akıncılar Turkey
150 G5 Akita Japan
176 A3 Akjoujt Mauritania
138 E2 Akkabak Kazakh.
158 L2 Akkajaure l. Sweden
Akkala Uzbek. see Oqqal'a
138 E2 Akkarga Kazakh.
139 G3 Akkense Kazakh.
138 D2 Akkermanovka Russia
150 I3 Akkeshi Japan
138 B3 Akkistau Kazakh.
136 E5 'Akko Israel
139 G2 Akkol' Akmolinskaya Oblast' Kazakh.
139 H3 Akkol' Almatinskaya Oblast' Kazakh.
138 B3 Akkol' Atyrauskaya Oblast' Kazakh.
139 G4 Akkol' Zhambylskaya Oblast' Kazakh.
139 G4 Akkol', Ozero salt l. Kazakh.
139 I2 Akku Kazakh.
138 F3 Akkum Kazakh.
136 F1 Akkuş Turkey
Akkyr, Gory hills Turkm. see Akgyr Erezi
144 D4 Aklera India
159 M4 Akmeņrags pt Latvia
144 D1 Akmeqit China
Akmola Kazakh. see Astana
139 G2 Akmolinskaya Oblast' admin. div. Kazakh.
139 I4 Ak-Moyun Kyrg.
151 D7 Akō Japan
177 F4 Akobo South Sudan
144 D5 Akola India
139 I4 Akongkür China
178 D2 Akordat Eritrea
136 D3 Akören Turkey
144 D5 Akot India
139 H2 Akoy Kazakh.
189 G1 Akpatok Island Canada
139 I4 Akqi China
158 B2 Akranes Iceland
159 I4 Åkrehamn Norway
194 G3 Akron CO U.S.A.
202 C4 Akron OH U.S.A.
202 C4 Akron City Reservoir U.S.A.
144 D2 Aksai Chin terr. Asia
136 E2 Aksaray Turkey
139 H4 Ak-Say r. Kyrg.
173 F6 Aksay Russia
144 D2 Aksayqin Hu l. China
136 C2 Akşehir Turkey
136 C2 Akşehir Gölü l. Turkey
136 C3 Akseki Turkey
138 C1 Aksenovo Russia
140 D4 Aks-e Rostam r. Iran
138 C2 Akshatau Aktyubinskaya Oblast' Kazakh.
139 H3 Akshatau Karagandinskaya Oblast' Kazakh.
139 I4 Akshi Kazakh.
138 E2 Akshiganak Kazakh.
138 B4 Akshukyr Kazakh.
138 C3 Akshymyrau Kazakh.
139 J4 Aksu Xinjiang Uygur Zizhiqu China
139 J4 Aksu Xinjiang Uygur Zizhiqu China
139 G1 Aksu Akmolinskaya Oblast' Kazakh.
139 I3 Aksu Almatinskaya Oblast' Kazakh.
139 I1 Aksu Pavlodarskaya Oblast' Kazakh.
139 G4 Aksu Yuzhnyy Kazakhstan Kazakh.
138 C2 Aksu Zapadnyy Kazakhstan Kazakh.
139 I3 Aksu r. Kazakh.
136 C3 Aksu r. Turkey
138 F2 Aksuat Kostanayskaya Oblast' Kazakh.
139 J3 Aksuat Vostochnyy Kazakhstan Kazakh.
139 H2 Aksu-Ayuly Kazakh.
139 J4 Aksu He r. China
178 D2 Āksum Eth.
139 F3 Aksumbe Kazakh.
139 H3 Aksuyek Kazakh.
145 F1 Aktag mt. China
138 F2 Aktas Kazakh.
137 J2 Aktas Dağı mt. Turkey
137 I1 Aktaş Gölü l. Georgia
Aktash Uzbek. see Oqtosh
139 G3 Aktau Karagandinskaya Oblast' Kazakh.
139 H2 Aktau Karagandinskaya Oblast' Kazakh.
138 B4 Aktau Mangystauskaya Oblast' Kazakh.
139 I5 Akto China
138 D2 Aktobe Kazakh.
139 H2 Aktogay Karagandinskaya Oblast' Kazakh.
139 H1 Aktogay Pavlodarskaya Oblast' Kazakh.
139 I3 Aktogay Vostochnyy Kazakhstan Kazakh.
169 N4 Aktsyabrski Belarus
139 F2 Aktuma (abandoned) Kazakh.
138 D3 Aktumsyk Kazakh.
138 D3 Aktumsyk, Mys pt Uzbek.
139 H4 Ak-Tüz Kyrg.
138 D2 Aktyubinskaya Oblast' admin. div. Kazakh.
151 B8 Akune Japan
176 C4 Akure Nigeria
158 C2 Akureyri Iceland
145 G1 Akxokesay China
Akyab Myanmar see Sittwe
139 H3 Akzhal Karagandinskaya Oblast' Kazakh.
139 J2 Akzhal Vostochnyy Kazakhstan Kazakh.
138 D2 Akzhar Aktyubinskaya Oblast' Kazakh.
138 F3 Akzhar Kyzylordinskaya Oblast' Kazakh.
139 J3 Akzhar Vostochnyy Kazakhstan Kazakh.
139 G4 Akzhar Zhambylskaya Oblast' Kazakh.
139 F3 Akzhaykyn, Ozero salt l. Kazakh.
136 G3 Akziyaret Turkey
159 J3 Ål Norway
140 C5 Al 'Abā Saudi Arabia
201 C6 Alabama r. U.S.A.
201 C5 Alabama state U.S.A.
201 C5 Alabaster U.S.A.
153 B3 Alabat i. Phil.
137 J7 Al 'Abṭīyah well Iraq
139 G4 Ala-Buka Kyrg.
177 E1 Al Abyār Libya
136 E1 Alaca Turkey
136 F2 Alacahan Turkey
136 E1 Alaçam Turkey
136 B2 Alaçam Dağları mts Turkey
207 G3 Alacrán, Arrecife reef Mex.
137 I2 Ala Dag mt. Turkey
137 I2 Ala Dağlar mts Turkey
136 E3 Ala Dağları mts Turkey
173 H7 Alagir Russia
211 K6 Alagoinhas Brazil
167 F2 Alagón Spain
153 C5 Alah r. Phil.
158 M3 Alahärmä Fin.
137 K7 Al Aḩmadī Kuwait
140 D5 Al Ain, Cultural Sites of tourist site U.A.E.
139 G5 Alai Range mts Asia
158 M3 Alajärvi Fin.
206 H6 Alajuela Costa Rica
137 K2 Ālājūjeh Iran
144 D3 Alaknanda r. India
139 J3 Alakol', Ozero salt l. Kazakh.
158 O2 Alakurtti Russia
136 B6 Al 'Alamayn Egypt
210 F4 Alalaú r. Brazil
140 B5 Al 'Amār Saudi Arabia
137 K6 Al 'Amārah Iraq
Alamdo China see Alando
137 J7 Al Amghar waterhole Iraq
153 A2 Alaminos Phil.
136 B6 Al 'Āmirīyah Egypt
206 D2 Alamítos, Sierra de los mt. Mex.
197 E3 Alamo U.S.A.
197 F4 Alamo Dam U.S.A.
195 F5 Alamogordo U.S.A.
199 D6 Alamo Heights U.S.A.
195 E6 Alamos Sonora Mex.
206 B2 Alamos Sonora Mex.
195 F4 Alamosa U.S.A.
143 B3 Alampur India
158 K2 Alanäs Sweden
Åland is Fin. see Åland Islands
165 J1 Aland r. Germany
143 B2 Aland India
140 B2 Aland r. Iran
159 L3 Åland Islands Fin.
145 H3 Alando China
154 B5 Alang Besar i. Indon.
Alaniya aut. rep. Russia see Severnaya Osetiya-Alaniya, Respublika
190 E3 Alanson U.S.A.
136 D3 Alanya Turkey
140 D4 'Alā' od Dīn Iran
136 C1 Alaplı Turkey
143 B4 Alappuzha India
136 E7 Al 'Aqabah Jordan
141 F3 'Alāqahdārī Gulistān Afgh.
140 C6 Al 'Āqūlah well Saudi Arabia
167 E3 Alarcón, Embalse de resr Spain
136 D6 Al 'Arīsh Egypt
142 C4 Al Arṭāwīyah Saudi Arabia
155 E4 Alas Indon.
136 B2 Alaşehir Turkey
137 I6 Al 'Āshūrīyah well Iraq
184 D3 Alaska state U.S.A.
184 D4 Alaska, Gulf of U.S.A.
186 E3 Alaska Highway Canada/U.S.A.
184 B4 Alaska Peninsula U.S.A.
184 D3 Alaska Range mts U.S.A.
137 L2 Älät Azer.
Alat Uzbek. see Olot
137 I6 Al 'Athāmīn hills Iraq
172 H4 Alatyr' Russia
172 H4 Alatyr' r. Russia
210 C4 Alausí Ecuador
137 J1 Alaverdi Armenia
158 N2 Alavieska Fin.
158 M3 Alavus Fin.
126 D5 Alawoona Australia
137 K1 Alazani r. Azer./Georgia
137 J5 Al 'Azīzīyah Iraq
177 D1 Al 'Azīzīyah Libya
170 C2 Alba Italy
136 F3 Al Bāb Syria
167 F3 Albacete Spain
126 D5 Albacutya, Lake dry lake Australia
137 J6 Al Bādiyah al Janūbīyah des. Iraq
171 J1 Alba Iulia Romania
188 F3 Albanel, Lac Canada
171 I4 Albania country Europe
124 B5 Albany Australia
188 C3 Albany r. Canada
201 C6 Albany GA U.S.A.
190 E5 Albany IN U.S.A.
200 C4 Albany KY U.S.A.
203 G3 Albany NY U.S.A.
194 B2 Albany OR U.S.A.
127 H1 Albany Downs Australia
140 B5 Al Barrah Saudi Arabia
Al Başrah Iraq see Basra
137 J6 Al Baţḩa' marsh Iraq
124 E3 Albatross Bay Australia
127 F8 Albatross Island Australia
177 E2 Al Bawītī Egypt
177 E1 Al Bayḑā' Libya
210 □ Albemarle, Punta pt Galapagos Is Ecuador
201 E5 Albemarle Sound sea chan. U.S.A.
170 C2 Albenga Italy
167 D3 Alberche r. Spain
124 D4 Alberga watercourse Australia
167 B2 Albergaria-a-Velha Port.
127 G4 Albert Australia
166 F2 Albert France
126 C5 Albert, Lake Australia
178 D3 Albert, Lake Dem. Rep. Congo/Uganda
186 F4 Alberta prov. Canada
202 E6 Alberta U.S.A.
186 F4 Alberta, Mount Canada
180 D7 Albertinia S. Africa
164 D4 Albert Kanaal canal Belgium
198 E3 Albert Lea U.S.A.
178 D3 Albert Nile r. South Sudan/Uganda
212 B8 Alberto de Agostini, Parque Nacional nat. park Chile
181 H3 Alberton S. Africa
166 H4 Albertville France
164 E6 Albestroff France
166 F5 Albi France
211 H2 Albina Suriname
196 A2 Albion CA U.S.A.
203 I2 Albion ME U.S.A.
190 E4 Albion MI U.S.A.
202 D3 Albion NY U.S.A.
167 E5 Alborán, Isla de i. Spain
167 D4 Alboran Sea Europe
Ålborg Denmark see Aalborg
Ålborg Bugt b. Denmark see Aalborg Bugt
Alborz, Reshteh-ye mts Iran see Elburz Mountains
186 F4 Albreda Canada
140 C5 Al Budayyi' Bahrain
167 B4 Albufeira Port.
195 F5 Albuquerque U.S.A.
206 I5 Albuquerque, Cayos de is Col.
142 E5 Al Buraymī Oman
167 C3 Alburquerque Spain
127 G6 Albury Australia
137 H4 Al Buşayrah Syria
136 G7 Al Busayṭā' plain Saudi Arabia
137 K6 Al Buşayyah Iraq
140 B4 Al Bushūk well Saudi Arabia
167 B3 Alcácer do Sal Port.
167 E2 Alcalá de Henares Spain
167 E4 Alcalá la Real Spain
170 E6 Alcamo Sicily Italy
167 F2 Alcañiz Spain
167 C3 Alcántara Spain
167 E3 Alcaraz Spain
167 D4 Alcaudete Spain
167 E3 Alcázar de San Juan Spain
173 F5 Alchevs'k Ukr.
215 D2 Alcira Arg.
214 E2 Alcobaça Brazil
215 E2 Alcorta Arg.
Alcoy Spain see Alcoy-Alcoi
167 F3 Alcoy-Alcoi Spain
167 H3 Alcúdia Spain
179 E4 Aldabra Islands Seychelles
206 C1 Aldama Chihuahua Mex.
207 E3 Aldama Tamaulipas Mex.
133 N4 Aldan Russia
133 O3 Aldan r. Russia
164 D1 Aldeboarn Neth.
161 I5 Aldeburgh U.K.
166 D2 Alderney i. U.K.
196 B4 Alder Peak U.S.A.
161 G6 Aldershot U.K.
202 C6 Alderson U.S.A.
140 D6 Al Dhafrah reg. U.A.E.
160 D3 Aldingham U.K.
161 F5 Aldridge U.K.
190 B5 Aledo U.S.A.
176 A3 Aleg Mauritania
214 E3 Alegre Brazil
212 E3 Alegrete Brazil
215 E2 Alejandro Korn Arg.
172 E2 Alekhovshchina Russia
138 B4 Aleksandra Bekovicha-Cherkasskogo, Zaliv b. Kazakh.
172 F3 Aleksandrov Russia
173 I5 Aleksandrov Gay Russia
138 C1 Aleksandrovka Orenburgskaya Oblast' Russia
138 D1 Aleksandrovka Respublika Bashkortostan Russia
173 H6 Aleksandrovskoye Russia
133 P4 Aleksandrovsk-Sakhalinskiy Russia
132 F1 Aleksandry, Zemlya i. Russia
139 G1 Alekseyevka Kazakh.
173 F5 Alekseyevka Belgorodskaya Oblast' Russia
173 F5 Alekseyevka Belgorodskaya Oblast' Russia
173 G5 Alekseyevskaya Russia
172 F4 Aleksin Russia
171 I3 Aleksinac Serbia
178 B4 Alèmbé Gabon
136 E1 Alembeyli Turkey
214 D3 Além Paraíba Brazil
158 J3 Ålen Norway
166 E2 Alençon France
211 H4 Alenquer Brazil
196 □2 'Alenuihāhā Channel U.S.A.
136 F3 Aleppo Syria
185 M1 Alert Canada
210 D6 Alerta Peru
186 D4 Alert Bay Canada
166 G4 Alès France
169 K7 Aleşd Romania
170 C2 Alessandria Italy
158 I3 Ålesund Norway
216 G2 Aleutian Basin sea feature Bering Sea
182 C2 Aleutian Islands U.S.A.
184 C4 Aleutian Range mts U.S.A.
216 H2 Aleutian Trench sea feature N. Pacific Ocean
133 Q4 Alevina, Mys c. Russia
203 J2 Alexander U.S.A.
186 B3 Alexander Archipelago is U.S.A.
180 B4 Alexander Bay b. Namibia/S. Africa
180 B4 Alexander Bay S. Africa
201 C5 Alexander City U.S.A.
129 B3 Alexander Island i. Antarctica
127 F6 Alexandra Australia
128 B6 Alexandra N.Z.
212 □ Alexandra, Cape Atlantic Ocean
171 J4 Alexandreia Greece
203 F2 Alexandria Canada
177 E1 Alexandria Egypt
171 K3 Alexandria Romania
181 G6 Alexandria S. Africa
162 D5 Alexandria U.K.
190 E5 Alexandria IN U.S.A.
199 E6 Alexandria LA U.S.A.
198 E2 Alexandria MN U.S.A.
202 E5 Alexandria VA U.S.A.
203 F2 Alexandria Bay U.S.A.
126 C5 Alexandrina, Lake Australia
171 K4 Alexandroupoli Greece
189 I3 Alexis r. Canada
190 B5 Alexis U.S.A.
186 E4 Alexis Creek Canada
139 J1 Aley r. Russia
139 J1 Aleysk Russia
164 F4 Alf Germany
167 F1 Alfaro Spain
137 K7 Al Farwānīyah Kuwait
137 I4 Al Fatḩah Iraq
137 L7 Al Fāw Iraq
177 F2 Al Fayyūm Egypt
165 H3 Alfeld (Leine) Germany
214 D3 Alfenas Brazil
137 L7 Al Fintās Kuwait
169 J7 Alföld plain Hungary
161 H4 Alford U.K.
203 F2 Alfred Canada
203 H3 Alfred U.S.A.
137 L7 Al Fuḩayḩīl Kuwait
Al Fujayrah U.A.E. see Fujairah
Al Furāt r. Iraq/Syria see Euphrates
138 D2 Alga Kazakh.
138 C2 Algabas Kazakh.
159 I4 Ålgård Norway
215 C3 Algarrobo del Aguilla Arg.
167 B4 Algarve reg. Port.
172 G4 Algasovo Russia
167 D4 Algeciras Spain

Apurahuan

153 A4 Apurahuan Phil.
213 D3 Apure r. Venez.
210 D6 Apurímac r. Peru
177 F2 Aqaba, Gulf of Asia
137 I6 'Aqabah, Birkat al well Iraq
139 I4 Aqal China
140 D2 Aqbana Iran
141 G2 Āqchah Afgh.
140 B2 Aq Chai r. Iran
140 D3 'Aqdā Iran
140 B2 Aqdoghmish r. Iran
137 J3 Āq Kān Dāgh, Kūh-e mt. Iran
138 C5 Āq Qalā Iran
141 G3 Āq Rabat, Kōtal-e Afgh.
137 I3 'Aqrah Iraq
197 F4 Aquarius Mountains U.S.A.
197 G3 Aquarius Plateau U.S.A.
214 A3 Aquidauana Brazil
214 A2 Aquidauana r. Brazil
206 D4 Aquila Mex.
213 D4 Aquio r. Col.
207 E3 Aquismón Mex.
166 D4 Aquitaine reg. France
141 G4 'Arab Afgh.
201 C5 Arab U.S.A.
177 E3 Arab, Bahr el watercourse South Sudan
136 B6 'Arab, Khalīj al b. Egypt
141 E3 'Arabābād Iran
218 I4 Arabian Basin sea feature Indian Ocean
Arabian Gulf Asia see The Gulf
142 B4 Arabian Peninsula Saudi Arabia
134 E5 Arabian Sea Indian Ocean
213 E3 Arabopó Venez.
213 E3 Arabopó r. Venez.
136 D1 Araç Turkey
213 E4 Araça r. Brazil
211 K6 Aracaju Brazil
213 D4 Aracamuni, Cerro h. Venez.
214 A4 Aracanguy, Montes de hills Para.
211 K4 Aracati Brazil
214 E1 Aracatu Brazil
214 B3 Araçatuba Brazil
167 C4 Aracena Spain
214 E2 Aracruz Brazil
214 D2 Araçuaí Brazil
214 D2 Araçuaí r. Brazil
171 I1 Arad Romania
177 E3 Arada Chad
124 D2 Arafura Sea Australia/Indon.
216 D6 Arafura Shelf sea feature Australia/Indon.
214 B1 Aragarças Brazil
137 I1 Aragats Armenia
137 J1 Aragats Lerr mt. Armenia
167 F2 Aragón aut. comm. Spain
167 F1 Aragón r. Spain
211 I5 Araguacema Brazil
213 D2 Aragua de Barcelona Venez.
211 I5 Araguaia r. Brazil
211 H6 Araguaia, Parque Indígena nat. park Brazil
211 H6 Araguaia, Parque Nacional do nat. park Brazil
211 I5 Araguaína Brazil
213 E2 Araguao, Boca r. mouth Venez.
213 E2 Araguao, Caño r. Venez.
214 C2 Araguari Brazil
214 C2 Araguari r. Brazil
211 I5 Araguatins Brazil
173 H7 Aragvi r. Georgia
Arai Japan see Myōkō
Árainn Mhór Ireland see Arranmore Island
211 J4 Araioses Brazil
176 C2 Arak Alg.
140 C3 Ārāk Iran
145 H5 Arakan Yoma mts Myanmar
143 B3 Arakkonam India
139 J4 Aral China
137 J2 Aralık Turkey
138 D3 Aral Sea salt l. Kazakh./Uzbek.
138 E3 Aral'sk Kazakh.
Aral'skoye More salt l. Kazakh./Uzbek. see Aral Sea
138 B2 Aralsor, Ozero l. Kazakh.
138 C2 Aralsor, Ozero salt l. Kazakh.
140 B5 Aramah plat. Saudi Arabia
207 E2 Aramberri Mex.
144 D6 Aran r. India
167 E2 Aranda de Duero Spain
137 K4 Ārandān Iran
171 I2 Aranđelovac Serbia
143 B3 Arani India
163 B4 Aran Islands Ireland
167 E2 Aranjuez Spain
179 B6 Aranos Namibia
199 D7 Aransas Pass U.S.A.
214 B2 Arantes r. Brazil
125 H1 Aranuka atoll Kiribati
154 B2 Aranyaprathet Thai.
151 B8 Arao Japan
176 B3 Araouane Mali
198 D3 Arapahoe U.S.A.
213 E4 Arapari r. Brazil
215 F1 Arapey Grande r. Uruguay
136 G2 Arapgir Turkey
211 K5 Arapiraca Brazil
171 K4 Arapis, Akrotirio pt Greece
214 B3 Arapongas Brazil
145 F4 A Rapti Doon r. Nepal
142 B3 'Ar'ar Saudi Arabia
137 I6 'Ar'ar, Wādī watercourse Iraq/Saudi Arabia
212 G3 Araranguá Brazil
214 C3 Araraquara Brazil
211 H5 Araras Brazil
214 B4 Araras, Serra das mts Brazil
137 J2 Ararat Armenia
126 E6 Ararat Australia
137 J2 Ararat, Mount Turkey
145 F4 Araria India
214 D3 Araruama, Lago de lag. Brazil
137 I2 Aras Turkey
137 I1 Aras r. Turkey alt. Araks (Armenia/Turkey), alt. Araz (Azerbaijan)
214 E1 Arataca Brazil
213 C3 Arauca Col.
213 C3 Arauca r. Venez.
215 B3 Araucanía admin. reg. Chile
215 B3 Arauco Chile
213 C3 Arauquita Col.
213 C2 Araure Venez.
144 C4 Aravalli Range mts India
159 N4 Aravete Estonia
125 F2 Arawa P.N.G.
214 C2 Araxá Brazil
213 D2 Araya, Península de pen. Venez.
213 D2 Araya, Punta de pt Venez.
136 C2 Arayıt Dağı mt. Turkey
137 L2 Araz r. Asia alt. Araks (Armenia/Turkey), alt. Aras (Turkey)
172 I3 Arbazh Russia
137 J3 Arbīl/Hewlêr Iraq
159 K4 Arboga Sweden
187 I4 Arborfield Canada
162 F4 Arbroath U.K.
196 A2 Arbuckle U.S.A.
141 F4 Arbū-ye Shamālī, Dasht-e des. Afgh.
166 D4 Arcachon France
201 D7 Arcadia U.S.A.
194 A3 Arcata U.S.A.
196 D2 Arc Dome mt. U.S.A.
207 D4 Arcelia Mex.
172 G1 Archangel Russia
124 E3 Archer r. Australia
197 H2 Arches National Park U.S.A.
Archman Turkm. see Arçman
137 L2 Ărçivan Azer.
126 A2 Arckaringa watercourse Australia
138 D5 Arçman Turkm.
194 D3 Arco U.S.A.
167 D4 Arcos de la Frontera Spain
185 J2 Arctic Bay Canada
220 B1 Arctic Mid-Ocean Ridge sea feature Arctic Ocean
220 Arctic Ocean
184 E3 Arctic Red r. Canada
129 E2 Arctowski research stn Antarctica
140 C2 Ardabīl Iran
137 I1 Ardahan Turkey
140 C4 Ardakān Fārs Iran
140 D3 Ardakān Yazd Iran
140 C4 Ardal Iran
159 I3 Årdalstangen Norway
163 C3 Ardara Ireland
171 K4 Ardas r. Bulg.
172 G4 Ardatov Nizhegorodskaya Oblast' Russia
172 H4 Ardatov Respublika Mordoviya Russia
191 G3 Ardbeg Canada
163 E4 Ardee Ireland
126 B4 Arden, Mount h. Australia
164 D5 Ardennes plat. Belgium
164 C5 Ardennes, Canal des France
140 D3 Ardestān Iran
163 F3 Ardglass U.K.
167 C3 Ardila r. Port.
127 G5 Ardlethan Australia
199 D5 Ardmore U.S.A.
162 B4 Ardnamurchan, Point of U.K.
162 C4 Ardrishaig U.K.
126 B5 Ardrossan Australia
162 D5 Ardrossan U.K.
162 C3 Ardvasar U.K.
215 E2 Areco r. Arg.
212 E3 Areguá Para.
211 K4 Areia Branca Brazil
164 E4 Aremberg h. Germany
153 B4 Arena reef Phil.
196 A2 Arena, Point U.S.A.
206 B3 Arena, Punta pt Mex.
206 H5 Arenal Hond.
167 D2 Arenas de San Pedro Spain
159 J4 Arendal Norway
165 J2 Arendsee (Altmark) Germany
161 D5 Arenig Fawr h. U.K.
171 J6 Areopoli Greece
206 C2 Areponapuchi Mex.
210 D7 Arequipa Peru
211 H4 Arere Brazil
167 D2 Arévalo Spain
170 D3 Arezzo Italy
136 G6 'Arfajah well Saudi Arabia
148 D1 Argalant Mongolia
167 E2 Arganda del Rey Spain
153 B4 Argao Phil.
170 D2 Argenta Italy
166 D2 Argentan France
170 D3 Argentario, Monte h. Italy
170 B2 Argentera, Cima dell' mt. Italy
164 F5 Argenthal Germany
212 C5 Argentina country S. America
129 C4 Argentina Range mts Antarctica
219 F9 Argentine Abyssal Plain sea feature S. Atlantic Ocean
219 G8 Argentine Basin sea feature S. Atlantic Ocean
219 F8 Argentine Rise sea feature S. Atlantic Ocean
212 B8 Argentino, Lago l. Arg.
171 K2 Argeș r. Romania
141 G4 Arghandāb Rōd r. Afgh.
136 C2 Argıthanı Turkey
171 J6 Argolikos Kolpos b. Greece
171 J6 Argos Greece
171 I5 Argostoli Greece
167 F1 Arguis Spain
146 E1 Argun' r. China/Russia
173 H7 Argun Russia
129 D5 Argus, Dome ice feature Antarctica
196 D4 Argus Range mts U.S.A.
190 C4 Argyle U.S.A.
124 C3 Argyle, Lake Australia
162 C4 Argyll reg. U.K.
128 E3 Aria N.Z.
127 G5 Ariah Park Australia
151 B8 Ariake-kai b. Japan
179 B6 Ariamsvlei Namibia
170 F4 Ariano Irpino Italy
213 B4 Ariari r. Col.
215 D2 Arias Arg.
135 F6 Ari Atholhu Maldives
213 E2 Aribí r. Venez.
176 B3 Aribinda Burkina Faso
212 B1 Arica Chile
162 C4 Arienas, Loch l. U.K.
136 F4 Arīḩā Syria
194 G4 Arikaree r. U.S.A.
213 E2 Arima Trin. and Tob.
214 C1 Arinos Brazil
211 G6 Arinos r. Brazil
206 D4 Ario de Rosáles Mex.
213 C3 Ariporo r. Col.
210 F5 Aripuanã Brazil
210 F5 Aripuanã r. Brazil
210 G6 Aripuanã, Parque Indígena nat. park Brazil
210 F5 Ariquemes Brazil
214 B2 Ariranhá r. Brazil
180 B1 Aris Namibia
162 C4 Arisaig U.K.
162 C4 Arisaig, Sound of sea chan. U.K.
186 D4 Aristazabal Island Canada
212 C2 Arizaro, Salar de salt flat Arg.
197 G4 Arizona state U.S.A.
192 D5 Arizpe Mex.
140 B5 'Arjah Saudi Arabia
158 L2 Arjeplog Sweden
213 B2 Arjona Col.
155 D4 Arjuna, Gunung vol. Indon.
173 G5 Arkadak Russia
199 E5 Arkadelphia U.S.A.
162 C4 Arkaig, Loch l. U.K.
139 F2 Arkalyk Kazakh.
199 F5 Arkansas r. U.S.A.
199 E5 Arkansas state U.S.A.
199 D4 Arkansas City U.S.A.
145 G1 Arka Tag mts China
172 G2 Arkhangel'skaya Oblast' admin. div. Russia
172 F4 Arkhangel'skoye Russia
150 C3 Arkhipovka Russia
163 E5 Arklow Ireland
171 L6 Arkoi i. Greece
168 F3 Arkona, Kap c. Germany
132 J2 Arkticheskogo Instituta, Ostrova is Russia
203 F3 Arkville U.S.A.
166 G5 Arles France
181 G4 Arlington S. Africa
194 B2 Arlington OR U.S.A.
198 D2 Arlington SD U.S.A.
202 E5 Arlington VA U.S.A.
190 D4 Arlington Heights U.S.A.
176 C3 Arlit Niger
164 D5 Arlon Belgium
153 C5 Armadores i. Indon.
163 E3 Armagh U.K.
177 F2 Armant Egypt
137 J1 Armavir Armenia
173 G6 Armavir Russia
137 J1 Armenia country Asia
213 B3 Armenia Col.
213 B3 Armero (abandoned) Col.
127 I3 Armidale Australia
187 K2 Armit Lake Canada
144 E5 Armori India
163 E2 Armoy U.K.
186 F4 Armstrong B.C. Canada
188 C3 Armstrong Ont. Canada
150 E1 Armu r. Russia
143 B2 Armur India
173 E6 Armyans'k Crimea
Arnaoutis, Cape Cyprus see Arnauti, Cape
189 F1 Arnaud r. Canada
136 D4 Arnauti, Cape Cyprus
159 J3 Årnes Norway
199 D4 Arnett U.S.A.
164 D3 Arnhem Neth.
124 D3 Arnhem, Cape Australia
124 D3 Arnhem Bay Australia
124 D3 Arnhem Land reg. Australia
170 D3 Arno r. Italy
126 B4 Arno Bay Australia
161 F4 Arnold U.K.
190 D2 Arnold U.S.A.
191 H1 Arnoux, Lac l. Canada
191 I3 Arnprior Canada
165 G3 Arnsberg Germany
165 I4 Arnstadt Germany
191 H3 Arnstein Canada
165 H5 Arnstein Germany
191 H1 Arntfield Canada
213 E3 Aro r. Venez.
179 B6 Aroab Namibia
165 H3 Arolsen Germany
170 C2 Arona Italy
203 J1 Aroostook Canada
203 I1 Aroostook r. Canada/U.S.A.
125 H2 Arorae i. Kiribati
153 B3 Aroroy Phil.
173 G7 Arpa r. Armenia/Turkey
137 I1 Arpaçay Turkey
141 G5 Arra r. Pak.
145 F4 Arrah India
137 I5 Ar Raḩḩālīyah Iraq
137 I5 Ar Ramādī Iraq
136 E7 Ar Ramlah Jordan
162 C5 Arran i. U.K.
163 C3 Arranmore Island Ireland
137 G4 Ar Raqqah Syria
166 F1 Arras France
140 A5 Ar Rass Al Qaşīm Saudi Arabia
142 B4 Ar Rass Al Qaşīm Saudi Arabia
136 F4 Ar Rastan Syria
137 I7 Ar Rawḑ well Saudi Arabia
140 C5 Ar Rayyān Qatar
213 C4 Arrecifal Col.
215 E2 Arrecifes Arg.
207 F4 Arriagá Mex.
206 D3 Arriaga Mex.
215 E2 Arribeños Arg.
137 K6 Ar Rifā'ī Iraq
137 J6 Ar Rihāb salt flat Iraq
142 D5 Ar Rimāl reg. Saudi Arabia
197 H3 Arriola U.S.A.
Ar Riyāḑ Saudi Arabia see Riyadh
162 D4 Arrochar U.K.
215 G2 Arroio Grande Brazil
214 D1 Arrojado r. Brazil
163 C3 Arrow, Lough l. Ireland
190 B1 Arrow Lake Canada
194 D3 Arrowrock Reservoir U.S.A.
128 C5 Arrowsmith, Mount N.Z.
196 B4 Arroyo Grande U.S.A.
215 E2 Arroyo Seco Arg.
207 E3 Arroyo Seco Mex.
140 B5 Ar Rubay'iyah Saudi Arabia
214 A1 Arruda Brazil
137 J6 Ar Rumaythah Iraq
141 E6 Ar Rustāq Oman
137 H5 Ar Ruţbah Iraq
140 B6 Ar Ruwayḑah Saudi Arabia
Års Denmark see Aars
140 B2 Ars Iran
140 D4 Arsanajān Iran
150 C2 Arsen'yev Russia
139 H2 Arshaly Akmolinskaya Oblast' Kazakh.
139 J2 Arshaly Vostochnyy Kazakhstan Kazakh.
143 B3 Arsikere India
172 I3 Arsk Russia
136 E3 Arslanköy Turkey
178 E2 Arta Djibouti
171 I5 Arta Greece
137 J2 Artashat Armenia
206 D4 Arteaga Mex.
150 C3 Artem Russia
205 H4 Artemisa Cuba
173 F5 Artemivs'k Ukr.
150 C3 Artemovskiy Russia
166 E2 Artenay France
195 F5 Artesia U.S.A.
191 G4 Arthur Canada
126 B3 Arthur, Lake salt flat Australia
202 C4 Arthur, Lake U.S.A.
127 G8 Arthur Lake Australia
124 F4 Arthur Point Australia
128 C5 Arthur's Pass N.Z.
128 C5 Arthur's Pass National Park N.Z.
201 F7 Arthur's Town Bahamas
129 E2 Artigas research stn Antarctica
215 F1 Artigas Uruguay
137 I1 Art'ik Armenia
187 H2 Artillery Lake Canada
181 G2 Artisia Botswana
166 F1 Artois reg. France
164 A4 Artois, Collines d' hills France
137 I2 Artos Dağı mt. Turkey
136 F1 Artova Turkey
173 D6 Artsyz Ukr.
129 B2 Arturo Prat research stn Antarctica
139 I5 Artux China
137 H1 Artvin Turkey
147 F7 Aru, Kepulauan is Indon.
178 D3 Arua Uganda
214 B1 Aruanã Brazil
213 C1 Aruba terr. Caribbean Sea
210 F4 Arumã Brazil
145 F4 Arun r. Nepal
145 H3 Arunachal Pradesh state India
161 G7 Arundel U.K.
178 D4 Arusha Tanz.
198 B4 Arvada U.S.A.
163 D4 Arvagh Ireland
146 C2 Arvayheer Mongolia
144 D5 Arvi India
187 K2 Arviat Canada
189 F4 Arvida Canada
158 L2 Arvidsjaur Sweden
159 K4 Arvika Sweden
196 C4 Arvin U.S.A.
140 B6 Arwā' Saudi Arabia
141 E3 Āryanshahr Iran
139 G1 Arykbalyk Kazakh.
139 G4 Arys Kazakh.
139 G4 Arys' r. Kazakh.
138 F3 Arys, Ozero salt l. Kazakh.
172 G4 Arzamas Russia
165 K4 Arzberg Germany
167 F5 Arzew Alg.
173 H6 Arzgir Russia
165 K4 Aš Czech Rep.
213 E3 Asa r. Venez.
176 C4 Asaba Nigeria
136 G3 Asad, Buḩayrat al resr Syria
141 H3 Asadābād Afgh.
140 C3 Asadābād Hamadān Iran
141 E3 Asadābād Khorāsān-e Razavī Iran
140 D4 Asadābād Yazd Iran
154 A5 Asahan r. Indon.
150 H3 Asahi-dake vol. Japan
151 C7 Asahi-gawa r. Japan
150 H3 Asahikawa Japan
139 H4 Asaka Uzbek.
140 C2 Asālem Iran
152 D5 Asan-man b. S. Korea
145 F5 Asansol India
164 F4 Asbach Germany
189 F4 Asbestos Canada
180 E4 Asbestos Mountains S. Africa
203 F4 Asbury Park U.S.A.
170 F4 Ascea Italy
210 F7 Ascensión Bol.
175 C5 Ascension i. S. Atlantic Ocean
207 H4 Ascensión, Bahía de la b. Mex.
165 H5 Aschaffenburg Germany
164 F3 Ascheberg Germany
165 J3 Aschersleben Germany
170 E3 Ascoli Piceno Italy
159 K4 Åseda Sweden
158 L2 Åsele Sweden
171 K3 Asenovgrad Bulg.
138 D5 Aşgabat Turkm.
140 B5 Asharat Saudi Arabia
124 B4 Ashburton watercourse Australia
128 C5 Ashburton N.Z.
190 D1 Ashburton Bay Canada
139 F3 Ashchikol', Ozero salt l. Kazakh.
139 G4 Ashchysay Kazakh.
186 E4 Ashcroft Canada
136 E6 Ashdod Israel
199 E5 Ashdown U.S.A.
201 E5 Asheboro U.S.A.
201 D5 Asheville U.S.A.
127 I2 Ashford Australia
161 H6 Ashford U.K.
197 F4 Ash Fork U.S.A.
Ashgabat Turkm. see Aşgabat
150 H3 Ashibetsu Japan
151 F6 Ashikaga Japan
160 F2 Ashington U.K.
172 I3 Ashit r. Russia
151 C8 Ashizuri-misaki pt Japan
140 D4 Ashkezar Iran
199 D4 Ashland KS U.S.A.
202 B5 Ashland KY U.S.A.
203 I1 Ashland ME U.S.A.
194 F2 Ashland MT U.S.A.
203 H3 Ashland NH U.S.A.
202 B4 Ashland OH U.S.A.
194 B3 Ashland OR U.S.A.
202 E6 Ashland VA U.S.A.
190 B2 Ashland WI U.S.A.
127 H2 Ashley Australia
198 D2 Ashley U.S.A.
124 C3 Ashmore and Cartier Islands terr. Australia
172 C4 Ashmyany Belarus
197 H5 Ash Peak U.S.A.
136 E6 Ashqelon Israel
137 I6 Ash Shabakah Iraq
137 H3 Ash Shaddādah Syria
137 J6 Ash Shanāfīyah Iraq
137 H7 Ash Shaqīq well Saudi Arabia
140 B5 Ash Sha'rā' Saudi Arabia
136 E6 Ash Sharāh reg. Jordan
142 E4 Ash Shāriqah U.A.E.
137 I4 Ash Sharqāţ Iraq
137 K6 Ash Shaţrah Iraq
136 D7 Ash Shaţţ Egypt
136 E6 Ash Shawbak Jordan
142 C7 Ash Shiḩr Yemen
140 E5 Ash Şhināş Oman
140 B4 Ash Shu'bah Saudi Arabia
140 B5 Ash Shumlūl Saudi Arabia
202 C4 Ashtabula U.S.A.
137 J1 Ashtarak Armenia
143 A2 Ashti Maharashtra India
144 D5 Ashti Maharashtra India
140 C3 Āshtīān Iran
180 D6 Ashton S. Africa
194 E2 Ashton U.S.A.
160 E4 Ashton-under-Lyne U.K.
185 L4 Ashuanipi Lake Canada
188 F4 Ashuapmushuan r. Canada
188 F4 Ashuapmushuan, Réserve Faunique nature res. Canada
201 C5 Ashville U.S.A.
136 F4 'Āşī, Nahr al r. Asia
130 Asia
206 D3 Asientos Mex.
143 B2 Asifabad India
143 D2 Asika India
170 C4 Asinara, Golfo dell' b. Sardinia Italy
132 J4 Asino Russia
172 D4 Asipovichy Belarus
142 B5 'Asīr reg. Saudi Arabia
137 H2 Aşkale Turkey
138 D1 Askarovo Russia
159 J4 Asker Norway
159 K4 Askersund Sweden
159 J4 Askim Norway
137 I3 Askī Mawşil Iraq
146 B1 Askiz Russia
137 K2 Aşlāndūz Iran
178 D2 Asmara Eritrea
159 K4 Åsnen l. Sweden
144 C4 Asop India
137 L3 Aspar Iran
139 H4 Aspara Kazakh.
160 D3 Aspatria U.K.
195 F4 Aspen U.S.A.
165 H6 Asperg Germany
199 C5 Aspermont U.S.A.
128 B6 Aspiring, Mount N.Z.
187 H4 Asquith Canada
139 G4 Assa Kazakh.
136 F4 As Sa'an Syria
178 E2 Assab Eritrea
140 C5 As Sabsab well Saudi Arabia
136 C7 Aş Şaff Egypt
136 E6 Aş Şāfī Jordan
136 F3 As Safīrah Syria
Aş Şaḩrā' al Gharbīyah Egypt see Western Desert
Aş Şaḩrā' ash Sharqīyah des. Egypt see Eastern Desert
140 C5 As Saji well Saudi Arabia
138 D4 Assake-Audan, Vpadina depr. Uzbek.
140 B5 As Salamiyah Saudi Arabia
136 D6 Aş Şāliḩīyah Egypt
137 H4 Aş Şālihīyah Syria
137 J6 As Salmān Iraq
136 E5 As Salţ Jordan
145 H4 Assam state India
137 J6 As Samāwah Iraq
136 F5 Aş Şanamayn Syria
177 E2 As Sarīr reg. Libya
203 F5 Assateague Island U.S.A.
203 F6 Assateague Island National Seashore nature res. U.S.A.
164 E1 Assen Neth.
164 B3 Assenede Belgium
164 D4 Assesse Belgium
145 F5 Assia Hills India
177 D1 As Sidrah Libya
187 H5 Assiniboia Canada
187 J5 Assiniboine r. Canada
186 F4 Assiniboine, Mount Canada
214 B3 Assis Brazil
170 E3 Assisi Italy
165 G4 Aßlar Germany
137 K7 Aş Şubayḩīyah Kuwait
140 B4 Aş Şufayrī well Saudi Arabia
137 G4 As Sukhnah Syria
137 J4 As Sulaymānīyah/Slêmānî Iraq
142 C5 As Sulayyil Saudi Arabia
140 C5 Aş Şulb reg. Saudi Arabia
140 B5 Aş Şummān plat. Saudi Arabia
142 B5 As Sūq Saudi Arabia
137 H4 Aş Şuwar Syria
136 F5 As Suwaydā' Syria
141 E6 As Suwayq Oman
137 J5 Aş Şuwayrah Iraq
As Suways Egypt see Suez
162 C2 Assynt, Loch l. U.K.
171 L7 Astakida i. Greece
134 F1 Astana Kazakh.
137 L3 Āstāneh-ye Ashrafīyeh Iran
137 L2 Āstārā Azer.
170 C2 Asti Italy
196 A2 Asti U.S.A.
215 C1 Astica Arg.
141 F5 Astola Island Pak.
144 C2 Astor Pak.
144 C2 Astor r. Pak.
167 C1 Astorga Spain
194 B2 Astoria U.S.A.
159 K4 Åstorp Sweden
134 C2 Astrakhan' Russia
173 H6 Astrakhanskaya Oblast' admin. div. Russia
172 C4 Astravyets Belarus
129 D3 Astrid Ridge sea feature Southern Ocean
167 C1 Asturias aut. comm. Spain
171 L6 Astypalaia i. Greece
139 J2 Asubulak Kazakh.
212 E3 Asunción Para.
177 F2 Aswān Egypt
140 A5 Asyāḩ, Safrā' al esc. Saudi Arabia
177 F2 Asyūţ Egypt
125 I4 Ata i. Tonga
213 D4 Atabapo r. Col./Venez.
139 G4 Atabay Kazakh.
Atabayeva, imeni Turkm. see Māne
Atacama, Desierto de des. Chile see Atacama Desert
212 C2 Atacama, Salar de salt flat Chile
212 C2 Atacama Desert Chile
125 I2 Atafu atoll Tokelau
139 G4 Atakent Kazakh.
176 C4 Atakpamé Togo
171 J5 Atalanti Greece
206 I7 Atalaya Panama
210 D6 Atalaya Peru
138 F5 Atamyrat Turkm.
139 G1 Atansor, Ozero salt l. Kazakh.
176 A2 Atâr Mauritania
154 A1 Ataran r. Myanmar
197 H4 Atarque U.S.A.
196 B4 Atascadero U.S.A.
139 G2 Atasu Kazakh.
147 E7 Ataúro, Ilha de i. East Timor
171 L6 Atavyros mt. Greece
138 D4 Ataýap Turkm.
177 F3 Atbara Sudan
177 F3 Atbara r. Sudan
139 G2 Atbasar Kazakh.
139 H4 At-Bashy Kyrg.
199 F6 Atchafalaya Bay U.S.A.
198 E4 Atchison U.S.A.
206 C3 Atenguillo Mex.
170 E3 Aterno r. Italy
170 F3 Atessa Italy
164 B4 Ath Belgium
186 G4 Athabasca Canada
184 G4 Athabasca r. U.S.A.
187 G3 Athabasca, Lake Canada
137 I6 'Athāmīn, Birkat al well Iraq
163 E4 Athboy Ireland
163 C4 Athenry Ireland
191 J3 Athens Canada
171 J6 Athens Greece (City Plan 107)
201 C5 Athens AL U.S.A.
201 D5 Athens GA U.S.A.
202 B5 Athens OH U.S.A.
201 C5 Athens TN U.S.A.
199 E5 Athens TX U.S.A.
161 F5 Atherstone U.K.
164 A5 Athies France
Athina Greece see Athens
163 C4 Athleague Ireland
163 D4 Athlone Ireland
143 A2 Athni India
128 B6 Athol N.Z.
203 G3 Athol U.S.A.
162 E4 Atholl, Forest of reg. U.K.
171 K4 Athos mt. Greece
136 E7 Ath Thamad Egypt
163 E5 Athy Ireland
177 D3 Ati Chad
210 D7 Atico Peru
188 B4 Atikokan Canada
189 H3 Atikonak Lake Canada
153 B3 Atimonan Phil.
143 B4 Atirampattinam India
207 G5 Atitlán Guat.
207 G5 Átitlán, Volcán vol. Guat.
140 B5 'Atk, Wādī al watercourse Saudi Arabia
133 Q3 Atka Russia
173 H5 Atkarsk Russia
207 E4 Atlacomulco Mex.
201 C5 Atlanta GA U.S.A.
190 C5 Atlanta IL U.S.A.
191 E3 Atlanta MI U.S.A.
136 D2 Atlantı Turkey
198 E3 Atlantic U.S.A.
203 F5 Atlantic City U.S.A.
218 D9 Atlantic-Indian-Antarctic Basin sea feature S. Atlantic Ocean
218 D8 Atlantic-Indian Ridge sea feature Southern Ocean
219 Atlantic Ocean
180 C6 Atlantis S. Africa
173 B1 Atlas Mountains Africa
176 C1 Atlas Saharien mts Alg.
186 C3 Atlin Canada
186 C3 Atlin Lake Canada
186 C3 Atlin Provincial Park Canada
136 E5 'Atlit Israel
207 E4 Atlixco Mex.
143 B3 Atmakur Andhra Pradesh India
143 B3 Atmakur Andhra Pradesh India
199 G6 Atmore U.S.A.
199 D5 Atoka U.S.A.
206 D3 Atotonilco el Alto Mex.
154 C1 Atouat mt. Laos
207 D4 Atoyac de Álvarez Mex.
145 G4 Atrai r. India
140 E2 Atrak, Rūd-e r. Iran/Turkm. alt. Atrek, alt. Etrek
213 A3 Atrato r. Col.
140 D2 Atrek r. Iran/Turkm. alt. Atrak, Rūd-e, alt. Etrek
203 F5 Atsion U.S.A.
136 E6 Aţ Ţafīlah Jordan
142 B5 Aţ Ţā'if Saudi Arabia
201 C5 Attalla U.S.A.
154 C2 Attapu Laos
188 D3 Attawapiskat Canada
188 C3 Attawapiskat r. Canada
188 C3 Attawapiskat Lake Canada
137 G7 Aţ Ţawīl mts Saudi Arabia
140 A4 At Taysīyah plat. Saudi Arabia
165 F3 Attendorn Germany
168 F7 Attersee l. Austria
190 D5 Attica IN U.S.A.
202 B4 Attica OH U.S.A.
164 C5 Attigny France
203 H3 Attleboro U.S.A.
161 I5 Attleborough U.K.
136 F7 Aţ Ţubayq reg. Saudi Arabia
216 G2 Attu Island U.S.A.
140 B5 Aţ Ţulayḩī well Saudi Arabia
177 F2 Aţ Ţūr Egypt
143 B4 Attur India
215 C2 Atuel r. Arg.
215 C3 Atuel, Bañados del marsh Arg.
159 K4 Åtvidaberg Sweden
202 C4 Atwood Lake U.S.A.
138 B3 Atyrau Kazakh.
138 B3 Atyrauskaya Oblast' admin. div. Kazakh.
165 I5 Aub Germany
166 G5 Aubagne France
164 D5 Aubange Belgium
153 B2 Aubarede Point Phil.
166 G4 Aubenas France
164 D5 Auboué France
197 F4 Aubrey Cliffs mts U.S.A.
184 F3 Aubry Lake Canada
126 C5 Auburn Australia
191 G4 Auburn Canada
201 C5 Auburn AL U.S.A.
196 B2 Auburn CA U.S.A.
190 E5 Auburn IN U.S.A.
203 H2 Auburn ME U.S.A.
198 E3 Auburn NE U.S.A.
202 E3 Auburn NY U.S.A.
194 B2 Auburn WA U.S.A.
166 F4 Aubusson France
215 C3 Auca Mahuida, Sierra de mt. Arg.
166 E5 Auch France
162 E4 Auchterarder U.K.
128 E2 Auckland N.Z. (City Plan 102)
125 G7 Auckland Islands N.Z.
203 H2 Audet Canada
161 I7 Audresselles France
164 A4 Audruicq France
165 K4 Aue Germany
165 K4 Auerbach Germany
165 J5 Auerbach in der Oberpfalz Germany
165 K4 Auersberg mt. Germany
139 J2 Auezov Kazakh.
163 D3 Augher U.K.
163 E3 Aughnacloy U.K.
163 E5 Aughrim Ireland
180 D4 Augrabies S. Africa
180 D4 Augrabies Falls S. Africa
180 D4 Augrabies Falls National Park S. Africa
191 F3 Au Gres U.S.A.
168 E6 Augsburg Germany
170 F6 Augusta Sicily Italy
201 D5 Augusta GA U.S.A.
199 D4 Augusta KS U.S.A.
203 I2 Augusta ME U.S.A.
190 B3 Augusta WI U.S.A.
169 K4 Augustowska, Puszcza for. Poland
124 B4 Augustus, Mount Australia
138 F1 Auliyekol' Kazakh.
164 B4 Aulnoye-Aymeries France
161 I7 Ault France
Auminzatau, Gory hill Uzbek. see Ovminzatov tog'lari
179 B6 Auob watercourse Namibia
189 G2 Aupaluk Canada
154 C5 Aur i. Malaysia
159 M3 Aura Fin.
144 D4 Auraiya India
144 C6 Aurangabad India
164 F1 Aurich Germany
214 B2 Aurilândia Brazil
166 F4 Aurillac France
155 D3 Aurkuning Indon.
153 B5 Aurora Phil.
194 F4 Aurora CO U.S.A.
190 C5 Aurora IL U.S.A.
203 I2 Aurora ME U.S.A.
199 E4 Aurora MO U.S.A.
179 B6 Aus Namibia
191 F3 Au Sable U.S.A.
191 E3 Au Sable r. U.S.A.
203 G2 Ausable r. U.S.A.
203 G2 Au Sable Forks U.S.A.
190 D2 Au Sable Point MI U.S.A.
191 F3 Au Sable Point MI U.S.A.
162 F1 Auskerry i. U.K.
158 C2 Austari-Jökulsá r. Iceland
198 E3 Austin MN U.S.A.
196 D2 Austin NV U.S.A.
199 D6 Austin TX U.S.A.
Australes, Îles is Fr. Polynesia see Tubuai Islands
124 C4 Australia country Oceania
219 P9 Australian-Antarctic Basin sea feature Southern Ocean
129 B7 Australian Antarctic Territory reg. Antarctica
127 H5 Australian Capital Territory admin. div. Australia
127 G9 Australian Convict Sites tourist site Australia
168 F7 Austria country Europe
158 K1 Austvågøy i. Norway
206 C4 Autlán Mex.
158 N2 Autti Fin.
166 G3 Autun France
166 F4 Auvergne reg. France
166 F3 Auxerre France
164 A4 Auxi-le-Château France
166 G3 Auxonne France
203 F3 Ava U.S.A.
137 L4 Āvaj Iran
166 F3 Avallon France
196 C5 Avalon U.S.A.
189 J4 Avalon Peninsula Canada
206 D2 Ávalos Mex.
140 B2 Avān Iran
136 E2 Avanos Turkey
214 C3 Avaré Brazil
137 K2 Āvārsīn Iran
196 D4 Avawatz Mountains U.S.A.
141 F3 Āvāz Iran
211 G4 Aveiro Brazil
167 B2 Aveiro Port.
167 B2 Aveiro, Ria de est. Port.
215 E2 Avellaneda Arg.
170 F4 Avellino Italy
196 B3 Avenal U.S.A.
126 F6 Avenel Australia
170 F4 Aversa Italy
164 B4 Avesnes-sur-Helpe France
159 L3 Avesta Sweden
166 F4 Aveyron r. France
170 E3 Avezzano Italy
162 E3 Aviemore U.K.
170 F4 Avigliano Italy
166 G5 Avignon France
167 D2 Ávila Spain
167 D1 Avilés Spain
164 A4 Avion France
143 C5 Avissawella Sri Lanka
172 H2 Avnyugskiy Russia
127 G8 Avoca Tas. Australia
126 E6 Avoca Vic. Australia
126 E6 Avoca r. Australia
163 E5 Avoca Ireland
198 E3 Avoca U.S.A.
170 F6 Avola Sicily Italy
161 E6 Avon r. England U.K.
161 F5 Avon r. England U.K.
161 F7 Avon r. England U.K.
190 B5 Avon U.S.A.
197 F5 Avondale U.S.A.
161 E6 Avonmouth U.K.
201 D7 Avon Park U.S.A.
166 D2 Avranches France
164 A5 Avre r. France
125 G2 Avuavu Solomon Is
151 D7 Awaji-shima i. Japan
128 E3 Awakino N.Z.
140 C5 'Awālī Bahrain
128 D1 Awanui N.Z.
128 B6 Awarua Point N.Z.
178 E3 Āwash Eth.
178 D3 Āwash r. Eth.
150 F5 Awa-shima i. Japan
178 D3 Āwash National Park Eth.
180 A2 Awasib Mountains Namibia
139 J4 Awat China
128 D4 Awatere r. N.Z.
177 D2 Awbārī Libya
176 D2 Awbārī, Idhān des. Libya
163 C5 Awbeg r. Ireland
137 K6 'Awdah, Hawr al imp. l. Iraq
178 E3 Aw Dheegle Somalia
162 C4 Awe, Loch l. U.K.
177 E4 Aweil South Sudan
176 C4 Awka Nigeria
153 C6 Awu vol. Indon.
126 F6 Axedale Australia
185 I2 Axel Heiberg Island Canada
176 B4 Axim Ghana
161 E7 Axminster U.K.
164 C5 Ay France
139 J3 Ay Kazakh.
151 D7 Ayabe Japan
215 E3 Ayacucho Arg.
210 D6 Ayacucho Peru
139 J3 Ayagoz Kazakh.
139 I3 Ayagoz watercourse Kazakh.
Ayakkuduk Uzbek. see Oyoqquduq
146 A3 Ayakkum Hu salt l. China
167 C4 Ayamonte Spain
146 F1 Ayan Russia
173 E7 Ayancık Turkey
152 C4 Ayang N. Korea
133 R3 Ayanka Russia
213 B2 Ayapel Col.
136 D1 Ayaş Turkey
210 D6 Ayaviri Peru
139 G1 Aydabol Kazakh.
173 F5 Aydar r. Ukr.

Bârlad

139 F4 Aydarko'l ko'li l. Uzbek.
Aydarkul', Ozero l. Uzbek. see Aydarko'l ko'li
138 F3 Aydarly Kazakh.
136 A3 Aydın Turkey
136 A2 Aydın Dağları mts Turkey
138 C5 Aýdyň Turkm.
138 D2 Aydyrlinskiy Russia
154 □ Ayer Chawan, Pulau i. Sing.
154 □ Ayer Merbau, Pulau i. Sing.
Ayers Rock h. Australia see Uluṟu
139 J2 Aygyrzhal Kazakh.
138 E2 Ayke, Ozero l. Kazakh.
133 M3 Aykhal Russia
172 I2 Aykino Russia
139 J4 Aykol China
128 D5 Aylesbury N.Z.
161 G6 Aylesbury U.K.
202 E6 Aylett U.S.A.
167 E2 Ayllón Spain
191 G4 Aylmer Canada
187 H2 Aylmer Lake Canada
139 I3 Aynabulak Kazakh.
140 C4 'Ayn al 'Abd well Saudi Arabia
137 G3 'Ayn al 'Arab Syria
139 G5 Ayní Tajik.
136 G3 'Ayn 'Īsá Syria
177 F4 Ayod South Sudan
133 R3 Ayon, Ostrov i. Russia
176 B3 'Ayoûn el 'Atroûs Mauritania
124 E3 Ayr Australia
162 D5 Ayr U.K.
162 D5 Ayr r. U.K.
136 D3 Ayrancı Turkey
160 C3 Ayre, Point of Isle of Man
139 G3 Ayshyrak Kazakh.
138 E3 Ayteke Bi Kazakh.
171 L3 Aytos Bulg.
154 D2 A Yun Pa Vietnam
154 B2 Ayutthaya Thai.
171 L5 Ayvacık Turkey
136 F2 Ayvalı Turkey
171 L5 Ayvalık Turkey
206 H5 Azacualpa Hond.
145 E4 Azamgarh India
Azania reg. Somalia see Jubaland
176 B3 Azaouâd reg. Mali
176 C3 Azaouagh, Vallée de watercourse Mali/Niger
139 G3 Azat, Gory h. Kazakh.
176 B3 Azawad reg. Mali
Azbine mts Niger see Aïr, Massif de l'
136 D1 Azdavay Turkey
137 K1 Azerbaijan country Asia
140 B2 Āzghān Iran
138 E3 Azhar Kazakh.
139 G2 Azhibeksor, Ozero salt l. Kazakh.
191 G2 Azilda Canada
203 H2 Aziscohos Lake U.S.A.
210 C4 Azogues Ecuador
132 F3 Azopol'ye Russia
156 A6 Azores terr. N. Atlantic Ocean
219 H3 Azores-Biscay Rise sea feature N. Atlantic Ocean
173 F6 Azov Russia
173 F6 Azov, Sea of Russia/Ukr.
Azraq, Bahr el r. Eth./Sudan see Blue Nile
136 F6 Azraq, Qaşr al Jordan
176 B1 Azrou Morocco
195 F4 Aztec U.S.A.
167 D3 Azuaga Spain
212 B3 Azúcar r. Chile
206 I7 Azuero, Península de pen. Panama
215 E3 Azul Arg.
207 G4 Azul r. Mex.
215 B4 Azul, Cerro mt. Arg.
210 C5 Azul, Cordillera mts Peru
214 A1 Azul, Serra hills Brazil
151 G6 Azuma-san vol. Japan
166 H5 Azur, Côte d' coastal area France
210 F8 Azurduy Bol.
140 C5 Az̧ Za'āyin Qatar
170 B6 Azzaba Alg.
136 F5 Az Zabadānī Syria
137 I6 Az̧ Z̧afīrī reg. Iraq
Az̧ Z̧ahrān Saudi Arabia see Dhahran
177 F1 Az Zaqāzīq Egypt
136 F5 Az Zarqā' Jordan
177 D1 Az Zāwiyah Libya
137 J3 Az Zībār Iraq
140 B5 Az Zilfī Saudi Arabia
137 K6 Az Zubayr Iraq

B

154 D2 Ba, Sông r. Vietnam
136 E5 Baabda Lebanon
136 F4 Ba'albek Lebanon
127 H3 Baan Baa Australia
178 E3 Baardheere Somalia
141 H3 Bābā, Kōh-e mts Afgh.
171 L5 Baba Burnu pt Turkey
137 L1 Babadağ mt. Azer.
171 M2 Babadag Romania
Babadaykhan Ahal Turkm. see Badabaýhan
Babadaykhan Ahal Turkm. see Badabaýhan
138 D5 Babadurmaz Turkm.
173 C7 Babaeski Turkey
210 C4 Babahoyo Ecuador
143 B1 Babai India
145 E3 Babai r. Nepal
148 B1 Babai Gaxun China
137 K2 Bābājān Iran
153 C5 Babak Phil.
178 E2 Bāb al Mandab str. Africa/Asia
147 E7 Babar i. Indon.
139 H4 Babash-Ata, Khrebet mt. Kyrg.
178 D4 Babati Tanz.
172 E3 Babayevo Russia
173 H7 Babayurt Russia
190 B2 Babbitt U.S.A.
127 H7 Babel Island Australia
184 F4 Babine r. Canada
186 D4 Babine Lake Canada
147 F7 Babo Indon.
140 D2 Bābol Iran
138 C5 Bābolsar Iran
180 C6 Baboon Point S. Africa
197 G6 Baboquivari Peak U.S.A.
178 B3 Baboua C.A.R.
172 D4 Babruysk Belarus
144 B4 Babuhri India
144 C2 Babusar Pass Pak.
172 G3 Babushkina, imeni Russia
153 A4 Babuyan Phil.
153 B2 Babuyan i. Phil.
149 F7 Babuyan Channel Phil.
153 B2 Babuyan Islands Phil.
137 J5 Babylon tourist site Iraq
211 J4 Bacabal Brazil
136 C1 Bacakliyayla Tepesi mt. Turkey
207 G4 Bacalar Mex.
147 E7 Bacan i. Indon.
153 B2 Bacarra Phil.
169 M7 Bacău Romania
126 F6 Bacchus Marsh Australia
149 C6 Băc Giang Vietnam
206 C1 Bachiniva Mex.
149 C6 Bach Long Vi, Đao i. Vietnam
139 I5 Bachu China
139 I5 Bachu Liuchang China
187 I1 Back r. Canada
149 B6 Băc Kan Vietnam
171 H2 Bačka Palanka Serbia
186 D2 Backbone Ranges mts Canada
158 L3 Backe Sweden
126 B5 Backstairs Passage sea chan. Australia
162 E4 Backwater Reservoir U.K.
154 C3 Bac Liêu Vietnam
149 C6 Băc Ninh Vietnam
153 B3 Baco, Mount Phil.
153 B4 Bacolod Phil.
Băc Quang Vietnam see Việt Quang
188 F2 Bacqueville, Lac l. Canada
138 E5 Badabaýhan Ahal Turkm.
138 E5 Badabaýhan Ahal Turkm.
165 K6 Bad Abbach Germany
148 A1 Badain Jaran Shamo des. China
210 F4 Badajós, Lago l. Brazil
167 C3 Badajoz Spain
143 A3 Badami India
138 D2 Badamsha Kazakh.
137 H6 Badanah Saudi Arabia
145 H4 Badarpur India
191 F4 Bad Axe U.S.A.
165 G1 Bad Bederkesa Germany
165 K2 Bad Belzig Germany
165 F5 Bad Bergzabern Germany
165 G3 Bad Berleburg Germany
165 I1 Bad Bevensen Germany
165 J4 Bad Blankenburg Germany
165 G4 Bad Camberg Germany
189 H4 Baddeck Canada
141 G4 Baddo r. Pak.
165 H3 Bad Driburg Germany
165 K3 Bad Düben Germany
165 G5 Bad Dürkheim Germany
165 K3 Bad Dürrenberg Germany
136 C3 Bademli Geçidi pass Turkey
165 F4 Bad Ems Germany
168 H6 Baden Austria
168 D7 Baden Switz.
168 D6 Baden-Baden Germany
162 D4 Badenoch reg. U.K.
165 G5 Baden-Württemberg land Germany
165 G2 Bad Essen Germany
165 H2 Bad Fallingbostel Germany
189 I4 Badger Canada
165 I3 Bad Grund (Harz) Germany
165 I3 Bad Harzburg Germany
165 H4 Bad Hersfeld Germany
168 F7 Bad Hofgastein Austria
165 G4 Bad Homburg vor der Höhe Germany
170 D2 Badia Polesine Italy
144 B4 Badin Pak.
206 C2 Badiraguato Mex.
168 F7 Bad Ischl Austria
Bādiyat ash Shām des. Asia see Syrian Desert
165 I4 Bad Kissingen Germany
165 J3 Bad Kösen Germany
165 K5 Bad Kötzting Germany
165 F5 Bad Kreuznach Germany
165 G4 Bad Laasphe Germany
198 C2 Badlands reg. U.S.A.
198 C3 Badlands National Park U.S.A.
165 I3 Bad Langensalza Germany
165 I3 Bad Lauterberg im Harz Germany
165 G3 Bad Lippspringe Germany
165 F4 Bad Marienberg (Westerwald) Germany
165 H5 Bad Mergentheim Germany
165 G4 Bad Nauheim Germany
164 F4 Bad Neuenahr-Ahrweiler Germany
165 I4 Bad Neustadt an der Saale Germany
165 I1 Bad Oldesloe Germany
148 D4 Badong China
154 C3 Ba Đông Vietnam
165 H3 Bad Pyrmont Germany
137 J5 Badrah Iraq
168 F7 Bad Reichenhall Germany
165 I3 Bad Sachsa Germany
165 I2 Bad Salzdetfurth Germany
165 G2 Bad Salzuflen Germany
165 I4 Bad Salzungen Germany
165 G4 Bad Schwalbach Germany
168 E4 Bad Schwartau Germany
168 E4 Bad Segeberg Germany
165 F5 Bad Sobernheim Germany
165 I4 Bad Staffelstein Germany
124 E3 Badu Island Australia
143 C5 Badulla Sri Lanka
165 G4 Bad Vilbel Germany
165 J2 Bad Wilsnack Germany
165 I5 Bad Windsheim Germany
165 G1 Bad Zwischenahn Germany
158 B1 Bæir Iceland
152 C5 Baengnyeong-do i. N. Korea
127 I4 Baerami Australia
164 E4 Baesweiler Germany
167 E4 Baeza Spain
176 D4 Bafang Cameroon
176 A3 Bafatá Guinea-Bissau
220 T2 Baffin Basin sea feature Arctic Ocean
185 L2 Baffin Bay sea Canada/Greenland
185 K2 Baffin Island Canada
176 D4 Bafia Cameroon
176 A3 Bafing, Réserve du nature res. Mali
176 A3 Bafoulabé Mali
176 D4 Bafoussam Cameroon
140 D4 Bāfq Iran
136 E1 Bafra Turkey
173 E7 Bafra Burnu pt Turkey
140 E4 Bāft Iran
178 C3 Bafwasende Dem. Rep. Congo
145 F4 Bagaha India
153 A5 Bagahak, Gunung h. Sabah Malaysia
143 A2 Bagalkot India
178 D4 Bagamoyo Tanz.
155 B2 Bagan Datuk Malaysia
179 C5 Bagani Namibia
154 B4 Bagan Serai Malaysia
154 B5 Bagansiapiapi Indon.
197 F4 Bagdad U.S.A.
215 F1 Bagé Brazil
163 E5 Bagenalstown Ireland
145 G5 Bagerhat Bangl.
144 D3 Bageshwar India
194 F3 Baggs U.S.A.
161 C6 Baggy Point U.K.
144 C5 Bagh India
140 D4 Bāgh, Chāh-e well Iran
141 F2 Baghbaghū Iran
141 E4 Bāghbāghū'īyeh Iran
137 J5 Baghdād Iraq
140 C4 Bāgh-e Malek Iran
141 H2 Baghlān Afgh.
141 G3 Baghrān Afgh.
198 E2 Bagley U.S.A.
145 E3 Baglung Nepal
167 G1 Bagnères-de-Luchon France
166 G4 Bagnols-sur-Cèze France
145 F4 Bagnuiti r. Nepal
148 C2 Bag Nur l. China
153 B4 Bago Phil.
169 J3 Bagrationovsk Russia
153 B2 Baguio Benguet Phil.
153 C5 Baguio Davao del Sur Phil.
144 D3 Bahadurgarh India
205 I3 Bahamas, The country Caribbean Sea
145 G4 Baharampur India
Bahariya Oasis Egypt see Bahrīyah, Wāḩāt al
138 D5 Baharly Turkm.
155 B2 Bahau Malaysia
144 C3 Bahawalnagar Pak.
144 B3 Bahawalpur Pak.
136 F3 Bahçe Turkey
148 C4 Ba He r. China
144 D3 Baheri India
178 D4 Bahi Tanz.
214 E1 Bahia state Brazil
206 H4 Bahía, Islas de la is Hond.
215 D3 Bahía Blanca Arg.
206 B1 Bahía Kino Mex.
212 C7 Bahía Laura Arg.
212 E2 Bahía Negra Para.
206 A2 Bahía Tortugas Mex.
178 D2 Bahir Dar Eth.
142 E5 Bahlā Oman
140 C4 Bahman Yārī Iran
145 E4 Bahraich India
140 C5 Bahrain country Asia
140 C5 Bahrain, Gulf of Asia
137 L3 Bahrāmābād Iran
137 L3 Bahrām Beyg Iran
140 E4 Bahrāmjerd Iran
177 E2 Bahrīyah, Wāḩāt al oasis Egypt
210 E6 Bahuaja-Sonene, Parque Nacional nat. park Peru
141 F5 Bāhū Kālāt Iran
169 K7 Baia Mare Romania
146 E2 Baicheng Jilin China
139 J4 Baicheng Xinjiang Uygur Zizhiqu China
189 G4 Baie-Comeau Canada
Baie-du-Poste Canada see Mistissini
189 F4 Baie-St-Paul Canada
189 I4 Baie Verte Canada
148 E2 Baigou He r. China
144 E5 Baihar India
152 E2 Baihe Jilin China
148 D3 Baihe Shaanxi China
148 E1 Bai He r. China
146 C1 Baikal, Lake Russia
Baile an Bhuinneánaigh Ireland see Ballybunion
Baile an Chinnéidigh Ireland see Newtown Mount Kennedy
162 A3 Baile Mhartainn U.K.
163 C3 Baile na Finne Ireland
171 J2 Băileşti Romania
171 J2 Băileştilor, Câmpia plain Romania
163 E4 Bailieborough Ireland
148 D1 Bailingmiao China
164 A4 Bailleul France
187 H2 Baillie r. Canada
148 B3 Bailong Jiang r. China
146 C3 Baima China
148 E4 Baima Jian mt. China
161 G4 Bain r. U.K.
201 C6 Bainbridge GA U.S.A.
203 F3 Bainbridge NY U.S.A.
Baingoin China see Porong
136 F6 Bā'ir Jordan
136 F6 Bā'ir, Wādī watercourse Jordan
145 E2 Bairab Co l. China
145 F4 Bairagnia India
184 C3 Baird Mountains U.S.A.
123 G3 Bairiki Kiribati
148 F1 Bairin Qiao China
127 G6 Bairnsdale Australia
153 B4 Bais Phil.
149 C6 Baise China
149 C7 Baisha Hainan China
149 E5 Baisha Jiangxi China
148 C4 Baisha Sichuan China
152 D2 Baishan Jilin China
152 D3 Baishan Jilin China
148 B3 Baishui Jiang r. China
149 B7 Bai Thương Vietnam
152 A2 Baixingt China
148 B2 Baiyin China
177 F3 Baiyuda Desert Sudan
171 H1 Baja Hungary
206 A2 Baja California pen. Mex.
192 C6 Baja California state Mex.
206 A2 Baja California Sur state Mex.
137 L3 Bājalān Iran
206 D2 Bajan Mex.
144 E3 Bajang Nepal
145 G5 Baj Baj India
141 E3 Bajestān Iran
141 E2 Bājgīrān Iran
213 A3 Bajo Baudó Col.
206 I6 Bajo Boquete Panama
215 D1 Bajo Hondo Arg.
139 I3 Bakanas Kazakh.
139 I3 Bakanas watercourse Kazakh.
139 G4 Bakay-Ata Kyrg.
176 A3 Bakel Senegal
196 D4 Baker CA U.S.A.
194 F2 Baker MT U.S.A.
197 E2 Baker NV U.S.A.
194 B1 Baker, Mount vol. U.S.A.
197 G4 Baker Butte mt. U.S.A.
194 C2 Baker City U.S.A.
125 I1 Baker Island terr. Pacific Ocean
186 C3 Baker Island U.S.A.
187 J2 Baker Lake Canada
187 J2 Baker Lake l. Canada
188 E2 Baker's Dozen Islands Canada
196 C4 Bakersfield U.S.A.
154 C2 Bâ Kêv Cambodia
Bakhardok Turkm. see Bokurdak
141 F3 Bākharz, Kūhhā-ye mts Iran
144 B4 Bakhasar India
173 E6 Bakhchysaray Crimea
Bakherden Turkm. see Baharly
173 E5 Bakhmach Ukr.
140 D4 Bakhtegan, Daryācheh-ye l. Iran
Bakı Azer. see Baku
178 E2 Baki Somalia
136 B1 Bakırköy Turkey
178 D3 Bako Eth.
178 C3 Bakouma C.A.R.
178 B4 Bakoumba Gabon
173 G7 Baksan Russia
139 J3 Bakty Kazakh.
137 L1 Baku Azer.
178 D3 Baku Dem. Rep. Congo
136 D2 Balâ Turkey
161 D5 Bala U.K.
210 E6 Bala, Cerros de mts Bol.
153 A4 Balabac Phil.
153 A5 Balabac i. Phil.
155 E1 Balabac Strait Malaysia/Phil.
137 J4 Balad Iraq
140 C4 Bālā Deh Iran
140 C2 Baladeh Māzandarān Iran
140 C2 Baladeh Māzandarān Iran
Balagar Gaole China see Bayan Ul
144 E5 Balaghat India
143 A2 Balaghat Range hills India
141 E4 Bālā Ḩowz Iran
137 K1 Balakän Azer.
172 G3 Balakhna Russia
126 C5 Balaklava Australia
173 E6 Balaklava Crimea
173 F5 Balakliya Ukr.
173 H4 Balakovo Russia
161 D5 Bala Lake U.K.
155 E1 Balambangan i. Sabah Malaysia
141 F3 Bālā Murghāb Afgh.
144 B4 Balan India
173 H5 Balanda r. Russia
136 B3 Balan Dağı h. Turkey
153 B3 Balanga Phil.
143 C1 Balangir India
143 C5 Balangoda Sri Lanka
138 B2 Balashi Russia
173 G5 Balashov Russia
144 C5 Balasinor India
168 H7 Balaton, Lake Hungary
168 H7 Balatonboglár Hungary
168 H7 Balatonfüred Hungary
211 G4 Balbina, Represa de resr Brazil
163 E4 Balbriggan Ireland
126 C3 Balcanoona Australia
215 E3 Balcarce Arg.
171 M3 Balchik Bulg.
141 G3 Bal Chirāgh Afgh.
128 B7 Balclutha N.Z.
199 F5 Bald Knob U.S.A.
197 E3 Bald Mountain U.S.A.
187 J3 Baldock Lake Canada
191 H3 Baldwin Canada
201 D6 Baldwin FL U.S.A.
190 E4 Baldwin MI U.S.A.
190 A3 Baldwin WI U.S.A.
203 E3 Baldwinsville U.S.A.
197 H5 Baldy Peak U.S.A.
Baleares, Islas is Spain see Balearic Islands
167 H3 Balearic Islands is Spain
155 D2 Baleh r. Sarawak Malaysia
214 E2 Baleia, Ponta da pt Brazil
188 F3 Baleine, Grande Rivière de la r. Canada
188 E2 Baleine, Petite Rivière de la r. Canada
189 G2 Baleine, Rivière à la r. Canada
178 D3 Bale Mountains National Park Eth.
153 B3 Baler Phil.
153 B3 Baler Bay Phil.
145 F5 Baleshwar India
159 I3 Balestrand Norway
170 C4 Balestrieri, Punta mt. Sardinia Italy
128 B6 Balfour N.Z.
155 E4 Bali i. Indon.
176 D4 Bali Nigeria
155 E4 Bali, Laut sea Indon.
155 A2 Balige Indon.
143 C1 Baligurha India
148 F1 Balihan China
136 A2 Balıkesir Turkey
155 E3 Balikpapan Indon.
143 C2 Balimila Reservoir India
124 E2 Balimo P.N.G.
168 D6 Balingen Germany
153 B2 Balintang Channel Phil.
162 E3 Balintore U.K.
Bali Sea Indon. see Bali, Laut
153 B5 Baliungan i. Phil.
139 G5 Baljuvon Tajik.
164 D2 Balk Neth.
138 C5 Balkanabat Turkm.
171 J3 Balkan Mountains Bulg./Serbia
139 H3 Balkash Kazakh.
139 G1 Balkashino Kazakh.
141 G3 Balkh r. Afgh.
139 H3 Balkhash, Lake Kazakh.
138 A3 Balkuduk Kazakh.
162 C4 Ballachulish U.K.
124 C5 Balladonia Australia
127 H3 Balladoran Australia
163 C4 Ballaghaderreen Ireland
126 F6 Ballan Australia
158 L1 Ballangen Norway
194 E2 Ballantine U.S.A.
162 D5 Ballantrae U.K.
126 E6 Ballarat Australia
124 C4 Ballard, Lake salt flat Australia
143 B3 Ballari India
144 D6 Ballarpur India
162 E3 Ballater U.K.
176 B3 Ballé Mali
212 B3 Ballena, Punta pt Chile
129 B6 Balleny Islands is Antarctica
145 F4 Ballia India
127 J2 Ballina Australia
163 B3 Ballina Ireland
163 C3 Ballinafad Ireland
163 D4 Ballinalack Ireland
163 D3 Ballinamore Ireland
163 C4 Ballinasloe Ireland
163 C4 Ballindine Ireland
199 D6 Ballinger U.S.A.
162 E4 Ballinluig U.K.
163 B4 Ballinrobe Ireland
203 G3 Ballston Spa U.S.A.
163 E3 Ballybay Ireland
Ballybrack Ireland see An Baile Breac
163 B5 Ballybunion Ireland
163 E5 Ballycanew Ireland
163 B3 Ballycastle Ireland
163 E2 Ballycastle U.K.
163 F3 Ballyclare U.K.
163 A4 Ballyconneely Bay Ireland
163 D3 Ballyconnell Ireland
163 C4 Ballygar Ireland
163 D3 Ballygawley U.K.
163 D2 Ballygorman Ireland
163 C4 Ballyhaunis Ireland
163 B5 Ballyheigue Ireland
163 C5 Ballyhoura Mountains hills Ireland
163 D2 Ballykelly U.K.
163 D5 Ballylynan Ireland
163 D5 Ballymacmague Ireland
163 D4 Ballymahon Ireland
163 E3 Ballymena U.K.
163 E2 Ballymoney U.K.
163 C3 Ballymote Ireland
163 F3 Ballynahinch U.K.
163 C3 Ballyshannon Ireland
163 E5 Ballyteige Bay Ireland
163 B4 Ballyvaughan Ireland
163 E3 Ballyward U.K.
126 D6 Balmoral Australia
199 C6 Balmorhea U.S.A.
141 G4 Balochistan prov. Pak.
134 E4 Balochistan reg. Pak.
144 E5 Balod India
143 C1 Baloda Bazar India
127 H2 Balonne r. Australia
144 C4 Balotra India
139 I3 Balpyk Bi Kazakh.
145 E4 Balrampur India
126 E5 Balranald Australia
171 K2 Balş Romania
191 H2 Balsam Creek Canada
211 I5 Balsas Brazil
207 E4 Balsas Mex.
206 D4 Balsas r. Mex.
173 D6 Balta Ukr.
172 I3 Baltasi Russia
162 □ Baltasound U.K.
173 C6 Bălţi Moldova
159 L5 Baltic Sea g. Europe
136 C6 Balţīm Egypt
181 H1 Baltimore S. Africa
202 E5 Baltimore U.S.A.
163 E5 Baltinglass Ireland
144 C2 Baltistan reg. Pak.
169 I3 Baltiysk Russia
144 D2 Baltoro Glacier Pak.
141 E4 Baluch Ab well Iran
145 G4 Balurghat India
153 C5 Balut i. Phil.
165 F3 Balve Germany
159 N4 Balvi Latvia
171 L5 Balya Turkey
139 I4 Balykchy Kyrg.
138 B3 Balykshi Kazakh.
141 E4 Bam Iran
141 E2 Bām Iran
149 C5 Bama China
124 E3 Bamaga Australia
188 B3 Bamaji Lake Canada
176 B3 Bamako Mali
176 B3 Bamba Mali
153 B2 Bambang Phil.
178 C3 Bambari C.A.R.
154 A5 Bambel Indon.
165 I5 Bamberg Germany
201 D5 Bamberg U.S.A.
178 C3 Bambili Dem. Rep. Congo
181 G5 Bamboesberg mts S. Africa
178 C3 Bambouti C.A.R.
214 D3 Bambuí Brazil
137 L6 Bāmdezh Iran
176 D4 Bamenda Cameroon
Bami Turkm. see Bamy
152 C2 Bamiancheng China
178 C3 Bamingui-Bangoran, Parc National du nat. park C.A.R.
141 F5 Bamposht reg. Iran
161 D7 Bampton U.K.
141 F5 Bampūr Iran
141 E5 Bampūr watercourse Iran
141 F3 Bamrūd Iran
138 D5 Bamy Turkm.
141 G3 Bāmyān Afgh.
125 G2 Banaba i. Kiribati
211 K5 Banabuiu, Açude resr Brazil
163 D4 Banagher Ireland
178 C3 Banalia Dem. Rep. Congo
181 J1 Banamana, Lagoa l. Moz.
176 B3 Banamba Mali
149 C4 Banan China
211 H6 Bananal, Ilha do i. Brazil
143 D2 Banapur India
144 D4 Banas r. India
136 B2 Banaz Turkey
154 B1 Ban Ban Laos
Banbar China see Domartang
163 E3 Banbridge U.K.
154 B2 Ban Bua Yai Thai.
161 F5 Banbury U.K.
153 A4 Bancalan i. Phil.
126 D3 Bancannia Lake salt flat Australia
176 A2 Banc d'Arguin, Parc National du nat. park Mauritania
162 F3 Banchory U.K.
153 A5 Bancoran i. Phil.
191 I3 Bancroft Canada
178 C3 Banda Dem. Rep. Congo
144 E4 Banda India
147 E7 Banda, Kepulauan is Indon.
147 F7 Banda, Laut sea Indon.
155 A1 Banda Aceh Indon.
127 J3 Banda Banda, Mount Australia
144 B2 Banda Daud Shah Pak.
154 A5 Bandahara, Gunung mt. Indon.
151 F6 Bandai-Asahi Kokuritsu-kōen nat. park Japan
141 F4 Bandān Iran
141 F4 Bandān Kūh mts Iran
145 H5 Bandarban Bangl.
140 E5 Bandar-e 'Abbās Iran
140 C2 Bandar-e Anzalī Iran
140 C4 Bandar-e Būshehr Iran
140 D5 Bandar-e Chārak Iran
140 C5 Bandar-e Dayyer Iran
140 C4 Bandar-e Deylam Iran
140 C4 Bandar-e Emām Khomeynī Iran
140 C4 Bandar-e Ganāveh Iran
140 B2 Bandar-e Ḩeydarābād Iran
141 E5 Bandar-e Jāsk Iran
140 D5 Bandar-e Kangān Iran
140 D5 Bandar-e Khamīr Iran
140 D5 Bandar-e Lengeh Iran
140 C4 Bandar-e Māhshahr Iran
140 D5 Bandar-e Moghūyeh Iran
140 D5 Bandar-e Moqām Iran
140 C4 Bandar-e Rīg Iran
140 D2 Bandar-e Torkaman Iran
155 C4 Bandar Lampung Indon.
144 D3 Bandarpunch mt. India
155 D1 Bandar Seri Begawan Brunei
Banda Sea Indon. see Banda, Laut
Band-e Amir r. Afgh. see Balkh
141 F3 Band-e Bābā, Silsilah-ye Kōh-e mts Afgh.
141 F5 Band-e Bamposht, Kūh-e mts Iran
214 B1 Bandeirante Brazil
214 E3 Bandeiras, Pico de mt. Brazil
181 H1 Bandelierkop S. Africa
206 C3 Banderas, Bahía de b. Mex.
140 D3 Band-e Sar Qom Iran
144 C4 Bandi r. Rajasthan India
144 C4 Bandi r. Rajasthan India
144 E6 Bandia r. India
176 B3 Bandiagara Mali
177 F4 Bandingilo National Park S. Sudan
141 E5 Bandīnī Iran
136 A1 Bandırma Turkey
163 C6 Bandon Ireland
163 C6 Bandon r. Ireland
154 A3 Ban Don, Ao b. Thai.
137 L2 Bändovan Burnu pt Azer.
137 L6 Band Qīr Iran
178 B4 Bandundu Dem. Rep. Congo
155 C4 Bandung Indon.
140 B3 Bāneh Iran
205 I4 Banes Cuba
186 F4 Banff Canada
162 F3 Banff U.K.
186 F4 Banff National Park Canada
176 B3 Banfora Burkina Faso
178 C4 Banga Dem. Rep. Congo
153 C5 Banga Phil.
153 C5 Bangai Point Phil.
Bangalore India see Bengaluru
144 D4 Banganga r. India
145 G5 Bangaon India
153 B2 Bangar Phil.
178 C3 Bangassou C.A.R.
145 E2 Bangdag Co salt l. China
154 C1 Bangfai, Xé r. Laos
124 C2 Banggai Indon.
147 E7 Banggai, Kepulauan is Indon.
155 E1 Banggi i. Sabah Malaysia
154 C1 Banghiang, Xé r. Laos
155 C3 Bangka i. Indon.
155 D4 Bangkalan Indon.
154 A5 Bangkaru i. Indon.
155 B3 Bangko Indon.
154 B2 Bangkok Thai. (City Plan 103)
154 B2 Bangkok, Bight of b. Thai.
145 G5 Bangladesh country Asia
154 D3 Ba Ngoi Vietnam
176 B4 Bangolo Côte d'Ivoire
144 D2 Bangong Co salt l. China
144 D2 Bangong Co l. India
163 F3 Bangor Northern Ireland U.K.
161 C4 Bangor Wales U.K.
203 I2 Bangor ME U.S.A.
190 D4 Bangor MI U.S.A.
203 F4 Bangor PA U.S.A.
163 B3 Bangor Erris Ireland
197 F3 Bangs, Mount U.S.A.
154 A3 Bang Saphan Yai Thai.
158 J2 Bangsund Norway
153 B2 Bangued Phil.
178 B3 Bangui C.A.R.
153 B2 Bangui Phil.
154 A5 Bangunpurba Indon.
179 C5 Bangweulu, Lake Zambia
136 C6 Banhā Egypt
179 D6 Banhine, Parque Nacional de nat. park Moz.
154 B1 Ban Hin Heup Laos
178 C3 Bani C.A.R.
153 A2 Bani Phil.
178 B3 Bania C.A.R.
144 C2 Banihal Pass and Tunnel India
202 D6 Banister r. U.S.A.
177 F2 Banī Suwayf Egypt
177 D1 Banī Walīd Libya
140 C5 Banī Wuţayfān well Saudi Arabia
136 E5 Bāniyās HaZafon Syria
136 E4 Bāniyās Ţarţūs Syria
170 G2 Banja Luka Bos. & Herz.
144 D3 Banjar India
155 D3 Banjarmasin Indon.
176 A3 Banjul Gambia
137 L2 Bankä Azer.
145 F4 Banka India
143 A3 Bankapur India
176 B3 Bankass Mali
154 A2 Ban Khao Yoi Thai.
154 A3 Ban Khok Kloi Thai.
145 F5 Banki India
184 E4 Banks Island B.C. Canada
184 F2 Banks Island N.W.T. Canada
125 G3 Banks Islands Vanuatu
187 K2 Banks Lake Canada
194 C2 Banks Lake U.S.A.
128 D5 Banks Peninsula N.Z.
127 H8 Banks Strait Australia
145 F5 Bankura India
154 B1 Ban Mouang Laos
163 E5 Bann r. Ireland
163 E3 Bann r. U.K.
154 C1 Ban Nakham Laos
154 A3 Ban Na San Thai.
190 C5 Banner U.S.A.
201 E7 Bannerman Town Bahamas
196 D5 Banning U.S.A.
154 C1 Ban Nonghèt Laos
215 B3 Baños Maule Chile
154 B1 Ban Pak-Leng Laos
154 C1 Ban Phaeng Thai.
154 B1 Ban Phai Thai.
Ban Phôn Laos see Xékong
154 B1 Ban Phôn-Hông Laos
154 A2 Banphot Phisai Thai.
154 A2 Ban Pong Thai.
154 A3 Ban Sawi Thai.
145 E4 Bansi India
169 I6 Banská Bystrica Slovakia
141 F5 Bānsont Iran
154 A1 Ban Sut Ta Thai.
154 C2 Ban Suwan Wari Thai.
143 B2 Banswada India
144 C5 Banswara India
153 B4 Bantayan i. Phil.
163 C5 Banteer Ireland
154 A3 Ban Tha Chang Thai.
154 A3 Ban Tha Kham Thai.
154 A1 Ban Tha Song Yang Thai.
154 B2 Ban Tha Tako Thai.
154 A1 Ban Tha Ton Thai.
154 B2 Ban Tha Tum Thai.
154 A2 Ban Thung Luang Thai.
153 B3 Banton i. Phil.
154 C1 Ban Tôp Laos
163 B6 Bantry Ireland
163 B6 Bantry Bay Ireland
143 A3 Bantval India
154 B1 Ban Woen Laos
155 A2 Banyak, Pulau-pulau is Indon.
176 D4 Banyo Cameroon
167 H1 Banyoles Spain
155 D4 Banyuwangi Indon.
218 J8 Banzare Seamount sea feature Indian Ocean
165 J1 Banzkow Germany
148 B3 Bao'an China
148 E1 Baochang China
148 E2 Baoding China
148 D3 Baofeng China
148 C3 Baoji China
149 C4 Baojing China
148 D4 Baokang Hubei China
152 B1 Baokang Nei Mongol Zizhiqu China
149 B6 Bao Lac Vietnam
152 B2 Baoli China
152 E1 Baolin China
154 C3 Bao Lôc Vietnam
150 C1 Baoqing China
146 B4 Baoshan China
148 D1 Baotou China
149 B4 Baoxing China
148 F3 Baoying China
144 C4 Bap India
143 C3 Bapatla India
164 A4 Bapaume France
191 H3 Baptiste Lake Canada
145 H2 Baqên Xizang Zizhiqu China
145 H3 Baqên Xizang Zizhiqu China
149 E5 Baqiu China
137 J5 Ba'qūbah Iraq
Baquerizo Moreno Galapagos Is Ecuador see Puerto Baquerizo Moreno
171 H3 Bar Montenegro
177 F3 Bara Sudan
178 E3 Baraawe Somalia
145 F4 Barabar Hills India
190 C4 Baraboo U.S.A.
190 B4 Baraboo r. U.S.A.
205 J4 Baracoa Cuba
215 E2 Baradero Arg.
127 H3 Baradine Australia
127 H3 Baradine r. Australia
190 C2 Baraga U.S.A.
213 C2 Baragua Venez.
205 J5 Barahona Dom. Rep.
145 H4 Barail Range mts India
145 H4 Barak r. India
177 F3 Baraka watercourse Eritrea/Sudan
167 E1 Barakaldo Spain
141 H3 Barakī Barak Afgh.
143 D1 Barakot India
144 D2 Bara Lacha La India
187 J3 Baralzon Lake Canada
143 A2 Baramati India
144 D4 Baran India
144 B4 Baran r. Pak.
141 F3 Bārān, Kūh-e mts Iran
172 C4 Baranavichy Belarus
133 R3 Baranikha Russia
173 C5 Baranivka Ukr.
213 B2 Baranoa Col.
186 B3 Baranof Island U.S.A.
138 A1 Baranovka Russia
214 A2 Barão de Melgaço Brazil
176 B3 Baraouéli Mali
164 D4 Baraque de Fraiture h. Belgium
147 E7 Barat Daya, Kepulauan is Indon.
126 C4 Baratta (abandoned) Australia
144 D3 Baraut India
213 B4 Baraya Col.
214 D3 Barbacena Brazil
213 A4 Barbacoas Col.
205 M6 Barbados country Caribbean Sea
167 G1 Barbastro Spain
167 D4 Barbate Spain
153 B4 Barbaza Phil.
206 C2 Barbechitos Mex.
Barber's Point U.S.A. see Kalaeloa
181 I2 Barberton S. Africa
202 C4 Barberton U.S.A.
166 D4 Barbezieux-St-Hilaire France
213 B3 Barbosa Col.
187 K2 Barbour Bay Canada
202 B6 Barbourville U.S.A.
205 L5 Barbuda i. Antigua and Barbuda
165 J3 Barby Germany
124 E4 Barcaldine Australia
167 H2 Barcelona Spain (City Plan 112)
213 D2 Barcelona Venez.
210 F4 Barcelos Brazil
165 I4 Barchfeld Germany
176 B4 Barclayville Liberia
170 G2 Barcs Hungary
137 K1 Bärdä Azer.
177 D2 Bardaï Chad
158 C2 Bárðarbunga mt. Iceland
215 C2 Bardas Blancas Arg.
136 D6 Bardawīl, Sabkhat al lag. Egypt
145 F5 Barddhaman India
169 J6 Bardejov Slovakia
Bar Đôn Vietnam see Buôn Đôn
161 C5 Bardsey Island U.K.
140 E4 Bardsīr Iran
200 C4 Bardstown U.S.A.
202 B5 Bardwell U.S.A.
144 D3 Bareilly India
132 C2 Barentsburg Svalbard
132 D2 Barentsøya i. Svalbard
132 F2 Barents Sea Arctic Ocean
178 D2 Barentu Eritrea
144 E3 Barga China
143 C1 Bargarh India
144 D5 Bargi India
162 D5 Bargrennan U.K.
165 I1 Bargteheide Germany
145 G5 Barguna Bangl.
203 I2 Bar Harbor U.S.A.
170 G4 Bari Italy
154 C3 Ba Ria Vietnam
179 D4 Bariadi Tanz.
144 C3 Bari Doab lowland Pak.
145 E3 Barikot Nepal
213 E2 Barima r. Venez.
213 C2 Barinas Venez.
145 G5 Barisal Bangl.
155 B3 Barisan, Pegunungan mts Indon.
155 D3 Barito r. Indon.
210 F8 Baritú, Parque Nacional nat. park Arg.
141 E6 Barkā Oman
148 B4 Barkam China
140 C4 Barkan, Ra's-e pt Iran
159 N4 Barkava Latvia
186 E4 Barkerville Canada
200 C4 Barkley, Lake U.S.A.
186 D5 Barkley Sound inlet Canada
181 G5 Barkly East S. Africa
124 D3 Barkly Tableland reg. Australia
180 F4 Barkly West S. Africa
146 B2 Barkol China
144 D3 Barkot India
169 M7 Bârlad Romania

Bar-le-Duc

166 G2 **Bar-le-Duc** France
124 B4 **Barlee, Lake** *salt flat* Australia
170 G4 **Barletta** Italy
127 G5 **Barmedman** Australia
144 B4 **Barmer** India
126 D5 **Barmera** Australia
161 C5 **Barmouth** U.K.
144 C3 **Barnala** India
160 F3 **Barnard Castle** U.K.
127 F3 **Barnato** Australia
132 J4 **Barnaul** Russia
203 F5 **Barnegat** U.S.A.
203 F5 **Barnegat Bay** U.S.A.
202 D4 **Barnesboro** U.S.A.
185 K2 **Barnes Icecap** Canada
164 D2 **Barneveld** Neth.
126 F4 **Barneys Lake** *imp. l.* Australia
197 G3 **Barney Top** *mt.* U.S.A.
199 C6 **Barnhart** U.S.A.
160 F4 **Barnsley** U.K.
161 C6 **Barnstaple** U.K.
161 C6 **Barnstaple Bay** U.K.
165 G2 **Barnstorf** Germany
201 D5 **Barnwell** U.S.A.
Baroda India *see* **Vadodara**
145 H4 **Barpathar** India
145 G4 **Barpeta** India
190 D3 **Barques, Point Aux** *MI* U.S.A.
191 F3 **Barques, Point Aux** *MI* U.S.A.
213 C2 **Barquisimeto** Venez.
211 J6 **Barra** Brazil
162 A4 **Barra** *i.* U.K.
162 A3 **Barra, Sound of** *sea chan.* U.K.
127 I3 **Barraba** Australia
180 D7 **Barracouta, Cape** S. Africa
211 G6 **Barra do Bugres** Brazil
211 I5 **Barra do Corda** Brazil
214 B1 **Barra do Garças** Brazil
211 G5 **Barra do São Manuel** Brazil
210 C6 **Barranca** *Lima* Peru
210 C4 **Barranca** *Loreto* Peru
213 B3 **Barrancabermeja** Col.
215 B3 **Barrancas** *r.* Arg.
213 B2 **Barrancas** Col.
213 E2 **Barrancas** Venez.
212 E3 **Barranqueras** Arg.
213 B2 **Barranquilla** Col.
203 G2 **Barre** U.S.A.
215 C1 **Barreal** Arg.
211 J6 **Barreiras** Brazil
211 G4 **Barreirinha** Brazil
211 J4 **Barreirinhas** Brazil
214 B1 **Barreiro** *r.* Brazil
167 B3 **Barreiro** Port.
211 K5 **Barreiros** Brazil
214 C3 **Barretos** Brazil
186 G4 **Barrhead** Canada
162 D5 **Barrhead** U.K.
191 H3 **Barrie** Canada
191 F3 **Barrie Island** Canada
186 E4 **Barrière** Canada
126 D3 **Barrier Range** *hills* Australia
207 H4 **Barrier Reef** Belize
127 I4 **Barrington, Mount** Australia
187 I3 **Barrington Lake** Canada
127 F2 **Barringun** Australia
190 B3 **Barron** U.S.A.
206 D2 **Barroterán** Mex.
215 E3 **Barrow** Arg.
163 E5 **Barrow** *r.* Ireland
184 C2 **Barrow** U.S.A.
184 C2 **Barrow, Point** U.S.A.
124 D4 **Barrow Creek** Australia
160 D3 **Barrow-in-Furness** U.K.
124 B4 **Barrow Island** Australia
185 I2 **Barrow Strait** Canada
161 D6 **Barry** U.K.
180 D6 **Barrydale** S. Africa
191 I3 **Barrys Bay** Canada
138 D3 **Barsakel'mes, Poluostrov** *pen.* Kazakh.
Barsa-Kel'mes, Shor *salt marsh* Uzbek. *see* **Borsakelmas sho'rxogi**
144 C3 **Barsalpur** India
139 I2 **Barshatas** Kazakh.
143 A2 **Barsi** India
165 H2 **Barsinghausen** Germany
144 D5 **Barsi Takli** India
196 D4 **Barstow** U.S.A.
166 G2 **Bar-sur-Aube** France
168 F3 **Barth** Germany
211 G2 **Bartica** Guyana
136 D1 **Bartın** Turkey
124 E3 **Bartle Frere, Mount** Australia
197 G2 **Bartles, Mount** U.S.A.
193 G4 **Bartlesville** U.S.A.
198 D3 **Bartlett** *NE* U.S.A.
203 H2 **Bartlett** *NH* U.S.A.
186 F2 **Bartlett Lake** Canada
203 G2 **Barton** U.S.A.
160 G4 **Barton-upon-Humber** U.K.
169 J3 **Bartoszyce** Poland
206 I6 **Barú, Volcán** *vol.* Panama
155 B2 **Barumun** *r.* Indon.
155 D4 **Barung** *i.* Indon.
154 A5 **Barus** Indon.
Baruunsuu Mongolia *see* **Tsogttsetsiy**
146 D2 **Baruun-Urt** Mongolia
144 D5 **Barwah** India
144 C3 **Barwala** India
144 C5 **Barwani** India
127 H2 **Barwon** *r.* Australia
172 D4 **Barysaw** Belarus
172 H4 **Barysh** Russia
172 H4 **Barysh** *r.* Russia
140 C3 **Barzok** Iran
140 D5 **Bāsa'īdū** Iran
154 C3 **Basăk, Tônlé** *r.* Cambodia
196 C2 **Basalt** U.S.A.
149 □ **Basalt Island** *Hong Kong* China
178 B3 **Basankusu** Dem. Rep. Congo
143 B2 **Basar** India
171 M2 **Basarabi** Romania
215 E2 **Basavilbaso** Arg.
153 B4 **Basay** Phil.
153 B1 **Basco** Phil.
168 C7 **Basel** Switz.
141 E5 **Bashākerd, Kūhhā-ye** *mts* Iran
186 G4 **Bashaw** Canada
149 F6 **Bashi Channel** Phil./Taiwan
172 G4 **Bashmakovo** Russia
140 C4 **Bāsht** Iran
173 E6 **Bashtanka** Ukr.
144 D4 **Basi** India
143 D1 **Basia** India
153 B5 **Basilan** *i.* Phil.
153 B5 **Basilan Strait** Phil.
161 H6 **Basildon** U.K.
194 E2 **Basin** U.S.A.
161 F6 **Basingstoke** U.K.
137 J4 **Bāsīra** *r.* Iraq
145 G5 **Basirhat** India
203 J2 **Baskahegan Lake** U.S.A.
137 J2 **Başkale** Turkey
191 J2 **Baskatong, Réservoir** *resr* Canada
173 H5 **Baskunchak, Ozero** *l.* Russia
Basle Switz. *see* **Basel**
144 D5 **Basoda** India
178 C3 **Basoko** Dem. Rep. Congo
141 G5 **Basol** *r.* Pak.
137 K6 **Basra** Iraq
170 D2 **Bassano del Grappa** Italy
176 C4 **Bassar** Togo
176 A3 **Bassari Country** *tourist site* Senegal
179 D6 **Bassas da India** *reef* Indian Ocean
147 B5 **Bassein** Myanmar
160 D3 **Bassenthwaite Lake** U.K.
176 A3 **Basse Santa Su** Gambia
205 L5 **Basse-Terre** Guadeloupe
205 L5 **Basseterre** St Kitts and Nevis
198 D3 **Bassett** U.S.A.
197 G5 **Bassett Peak** U.S.A.
203 I2 **Bass Harbor** U.S.A.
176 B3 **Bassikounou** Mauritania
176 C4 **Bassila** Benin
162 F4 **Bass Rock** *i.* U.K.
124 E5 **Bass Strait** Australia
165 G2 **Bassum** Germany
190 B1 **Basswood Lake** U.S.A.
159 K4 **Båstad** Sweden
140 D5 **Bastak** Iran
165 I4 **Bastheim** Germany
145 E4 **Basti** India
170 C3 **Bastia** *Corsica* France
164 D4 **Bastogne** Belgium
199 F5 **Bastrop** *LA* U.S.A.
199 D6 **Bastrop** *TX* U.S.A.
176 C4 **Bata** Equat. Guinea
205 H4 **Batabanó, Golfo de** *b.* Cuba
153 B2 **Batac** Phil.
153 C3 **Batag** *i.* Phil.
133 O3 **Batagay** Russia
144 B2 **Batai Pass** Pak.
144 C3 **Batala** India
167 B3 **Batalha** Port.
155 F2 **Batam** Indon.
154 C5 **Batam** *i.* Indon.
133 N3 **Batamay** Russia
153 B1 **Batan** *i.* Phil.
178 B3 **Batangafo** C.A.R.
153 B3 **Batangas** Phil.
155 B3 **Batanghari** *r.* Indon.
154 A5 **Batangtoru** Indon.
153 B1 **Batan Islands** Phil.
214 C3 **Batatais** Brazil
190 C5 **Batavia** *IL* U.S.A.
202 D3 **Batavia** *NY* U.S.A.
173 F6 **Bataysk** Russia
191 E2 **Batchawana** Canada
191 E2 **Batchawana** *r.* Canada
190 E2 **Batchawana Bay** Canada
188 D4 **Batchawana Mountain** *h.* Canada
124 D3 **Batchelor** Australia
154 B2 **Bătdâmbâng** Cambodia
127 I5 **Batemans Bay** Australia
127 I5 **Batemans Bay** *b.* Australia
199 F5 **Batesville** *AR* U.S.A.
199 F5 **Batesville** *MS* U.S.A.
172 D3 **Batetskiy** Russia
189 G4 **Bath** *N.B.* Canada
191 I3 **Bath** *Ont.* Canada
161 E6 **Bath** U.K.
203 I3 **Bath** *ME* U.S.A.
202 E3 **Bath** *NY* U.S.A.
162 E5 **Bathgate** U.K.
144 C3 **Bathinda** India
127 H4 **Bathurst** Australia
189 G4 **Bathurst** Canada
181 G6 **Bathurst** S. Africa
127 H5 **Bathurst, Lake** Australia
184 H3 **Bathurst Inlet** *inlet* Canada
184 H3 **Bathurst Inlet (abandoned)** Canada
124 D3 **Bathurst Island** Australia
185 I2 **Bathurst Island** Canada
137 K7 **Bāţin, Wādī al** *watercourse* Asia
139 G4 **Batken** *admin. div.* Kyrg.
140 D3 **Bāţlāq-e Gavkhūnī** *marsh* Iran
160 F4 **Batley** U.K.
127 H5 **Batlow** Australia
137 H3 **Batman** Turkey
176 C1 **Batna** Alg.
154 □ **Batok, Bukit** *h.* Sing.
154 A4 **Batong, Ko** *i.* Thai.
199 F6 **Baton Rouge** U.S.A.
206 C2 **Batopilas** Mex.
177 D4 **Batouri** Cameroon
214 B1 **Batovi** Brazil
136 E4 **Batroûn** Lebanon
158 O1 **Båtsfjord** Norway
143 C5 **Batticaloa** Sri Lanka
170 F4 **Battipaglia** Italy
187 G4 **Battle** *r.* Canada
190 E4 **Battle Creek** U.S.A.
187 H4 **Battleford** Canada
194 C3 **Battle Mountain** U.S.A.
144 C1 **Battura Glacier** Pak.
155 A3 **Batu, Pulau-pulau** *is* Indon.
154 B4 **Batu Gajah** Malaysia
153 C5 **Batulaki** Phil.
137 H1 **Bat'umi** Georgia
155 B2 **Batu Pahat** Malaysia
154 B4 **Batu Putih, Gunung** *mt.* Malaysia
147 E7 **Baubau** Indon.
176 C3 **Bauchi** Nigeria
198 E1 **Baudette** U.S.A.
213 A3 **Baudo, Serranía de** *mts* Col.
166 D3 **Baugé-en-Anjou** France
165 H5 **Bauland** *reg.* Germany
189 J3 **Bauld, Cape** Canada
166 H3 **Baume-les-Dames** France
214 C3 **Bauru** Brazil
214 B2 **Baús** Brazil
164 E4 **Bausendorf** Germany
159 N4 **Bauska** Latvia
138 B3 **Bautino** Kazakh.
168 G5 **Bautzen** Germany
139 G4 **Bauyrzhan Momyshuly** Kazakh.
154 B2 **Bâvêl** Cambodia
180 E6 **Baviaanskloofberge** *mts* S. Africa
192 E6 **Bavispe** *r.* Mex.
127 G6 **Baw Baw National Park** Australia
161 I5 **Bawdeswell** U.K.
155 D4 **Bawean** *i.* Indon.
164 F2 **Bawinkel** Germany
176 B3 **Bawku** Ghana
154 A1 **Bawlake** Myanmar
149 A4 **Bawolung** China
148 B3 **Baxi** China
201 D6 **Baxley** U.S.A.
153 B3 **Bay, Laguna de** *lag.* Phil.
205 I4 **Bayamo** Cuba
144 D4 **Bayana** India
139 H2 **Bayanauyl** Kazakh.
148 B1 **Bayandalay** Mongolia
146 B3 **Bayan Har Shan** *mts* China
146 C2 **Bayanhongor** Mongolia
148 B2 **Bayan Hot** China
152 A1 **Bayan Huxu** China
140 B3 **Bayānlū** Iran
148 C1 **Bayannur** China
148 B1 **Bayan Nurun** China
148 C1 **Bayan Obo** China
148 C1 **Bayan-Ovoo** Mongolia
152 A1 **Bayan Qagan** China
148 D1 **Bayan Shutu** China
146 D2 **Bayan Ul** China
146 D2 **Bayan-Uul** Mongolia
140 D4 **Bayāẕ** Iran
140 D3 **Bayāẕīyeh** Iran
153 C4 **Baybay** Phil.
137 H1 **Bayburt** Turkey
191 F4 **Bay City** *MI* U.S.A.
199 D6 **Bay City** *TX* U.S.A.
132 H3 **Baydaratskaya Guba** Russia
178 E3 **Baydhabo** Somalia
165 K5 **Bayerischer Wald** *mts* Germany
165 I5 **Bayern** *land* Germany
139 J1 **Bayevo** Russia
190 B2 **Bayfield** U.S.A.
138 F3 **Baygekum** Kazakh.
138 E1 **Baygora** Kazakh.
171 L5 **Bayındır** Turkey
137 I4 **Bayjī** Iraq
Baykal, Ozero *l.* Russia *see* **Baikal, Lake**
146 C1 **Baykal'skiy Khrebet** *mts* Russia
137 H2 **Baykan** Turkey
138 F3 **Baykonur** Kazakh.
138 E3 **Baykonyr** Kazakh.
138 E3 **Baykozha** Kazakh.
139 H5 **Baykurt** China
138 D1 **Baymak** Russia
140 D6 **Baynūna'h** *reg.* U.A.E.
153 B2 **Bayombong** Phil.
166 D5 **Bayonne** France
153 B4 **Bayo Point** Phil.
138 E5 **Baýramaly** Turkm.
171 L5 **Bayramiç** Turkey
165 J5 **Bayreuth** Germany
199 F6 **Bay St Louis** U.S.A.
138 C3 **Bayshonas** Kazakh.
203 G4 **Bay Shore** U.S.A.
161 E5 **Bayston Hill** U.K.
Baysun Uzbek. *see* **Boysun**
139 F5 **Baysuntau, Gory** *mts* Uzbek.
199 E6 **Baytown** U.S.A.
128 F3 **Bay View** N.Z.
139 G4 **Bayyrkum** Kazakh.
139 G4 **Bayzhansay** Kazakh.
167 E4 **Baza** Spain
139 H5 **Bāzā'ī Gunbad** Afgh.
139 J3 **Bazar** *watercourse* Kazakh.
141 H3 **Bāzārak** Afgh.
Bazardyuzi, Gora *mt.* Azer./Russia *see* **Bazardyuzyu, Gora**
137 K1 **Bazardyuzyu, Gora** *mt.* Azer./Russia
137 L3 **Bāzār-e Jom'eh** Iran
141 G3 **Bāzār-e Mālistān** Afgh.
140 C2 **Bāzār-e Māsāl** Iran
137 J2 **Bāzargān** Iran
173 H4 **Bazarnyy Karabulak** Russia
138 B2 **Bazarsholan** Kazakh.
138 B2 **Bazartobe** Kazakh.
179 D6 **Bazaruto, Ilha do** *i.* Moz.
141 G5 **Bazdar** Pak.
148 C4 **Bazhong** China
148 E2 **Bazhou** China
141 F5 **Bazmān** Iran
141 F4 **Bazmān, Kūh-e** *mt.* Iran
140 C3 **Bāzoft, Āb-e** *r.* Iran
136 E4 **Bcharré** Lebanon
179 E5 **Bé, Nosy** *i.* Madag.
154 C3 **Be, Sông** *r.* Vietnam
198 C2 **Beach** U.S.A.
191 I3 **Beachburg** Canada
203 F5 **Beach Haven** U.S.A.
126 D6 **Beachport** Australia
203 F5 **Beachwood** U.S.A.
161 H7 **Beachy Head** U.K.
203 G4 **Beacon** U.S.A.
181 G6 **Beacon Bay** S. Africa
149 □ **Beacon Hill** *Hong Kong* China
161 G6 **Beaconsfield** U.K.
212 C8 **Beagle, Canal** *sea chan.* Arg.
124 C3 **Beagle Gulf** Australia
179 E5 **Bealanana** Madag.
163 B3 **Béal an Mhuirthead** Ireland
161 E7 **Beaminster** U.K.
194 E3 **Bear** *r.* U.S.A.
187 M2 **Bear Cove** *b.* Canada
188 C4 **Beardmore** Canada
Beardmore Reservoir Australia *see* **Kajarabie, Lake**
190 B5 **Beardstown** U.S.A.
188 D3 **Bear Island** Canada
186 D3 **Bear Lake** Canada
194 E3 **Bear Lake** *l.* U.S.A.
144 D4 **Bearma** *r.* India
194 E1 **Bear Paw Mountain** U.S.A.
188 B3 **Bearskin Lake** Canada
196 B2 **Bear Valley** U.S.A.
144 C3 **Beas** *r.* India
144 C3 **Beas Dam** India
205 J5 **Beata, Cabo** *c.* Dom. Rep.
205 J5 **Beata, Isla** *i.* Dom. Rep.
198 D3 **Beatrice** U.S.A.
186 E3 **Beatton** *r.* Canada
186 E3 **Beatton River** Canada
196 D3 **Beatty** U.S.A.
188 E4 **Beattyville** Canada
166 G5 **Beaucaire** France
212 E8 **Beauchene Island** Falkland Is
126 E6 **Beaufort** Australia
155 E1 **Beaufort** *Sabah* Malaysia
201 D5 **Beaufort** U.S.A.
184 D2 **Beaufort Sea** Canada/U.S.A.
180 E6 **Beaufort West** S. Africa
188 F4 **Beauharnois** Canada
162 D3 **Beauly** U.K.
162 D3 **Beauly Firth** *est.* U.K.
161 C4 **Beaumaris** U.K.
164 C4 **Beaumont** Belgium
128 B6 **Beaumont** N.Z.
199 F6 **Beaumont** *MS* U.S.A.
202 B5 **Beaumont** *OH* U.S.A.
199 E6 **Beaumont** *TX* U.S.A.
166 G3 **Beaune** France
166 D3 **Beaupréau** France
164 A4 **Beauquesne** France
164 C4 **Beauraing** Belgium
187 J4 **Beauséjour** Canada
166 F2 **Beauvais** France
187 H3 **Beauval** Canada
164 A4 **Beauval** France
184 H4 **Beaver** *r. Alta* Canada
188 C2 **Beaver** *r. Ont.* Canada
186 D2 **Beaver** *r. Y.T.* Canada
197 F2 **Beaver** U.S.A.
197 F2 **Beaver** *r.* U.S.A.
186 A2 **Beaver Creek** Canada
200 C4 **Beaver Dam** *KY* U.S.A.
190 C4 **Beaver Dam** *WI* U.S.A.
202 C4 **Beaver Falls** U.S.A.
194 D2 **Beaverhead Mountains** U.S.A.
187 J4 **Beaver Hill Lake** Canada
187 I2 **Beaverhill Lake** Canada
190 E3 **Beaver Island** U.S.A.
199 E4 **Beaver Lake** *resr* U.S.A.
186 F3 **Beaverlodge** Canada
202 D4 **Beaver Run Reservoir** U.S.A.
144 C4 **Beawar** India
215 C2 **Beazley** Arg.
214 C3 **Bebedouro** Brazil
161 D4 **Bebington** U.K.
165 H4 **Bebra** Germany
188 F1 **Bécard, Lac** *l.* Canada
161 I5 **Beccles** U.K.
171 I2 **Bečej** Serbia
167 C1 **Becerreá** Spain
176 B1 **Béchar** Alg.
165 I5 **Bechhofen** Germany
202 C6 **Beckley** U.S.A.
165 G3 **Beckum** Germany
165 K4 **Bečov nad Teplou** Czech Rep.
160 F3 **Bedale** U.K.
164 E4 **Bedburg** Germany
203 I2 **Beddington** U.S.A.
178 D3 **Bedelē** Eth.
139 I4 **Bedel Pass** China/Kyrg.
203 G2 **Bedford** Canada
181 I4 **Bedford** S. Africa
161 G5 **Bedford** U.K.
200 C4 **Bedford** *IN* U.S.A.
203 H3 **Bedford** *MA* U.S.A.
202 D4 **Bedford** *PA* U.S.A.
202 D6 **Bedford** *VA* U.S.A.
161 G5 **Bedford Level (North Level)** *lowland* U.K.
127 G4 **Bedgerebong** Australia
160 F2 **Bedlington** U.K.
154 □ **Bedok** Sing.
154 □ **Bedok Reservoir** Sing.
197 H2 **Bedrock** U.S.A.
164 E1 **Bedum** Neth.
161 F5 **Bedworth** U.K.
202 B5 **Beech Fork Lake** U.S.A.
190 C2 **Beechwood** U.S.A.
127 G6 **Beechworth** Australia
127 I5 **Beecroft Peninsula** Australia
165 K2 **Beelitz** Germany
127 J1 **Beenleigh** Australia
163 A5 **Beenoskee** *h.* Ireland
164 B3 **Beernem** Belgium
136 E6 **Beersheba** Israel
180 E6 **Beervlei Dam** S. Africa
127 J1 **Beerwah** Australia
165 K2 **Beetzsee** *l.* Germany
199 D6 **Beeville** U.S.A.
178 C3 **Befale** Dem. Rep. Congo
179 E5 **Befandriana Avaratra** Madag.
127 H6 **Bega** Australia
144 B3 **Begari** *r.* Pak.
167 H2 **Begur, Cap de** *c.* Spain
145 F4 **Begusarai** India
141 E3 **Behābād** *Khorāsān-e Jonūbī* Iran
140 D4 **Behābād** *Yazd* Iran
211 H3 **Béhague, Pointe** *pt* Fr. Guiana
140 C4 **Behbahān** Iran
186 F2 **Behchokò** Canada
186 C3 **Behm Canal** *sea chan.* U.S.A.
140 D4 **Behrūsī** Iran
140 D2 **Behshahr** Iran
146 E2 **Bei'an** China
149 C4 **Beibei** China
149 F6 **Beigang** Taiwan
149 C6 **Beihai** China
149 D6 **Bei Jiang** *r.* China
148 E2 **Beijing** China (City Plan **103**)
148 E1 **Beijing** *mun.* China
164 E2 **Beilen** Neth.
149 C7 **Beili** China
149 D6 **Beiliu** China
165 J5 **Beilngries** Germany
162 C5 **Beinn an Oir** *h.* U.K.
162 D3 **Beinn Dearg** *mt.* U.K.
149 C5 **Beipan Jiang** *r.* China
152 A3 **Beipiao** China
179 D5 **Beira** Moz.
148 E3 **Beiru He** *r.* China
136 E5 **Beirut** Lebanon
148 D2 **Beitai Ding** *mt.* China
179 C6 **Beitbridge** Zimbabwe
162 D5 **Beith** U.K.
169 K7 **Beiuş** Romania
152 A3 **Beizhen** China
167 C3 **Beja** Port.
176 C1 **Béja** Tunisia
176 C1 **Bejaïa** Alg.
167 D2 **Béjar** Spain
144 B3 **Beji** *r.* Pak.
138 E3 **Bekbauly** Kazakh.
138 C3 **Bekbike** Kazakh.
Bekdash Turkm. *see* **Garabogaz**
169 J7 **Békés** Hungary
169 J7 **Békéscsaba** Hungary
179 E6 **Bekily** Madag.
176 B4 **Bekwai** Ghana
145 E4 **Bela** India
141 G5 **Bela** Pak.
144 B3 **Belab** *r.* Pak.
181 H2 **Bela-Bela** S. Africa
177 D4 **Bélabo** Cameroon
171 I2 **Bela Crkva** Serbia
139 J2 **Bel'agash** Kazakh.
143 A3 **Belagavi** India
203 E5 **Bel Air** U.S.A.
167 D3 **Belalcázar** Spain
165 K5 **Bělá nad Radbuzou** Czech Rep.
Belaraboon Australia *see* **Paddington**
169 M4 **Belarus** *country* Europe
214 A3 **Bela Vista** Brazil
179 D6 **Bela Vista** Moz.
154 A5 **Belawan** Indon.
133 S3 **Belaya** *r.* Russia
173 G6 **Belaya Glina** Russia
173 G5 **Belaya Kalitva** Russia
172 I3 **Belaya Kholunitsa** Russia
169 I5 **Bełchatów** Poland
202 B6 **Belcher** U.S.A.
185 J4 **Belcher Islands** Canada
136 F2 **Belcik** Turkey
163 D3 **Belcoo** U.K.
191 I1 **Belcourt** Canada
196 B1 **Belden** U.S.A.
178 E3 **Beledweyne** Somalia
138 C5 **Belek** Turkm.
211 I4 **Belém** Brazil
212 C3 **Belén** Arg.
136 F3 **Belen** Turkey
195 F5 **Belen** U.S.A.
125 G3 **Belep, Îles** *is* New Caledonia
138 D3 **Beleuli** *tourist site* Uzbek.
172 F4 **Belev** Russia
128 D5 **Belfast** N.Z.
163 F3 **Belfast** U.K.
203 I2 **Belfast** U.S.A.
163 F3 **Belfast Lough** *inlet* U.K.
198 C2 **Belfield** U.S.A.
160 F2 **Belford** U.K.
166 H3 **Belfort** France
Belgaum India *see* **Belagavi**
165 L3 **Belgern** Germany
164 C4 **Belgium** *country* Europe
173 F5 **Belgorod** Russia
173 F5 **Belgorodskaya Oblast'** *admin. div.* Russia
171 I2 **Belgrade** Serbia
194 E2 **Belgrade** U.S.A.
129 C3 **Belgrano II** *research stn* Antarctica
170 E6 **Belice** *r. Sicily* Italy
172 G4 **Belinskiy** Russia
155 C3 **Belinyu** Indon.
155 C3 **Belitung** *i.* Indon.
207 G4 **Belize** Belize
207 G4 **Belize** *country* Central America
150 E2 **Belkina, Mys** *pt* Russia
133 O2 **Bel'kovskiy, Ostrov** *i.* Russia
127 I1 **Bell** Australia
127 H4 **Bell** *r.* Australia
186 D4 **Bella Bella** Canada
166 E3 **Bellac** France
186 D4 **Bella Coola** Canada
199 E6 **Bellaire** U.S.A.
Bellary India *see* **Ballari**
127 H2 **Bellata** Australia
215 F1 **Bella Unión** Uruguay
127 J3 **Bellbrook** Australia
202 B4 **Bellefontaine** U.S.A.
202 E4 **Bellefonte** U.S.A.
198 C2 **Belle Fourche** U.S.A.
198 C2 **Belle Fourche** *r.* U.S.A.
166 G3 **Bellegarde-sur-Valserine** France
201 D7 **Belle Glade** U.S.A.
166 C3 **Belle-Île** *i.* France
189 J3 **Belle Isle** *i.* Canada
189 I3 **Belle Isle, Strait of** Canada
197 G4 **Bellemont** U.S.A.
190 A5 **Belle Plaine** U.S.A.
191 H2 **Belleterre** Canada
191 I3 **Belleville** Canada
198 D4 **Belleville** U.S.A.
190 B4 **Bellevue** *IA* U.S.A.
194 D3 **Bellevue** *ID* U.S.A.
202 B4 **Bellevue** *OH* U.S.A.
194 B2 **Bellevue** *WA* U.S.A.
127 J3 **Bellingen** Australia
160 E2 **Bellingham** U.K.
194 B1 **Bellingham** U.S.A.
129 E2 **Bellingshausen** *research stn* Antarctica
129 B3 **Bellingshausen Sea** *sea* Antarctica
168 D7 **Bellinzona** Switz.
213 B3 **Bello** Col.
203 G3 **Bellows Falls** U.S.A.
144 B3 **Bellpat** Pak.
162 F4 **Bell Rock** *i.* U.K.
203 F5 **Belltown** U.S.A.
170 E1 **Belluno** Italy
215 D2 **Bell Ville** Arg.
180 C6 **Bellville** S. Africa
165 G2 **Belm** Germany
180 F4 **Belmont** S. Africa
162 □ **Belmont** U.K.
202 D3 **Belmont** U.S.A.
214 E1 **Belmonte** Brazil
207 G4 **Belmopan** Belize
127 J2 **Belmore, Mount** *h.* Australia
Belmullet Ireland *see* **Béal an Mhuirthead**
164 B4 **Belœil** Belgium
203 G2 **Belœil** Canada
146 E1 **Belogorsk** Russia
179 E6 **Beloha** Madag.
214 D2 **Belo Horizonte** Brazil
198 D4 **Beloit** *KS* U.S.A.
190 C4 **Beloit** *WI* U.S.A.
139 K2 **Belokurikha** Russia
172 E1 **Belomorsk** Russia
145 G5 **Belonia** India
173 F6 **Belorechensk** Russia
136 F3 **Belören** Turkey
138 D1 **Beloretsk** Russia
Belorussia *country* Europe *see* **Belarus**
179 E5 **Belo Tsiribihina** Madag.
139 J2 **Belousovka** Kazakh.
172 F1 **Beloye (abandoned)** Russia
172 F2 **Beloye, Ozero** *l.* Russia
Beloye More *sea* Russia *see* **White Sea**
172 F2 **Belozersk** Russia
202 C5 **Belpre** U.S.A.
194 E2 **Belt** U.S.A.
126 C3 **Beltana** Australia
126 B2 **Belt Bay** *salt flat* Australia
196 D3 **Belted Range** *mts* U.S.A.
199 D6 **Belton** U.S.A.
143 A3 **Belur** India
153 A5 **Beluran** *Sabah* Malaysia
190 C4 **Belvidere** U.S.A.
138 D2 **Belyayevka** Russia
172 H3 **Belyshevo** Russia
172 E4 **Belyy** Russia
132 I2 **Belyy, Ostrov** *i.* Russia
179 E5 **Bemaraha, Parc National de** Madag.
190 C6 **Bement** U.S.A.
198 E2 **Bemidji** U.S.A.
178 C4 **Bena Dibele** Dem. Rep. Congo
162 D4 **Ben Alder** *mt.* U.K.
127 F6 **Benalla** Australia
170 D6 **Ben Arous** Tunisia
167 D1 **Benavente** Spain
162 E3 **Ben Avon** *mt.* U.K.
163 B4 **Benbaun** *h.* Ireland
162 A3 **Benbecula** *i.* U.K.
163 C3 **Benbulben** *h.* Ireland
163 E3 **Benburb** U.K.
162 C4 **Ben Cruachan** *mt.* U.K.
194 B2 **Bend** U.S.A.
181 G5 **Bendearg** *mt.* S. Africa
127 I3 **Bendemeer** Australia
173 D6 **Bender** Moldova
178 E3 **Bender-Bayla** Somalia
126 F6 **Bendigo** Australia
127 H6 **Bendoc** Australia
179 D5 **Bene** Moz.
189 I3 **Benedict, Mount** *h.* Canada
203 I2 **Benedicta** U.S.A.
179 E6 **Benenitra** Madag.
168 G6 **Benešov** Czech Rep.
164 E6 **Bénestroff** France
170 F4 **Benevento** Italy
135 G5 **Bengal, Bay of** *sea* Asia
143 B3 **Bengaluru** India
178 C3 **Bengamisa** Dem. Rep. Congo
148 E3 **Bengbu** China
177 E1 **Benghazi** Libya
148 F3 **Beng He** *r.* China
154 B5 **Bengkalis** Indon.
155 B3 **Bengkulu** Indon.
159 K4 **Bengtsfors** Sweden
179 B5 **Benguela** Angola
162 B4 **Ben Hiant** *h.* U.K.
162 D2 **Ben Hope** *h.* U.K.
210 E6 **Beni** *r.* Bol.
178 C3 **Beni** Dem. Rep. Congo
176 B1 **Beni Abbès** Alg.
167 F3 **Benidorm** Spain
176 B1 **Beni Mellal** Morocco
176 C4 **Benin** *country* Africa
176 C4 **Benin, Bight of** *g.* Africa
176 C4 **Benin City** Nigeria
176 B1 **Beni Saf** Alg.
215 E3 **Benito Juárez** Arg.
153 B2 **Benito Soliven** Phil.
210 E4 **Benjamin Constant** Brazil
204 B2 **Benjamín Hill** Mex.
124 D2 **Benjina** Indon.
198 C3 **Benkelman** U.S.A.
162 D2 **Ben Klibreck** *h.* U.K.
162 D4 **Ben Lawers** *mt.* U.K.
127 I3 **Ben Lomond** *mt.* Australia
162 D4 **Ben Lomond** *h.* U.K.
127 G8 **Ben Lomond National Park** Australia
162 D2 **Ben Loyal** *h.* U.K.
162 D4 **Ben Lui** *mt.* U.K.
162 E3 **Ben Macdui** *mt.* U.K.
162 B4 **Ben More** *h.* U.K.
162 D4 **Ben More** *mt.* U.K.
128 C6 **Benmore, Lake** N.Z.
162 D2 **Ben More Assynt** *h.* U.K.
158 M3 **Bennäs** Fin.
133 P2 **Bennetta, Ostrov** *i.* Russia
162 C4 **Ben Nevis** *mt.* U.K.
203 G3 **Bennington** U.S.A.
181 H3 **Benoni** S. Africa
177 D4 **Bénoué, Parc National de la** *nat. park* Cameroon
165 G5 **Bensheim** Germany
197 G6 **Benson** *AZ* U.S.A.
198 E2 **Benson** *MN* U.S.A.
141 E5 **Bent** Iran
155 B2 **Benta Seberang** Malaysia
202 D6 **Bent Creek** U.S.A.
147 E7 **Benteng** Indon.
124 D3 **Bentinck Island** Australia
154 A3 **Bentinck Island** Myanmar
178 C3 **Bentiu** South Sudan
160 F4 **Bentley** U.K.
203 J2 **Benton** Canada
199 E5 **Benton** *AR* U.S.A.
196 C3 **Benton** *CA* U.S.A.
200 B4 **Benton** *IL* U.S.A.
190 D4 **Benton Harbor** U.S.A.
154 C3 **Bên Tre** Vietnam
154 B5 **Bentung** Malaysia
176 D4 **Benue** *r.* Nigeria
162 D4 **Ben Vorlich** *h.* U.K.
163 B3 **Benwee Head** Ireland
162 D3 **Ben Wyvis** *mt.* U.K.
152 B3 **Benxi** *Liaoning* China
152 C3 **Benxi** *Liaoning* China
153 C5 **Beo** Indon.
Beograd Serbia *see* **Belgrade**
144 E5 **Beohari** India
176 B4 **Béoumi** Côte d'Ivoire
151 B8 **Beppu** Japan
125 H3 **Beqa** *i.* Fiji
144 C4 **Berach** *r.* India
171 H3 **Berane** Montenegro
189 G2 **Bérard, Lac** *l.* Canada
144 D5 **Berasia** India
154 A5 **Berastagi** Indon.
171 H4 **Berat** Albania
155 E3 **Beratus, Gunung** *mt.* Indon.
147 F7 **Berau, Teluk** *b.* Indon.
177 F3 **Berber** Sudan
178 E2 **Berbera** Somalia
178 B3 **Berbérati** C.A.R.
166 E1 **Berck** France
137 J1 **Berd** Armenia
133 N3 **Berdigestyakh** Russia
146 A1 **Berdsk** Russia
173 F6 **Berdyans'k** Ukr.
173 D5 **Berdychiv** Ukr.
202 A6 **Berea** U.S.A.
173 B5 **Berehove** Ukr.
124 E2 **Bereina** P.N.G.
138 C5 **Bereket** Turkm.
139 K2 **Berel'** Kazakh.
187 J4 **Berens** *r.* Canada
187 J4 **Berens River** Canada
198 D3 **Beresford** U.S.A.
173 C5 **Berezhany** Ukr.
173 D6 **Berezivka** Ukr.
173 C5 **Berezne** Ukr.
172 G2 **Bereznik** Russia
138 D1 **Berezovka** Russia
132 H3 **Berezovo** Russia
165 J3 **Berga** Germany
167 G1 **Berga** Spain
171 L5 **Bergama** Turkey
170 C2 **Bergamo** Italy
159 L3 **Bergby** Sweden
165 H2 **Bergen** Germany
159 I3 **Bergen** Norway
168 F3 **Bergen auf Rügen** Germany
164 C3 **Bergen op Zoom** Neth.
166 E4 **Bergerac** France
164 C6 **Bergères-lès-Vertus** France
164 E4 **Bergheim** Germany
164 F4 **Bergisches Land** *reg.* Germany
164 F4 **Bergisch Gladbach** Germany
180 B1 **Bergland** Namibia
190 C2 **Bergland** U.S.A.
159 L3 **Bergsjö** Sweden
158 M2 **Bergsviken** Sweden
165 I5 **Bergtheim** Germany
164 A4 **Bergues** France
Bergum Neth. *see* **Burgum**
181 H4 **Bergville** S. Africa
155 B3 **Berhala, Selat** *sea chan.* Indon.
133 R4 **Beringa, Ostrov** *i.* Russia
164 D3 **Beringen** Belgium
133 S3 **Beringovskiy** Russia
133 S4 **Bering Sea** Pacific Ocean
184 B3 **Bering Strait** Russia/U.S.A.
158 J3 **Berkåk** Norway
164 E2 **Berkel** *r.* Neth.
196 A3 **Berkeley** U.S.A.
202 D5 **Berkeley Springs** U.S.A.
164 D2 **Berkhout** Neth.
129 C3 **Berkner Sub-glacial Island** *i.* Antarctica
171 J3 **Berkovitsa** Bulg.
161 F6 **Berkshire Downs** *hills* U.K.
164 C3 **Berlare** Belgium
158 O1 **Berlevåg** Norway
165 L2 **Berlin** Germany
203 F5 **Berlin** *MD* U.S.A.
203 H2 **Berlin** *NH* U.S.A.
202 D5 **Berlin** *PA* U.S.A.
190 C4 **Berlin** *WI* U.S.A.
185 J2 **Berlinguet Inlet** Canada
202 C4 **Berlin Lake** U.S.A.
127 I6 **Bermagui** Australia
215 D4 **Bermeja, Punta** *pt* Arg.
206 D2 **Bermejíllo** Mex.
215 C1 **Bermejo** *r.* Arg.
212 D2 **Bermejo** *r.* Arg./Bol.
210 F8 **Bermejo** Bol.
205 M2 **Bermuda** *terr.* Atlantic Ocean
219 E4 **Bermuda Rise** *sea feature* N. Atlantic Ocean
168 C7 **Bern** Switz.
195 F5 **Bernalillo** U.S.A.
129 E2 **Bernardo O'Higgins** *research stn* Antarctica
212 A7 **Bernardo O'Higgins, Parque Nacional** *nat. park* Chile
215 D3 **Bernasconi** Arg.
165 J3 **Bernburg (Saale)** Germany
165 G1 **Berne** Germany
190 E5 **Berne** U.S.A.
168 C7 **Berner Alpen** *mts* Switz.
162 A3 **Berneray** *i. Scotland* U.K.
162 A4 **Berneray** *i. Scotland* U.K.
185 J2 **Bernier Bay** Canada
124 B4 **Bernier Island** Australia
168 E7 **Bernina Pass** Switz.
164 F5 **Bernkastel-Kues** Germany
179 E6 **Beroroha** Madag.
168 G6 **Beroun** Czech Rep.
168 F5 **Berounka** *r.* Czech Rep.
126 D5 **Berri** Australia
162 E2 **Berriedale** U.K.
127 F5 **Berrigan** Australia
127 I5 **Berrima** Australia
167 H4 **Berrouaghia** Alg.
127 I5 **Berry** Australia
166 E3 **Berry** *reg.* France
196 A2 **Berryessa, Lake** U.S.A.
201 E7 **Berry Islands** Bahamas
180 B3 **Berseba** Namibia
165 F2 **Bersenbrück** Germany
173 D5 **Bershad'** Ukr.
138 E1 **Bersuat** Russia
155 B1 **Bertam** Malaysia
211 J5 **Bertolínia** Brazil
177 D4 **Bertoua** Cameroon
163 B4 **Bertraghboy Bay** Ireland
125 H2 **Beru** *atoll* Kiribati
Beruni Uzbek. *see* **Beruniy**
138 E4 **Beruniy** Uzbek.
210 F4 **Beruri** Brazil
126 F7 **Berwick** Australia
203 E4 **Berwick** U.S.A.
160 E2 **Berwick-upon-Tweed** U.K.
186 F3 **Berwyn** Canada
161 D5 **Berwyn** *hills* U.K.
173 E6 **Beryslav** Ukr.
179 E5 **Besalampy** Madag.
166 H3 **Besançon** France
138 C3 **Besbay** Kazakh.
139 G4 **Beshariq** Uzbek.
Besharyk Uzbek. *see* **Beshariq**
Beshir Turkm. *see* **Beşir**
138 F5 **Beshkent** Uzbek.
140 D4 **Beshneh** Iran
138 F5 **Beşir** Turkm.
137 H3 **Beşiri** Turkey
173 H7 **Beslan** Russia
187 H3 **Besnard Lake** Canada
136 F3 **Besni** Turkey
139 H2 **Besoba** Kazakh.
163 E3 **Bessbrook** U.K.
201 C5 **Bessemer** *AL* U.S.A.
190 B2 **Bessemer** *MI* U.S.A.
138 C3 **Besshoky, Gora** *h.* Kazakh.
138 C2 **Bestamak** *Aktyubinskaya Oblast'* Kazakh.
139 I2 **Bestamak** *Vostochnyy Kazakhstan* Kazakh.
139 H1 **Bestobe** Kazakh.
145 H5 **Betalongchhip** *mt.* India
179 E6 **Betanty** Madag.
167 B1 **Betanzos** Spain
177 D4 **Bétaré Oya** Cameroon
181 H3 **Bethal** S. Africa
180 B3 **Bethanie** Namibia
198 E3 **Bethany** *MO* U.S.A.
199 D5 **Bethany** *OK* U.S.A.
184 B3 **Bethel** *AK* U.S.A.
203 H2 **Bethel** *ME* U.S.A.
190 A6 **Bethel** *MO* U.S.A.
202 A5 **Bethel** *OH* U.S.A.
202 D4 **Bethel Park** U.S.A.
161 C4 **Bethesda** U.K.
202 E5 **Bethesda** *MD* U.S.A.
202 C4 **Bethesda** *OH* U.S.A.
180 F5 **Bethesdaweg** S. Africa
181 H4 **Bethlehem** S. Africa
203 F4 **Bethlehem** U.S.A.
136 E6 **Bethlehem** West Bank
181 F5 **Bethulie** S. Africa
164 A4 **Béthune** France
213 C2 **Betijoque** Venez.
179 E6 **Betioky** Madag.
154 B4 **Betong** Thai.
139 G3 **Betpak-Dala** Kazakh.
139 G3 **Betpakdala** *plain* Kazakh.
179 E6 **Betroka** Madag.
136 E5 **Bet She'an** Israel
189 G4 **Betsiamites** Canada
189 G4 **Betsiamites** *r.* Canada
179 E5 **Betsiboka** *r.* Madag.
190 D3 **Betsie, Point** U.S.A.
150 I3 **Betsukai** Japan
190 E2 **Betsy Lake** U.S.A.
190 B5 **Bettendorf** U.S.A.
145 F4 **Bettiah** India
162 D2 **Bettyhill** U.K.
163 E4 **Bettystown** Ireland
144 D5 **Betul** India
155 D2 **Betung Kerihun, Taman Nasional** *nat. park* Indon./Malaysia
164 D3 **Betuwe** *reg.* Neth.
144 D4 **Betwa** *r.* India
161 D4 **Betws-y-coed** U.K.
165 F4 **Betzdorf** Germany
126 E5 **Beulah** Australia
190 D3 **Beulah** U.S.A.
161 H6 **Beult** *r.* U.K.
160 G4 **Beverley** U.K.
184 C4 **Beverley, Lake** U.S.A.
203 H3 **Beverly** *MA* U.S.A.

228

Catamarca

Corinna

179 C5 Chitokoloki Zambia
150 G3 Chitose Japan
143 B3 Chitradurga India
144 B2 Chitral Pak.
144 B2 Chitral r. Pak.
206 I7 Chitré Panama
145 G5 Chittagong Bangl.
145 F5 Chittaranjan India
144 C4 Chittaurgarh India
143 B3 Chittoor India
143 B4 Chittur India
179 D5 Chitungulu Zambia
179 D5 Chitungwiza Zimbabwe
179 C5 Chiume Angola
206 A2 Chívato, Punta pt Mex.
179 D5 Chivhu Zimbabwe
215 E2 Chivilcoy Arg.
149 D6 Chixixu China
137 J4 Chiyā Surkh Iraq
149 E4 Chizhou China
151 D7 Chizu Japan
139 G1 Chkalovo Kazakh.
172 G3 Chkalovsk Russia
150 C2 Chkalovskoye Russia
176 C1 Chlef Alg.
167 G4 Chlef, Oued r. Alg.
154 □ Choa Chu Kang Sing.
154 □ Choa Chu Kang h. Sing.
154 C2 Chŏâm Khsant Cambodia
215 B1 Choapa r. Chile
179 C5 Chobe National Park Botswana
197 E5 Chocolate Mountains U.S.A.
213 B3 Chocontá Col.
152 C4 Cho-do i. N. Korea
152 D6 Cho-do i. S. Korea
165 K4 Chodov Czech Rep.
215 D3 Choele Choel Arg.
144 C2 Chogo Lungma Glacier Pak.
173 H6 Chograyskoye Vodokhranilishche resr Russia
187 I4 Choiceland Canada
125 F2 Choiseul i. Solomon Is
212 E8 Choiseul Sound sea chan. Falkland Is
206 B2 Choix Mex.
168 H4 Chojnice Poland
150 G5 Chōkai-san vol. Japan
178 D2 Ch'ok'ē Eth.
199 D6 Choke Canyon Lake U.S.A.
178 D2 Ch'ok'ē Terara mt. Eth.
145 F3 Choksum China
133 P2 Chokurdakh Russia
179 D6 Chókwè Moz.
166 D3 Cholet France
215 B4 Cholila Arg.
139 H4 Cholpon Kyrg.
139 I4 Cholpon-Ata Kyrg.
206 H5 Choluteca Hond.
179 C5 Choma Zambia
145 G4 Chomo Lhari mt. Bhutan
154 A1 Chom Thong Thai.
168 F5 Chomutov Czech Rep.
133 L3 Chona r. Russia
154 B2 Chon Buri Thai.
152 D3 Ch'ŏnch'ŏn N. Korea
210 B4 Chone Ecuador
152 C4 Ch'ŏngch'ŏn-gang r. N. Korea
152 E3 Ch'ŏngjin N. Korea
152 C4 Chŏngju N. Korea
Ch'ŏngju S. Korea see Cheongju
154 B2 Chŏng Kal Cambodia
152 D4 Chŏngp'yŏng N. Korea
149 C4 Chongqing China
149 C4 Chongqing mun. China
149 E5 Chongren China
181 J2 Chonguene Moz.
179 C5 Chongwe Zambia
149 D4 Chongyang China
149 F5 Chongyang Xi r. China
149 E5 Chongyi China
149 C6 Chongzuo China
212 B7 Chonos, Archipiélago de los is Chile
145 F3 Cho Oyu mt. China
214 B4 Chopim r. Brazil
214 B4 Chopinzinho Brazil
203 F5 Choptank r. U.S.A.
144 B4 Chor Pak.
171 K7 Chora Sfakion Greece
160 E4 Chorley U.K.
173 D5 Chornobyl' Ukr.
173 E6 Chornomors'ke Crimea
173 C5 Chortkiv Ukr.
139 G4 Chorvoq suv ombori resr Kazakh./Uzbek.
152 C3 Ch'osan N. Korea
151 G7 Chōshi Japan
215 B3 Chos Malal Arg.
168 G4 Choszczno Poland
210 C5 Chota Peru
194 D2 Choteau U.S.A.
144 B3 Choti Pak.
176 A2 Choûm Mauritania
196 B3 Chowchilla U.S.A.
186 F4 Chown, Mount Canada
139 K2 Choya Russia
146 D2 Choybalsan Mongolia
146 C2 Choyr Mongolia
168 H6 Chřiby hills Czech Rep.
190 D6 Chrisman U.S.A.
181 I3 Chrissiesmeer S. Africa
128 D5 Christchurch N.Z.
161 F7 Christchurch U.K.
185 L2 Christian, Cape Canada
181 F3 Christiana S. Africa
191 G3 Christian Island Canada
202 C6 Christiansburg U.S.A.
Christianshåb Greenland see Qasigiannguit
186 C3 Christian Sound sea chan. U.S.A.
187 G3 Christina r. Canada
147 C8 Christmas Island terr. Indian Ocean
168 G6 Chrudim Czech Rep.
145 G5 Chuadanga Bangl.
181 J2 Chuali, Lago l. Moz.
148 C1 Chuanjing China
148 F4 Chuansha China
194 D3 Chubbuck U.S.A.
151 E6 Chūbu-Sangaku Kokuritsu-kōen nat. park Japan
215 C4 Chubut prov. Arg.
212 C6 Chubut r. Arg.
197 E5 Chuckwalla Mountains U.S.A.
173 D5 Chudniv Ukr.
172 D3 Chudovo Russia
184 C4 Chugach Mountains U.S.A.
151 C7 Chūgoku-sanchi mts Japan
150 C2 Chuguyevka Russia
194 F3 Chugwater U.S.A.
173 F5 Chuhuyiv Ukr.
197 G5 Chuichu U.S.A.
146 F1 Chukchagirskoye, Ozero l. Russia
220 M1 Chukchi Plateau sea feature Arctic Ocean
133 U3 Chukchi Sea Russia/U.S.A.
172 G3 Chukhloma Russia
133 T3 Chukotskiy Poluostrov pen. Russia
172 H1 Chulasa Russia
196 D5 Chula Vista U.S.A.
132 J4 Chulym Russia
145 G4 Chumbi China
212 C3 Chumbicha Arg.
139 K2 Chumek Kazakh.
146 F1 Chumikan Russia
154 B1 Chum Phae Thai.
154 A3 Chumphon Thai.
154 B2 Chum Saeng Thai.
133 K4 Chuna r. Russia
149 F4 Chun'an China
152 D5 Chuncheon S. Korea
141 H3 Chūnghar, Kōh-e h. Afgh.
152 D5 Chungju S. Korea
Chungking China see Chongqing
152 C4 Chŭngsan N. Korea
Chungur, Koh-i- hill Afgh. see Chūnghar, Kōh-e
152 F2 Chunhua China
207 G4 Chunhuhux Mex.
133 L3 Chunya r. Russia
137 K3 Chūplū Iran
210 D7 Chuquibamba Peru
212 C2 Chuquicamata Chile
168 D7 Chur Switz.
133 O3 Churapcha Russia
187 K3 Churchill Canada
187 J3 Churchill r. Man. Canada
189 H3 Churchill r. Nfld and Lab. Canada
187 K3 Churchill, Cape Canada
189 H3 Churchill Falls Canada
187 H3 Churchill Lake Canada
186 D3 Churchill Peak Canada
188 E2 Churchill Sound sea chan. Canada
198 D1 Churchs Ferry U.S.A.
202 D5 Churchville U.S.A.
145 F4 Churia Ghati Hills Nepal
172 H3 Churov Russia
144 C3 Churu India
Churubay Nura Kazakh. see Abay
213 C2 Churuguara Venez.
154 D2 Chư Sê Vietnam
144 D2 Chushul India
197 H3 Chuska Mountains U.S.A.
139 G4 Chust Uzbek.
189 F4 Chute-des-Passes Canada
191 I2 Chute-Rouge Canada
191 J2 Chute-St-Philippe Canada
123 E2 Chuuk is Micronesia
172 H4 Chuvashskaya Respublika aut. rep. Russia
149 A5 Chuxiong China
148 F3 Chuzhou Anhui China
148 F3 Chuzhou Jiangsu China
137 J4 Chwarta Iraq
173 D6 Ciadîr-Lunga Moldova
155 C4 Ciamis Indon.
155 C4 Cianjur Indon.
214 B3 Cianorte Brazil
195 E6 Cibuta Mex.
170 F2 Čićarija mts Croatia
136 E2 Çiçekdağı Turkey
173 E7 Cide Turkey
169 J4 Ciechanów Poland
205 I4 Ciego de Ávila Cuba
213 B2 Ciénaga Col.
207 D2 Ciénega de Flores Mex.
205 H4 Cienfuegos Cuba
167 F3 Cieza Spain
167 E2 Cifuentes Spain
137 L2 Çigil Adası i. Azer.
167 E3 Cigüela r. Spain
136 D2 Cihanbeyli Turkey
206 C4 Cihuatlán Mex.
167 D3 Cíjara, Embalse de resr Spain
155 C4 Cilacap Indon.
137 I1 Çıldır Turkey
137 I1 Çıldır Gölü l. Turkey
149 D4 Cili China
138 C4 Çilmämmetgum des. Turkm.
137 J3 Cilo Dağı mt. Turkey
137 M1 Çilov Adası i. Azer.
197 E4 Cima U.S.A.
195 F4 Cimarron U.S.A.
199 D4 Cimarron r. U.S.A.
173 D6 Cimişlia Moldova
170 D2 Cimone, Monte mt. Italy
137 H3 Çınar Turkey
213 C3 Cinaruco r. Venez.
167 G2 Cinca r. Spain
202 A5 Cincinnati U.S.A.
203 F3 Cincinnatus U.S.A.
215 D4 Cinco Chañares Arg.
215 C3 Cinco Saltos Arg.
161 E6 Cinderford U.K.
136 B3 Çine Turkey
164 D4 Ciney Belgium
207 F4 Cintalapa Mex.
166 I5 Cinto, Monte mt. France
214 B3 Cinzas r. Brazil
149 E5 Ciping China
215 C3 Cipolletti Arg.
Circe, Dome ice feature Antarctica see Charlie, Dome
184 D3 Circle AK U.S.A.
194 F2 Circle MT U.S.A.
202 B5 Circleville OH U.S.A.
197 F2 Circleville UT U.S.A.
155 C4 Cirebon Indon.
161 F6 Cirencester U.K.
170 B2 Ciriè Italy
170 G5 Cirò Marina Italy
189 H2 Cirque Mountain Canada
190 C6 Cisco IL U.S.A.
199 D5 Cisco TX U.S.A.
197 H2 Cisco (abandoned) U.S.A.
205 H5 Cisne, Islas del Hond.
213 B3 Cisneros Col.
201 E7 Cistern Point Bahamas
170 G3 Čitluk Bos. & Herz.
180 C6 Citrusdal S. Africa
170 E3 Città di Castello Italy
171 K2 Ciucaş, Vârful mt. Romania
206 D1 Ciudad Acuña Mex.
206 D4 Ciudad Altamirano Mex.
213 E3 Ciudad Bolívar Venez.
206 C2 Ciudad Camargo Mex.
206 B2 Ciudad Constitución Mex.
206 I6 Ciudad Cortés Costa Rica
207 G5 Ciudad Cuauhtémoc Mex.
206 H5 Ciudad Darío Nicaragua
207 G4 Ciudad del Carmen Mex.
214 A4 Ciudad del Este Para.
206 C1 Ciudad Delicias Mex.
207 E3 Ciudad del Maíz Mex.
213 C2 Ciudad de Nutrias Venez.
207 E3 Ciudad de Valles Mex.
213 E2 Ciudad Guayana Venez.
206 C1 Ciudad Guerrero Mex.
206 D4 Ciudad Guzmán Mex.
206 D4 Ciudad Hidalgo Mex.
207 F4 Ciudad Ixtepec Mex.
204 C2 Ciudad Juárez Mex.
206 D2 Ciudad Lerdo Mex.
207 E3 Ciudad Madero Mex.
207 E3 Ciudad Mante Mex.
207 E4 Ciudad Mendoza Mex.
207 E2 Ciudad Mier Mex.
206 B2 Ciudad Obregón Mex.
213 E3 Ciudad Piar Venez.
167 E3 Ciudad Real Spain
207 E2 Ciudad Río Bravo Mex.
167 C2 Ciudad Rodrigo Spain
207 E3 Ciudad Victoria Mex.
167 H2 Ciutadella Spain
136 F1 Cıva Burnu pt Turkey
136 B2 Cıvan Dağ mt. Turkey
170 E1 Cividale del Friuli Italy
170 E3 Civita Castellana Italy
170 E3 Civitanova Marche Italy
170 D3 Civitavecchia Italy
136 B2 Çivril Turkey
149 F4 Cixi China
148 E2 Cixian China
137 I3 Cizre Turkey
161 I6 Clacton-on-Sea U.K.
163 D3 Clady U.K.
187 G3 Claire, Lake Canada
194 B3 Clair Engle Lake resr U.S.A.
202 D4 Clairton U.S.A.
166 F3 Clamecy France
196 D2 Clan Alpine Mountains U.S.A.
163 E4 Clane Ireland
201 C5 Clanton U.S.A.
180 C6 Clanwilliam S. Africa
163 D4 Clara Ireland
154 A3 Clara Island Myanmar
126 E4 Clare N.S.W. Australia
126 C4 Clare S.A. Australia
163 C4 Clare r. Ireland
190 E4 Clare U.S.A.
163 C5 Clarecastle Ireland
163 A4 Clare Island Ireland
203 G3 Claremont U.S.A.
199 E4 Claremore U.S.A.
163 C4 Claremorris Ireland
127 J2 Clarence r. Australia
128 D5 Clarence N.Z.
201 F7 Clarence Town Bahamas
199 C5 Clarendon U.S.A.
189 J4 Clarenville Canada
186 G5 Claresholm Canada
198 E3 Clarinda U.S.A.
202 C5 Clarington U.S.A.
202 D4 Clarion U.S.A.
202 D4 Clarion r. U.S.A.
217 L4 Clarión, Isla i. Mex.
198 D2 Clark U.S.A.
181 H5 Clarkebury S. Africa
127 H8 Clarke Island Australia
201 D5 Clark Hill Reservoir U.S.A.
197 E4 Clark Mountain U.S.A.
191 G3 Clark Point Canada
202 C5 Clarksburg U.S.A.
199 F5 Clarksdale U.S.A.
192 D2 Clarks Fork r. U.S.A.
203 F4 Clarks Summit U.S.A.
194 C2 Clarkston U.S.A.
199 E5 Clarksville AR U.S.A.
190 A4 Clarksville IA U.S.A.
201 C4 Clarksville TN U.S.A.
214 B2 Claro r. Goiás Brazil
214 B1 Claro r. Mato Grosso Brazil
163 D5 Clashmore Ireland
163 D3 Claudy U.K.
153 B2 Claveria Phil.
164 D4 Clavier Belgium
203 G2 Clayburg U.S.A.
198 D4 Clay Center U.S.A.
197 F3 Clayhole Wash watercourse U.S.A.
201 D5 Clayton GA U.S.A.
195 G4 Clayton NM U.S.A.
203 E2 Clayton NY U.S.A.
203 I1 Clayton Lake U.S.A.
202 C6 Claytor Lake U.S.A.
163 B6 Clear, Cape Ireland
191 G4 Clear Creek Canada
197 G4 Clear Creek r. U.S.A.
184 D4 Cleare, Cape U.S.A.
202 D4 Clearfield PA U.S.A.
194 E3 Clearfield UT U.S.A.
202 B4 Clear Fork Reservoir U.S.A.
186 F3 Clear Hills Canada
198 E3 Clear Lake IA U.S.A.
190 A3 Clear Lake WI U.S.A.
196 A2 Clear Lake l. CA U.S.A.
197 F2 Clear Lake l. UT U.S.A.
194 B3 Clear Lake Reservoir U.S.A.
186 F4 Clearwater r. Alta Canada
187 H3 Clearwater r. Sask. Canada
201 D7 Clearwater U.S.A.
149 □ Clear Water Bay Hong Kong China
194 D2 Clearwater Mountains U.S.A.
187 H3 Clearwater River Provincial Park Canada
199 D5 Cleburne U.S.A.
194 B2 Cle Elum U.S.A.
160 G4 Cleethorpes U.K.
154 □ Clementi Sing.
202 C5 Clendenin U.S.A.
202 C4 Clendening Lake U.S.A.
153 A4 Cleopatra Needle mt. Phil.
191 H1 Cléricy Canada
124 E4 Clermont Australia
164 A5 Clermont France
201 D6 Clermont U.S.A.
164 D5 Clermont-en-Argonne France
166 F4 Clermont-Ferrand France
164 E4 Clervaux Lux.
170 D1 Cles Italy
126 B4 Cleve Australia
161 E6 Clevedon U.K.
199 F5 Cleveland MS U.S.A.
202 C4 Cleveland OH U.S.A.
201 C5 Cleveland TN U.S.A.
194 D1 Cleveland, Mount U.S.A.
190 D2 Cleveland Cliffs Basin l. U.S.A.
160 F3 Cleveland Hills U.K.
160 D4 Cleveleys U.K.
163 B4 Clew Bay Ireland
201 D7 Clewiston U.S.A.
163 A4 Clifden Ireland
197 H5 Cliff U.S.A.
163 C3 Cliffoney Ireland
128 E4 Clifford Bay N.Z.
127 I1 Clifton Australia
197 H5 Clifton U.S.A.
202 D6 Clifton Forge U.S.A.
202 B6 Clinch r. U.S.A.
202 B6 Clinch Mountain mts U.S.A.
186 E4 Clinton B.C. Canada
191 G4 Clinton Ont. Canada
203 G4 Clinton CT U.S.A.
190 B5 Clinton IA U.S.A.
190 C5 Clinton IL U.S.A.
203 H3 Clinton MA U.S.A.
203 I2 Clinton ME U.S.A.
198 E4 Clinton MO U.S.A.
199 F5 Clinton MS U.S.A.
201 E5 Clinton NC U.S.A.
199 D5 Clinton OK U.S.A.
203 F4 Clinton PA U.S.A.
187 H2 Clinton-Colden Lake Canada
190 C5 Clinton Lake U.S.A.
190 C3 Clintonville U.S.A.
197 G4 Clints Well U.S.A.
204 C6 Clipperton, Île terr. Pacific Ocean
162 B3 Clisham h. U.K.
160 E4 Clitheroe U.K.
181 G4 Clocolan S. Africa
163 D4 Cloghan Ireland
163 C6 Clonakilty Ireland
163 C6 Clonakilty Bay Ireland
163 C4 Clonbern Ireland
124 E4 Cloncurry Australia
163 D3 Clones Ireland
163 D5 Clonmel Ireland
163 D4 Clonygowan Ireland
163 B5 Cloonbannin Ireland
163 D4 Clooneagh Ireland
165 G2 Cloppenburg Germany
190 A2 Cloquet U.S.A.
194 F2 Cloud Peak U.S.A.
128 E4 Cloudy Bay N.Z.
149 □ Cloudy Hill Hong Kong China
191 J1 Clova Canada
196 A2 Cloverdale U.S.A.
199 C5 Clovis U.S.A.
191 I3 Cloyne Canada
162 C3 Cluanie, Loch l. U.K.
187 H3 Cluff Lake Mine Canada
169 K7 Cluj-Napoca Romania
161 D5 Clun U.K.
126 E6 Clunes Australia
166 H3 Cluses France
161 D4 Clwydian Range hills U.K.
186 G4 Clyde Canada
162 D5 Clyde r. U.K.
202 E3 Clyde NY U.S.A.
202 B4 Clyde OH U.S.A.
162 D5 Clyde, Firth of est. U.K.
162 D5 Clydebank U.K.
185 L2 Clyde River Canada
195 C5 Coachella U.S.A.
206 D4 Coahuayutla de Guerrero Mex.
206 D2 Coahuila state Mex.
186 D2 Coal r. Canada
190 C5 Coal City U.S.A.
206 D4 Coalcomán Mex.
196 D3 Coaldale (abandoned) U.S.A.
199 D5 Coalgate U.S.A.
196 B3 Coalinga U.S.A.
186 D3 Coal River Canada
161 F5 Coalville U.K.
210 F4 Coari Brazil
210 F5 Coari r. Brazil
193 I5 Coastal Plain U.S.A.
186 D4 Coast Mountains Canada
194 B2 Coast Ranges mts U.S.A.
162 E5 Coatbridge U.K.
207 G5 Coatepeque Guat.
203 F5 Coatesville U.S.A.
189 F4 Coaticook Canada
185 J3 Coats Island Canada
129 C3 Coats Land reg. Antarctica
207 F4 Coatzacoalcos Mex.
191 H2 Cobalt Canada
207 G5 Cobán Guat.
127 F3 Cobar Australia
127 H6 Cobargo Australia
127 H6 Cobberas, Mount Australia
126 E7 Cobden Australia
191 I3 Cobden Canada
163 C6 Cobh Ireland
187 J4 Cobham r. Canada
210 E6 Cobija Bol.
203 F3 Cobleskill U.S.A.
191 H4 Cobourg Canada
124 D3 Cobourg Peninsula Australia
127 F5 Cobram Australia
165 I4 Coburg Germany
210 C4 Coca Ecuador
167 D2 Coca Spain
214 B1 Cocalinho Brazil
210 E7 Cochabamba Bol.
215 B4 Cochamó Chile
164 F4 Cochem Germany
Cochin India see Kochi
197 H5 Cochise U.S.A.
186 G4 Cochrane Alta Canada
188 D4 Cochrane Ont. Canada
187 I3 Cochrane r. Canada
212 B7 Cochrane Chile
126 D4 Cockburn Australia
191 F3 Cockburn Island Canada
162 F5 Cockburnspath U.K.
201 F7 Cockburn Town Bahamas
Cockburn Town Turks and Caicos Is see Grand Turk
160 D3 Cockermouth U.K.
180 F6 Cockscomb mt. S. Africa
206 I6 Coclé del Norte Panama
206 H5 Coco r. Hond./Nicaragua
204 G7 Coco, Isla de i. Col.
213 A4 Coco, Punta pt Col.
197 F4 Coconino Plateau U.S.A.
127 G5 Cocopara National Park Australia
127 G4 Cocoparra Range hills Australia
213 B3 Cocorná Col.
214 D1 Cocos Brazil
147 B8 Cocos (Keeling) Islands terr. Indian Ocean
218 K4 Cocos Basin sea feature Indian Ocean
217 N5 Cocos Ridge sea feature N. Pacific Ocean
206 D3 Cocula Mex.
213 B3 Cocuy, Sierra Nevada del mt. Col.
203 H4 Cod, Cape U.S.A.
210 F4 Codajás Brazil
213 D2 Codera, Cabo c. Venez.
128 A7 Codfish Island N.Z.
170 E2 Codigoro Italy
189 H2 Cod Island Canada
171 K2 Codlea Romania
211 J4 Codó Brazil
161 E5 Codsall U.K.
163 A6 Cod's Head Ireland
194 E2 Cody U.S.A.
124 E3 Coen Australia
164 F3 Coesfeld Germany
175 I5 Coëtivy i. Seychelles
194 C2 Coeur d'Alene U.S.A.
194 C2 Coeur d'Alene Lake U.S.A.
164 E2 Coevorden Neth.
181 H5 Coffee Bay S. Africa
213 B3 Coffee Cultural Landscape of Colombia tourist site Col.
199 E4 Coffeyville U.S.A.
126 A5 Coffin Bay Australia
126 A5 Coffin Bay Australia
127 J3 Coffs Harbour Australia
181 G6 Cofimvaba S. Africa
190 B4 Coggon U.S.A.
166 D4 Cognac France
176 C4 Cogo Equat. Guinea
202 E3 Cohocton r. U.S.A.
203 G3 Cohoes U.S.A.
126 F5 Cohuna Australia
206 I7 Coiba, Isla de i. Panama
206 I7 Coiba, Parque Nacional nat. park Panama
212 C8 Coig r. Arg.
162 C2 Coigeach, Rubha pt U.K.
212 B7 Coihaique Chile
Coillan Chollaigh Ireland see Bailieborough
143 B4 Coimbatore India
167 B2 Coimbra Port.
167 D4 Coín Spain
210 E7 Coipasa, Salar de salt flat Bol.
213 C2 Cojedes r. Venez.
206 G5 Cojutepeque El Salvador
194 E3 Cokeville U.S.A.
126 E7 Colac Australia
214 E2 Colatina Brazil
165 J2 Colbitz Germany
198 C4 Colby U.S.A.
210 D7 Colca r. Peru
161 H6 Colchester U.K.
190 B5 Colchester U.S.A.
162 F5 Coldingham U.K.
165 K3 Colditz Germany
187 G4 Cold Lake Canada
187 G4 Cold Lake l. Canada
162 F5 Coldstream U.K.
199 D4 Coldwater KS U.S.A.
190 E5 Coldwater MI U.S.A.
190 D1 Coldwell Canada
203 H2 Colebrook U.S.A.
190 E4 Coleman MI U.S.A.
199 D6 Coleman TX U.S.A.
181 H4 Colenso S. Africa
126 D6 Coleraine Australia
163 E2 Coleraine U.K.
128 C5 Coleridge, Lake N.Z.
127 H9 Coles Bay Australia
180 F5 Colesberg S. Africa
196 B2 Colfax CA U.S.A.
194 C2 Colfax WA U.S.A.
162 □ Colgrave Sound str. U.K.
181 G3 Coligny S. Africa
206 D4 Colima Mex.
206 D4 Colima state Mex.
206 D4 Colima, Nevado de vol. Mex.
162 B4 Coll i. U.K.
167 E2 Collado Villalba Spain
127 H2 Collarenebri Australia
201 C5 College Park U.S.A.
199 D6 College Station U.S.A.
127 G2 Collerina Australia
127 H3 Collie Australia
124 C3 Collier Bay Australia
191 G3 Collingwood Canada
128 D4 Collingwood N.Z.
199 F6 Collins U.S.A.
200 B4 Collinsville U.S.A.
215 B3 Collipulli Chile
163 C3 Collooney Ireland
166 H2 Colmar France
167 E2 Colmenar Viejo Spain
162 D5 Colmonell U.K.
161 H6 Colne r. U.K.
127 I4 Colo r. Australia
164 F4 Cologne Germany
190 C3 Coloma U.S.A.
214 C3 Colômbia Brazil
207 E2 Colombia Mex.
213 B3 Colombia country S. America
219 D5 Colombian Basin sea feature S. Atlantic Ocean
143 B5 Colombo Sri Lanka
166 E5 Colomiers France
215 E2 Colón Buenos Aires Arg.
215 E2 Colón Entre Ríos Arg.
205 H4 Colón Cuba
206 J6 Colón Panama
195 C6 Colonet, Cabo c. Mex.
214 E1 Colônia r. Brazil
215 D3 Colonia Choele Choel, Isla i. Arg.
215 F2 Colonia del Sacramento Uruguay
215 C3 Colonia Emilio Mitre Arg.
215 F1 Colonia Lavalleja Uruguay
202 E6 Colonial Heights U.S.A.
197 F6 Colonia Reforma Mex.
170 G5 Colonna, Capo c. Italy
217 M5 Colon Ridge sea feature Pacific Ocean
162 B4 Colonsay i. U.K.
215 D3 Colorada Grande, Salina salt pan Arg.
215 D3 Colorado r. La Pampa Arg.
215 C1 Colorado r. San Juan Arg.
197 E5 Colorado r. Mex./U.S.A.
199 D6 Colorado r. U.S.A.
195 F4 Colorado state U.S.A.
215 D3 Colorado, Delta del Río Arg.
197 F3 Colorado City AZ U.S.A.
199 C5 Colorado City TX U.S.A.
196 D5 Colorado Desert U.S.A.
197 H2 Colorado National Monument nat. park U.S.A.
197 G3 Colorado Plateau U.S.A.
197 E4 Colorado River Aqueduct canal U.S.A.
195 F4 Colorado Springs U.S.A.
206 D3 Colotlán Mex.
165 L1 Cölpin Germany
161 G5 Colsterworth U.K.
161 I5 Coltishall U.K.
196 D4 Colton CA U.S.A.
203 F2 Colton NY U.S.A.
197 G2 Colton (abandoned) U.S.A.
194 B2 Columbia r. Canada/U.S.A.
202 E5 Columbia MD U.S.A.
198 E4 Columbia MO U.S.A.
199 F6 Columbia MS U.S.A.
202 E4 Columbia PA U.S.A.
201 D5 Columbia SC U.S.A.
201 C5 Columbia TN U.S.A.
185 K1 Columbia, Cape Canada
202 E5 Columbia, District of admin. dist. U.S.A.
186 F4 Columbia, Mount Canada
190 E5 Columbia City U.S.A.
203 J2 Columbia Falls ME U.S.A.
194 D1 Columbia Falls MT U.S.A.
186 F4 Columbia Mountains Canada
194 C2 Columbia Plateau U.S.A.
180 B6 Columbine, Cape S. Africa
201 C5 Columbus GA U.S.A.
200 C4 Columbus IN U.S.A.
199 F5 Columbus MS U.S.A.
194 E2 Columbus MT U.S.A.
198 D3 Columbus NE U.S.A.
195 F6 Columbus NM U.S.A.
202 B5 Columbus OH U.S.A.
199 D6 Columbus TX U.S.A.
190 C4 Columbus WI U.S.A.
190 B5 Columbus Junction U.S.A.
201 F7 Columbus Point Bahamas
196 D2 Columbus Salt Marsh U.S.A.
196 A2 Colusa U.S.A.
128 E2 Colville N.Z.
194 C1 Colville U.S.A.
184 C3 Colville r. U.S.A.
128 E2 Colville Channel N.Z.
184 F3 Colville Lake Canada
161 D4 Colwyn Bay U.K.
170 E2 Comacchio Italy
170 E2 Comacchio, Valli di lag. Italy
145 G3 Comai China
215 B4 Comallo r. Arg.
199 D6 Comanche U.S.A.
129 E2 Comandante Ferraz research stn Antarctica
215 C2 Comandante Salas Arg.
169 M7 Comănești Romania
206 H5 Comayagua Hond.
215 B1 Combarbalá Chile
163 F3 Comber U.K.
191 I3 Combermere Canada
145 H6 Combermere Bay Myanmar
164 A4 Combles France
181 J1 Combomune Moz.
127 J3 Comboyne Australia
188 E3 Comencho, Lac l. Canada
163 D5 Comeragh Mountains hills Ireland
199 D6 Comfort U.S.A.
145 G5 Comilla Bangl.
164 A4 Comines Belgium
170 C4 Comino, Capo c. Sardinia Italy
207 F4 Comitán de Domínguez Mex.
203 G4 Commack U.S.A.
191 H3 Commanda Canada
185 J3 Committee Bay Canada
129 B6 Commonwealth Bay b. Antarctica
170 C2 Como Italy
170 C2 Como, Lake Italy
145 G3 Como Chamling l. China
212 C7 Comodoro Rivadavia Arg.
176 B4 Comoé, Parc National de la nat. park Côte d'Ivoire
143 B4 Comorin, Cape India
179 E5 Comoros country Africa
166 F2 Compiègne France
206 C3 Compostela Mex.
153 C5 Compostela Phil.
214 C4 Comprida, Ilha i. Brazil
190 C5 Compton U.S.A.
173 D6 Comrat Moldova
162 E4 Comrie U.K.
199 C6 Comstock U.S.A.
154 C1 Con, Sông r. Vietnam
145 H4 Cona China
176 A4 Conakry Guinea
215 C4 Cona Niyeo Arg.
127 G8 Conara Australia
214 C2 Conceição r. Brazil
214 E2 Conceição da Barra Brazil
211 I5 Conceição do Araguaia Brazil
212 C3 Concepción Arg.
210 F7 Concepción Bol.
215 B3 Concepción Chile
Concepción Panama see La Concepción
212 E2 Concepción Para.
215 E2 Concepción del Uruguay Arg.
196 B4 Conception, Point U.S.A.
189 J4 Conception Bay South Canada
201 F7 Conception Island Bahamas
214 C3 Conchas Brazil
195 F5 Conchas Lake U.S.A.
197 H4 Concho U.S.A.
206 C2 Conchos r. Chihuahua Mex.
207 E2 Conchos r. Nuevo León/Tamaulipas Mex.
196 A3 Concord CA U.S.A.
201 D5 Concord NC U.S.A.
203 H3 Concord NH U.S.A.
129 C6 Concordia research stn Antarctica
215 F1 Concordia Arg.
180 B4 Concordia S. Africa
198 D4 Concordia U.S.A.
139 H5 Concord Peak Afgh.
127 I1 Condamine Australia
154 C3 Côn Đao Vietnam
206 H5 Condega Nicaragua
214 E1 Condeúba Brazil
127 G4 Condobolin Australia
166 E5 Condom France
194 B2 Condon U.S.A.
164 D4 Condroz reg. Belgium
201 C6 Conecuh r. U.S.A.
170 E2 Conegliano Italy
206 D2 Conejos Mex.
202 D4 Conemaugh r. U.S.A.
191 G4 Conestogo Lake Canada
202 E3 Conesus Lake U.S.A.
Coney Island Sing. see Serangoon, Pulau
203 G4 Coney Island U.S.A.
124 F3 Conflict Group is P.N.G.
166 E3 Confolens France
197 F2 Confusion Range mts U.S.A.
145 F3 Congdü China
149 D6 Conghua China
149 C5 Congjiang China
161 E4 Congleton U.K.
178 B4 Congo country Africa
178 B3 Congo r. Africa
178 C4 Congo, Democratic Republic of the country Africa
219 J6 Congo Cone sea feature S. Atlantic Ocean
214 D3 Congonhas Brazil
197 F4 Congress U.S.A.
215 B3 Conguillo, Parque Nacional nat. park Chile
161 G4 Coningsby U.K.
188 D4 Coniston Canada
160 D3 Coniston U.K.
187 G3 Conklin Canada
122 B4 Conkouati-Douli, Parc National de nat. park Congo
215 D2 Conlara Arg.
215 D2 Conlara r. Arg.
163 B3 Conn, Lough l. Ireland
202 C4 Conneaut U.S.A.
200 F3 Connecticut r. U.S.A.
203 G4 Connecticut state U.S.A.
202 D4 Connellsville U.S.A.
163 B4 Connemara reg. Ireland
203 I1 Conners Canada
200 C4 Connersville U.S.A.
126 F4 Conoble Australia
Co Nôi Vietnam see Yên Châu
203 E5 Conowingo U.S.A.
194 E1 Conrad U.S.A.
219 L9 Conrad Rise sea feature Southern Ocean
199 E6 Conroe U.S.A.
214 D3 Conselheiro Lafaiete Brazil
214 E2 Conselheiro Pena Brazil
160 F3 Consett U.K.
154 C3 Côn Sơn, Đao i. Vietnam
187 G4 Consort Canada
168 D7 Constance, Lake Germany/Switz.
210 F5 Constância dos Baetas Brazil
171 M2 Constanța Romania
167 D4 Constantina Spain
176 C1 Constantine Alg.
190 E5 Constantine U.S.A.
197 E6 Constitución de 1857, Parque Nacional nat. park Mex.
194 D3 Contact U.S.A.
210 C5 Contamana Peru
214 E1 Contas r. Brazil
197 G6 Continental U.S.A.
203 H3 Contoocook r. U.S.A.
187 G1 Contwoyto Lake Canada
199 E5 Conway AR U.S.A.
203 H3 Conway NH U.S.A.
201 E5 Conway SC U.S.A.
126 A2 Conway, Lake salt flat Australia
161 D4 Conwy U.K.
161 D4 Conwy r. U.K.
124 D4 Coober Pedy Australia
190 A2 Cook U.S.A.
186 D4 Cook, Cape Canada
125 G3 Cook, Grand Récif de reef New Caledonia
Cook, Mount mt. N.Z. see Aoraki/Mount Cook
201 C4 Cookeville U.S.A.
181 F6 Cookhouse S. Africa
184 C3 Cook Inlet sea chan. U.S.A.
123 I5 Cook Islands Pacific Ocean
203 F3 Cooksburg U.S.A.
189 I3 Cook's Harbour Canada
163 E3 Cookstown U.K.
128 E4 Cook Strait N.Z.
124 E3 Cooktown Australia
127 G3 Coolabah Australia
127 H3 Coolah Australia
127 G5 Coolamon Australia
127 J2 Coolangatta Australia
124 C5 Coolgardie Australia
197 G5 Coolidge U.S.A.
197 G5 Coolidge Dam U.S.A.
127 H6 Cooma Australia
163 A6 Coomacarrea h. Ireland
126 D4 Coombah Australia
163 B6 Coomnadiha h. Ireland
126 C5 Coonalpyn Australia
127 H3 Coonamble Australia
126 D6 Coonawarra Australia
126 A3 Coondambo Australia
127 F1 Coongoola Australia
126 C2 Cooper Creek watercourse Australia
127 J3 Coopernook Australia
203 I2 Coopers Mills U.S.A.
201 E7 Cooper's Town Bahamas
198 D2 Cooperstown ND U.S.A.
203 F3 Cooperstown NY U.S.A.
194 A3 Coos Bay U.S.A.
127 H5 Cootamundra Australia
163 D3 Cootehill Ireland
215 B3 Copahue, Volcán vol. Chile
207 F4 Copainalá Mex.
207 E4 Copala Mex.
207 E4 Copalillo Mex.
207 G5 Copán tourist site Hond.
194 G4 Cope U.S.A.
159 K5 Copenhagen Denmark
127 I2 Copeton Reservoir Australia
154 C1 Cô Pi, Phou mt. Laos/Vietnam
212 B3 Copiapó Chile
212 B3 Copiapo r. Chile
126 C3 Copley Australia
170 D2 Copparo Italy
191 G2 Copper Cliff Canada
190 D2 Copper Harbor U.S.A.
Coppermine Canada see Kugluktuk
184 G3 Coppermine r. Canada
190 E2 Coppermine Point Canada
180 E4 Copperton S. Africa
145 F3 Coqên China
215 B1 Coquimbo Chile
215 B1 Coquimbo admin. reg. Chile
171 K3 Corabia Romania
214 D2 Coração de Jesus Brazil
210 D7 Coracora Peru
127 J2 Coraki Australia
124 B4 Coral Bay Australia
201 D7 Coral Gables U.S.A.
185 J3 Coral Harbour Canada
125 F3 Coral Sea Coral Sea Is Terr.
216 F6 Coral Sea Basin S. Pacific Ocean
124 F3 Coral Sea Islands Territory terr. Pacific Ocean
190 B5 Coralville Reservoir U.S.A.
126 E7 Corangamite, Lake Australia
211 G3 Corantijn r. Suriname
137 L1 Corat Azer.
164 B5 Corbeny France
215 E2 Corbett Arg.
187 K2 Corbett Inlet Canada
164 A5 Corbie France
202 A6 Corbin U.S.A.
161 G5 Corby U.K.
196 C3 Corcoran U.S.A.
212 B6 Corcovado, Golfo de sea chan. Chile
206 I6 Corcovado, Parque Nacional nat. park Costa Rica
201 D6 Cordele U.S.A.
213 B4 Cordillera de los Picachos, Parque Nacional nat. park Col.
153 B4 Cordilleras Range mts Phil.
215 D1 Córdoba Córdoba Arg.
215 C4 Córdoba Río Negro Arg.
215 D2 Córdoba prov. Arg.
206 D2 Córdoba Durango Mex.
207 E4 Córdoba Veracruz Mex.
167 D4 Córdoba Spain
215 D2 Córdoba, Sierras de mts Arg.
184 D3 Cordova U.S.A.
186 C4 Cordova Bay U.S.A.
203 J2 Corea U.S.A.
171 H5 Corfu i. Greece
167 C3 Coria Spain
127 I4 Coricudgy mt. Australia
170 G5 Corigliano Calabro Italy
127 F8 Corinna Australia

Corinna

203 I2 Corinna U.S.A.
187 I4 Corinne Canada
171 J6 Corinth Greece
199 F5 Corinth MS U.S.A.
203 G3 Corinth NY U.S.A.
171 J5 Corinth, Gulf of sea chan. Greece
214 D2 Corinto Brazil
211 G7 Corixa Grande r. Bol./Brazil
214 A2 Corixinha r. Brazil
163 C6 Cork Ireland
170 E6 Corleone Sicily Italy
136 A1 Çorlu Turkey
187 I4 Cormorant Canada
181 H3 Cornelia S. Africa
214 B3 Cornélio Procópio Brazil
190 B3 Cornell U.S.A.
189 I4 Corner Brook Canada
127 G7 Corner Inlet b. Australia
219 F3 Corner Seamounts sea feature N. Atlantic Ocean
164 C5 Cornillet, Mont h. France
196 A2 Corning CA U.S.A.
202 E3 Corning NY U.S.A.
Corn Islands is Nicaragua see Maíz, Islas del
170 E3 Corno Grande mt. Italy
188 F4 Cornwall Canada
185 I2 Cornwallis Island Canada
126 B5 Corny Point Australia
213 C2 Coro Venez.
211 J4 Coroatá Brazil
210 E7 Corocoro Bol.
163 B5 Corofin Ireland
210 E7 Coroico Bol.
214 C2 Coromandel Brazil
135 G5 Coromandel Coast India
128 E2 Coromandel Peninsula N.Z.
128 E2 Coromandel Range hills N.Z.
153 B3 Coron Phil.
126 D3 Corona Australia
196 D5 Corona U.S.A.
196 D5 Coronado U.S.A.
206 I6 Coronado, Bahía de b. Costa Rica
215 B4 Coronados, Golfo de los b. Chile
187 G4 Coronation Canada
184 G3 Coronation Gulf Canada
129 C2 Coronation Island i. S. Atlantic Ocean
186 C3 Coronation Island U.S.A.
153 B4 Coron Bay Phil.
215 E1 Coronda Arg.
215 E2 Coronel Brandsen Arg.
215 E3 Coronel Dorrego Arg.
212 E3 Coronel Oviedo Para.
214 A1 Coronel Ponce Brazil
215 E3 Coronel Pringles Arg.
214 A3 Coronel Sapucaia Brazil
215 E3 Coronel Suárez Arg.
215 F3 Coronel Vidal Arg.
210 D7 Coropuna, Nudo mt. Peru
171 I4 Çorovodë Albania
127 G5 Corowa Australia
207 G4 Corozal Belize
199 D7 Corpus Christi U.S.A.
199 D6 Corpus Christi, Lake U.S.A.
210 E7 Corque Bol.
167 D3 Corral de Cantos mt. Spain
215 C1 Corral de Isaac Arg.
211 I6 Corrente Brazil
214 D1 Corrente r. Bahia Brazil
214 C1 Corrente r. Goiás Brazil
214 B2 Corrente r. Minas Gerais Brazil
214 A2 Correntes Brazil
214 A2 Correntes r. Brazil
214 D1 Correntina Brazil
163 B4 Corrib, Lough l. Ireland
212 E3 Corrientes Arg.
212 E3 Corrientes r. Arg.
215 F3 Corrientes, Cabo c. Arg.
213 A3 Corrientes, Cabo c. Col.
206 C3 Corrientes, Cabo Mex.
199 E6 Corrigan U.S.A.
161 D5 Corris U.K.
202 D4 Corry U.S.A.
127 G6 Corryong Australia
Corse i. France see Corsica
170 C3 Corse, Cap c. Corsica France
161 E6 Corsham U.K.
166 I5 Corsica i. France
199 D5 Corsicana U.S.A.
170 C3 Corte Corsica France
167 C4 Cortegana Spain
197 H3 Cortez U.S.A.
196 D1 Cortez Mountains U.S.A.
170 E1 Cortina d'Ampezzo Italy
203 E3 Cortland U.S.A.
161 I5 Corton U.K.
170 D3 Cortona Italy
167 B3 Coruche Port.
137 H1 Çoruh r. Turkey
136 E1 Çorum Turkey
211 G7 Corumbá Brazil
214 C2 Corumbá r. Brazil
214 C2 Corumbaíba Brazil
213 E3 Corumo r. Venez.
194 B2 Corvallis U.S.A.
161 D5 Corwen U.K.
206 C2 Cosalá Mex.
170 G5 Cosenza Italy
202 C4 Coshocton U.S.A.
166 F3 Cosne-Cours-sur-Loire France
215 D1 Cosquín Arg.
167 F3 Costa Blanca coastal area Spain
167 H2 Costa Brava coastal area France/Spain
167 C5 Costa de la Luz coastal area Spain
167 D4 Costa del Sol coastal area Spain
206 H6 Costa Rica country Central America
206 C2 Costa Rica Mex.
171 K2 Costești Romania
203 I2 Costigan U.S.A.
165 K3 Coswig (Anhalt) Germany
153 C5 Cotabato Phil.
213 A4 Cotacachi, Cerro mt. Ecuador
210 E8 Cotagaita Bol.
214 E2 Cotaxé r. Brazil
186 C3 Cote, Mount U.S.A.
176 B4 Côte d'Ivoire country Africa
161 D5 Cothi r. U.K.
167 G1 Cotiella mt. Spain
213 E3 Cotingo r. Brazil
176 C4 Cotonou Benin
210 C4 Cotopaxi, Volcán vol. Ecuador
161 E6 Cotswold Hills U.K.
194 B3 Cottage Grove U.S.A.
168 G5 Cottbus Germany
143 B3 Cottellar r. India
161 H5 Cottenham U.K.
190 D3 Cotton City U.S.A.
197 F4 Cottonwood U.S.A.
197 G4 Cottonwood Wash watercourse U.S.A.
199 D6 Cotulla U.S.A.
202 D4 Coudersport U.S.A.
126 B6 Couedic, Cape du Australia
129 B5 Coulman Island i. Antarctica
166 F2 Coulommiers France
191 I2 Coulonge r. Canada
196 B3 Coulterville U.S.A.
194 C2 Council U.S.A.
198 E3 Council Bluffs U.S.A.
126 F7 Councillor Island Australia
187 G2 Courageous Lake Canada
159 M5 Courland Lagoon b. Lith./Russia
186 E5 Courtenay Canada
163 C6 Courtmacsherry Ireland
163 E5 Courtown Ireland
199 E5 Coushatta U.S.A.
166 D2 Coutances France
188 E2 Couture, Lac l. Canada
164 C4 Couvin Belgium
197 F2 Cove Fort U.S.A.
191 G3 Cove Island Canada
202 E5 Cove Mountains hills U.S.A.
161 F5 Coventry U.K.
203 E5 Cove Point U.S.A.
167 C2 Covilhã Port.
201 D5 Covington GA U.S.A.
190 D5 Covington IN U.S.A.
202 A5 Covington KY U.S.A.
201 B5 Covington TN U.S.A.
202 D6 Covington VA U.S.A.
191 F2 Cow r. Canada
127 G4 Cowal, Lake dry lake Australia
124 C5 Cowan, Lake salt flat Australia
203 G2 Cowansville Canada
162 E4 Cowdenbeath U.K.
126 B4 Cowell Australia
126 F7 Cowes Australia
161 F7 Cowes U.K.
160 E3 Cow Green Reservoir U.K.
202 D5 Cowpasture r. U.S.A.
127 H4 Cowra Australia
214 D1 Coxá r. Brazil
215 F1 Coxilha de Santana hills Brazil/Uruguay
214 A2 Coxim Brazil
214 A2 Coxim r. Brazil
203 G3 Coxsackie U.S.A.
145 H5 Cox's Bazar Bangl.
206 B2 Coyote, Punta pt Mex.
196 D4 Coyote Lake U.S.A.
197 E5 Coyote Peak h. U.S.A.
196 C3 Coyote Peak U.S.A.
206 C3 Coyotitán Mex.
207 D4 Coyuca de Benítez Mex.
145 F2 Cozhê Xizang Zizhiqu China
145 F3 Cozhê Xizang Zizhiqu China
171 K2 Cozia, Vârful mt. Romania
207 H3 Cozumel Mex.
207 H3 Cozumel, Isla de i. Mex.
127 H4 Craboon Australia
127 G8 Cradle Mountain Australia
127 G8 Cradle Mountain Lake St Clair National Park Australia
126 C3 Cradock Australia
181 F6 Cradock S. Africa
162 C3 Craig U.K.
186 C3 Craig AL U.S.A.
194 F3 Craig CO U.S.A.
163 E3 Craigavon U.K.
126 F6 Craigieburn Australia
202 D5 Craigsville U.S.A.
162 F4 Crail U.K.
165 I5 Crailsheim Germany
171 J2 Craiova Romania
160 F2 Cramlington U.K.
203 F2 Cranberry Lake U.S.A.
203 F2 Cranberry Lake l. U.S.A.
126 F7 Cranbourne Australia
186 F5 Cranbrook Canada
190 C3 Crandon U.S.A.
194 C3 Crane OR U.S.A.
199 C6 Crane TX U.S.A.
190 A1 Crane Lake U.S.A.
203 H4 Cranston U.S.A.
129 B5 Crary Ice Rise ice feature Antarctica
129 B4 Crary Mountains mts Antarctica
194 B3 Crater Lake U.S.A.
194 B3 Crater Lake National Park U.S.A.
194 D3 Craters of the Moon National Monument nat. park U.S.A.
211 J5 Crateús Brazil
211 K5 Crato Brazil
213 C3 Cravo Norte Col.
213 C3 Cravo Sur r. Col.
198 C3 Crawford U.S.A.
190 D5 Crawfordsville U.S.A.
201 C6 Crawfordville U.S.A.
161 G6 Crawley U.K.
194 E2 Crazy Mountains U.S.A.
162 D4 Creag Meagaidh mt. U.K.
187 H4 Crean Lake Canada
161 E5 Credenhill U.K.
161 D7 Crediton U.K.
187 H3 Cree r. Canada
206 C2 Creel Mex.
187 H3 Cree Lake Canada
187 I4 Creighton Canada
164 A5 Creil France
164 D2 Creil Neth.
165 I2 Cremlingen Germany
170 D2 Cremona Italy
166 F2 Crépy-en-Valois France
170 F2 Cres i. Croatia
194 A3 Crescent City U.S.A.
149 □ Crescent Island Hong Kong China
197 H2 Crescent Junction U.S.A.
196 B1 Crescent Mills U.S.A.
197 E4 Crescent Peak U.S.A.
190 A4 Cresco U.S.A.
215 E2 Crespo Arg.
126 E7 Cressy Australia
186 F5 Creston Canada
198 E3 Creston IA U.S.A.
194 F3 Creston WY U.S.A.
201 C6 Crestview U.S.A.
203 F5 Crestwood Village U.S.A.
126 E6 Creswick Australia
171 K7 Crete i. Greece
167 H1 Creus, Cap de c. Spain
166 E3 Creuse r. France
165 J5 Creußen Germany
164 E5 Creutzwald France
165 I3 Creuzburg Germany
161 E4 Crewe U.K.
202 D6 Crewe U.S.A.
161 E7 Crewkerne U.K.
162 D4 Crianlarich U.K.
161 C5 Criccieth U.K.
212 G3 Criciúma Brazil
162 E4 Crieff U.K.
162 E6 Criffel h. U.K.
Criffell hill U.K. see Criffel
170 F2 Crikvenica Croatia
173 E6 Crimea disp. terr. Europe
165 K4 Crimmitschau Germany
162 G3 Crimond U.K.
203 F6 Crisfield U.S.A.
214 C2 Cristalina Brazil
213 B2 Cristóbal Colón, Pico mt. Col.
214 C1 Crixás Brazil
214 C1 Crixás Açu r. Brazil
214 B1 Crixás Mirim r. Brazil
171 H3 Crna Gora aut. rep. Europe
170 F2 Črnomelj Slovenia
163 B4 Croagh Patrick h. Ireland
127 H6 Croajingolong National Park Australia
170 G2 Croatia country Europe
155 E2 Crocker, Banjaran mts Malaysia
199 E6 Crockett U.S.A.
203 F3 Croghan U.S.A.
164 A4 Croisilles France
124 D3 Croker Island Australia
162 D3 Cromarty U.K.
162 D3 Cromarty Firth est. U.K.
162 E3 Cromdale, Hills of U.K.
161 I5 Cromer U.K.
128 B6 Cromwell N.Z.
160 F3 Crook U.K.
202 D4 Crooked Creek Reservoir U.S.A.
205 J4 Crooked Island Bahamas
149 □ Crooked Island Hong Kong China
205 J4 Crooked Island Passage Bahamas
190 B1 Crooked Lake Canada/U.S.A.
198 D2 Crookston U.S.A.
127 H5 Crookwell Australia
163 C5 Croom Ireland
127 I2 Croppa Creek Australia
160 D4 Crosby U.K.
187 I5 Crosby U.S.A.
187 K2 Cross Bay Canada
201 D6 Cross City U.S.A.
203 J1 Cross Creek Canada
199 E5 Crossett U.S.A.
160 E3 Cross Fell h. U.K.
163 F3 Crossgar U.K.
161 C5 Cross Inn U.K.
187 J4 Cross Lake Canada
187 J4 Cross Lake l. Canada
202 E3 Cross Lake l. U.S.A.
128 D5 Crossley, Mount N.Z.
163 E3 Crossmaglen U.K.
197 E4 Crossman Peak U.S.A.
186 B3 Cross Sound sea chan. U.S.A.
190 E3 Cross Village U.S.A.
201 C5 Crossville U.S.A.
191 F4 Croswell U.S.A.
170 G5 Crotone Italy
161 H6 Crouch r. U.K.
126 B3 Crowal watercourse Australia
161 H6 Crowborough U.K.
127 F4 Crowl watercourse Australia
161 G5 Crowland U.K.
199 E6 Crowley U.S.A.
196 C3 Crowley, Lake U.S.A.
190 D5 Crown Point IN U.S.A.
203 G3 Crown Point NY U.S.A.
127 J1 Crows Nest Australia
186 G5 Crowsnest Pass Canada
161 G6 Croydon U.K.
218 H8 Crozet, Îles is Indian Ocean
219 N8 Crozet Basin sea feature Indian Ocean
218 G7 Crozet Plateau sea feature Indian Ocean
184 G2 Crozier Channel Canada
166 B2 Crozon France
213 B4 Cruces, Paso de las mt. Col.
162 G3 Cruden Bay U.K.
207 E2 Cruillas Mex.
163 E3 Crumlin U.K.
163 C5 Crusheen Ireland
205 I5 Cruz, Cabo c. Cuba
212 F3 Cruz Alta Brazil
215 D1 Cruz del Eje Arg.
214 D3 Cruzeiro Brazil
210 D5 Cruzeiro do Sul Brazil
197 H5 Cruzville U.S.A.
186 E3 Crysdale, Mount Canada
126 C4 Crystal Brook Australia
199 D6 Crystal City U.S.A.
190 C2 Crystal Falls U.S.A.
190 C4 Crystal Lake U.S.A.
169 J7 Csongrád Hungary
137 J5 Ctesiphon tourist site Iraq
213 D2 Cúa Venez.
154 C3 Cửa Lớn, Sông r. Vietnam
179 C5 Cuando r. Angola/Zambia
179 B5 Cuangar Angola
178 B4 Cuango r. Angola/Dem. Rep. Congo
179 B4 Cuanza r. Angola
213 D3 Cuao r. Venez.
215 F1 Cuaró r. Uruguay
215 D2 Cuarto r. Arg.
206 D2 Cuatro Ciénegas Mex.
206 C1 Cuauhtémoc Mex.
207 E4 Cuautla Mex.
205 I4 Cuba country Caribbean Sea
190 B5 Cuba IL U.S.A.
195 F4 Cuba NM U.S.A.
197 F6 Cubabi, Cerro mt. Mex.
179 B5 Cubal Angola
179 B5 Cubango r. Angola/Namibia
213 B3 Cubará Col.
187 I4 Cub Hills Canada
136 D1 Çubuk Turkey
215 F1 Cuchilla Grande hills Uruguay
215 F1 Cuchilla Grande Inferior hills Uruguay
215 D3 Cuchillo-Có Arg.
213 D3 Cuchivero r. Venez.
202 E6 Cuckoo U.S.A.
213 D4 Cucuí Brazil
213 B3 Cúcuta Col.
143 B4 Cuddalore India
Cuddapah India see Kadapa
187 H4 Cudworth Canada
167 D2 Cuéllar Spain
179 B5 Cuemba Angola
210 C4 Cuenca Ecuador
167 E2 Cuenca Spain
167 E2 Cuenca, Serranía de mts Spain
206 D2 Cuencamé Mex.
207 E4 Cuernavaca Mex.
199 D6 Cuero U.S.A.
196 B4 Cuesta Pass U.S.A.
207 E3 Cuetzalán Mex.
213 C2 Cueva de la Quebrada del Toro, Parque Nacional nat. park Venez.
171 J2 Cugir Romania
211 G5 Cuiabá Amazonas Brazil
214 A1 Cuiabá Mato Grosso Brazil
214 A2 Cuiabá r. Brazil
214 A1 Cuiabá de Larga Brazil
207 E4 Cuicatlan Mex.
164 D3 Cuijk Neth.
207 G5 Cuilapa Guat.
163 D3 Cuilcagh h. Ireland/U.K.
162 B3 Cuillin Hills U.K.
162 B3 Cuillin Sound sea chan. U.K.
179 B4 Cuilo Angola
214 E2 Cuité r. Brazil
179 B5 Cuito r. Angola
179 B5 Cuito Cuanavale Angola
206 D4 Cuitzeo, Laguna de l. Mex.
155 B2 Cukai Malaysia
137 I3 Çukurca Turkey
194 F1 Culbertson MT U.S.A.
198 C3 Culbertson NE U.S.A.
127 G5 Culcairn Australia
167 C2 Culebra, Sierra de la mts Spain
137 J2 Culfa Azer.
127 G2 Culgoa r. Australia
206 C2 Culiacán Mex.
153 A4 Culion Phil.
153 A4 Culion i. Phil.
162 F3 Cullen U.K.
167 F3 Cullera Spain
162 □ Cullivoe U.K.
201 C5 Cullman U.S.A.
137 H2 Çullu Turkey
163 E3 Cullybackey U.K.
162 C2 Cul Mòr h. U.K.
202 D5 Culpeper U.S.A.
211 H6 Culuene r. Brazil
128 D5 Culverden N.Z.
162 D5 Culzean Bay U.K.
213 D2 Cumaná Venez.
213 B4 Cumare, Cerro h. Col.
213 A4 Cumbal, Nevado de vol. Col.
202 D5 Cumberland MD U.S.A.
190 A3 Cumberland WI U.S.A.
200 C4 Cumberland r. U.S.A.
187 I4 Cumberland House Canada
187 I4 Cumberland Lake Canada
202 B6 Cumberland Mountains U.S.A.
185 L3 Cumberland Peninsula Canada
200 C4 Cumberland Plateau U.S.A.
190 C2 Cumberland Point U.S.A.
185 L3 Cumberland Sound sea chan. Canada
162 E5 Cumbernauld U.K.
206 D2 Cumbres de Monterey, Parque Nacional nat. park Mex.
165 J1 Cumlosen Germany
196 A2 Cummings U.S.A.
126 A5 Cummins Australia
162 D5 Cumnock U.K.
136 D3 Çumra Turkey
206 B1 Cumuripa Mex.
207 F4 Cunduacán Mex.
207 G5 Cunén Guat.
179 B5 Cunene r. Angola/Namibia
alt. Kunene
170 B2 Cuneo Italy
126 A4 Cungena Australia
154 D2 Cung Sơn Vietnam
137 G2 Çüngüş Turkey
127 F2 Cunnamulla Australia
162 □ Cunningsburgh U.K.
213 D4 Cunucunuma r. Venez.
170 B2 Cuorgnè Italy
162 E4 Cupar U.K.
213 A3 Cupica Col.
213 A3 Cupica, Golfo de b. Col.
206 B2 Cupula, Pico mt. Mex.
211 K5 Curaçá Brazil
205 K6 Curaçao terr. West Indies
215 B3 Curacautín Chile
215 D3 Curacó r. Arg.
215 B3 Curanilahue Chile
210 D4 Curaray r. Ecuador
215 B2 Curaumilla, Punta pt Chile
126 B3 Curdlawidny Lagoon salt flat Australia
195 F4 Curecanti National Recreation Area park U.S.A.
215 B2 Curicó Chile
213 D5 Curicuriari, Serra h. Brazil
213 D5 Curieuriari r. Brazil
214 C4 Curitiba Brazil
126 C3 Curnamona Australia
127 I3 Currabubula Australia
211 K5 Currais Novos Brazil
176 □ Curral Velho Cape Verde
191 F3 Curran U.S.A.
163 A6 Currane, Lough l. Ireland
197 E2 Currant U.S.A.
126 F3 Curranyalpa Australia
201 E7 Current Bahamas
127 E7 Currie Australia
197 E1 Currie U.S.A.
127 I5 Currockbilly, Mount Australia
127 G7 Curtis Group is Australia
124 F4 Curtis Island Australia
211 H5 Curuá r. Brazil
211 I4 Curuçá Brazil
155 B3 Curup Indon.
213 D4 Curupira, Serra mts Brazil/Venez.
211 J4 Cururupu Brazil
213 E3 Curutú, Cerro mt. Venez.
214 D2 Curvelo Brazil
210 D6 Cusco Peru
163 E2 Cushendall U.K.
163 E2 Cushendun U.K.
199 D4 Cushing U.S.A.
213 C3 Cusiana r. Col.
206 C1 Cusihuiráchic Mex.
201 C5 Cusseta U.S.A.
190 A1 Cusson U.S.A.
188 E1 Cusson, Pointe pt Canada
194 F2 Custer MT U.S.A.
198 C3 Custer SD U.S.A.
213 A4 Cutanga, Pico de mt. Col.
194 D1 Cut Bank U.S.A.
201 C6 Cuthbert U.S.A.
187 H4 Cut Knife Canada
203 J2 Cutler U.S.A.
201 D7 Cutler Ridge U.S.A.
215 C3 Cutral-Có Arg.
145 F5 Cuttack India
190 D5 Cutter U.S.A.
165 G1 Cuxhaven Germany
202 C4 Cuyahoga Falls U.S.A.
202 C4 Cuyahoga Valley National Park U.S.A.
196 C4 Cuyama r. U.S.A.
153 B3 Cuyapo Phil.
153 B4 Cuyo Phil.
153 B4 Cuyo i. Phil.
153 B4 Cuyo East Passage Phil.
153 B4 Cuyo Islands Phil.
153 B4 Cuyo West Passage Phil.
213 E3 Cuyuni r. Guyana
Cuzco Peru see Cusco
161 D6 Cwmbrân U.K.
178 C4 Cyangugu Rwanda
171 K6 Cyclades is Greece
127 G9 Cygnet Australia
202 A5 Cynthiana U.S.A.
187 G5 Cypress Hills Canada
136 D4 Cyprus country Asia
187 G4 Czar Canada
168 G6 Czech Republic country Europe
168 H4 Czersk Poland
169 I5 Częstochowa Poland

D

Đa, Sông r. Vietnam see Black
152 C1 Da'an China
213 C2 Dabajuro Venez.
176 B4 Dabakala Côte d'Ivoire
148 F1 Daban China
148 A2 Daban Shan mts China
148 C3 Daba Shan mts China
213 B3 Dabeiba Col.
165 J1 Dabel Germany
144 C5 Dabhoi India
143 A2 Dabhol India
148 E4 Dabie Shan mts China
144 D4 Daboh India
176 A3 Dabola Guinea
176 B4 Daboya Ghana
148 C2 Dabqig China
144 D4 Dabra India
169 I5 Dąbrowa Górnicza Poland
152 B1 Dabs Nur l. China
149 E5 Dabu China
Dacca Bangl. see Dhaka
168 E6 Dachau Germany
148 A2 Dachechang China
Dachengzi China see Harqin
143 B2 Dachepalle India
Đắc Lắc, Cao Nguyên plat. Vietnam see Đắk Lắk, Cao Nguyên
191 I3 Dacre Canada
178 E3 Dadaab Kenya
136 D1 Daday Turkey
201 D6 Dade City U.S.A.
144 C5 Dadra India
144 C5 Dadra and Nagar Haveli union terr. India
144 A4 Dadu Pak.
149 B4 Dadu He r. China
152 D5 Daecheong-do i. N. Korea
152 E6 Daegu S. Korea
152 C6 Daeheuksan-gundo is S. Korea
152 D5 Daejeon S. Korea
152 D7 Daejeong S. Korea
153 B3 Daet Phil.
149 B5 Dafang China
148 F3 Dafeng China
145 H4 Dafla Hills India
176 A3 Dagana Senegal
173 H7 Dagestan, Respublika aut. rep. Russia
Dağlıq Qarabağ disp. terr. Azer. see Nagorno-Karabakh
149 B5 Daguan China
148 F2 Dagu He r. China
149 □ D'Aguilar Peak h. Hong Kong China
153 B2 Dagupan Phil.
145 H1 Dagur China
145 G3 Dagzê China
145 F3 Dagzê Co salt l. China
144 C6 Dahanu India
150 C1 Dahe China
148 D1 Dahei He r. China
152 C2 Dahei Shan mts China
146 D2 Da Hinggan Ling mts China
178 E2 Dahlak Archipelago is Eritrea
178 E2 Dahlak Marine National Park Eritrea
164 E4 Dahlem Germany
165 I1 Dahlenburg Germany
170 C7 Dahmani Tunisia
165 F5 Dahn Germany
144 C5 Dahod India
144 D2 Dahongliutan China
165 I2 Dähre Germany
137 I3 Dahūk/Dihok Iraq
152 C3 Dahuofang Shuiku resr China
152 B3 Dahushan China
148 D1 Dai Hai l. China
155 B3 Daik Indon.
154 D2 Đại Lanh, Mui pt Vietnam
162 D5 Dailly U.K.
151 C6 Daimanji-san h. Japan
167 E3 Daimiel Spain
163 A5 Daingean Uí Chúis Ireland
215 E3 Daireaux Arg.
190 A2 Dairyland U.S.A.
151 C7 Dai-sen vol. Japan
150 H3 Daisetsu-zan National Park Japan
149 G4 Daishan China
149 F5 Daiyun Shan mts China
124 D4 Dajarra Australia
148 A4 Dajin Chuan r. China
148 B2 Dajing China
145 H1 Da Juh China
176 A3 Dakar Senegal
145 G3 Dakelangsi China
177 E2 Dākhilah, Wāḥāt ad oasis Egypt
145 G5 Dakhin Shahbazpur Island Bangl.
176 A2 Dakhla W. Sahara
Dakhla Oasis Egypt see Dākhilah, Wāḥāt ad
Dak Kon Vietnam see Plei Kân
154 D2 Đăk Lăk, Cao Nguyên plat. Vietnam
172 D4 Dakol'ka r. Belarus
198 D3 Dakota City U.S.A.
Đakovica Serbia see Gjakovë
171 H2 Đakovo Croatia
179 C5 Dala Angola
176 A3 Dalaba Guinea
148 E1 Dalain Hob China
148 E1 Dalai Nur l. China
137 K4 Dālā Khānī, Kūh-e mt. Iraq
140 C4 Dalaki, Rūd-e r. Iran
148 D1 Dalamamiao China
136 B3 Dalaman Turkey
136 B3 Dalaman r. Turkey
146 C2 Dalandzadgad Mongolia
153 B4 Dalanganem Islands Phil.
154 D3 Đa Lat Vietnam
Dalay Mongolia see Bayandalay
141 G4 Dalbandin Pak.
162 E6 Dalbeattie U.K.
127 I1 Dalby Australia
160 C3 Dalby U.K.
158 I3 Dale Hordaland Norway
159 I3 Dale Sogn og Fjordane Norway
202 E5 Dale City U.S.A.
199 G4 Dale Hollow Lake U.S.A.
164 E2 Dalen Neth.
145 H6 Dalet Myanmar
145 H5 Daletme Myanmar
159 K3 Dalfors Sweden
141 E5 Dalgān Iran
126 D4 Dalgety Australia
199 C4 Dalhart U.S.A.
189 G4 Dalhousie Canada
148 D3 Dali Shaanxi China
146 C4 Dali Yunnan China
152 A4 Dalian China
149 B4 Daliang Shan mts China
152 B2 Dalin China
148 F1 Daling He r. China
152 D3 Dalizi China
162 E5 Dalkeith U.K.
145 F4 Dalkola India
203 F4 Dallas PA U.S.A.
199 D5 Dallas TX U.S.A.
194 B2 Dalles City U.S.A.
186 C4 Dall Island U.S.A.
140 D5 Dalmā i. U.A.E.
215 D2 Dalmacio Vélez Sarsfield Arg.
170 G3 Dalmatia reg. Bos. & Herz./Croatia
144 E4 Dalmau India
162 D5 Dalmellington U.K.
150 D2 Dal'negorsk Russia
150 C2 Dal'nerechensk Russia
176 B4 Daloa Côte d'Ivoire
149 C5 Dalou Shan mts China
140 B5 Dalqān well Saudi Arabia
162 D5 Dalry U.K.
162 D5 Dalrymple U.K.
124 E4 Dalrymple, Lake Australia
124 E4 Dalrymple, Mount Australia
191 E1 Dalton Canada
181 I4 Dalton S. Africa
201 C5 Dalton GA U.S.A.
203 G3 Dalton MA U.S.A.
145 F4 Daltonganj India
160 D3 Dalton-in-Furness U.K.
191 E1 Dalton Mills Canada
163 C4 Dalua r. Ireland
153 B2 Dalupiri i. Phil.
153 C3 Dalupiri i. Phil.
158 C2 Dalvík Iceland
124 D3 Daly r. Australia
196 A3 Daly City U.S.A.
124 D3 Daly Waters Australia
144 C5 Daman India
144 C5 Daman and Diu union terr. India
177 F1 Damanhūr Egypt
140 C3 Damaq Iran
148 E1 Damaqun Shan mts China
153 C6 Damar Indon.
147 E7 Damar i. Indon.
215 B2 Damas, Paso de las pass Arg./Chile
136 F5 Damascus Syria
176 D3 Damaturu Nigeria
140 D3 Damāvand Iran
140 D3 Damāvand, Qolleh-ye mt. Iran
143 C5 Dambulla Sri Lanka
138 F2 Damdy Kazakh.
140 D2 Dāmghān Iran
Damietta Egypt see Dumyāṭ
148 E2 Daming China
149 C6 Daming Shan mt. China
145 H2 Damjong China
153 B5 Dammai i. Phil.
140 C5 Dammam Saudi Arabia
164 B3 Damme Belgium
165 G2 Damme Germany
144 D4 Damoh India
176 B4 Damongo Ghana
136 E5 Damour Lebanon
124 E2 Dampier Strait P.N.G.
147 F7 Dampir, Selat sea chan. Indon.
145 E3 Damqog Zangbo r. China
145 H2 Dam Qu r. China
154 C3 Dâmrei, Chuŏr Phnum mts Cambodia
145 H3 Damroh India
164 E1 Damwâld Neth.
178 E2 Dankalil des. Eritrea
176 B4 Danané Côte d'Ivoire
154 D1 Đa Nẵng Vietnam
148 A4 Danba China
203 G4 Danbury CT U.S.A.
203 H3 Danbury NH U.S.A.
203 G3 Danby U.S.A.
197 E4 Danby Lake U.S.A.
148 E3 Dancheng China
178 D3 Dande Eth.
143 B3 Dandeli India
126 E6 Dandenong Australia
152 C3 Dandong China
161 E4 Dane r. U.K.
185 P2 Daneborg Greenland
203 J2 Danforth U.S.A.
154 C1 Đằng, Đa r. Vietnam
149 E6 Dangan Liedao is China
145 E2 Dangbe La pass China
150 B2 Dangbi Russia
148 B3 Dangchang China
Danger Islands atoll Cook Is see Pukapuka
180 C7 Danger Point S. Africa
178 D2 Dangila Eth.
145 G3 Dangqên China
207 G4 Dangriga Belize
148 E3 Dangshan China
148 F4 Dangtu China
149 D4 Dangyang China
194 E3 Daniel U.S.A.
180 E4 Daniëlskuil S. Africa
172 G3 Danilov Russia
139 G1 Danilovka Kazakh.
173 H5 Danilovka Russia
172 G3 Danilovskaya Vozvyshennost' hills Russia
148 D2 Daning China
148 D3 Danjiangkou China
148 D3 Danjiangkou Shuiku resr China
140 E6 Đank Oman
144 D2 Dankhar India
172 F4 Dankov Russia
139 I4 Dan'kova, Pik mt. Kyrg.
206 H5 Danlí Hond.
149 B4 Danling China
203 G2 Dannemora U.S.A.
165 J1 Dannenberg (Elbe) Germany
165 J1 Dannenwalde Germany
128 F4 Dannevirke N.Z.
181 I4 Dannhauser S. Africa
154 B1 Dan Sai Thai.
149 F5 Danshui Taiwan
202 E3 Dansville U.S.A.
144 C4 Danta India
143 C2 Dantewada India
171 L3 Danube r. Europe
alt. Donau (Austria/Germany),
alt. Duna (Hungary),
alt. Dunaj (Slovakia),
alt. Dunărea (Romania),
alt. Dunav (Serbia)
171 M2 Danube Delta Romania
190 D5 Danville IL U.S.A.
190 D6 Danville IN U.S.A.
200 C4 Danville KY U.S.A.
191 I5 Danville PA U.S.A.
202 D6 Danville VA U.S.A.
148 F4 Danyang China
152 E5 Danyang S. Korea
149 C5 Danzhai China
149 C7 Danzhou China
176 B4 Daoukro Côte d'Ivoire
149 D5 Daoxian China
149 C4 Daozhen China
153 C4 Dapa Phil.
176 C3 Dapaong Togo
145 I4 Dapha Bum mt. India
136 D6 Daphnae tourist site Egypt
153 B4 Dapiak, Mount Phil.
153 B4 Dapitan Phil.
135 H3 Da Qaidam China
146 E2 Daqing China
148 D1 Daqing Shan mts China
152 A2 Daqin Tal China
149 F5 Daqiu China
140 D4 Daqq-e Dombūn Iran
137 J4 Dāqūq Iraq
149 G4 Daqu Shan i. China
136 F5 Dar'ā Syria
140 D4 Dārāb Iran
153 B4 Daraga Phil.
169 N4 Darahanava Belarus
141 E4 Dārākūyeh Iran
153 C4 Daram i. Phil.
140 D3 Darang, Kūh-e h. Iran
Đa Răng, Sông r. Vietnam see Ba, Sông
133 M4 Darasun Russia
138 F2 Darat Kazakh.
139 H5 Daraut-Korgon Kyrg.
172 G3 Daravka Russia
140 E4 Darband Iran
139 F5 Darband Uzbek.
145 F4 Darbhanga India
196 C2 Dardanelle U.S.A.
199 E5 Dardanelle, Lake U.S.A.
171 L4 Dardanelles str. Turkey
165 I3 Dardesheim Germany
136 F2 Darende Turkey
178 D4 Dar es Salaam Tanz.
170 D2 Darfo Boario Terme Italy
177 E3 Darfur reg. Sudan
144 B2 Dargai Pak.
128 D1 Dargaville N.Z.
141 E2 Dargaz Iran
127 G6 Dargo Australia
146 C2 Darhan Mongolia
148 D1 Darhan Ul China
201 D6 Darien U.S.A.
213 A2 Darién, Golfo del g. Col.
206 J7 Darién, Parque Nacional de nat. park Panama
206 J6 Darién, Serranía del mts Panama
138 B2 Dar'inskoye Kazakh.
139 H2 Dariya Kazakh.
Darjeeling India see Darjiling
145 G4 Darjiling India
126 B4 Darke Peak Australia
140 C4 Darkhazīneh Iran
126 E4 Darling r. Australia
127 H2 Darling Downs hills Australia
124 B5 Darling Range hills Australia
160 F3 Darlington U.K.
190 B4 Darlington U.S.A.
127 G5 Darlington Point Australia
168 H3 Darłowo Poland
140 B5 Darmā Saudi Arabia
145 E3 Darma Pass China/India
143 B2 Darmaraopet India
140 E4 Dar Mazār Iran
165 G5 Darmstadt Germany
144 C5 Darna r. India
177 E1 Darnah Libya
181 I4 Darnall S. Africa
126 E4 Darnick Australia
129 E5 Darnley, Cape c. Antarctica
184 F3 Darnley Bay Canada
167 F2 Daroca Spain
172 H3 Darovskoy Russia
215 D3 Darregueira Arg.
140 E3 Darreh Bid Iran
143 B3 Darsi India
161 D7 Dart r. U.K.
Darta Turkm. see Tarta
161 H6 Dartford U.K.
126 D6 Dartmoor Australia
161 C7 Dartmoor hills U.K.
161 D7 Dartmoor National Park U.K.
189 H5 Dartmouth Canada
161 D7 Dartmouth U.K.
160 F4 Darton U.K.
124 E2 Daru P.N.G.
176 A4 Daru Sierra Leone
145 G3 Darum Tso l. China
170 G2 Daruvar Croatia
Darvaza Turkm. see Içoguz
140 C4 Darvīshī Iran
141 G4 Darwāzagêy Afgh.
160 E4 Darwen U.K.
124 D3 Darwin Australia
210 □ Darwin, Isla i. Galapagos Is Ecuador
212 C8 Darwin, Monte mt. Chile
144 B3 Darya Khan Pak.
138 F3 Dar'yalyktakyr, Ravnina plain Kazakh.
141 G3 Darzāb Afgh.
141 E4 Dārzīn Iran
140 D5 Dās i. U.A.E.
152 B3 Dashiqiao China
Dashoguz Turkm. see Daşoguz
140 E2 Dasht Iran
141 F5 Dasht r. Pak.
140 C4 Dasht-e Palang r. Iran
141 F5 Dashtiari Iran
139 G5 Dashti Obburdon Tajik.
139 G4 Dashtobod Uzbek.
148 C2 Dashuikeng China
148 B2 Dashuitou China
144 C2 Daska Pak.
137 K1 Daşkäsän Azer.
141 F2 Daşköpri Turkm.
138 E4 Daşoguz Turkm.
144 C1 Daspar mt. Pak.
165 H3 Dassel Germany
180 C6 Dassen Island S. Africa
137 K2 Dastakert Armenia
140 E3 Dastgerdān Iran
152 F2 Dasuifen He r. China
171 L6 Datça Turkey
151 F6 Date Japan
197 F5 Dateland U.S.A.
144 D4 Datia India
149 E5 Datian China
148 A2 Datong Qinghai China
148 D1 Datong Shanxi China
148 B2 Datong He r. China

Donskoye

148 A2 **Datong Shan** *mts* China
155 C2 **Datu, Tanjung** *c.* Indon./Malaysia
153 C5 **Datu Piang** Phil.
172 C3 **Daugava** *r.* Belarus/Latvia
alt. **Zakhodnyaya Dzvina,**
alt. **Zapadnaya Dvina,**
conv. **Western Dvina**
159 N5 **Daugavpils** Latvia
144 C6 **Daulatabad** India
164 E4 **Daun** Germany
143 A2 **Daund** India
154 A2 **Daung Kyun** *i.* Myanmar
187 I4 **Dauphin** Canada
166 G4 **Dauphiné** *reg.* France
199 F6 **Dauphin Island** U.S.A.
187 J4 **Dauphin Lake** Canada
144 D4 **Dausa** India
162 E3 **Dava** U.K.
143 A3 **Davangere** India
153 C5 **Davao** Phil.
153 C5 **Davao Gulf** Phil.
140 E4 **Dāvarān** Iran
141 F5 **Dāvar Panāh** Iran
181 H3 **Davel** S. Africa
196 A3 **Davenport** *CA* U.S.A.
190 B5 **Davenport** *IA* U.S.A.
161 F5 **Daventry** U.K.
181 H3 **Daveyton** S. Africa
206 I6 **David** Panama
187 H4 **Davidson** Canada
187 I3 **Davin Lake** Canada
129 D5 **Davis** *research stn* Antarctica
196 B2 **Davis** U.S.A.
197 E4 **Davis Dam** U.S.A.
189 H2 **Davis Inlet (abandoned)** Canada
129 E6 **Davis Sea** *sea* Antarctica
185 M3 **Davis Strait** Canada/Greenland
168 D7 **Davos** Switz.
152 B3 **Dawa** China
148 A1 **Dawan** China
145 F3 **Dawaxung** China
148 B4 **Dawê** China
154 A2 **Dawei** Myanmar
148 E3 **Dawen He** *r.* China
137 G7 **Dawmat al Jandal** *Al Jawf*
Saudi Arabia
142 A4 **Dawmat al Jandal** *Al Jawf*
Saudi Arabia
154 A1 **Dawna Range** *mts* Myanmar/Thai.
142 D6 **Dawqah** Oman
184 E3 **Dawson** Canada
201 C6 **Dawson** *GA* U.S.A.
198 D2 **Dawson** *ND* U.S.A.
187 I4 **Dawson Bay** Canada
186 E3 **Dawson Creek** Canada
187 K2 **Dawson Inlet** Canada
186 B2 **Dawson Range** *mts* Canada
148 E4 **Dawu** *Hubei* China
146 C3 **Dawu** *Sichuan* China
149 F6 **Dawu** Taiwan
166 D5 **Dax** France
149 C6 **Daxin** China
148 E2 **Daxing** China
149 A4 **Da Xueshan** *mts* China
145 H4 **Dayang** *r.* India
152 B4 **Dayang He** *r.* China
149 D6 **Dayao Shan** *mts* China
149 E4 **Daye** China
149 B4 **Dayi** China
126 F6 **Daylesford** Australia
196 D3 **Daylight Pass** U.S.A.
215 F1 **Daymán** *r.* Uruguay
215 F1 **Daymán, Cuchilla del** *hills* Uruguay
137 H4 **Dayr az Zawr** Syria
202 A5 **Dayton** *OH* U.S.A.
201 C5 **Dayton** *TN* U.S.A.
194 C2 **Dayton** *WA* U.S.A.
201 D6 **Daytona Beach** U.S.A.
149 E5 **Dayu** China
149 D5 **Dayu Ling** *mts* China
194 C2 **Dayville** U.S.A.
148 C4 **Dazhou** China
149 D7 **Dazhou Dao** *i.* China
149 C4 **Dazhu** China
149 B4 **Dazu** China
186 B2 **Ddhaw Gro Habitat Protection Area**
nature res. Canada
180 F5 **De Aar** S. Africa
203 H2 **Dead** *r. ME* U.S.A.
190 D2 **Dead** *r. MI* U.S.A.
201 F7 **Deadman's Cay** Bahamas
197 E4 **Dead Mountains** U.S.A.
136 E6 **Dead Sea** *salt l.* Asia
161 I6 **Deal** U.K.
181 F4 **Dealesville** S. Africa
186 D4 **Dean** *r.* Canada
149 E4 **De'an** China
161 E6 **Dean, Forest of** U.K.
215 D1 **Deán Funes** Arg.
191 F4 **Dearborn** U.S.A.
141 G4 **Dê Arghistān Rōd** *r.* Afgh.
186 D3 **Dease** *r.* Canada
186 C3 **Dease Lake** Canada
184 H3 **Dease Strait** Canada
196 D3 **Death Valley** *depr.* U.S.A.
196 D3 **Death Valley Junction** U.S.A.
196 D3 **Death Valley National Park** U.S.A.
166 E2 **Deauville** France
155 D2 **Debak** *Sarawak* Malaysia
149 C6 **Debao** China
171 I4 **Debar** Macedonia
187 H4 **Debden** Canada
161 I5 **Debenham** U.K.
197 H2 **De Beque** U.S.A.
164 C3 **De Biesbosch, Nationaal Park**
nat. park Neth.
203 I2 **Deblois** U.S.A.
178 D3 **Debre Birhan** Eth.
169 J7 **Debrecen** Hungary
178 D2 **Debre Markos** Eth.
178 D2 **Debre Tabor** Eth.
178 D3 **Debre Zeyit** Eth.
171 I3 **Deçan** Kosovo
201 C5 **Decatur** *AL* U.S.A.
201 C5 **Decatur** *GA* U.S.A.
190 C6 **Decatur** *IL* U.S.A.
190 E5 **Decatur** *IN* U.S.A.
190 E4 **Decatur** *MI* U.S.A.
143 B2 **Deccan** *plat.* India
191 H2 **Decelles, Lac** *resr* Canada
127 J1 **Deception Bay** Australia
168 G5 **Děčín** Czech Rep.
190 B4 **Decorah** U.S.A.
161 F6 **Deddington** U.K.
165 I2 **Dedeleben** Germany
165 I2 **Dedelstorf** Germany
164 E2 **Dedemsvaart** Neth.
214 C4 **Dedo de Deus** *mt.* Brazil
180 C6 **De Doorns** S. Africa
137 K1 **Dedoplists'q'aro** Georgia
176 B3 **Dédougou** Burkina Faso
172 D3 **Dedovichi** Russia
179 D5 **Dedza** Malawi
161 D4 **Dee** *est.* U.K.
161 E4 **Dee** *r. England/Wales* U.K.
162 F3 **Dee** *r. Scotland* U.K.
163 C5 **Deel** *r.* Ireland
163 D3 **Deele** *r.* Ireland
149 □ **Deep Bay** *Hong Kong* China
202 D5 **Deep Creek Lake** U.S.A.
197 F2 **Deep Creek Range** *mts* U.S.A.
191 I2 **Deep River** Canada
203 G4 **Deep River** U.S.A.
187 J1 **Deep Rose Lake** Canada
196 D3 **Deep Springs** U.S.A.
127 I2 **Deepwater** Australia
202 B5 **Deer Creek Lake** U.S.A.
203 J2 **Deer Island** Canada
203 I2 **Deer Island** U.S.A.
203 I2 **Deer Isle** U.S.A.
189 I4 **Deer Lake** *Nfld and Lab.* Canada
188 B3 **Deer Lake** *Ont.* Canada
188 B3 **Deer Lake** *l.* Canada
194 D2 **Deer Lodge** U.S.A.
212 D2 **Defensores del Chaco, Parque**
Nacional *nat. park* Para.
202 A4 **Defiance** U.S.A.
201 C6 **De Funiak Springs** U.S.A.
146 B3 **Dêgê** China
178 E3 **Degeh Bur** Eth.
165 K6 **Deggendorf** Germany
144 C3 **Degh** *r.* Pak.
164 C2 **De Goorn** Neth.
164 B3 **De Haan** Belgium
140 D4 **Dehaj** Iran
141 F5 **Dehak** Iran
141 F4 **Dehak Seydābād** Iran
140 C3 **Dehaq** Iran
140 C4 **Dehdasht** Iran
141 F4 **Deh-e Shū** Afgh.
140 C2 **Dehgāh** Iran
140 B3 **Dehgolān** Iran
143 B5 **Dehiwala-Mount Lavinia** Sri Lanka
140 D5 **Dehkūyeh** Iran
140 B3 **Dehlorān** Iran
139 F5 **Dehqonobod** Uzbek.
144 D3 **Dehra Dun** India
145 F4 **Dehri** India
141 E4 **Deh Salm** Iran
140 E4 **Deh Sard** Iran
137 J4 **Deh Sheykh** Iran
149 F5 **Dehua** China
152 C1 **Dehui** China
164 B4 **Deinze** Belgium
169 K7 **Dej** Romania
149 C4 **Dejiang** China
190 C5 **DeKalb** U.S.A.
199 E5 **De Kalb** U.S.A.
203 F2 **De Kalb Junction** U.S.A.
142 A6 **Dekemhare** Eritrea
178 C4 **Dekese** Dem. Rep. Congo
Dekhkanabad Uzbek. *see*
Dehqonobod
164 C1 **De Koog** Neth.
164 C2 **De Kooy** Neth.
197 E3 **Delamar Lake** U.S.A.
196 C4 **Delano** U.S.A.
197 F2 **Delano Peak** U.S.A.
123 G2 **Delap-Uliga-Djarrit** Marshall Is
181 F3 **Delareyville** S. Africa
187 H4 **Delaronde Lake** Canada
190 C5 **Delavan** *IL* U.S.A.
190 C4 **Delavan** *WI* U.S.A.
202 B4 **Delaware** U.S.A.
203 F4 **Delaware** *r.* U.S.A.
203 F5 **Delaware** *state* U.S.A.
203 F5 **Delaware Bay** U.S.A.
202 B4 **Delaware Lake** U.S.A.
203 F4 **Delaware Water Gap National**
Recreational Area *park* U.S.A.
165 G3 **Delbrück** Germany
127 H6 **Delegate** Australia
168 C7 **Delémont** Switz.
164 C2 **Delft** Neth.
143 B4 **Delft Island** Sri Lanka
164 E1 **Delfzijl** Neth.
179 E5 **Delgado, Cabo** *c.* Moz.
146 C2 **Delgerhaan** Mongolia
191 G4 **Delhi** Canada
144 D3 **Delhi** India
(City Plan **106**)
195 F4 **Delhi** *CO* U.S.A.
203 F3 **Delhi** *NY* U.S.A.
137 I2 **Deli** *r.* Turkey
136 E2 **Delice** Turkey
136 E1 **Delice** *r.* Turkey
140 C3 **Delījān** Iran
186 E1 **Délįne** Canada
146 B3 **Delingha** China
187 H4 **Delisle** Canada
165 K3 **Delitzsch** Germany
165 H3 **Delligsen** Germany
198 D3 **Dell Rapids** U.S.A.
167 H4 **Dellys** Alg.
196 D5 **Del Mar** U.S.A.
165 G1 **Delmenhorst** Germany
133 Q2 **De-Longa, Ostrova** *is* Russia
184 B3 **De Long Mountains** U.S.A.
187 I5 **Deloraine** Canada
171 J5 **Delphi** *tourist site* Greece
190 D5 **Delphi** U.S.A.
202 A4 **Delphos** U.S.A.
180 F4 **Delportshoop** S. Africa
201 D7 **Delray Beach** U.S.A.
195 E6 **Del Río** Mex.
199 C6 **Del Rio** U.S.A.
159 L3 **Delsbo** Sweden
197 H2 **Delta** *CO* U.S.A.
190 A5 **Delta** *IA* U.S.A.
197 F2 **Delta** *UT* U.S.A.
184 D3 **Delta Junction** U.S.A.
203 F3 **Delta Reservoir** U.S.A.
201 D6 **Deltona** U.S.A.
127 I2 **Delungra** Australia
163 D4 **Delvin** Ireland
171 I5 **Delvinë** Albania
138 C1 **Dema** *r.* Russia
167 E1 **Demanda, Sierra de la** *mts* Spain
178 C4 **Demba** Dem. Rep. Congo
178 D3 **Dembī Dolo** Eth.
219 F5 **Demerara Abyssal Plain** *sea feature*
S. Atlantic Ocean
172 D4 **Demidov** Russia
195 F5 **Deming** U.S.A.
213 E4 **Demini** *r.* Brazil
136 B2 **Demirci** Turkey
171 L4 **Demirköy** Turkey
168 F4 **Demmin** Germany
201 C5 **Demopolis** U.S.A.
190 D5 **DeMotte** U.S.A.
155 B3 **Dempo, Gunung** *vol.* Indon.
144 D2 **Dêmqog** China/India
141 G3 **Dê Mūsá Qal'ah Rōd** *r.* Afgh.
172 H2 **Dem'yanovo** Russia
169 P2 **Demyansk** Russia
180 D5 **De Naawte** S. Africa
178 E3 **Denan** Eth.
187 I4 **Denare Beach** Canada
Denau Uzbek. *see* **Denov**
191 I3 **Denbigh** Canada
161 D4 **Denbigh** U.K.
164 C1 **Den Burg** Neth.
154 B1 **Den Chai** Thai.
155 C3 **Dendang** Indon.
164 C3 **Dendermonde** Belgium
Dendron S. Africa *see* **Mogwadi**
148 D3 **Dengfeng** China
148 C1 **Dengkou** China
145 H3 **Dêngqên** China
148 D3 **Dengzhou** China
Den Haag Neth. *see* **The Hague**
124 B4 **Denham** Australia
164 E2 **Den Ham** Neth.
164 C2 **Den Helder** Neth.
167 G3 **Dénia** Spain
126 F5 **Deniliquin** Australia
194 C3 **Denio** U.S.A.
198 E3 **Denison** *IA* U.S.A.
199 D5 **Denison** *TX* U.S.A.
138 E1 **Denisovka** Kazakh.
136 B3 **Denizli** Turkey
127 I4 **Denman** Australia
129 D6 **Denman Glacier** *glacier* Antarctica
124 B5 **Denmark** Australia
159 J4 **Denmark** *country* Europe
185 P3 **Denmark Strait** Greenland/Iceland
197 H3 **Dennehotso** U.S.A.
203 H4 **Dennis Port** U.S.A.
162 E4 **Denny** U.K.
203 J2 **Dennysville** U.S.A.
139 F5 **Denov** Uzbek.
155 E4 **Denpasar** Indon.
203 F5 **Denton** *MD* U.S.A.
199 D5 **Denton** *TX* U.S.A.
124 B5 **D'Entrecasteaux, Point** Australia
125 G3 **D'Entrecasteaux, Récifs** *reef*
New Caledonia
124 F2 **D'Entrecasteaux Islands** P.N.G.
194 F4 **Denver** U.S.A.
145 F4 **Deo** India
144 D3 **Deoband** India
143 D1 **Deogarh** India
145 E5 **Deogarh** *mt.* India
145 F4 **Deoghar** India
143 I2 **Deomali** *mt.* India
144 D5 **Deori** India
145 E4 **Deoria** India
144 C2 **Deosai, Plains of** Pak.
145 E5 **Deosil** India
164 A3 **De Panne** Belgium
164 D3 **De Peel** *reg.* Neth.
190 C3 **De Pere** U.S.A.
203 F3 **Deposit** U.S.A.
191 I2 **Dépôt-Forbes** Canada
191 I2 **Dépôt-Rowanton** Canada
190 C5 **Depue** U.S.A.
133 O3 **Deputatskiy** Russia
145 G3 **Dêqên** *Xizang Zizhiqu* China
146 B4 **Dêqên** *Yunnan* China
149 D6 **Deqing** *Guangdong* China
149 F4 **Deqing** *Zhejiang* China
199 E5 **De Queen** U.S.A.
144 B3 **Dera Bugti** Pak.
144 B3 **Dera Ghazi Khan** Pak.
144 B3 **Dera Ismail Khan** Pak.
144 B3 **Derawar Fort** Pak.
173 I7 **Derbent** Russia
Derbent Uzbek. *see* **Darband**
127 G8 **Derby** *Tas.* Australia
124 C3 **Derby** *W.A.* Australia
161 F5 **Derby** U.K.
203 G4 **Derby** *CT* U.S.A.
199 D4 **Derby** *KS* U.S.A.
161 H5 **Dereham** U.K.
163 D3 **Derg** *r.* Ireland/U.K.
163 C5 **Derg, Lough** *l.* Ireland
173 I5 **Dergachi** Russia
173 F5 **Derhachi** Ukr.
199 E6 **DeRidder** U.S.A.
137 H3 **Derik** Turkey
136 E2 **Derinkuyu** Turkey
173 F5 **Derkul** *r.* Russia/Ukr.
180 C1 **Derm** Namibia
163 D4 **Derravaragh, Lough** *l.* Ireland
163 E5 **Derry** *r.* Ireland
Derry U.K. *see* **Londonderry**
203 H3 **Derry** U.S.A.
163 C3 **Derryveagh Mountains** *hills* Ireland
148 A1 **Derstei** China
144 D2 **Dêrub** China
177 F3 **Derudeb** Sudan
180 E6 **De Rust** S. Africa
170 G2 **Derventa** Bos. & Herz.
127 G9 **Derwent** *r.* Australia
160 G4 **Derwent** *r. England* U.K.
161 F4 **Derwent** *r. England* U.K.
162 G6 **Derwent Reservoir** U.K.
160 D3 **Derwent Water** *l.* U.K.
138 C1 **Derzhavino** Russia
138 F2 **Derzhavinsk** Kazakh.
215 C2 **Desaguadero** *r.* Arg.
210 E7 **Desaguadero** *r.* Bol.
123 J5 **Désappointement, Îles du** *is*
Fr. Polynesia
196 D2 **Desatoya Mountains** U.S.A.
191 F2 **Desbarats** Canada
187 I4 **Deschambault Lake** Canada
187 I3 **Deschambault Lake** *l.* Canada
194 B2 **Deschutes** *r.* U.S.A.
178 D2 **Desē** Eth.
212 C7 **Deseado** *r.* Arg.
197 F1 **Deseret Peak** U.S.A.
191 I3 **Deseronto** Canada
144 B3 **Desert Canal** Pak.
197 E5 **Desert Center** U.S.A.
186 G3 **Desmarais** Canada
198 E3 **Des Moines** *IA* U.S.A.
195 G4 **Des Moines** *NM* U.S.A.
190 A5 **Des Moines** *r.* U.S.A.
172 E5 **Desna** *r.* Russia
173 D5 **Desna** Ukr.
172 E4 **Desnogorsk** Russia
153 C4 **Desolation Point** Phil.
190 D4 **Des Plaines** U.S.A.
165 K3 **Dessau-Roßlau** Germany
164 B3 **Destelbergen** Belgium
191 H1 **Destor** Canada
126 B5 **D'Estrees Bay** Australia
186 B2 **Destruction Bay** Canada
208 F4 **Desventuradas, Islas** *is* Chile
171 I2 **Deta** Romania
186 G2 **Detah** Canada
179 C5 **Dete** Zimbabwe
165 G3 **Detmold** Germany
190 D3 **Detour, Point** U.S.A.
191 F3 **De Tour Village** U.S.A.
191 F4 **Detroit** U.S.A.
198 E2 **Detroit Lakes** U.S.A.
127 H5 **Deua National Park** Australia
165 K3 **Deuben** Germany
164 D3 **Deurne** Neth.
170 F1 **Deutschlandsberg** Austria
165 K3 **Deutzen** Germany
191 H2 **Deux-Rivières** Canada
171 J2 **Deva** Romania
143 B2 **Devarkonda** India
136 E2 **Develi** Turkey
164 E2 **Deventer** Neth.
168 H6 **Devét skal** *h.* Czech Rep.
144 B4 **Devikot** India
163 D5 **Devil's Bit Mountain** *h.* Ireland
161 D5 **Devil's Bridge** U.K.
196 C4 **Devils Den** U.S.A.
196 C2 **Devils Gate** *pass* U.S.A.
190 B2 **Devils Island** U.S.A.
198 D1 **Devils Lake** U.S.A.
196 C3 **Devils Peak** U.S.A.
201 F7 **Devil's Point** Bahamas
196 C3 **Devils Postpile National Monument**
nat. park U.S.A.
161 F6 **Devizes** U.K.
144 C4 **Devli** India
171 L3 **Devnya** Bulg.
186 G4 **Devon** Canada
161 G5 **Devon** *r.* U.K.
185 I2 **Devon Island** Canada
127 G8 **Devonport** Australia
136 C1 **Devrek** Turkey
136 D1 **Devrekâni** Turkey
136 E1 **Devrez** *r.* Turkey
143 A2 **Devrukh** India
155 A2 **Dewa, Tanjung** *pt* Indon.
144 D5 **Dewas** India
164 E2 **De Weerribben-Wieden, Nationaal**
Park *nat. park* Neth.
181 G4 **Dewetsdorp** S. Africa
202 B6 **Dewey Lake** U.S.A.
199 F5 **De Witt** *AR* U.S.A.
190 B5 **De Witt** *IA* U.S.A.
160 F4 **Dewsbury** U.K.
149 E4 **Dexing** China
203 I2 **Dexter** *ME* U.S.A.
199 F4 **Dexter** *MO* U.S.A.
203 E2 **Dexter** *NY* U.S.A.
148 B4 **Deyang** China
140 E3 **Deyhūk** Iran
137 L3 **Deylamān** Iran
141 E3 **Deym** Iran
124 D2 **Deyong, Tanjung** *pt* Indon.
137 L6 **Dez** *r.* Iran
137 L5 **Dez, Sadd-e** *resr* Iran
140 C3 **Dezfūl** Iran
148 E2 **Dezhou** China
140 B5 **Dhahlān, Jabal** *h.* Saudi Arabia
142 D4 **Dhahran** Saudi Arabia
145 G5 **Dhaka** Bangl.
145 G5 **Dhaleswari** *r.* Bangl.
145 H4 **Dhaleswari** *r.* India
142 B7 **Dhamār** Yemen
145 F5 **Dhamara** India
144 C5 **Dhamnod** India
143 C1 **Dhamtari** India
144 B3 **Dhana Sar** Pak.
145 F5 **Dhanbad** India
144 C5 **Dhandhuka** India
145 E3 **Dhang Range** *mts* Nepal
144 C5 **Dhar** India
144 D2 **Dharamsala** India
145 F4 **Dharan** Nepal
143 B4 **Dharapuram** India
144 B5 **Dhari** India
143 B3 **Dharmapuri** India
143 B3 **Dharmavaram** India
143 A3 **Dharwad** India
144 D4 **Dhasan** *r.* India
145 E3 **Dhaulagiri I** *mt.* Nepal
Dhaulpur India *see* **Dholpur**
Dhebar Lake India *see*
Jaisamand Lake
145 H4 **Dhekiajuli** India
136 E6 **Dhībān** Jordan
145 H4 **Dhing** India
144 D4 **Dholpur** India
143 B3 **Dhone** India
144 B5 **Dhoraji** India
144 B5 **Dhrangadhra** India
144 C5 **Dhule** India
145 F4 **Dhulian** India
145 F4 **Dhunche** Nepal
144 D4 **Dhund** *r.* India
178 E3 **Dhuusa Marreeb** Somalia
171 K7 **Dia** *i.* Greece
196 B3 **Diablo, Mount** U.S.A.
204 A2 **Diablo, Picacho del** *mt.* Mex.
196 B3 **Diablo Range** *mts* U.S.A.
215 E2 **Diamante** Arg.
215 C2 **Diamante** *r.* Arg.
124 D4 **Diamantina** *watercourse* Australia
214 D2 **Diamantina** Brazil
211 J6 **Diamantina, Chapada** *plat.* Brazil
218 K7 **Diamantina Deep** *sea feature*
Indian Ocean
214 A1 **Diamantino** Brazil
196 □1 **Diamond Head** U.S.A.
197 E2 **Diamond Peak** U.S.A.
149 D6 **Dianbai** China
149 B5 **Dian Chi** *l.* China
149 C4 **Dianjiang** China
211 I6 **Dianópolis** Brazil
176 B4 **Dianra** Côte d'Ivoire
152 B2 **Diaobingshan** China
150 B2 **Diaoling** China
176 C3 **Diapaga** Burkina Faso
141 E6 **Ḍibab** Oman
145 H4 **Dibang** *r.* India
178 C4 **Dibaya** Dem. Rep. Congo
180 E3 **Dibeng** S. Africa
181 G1 **Dibete** Botswana
145 H4 **Dibrugarh** India
199 C5 **Dickens** U.S.A.
203 I1 **Dickey** U.S.A.
198 C2 **Dickinson** U.S.A.
201 C4 **Dickson** U.S.A.
203 F4 **Dickson City** U.S.A.
137 H3 **Dicle** *r.* Turkey
alt. **Dijlah, Nahr (Iraq/Syria),**
conv. **Tigris**
153 B2 **Didicas** *i.* Phil.
144 C4 **Didwana** India
171 L4 **Didymoteicho** Greece
166 G4 **Die** France
164 F4 **Dieblich** Germany
176 B3 **Diébougou** Burkina Faso
165 G5 **Dieburg** Germany
187 H4 **Diefenbaker, Lake** Canada
218 I5 **Diego Garcia** *atoll*
British Indian Ocean Terr.
164 E5 **Diekirch** Lux.
176 B3 **Diéma** Mali
165 H3 **Diemel** *r.* Germany
149 B6 **Điên Biên Phu** Vietnam
154 C1 **Diên Châu** Vietnam
154 D2 **Diên Khanh** Vietnam
165 G2 **Diepholz** Germany
166 E2 **Dieppe** France
164 D3 **Diessen** Neth.
164 D4 **Diest** Belgium
168 D7 **Dietikon** Switz.
165 G4 **Diez** Germany
177 D3 **Diffa** Niger
143 D2 **Digapahandi** India
189 G5 **Digby** Canada
145 F5 **Digha** India
166 H4 **Digne-les-Bains** France
166 F3 **Digoin** France
153 C5 **Digos** Phil.
144 D5 **Digras** India
144 B4 **Digri** Pak.
147 F7 **Digul** *r.* Indon.
176 B4 **Digya National Park** Ghana
145 G4 **Dihang** *r.* Asia
alt. **Dihang (India),**
conv. **Brahmaputra**
138 E3 **Diirmentobe** Kazakh.
137 J5 **Dijlah, Nahr** *r.* Iraq/Syria
alt. **Dicle (Turkey),**
conv. **Tigris**
166 G3 **Dijon** France
178 E2 **Dikhil** Djibouti
171 L5 **Dikili** Turkey
164 A3 **Diksmuide** Belgium
132 J2 **Dikson** Russia
177 D3 **Dikwa** Nigeria
178 D3 **Dīla** Eth.
141 F3 **Dilārām** Afgh.
141 E4 **Dilaram** Iran
124 C2 **Dili** East Timor
137 J1 **Dilijan** Armenia
154 D3 **Di Linh** Vietnam
165 G4 **Dillenburg** Germany
199 D6 **Dilley** U.S.A.
168 E6 **Dillingen an der Donau**
Germany
164 E5 **Dillingen/Saar** Germany
184 C4 **Dillingham** U.S.A.
187 H3 **Dillon** Canada
194 D2 **Dillon** *MT* U.S.A.
201 E5 **Dillon** *SC* U.S.A.
179 C5 **Dilolo** Dem. Rep. Congo
164 D3 **Dilsen** Belgium
137 J5 **Diltāwa** Iraq
145 H4 **Dimapur** India
Dimashq Syria *see* **Damascus**
178 C4 **Dimbelenge** Dem. Rep. Congo
176 B4 **Dimbokro** Côte d'Ivoire
126 E6 **Dimboola** Australia
171 K3 **Dimitrovgrad** Bulg.
172 I4 **Dimitrovgrad** Russia
136 E6 **Dimona** Israel
180 D2 **Dimpho Pan** *salt pan* Botswana
153 C4 **Dinagat** *i.* Phil.
145 G4 **Dinajpur** Bangl.
166 C2 **Dinan** France
144 C2 **Dinanagar** India
164 C4 **Dinant** Belgium
145 F4 **Dinapur** India
136 C2 **Dinar** Turkey
140 C4 **Dīnār, Kūh-e** *mt.* Iran
Dinara Planina *mts* Europe *see*
Dinaric Alps
170 G2 **Dinaric Alps** *mts* Europe
177 F3 **Dinder National Park** Sudan
143 B4 **Dindigul** India
181 J1 **Dindiza** Moz.
144 E5 **Dindori** India
136 D3 **Dinek** Turkey
148 C2 **Dingbian** China
178 B4 **Dinge** Angola
165 I3 **Dingelstädt** Germany
145 F3 **Dinggyê** China
145 F4 **Dingla** Nepal
Dingle Ireland *see*
Daingean Uí Chúis
163 A5 **Dingle Bay** Ireland
149 E5 **Dingnan** China
153 B2 **Dingras** Phil.
148 E3 **Dingtao** China
176 A3 **Dinguiraye** Guinea
162 D3 **Dingwall** U.K.
148 B3 **Dingxi** China
148 E2 **Dingxing** China
148 E3 **Dingyuan** China
148 E2 **Dingzhou** China
148 F2 **Dingzi Gang** *b.* China
Dinh, Mui *hd* Vietnam *see*
Ca Na, Mui
149 C6 **Dinh Lâp** Vietnam
165 I5 **Dinkelsbühl** Germany
197 G3 **Dinnebito Wash** *watercourse* U.S.A.
181 G1 **Dinokwe** Botswana
187 K5 **Dinorwic** U.S.A.
197 H1 **Dinosaur** U.S.A.
194 E3 **Dinosaur National Monument**
nat. park U.S.A.
164 E3 **Dinslaken** Germany
176 B3 **Dioïla** Mali
214 B4 **Dionísio Cerqueira** Brazil
176 A3 **Diourbel** Senegal
144 E3 **Dipayal** Nepal
145 H4 **Diphu** India
Dipkarpaz Cyprus *see* **Rizokarpason**
144 B4 **Diplo** Pak.
153 B4 **Dipolog** Phil.
128 B6 **Dipton** N.Z.
136 F2 **Dirckli** Turkey
176 B3 **Diré** Mali
124 E3 **Direction, Cape** Australia
178 E3 **Dirē Dawa** Eth.
179 C5 **Dirico** Angola
176 D1 **Dirj** Libya
124 B4 **Dirk Hartog Island** Australia
127 H2 **Dirranbandi** Australia
137 L6 **Dīrsīyeh** Iran
197 G2 **Dirty Devil** *r.* U.S.A.
144 C4 **Disa** India
194 A2 **Disappointment, Cape** U.S.A.
124 C4 **Disappointment, Lake** *salt flat*
Australia
127 H6 **Disaster Bay** Australia
126 D7 **Discovery Bay** Australia
149 □ **Discovery Bay** *Hong Kong* China
219 J8 **Discovery Seamounts** *sea feature*
S. Atlantic Ocean
Disko *i.* Greenland *see* **Qeqertarsuaq**
203 E6 **Dismal Swamp** U.S.A.
145 G4 **Dispur** India
161 I5 **Diss** U.K.
214 C1 **Distrito Federal** *admin. dist.* Brazil
136 C6 **Disūq** Egypt
153 B4 **Dit** *i.* Phil.
180 E4 **Ditloung** S. Africa
170 F6 **Dittaino** *r. Sicily* Italy
153 C4 **Diuata Mountains** Phil.
153 C4 **Diuata Point** Phil.
140 B3 **Dīvāndarreh** Iran
172 G4 **Diveyevo** Russia
153 B2 **Divilican Bay** Phil.
214 D3 **Divinópolis** Brazil
173 G6 **Divnoye** Russia
176 B4 **Divo** Côte d'Ivoire
136 G2 **Divriği** Turkey
141 G5 **Diwana** Pak.
203 H2 **Dixfield** U.S.A.
203 I2 **Dixmont** U.S.A.
196 B2 **Dixon** *CA* U.S.A.
190 C5 **Dixon** *IL* U.S.A.
186 C4 **Dixon Entrance** *sea chan.*
Canada/U.S.A.
201 F7 **Dixon's** Bahamas
186 F3 **Dixonville** Canada
203 H2 **Dixville** Canada
137 I2 **Diyadin** Turkey
137 J5 **Diyālá, Nahr** *r.* Iraq
137 H3 **Diyarbakır** Turkey
144 B4 **Diyodar** India
140 D3 **Diz Chah** Iran
177 D2 **Djado** Niger
177 D2 **Djado, Plateau du** Niger
178 B4 **Djambala** Congo
176 C2 **Djanet** Alg.
176 C1 **Djelfa** Alg.
178 C3 **Djéma** C.A.R.
176 B3 **Djenné** Mali
177 D4 **Djibloho** Equat. Guinea
176 B3 **Djibo** Burkina Faso
178 E2 **Djibouti** *country* Africa
178 E2 **Djibouti** Djibouti
163 E4 **Djouce Mountain** *h.* Ireland
176 C4 **Djougou** Benin
177 D3 **Djourab, Erg du** *des.* Chad
158 D2 **Djúpivogur** Iceland
159 K3 **Djurås** Sweden
137 J1 **Dmanisi** Georgia
133 P2 **Dmitriya Lapteva, Proliv** *sea chan.*
Russia
150 C2 **Dmitriyevka** *Primorskiy Kray* Russia
139 K1 **Dmitriyevka** *Respublika Altay* Russia
172 G4 **Dmitriyevka** *Tambovskaya Oblast'*
Russia
173 E4 **Dmitriyev-L'govskiy** Russia
172 F3 **Dmitrov** Russia
173 E6 **Dnepr** *r.* Russia
alt. **Dnipro (Ukraine),**
alt. **Dnyapro (Belarus),**
conv. **Dnieper**
169 O6 **Dnieper** *r.* Europe
alt. **Dnepr (Russia),**
alt. **Dnipro (Ukraine),**
alt. **Dnyapro (Belarus)**
169 O6 **Dnipro** *r.* Ukr.
alt. **Dnepr (Russia),**
alt. **Dnyapro (Belarus),**
conv. **Dnieper**
173 E5 **Dniprodzerzhyns'k** Ukr.
173 E5 **Dnipropetrovs'k** Ukr.
173 E6 **Dniprorudne** Ukr.
169 M6 **Dnister** *r.* Ukr.
alt. **Nistru (Moldova),**
conv. **Dniester**
172 D3 **Dno** Russia
169 O4 **Dnyapro** *r.* Belarus
alt. **Dnepr (Russia),**
alt. **Dnipro (Ukraine),**
conv. **Dnieper**
177 D4 **Doba** Chad
191 G3 **Dobbinton** Canada
159 M4 **Dobele** Latvia
165 L3 **Döbeln** Germany
147 F7 **Doberai, Jazirah** *pen.* Indon.
215 D3 **Doblas** Arg.
147 F7 **Dobo** Indon.
171 H2 **Doboj** Bos. & Herz.
165 J4 **Döbraberg** *h.* Germany
171 L3 **Dobrich** Bulg.
173 G4 **Dobrinka** Russia
171 M2 **Dobruja** *reg.* Romania
173 D4 **Dobrush** Belarus
139 J4 **Dobyn** Kazakh.
153 A5 **Doc Can** *reef* Phil.
214 E2 **Doce** *r.* Brazil
161 H5 **Docking** U.K.
207 D3 **Doctor Arroyo** Mex.
206 C1 **Doctor Belisario Domínguez** Mex.
212 D2 **Doctor Pedro P. Peña** Para.
143 B3 **Dod Ballapur** India
171 L6 **Dodecanese** *is* Greece
Dodekanisa *is* Greece *see*
Dodecanese
194 C2 **Dodge** U.S.A.
190 A3 **Dodge Center** U.S.A.
199 C4 **Dodge City** U.S.A.
127 G9 **Dodges Ferry** Australia
190 B4 **Dodgeville** U.S.A.
161 C7 **Dodman Point** U.K.
178 D4 **Dodoma** Tanz.
164 E3 **Doetinchem** Neth.
147 E7 **Dofa** Indon.
145 G2 **Dogai Coring** *salt l.* China
145 G2 **Dogaicoring Qangco** *salt l.* China
136 F2 **Doğanşehir** Turkey
186 E4 **Dog Creek** Canada
145 G3 **Dogên Co** *l.* China
189 H2 **Dog Island** Canada
187 J4 **Dog Lake** *Man.* Canada
191 E1 **Dog Lake** *Ont.* Canada
151 C6 **Dōgo** *i.* Japan
139 F5 **D'og'ob** Uzbek.
140 C4 **Do Gonbadān** Iran
176 C3 **Dogondoutchi** Niger
151 C7 **Dōgo-yama** *mt.* Japan
137 J2 **Doğubeyazıt** Turkey
145 F3 **Dogxung Zangbo** *r.* China
145 G3 **Do'gyaling** China
140 C5 **Doha** Qatar
145 H5 **Dohazari** Bangl.
145 G3 **Doilungdêqên** China
154 A1 **Doi Saket** Thai.
211 J5 **Dois Irmãos, Serra dos** *hills* Brazil
171 J4 **Dojran, Lake** Greece/Macedonia
137 J4 **Dokan, Sadd** Iraq
Dok-do *i.* N. Pacific Ocean *see*
Liancourt Rocks
159 J3 **Dokka** Norway
164 E1 **Dokkum** Neth.
144 B4 **Dokri** Pak.
169 M3 **Dokshytsy** Belarus
173 F6 **Dokuchayevs'k** Ukr.
189 F4 **Dolbeau-Mistassini** Canada
161 C5 **Dolbenmaen** U.K.
166 D2 **Dol-de-Bretagne** France
166 G3 **Dole** France
161 D5 **Dolgellau** U.K.
165 L1 **Dolgen** Germany
203 F3 **Dolgeville** U.S.A.
173 F4 **Dolgorukovo** Russia
173 F4 **Dolgoye** Russia
170 C5 **Dolianova** *Sardinia* Italy
146 G2 **Dolinsk** Russia
178 B4 **Dolisie** Congo
165 J6 **Dollnstein** Germany
139 G1 **Dolmatovo** Kazakh.
147 F7 **Dolok, Pulau** *i.* Indon.
170 D1 **Dolomites** *mts* Italy
Dolonnur China *see* **Duolun**
178 E3 **Dolo Odo** Eth.
215 F3 **Dolores** Arg.
207 G4 **Dolores** Guat.
206 B2 **Dolores** Mex.
215 E2 **Dolores** Uruguay
197 H2 **Dolores** *r.* U.S.A.
206 D3 **Dolores Hidalgo** Mex.
184 G3 **Dolphin and Union Strait** Canada
152 D6 **Dolsan-do** *i.* S. Korea
149 B7 **Đô Lương** Vietnam
173 B5 **Dolyna** Ukr.
136 B2 **Domaniç** Turkey
144 E2 **Domar** China
145 H3 **Domartang** China
168 F6 **Domažlice** Czech Rep.
145 H2 **Domba** China
140 B3 **Dom Bākh** Iran
138 D2 **Dombarovskiy** Russia
159 J3 **Dombås** Norway
168 I7 **Dombóvár** Hungary
186 E4 **Dome Creek** Canada
129 D4 **Dome Fuji** *research stn* Antarctica
186 D2 **Dome Peak** Canada
197 E5 **Dome Rock Mountains** U.S.A.
166 D2 **Domfront** France
205 L5 **Dominica** *country* Caribbean Sea
206 I6 **Dominical** Costa Rica
205 J5 **Dominican Republic** *country*
Caribbean Sea
165 J1 **Dömitz** Germany
154 C2 **Dom Noi, Lam** *r.* Thai.
170 C1 **Domodossola** Italy
171 J5 **Domokos** Greece
215 F1 **Dom Pedrito** Brazil
155 E4 **Dompu** Indon.
215 B3 **Domuyo, Volcán** *vol.* Arg.
127 I2 **Domville, Mount** *h.* Australia
143 B2 **Don** *r.* India
206 B2 **Don** Mex.
173 G5 **Don** *r.* Russia
162 F3 **Don** *r.* U.K.
154 C2 **Don, Xé** *r.* Laos
163 F3 **Donaghadee** U.K.
163 E3 **Donaghmore** U.K.
126 E6 **Donald** Australia
168 G6 **Donau** *r.* Austria/Germany
alt. **Duna (Hungary),**
alt. **Dunaj (Slovakia),**
alt. **Dunărea (Romania),**
alt. **Dunav (Serbia),**
conv. **Danube**
168 D7 **Donaueschingen** Germany
168 E6 **Donauwörth** Germany
167 D3 **Don Benito** Spain
160 F4 **Doncaster** U.K.
179 B4 **Dondo** Angola
179 D5 **Dondo** Moz.
153 B4 **Dondonay** *i.* Phil.
143 C5 **Dondra Head** Sri Lanka
163 C3 **Donegal** Ireland
163 C3 **Donegal Bay** Ireland
139 J2 **Donenbay** Kazakh.
173 F6 **Donets'k** Ukr.
173 F5 **Donets'kyy Kryazh** *hills* Russia/Ukr.
149 D5 **Dong'an** China
124 B4 **Dongara** Australia
144 E5 **Dongargarh** India
146 E2 **Dongbei** *reg.* China
149 B5 **Dongchuan** China
145 F2 **Dongco** China
152 D5 **Dongducheon** S. Korea
149 C7 **Dongfang** China
150 C1 **Dongfanghong** China
152 C2 **Dongfeng** China
155 E3 **Donggala** Indon.
152 C4 **Donggang** *Liaoning* China
148 F3 **Donggang** *Shandong* China
Donggar China *see* **Doilungdêqên**
149 E5 **Donggu** China
149 D6 **Dongguan** China
154 C1 **Đông Ha** Vietnam
152 E5 **Donghae** S. Korea
148 F3 **Donghai** China
149 D6 **Donghai Dao** *i.* China
152 C1 **Dong Haxat** China
148 C3 **Dong He** *r.* China
154 C1 **Đông Hơi** Vietnam
148 B2 **Donghu** China
152 E1 **Dongjingcheng** China
145 H3 **Dongjug** *Xizang Zizhiqu* China
145 H3 **Dongjug** *Xizang Zizhiqu* China
149 D5 **Dongkou** China
145 G4 **Dongkya La** *pass* India
149 C5 **Donglan** China
148 A2 **Dongle** China
152 C2 **Dongliao He** *r.* China
152 B1 **Dongminzhutun** China
152 E6 **Dongnae** S. Korea
152 F2 **Dongning** China
179 B5 **Dongo** Angola
177 F3 **Dongola** Sudan
178 B3 **Dongou** Congo
154 B2 **Dong Phraya Yen** *esc.* Thai.
149 D6 **Dongping** *Guangdong* China
Dongping *Shandong* China *see*
Zhoucheng
145 G3 **Dongqiao** China
149 E6 **Dongshan** China
149 E6 **Dongshan Dao** *i.* China
148 D2 **Dongsheng** China
148 F3 **Dongtai** China
148 F3 **Dongtai He** *r.* China
149 D4 **Dongting Hu** *l.* China
149 F5 **Dongtou** China
148 B3 **Dongxiang** *Gansu* China
149 E4 **Dongxiang** *Jiangxi* China
154 C3 **Đông Xoai** Vietnam
149 F4 **Dongyang** China
148 F2 **Dongying** China
149 E4 **Dongzhi** China
186 B2 **Donjek** *r.* Canada
164 E1 **Donkerbroek** Neth.
154 C3 **Don Kêv** Cambodia
145 G5 **Donmanick Islands** Bangl.
189 F4 **Donnacona** Canada
186 F3 **Donnelly** Canada
128 D1 **Donnellys Crossing** N.Z.
196 B2 **Donner Pass** U.S.A.
Donostia Spain *see* **San Sebastián**
171 K6 **Donousa** *i.* Greece
172 F4 **Donskoy** Russia
173 G6 **Donskoye** Russia

Donsol

153 B3 Donsol Phil.
138 D3 Donyztau, Sor dry lake Kazakh.
163 A4 Dooagh Ireland
162 D5 Doon, Loch l. U.K.
163 B5 Doonbeg r. Ireland
164 D2 Doorn Neth.
190 D3 Door Peninsula U.S.A.
164 D3 Doorwerth Neth.
199 C5 Dora U.S.A.
170 C2 Dora Baltea r. Italy
140 C5 Dorāhak Iran
161 E7 Dorchester U.K.
179 B6 Dordabis Namibia
166 E4 Dordogne r. France
164 C3 Dordrecht Neth.
181 G5 Dordrecht S. Africa
180 C1 Doreenville Namibia
187 H4 Doré Lake Canada
187 H4 Doré Lake l. Canada
170 C4 Dorgali Sardinia Italy
145 H2 Dorgê Co l. China
146 B2 Dörgön Nuur salt l. Mongolia
176 B3 Dori Burkina Faso
180 C5 Doring r. S. Africa
161 G6 Dorking U.K.
164 E3 Dormagen Germany
164 B5 Dormans France
162 D3 Dornoch Firth est. U.K.
148 C1 Dornogovĭ prov. Mongolia
164 F1 Dornum Germany
179 B6 Dorob National Park Namibia
172 E4 Dorogobuzh Russia
141 F3 Doroḩ Iran
169 M7 Dorohoi Romania
158 L2 Dorotea Sweden
124 B4 Dorre Island Australia
127 J3 Dorrigo Australia
194 B3 Dorris U.S.A.
191 H3 Dorset Canada
161 D7 Dorset and East Devon Coast tourist site U.K.
164 F3 Dortmund Germany
202 B6 Dorton U.S.A.
136 F3 Dörtyol Turkey
140 C3 Dorūd Iran
165 G1 Dorum Germany
178 C3 Doruma Dem. Rep. Congo
140 E3 Dorūneh Iran
165 H2 Dörverden Germany
141 E4 Do Sārī Iran
212 C6 Dos Bahías, Cabo c. Arg.
197 H5 Dos Cabezas U.S.A.
210 C5 Dos de Mayo Peru
141 H3 Dōshī Afgh.
149 C6 Đô Sơn Vietnam
196 B3 Dos Palos U.S.A.
165 K2 Dosse r. Germany
176 C3 Dosso Niger
138 C3 Dossor Kazakh.
139 G4 Do'stlik Uzbek.
139 J3 Dostyk Kazakh.
201 C6 Dothan U.S.A.
166 F1 Douai France
176 C4 Douala Cameroon
166 B2 Douarnenez France
149 □ Double Island Hong Kong China
196 C4 Double Peak U.S.A.
166 H3 Doubs r. France
128 A6 Doubtful Sound inlet N.Z.
128 D1 Doubtless Bay N.Z.
176 B3 Douentza Mali
160 C3 Douglas Isle of Man
180 E4 Douglas S. Africa
162 E5 Douglas U.K.
186 C3 Douglas AK U.S.A.
197 H6 Douglas AZ U.S.A.
201 D6 Douglas GA U.S.A.
194 F3 Douglas WY U.S.A.
127 H8 Douglas-Apsley National Park Australia
186 D4 Douglas Channel Canada
197 H2 Douglas Creek r. U.S.A.
149 F6 Douliu Taiwan
166 F1 Doullens France
162 D4 Doune U.K.
214 C2 Dourada, Cachoeira waterfall Brazil
214 B2 Dourada, Serra hills Brazil
214 C1 Dourada, Serra mts Brazil
214 A3 Dourados Brazil
214 A3 Dourados r. Brazil
214 B3 Dourados, Serra dos hills Brazil
167 C2 Douro r. Port. alt. Duero (Spain)
164 D5 Douzy France
161 F4 Dove r. England U.K.
161 I5 Dove r. England U.K.
189 I3 Dove Brook Canada
197 H3 Dove Creek U.S.A.
127 G9 Dover Australia
161 I6 Dover U.K.
203 F5 Dover DE U.S.A.
203 H3 Dover NH U.S.A.
203 F4 Dover NJ U.S.A.
202 C4 Dover OH U.S.A.
161 I7 Dover, Strait of France/U.K.
203 I2 Dover-Foxcroft U.S.A.
161 D5 Dovey r. U.K.
140 B3 Doveyrich r. Iran/Iraq
190 D5 Dowagiac U.S.A.
140 D4 Dow Chāhī Iran
141 E2 Dowghā'ī Iran
154 A5 Dowi, Tanjung pt Indon.
141 G2 Dowlātābād Afgh.
141 F3 Dowlatābād Farāh Afgh.
141 G2 Dowlatābād Fāryāb Afgh.
140 D4 Dowlatābād Fārs Iran
140 D4 Dowlatābād Fārs Iran
140 E4 Dowlatābād Kermān Iran
141 F2 Dowlatābād Khorāsān-e Razavī Iran
141 G3 Dowlatyār Afgh.
196 B2 Downieville U.S.A.
163 F3 Downpatrick U.K.
203 F3 Downsville U.S.A.
137 K4 Dow Sar Iran
196 B1 Doyle U.S.A.
203 F4 Doylestown U.S.A.
151 C6 Dōzen is Japan
191 I2 Dozois, Réservoir resr Canada
176 B2 Drâa, Hamada du plat. Alg.
214 B3 Dracena Brazil
164 E1 Drachten Neth.
171 K2 Drăgănești-Olt Romania
171 K2 Drăgășani Romania
213 E2 Dragon's Mouths str. Trin. and Tob./Venez.
159 M3 Dragsfjärd Fin.
166 H5 Draguignan France
173 C4 Drahichyn Belarus
127 J2 Drake Australia
197 F4 Drake AR U.S.A.
187 I5 Drake ND U.S.A.
181 H5 Drakensberg mts Lesotho/S. Africa
181 I2 Drakensberg mts S. Africa
219 E9 Drake Passage sea chan. S. Atlantic Ocean
171 K4 Drama Greece
159 J4 Drammen Norway
159 J4 Drangedal Norway
141 G5 Drangjuk h. Pak.
165 H3 Dransfeld Germany
163 E3 Draperstown U.K.
144 C2 Dras India
168 F7 Drau r. Austria
186 G4 Drayton Valley Canada
170 B6 Dréan Alg.
165 H4 Dreistelzberge h. Germany
168 F5 Dresden Germany
172 D4 Dretun' Belarus
166 E2 Dreux France
159 K3 Drevsjø Norway
160 G3 Driffield U.K.
202 D4 Driftwood U.S.A.
163 B6 Drimoleague Ireland
170 G3 Drniš Croatia
165 H1 Drochtersen Germany
163 E4 Drogheda Ireland
173 B5 Drohobych Ukr.
161 E5 Droitwich Spa U.K.
145 G4 Drokung India
165 I2 Drömling reg. Germany
163 D4 Dromod Ireland
163 D3 Dromore Northern Ireland U.K.
163 E3 Dromore Northern Ireland U.K.
161 F4 Dronfield U.K.
185 P2 Dronning Louise Land reg. Greenland
164 D2 Dronten Neth.
144 B2 Drosh Pak.
173 F4 Droskovo Russia
127 F7 Drouin Australia
186 G4 Drumheller Canada
194 D2 Drummond MT U.S.A.
190 B2 Drummond WI U.S.A.
191 F3 Drummond Island U.S.A.
189 F4 Drummondville Canada
162 D6 Drummore U.K.
162 D4 Drumochter, Pass of U.K.
159 N5 Druskininkai Lith.
133 P3 Druzhina Russia
171 K3 Dryanovo Bulg.
186 B3 Dry Bay U.S.A.
187 K5 Dryberry Lake Canada
190 E2 Dryburg U.S.A.
188 B4 Dryden Canada
196 D2 Dry Lake U.S.A.
162 D4 Drymen U.K.
124 C3 Drysdale r. Australia
140 C3 Dūāb r. Iran
149 C6 Du'an China
203 F2 Duane U.S.A.
145 G4 Duars reg. India
205 J5 Duarte, Pico mt. Dom. Rep.
134 B4 Ḑubā Saudi Arabia
142 E4 Dubai U.A.E.
169 N7 Dubăsari Moldova
187 I2 Dubawnt r. Canada
187 I2 Dubawnt Lake Canada
Dubayy U.A.E. see Dubai
134 B4 Dubbagh, Jabal ad mt. Saudi Arabia
127 H4 Dubbo Australia
190 D1 Dublin Canada
163 E4 Dublin Ireland
201 D5 Dublin U.S.A.
172 F3 Dubna Russia
173 C5 Dubno Ukr.
194 D2 Dubois ID U.S.A.
202 D4 Du Bois U.S.A.
194 E3 Dubois WY U.S.A.
173 H5 Dubovka Russia
173 G6 Dubovskoye Russia
176 A4 Dubréka Guinea
171 H3 Dubrovnik Croatia
173 C5 Dubrovytsya Ukr.
172 D4 Dubrowna Belarus
190 B4 Dubuque U.S.A.
159 M5 Dubysa r. Lith.
154 C3 Đưc Bôn Vietnam
123 J6 Duc de Gloucester, Îles du is Fr. Polynesia
149 E4 Duchang China
197 G1 Duchesne U.S.A.
123 J7 Ducie Island atoll Pitcairn Is
201 C5 Duck r. U.S.A.
187 I4 Duck Bay Canada
187 H4 Duck Lake Canada
190 E4 Duck Lake U.S.A.
197 E2 Duckwater U.S.A.
197 E2 Duckwater Peak U.S.A.
154 C3 Đưc Linh Vietnam
154 D2 Đưc Phô Vietnam
Đưc Tai Vietnam see Đưc Linh
154 C1 Duc Tho Vietnam
Đưc Trong Vietnam see Liên Nghia
213 B4 Duda r. Col.
164 E5 Dudelange Lux.
165 I3 Duderstadt Germany
145 E4 Dudhi India
145 G4 Dudhnai India
132 J3 Dudinka Russia
161 E5 Dudley U.K.
144 D6 Dudna r. India
162 F3 Dudwick, Hill of U.K.
176 B4 Duékoué Côte d'Ivoire
167 C2 Duero r. Spain alt. Douro (Portugal)
191 H1 Dufault, Lac l. Canada
164 C3 Duffel Belgium
188 E2 Dufferin, Cape Canada
202 B6 Duffield U.S.A.
125 G2 Duff Islands Solomon Is
162 E3 Dufftown U.K.
170 B2 Dufourspitze mt. Italy/Switz.
188 E1 Dufrost, Pointe pt Canada
170 F3 Dugi Otok i. Croatia
148 D3 Du He r. China
213 D4 Duida, Cerro mt. Venez.
210 E3 Duida-Marahuaca, Parque Nacional Venez.
164 E3 Duisburg Germany
213 B3 Duitama Col.
148 B4 Dujiangyan China
181 G5 Dukathole S. Africa
186 C4 Duke Island U.S.A.
140 C5 Dukhān Qatar
169 P3 Dukhovshchina Russia
144 B3 Duki Pak.
159 N5 Dūkštas Lith.
141 E4 Dūlab Iran
146 B3 Dulan China
212 D3 Dulce r. Arg.
206 I6 Dulce, Golfo b. Costa Rica
206 H5 Dulce Nombre de Culmí Hond.
145 E2 Dulishi Hu salt l. China
181 I2 Dullstroom S. Africa
164 F3 Dülmen Germany
171 L3 Dulovo Bulg.
190 A2 Duluth U.S.A.
190 A2 Duluth/Superior airport U.S.A.
161 D6 Dulverton U.K.
136 F5 Dūmā Syria
153 B4 Dumaguete Phil.
155 B2 Dumai Indon.
153 B4 Dumaran i. Phil.
199 F5 Dumas AR U.S.A.
199 C5 Dumas TX U.S.A.
136 F5 Ḑumayr Syria
162 D5 Dumbarton U.K.
181 I3 Dumbe S. Africa
169 I6 Ďumbier mt. Slovakia
144 D2 Dumchele India
145 G5 Dum-Dum India
145 H4 Dum Duma India
162 E5 Dumfries U.K.
145 F4 Dumka India
165 G2 Dümmer l. Germany
188 E4 Dumoine, Lac Canada
129 C6 Dumont d'Urville research stn Antarctica
129 C6 Dumont d'Urville Sea sea Antarctica
164 E4 Dümpelfeld Germany
177 F1 Dumyāṭ Egypt
165 I3 Dün ridge Germany
171 H1 Duna r. Hungary alt. Donau (Austria/Germany), alt. Dunaj (Slovakia), alt. Dunărea (Romania), alt. Dunav (Serbia), conv. Danube
171 L3 Dunaj r. Slovakia alt. Donau (Austria/Germany), alt. Duna (Hungary), alt. Dunărea (Romania), alt. Dunav (Serbia), conv. Danube
168 H7 Dunajská Streda Slovakia
169 I7 Dunakeszi Hungary
127 G9 Dunalley Australia
163 E4 Dunany Point Ireland
171 L3 Dunărea r. Romania alt. Donau (Austria/Germany), alt. Duna (Hungary), alt. Dunaj (Slovakia), alt. Dunav (Serbia), conv. Danube
169 I7 Dunaújváros Hungary
171 L3 Dunav r. alt. Donau (Austria/Germany), alt. Duna (Hungary), alt. Dunaj (Slovakia), alt. Dunărea (Romania), conv. Danube
173 C5 Dunayivtsi Ukr.
128 C6 Dunback N.Z.
162 F4 Dunbar U.K.
162 E4 Dunblane U.K.
163 E4 Dunboyne Ireland
186 E5 Duncan Canada
197 H5 Duncan AZ U.S.A.
199 D5 Duncan OK U.S.A.
188 D3 Duncan, Cape Canada
188 E3 Duncan, Lac l. Canada
190 B5 Duncan Mills U.S.A.
202 E4 Duncannon U.S.A.
162 E2 Duncansby Head U.K.
163 E5 Duncormick Ireland
159 M4 Dundaga Latvia
191 G3 Dundalk Canada
163 E3 Dundalk Ireland
202 E5 Dundalk U.S.A.
163 E4 Dundalk Bay Ireland
186 C4 Dundas Island Canada
Dún Dealgan Ireland see Dundalk
181 I4 Dundee S. Africa
162 F4 Dundee U.K.
191 F5 Dundee MI U.S.A.
202 E3 Dundee NY U.S.A.
163 F3 Dundonald U.K.
127 F1 Dundoo Australia
162 E6 Dundrennan U.K.
163 F3 Dundrum U.K.
163 F3 Dundrum Bay U.K.
145 E4 Dundwa Range mts India/Nepal
188 F2 Dune, Lac l. Canada
128 C6 Dunedin N.Z.
201 D6 Dunedin U.S.A.
127 H4 Dunedoo Australia
162 E4 Dunfermline U.K.
163 E3 Dungannon U.K.
144 C5 Dungarpur India
163 D5 Dungarvan Ireland
161 H7 Dungeness hd U.K.
212 C8 Dungeness, Punta pt Arg.
164 F4 Düngenheim Germany
163 E3 Dungiven U.K.
Dungloe Ireland see An Clochán Liath
127 I4 Dungog Australia
178 C3 Dungu Dem. Rep. Congo
155 B2 Dungun Malaysia
177 F2 Dungunab Sudan
152 E2 Dunhua China
146 B2 Dunhuang China
126 E6 Dunkeld Australia
162 E4 Dunkeld U.K.
Dunkerque France see Dunkirk
161 D6 Dunkery Hill U.K.
166 F1 Dunkirk France
202 D3 Dunkirk U.S.A.
176 B4 Dunkwa Ghana
163 E4 Dún Laoghaire Ireland
163 E4 Dunlavin Ireland
163 E4 Dunleer Ireland
163 E2 Dunloy U.K.
163 B6 Dunmanus Bay Ireland
163 B6 Dunmanway Ireland
163 C4 Dunmore Ireland
201 E7 Dunmore Town Bahamas
196 D3 Dunmovin U.S.A.
163 F3 Dunmurry U.K.
201 E5 Dunn U.S.A.
162 E2 Dunnet Bay U.K.
162 E2 Dunnet Head U.K.
196 B2 Dunnigan U.S.A.
198 C3 Dunning U.S.A.
191 H4 Dunnville Canada
126 E6 Dunolly Australia
162 D5 Dunoon U.K.
162 F5 Duns U.K.
198 C1 Dunseith U.S.A.
194 B3 Dunsmuir U.S.A.
161 G6 Dunstable U.K.
128 B6 Dunstan Mountains N.Z.
164 D5 Dun-sur-Meuse France
128 C6 Duntroon N.Z.
162 B3 Dunvegan, Loch b. U.K.
144 B3 Dunyapur Pak.
148 E1 Duolun China
154 C3 Dương Đông Vietnam
149 D5 Dupang Ling mts China
191 H1 Duparquet, Lac l. Canada
171 J3 Dupnitsa Bulg.
198 C2 Dupree U.S.A.
200 B4 Du Quoin U.S.A.
124 C3 Durack r. Australia
136 E1 Durağan Turkey
166 G5 Durance r. France
191 F4 Durand MI U.S.A.
190 B3 Durand WI U.S.A.
206 C2 Durango Mex.
206 C2 Durango state Mex.
167 E1 Durango Spain
195 F4 Durango U.S.A.
199 D5 Durant U.S.A.
215 F2 Durazno Uruguay
215 F1 Durazno, Cuchilla Grande del hills Uruguay
181 I4 Durban S. Africa
166 F5 Durban-Corbières France
180 C6 Durbanville S. Africa
202 D5 Durbin U.S.A.
164 D4 Durbuy Belgium
164 E4 Düren Germany
144 E5 Durg India
145 F5 Durgapur India
191 G3 Durham Canada
160 F3 Durham U.K.
196 B2 Durham CA U.S.A.
201 E4 Durham NC U.S.A.
203 H3 Durham NH U.S.A.
141 G4 Dūrī Rōd r. Afgh.
173 D6 Durlești Moldova
165 G6 Durmersheim Germany
171 H3 Durmitor mt. Montenegro
162 D2 Durness U.K.
171 H4 Durrës Albania
161 F6 Durrington U.K.
163 A6 Dursey Island Ireland
136 B2 Dursunbey Turkey
136 F5 Durūz, Jabal ad mt. Syria
124 D2 D'Urville, Tanjung pt Indon.
128 D4 D'Urville Island N.Z.
138 D5 Duşak Turkm.
141 G4 Dushai Pak.
Dushak Turkm. see Duşak
149 C5 Dushan China
139 G5 Dushanbe Tajik.
173 H7 Dusheti Georgia
128 A6 Dusky Sound inlet N.Z.
164 E3 Düsseldorf Germany
Dustlik Uzbek. see Do'stlik
197 F1 Dutch Mountain U.S.A.
180 E1 Dutlwe Botswana
176 C3 Dutse Nigeria
126 B3 Dutton, Lake salt flat Australia
197 F2 Dutton, Mount U.S.A.
181 H6 Dutywa S. Africa
172 H3 Duvannoye Russia
189 F2 Duvert, Lac l. Canada
140 C5 Duweihin, Khor b. Saudi Arabia/U.A.E.
149 C5 Duyun China
141 F5 Duzab Pak.
136 C1 Düzce Turkey
173 F5 Dvorichna Ukr.
150 B2 Dvoryanka Russia
144 B5 Dwarka India
181 G2 Dwarsberg S. Africa
190 C5 Dwight U.S.A.
164 E2 Dwingelderveld, Nationaal Park nat. park Neth.
194 C2 Dworshak Reservoir U.S.A.
180 D6 Dwyka S. Africa
Dyanev Turkm. see Galkynyş
172 E4 Dyat'kovo Russia
162 F3 Dyce U.K.
190 D5 Dyer IN U.S.A.
196 C3 Dyer NV U.S.A.
185 L3 Dyer, Cape Canada
191 G3 Dyer Bay Canada
201 B4 Dyersburg U.S.A.
190 B4 Dyersville U.S.A.
162 E3 Dyke U.K.
165 K5 Dyleň h. Czech Rep.
169 I4 Dylewska Góra h. Poland
126 F2 Dynevor Downs Australia
181 H5 Dyoki S. Africa
190 A4 Dysart U.S.A.
180 E6 Dysselsdorp S. Africa
146 D2 Dzamïn Üüd Mongolia
177 D4 Dzanga-Ndoki, Parc National de nat. park C.A.R.
177 D4 Dzanga-Ndoki, Parc National de nat. park C.A.R.
179 E5 Dzaoudzi Africa
172 G3 Dzerzhinsk Russia
169 M5 Dzerzhyns'k Ukr.
146 E1 Dzhagdy, Khrebet mts Russia
Dzhalal-Abad Kyrg. see Jalal-Abad
Dzhanga Turkm. see Jaňňa
Dzhangel'dy Uzbek. see Jongeldi
173 E6 Dzhankoy Crimea
Dzharkurgan Uzbek. see Jarqo'rg'on
Dzhebel Turkm. see Jebel
Dzhigirbent Turkm. see Jigerbent
Dzhizak Uzbek. see Jizzax
146 F1 Dzhugdzhur, Khrebet mts Russia
Dzhuma Uzbek. see Juma
139 I2 Dzhusaly Kazakh.
169 J4 Działdowo Poland
207 G4 Dzibalchén Mex.
207 G3 Dzilam de Bravo Mex.
Dzungarian Basin China see Junggar Pendi
139 J3 Dzungarian Gate pass China/Kazakh.
146 C2 Dzuunmod Mongolia
172 C4 Dzyaniskavichy Belarus
172 C4 Dzyarzhynsk Belarus
169 M4 Dzyatlavichy Belarus

E

188 C3 Eabamet Lake Canada
197 H4 Eagar U.S.A.
189 I3 Eagle r. Canada
195 F4 Eagle U.S.A.
203 F3 Eagle Bay U.S.A.
196 D4 Eagle Crags mt. U.S.A.
187 H4 Eagle Creek r. Canada
187 K5 Eagle Lake l. Canada
203 I1 Eagle Lake U.S.A.
194 B3 Eagle Lake l. CA U.S.A.
203 I1 Eagle Lake l. ME U.S.A.
190 B2 Eagle Mountain h. U.S.A.
199 C6 Eagle Pass U.S.A.
184 D3 Eagle Plain Canada
190 C2 Eagle River MI U.S.A.
190 C3 Eagle River WI U.S.A.
186 F3 Eaglesham Canada
197 F5 Eagle Tail Mountains U.S.A.
188 B3 Ear Falls Canada
196 C4 Earlimart U.S.A.
162 F5 Earlston U.K.
191 H2 Earlton Canada
162 E4 Earn r. U.K.
162 D4 Earn, Loch l. U.K.
199 C5 Earth U.S.A.
160 H4 Easington U.K.
201 D5 Easley U.S.A.
129 D5 East Antarctica reg. Antarctica
203 F4 East Ararat U.S.A.
202 D3 East Aurora U.S.A.
199 F6 East Bay U.S.A.
203 G2 East Berkshire U.S.A.
161 H7 Eastbourne U.K.
202 D4 East Branch Clarion River Reservoir U.S.A.
203 H4 East Brooklyn U.S.A.
128 G2 East Cape N.Z.
197 G2 East Carbon City U.S.A.
216 E5 East Caroline Basin sea feature N. Pacific Ocean
190 D5 East Chicago U.S.A.
146 E3 East China Sea Asia
128 E2 East Coast Bays N.Z.
203 G2 East Corinth U.S.A.
East Dereham U.K. see Dereham
208 C5 Easter Island S. Pacific Ocean
181 G5 Eastern Cape prov. S. Africa
177 F2 Eastern Desert Egypt
143 C2 Eastern Ghats mts India
144 B4 Eastern Nara canal Pak.
Eastern Transvaal prov. S. Africa see Mpumalanga
187 J4 Easterville Canada
212 E8 East Falkland i. Falkland Is
203 H4 East Falmouth U.S.A.
164 E1 East Frisian Islands Germany
196 D2 Eastgate U.S.A.
198 D2 East Grand Forks U.S.A.
161 G6 East Grinstead U.K.
203 G3 Easthampton U.S.A.
203 G4 East Hampton U.S.A.
203 G3 East Hebron U.S.A.
202 D4 East Hickory U.S.A.
218 K6 East Indiaman Ridge sea feature Indian Ocean
203 G3 East Jamaica U.S.A.
190 E3 East Jordan U.S.A.
162 D5 East Kilbride U.K.
190 D3 East Lake U.S.A.
149 □ East Lamma Channel Hong Kong China
161 F7 Eastleigh U.K.
202 C4 East Liverpool U.S.A.
162 B3 East Loch Tarbert inlet U.K.
181 G6 East London S. Africa
202 B5 East Lynn Lake U.S.A.
188 E3 Eastmain Canada
188 F3 Eastmain r. Canada
203 G2 Eastman Canada
201 D5 Eastman U.S.A.
216 F5 East Mariana Basin sea feature Pacific Ocean
203 I2 East Millinocket U.S.A.
190 B5 East Moline U.S.A.
190 C5 Easton IL U.S.A.
203 E5 Easton MD U.S.A.
203 F4 Easton PA U.S.A.
217 L8 East Pacific Ridge sea feature S. Pacific Ocean
217 L4 East Pacific Rise sea feature N. Pacific Ocean
196 A2 East Park Reservoir U.S.A.
189 H4 East Point pt Canada
201 C5 East Point U.S.A.
203 J2 Eastport ME U.S.A.
190 E3 Eastport MI U.S.A.
196 D1 East Range mts U.S.A.
200 B4 East St Louis U.S.A.
East Sea Pacific Ocean see Japan, Sea of
133 Q2 East Siberian Sea Russia
127 H7 East Sister Island Australia
147 E7 East Timor country Asia
145 F4 East Tons r. India
127 F3 East Toorale Australia
190 C4 East Troy U.S.A.
203 F6 Eastville U.S.A.
196 C2 East Walker r. U.S.A.
203 G3 East Wallingford U.S.A.
201 D5 Eatonton U.S.A.
190 B3 Eau Claire U.S.A.
190 B3 Eau Claire r. U.S.A.
188 F2 Eau Claire, Lac à l' l. Canada
147 G6 Eauripik atoll Micronesia
216 E5 Eauripik Rise-New Guinea Rise sea feature N. Pacific Ocean
207 E3 Ebano Mex.
161 D6 Ebbw Vale U.K.
176 D4 Ebebiyin Equat. Guinea
180 B2 Ebenerde Namibia
202 D4 Ebensburg U.S.A.
136 C2 Eber Gölü l. Turkey
165 I3 Ebergötzen Germany
168 F4 Eberswalde Germany
191 F4 Eberts Canada
150 G3 Ebetsu Japan
149 B4 Ebian China
139 J3 Ebinur Hu salt l. China
170 F4 Eboli Italy
176 D4 Ebolowa Cameroon
137 J3 Ebrāhim Ḩeṣār Iran
167 G2 Ebro r. Spain
165 I1 Ebstorf Germany
171 L4 Eceabat Turkey
153 B2 Echague Phil.
167 E1 Echegárate, Puerto pass Spain
206 A1 Echeverria, Pico mt. Mex.
151 E7 Echizen Japan
127 G9 Echo, Lake Australia
186 F1 Echo Bay N.W.T. Canada
191 E2 Echo Bay Ont. Canada
197 G3 Echo Cliffs U.S.A.
188 B3 Echoing r. Canada
191 J2 Échouani, Lac l. Canada
164 D3 Echt Neth.
164 E5 Echternach Lux.
126 F6 Echuca Australia
165 G4 Echzell Germany
167 D4 Écija Spain
165 J5 Eckental Germany
190 E2 Eckerman U.S.A.
168 D3 Eckernförde Germany
185 K2 Eclipse Sound sea chan. Canada
166 H4 Écrins, Massif des mts France
210 C4 Ecuador country S. America
188 E2 Écueils, Pointe aux pt Canada
178 E2 Ed Eritrea
159 J4 Ed Sweden
187 H4 Edam Canada
164 D2 Edam Neth.
162 F1 Eday i. U.K.
177 E3 Ed Da'ein Sudan
177 F3 Ed Damazin Sudan
177 F3 Ed Damer Sudan
177 F3 Ed Debba Sudan
177 F3 Ed Dueim Sudan
127 H8 Eddystone Point Australia
164 D2 Ede Neth.
176 D4 Edéa Cameroon
187 J2 Edehon Lake Canada
214 C2 Edéia Brazil
127 H6 Eden Australia
160 E3 Eden r. U.K.
199 D6 Eden U.S.A.
181 F4 Edenburg S. Africa
128 B7 Edendale N.Z.
163 D4 Edenderry Ireland
126 D6 Edenhope Australia
201 E4 Edenton U.S.A.
181 G3 Edenville S. Africa
171 J4 Edessa Greece
165 F1 Edewecht Germany
203 H4 Edgartown U.S.A.
198 D2 Edgeley U.S.A.
198 C3 Edgemont U.S.A.
190 C4 Edgerton U.S.A.
163 D4 Edgeworthstown Ireland
139 K2 Edigan Russia
190 A5 Edina U.S.A.
199 D7 Edinburg U.S.A.
162 E5 Edinburgh U.K.
169 M6 Edineț Moldova
173 C7 Edirne Turkey
186 F4 Edith Cavell, Mount Canada
194 B2 Edmonds U.S.A.
186 G4 Edmonton Canada
187 J5 Edmore U.S.A.
190 B4 Edmund U.S.A.
187 K4 Edmund Lake Canada
189 G4 Edmundston Canada
199 D6 Edna U.S.A.
186 C3 Edna Bay U.S.A.
171 L5 Edremit Turkey
159 K3 Edsbyn Sweden
186 F4 Edson Canada
215 D2 Eduardo Castex Arg.
126 F5 Edward r. Australia
178 C4 Edward, Lake Dem. Rep. Congo/Uganda
190 C1 Edward Island Canada
203 F2 Edwards U.S.A.
126 A2 Edward's Creek Australia
199 C6 Edwards Plateau U.S.A.
200 B4 Edwardsville U.S.A.
129 B5 Edward VII Peninsula pen. Antarctica
186 C3 Edziza, Mount Canada
164 B3 Eeklo Belgium
196 A1 Eel r. U.S.A.
196 A2 Eel, South Fork r. U.S.A.
164 E1 Eemshaven pt Neth.
179 B5 Eenhana Namibia
164 E1 Eenrum Neth.
180 D3 Eenzamheid Pan salt pan S. Africa
125 G3 Éfaté i. Vanuatu
Efes tourist site Turkey see Ephesus
200 B4 Effingham U.S.A.
136 D1 Eflâni Turkey
197 E2 Egan Range mts U.S.A.
191 I3 Eganville Canada
169 J7 Eger Hungary
159 I4 Egersund Norway
165 G3 Eggegebirge hills Germany
165 J5 Eggolsheim Germany
164 C4 Eghezée Belgium
158 D2 Egilsstaðir Iceland
136 C3 Eğirdir Turkey
136 C3 Eğirdir Gölü l. Turkey
166 F4 Égletons France
163 D2 Eglinton U.K.
184 F2 Eglinton Island Canada
164 C2 Egmond aan Zee Neth.
128 D3 Egmont, Cape N.Z.
Egmont, Mount vol. N.Z. see Taranaki, Mount
128 E3 Egmont National Park N.Z.
136 B2 Eğrigöz Dağı mts Turkey
160 G3 Egton U.K.
214 D1 Éguas r. Brazil
133 U3 Egvekinot Russia
177 E2 Egypt country Africa
148 A2 Ehen Hudag China
168 D6 Ehingen (Donau) Germany
165 I2 Ehra-Lessien Germany
197 E5 Ehrenberg U.S.A.
165 I5 Eibelstadt Germany
164 E2 Eibergen Neth.
165 H4 Eichenzell Germany
165 J6 Eichstätt Germany
159 I3 Eidfjord Norway
159 J3 Eidsvoll Norway
164 E4 Eifel hills Germany
162 B4 Eigg i. U.K.
143 A4 Eight Degree Channel India/Maldives
124 C3 Eighty Mile Beach Australia
136 E7 Eilat Israel
127 F6 Eildon Australia
127 F6 Eildon, Lake Australia
187 H2 Eileen Lake Canada
165 K3 Eilenburg Germany
165 I2 Eimke Germany
165 H3 Einbeck Germany
164 D3 Eindhoven Neth.
168 D7 Einsiedeln Switz.
219 G2 Eirik Ridge sea feature N. Atlantic Ocean
210 E5 Eirunepé Brazil
165 H3 Eisberg h. Germany
179 C5 Eiseb watercourse Namibia
165 I4 Eisenach Germany
165 J4 Eisenberg Germany
168 G4 Eisenhüttenstadt Germany
168 H7 Eisenstadt Austria
165 I4 Eisfeld Germany
162 C3 Eishort, Loch inlet U.K.
165 J3 Eisleben, Lutherstadt Germany
165 H4 Eiterfeld Germany
Eivissa Spain see Ibiza
Eivissa i. Spain see Ibiza
167 F1 Ejea de los Caballeros Spain
179 E6 Ejeda Madag.
207 E4 Ejutla Mex.
159 M4 Ekenäs Fin.
138 C5 Ekerem Turkm.
164 C3 Ekeren Belgium
128 E4 Eketahuna N.Z.
133 L3 Ekonda Russia
159 K3 Ekshärad Sweden
159 K4 Eksjö Sweden
180 B4 Eksteenfontein S. Africa
178 C4 Ekuku Dem. Rep. Congo
188 D3 Ekwan r. Canada
188 D3 Ekwan Point Canada
171 J6 Elafonisou, Steno sea chan. Greece
181 H2 Elands r. S. Africa
181 H2 Elandsdoorn S. Africa
170 B7 El Aouinet Alg.
167 H4 El Arba, Tizi h. Alg.
206 A1 El Arco Mex.
171 J5 Elassona Greece
137 G2 Elazığ Turkey
170 D3 Elba, Isola d' i. Italy
146 F1 El'ban Russia
213 B2 El Banco Col.
192 E5 El Barreal salt l. Mex.
171 I4 Elbasan Albania
136 E2 Elbaşı Turkey
213 C2 El Baúl Venez.
El Bawîti Egypt see Al Bawīṭī
176 C1 El Bayadh Alg.
165 I1 Elbe r. Germany alt. Labe (Czech Rep.)
195 F4 Elbert, Mount U.S.A.
190 D3 Elberta MI U.S.A.
197 G2 Elberta UT U.S.A.
201 D5 Elberton U.S.A.
166 E2 Elbeuf France
136 F2 Elbistan Turkey
169 I3 Elbląg Poland
215 B4 El Bolsón Arg.
201 E7 Elbow Cay i. Bahamas
173 G7 El'brus mt. Russia
164 D2 Elburg Neth.
167 E2 El Burgo de Osma Spain
140 C2 Elburz Mountains Iran
215 C4 El Caín Arg.
196 D5 El Cajon U.S.A.
212 B8 El Calafate Arg.
213 E3 El Callao Venez.
199 D6 El Campo U.S.A.
195 F5 El Capitan Mountain U.S.A.
213 B2 El Carmen de Bolívar Col.
197 E5 El Centro U.S.A.
210 F7 El Cerro Bol.
213 D2 El Chaparro Venez.
Elche Spain see Elche-Elx
167 F3 Elche-Elx Spain
207 F4 El Chichónal vol. Mex.
206 C1 El Chilicote Mex.
124 D3 Elcho Island Australia
213 B3 El Cocuy Col.
213 B3 El Cocuy, Parque Nacional nat. park Col.
207 H3 El Cuyo Mex.
167 F3 Elda Spain
165 J1 Elde r. Germany
191 H2 Eldee Canada
126 D3 Elder, Lake Australia
206 D2 El Diamante Mex.
213 B2 El Difícil Col.
133 O3 El'dikan Russia
213 A4 El Diviso Col.
197 E6 El Doctor Mex.
190 A5 Eldon IA U.S.A.
198 E4 Eldon MO U.S.A.
212 F3 Eldorado Arg.
206 C2 El Dorado Mex.
199 E5 El Dorado AR U.S.A.
199 D4 El Dorado KS U.S.A.
199 C6 Eldorado U.S.A.
213 E3 El Dorado Venez.
178 D3 Eldoret Kenya
194 E2 Electric Peak U.S.A.
176 B2 El Eglab plat. Alg.
167 E4 El Ejido Spain
172 F4 Elektrostal' Russia
210 D4 El Encanto Col.
165 I3 Elend Germany
143 A2 Elephanta Caves tourist site India
195 F5 Elephant Butte Reservoir U.S.A.
129 B2 Elephant Island i. Antarctica
145 H5 Elephant Point Bangl.
137 I2 Eleşkirt Turkey
207 G5 El Estor Guat.
176 C1 El Eulma Alg.
201 E7 Eleuthera i. Bahamas
170 C6 El Fahs Tunisia
177 E3 El Fasher Sudan
165 H4 Elfershausen Germany
206 B2 El Fuerte Mex.
177 E3 El Fula West Kordofan Sudan
178 C2 El Fula West Kordofan Sudan
177 E3 El Geneina Sudan
177 F3 El Geteina Sudan
162 E3 Elgin U.K.
190 C4 Elgin IL U.S.A.
198 C2 Elgin ND U.S.A.
197 E3 Elgin NV U.S.A.
197 G2 Elgin (abandoned) U.S.A.
133 P3 El'ginskiy Russia
206 D3 El Gogorrón, Parque Nacional nat. park Mex.
176 C1 El Goléa Alg.
177 F4 Elgon, Mount Uganda
170 B6 El Hadjar Alg.
176 A2 El Hierro i. Canary Is
207 E3 El Higo Mex.
176 C2 El Homr Alg.
171 L3 Elhovo Bulg.
162 F4 Elie U.K.
128 C5 Elie de Beaumont, Mount mt. N.Z.
184 B3 Elim U.S.A.
189 H2 Eliot, Mount Canada
173 H6 Elista Russia
190 B4 Elizabeth IL U.S.A.
203 F4 Elizabeth NJ U.S.A.
202 C5 Elizabeth WV U.S.A.
201 E4 Elizabeth City U.S.A.
203 H4 Elizabeth Islands U.S.A.
201 D4 Elizabethton U.S.A.
200 C4 Elizabethtown KY U.S.A.
201 E5 Elizabethtown NC U.S.A.
203 G2 Elizabethtown NY U.S.A.
202 E4 Elizabethtown PA U.S.A.
167 F1 Elizondo Spain
176 B1 El Jadida Morocco
206 C2 El Jaralito Mex.
170 D7 El Jem Tunisia
206 H5 El Jicaral Nicaragua
186 G4 Elk r. Canada
169 K4 Ełk Poland
196 A2 Elk U.S.A.
202 C5 Elk r. U.S.A.
170 C6 El Kala Alg.
177 F3 El Kamlin Sudan
199 D5 Elk City U.S.A.
196 A2 Elk Creek U.S.A.
196 B2 Elk Grove U.S.A.

Ferkessédougou

190 E5 Elkhart U.S.A.
176 B2 El Khnâchîch esc. Mali
190 C4 Elkhorn U.S.A.
198 D3 Elkhorn r. U.S.A.
202 D5 Elkins U.S.A.
186 G4 Elk Island National Park Canada
191 G2 Elk Lake Canada
190 E3 Elk Lake l. U.S.A.
202 E4 Elkland U.S.A.
186 F5 Elko Canada
194 D3 Elko U.S.A.
187 G4 Elk Point Canada
198 E2 Elk River U.S.A.
203 F5 Elkton MD U.S.A.
202 D5 Elkton VA U.S.A.
187 L2 Ell Bay Canada
185 H2 Ellef Ringnes Island Canada
197 G2 Ellen, Mount U.S.A.
144 C3 Ellenabad India
198 D2 Ellendale U.S.A.
194 B2 Ellensburg U.S.A.
203 F4 Ellenville U.S.A.
127 H6 Ellery, Mount Australia
128 D5 Ellesmere, Lake N.Z.
185 J2 Ellesmere Island Canada
161 E4 Ellesmere Port U.K.
184 H3 Ellice r. Canada
202 D3 Ellicottville U.S.A.
207 E3 El Limón Mex.
165 I5 Ellingen Germany
181 G5 Elliot S. Africa
181 H5 Elliotdale S. Africa
191 F2 Elliot Lake Canada
194 D2 Ellis U.S.A.
Ellisras S. Africa see Lephalale
126 A4 Elliston Australia
162 F3 Ellon U.K.
144 C5 Ellora Caves tourist site India
203 I2 Ellsworth ME U.S.A.
190 A3 Ellsworth WI U.S.A.
129 B3 Ellsworth Land reg. Antarctica
129 B3 Ellsworth Mountains mts Antarctica
165 I6 Ellwangen (Jagst) Germany
136 B3 Elmalı Turkey
196 D6 El Maneadero Mex.
213 E3 El Manteco Venez.
176 C1 El Meghaïer Alg.
213 E3 El Miamo Venez.
136 E4 El Mîna Lebanon
190 E3 Elmira MI U.S.A.
202 E3 Elmira NY U.S.A.
197 F5 El Mirage U.S.A.
167 E4 El Moral Spain
126 F6 Elmore Australia
215 D2 El Morro mt. Arg.
176 B2 El Mreyyé reg. Mauritania
165 H1 Elmshorn Germany
177 E3 El Muglad Sudan
191 G3 Elmwood Canada
190 C5 Elmwood IL U.S.A.
190 A3 Elmwood WI U.S.A.
158 I3 Elnesvågen Norway
213 B3 El Nevado, Cerro mt. Col.
153 A4 El Nido Phil.
177 F3 El Obeid Sudan
206 D2 El Oro Mex.
213 C3 Elorza Venez.
176 C1 El Oued Alg.
197 G5 Eloy U.S.A.
206 C2 El Palmito Mex.
213 E2 El Pao Bolívar Venez.
213 C2 El Pao Cojedes Venez.
190 C5 El Paso IL U.S.A.
195 F6 El Paso TX U.S.A.
162 C2 Elphin U.K.
196 C3 El Portal U.S.A.
206 J6 El Porvenir Panama
167 H2 El Prat de Llobregat Spain
El Progreso Guat. see Guastatoya
207 H5 El Progreso Hond.
206 B2 El Puerto, Cerro mt. Mex.
167 C4 El Puerto de Santa María Spain
El Quds Israel/West Bank see Jerusalem
206 J6 El Real de Santa María Panama
199 D5 El Reno U.S.A.
207 D3 El Retorno Mex.
190 B4 Elroy U.S.A.
206 D3 El Rucio Mex.
186 B2 Elsa Canada
206 D2 El Salado Mex.
206 C3 El Salto Mex.
207 G5 El Salvador country Central America
206 D2 El Salvador Mex.
153 C4 El Salvador Phil.
213 C3 El Samán de Apure Venez.
191 F1 Elsas Canada
206 C1 El Sauz Mex.
165 G2 Else r. Germany
213 D2 El Sombrero Venez.
215 C2 El Sosneado Arg.
207 E3 El Tajín tourist site Mex.
213 B3 El Tama, Parque Nacional nat. park Venez.
170 C6 El Tarf Alg.
167 C1 El Teleno mt. Spain
207 E4 El Tepozteco, Parque Nacional nat. park Mex.
213 D2 El Tigre Venez.
207 G4 El Tigre, Parque Nacional nat. park Guat.
165 I5 Eltmann Germany
213 C2 El Tocuyo Venez.
173 H5 El'ton Russia
173 H5 El'ton, Ozero l. Russia
194 C2 Eltopia U.S.A.
213 E2 El Toro Venez.
215 E2 El Trébol Arg.
206 B3 El Triunfo Mex.
213 C3 El Tuparro, Parque Nacional nat. park Col.
212 B8 El Turbio Arg.
143 C2 Eluru India
159 N4 Elva Estonia
213 A3 El Valle Col.
162 E5 Elvanfoot U.K.
167 C3 Elvas Port.
159 J3 Elverum Norway
213 B3 El Viejo mt. Col.
213 C2 El Vigía Venez.
210 D5 Elvira Brazil
178 E3 El Wak Kenya
190 E5 Elwood U.S.A.
165 I3 Elxleben Germany
161 H5 Ely U.K.
190 B2 Ely MN U.S.A.
197 E2 Ely NV U.S.A.
202 B4 Elyria U.S.A.
165 G4 Elz Germany
165 H2 Elze Germany
125 G3 Émaé i. Vanuatu
181 I2 eMakhazeni S. Africa
181 H2 eMalahleni S. Africa
137 K5 Emāmzādeh Naşrod Dīn Iran
159 L4 Emån r. Sweden
181 I5 eManzimtoti S. Africa
214 B2 Emas, Parque Nacional das nat. park Brazil
139 J3 Emazar Kazakh.
138 D2 Emba Kazakh.
181 H3 Embalenhle S. Africa
187 G3 Embarras Portage Canada
214 C2 Emborcação, Represa de resr Brazil
203 F2 Embrun Canada
178 D4 Embu Kenya
164 F1 Emden Germany
149 B4 Emeishan China
149 B4 Emei Shan mt. China
124 E4 Emerald Qld Australia
126 F6 Emerald Vic. Australia
189 G3 Emeril Canada
187 J5 Emerson Canada
136 B2 Emet Turkey
181 I2 Emgwenya S. Africa
181 I2 eMgwenya S. Africa
197 E3 Emigrant Valley U.S.A.
177 D3 Emi Koussi mt. Chad
206 C2 Emiliano Martínez Mex.
207 G4 Emiliano Zapata Mex.
139 J3 Emin China
171 L3 Emine, Nos pt Bulg.
139 J3 Emin He r. China
171 L3 Eminska Planina hills Bulg.
136 C2 Emirdağ Turkey
136 C2 Emir Dağı mt. Turkey
127 G8 Emita Australia
181 I2 eMjindini S. Africa
181 I3 eMkhondo S. Africa
159 K4 Emmaboda Sweden
159 M4 Emmaste Estonia
127 I2 Emmaville Australia
164 D2 Emmeloord Neth.
164 F4 Emmelshausen Germany
164 E2 Emmen Neth.
168 D7 Emmen Switz.
164 E3 Emmerich am Rhein Germany
143 B3 Emmiganuru India
181 I3 eMondlo S. Africa
199 C6 Emory Peak U.S.A.
206 B2 Empalme Mex.
181 I4 Empangeni S. Africa
212 E3 Empedrado Arg.
216 G2 Emperor Seamount Chain sea feature N. Pacific Ocean
216 G2 Emperor Trough sea feature N. Pacific Ocean
170 D3 Empoli Italy
198 D4 Emporia KS U.S.A.
202 E6 Emporia VA U.S.A.
202 D4 Emporium U.S.A.
187 G4 Empress Canada
164 F2 Ems r. Germany
191 H3 Emsdale Canada
164 F2 Emsdetten Germany
164 F1 Ems-Jade-Kanal canal Germany
164 F2 Emsland reg. Germany
181 H3 eMzinoni S. Africa
158 K3 Enafors Sweden
147 F7 Enarotali Indon.
151 E7 Ena-san mt. Japan
215 G1 Encantadas, Serra das hills Brazil
206 A2 Encantado, Cerro mt. Mex.
153 B3 Encanto, Cape Phil.
206 D3 Encarnación Mex.
212 E3 Encarnación Para.
199 D6 Encinal U.S.A.
196 D5 Encinitas U.S.A.
195 F5 Encino U.S.A.
126 C5 Encounter Bay Australia
214 E1 Encruzilhada Brazil
215 G1 Encruzilhada do Sul Brazil
186 D4 Endako Canada
147 E7 Ende Indon.
124 E3 Endeavour Strait Australia
Endeh Indon. see Ende
219 L9 Enderby Abyssal Plain sea feature Southern Ocean
129 E4 Enderby Land reg. Antarctica
203 E3 Endicott U.S.A.
186 C3 Endicott Arm est. U.S.A.
184 C3 Endicott Mountains U.S.A.
138 D2 Energetik Russia
215 E3 Energía Arg.
173 E6 Enerhodar Ukr.
216 G6 Enewetak atoll Marshall Is
170 D6 Enfidaville Tunisia
203 G3 Enfield U.S.A.
190 E2 Engadine U.S.A.
158 J3 Engan Norway
153 B2 Engaño, Cape Phil.
150 H2 Engaru Japan
201 F5 Engelhard U.S.A.
173 H5 Engel's Russia
164 C1 Engelschmangat sea chan. Neth.
126 A2 Engenina watercourse Australia
155 B4 Enggano i. Indon.
164 C4 Enghien Belgium
161 E5 England admin. div. U.K.
189 I3 Englee Canada
191 H2 Englehart Canada
193 H1 English r. Canada
161 D7 English Channel France/U.K.
173 G7 Enguri r. Georgia
181 I4 Enhlalakahle S. Africa
199 D4 Enid U.S.A.
150 G3 Eniwa Japan
164 D2 Enkhuizen Neth.
159 L4 Enköping Sweden
170 F6 Enna Sicily Italy
187 I2 Ennadai Lake Canada
177 E3 En Nahud Sudan
177 E3 Ennedi, Massif mts Chad
163 D4 Ennell, Lough l. Ireland
127 F2 Enngonia Australia
198 C2 Enning U.S.A.
163 C5 Ennis Ireland
194 E2 Ennis MT U.S.A.
199 D5 Ennis TX U.S.A.
163 E5 Enniscorthy Ireland
163 D3 Enniskillen U.K.
163 B5 Ennistymon Ireland
168 G7 Enns r. Austria
158 O3 Eno Fin.
197 F3 Enoch U.S.A.
158 M1 Enontekiö Fin.
149 D6 Enping China
153 B2 Enrile Phil.
164 D2 Ens Neth.
127 G6 Ensay Australia
164 E2 Enschede Neth.
165 G3 Ense Germany
215 F2 Ensenada Arg.
204 A2 Ensenada Mex.
149 C4 Enshi China
186 F2 Enterprise N.W.T. Canada
191 I3 Enterprise Ont. Canada
201 C6 Enterprise AL U.S.A.
194 C2 Enterprise OR U.S.A.
197 F3 Enterprise UT U.S.A.
186 F4 Entrance Canada
215 E2 Entre Ríos prov. Arg.
210 F8 Entre Ríos Bol.
167 B3 Entroncamento Port.
176 C4 Enugu Nigeria
133 U3 Enurmino Russia
210 D5 Envira Brazil
210 D5 Envira r. Brazil
128 C5 Enys, Mount N.Z.
164 D2 Epe Neth.
164 B5 Épernay France
171 L6 Ephesus tourist site Turkey
197 G2 Ephraim U.S.A.
203 E4 Ephrata PA U.S.A.
194 C2 Ephrata WA U.S.A.
125 G3 Épi i. Vanuatu
166 H2 Épinal France
136 D4 Episkopi Cyprus
170 E4 Epomeo, Monte vol. Italy
161 H6 Epping U.K.
165 G4 Eppstein Germany
161 D5 Eppynt, Mynydd hills U.K.
161 G6 Epsom U.K.
215 D3 Epu-pel Arg.
140 D4 Eqlīd Iran
176 C4 Equatorial Guinea country Africa
213 E3 Equeipa Venez.
153 A4 Eran Bay Phil.
136 F1 Erbaa Turkey
165 K5 Erbendorf Germany
164 F5 Erbeskopf h. Germany
137 J4 Erbil Iraq
137 I2 Erçek Turkey
137 I2 Erciş Turkey
136 E2 Erciyes Dağı mt. Turkey
169 I7 Érd Hungary
145 H2 Erdaogou Bingzhan China
152 D2 Erdao Jiang r. China
136 A1 Erdek Turkey
136 E3 Erdemli Turkey
Erdenetsogt Mongolia see Bayan-Ovoo
177 E3 Erdi reg. Chad
173 H6 Erdniyevskiy Russia
214 B4 Eré, Campos hills Brazil
213 D3 Erebato r. Venez.
129 B5 Erebus, Mount vol. Antarctica
137 J6 Erech tourist site Iraq
212 F3 Erechim Brazil
146 D2 Ereentsav Mongolia
136 E3 Ereğli Konya Turkey
136 C1 Ereğli Zonguldak Turkey
170 F6 Erei, Monti mts Sicily Italy
148 D1 Erenhot China
140 E3 Eresk Iran
167 D2 Eresma r. Spain
171 J5 Eretria Greece
165 J4 Erfurt Germany
137 G2 Ergani Turkey
176 B2 'Erg Chech des. Alg./Mali
Ergel Mongolia see Hatanbulag
171 L4 Ergene r. Turkey
159 N4 Ērgļi Latvia
150 A1 Ergu China
152 C3 Erhulai China
162 D2 Eriboll, Loch inlet U.K.
162 D4 Ericht, Loch l. U.K.
190 B5 Erie IL U.S.A.
199 E4 Erie KS U.S.A.
202 C3 Erie PA U.S.A.
191 G4 Erie, Lake Canada/U.S.A.
150 H3 Erimo Japan
150 H4 Erimo-misaki c. Japan
162 A3 Eriskay i. U.K.
178 D2 Eritrea country Africa
139 H5 Erkech-Tam Kyrg.
136 E2 Erkilet Turkey
165 J5 Erlangen Germany
124 D4 Erldunda Australia
152 E2 Erlong Shan mt. China
152 C2 Erlongshan Shuiku resr China
164 D2 Ermelo Neth.
181 H3 Ermelo S. Africa
136 D3 Ermenek Turkey
171 K6 Ermoupoli Greece
143 B4 Ernakulam India
143 B4 Erode India
180 A1 Erongo admin. reg. Namibia
164 D3 Erp Neth.
176 B1 Er Rachidia Morocco
177 F3 Er Rahad Sudan
179 D5 Errego Moz.
170 D7 Er Remla Tunisia
163 C2 Errigal h. Ireland
163 A3 Erris Head Ireland
203 H2 Errol U.S.A.
125 G3 Erromango i. Vanuatu
171 I4 Ersekë Albania
198 D2 Erskine U.S.A.
158 M3 Ersmark Sweden
173 G5 Ertil' Russia
126 C3 Erudina Australia
137 I3 Eruh Turkey
202 D5 Erwin U.S.A.
165 G3 Erwitte Germany
165 J2 Erxleben Sachsen-Anhalt Germany
165 J2 Erxleben Sachsen-Anhalt Germany
165 K4 Erzgebirge mts Czech Rep./Germany
136 F3 Erzin Turkey
137 G2 Erzincan Turkey
137 H2 Erzurum Turkey
150 G4 Esan-misaki pt Japan
150 G4 Esashi Hokkaidō Japan
150 H2 Esashi Hokkaidō Japan
159 J5 Esbjerg Denmark
197 G3 Escalante U.S.A.
197 G3 Escalante r. U.S.A.
197 F3 Escalante Desert U.S.A.
206 C2 Escalón Mex.
190 D3 Escanaba U.S.A.
207 G4 Escárcega Mex.
153 B2 Escarpada Point Phil.
167 F2 Escatrón Spain
164 B4 Escaut r. Belgium
164 D3 Esch Neth.
164 E2 Esche Germany
165 I2 Eschede Germany
164 D5 Esch-sur-Alzette Lux.
165 I3 Eschwege Germany
164 E4 Eschweiler Germany
196 D5 Escondido U.S.A.
206 C3 Escuinapa Mex.
207 G5 Escuintla Guat.
207 F5 Escuintla Mex.
136 B3 Eşen Turkey
138 C5 Esenguly Turkm.
164 F1 Esens Germany
140 C3 Eşfahān Iran
140 D4 Esfandārān Iran
140 E2 Esfarayen, Reshteh-ye mts Iran
140 C4 Esfarjān Iran
140 D5 Eshkanān Iran
181 I4 Eshowe S. Africa
141 E3 'Eshqābād Iran
140 C3 Eshtehārd Iran
179 C6 Esigodini Zimbabwe
181 J4 eSikhaleni S. Africa
Esikhawini S. Africa see eSikhaleni
127 J1 Esk Australia
127 G8 Esk r. Australia
160 D2 Esk r. U.K.
162 E5 Eskdalemuir U.K.
189 G3 Esker Canada
158 D2 Eskifjörður Iceland
136 B2 Eski Gediz Turkey
159 L4 Eskilstuna Sweden
184 E3 Eskimo Lakes Canada
139 H4 Eski-Nookat Kyrg.
136 D1 Eskipazar Turkey
136 C2 Eskişehir Turkey
167 D1 Esla r. Spain
137 L4 Eslāmābād Iran
140 B3 Eslāmābād-e Gharb Iran
136 B3 Esler Dağı mt. Turkey
165 G3 Eslohe (Sauerland) Germany
159 K5 Eslöv Sweden
136 B2 Eşme Turkey
210 C3 Esmeraldas Ecuador
190 E1 Esnagi Lake Canada
164 B4 Esnes France
141 F5 Espakeh Iran
166 F4 Espalion France
191 G2 Espanola Canada
195 F4 Espanola U.S.A.
210 □ Española, Isla i. Galapagos Is Ecuador
196 A2 Esparto U.S.A.
165 G2 Espelkamp Germany
124 C5 Esperance Australia
129 E2 Esperanza research stn Antarctica
215 E1 Esperanza Arg.
206 B2 Esperanza Mex.
153 C4 Esperanza Phil.
206 H5 Esperanza, Sierra de la mts Hond.
167 B3 Espichel, Cabo c. Port.
167 D1 Espigüete mt. Spain
206 D2 Espinazo Mex.
214 D2 Espinhaço, Serra do mts Brazil
214 D1 Espinosa Brazil
214 E2 Espírito Santo state Brazil
153 B2 Espiritu Phil.
125 G3 Espiritu Santo i. Vanuatu
207 H4 Espíritu Santo, Bahía del b. Mex.
206 B2 Espíritu Santo, Isla i. Mex.
159 N3 Espoo Fin.
167 F4 Espuña mt. Spain
212 B6 Esquel Arg.
186 E5 Esquimalt Canada
153 C5 Essang Indon.
176 B1 Essaouira Morocco
164 C3 Essen Belgium
164 F3 Essen Germany
165 F2 Essen (Oldenburg) Germany
211 G3 Essequibo r. Guyana
191 F4 Essex Canada
197 E4 Essex U.S.A.
203 G2 Essex Junction U.S.A.
191 F4 Essexville U.S.A.
176 A2 Es-Smara W. Sahara
133 Q4 Esso Russia
189 H4 Est, Île de l' i. Canada
203 I1 Est, Lac de l' l. Canada
212 D8 Estados, Isla de los i. Arg.
140 D4 Estahbān Iran
191 G2 Estaire Canada
211 K6 Estância Brazil
167 G1 Estats, Pic d' mt. France/Spain
181 H4 Estcourt S. Africa
165 H1 Este r. Germany
206 H5 Estelí Nicaragua
167 E1 Estella Spain
167 D4 Estepa Spain
167 D4 Estepona Spain
187 I4 Esterhazy Canada
196 B4 Estero Bay U.S.A.
212 D2 Esteros Para.
187 I5 Estevan Canada
198 E3 Estherville U.S.A.
201 D5 Estill U.S.A.
159 N4 Estonia country Europe
164 A5 Estrées-St-Denis France
167 C2 Estrela, Serra da mts Port.
167 E3 Estrella mt. Spain
197 F5 Estrella, Sierra mts U.S.A.
167 C3 Estremoz Port.
211 I5 Estrondo, Serra hills Brazil
137 L4 Estūh Iran
126 C2 Etadunna Australia
144 D4 Etah India
164 D5 Étain France
166 F2 Étampes France
166 E1 Étaples France
144 D4 Etawah India
181 I3 Ethandakukhanya S. Africa
180 E4 E'Thembini S. Africa
178 D3 Ethiopia country Africa
136 D2 Etimesgut Turkey
162 C4 Etive, Loch inlet U.K.
170 F6 Etna, Mount vol. Sicily Italy
159 I4 Etne Norway
186 C3 Etolin Island U.S.A.
179 B5 Etosha National Park Namibia
179 B5 Etosha Pan salt pan Namibia
Etrek r. Iran/Turkm. see Atrek
138 C5 Etrek Turkm.
171 K3 Etropole Bulg.
143 B4 Ettaiyapuram India
164 E5 Ettelbruck Lux.
164 C3 Etten-Leur Neth.
165 G6 Ettlingen Germany
162 E5 Ettrick Forest reg. U.K.
Etxarri Spain see Etxarri-Aranatz
167 E1 Etxarri-Aranatz Spain
206 C3 Etzatlán Mex.
127 G4 Euabalong Australia
124 C5 Eucla Australia
202 C4 Euclid U.S.A.
211 K6 Euclides da Cunha Brazil
127 H6 Eucumbene, Lake Australia
126 C5 Eudunda Australia
201 C6 Eufaula U.S.A.
199 E5 Eufaula Lake resr U.S.A.
194 B2 Eugene U.S.A.
206 A2 Eugenia, Punta pt Mex.
127 H4 Eugowra Australia
127 F2 Eulo Australia
127 H3 Eumungerie Australia
199 E6 Eunice U.S.A.
164 E4 Eupen Belgium
137 J6 Euphrates r. Asia alt. Al Furāt (Iraq/Syria), alt. Fırat (Turkey)
159 M3 Eura Fin.
166 E2 Eure r. France
194 A3 Eureka CA U.S.A.
194 D1 Eureka MT U.S.A.
197 E2 Eureka NV U.S.A.
126 D3 Eurinilla watercourse Australia
126 D3 Euriowie Australia
127 F6 Euroa Australia
179 E6 Europa, Île i. Indian Ocean
167 D4 Europa Point Gibraltar
156 Europe
164 E4 Euskirchen Germany
126 E5 Euston Australia
201 C5 Eutaw U.S.A.
186 D4 Eutsuk Lake Canada
165 K3 Eutzsch Germany
181 H3 Evander S. Africa
188 E3 Evans, Lac l. Canada
195 F4 Evans, Mount U.S.A.
186 F4 Evansburg Canada
127 J2 Evans Head Australia
185 J3 Evans Strait Canada
190 D4 Evanston IL U.S.A.
194 E3 Evanston WY U.S.A.
191 F3 Evansville Canada
200 C4 Evansville IN U.S.A.
190 C4 Evansville WI U.S.A.
194 F3 Evansville WY U.S.A.
190 E4 Evart U.S.A.
181 G3 Evaton S. Africa
140 D5 Evaz Iran
190 A2 Eveleth U.S.A.
133 Q3 Evensk Russia
126 A3 Everard, Lake salt flat Australia
124 D4 Everard Range hills Australia
164 D3 Everdingen Neth.
145 F4 Everest, Mount China
203 J1 Everett Canada
194 B1 Everett U.S.A.
164 B3 Evergem Belgium
201 D7 Everglades swamp U.S.A.
201 D7 Everglades National Park U.S.A.
199 G6 Evergreen U.S.A.
161 F5 Evesham U.K.
161 F5 Evesham, Vale of val. U.K.
158 M3 Evijärvi Fin.
176 D4 Evinayong Equat. Guinea
159 I4 Evje Norway
167 C3 Évora Port.
146 F1 Evoron, Ozero l. Russia
137 J2 Evowghlī Iran
166 E2 Évreux France
171 J6 Evrotas r. Greece
136 D4 Evrychou Cyprus
171 K5 Evvoia i. Greece
196 □1 'Ewa Beach U.S.A.
178 D3 Ewaso Ngiro r. Kenya
162 C3 Ewe, Loch b. U.K.
178 B4 Ewo Congo
210 E6 Exaltación Bol.
181 G4 Excelsior S. Africa
196 C2 Excelsior Mountain U.S.A.
196 C2 Excelsior Mountains U.S.A.
198 E4 Excelsior Springs U.S.A.
161 D6 Exe r. U.K.
129 B4 Executive Committee Range mts Antarctica
127 I5 Exeter Australia
191 G4 Exeter Canada
161 D7 Exeter U.K.
196 C3 Exeter CA U.S.A.
203 H3 Exeter NH U.S.A.
164 E2 Exloo Neth.
161 D7 Exminster U.K.
161 D6 Exmoor hills U.K.
161 D6 Exmoor National Park U.K.
203 F6 Exmore U.S.A.
161 D7 Exmouth U.K.
127 H3 Exmouth, Mount Australia
124 B4 Exmouth Gulf Australia
218 L6 Exmouth Plateau sea feature Indian Ocean
167 D3 Extremadura aut. comm. Spain
201 E7 Exuma Sound sea chan. Bahamas
178 D4 Eyasi, Lake salt l. Tanz.
161 I5 Eye U.K.
162 F5 Eyemouth U.K.
162 B2 Eye Peninsula U.K.
158 C3 Eyjafjallajökull ice cap Iceland
158 C1 Eyjafjörður inlet Iceland
178 E3 Eyl Somalia
161 F6 Eynsham U.K.
128 B6 Eyre Mountains N.Z.
126 A4 Eyre Peninsula Australia
165 H2 Eystrup Germany
158 □ Eysturoy i. Faroe Is
181 I4 Ezakheni S. Africa
181 H3 Ezenzeleni S. Africa
215 C3 Ezequiel Ramos Mexía, Embalse resr Arg.
149 E4 Ezhou China
172 I2 Ezhva Russia
171 L5 Ezine Turkey
136 F1 Ezinepazar Turkey

F

159 J5 Faaborg Denmark
199 B6 Fabens U.S.A.
154 □ Faber, Mount h. Sing.
186 F2 Faber Lake Canada
Fåborg Denmark see Faaborg
170 E3 Fabriano Italy
213 B3 Facatativá Col.
164 B4 Faches-Thumesnil France
176 D3 Fachi Niger
203 F4 Factoryville U.S.A.
212 B7 Facundo Arg.
177 E3 Fada Chad
176 C3 Fada-N'Gourma Burkina Faso
137 H4 Fadghāmī Syria
170 D2 Faenza Italy
Faeroes terr. Atlantic Ocean see Faroe Islands
147 F7 Fafanlap Indon.
178 E3 Fafen Shet' watercourse Eth.
171 K2 Făgăraş Romania
159 J3 Fagernes Norway
159 K4 Fagersta Sweden
212 C8 Fagnano, Lago l. Arg./Chile
164 C4 Fagne reg. Belgium
176 B3 Faguibine, Lac l. Mali
158 C3 Fagurhólsmýri Iceland
177 F4 Fagwir South Sudan
140 C4 Fahlīān, Rūdkhāneh-ye watercourse Iran
141 E4 Fahraj Iran
136 D6 Fā'id Egypt
184 D3 Fairbanks U.S.A.
202 B5 Fairborn U.S.A.
198 D3 Fairbury U.S.A.
202 E5 Fairfax U.S.A.
196 A2 Fairfield CA U.S.A.
190 B5 Fairfield IA U.S.A.
200 C4 Fairfield OH U.S.A.
199 D6 Fairfield TX U.S.A.
203 G3 Fair Haven U.S.A.
163 E2 Fair Head U.K.
153 A4 Fairie Queen Shoal sea feature Phil.
162 G1 Fair Isle i. U.K.
128 C7 Fairlie N.Z.
198 E3 Fairmont MN U.S.A.
202 C5 Fairmont WV U.S.A.
195 F4 Fairplay U.S.A.
190 D3 Fairport U.S.A.
202 C4 Fairport Harbor U.S.A.
186 F3 Fairview Canada
191 E3 Fairview MI U.S.A.
199 D4 Fairview OK U.S.A.
197 G2 Fairview UT U.S.A.
149 □ Fairview Park Hong Kong China
186 B3 Fairweather, Cape U.S.A.
186 B3 Fairweather, Mount Canada/U.S.A.
147 G6 Fais i. Micronesia
144 C3 Faisalabad Pak.
164 C5 Faissault France
198 C2 Faith U.S.A.
141 H2 Faīẕābād Afgh.
145 E4 Faizabad India
125 I2 Fakaofo atoll Tokelau
161 H5 Fakenham U.K.
158 K3 Fåker Sweden
147 F7 Fakfak Indon.
140 D4 Fakhrābād Iran
152 B2 Faku China
161 C7 Fal r. U.K.
176 A4 Falaba Sierra Leone
166 D2 Falaise France
145 G4 Falakata India
145 H5 Falam Myanmar
140 C3 Falāvarjān Iran
199 D7 Falcon Lake Mex./U.S.A.
199 D7 Falfurrias U.S.A.
186 F3 Falher Canada
159 K4 Falkenberg Sweden
165 L3 Falkenberg/Elster Germany
165 K1 Falkenhagen Germany
165 K3 Falkenhain Germany
165 L2 Falkensee Germany
165 K5 Falkenstein Germany
162 E5 Falkirk U.K.
162 E4 Falkland U.K.
219 F9 Falkland Escarpment sea feature S. Atlantic Ocean
212 E8 Falkland Islands terr. Atlantic Ocean
219 F9 Falkland Plateau sea feature S. Atlantic Ocean
212 D8 Falkland Sound sea chan. Falkland Is
159 K4 Falköping Sweden
196 D5 Fallbrook U.S.A.
196 C2 Fallon U.S.A.
203 H4 Fall River U.S.A.
194 F3 Fall River Pass U.S.A.
198 E3 Falls City U.S.A.
161 B7 Falmouth U.K.
202 A5 Falmouth KY U.S.A.
203 H3 Falmouth ME U.S.A.
190 E3 Falmouth MI U.S.A.
180 C7 False Bay S. Africa
206 B3 Falso, Cabo c. Mex.
159 J5 Falster i. Denmark
169 M7 Fălticeni Romania
159 K3 Falun Sweden
136 D4 Famagusta Cyprus
164 E5 Fameck France
140 C3 Fāmenīn Iran
164 D4 Famenne val. Belgium
187 J4 Family Lake Canada
148 F4 Fanchang China
163 E4 Fane r. Ireland
154 A1 Fang Thai.
148 D3 Fangcheng China
149 C4 Fangdou Shan mts China
149 F6 Fangliao Taiwan
148 E2 Fangshan Beijing China
148 D2 Fangshan Shanxi China
149 F6 Fangshan Taiwan
148 D3 Fangxian China
150 A2 Fangzheng China
149 □ Fanling Hong Kong China
162 C3 Fannich, Loch l. U.K.
141 E5 Fannūj Iran
170 E3 Fano Italy
149 F5 Fanshan China
148 D2 Fanshi China
Fan Si Pan mt. Vietnam see Phăng Xi Păng
178 C3 Faradje Dem. Rep. Congo
179 E6 Farafangana Madag.
177 E2 Farāfirah, Wāḩāt al oasis Egypt
Farafra Oasis Egypt see Farāfirah, Wāḩāt al
141 F3 Farāh Afgh.
141 F4 Farāh Rōd watercourse Afgh.
213 A4 Farallones de Cali, Parque Nacional nat. park Col.
176 A3 Faranah Guinea
138 E5 Farap Turkm.
142 B6 Farasān, Jazā'ir is Saudi Arabia
147 G6 Faraulep atoll Micronesia
161 F7 Fareham U.K.
185 N4 Farewell, Cape Greenland
128 D4 Farewell, Cape N.Z.
128 D4 Farewell Spit N.Z.
159 K4 Färgelanda Sweden
198 D2 Fargo U.S.A.
139 G4 Farg'ona Uzbek.
198 E2 Faribault U.S.A.
189 F2 Faribault, Lac l. Canada
144 D3 Faridabad India
144 C3 Faridkot India
145 G5 Faridpur Bangl.
176 A3 Farim Guinea-Bissau
141 E3 Farīmān Iran
159 L4 Färjestaden Sweden
139 G5 Farkhor Tajik.
137 L4 Farmahīn Iran
190 C5 Farmer City U.S.A.
188 D2 Farmer Island Canada
186 E3 Farmington Canada
190 B5 Farmington IA U.S.A.
190 B5 Farmington IL U.S.A.
203 H2 Farmington ME U.S.A.
203 H3 Farmington NH U.S.A.
197 H3 Farmington NM U.S.A.
194 E3 Farmington UT U.S.A.
186 D4 Far Mountain Canada
202 D6 Farmville U.S.A.
161 G6 Farnborough U.K.
160 F2 Farne Islands U.K.
161 G6 Farnham U.K.
186 F4 Farnham, Mount Canada
211 G4 Faro Brazil
186 C2 Faro Canada
167 C4 Faro Port.
159 L4 Fårö i. Sweden
158 □2 Faroe Islands terr. N. Atlantic Ocean
159 L4 Fårösund Sweden
175 I5 Farquhar, Atoll de is Seychelles
Farquhar Islands Seychelles see Farquhar, Atoll de
140 D4 Farrāshband Iran
202 C4 Farrell U.S.A.
191 J3 Farrellton Canada
141 E3 Farrokhī Iran
140 D3 Farsakh Iran
171 J5 Farsala Greece
194 E3 Farson U.S.A.
159 I4 Farsund Norway
138 D5 Fārūj Iran
Farvel, Kap c. Greenland see Farewell, Cape
199 C5 Farwell U.S.A.
140 E5 Fāryāb Iran
140 D4 Fasā Iran
170 G4 Fasano Italy
165 I2 Faßberg Germany
202 E4 Fassett U.S.A.
173 D5 Fastiv Ukr.
144 D4 Fatehgarh India
144 C4 Fatehpur Rajasthan India
144 E4 Fatehpur Uttar Pradesh India
144 D4 Fatehpur Sikri India
140 D4 Fatḩābād Iran
191 G3 Fathom Five National Marine Park Canada
176 A3 Fatick Senegal
166 H2 Faulquemont France
181 F4 Fauresmith S. Africa
158 K2 Fauske Norway
197 F1 Faust U.S.A.
170 E6 Favignana, Isola i. Sicily Italy
186 G4 Fawcett Canada
161 F7 Fawley U.K.
188 C3 Fawn r. Canada
158 B2 Faxaflói b. Iceland
158 L3 Faxälven r. Sweden
177 D3 Faya Chad
190 D3 Fayette (abandoned) U.S.A.
199 E4 Fayetteville AR U.S.A.
201 E5 Fayetteville NC U.S.A.
201 C5 Fayetteville TN U.S.A.
137 L7 Faylakah i. Kuwait
176 C4 Fazao Malfakassa, Parc National de nat. park Togo
144 C3 Fazilka India
140 C5 Fazrān, Jabal h. Saudi Arabia
176 A2 Fdérik Mauritania
163 B5 Feale r. Ireland
201 E5 Fear, Cape U.S.A.
196 B2 Feather, North Fork r. U.S.A.
196 B2 Feather Falls U.S.A.
128 E4 Featherston N.Z.
127 G6 Feathertop, Mount Australia
166 E2 Fécamp France
215 F1 Federación Arg.
212 E4 Federal Arg.
138 E1 Fedorovka Kostanayskaya Oblast' Kazakh.
139 I1 Fedorovka Pavlodarskaya Oblast' Kazakh.
138 B2 Fedorovka Zapadnyy Kazakhstan Kazakh.
138 C1 Fedorovka Russia
168 E3 Fehmarn i. Germany
165 K2 Fehrbellin Germany
214 E3 Feia, Lagoa lag. Brazil
148 E4 Feidong China
148 F3 Feihuanghe Kou r. mouth China
210 D5 Feijó Brazil
128 E4 Feilding N.Z.
211 K6 Feira de Santana Brazil
148 E4 Feixi China
136 E3 Feke Turkey
167 H3 Felanitx Spain
190 D3 Felch U.S.A.
165 L1 Feldberg Germany
168 D7 Feldberg mt. Germany
168 D7 Feldkirch Austria
168 G7 Feldkirchen in Kärnten Austria
215 E1 Feliciano r. Arg.
207 G4 Felipe C. Puerto Mex.
214 D2 Felixlândia Brazil
161 I6 Felixstowe U.K.
170 D1 Feltre Italy
159 J3 Femunden l. Norway
159 K3 Femundsmarka Nasjonalpark nat. park Norway
170 D3 Fenaio, Punta del pt Italy
197 H4 Fence Lake U.S.A.
191 H3 Fenelon Falls Canada
171 K4 Fengari mt. Greece
149 E4 Fengcheng Jiangxi China
152 C3 Fengcheng Liaoning China
149 C4 Fengdu China
149 C5 Fenggang China
152 D1 Fengguang China
149 F4 Fenghua China
149 C5 Fenghuang China
148 C4 Fengjie China
149 D6 Fengkai China
149 F6 Fenglin Taiwan
152 D2 Fengman China
148 F2 Fengnan China
148 E1 Fengning China
148 E3 Fengqiu China
149 C5 Fengshan China
149 E6 Fengshun China
148 E3 Fengtai China
149 E4 Fengxin China
148 E3 Fengyang China
148 D1 Fengzhen China
148 D2 Fen He r. China
145 G5 Feni Bangl.
125 F2 Feni Islands P.N.G.
166 F5 Fenille, Col de la pass France
190 B4 Fennimore U.S.A.
179 E5 Fenoarivo Atsinanana Madag.
191 F4 Fenton U.S.A.
148 D2 Fenxi China
148 D2 Fenyang China
149 E5 Fenyi China
173 E6 Feodosiya Crimea
170 B6 Fer, Cap de c. Alg.
141 E3 Ferdows Iran
Fergana Uzbek. see Farg'ona
139 H4 Fergana Too Tizmegi mts Kyrg.
191 G4 Fergus Canada
198 D2 Fergus Falls U.S.A.
124 F2 Fergusson Island P.N.G.
170 C7 Fériana Tunisia
171 I3 Ferizaj Kosovo
176 B4 Ferkessédougou Côte d'Ivoire

Fermo

170 E3 Fermo Italy
189 G3 Fermont Canada
167 C2 Fermoselle Spain
163 C5 Fermoy Ireland
210 □ Fernandina, Isla *i. Galapagos Is* Ecuador
201 D6 Fernandina Beach U.S.A.
212 B8 Fernando de Magallanes, Parque Nacional *nat. park* Chile
219 G6 Fernando de Noronha *i.* Brazil
214 B3 Fernandópolis Brazil
194 B1 Ferndale U.S.A.
161 F7 Ferndown U.K.
186 F5 Fernie Canada
127 G2 Fernlee Australia
196 C2 Fernley U.S.A.
203 F4 Fernridge U.S.A.
163 E5 Ferns Ireland
194 C2 Fernwood U.S.A.
170 D2 Ferrara Italy
214 B3 Ferreiros Brazil
199 F6 Ferriday U.S.A.
170 C4 Ferro, Capo *c. Sardinia* Italy
167 B1 Ferrol Spain
197 G2 Ferron U.S.A.
138 D1 Fershampenuaz Russia
164 D1 Ferwerd Neth.
Ferwert Neth. *see* Ferwerd
176 B1 Fès Morocco
178 B4 Feshi Dem. Rep. Congo
187 J5 Fessenden U.S.A.
198 F4 Festus U.S.A.
162 □ Fethaland, Point of U.K.
163 D5 Fethard Ireland
136 B3 Fethiye Turkey
138 C4 Fetisovo Kazakh.
162 □ Fetlar *i.* U.K.
162 F4 Fettercairn U.K.
165 J5 Feucht Germany
165 I5 Feuchtwangen Germany
189 F2 Feuilles, Rivière aux *r.* Canada
136 F3 Fevzipaşa Turkey
141 E3 Feyẕābād Iran
177 D2 Fezzan *reg.* Libya
161 D5 Ffestiniog U.K.
179 E6 Fianarantsoa Madag.
178 D3 Fichē Eth.
165 K4 Fichtelgebirge *hills* Germany
181 G4 Ficksburg S. Africa
186 F4 Field *B.C.* Canada
191 G2 Field *Ont.* Canada
171 H4 Fier Albania
190 E3 Fife Lake U.S.A.
162 F4 Fife Ness *pt* U.K.
127 G4 Fifield Australia
190 B3 Fifield U.S.A.
166 F4 Figeac France
167 B2 Figueira da Foz Port.
167 H1 Figueres Spain
176 B1 Figuig Morocco
125 H3 Fiji *country* Pacific Ocean
206 H6 Filadelfia Costa Rica
212 D2 Filadelfia Para.
129 C3 Filchner Ice Shelf *ice feature* Antarctica
160 G3 Filey U.K.
171 I5 Filippiada Greece
159 K4 Filipstad Sweden
158 J3 Fillan Norway
196 C4 Fillmore *CA* U.S.A.
197 F2 Fillmore *UT* U.S.A.
129 D3 Fimbul Ice Shelf *ice feature* Antarctica
203 F2 Finch Canada
162 E3 Findhorn *r.* U.K.
137 H3 Fındık Turkey
202 B4 Findlay U.S.A.
127 H8 Fingal Australia
188 E5 Finger Lakes U.S.A.
179 D5 Fingoè Moz.
136 C3 Finike Turkey
136 C3 Finike Körfezi *b.* Turkey
167 B1 Finisterre, Cape Spain
172 S5 Finland *country* Europe
159 M4 Finland, Gulf of Europe
186 D3 Finlay *r.* Canada
186 D3 Finlay, Mount Canada
127 F5 Finley Australia
165 J3 Finne *ridge* Germany
126 A4 Finniss, Cape Australia
158 L1 Finnsnes Norway
159 K4 Finspång Sweden
163 D3 Fintona U.K.
Fintown Ireland *see* Baile na Finne
162 C3 Fionn Loch *l.* U.K.
162 B4 Fionnphort U.K.
128 A6 Fiordland National Park N.Z.
Fırat *r.* Turkey *see* Euphrates
196 B3 Firebaugh U.S.A.
187 I2 Firedrake Lake Canada
203 G4 Fire Island National Seashore *nature res.* U.S.A.
Firenze Italy *see* Florence
137 J6 Firk, Sha'īb *watercourse* Iraq
215 E2 Firmat Arg.
166 G4 Firminy France
165 I6 Firngrund *reg.* Germany
169 P2 Firovo Russia
144 B3 Firoz Pak.
144 D4 Firozabad India
141 G3 Firozkoh *reg.* Afgh.
144 C3 Firozpur India
203 H2 First Connecticut Lake U.S.A.
140 D4 Fīrūzābād Iran
164 F5 Fischbach Germany
179 B6 Fish *watercourse* Namibia
180 D5 Fish *r.* S. Africa
129 B6 Fisher Bay *b.* Antarctica
203 F6 Fisherman Island U.S.A.
203 H4 Fishers Island U.S.A.
187 M2 Fisher Strait Canada
161 C6 Fishguard U.K.
186 E2 Fish Lake Canada
190 A2 Fish Lake *MN* U.S.A.
197 G2 Fish Lake *UT* U.S.A.
191 F4 Fish Point U.S.A.
129 C3 Fiske, Cape *c.* Antarctica
164 B5 Fismes France
167 B1 Fisterra Spain
Fisterra, Cabo *c.* Spain *see* Finisterre, Cape
203 H3 Fitchburg U.S.A.
187 G3 Fitzgerald Canada
201 D6 Fitzgerald U.S.A.
126 B4 Fitzgerald Bay Australia
212 C7 Fitz Roy Arg.
124 C3 Fitzroy Crossing Australia
191 G3 Fitzwilliam Island Canada
163 D3 Fivemiletown U.K.
170 D2 Fivizzano Italy
178 C4 Fizi Dem. Rep. Congo
159 J3 Flå Norway
181 H5 Flagstaff S. Africa
197 G4 Flagstaff U.S.A.
203 H2 Flagstaff Lake U.S.A.
188 E2 Flaherty Island Canada
190 B3 Flambeau *r.* U.S.A.
160 G3 Flamborough Head U.K.
165 K2 Fläming *hills* Germany
194 E3 Flaming Gorge Reservoir U.S.A.
180 D5 Flaminksvlei *salt pan* S. Africa
164 A3 Flanders *reg.* Europe
164 A4 Flandre *reg.* France
162 A2 Flannan Isles U.K.
158 K2 Flåsjön *l.* Sweden
190 E4 Flat *r.* U.S.A.
194 D2 Flathead Lake U.S.A.
128 E4 Flat Point N.Z.
124 E3 Flattery, Cape Australia
194 A1 Flattery, Cape U.S.A.
165 J2 Fleetmark Germany
160 D4 Fleetwood U.K.
203 F4 Fleetwood U.S.A.
159 I4 Flekkefjord Norway
202 E3 Fleming U.S.A.
202 B5 Flemingsburg U.S.A.
219 G2 Flemish Cap *sea feature* N. Atlantic Ocean
159 L4 Flen Sweden
168 D3 Flensburg Germany
166 D2 Flers France
191 G3 Flesherton Canada
187 H2 Fletcher Lake Canada
191 F3 Fletcher Pond *l.* U.S.A.
124 E3 Flinders *r.* Australia
124 B5 Flinders Bay Australia
126 B5 Flinders Chase National Park Australia
126 A4 Flinders Island *S.A.* Australia
127 H7 Flinders Island *Tas.* Australia
126 C3 Flinders Ranges *mts* Australia
126 C3 Flinders Ranges National Park Australia
187 I4 Flin Flon Canada
161 D4 Flint U.K.
191 F4 Flint U.S.A.
201 C6 Flint *r. GA* U.S.A.
191 F4 Flint *r. MI* U.S.A.
217 I5 Flint Island Kiribati
127 H1 Flinton Australia
159 K3 Flisa Norway
160 E2 Flodden U.K.
165 L4 Flöha Germany
165 L4 Flöha *r.* Germany
129 B4 Flood Range *mts* Antarctica
190 A2 Floodwood U.S.A.
200 B4 Flora U.S.A.
166 F4 Florac France
164 E5 Florange France
210 □ Floreana, Isla *i. Galapagos Is* Ecuador
191 F4 Florence Canada
170 D3 Florence Italy
201 C5 Florence *AL* U.S.A.
197 G5 Florence *AZ* U.S.A.
198 D4 Florence *KS* U.S.A.
202 C5 Florence *OH* U.S.A.
194 A3 Florence *OR* U.S.A.
201 E5 Florence *SC* U.S.A.
197 G5 Florence Junction U.S.A.
203 J1 Florenceville Canada
213 B4 Florencia Col.
164 C4 Florennes Belgium
212 C6 Florentino Ameghino, Embalse *resr* Arg.
215 E2 Flores *r.* Arg.
156 A6 Flores *i.* Azores
207 G4 Flores Guat.
147 E7 Flores *i.* Indon.
147 D7 Flores, Laut *sea* Indon.
214 C1 Flores de Goiás Brazil
Flores Sea Indon. *see* Flores, Laut
211 K5 Floresta Brazil
211 J5 Floriano Brazil
212 G3 Florianópolis Brazil
215 F2 Florida Uruguay
201 D6 Florida *state* U.S.A.
205 H4 Florida, Straits of Bahamas/U.S.A.
201 D7 Florida Bay U.S.A.
201 D7 Florida City U.S.A.
125 G2 Florida Islands Solomon Is
193 J7 Florida Keys *is* U.S.A.
171 I4 Florina Greece
159 I3 Florø Norway
189 H3 Flour Lake Canada
190 A4 Floyd *IA* U.S.A.
202 C6 Floyd *VA* U.S.A.
197 F4 Floyd, Mount U.S.A.
199 C5 Floydada U.S.A.
164 D2 Fluessen *l.* Neth.
124 E2 Fly *r.* P.N.G.
202 C5 Fly U.S.A.
171 H3 Foča Bos. & Herz.
162 E3 Fochabers U.K.
181 G3 Fochville S. Africa
171 L2 Focşani Romania
149 D6 Fogang China
170 F4 Foggia Italy
176 □ Fogo *i.* Cape Verde
189 J4 Fogo Island Canada
162 D2 Foinaven *h.* U.K.
166 E5 Foix France
158 K2 Folda *sea chan.* Norway
158 K2 Foldereid Norway
158 J2 Foldfjorden *sea chan.* Norway
171 K6 Folegandros *i.* Greece
191 F1 Foleyet Canada
170 E3 Foligno Italy
161 I6 Folkestone U.K.
161 G5 Folkingham U.K.
201 D6 Folkston U.S.A.
159 J3 Folldal Norway
170 D3 Follonica Italy
196 B2 Folsom Lake U.S.A.
173 G6 Fomin Russia
172 I2 Fominskiy Russia
187 H3 Fond-du-Lac Canada
187 I3 Fond du Lac *r.* Canada
190 C4 Fond du Lac U.S.A.
167 B2 Fondevila Spain
170 E4 Fondi Italy
125 H2 Fongafale *i.* Tuvalu
170 C4 Fonni *Sardinia* Italy
206 H5 Fonseca, Golfo do *b.* Central America
189 F3 Fontanges Canada
186 E3 Fontas Canada
186 E3 Fontas *r.* Canada
210 E4 Fonte Boa Brazil
166 D3 Fontenay-le-Comte France
158 D1 Fontur *pt* Iceland
191 H3 Foot's Bay Canada
148 C3 Foping China
127 H4 Forbes Australia
194 C1 Forbes, Mount Canada
165 J5 Forchheim Germany
189 G2 Ford *r.* Canada
190 D2 Ford *r.* U.S.A.
159 I3 Førde Norway
187 J2 Forde Lake Canada
161 H5 Fordham U.K.
161 F7 Fordingbridge U.K.
129 B4 Ford Range *mts* Antarctica
127 F2 Fords Bridge Australia
199 E5 Fordyce U.S.A.
176 A4 Forécariah Guinea
161 F7 Foreland *hd* U.K.
161 D6 Foreland Point U.K.
186 D4 Foresight Mountain Canada
191 G4 Forest Canada
199 F5 Forest *MS* U.S.A.
202 B4 Forest *OH* U.S.A.
203 G3 Forest Dale U.S.A.
127 G5 Forest Hill Australia
196 B2 Foresthill U.S.A.
127 H9 Forestier, Cape Australia
127 H9 Forestier Peninsula Australia
190 A3 Forest Lake U.S.A.
201 C5 Forest Park U.S.A.
189 G4 Forestville Canada
162 F4 Forfar U.K.
194 A2 Forks U.S.A.
202 E4 Forksville U.S.A.
170 E2 Forlì Italy
160 D4 Formby U.K.
167 G3 Formentera *i.* Spain
167 H3 Formentor, Cap de *c.* Spain
214 D3 Formiga Brazil
212 E3 Formosa Arg.
214 C1 Formosa Brazil
211 G6 Formosa, Serra *hills* Brazil
214 D1 Formoso *r.* Brazil
162 E3 Forres U.K.
126 E7 Forrest Australia
190 C5 Forrest U.S.A.
199 F5 Forrest City U.S.A.
190 C4 Forreston U.S.A.
158 L3 Fors Sweden
124 E3 Forsayth Australia
158 M2 Forsnäs Sweden
159 M3 Forssa Fin.
127 J4 Forster Australia
199 E4 Forsyth *MO* U.S.A.
194 F2 Forsyth *MT* U.S.A.
191 I1 Forsythe Canada
144 C3 Fort Abbas Pak.
188 D3 Fort Albany Canada
211 K4 Fortaleza Brazil
197 H5 Fort Apache U.S.A.
186 G4 Fort Assiniboine Canada
190 C4 Fort Atkinson U.S.A.
162 D3 Fort Augustus U.K.
181 G6 Fort Beaufort S. Africa
194 E2 Fort Benton U.S.A.
187 H3 Fort Black Canada
196 A2 Fort Bragg U.S.A.
Fort Chimo Canada *see* Kuujjuaq
187 G3 Fort Chipewyan Canada
199 D5 Fort Cobb Reservoir U.S.A.
194 F3 Fort Collins U.S.A.
191 I3 Fort-Coulonge Canada
203 F2 Fort Covington U.S.A.
199 C6 Fort Davis U.S.A.
205 L6 Fort-de-France Martinique
201 C5 Fort Deposit U.S.A.
198 E3 Fort Dodge U.S.A.
198 E1 Fort Frances U.S.A.
Fort George Canada *see* Chisasibi
184 F3 Fort Good Hope Canada
162 D4 Forth *r.* U.K.
162 F4 Forth, Firth of *est.* U.K.
197 E2 Fortification Range *mts* U.S.A.
212 D2 Fortín Capitán Demattei Para.
212 D2 Fortín General Mendoza Para.
212 E2 Fortín Madrejón Para.
212 D2 Fortín Pilcomayo Arg.
210 F7 Fortín Ravelo Bol.
210 F7 Fortín Suárez Arana Bol.
203 I1 Fort Kent U.S.A.
201 D7 Fort Lauderdale U.S.A.
186 E2 Fort Liard Canada
187 G3 Fort Mackay Canada
186 G5 Fort Macleod Canada
190 B5 Fort Madison U.S.A.
190 B3 Fort McCoy U.S.A.
187 G3 Fort McMurray Canada
184 E3 Fort McPherson Canada
194 G3 Fort Morgan U.S.A.
201 D7 Fort Myers U.S.A.
186 E3 Fort Nelson Canada
186 E3 Fort Nelson *r.* Canada
Fort Norman Canada *see* Tulita
201 C5 Fort Payne U.S.A.
194 F1 Fort Peck U.S.A.
194 F2 Fort Peck Reservoir U.S.A.
201 D7 Fort Pierce U.S.A.
198 C2 Fort Pierre U.S.A.
186 F2 Fort Providence Canada
187 I4 Fort Qu'Appelle Canada
186 G2 Fort Resolution Canada
128 B7 Fortrose N.Z.
162 D3 Fortrose U.K.
196 A2 Fort Ross U.S.A.
Fort Rupert Canada *see* Waskaganish
186 E4 Fort St James Canada
186 E3 Fort St John Canada
186 G4 Fort Saskatchewan Canada
199 E4 Fort Scott U.S.A.
188 C2 Fort Severn Canada
138 B3 Fort-Shevchenko Kazakh.
186 E2 Fort Simpson Canada
187 G2 Fort Smith Canada
199 E5 Fort Smith U.S.A.
199 C6 Fort Stockton U.S.A.
145 F4 Fort Sumeshwar *mt.* India
195 F5 Fort Sumner U.S.A.
194 A3 Fortuna *CA* U.S.A.
198 C1 Fortuna *ND* U.S.A.
189 I4 Fortune Bay Canada
186 F3 Fort Vermilion Canada
201 C6 Fort Walton Beach U.S.A.
190 E5 Fort Wayne U.S.A.
162 C4 Fort William U.K.
199 D5 Fort Worth U.S.A.
184 D3 Fort Yukon U.S.A.
140 D5 Forūr-e Bozorg, Jazīreh-ye *i.* Iran
140 D5 Forūr-e Kūchek, Jazīreh-ye *i.* Iran
158 K2 Forvik Norway
149 D6 Foshan China
170 B2 Fossano Italy
127 G7 Foster Australia
186 B3 Foster, Mount Canada/U.S.A.
185 P2 Foster Bugt *b.* Greenland
202 B4 Fostoria U.S.A.
161 G4 Fotherby U.K.
166 D2 Fougères France
162 □ Foula *i.* U.K.
161 H6 Foulness Point U.K.
143 C4 Foul Point Sri Lanka
128 C4 Foulwind, Cape N.Z.
176 D4 Foumban Cameroon
129 C4 Foundation Ice Stream *glacier* Antarctica
176 A3 Foundiougne Senegal
190 A4 Fountain U.S.A.
160 F3 Fountains Abbey and Studley Royal Water Garden *tourist site* U.K.
166 G2 Fourches, Mont des *h.* France
196 D4 Four Corners U.S.A.
181 H4 Fouriesburg S. Africa
164 C4 Fourmies France
171 L6 Fournoi *i.* Greece
190 C2 Fourteen Mile Point U.S.A.
176 A3 Fouta Djallon *reg.* Guinea
128 A7 Foveaux Strait N.Z.
201 E7 Fowl Cay *i.* Bahamas
195 F4 Fowler *CO* U.S.A.
190 D5 Fowler *IN* U.S.A.
190 E4 Fowler *MI* U.S.A.
129 B3 Fowler Ice Rise *ice feature* Antarctica
124 D5 Fowlers Bay Australia
187 K3 Fox *r.* Canada
190 C4 Fox *r.* U.S.A.
186 F4 Fox Creek Canada
160 C3 Foxdale U.K.
185 J3 Foxe Basin *g.* Canada
185 J3 Foxe Channel Canada
185 K3 Foxe Peninsula Canada
128 C5 Fox Glacier N.Z.
186 G3 Fox Lake Canada
190 C4 Fox Lake U.S.A.
128 E4 Foxton N.Z.
162 D3 Foyers U.K.
163 D3 Foyle *r.* Ireland/U.K.
163 D2 Foyle, Lough *b.* Ireland/U.K.
163 B5 Foynes Ireland
179 B5 Foz do Cunene Angola
214 A4 Foz do Iguaçu Brazil
167 G2 Fraga Spain
214 C3 Franca Brazil
125 G3 Français, Récif des *reef* New Caledonia
166 F3 France *country* Europe
126 D6 Frances Australia
186 D2 Frances *r.* Canada
186 D2 Frances Lake Canada
186 D2 Frances Lake *l.* Canada
190 D5 Francesville U.S.A.
178 B4 Franceville Gabon
203 H2 Francis, Lake U.S.A.
198 D3 Francis Case, Lake U.S.A.
206 D2 Francisco I. Madero *Coahuila* Mex.
206 C2 Francisco I. Madero *Durango* Mex.
214 D2 Francisco Sá Brazil
179 C6 Francistown Botswana
186 D4 François Lake Canada
194 E3 Francs Peak U.S.A.
164 D1 Franeker Neth.
165 G3 Frankenberg (Eder) Germany
165 L4 Frankenberg/Sachsen Germany
191 F4 Frankenmuth U.S.A.
165 G5 Frankenthal (Pfalz) Germany
165 J4 Frankenwald *mts* Germany
181 H3 Frankfort S. Africa
190 D5 Frankfort *IN* U.S.A.
200 C4 Frankfort *KY* U.S.A.
190 D3 Frankfort *MI* U.S.A.
168 G4 Frankfurt (Oder) Germany
165 G4 Frankfurt am Main Germany
197 E1 Frankin Lake U.S.A.
165 J5 Fränkische Alb *hills* Germany
165 J5 Fränkische Schweiz *reg.* Germany
194 E3 Franklin *ID* U.S.A.
200 C4 Franklin *IN* U.S.A.
199 F6 Franklin *LA* U.S.A.
203 H3 Franklin *MA* U.S.A.
201 D5 Franklin *NC* U.S.A.
203 H3 Franklin *NH* U.S.A.
203 F4 Franklin *NJ* U.S.A.
202 D4 Franklin *PA* U.S.A.
201 C5 Franklin *TN* U.S.A.
202 E6 Franklin *VA* U.S.A.
202 D5 Franklin *WV* U.S.A.
184 F3 Franklin Bay Canada
194 C1 Franklin D. Roosevelt Lake *resr* U.S.A.
127 F9 Franklin-Gordon National Park Australia
126 B4 Franklin Harbor *b.* Australia
186 E2 Franklin Mountains Canada
128 A6 Franklin Mountains N.Z.
127 G8 Franklin Sound *sea chan.* Australia
185 I2 Franklin Strait Canada
126 F7 Frankston Australia
159 L3 Fränsta Sweden
132 G2 Frantsa-Iosifa, Zemlya *is* Russia
190 E1 Franz Canada
128 C5 Franz Josef Glacier N.Z.
170 C5 Frasca, Capo della *c. Sardinia* Italy
170 E4 Frascati Italy
186 E4 Fraser *r. B.C.* Canada
189 H2 Fraser *r. Nfld and Lab.* Canada
180 D5 Fraserburg S. Africa
162 F3 Fraserburgh U.K.
188 D4 Fraserdale Canada
125 F4 Fraser Island Australia
186 E4 Fraser Lake Canada
186 E4 Fraser Plateau Canada
128 F3 Frasertown N.Z.
190 E2 Frater Canada
168 D7 Frauenfeld Switz.
215 E2 Fray Bentos Uruguay
164 E4 Frechen Germany
160 E4 Freckleton U.K.
190 E3 Frederic *MI* U.S.A.
190 A3 Frederic *WI* U.S.A.
159 J5 Fredericia Denmark
202 E5 Frederick *MD* U.S.A.
199 D5 Frederick *OK* U.S.A.
199 D6 Fredericksburg *TX* U.S.A.
202 E5 Fredericksburg *VA* U.S.A.
186 C3 Frederick Sound *sea chan.* U.S.A.
199 F4 Fredericktown U.S.A.
189 G4 Fredericton Canada
Frederikshåb Greenland *see* Paamiut
159 J4 Frederikshavn Denmark
159 K5 Frederiksværk Denmark
197 F3 Fredonia *AZ* U.S.A.
202 D3 Fredonia *NY* U.S.A.
158 L2 Fredrika Sweden
159 J4 Fredrikstad Norway
203 F4 Freehold U.S.A.
203 F4 Freeland U.S.A.
126 C3 Freeling Heights *h.* Australia
196 C2 Freel Peak U.S.A.
198 D3 Freeman U.S.A.
190 D5 Freeman, Lake U.S.A.
201 E7 Freeport Bahamas
190 C4 Freeport *IL* U.S.A.
203 H3 Freeport *ME* U.S.A.
203 G4 Freeport *NY* U.S.A.
199 E6 Freeport *TX* U.S.A.
199 D7 Freer U.S.A.
181 G4 Free State *prov.* S. Africa
176 A4 Freetown Sierra Leone
167 C3 Fregenal de la Sierra Spain
166 C2 Fréhel, Cap *c.* France
129 E2 Frei *research stn* Antarctica
168 C6 Freiburg im Breisgau Germany
164 F5 Freisen Germany
168 E6 Freising Germany
168 G6 Freistadt Austria
166 H5 Fréjus France
124 B5 Fremantle Australia
190 E4 Fremont *MI* U.S.A.
198 D3 Fremont *NE* U.S.A.
202 B4 Fremont *OH* U.S.A.
197 G2 Fremont *r.* U.S.A.
202 B6 Frenchburg U.S.A.
202 C4 French Creek *r.* U.S.A.
211 H3 French Guiana *terr.* S. America
126 F7 French Island Australia
187 H5 Frenchman *r.* Canada/U.S.A.
196 C2 Frenchman U.S.A.
196 B2 Frenchman Lake *CA* U.S.A.
197 E3 Frenchman Lake *NV* U.S.A.
127 F9 Frenchman's Cap *mt.* Australia
163 C4 Frenchpark Ireland
128 D4 French Pass N.Z.
123 I5 French Polynesia *terr.* Pacific Ocean
121 French Southern and Antarctic Lands *terr.* Indian Ocean
203 I1 Frenchville U.S.A.
164 F2 Freren Germany
163 D5 Freshford Ireland
197 G6 Fresnal Canyon U.S.A.
206 D3 Fresnillo Mex.
196 C3 Fresno U.S.A.
196 C3 Fresno *r.* U.S.A.
167 H3 Freu, Cap des *c.* Spain
165 F4 Freudenberg Germany
168 D6 Freudenstadt Germany
164 A4 Frévent France
127 H9 Freycinet National Park Australia
127 H9 Freycinet Peninsula Australia
165 K1 Freyenstein Germany
166 H2 Freyming-Merlebach France
215 D1 Freyre Arg.
176 A3 Fria Guinea
196 C3 Friant U.S.A.
212 C3 Frías Arg.
168 C7 Fribourg Switz.
165 F1 Friedeburg Germany
165 L1 Friedland Germany
168 D7 Friedrichshafen Germany
203 I3 Friendship U.S.A.
165 K2 Friesack Germany
164 D1 Friese Wad *tidal flat* Neth.
165 F1 Friesoythe Germany
161 I6 Frinton-on-Sea U.K.
199 D6 Frio *r.* U.S.A.
162 B4 Frisa, Loch *l.* U.K.
197 F2 Frisco Mountain U.S.A.
165 H3 Fritzlar Germany
185 L3 Frobisher Bay Canada
187 H3 Frobisher Lake Canada
158 J3 Frohavet *b.* Norway
165 K3 Frohburg Germany
164 A5 Froissy France
173 G5 Frolovo Russia
172 J2 Frolovsk Russia
126 C2 Frome *watercourse* Australia
161 E6 Frome U.K.
126 C3 Frome, Lake *salt flat* Australia
126 C3 Frome Downs Australia
165 F3 Fröndenberg/Ruhr Germany
207 F4 Frontera Mex.
207 F4 Frontera, Punta *pt* Mex.
202 D5 Front Royal U.S.A.
170 E4 Frosinone Italy
202 D5 Frostburg U.S.A.
129 C6 Frost Glacier *glacier* Antarctica
158 J3 Frøya *i.* Norway
164 A4 Fruges France
197 H2 Fruita U.S.A.
197 G1 Fruitland U.S.A.
Frunze Kyrg. *see* Bishkek
168 C7 Frutigen Switz.
169 I6 Frýdek-Místek Czech Rep.
203 H2 Fryeburg U.S.A.
149 F5 Fu'an China
149 D5 Fuchuan China
149 F4 Fuchun Jiang *r.* China
162 A3 Fuday *i.* U.K.
149 E5 Fude China
149 F5 Fuding China
167 E2 Fuenlabrada Spain
167 D3 Fuente Obejuna Spain
152 D2 Fu'er He *r.* China
212 E2 Fuerte Olimpo Para.
176 A2 Fuerteventura *i.* Canary Is
153 B2 Fuga *i.* Phil.
148 E3 Fugou China
148 D2 Fugu China
137 I4 Fuḩaymī Iraq
142 E4 Fujairah U.A.E.
151 F7 Fuji Japan
149 E5 Fujian *prov.* China
148 C4 Fu Jiang *r.* China
151 F7 Fuji-Hakone-Izu Kokuritsu-kōen *nat. park* Japan
150 B1 Fujin China
151 F7 Fujinomiya Japan
151 F7 Fuji-san *vol.* Japan
150 H3 Fukagawa Japan
151 D7 Fukuchiyama Japan
151 A8 Fukue-jima *i.* Japan
151 E6 Fukui Japan
151 B8 Fukuoka Japan
151 G6 Fukushima Japan
151 B9 Fukuyama Japan
140 D2 Fūlād Maḩalleh Iran
165 H4 Fulda Germany
165 H3 Fulda *r.* Germany
161 G6 Fulham U.K.
148 E3 Fuli China
149 C4 Fuling China
187 L2 Fullerton, Cape Canada
190 B5 Fulton *IL* U.S.A.
200 B4 Fulton *KY* U.S.A.
198 F4 Fulton *MO* U.S.A.
203 E3 Fulton *NY* U.S.A.
137 L3 Fūman Iran
181 J2 Fumane Moz.
164 C5 Fumay France
151 F7 Funabashi Japan
125 H2 Funafuti *atoll* Tuvalu
176 A1 Funchal Madeira
213 B2 Fundación Col.
167 C2 Fundão Port.
206 B2 Fundición Mex.
189 G5 Fundy, Bay of *g.* Canada
189 G4 Fundy National Park Canada
196 D3 Funeral Peak U.S.A.
179 D6 Funhalouro Moz.
148 F3 Funing *Jiangsu* China
149 B6 Funing *Yunnan* China
148 D3 Funiu Shan *mts* China
176 C3 Funtua Nigeria
162 □ Funzie U.K.
149 F5 Fuqing China
150 H3 Furano Japan
140 E5 Fürgun, Kūh-e *mt.* Iran
172 G3 Furmanov Russia
150 D3 Furmanovo Russia
196 D3 Furnace Creek U.S.A.
167 G3 Furnás *h.* Spain
214 C3 Furnas, Represa *resr* Brazil
124 E6 Furneaux Group *is* Australia
165 F2 Fürstenau Germany
165 L1 Fürstenberg/Havel Germany
168 G4 Fürstenwalde/Spree Germany
165 I5 Fürth Germany
165 K5 Furth im Wald Germany
150 G3 Furubira Japan
185 J3 Fury and Hecla Strait Canada
213 B3 Fusagasugá Col.
149 C7 Fushan *Hainan* China
152 A5 Fushan *Shandong* China
152 B3 Fushun *Liaoning* China
149 B4 Fushun *Sichuan* China
152 D2 Fusong China
149 C6 Fusui China
151 B8 Futago-san *vol.* Japan
125 H3 Futuna *i.* Vanuatu
149 E5 Futun Xi *r.* China
148 C3 Fuxian China
149 B5 Fuxian Hu *l.* China
152 A2 Fuxin *Liaoning* China
152 A2 Fuxin *Liaoning* China
150 F5 Fuya Japan
148 E3 Fuyang *Anhui* China
149 F4 Fuyang *Zhejiang* China
148 E2 Fuyang He *r.* China
146 E2 Fuyu *Heilongjiang* China
152 D1 Fuyu *Jilin* China
149 B5 Fuyuan China
149 F5 Fuzhou *Fujian* China
149 E5 Fuzhou *Jiangxi* China
152 A4 Fuzhou Wan *b.* China
137 K2 Füzuli Azer.
159 J5 Fyn *i.* Denmark
162 C5 Fyne, Loch *inlet* U.K.
F.Y.R.O.M. (Former Yugoslav Republic of Macedonia) *country* Europe *see* Macedonia

G

170 C6 Gaâfour Tunisia
178 E3 Gaalkacyo Somalia
138 E5 Gabakly Turkm.
181 F2 Gabane Botswana
196 D2 Gabbs U.S.A.
196 C2 Gabbs Valley Range *mts* U.S.A.
179 B5 Gabela Angola
176 D1 Gabès Tunisia
177 D1 Gabès, Golfe de *g.* Tunisia
139 H2 Gabiden Mustafin Kazakh.
127 H6 Gabo Island Australia
178 B4 Gabon *country* Africa
179 C6 Gaborone Botswana
141 E5 Gābrīk Iran
141 E5 Gābrīk *watercourse* Iran
171 K3 Gabrovo Bulg.
176 A3 Gabú Guinea-Bissau
140 C2 Gachsar Iran
143 A3 Gadag-Betigeri India
144 E5 Gadchiroli India
158 K2 Gäddede Sweden
165 J1 Gadebusch Germany
144 B5 Gadhda India
144 B4 Gadra Pak.
201 C5 Gadsden U.S.A.
143 B2 Gadwal India
138 E5 Gadyn Turkm.
Gæi'dnuvuop'pi Norway *see* Geaidnovuohppi
161 D6 Gaer U.K.
171 K2 Găeşti Romania
170 E4 Gaeta Italy
170 E4 Gaeta, Golfo di *g.* Italy
216 E5 Gaferut *i.* Micronesia
201 D5 Gaffney U.S.A.
176 C1 Gafsa Tunisia
172 E4 Gagarin Russia
139 G4 Gagarin Uzbek.
172 H4 Gagino Russia
176 B4 Gagnoa Côte d'Ivoire
189 G3 Gagnon Canada
173 G7 Gagra Georgia
137 K4 Gahvāreh Iran
180 C3 Gaiab *watercourse* Namibia
145 G4 Gaibandha Bangl.
171 K7 Gaïdouronisi *i.* Greece
165 H6 Gaildorf Germany
166 E5 Gaillac France
201 D6 Gainesville *FL* U.S.A.
201 D5 Gainesville *GA* U.S.A.
199 D5 Gainesville *TX* U.S.A.
161 G4 Gainsborough U.K.
126 A3 Gairdner, Lake *salt flat* Australia
162 C3 Gairloch U.K.
162 C3 Gair Loch *b.* U.K.
152 B3 Gaizhou China
143 C2 Gajapatinagaram India
141 G5 Gajar Pak.
180 E3 Gakarosa *mt.* S. Africa
144 C1 Gakuch Pak.
145 G3 Gala China
Galaasiya Uzbek. *see* Galaosiyo
178 D4 Galana *r.* Kenya
138 F5 Galaosiyo Uzbek.
210 □ Galápagos, Parque Nacional *nat. park* Ecuador
210 □ Galapagos Islands Pacific Ocean
217 M6 Galapagos Rise *sea feature* Pacific Ocean
162 F5 Galashiels U.K.
171 L3 Galata, Nos *pt* Bulg.
171 M2 Galaţi Romania
171 H4 Galatina Italy
202 C6 Galax U.S.A.
141 F3 Galaýmor Turkm.
163 C5 Galbally Ireland
159 J3 Galdhøpiggen *mt.* Norway
207 D2 Galeana Mex.
140 D5 Galeh Dār Iran
190 B4 Galena U.S.A.
213 E2 Galeota Point Trin. and Tob.
215 B4 Galera, Punta *pt* Chile
207 E5 Galera, Punta *pt* Mex.
213 E2 Galera Point Trin. and Tob.
190 B5 Galesburg U.S.A.
180 F4 Galeshewe S. Africa
190 B3 Galesville U.S.A.
202 E4 Galeton U.S.A.
173 G7 Gali Georgia
172 G3 Galich Russia
172 G2 Galichskaya Vozvyshennost' *hills* Russia
167 C1 Galicia *aut. comm.* Spain
136 E5 Galilee, Sea of Israel
202 B4 Galion U.S.A.
170 C6 Galite, Canal de la *sea chan.* Tunisia
197 G5 Galiuro Mountains U.S.A.
138 E5 Galkynyş Turkm.
177 F3 Gallabat Sudan
139 F4 G'allaorol Uzbek.
201 C4 Gallatin U.S.A.
194 E2 Gallatin *r.* U.S.A.
143 C5 Galle Sri Lanka
217 L6 Gallego Rise *sea feature* Pacific Ocean
212 B8 Gallegos *r.* Arg.
213 C1 Gallinas, Punta *pt* Col.
171 L4 Gallipoli Turkey
202 B5 Gallipolis U.S.A.
158 M2 Gällivare Sweden
158 K3 Gällö Sweden
203 E3 Gallo Island U.S.A.
197 H4 Gallo Mountains U.S.A.
197 H4 Gallup U.S.A.
Gallyaaral Uzbek. *see* G'allaorol
162 B4 Galmisdale U.K.
178 E3 Galmudug *reg.* Somalia
127 H5 Galong Australia
143 C4 Galoya Sri Lanka
143 C5 Gal Oya *r.* Sri Lanka
162 D5 Galston U.K.
196 B2 Galt U.S.A.
176 A2 Galtat-Zemmour W. Sahara
163 C5 Galtee Mountains *hills* Ireland
163 C5 Galtymore *h.* Ireland
141 E3 Galūgāh-e Āsīyeh Iran
190 B5 Galva U.S.A.
199 E6 Galveston U.S.A.
199 E6 Galveston Bay U.S.A.
215 E2 Gálvez Arg.
145 E3 Galwa Nepal
163 B4 Galway Ireland
163 B4 Galway Bay Ireland
149 B6 Gâm, Sông *r.* Vietnam
161 I8 Gamaches France
181 I5 Gamalakhe S. Africa
213 B2 Gamarra Col.
145 G3 Gamba China
178 D3 Gambēla Eth.
178 D3 Gambēla National Park Eth.
184 A3 Gambell U.S.A.
144 D4 Gambhir *r.* India
176 A3 Gambia *r.* Gambia
176 A3 Gambia, The *country* Africa
123 J6 Gambier, Îles *is* Fr. Polynesia
126 B5 Gambier Islands Australia
189 J4 Gambo Canada
178 B4 Gamboma Congo
197 H4 Gamerco U.S.A.
186 F2 Gamêtî Canada
159 L4 Gamleby Sweden
158 M2 Gammelstaden Sweden
180 C4 Gamoep S. Africa
150 B3 Gamova, Mys *pt* Russia
143 C5 Gampola Sri Lanka
141 F4 Gamshadzai Kūh *mts* Iran
171 J3 Gamzigrad-Romuliana *tourist site*
148 A3 Gana China
197 H4 Ganado U.S.A.
181 H3 Ga-Nala S. Africa
191 I3 Gananoque Canada
137 K1 Gäncä Azer.
149 C7 Gancheng China
155 E3 Gandadiwata, Bukit *mt.* Indon.
145 G3 Gandaingoin China
178 C4 Gandajika Dem. Rep. Congo
145 E4 Gandak Barrage *dam* Nepal
144 B3 Gandari Mountain Pak.
144 A3 Gandava Pak.
189 J4 Gander Canada
165 G1 Ganderkesee Germany
167 G2 Gandesa Spain
144 C5 Gandevi India
144 B5 Gandhidham India
144 C5 Gandhinagar India
144 C4 Gandhi Sagar *resr* India
144 C4 Gandhi Sagar Dam India
167 F3 Gandia Spain
214 E1 Gandu Brazil
144 E4 Ganga *r.* Bangl./India *alt.* Padma, *conv.* Ganges
143 C5 Ganga *r.* Sri Lanka
215 C4 Gangán Arg.
144 C3 Ganganagar India
144 D4 Gangapur India
145 H5 Gangaw Myanmar
143 B3 Gangawati India
148 A2 Gangca China
144 E3 Gangdisê Shan *mts* China
144 E4 Ganges *r.* Bangl./India *alt.* Ganga, *alt.* Padma
166 F5 Ganges France
145 G5 Ganges, Mouths of the Bangl./India
218 J3 Ganges Cone *sea feature* Indian Ocean
152 D5 Ganghwa S. Korea
152 D5 Ganghwa-do *i.* S. Korea
152 E5 Gangneung S. Korea
144 D3 Gangoh India
144 D3 Gangotri Group *mts* India
145 G4 Gangtok India
148 B3 Gangu China
143 D2 Ganjam India
140 C4 Ganjgūn Iran
149 E4 Gan Jiang *r.* China
152 B2 Ganjig China
149 B4 Ganluo China
127 G5 Ganmain Australia
166 F3 Gannat France
194 E3 Gannett Peak U.S.A.
144 C5 Ganora India
148 C2 Ganquan China
180 C7 Gansbaai S. Africa
152 E4 Ganseong S. Korea
148 B3 Gansu *prov.* China
148 B2 Gantang China
126 B6 Gantheaume, Cape Australia
173 G7 Gantiadi Georgia
149 E5 Ganxian China
180 F3 Ganyesa S. Africa
148 F3 Ganyu China
138 B3 Ganyushkino Kazakh.
149 E5 Ganzhou China
177 F4 Ganzi South Sudan
176 B3 Gao Mali

Graham Lake

149 E4 Gao'an China
148 E2 Gaocheng China
148 F4 Gaochun China
148 B2 Gaolan China
148 F2 Gaomi China
149 D5 Gaomudang China
148 D3 Gaoping China
148 A2 Gaotai China
148 E2 Gaotang China
163 C2 Gaoth Dobhair Ireland
148 C2 Gaotouyao China
176 B3 Gaoua Burkina Faso
176 A3 Gaoual Guinea
Gaoxian China see Wenjiang
149 F6 Gaoxiong Taiwan
148 E2 Gaoyang China
148 E2 Gaoyi China
148 F3 Gaoyou China
148 F3 Gaoyou Hu l. China
149 D6 Gaozhou China
166 H4 Gap France
153 B3 Gapan Phil.
152 D5 Gapyeong S. Korea
144 E2 Gar China
163 C4 Gara, Lough l. Ireland
Garabekevyul Turkm. see Garabekewül
138 F5 Garabekewül Turkm.
141 F2 Garabil Belentligi hills Turkm.
138 C4 Garabogaz Turkm.
138 C4 Garabogazköl Turkm.
138 C4 Garabogazköl Aýlagy b. Turkm.
206 J6 Garachiné Panama
141 F4 Garāgheh Iran
Garagum des. Turkm. see Karakum Desert
138 E5 Garagum Kanaly canal Turkm.
127 H2 Garah Australia
138 F5 Garamätnyýaz Turkm.
178 C3 Garamba r. Dem. Rep. Congo
178 C3 Garamba, Parc National de la nat. park Dem. Rep. Congo
211 K5 Garanhuns Brazil
181 G2 Ga-Rankuwa S. Africa
178 D3 Garba Tula Kenya
196 A1 Garberville U.S.A.
165 H2 Garbsen Germany
214 C3 Garça Brazil
214 B1 Garças, Rio das r. Brazil
145 G2 Garco China
170 D2 Garda, Lake Italy
137 J1 Gardabani Georgia
170 B6 Garde, Cap de c. Alg.
165 J2 Gardelegen Germany
198 C4 Garden City U.S.A.
190 D3 Garden Corners U.S.A.
196 C5 Garden Grove U.S.A.
187 K4 Garden Hill Canada
190 E3 Garden Island U.S.A.
180 E6 Garden Route National Park nat. park S. Africa
141 H3 Gardēz Afgh.
203 I2 Gardiner ME U.S.A.
194 E2 Gardiner MT U.S.A.
203 G4 Gardiners Island U.S.A.
Gardīz Afgh. see Gardēz
190 C5 Gardner U.S.A.
203 J2 Gardner Lake U.S.A.
123 H2 Gardner Pinnacles is U.S.A.
196 C2 Gardnerville U.S.A.
162 D4 Garelochhead U.K.
190 E2 Gargantua, Cape Canada
137 L6 Gargar Iran
159 M5 Gargždai Lith.
144 D5 Garhakota India
144 A3 Garhi Khairo Pak.
144 D4 Garhi Malehra India
186 E5 Garibaldi, Mount Canada
186 E5 Garibaldi Provincial Park Canada
181 F5 Gariep Dam resr S. Africa
180 B5 Garies S. Africa
170 E4 Garigliano r. Italy
178 D4 Garissa Kenya
159 N4 Garkalne Latvia
202 D4 Garland PA U.S.A.
199 D5 Garland TX U.S.A.
168 E7 Garmisch-Partenkirchen Germany
Garmo, Qullai mt. Tajik. see Ismoili Somoní, Qullai
140 D3 Garmsār Iran
141 F4 Garm Sēr reg. Afgh.
198 E4 Garnett U.S.A.
126 E4 Garnpung Lake imp. l. Australia
145 G4 Garo Hills India
166 D4 Garonne r. France
178 E3 Garoowe Somalia
212 G3 Garopaba Brazil
177 D4 Garoua Cameroon
215 D3 Garré Arg.
197 E2 Garrison U.S.A.
163 F2 Garron Point U.K.
141 G4 Garruk Pak.
162 D4 Garry, Loch l. U.K.
187 I1 Garry Lake Canada
162 B2 Garrynahine U.K.
178 E4 Garsen Kenya
138 C4 Garşy Turkm.
161 D5 Garth U.K.
165 J1 Gartow Germany
180 B3 Garub Namibia
155 C4 Garut Indon.
163 E3 Garvagh U.K.
162 D3 Garve U.K.
190 D5 Gary U.S.A.
144 E3 Garyarsa China
151 C7 Garyū-zan mt. Japan
144 D2 Gar Zangbo r. China
146 B3 Garzê China
213 B4 Garzón Col.
Gascogne, Golfe de g. France/Spain see Gascony, Gulf of
198 E4 Gasconade r. U.S.A.
166 D5 Gascony reg. France
166 C4 Gascony, Gulf of France/Spain
124 B4 Gascoyne r. Australia
144 D2 Gasherbrum I mt. China/Pak.
141 F5 Gasht Iran
176 D3 Gashua Nigeria
141 E3 Gask Iran
155 C3 Gaspar, Selat sea chan. Indon.
189 H4 Gaspé Canada
189 H4 Gaspé, Cap c. Canada
189 G4 Gaspésie, Parc de Conservation de la nature res. Canada
189 G4 Gaspésie, Péninsule de la pen. Canada
164 E2 Gasselte Neth.
201 D5 Gastonia U.S.A.
215 C4 Gastre Arg.
167 E4 Gata, Cabo de c. Spain
136 D4 Gata, Cape Cyprus
172 D3 Gatchina Russia
202 B6 Gate City U.S.A.
162 D6 Gatehouse of Fleet U.K.
160 F3 Gateshead U.K.
199 D6 Gatesville U.S.A.
197 H2 Gateway U.S.A.
203 F4 Gateway National Recreational Area park U.S.A.
191 J3 Gatineau Canada
191 J2 Gatineau r. Canada
127 J1 Gatton Australia
206 I6 Gatún, Lago l. Panama
137 L5 Gatvand Iran
125 H3 Gau i. Fiji
187 J3 Gauer Lake Canada
158 J3 Gaula r. Norway
202 C5 Gauley Bridge U.S.A.
164 D5 Gaume reg. Belgium
145 F4 Gauri Sankar mt. China
181 G3 Gauteng prov. S. Africa
137 J1 Gavarr Armenia
141 F5 Gavāter Iran
141 H3 Gāv Band Afgh.
140 D5 Gāvbūs, Kūh-e mts Iran
171 K7 Gavdos i. Greece
140 B3 Gāveh Rūd r. Iran
214 E1 Gavião r. Brazil
137 K4 Gavīleh Iran
196 B4 Gaviota U.S.A.
159 L3 Gävle Sweden
172 F3 Gavrilov-Yam Russia
180 B3 Gawachab Namibia
141 G3 Gāw Jān Afgh.
126 C5 Gawler Australia
126 A4 Gawler Ranges hills Australia
148 A1 Gaxun Nur salt l. China
138 D2 Gay Russia
145 F4 Gaya India
176 C3 Gaya Niger
152 E2 Gaya He r. China
190 E3 Gaylord U.S.A.
136 E6 Gaza disp. terr. Asia
136 E6 Gaza Gaza
181 J1 Gaza prov. Moz.
Gaz-Achak Turkm. see Gazojak
139 G4 G'azalkent Uzbek.
Gazandzhyk Turkm. see Bereket
Gazgan Uzbek. see G'ozg'on
136 F3 Gaziantep Turkey
141 F3 Gazīk Iran
Gazimağusa Cyprus see Famagusta
136 D3 Gazipaşa Turkey
138 E4 Gazli Uzbek.
141 E5 Gaz Māhū Iran
138 E4 Gazojak Turkm.
178 C3 Gbadolite Dem. Rep. Congo
176 A4 Gbangbatok Sierra Leone
176 B4 Gbarnga Liberia
176 C4 Gboko Nigeria
181 H6 Gcuwa S. Africa
169 I3 Gdańsk Poland
169 I3 Gdańsk, Gulf of Poland/Russia
172 C3 Gdov Russia
169 I3 Gdynia Poland
158 M1 Geaidnovuohppi Norway
162 C1 Gealldruig Mhòr i. U.K.
165 I3 Gebesee Germany
177 F3 Gedaref Sudan
165 H4 Gedern Germany
164 C5 Gedinne Belgium
136 A2 Gediz r. Turkey
161 H5 Gedney Drove End U.K.
159 J5 Gedser Denmark
164 D3 Geel Belgium
126 F7 Geelong Australia
180 D4 Geel Vloer salt pan S. Africa
164 F2 Geeste Germany
165 I1 Geesthacht Germany
127 G9 Geeveston Australia
176 D3 Geidam Nigeria
165 H5 Geiersberg h. Germany
187 I3 Geikie r. Canada
164 E4 Geilenkirchen Germany
159 J3 Geilo Norway
159 I3 Geiranger Norway
190 E6 Geist Reservoir U.S.A.
179 D4 Geita Tanz.
165 K3 Geithain Germany
149 B6 Gejiu China
170 F6 Gela Sicily Italy
178 E3 Geladī Eth.
154 B4 Gelang, Tanjung pt Malaysia
164 E3 Geldern Germany
173 F6 Gelendzhik Russia
169 K3 Gelgaudiškis Lith.
Gelibolu Turkey see Gallipoli
136 C2 Gelincik Dağı mt. Turkey
165 H4 Gelnhausen Germany
164 F3 Gelsenkirchen Germany
154 B5 Gemas Malaysia
153 C5 Gemeh Indon.
178 B3 Gemena Dem. Rep. Congo
136 F2 Gemerek Turkey
136 B1 Gemlik Turkey
170 E1 Gemona del Friuli Italy
179 C6 Gemsbok National Park Botswana
180 D3 Gemsbokplein well S. Africa
178 E3 Genalē Wenz r. Eth.
164 C4 Genappe Belgium
215 D3 General Acha Arg.
215 E3 General Alvear Buenos Aires Arg.
215 E1 General Alvear Entre Ríos Arg.
215 C2 General Alvear Mendoza Arg.
215 E2 General Belgrano Arg.
207 E2 General Bravo Mex.
212 B7 General Carrera, Lago l. Chile
206 D2 General Cepeda Mex.
215 F3 General Conesa Buenos Aires Arg.
215 D4 General Conesa Río Negro Arg.
215 F3 General Guido Arg.
215 F3 General Juan Madariaga Arg.
215 E3 General La Madrid Arg.
215 F3 General Lavalle Arg.
215 D2 General Levalle Arg.
153 C4 General Luna Phil.
153 C4 General MacArthur Phil.
215 D2 General Pico Arg.
215 E2 General Pinto Arg.
215 C3 General Roca Arg.
153 C5 General Santos Phil.
207 E2 General Terán Mex.
215 D2 General Villegas Arg.
202 D3 Genesee r. U.S.A.
190 B5 Geneseo IL U.S.A.
202 E3 Geneseo NY U.S.A.
181 G3 Geneva S. Africa
168 C7 Geneva Switz.
190 C5 Geneva IL U.S.A.
198 D3 Geneva NE U.S.A.
202 E3 Geneva NY U.S.A.
202 C4 Geneva OH U.S.A.
166 H3 Geneva, Lake France/Switz.
190 C4 Geneva, Lake U.S.A.
Genève Switz. see Geneva
149 F4 Genglou China
167 D4 Genil r. Spain
164 D4 Genk Belgium
164 D3 Gennep Neth.
127 H6 Genoa Australia
170 C2 Genoa Italy
170 C2 Genoa, Gulf of Italy
Genova Italy see Genoa
Gent Belgium see Ghent
165 K2 Genthin Germany
152 D6 Geochang S. Korea
124 B5 Geographe Bay Australia
152 E6 Geoje-do i. S. Korea
152 E6 Geongju S. Korea
132 F2 Georga, Zemlya i. Russia
189 G2 George r. Canada
180 E6 George S. Africa
127 H5 George, Lake N.S.W. Australia
126 C6 George, Lake S.A. Australia
201 D6 George, Lake FL U.S.A.
203 G3 George, Lake NY U.S.A.
128 A6 George Sound inlet N.Z.
126 C4 Georgetown Australia
127 G8 George Town Australia
201 F7 George Town Bahamas
191 H4 Georgetown Canada
211 G2 Georgetown Guyana
155 B1 George Town Malaysia
203 F5 Georgetown DE U.S.A.
190 D6 Georgetown IL U.S.A.
200 C4 Georgetown KY U.S.A.
202 B5 Georgetown OH U.S.A.
201 E5 Georgetown SC U.S.A.
199 D6 Georgetown TX U.S.A.
129 C6 George V Land reg. Antarctica
199 D6 George West U.S.A.
173 G7 Georgia country Asia
201 D5 Georgia state U.S.A.
186 E5 Georgia, Strait of Canada
191 G3 Georgian Bay Canada
191 H3 Georgian Bay Islands National Park Canada
124 D4 Georgina watercourse Australia
139 J2 Georgiyevka Vostochnyy Kazakhstan Kazakh.
139 G4 Georgiyevka Yuzhnyy Kazakhstan Kazakh.
173 G6 Georgiyevsk Russia
172 H3 Georgiyevskoye Russia
165 K4 Gera Germany
164 B4 Geraardsbergen Belgium
211 I6 Geral de Goiás, Serra hills Brazil
128 C6 Geraldine N.Z.
214 C1 Geral do Paraná, Serra hills Brazil
124 B4 Geraldton Australia
140 D5 Gerāsh Iran
137 H3 Gercüş Turkey
136 D1 Gerede Turkey
136 D1 Gerede r. Turkey
154 B4 Gerik Malaysia
198 C3 Gering U.S.A.
194 C3 Gerlach U.S.A.
168 C3 German Bight g. Denmark/Germany
186 E3 Germansen Landing Canada
202 E5 Germantown U.S.A.
168 E5 Germany country Europe
165 G5 Germersheim Germany
140 C2 Germī Iran
181 H3 Germiston S. Africa
165 G5 Gernsheim Germany
164 E4 Gerolstein Germany
165 I5 Gerolzhofen Germany
197 G5 Geronimo (abandoned) U.S.A.
127 I5 Gerringong Australia
165 H4 Gersfeld (Rhön) Germany
165 I4 Gerstungen Germany
165 J2 Gerwisch Germany
145 F2 Gêrzê China
173 E7 Gerze Turkey
164 F3 Gescher Germany
178 E3 Gestro Wenz, Wabē r. Eth.
164 D4 Gete r. Belgium
202 E5 Gettysburg PA U.S.A.
198 D2 Gettysburg SD U.S.A.
202 E5 Gettysburg National Military Park nat. park U.S.A.
149 C5 Getu He r. China
129 B4 Getz Ice Shelf ice feature Antarctica
155 A2 Geumapang r. Indon.
152 D6 Geumeo-do i. S. Korea
152 D5 Geum-gang r. S. Korea
152 E6 Geumho-gang r. S. Korea
127 H4 Geurie Australia
137 I2 Gevaş Turkey
171 J4 Gevgelija Macedonia
141 G4 Gêwārām Band Afgh.
154 □ Geylang Sing.
181 F3 Geysdorp S. Africa
136 C1 Geyve Turkey
180 F2 Ghaap Plateau S. Africa
137 I5 Ghadaf, Wādī al watercourse Iraq
176 C1 Ghadāmis Libya
139 G4 Ghafurov Tajik.
144 E4 Ghaghara r. India
145 F5 Ghaghra India
176 B4 Ghana country Africa
140 D5 Ghanādah, Rās pt U.A.E.
144 C4 Ghanliala India
179 C6 Ghanzi Botswana
180 E1 Ghanzi admin. dist. Botswana
140 C5 Ghār, Ras al pt Saudi Arabia
136 E6 Gharandal Jordan
176 C1 Ghardaïa Alg.
Ghârib, Gebel mt. Egypt see Ghārib, Jabal
177 F2 Ghārib, Jabal mt. Egypt
139 G5 Gharm Tajik.
177 D1 Gharyān Libya
136 F5 Gharz, Wādī al watercourse Syria
176 D2 Ghāt Libya
144 B3 Ghauspur Pak.
177 D3 Ghazal, Bahr el watercourse Chad
176 B1 Ghazaouet Alg.
144 D3 Ghaziabad India
145 E4 Ghazipur India
144 A3 Ghazluna Pak.
141 H3 Ghaznī Afgh.
141 H3 Ghaznī Rōd r. Afgh.
164 B3 Ghent Belgium
169 L7 Gheorgheni Romania
169 K7 Gherla Romania
170 C3 Ghisonaccia Corsica France
144 C1 Ghizar Pak.
143 A2 Ghod r. India
145 G4 Ghoraghat Bangl.
141 H3 Ghōr Band, Daryā-ye r. Afgh.
141 F3 Ghōriyān Afgh.
144 B4 Ghotaru India
144 B4 Ghotki Pak.
139 H5 Ghŭdara Tajik.
145 F4 Ghugri r. India
144 D6 Ghugus India
144 B4 Ghulam Muhammad Barrage Pak.
140 D4 Ghūrī Iran
164 A3 Ghyvelde France
Gia Đinh Vietnam see Thu Đuc
173 G6 Giaginskaya Russia
154 C2 Gia Nghia Vietnam
171 J4 Giannitsa Greece
181 H4 Giant's Castle mt. S. Africa
163 E2 Giant's Causeway lava field U.K.
155 E4 Gianyar Indon.
154 C3 Gia Rai Vietnam
170 F6 Giarre Sicily Italy
170 B2 Giaveno Italy
180 B2 Gibeon Namibia
167 D4 Gibraltar Europe
167 C5 Gibraltar, Strait of Morocco/Spain
190 C5 Gibson City U.S.A.
124 C4 Gibson Desert Australia
146 B2 Gichgeniyn Nuruu mts Mongolia
143 B3 Giddalur India
178 D3 Gīdolē Eth.
166 F3 Gien France
165 G4 Gießen Germany
165 I2 Gifhorn Germany
186 F3 Gift Lake Canada
151 E7 Gifu Japan
213 B4 Gigante Col.
162 C5 Gigha i. U.K.
138 F4 G'ijduvon Uzbek.
167 D1 Gijón/Xixón Spain
197 F5 Gila r. U.S.A.
197 F5 Gila Bend U.S.A.
197 F5 Gila Bend Mountains U.S.A.
197 E5 Gila Mountains U.S.A.
137 J4 Gīlān-e Gharb Iran
137 L1 Giläzi Azer.
124 E3 Gilbert r. Australia
197 G5 Gilbert AZ U.S.A.
202 C6 Gilbert WV U.S.A.
125 H2 Gilbert Islands Kiribati
216 G6 Gilbert Ridge sea feature Pacific Ocean
211 I5 Gilbués Brazil
140 E3 Gil Chashmeh Iran
194 E1 Gildford U.S.A.
186 D4 Gilford Island Canada
127 I2 Gilgai Australia
127 H3 Gilgandra Australia
178 D4 Gilgil Kenya
127 H2 Gil Gil Creek r. Australia
144 C2 Gilgit Pak.
144 C2 Gilgit r. Pak.
144 C1 Gilgit-Baltistan admin. div. Pak.
127 G4 Gilgunnia Australia
186 D4 Gil Island Canada
187 K3 Gillam Canada
126 B4 Gilles, Lake salt flat Australia
190 C3 Gillett U.S.A.
194 F2 Gillette U.S.A.
161 E6 Gillingham England U.K.
161 H6 Gillingham England U.K.
160 F3 Gilling West U.K.
190 D3 Gills Rock U.S.A.
190 D5 Gilman IL U.S.A.
190 B3 Gilman WI U.S.A.
188 E2 Gilmour Island Canada
196 B3 Gilroy U.S.A.
203 G3 Gilsum U.S.A.
177 E3 Gimbala, Jebel mt. Sudan
178 D3 Gīmbī Eth.
152 E5 Gimcheon S. Korea
152 D4 Gimhwa S. Korea
152 D6 Gimje S. Korea
187 J4 Gimli Canada
210 E6 Ginebra, Laguna l. Bol.
143 C5 Gin Ganga r. Sri Lanka
143 B3 Gingee India
186 D3 Gingolx Canada
178 E3 Gīnīr Eth.
170 G4 Ginosa Italy
170 G4 Gioia del Colle Italy
127 G6 Gippsland reg. Australia
144 B4 Girab India
141 E5 Gīrān Iran
141 E4 Gīrān Rīg mt. Iran
202 C3 Girard U.S.A.
144 B3 Girdao Pak.
141 G5 Girdar Dhor r. Pak.
141 F4 Gīrdī Iran
136 G1 Giresun Turkey
144 B5 Gir Forest India
145 F4 Giridih India
127 G3 Girilambone Australia
141 G4 Girishk Afgh.
144 C5 Girna r. India
167 H2 Girona Spain
166 D4 Gironde est. France
127 G4 Girral Australia
162 D5 Girvan U.K.
172 E2 Girvas Russia
144 E4 Girwan India
128 G3 Gisborne N.Z.
186 E4 Giscome Canada
159 K4 Gislaved Sweden
139 F5 Gissar Range mts Tajik./Uzbek.
173 G7 Gistola, Gora mt. Georgia/Russia
178 C4 Gitarama Rwanda
140 D3 Gītcheh, Kūh-e hills Iran
178 C4 Gitega Burundi
170 E3 Giulianova Italy
171 K3 Giurgiu Romania
171 K2 Giuvala, Pasul pass Romania
164 C4 Givet France
166 G4 Givors France
164 C6 Givry-en-Argonne France
181 I1 Giyani S. Africa
177 F2 Giza Egypt
137 K4 Gīzeh Rūd r. Iran
Gizhduvan Uzbek. see G'ijduvon
133 R3 Gizhiga Russia
171 I3 Gjakovë Kosovo
171 I3 Gjilan Kosovo
171 I4 Gjirokastër Albania
185 I3 Gjoa Haven Canada
158 J3 Gjøra Norway
159 J3 Gjøvik Norway
171 M6 Gkinas, Akrotirio pt Greece
189 I4 Glace Bay Canada
186 B3 Glacier Bay U.S.A.
186 B3 Glacier Bay National Park and Preserve U.S.A.
186 F4 Glacier National Park Canada
194 D1 Glacier National Park U.S.A.
194 B1 Glacier Peak vol. U.S.A.
158 J2 Gladstad Norway
124 F4 Gladstone Qld Australia
126 C4 Gladstone S.A. Australia
127 H8 Gladstone Tas. Australia
190 D3 Gladstone U.S.A.
190 E4 Gladwin U.S.A.
162 E4 Glamis U.K.
164 F5 Glan r. Germany
153 C5 Glan Phil.
163 B5 Glanaruddery Mountains hills Ireland
165 G2 Glandorf Germany
160 F2 Glanton U.K.
191 G4 Glanworth Canada
162 D5 Glasgow U.K.
200 C4 Glasgow KY U.S.A.
194 F1 Glasgow MT U.S.A.
202 D6 Glasgow VA U.S.A.
187 H4 Glaslyn Canada
196 C3 Glass Mountain U.S.A.
161 E6 Glastonbury U.K.
165 K4 Glauchau Germany
132 G4 Glazov Russia
173 F4 Glazunovka Russia
169 O3 Glazunovo Russia
203 H2 Glen U.S.A.
162 C3 Glen Affric val. U.K.
191 G2 Glen Afton Canada
128 E2 Glen Afton N.Z.
181 H1 Glen Alpine Dam S. Africa
163 C4 Glenamaddy Ireland
190 E3 Glen Arbor U.S.A.
128 C6 Glenavy N.Z.
162 C3 Glen Cannich val. U.K.
195 E4 Glen Canyon gorge U.S.A.
197 G3 Glen Canyon National Recreation Area park U.S.A.
162 E4 Glen Clova val. U.K.
126 D6 Glencoe Australia
191 G4 Glencoe Canada
181 I4 Glencoe S. Africa
162 C4 Glen Coe val. U.K.
191 E2 Glendale Canada
197 F5 Glendale AZ U.S.A.
196 C4 Glendale CA U.S.A.
197 E3 Glendale NV U.S.A.
197 F3 Glendale UT U.S.A.
202 D4 Glendale Lake U.S.A.
127 I4 Glen Davis Australia
194 F2 Glendive U.S.A.
187 G4 Glendon Canada
194 F3 Glendo Reservoir U.S.A.
126 D6 Glenelg r. Australia
162 F4 Glen Esk val. U.K.
162 A5 Glengad Head Ireland
162 C3 Glen Garry val. Scotland U.K.
162 D4 Glen Garry val. Scotland U.K.
163 D3 Glengavlen Ireland
127 I2 Glen Innes Australia
162 D6 Glenluce U.K.
162 D4 Glen Lyon val. U.K.
162 D3 Glen More val. U.K.
127 H1 Glenmorgan Australia
162 D3 Glen Moriston val. U.K.
197 G6 Glenn, Mount U.S.A.
184 D3 Glennallen U.S.A.
162 C4 Glen Nevis val. U.K.
191 F3 Glennie U.S.A.
202 E6 Glenns U.S.A.
186 C3 Glenora Canada
203 F2 Glen Robertson Canada
162 E4 Glenrothes U.K.
203 G3 Glens Falls U.S.A.
162 E4 Glen Shee val. U.K.
162 C3 Glen Shiel val. U.K.
163 C3 Glenties Ireland
163 D2 Glenveagh National Park Ireland
202 C5 Glenville U.S.A.
199 E5 Glenwood AR U.S.A.
197 H5 Glenwood NM U.S.A.
195 F4 Glenwood Springs U.S.A.
190 B2 Glidden U.S.A.
165 I1 Glinde Germany
169 I5 Gliwice Poland
197 G5 Globe U.S.A.
168 H5 Głogów Poland
158 K2 Glomfjord Norway
159 J4 Glomma r. Norway
179 E5 Glorieuses, Îles is Indian Ocean
127 I3 Gloucester Australia
161 E6 Gloucester U.K.
203 H3 Gloucester MA U.S.A.
202 E6 Gloucester VA U.S.A.
203 F3 Gloversville U.S.A.
165 K2 Glöwen Germany
150 D1 Glubinnoye Russia
173 G6 Glubokiy Russia
139 J2 Glubokoye Kazakh.
165 H1 Glückstadt Germany
158 □ Gluggarnir h. Faroe Is
160 F4 Glusburn U.K.
173 H5 Gmelinka Russia
168 G6 Gmünd Austria
168 F7 Gmunden Austria
159 L3 Gnarp Sweden
165 H1 Gnarrenburg Germany
168 H4 Gniezno Poland
143 A3 Goa India
143 A3 Goa state India
180 B3 Goageb Namibia
127 I6 Goalen Head Australia
145 G4 Goalpara India
162 C5 Goat Fell h. U.K.
178 E3 Goba Eth.
179 B6 Gobabis Namibia
180 C3 Gobas Namibia
215 E1 Gobernador Crespo Arg.
215 C3 Gobernador Duval Arg.
212 B7 Gobernador Gregores Arg.
146 C2 Gobi Desert Mongolia
151 D8 Gobō Japan
137 L1 Gobustan Rock Art tourist site Azer.
164 E3 Goch Germany
152 D6 Gochang S. Korea
179 B6 Gochas Namibia
154 C3 Go Công Vietnam
161 G6 Godalming U.K.
143 C2 Godavari r. India
143 C2 Godavari, Mouths of the India
189 G4 Godbout Canada
196 C3 Goddard, Mount U.S.A.
178 E3 Godere Eth.
191 G4 Goderich Canada
144 C5 Godhra India
215 C2 Godoy Cruz Arg.
187 K3 Gods r. Canada
187 K4 Gods Lake Canada
187 L2 God's Mercy, Bay of Canada
Godthåb Greenland see Nuuk
Godwin-Austen, Mount mt. China/Pak. see K2
164 B3 Goedereede Neth.
188 E4 Goéland, Lac au l. Canada
189 H2 Goélands, Lac aux l. Canada
164 B3 Goes Neth.
191 E2 Goetzville U.S.A.
197 E4 Goffs U.S.A.
191 G2 Gogama Canada
190 C2 Gogebic, Lake U.S.A.
190 C2 Gogebic Range hills U.S.A.
144 D4 Gohad India
152 D6 Goheung S. Korea
211 L5 Goiana Brazil
214 C2 Goiandira Brazil
214 C2 Goiânia Brazil
214 B1 Goiás Brazil
214 B2 Goiás state Brazil
214 B4 Goioerê Brazil
144 C3 Gojra Pak.
143 A2 Gokak India
173 C7 Gökçeada i. Turkey
136 B2 Gökçedağ Turkey
145 G3 Gokhar La pass China
136 E1 Gökirmak r. Turkey
138 D4 Goklenkuy, Solonchak salt l. Turkm.
141 F5 Gokprosh Hills Pak.
136 F2 Göksun Turkey
136 E3 Göksu Nehri r. Turkey
179 C5 Gokwe Zimbabwe
159 J3 Gol Norway
144 E3 Gola India
145 H4 Golaghat India
141 E4 Golbāf Iran
136 F3 Gölbaşı Turkey
136 B1 Gölcük Turkey
169 K3 Gołdap Poland
165 K1 Goldberg Germany
127 J2 Gold Coast Australia
176 B4 Gold Coast coastal area Ghana
186 F4 Golden Canada
128 D4 Golden Bay N.Z.
165 I3 Goldene Aue reg. Germany
196 A3 Golden Gate National Recreation Area park U.S.A.
186 D5 Golden Hinde mt. Canada
165 G2 Goldenstedt Germany
163 C5 Golden Vale lowland Ireland
196 D3 Goldfield U.S.A.
196 D3 Gold Point (abandoned) U.S.A.
201 E5 Goldsboro U.S.A.
199 D6 Goldthwaite U.S.A.
137 I1 Göle Turkey
196 C4 Goleta U.S.A.
206 I6 Golfito Costa Rica
199 D6 Goliad U.S.A.
152 A1 Golin Baixing China
136 F1 Gölköy Turkey
165 K2 Golm Germany
137 J3 Golmānkhāneh Iran
146 B3 Golmud China
145 H1 Golmud He r. China
153 B3 Golo i. Phil.
150 I3 Golovnino Russia
140 C3 Golpāyegān Iran
136 C1 Gölpazarı Turkey
162 E3 Golspie U.K.
139 H1 Golubovka Kazakh.
141 F3 Gol Vardeh Iran
171 K4 Golyama Syutkya mt. Bulg.
171 K4 Golyam Persenk mt. Bulg.
165 K2 Golzow Germany
178 C4 Goma Dem. Rep. Congo
145 G3 Gomang Co salt l. China
144 E4 Gomati r. India
154 □ Gombak, Bukit h. Sing.
176 D3 Gombe Nigeria
178 D4 Gombe r. Tanz.
177 D3 Gombi Nigeria
206 D2 Gómez Palacio Mex.
140 D2 Gomīsh Tappeh Iran
165 J2 Gommern Germany
145 F2 Gomo Co salt l. China
141 E2 Gonābād Khorāsān-e Razavī Iran
141 E3 Gonābād Khorāsān-e Razavī Iran
205 J5 Gonaïves Haiti
181 I1 Gonarezhou National Park Zimbabwe
205 J5 Gonâve, Île de la i. Haiti
140 D2 Gonbad-e Kāvūs Iran
145 E4 Gonda India
144 B5 Gondal India
178 D2 Gonder Eth.
144 E5 Gondiya India
136 A1 Gönen Turkey
149 D4 Gong'an China
Gongbalou China see Gamba
149 D5 Gongcheng China
149 A4 Gongga Shan mt. China
148 A2 Gonghe China
148 E1 Gonghui China
152 D5 Gongju S. Korea
139 J4 Gongliu China
214 E1 Gongogi r. Brazil
176 D3 Gongola r. Nigeria
127 G3 Gongolgon Australia
149 B4 Gongquan China
149 B5 Gongwang Shan mts China
Gongxian China see Gongquan
148 D3 Gongyi China
152 C2 Gongzhuling China
181 H6 Gonubie S. Africa
207 E3 Gonzáles Mex.
196 B3 Gonzales CA U.S.A.
199 D6 Gonzales TX U.S.A.
215 D2 González Moreno Arg.
202 E6 Goochland U.S.A.
129 C6 Goodenough, Cape c. Antarctica
124 F2 Goodenough Island P.N.G.
191 H3 Gooderham Canada
190 E3 Good Harbor Bay U.S.A.
180 C7 Good Hope, Cape of S. Africa
194 D3 Gooding U.S.A.
198 C4 Goodland U.S.A.
127 G2 Goodooga Australia
160 G4 Goole U.K.
127 F5 Goolgowi Australia
127 H4 Goolma Australia
127 H4 Gooloogong Australia
126 C5 Goolwa Australia
127 F2 Goombalie Australia
127 I2 Goondiwindi Australia
189 H3 Goose r. Canada
194 B3 Goose Lake U.S.A.
143 B3 Gooty India
168 D6 Göppingen Germany
145 E4 Gorakhpur India
171 H3 Goražde Bos. & Herz.
172 G3 Gorchukha Russia
206 I5 Gorda, Punta pt Nicaragua
201 E7 Gorda Cay i. Bahamas
136 B2 Gördes Turkey
169 O4 Gordeyevka Russia
127 F9 Gordon r. Australia
162 F5 Gordon U.K.
127 G9 Gordon, Lake Australia
186 G2 Gordon Lake Canada
202 D5 Gordon Lake U.S.A.
202 D5 Gordonsville U.S.A.
177 D4 Goré Chad
178 D3 Gorē Eth.
128 B7 Gore N.Z.
191 F3 Gore Bay Canada
162 E5 Gorebridge U.K.
136 E2 Göreme Milli Parkı nat. park Turkey
163 E5 Gorey Ireland
141 E4 Gorg Iran
140 D2 Gorgān Iran
213 A4 Gorgona, Isla i. Col.
203 H2 Gorham U.S.A.
173 H7 Gori Georgia
164 C3 Gorinchem Neth.
137 K2 Goris Armenia
170 E2 Gorizia Italy
Gor'kiy Russia see Nizhniy Novgorod
172 G3 Gor'kovskoye Vodokhranilishche resr Russia
139 J1 Gor'koye, Ozero salt l. Russia
169 J6 Gorlice Poland
168 G5 Görlitz Germany
144 D4 Gormi India
171 K3 Gorna Oryahovitsa Bulg.
171 I2 Gornji Milanovac Serbia
170 G3 Gornji Vakuf Bos. & Herz.
139 K2 Gorno-Altaysk Russia
150 G1 Gornozavodsk Russia
139 J2 Gornyak Russia
150 C2 Gornyy Primorskiy Kray Russia
173 I5 Gornyy Saratovskaya Oblast' Russia
173 H5 Gornyy Balykley Russia
150 C2 Gornyye Klyuchi Russia
172 G3 Gorodets Russia
173 H5 Gorodishche Russia
173 G6 Gorodovikovsk Russia
124 E2 Goroka P.N.G.
126 D6 Goroke Australia
172 G3 Gorokhovets Russia
176 B3 Gorom Gorom Burkina Faso
179 D5 Gorongosa Moz.
179 D5 Gorongosa, Parque Nacional da nat. park Moz.
147 E6 Gorontalo Indon.
173 F5 Gorshechnoye Russia
163 C4 Gort Ireland
Gortahork Ireland see Gort an Choirce
163 C2 Gort an Choirce Ireland
141 E4 Gorūh Iran
214 D1 Gorutuba r. Brazil
173 F6 Goryachiy Klyuch Russia
152 E6 Goryeong S. Korea
165 K2 Görzke Germany
168 G4 Gorzów Wielkopolski Poland
127 I4 Gosford Australia
160 F2 Gosforth U.K.
190 E5 Goshen IN U.S.A.
203 F4 Goshen NY U.S.A.
150 G4 Goshogawara Japan
165 I3 Goslar Germany
138 C4 Goşoba Turkm.
170 F2 Gospić Croatia
161 F7 Gosport U.K.
171 I4 Gostivar Macedonia
Göteborg Sweden see Gothenburg
159 K4 Götene Sweden
165 I4 Gotha Germany
159 J4 Gothenburg Sweden
198 C3 Gothenburg U.S.A.
159 L4 Gotland i. Sweden
151 A8 Gotō Japan
171 J4 Gotse Delchev Bulg.
159 L4 Gotska Sandön i. Sweden
151 C7 Gōtsu Japan
165 H3 Göttingen Germany
186 E4 Gott Peak Canada
138 C5 Goturdepe Turkm.
152 A3 Goubangzi China
164 C2 Gouda Neth.
176 A3 Goudiri Senegal
176 D3 Goudoumaria Niger
190 E1 Goudreau Canada
219 I8 Gough Island S. Atlantic Ocean
188 F4 Gouin, Réservoir resr Canada
190 E2 Goulais River Canada
127 H5 Goulburn Australia
127 I4 Goulburn r. N.S.W. Australia
126 F6 Goulburn r. Vic. Australia
124 D3 Goulburn Islands Australia
190 E2 Gould City U.S.A.
176 B3 Goundam Mali
167 G4 Gouraya Alg.
176 D3 Gouré Niger
180 D7 Gourits r. S. Africa
176 B3 Gourma-Rharous Mali
166 E2 Gournay-en-Bray France
127 H6 Gourock Range mts Australia
164 A5 Goussainville France
203 F2 Gouverneur U.S.A.
187 H5 Govenlock Canada
214 E2 Governador Valadares Brazil
153 C5 Governor Generoso Phil.
201 E7 Governor's Harbour Bahamas
146 B2 Govĭ Altayn Nuruu mts Mongolia
145 E4 Govind Ballash Pant Sagar resr India
144 D3 Govind Sagar resr India
Govurdak Turkm. see Magdanly
202 D3 Gowanda U.S.A.
140 D4 Gowd-e Aḥmar Iran
161 C6 Gower pen. U.K.
191 G2 Gowganda Canada
163 D4 Gowna, Lough l. Ireland
212 E3 Goya Arg.
137 K1 Göyçay Azer.
138 C4 Goýmatdag hills Turkm.
137 H2 Göynük Turkey
150 G5 Goyō-zan mt. Japan
137 L2 Göytäpä Azer.
Gożareh Afgh. see Guzarah
136 G2 Gözene Turkey
138 F4 G'ozg'on Uzbek.
144 E2 Gozha Co salt l. China
170 F6 Gozo i. Malta
180 F6 Graaff-Reinet S. Africa
180 C6 Graafwater S. Africa
165 I4 Grabfeld plain Germany
176 B4 Grabo Côte d'Ivoire
180 C7 Grabouw S. Africa
165 J1 Grabow Germany
170 F2 Gračac Croatia
191 I2 Gracefield Canada
138 C1 Grachevka Russia
139 I2 Grachi (abandoned) Kazakh.
206 G5 Gracias Hond.
165 K3 Gräfenhainichen Germany
165 J5 Grafenwöhr Germany
127 J2 Grafton Australia
198 D1 Grafton ND U.S.A.
190 D4 Grafton WI U.S.A.
202 C5 Grafton WV U.S.A.
197 E2 Grafton, Mount U.S.A.
199 D5 Graham U.S.A.
197 H5 Graham, Mount U.S.A.
Graham Bell Island Russia see Greem-Bell, Ostrov
186 C4 Graham Island B.C. Canada
185 I2 Graham Island Nunavut Canada
203 I2 Graham Lake U.S.A.

H

Hitzacker (Elbe)

149 C7 Haitangwan China
205 J5 Haiti country Caribbean Sea
149 C7 Haitou China
154 D2 Hai Triêu Vietnam
197 G5 Haivana Nakya U.S.A.
196 D3 Haiwee Reservoir U.S.A.
148 E2 Haixing China
177 F3 Haiya Sudan
148 A2 Haiyan Qinghai China
149 F4 Haiyan Zhejiang China
152 A5 Haiyang China
152 B4 Haiyang Dao i. China
148 F3 Haizhou Wan b. China
169 J7 Hajdúböszörmény Hungary
170 C7 Hajeb El Ayoun Tunisia
142 D7 Hajhir mt. Yemen
140 D3 Haji Abdulla, Chāh well Iran
150 F5 Hajiki-zaki pt Japan
145 F4 Hajipur India
140 D3 Ḥājj 'Alī Qolī, Kavīr-e salt l. Iran
140 D4 Ḥājjīābād Fārs Iran
140 D4 Ḥājjīābād Hormozgān Iran
145 H5 Haka Myanmar
196 □2 Hakalau U.S.A.
215 C4 Hakelhuincul, Altiplanicie de plat. Arg.
137 I3 Hakkâri Turkey
158 M2 Hakkas Sweden
151 D7 Hakken-zan mt. Japan
150 H2 Hako-dake mt. Japan
150 G4 Hakodate Japan
180 B1 Hakos Mountains Namibia
144 C3 Hakra Right Distributary watercourse Pak.
180 D3 Hakseen Pan salt pan S. Africa
151 E6 Hakui Japan
151 E6 Haku-san vol. Japan
151 E6 Haku-san Kokuritsu-kōen nat. park Japan
144 B4 Hala Pak.
Ḥalab Syria see Aleppo
140 B6 Halabān Saudi Arabia
137 J4 Ḥalabjah/Hełebce Iraq
138 F5 Halaç Turkm.
152 C1 Halahai China
177 F2 Ḥalā'ib Sudan
154 D2 Ha Lam Vietnam
142 E6 Ḥalāniyāt, Juzur al is Oman
196 □2 Hālawa U.S.A.
136 F4 Halba Lebanon
Halban Mongolia see Tsetserleg
165 J3 Halberstadt Germany
153 B3 Halcon, Mount Phil.
158 □ Haldarsvik Faroe Is
159 J4 Halden Norway
165 J2 Haldensleben Germany
145 G5 Haldi r. India
145 G5 Haldia India
145 G4 Haldibari India
144 D3 Haldwani India
191 F3 Hale U.S.A.
140 D5 Hāleh Iran
196 □1 Hale'iwa U.S.A.
161 E5 Halesowen U.K.
161 I5 Halesworth U.K.
140 C4 Haleyleh Iran
136 F3 Halfeti Turkey
128 B7 Halfmoon Bay N.Z.
186 E3 Halfway r. Canada
163 C6 Halfway Ireland
164 C2 Halfweg Neth.
145 E4 Halia India
137 G4 Ḥalībīyah Syria
191 H3 Haliburton Canada
189 H5 Halifax Canada
160 F4 Halifax U.K.
202 D6 Halifax U.S.A.
148 C1 Haliut China
162 E2 Halkirk U.K.
158 L3 Hälla Sweden
152 D7 Halla-san mt. S. Korea
152 D7 Halla-san National Park nat. park S. Korea
126 A5 Hall Bay Australia
185 J3 Hall Beach Canada
164 C4 Halle Belgium
164 E3 Halle Neth.
165 J3 Halle (Saale) Germany
159 K4 Hällefors Sweden
168 F7 Hallein Austria
165 J3 Halle-Neustadt Germany
129 C3 Halley research stn Antarctica
122 E2 Hall Islands Micronesia
158 L2 Hällnäs Sweden
198 D1 Hallock U.S.A.
185 L3 Hall Peninsula Canada
159 K4 Hallsberg Sweden
124 C3 Halls Creek Australia
191 H3 Halls Lake Canada
164 B4 Halluin France
158 K3 Hallviken Sweden
147 E6 Halmahera i. Indon.
159 K4 Halmstad Sweden
144 C5 Halol India
149 C6 Ha Long Vietnam
159 J4 Hals Denmark
159 L3 Hälsingland, Decorated Farmhouses of tourist site Sweden
158 D2 Hálslón resr Iceland
158 N3 Halsua Fin.
164 F3 Haltern am See Germany
160 E3 Haltwhistle U.K.
140 D5 Ḥālūl i. Qatar
164 F3 Halver Germany
164 B5 Ham France
151 C7 Hamada Japan
140 C3 Hamadān Iran
136 F4 Ḥamāh Syria
150 G3 Hamamasu Japan
151 E7 Hamamatsu Japan
159 J3 Hamar Norway
Ḥamâṭa, Gebel mt. Egypt see Ḥamāṭah, Jabal
177 F2 Ḥamāṭah, Jabal mt. Egypt
150 H2 Hamatonbetsu Japan
143 C5 Hambantota Sri Lanka
165 G1 Hambergen Germany
160 F3 Hambleton Hills U.K.
165 H1 Hamburg Germany
181 G6 Hamburg S. Africa
199 F5 Hamburg AR U.S.A.
202 D3 Hamburg NY U.S.A.
203 F4 Hamburg PA U.S.A.
165 G1 Hamburgisches Wattenmeer, Nationalpark nat. park Germany
203 G4 Hamden U.S.A.
159 N3 Hämeenlinna Fin.
165 H2 Hameln Germany
124 B4 Hamersley Range mts Australia
152 D4 Hamhŭng N. Korea
146 B2 Hami China
140 C4 Ḥamīd Iran
177 F2 Hamid Sudan
126 E6 Hamilton Australia
205 L2 Hamilton Bermuda
191 H4 Hamilton Canada
128 E2 Hamilton N.Z.
162 D5 Hamilton U.K.
201 C5 Hamilton AL U.S.A.
190 B5 Hamilton IL U.S.A.
194 D2 Hamilton MT U.S.A.
203 F3 Hamilton NY U.S.A.
202 A5 Hamilton OH U.S.A.
196 B3 Hamilton, Mount CA U.S.A.
197 E2 Hamilton, Mount NV U.S.A.
196 A2 Hamilton City U.S.A.
159 N3 Hamina Fin.
137 H6 Ḥāmir, Wādī al watercourse Saudi Arabia
144 D3 Hamirpur India
152 D4 Hamju N. Korea
126 C5 Hamley Bridge Australia
190 D3 Hamlin Lake U.S.A.
165 F3 Hamm Germany
137 I3 Ḥammām al 'Alīl Iraq
170 D6 Hammamet Tunisia
177 D1 Hammamet, Golfe de g. Tunisia
137 K6 Ḥammār, Hawr al imp. l. Iraq
158 L3 Hammarstrand Sweden
165 H4 Hammelburg Germany
158 K3 Hammerdal Sweden
158 M1 Hammerfest Norway
164 E3 Hamminkeln Germany
126 C4 Hammond Australia
190 D5 Hammond IN U.S.A.
199 F6 Hammond LA U.S.A.
194 F2 Hammond MT U.S.A.
191 E3 Hammond Bay U.S.A.
202 E3 Hammondsport U.S.A.
203 F5 Hammonton U.S.A.
164 D4 Hamoir Belgium
128 C6 Hampden N.Z.
143 B3 Hampi India
161 F6 Hampshire Downs hills U.K.
189 G4 Hampton Canada
199 E5 Hampton AR U.S.A.
203 H3 Hampton NH U.S.A.
203 E6 Hampton VA U.S.A.
177 D2 Ḥamrā', Al Ḥamādah al plat. Libya
137 J4 Ḥamrīn, Jabal hills Iraq
154 C3 Ham Tân Vietnam
144 D2 Hamta Pass India
141 F4 Hāmūn Ṣāberī, Daryācheh-ye marsh Afgh./Iran
137 I2 Hamur Turkey
139 G4 Hamza Uzbek.
164 D4 Han, Grotte de tourist site Belgium
196 □2 Hāna U.S.A.
180 E1 Hanahai watercourse Botswana/Namibia
196 □2 Hanalei U.S.A.
150 G5 Hanamaki Japan
165 G4 Hanau Germany
146 C2 Hanbogd Mongolia
148 D3 Hancheng China
202 D5 Hancock MD U.S.A.
190 C2 Hancock MI U.S.A.
203 F4 Hancock NY U.S.A.
162 C2 Handa Island U.K.
148 E2 Handan China
178 D4 Handeni Tanz.
153 C4 Handig Point Phil.
196 C3 Hanford U.S.A.
143 A3 Hangal India
152 D5 Han-gang r. S. Korea
146 B2 Hangayn Nuruu mts Mongolia
144 B2 Hangu Pak.
149 D5 Hanguang China
149 F4 Hangzhou China
149 F4 Hangzhou Wan b. China
137 H2 Hani Turkey
140 C5 Ḥanīdh Saudi Arabia
148 B2 Hanjiaoshui China
165 I2 Hankensbüttel Germany
180 F6 Hankey S. Africa
159 M4 Hanko Fin.
197 G2 Hanksville U.S.A.
144 D2 Hanle India
128 D5 Hanmer Springs N.Z.
187 G4 Hanna Canada
188 D3 Hannah Bay Canada
190 B6 Hannibal U.S.A.
165 H2 Hannover Germany
165 H3 Hannoversch Münden Germany
164 D4 Hannut Belgium
159 K5 Hanöbukten b. Sweden
149 B6 Ha Nôi Vietnam
191 G3 Hanover Canada
180 F5 Hanover S. Africa
203 G3 Hanover NH U.S.A.
202 E5 Hanover PA U.S.A.
129 E5 Hansen Mountains mts Antarctica
149 D4 Hanshou China
148 E4 Han Shui r. China
144 D3 Hansi India
158 L1 Hansnes Norway
126 B3 Hanson, Lake salt flat Australia
202 B6 Hansonville U.S.A.
159 J4 Hanstholm Denmark
164 E6 Han-sur-Nied France
172 C4 Hantsavichy Belarus
144 C3 Hanumangarh India
127 G5 Hanwood Australia
148 C3 Hanyin China
149 B4 Hanyuan China
141 F5 Hanzaram Iran
148 C3 Hanzhong China
123 J6 Hao atoll Fr. Polynesia
145 G5 Haora India
158 N2 Haparanda Sweden
145 H4 Hapoli India
189 H3 Happy Valley-Goose Bay Canada
152 E3 Hapsu N. Korea
144 D3 Hapur India
143 C5 Haputale Sri Lanka
140 C5 Ḥaraḍ well Saudi Arabia
140 C5 Ḥaraḍh Saudi Arabia
172 D4 Haradok Belarus
151 G6 Haramachi Japan
144 C2 Haramukh mt. India
144 C3 Harappa Road Pak.
179 D5 Harare Zimbabwe
142 E6 Ḥarāsīs, Jiddat al des. Oman
176 A4 Harbel Liberia
146 E2 Harbin China
191 F4 Harbor Beach U.S.A.
190 E3 Harbor Springs U.S.A.
189 I4 Harbour Breton Canada
212 E8 Harbours, Bay of Falkland Is
197 F5 Harcuvar Mountains U.S.A.
144 D5 Harda India
159 I4 Hardangerfjorden sea chan. Norway
159 I3 Hardangervidda plat. Norway
159 I3 Hardangervidda Nasjonalpark nat. park Norway
180 B2 Hardap admin. reg. Namibia
180 B2 Hardap Dam Namibia
155 E2 Harden, Bukit mt. Indon.
164 E2 Hardenberg Neth.
164 D2 Harderwijk Neth.
180 C5 Hardeveld mts S. Africa
165 H5 Hardheim Germany
194 F2 Hardin U.S.A.
181 H5 Harding S. Africa
187 G4 Hardisty Canada
186 F2 Hardisty Lake Canada
144 E4 Hardoi India
203 G2 Hardwick U.S.A.
126 B5 Hardwicke Bay Australia
199 F4 Hardy U.S.A.
Hardy, Mount N.Z. see Rangipoua
190 E4 Hardy Reservoir U.S.A.
164 B4 Harelbeke Belgium
164 E1 Haren Neth.
164 F2 Haren (Ems) Germany
178 E3 Hārer Eth.
203 F4 Harford U.S.A.
178 E3 Hargeysa Somalia
169 L7 Harghita-Mădăraș, Vârful mt. Romania
137 H2 Harhal Dağları mts Turkey
148 C2 Harhatan China
146 B3 Har Hu l. China
176 B2 Ḥaricha, Ḥamâda El des. Mali
144 D3 Haridwar India
143 A3 Harihar India
128 C5 Harihari N.Z.
151 D7 Harima-nada b. Japan
145 G5 Haringhat r. Bangl.
164 C3 Haringvliet est. Neth.
141 G3 Harī Rōd r. Afgh./Iran
159 M3 Harjavalta Fin.
198 E3 Harlan IA U.S.A.
202 B6 Harlan KY U.S.A.
161 C5 Harlech U.K.
194 E1 Harlem U.S.A.
161 I5 Harleston U.K.
164 D1 Harlingen Neth.
199 D7 Harlingen U.S.A.
161 H6 Harlow U.K.
194 E2 Harlowton U.S.A.
164 B5 Harly France
171 K4 Harmanli Bulg.
203 I2 Harmony ME U.S.A.
190 A4 Harmony MN U.S.A.
165 I1 Harmsdorf Germany
144 A3 Harnai Pak.
164 A4 Harnes France
194 B3 Harney Basin U.S.A.
194 C3 Harney Lake U.S.A.
159 L3 Härnösand Sweden
146 E2 Har Nur China
146 B2 Har Nuur l. Mongolia
162 □ Haroldswick U.K.
176 B4 Harper Liberia
196 D4 Harper Lake U.S.A.
202 E5 Harpers Ferry U.S.A.
189 H2 Harp Lake Canada
165 G2 Harpstedt Germany
137 G2 Harput Turkey
148 F1 Harqin China
197 F5 Harquahala Mountains U.S.A.
137 G3 Harran Turkey
188 E3 Harricana, Rivière d' r. Canada
201 C5 Harriman U.S.A.
203 G3 Harriman Reservoir U.S.A.
127 J3 Harrington Australia
203 F5 Harrington U.S.A.
189 I3 Harrington Harbour Canada
162 B3 Harris reg. U.K.
126 A3 Harris, Lake salt flat Australia
162 A3 Harris, Sound of sea chan. U.K.
200 B4 Harrisburg IL U.S.A.
202 E4 Harrisburg PA U.S.A.
181 H4 Harrismith S. Africa
199 E4 Harrison AR U.S.A.
190 E3 Harrison MI U.S.A.
189 I3 Harrison, Cape Canada
184 C2 Harrison Bay U.S.A.
202 D5 Harrisonburg U.S.A.
186 E5 Harrison Lake Canada
198 E4 Harrisonville U.S.A.
191 F3 Harrisville MI U.S.A.
203 F2 Harrisville NY U.S.A.
202 C5 Harrisville WV U.S.A.
160 F4 Harrogate U.K.
165 H1 Harsefeld Germany
140 B3 Harsīn Iran
136 G1 Harşit r. Turkey
171 L2 Hârșova Romania
158 L1 Harstad Norway
165 H2 Harsum Germany
190 D4 Hart U.S.A.
126 B3 Hart, Lake salt flat Australia
180 D4 Hartbees watercourse S. Africa
168 G7 Hartberg Austria
159 I3 Harteigan mt. Norway
162 E5 Hart Fell h. U.K.
203 G4 Hartford CT U.S.A.
190 D4 Hartford MI U.S.A.
198 D3 Hartford SD U.S.A.
190 C4 Hartford WI U.S.A.
186 E3 Hart Highway Canada
189 G4 Hartland Canada
161 C7 Hartland U.K.
203 I2 Hartland U.S.A.
161 C6 Hartland Point U.K.
160 F3 Hartlepool U.K.
199 C5 Hartley U.S.A.
186 D4 Hartley Bay Canada
159 N3 Hartola Fin.
186 E4 Hart Ranges mts Canada
168 E6 Härtsfeld hills Germany
180 F3 Hartswater S. Africa
201 D5 Hartwell Reservoir U.S.A.
146 B2 Har Us Nuur l. Mongolia
141 F3 Hārūt r. Afgh.
141 F3 Hārūt watercourse Afgh.
190 C4 Harvard U.S.A.
195 F4 Harvard, Mount U.S.A.
203 J2 Harvey Canada
190 D2 Harvey MI U.S.A.
198 C2 Harvey ND U.S.A.
161 I6 Harwich U.K.
127 J2 Harwood Australia
144 C3 Haryana state India
165 I3 Harz hills Germany
136 E6 Ḥasā, Qal'at al tourist site Jordan
136 F6 Ḥaşāh, Wādī al watercourse Jordan
139 I5 Hasalbag China
136 E2 Hasan Dağı mts Turkey
137 H3 Hasankeyf Turkey
140 E5 Ḥasan Langī Iran
143 B2 Hasanparti India
140 B2 Ḥasan Sālārān Iran
138 D5 Hasardag mt. Turkm.
136 E5 Hasbani r. Lebanon
136 E2 Hasbek Turkey
143 C1 Hasdo r. India
165 F2 Hase r. Germany
164 F2 Haselünne Germany
165 I4 Hasenkopf h. Germany
140 C3 Hashtgerd Iran
140 B2 Hashtrūd Iran
140 E3 Hasht Tekkeh, Gowd-e waterhole Iran
199 D5 Haskell U.S.A.
171 K4 Haskovo Bulg.
161 G6 Haslemere U.K.
169 L7 Hășmașul Mare mt. Romania
143 B3 Hassan India
137 J4 Hassan Iraq
144 C2 Hassan Abdal Pak.
197 F5 Hassayampa watercourse U.S.A.
165 I4 Haßberge hills Germany
164 D4 Hasselt Belgium
164 E2 Hasselt Neth.
176 C1 Hassi Messaoud Alg.
159 K4 Hässleholm Sweden
126 F7 Hastings Australia
127 J3 Hastings r. Australia
128 F3 Hastings N.Z.
161 H7 Hastings U.K.
190 E4 Hastings MI U.S.A.
190 A3 Hastings MN U.S.A.
198 D3 Hastings NE U.S.A.
148 C1 Hatanbulag Mongolia
197 F3 Hatch U.S.A.
187 I3 Hatchet Lake Canada
201 B5 Hatchie r. U.S.A.
126 E4 Hatfield Australia
160 G4 Hatfield U.K.
146 C1 Hatgal Mongolia
144 D4 Hathras India
145 F4 Hatia Nepal
154 C3 Ha Tiên Vietnam
154 C1 Ha Tinh Vietnam
137 I4 Hatra Iraq
126 E5 Hattah Australia
126 E5 Hattah-Kulkyne National Park Australia
201 F5 Hatteras, Cape U.S.A.
219 E4 Hatteras Abyssal Plain sea feature S. Atlantic Ocean
158 K2 Hattfjelldal Norway
143 C2 Hatti r. India
201 B6 Hattiesburg U.S.A.
164 F3 Hattingen Germany
154 B4 Hat Yai Thai.
154 C3 Hâu, Sông r. Vietnam
178 E3 Haud reg. Eth.
159 I4 Hauge Norway
159 I4 Haugesund Norway
Hâu Giang, Sông r. Vietnam see Hâu, Sông
128 E3 Hauhungaroa mt. N.Z.
159 I4 Haukeligrend Norway
158 N2 Haukipudas Fin.
159 O3 Haukivesi l. Fin.
187 H3 Haultain r. Canada
128 E2 Hauraki Gulf N.Z.
128 A7 Hauroko, Lake N.Z.
203 I3 Haut, Isle au i. U.S.A.
176 B1 Haut Atlas mts Morocco
189 G4 Hauterive Canada
176 B1 Hauts Plateaux Alg.
196 □1 Hau'ula U.S.A.
205 H4 Havana Cuba
190 B5 Havana U.S.A.
161 G7 Havant U.K.
197 E4 Havasu, Lake U.S.A.
165 K2 Havel r. Germany
164 D4 Havelange Belgium
165 K2 Havelberg Germany
165 K2 Havelländisches Luch marsh Germany
191 I3 Havelock Canada
201 E5 Havelock U.S.A.
128 F3 Havelock North N.Z.
161 C6 Haverfordwest U.K.
203 H3 Haverhill U.S.A.
143 A3 Haveri India
164 D4 Haversin Belgium
164 F3 Havixbeck Germany
168 G6 Havlíčkův Brod Czech Rep.
158 N1 Havøysund Norway
171 L5 Havran Turkey
194 E1 Havre U.S.A.
189 H4 Havre Aubert, Île du i. Canada
203 E5 Havre de Grace U.S.A.
189 H3 Havre-St-Pierre Canada
171 L4 Havsa Turkey
136 E1 Havza Turkey
196 □2 Hawai'i i. U.S.A.
196 □1 Hawai'ian Islands N. Pacific Ocean
216 H4 Hawaiian Ridge sea feature N. Pacific Ocean
196 □2 Hawai'i Volcanoes National Park U.S.A.
137 K7 Ḥawallī Kuwait
161 D4 Hawarden U.K.
128 B6 Hawea, Lake N.Z.
128 E3 Hawera N.Z.
160 E3 Hawes U.K.
196 □2 Hāwī U.S.A.
162 F5 Hawick U.K.
137 K6 Ḥawīzah, Hawr al imp. l. Iraq
128 B6 Hawkdun Range mts N.Z.
128 F3 Hawke Bay N.Z.
189 I3 Hawke Island Canada
126 C3 Hawker Australia
126 D2 Hawkers Gate Australia
203 F2 Hawkesbury Canada
197 F3 Hawkins Peak U.S.A.
191 F3 Hawks U.S.A.
203 J2 Hawkshaw Canada
203 F4 Hawley U.S.A.
137 I5 Ḥawrān, Wādī watercourse Iraq
140 B6 Ḥawshah, Jibāl al mts Saudi Arabia
180 C7 Hawston S. Africa
196 C2 Hawthorne U.S.A.
160 F3 Haxby U.K.
126 F5 Hay Australia
186 F2 Hay r. Canada
190 B3 Hay r. U.S.A.
150 G5 Hayachine-san mt. Japan
197 G5 Hayden AZ U.S.A.
194 C2 Hayden ID U.S.A.
187 K3 Hayes r. Man. Canada
185 I3 Hayes r. Nunavut Canada
185 L2 Hayes Halvø pen. Greenland
161 B7 Hayle U.K.
142 E6 Haymā' Oman
136 D2 Haymana Turkey
202 E5 Haymarket U.S.A.
203 I2 Haynesville U.S.A.
161 D5 Hay-on-Wye U.K.
173 C7 Hayrabolu Turkey
186 F2 Hay River Canada
198 D4 Hays U.S.A.
173 D5 Haysyn Ukr.
196 A3 Hayward CA U.S.A.
190 B2 Hayward WI U.S.A.
161 G7 Haywards Heath U.K.
138 C5 Hazar Turkm.
141 G3 Hazārah Jāt reg. Afgh.
202 B6 Hazard U.S.A.
145 F5 Hazaribagh India
145 E5 Hazaribagh Range mts India
164 A4 Hazebrouck France
186 D3 Hazelton Canada
184 G2 Hazen Strait Canada
164 C2 Hazerswoude-Rijndijk Neth.
203 F4 Hazleton U.S.A.
138 E4 Hazorasp Uzbek.
141 G2 Ḥazrat-e Sulṭān Afgh.
137 H2 Hazro Turkey
215 D2 H. Bouchard Arg.
163 B4 Headford Ireland
196 A2 Healdsburg U.S.A.
126 F6 Healesville Australia
161 F4 Heanor U.K.
218 I8 Heard Island Indian Ocean
121 Heard Island and McDonald Islands terr. Indian Ocean
199 D6 Hearne U.S.A.
188 D4 Hearst Canada
161 H7 Heathfield U.K.
203 E6 Heathsville U.S.A.
199 D7 Hebbronville U.S.A.
148 E2 Hebei prov. China
127 G2 Hebel Australia
192 D3 Heber City U.S.A.
199 E5 Heber Springs U.S.A.
Hebi China see Shancheng
189 H2 Hebron Canada
190 D5 Hebron IN U.S.A.
198 D3 Hebron NE U.S.A.
136 E6 Hebron West Bank
189 H2 Hebron Fiord inlet Canada
186 C4 Hecate Strait Canada
207 G3 Hecelchakán Mex.
186 C3 Heceta Island U.S.A.
149 C5 Hechi China
149 C4 Hechuan China
159 K3 Hede Sweden
159 K3 Hedemora Sweden
194 C2 He Devil Mountain U.S.A.
149 D6 Hedi Shuiku resr China
190 A5 Hedrick U.S.A.
164 D2 Heeg Neth.
164 F2 Heek Germany
164 C4 Heer Belgium
164 E2 Heerde Neth.
164 D2 Heerenveen Neth.
164 C2 Heerhugowaard Neth.
164 D4 Heerlen Neth.
Ḥefa Israel see Haifa
148 E4 Hefei China
149 D4 Hefeng China
150 B1 Hegang China
151 E6 Hegura-jima i. Japan
165 J3 Heidberg h. Germany
168 D3 Heide Germany
179 B6 Heide Namibia
165 G5 Heidelberg Germany
181 H3 Heidelberg Gauteng S. Africa
180 D7 Heidelberg Western Cape S. Africa
181 G3 Heilbron S. Africa
165 H5 Heilbronn Germany
168 E3 Heiligenhafen Germany
149 □ Hei Ling Chau i. Hong Kong China
152 E1 Heilongjiang prov. China
146 E2 Heilong Jiang r. China/Russia alt. Amur
165 I5 Heilsbronn Germany
158 J3 Heimdal Norway
159 N3 Heinola Fin.
154 A2 Heinze Islands Myanmar
152 B3 Heishan China
164 C3 Heist-op-den-Berg Belgium
148 E2 Hejian China
149 B4 Hejiang China
149 D6 He Jiang r. China
148 D3 Hejin China
136 F2 Hekimhan Turkey
158 C3 Hekla vol. Iceland
148 B2 Hekou Gansu China
149 B6 Hekou Yunnan China
158 K3 Helagsfjället mt. Sweden
148 B2 Helan Shan mts China
165 J3 Helbra Germany
145 H4 Helem India
196 D3 Helen, Mount U.S.A.
199 F5 Helena AR U.S.A.
194 E2 Helena MT U.S.A.
162 D4 Helensburgh U.K.
136 E6 Ḥelez Israel
168 C3 Helgoland i. Germany
168 D3 Helgoländer Bucht g. Germany
127 J1 Helidon Australia
158 B3 Hella Iceland
158 L1 Helland Norway
140 C4 Helleh r. Iran
164 C3 Hellevoetsluis Neth.
158 M1 Helligskogen Norway
167 F3 Hellín Spain
194 C2 Hells Canyon gorge U.S.A.
141 F4 Helmand r. Afgh.
141 F4 Helmand reg. Afgh.
141 F4 Helmand, Hāmūn salt flat Afgh./Iran
165 J4 Helmbrechts Germany
165 I3 Helme r. Germany
179 B6 Helmeringhausen Namibia
164 D3 Helmond Neth.
162 E2 Helmsdale U.K.
162 E2 Helmsdale r. U.K.
165 J2 Helmstedt Germany
152 E2 Helong China
197 G2 Helper U.S.A.
159 K4 Helsingborg Sweden
Helsingfors Fin. see Helsinki
159 K4 Helsingør Denmark
159 N3 Helsinki Fin.
161 B7 Helston U.K.
160 D3 Helvellyn h. U.K.
163 D5 Helvick Head Ireland
161 G6 Hemel Hempstead U.K.
196 D5 Hemet U.S.A.
202 E3 Hemlock Lake U.S.A.
165 H2 Hemmingen Germany
203 G2 Hemmingford Canada
165 H1 Hemmoor Germany
199 D6 Hempstead U.S.A.
161 I5 Hemsby U.K.
159 L4 Hemse Sweden
148 A3 Henan China
148 D3 Henan prov. China
167 E2 Henares r. Spain
150 F4 Henashi-zaki pt Japan
136 C1 Hendek Turkey
215 E3 Henderson Arg.
200 C4 Henderson KY U.S.A.
201 E4 Henderson NC U.S.A.
197 E3 Henderson NV U.S.A.
203 E3 Henderson NY U.S.A.
199 E5 Henderson TX U.S.A.
123 J7 Henderson Island Pitcairn Is
201 D5 Hendersonville NC U.S.A.
201 C4 Hendersonville TN U.S.A.
140 C4 Hendījān Iran
161 G6 Hendon U.K.
140 D5 Hendorābī, Jazīreh-ye i. Iran
141 E5 Hengām Iran
146 B4 Hengduan Shan mts China
164 E2 Hengelo Neth.
152 F1 Hengshan Heilongjiang China
149 D5 Hengshan Hunan China
148 C2 Hengshan Shaanxi China
149 D5 Heng Shan mt. China
148 D2 Heng Shan mts China
148 E2 Hengshui China
149 C6 Hengxian China
149 D5 Hengyang Hunan China
149 D5 Hengyang Hunan China
173 E6 Heniches'k Ukr.
128 C6 Henley N.Z.
161 G6 Henley-on-Thames U.K.
203 F5 Henlopen, Cape U.S.A.
164 F4 Hennef (Sieg) Germany
181 G3 Hennenman S. Africa
165 L2 Hennigsdorf Germany
203 H3 Henniker U.S.A.
199 D5 Henrietta U.S.A.
188 D2 Henrietta Maria, Cape Canada
197 G3 Henrieville U.S.A.
190 C5 Henry U.S.A.
129 C3 Henry Ice Rise ice feature Antarctica
185 L3 Henry Kater, Cape Canada
197 G2 Henry Mountains U.S.A.
191 G4 Hensall Canada
165 H1 Henstedt-Ulzburg Germany
179 B6 Hentiesbaai Namibia
127 G5 Henty Australia
Henzada Myanmar see Hinthada
187 H4 Hepburn Canada
149 E5 Heping China
149 C6 Hepu China
148 D2 Hequ China
141 F3 Herāt Afgh.
166 F5 Hérault r. France
187 H4 Herbert Canada
165 G4 Herborn Germany
165 H4 Herbstein Germany
129 C4 Hercules Dome ice feature Antarctica
164 F3 Herdecke Germany
165 F4 Herdorf Germany
206 H6 Heredia Costa Rica
161 E5 Hereford U.K.
199 C5 Hereford U.S.A.
123 J6 Hereheretue atoll Fr. Polynesia
164 C4 Herent Belgium
165 G2 Herford Germany
165 I4 Heringen (Werra) Germany
198 D4 Herington U.S.A.
140 B2 Herīs Iran
168 D7 Herisau Switz.
203 F3 Herkimer U.S.A.
165 I3 Herleshausen Germany
206 D2 Hermanas Mex.
162 □ Herma Ness hd U.K.
165 I2 Hermannsburg Germany
180 C7 Hermanus S. Africa
181 H5 Hermes, Cape S. Africa
127 G3 Hermidale Australia
194 C2 Hermiston U.S.A.
212 C9 Hermite, Islas is Chile
124 E2 Hermit Islands P.N.G.
136 E5 Hermon, Mount Lebanon/Syria
206 B1 Hermosillo Mex.
212 F3 Hernandarias Para.
164 F3 Herne Germany
161 I6 Herne Bay U.K.
159 J4 Herning Denmark
190 D1 Heron Bay Canada
206 D3 Herradura Mex.
167 D3 Herrera del Duque Spain
127 G8 Herrick Australia
165 I5 Herrieden Germany
202 E4 Hershey U.S.A.
161 G6 Hertford U.K.
181 F4 Hertzogville S. Africa
215 G2 Herval Brazil
164 D4 Herve Belgium
125 F4 Hervey Bay Australia
217 I7 Hervey Islands Cook Is
165 K2 Herzberg Germany
165 L3 Herzberg (Elster) Germany
164 F2 Herzlake Germany
165 I5 Herzogenaurach Germany
165 K1 Herzsprung Germany
137 L3 Ḥeṣār Iran
137 L4 Ḥeṣār-e Valī-ye 'Asr Iran
164 C4 Hesbaye reg. Belgium
164 F1 Hesel Germany
149 C6 Heshan China
148 C3 Heshui China
148 D2 Heshun China
196 D4 Hesperia U.S.A.
186 C2 Hess r. Canada
165 I5 Heßdorf Germany
165 I5 Hesselberg h. Germany
165 H4 Hessen land Germany
165 H3 Hessisch Lichtenau Germany
149 B6 Het r. Laos
196 B3 Hetch Hetchy Aqueduct canal U.S.A.
164 D3 Heteren Neth.
164 D2 Het Loo, Paleis tourist site Neth.
198 C2 Hettinger U.S.A.
160 E3 Hetton U.K.
165 J3 Hettstedt Germany
160 E3 Hexham U.K.
148 F4 Hexian China
148 B2 Hexipu China
180 C6 Hex River Pass S. Africa
148 D3 Heyang China
140 E4 Ḥeydarābād Kermān Iran
141 F4 Ḥeydarābād Khorāsān-e Jonūbī Iran
160 E3 Heysham U.K.
149 E6 Heyuan China
126 D7 Heywood Australia
160 E4 Heywood U.K.
190 C5 Heyworth U.S.A.
148 E3 Heze China
149 B5 Hezhang China
148 B3 Hezheng China
149 D5 Hezhou China
148 B3 Hezuo China
201 D7 Hialeah U.S.A.
198 E4 Hiawatha U.S.A.
190 A2 Hibbing U.S.A.
127 F9 Hibbs, Point Australia
201 D5 Hickory U.S.A.
128 G2 Hicks Bay N.Z.
207 G4 Hicks Cayes is Belize
187 J2 Hicks Lake Canada
202 A4 Hicksville U.S.A.
199 D5 Hico U.S.A.
150 H3 Hidaka Japan
150 H3 Hidaka-sanmyaku mts Japan
207 E2 Hidalgo Mex.
207 E3 Hidalgo state Mex.
206 C2 Hidalgo del Parral Mex.
214 C2 Hidrolândia Brazil
151 C7 Higashihiroshima Japan
150 G5 Higashine Japan
151 D7 Higashi-Ōsaka Japan
151 A8 Higashi-suidō sea chan. Japan
203 F3 Higgins Bay U.S.A.
190 E3 Higgins Lake U.S.A.
194 B3 High Desert U.S.A.
190 C3 High Falls Reservoir U.S.A.
190 E3 High Island U.S.A.
149 □ High Island Reservoir Hong Kong China
190 D4 Highland Park U.S.A.
196 C2 Highland Peak CA U.S.A.
197 E3 Highland Peak NV U.S.A.
186 F3 High Level Canada
145 F5 High Level Canal India
201 E5 High Point U.S.A.
186 F3 High Prairie Canada
186 G4 High River Canada
201 E7 High Rock Bahamas
187 I3 Highrock Lake Canada
127 F9 High Rocky Point Australia
160 E3 High Seat h. U.K.
203 F4 Hightstown U.S.A.
161 G6 High Wycombe U.K.
206 B2 Higuera de Zaragoza Mex.
213 D2 Higuerote Venez.
159 M4 Hiiumaa i. Estonia
142 A4 Hijaz reg. Saudi Arabia
197 E3 Hiko U.S.A.
151 E7 Hikone Japan
128 G2 Hikurangi mt. N.Z.
197 F3 Hildale U.S.A.
165 I4 Hildburghausen Germany
165 I4 Hilders Germany
165 H2 Hildesheim Germany
145 G4 Hili Bangl.
198 D4 Hill City U.S.A.
197 H2 Hill Creek r. U.S.A.
164 C2 Hillegom Neth.
159 K5 Hillerød Denmark
198 D2 Hillsboro ND U.S.A.
203 H3 Hillsboro NH U.S.A.
202 B5 Hillsboro OH U.S.A.
199 D5 Hillsboro TX U.S.A.
190 B4 Hillsboro WI U.S.A.
202 C5 Hillsboro WV U.S.A.
190 E5 Hillsdale MI U.S.A.
203 G3 Hillsdale NY U.S.A.
202 E4 Hillsgrove U.S.A.
162 F4 Hillside U.K.
197 F4 Hillside U.S.A.
127 F4 Hillston Australia
202 C6 Hillsville U.S.A.
127 I5 Hill Top Australia
196 □2 Hilo U.S.A.
181 I4 Hilton S. Africa
202 E3 Hilton U.S.A.
191 F2 Hilton Beach Canada
201 D5 Hilton Head Island U.S.A.
137 G3 Hilvan Turkey
164 D2 Hilversum Neth.
144 D3 Himachal Pradesh state India
144 D2 Himalaya mts Asia
145 F3 Himalchul mt. Nepal
158 M2 Himanka Fin.
171 H4 Himarë Albania
144 C5 Himatnagar India
151 D7 Himeji Japan
150 G5 Himekami-dake mt. Japan
181 H4 Himeville S. Africa
151 E6 Himi Japan
136 F4 Ḥimş Syria
153 C4 Hinatuan Phil.
169 N7 Hîncești Moldova
124 E3 Hinchinbrook Island Australia
161 F5 Hinckley U.K.
190 A2 Hinckley MN U.S.A.
197 F2 Hinckley UT U.S.A.
203 F3 Hinckley Reservoir U.S.A.
144 D3 Hindan r. India
144 D4 Hindaun India
160 G3 Hinderwell U.K.
160 E4 Hindley U.K.
202 B6 Hindman U.S.A.
126 D6 Hindmarsh, Lake dry lake Australia
143 D1 Hindola India
141 G3 Hindu Kush mts Afgh./Pak.
143 B3 Hindupur India
186 F3 Hines Creek Canada
201 D6 Hinesville U.S.A.
144 D5 Hinganghat India
141 G5 Hinglaj Pak.
141 G5 Hingol r. Pak.
144 D6 Hingoli India
137 H2 Hınıs Turkey
196 D4 Hinkley U.S.A.
158 K1 Hinnøya i. Norway
153 B4 Hinoba-an Phil.
167 D3 Hinojosa del Duque Spain
151 C7 Hino-misaki pt Japan
203 G3 Hinsdale U.S.A.
164 F1 Hinte Germany
147 B5 Hinthada Myanmar
186 F4 Hinton Canada
202 C6 Hinton U.S.A.
164 C2 Hippolytushoef Neth.
137 J2 Hirabit Dağ mt. Turkey
151 A8 Hirado Japan
151 A8 Hirado-shima i. Japan
150 G5 Hiraizumi tourist site Japan
143 C1 Hirakud Reservoir India
150 H3 Hiroo Japan
150 G4 Hirosaki Japan
151 C7 Hiroshima Japan
165 J5 Hirschaid Germany
165 J4 Hirschberg Germany
168 E7 Hirschberg mt. Germany
166 G2 Hirson France
159 J4 Hirtshals Denmark
144 C3 Hisar India
141 G3 Ḥiṣār, Kōh-e mts Afgh.
136 D1 Hisarönü Turkey
137 J6 Ḥisb, Sha'īb watercourse Iraq
139 G5 Hisor Tajik.
205 J4 Hispaniola i. Caribbean Sea
145 F4 Hisua India
137 I5 Hīt Iraq
151 G6 Hitachi Japan
151 G6 Hitachiōta Japan
151 B8 Hitoyoshi Japan
158 J3 Hitra i. Norway
165 J1 Hitzacker (Elbe) Germany

Hiuchi-nada

151 C7 Hiuchi-nada b. Japan
123 J5 Hiva Oa i. Fr. Polynesia
186 E4 Hixon Canada
137 I2 Hizan Turkey
159 K4 Hjälmaren l. Sweden
187 H2 Hjalmar Lake Canada
159 J3 Hjerkinn Norway
159 K4 Hjo Sweden
159 J4 Hjørring Denmark
181 I4 Hlabisa S. Africa
181 I3 Hlatikulu Swaziland
173 E5 Hlobyne Ukr.
181 G4 Hlohlowane S. Africa
181 H4 Hlotse Lesotho
181 J4 Hluhluwe S. Africa
173 E5 Hlukhiv Ukr.
169 N4 Hlusha Belarus
172 C4 Hlybokaye Belarus
176 C4 Ho Ghana
149 B6 Hoa Binh Hoa Binh Vietnam
154 C1 Hoa Binh Nghê An Vietnam
179 B6 Hoachanas Namibia
Hoan Lao Vietnam see Bô Trach
127 G9 Hobart Australia
199 D5 Hobart U.S.A.
199 C5 Hobbs U.S.A.
201 D7 Hobe Sound U.S.A.
148 D1 Hobor China
159 J4 Hobro Denmark
178 E3 Hobyo Somalia
165 H5 Höchberg Germany
165 I3 Hochharz, Nationalpark nat. park Germany
154 C3 Ho Chi Minh City Vietnam
168 G7 Hochschwab mt. Austria
165 G5 Hockenheim Germany
202 B5 Hocking r. U.S.A.
207 G3 Hoctúm Mex.
144 D4 Hodal India
160 E4 Hodder r. U.K.
161 G6 Hoddesdon U.K.
142 B7 Hodeidah Yemen
203 J1 Hodgdon U.S.A.
169 J7 Hódmezővásárhely Hungary
167 I5 Hodna, Chott el salt l. Alg.
152 D4 Hodo-dan pt N. Korea
149 B6 Ho Dynasty, Citadel of the tourist site Vietnam
Hoek van Holland Neth. see Hook of Holland
164 D4 Hoensbroek Neth.
152 E2 Hoeryŏng N. Korea
152 D4 Hoeyang N. Korea
165 J4 Hof Germany
165 I4 Hofheim in Unterfranken Germany
181 F5 Hofmeyr S. Africa
158 D2 Höfn Iceland
159 L3 Hofors Sweden
158 C2 Hofsjökull ice cap Iceland
151 B7 Hōfu Japan
159 K4 Höganäs Sweden
127 G7 Hogan Group is Australia
203 F6 Hog Island U.S.A.
159 L4 Högsby Sweden
159 I3 Høgste Breakulen mt. Norway
165 H5 Hohenloher Ebene plain Germany
165 K3 Hohenmölsen Germany
165 K2 Hohennauen Germany
165 J4 Hohenwartetalsperre resr Germany
165 H4 Hohe Rhön mts Germany
168 F7 Hohe Tauern mts Austria
164 E4 Hohe Venn moorland Belgium
148 D1 Hohhot China
145 H2 Hoh Sai Hu l. China
145 G2 Hoh Xil Hu salt l. China
145 G2 Hoh Xil Shan mts China
154 D2 Hôi An Vietnam
178 D3 Hoima Uganda
145 H4 Hojai India
138 F5 Hojambaz Turkm.
151 C8 Hōjo Japan
128 D1 Hokianga Harbour N.Z.
128 C5 Hokitika N.Z.
150 H3 Hokkaidō i. Japan
159 J4 Hokksund Norway
Hoktemberyan Armenia see Armavir
159 J3 Hol Norway
143 B3 Holalkere India
159 J5 Holbæk Denmark
161 H5 Holbeach U.K.
197 G4 Holbrook U.S.A.
190 B3 Holcombe Flowage resr U.S.A.
187 G4 Holden Canada
197 F2 Holden U.S.A.
199 D5 Holdenville U.S.A.
198 D3 Holdrege U.S.A.
143 B3 Hole Narsipur India
205 I4 Holguín Cuba
152 B1 Holin He r. China
159 K3 Höljes Sweden
Holland country Europe see Netherlands
190 D4 Holland U.S.A.
202 D4 Hollidaysburg U.S.A.
186 C3 Hollis AL U.S.A.
199 D5 Hollis OK U.S.A.
196 B3 Hollister U.S.A.
191 F4 Holly U.S.A.
199 F5 Holly Springs U.S.A.
196 C4 Hollywood CA U.S.A.
201 D7 Hollywood FL U.S.A.
158 K2 Holm Norway
Holman Canada see Ulukhaktok
159 J4 Holmestrand Norway
158 M3 Holmön i. Sweden
158 M3 Holmsund Sweden
180 B3 Holoog Namibia
159 J4 Holstebro Denmark
201 D4 Holston r. U.S.A.
202 C6 Holston Lake U.S.A.
161 C7 Holsworthy U.K.
161 I5 Holt U.K.
190 E4 Holt U.S.A.
198 E4 Holton U.S.A.
164 D1 Holwerd Neth.
163 D5 Holycross Ireland
161 C4 Holyhead U.K.
161 C4 Holyhead Bay U.K.
160 F2 Holy Island England U.K.
161 C4 Holy Island Wales U.K.
203 G3 Holyoke U.S.A.
161 D4 Holywell U.K.
165 K3 Holzhausen Germany
168 E7 Holzkirchen Germany
165 H3 Holzminden Germany
165 H3 Homberg (Efze) Germany
176 B3 Hombori Mali
164 F5 Homburg Germany
185 L3 Home Bay Canada
164 D5 Homécourt France
199 E5 Homer U.S.A.
201 D6 Homerville U.S.A.
201 D7 Homestead U.S.A.
201 C5 Homewood U.S.A.
143 B2 Homnabad India
Homs Syria see Ḩimş
173 D4 Homyel' Belarus
143 A3 Honavar India
213 B3 Honda Col.
153 A4 Honda Bay Phil.
197 H4 Hon Dah U.S.A.
180 B5 Hondeklipbaai S. Africa
148 C1 Hondlon Ju China
207 G4 Hondo r. Belize/Mex.
199 D6 Hondo U.S.A.
164 E1 Hondsrug reg. Neth.
206 H5 Honduras country Central America
206 H4 Honduras, Gulf of Belize/Hond.
159 J3 Hønefoss Norway
203 F4 Honesdale U.S.A.
196 B1 Honey Lake salt l. U.S.A.
203 E3 Honeyoye Lake U.S.A.
166 E2 Honfleur France
Hông, Sông r. Vietnam see Red
148 E4 Hong'an China
152 D5 Hongcheon S. Korea
Hông Gai Vietnam see Ha Long
149 E6 Honghai Wan b. China
149 B6 Honghe China
148 E3 Hong He r. China
149 B6 Honghe Hani Rice Terraces tourist site China
149 D4 Honghu China
149 C5 Hongjiang Hunan China
149 C5 Hongjiang Hunan China
149 E6 Hong Kong Hong Kong China (City Plan 103)
149 □ Hong Kong aut. reg. China
149 □ Hong Kong Island Hong Kong China
148 C2 Hongliu He r. China
148 B2 Hongliuyuan China
154 C3 Hông Ngư Vietnam
Hongqizhen China see Wuzhishan
148 D4 Hongshan China
148 B2 Hongshansi China
152 D2 Hongshilazi China
149 D6 Hongshui He r. China
148 D2 Hongtong China
189 G4 Honguedo, Détroit d' sea chan. Canada
152 D3 Hongwŏn N. Korea
152 B1 Hongxing China
148 B3 Hongyuan China
148 F3 Hongze China
148 F3 Hongze Hu l. China
125 F2 Honiara Solomon Is
161 D7 Honiton U.K.
159 M3 Honkajoki Fin.
143 A3 Honnali India
158 N1 Honningsvåg Norway
196 □2 Honoka'a U.S.A.
196 □1 Honolulu U.S.A.
151 D6 Honshū i. Japan
194 B2 Hood, Mount vol. U.S.A.
124 B5 Hood Point Australia
164 E2 Hoogeveen Neth.
164 E1 Hoogezand-Sappemeer Neth.
199 C4 Hooker U.S.A.
163 E5 Hook Head Ireland
164 C3 Hook of Holland Neth.
186 B3 Hoonah U.S.A.
184 B3 Hooper Bay U.S.A.
203 E5 Hooper Island U.S.A.
190 D5 Hoopeston U.S.A.
181 F3 Hoopstad S. Africa
159 K5 Höör Sweden
164 D2 Hoorn Neth.
203 G3 Hoosick U.S.A.
197 E3 Hoover Dam U.S.A.
202 B4 Hoover Memorial Reservoir U.S.A.
137 H1 Hopa Turkey
203 F4 Hop Bottom U.S.A.
186 E5 Hope Canada
128 D5 Hope r. N.Z.
197 F5 Hope AR U.S.A.
199 E5 Hope AR U.S.A.
126 C2 Hope, Lake salt flat Australia
184 B3 Hope, Point U.S.A.
189 I2 Hopedale Canada
180 C6 Hopefield S. Africa
207 G4 Hopelchén Mex.
189 H3 Hope Mountains Canada
132 D2 Hopen i. Svalbard
128 D4 Hope Saddle pass N.Z.
189 G2 Hopes Advance, Baie b. Canada
126 E5 Hopetoun Australia
180 F4 Hopetown S. Africa
202 E6 Hopewell U.S.A.
188 E2 Hopewell Islands Canada
124 C4 Hopkins, Lake salt flat Australia
200 C4 Hopkinsville U.S.A.
196 A2 Hopland U.S.A.
194 B2 Hoquiam U.S.A.
148 A3 Hor China
137 K2 Horadiz Azer.
137 I1 Horasan Turkey
159 K5 Hörby Sweden
206 C1 Horcasitas Mex.
139 J3 Horgos Kou'an China
148 B1 Hörhiyn Nuruu mts Mongolia
190 C4 Horicon U.S.A.
148 D1 Horinger China
216 H7 Horizon Deep sea feature S. Pacific Ocean
172 D4 Horki Belarus
129 B4 Horlick Mountains mts Antarctica
173 F5 Horlivka Ukr.
141 F4 Hormak Iran
140 E5 Hormoz, Jazīreh-ye i. Iran
140 E5 Hormuz, Strait of Iran/Oman
168 G6 Horn Austria
186 F2 Horn r. Canada
158 B1 Horn c. Iceland
212 C9 Horn, Cape Chile
125 I3 Horn, Îles de is Wallis and Futuna Is
158 L2 Hornavan l. Sweden
199 E6 Hornbeck U.S.A.
165 I2 Hornburg Germany
161 G4 Horncastle U.K.
159 L3 Horndal Sweden
165 H1 Horneburg Germany
158 L3 Hörnefors Sweden
202 E3 Hornell U.S.A.
188 D4 Hornepayne Canada
201 B6 Horn Island U.S.A.
180 B1 Hornkranz Namibia
215 B4 Hornopiren, Volcán vol. Chile
Hornos, Cabo de c. Chile see Horn, Cape
127 I4 Hornsby Australia
160 G4 Hornsea U.K.
159 L3 Hornslandet pen. Sweden
169 L6 Horodenka Ukr.
173 D5 Horodnya Ukr.
173 C5 Horodok Khmel'nyts'ka Oblast' Ukr.
173 B5 Horodok L'vivs'ka Oblast' Ukr.
150 H2 Horokanai Japan
169 L5 Horokhiv Ukr.
150 H3 Horoshiri-dake mt. Japan
152 A2 Horqin Shadi reg. China
161 C7 Horrabridge U.K.
145 G3 Horru China
186 E4 Horsefly Canada
202 E3 Horseheads U.S.A.
189 I3 Horse Islands Canada
163 C4 Horseleap Ireland
159 J5 Horsens Denmark
194 C3 Horseshoe Bend U.S.A.
219 H3 Horseshoe Seamounts sea feature N. Atlantic Ocean
126 E6 Horsham Australia
161 G6 Horsham U.K.
165 K5 Horšovský Týn Czech Rep.
165 H4 Horst h. Germany
164 F2 Hörstel Germany
159 J4 Horten Norway
184 F3 Horton r. Canada
191 F1 Horwood Lake Canada
169 M5 Horyn' r. Ukr.
151 D7 Hōryūji tourist site Japan
178 D3 Hosa'ina Eth.
143 B3 Hosapete India
165 H4 Hösbach Germany
143 B3 Hosdurga India
137 K4 Ḩoseynābād Iran
140 C4 Ḩoseynīyeh Iran
141 F5 Hoshab Pak.
144 D5 Hoshangabad India
144 C3 Hoshiarpur India
149 B6 Hô Sông Đa resr Vietnam
163 C5 Hospital Ireland
215 F1 Hospital, Cuchilla del hills Uruguay
212 C9 Hoste, Isla i. Chile
158 K3 Hotagen r. Sweden
139 J5 Hotan China
139 J5 Hotan He watercourse China
180 E3 Hotazel S. Africa
197 G4 Hotevilla U.S.A.
127 G6 Hotham, Mount Australia
158 L2 Hoting Sweden
199 E5 Hot Springs AR U.S.A.
198 C3 Hot Springs SD U.S.A.
186 F1 Hottah Lake Canada
205 J5 Hotte, Massif de la mts Haiti
164 D4 Houffalize Belgium
154 □ Hougang Sing.
190 C2 Houghton U.S.A.
190 E3 Houghton Lake U.S.A.
190 E3 Houghton Lake l. U.S.A.
160 F3 Houghton le Spring U.K.
203 J1 Houlton U.S.A.
148 D3 Houma China
199 F6 Houma U.S.A.
162 C3 Hourn, Loch inlet U.K.
203 G3 Housatonic U.S.A.
197 F2 House Range mts U.S.A.
186 D4 Houston Canada
199 F4 Houston MO U.S.A.
199 F5 Houston MS U.S.A.
199 E6 Houston TX U.S.A.
124 B4 Houtman Abrolhos is Australia
162 E2 Houton U.K.
180 E5 Houwater S. Africa
146 B2 Hovd Mongolia
161 G7 Hove U.K.
161 I5 Hoveton U.K.
140 C4 Hoveyzeh Iran
159 K4 Hovmantorp Sweden
148 C1 Hövsgöl Mongolia
146 C1 Hövsgöl Nuur l. Mongolia
Hövüün Mongolia see Noyon
177 E3 Howar, Wadi watercourse Sudan
190 E4 Howard City U.S.A.
187 H2 Howard Lake Canada
160 G4 Howden U.K.
127 H6 Howe, Cape Australia
191 F4 Howell U.S.A.
198 C2 Howes U.S.A.
203 G2 Howick Canada
181 I4 Howick S. Africa
126 C1 Howitt, Lake salt flat Australia
127 G6 Howitt, Mount Australia
203 I2 Howland U.S.A.
125 I1 Howland Island terr. Pacific Ocean
127 G5 Howlong Australia
163 E4 Howth Ireland
140 D3 Ḩowz-e Dūmatu Iran
140 E4 Ḩowz-e Panj Iran
154 C1 Hô Xa Vietnam
165 H3 Höxter Germany
162 E2 Hoy i. U.K.
165 H2 Hoya Germany
159 I3 Høyanger Norway
168 G5 Hoyerswerda Germany
158 K2 Høylandet Norway
165 J3 Hoym Germany
158 O3 Höytiäinen l. Fin.
137 G2 Hozat Turkey
154 A1 Hpa-an Myanmar
154 A1 Hpapun Myanmar
168 G5 Hradec Králové Czech Rep.
165 L4 Hradiště h. Czech Rep.
171 H3 Hrasnica Bos. & Herz.
137 J1 Hrazdan Armenia
173 E5 Hrebinka Ukr.
172 B4 Hrodna Belarus
135 H4 Hsipaw Myanmar
149 E5 Hua'an China
213 D4 Huachamacari, Cerro mt. Venez.
148 C2 Huachi China
210 C6 Huacho Peru
150 B1 Huachuan China
197 G6 Huachuca City U.S.A.
215 C1 Huaco Arg.
148 D1 Huade China
152 D2 Huadian China
149 D6 Huadu China
154 A2 Hua Hin Thai.
148 E1 Huai'an Hebei China
148 F3 Huai'an Jiangsu China
148 E3 Huaibei China
148 E3 Huaibin China
Huaicheng China see Chuzhou
152 C2 Huaide China
148 F3 Huai He r. China
149 C5 Huaihua China
149 D6 Huaiji China
148 E1 Huailai China
148 E3 Huainan China
149 E4 Huaining China
148 D2 Huairen China
148 E3 Huaiyang China
148 F3 Huaiyin Jiangsu China
Huaiyin Jiangsu China see Huai'an
148 E3 Huaiyuan Anhui China
149 C5 Huaiyuan Guangxi Zhuangzu Zizhiqu China
148 B3 Huajialing China
207 E4 Huajuápan de León Mex.
147 E7 Huaki Indon.
197 F4 Hualapai Peak U.S.A.
149 F5 Hualian Taiwan
210 C5 Huallaga r. Peru
148 B2 Hualong China
179 B5 Huambo Angola
150 B1 Huanan China
215 C4 Huancache, Sierra mts Arg.
210 C6 Huancayo Peru
148 E2 Huangbizhuang Shuiku resr China
148 A2 Huangcheng China
148 E3 Huangchuan China
149 E4 Huanggang China
Huang Hai sea Pacific Ocean see Yellow Sea
Huang He r. China see Yellow
148 F2 Huanghe Kou r. mouth China
145 H2 Huanghetan China
148 E2 Huanghua China
148 C3 Huangling China
149 C7 Huangliu China
149 E4 Huangmei China
152 D2 Huangnihe China
149 E4 Huangpi China
149 C5 Huangping China
148 D1 Huangqi Hai l. China
149 F4 Huangshan China
149 E4 Huangshi China
148 B2 Huang Shui r. China
148 C2 Huangtu Gaoyuan plat. China
149 F4 Huangyan China
148 A2 Huangyuan China
Huangzhou China see Huanggang
149 C5 Huanjiang China
148 C2 Huan Jiang r. China
152 C3 Huanren China
148 F2 Huantai China
210 C5 Huánuco Peru
210 E7 Huanuni Bol.
148 C2 Huanxian China
149 G5 Huaping Yu i. Taiwan
210 C5 Huaraz Peru
210 C6 Huarmey Peru
149 D4 Huarong China
210 C5 Huascarán, Nevado de mt. Peru
210 C5 Huascarán, Parque Nacional nat. park Peru
212 B3 Huasco Chile
212 B3 Huasco r. Chile
152 D2 Huashulinzi China
206 B2 Huatabampo Mex.
148 C3 Huating China
152 A3 Huatong China
207 E4 Huatusco Mex.
207 E3 Huauchinango Mex.
207 E4 Huautla Mex.
148 E3 Huaxian China
149 C4 Huaying China
149 C4 Huayuan China
149 D6 Huazhou China
143 A3 Hubballi India
186 B2 Hubbard, Mount Canada/U.S.A.
189 G2 Hubbard, Pointe pt Canada
191 F3 Hubbard Lake U.S.A.
148 D4 Hubei prov. China
Hubli India see Hubballi
152 D3 Huch'ang N. Korea
164 E3 Hückelhoven Germany
161 F4 Hucknall U.K.
Ḩudaydah Yemen see Hodeidah
160 F4 Huddersfield U.K.
202 B6 Huddy U.S.A.
159 L3 Hudiksvall Sweden
190 E5 Hudson MI U.S.A.
203 G3 Hudson NY U.S.A.
190 A3 Hudson WI U.S.A.
200 F3 Hudson r. U.S.A.
187 I4 Hudson Bay Canada
185 J4 Hudson Bay sea Canada
203 G3 Hudson Falls U.S.A.
185 P2 Hudson Land reg. Greenland
129 B3 Hudson Mountains mts Antarctica
186 E3 Hudson's Hope Canada
185 K3 Hudson Strait Canada
154 C1 Huê Vietnam
215 A4 Huechucuicui, Punta pt Chile
207 G5 Huehuetenango Guat.
206 C2 Huehueto, Cerro mt. Mex.
207 E4 Huejotzingo Mex.
207 E3 Huejutla Mex.
167 C4 Huelva Spain
215 B1 Huentelauquén Chile
215 B4 Huequi, Volcán vol. Chile
167 F4 Huércal-Overa Spain
167 F1 Huesca Spain
167 E4 Huéscar Spain
206 D4 Huétamo Mex.
202 E4 Hughesville U.S.A.
145 F5 Hugli r. mouth India
145 G5 Hugli-Chinsurah India
199 E5 Hugo U.S.A.
199 C4 Hugoton U.S.A.
148 D2 Huguan China
180 F3 Huhudi S. Africa
149 F5 Hui'an China
148 C2 Hui'anpu China
128 F3 Huiarau Range mts N.Z.
180 B3 Huib-Hoch Plateau Namibia
149 E5 Huichang China
152 D3 Huich'ŏn N. Korea
149 E6 Huidong Guangdong China
149 B5 Huidong Sichuan China
152 D2 Huifa He r. China
164 C3 Huijbergen Neth.
148 E3 Huiji He r. China
213 B4 Huila, Nevado de vol. Col.
149 E6 Huilai China
149 B5 Huili China
207 F4 Huimanguillo Mex.
148 E2 Huimin China
152 D2 Huinan China
215 D2 Huinca Renancó Arg.
148 B3 Huining China
149 C5 Huishui China
145 G2 Huiten Nur l. China
149 C5 Huitong China
159 M3 Huittinen Fin.
207 E4 Huitzuco Mex.
148 C3 Huixian Gansu China
148 D3 Huixian Henan China
207 F5 Huixtla Mex.
149 B5 Huize China
149 E6 Huizhou China
Hujirt Mongolia see Delgerhaan
149 E4 Hukou China
141 G3 Ḩukūmatī Gīzāb Afgh.
180 D1 Hukuntsi Botswana
190 E2 Hulbert Lake U.S.A.
140 B3 Hulīlan Iran
150 C2 Hulin China
191 J3 Hull Canada
159 K4 Hultsfred Sweden
152 A3 Huludao China
146 D2 Hulun Buir China
146 D2 Hulun Nur l. China
177 F2 Ḩulwān Egypt
173 F6 Hulyaypole Ukr.
146 E1 Huma China
212 C2 Humahuaca Arg.
210 F5 Humaitá Brazil
180 F7 Humansdorp S. Africa
140 B5 Humayyān, Jabal h. Saudi Arabia
160 H4 Humber, Mouth of the U.K.
187 H4 Humboldt Canada
194 C3 Humboldt r. U.S.A.
194 A3 Humboldt Bay U.S.A.
196 C1 Humboldt Lake U.S.A.
196 C1 Humboldt Range mts U.S.A.
196 D2 Humbolt Salt Marsh U.S.A.
127 F1 Humeburn Australia
149 D6 Hu Men sea chan. China
169 J6 Humenné Slovakia
127 G6 Hume Reservoir Australia
196 C3 Humphreys, Mount U.S.A.
197 G4 Humphreys Peak U.S.A.
177 D2 Hūn Libya
158 B2 Húnaflói b. Iceland
149 D5 Hunan prov. China
152 F2 Hunchun China
152 F2 Hunchun He r. China
165 K3 Hundeluft Germany
159 J5 Hundested Denmark
171 J2 Hunedoara Romania
165 H4 Hünfeld Germany
169 I7 Hungary country Europe
126 F2 Hungerford Australia
152 D4 Hŭngnam N. Korea
194 D1 Hungry Horse Reservoir U.S.A.
149 □ Hung Shui Kiu Hong Kong China
149 C6 Hưng Yên Vietnam
152 B3 Hun He r. China
162 B3 Hunish, Rubha pt U.K.
152 C3 Hun Jiang r. China
180 B3 Huns Mountains Namibia
164 F5 Hunsrück hills Germany
161 H5 Hunstanton U.K.
143 B3 Hunsur India
197 H4 Hunt U.S.A.
165 G2 Hunte r. Germany
127 I4 Hunter r. Australia
203 F3 Hunter U.S.A.
127 F8 Hunter Island Australia
186 D4 Hunter Island Canada
125 H4 Hunter Island New Caledonia
127 F8 Hunter Islands Australia
145 H6 Hunter's Bay Myanmar
203 F2 Huntingdon Canada
161 G5 Huntingdon U.K.
202 E4 Huntingdon U.S.A.
190 E5 Huntington IN U.S.A.
197 G2 Huntington UT U.S.A.
202 B5 Huntington WV U.S.A.
196 D5 Huntington Beach U.S.A.
128 E2 Huntly N.Z.
162 F3 Huntly U.K.
126 B2 Hunt Peninsula Australia
191 H3 Huntsville Canada
201 C5 Huntsville AL U.S.A.
199 E6 Huntsville TX U.S.A.
136 D6 Hunū, Kathīb al des. Egypt
148 D2 Hunyuan China
144 C1 Hunza Pak.
144 C2 Hunza r. Pak.
139 J3 Huocheng China
154 C1 Hương Khê Vietnam
Hương Thuy Vietnam see Phu Bai
124 E2 Huon Peninsula P.N.G.
127 G9 Huonville Australia
148 E3 Huoqiu China
148 E4 Huoshan China
Huoshao Tao i. Taiwan see Lü Dao
148 D2 Huozhou China
140 E4 Ḩūr Iran
136 D6 Ḩurayḑīn, Wādī watercourse Egypt
191 G3 Hurd, Cape Canada
152 A2 Hure China
148 C1 Hure Jadgai China
177 F2 Hurghada Egypt
190 C1 Hurkett Canada
163 C5 Hurler's Cross Ireland
190 B2 Hurley U.S.A.
198 D2 Huron U.S.A.
191 F3 Huron, Lake Canada/U.S.A.
190 C2 Huron Bay U.S.A.
190 D2 Huron Mountains hills U.S.A.
197 F3 Hurricane U.S.A.
161 F6 Hursley U.K.
161 H6 Hurst Green U.K.
128 D5 Hurunui r. N.Z.
158 C1 Húsavík Norðurland eystra Iceland
158 B2 Húsavík Vestfirðir Iceland
169 N7 Huşi Romania
159 K4 Huskvarna Sweden
184 C3 Huslia U.S.A.
159 I4 Husnes Norway
145 F4 Hussainabad India
168 D3 Husum Germany
158 L3 Husum Sweden
Hutag Mongolia see Hutag-Öndör
146 C2 Hutag-Öndör Mongolia
198 D4 Hutchinson U.S.A.
197 G4 Hutch Mountain U.S.A.
154 A1 Huthi Myanmar
150 C2 Hutou China
187 M2 Hut Point Canada
202 D5 Huttonsville U.S.A.
148 D2 Hutuo He r. China
Hüvek Turkey see Bozova
148 C3 Huxian China
148 F4 Huzhou China
148 A2 Huzhu China
158 C2 Hvannadalshnúkur vol. Iceland
170 G3 Hvar i. Croatia
173 E6 Hvardiys'ke Crimea
158 B2 Hveragerði Iceland
159 J4 Hvide Sande Denmark
158 B3 Hvíta r. Iceland
152 E3 Hwadae N. Korea
179 C5 Hwange Zimbabwe
179 C5 Hwange National Park Zimbabwe
152 C4 Hwangju N. Korea
179 D5 Hwedza Zimbabwe
203 H4 Hyannis MA U.S.A.
198 C3 Hyannis NE U.S.A.
146 B2 Hyargas Nuur salt l. Mongolia
186 C3 Hydaburg U.S.A.
128 C6 Hyde N.Z.
124 B5 Hyden Australia
202 B6 Hyden U.S.A.
203 G4 Hyde Park U.S.A.
197 F5 Hyder U.S.A.
143 B2 Hyderabad India
144 B4 Hyderabad Pak.
166 H5 Hyères France
166 H5 Hyères, Îles d' is France
152 E3 Hyesan N. Korea
186 D2 Hyland r. Canada
127 J3 Hyland, Mount Australia
159 I3 Hyllestad Norway
159 K4 Hyltebruk Sweden
126 D6 Hynam Australia
151 D7 Hyōno-sen mt. Japan
158 O2 Hyrynsalmi Fin.
186 F3 Hythe Canada
161 I6 Hythe U.K.
151 B8 Hyūga Japan
159 N3 Hyvinkää Fin.

I

210 E6 Iaco r. Brazil
211 J6 Iaçu Brazil
179 E6 Iakora Madag.
171 L2 Ialomiţa r. Romania
171 L2 Ianca Romania
169 M7 Iaşi Romania
153 A3 Iba Phil.
176 C4 Ibadan Nigeria
213 B3 Ibagué Col.
197 F1 Ibapah U.S.A.
210 C3 Ibarra Ecuador
142 B7 Ibb Yemen
165 F2 Ibbenbüren Germany
212 E3 Iberá, Esteros del marsh Arg.
188 F2 Iberville, Lac d' l. Canada
154 A4 Ibi Indon.
176 C4 Ibi Nigeria
214 C2 Ibiá Brazil
211 J4 Ibiapaba, Serra da hills Brazil
215 F1 Ibicuí da Cruz r. Brazil
214 E2 Ibiraçu Brazil
167 G3 Ibiza Spain
167 G3 Ibiza i. Spain
170 F6 Iblei, Monti mts Sicily Italy
140 B5 Ibn Buşayyiş well Saudi Arabia
211 J6 Ibotirama Brazil
142 E5 Ibrā' Oman
142 E5 Ibrī Oman
153 B1 Ibuhos i. Phil.
151 B9 Ibusuki Japan
210 C6 Ica Peru
207 G4 Icaiché Mex.
213 D4 Içana Brazil
213 D4 Içana r. Brazil
197 E3 Iceberg Canyon gorge U.S.A.
İçel Turkey see Mersin
158 □ Iceland country Europe
219 H2 Iceland Basin sea feature N. Atlantic Ocean
219 I1 Icelandic Plateau sea feature N. Atlantic Ocean
143 A2 Ichalkaranji India
143 D2 Ichchapuram India
152 D5 Icheon S. Korea
151 B8 Ichifusa-yama mt. Japan
151 B9 Ichiki-Kushikino Japan
150 G5 Ichinoseki Japan
133 Q4 Ichinskaya Sopka, Vulkan vol. Russia
173 E5 Ichnya Ukr.
152 D4 Ich'ŏn N. Korea
164 B3 Ichtegem Belgium
165 I4 Ichtershausen Germany
138 D4 Içoguz Turkm.
186 B3 Icy Point U.S.A.
186 B3 Icy Strait U.S.A.
199 E5 Idabel U.S.A.
194 D2 Idaho state U.S.A.
194 D3 Idaho City U.S.A.
194 D3 Idaho Falls U.S.A.
164 F5 Idar-Oberstein Germany
177 F2 Idfū Egypt
178 B4 Idiofa Dem. Rep. Congo
184 C3 Iditarod (abandoned) U.S.A.
158 M1 Idivuoma Sweden
136 C6 Idkū Egypt
136 F4 Idlib Syria
159 K3 Idre Sweden
170 F1 Idrija Slovenia
165 G4 Idstein Germany
Idutywa S. Africa see Dutywa
159 N4 Iecava Latvia
214 B3 Iepê Brazil
164 A4 Ieper Belgium
171 K7 Ierapetra Greece
158 N1 Iešjávri l. Norway
179 D4 Ifakara Tanz.
179 E6 Ifanadiana Madag.
176 C4 Ife Nigeria
158 N1 Ifjord Norway
176 C3 Ifôghas, Adrar des hills Mali
155 D2 Igan Sarawak Malaysia
214 C3 Igarapava Brazil
214 D3 Igarapé Brazil
132 J3 Igarka Russia
144 C6 Igatpuri India
137 J2 Iğdır Turkey
159 L3 Iggesund Sweden
170 C5 Iglesias Sardinia Italy
185 J3 Igloolik Canada
188 B4 Ignace Canada
159 N5 Ignalina Lith.
173 C7 İğneada Turkey
171 M4 İğneada Burnu pt Turkey
169 P3 Igorevskaya Russia
171 I5 Igoumenitsa Greece
132 H3 Igrim Russia
214 B4 Iguaçu r. Brazil
214 A4 Iguaçu, Parque Nacional do nat. park Brazil
212 F3 Iguaçu Falls Arg./Brazil
214 E1 Iguaí Brazil
213 B4 Iguaje, Mesa de hills Col.
207 E4 Iguala Mex.
167 G2 Igualada Spain
214 C4 Iguape Brazil
214 A3 Iguatemi Brazil
214 A3 Iguatemi r. Brazil
211 K5 Iguatu Brazil
214 B4 Iguazú, Parque Nacional del nat. park Arg.
178 A4 Iguéla Gabon
176 B2 Iguidi, Erg des. Alg./Mauritania
178 D4 Igunga Tanz.
179 E5 Iharaña Madag.
Ihbulag Mongolia see Hanbogd
179 E6 Ihosy Madag.
152 B2 Ih Tal China
171 J3 Ihtiman Bulg.
151 F6 Iide-san mt. Japan
158 N1 Iijärvi Fin.
158 N2 Iijoki r. Fin.
158 N3 Iisalmi Fin.
151 B8 Iizuka Japan
176 C4 Ijebu-Ode Nigeria
137 J1 Ijevan Armenia
164 C2 IJmuiden Neth.
164 D2 IJssel r. Neth.
164 D2 IJsselmeer l. Neth.
159 M3 Ikaalinen Fin.
181 G2 Ikageleng S. Africa
181 G3 Ikageng S. Africa
171 L6 Ikaria i. Greece
159 J4 Ikast Denmark
150 H3 Ikeda Japan
178 C4 Ikela Dem. Rep. Congo
180 F4 Ikhutseng S. Africa
173 H6 Iki-Burul Russia
151 A8 Iki-shima i. Japan
176 C4 Ikom Nigeria
179 E6 Ikongo Madag.
173 H6 Ikryanoye Russia
152 D6 Iksan S. Korea
178 D4 Ikungu Tanz.
153 B2 Ilagan Phil.
178 D3 Ilaisamis Kenya
140 B3 Īlām Iran
145 F4 Ilam Nepal
176 C4 Ilaro Nigeria
169 I4 Iława Poland
187 H3 Île-à-la-Crosse Canada
187 H3 Île-à-la-Crosse, Lac l. Canada
178 C4 Ilebo Dem. Rep. Congo
138 C2 Ilek Kazakh.
138 C2 Ilek r. Russia
178 D3 Ileret Kenya
172 G2 Ileza Russia
187 J3 Ilford Canada
161 H6 Ilford U.K.
161 C6 Ilfracombe U.K.
136 D1 Ilgaz Turkey
136 D1 Ilgaz Dağları mts Turkey
136 C2 Ilgın Turkey
213 D5 Ilha Grande Brazil
214 B3 Ilha Grande resr Brazil
214 D3 Ilha Grande, Baía da b. Brazil
181 J2 Ilhas da Inhaca e dos Portugueses nature res. S. Africa
214 B3 Ilha Solteíra, Represa resr Brazil
167 B2 Ílhavo Port.
214 E1 Ilhéus Brazil
139 J4 Ili r. China
139 I3 Ili r. Kazakh.
184 C4 Iliamna Lake U.S.A.
136 G2 İliç Turkey
153 C4 Iligan Phil.
153 C4 Iligan Bay Phil.
138 D2 Il'inka Kazakh.
172 H2 Il'insko-Podomskoye Russia
203 F3 Ilion U.S.A.
143 B3 Ilkal India
161 F5 Ilkeston U.K.
160 F4 Ilkley U.K.
153 B5 Illana Bay Phil.
215 B1 Illapel Chile
215 B1 Illapel r. Chile
168 E7 Iller r. Germany
173 D6 Illichivs'k Ukr.
210 E7 Illimani, Nevado de mt. Bol.
190 C5 Illinois r. U.S.A.
190 C5 Illinois state U.S.A.
190 B5 Illinois and Mississippi Canal U.S.A.
173 D5 Illintsi Ukr.
176 C2 Illizi Alg.
165 J4 Ilm r. Germany
158 M3 Ilmajoki Fin.
172 D3 Il'men', Ozero l. Russia
165 I4 Ilmenau Germany
165 I1 Ilmenau r. Germany
161 E7 Ilminster U.K.
210 D7 Ilo Peru
153 A4 Iloc i. Phil.
153 B4 Iloilo Phil.
158 O3 Ilomantsi Fin.
176 C4 Ilorin Nigeria
173 F6 Ilovays'k Ukr.
173 G5 Ilovlya Russia
173 H5 Ilovlya r. Russia
165 I2 Ilsede Germany
127 J2 Iluka Australia
185 M3 Ilulissat Greenland
151 C7 Imabari Japan
Imaichi Japan see Nikkō
137 J6 Imām al Ḩamzah Iraq
137 J5 Imām Ḩamīd Iraq
136 E3 İmamoğlu admin. dist. Turkey
141 H2 Imām Şāḩib Afgh.
150 D2 Iman r. Russia
151 A8 Imari Japan
213 E3 Imataca, Serranía de mts Venez.
159 O3 Imatra Fin.
151 E7 Imazu Japan
212 G3 Imbituba Brazil
214 B4 Imbituva Brazil
178 E3 Īmī Eth.
137 L2 İmişli Azer.
152 D6 Imja-do i. S. Korea
152 D4 Imjin-gang r. N. Korea
170 D2 Imola Italy
181 H4 Impendle S. Africa
211 I5 Imperatriz Brazil
170 C3 Imperia Italy
198 C3 Imperial U.S.A.
196 D5 Imperial Beach U.S.A.
197 E5 Imperial Valley plain U.S.A.
178 B3 Impfondo Congo
145 H4 Imphal India
171 K4 İmroz Turkey
152 D6 Imsil S. Korea
136 F5 Imtān Syria
153 A4 Imuruan Bay Phil.
151 E7 Ina Japan
210 E6 Inambari r. Peru
176 C2 In Aménas Alg.
181 I4 Inanda S. Africa
128 C4 Inangahua Junction N.Z.
147 F7 Inanwatan Indon.
158 N1 Inari Fin.
158 N1 Inarijärvi l. Fin.
158 N1 Inarijoki r. Fin./Norway
167 H3 Inca Spain
173 C7 İnce Burnu pt Turkey
173 E7 İnce Burun pt Turkey
136 D3 İncekum Burnu pt Turkey
136 E2 İncesu Turkey
163 E5 Inch Ireland
162 C2 Inchard, Loch b. U.K.
Inchcape Rock i. U.K. see Bell Rock
152 D5 Incheon S. Korea
162 E4 Inchkeith i. U.K.
181 J2 Incomati r. Moz.
162 B5 Indaal, Loch b. U.K.
214 D2 Indaiá r. Brazil
214 B2 Indaiá Grande r. Brazil

Khomas Highland

137 H2 Kara r. Turkey
171 L5 Kara Ada i. Turkey
136 D2 Karaali Turkey
139 I2 Karaauyl Kazakh.
139 H4 Kara-Balta Kyrg.
138 E1 Karabalyk Kazakh.
139 H2 Karabas Kazakh.
138 C2 Karabau Kazakh.
138 C4 Karabaur, Uval hills Uzbek.
Karabil', Vozvyshennost' hills Turkm. see Garabil Belentligi
Kara-Bogaz-Gol, Zaliv b. Turkm. see Garabogazköl Aýlagy
Karabogazkel' Turkm. see Garabogazköl
136 D1 Karabük Turkey
139 I3 Karabulak Almatinskaya Oblast' Kazakh.
139 K3 Karabulak Vostochnyy Kazakhstan Kazakh.
139 H2 Karabulakskaya (abandoned) Kazakh.
138 E2 Karabutak Kazakh.
136 B1 Karacabey Turkey
137 G3 Karacadağ Turkey
136 D3 Karacadağ mts Turkey
136 B1 Karacaköy Turkey
137 G3 Karacalı Dağ mt. Turkey
136 B3 Karacasu Turkey
136 C3 Karaca Yarımadası pen. Turkey
173 G7 Karachayevo-Cherkesskaya Respublika aut. rep. Russia
173 G7 Karachayevsk Russia
172 E4 Karachev Russia
141 G5 Karachi Pak. (City Plan 103)
137 I2 Karaçoban Turkey
143 A2 Karad India
136 D3 Kara Dağ mt. Turkey
137 I3 Kara Dağ mt. Turkey
139 H4 Kara-Daryya r. Kyrg.
139 G2 Karagandinskaya Oblast' admin. div. Kazakh.
139 H2 Karagandy Kazakh.
139 H2 Karagayly Kazakh.
133 R4 Karaginskiy Zaliv b. Russia
138 B4 Karagiye, Vpadina depr. Kazakh.
136 B2 Karahallı Turkey
136 E2 Karahasanlı Turkey
143 B4 Karaikal India
143 B4 Karaikkudi India
136 E3 Karaisalı Turkey
143 B4 Karaitivu i. Sri Lanka
140 C3 Karaj Iran
140 C3 Karaj r. Iran
Karakalpakiya Uzbek. see Qoraqalpog'iston
127 E6 Kara Kara National Park Australia
Karakatinskaya, Vpadina depr. Uzbek. see Qoraqata botig'i
144 E1 Karakax He r. China
137 G3 Karakeçi Turkey
136 D2 Karakeçili Turkey
147 E6 Karakelong i. Indon.
138 F3 Karaketken Kazakh.
137 H2 Karakoçan Turkey
138 C2 Karakol' Kazakh.
139 H4 Kara-Köl Kyrg.
139 I4 Karakol Ysyk-Köl Kyrg.
139 I4 Karakol Ysyk-Köl Kyrg.
144 D2 Karakoram Pass China/India
135 F3 Karakoram Range mts Asia
178 D2 Kara K'orē Eth.
139 G3 Karakoyyn, Ozero salt l. Kazakh.
139 J2 Karakozha Kazakh.
Karakul' Uzbek. see Qorako'l
138 E1 Karakul'skoye Russia
139 I3 Karakum Kazakh.
138 C3 Karakum, Peski des. Kazakh.
141 F2 Karakum Desert Turkm.
Karakumskiy Kanal canal Turkm. see Garagum Kanaly
137 I1 Karakurt Turkey
159 M4 Karala Estonia
136 D3 Karaman Turkey
136 B3 Karamanlı Turkey
135 G2 Karamay China
144 C1 Karambar Pass Afgh./Pak.
128 D4 Karamea N.Z.
128 C4 Karamea Bight b. N.Z.
138 F2 Karamendy Kazakh.
Karamet-Niyaz Turkm. see Garamätnyýaz
145 F1 Karamiran China
145 F1 Karamiran Shankou pass China
136 B1 Karamürsel Turkey
172 D3 Karamyshevo Russia
140 C5 Karān i. Saudi Arabia
144 D5 Karanja India
143 B2 Karanja r. India
145 F5 Karanjia India
144 C3 Karanpura India
139 I1 Karaoba Kazakh.
139 H3 Karaoy (abandoned) Almatinskaya Oblast' Kazakh.
139 H3 Karaoy (abandoned) Almatinskaya Oblast' Kazakh.
138 F3 Karaozek Kazakh.
136 D3 Karapınar Turkey
139 I4 Karaqi China
180 B3 !Karas admin. reg. Namibia
180 B3 Karas watercourse Namibia
139 I4 Kara-Say Kyrg.
179 B6 Karasburg Namibia
132 I2 Kara Sea Russia
139 H2 Karashoky Kazakh.
Kárášjohka Norway see Karasjok
158 N1 Karasjok Norway
139 H2 Karasor Kazakh.
139 H1 Karasor, Ozero salt l. Kazakh.
139 H2 Karasor, Ozero salt l. Kazakh.
139 H3 Karasu Karagandinskaya Oblast' Kazakh.
138 F1 Karasu Kostanayskaya Oblast' Kazakh.
139 H1 Karasu r. Kazakh.
136 C1 Karasu Turkey
137 I2 Karasu r. Turkey
139 I1 Karasuk Russia
139 H4 Kara-Suu Kyrg.
139 K3 Karatal Kazakh.
136 E3 Karataş Turkey
136 E3 Karataş Burun pt Turkey
139 G4 Karatau Kazakh.
139 F3 Karatau, Khrebet mts Kazakh.
144 E2 Karatax Shan mts China
154 A3 Karathuri Myanmar
138 C2 Karatobe Kazakh.
138 D3 Karatobe, Mys pt Kazakh.
138 D2 Karatogay Kazakh.
139 I3 Karatol r. Kazakh.
138 E1 Karatomarskoye Vodokhranilishche resr Kazakh.
138 C3 Karaton Kazakh.
145 G4 Karatoya r. Bangl.
151 A8 Karatsu Japan
153 C5 Karatung i. Indon.
138 F2 Kara-Turgay r. Kazakh.
Karaulbazar Uzbek. see Qorovulbozor
144 D4 Karauli India
137 I1 Karaurgan Turkey
138 C2 Karauylkel'dy Kazakh.
155 C4 Karawang Indon.
139 K3 Kara Yertis r. Kazakh.
139 J4 Karayulgun China
139 G2 Karazhal Kazakh.
138 B3 Karazhambas Kazakh.
Karazhar Uzbek. see Qorajar
139 H3 Karazhingil (abandoned) Kazakh.
137 J5 Karbalā' Iraq
165 G4 Karben Germany
140 C3 Karbūsh, Kūh-e mt. Iran
169 J7 Karcag Hungary
164 F4 Karden Germany
171 I5 Karditsa Greece
159 M4 Kärdla Estonia
171 K4 Kardzhali Bulg.
181 G4 Karee S. Africa
180 D5 Kareeberge mts S. Africa
177 F3 Kareima Sudan
173 G7 Kareli Georgia
144 D5 Kareli India
172 E2 Kareliya, Respublika aut. rep. Russia
146 D1 Karenga r. Russia
144 D4 Karera India
158 M1 Karesuando Sweden
141 F5 Kārevāndar Iran
141 F3 Kārēz Afgh.
141 F3 Kārēz Ilyās Afgh.
173 H7 Kargalinskaya Russia
138 D2 Kargaly Aktyubinskaya Oblast' Kazakh.
139 H2 Kargaly Karagandinskaya Oblast' Kazakh.
139 J2 Kargaly Vostochnyy Kazakhstan Kazakh.
137 H2 Kargapazarı Dağları mts Turkey
136 E1 Kargı Turkey
144 D2 Kargil India
172 F2 Kargopol' Russia
140 E5 Kargūshkī Iran
179 C5 Kariba Zimbabwe
179 C5 Kariba, Lake resr Zambia/Zimbabwe
150 F3 Kariba-yama vol. Japan
180 E6 Kariega r. S. Africa
158 N1 Karigasniemi Fin.
159 M3 Karijoki Fin.
128 D1 Karikari, Cape N.Z.
140 D3 Karīmābād Iran
155 C3 Karimata, Pulau-pulau is Indon.
155 C3 Karimata, Selat str. Indon.
143 B2 Karimnagar India
155 D4 Karimunjawa, Pulau-pulau is Indon.
178 E2 Karin Somalia
143 A2 Karjat India
145 F5 Karkai r. India
143 A3 Karkal India
153 C5 Karkaralong, Kepulauan is Indon.
139 H2 Karkaraly Kazakh.
124 E2 Karkar Island P.N.G.
140 C4 Karkheh, Rūdkhāneh-ye r. Iran
173 E6 Karkinits'ka Zatoka g. Crimea
159 N3 Kärkölä Fin.
159 N4 Karksi-Nuia Estonia
Kar Lake l. India see Tsokar Chumo
159 L3 Karlholmsbruk Sweden
137 H2 Karlıova Turkey
173 E5 Karlivka Ukr.
Karl-Marx-Stadt Germany see Chemnitz
170 F2 Karlovac Croatia
171 K3 Karlovo Bulg.
168 F5 Karlovy Vary Czech Rep.
165 G6 Karlsbad Germany
159 K4 Karlsborg Sweden
159 K4 Karlshamn Sweden
159 K4 Karlskoga Sweden
159 K4 Karlskrona Sweden
165 G5 Karlsruhe Germany
159 K4 Karlstad Sweden
198 D1 Karlstad U.S.A.
165 H5 Karlstadt Germany
172 D4 Karma Belarus
143 A2 Karmala India
Karmanovka Kazakh. see Kyrkopa
159 I4 Karmøy i. Norway
144 D3 Karnal India
145 E3 Karnali r. Nepal
145 H5 Karnaphuli Reservoir Bangl.
143 A3 Karnataka state India
171 L3 Karnobat Bulg.
141 G5 Karodi Pak.
179 C5 Karoi Zimbabwe
145 G3 Karo La pass China
145 H4 Karong India
179 D4 Karonga Malawi
139 I4 Karool-Döbö Kyrg.
180 E6 Karoo National Park S. Africa
126 C5 Karoonda Australia
144 B3 Karor Pak.
178 D2 Karora Eritrea
165 K1 Karow Germany
171 L7 Karpathos i. Greece
171 L6 Karpathou, Steno sea chan. Greece
171 I5 Karpenisi Greece
172 H1 Karpogory Russia
124 B4 Karratha Australia
140 C4 Karrī Iran
137 I1 Kars Turkey
158 N3 Kärsämäki Fin.
159 N4 Kārsava Latvia
Karshi Turkm. see Garşy
Karshi Uzbek. see Qarshi
145 G4 Karsiyang India
132 G3 Karskiye Vorota, Proliv str. Russia
Karskoye More sea Russia see Kara Sea
165 J1 Karstädt Germany
158 N3 Karstula Fin.
136 B1 Kartal Turkey
138 E1 Kartaly Russia
158 N3 Karttula Fin.
141 F3 Karukh Afgh.
140 C4 Kārūn, Kūh-e h. Iran
140 C4 Kārūn, Rūd-e r. Iran
143 B4 Karur India
159 M3 Karvia Fin.
159 M3 Karvianjoki r. Fin.
143 A3 Karwar India
171 K4 Karyes Greece
146 D1 Karymskoye Russia
138 C4 Karynzharyk, Peski des. Kazakh.
171 K5 Karystos Greece
136 B3 Kaş Turkey
188 C3 Kasabonika Canada
188 C3 Kasabonika Lake Canada
141 F3 Kāsah Murgh mts Afgh.
178 B4 Kasaï r. Dem. Rep. Congo
179 C5 Kasaji Dem. Rep. Congo
179 D5 Kasama Zambia
Kasan Uzbek. see Koson
179 C5 Kasane Botswana
178 B4 Kasangulu Dem. Rep. Congo
Kasansay Uzbek. see Kosonsoy
143 A3 Kasaragod India
187 I2 Kasba Lake Canada
176 B1 Kasba Tadla Morocco
137 K4 Kāseh Garān Iran
179 C5 Kasempa Zambia
179 C5 Kasenga Dem. Rep. Congo
178 C4 Kasese Dem. Rep. Congo
178 D3 Kasese Uganda
144 D4 Kasganj India
140 C3 Kāshān Iran
188 D3 Kashechewan Canada
Kashgar China see Kashi
139 I5 Kashi China
151 D7 Kashihara Japan
151 B8 Kashima Japan
151 G6 Kashima-nada b. Japan
172 F3 Kashin Russia
144 D3 Kashipur India
151 F6 Kashiwazaki Japan
137 K5 Kashkan r. Iran
139 H3 Kashkanteniz Kazakh.
140 D4 Kashkū'īyeh Iran
141 E3 Kāshmar Iran
144 C2 Kashmir reg. Asia
144 C2 Kashmir, Vale of reg. India
144 B3 Kashmore Pak.
141 H3 Kashmund Ghar reg. Afgh.
139 I1 Kashyr Kazakh.
178 C4 Kashyukulu Dem. Rep. Congo
172 G4 Kasimov Russia
200 B4 Kaskaskia r. U.S.A.
187 K3 Kaskattama r. Canada
139 I4 Kaskelen Kazakh.
159 M3 Kaskinen Fin.
178 C4 Kasongo Dem. Rep. Congo
178 B4 Kasongo-Lunda Dem. Rep. Congo
171 L7 Kasos i. Greece
171 L7 Kasou, Steno sea chan. Greece
173 H7 K'asp'i Georgia
173 H7 Kaspiysk Russia
169 O3 Kasplya Russia
177 F3 Kassala Sudan
171 J4 Kassandras, Chersonisos pen. Greece
171 J4 Kassandras, Kolpos b. Greece
165 H3 Kassel Germany
176 C1 Kasserine Tunisia
190 A3 Kasson U.S.A.
136 D1 Kastamonu Turkey
164 F4 Kastellaun Germany
171 J7 Kastellia Greece
164 C3 Kasterlee Belgium
171 I4 Kastoria Greece
172 E4 Kastsyukovichy Belarus
151 E7 Kasugai Japan
178 D4 Kasulu Tanz.
151 G6 Kasumiga-ura l. Japan
173 I7 Kasumkent Russia
179 D5 Kasungu Malawi
144 C3 Kasur Pak.
203 I2 Katahdin, Mount U.S.A.
141 G3 Katah Sang Srah Afgh.
144 D2 Kataklik India
178 C4 Katako-Kombe Dem. Rep. Congo
144 D5 Katangi India
124 B5 Katanning Australia
178 C4 Katea Dem. Rep. Congo
171 J4 Katerini Greece
186 C3 Kate's Needle mt. Canada/U.S.A.
179 D5 Katete Zambia
143 C1 Katghora India
146 B4 Katha Myanmar
124 D3 Katherine r. Australia
144 B5 Kathiawar pen. India
143 C4 Kathiraveli Sri Lanka
145 F4 Kathmandu Nepal
180 E3 Kathu S. Africa
144 C2 Kathua India
176 B3 Kati Mali
145 F4 Katihar India
128 E2 Katikati N.Z.
181 G6 Katikati S. Africa
179 C5 Katima Mulilo Namibia
176 B4 Katiola Côte d'Ivoire
126 B2 Kati Thanda-Lake Eyre (North) salt flat Australia
126 B2 Kati Thanda-Lake Eyre (South) salt flat Australia
126 B2 Kati Thanda-Lake Eyre National Park Australia
180 D4 Katkop Hills S. Africa
181 H3 Katlehong S. Africa
144 E5 Katni India
171 I5 Kato Achaïa Greece
144 D5 Katol India
154 □ Katong Sing.
139 K2 Katonkaragay Kazakh.
127 I4 Katoomba Australia
169 I5 Katowice Poland
145 G5 Katoya India
162 D4 Katrine, Loch l. U.K.
159 L4 Katrineholm Sweden
176 C3 Katsina Nigeria
176 C4 Katsina-Ala Nigeria
151 G7 Katsuura Japan
151 E6 Katsuyama Japan
189 G2 Kattaktoc, Cap c. Canada
Kattakurgan Uzbek. see Kattaqo'rg'on
138 F5 Kattaqo'rg'on Uzbek.
159 J4 Kattegat str. Denmark/Sweden
139 K1 Katun' r. Russia
144 B3 Katuri Pak.
164 C2 Katwijk aan Zee Neth.
165 H5 Katzenbuckel h. Germany
196 □2 Kaua'i i. U.S.A.
196 □2 Kaua'i Channel U.S.A.
165 F4 Kaub Germany
165 H3 Kaufungen Germany
159 M3 Kauhajoki Fin.
158 M3 Kauhava Fin.
158 N2 Kaukonen Fin.
196 □2 Ka'ula i. U.S.A.
196 □2 Kaulakahi Channel U.S.A.
189 H2 Kaumajet Mountains Canada
196 □2 Kaunakakai U.S.A.
159 M5 Kaunas Lith.
159 N4 Kaunata Latvia
138 C4 Kaundy, Vpadina depr. Kazakh.
176 C3 Kaura-Namoda Nigeria
149 □ Kau Sai Chau i. Hong Kong China
158 M3 Kaustinen Fin.
158 M1 Kautokeino Norway
154 A3 Kau-ye Kyun i. Myanmar
171 J4 Kavadarci Macedonia
136 F1 Kavak Turkey
171 K4 Kavala Greece
150 D2 Kavalerovo Russia
143 C3 Kavali India
179 C5 Kavango Zambezi Transfrontier Conservation Area nat. park Africa
140 D4 Kavār Iran
143 A4 Kavaratti atoll India
171 M3 Kavarna Bulg.
143 B4 Kaveri r. India
140 E3 Kavīr, Chāh-e well Iran
140 D3 Kavīr, Dasht-e des. Iran
151 F7 Kawagoe Japan
151 F7 Kawaguchi Japan
196 □2 Kawaihae U.S.A.
128 E1 Kawakawa N.Z.
179 C4 Kawambwa Zambia
190 H3 Kawartha Highlands Signature Site res. Canada
188 E5 Kawartha Lakes Canada
151 F7 Kawasaki Japan
128 E2 Kawau Island N.Z.
189 G2 Kawawachikamach Canada
128 F3 Kawerau N.Z.
128 E3 Kawhia N.Z.
128 E3 Kawhia Harbour N.Z.
196 D3 Kawich Range mts U.S.A.
154 A1 Kawkareik Myanmar
154 A1 Kawludo Myanmar
140 E6 Kawr, Jabal mt. Oman
154 A3 Kawthaung Myanmar
139 I5 Kaxgar He r. China
139 J4 Kax He r. China
144 D1 Kaxtexi China
176 B3 Kaya Burkina Faso
136 F2 Kayadibi Turkey
155 E2 Kayan r. Indon.
143 B4 Kayankulam India
155 E2 Kayan Mentarang, Taman Nasional nat. park Indon.
178 C4 Kayanza Burundi
194 F3 Kaycee U.S.A.
138 C3 Kaydak, Sor dry lake Kazakh.
179 C4 Kayembe-Mukulu Dem. Rep. Congo
197 G3 Kayenta U.S.A.
176 A3 Kayes Mali
138 F2 Kayga Kazakh.
176 A4 Kayima Sierra Leone
139 H1 Kaymanachikha Kazakh.
139 I2 Kaynar Vostochnyy Kazakhstan Kazakh.
139 H4 Kaynar Zhambylskaya Oblast' Kazakh.
136 F2 Kaynar Turkey
136 F3 Kaypak Turkey
173 H5 Kaysatskoye Russia
136 E2 Kayseri Turkey
143 B4 Kayts Island Sri Lanka
155 B3 Kayuagung Indon.
132 J3 Kayyerkan Russia
138 B2 Kayyndy Kazakh.
139 H4 Kayyngdy Kyrg.
133 O2 Kazach'ye Russia
Kazakhdar'ya Uzbek. see Qozoqdaryo
138 C4 Kazakhskiy Zaliv b. Kazakh.
138 D3 Kazakhstan country Asia
138 E3 Kazaly Kazakh.
187 J2 Kazan r. Canada
172 I4 Kazan' Russia
136 D3 Kazancı Turkey
172 I4 Kazanka r. Russia
171 K3 Kazanlak Bulg.
Kazan-rettō is Japan see Volcano Islands
173 G5 Kazanskaya Russia
139 H4 Kazarman Kyrg.
138 D2 Kazatskiy Kazakh.
173 H7 Kazbek mt. Georgia/Russia
171 L5 Kaz Dağı mts Turkey
140 C4 Kāzerūn Iran
141 F5 Kazhmak r. Pak.
172 I2 Kazhym Russia
169 J6 Kazincbarcika Hungary
145 H4 Kaziranga National Park India
173 H7 K'azreti Georgia
138 B2 Kaztalovka Kazakh.
150 G4 Kazuno Japan
139 G4 Kazygurt Kazakh.
132 H3 Kazym-Mys Russia
163 E3 Keady U.K.
196 □2 Kealakekua Bay U.S.A.
197 G4 Keams Canyon U.S.A.
198 D3 Kearney U.S.A.
197 G5 Kearny U.S.A.
136 G2 Keban Turkey
136 G2 Keban Barajı resr Turkey
176 A3 Kébémèr Senegal
136 F4 Kebīr, Nahr al r. Lebanon/Syria
177 E3 Kebkabiya Sudan
158 L2 Kebnekaise mt. Sweden
162 B2 Kebock Head U.K.
178 E3 K'ebrī Dehar Eth.
155 C4 Kebumen Indon.
186 D3 Kechika r. Canada
136 C3 Keçiborlu Turkey
169 I7 Kecskemét Hungary
137 H1 Keda Georgia
159 M5 Kdainiai Lith.
144 D3 Kedar Kantha mt. India
144 D3 Kedarnath Peak India
189 G4 Kedgwick Canada
155 D4 Kediri Indon.
176 A3 Kédougou Senegal
186 D2 Keele r. Canada
186 C2 Keele Peak Canada
195 C4 Keeler U.S.A.
Keeling Islands terr. Indian Ocean see Cocos (Keeling) Islands
Keelung Taiwan see Jilong
162 F4 Keen, Mount h. U.K.
153 A5 Keenapusan i. Phil.
203 G3 Keene U.S.A.
127 I3 Keepit, Lake resr Australia
164 C3 Keerbergen Belgium
179 B6 Keetmanshoop Namibia
187 K6 Keewatin Canada
187 K5 Keewatin U.S.A.
Kefallonia i. Greece see Cephalonia
147 E7 Kefamenanu Indon.
158 B2 Keflavík Iceland
143 C5 Kegalla Sri Lanka
139 I4 Kegen Kazakh.
138 D4 Kegeyli Uzbek.
189 G2 Keglo, Baie de b. Canada
173 H6 Kegul'ta Russia
159 N4 Kehra Estonia
160 F4 Keighley U.K.
159 N4 Keila Estonia
180 D4 Keimoes S. Africa
158 N3 Keitele Fin.
158 N3 Keitele l. Fin.
126 D6 Keith Australia
162 F3 Keith U.K.
186 E1 Keith Arm b. Canada
189 G5 Kejimkujik National Park Canada
196 □2 Kekaha U.S.A.
169 J7 Kékes mt. Hungary
144 C4 Kekri India
135 F6 Kelaa i. Maldives
148 D2 Kelan China
Kelang Malaysia see Klang
154 B4 Kelantan r. Malaysia
164 E4 Kelberg Germany
139 J3 Kel'demurat Kazakh.
139 G4 Keles Uzbek.
165 J6 Kelheim Germany
170 D6 Kelibia Tunisia
138 F5 Kelif Turkm.
Kelifskiy Uzboy marsh Turkm. see Kelif Uzboýy
138 E5 Kelif Uzboýy marsh Turkm.
165 G4 Kelkheim (Taunus) Germany
137 G1 Kelkit Turkey
136 F1 Kelkit r. Turkey
186 E2 Keller Lake Canada
139 G1 Kellerovka Kazakh.
202 B4 Kelleys Island U.S.A.
194 C2 Kellogg U.S.A.
158 O2 Kelloselkä Fin.
163 E4 Kells Ireland
159 M5 Kelm Lith.
164 E4 Kelmis Belgium
177 D4 Kélo Chad
186 F5 Kelowna Canada
196 A2 Kelseyville U.S.A.
162 F5 Kelso U.K.
194 B2 Kelso U.S.A.
197 E4 Kelso (abandoned) U.S.A.
155 B2 Keluang Malaysia
187 I4 Kelvington Canada
172 E1 Kem' Russia
172 E1 Kem' r. Russia
137 G2 Kemah Turkey
136 G2 Kemaliye Turkey
171 L5 Kemalpaşa Turkey
186 D4 Kemano (abandoned) Canada
136 C3 Kemer Antalya Turkey
136 B3 Kemer Muğla Turkey
136 B3 Kemer Barajı resr Turkey
146 A1 Kemerovo Russia
158 N2 Kemi Fin.
158 N2 Kemijärvi Fin.
158 N2 Kemijärvi l. Fin.
158 O2 Kemijoki r. Fin.
139 H4 Kemin Kyrg.
194 E3 Kemmerer U.S.A.
165 J5 Kemnath Germany
162 F3 Kemnay U.K.
199 D5 Kemp, Lake U.S.A.
158 N2 Kempele Fin.
164 C3 Kempen reg. Belgium
164 E3 Kempen Germany
129 D5 Kemp Land pen. Antarctica
129 C3 Kemp Peninsula pen. Antarctica
201 E7 Kemp's Bay Bahamas
127 J3 Kempsey Australia
188 F4 Kempt, Lac l. Canada
168 E7 Kempten (Allgäu) Germany
127 G9 Kempton Australia
181 H3 Kempton Park S. Africa
191 J3 Kemptville Canada
155 D4 Kemujan i. Indon.
144 E4 Ken r. India
184 C3 Kenai U.S.A.
184 C4 Kenai Mountains U.S.A.
160 E3 Kendal U.K.
127 J3 Kendall Australia
187 L2 Kendall, Cape Canada
190 E5 Kendallville U.S.A.
155 C4 Kendang, Gunung vol. Indon.
147 E7 Kendari Indon.
155 D3 Kendawangan Indon.
177 D3 Kendégué Chad
138 C4 Kendirli-Kiyasan, Plato plat. Kazakh.
145 F5 Kendrapara India
194 C2 Kendrick U.S.A.
197 G4 Kendrick Peak U.S.A.
139 H4 Kendyktas mts Kazakh.
138 C4 Kendyrlisor, Solonchak salt l. Kazakh.
127 H3 Kenebri Australia
199 D6 Kenedy U.S.A.
176 A4 Kenema Sierra Leone
Keneurgench Turkm. see Köneürgenç
178 B4 Kenge Dem. Rep. Congo
138 D4 Keng-Peli Uzbek.
147 B4 Kengtung Myanmar
180 D4 Kenhardt S. Africa
176 A3 Kéniéba Mali
176 B1 Kenitra Morocco
148 F2 Kenli China
163 B6 Kenmare Ireland
198 C1 Kenmare U.S.A.
163 A6 Kenmare River inlet Ireland
164 E5 Kenn Germany
195 G5 Kenna U.S.A.
203 I2 Kennebec r. U.S.A.
203 H3 Kennebunk U.S.A.
203 H3 Kennebunkport U.S.A.
199 F6 Kenner U.S.A.
161 F6 Kennet r. U.K.
199 F4 Kennett U.S.A.
194 C2 Kennewick U.S.A.
191 G1 Kenogami Lake Canada
191 G1 Kenogamissi Lake Canada
186 B2 Keno Hill Canada
187 K5 Kenora Canada
190 D4 Kenosha U.S.A.
172 F2 Kenozero, Ozero l. Russia
160 E3 Kent r. U.K.
203 G4 Kent CT U.S.A.
199 B6 Kent TX U.S.A.
194 B2 Kent WA U.S.A.
139 G4 Kentau Kazakh.
127 G7 Kent Group is Australia
190 D5 Kentland U.S.A.
202 B4 Kenton U.S.A.
193 J4 Kentucky r. U.S.A.
202 A6 Kentucky state U.S.A.
201 B4 Kentucky Lake U.S.A.
189 H4 Kentville Canada
199 F6 Kentwood LA U.S.A.
190 E4 Kentwood MI U.S.A.
178 D3 Kenya country Africa
178 D3 Kenya, Mount Kenya
190 A3 Kenyon U.S.A.
139 G2 Kenzharyk Kazakh.
196 □2 Kēōkea U.S.A.
190 B5 Keokuk U.S.A.
144 D4 Keoladeo National Park India
Keo Neua Pass pass Laos/Vietnam see Keo Nưa, Đeo
154 C1 Keo Nưa, Đeo pass Laos/Vietnam
190 B5 Keosauqua U.S.A.
124 F4 Keppel Bay Australia
154 □ Keppel Harbour sea chan. Sing.
136 B2 Kepsut Turkey
141 E4 Kerāh Iran
143 A4 Kerala state India
176 C4 Kéran, Parc National de la nat. park Togo
126 E5 Kerang Australia
159 N3 Kerava Fin.
167 G4 Kerba Alg.
139 G4 Kerben Kyrg.
173 F6 Kerch Crimea
124 E2 Kerema P.N.G.
186 F5 Keremeos Canada
173 E7 Kerempe Burun pt Turkey
178 D2 Keren Eritrea
140 B3 Kerend-e Gharb Iran
Kerepakupai Merú Venez. see Angel Falls
139 G2 Kerey watercourse Kazakh.
139 G2 Kerey, Ozero salt l. Kazakh.
138 D5 Kergeli Turkm.
218 I8 Kerguelen, Îles is Indian Ocean
218 I8 Kerguelen Plateau sea feature Indian Ocean
178 D4 Kericho Kenya
128 D1 Kerikeri N.Z.
159 O3 Kerimäki Fin.
141 E3 Kerīmonj Iran
155 B3 Kerinci, Gunung vol. Indon.
155 B3 Kerinci Seblat, Taman Nasional Indon.
139 J5 Keriya He watercourse China
145 E2 Keriya Shankou pass China
164 E3 Kerken Germany
Kerki Turkm. see Atamyrat
Kerkichi Turkm. see Kerkiçi
138 F5 Kerkiçi Turkm.
171 J4 Kerkini, Limni l. Greece
171 H5 Kerkyra Greece
Kerkyra i. Greece see Corfu
177 F3 Kerma Sudan
123 H5 Kermadec Islands S. Pacific Ocean
216 H8 Kermadec Trench sea feature S. Pacific Ocean
140 E4 Kermān Iran
196 B3 Kerman U.S.A.
141 E4 Kermān, Bīābān-e des. Iran
Kermān Desert Iran see Kermān, Bīābān-e
140 B3 Kermānshāh Kermānshāh Iran
140 D4 Kermānshāh Yazd Iran
199 C6 Kermit U.S.A.
195 C5 Kern r. U.S.A.
196 C4 Kern, South Fork r. U.S.A.
189 G2 Kernertut, Cap c. Canada
196 C4 Kernville U.S.A.
172 J2 Keros Russia
171 K6 Keross i. Greece
176 B4 Kérouané Guinea
164 E4 Kerpen Germany
129 B5 Kerr, Cape c. Antarctica
187 H4 Kerrobert Canada
199 D6 Kerrville U.S.A.
163 B5 Kerry Head Ireland
154 B4 Kerteh Malaysia
159 J5 Kerteminde Denmark
Keryneia Cyprus see Kyrenia
172 H3 Kerzhenets r. Russia
188 D3 Kesagami Lake Canada
159 O3 Kesälahti Fin.
173 C7 Keşan Turkey
136 G1 Keşap Turkey
150 G5 Kesennuma Japan
144 B5 Keshod India
137 L5 Keshvar Iran
136 D2 Keskin Turkey
172 E2 Keskozero Russia
164 E3 Kessel Neth.
181 H4 Kestell S. Africa
158 O2 Kesten'ga Russia
158 N2 Kestilä Fin.
191 H3 Keswick Canada
160 D3 Keswick U.K.
168 H7 Keszthely Hungary
132 J4 Ket' r. Russia
176 C4 Keta Ghana
154 □ Ketam, Pulau i. Sing.
155 D3 Ketapang Indon.
186 C3 Ketchikan U.S.A.
164 D2 Ketelmeer l. Neth.
141 G5 Keti Bandar Pak.
139 J4 Ketmen', Khrebet mts China/Kazakh.
161 G5 Kettering U.K.
202 A5 Kettering U.S.A.
186 F5 Kettle r. Canada
190 A2 Kettle r. U.S.A.
202 E4 Kettle Creek r. U.S.A.
196 C3 Kettleman City U.S.A.
194 C1 Kettle River Range mts U.S.A.
202 E3 Keuka Lake U.S.A.
159 N3 Keuruu Fin.
190 C5 Kewanee U.S.A.
190 D3 Kewaunee U.S.A.
190 C2 Keweenaw Bay U.S.A.
190 C2 Keweenaw Peninsula U.S.A.
190 D2 Keweenaw Point U.S.A.
213 E3 Keweigek Guyana
163 C3 Key, Lough l. Ireland
188 F3 Keyano Canada
191 G3 Key Harbour Canada
139 J4 Keyi China
201 D7 Key Largo U.S.A.
161 E6 Keynsham U.K.
202 D5 Keyser U.S.A.
202 D5 Keysers Ridge U.S.A.
197 G6 Keystone Peak U.S.A.
202 D6 Keysville U.S.A.
137 L4 Keytū Iran
201 D7 Key West FL U.S.A.
190 B4 Key West IA U.S.A.
203 H3 Kezar Falls U.S.A.
179 C6 Kezi Zimbabwe
169 J6 Kežmarok Slovakia
180 D2 Kgalagadi admin. dist. Botswana
180 D2 Kgalagadi Transfrontier Park nat. park Botswana/S. Africa
181 G2 Kgatleng admin. dist. Botswana
180 D1 Kgomofatshe Pan salt pan Botswana
180 F2 Kgoro Pan salt pan Botswana
181 G3 Kgotsong S. Africa
146 F2 Khabarovsk Russia
139 I1 Khabary Russia
137 H4 Khābūr, Nahr al r. Syria
137 I7 Khadd, Wādī al watercourse Saudi Arabia
141 G3 Khadīr Afgh.
140 B6 Khafs Daghrah Saudi Arabia
144 E4 Khaga India
145 G5 Khagrachari Bangl.
144 B3 Khairgarh Pak.
144 B4 Khairpur Pak.
144 D4 Khajuraho India
179 C6 Khakhea Botswana
141 G4 Khākrēz Afgh.
141 G4 Khākrēz reg. Afgh.
Khalach Turkm. see Halaç
140 C3 Khalajestan reg. Iran
144 D2 Khalatse India
137 L3 Khāleh Sarāy Iran
144 A3 Khalifat mt. Pak.
141 E3 Khalīlābād Iran
Khalkabad Uzbek. see Xalqobod
140 C2 Khalkhāl Iran
143 D2 Khallikot India
172 D4 Khalopyenichy Belarus
146 C1 Khamar-Daban, Khrebet mts Russia
144 C5 Khambhat India
144 B5 Khambhat, Gulf of India
144 D5 Khamgaon India
154 C1 Khamkeut Laos
140 B5 Khamma well Saudi Arabia
143 C2 Khammam India
133 M3 Khamra Russia
140 C3 Khamseh reg. Iran
Khamza Uzbek. see Hamza
154 B1 Khan, Nâm r. Laos
141 H2 Khānābād Afgh.
Khanabad Uzbek. see Xonobod
137 I5 Khān al Baghdādī Iraq
137 J5 Khān al Maḩāwīl Iraq
137 J5 Khān al Mashāhidah Iraq
137 J5 Khān al Muşallá Iraq
143 A3 Khanapur India
140 B2 Khānaqāh Iran
137 J4 Khānaqīn Iraq
137 J6 Khān ar Raḩbah Iraq
137 J2 Khanasur Pass Iran/Turkey
136 F6 Khān az Zabīb tourist site Jordan
144 C2 Khanbari Pass Pak.
127 H6 Khancoban Australia
144 B2 Khand Pass Afgh./Pak.
139 H5 Khandūd Afgh.
144 D5 Khandwa India
133 O3 Khandyga Russia
144 B3 Khanewal Pak.
144 D4 Khaniadhana India
140 D4 Khānī Yek Iran
137 J5 Khān Jadwal Iraq
150 C2 Khanka, Lake China/Russia
144 C2 Khanki Weir Pak.
144 D3 Khanna India
138 A2 Khan Ordasy Kazakh.
144 B3 Khanpur Balochistan Pak.
144 B3 Khanpur Punjab Pak.
136 F4 Khān Shaykhūn Syria
139 H3 Khantau Kazakh.
132 K3 Khantayskoye, Ozero l. Russia
139 J4 Khan-Tengri, Pik mt. Kyrg.
132 H3 Khanty-Mansiysk Russia
136 E6 Khān Yūnus Gaza
154 A3 Khao Chum Thong Thai.
144 D5 Khapa India
173 H6 Kharabali Russia
145 F5 Kharagpur India
140 E2 Kharakī Iran
140 D4 Kharāmeh Iran
140 E5 Khārān r. Iran
141 G4 Kharan Pak.
140 D3 Kharānaq Iran
140 D3 Kharānaq, Kūh-e mt. Iran
144 B2 Kharbin Pass Afgh.
144 C6 Khardi India
144 D2 Khardung La pass India
137 K6 Kharfiyah Iraq
140 C4 Kharg Islands Iran
144 C5 Khargone India
144 C4 Khari r. Rajasthan India
144 C4 Khari r. Rajasthan India
144 C2 Kharian Pak.
143 C1 Khariar India
177 F2 Khārijah, Wāḩāt al oasis Egypt
173 F5 Kharkiv Ukr.
172 G3 Kharovsk Russia
140 C3 Khar Rūd r. Iran
143 C1 Kharsia India
177 F3 Khartoum Sudan
Khasardag, Gora mt. Turkm. see Hasardag
173 H7 Khasavyurt Russia
141 F4 Khāsh Iran
141 F4 Khāsh, Dasht-e Afgh.
141 F4 Khāsh Rōd Afgh.
141 F4 Khāsh Rōd r. Afgh.
173 G7 Khashuri Georgia
145 G4 Khasi Hills India
133 L2 Khatanga Russia
133 L2 Khatangskiy Zaliv b. Russia
Khatmia Pass Egypt see Khutmīyah, Mamarr al
133 S3 Khatyrka Russia
Khavast Uzbek. see Xovos
144 B5 Khavda India
141 H3 Khāwāk, Kōtal-e Afgh.
140 E5 Khawr Fakkan U.A.E.
154 A2 Khawsa Myanmar
181 F5 Khayamnandi S. Africa
145 H4 Khayang mt. India
139 G5 Khaydarken Kyrg.
180 C7 Khayelitsha S. Africa
Khazarasp Uzbek. see Hazorasp
137 I3 Khāzir, Nahr al r. Iraq
Khê Bo Vietnam see Hoa Binh
143 A2 Khed India
144 C4 Khedbrahma India
144 E3 Khela India
167 H4 Khemis Miliana Alg.
154 C1 Khemmarat Thai.
176 C1 Khenchela Alg.
176 B1 Khenifra Morocco
140 C4 Khersan r. Iran
173 E6 Kherson Ukr.
140 C4 Khesht Iran
133 K2 Kheta r. Russia
140 D4 Kheyrābād Iran
140 D2 Khezerābād Iran
141 E3 Khezrī Dasht-e Bayāz Iran
144 D4 Khilchipur India
144 B4 Khipro Pak.
136 F4 Khirbat Isrīyah Syria
141 G3 Khisrow Afgh.
144 D2 Khitai Dawan China
Khiva Uzbek. see Xiva
140 B2 Khīyāv Iran
159 O3 Khiytola Russia
154 B2 Khlong, Mae r. Thai.
173 C5 Khmel'nyts'kyy Ukr.
173 C5 Khmil'nyk Ukr.
154 C3 Khoai, Hon i. Vietnam
140 B2 Khodā Āfarīn Iran
Khodzhambaz Turkm. see Hojambaz
Khodzheyli Uzbek. see Xo'jayli
180 D2 Khokhowe Pan salt pan Botswana
144 B4 Khokhropar Pak.
172 G1 Kholmogory Russia
146 G2 Kholmsk Russia
169 P3 Kholm-Zhirkovskiy Russia
137 L3 Khomām Iran
180 B1 Khomas admin. reg. Namibia
180 A1 Khomas Highland hills Namibia

Lake Superior National Marine Conservation Area

Lūmār

Medvednica

190 D3 **Manistee** U.S.A.
190 E3 **Manistee** r. U.S.A.
190 D3 **Manistique** U.S.A.
190 E2 **Manistique Lake** U.S.A.
188 B2 **Manitoba** prov. Canada
187 J4 **Manitoba, Lake** Canada
187 H4 **Manito Lake** Canada
187 J5 **Manitou** Canada
191 G3 **Manitou, Lake** Canada
202 E3 **Manitou Beach** U.S.A.
188 B3 **Manitou Falls** Canada
190 D2 **Manitou Island** U.S.A.
200 C2 **Manitou Islands** U.S.A.
191 F3 **Manitoulin Island** Canada
191 G3 **Manitowaning** Canada
190 E1 **Manitowik Lake** Canada
190 D3 **Manitowoc** U.S.A.
191 J2 **Maniwaki** Canada
213 B3 **Manizales** Col.
179 E6 **Manja** Madag.
181 J2 **Manjacaze** Moz.
143 B4 **Manjeri** India
152 D3 **Man Jiang** r. China
137 L3 **Manjil** Iran
143 B2 **Manjra** r. India
198 E2 **Mankato** U.S.A.
181 I3 **Mankayane** Swaziland
176 B4 **Mankono** Côte d'Ivoire
143 C4 **Mankulam** Sri Lanka
181 K2 **Manlay** Mongolia
127 I4 **Manly** Australia
144 C5 **Manmad** India
155 B3 **Manna** Indon.
126 C4 **Mannahill** Australia
143 B4 **Mannar** Sri Lanka
143 B4 **Mannar, Gulf of** India/Sri Lanka
143 B3 **Manneru** r. India
165 G5 **Mannheim** Germany
163 A4 **Mannin Bay** Ireland
186 F3 **Manning** Canada
201 D5 **Manning** U.S.A.
161 I6 **Manningtree** U.K.
170 C4 **Mannu, Capo** c. Sardinia Italy
126 C5 **Mannum** Australia
214 E1 **Manoel Vitorino** Brazil
147 F7 **Manokwari** Indon.
178 C4 **Manono** Dem. Rep. Congo
154 A3 **Manoron** Myanmar
166 G5 **Manosque** France
191 H2 **Manouane, Lac** l. Canada
178 C3 **Manovo-Gounda Saint Floris, Parc National du** nat. park C.A.R.
152 D3 **Manp'o** N. Korea
125 I2 **Manra** i. Kiribati
167 G2 **Manresa** Spain
144 C3 **Mansa** India
179 C5 **Mansa** Zambia
176 A3 **Mansa Konko** Gambia
144 C2 **Mansehra** Pak.
185 K3 **Mansel Island** Canada
127 G6 **Mansfield** Australia
161 F4 **Mansfield** U.K.
199 E5 **Mansfield** LA U.S.A.
202 B4 **Mansfield** OH U.S.A.
202 E4 **Mansfield** PA U.S.A.
186 E3 **Manson Creek** Canada
137 L6 **Manşūrī** Iran
136 E3 **Mansurlu** Turkey
210 B4 **Manta** Ecuador
210 B4 **Manta, Bahía de** b. Ecuador
153 A4 **Mantalingajan, Mount** Phil.
196 B3 **Manteca** U.S.A.
213 C3 **Mantecal** Venez.
165 K5 **Mantel** Germany
201 F5 **Manteo** U.S.A.
166 E2 **Mantes-la-Jolie** France
143 B2 **Manthani** India
197 G2 **Manti** U.S.A.
214 D3 **Mantiqueira, Serra da** mts Brazil
190 E3 **Manton** U.S.A.
Mantova Italy see **Mantua**
159 N3 **Mäntsälä** Fin.
159 N3 **Mänttä** Fin.
170 D2 **Mantua** Italy
172 H3 **Manturovo** Russia
159 N3 **Mäntyharju** Fin.
158 N2 **Mäntyjärvi** Fin.
210 D6 **Manu, Parque Nacional del** nat. park Peru
217 I7 **Manuae** atoll Fr. Polynesia
Manua Islands American Samoa see **Manu'a Islands**
123 H4 **Manu'a Islands** American Samoa
197 H4 **Manuelito** U.S.A.
215 F2 **Manuel J. Cobo** Arg.
211 H5 **Manuelzinho** Brazil
147 E7 **Manui** i. Indon.
141 E5 **Manūjān** Iran
153 B4 **Manukan** Phil.
128 E2 **Manukau** N.Z.
128 E2 **Manukau Harbour** N.Z.
153 A5 **Manuk Manka** i. Phil.
126 C4 **Manunda** watercourse Australia
124 E2 **Manus Island** P.N.G.
143 B3 **Manvi** India
181 I2 **Manyakatana** S. Africa
181 F2 **Manyana** Botswana
197 H3 **Many Farms** U.S.A.
178 D4 **Manyoni** Tanz.
167 E3 **Manzanares** Spain
205 I4 **Manzanillo** Cuba
206 C4 **Manzanillo** Mex.
206 J6 **Manzanillo, Punta** pt Panama
140 C3 **Manzarīyeh** Iran
146 D2 **Manzhouli** China
136 D6 **Manzilah, Buḩayrat al** lag. Egypt
181 I3 **Manzini** Swaziland
177 D3 **Mao** Chad
167 I3 **Maó** Spain
148 C2 **Maojiachuan** China
147 F7 **Maoke, Pegunungan** mts Indon.
181 G3 **Maokeng** S. Africa
152 B3 **Maokui Shan** mt. China
152 B2 **Maolin** China
148 B2 **Maomao Shan** mt. China
149 D6 **Maoming** China
149 □ **Ma On Shan** h. Hong Kong China
179 D6 **Mapai** Moz.
144 E3 **Mapam Yumco** l. China
124 C2 **Mapane** Indon.
178 B3 **Mapé, Retenue de la** resr Cameroon
181 F5 **Maphodi** S. Africa
206 D2 **Mapimí** Mex.
206 C2 **Mapimí, Bolsón de** des. Mex.
179 D6 **Mapinhane** Moz.
213 D3 **Mapire** Venez.
190 E4 **Maple** r. U.S.A.
187 H5 **Maple Creek** Canada
216 G4 **Mapmaker Seamounts** sea feature N. Pacific Ocean
181 G4 **Mapoteng** Lesotho
211 G4 **Mapuera** r. Brazil
181 J2 **Mapulanguene** Moz.
181 H1 **Mapungubwe National Park** S. Africa
179 D6 **Maputo** Moz.
181 J2 **Maputo** prov. Moz.
181 J3 **Maputo** r. Moz.
181 G4 **Maputsoe** Lesotho
137 H6 **Maqar an Na'am** well Iraq
148 B3 **Maqu** China
Maquan He r. China see **Damqoq Zangbo**
178 B4 **Maquela do Zombo** Angola
215 C4 **Maquinchao** Arg.
215 C4 **Maquinchao** r. Arg.
190 B4 **Maquoketa** U.S.A.
190 B4 **Maquoketa** r. U.S.A.
141 G5 **Mar** r. Pak.
214 D3 **Mar, Serra do** mts Brazil
187 H1 **Mara** r. Canada
145 E5 **Mara** India
181 H1 **Mara** S. Africa
210 E4 **Maraã** Brazil
211 I5 **Marabá** Brazil
211 H3 **Maracá, Ilha de** i. Brazil
213 C2 **Maracaibo** Venez.
213 C2 **Maracaibo, Lake** inlet Venez.
214 A3 **Maracaju** Brazil
214 A3 **Maracaju, Serra de** hills Brazil
214 E1 **Maracás, Chapada de** hills Brazil
213 D2 **Maracay** Venez.
177 D2 **Marādah** Libya
176 C3 **Maradi** Niger
140 B2 **Marāgheh** Iran
214 E1 **Maragogipe** Brazil
153 B3 **Maragondon** Phil.
213 D4 **Marahuaca, Cerro** mt. Venez.
211 I4 **Marajó, Baía de** est. Brazil
211 I3 **Marajó, Ilha de** i. Brazil
137 J2 **Marakān** Iran
181 G2 **Marakele National Park** S. Africa
143 B3 **Marakkanam** India
178 D3 **Maralal** Kenya
144 C2 **Marala Weir** Pak.
137 I1 **Maralik** Armenia
124 D5 **Maralinga** Australia
125 G2 **Maramasike** i. Solomon Is
129 E2 **Marambio** research stn Antarctica
153 C5 **Marampit** i. Indon.
197 G5 **Marana** U.S.A.
140 B2 **Marand** Iran
154 B4 **Marang** Malaysia
154 A3 **Marang** Myanmar
214 C1 **Maranhão** r. Brazil
210 D4 **Marañón** r. Peru
181 K2 **Marão** Moz.
167 C2 **Marão** mt. Port.
213 D4 **Marari** r. Brazil
128 A6 **Mararoa** r. N.Z.
190 D1 **Marathon** Canada
201 D7 **Marathon** FL U.S.A.
199 C6 **Marathon** TX U.S.A.
214 E1 **Maraú** Brazil
155 D3 **Marau** Indon.
213 D4 **Marauiá** r. Brazil
140 D2 **Marāveh Tappeh** Iran
153 C4 **Marawi** Phil.
167 D4 **Marbella** Spain
124 B4 **Marble Bar** Australia
197 G3 **Marble Canyon** U.S.A.
197 G3 **Marble Canyon** gorge U.S.A.
181 H2 **Marble Hall** S. Africa
203 H3 **Marblehead** U.S.A.
187 K2 **Marble Island** Canada
165 G4 **Marburg** Germany
181 I5 **Marburg** S. Africa
202 E5 **Marburg, Lake** U.S.A.
168 H7 **Marcali** Hungary
161 H5 **March** U.K.
126 C4 **Marchant Hill** Australia
164 D4 **Marche-en-Famenne** Belgium
167 D4 **Marchena** Spain
210 □ **Marchena, Isla** i. Galapagos Is Ecuador
Mar Chiquita, Lago l. Arg. see **Mar Chiquita, Laguna**
215 D1 **Mar Chiquita, Laguna** l. Arg.
168 G6 **Marchtrenk** Austria
201 D7 **Marco** U.S.A.
164 B4 **Marcoing** France
188 E2 **Marcopeet Islands** Canada
215 D2 **Marcos Juárez** Arg.
203 G2 **Marcy, Mount** U.S.A.
144 C2 **Mardan** Pak.
215 F3 **Mar del Plata** Arg.
137 H3 **Mardin** Turkey
125 G4 **Maré** i. New Caledonia
162 C3 **Maree, Loch** l. U.K.
190 A5 **Marengo** IA U.S.A.
190 C4 **Marengo** IL U.S.A.
170 E6 **Marettimo, Isola** i. Sicily Italy
172 E3 **Marevo** Russia
199 B6 **Marfa** U.S.A.
143 A3 **Margao** India
126 B2 **Margaret** watercourse Australia
124 B5 **Margaret River** Australia
213 E2 **Margarita, Isla de** i. Venez.
150 D3 **Margaritovo** Russia
127 G9 **Margate** Australia
181 I5 **Margate** S. Africa
161 I6 **Margate** U.K.
178 C3 **Margherita Peak** mt. Dem. Rep. Congo/Uganda
Margilan Uzbek. see **Marg'ilon**
139 G4 **Marg'ilon** Uzbek.
141 F4 **Mārgō, Dasht-e** des. Afgh.
Margo, Dasht-i des. Afgh. see **Mārgō, Dasht-e**
153 B5 **Margosatubig** Phil.
164 D4 **Margraten** Neth.
190 E3 **Margrethe, Lake** U.S.A.
186 E4 **Marguerite** Canada
129 B2 **Marguerite Bay** b. Antarctica
145 G3 **Margyang** China
137 K5 **Marhaj Khalīl** Iraq
139 H4 **Marhamat** Uzbek.
137 I3 **Marhan Dāgh** h. Iraq
173 E6 **Marhanets'** Ukr.
217 I7 **Maria** atoll Fr. Polynesia
212 C2 **María Elena** Chile
215 E3 **María Ignacia** Arg.
124 D3 **Maria Island** N.T. Australia
127 H9 **Maria Island** Tas. Australia
216 E4 **Mariana Ridge** sea feature N. Pacific Ocean
216 E5 **Mariana Trench** sea feature N. Pacific Ocean
145 H4 **Mariani** India
186 F2 **Marian Lake** Canada
199 E5 **Marianna** AR U.S.A.
201 C6 **Marianna** FL U.S.A.
168 F6 **Mariánské Lázně** Czech Rep.
206 C3 **Marías, Islas** is Mex.
206 I7 **Mariato, Punta** pt Panama
128 D1 **Maria van Diemen, Cape** N.Z.
170 F1 **Maribor** Slovenia
197 F5 **Maricopa** AZ U.S.A.
196 C4 **Maricopa** CA U.S.A.
197 F5 **Maricopa Mountains** U.S.A.
177 E4 **Maridi** watercourse South Sudan
129 B4 **Marie Byrd Land** reg. Antarctica
205 L5 **Marie-Galante** i. Guadeloupe
159 L3 **Mariehamn** Fin.
214 B1 **Mariembero** r. Brazil
165 L4 **Marienberg** Germany
164 F1 **Marienhafe** Germany
179 B6 **Mariental** Namibia
159 K4 **Mariestad** Sweden
201 C5 **Marietta** GA U.S.A.
202 C5 **Marietta** OH U.S.A.
166 G5 **Marignane** France
146 G1 **Marii, Mys** pt Russia
146 A1 **Mariinsk** Russia
138 E1 **Mariinskiy** Russia
159 M5 **Marijampolė** Lith.
214 C3 **Marília** Brazil
207 D2 **Marín** Mex.
167 B1 **Marín** Spain
141 G4 **Marin** mt. Pak.
170 G5 **Marina di Gioiosa Ionica** Italy
172 D4 **Mar''ina Horka** Belarus
153 B3 **Marinduque** i. Phil.
190 D3 **Marinette** U.S.A.
214 B3 **Maringá** Brazil
167 B3 **Marinha Grande** Port.
200 B4 **Marion** IL U.S.A.
190 E5 **Marion** IN U.S.A.
203 J2 **Marion** ME U.S.A.
202 B4 **Marion** OH U.S.A.
201 E5 **Marion** SC U.S.A.
202 C6 **Marion** VA U.S.A.
201 D5 **Marion, Lake** U.S.A.
126 B5 **Marion Bay** Australia
213 D3 **Maripa** Venez.
196 C3 **Mariposa** U.S.A.
212 D2 **Mariscal José Félix Estigarribia** Para.
166 H4 **Maritime Alps** mts France/Italy
171 K3 **Maritsa** r. Bulg.
172 I3 **Mari-Turek** Russia
173 F6 **Mariupol'** Ukr.
213 E2 **Mariusa, Caño** r. Venez.
140 B3 **Marīvān** Iran
172 I3 **Mariy El, Respublika** aut. rep. Russia
178 E3 **Marka** Somalia
139 K2 **Markakol', Ozero** l. Kazakh.
143 B3 **Markapur** India
159 K4 **Markaryd** Sweden
141 H3 **Markaz-e Sayyidābād** Afgh.
191 G3 **Markdale** Canada
181 H1 **Marken** S. Africa
164 D2 **Markermeer** l. Neth.
161 G5 **Market Deeping** U.K.
161 E5 **Market Drayton** U.K.
161 G5 **Market Harborough** U.K.
163 E3 **Markethill** U.K.
160 G4 **Market Weighton** U.K.
133 M3 **Markha** r. Russia
191 H4 **Markham** Canada
Markhamet Uzbek. see **Marhamat**
139 I5 **Markit** China
173 F5 **Markivka** Ukr.
165 K3 **Markkleeberg** Germany
165 H2 **Marklohe** Germany
148 A3 **Markog Qu** r. China
165 K3 **Markranstädt** Germany
173 H5 **Marks** Russia
165 H5 **Marktheidenfeld** Germany
168 E7 **Marktoberdorf** Germany
165 K4 **Marktredwitz** Germany
190 B6 **Mark Twain Lake** U.S.A.
164 F3 **Marl** Germany
203 H3 **Marlborough** U.S.A.
161 F6 **Marlborough Downs** hills U.K.
164 B5 **Marle** France
199 D6 **Marlin** U.S.A.
202 C5 **Marlinton** U.S.A.
127 H6 **Marlo** Australia
166 E4 **Marmande** France
136 B1 **Marmara, Sea of** g. Turkey
Marmara Denizi g. Turkey see **Marmara, Sea of**
136 B2 **Marmara Gölü** l. Turkey
136 B3 **Marmaris** Turkey
198 C2 **Marmarth** U.S.A.
202 C5 **Marmet** U.S.A.
188 B4 **Marmion Lake** Canada
170 D1 **Marmolada** mt. Italy
166 F2 **Marne-la-Vallée** France
137 J1 **Marneuli** Georgia
165 J1 **Marnitz** Germany
126 E6 **Marnoo** Australia
179 E5 **Maroantsetra** Madag.
165 I4 **Maroldsweisach** Germany
179 E5 **Maromokotro** mt. Madag.
179 D5 **Marondera** Zimbabwe
211 H2 **Maroni** r. Fr. Guiana
127 J1 **Maroochydore** Australia
123 I6 **Marotiri** is Fr. Polynesia
177 D3 **Maroua** Cameroon
179 E5 **Marovoay** Madag.
137 H4 **Marqadah** Syria
181 G4 **Marquard** S. Africa
123 J5 **Marquesas Islands** Fr. Polynesia
201 D7 **Marquesas Keys** is U.S.A.
190 D2 **Marquette** U.S.A.
164 B4 **Marquion** France
Marquises, Îles is Fr. Polynesia see **Marquesas Islands**
126 E3 **Marra** Australia
127 G3 **Marra** r. Australia
177 E3 **Marra, Jebel** Sudan
181 J2 **Marracuene** Moz.
176 B1 **Marrakech** Morocco
181 K2 **Marrangua, Lagoa** l. Moz.
127 G5 **Marrar** Australia
177 F8 **Marrawah** Australia
126 C2 **Marree** Australia
199 F6 **Marrero** U.S.A.
179 D5 **Marromeu** Moz.
179 D5 **Marrupa** Moz.
177 F2 **Marsá al 'Alam** Egypt
177 D1 **Marsá al Burayqah** Libya
178 D3 **Marsabit** Kenya
170 E6 **Marsala** Sicily Italy
177 E1 **Marsá Maţrūḩ** Egypt
165 G3 **Marsberg** Germany
170 E3 **Marsciano** Italy
127 G4 **Marsden** Australia
164 C2 **Marsdiep** sea chan. Neth.
166 G5 **Marseille** France
190 C5 **Marseilles** U.S.A.
158 K2 **Marsfjället** mt. Sweden
187 H4 **Marshall** Canada
199 E5 **Marshall** AR U.S.A.
200 C4 **Marshall** IL U.S.A.
190 E4 **Marshall** MI U.S.A.
198 E2 **Marshall** MN U.S.A.
198 E4 **Marshall** MO U.S.A.
199 E5 **Marshall** TX U.S.A.
127 G7 **Marshall Bay** Australia
123 F2 **Marshall Islands** country N. Pacific Ocean
198 E3 **Marshalltown** U.S.A.
190 B3 **Marshfield** U.S.A.
201 E7 **Marsh Harbour** Bahamas
203 J1 **Mars Hill** U.S.A.
199 E6 **Marsh Island** U.S.A.
186 C2 **Marsh Lake** Canada
137 L3 **Marshūn** Iran
194 C3 **Marsing** U.S.A.
159 L4 **Märsta** Sweden
145 F4 **Marsyangdi** r. Nepal
Martaban Myanmar see **Mottama**
155 D3 **Martapura** Kalimantan Selatan Indon.
155 B3 **Martapura** Sumatera Selatan Indon.
191 H2 **Marten River** Canada
187 H4 **Martensville** Canada
207 E2 **Marte R. Gómez, Presa** resr Mex.
203 H4 **Martha's Vineyard** i. U.S.A.
168 C7 **Martigny** Switz.
169 I6 **Martin** Slovakia
198 C3 **Martin** SD U.S.A.
201 B4 **Martin** TN U.S.A.
201 C5 **Martin, Lake** U.S.A.
207 E3 **Martínez** Mex.
197 E5 **Martinez Lake** U.S.A.
205 L6 **Martinique** terr. Caribbean Sea
129 B4 **Martin Peninsula** pen. Antarctica
202 D4 **Martinsburg** PA U.S.A.
202 E5 **Martinsburg** WV U.S.A.
202 C4 **Martins Ferry** U.S.A.
202 D6 **Martinsville** U.S.A.
219 H7 **Martin Vaz, Ilhas** is S. Atlantic Ocean
138 D2 **Martok** Kazakh.
128 E4 **Marton** N.Z.
167 G2 **Martorell** Spain
167 E4 **Martos** Spain
137 J1 **Martuni** Armenia
151 C7 **Marugame** Japan
128 D5 **Maruia** r. N.Z.
211 K6 **Maruim** Brazil
173 G7 **Marukhis Ugheltekhili** pass Georgia/Russia
127 H5 **Marulan** Australia
139 K1 **Marushka** Russia
140 D4 **Marvast** Iran
166 F4 **Marvejols** France
197 G2 **Marvine, Mount** U.S.A.
187 G4 **Marwayne** Canada
141 F2 **Mary** Turkm.
125 F4 **Maryborough** Qld Australia
126 E6 **Maryborough** Vic. Australia
180 H3 **Marydale** S. Africa
172 I4 **Mar'yevka** Russia
187 H2 **Mary Frances Lake** Canada
203 E5 **Maryland** state U.S.A.
160 D3 **Maryport** U.K.
189 I3 **Mary's Harbour** Canada
189 J4 **Marystown** Canada
197 F2 **Marysvale** U.S.A.
189 G4 **Marysville** Canada
196 B2 **Marysville** CA U.S.A.
198 D4 **Marysville** KS U.S.A.
202 B4 **Marysville** OH U.S.A.
198 E3 **Maryville** MO U.S.A.
201 C5 **Maryville** TN U.S.A.
165 K2 **Marzahna** Germany
206 H6 **Masachapa** Nicaragua
136 E6 **Masada** tourist site Israel
140 D4 **Masāhūn, Kūh-e** mt. Iran
178 D4 **Masaka** Uganda
181 G5 **Masakhane** S. Africa
137 L2 **Masallı** Azer.
124 C2 **Masamba** Indon.
152 E6 **Masan** S. Korea
203 I1 **Masardis** U.S.A.
179 D5 **Masasi** Tanz.
210 F7 **Masavi** Bol.
206 H6 **Masaya** Nicaragua
153 B3 **Masbate** Phil.
153 B4 **Masbate** i. Phil.
176 C1 **Mascara** Alg.
218 H6 **Mascarene Basin** sea feature Indian Ocean
218 H6 **Mascarene Plain** sea feature Indian Ocean
218 H5 **Mascarene Ridge** sea feature Indian Ocean
203 G2 **Mascouche** Canada
181 G4 **Maseru** Lesotho
181 H4 **Mashai** Lesotho
149 C6 **Mashan** China
144 D2 **Masherbrum** mt. Pak.
141 E2 **Mashhad** Iran
144 C4 **Mashi** r. India
137 K2 **Mashīrān** Iran
181 I2 **Mashishing** S. Africa
141 F4 **Mashkel, Hamun-i-** salt flat Pak.
141 F5 **Mashkel, Rudi-i** r. Pak.
141 F4 **Mashki Chah** Pak.
141 F5 **Māshkīd, Rūdkhāneh-ye** r. Iran
158 M1 **Masi** Norway
206 B2 **Masiáca** Mex.
181 G5 **Masibambane** S. Africa
181 G4 **Masilo** S. Africa
178 D3 **Masindi** Uganda
153 A3 **Masinloc** Phil.
180 E5 **Masinyusane** S. Africa
Masīrah i. Oman see **Maşīrah, Jazīrat**
142 E5 **Maşīrah, Jazīrat** i. Oman
142 E6 **Maşīrah, Khalīj** b. Oman
137 J1 **Masis** Armenia
140 C4 **Masjed Soleymān** Iran
163 B4 **Mask, Lough** l. Ireland
136 G3 **Maskanah** Syria
164 D3 **Maskūtān** Iran
141 G4 **Maslti** Pak.
179 E5 **Masoala, Parc National** nat. park Madag.
179 F5 **Masoala, Tanjona** c. Madag.
190 E4 **Mason** MI U.S.A.
196 C2 **Mason** NV U.S.A.
199 D6 **Mason** TX U.S.A.
128 A7 **Mason Bay** N.Z.
198 E3 **Mason City** IA U.S.A.
190 C5 **Mason City** IL U.S.A.
202 D5 **Masontown** U.S.A.
Masqaţ Oman see **Muscat**
170 D2 **Massa** Italy
203 G3 **Massachusetts** state U.S.A.
203 H3 **Massachusetts Bay** U.S.A.
197 H1 **Massadona** U.S.A.
170 G4 **Massafra** Italy
177 D3 **Massakory** Chad
170 D3 **Massa Marittima** Italy
179 D6 **Massangena** Moz.
179 B4 **Massango** Angola
178 D2 **Massawa** Eritrea
203 G2 **Massawippi, Lac** l. Canada
203 F2 **Massena** U.S.A.
177 D3 **Massenya** Chad
186 C4 **Masset** Canada
191 F2 **Massey** Canada
166 F4 **Massif Central** mts France
202 C4 **Massillon** U.S.A.
179 D6 **Massinga** Moz.
179 D6 **Massingir** Moz.
181 J1 **Massingir, Barragem de** resr Moz.
181 J2 **Massintonto** r. Moz./S. Africa
191 J3 **Masson-Angers** Canada
137 L1 **Maştağa** Azer.
139 G5 **Mastchoh** Tajik.
138 B2 **Masteksay** Kazakh.
128 E4 **Masterton** N.Z.
201 E7 **Mastic Point** Bahamas
144 C1 **Mastuj** Pak.
141 G4 **Mastung** Pak.
172 C4 **Masty** Belarus
151 B7 **Masuda** Japan
137 L3 **Māsūleh** Iran
179 D6 **Masvingo** Zimbabwe
136 F4 **Maşyāf** Syria
191 G2 **Matachewan** Canada
206 C1 **Matachic** Mex.
213 D4 **Matacuni** r. Venez.
146 D2 **Matad** Mongolia
178 B4 **Matadi** Dem. Rep. Congo
206 H5 **Matagalpa** Nicaragua
188 E4 **Matagami** Canada
188 E4 **Matagami, Lac** l. Canada
199 D6 **Matagorda Island** U.S.A.
148 C2 **Mataigou** China
154 C5 **Matak** i. Indon.
139 H2 **Matak** Kazakh.
128 F2 **Matakana Island** N.Z.
179 B5 **Matala** Angola
143 C5 **Matale** Sri Lanka
176 A3 **Matam** Senegal
206 D2 **Matamoros** Coahuila Mex.
207 E2 **Matamoros** Tamaulipas Mex.
153 B4 **Matanal Point** Phil.
179 D4 **Matandu** r. Tanz.
189 G4 **Matane** Canada
144 B2 **Matanni** Pak.
205 H4 **Matanzas** Cuba
189 G4 **Matapédia** r. Canada
215 B2 **Mataquito** r. Chile
143 C5 **Matara** Sri Lanka
155 E4 **Mataram** Indon.
210 D7 **Matarani** Peru
124 D3 **Mataranka** Australia
167 H2 **Mataró** Spain
181 H5 **Matatiele** S. Africa
128 B7 **Mataura** N.Z.
128 B7 **Mataura** r. N.Z.
125 J3 **Matā'utu** Wallis and Futuna Is
213 C3 **Mataveni** r. Col.
128 F3 **Matawai** N.Z.
210 E6 **Mategua** Bol.
206 D3 **Matehuala** Mex.
179 D5 **Matemanga** Tanz.
170 G4 **Matera** Italy
170 C6 **Mateur** Tunisia
188 D4 **Matheson** Canada
199 D6 **Mathis** U.S.A.
126 F5 **Mathoura** Australia
144 D4 **Mathura** India
153 C5 **Mati** Phil.
145 G4 **Matiali** India
149 D5 **Matian** China
144 B4 **Matiari** Pak.
207 F4 **Matías Romero** Mex.
189 G3 **Matimekosh** Canada
191 F2 **Matinenda Lake** Canada
203 I3 **Matinicus Island** U.S.A.
145 G5 **Matla** r. India
181 G2 **Matlabas** S. Africa
181 G2 **Matlabas** r. S. Africa
144 B4 **Matli** Pak.
161 F4 **Matlock** U.K.
213 D3 **Mato** r. Venez.
213 D3 **Mato, Cerro** mt. Venez.
214 A1 **Mato Grosso** state Brazil
214 A1 **Mato Grosso, Planalto do** plat. Brazil
214 A3 **Mato Grosso do Sul** state Brazil
179 D6 **Matola** Maputo Moz.
181 J2 **Matola** Maputo Moz.
167 B2 **Matosinhos** Port.
142 E5 **Maţrah** Oman
180 C6 **Matroosberg** mt. S. Africa
151 C7 **Matsue** Japan
150 G4 **Matsumae** Japan
151 E6 **Matsumoto** Japan
151 E7 **Matsusaka** Japan
151 C8 **Matsuyama** Japan
188 D4 **Mattagami** r. Canada
191 H2 **Mattawa** Canada
203 I2 **Mattawamkeag** U.S.A.
168 C7 **Matterhorn** mt. Italy/Switz.
194 D3 **Matterhorn** mt. U.S.A.
123 G2 **Matthew Island** S. Pacific Ocean
213 E3 **Matthews Ridge** Guyana
205 J4 **Matthew Town** Bahamas
140 D6 **Maţţī, Sabkhat** salt pan Saudi Arabia
200 B4 **Mattoon** U.S.A.
143 C5 **Matugama** Sri Lanka
125 H3 **Matuku** i. Fiji
213 E2 **Maturín** Venez.
153 C5 **Matutuang** i. Indon.
181 G4 **Matwabeng** S. Africa
144 E4 **Mau** India
145 E4 **Mau Aimma** India
164 B4 **Maubeuge** France
166 E5 **Maubourguet** France
162 D5 **Mauchline** U.K.
219 J10 **Maud Seamount** sea feature S. Atlantic Ocean
211 G4 **Maués** Brazil
144 E4 **Mauganj** India
196 □² **Maui** i. U.S.A.
165 G6 **Maulbronn** Germany
215 B2 **Maule** admin. reg. Chile
215 B2 **Maule** r. Chile
215 B4 **Maullín** Chile
163 B3 **Maumakeogh** h. Ireland
202 B4 **Maumee** U.S.A.
202 B4 **Maumee** r. U.S.A.
191 F5 **Maumee Bay** U.S.A.
163 B4 **Maumtrasna** h. Ireland
163 B4 **Maumturk Mountains** hills Ireland
179 C5 **Maun** Botswana
196 □² **Mauna Kea** vol. U.S.A.
196 □² **Mauna Loa** vol. U.S.A.
196 □¹ **Maunalua Bay** U.S.A.
145 E4 **Maunath Bhanjan** India
181 G1 **Maunatlala** Botswana
128 E2 **Maungaturoto** N.Z.
145 H5 **Maungdaw** Myanmar
154 A2 **Maungmagan Islands** Myanmar
184 F3 **Maunoir, Lac** l. Canada
126 B5 **Maupertuis Bay** Australia
124 D4 **Maurice, Lake** salt flat Australia
164 D3 **Maurik** Neth.
176 A3 **Mauritania** country Africa
175 I6 **Mauritius** country Indian Ocean
190 B4 **Mauston** U.S.A.
213 D4 **Mavaca** r. Venez.
179 C5 **Mavinga** Angola
181 G5 **Mavuya** S. Africa
144 D3 **Mawana** India
178 B4 **Mawanga** Dem. Rep. Congo
149 D4 **Ma Wang Dui** tourist site China
154 A3 **Mawdaung Pass** Myanmar/Thai.
128 G3 **Mawhai Point** N.Z.
154 A1 **Mawlamyaing** Myanmar
129 E5 **Mawson** research stn Antarctica
129 D5 **Mawson Escarpment** esc. Antarctica
129 B6 **Mawson Peninsula** pen. Antarctica
154 A3 **Maw Taung** mt. Myanmar
198 C2 **Max** U.S.A.
207 G3 **Maxcanú** Mex.
170 C5 **Maxia, Punta** mt. Sardinia Italy
190 D5 **Maxinkuckee, Lake** U.S.A.
158 M3 **Maxmo** Fin.
191 F2 **Maxton** U.S.A.
139 J5 **Maxūt** China
196 A2 **Maxwell** U.S.A.
162 F4 **May, Isle of** i. U.K.
155 C3 **Maya** i. Indon.
146 F1 **Maya** r. Russia
205 J4 **Mayaguana** i. Bahamas
205 K5 **Mayagüez** Puerto Rico
176 C3 **Mayahi** Niger
139 H5 **Mayakovskiy, Qullai** mt. Tajik.
139 G4 **Mayakum** Kazakh.
178 B4 **Mayama** Congo
140 D2 **Mayāmey** Iran
207 G4 **Maya Mountains** Belize
149 C5 **Mayang** China
148 B3 **Mayanhe** China
150 F5 **Mayang-do** i. N. Korea
162 D5 **Maybole** U.K.
137 J4 **Maydān Sarāy** Iraq
Maydān Shahr Afgh. see **Maidān Shahr**
127 G9 **Maydena** Australia
164 F4 **Mayen** Germany
166 D2 **Mayenne** France
166 D2 **Mayenne** r. France
197 F4 **Mayer** U.S.A.
186 F4 **Mayerthorpe** Canada
128 C5 **Mayfield** N.Z.
200 B4 **Mayfield** U.S.A.
195 F5 **Mayhill** U.S.A.
152 E1 **Mayi He** r. China
139 I3 **Maykamys** Kazakh.
139 H2 **Maykayyn** Kazakh.
139 G5 **Maykhura** Tajik.
173 G6 **Maykop** Russia
139 H4 **Mayluu-Suu** Kyrg.
138 E3 **Maylybas** Kazakh.
139 K1 **Mayma** Russia
139 G4 **Maymak** Kazakh.
Maymyo Myanmar see **Pyin-U-Lwin**
146 B1 **Mayna** Russia
143 A2 **Mayni** India
191 I3 **Maynooth** Canada
186 B2 **Mayo** Canada
153 C5 **Mayo Bay** Phil.
178 B4 **Mayoko** Congo
186 B2 **Mayo Lake** Canada
153 B3 **Mayon** vol. Phil.
215 D3 **Mayor Buratovich** Arg.
128 F2 **Mayor Island** N.Z.
212 D1 **Mayor Pablo Lagerenza** Para.
179 E5 **Mayotte** terr. Africa
153 B2 **Mayraira Point** Phil.
146 E1 **Mayskiy** Russia
202 B5 **Maysville** U.S.A.
178 B4 **Mayumba** Gabon
145 E3 **Mayum La** pass China
143 B4 **Mayuram** India
191 F4 **Mayville** MI U.S.A.
198 D2 **Mayville** ND U.S.A.
202 D3 **Mayville** NY U.S.A.
190 C4 **Mayville** WI U.S.A.
198 C3 **Maywood** U.S.A.
215 D3 **Maza** Arg.
172 F3 **Maza** Russia
179 C5 **Mazabuka** Zambia
211 H4 **Mazagão** Brazil
166 F5 **Mazamet** France
144 D1 **Mazar** China
141 G3 **Mazār, Kōh-e** mt. Afgh.
170 E6 **Mazara del Vallo** Sicily Italy
141 G2 **Mazār-e Sharīf** Afgh.
213 E3 **Mazaruni** r. Guyana
206 B1 **Mazatán** Mex.
207 G5 **Mazatenango** Guat.
206 C3 **Mazatlán** Mex.
197 G4 **Mazatzal Peak** U.S.A.
140 C3 **Mazdaj** Iran
141 F2 **Mazdāvand** Iran
159 M4 **Mažeikiai** Lith.
137 G2 **Mazgirt** Turkey
140 A5 **Maẕhūr, 'Irq al** des. Saudi Arabia
159 M4 **Mazirbe** Latvia
178 D4 **Mazomora** Tanz.
169 J4 **Mazowiecka, Nizina** lowland Poland
137 L3 **Mazr'eh** Iran
137 L3 **Māzū** Iran
149 F5 **Mazu Dao** i. Taiwan
179 C6 **Mazunga** Zimbabwe
173 D4 **Mazyr** Belarus
181 I3 **Mbabane** Swaziland
176 B4 **Mbahiakro** Côte d'Ivoire
178 B3 **Mbaïki** C.A.R.
179 D4 **Mbala** Zambia
178 D3 **Mbale** Uganda
176 D4 **Mbalmayo** Cameroon
178 B4 **Mbandaka** Dem. Rep. Congo
176 C4 **Mbanga** Cameroon
178 B4 **M'banza Congo** Angola
178 D4 **Mbarara** Uganda
178 C3 **Mbari** r. C.A.R.
181 J3 **Mbaswana** S. Africa
176 D4 **Mbengwi** Cameroon
179 D4 **Mbeya** Tanz.
181 H6 **Mbhashe** r. S. Africa
179 D5 **Mbinga** Tanz.
179 D6 **Mbizi** Zimbabwe
181 I2 **Mbombela** S. Africa
178 B3 **Mbomo** Congo
176 D4 **Mbouda** Cameroon
176 A3 **Mbour** Senegal
176 A3 **Mbout** Mauritania
179 D4 **Mbozi** Tanz.
178 C4 **Mbuji-Mayi** Dem. Rep. Congo
178 D4 **Mbulu** Tanz.
178 D4 **Mbuyuni** Tanz.
203 J2 **McAdam** Canada
199 E5 **McAlester** U.S.A.
202 E4 **McAlevys Fort** U.S.A.
127 H5 **McAlister** mt. Australia
199 D7 **McAllen** U.S.A.
202 B5 **McArthur** U.S.A.
191 I3 **McArthur Mills** Canada
186 E4 **McBride** Canada
194 C2 **McCall** U.S.A.
199 C6 **McCamey** U.S.A.
194 D3 **McCammon** U.S.A.
186 C4 **McCauley Island** Canada
184 H2 **McClintock Channel** Canada
196 B3 **McClure, Lake** U.S.A.
184 F2 **McClure Strait** Canada
199 F6 **McComb** U.S.A.
198 C3 **McConaughy, Lake** U.S.A.
202 E5 **McConnellsburg** U.S.A.
202 C5 **McConnelsville** U.S.A.
198 C3 **McCook** U.S.A.
187 J4 **McCreary** Canada
197 E4 **McCullough Range** mts U.S.A.
186 D3 **McDame (abandoned)** Canada
194 C3 **McDermitt** U.S.A.
218 I8 **McDonald Islands** Indian Ocean
194 D2 **McDonald Peak** U.S.A.
126 C2 **McDonnell Creek** watercourse Australia
180 B4 **McDougall's Bay** S. Africa
197 G5 **McDowell Peak** U.S.A.
196 C4 **McFarland** U.S.A.
187 H3 **McFarlane** r. Canada
197 E2 **McGill** U.S.A.
184 C3 **McGrath** U.S.A.
186 E4 **McGregor** r. Canada
180 C6 **McGregor** S. Africa
190 A2 **McGregor** U.S.A.
191 G2 **McGregor Bay** Canada
194 D2 **McGuire, Mount** U.S.A.
179 D4 **Mchinga** Tanz.
203 G2 **McIndoe Falls** U.S.A.
198 C2 **McIntosh** U.S.A.
125 I2 **McKean** i. Kiribati
202 A6 **McKee** U.S.A.
202 D4 **McKeesport** U.S.A.
203 F3 **McKeever** U.S.A.
201 B4 **McKenzie** U.S.A.
184 C3 **McKinley, Mount** U.S.A.
199 D5 **McKinney** U.S.A.
196 C4 **McKittrick** U.S.A.
198 C2 **McLaughlin** U.S.A.
186 F3 **McLennan** Canada
186 F4 **McLeod** r. Canada
186 E3 **McLeod Lake** Canada
194 B3 **McLoughlin, Mount** U.S.A.
190 E2 **McMillan** U.S.A.
194 B2 **McMinnville** OR U.S.A.
201 C5 **McMinnville** TN U.S.A.
129 B5 **McMurdo** research stn Antarctica
197 H4 **McNary** U.S.A.
186 F4 **McNaughton Lake** Canada
197 H6 **McNeal** U.S.A.
198 D4 **McPherson** U.S.A.
127 J2 **McPherson Range** mts Australia
186 B2 **McQuesten** r. Canada
201 D5 **McRae** U.S.A.
186 E1 **McVicar Arm** b. Canada
181 G6 **Mdantsane** S. Africa
170 B6 **M'Daourouch** Alg.
154 D2 **M'Đrăk** Vietnam
154 C1 **Mê, Hon** i. Vietnam
197 E3 **Mead, Lake** resr U.S.A.
199 C4 **Meade** U.S.A.
187 H4 **Meadow Lake** Canada
187 H4 **Meadow Lake Provincial Park** Canada
197 E3 **Meadow Valley Wash** r. U.S.A.
202 C4 **Meadville** U.S.A.
191 G3 **Meaford** Canada
150 I3 **Meaken-dake** vol. Japan
162 A2 **Mealasta Island** U.K.
167 B2 **Mealhada** Port.
162 D4 **Meall a' Bhuiridh** mt. U.K.
189 I3 **Mealy Mountains** Canada
127 H1 **Meandarra** Australia
186 F3 **Meander River** Canada
153 C5 **Meares** i. Indon.
166 F2 **Meaux** France
178 B4 **Mebridege** r. Angola
142 A5 **Mecca** Saudi Arabia
203 H2 **Mechanic Falls** U.S.A.
202 B4 **Mechanicsburg** U.S.A.
190 B5 **Mechanicsville** U.S.A.
164 C3 **Mechelen** Belgium
164 D4 **Mechelen** Neth.
176 B1 **Mecheria** Alg.
164 E4 **Mechernich** Germany
136 E1 **Mecitözü** Turkey
164 F4 **Meckenheim** Germany
168 E3 **Mecklenburger Bucht** b. Germany
165 J1 **Mecklenburgische Seenplatte** reg. Germany
165 K1 **Mecklenburg-Vorpommern** land Germany
179 D5 **Mecula** Moz.
167 C2 **Meda** Port.
143 B2 **Medak** India
155 A2 **Medan** Indon.
215 D3 **Médanos** Arg.
212 C7 **Medanosa, Punta** pt Arg.
143 C4 **Medawachchiya** Sri Lanka
143 B2 **Medchal** India
203 J2 **Meddybemps Lake** U.S.A.
167 H4 **Médéa** Alg.
165 G3 **Medebach** Germany
213 B3 **Medellín** Col.
161 F4 **Meden** r. U.K.
176 D1 **Medenine** Tunisia
176 A3 **Mederdra** Mauritania
194 B3 **Medford** OR U.S.A.
190 B3 **Medford** WI U.S.A.
203 F5 **Medford Farms** U.S.A.
171 M2 **Medgidia** Romania
190 B5 **Media** U.S.A.
215 C2 **Media Luna** Arg.
169 L7 **Mediaş** Romania
194 C2 **Medical Lake** U.S.A.
194 F3 **Medicine Bow** U.S.A.
194 F3 **Medicine Bow Mountains** U.S.A.
194 F3 **Medicine Bow Peak** U.S.A.
187 G4 **Medicine Hat** Canada
199 D4 **Medicine Lodge** U.S.A.
214 E2 **Medina** Brazil
142 A5 **Medina** Saudi Arabia
202 D3 **Medina** NY U.S.A.
202 C4 **Medina** OH U.S.A.
167 E2 **Medinaceli** Spain
167 D2 **Medina del Campo** Spain
167 D2 **Medina de Rioseco** Spain
145 F5 **Medinipur** India
156 F5 **Mediterranean Sea** Africa/Europe
170 B6 **Medjerda, Monts de la** mts Alg.
138 D2 **Mednogorsk** Russia
166 D4 **Médoc** reg. France
172 H3 **Medvedevo** Russia
173 H5 **Medveditsa** r. Russia
170 F2 **Medvednica** mts Croatia

Nunavik

188 E2 **Nunavik** *reg.* U.S.A.
185 H3 **Nunavut** *admin. div.* Canada
202 E3 **Nunda** U.S.A.
127 I3 **Nundle** Australia
161 F5 **Nuneaton** U.K.
188 B3 **Nungesser Lake** Canada
184 B4 **Nunivak Island** U.S.A.
144 D2 **Nunkun** *mt.* India
133 T3 **Nunligran** Russia
167 C2 **Nuñomoral** Spain
164 D2 **Nunspeet** Neth.
170 C4 **Nuoro** *Sardinia* Italy
125 G3 **Nupani** *i.* Solomon Is
142 B4 **Nuqrah** Saudi Arabia
213 A3 **Nuquí** Col.
144 E1 **Nur** China
140 C2 **Nūr** Iran
139 H2 **Nura** Kazakh.
139 G2 **Nura** *r.* Kazakh.
140 C4 **Nūrābād** Iran
Nurata Uzbek. *see* **Nurota**
Nuratau, Khrebet *mts* Uzbek. *see* **Nurota tizmasi**
165 J5 **Nuremberg** Germany
141 H3 **Nūrestān** *reg.* Afgh.
137 I2 **Nurettin** Turkey
206 B1 **Nuri** Mex.
126 C5 **Nuriootpa** Australia
172 I4 **Nurlaty** Russia
158 O3 **Nurmes** Fin.
158 M3 **Nurmo** Fin.
Nürnberg Germany *see* **Nuremberg**
138 F4 **Nurota** Uzbek.
139 F4 **Nurota tizmasi** *mts* Uzbek.
127 G3 **Nurri, Mount** *h.* Australia
140 D2 **Nūr Rūd** *r.* Iran
145 H1 **Nur Turu** China
137 H3 **Nusaybin** Turkey
136 F4 **Nuşayrīyah, Jabal an** *mts* Syria
140 C3 **Nūshābād** Iran
141 G4 **Nushki** Pak.
189 H2 **Nutak** Canada
197 H5 **Nutrioso** U.S.A.
144 B3 **Nuttal** Pak.
220 U2 **Nuuk** Greenland
158 N2 **Nuupas** Fin.
185 M2 **Nuussuaq** Greenland
185 M2 **Nuussuaq** *pen.* Greenland
143 C5 **Nuwara Eliya** Sri Lanka
180 C5 **Nuwerus** S. Africa
180 D6 **Nuweveldberge** *mts* S. Africa
137 J4 **Nuzi** *tourist site* Iraq
181 I1 **Nwanedi Nature Reserve** S. Africa
132 H3 **Nyagan'** Russia
126 E5 **Nyah West** Australia
145 G3 **Nyainqêntanglha Feng** *mt.* China
145 G3 **Nyainqêntanglha Shan** *mts* China
145 H2 **Nyainrong** China
158 L3 **Nyåker** Sweden
177 E3 **Nyala** Sudan
Nyalam China *see* **Congdü**
179 C5 **Nyamandhlovu** Zimbabwe
172 G2 **Nyandoma** Russia
172 F2 **Nyandomskaya Vozvyshennost'** *hills* Russia
178 B4 **Nyanga** *r.* Gabon
179 D5 **Nyanga** Zimbabwe
145 G3 **Nyang Qu** *r. Xizang Zizhiqu* China
145 H3 **Nyang Qu** *r. Xizang Zizhiqu* China
144 D3 **Nyar** *r.* India
179 D5 **Nyasa, Lake** Africa
172 C4 **Nyasvizh** Belarus
159 J5 **Nyborg** Denmark
158 O1 **Nyborg** Norway
159 K4 **Nybro** Sweden
185 M1 **Nyeboe Land** *reg.* Greenland
145 G3 **Nyêmo** China
178 D4 **Nyeri** Kenya
146 B4 **Nyingchi** China
169 J7 **Nyíregyháza** Hungary
158 M3 **Nykarleby** Fin.
159 J5 **Nykøbing Falster** Denmark
159 J5 **Nykøbing Sjælland** Denmark
159 L4 **Nyköping** Sweden
158 L3 **Nyland** Sweden
Nylstroom S. Africa *see* **Modimolle**
127 G4 **Nymagee** Australia
127 J2 **Nymboida** Australia
127 J2 **Nymboida** *r.* Australia
159 L4 **Nynäshamn** Sweden
127 G3 **Nyngan** Australia
169 K4 **Nyoman** *r.* Belarus/Lith.
168 C7 **Nyon** Switz.
145 F3 **Nyonni Ri** *mt.* China
166 G4 **Nyons** France
132 G3 **Nyrob** Russia
168 H5 **Nysa** Poland
172 I2 **Nyuchpas** Russia
150 F5 **Nyūdō-zaki** *pt* Japan
178 C4 **Nyunzu** Dem. Rep. Congo
133 M3 **Nyurba** Russia
172 I2 **Nyuvchim** Russia
173 E6 **Nyzhn'ohirs'kyy** Crimea
178 D4 **Nzega** Tanz.
176 B4 **Nzérékoré** Guinea
178 B4 **N'zeto** Angola
181 I1 **Nzhelele Dam** S. Africa

O

198 C2 **Oahe, Lake** U.S.A.
196 □1 **O'ahu** *i.* U.S.A.
Oahu *i.* U.S.A. *see* **O'ahu**
126 D4 **Oakbank** Australia
197 F2 **Oak City** U.S.A.
199 E6 **Oakdale** U.S.A.
198 D2 **Oakes** U.S.A.
127 I1 **Oakey** Australia
161 G5 **Oakham** U.K.
194 B1 **Oak Harbor** U.S.A.
202 C6 **Oak Hill** U.S.A.
196 C3 **Oakhurst** U.S.A.
190 B2 **Oak Island** U.S.A.
196 A3 **Oakland** *CA* U.S.A.
202 D5 **Oakland** *MD* U.S.A.
198 D3 **Oakland** *NE* U.S.A.
194 B3 **Oakland** *OR* U.S.A.
127 G5 **Oaklands** Australia
190 D5 **Oak Lawn** U.S.A.
198 C4 **Oakley** U.S.A.
124 C4 **Oakover** *r.* Australia
194 B3 **Oakridge** U.S.A.
201 C4 **Oak Ridge** U.S.A.
126 D4 **Oakvale** Australia
191 H4 **Oakville** Canada
128 C6 **Oamaru** N.Z.
128 D5 **Oaro** N.Z.
153 B3 **Oas** Phil.
194 D3 **Oasis** U.S.A.
129 B6 **Oates Land** *reg.* Antarctica
127 G9 **Oatlands** Australia
197 E4 **Oatman** U.S.A.
207 E4 **Oaxaca** Mex.
207 E4 **Oaxaca** *state* Mex.
132 H3 **Ob'** *r.* Russia
139 J2 **Oba** *r.* Kazakh.
176 D4 **Obala** Cameroon
151 D7 **Obama** Japan
162 C4 **Oban** U.K.
150 G5 **Obanazawa** Japan
167 C1 **O Barco** Spain
188 F4 **Obatogamau, Lac** Canada
186 F4 **Obed** Canada
141 F3 **Ōbêh** Afgh.
128 B6 **Obelisk** *mt.* N.Z.
165 H4 **Oberaula** Germany
165 I3 **Oberdorla** Germany
164 E3 **Oberhausen** Germany
198 C4 **Oberlin** *KS* U.S.A.
202 B4 **Oberlin** *OH* U.S.A.
165 F5 **Obermoschel** Germany
127 H4 **Oberon** Australia
165 K5 **Oberpfälzer Wald** *mts* Germany
165 H4 **Obersinn** Germany
165 H4 **Oberthulba** Germany
165 G4 **Obertshausen** Germany
165 H3 **Oberwälder Land** *reg.* Germany
147 E7 **Obi** *i.* Indon.
211 G4 **Óbidos** Brazil
139 G5 **Obigarm** Tajik.
150 H3 **Obihiro** Japan
173 H6 **Obil'noye** Russia
213 C2 **Obispos** Venez.
146 F2 **Obluch'ye** Russia
172 F4 **Obninsk** Russia
178 C3 **Obo** C.A.R.
148 A2 **Obo** China
178 E2 **Obock** Djibouti
152 E3 **Ŏbŏk** N. Korea
178 C4 **Obokote** Dem. Rep. Congo
178 B4 **Obouya** Congo
173 F5 **Oboyan'** Russia
172 G2 **Obozerskiy** Russia
145 E4 **Obra** India
145 E4 **Obra Dam** India
206 B1 **Obregón, Presa** *resr* Mex.
171 I2 **Obrenovac** Serbia
136 D2 **Obruk** Turkey
138 B2 **Obshchiy Syrt** *hills* Russia
132 I2 **Obskaya Guba** *sea chan.* Russia
176 B4 **Obuasi** Ghana
173 D5 **Obukhiv** Ukr.
172 I2 **Ob''yachevo** Russia
201 D6 **Ocala** U.S.A.
213 D4 **Ocamo** *r.* Venez.
206 D2 **Ocampo** Mex.
213 B2 **Ocaña** Col.
167 E3 **Ocaña** Spain
210 E7 **Occidental, Cordillera** *mts* Chile
213 A4 **Occidental, Cordillera** *mts* Col.
210 C6 **Occidental, Cordillera** *mts* Peru
186 B3 **Ocean Cape** U.S.A.
203 F5 **Ocean City** *MD* U.S.A.
203 F5 **Ocean City** *NJ* U.S.A.
186 D4 **Ocean Falls** Canada
196 D5 **Oceanside** U.S.A.
199 F6 **Ocean Springs** U.S.A.
173 D6 **Ochakiv** Ukr.
173 G7 **Ochamchire** Georgia
162 E4 **Ochil Hills** U.K.
144 C1 **Ochili Pass** Afgh.
165 I5 **Ochsenfurt** Germany
164 F2 **Ochtrup** Germany
159 L3 **Ockelbo** Sweden
169 L7 **Ocolaşul Mare, Vârful** *mt.* Romania
193 J5 **Oconee** *r.* U.S.A.
190 C4 **Oconomowoc** U.S.A.
190 D3 **Oconto** U.S.A.
207 F4 **Ocosingo** Mex.
206 H5 **Ocotal** Nicaragua
196 D5 **Ocotillo Wells** U.S.A.
206 D3 **Ocotlán** Mex.
176 B4 **Oda** Ghana
151 C7 **Ōda** Japan
158 C2 **Ódáðahraun** *lava field* Iceland
152 E3 **Ŏdaejin** N. Korea
150 G4 **Ōdate** Japan
151 F7 **Odawara** Japan
159 I3 **Odda** Norway
187 J3 **Odei** *r.* Canada
190 C5 **Odell** U.S.A.
167 B4 **Odemira** Port.
136 A2 **Ödemiş** Turkey
181 G3 **Odendaalsrus** S. Africa
159 J5 **Odense** Denmark
165 G5 **Odenwald** *reg.* Germany
165 I3 **Oder** *r.* Germany *alt.* **Odra (Poland)**
168 G3 **Oderbucht** *b.* Germany
Odesa Ukr. *see* **Odessa**
159 K4 **Ödeshög** Sweden
173 D6 **Odessa** Ukr.
199 C6 **Odessa** U.S.A.
139 H1 **Odesskoye** Russia
167 C4 **Odiel** *r.* Spain
176 B4 **Odienné** Côte d'Ivoire
172 F4 **Odintsovo** Russia
143 D1 **Odisha** *state* India
154 C3 **Ŏdŏngk** Cambodia
168 G4 **Odra** *r.* Poland *alt.* **Oder (Germany)**
211 J5 **Oeiras** Brazil
198 C3 **Oelrichs** U.S.A.
165 K4 **Oelsnitz/Vogtland** Germany
190 B4 **Oelwein** U.S.A.
164 D1 **Oenkerk** Neth.
137 H1 **Of** Turkey
170 G4 **Ofanto** *r.* Italy
165 G4 **Offenbach am Main** Germany
164 F6 **Offenburg** Germany
171 L6 **Ofidoussa** *i.* Greece
150 G5 **Ōfunato** Japan
150 F5 **Oga** Japan
178 E3 **Ogadēn** *reg.* Eth.
150 F5 **Oga-hantō** *pen.* Japan
151 E7 **Ōgaki** Japan
198 C3 **Ogallala** U.S.A.
Ogasawara-shotō *is* Japan *see* **Bonin Islands**
191 H2 **Ogascanane, Lac** *l.* Canada
Ogbomosho Nigeria *see* **Ogbomoso**
176 C4 **Ogbomoso** Nigeria
198 E3 **Ogden** *IA* U.S.A.
194 E3 **Ogden** *UT* U.S.A.
186 C3 **Ogden, Mount** Canada
203 F2 **Ogdensburg** U.S.A.
184 E3 **Ogilvie** *r.* Canada
184 E3 **Ogilvie Mountains** Canada
138 C5 **Oglanly** Turkm.
201 C5 **Oglethorpe, Mount** U.S.A.
170 D1 **Oglio** *r.* Italy
176 C4 **Ogoja** Nigeria
188 C3 **Ogoki** *r.* Canada
188 C3 **Ogoki Reservoir** Canada
171 J3 **Ogosta** *r.* Bulg.
159 N4 **Ogre** Latvia
170 F2 **Ogulin** Croatia
Ogurchinskiy, Ostrov *i.* Turkm. *see* **Ogurjaly Adasy**
138 C5 **Ogurjaly Adasy** *i.* Turkm.
137 K1 **Oğuz** Azer.
128 A6 **Ohai** N.Z.
128 E3 **Ohakune** N.Z.
150 G4 **Ōhata** Japan
128 B6 **Ohau, Lake** N.Z.
215 B2 **O'Higgins** *admin. reg.* Chile
212 B7 **O'Higgins, Lago** *l.* Chile
200 C4 **Ohio** *r.* U.S.A.
202 B4 **Ohio** *state* U.S.A.
165 G4 **Ohm** *r.* Germany
165 I4 **Ohrdruf** Germany
165 K4 **Ohře** *r.* Czech Rep.
165 J2 **Ohre** *r.* Germany
171 I4 **Ohrid** Macedonia
171 I4 **Ohrid, Lake** Albania/Macedonia
181 I2 **Ohrigstad** S. Africa
165 H5 **Öhringen** Germany
128 E3 **Ohura** N.Z.
211 H3 **Oiapoque** Brazil
162 D3 **Oich, Loch** *l.* U.K.
145 H3 **Oiga** China
164 A4 **Oignies** France
202 D4 **Oil City** U.S.A.
196 C4 **Oildale** U.S.A.
166 F2 **Oise** *r.* France
164 B5 **Oise à l'Aisne, Canal de l'** France
151 B8 **Ōita** Japan
171 J5 **Oiti** *mt.* Greece
196 C4 **Ojai** U.S.A.
215 D2 **Ojeda** Arg.
190 B3 **Ojibwa** U.S.A.
204 D3 **Ojinaga** Mex.
207 E4 **Ojitlán** Mex.
151 F6 **Ojiya** Japan
206 A2 **Ojo de Liebre, Lago** *b.* Mex.
212 C3 **Ojos del Salado, Nevado** *mt.* Arg.
172 G4 **Oka** *r.* Russia
179 B6 **Okahandja** Namibia
128 E3 **Okahukura** N.Z.
179 B6 **Okakarara** Namibia
189 H2 **Okak Islands** Canada
186 F5 **Okanagan Falls** Canada
186 F4 **Okanagan Lake** Canada
194 C1 **Okanogan** *r.* Canada/U.S.A.
186 F5 **Okanogan** U.S.A.
194 B1 **Okanogan Range** *mts* U.S.A.
178 C3 **Okapi, Parc National de la** *nat. park* Dem. Rep. Congo
144 C3 **Okara** Pak.
Okarem Turkm. *see* **Ekerem**
179 B5 **Okaukuejo** Namibia
179 C5 **Okavango** *r.* Botswana/Namibia
179 C5 **Okavango Delta** *swamp* Botswana
151 F6 **Okaya** Japan
151 C7 **Okayama** Japan
151 E7 **Okazaki** Japan
201 D7 **Okeechobee** U.S.A.
201 D7 **Okeechobee, Lake** U.S.A.
201 D6 **Okefenokee Swamp** U.S.A.
161 C7 **Okehampton** U.K.
176 C4 **Okene** Nigeria
165 I2 **Oker** *r.* Germany
144 B5 **Okha** India
146 G1 **Okha** Russia
145 F4 **Okhaldhunga** Nepal
144 B5 **Okha Rann** *marsh* India
133 P3 **Okhota** *r.* Russia
133 P4 **Okhotsk** Russia
133 P4 **Okhotsk, Sea of** Russia
Okhotskoye More *sea* Russia *see* **Okhotsk, Sea of**
173 E5 **Okhtyrka** Ukr.
146 E4 **Okinawa** *i.* Japan
Okinawa-guntō *is* Japan *see* **Okinawa-shotō**
146 E4 **Okinawa-shotō** *is* Japan
151 C6 **Okinoshima** Japan
151 B7 **Okino-shima** *i.* Japan
151 C6 **Oki-shotō** *is* Japan
199 D5 **Oklahoma** *state* U.S.A.
199 D5 **Oklahoma City** U.S.A.
199 D5 **Okmulgee** U.S.A.
178 B4 **Okondja** Gabon
186 G4 **Okotoks** Canada
172 E4 **Okovskiy Les** *for.* Russia
178 B4 **Okoyo** Congo
138 B3 **Okpan, Gora** *h.* Kazakh.
139 J3 **Okpekty, Gora** *mt.* Kazakh.
158 M1 **Øksfjord** Norway
172 F2 **Oksovskiy** Russia
139 G5 **Oktyabr** Tajik.
172 I4 **Oktyabr'sk** Russia
Oktyabr'sk Turkm. *see* **Saparmyrat Türkmenbaşy**
172 G2 **Oktyabr'skiy** *Arkhangel'skaya Oblast'* Russia
146 H1 **Oktyabr'skiy** *Kamchatskiy Kray* Russia
132 G4 **Oktyabr'skiy** *Respublika Bashkortostan* Russia
173 G6 **Oktyabr'skiy** *Volgogradskaya Oblast'* Russia
139 F5 **Oktyabr'skiy** Uzbek.
138 F1 **Oktyabr'skoye** Kazakh.
138 E1 **Oktyabr'skoye** *Chelyabinskaya Oblast'* Russia
132 H3 **Oktyabr'skoye** *Khanty-Mansiyskiy Avtonomnyy Okrug-Yugra* Russia
138 C1 **Oktyabr'skoye** *Orenburgskaya Oblast'* Russia
133 K2 **Oktyabr'skoy Revolyutsii, Ostrov** *i.* Russia
172 E3 **Okulovka** Russia
150 F3 **Okushiri-tō** *i.* Japan
180 E1 **Okwa** *watercourse* Botswana
158 B2 **Ólafsvík** Iceland
196 C3 **Olancha** U.S.A.
196 C3 **Olancha Peak** U.S.A.
206 H5 **Olanchito** Hond.
159 L4 **Öland** *i.* Sweden
158 O2 **Olanga** Russia
126 D4 **Olary** Australia
126 D4 **Olary** *watercourse* Australia
198 E4 **Olathe** U.S.A.
215 E3 **Olavarría** Arg.
168 H5 **Oława** Poland
197 G5 **Olberg** U.S.A.
170 C4 **Olbia** *Sardinia* Italy
202 D3 **Olcott** U.S.A.
127 H6 **Old Adaminaby** Australia
127 J3 **Old Bar** Australia
143 C2 **Old Bastar** India
163 D4 **Oldcastle** Ireland
184 E3 **Old Crow** Canada
Oldeboorn Neth. *see* **Aldeboarn**
165 G1 **Oldenburg** Germany
168 E3 **Oldenburg in Holstein** Germany
164 E2 **Oldenzaal** Neth.
158 M1 **Olderdalen** Norway
203 F3 **Old Forge** *NY* U.S.A.
203 F4 **Old Forge** *PA* U.S.A.
160 E4 **Oldham** U.K.
163 C6 **Old Head of Kinsale** Ireland
186 G4 **Oldman** *r.* Canada
162 F3 **Oldmeldrum** U.K.
203 H3 **Old Orchard Beach** U.S.A.
189 J4 **Old Perlican** Canada
186 G4 **Olds** Canada
203 I2 **Old Town** U.S.A.
187 H4 **Old Wives Lake** Canada
197 E4 **Old Woman Mountains** U.S.A.
202 D3 **Olean** U.S.A.
169 K3 **Olecko** Poland
133 N4 **Olekma** *r.* Russia
133 N3 **Olekminsk** Russia
173 E5 **Oleksandriya** Ukr.
172 H1 **Olema** Russia
159 I4 **Ølen** Norway
158 P1 **Olenegorsk** Russia
133 M3 **Olenek** Russia
133 N2 **Olenek** *r.* Russia
133 N2 **Olenekskiy Zaliv** *b.* Russia
172 E3 **Olenino** Russia
138 C2 **Olenti** *r.* Kazakh.
139 H1 **Olenty** *r.* Kazakh.
173 C5 **Olevs'k** Ukr.
150 D3 **Ol'ga** Russia
167 C4 **Olhão** Port.
180 C2 **Olifants** *watercourse* Namibia
181 I1 **Olifants** S. Africa
180 C5 **Olifants** *r. Western Cape* S. Africa
180 D6 **Olifants** *r. Western Cape* S. Africa
180 E3 **Olifantshoek** S. Africa
180 C6 **Olifantsrivierberge** *mts* S. Africa
215 F2 **Olimar Grande** *r.* Uruguay
214 C3 **Olímpia** Brazil
207 E4 **Olinalá** Mex.
211 L5 **Olinda** Brazil
179 D5 **Olinga** Moz.
181 G2 **Oliphants Drift** Botswana
215 D2 **Oliva** Arg.
167 F3 **Oliva** Spain
212 C3 **Oliva, Cordillera de** *mts* Arg./Chile
215 C1 **Olivares, Cerro de** *mt.* Chile
202 B5 **Olive Hill** U.S.A.
214 D3 **Oliveira** Brazil
167 C3 **Olivenza** Spain
198 E2 **Olivia** U.S.A.
148 B1 **Olji** *Nei Mongol Zizhiqu* China
148 C1 **Olji** *Nei Mongol Zizhiqu* China
138 E2 **Ol'keyyek** *r.* Kazakh.
172 G4 **Ol'khi** Russia
212 C2 **Ollagüe** Chile
215 B1 **Ollita, Cordillera de** *mts* Arg./Chile
215 B1 **Ollitas** *mt.* Arg.
139 G4 **Olmaliq** Uzbek.
210 C5 **Olmos** Peru
203 G3 **Olmstedville** U.S.A.
161 G5 **Olney** U.K.
200 C4 **Olney** U.S.A.
159 K4 **Olofström** Sweden
168 H6 **Olomouc** Czech Rep.
172 E2 **Olonets** Russia
153 B3 **Olongapo** Phil.
166 D5 **Oloron-Ste-Marie** France
167 H1 **Olot** Spain
138 E5 **Olot** Uzbek.
146 D1 **Olovyannaya** Russia
133 R3 **Oloy** *r.* Russia
144 C5 **Olpad** India
165 F3 **Olpe** Germany
169 J4 **Olsztyn** Poland
168 C7 **Olten** Switz.
171 L2 **Olteniţa** Romania
137 H1 **Oltu** Turkey
153 B5 **Olutanga** *i.* Phil.
171 I6 **Olympia** *tourist site* Greece
194 B2 **Olympia** U.S.A.
194 A2 **Olympic National Park** U.S.A.
136 C3 **Olympos** *tourist site* Turkey
136 D4 **Olympus, Mount** Cyprus
171 J4 **Olympus, Mount** Greece
194 B2 **Olympus, Mount** U.S.A.
133 S4 **Olyutorskiy, Mys** *c.* Russia
133 R4 **Olyutorskiy Zaliv** *b.* Russia
145 E2 **Oma** China
150 G4 **Ōma** Japan
151 E6 **Ōmachi** Japan
151 F7 **Omae-zaki** *pt* Japan
163 D3 **Omagh** U.K.
198 E3 **Omaha** U.S.A.
180 C1 **Omaheke** *admin. reg.* Namibia
194 C1 **Omak** U.S.A.
142 E6 **Oman** *country* Asia
141 E5 **Oman, Gulf of** Asia
128 B6 **Omarama** N.Z.
179 B6 **Omaruru** Namibia
179 B5 **Omatako** *watercourse* Namibia
210 D7 **Omate** Peru
180 E2 **Omaweneno** Botswana
150 G4 **Ōma-zaki** *c.* Japan
178 A4 **Omboué** Gabon
170 D3 **Ombrone** *r.* Italy
145 F3 **Ombu** China
180 E5 **Omdraaisvlei** S. Africa
177 F3 **Omdurman** Sudan
170 C2 **Omegna** Italy
127 G6 **Omeo** Australia
206 H6 **Ometepe, Isla de** *i.* Nicaragua
178 D2 **Om Hajēr** Eritrea
140 C4 **Omīdīyeh** Iran
186 D3 **Omineca Mountains** Canada
180 C1 **Omitara** Namibia
186 C3 **Ommaney, Cape** U.S.A.
164 E2 **Ommen** Neth.
148 B1 **Ömnögovĭ** *prov.* Mongolia
133 R3 **Omolon** Russia
133 Q3 **Omolon** *r.* Russia
178 D3 **Omo National Park** Eth.
148 A1 **Omon Gol** *watercourse* China
150 G5 **Omono-gawa** *r.* Japan
141 E3 **'Omrānī** Iran
132 I4 **Omsk** Russia
133 Q3 **Omsukchan** Russia
150 H2 **Ōmu** Japan
171 K2 **Omu, Vârful** *mt.* Romania
151 A8 **Ōmura** Japan
179 B5 **Omuthiya** Namibia
190 B4 **Onalaska** U.S.A.
203 F6 **Onancock** U.S.A.
188 D4 **Onaping Lake** Canada
206 B1 **Onavas** Mex.
191 E3 **Onaway** U.S.A.
141 H3 **Ōnay, Kōtal-e** Afgh.
154 A2 **Onbingwin** Myanmar
215 D1 **Oncativo** Arg.
160 C3 **Onchan** U.K.
179 B5 **Oncócua** Angola
179 B5 **Ondangwa** Namibia
180 B1 **Ondekaremba** Namibia
180 D5 **Onderstedorings** S. Africa
179 B5 **Ondjiva** Angola
176 C4 **Ondo** Nigeria
146 D2 **Öndörhaan** Mongolia
152 A1 **Ondor Had** China
148 B1 **Ondor Mod** China
148 D1 **Ondor Sum** China
172 E2 **Ondozero** Russia
180 D1 **One** Botswana
172 F2 **Onega** Russia
172 F2 **Onega** *r.* Russia
172 E2 **Onega, Lake** Russia
203 F3 **Oneida** U.S.A.
203 F3 **Oneida Lake** U.S.A.
198 D3 **O'Neill** U.S.A.
146 H2 **Onekotan, Ostrov** *i.* Russia
203 F3 **Oneonta** U.S.A.
128 E2 **Oneroa** N.Z.
169 M7 **Oneşti** Romania
172 E1 **Onezhskaya Guba** *g.* Russia
132 E3 **Onezhskoye Ozero** Russia
Onezhskoye Ozero *l.* Russia *see* **Onega, Lake**
143 C1 **Ong** *r.* India
178 B4 **Onga** Gabon
128 F3 **Ongaonga** N.Z.
180 E4 **Ongers** *watercourse* S. Africa
152 C5 **Ongjin** N. Korea
143 C3 **Ongole** India
148 B1 **Ongt Gol** China
139 K2 **Onguday** Russia
173 G7 **Oni** Georgia
179 E6 **Onilahy** *r.* Madag.
176 C4 **Onitsha** Nigeria
180 B1 **Onjati Mountain** Namibia
151 E7 **Ōno** Japan
125 I4 **Ono-i-Lau** *i.* Fiji
151 C7 **Onomichi** Japan
125 H2 **Onotoa** *atoll* Kiribati
186 G4 **Onoway** Canada
180 C4 **Onseepkans** S. Africa
124 B4 **Onslow** Australia
201 E5 **Onslow Bay** U.S.A.
152 F2 **Onsŏng** N. Korea
164 F1 **Onstwedde** Neth.
151 E7 **Ontake-san** *vol.* Japan
188 B3 **Ontario** *prov.* Canada
194 C2 **Ontario** U.S.A.
191 H4 **Ontario, Lake** Canada/U.S.A.
190 C2 **Ontonagon** U.S.A.
125 F2 **Ontong Java Atoll** Solomon Is
124 D4 **Oodnadatta** Australia
126 F5 **Oolambeyan National Park** Australia
199 E4 **Oologah Lake** *resr* U.S.A.
164 B3 **Oostburg** Neth.
Oostende Belgium *see* **Ostend**
164 D2 **Oostendorp** Neth.
164 C3 **Oosterhout** Neth.
164 B3 **Oosterschelde** *est.* Neth.
164 E2 **Oosterwolde** Neth.
164 A4 **Oostvleteren** Belgium
164 D1 **Oost-Vlieland** Neth.
186 D4 **Ootsa Lake** Canada
186 D4 **Ootsa Lake** *l.* Canada
202 E5 **Opal** U.S.A.
178 C4 **Opala** Dem. Rep. Congo
172 I3 **Oparino** Russia
188 B3 **Opasquia** Canada
188 B3 **Opasquia Provincial Park** Canada
188 F3 **Opataca, Lac** *l.* Canada
168 H6 **Opava** Czech Rep.
201 C5 **Opelika** U.S.A.
199 E6 **Opelousas** U.S.A.
194 F1 **Opheim** U.S.A.
191 F2 **Ophir** Canada
155 B2 **Ophir, Gunung** *vol.* Indon.
128 C6 **Opihi** *r.* N.Z.
188 E3 **Opinaca** *r.* Canada
188 E3 **Opinaca, Réservoir** *resr* Canada
188 D3 **Opinnagau** *r.* Canada
137 J5 **Opis** *tourist site* Iraq
189 G3 **Opiscotéo, Lac** *l.* Canada
164 C2 **Opmeer** Neth.
172 D3 **Opochka** Russia
168 H5 **Opole** Poland
167 B2 **Oporto** Port.
128 F3 **Opotiki** N.Z.
201 C6 **Opp** U.S.A.
158 J3 **Oppdal** Norway
158 K1 **Oppeid** Norway
128 D3 **Opunake** N.Z.
179 B5 **Opuwo** Namibia
138 B3 **Opytnoye** Kazakh.
138 D4 **Oqqal'a** Uzbek.
139 H5 **Oqsu** *r.* Tajik.
138 F5 **Oqtosh** Uzbek.
190 B5 **Oquawka** U.S.A.
203 H2 **Oquossoc** U.S.A.
138 D2 **Or'** *r.* Russia
197 G5 **Oracle** U.S.A.
197 G5 **Oracle Junction** U.S.A.
169 J7 **Oradea** Romania
158 C2 **Öræfajökull** *glacier* Iceland
144 D4 **Orai** India
176 B1 **Oran** Alg.
212 D2 **Orán** Arg.
152 E3 **Ŏrang** N. Korea
127 H4 **Orange** Australia
166 G4 **Orange** France
180 B4 **Orange** *r.* Namibia/S. Africa
203 G3 **Orange** *MA* U.S.A.
199 E6 **Orange** *TX* U.S.A.
202 D5 **Orange** *VA* U.S.A.
211 H3 **Orange, Cabo** *c.* Brazil
201 D5 **Orangeburg** U.S.A.
219 J8 **Orange Cone** *sea feature* S. Atlantic Ocean
Orange Free State *prov.* S. Africa *see* **Free State**
191 G3 **Orangeville** Canada
197 G2 **Orangeville** U.S.A.
207 G4 **Orange Walk** Belize
153 B3 **Orani** Phil.
165 L2 **Oranienburg** Germany
179 B6 **Oranjemund** Namibia
213 C1 **Oranjestad** Aruba
163 C4 **Oranmore** Ireland
179 C6 **Orapa** Botswana
153 C3 **Oras** Phil.
171 J2 **Orăştie** Romania
158 M3 **Oravais** Fin.
171 I2 **Oraviţa** Romania
144 E2 **Orba Co** *l.* China
170 D3 **Orbetello** Italy
167 D1 **Órbigo** *r.* Spain
127 H6 **Orbost** Australia
129 C2 **Orcadas** *research stn* S. Atlantic Ocean
197 H2 **Orchard Mesa** U.S.A.
213 D2 **Orchila, Isla** *i.* Venez.
196 B4 **Orcutt** U.S.A.
124 C3 **Ord** *r.* Australia
124 C3 **Ord, Mount** *h.* Australia
195 D4 **Orderville** U.S.A.
167 B1 **Ordes** Spain
196 D4 **Ord Mountain** U.S.A.
148 C2 **Ordos** *Nei Mongol Zizhiqu* China
Ordos *Nei Mongol Zizhiqu* China *see* **Dongsheng**
136 F1 **Ordu** Turkey
137 K2 **Ordubad** Azer.
195 G4 **Ordway** U.S.A.
Ordzhonikidze Russia *see* **Vladikavkaz**
173 E6 **Ordzhonikidze** Ukr.
196 C1 **Oreana** U.S.A.
154 C2 **O Reăng** Cambodia
159 K4 **Örebro** Sweden
190 C4 **Oregon** *IL* U.S.A.
202 B4 **Oregon** *OH* U.S.A.
190 C4 **Oregon** *WI* U.S.A.
194 B3 **Oregon** *state* U.S.A.
194 B2 **Oregon City** U.S.A.
172 F4 **Orekhovo-Zuyevo** Russia
139 K2 **Orel'** Kazakh.
172 F4 **Orel** Russia
146 F1 **Orel', Ozero** *l.* Russia
197 G1 **Orem** U.S.A.
136 A2 **Ören** *İzmir* Turkey
171 L6 **Ören** *Muğla* Turkey
138 C2 **Orenburg** Russia
138 C2 **Orenburgskaya Oblast'** *admin. div.* Russia
215 E3 **Orense** Arg.
128 A7 **Orepuki** N.Z.
159 K5 **Öresund** *str.* Denmark
128 B7 **Oreti** *r.* N.Z.
128 E2 **Orewa** N.Z.
164 D4 **Oreye** Belgium
171 J4 **Orfanou, Kolpos** *b.* Greece
127 G9 **Orford** Australia
161 I5 **Orford** U.K.
161 I5 **Orford Ness** *hd* U.K.
197 F5 **Organ Pipe Cactus National Monument** *nat. park* U.S.A.
136 B2 **Orhaneli** Turkey
173 D7 **Orhangazi** Turkey
169 N7 **Orhei** Moldova
172 I3 **Orichi** Russia
203 J2 **Orient** U.S.A.
210 E7 **Oriental, Cordillera** *mts* Bol.
213 B3 **Oriental, Cordillera** *mts* Col.
210 D6 **Oriental, Cordillera** *mts* Peru
215 E3 **Oriente** Arg.
167 F3 **Orihuela** Spain
173 E6 **Orikhiv** Ukr.
191 H3 **Orillia** Canada
159 N3 **Orimattila** Fin.
213 E2 **Orinoco** *r.* Col./Venez.
213 E2 **Orinoco, Delta del** Venez.
Orissa *state* India *see* **Odisha**
159 M4 **Orissaare** Estonia
170 C5 **Oristano** *Sardinia* Italy
159 N3 **Orivesi** Fin.
158 O3 **Orivesi** *l.* Fin.
211 G4 **Oriximiná** Brazil
207 E4 **Orizaba** Mex.
207 E4 **Orizaba, Pico de** *vol.* Mex.
158 J3 **Orkanger** Norway
159 K4 **Örkelljunga** Sweden
158 J3 **Orkla** *r.* Norway
181 G3 **Orkney** S. Africa
162 E1 **Orkney Islands** U.K.
199 C6 **Orla** U.S.A.
196 A2 **Orland** U.S.A.
214 C3 **Orlândia** Brazil
201 D6 **Orlando** U.S.A.
166 E3 **Orléans** France
203 I4 **Orleans** *MA* U.S.A.
203 G2 **Orleans** *VT* U.S.A.
172 I3 **Orlov** Russia
172 F4 **Orlovskaya Oblast'** *admin. div.* Russia
173 G6 **Orlovskiy** Russia
141 G5 **Ormara** Pak.
141 G5 **Ormara, Ras** *hd* Pak.
153 C4 **Ormoc** Phil.
201 D6 **Ormond Beach** U.S.A.
160 E4 **Ormskirk** U.K.
203 G2 **Ormstown** Canada
166 D2 **Orne** *r.* France
158 K2 **Ørnes** Norway
158 L3 **Örnsköldsvik** Sweden
152 D4 **Oro** N. Korea
213 C3 **Orocué** Col.
176 B3 **Orodara** Burkina Faso
194 C2 **Orofino** U.S.A.
195 F5 **Orogrande** U.S.A.
189 G4 **Oromocto** Canada
136 E6 **Oron** Israel
125 I2 **Orona** *atoll* Kiribati
203 I2 **Orono** U.S.A.
162 B4 **Oronsay** *i.* U.K.
153 B4 **Oroquieta** Phil.
211 K5 **Orós, Açude** *resr* Brazil
170 C4 **Orosei** *Sardinia* Italy
170 C4 **Orosei, Golfo di** *b. Sardinia* Italy
169 J7 **Orosháza** Hungary
197 G5 **Oro Valley** U.S.A.
196 B2 **Oroville** *CA* U.S.A.
194 C1 **Oroville** *WA* U.S.A.
196 B2 **Oroville, Lake** *resr* U.S.A.
126 C4 **Orroroo** Australia
159 K3 **Orsa** Sweden
172 D4 **Orsha** Belarus
138 D2 **Orsk** Russia
159 I3 **Ørsta** Norway
167 C1 **Ortegal, Cabo** *c.* Spain
166 D5 **Orthez** France
167 C1 **Ortigueira** Spain
206 B1 **Ortíz** Mex.
213 D2 **Ortíz** Venez.
170 D1 **Ortles** *mt.* Italy
160 E3 **Orton** U.K.
170 F3 **Ortona** Italy
198 D2 **Ortonville** U.S.A.
133 N3 **Orulgan, Khrebet** *mts* Russia
180 B1 **Orumbo** Namibia
Orūmīyeh Iran *see* **Urmia**
Orūmīyeh, Daryācheh-ye *salt l.* Iran *see* **Urmia, Lake**
210 E7 **Oruro** Bol.
164 D5 **Orval, Abbaye d'** *tourist site* Belgium
170 E3 **Orvieto** Italy
202 C4 **Orwell** *OH* U.S.A.
203 G3 **Orwell** *VT* U.S.A.
159 J3 **Os** Norway
206 I6 **Osa, Península de** Costa Rica
190 A4 **Osage** U.S.A.
198 E4 **Osage** *r.* U.S.A.
151 D7 **Ōsaka** Japan
139 H2 **Osakarovka** Kazakh.
150 G5 **Ōsaki** Japan
171 K3 **Osam** *r.* Bulg.
159 K4 **Osby** Sweden
199 F5 **Osceola** *AR* U.S.A.
198 E3 **Osceola** *IA* U.S.A.
165 L3 **Oschatz** Germany
165 J2 **Oschersleben (Bode)** Germany
170 C4 **Oschiri** *Sardinia* Italy
191 F3 **Oscoda** U.S.A.
172 F4 **Osetr** *r.* Russia
151 A8 **Ōse-zaki** *pt* Japan
191 J3 **Osgoode** Canada
139 H4 **Osh** Kyrg.
179 B5 **Oshakati** Namibia
150 G3 **Oshamanbe** Japan
191 H4 **Oshawa** Canada
150 G5 **Oshika-hantō** *pen.* Japan
150 F4 **Ō-shima** *i.* Japan
151 F7 **Ō-shima** *i.* Japan
198 C3 **Oshkosh** *NE* U.S.A.
190 C3 **Oshkosh** *WI* U.S.A.
140 B2 **Oshnavīyeh** Iran
137 L5 **Oshtorān Kūh** *mt.* Iran
137 L5 **Oshtorīnān** Iran
150 G5 **Ōshū** Japan
178 B4 **Oshwe** Dem. Rep. Congo
171 H2 **Osijek** Croatia
170 E3 **Osimo** Italy
144 C4 **Osiyan** India
181 I3 **oSizweni** S. Africa
170 G2 **Osječenica** *mts* Bos. & Herz.
158 K3 **Ösjön** *l.* Sweden
198 E3 **Oskaloosa** U.S.A.
159 L4 **Oskarshamn** Sweden
191 J1 **Oskélanéo** Canada
173 F5 **Oskol** *r.* Russia
159 J4 **Oslo** Norway
153 B4 **Oslob** Phil.
159 J4 **Oslofjorden** *sea chan.* Norway
143 B2 **Osmanabad** India
136 E1 **Osmancık** Turkey
136 B1 **Osmaneli** Turkey
136 F3 **Osmaniye** Turkey
159 O4 **Os'mino** Russia
165 G2 **Osnabrück** Germany
176 C4 **Osogbo** Nigeria
171 J3 **Osogovska Planina** *mts* Bulg./Macedonia
215 B4 **Osorno** Chile
167 D1 **Osorno** Spain
215 B4 **Osorno, Volcán** *vol.* Chile
186 F5 **Osoyoos** Canada
159 I3 **Osøyro** Norway
124 E3 **Osprey Reef** Coral Sea Is Terr.
164 D3 **Oss** Neth.
127 G8 **Ossa, Mount** Australia
190 B3 **Osseo** U.S.A.
191 F3 **Ossineke** U.S.A.
203 H3 **Ossipee Lake** U.S.A.
165 J3 **Oßmannstedt** Germany
189 H3 **Ossokmanuan Lake** Canada
164 D5 **Ossuaire, Cimetière d'** *tourist site* France
172 E3 **Ostashkov** Russia
165 F2 **Ostbevern** Germany
165 H1 **Oste** *r.* Germany
164 A3 **Ostend** Belgium
169 O5 **Oster** Ukr.
165 J2 **Osterburg (Altmark)** Germany
159 K4 **Österbymo** Sweden
159 K3 **Österdalälven** *l.* Sweden
159 J3 **Østerdalen** *val.* Norway
165 J3 **Osterfeld** Germany
165 G1 **Osterholz-Scharmbeck** Germany
165 I3 **Osterode am Harz** Germany
158 K3 **Östersund** Sweden
165 I3 **Osterwieck** Germany
164 F1 **Ostfriesland** *reg.* Germany
159 L3 **Östhammar** Sweden
168 I6 **Ostrava** Czech Rep.
169 I4 **Ostróda** Poland
173 F5 **Ostrogozhsk** Russia
165 K4 **Ostrov** Czech Rep.
172 D3 **Ostrov** Russia
169 J5 **Ostrowiec Świętokrzyski** Poland
169 J4 **Ostrów Mazowiecka** Poland
168 H5 **Ostrów Wielkopolski** Poland
151 B9 **Ōsumi-kaikyō** *sea chan.* Japan
151 B9 **Ōsumi-shotō** *is* Japan
167 D4 **Osuna** Spain
203 F2 **Oswegatchie** U.S.A.
190 C5 **Oswego** *IL* U.S.A.
202 E3 **Oswego** *NY* U.S.A.
203 E3 **Oswego** *r.* U.S.A.
161 D5 **Oswestry** U.K.
151 F6 **Ōta** Japan
128 C6 **Otago Peninsula** N.Z.
128 E4 **Otaki** N.Z.
158 N2 **Otanmäki** Fin.
139 H4 **Otar** Kazakh.
213 B4 **Otare, Cerro** *h.* Col.
150 G3 **Otaru** Japan
128 B7 **Otatara** N.Z.
210 C3 **Otavalo** Ecuador
179 B5 **Otavi** Namibia
151 G6 **Ōtawara** Japan
139 I4 **Otegen Batyr** Kazakh.
128 C6 **Otematata** N.Z.
159 N4 **Otepää** Estonia
138 C3 **Otes** Kazakh.
194 C2 **Othello** U.S.A.
181 I4 **oThongathi** S. Africa
206 C2 **Otinapa** Mex.
128 C5 **Otira** N.Z.
203 E3 **Otisco Lake** U.S.A.
189 F3 **Otish, Monts** *hills* Canada
179 B6 **Otjiwarongo** Namibia
160 F4 **Otley** U.K.
150 H2 **Otoineppu** Japan
128 E3 **Otorohanga** N.Z.
188 C3 **Otoskwin** *r.* Canada
138 B1 **Otradnyy** Russia
171 H4 **Otranto** Italy
171 H4 **Otranto, Strait of** Albania/Italy
190 E4 **Otsego** U.S.A.
190 E3 **Otsego Lake** *MI* U.S.A.
203 F3 **Otsego Lake** *NY* U.S.A.
203 F3 **Otselic** U.S.A.
151 D7 **Ōtsu** Japan
159 J3 **Otta** Norway
191 J3 **Ottawa** Canada
191 H2 **Ottawa** *r.* Canada
190 C5 **Ottawa** *IL* U.S.A.
198 E4 **Ottawa** *KS* U.S.A.
202 A4 **Ottawa** *OH* U.S.A.
188 D2 **Ottawa Islands** Canada
160 E2 **Otterburn** U.K.
197 G2 **Otter Creek Reservoir** U.S.A.
190 D1 **Otter Island** Canada
188 D3 **Otter Rapids** Canada
165 H1 **Ottersberg** Germany
161 C7 **Ottery** *r.* U.K.
164 C4 **Ottignies** Belgium

Peery Lake

185 J1 **Otto Fiord** *inlet* Canada
139 H4 **Ottuk** Kyrg.
190 A5 **Ottumwa** U.S.A.
164 F5 **Ottweiler** Germany
176 C4 **Otukpo** Nigeria
212 D3 **Otumpa** Arg.
210 C5 **Otuzco** Peru
126 E7 **Otway, Cape** Australia
149 B6 **Ou, Nâm** *r.* Laos
199 E5 **Ouachita** *r.* U.S.A.
199 E5 **Ouachita, Lake** U.S.A.
199 E5 **Ouachita Mountains** U.S.A.
176 A2 **Ouadâne** Mauritania
178 C3 **Ouadda** C.A.R.
177 E3 **Ouaddaï** *reg.* Chad
176 B3 **Ouagadougou** Burkina Faso
176 B3 **Ouahigouya** Burkina Faso
176 B3 **Oualâta** Mauritania
178 C3 **Ouanda Djallé** C.A.R.
176 B2 **Ouarâne** *reg.* Mauritania
176 C1 **Ouargla** Alg.
176 B1 **Ouarzazate** Morocco
180 F6 **Oubergpas** *pass* S. Africa
164 B4 **Oudenaarde** Belgium
164 F1 **Oude Pekela** Neth.
149 B6 **Oudômxai** Laos
180 E6 **Oudtshoorn** S. Africa
164 C3 **Oud-Turnhout** Belgium
167 F5 **Oued Tlélat** Alg.
176 B1 **Oued Zem** Morocco
170 B6 **Oued Zénati** Alg.
166 B2 **Ouessant, Île d'** *i.* France
178 B3 **Ouesso** Congo
176 C4 **Ouidah** Benin
206 B2 **Ouiriego** Mex.
176 B1 **Oujda** Morocco
158 N2 **Oulainen** Fin.
167 G4 **Ouled Farès** Alg.
158 N2 **Oulu** Fin.
158 N2 **Oulujärvi** *l.* Fin.
158 N2 **Oulujoki** *r.* Fin.
158 N2 **Oulunsalo** Fin.
166 H4 **Oulx** Italy
177 E3 **Oum-Chalouba** Chad
176 B4 **Oumé** Côte d'Ivoire
177 D3 **Oum-Hadjer** Chad
158 N2 **Ounasjoki** *r.* Fin.
161 G5 **Oundle** U.K.
177 E3 **Ounianga, Lakes of** *tourist site* Chad
177 E3 **Ounianga Kébir** Chad
164 D4 **Oupeye** Belgium
164 E5 **Our** *r.* Lux.
168 C6 **Our, Vallée de l'** *val.* Germany/Lux.
171 L5 **Oura, Akrotirio** *pt* Greece
195 F4 **Ouray** *CO* U.S.A.
197 H1 **Ouray** *UT* U.S.A.
167 C1 **Ourense** Spain
211 J5 **Ouricuri** Brazil
214 C3 **Ourinhos** Brazil
214 C1 **Ouro** *r.* Brazil
214 D3 **Ouro Preto** Brazil
164 D4 **Ourthe** *r.* Belgium
160 G4 **Ouse** *r. England* U.K.
161 H7 **Ouse** *r. England* U.K.
179 B5 **Outapi** Namibia
189 G3 **Outardes, Rivière aux** *r.* Canada
180 E6 **Outeniekpas** *pass* S. Africa
162 A2 **Outer Hebrides** *is* U.K.
190 B2 **Outer Island** U.S.A.
196 C5 **Outer Santa Barbara Channel** U.S.A.
179 B6 **Outjo** Namibia
184 H4 **Outlook** Canada
158 O3 **Outokumpu** Fin.
162 □ **Out Skerries** *is* U.K.
125 G4 **Ouvéa** *atoll* New Caledonia
149 D5 **Ouyanghai Shuiku** *resr* China
126 E5 **Ouyen** Australia
161 G5 **Ouzel** *r.* U.K.
170 C4 **Ovace, Punta d'** *mt. Corsica* France
137 G2 **Ovacık** Turkey
170 C2 **Ovada** Italy
125 H3 **Ovalau** *i.* Fiji
215 B1 **Ovalle** Chile
167 B2 **Ovar** Port.
215 D2 **Oveja** *mt.* Arg.
127 G6 **Ovens** *r.* Australia
164 F4 **Overath** Germany
158 M2 **Överkalix** Sweden
197 E3 **Overton** U.S.A.
158 M2 **Övertorneå** Sweden
159 L4 **Överum** Sweden
164 C2 **Overveen** Neth.
190 E4 **Ovid** U.S.A.
167 D1 **Oviedo** Spain
138 E4 **Ovminzatov tog'lari** *hills* Uzbek.
158 N1 **Øvre Anárjohka Nasjonalpark** *nat. park* Norway
158 L1 **Øvre Dividal Nasjonalpark** *nat. park* Norway
159 J3 **Øvre Rendal** Norway
173 D5 **Ovruch** Ukr.
128 B7 **Owaka** N.Z.
178 B4 **Owando** Congo
151 E7 **Owase** Japan
198 E2 **Owatonna** U.S.A.
203 E3 **Owego** U.S.A.
163 B3 **Owenmore** *r.* Ireland
128 D4 **Owen River** N.Z.
196 C3 **Owens** *r.* U.S.A.
200 C4 **Owensboro** U.S.A.
196 D3 **Owens Lake** U.S.A.
191 G3 **Owen Sound** Canada
191 G3 **Owen Sound** *inlet* Canada
124 E2 **Owen Stanley Range** *mts* P.N.G.
176 C4 **Owerri** Nigeria
186 D4 **Owikeno Lake** Canada
202 B5 **Owingsville** U.S.A.
203 I2 **Owls Head** U.S.A.
176 C4 **Owo** Nigeria
191 E4 **Owosso** U.S.A.
137 K4 **Owrāmān, Kūh-e** *mts* Iran/Iraq
194 C3 **Owyhee** U.S.A.
194 C3 **Owyhee** *r.* U.S.A.
194 C3 **Owyhee Mountains** U.S.A.
210 C6 **Oxapampa** Peru
158 C1 **Öxarfjörður** *b.* Iceland
187 I5 **Oxbow** Canada
203 I1 **Oxbow** U.S.A.
159 L4 **Oxelösund** Sweden
128 D5 **Oxford** N.Z.
161 F6 **Oxford** U.K.
191 F4 **Oxford** *MI* U.S.A.
199 F5 **Oxford** *MS* U.S.A.
203 F3 **Oxford** *NY* U.S.A.
203 F5 **Oxford** *PA* U.S.A.
187 J4 **Oxford House** Canada
187 J4 **Oxford Lake** Canada
126 F5 **Oxley** Australia
127 I3 **Oxleys Peak** Australia
163 C3 **Ox Mountains** *hills* Ireland
196 C4 **Oxnard** U.S.A.
191 H3 **Oxtongue Lake** Canada
158 K2 **Øya** Norway
151 F6 **Oyama** Japan
211 H3 **Oyapock** *r.* Brazil/Fr. Guiana
178 B3 **Oyem** Gabon
162 D3 **Oykel** *r.* U.K.
176 C4 **Oyo** Nigeria
166 G3 **Oyonnax** France
138 F4 **Oyoqog'itma botig'i** *depr.* Uzbek.
138 F4 **Oyoqquduq** Uzbek.
139 J3 **Oyshilik** Kazakh.
145 H5 **Oyster Island** Myanmar
139 H4 **Oy-Tal** Kyrg.
165 H1 **Oyten** Germany
145 F1 **Oyyaylak** China
139 G4 **Oyyk** Kazakh.
138 C2 **Oyyl** Kazakh.
138 C2 **Oyyl** *r.* Kazakh.
137 I2 **Özalp** Turkey
153 B4 **Ozamis** Phil.
201 C6 **Ozark** *AL* U.S.A.
190 E2 **Ozark** *MI* U.S.A.
199 E4 **Ozark Plateau** U.S.A.
198 E4 **Ozarks, Lake of the** U.S.A.
140 E3 **Ozbakūh** Iran
146 H1 **Ozernovskiy** Russia
138 E1 **Ozernoye** Kazakh.
138 B2 **Ozernoye** Russia
138 E2 **Ozernyy** *Orenburgskaya Oblast'* Russia
172 E4 **Ozernyy** *Smolenskaya Oblast'* Russia
169 K3 **Ozersk** Russia
172 F4 **Ozery** Russia
139 H4 **Özgön** Kyrg.
170 C4 **Ozieri** *Sardinia* Italy
138 B2 **Ozinki** Russia
199 C6 **Ozona** U.S.A.
151 B7 **Ozuki** Japan
173 G7 **Ozurgeti** Georgia

P

185 N3 **Paamiut** Greenland
Pa-an Myanmar *see* **Hpa-an**
180 C6 **Paarl** S. Africa
180 D4 **Paballelo** S. Africa
152 E3 **P'abal-li** N. Korea
162 A3 **Pabbay** *i. Scotland* U.K.
162 A4 **Pabbay** *i. Scotland* U.K.
169 I5 **Pabianice** Poland
145 G4 **Pabna** Bangl.
159 N5 **Pabrad** Lith.
141 G5 **Pab Range** *mts* Pak.
210 F6 **Pacaás Novos, Parque Nacional** *nat. park* Brazil
210 C5 **Pacasmayo** Peru
195 E6 **Pacheco** *Chihuahua* Mex.
206 D2 **Pacheco** *Zacatecas* Mex.
172 H2 **Pachikha** Russia
170 F6 **Pachino** *Sicily* Italy
143 B1 **Pachmarhi** India
144 D5 **Pachor** India
207 E3 **Pachuca** Mex.
217 I9 **Pacific-Antarctic Ridge** *sea feature* Pacific Ocean
216 **Pacific Ocean**
153 C4 **Pacijan** *i.* Phil.
155 D4 **Pacitan** Indon.
211 H4 **Pacoval** Brazil
214 D2 **Pacuí** *r.* Brazil
168 H5 **Paczków** Poland
153 C5 **Padada** Phil.
213 D4 **Padamo** *r.* Venez.
155 B3 **Padang** Indon.
154 B5 **Padang Endau** Malaysia
155 B3 **Padangpanjang** Indon.
155 A2 **Padangsidimpuan** Indon.
155 C3 **Padangtikar** *i.* Indon.
172 E2 **Padany** Russia
137 L5 **Padatha, Kūh-e** *mt.* Iran
213 D4 **Padauiri** *r.* Brazil
210 F8 **Padcaya** Bol.
127 F4 **Paddington** Australia
186 F3 **Paddle Prairie** Canada
202 C5 **Paden City** U.S.A.
165 G3 **Paderborn** Germany
171 J2 **Padeșu, Vârful** *mt.* Romania
210 F7 **Padilla** Bol.
158 L2 **Padjelanta nationalpark** *nat. park* Sweden
145 G5 **Padma** *r.* Bangl.
alt. **Ganga,**
conv. **Ganges**
Padova Italy *see* **Padua**
199 D7 **Padre Island** U.S.A.
170 C3 **Padro, Monte** *mt. Corsica* France
161 C7 **Padstow** U.K.
169 M3 **Padsvillye** Belarus
126 D6 **Padthaway** Australia
143 C2 **Padua** India
170 D2 **Padua** Italy
200 B4 **Paducah** *KY* U.S.A.
199 C5 **Paducah** *TX* U.S.A.
144 D2 **Padum** India
152 E3 **Paegam** N. Korea
128 E2 **Paeroa** N.Z.
153 B3 **Paete** Phil.
Pafos Cyprus *see* **Paphos**
181 I1 **Pafuri** Moz.
170 F2 **Pag** Croatia
170 F2 **Pag** *i.* Croatia
153 B5 **Pagadian** Phil.
155 B3 **Pagai Selatan** *i.* Indon.
155 B3 **Pagai Utara** *i.* Indon.
147 G5 **Pagan** *i.* N. Mariana Is
155 E3 **Pagatan** Indon.
197 G3 **Page** U.S.A.
159 M5 **Paggiai** Lith.
212 □ **Paget, Mount** Atlantic Ocean
195 F4 **Pagosa Springs** U.S.A.
145 G4 **Pagri** China
188 C3 **Pagwa River** Canada
196 □2 **Pāhala** U.S.A.
155 B2 **Pahang** *r.* Malaysia
145 G4 **Paharpur** *tourist site* Bangl.
144 B2 **Paharpur** Pak.
128 A7 **Pahia Point** N.Z.
196 □2 **Pāhoa** U.S.A.
201 D7 **Pahokee** U.S.A.
197 E3 **Pahranagat Range** *mts* U.S.A.
144 D4 **Pahuj** *r.* India
196 D3 **Pahute Mesa** *plat.* U.S.A.
154 A1 **Pai** Thai.
159 N4 **Paide** Estonia
161 D7 **Paignton** U.K.
159 N3 **Päijänne** *l.* Fin.
145 F3 **Paikü Co** *l.* China
154 B2 **Pailĭn** Cambodia
215 B4 **Paillaco** Chile
196 □2 **Pailolo Channel** U.S.A.
159 M3 **Paimio** Fin.
215 B2 **Paine** Chile
202 C4 **Painesville** U.S.A.
197 G3 **Painted Desert** U.S.A.
197 F5 **Painted Rock Reservoir** U.S.A.
126 C3 **Painter, Mount** *h.* Australia
187 J3 **Paint Lake Provincial Recreation Park** Canada
202 B6 **Paintsville** U.S.A.
191 G3 **Paisley** Canada
162 D5 **Paisley** U.K.
210 B5 **Paita** Peru
153 A5 **Paitan, Teluk** *b. Sabah* Malaysia
149 D4 **Paizhouwan** China
158 M2 **Pajala** Sweden
211 K5 **Pajeú** *r.* Brazil
154 B4 **Paka** Malaysia
213 E4 **Pakaraima Mountains** Brazil
210 F2 **Pakaraima Mountains** Guyana
152 C4 **Pakch'ŏn** N. Korea
191 G3 **Pakesley (abandoned)** Canada
133 R3 **Pakhachi** Russia
138 D2 **Pakhar'** Kazakh.
Pakhtaabad Uzbek. *see* **Paxtaobod**
141 G4 **Pakistan** *country* Asia
128 D1 **Pakotai** N.Z.
144 C3 **Pakpattan** Pak.
154 B3 **Pak Phanang** Thai.
154 B4 **Pak Phayun** Thai.
159 M5 **Pakruojis** Lith.
169 I7 **Paks** Hungary
154 B2 **Pak Thong Chai** Thai.
141 H3 **Paktīkā** *prov.* Afgh.
154 B1 **Pakxan** Laos
154 C2 **Pakxé** Laos
177 D4 **Pala** Chad
154 A2 **Pala** Myanmar
155 C4 **Palabuhanratu** Indon.
155 C4 **Palabuhanratu, Teluk** *b.* Indon.
170 G3 **Palagruža** *i.* Croatia
171 J7 **Palaiochora** Greece
166 F2 **Palaiseau** France
143 B4 **Palakkad** India
143 D1 **Pala Laharha** India
180 E1 **Palamakoloi** Botswana
167 H2 **Palamós** Spain
144 C4 **Palana** India
133 Q4 **Palana** Russia
153 B2 **Palanan** Phil.
153 B2 **Palanan Point** Phil.
140 B3 **Palangān** Iran
141 F4 **Palangān, Kūh-e** *mts* Iran
155 D3 **Palangkaraya** Indon.
143 B4 **Palani** India
144 C4 **Palanpur** India
141 G5 **Palantak** Pak.
153 C3 **Palapag** Phil.
179 C6 **Palapye** Botswana
143 B3 **Palar** *r.* India
145 G4 **Palasbari** India
133 Q3 **Palatka** Russia
147 F6 **Palau** *country* Pacific Ocean
153 B2 **Palaui** *i.* Phil.
153 A3 **Palauig** Phil.
216 D5 **Palau Islands** Palau
154 A2 **Palauk** Myanmar
216 D5 **Palau Trench** *sea feature* N. Pacific Ocean
154 A2 **Palaw** Myanmar
153 A4 **Palawan** *i.* Phil.
216 C5 **Palawan Trough** *sea feature* N. Pacific Ocean
153 B3 **Palayan** Phil.
159 N4 **Paldiski** Estonia
145 H5 **Pale** Myanmar
155 B3 **Palembang** Indon.
212 B6 **Palena** Chile
167 D1 **Palencia** Spain
207 G4 **Palenque** Mex.
170 E5 **Palermo** *Sicily* Italy
199 E6 **Palestine** U.S.A.
145 H5 **Paletwa** Myanmar
Palghat India *see* **Palakkad**
144 C4 **Pali** India
123 F2 **Palikir** Micronesia
153 C5 **Palimbang** Phil.
176 C4 **Palimé** Togo
170 F4 **Palinuro, Capo** *c.* Italy
197 H2 **Palisade** U.S.A.
164 D5 **Paliseul** Belgium
144 B5 **Palitana** India
159 M4 **Palivere** Estonia
143 B4 **Palk Bay** Sri Lanka
172 D3 **Palkino** Russia
143 C2 **Palkohda** India
143 B3 **Palkonda Range** *mts* India
143 B4 **Palk Strait** India/Sri Lanka
127 I2 **Pallamallawa** Australia
163 C5 **Pallas Grean New** Ireland
173 H5 **Pallasovka** Russia
158 M1 **Pallas-Yllästunturin kansallispuisto** *nat. park* Fin.
143 C3 **Pallavaram** India
143 B2 **Palleru** *r.* India
128 E4 **Palliser, Cape** N.Z.
128 E4 **Palliser Bay** N.Z.
144 C3 **Pallu** India
167 D4 **Palma del Río** Spain
167 H3 **Palma de Mallorca** Spain
213 B2 **Palmar** *r.* Venez.
213 C3 **Palmarito** Venez.
211 I6 **Palmas** Brazil
176 B4 **Palmas, Cape** Liberia
214 D1 **Palmas de Monte Alto** Brazil
201 D7 **Palm Bay** U.S.A.
201 D7 **Palm Beach** U.S.A.
196 C4 **Palmdale** U.S.A.
214 B4 **Palmeira** Brazil
211 K5 **Palmeira dos Índios** Brazil
211 J5 **Palmeirais** Brazil
129 E2 **Palmer** *research stn* Antarctica
184 D3 **Palmer** U.S.A.
123 I5 **Palmerston** *atoll* Cook Is
128 C6 **Palmerston** N.Z.
128 E4 **Palmerston North** N.Z.
203 F4 **Palmerton** U.S.A.
201 E7 **Palmetto Point** Bahamas
170 F5 **Palmi** Italy
207 E3 **Palmillas** Mex.
213 A4 **Palmira** Col.
206 C3 **Palmito del Verde, Isla** *i.* Mex.
196 D5 **Palm Springs** U.S.A.
Palmyra Syria *see* **Tadmur**
190 B6 **Palmyra** *MO* U.S.A.
202 E3 **Palmyra** *NY* U.S.A.
190 C4 **Palmyra** *WI* U.S.A.
123 I3 **Palmyra Atoll** *terr.* N. Pacific Ocean
145 F5 **Palmyras Point** India
196 A3 **Palo Alto** U.S.A.
213 A3 **Palo de las Letras** Col.
177 F3 **Paloich** South Sudan
158 M1 **Palojärvi** Fin.
158 N1 **Palomaa** Fin.
207 F4 **Palomares** Mex.
196 D5 **Palomar Mountain** U.S.A.
197 G6 **Palominas** U.S.A.
143 C2 **Paloncha** India
147 E7 **Palopo** Indon.
167 F4 **Palos, Cabo de** *c.* Spain
197 F5 **Palo Verde** *AR* U.S.A.
197 E5 **Palo Verde** *CA* U.S.A.
158 N2 **Paltamo** Fin.
147 D7 **Palu** Indon.
137 G2 **Palu** Turkey
153 B3 **Paluan** Phil.
138 F5 **Pal'vart** Turkm.
144 D3 **Palwal** India
133 S3 **Palyavaam** *r.* Russia
148 A4 **Pamai** China
143 B4 **Pamban Channel** India
127 H6 **Pambula** Australia
155 C4 **Pameungpeuk** Indon.
143 B3 **Pamidi** India
166 E5 **Pamiers** France
139 H5 **Pamir** *r.* Afgh./Tajik.
139 H5 **Pamir** *mts* Asia
201 E5 **Pamlico Sound** *sea chan.* U.S.A.
199 C5 **Pampa** U.S.A.
210 F7 **Pampa Grande** Bol.
215 D2 **Pampas** *reg.* Arg.
213 B3 **Pamplona** Col.
153 B4 **Pamplona** Phil.
167 F1 **Pamplona** Spain
165 J1 **Pampow** Germany
136 C1 **Pamukova** Turkey
202 E6 **Pamunkey** *r.* U.S.A.
144 D2 **Pamzal** India
200 B4 **Pana** U.S.A.
207 G3 **Panabá** Mex.
153 C5 **Panabo** Phil.
197 E3 **Panaca** U.S.A.
153 A4 **Panagtaran Point** Phil.
155 C4 **Panaitan** *i.* Indon.
143 A3 **Panaji** India
206 I6 **Panama** *country* Central America
206 J6 **Panamá, Bahía de** *b.* Panama
206 J6 **Panamá, Canal de** Panama
206 J7 **Panama, Gulf of** Panama
206 I6 **Panamá, Istmo de** *isth.* Panama
206 J6 **Panama City** Panama
201 C6 **Panama City** U.S.A.
196 D3 **Panamint Range** *mts* U.S.A.
196 D3 **Panamint Springs** U.S.A.
196 D3 **Panamint Valley** U.S.A.
153 C4 **Panaon** *i.* Phil.
145 G4 **Panar** *r.* India
170 F5 **Panarea, Isola** *i. Isole Lipari* Italy
155 C2 **Panarik** Indon.
153 B4 **Panay** *i.* Phil.
153 C3 **Panay** *i.* Phil.
153 B4 **Panay Gulf** Phil.
197 E2 **Pancake Range** *mts* U.S.A.
171 I2 **Pančevo** Serbia
153 B4 **Pandan** *Antique* Phil.
153 C3 **Pandan** *Catanduanes* Phil.
154 □ **Pandan, Selat** *str.* Sing.
153 B4 **Pandan Bay** Phil.
154 □ **Pandan Reservoir** Sing.
144 E5 **Pandaria** India
214 D1 **Pandeiros** *r.* Brazil
143 A2 **Pandharpur** India
144 D5 **Pandhurna** India
215 F2 **Pando** Uruguay
161 E6 **Pandy** U.K.
159 N5 **Panevžys** Lith.
144 C2 **Pangi Range** *mts* Pak.
155 D3 **Pangkalanbuun** Indon.
155 A2 **Pangkalansusu** Indon.
155 C3 **Pangkalpinang** Indon.
147 E7 **Pangkalsiang, Tanjung** *pt* Indon.
145 G3 **Pangkog Co** *salt l.* China
153 B4 **Panglao** *i.* Phil.
153 A5 **Panglima Sugala** Phil.
185 L3 **Pangnirtung** Canada
132 I3 **Pangody** Russia
215 B3 **Panguipulli** Chile
215 B3 **Panguipulli, Lago** *l.* Chile
197 F3 **Panguitch** U.S.A.
154 A5 **Pangururan** Indon.
153 B5 **Pangutaran** *i.* Phil.
153 B5 **Pangutaran Group** *is* Phil.
199 C5 **Panhandle** U.S.A.
178 C4 **Pania-Mwanga** Dem. Rep. Congo
144 B5 **Panikoita** *i.* India
173 G5 **Panino** Russia
144 D3 **Panipat** India
153 A4 **Panitian** Phil.
144 B1 **Panj** *r.* Afgh./Tajik.
139 G5 **Panj** Tajik.
141 G3 **Panjāb** Afgh.
139 F5 **Panjakent** Tajik.
154 D5 **Panjang** *i.* Indon.
154 □ **Panjang, Bukit** Sing.
137 K5 **Panjbarār** Iran
141 G5 **Panjgur** Pak.
144 C5 **Panjhra** *r.* India
Panjin China *see* **Panshan**
144 B2 **Panjkora** *r.* Pak.
144 B3 **Panjnad** *r.* Pak.
137 J4 **Panjwīn/Pênjwên** Iraq
158 O3 **Pankakoski** Fin.
176 C4 **Pankshin** Nigeria
152 F2 **Pan Ling** *mts* China
144 D4 **Panna** *reg.* India
124 B4 **Pannawonica** Australia
136 D4 **Pano Lefkara** Cyprus
214 B3 **Panorama** Brazil
143 B4 **Panruti** India
152 B3 **Panshan** China
152 D2 **Panshi** China
211 G7 **Pantanal Matogrossense, Parque Nacional do** *nat. park* Brazil
170 D6 **Pantelleria** *Sicily* Italy
170 E6 **Pantelleria, Isola di** *i. Sicily* Italy
153 C5 **Pantukan** Phil.
207 E3 **Pánuco** Mex.
207 E3 **Pánuco** *r.* Mex.
143 A2 **Panvel** India
Panxian China *see* **Chengguan**
149 D6 **Panyu** China
149 A5 **Panzhihua** China
178 B4 **Panzi** Dem. Rep. Congo
207 G5 **Panzos** Guat.
213 E3 **Pao** *r.* Venez.
170 G5 **Paola** Italy
200 C4 **Paoli** U.S.A.
178 B3 **Paoua** C.A.R.
Pap Uzbek. *see* **Pop**
168 H7 **Pápa** Hungary
170 F4 **Papa, Monte del** *mt.* Italy
128 E2 **Papakura** N.Z.
207 E3 **Papantla** Mex.
143 C2 **Paparhahandi** India
128 C5 **Paparoa National Park** N.Z.
128 C5 **Paparoa Range** *mts* N.Z.
162 □ **Papa Stour** *i.* U.K.
128 E2 **Papatoetoe** N.Z.
128 B7 **Papatowai** N.Z.
162 F1 **Papa Westray** *i.* U.K.
164 F1 **Papenburg** Germany
136 D4 **Paphos** Cyprus
192 E6 **Papigochic** *r.* Mex.
191 J2 **Papineau-Labelle, Réserve Faunique de** *nature res.* Canada
197 E3 **Papoose Lake** U.S.A.
165 I6 **Pappenheim** Germany
162 B5 **Paps of Jura** *hills* U.K.
124 E2 **Papua, Gulf of** P.N.G.
124 E2 **Papua New Guinea** *country* Oceania
Papun Myanmar *see* **Hpapun**
161 C7 **Par** U.K.
214 D2 **Pará** *r.* Brazil
172 G4 **Para** *r.* Russia
211 I4 **Pará, Rio do** *r.* Brazil
124 B4 **Paraburdoo** Australia
153 B3 **Paracale** Phil.
214 C2 **Paracatu** Brazil
214 D2 **Paracatu** *r.* Brazil
147 D5 **Paracel Islands** S. China Sea
126 C3 **Parachilna** Australia
171 I3 **Paraćin** Serbia
214 D2 **Pará de Minas** Brazil
191 I1 **Paradis** Canada
196 B2 **Paradise** *CA* U.S.A.
190 E2 **Paradise** *MI* U.S.A.
187 H4 **Paradise Hill** Canada
196 D2 **Paradise Peak** U.S.A.
189 I3 **Paradise River** Canada
199 F4 **Paragould** U.S.A.
210 F6 **Paragua** *r.* Bol.
213 E3 **Paragua** *r.* Venez.
211 G7 **Paraguai** *r.* Brazil
213 C2 **Paraguáipoa** Venez.
213 C1 **Paraguaná, Península de** *pen.* Venez.
212 E3 **Paraguay** *r.* Arg./Para.
212 E2 **Paraguay** *country* S. America
211 K5 **Paraíba** *r.* Brazil
214 D3 **Paraíba do Sul** *r.* Brazil
207 F4 **Paraíso** Mex.
176 C4 **Parakou** Benin
126 B3 **Parakylia** Australia
143 D2 **Paralakhemundi** India
144 E6 **Paralkot** India
143 B4 **Paramakkudi** India
211 G2 **Paramaribo** Suriname
213 B3 **Paramillo** *mt.* Col.
213 A3 **Paramillo, Parque Nacional** *nat. park* Col.
214 D1 **Paramirim** Brazil
213 A3 **Paramo Frontino** *mt.* Col.
203 F4 **Paramus** U.S.A.
146 H1 **Paramushir, Ostrov** *i.* Russia
215 E1 **Paraná** Arg.
211 I6 **Paranã** Brazil
214 C1 **Paraná** *r.* Brazil
214 B4 **Paraná** *state* Brazil
212 E4 **Paraná** *r.* S. America
214 C1 **Paraná, Serra do** *hills* Brazil
214 C4 **Paranaguá** Brazil
214 B2 **Paranaíba** Brazil
214 B2 **Paranaíba** *r.* Brazil
215 E2 **Paraná Ibicuy** *r.* Arg.
214 B3 **Paranapanema** *r.* Brazil
214 C4 **Paranapiacaba, Serra** *mts* Brazil
153 C4 **Paranas** Phil.
214 B3 **Paranavaí** Brazil
153 B5 **Parang** Phil.
143 B4 **Parangipettai** India
171 J2 **Parângul Mare, Vârful** *mt.* Romania
214 D2 **Paraopeba** *r.* Brazil
137 J4 **Pārapāra** Iraq
128 E4 **Paraparaumu** N.Z.
213 D3 **Paraque, Cerro** *mt.* Venez.
207 E2 **Paras** Mex.
144 D5 **Parasia** India
144 D5 **Paratwada** India
137 K4 **Parāū, Kūh-e** *mt.* Iraq
214 B2 **Paraúna** Brazil
166 G3 **Paray-le-Monial** France
144 D4 **Parbati** *r.* India
143 B2 **Parbhani** India
139 F1 **Parchevka** Kazakh.
165 J1 **Parchim** Germany
190 C4 **Pardeeville** U.S.A.
145 G2 **Parding** China
214 E1 **Pardo** *r. Bahia* Brazil
214 B3 **Pardo** *r. Mato Grosso do Sul* Brazil
214 D1 **Pardo** *r. Minas Gerais* Brazil
214 C3 **Pardo** *r. São Paulo* Brazil
168 G5 **Pardubice** Czech Rep.
144 D2 **Pare Chu** *r.* China
210 F6 **Parecis, Serra dos** *hills* Brazil
206 D2 **Paredón** Mex.
140 B2 **Pareh** Iran
128 D1 **Parengarenga Harbour** N.Z.
188 E4 **Parent, Lac** *l.* Canada
128 C6 **Pareora** N.Z.
155 E3 **Parepare** Indon.
215 D2 **Parera** Arg.
172 G3 **Parfen'yevo** Russia
169 O2 **Parfino** Russia
171 I5 **Parga** Greece
159 M3 **Pargas** Fin.
213 E2 **Paria, Gulf of** Trin. and Tob./Venez.
213 E2 **Paria, Península de** *pen.* Venez.
213 D2 **Pariaguán** Venez.
197 F3 **Paria Plateau** U.S.A.
159 O3 **Parikkala** Fin.
213 D4 **Parima, Serra** *mts* Brazil
213 D4 **Parima-Tapirapecó, Parque Nacional** *nat. park* Venez.
210 B4 **Pariñas, Punta** *pt* Peru
126 D5 **Paringa** Australia
211 G4 **Parintins** Brazil
191 G4 **Paris** Canada
166 F2 **Paris** France
(City Plan **110**)
202 A5 **Paris** *KY* U.S.A.
201 B4 **Paris** *TN* U.S.A.
199 E5 **Paris** *TX* U.S.A.
164 A5 **Paris (Charles de Gaulle)** *airport* France
190 E2 **Parisienne, Île** *i.* Canada
206 I7 **Parita** Panama
140 D4 **Pārīz** Iran
138 E1 **Parizh** Russia
163 D3 **Park** U.K.
143 B2 **Parkal** India
159 M3 **Parkano** Fin.
189 I3 **Parke Lake** Canada
139 G4 **Parkent** Uzbek.
197 E4 **Parker** U.S.A.
149 □ **Parker, Mount** *h. Hong Kong* China
197 E4 **Parker Dam** U.S.A.
187 J2 **Parker Lake** Canada
190 A4 **Parkersburg** *IA* U.S.A.
202 C5 **Parkersburg** *WV* U.S.A.
127 H4 **Parkes** Australia
190 B3 **Park Falls** U.S.A.
190 D5 **Park Forest** U.S.A.
191 F2 **Parkinson** Canada
198 E2 **Park Rapids** U.S.A.
186 E5 **Parksville** Canada
203 F4 **Parksville** U.S.A.
143 D2 **Parla Kimedi** India
143 B2 **Parli Vaijnath** India
170 D2 **Parma** Italy
194 C3 **Parma** *ID* U.S.A.
202 C4 **Parma** *OH* U.S.A.
213 D3 **Parmana** Venez.
211 J4 **Parnaíba** Brazil
211 J4 **Parnaíba** *r.* Brazil
128 D5 **Parnassus** N.Z.
Parnassus, Mount *mt.* Greece *see* **Liakoura**
126 B5 **Parndana** Australia
190 A5 **Parnell** U.S.A.
171 J6 **Parnonas** *mts* Greece
159 N4 **Pärnu** Estonia
159 N4 **Pärnu-Jaagupi** Estonia
171 K6 **Paroikia** Greece
126 F2 **Paroo** *watercourse* Australia
126 E3 **Paroo-Darling National Park** Australia
Paropamisus *mts* Afgh. *see* **Safēd Kōh, Silsilah-ye**
171 K6 **Paros** *i.* Greece
197 F3 **Parowan** U.S.A.
181 I1 **Parque Nacional do Limpopo** S. Africa
215 B3 **Parral** Chile
203 F6 **Parramore Island** U.S.A.
206 D2 **Parras** Mex.
215 F3 **Parravicini** Arg.
161 E6 **Parrett** *r.* U.K.
206 H6 **Parrita** Costa Rica
189 H4 **Parrsboro** Canada
184 F2 **Parry, Cape** Canada
184 G2 **Parry Islands** Canada
191 G3 **Parry Sound** Canada
140 D5 **Pārsīān** Iran
199 E4 **Parsons** *KS* U.S.A.
202 D5 **Parsons** *WV* U.S.A.
165 H4 **Partenstein** Germany
166 D3 **Parthenay** France
150 C3 **Partizansk** Russia
161 H4 **Partney** U.K.
163 B4 **Partry** Ireland
163 B4 **Partry Mountains** *hills* Ireland
211 H4 **Paru** *r.* Brazil
213 D3 **Parucito** *r.* Venez.
143 C2 **Parvatipuram** India
144 C4 **Parvatsar** India
144 D4 **Parwan** *r.* India
145 E3 **Paryang** China
181 G3 **Parys** S. Africa
140 D3 **Pās, Chāh** *well* Iran
196 C4 **Pasadena** *CA* U.S.A.
199 E6 **Pasadena** *TX* U.S.A.
210 B4 **Pasado, Cabo** *c.* Ecuador
154 B2 **Pa Sak, Mae Nam** *r.* Thai.
140 D4 **Pasargadae** *tourist site* Iran
155 B3 **Pasarseblat** Indon.
154 A1 **Pasawng** Myanmar
199 F6 **Pascagoula** U.S.A.
191 I1 **Pascalis** Canada
169 M7 **Pașcani** Romania
194 C2 **Pasco** U.S.A.
214 E2 **Pascoal, Monte** *h.* Brazil
Pascua, Isla de *i.* S. Pacific Ocean *see* **Easter Island**
Pas de Calais *str.* France/U.K. *see* **Dover, Strait of**
168 G4 **Pasewalk** Germany
187 H3 **Pasfield Lake** Canada
172 E2 **Pasha** Russia
153 B3 **Pasig** Phil.
137 H2 **Pasinler** Turkey
154 □ **Pasir Gudang** Malaysia
154 □ **Pasir Panjang** Sing.
155 B1 **Pasir Putih** Malaysia
196 A2 **Paskenta** U.S.A.
141 F5 **Paskūh** Iran
141 F5 **Pasni** Pak.
207 G4 **Paso Caballos** Guat.
215 F2 **Paso de los Toros** Uruguay
212 B7 **Paso Río Mayo** Arg.
196 B4 **Paso Robles** U.S.A.
187 I4 **Pasquia Hills** Canada
203 I2 **Passadumkeag** U.S.A.
190 C1 **Passage Island** U.S.A.
168 F6 **Passau** Germany
153 B4 **Passi** Phil.
212 F3 **Passo Fundo** Brazil
214 C3 **Passos** Brazil
172 C4 **Pastavy** Belarus
210 C4 **Pastaza** *r.* Peru
213 A4 **Pasto** Col.
197 H3 **Pastora Peak** U.S.A.
153 B2 **Pasuquin** Phil.
155 D4 **Pasuruan** Indon.
159 N4 **Pasvalys** Lith.
153 B5 **Pata** *i.* Phil.
212 B7 **Patagonia** *reg.* Arg.
197 G6 **Patagonia** U.S.A.
145 G4 **Patakata** India
144 C5 **Patan** *Gujarat* India
144 D5 **Patan** *Madhya Pradesh* India
145 F4 **Patan** Nepal
126 E5 **Patchewollock** Australia
128 E3 **Patea** N.Z.
128 E3 **Patea** *r.* N.Z.
160 F3 **Pateley Bridge** U.K.
145 G5 **Patenga Point** Bangl.
180 F6 **Patensie** S. Africa
170 F6 **Paternò** *Sicily* Italy
127 I4 **Paterson** Australia
127 G1 **Paterson** *r.* Australia
203 F4 **Paterson** U.S.A.
144 C2 **Pathankot** India
144 D4 **Pathena** India
194 F3 **Pathfinder Reservoir** U.S.A.
154 A3 **Pathiu** Thai.
143 B2 **Pathri** India
154 B2 **Pathum Thani** Thai.
155 D4 **Pati** Indon.
213 A4 **Patía** *r.* Col.
144 D3 **Patiala** India
171 L6 **Patmos** *i.* Greece
145 F4 **Patna** India
143 C1 **Patnagarh** India
153 B3 **Patnanongan** *i.* Phil.
137 I2 **Patnos** Turkey
144 E3 **Paton** India
171 H4 **Patos** Albania
211 K5 **Patos** Brazil
212 F4 **Patos, Lagoa dos** *l.* Brazil
214 C2 **Patos de Minas** Brazil
215 C1 **Patquía** Arg.
171 I5 **Patras** Greece
158 B2 **Patreksfjörður** Iceland
214 C2 **Patrocínio** Brazil
158 O1 **Patsoyoki** *r.* Europe
143 A2 **Pattadakal** *tourist site* India
154 B4 **Pattani** Thai.
154 B4 **Pattani, Mae Nam** *r.* Thai.
154 B2 **Pattaya** Thai.
203 I2 **Patten** U.S.A.
165 H2 **Pattensen** Germany
196 B3 **Patterson** U.S.A.
202 D5 **Patterson** *r.* U.S.A.
186 C2 **Patterson, Mount** Canada
190 E3 **Patterson, Point** U.S.A.
196 C3 **Patterson Mountain** U.S.A.
158 N2 **Pattijoki** Fin.
158 M1 **Pättikkä** Fin.
143 B3 **Pattikonda** India
186 D3 **Pattullo, Mount** Canada
145 G5 **Patuakhali** Bangl.
187 H3 **Patuanak** Canada
206 H5 **Patuca** *r.* Hond.
206 H5 **Patuca, Punta** *pt* Hond.
202 E5 **Patuxent** *r.* U.S.A.
206 D4 **Pátzcuaro** Mex.
166 D5 **Pau** France
166 D4 **Pauillac** France
145 H5 **Pauktaw** Myanmar
197 F4 **Paulden** U.S.A.
202 A4 **Paulding** U.S.A.
189 H2 **Paul Island** Canada
211 J5 **Paulistana** Brazil
211 K5 **Paulo Afonso** Brazil
181 I3 **Paulpietersburg** S. Africa
181 G4 **Paul Roux** S. Africa
203 F2 **Paul Smiths** U.S.A.
163 D5 **Paulstown** Ireland
199 D5 **Pauls Valley** U.S.A.
213 C3 **Pauto** *r.* Col.
214 E2 **Pavão** Brazil
140 B3 **Pāveh** Iran
170 C2 **Pavia** Italy
159 M4 **Pāvilosta** Latvia
172 H3 **Pavino** Russia
171 K3 **Pavlikeni** Bulg.
139 I1 **Pavlodar** Kazakh.
139 H2 **Pavlodarskaya Oblast'** *admin. div.* Kazakh.
139 H1 **Pavlogradka** Russia
173 E5 **Pavlohrad** Ukr.
139 H2 **Pavlovka** Kazakh.
172 H4 **Pavlovka** Russia
172 G4 **Pavlovo** Russia
173 G5 **Pavlovsk** Russia
173 F6 **Pavlovskaya** Russia
213 B4 **Pavón** Col.
144 E3 **Pawayan** India
190 E4 **Paw Paw** U.S.A.
203 H4 **Pawtucket** U.S.A.
154 A2 **Pawut** Myanmar
139 H4 **Paxtaobod** Uzbek.
190 C5 **Paxton** U.S.A.
155 B3 **Payakumbuh** Indon.
154 □ **Paya Lebar** Sing.
194 C2 **Payette** U.S.A.
132 H3 **Pay-Khoy, Khrebet** *hills* Russia
188 F2 **Payne, Lac** *l.* Canada
196 B1 **Paynes Creek** U.S.A.
215 E2 **Paysandú** Uruguay
197 G4 **Payson** *AZ* U.S.A.
197 G1 **Payson** *UT* U.S.A.
215 C3 **Payún, Cerro** *vol.* Arg.
136 D1 **Pazar** *Ankara* Turkey
137 H1 **Pazar** *Rize* Turkey
136 F3 **Pazarcık** Turkey
171 K3 **Pazardzhik** Bulg.
213 C3 **Paz de Ariporo** Col.
213 B3 **Paz de Río** Col.
170 E2 **Pazin** Croatia
186 G3 **Peace** *r.* Canada
186 F3 **Peace River** Canada
197 F4 **Peach Springs** U.S.A.
161 F4 **Peak District National Park** U.K.
126 A2 **Peake** *watercourse* Australia
189 G4 **Peaked Mountain** *h.* U.S.A.
153 A4 **Peaked Point** Phil.
127 H4 **Peak Hill** Australia
197 H2 **Peale, Mount** U.S.A.
197 H6 **Pearce (abandoned)** U.S.A.
190 C1 **Pearl** Canada
199 F6 **Pearl** *r.* U.S.A.
123 H1 **Pearl and Hermes Atoll** U.S.A.
196 □1 **Pearl City** U.S.A.
196 □1 **Pearl Harbor** *inlet* U.S.A.
199 D6 **Pearsall** U.S.A.
201 D6 **Pearson** U.S.A.
185 H2 **Peary Channel** Canada
188 C2 **Peawanuck** Canada
179 D5 **Pebane** Moz.
Peć Kosovo *see* **Pejë**
214 D2 **Peçanha** Brazil
158 O1 **Pechenga** Russia
132 G3 **Pechora** Russia
220 D2 **Pechora** *r.* Russia
172 C3 **Pechory** Russia
191 F4 **Peck** U.S.A.
186 E3 **Peck, Mount** Canada
154 C2 **Pe Cô, Krông** *r.* Vietnam
199 C6 **Pecos** U.S.A.
199 C6 **Pecos** *r.* U.S.A.
171 H1 **Pécs** Hungary
206 I7 **Pedasí** Panama
127 G9 **Pedder, Lake** Australia
181 G6 **Peddie** S. Africa
206 C1 **Pedernales** Mex.
Pêdo La *pass* China *see* **Pindu Pass**
214 E1 **Pedra Azul** Brazil
213 C3 **Pedraza la Vieja** Venez.
213 C2 **Pedregal** Venez.
214 C3 **Pedregulho** Brazil
211 J4 **Pedreiras** Brazil
206 D2 **Pedriceña** Mex.
143 C4 **Pedro, Point** Sri Lanka
211 I5 **Pedro Afonso** Brazil
213 C4 **Pedro Chico** Col.
212 C2 **Pedro de Valdivia** Chile
214 A2 **Pedro Gomes** Brazil
206 J6 **Pedro González, Isla** *i.* Panama
211 J4 **Pedro II** Brazil
213 D4 **Pedro II, Ilha** *reg.* Brazil
212 E2 **Pedro Juan Caballero** Para.
215 G1 **Pedro Osório** Brazil
162 E5 **Peebles** U.K.
201 E5 **Pee Dee** *r.* U.S.A.
203 G4 **Peekskill** U.S.A.
127 I3 **Peel** *r.* Australia
184 E3 **Peel** *r.* Canada
160 C3 **Peel** U.K.
164 D3 **Peer** Belgium
186 F4 **Peers** Canada
126 E3 **Peery Lake** *salt l.* Australia

177 D4 Poli Cameroon
168 G4 Police Poland
170 G4 Policoro Italy
166 G3 Poligny France
153 B3 Polillo i. Phil.
153 B3 Polillo Islands Phil.
153 B3 Polillo Strait Phil.
136 D4 Polis Cyprus
173 D5 Polis'ke (abandoned) Ukr.
168 H5 Polkowice Poland
183 B4 Pollachi India
165 H3 Polle Germany
167 H3 Pollença Spain
170 G5 Pollino, Monte mt. Italy
158 N1 Polmak Norway
158 O2 Polo Fin.
190 C5 Polo U.S.A.
173 F6 Polohy Ukr.
181 H1 Polokwane S. Africa
181 H1 Polokwane r. S. Africa
172 I3 Polom Russia
153 C5 Polomolok Phil.
143 C5 Polonnaruwa Sri Lanka
173 C5 Polonne Ukr.
161 C7 Polperro U.K.
194 D2 Polson U.S.A.
172 G1 Poltava r. Ukr.
173 E5 Poltava Ukr.
158 B2 Poltavka Russia
153 B4 Poltavskaya Russia
159 N4 Põltsamaa Estonia
159 N4 Põltsamaa Estonia
158 O3 Põlva Estonia
158 P1 Polyarnyy Russia
133 S3 Polyarnyy (abandoned) Russia
158 P2 Polyarnyy Zori Russia
171 J4 Polygyros Greece
171 J4 Polykastro Greece
216 H6 Polynesia is Oceania
159 M3 Pomarkku Fin.
167 B3 Pomba r. Brazil
167 B3 Pombal Port.
176 ☐ Pombal r. Brazil
168 G5 Pomeranian Bay Poland
212 G3 Pomerode Brazil
181 I4 Pomeroy S. Africa
163 E3 Pomeroy U.K.
202 B5 Pomeroy U.S.A.
170 E4 Pomezia Italy
180 E2 Pomfret S. Africa
124 F2 Pomio P.N.G.
196 D4 Pomona U.S.A.
171 L3 Pomorie Bulg.
Pomorska, Zatoka b. Poland see Pomeranian Bay
172 E1 Pomorskiy Bereg coastal area Russia
201 D7 Pompano Beach U.S.A.
170 F4 Pompei Italy
214 D2 Pompéu Brazil
172 H3 Pomozyrevo Russia
199 D4 Ponca City U.S.A.
205 K5 Ponce Puerto Rico
195 F4 Poncha Springs U.S.A.
188 E3 Poncheville, Lac l. Canada
Pondicherry India see Puducherry
185 K2 Pond Inlet Canada
189 I3 Ponds, Island of Canada
206 H5 Ponds, Island of Canada
167 C1 Poneloya Nicaragua
128 F4 Pongaroa N.Z.
177 E4 Pongo watercourse South Sudan
181 I3 Pongola r. S. Africa
181 I3 Pongolapoort Dam l. S. Africa
169 O3 Ponizov'ye Russia
143 B3 Ponnaiyar r. India
143 A4 Ponnani India
145 H5 Ponnyadaung Range mts Myanmar
186 G4 Ponoka Canada
138 C1 Ponomarevka Russia
156 A6 Ponta Delgada Azores
176 ☐ Ponta do Sol Cape Verde
214 B4 Ponta Grossa Brazil
166 H2 Pont-à-Mousson France
214 A3 Pontalina Brazil
166 H3 Pontarlier France
199 F6 Pontchartrain, Lake U.S.A.
161 D5 Pontcysyllte Aqueduct and Canal tourist site U.K.
164 C3 Ponte-de-Loup Belgium
167 B3 Ponte de Sor Port.
160 F4 Pontefract U.K.
160 F2 Ponteland U.K.
211 G7 Pontes e Lacerda Brazil
167 B1 Pontevedra Spain
191 F4 Pontiac IL U.S.A.
191 F4 Pontiac MI U.S.A.
155 C3 Pontianak Indon.
166 C2 Pontivy France
166 B3 Pont-l'Abbé France
166 F2 Pontoise France
187 J4 Ponton Canada
199 F5 Pontotoc U.S.A.
170 C2 Pontremoli Italy
191 H3 Pontypool Canada
161 D6 Pontypool U.K.
161 D6 Pontypridd U.K.
170 E4 Ponza, Isola di i. Italy
170 E4 Ponziane, Isole is Italy
126 A4 Poochera Australia
161 F7 Poole U.K.
Poona India see Pune
126 E4 Pooncarie Australia
126 F3 Poopelloe Lake salt l. Australia
210 E7 Poopó, Lago de l. Bol.
128 E1 Poor Knights Islands N.Z.
139 G4 Pop Uzbek.
213 A4 Popayán Col.
164 A4 Poperinge Belgium
133 L2 Popigay r. Russia
126 D4 Popiltah Australia
126 D4 Popilta Lake imp. l. Australia
187 J4 Poplar r. Canada
191 F4 Poplar U.S.A.
199 F4 Poplar Bluff U.S.A.
202 C6 Poplar Camp U.S.A.
199 F6 Poplarville U.S.A.
207 E4 Popocatépetl, Volcán vol. Mex.
178 B4 Popokabaka Dem. Rep. Congo
171 L3 Popovo Bulg.
165 I3 Poppenberg h. Germany
169 J6 Poprad Slovakia
141 G5 Porali r. Pak.
128 F4 Porangahau N.Z.
214 C1 Porangatu Brazil
142 C4 Porbandar India
213 B3 Porce r. Col.
186 C4 Porcher Island Canada
184 E3 Porcuna Spain
219 H2 Porcupine Abyssal Plain sea feature N. Atlantic Ocean
187 I4 Porcupine Hills Canada
190 C2 Porcupine Mountains U.S.A.
187 I4 Porcupine Provincial Forest nature res. Canada
213 C3 Pore Col.
170 E2 Poreč Croatia
172 H4 Poretskoye Russia
159 M3 Pori Fin.
128 F5 Porirua N.Z.
172 D3 Porkhov Russia
213 E2 Porlamar Venez.
166 C3 Pornic France
166 G3 Poronaysk Russia
145 G3 Porong China
171 J6 Poros Greece
172 E2 Porosozero Russia
158 N1 Porsangen sea chan. Norway see Porsangerfjorden
159 J4 Porsgrunn Norway

136 C2 Porsuk r. Turkey
126 C5 Port Adelaide Australia
163 E3 Portadown U.K.
163 F3 Portaferry U.K.
203 I1 Portage ME U.S.A.
190 E4 Portage MI U.S.A.
190 C4 Portage WI U.S.A.
187 J5 Portage la Prairie Canada
198 C1 Portal U.S.A.
186 E5 Port Alberni Canada
127 G7 Port Albert Australia
167 C3 Portalegre Port.
199 C5 Portales U.S.A.
186 C3 Port Alexander U.S.A.
181 G6 Port Alfred S. Africa
186 D4 Port Alice Canada
202 D4 Port Allegany U.S.A.
199 F6 Port Allen U.S.A.
194 B1 Port Angeles U.S.A.
163 D4 Portarlington Ireland
127 G9 Port Arthur Australia
199 E6 Port Arthur U.S.A.
162 B5 Port Askaig U.K.
126 B4 Port Augusta Australia
205 J5 Port-au-Prince Haiti
191 F3 Port Austin U.S.A.
189 I3 Port aux Choix Canada
163 F3 Portavogie U.K.
180 D7 Port Beaufort S. Africa
135 H5 Port Blair India
191 H3 Port Bolster Canada
167 H1 Portbou Spain
191 G4 Port Burwell Canada
126 E7 Port Campbell Australia
191 H3 Port Carling Canada
128 C6 Port Chalmers N.Z.
201 D7 Port Charlotte U.S.A.
203 G4 Port Chester U.S.A.
186 C4 Port Clements Canada
202 B4 Port Clinton U.S.A.
203 I3 Port Clyde U.S.A.
191 H4 Port Colborne Canada
186 E5 Port Coquitlam Canada
191 H4 Port Credit Canada
127 F9 Port Davey b. Australia
205 J5 Port-de-Paix Haiti
154 B5 Port Dickson Malaysia
202 C3 Port Dover Canada
190 D3 Porte des Morts lake channel U.S.A.
186 C4 Port Edward Canada
181 I5 Port Edward S. Africa
202 B4 Port Edwards U.S.A.
214 D1 Porteirinha Brazil
211 H4 Portel Brazil
191 G3 Port Elgin Canada
181 F6 Port Elizabeth S. Africa
162 B5 Port Ellen U.K.
126 C5 Port Elliot Australia
160 C3 Port Erin U.K.
187 H2 Porter Lake Canada
180 C6 Porterville S. Africa
196 C3 Porterville U.S.A.
126 E7 Port Fairy Australia
128 E2 Port Fitzroy N.Z.
136 D6 Port Fuad Egypt
178 A4 Port-Gentil Gabon
167 C3 Port Germein Australia
199 F6 Port Gibson U.S.A.
162 D5 Port Glasgow U.K.
176 C4 Port Harcourt Nigeria
186 D4 Port Hardy Canada
Port Harrison Canada see Inukjuak
189 H4 Port Hawkesbury Canada
161 D6 Porthcawl U.K.
124 B4 Port Hedland Australia
203 G2 Port Henry U.S.A.
161 B7 Porthleven U.K.
161 C6 Porthmadog U.K.
191 H4 Port Hope Canada
189 I3 Port Hope Simpson Canada
191 F4 Port Huron U.S.A.
167 B4 Portimão Port.
149 ☐ Port Island Hong Kong China
127 I4 Port Jackson inlet Australia
203 G4 Port Jefferson U.S.A.
203 F4 Port Jervis U.S.A.
210 G2 Port Kaituma Guyana
127 I5 Port Kembla Australia
127 H4 Portland N.S.W. Australia
126 D7 Portland Vic. Australia
190 E5 Portland IN U.S.A.
203 H3 Portland ME U.S.A.
194 B2 Portland OR U.S.A.
161 E7 Portland, Isle of pen. U.K.
186 C3 Portland Canal inlet Canada
128 F3 Portland Island N.Z.
163 D4 Portlaoise Ireland
199 D6 Port Lavaca U.S.A.
163 D5 Portlaw Ireland
162 F3 Portlethen U.K.
126 A5 Port Lincoln Australia
176 A4 Port Loko Sierra Leone
124 F3 Port MacDonnell Australia
127 J3 Port Macquarie Australia
189 H2 Port Manvers inlet Canada
186 D4 Port McNeill Canada
189 H4 Port-Menier Canada
184 B4 Port Moller b. U.S.A.
194 B1 Port Moody Canada
124 E2 Port Moresby P.N.G.
126 B2 Portnaguran U.K.
162 B5 Portnahaven U.K.
126 B5 Port Neill Australia
201 F7 Port Nelson Bahamas
Port Nis U.K. see Port of Ness
180 B4 Port Nolloth S. Africa
Port-Nouveau-Québec Canada see Kangiqsualujjuaq
Porto Port. see Oporto
210 E5 Porto Acre Brazil
214 B3 Porto Alegre Mato Grosso do Sul Brazil
212 F4 Porto Alegre Rio Grande do Sul Brazil
211 G6 Porto Artur Brazil
206 J6 Portobelo Panama
211 G6 Porto dos Gaúchos Óbidos Brazil
211 G7 Porto Esperidião Brazil
170 D3 Portoferraio Italy
162 B2 Port of Ness U.K.
211 I5 Porto Franco Brazil
213 E2 Port of Spain Trin. and Tob.
170 E2 Portogruaro Italy
214 A2 Porto Jofre Brazil
196 B2 Portola U.S.A.
170 C4 Portomaggiore Italy
214 A4 Porto Mendes Para.
211 G8 Porto Murtinho Brazil
211 I6 Porto Nacional Brazil
176 C4 Porto-Novo Benin
214 B3 Porto Primavera, Represa resr Brazil
214 A3 Porto Seguro Brazil
170 E2 Porto Tolle Italy
170 C4 Porto Torres Sardinia Italy
170 C4 Porto-Vecchio Corsica France
210 F5 Porto Velho Brazil
210 B4 Portoviejo Ecuador
162 C6 Portpatrick U.K.
161 H3 Port Perry Canada
161 F7 Port Pirie Australia
161 B7 Portreath U.K.
162 B3 Portree U.K.
186 E5 Port Renfrew Canada
191 G4 Port Rowan Canada
202 E5 Port Royal U.S.A.
161 C6 Portrush U.K.
136 C4 Port Said Egypt
201 C6 Port St Joe U.S.A.
181 H5 Port St Johns S. Africa
160 C3 Port St Mary U.K.
163 C3 Portsalon Ireland
191 F4 Port Sanilac U.S.A.
191 H3 Port Severn Canada
149 ☐ Port Shelter b. Hong Kong China

181 I5 Port Shepstone S. Africa
Port Simpson Canada see Lax Kw'alaams
161 F7 Portsmouth U.K.
203 H3 Portsmouth NH U.S.A.
202 B5 Portsmouth OH U.S.A.
203 E6 Portsmouth VA U.S.A.
162 F3 Portsoy U.K.
127 J4 Port Stephens b. Australia
163 E2 Portstewart U.K.
177 F3 Port Sudan Sudan
201 B6 Port Sulphur U.S.A.
161 D6 Port Talbot U.K.
158 N1 Porttipahdan tekojärvi resr Fin.
167 B3 Portugal country Europe
167 E1 Portugalete Spain
213 C2 Portuguesa r. Venez.
163 C4 Portumna Ireland
166 F5 Port-Vendres France
126 B5 Port Victoria Australia
125 G3 Port Vila Vanuatu
158 P1 Port-Vladimir Russia
128 E2 Port Waikato N.Z.
126 C5 Port Wakefield Australia
190 D4 Port Washington U.S.A.
162 D6 Port William U.K.
190 B2 Port Wing U.S.A.
215 D2 Porvenir Arg.
159 N3 Porvoo Fin.
167 D1 Posada Spain
212 E3 Posadas Arg.
171 H2 Posavina reg. Bos. & Herz./Croatia
191 F3 Posen U.S.A.
137 K5 Posht-e Kūh mts Iran
140 C2 Posht Kūh h. Iran
158 O2 Posio Fin.
147 E7 Poso Indon.
137 I1 Posof Turkey
139 J1 Pospelikha Russia
214 C1 Posse Brazil
129 B5 Possession Islands is Antarctica
165 J3 Pößneck Germany
199 C5 Post U.S.A.
Poste-de-la-Baleine Canada see Kuujjuarapik
180 E4 Postmasburg S. Africa
189 I3 Postville Canada
190 B4 Postville U.S.A.
170 G3 Posušje Bos. & Herz.
150 B3 Pos'yet Russia
181 G3 Potchefstroom S. Africa
199 E5 Poteau U.S.A.
211 K5 Potengi r. Brazil
170 F4 Potenza Italy
128 A7 Poteriteri, Lake N.Z.
180 F5 Potfontein S. Africa
Potgietersrus S. Africa see Mokopane
199 D6 Poth U.S.A.
211 J5 Poti r. Brazil
173 G7 Poti Georgia
143 C2 Potikhal India
176 D3 Potiskum Nigeria
194 D2 Pot Mountain U.S.A.
149 ☐ Po Toi i. Hong Kong China
202 E5 Potomac r. U.S.A.
202 D5 Potomac, South Branch r. U.S.A.
202 D5 Potomac, South Fork South Branch r. U.S.A.
210 E7 Potosí Bol.
198 F4 Potosi U.S.A.
197 E4 Potosí Mex.
153 B4 Pototan Phil.
207 H5 Potrerillos Hond.
165 L2 Potsdam Germany
203 F2 Potsdam U.S.A.
161 F6 Potters Bar U.K.
203 F4 Pottstown U.S.A.
203 E4 Pottsville U.S.A.
143 C5 Pottuvil Sri Lanka
186 E3 Pouce Coupe Canada
189 I4 Pouch Cove Canada
203 G4 Poughkeepsie U.S.A.
203 G3 Poultney U.S.A.
160 E4 Poulton-le-Fylde U.K.
214 D3 Pouso Alegre Brazil
154 B2 Poŭthĭsăt Cambodia
169 I6 Považská Bystrica Slovakia
172 E2 Povenets Russia
128 F3 Poverty Bay N.Z.
199 F5 Poverty Point tourist site U.S.A.
171 H2 Povlen mt. Serbia
167 B2 Póvoa de Varzim Port.
173 G5 Povorino Russia
150 C3 Povorotnyy, Mys hd Russia
196 D5 Poway U.S.A.
194 F3 Powder r. U.S.A.
194 F3 Powder River U.S.A.
194 E2 Powell U.S.A.
202 B6 Powell r. U.S.A.
197 G3 Powell, Lake resr U.S.A.
196 C2 Powell Mountain U.S.A.
201 E7 Powell Point Bahamas
186 E5 Powell River Canada
190 D3 Powers U.S.A.
202 E6 Powhatan U.S.A.
214 A1 Poxoréo Brazil
149 E4 Poyang China
149 E4 Poyang Hu l. China
154 ☐ Poyan Reservoir Sing.
126 D3 Poygan, Lake U.S.A.
141 F4 Pōzak, Jahīl-e marsh Afgh.
136 E3 Pozantı Turkey
171 I2 Požarevac Serbia
207 E3 Poza Rica Mex.
170 G2 Požega Croatia
171 I3 Požega Serbia
150 D1 Pozharskoye Russia
168 H4 Poznań Poland
167 D3 Pozoblanco Spain
206 B1 Pozo Nuevo Mex.
170 F4 Pozzuoli Italy
155 B3 Prabumulih Indon.
169 G6 Prachatice Czech Rep.
145 F6 Prachi r. India
154 B2 Prachin Buri Thai.
154 A3 Prachuap Khiri Khan Thai.
166 F5 Prades France
214 E2 Prado Brazil
168 G5 Prague Czech Rep.
Praha Czech Rep. see Prague
176 ☐ Praia Cape Verde
181 J2 Praia do Bilene Moz.
211 A1 Praia Rica Brazil
190 E5 Prairie Creek Reservoir U.S.A.
199 C5 Prairie Dog Town Fork r. U.S.A.
190 B4 Prairie du Chien U.S.A.
154 B2 Prakhon Chai Thai.
143 B2 Pranhita r. India
143 D2 Prantij India
155 A2 Prapat Indon.
171 L7 Prasonisi, Akrotirio pt Greece
214 C2 Prata Brazil
214 C2 Prata r. Brazil
170 D3 Prato Italy
199 D4 Pratt U.S.A.
201 C5 Prattville U.S.A.
143 I4 Pravara r. India
169 J3 Pravdinsk Russia
155 C2 Preăh Vihéar Cambodia
169 P3 Prechistoye Russia
187 I4 Preeceville Canada
172 B4 Pregolya r. Russia
159 N4 Preiļi Latvia
191 I1 Preissac, Lac l. Canada
166 F5 Premer Australia
203 H4 Prémery France
165 K2 Premnitz Germany
190 B4 Prentice U.S.A.
168 F4 Prenzlau Germany
150 C3 Preobrazheniye Russia
169 H6 Přerov Czech Rep.
203 H2 Prescott Canada

197 F4 Prescott U.S.A.
197 F4 Prescott Valley U.S.A.
161 C6 Preseli, Mynydd hills U.K.
171 I3 Preševo Serbia
198 C3 Presho U.S.A.
212 D3 Presidencia Roque Sáenz Peña Arg.
212 D3 Prunelli-di-Fiumorbo Corsica France
211 J5 Presidente Dutra Brazil
173 D6 Prut r. Moldova/Romania
210 F6 Presidente Hermes Brazil
129 E5 Prydz Bay b. Antarctica
153 B4 Presidente Manuel A Roxas Phil.
173 E5 Pryluky Ukr.
214 B3 Presidente Prudente Brazil
173 F6 Prymors'k Ukr.
214 B3 Presidente Venceslau Brazil
193 G4 Pryor U.S.A.
186 E3 Presidio U.S.A.
169 M4 Pryp"yat' r. Belarus
139 I1 Presnogor'kovka Kazakh.
alt. Pryp"yat' (Ukraine), conv. Pripet
171 I4 Presnovka Kazakh.
169 L5 Pryp"yat' r. Ukr.
203 J1 Presque Isle U.S.A.
alt. Prypyats' (Belarus), conv. Pripet
190 D2 Presque Isle Point U.S.A.
161 D5 Presteigne U.K.
161 K6 Przemyśl Poland
194 E3 Preston U.K.
169 K6 Przheval'sk Kyrg. see Karakol
194 A3 Preston ID U.S.A.
171 K5 Psara i. Greece
190 A4 Preston MN U.S.A.
173 G6 Psebay Russia
199 E4 Preston MO U.S.A.
173 F6 Pshish r. Russia
197 E2 Preston NV U.S.A.
172 D3 Pskov Russia
162 F5 Prestonpans U.K.
159 N4 Pskov, Lake Estonia/Russia
202 B6 Prestonsburg U.S.A.
172 D3 Pskovskaya Oblast' admin. div. Russia
162 E5 Prestwick U.K.
171 J4 Ptolemaïda Greece
214 E1 Preto r. Bahia Brazil
170 F1 Ptuj Slovenia
214 C2 Preto r. Minas Gerais Brazil
154 B1 Pua Thai.
181 H2 Pretoria S. Africa
215 D3 Puán Arg.
202 E5 Prettyboy Lake U.S.A.
206 D2 Puapua Samoa
165 K3 Pretzsch Germany
210 D5 Pucallpa Peru
171 I5 Preveza Greece
149 F5 Pucheng Fujian China
154 C3 Prey Vêng Cambodia
148 C3 Pucheng Shaanxi China
133 Q4 Priargun'skiy Karakum des. Kazakh.
172 G3 Puchezh Russia
133 U4 Pribilof Islands U.S.A.
153 B4 Pucio Point Phil.
171 H3 Priboj Serbia
168 I3 Puck Poland
189 G4 Price r. Canada
197 G2 Price U.S.A.
190 C4 Price Island Canada
201 B6 Prichard U.S.A.
194 M4 Priekule Latvia
215 B3 Pucón Chile
159 M4 Priekuļi Latvia
141 F4 Pūdah Tal, Shēlah-ye watercourse Afgh.
159 N5 Prienai Lith.
140 D3 Pūdanū Iran
180 E4 Prieska S. Africa
158 N2 Pudasjärvi Fin.
194 C1 Priest Lake U.S.A.
180 F3 Pudimoe S. Africa
194 C1 Priest River U.S.A.
148 F4 Pudong China
167 D1 Prieta, Peña mt. Spain
172 F2 Pudozh Russia
169 I6 Prievidza Slovakia
160 F4 Pudsey U.K.
165 K1 Prignitz reg. Germany
143 B4 Puducherry India
171 I3 Prijedor Bos. & Herz.
143 B4 Puducherry union terr. India
171 H3 Prijepolje Serbia
143 B4 Pudukkottai India
Prikaspiyskaya Nizmennost' lowland Kazakh./Russia see Caspian Lowland
207 H4 Puebla Mex.
207 F4 Puebla state Mex.
171 I4 Prilep Macedonia
167 C3 Puebla de Sanabria Spain
165 K5 Přimda Czech Rep.
195 F4 Pueblo U.S.A.
215 D2 Primero r. Arg.
213 C2 Pueblo Nuevo Venez.
127 G8 Prime Seal Island Australia
207 F4 Pueblo Viejo tourist site Mex.
159 O3 Primorsk Russia
215 D3 Puelches Arg.
150 C2 Primorsky Kray admin. div. Russia
215 C3 Puelén Arg.
173 F6 Primorsko-Akhtarsk Russia
215 C4 Puente Alto Chile
196 D5 Primo Tapia Mex.
207 E4 Puente de Ixtla Mex.
187 H4 Primrose Lake Canada
167 D4 Puente Genil Spain
187 H4 Prince Albert Canada
215 B3 Puerto Aisén Chile
180 E7 Prince Albert S. Africa
212 B7 Puerto Alegre Bol.
184 G2 Prince Albert National Park Canada
207 E5 Puerto Ángel Mex.
184 G2 Prince Albert Peninsula Canada
207 F5 Puerto Arista Mex.
180 D6 Prince Albert Road S. Africa
206 I6 Puerto Armuelles Panama
184 G2 Prince Albert Sound sea chan. Canada
213 A4 Puerto Asís Col.
180 D6 Prince Alfred, Cape Canada
213 D3 Puerto Ayacucho Venez.
184 F1 Prince Alfred, Cape Canada
210 ☐ Puerto Baquerizo Moreno Galápagos Is Ecuador
185 K3 Prince Charles Island Canada
206 G5 Puerto Barrios Guat.
129 D5 Prince Charles Mountains mts Antarctica
213 B3 Puerto Berrío Col.
189 H4 Prince Edward Island prov. Canada
213 C2 Puerto Berrío Col.
218 G8 Prince Edward Islands Indian Ocean
206 I5 Puerto Cabezas Nicaragua
191 I4 Prince Edward Point Canada
206 I5 Puerto Cabezas Nicaragua
202 E5 Prince Frederick U.S.A.
213 C2 Puerto Carreño Col.
186 E4 Prince George Canada
212 C2 Puerto Casado Para.
184 B3 Prince of Wales, Cape U.S.A.
212 B6 Puerto Cisnes Chile
185 I2 Prince of Wales Island Australia
212 C2 Puerto Coig (abandoned) Arg.
186 C3 Prince of Wales Island Canada
215 C8 Puerto Coig (abandoned) Arg.
184 G2 Prince of Wales Island Canada
213 B4 Puerto Concordia Col.
184 F2 Prince Patrick Island Canada
207 H5 Puerto Cortés Hond.
185 I2 Prince Regent Inlet sea chan. Canada
206 B2 Puerto Cortés Mex.
186 C4 Prince Rupert Canada
213 C2 Puerto Cumarebo Venez.
203 F5 Princess Anne U.S.A.
207 F5 Puerto de Morelos Mex.
124 E3 Princess Charlotte Bay Australia
215 B7 Puerto Deseado Arg.
129 D4 Princess Elisabeth research stn Antarctica
207 E5 Puerto Escondido Mex.
213 C1 Puerto Estrella Col.
129 D5 Princess Elizabeth Land reg. Antarctica
210 F6 Puerto Frey Bol.
187 J2 Princess Mary Lake Canada
212 E2 Puerto Guaraní Para.
184 D3 Princess Royal Island Canada
210 E6 Puerto Heath Bol.
186 E5 Princeton Canada
211 G7 Puerto Isabel Bol.
196 A2 Princeton CA U.S.A.
206 H6 Puerto Jesús Costa Rica
190 C6 Princeton IL U.S.A.
207 H4 Puerto Juárez Mex.
200 C4 Princeton IN U.S.A.
213 D2 Puerto La Cruz Venez.
203 J2 Princeton ME U.S.A.
210 D4 Puerto Leguízamo Col.
198 F4 Princeton MO U.S.A.
210 D4 Puerto Lempira Hond.
191 F4 Princeton NJ U.S.A.
206 I6 Puerto Limón Costa Rica
190 C4 Princeton WI U.S.A.
167 D3 Puertollano Spain
202 C5 Princeton WV U.S.A.
206 I6 Puerto Lobos Arg.
203 J2 Prince William Canada
207 F4 Puerto López Col.
184 D3 Prince William Sound b. U.S.A.
207 H5 Puerto Madero Mex.
176 C4 Príncipe i. São Tomé and Príncipe
215 D6 Puerto Madryn Arg.
194 B2 Prineville U.S.A.
210 E6 Puerto Maldonado Peru
212 C3 Prins Karls Forland i. Svalbard
213 D3 Puerto Máncora Peru
206 I5 Prinzapolka Nicaragua
213 B4 Puerto Miraña Venez.
172 D2 Priozersk Russia
206 H5 Puerto Montt Nicaragua
169 L5 Pripet r. Belarus/Ukr.
212 B8 Puerto Natales Chile
alt. Pryp"yat' (Ukraine), alt. Prypyats' (Belarus)
213 C5 Puerto Nuevo Col.
158 C1 Prirechnyy Russia
206 J6 Puerto Obaldía Panama
171 I3 Prishtinë Kosovo
213 D3 Puerto Ordaz Venez.
Prishtinê Kosovo see Prishtinë
213 D3 Puerto Páez Venez.
165 J1 Pritzier Germany
204 B2 Puerto Peñasco Mex.
165 K1 Pritzwalk Germany
212 C7 Puerto Pinasco Para.
166 G4 Privas France
213 C1 Puerto Píritu Venez.
170 G3 Privlaka Croatia
205 J5 Puerto Plata Dom. Rep.
172 G3 Privolzhsk Russia
210 D5 Puerto Portillo Peru
172 H4 Privolzhskaya Vozvyshennost' hills Russia
153 A4 Puerto Princesa Phil.
138 B1 Priyutnoye Russia
215 D2 Puerto Príncipe Arg.
173 G6 Priyutnoye Russia
205 K5 Puerto Rico terr. Caribbean Sea
173 D6 Prizren Kosovo
219 E4 Puerto Rico Trench sea feature Caribbean Sea
155 C4 Probolinggo Indon.
213 C3 Puerto Rondón Col.
165 J4 Probstzella Germany
206 J5 Puerto Sandino Nicaragua
161 C7 Probus U.K.
207 G5 Puerto San José Guat.
190 A2 Proctor MN U.S.A.
212 C7 Puerto Santa Cruz Arg.
203 G3 Proctor VT U.S.A.
215 C8 Puerto Santa Cruz Arg.
211 G3 Professor van Blommestein Meer resr Suriname
213 C2 Puerto Tejada Col.
Progreso Hond. see El Progreso
206 C3 Puerto Vallarta Mex.
206 D2 Progreso Coahuila Mex.
213 C5 Puerto Vázquez Guachi Bol.
207 E3 Progreso Hidalgo Mex.
215 B4 Puerto Varas Chile
207 G3 Progreso Yucatán Mex.
173 I4 Pugachev Russia
129 D5 Progress research stn Antarctica
142 C4 Pugal India
170 H4 Prokhladnyy Russia
149 E5 Puge China
173 J4 Prokop'yevsk Russia
140 D4 Pūhāl-e Khamīr, Kūh-e mts Iran
171 I3 Prokuplje Serbia
148 C2 Pu He r. China
173 G6 Proletarsk Russia
173 G6 Proletarskoye Vodokhranilishche l. Russia
140 C3 Pūhīpān Iran
141 I5 Puiju China
214 A2 Promissão Brazil
152 E3 Pujon-ho resr N. Korea
190 E1 Prophet r. Canada
152 E3 Pujujil Guat.
186 F3 Prophet River Canada
152 E3 Pŭkaki, Lake N.Z.
124 C4 Proserpine Australia
152 E3 Pukch'ŏng N. Korea
203 F3 Prospect U.S.A.
128 C6 Pukaki, Lake N.Z.
180 D7 Prosperidad Phil.
152 E3 Pukch'ŏng N. Korea
153 C4 Prosperidad Phil.
152 E3 Pukchin N. Korea
180 A4 Protivín Czech Rep.
128 F3 Pukehina N.Z.
166 H5 Provence reg. France
128 C6 Pukeuri Junction N.Z.
171 L3 Provadia Bulg.
152 E3 Pukhovichy Belarus
203 H3 Providence U.S.A.
216 H6 Pukapuka atoll Cook Is
206 I5 Providencia, Isla de i. Col.
190 D2 Pukaskwa National Park Canada
184 A3 Providenya Russia
152 E3 Pukč'ŏng N. Korea
202 E6 Provincetown U.S.A.
152 E3 Pukchin N. Korea
197 G1 Provo U.S.A.
152 E3 Pulandian Wan b. China
152 D3 Pulandian China
153 C5 Pulangi r. Phil.
203 E3 Pulaski NY U.S.A.

187 G4 Provost Canada
214 B4 Prudentópolis Brazil
184 D2 Prudhoe Bay U.S.A.
164 F4 Prüm Germany
164 E4 Prüm r. Germany
212 D3 Prunelli-di-Fiumorbo Corsica France
169 J4 Pruszków Poland
173 D6 Prut r. Moldova/Romania
129 E5 Prydz Bay b. Antarctica
173 E5 Pryluky Ukr.
173 F6 Prymors'k Ukr.
193 G4 Pryor U.S.A.
169 M4 Pryp"yat' r. Belarus
alt. Pryp"yat' (Ukraine), conv. Pripet
169 L5 Pryp"yat' r. Ukr.
alt. Prypyats' (Belarus), conv. Pripet
161 K6 Przemyśl Poland
169 K6 Przheval'sk Kyrg. see Karakol
171 K5 Psara i. Greece
173 G6 Psebay Russia
173 F6 Pshish r. Russia
172 D3 Pskov Russia
159 N4 Pskov, Lake Estonia/Russia
172 D3 Pskovskaya Oblast' admin. div. Russia
171 J4 Ptolemaïda Greece
170 F1 Ptuj Slovenia
154 B1 Pua Thai.
215 D3 Puán Arg.
149 B5 Pu'an Guizhou China
148 B4 Pu'an Sichuan China
149 C6 Pubei China
210 D5 Pucallpa Peru
149 F5 Pucheng Fujian China
148 C3 Pucheng Shaanxi China
172 G3 Puchezh Russia
153 B4 Pucio Point Phil.
168 I3 Puck Poland
190 C4 Puckaway Lake U.S.A.
215 B3 Pucón Chile
141 F4 Pūdah Tal, Shēlah-ye watercourse Afgh.
140 D3 Pūdanū Iran
158 N2 Pudasjärvi Fin.
180 F3 Pudimoe S. Africa
148 F4 Pudong China
172 F2 Pudozh Russia
160 F4 Pudsey U.K.
143 B4 Puducherry India
143 B4 Puducherry union terr. India
143 B4 Pudukkottai India
207 H4 Puebla Mex.
207 F4 Puebla state Mex.
167 C3 Puebla de Sanabria Spain
195 F4 Pueblo U.S.A.
213 C2 Pueblo Nuevo Venez.
207 F4 Pueblo Viejo tourist site Mex.
215 D3 Puelches Arg.
215 C3 Puelén Arg.
215 C4 Puente Alto Chile
207 E4 Puente de Ixtla Mex.
167 D4 Puente Genil Spain
213 C2 Puente Torres Venez.
212 B7 Puerto Alegre Bol.
207 E5 Puerto Ángel Mex.
207 F5 Puerto Arista Mex.
206 I6 Puerto Armuelles Panama
213 A4 Puerto Asís Col.
213 D3 Puerto Ayacucho Venez.
210 ☐ Puerto Baquerizo Moreno Galápagos Is Ecuador
206 G5 Puerto Barrios Guat.
213 B3 Puerto Berrío Col.
213 C2 Puerto Berrío Col.
206 I5 Puerto Cabello Venez.
206 I5 Puerto Cabezas Nicaragua
206 I6 Puerto Cabo Gracias a Dios Nicaragua
213 C2 Puerto Carreño Col.
212 C2 Puerto Casado Para.
212 B6 Puerto Cisnes Chile
212 C2 Puerto Coig (abandoned) Arg.
215 C8 Puerto Coig (abandoned) Arg.
213 B4 Puerto Concordia Col.
207 H5 Puerto Cortés Hond.
206 B2 Puerto Cortés Mex.
213 C2 Puerto Cumarebo Venez.
207 F5 Puerto de Morelos Mex.
215 B7 Puerto Deseado Arg.
207 E5 Puerto Escondido Mex.
213 C1 Puerto Estrella Col.
210 F6 Puerto Frey Bol.
212 E2 Puerto Guaraní Para.
210 E6 Puerto Heath Bol.
211 G7 Puerto Isabel Bol.
206 H6 Puerto Jesús Costa Rica
207 H4 Puerto Juárez Mex.
213 D2 Puerto La Cruz Venez.
210 D4 Puerto Leguízamo Col.
210 D4 Puerto Lempira Hond.
206 I6 Puerto Limón Costa Rica
167 D3 Puertollano Spain
206 I6 Puerto Lobos Arg.
207 F4 Puerto López Col.
207 H5 Puerto Madero Mex.
215 D6 Puerto Madryn Arg.
210 E6 Puerto Maldonado Peru
213 D3 Puerto Máncora Peru
213 B4 Puerto Miraña Venez.
206 H5 Puerto Morazán Nicaragua
212 B8 Puerto Natales Chile
213 C5 Puerto Nuevo Col.
206 J6 Puerto Obaldía Panama
213 D3 Puerto Ordaz Venez.
213 D3 Puerto Páez Venez.
204 B2 Puerto Peñasco Mex.
212 C7 Puerto Pinasco Para.
213 C1 Puerto Píritu Venez.
205 J5 Puerto Plata Dom. Rep.
210 D5 Puerto Portillo Peru
153 A4 Puerto Princesa Phil.
215 D2 Puerto Príncipe Arg.
205 K5 Puerto Rico terr. Caribbean Sea
219 E4 Puerto Rico Trench sea feature Caribbean Sea
213 C3 Puerto Rondón Col.
206 J5 Puerto Sandino Nicaragua
207 G5 Puerto San José Guat.
212 C7 Puerto Santa Cruz Arg.
215 C8 Puerto Santa Cruz Arg.
213 C2 Puerto Tejada Col.
206 C3 Puerto Vallarta Mex.
213 C5 Puerto Vázquez Guachi Bol.
215 B4 Puerto Varas Chile
173 I4 Pugachev Russia
142 C4 Pugal India
149 E5 Puge China
140 D4 Pūhāl-e Khamīr, Kūh-e mts Iran
148 C2 Pu He r. China
140 C3 Pūhīpān Iran
141 I5 Puigcerdà Spain
152 E3 Pujon-ho resr N. Korea
216 H6 Pukapuka atoll Cook Is
190 D2 Pukaskwa National Park Canada
152 E3 Pukchin N. Korea
128 C6 Pukaki, Lake N.Z.
152 E3 Pukch'ŏng N. Korea
128 F3 Pukehina N.Z.
128 C6 Pukeuri Junction N.Z.
152 E3 Pukhovichy Belarus
152 E3 Puksubaek-san mt. N. Korea
170 E2 Pula Croatia
210 E8 Pulacayo Bol.
152 B4 Pulandian China
152 D3 Pulandian Wan b. China
153 C5 Pulangi' r. Phil.
203 E3 Pulaski NY U.S.A.

201 C5 Pulaski TN U.S.A.
202 C5 Pulaski VA U.S.A.
190 C3 Pulaski WI U.S.A.
169 J5 Puławy Poland
141 H3 Pul-e 'Alam Afgh.
141 H3 Pul-e Khumrī Afgh.
139 G4 Pülgön Kyrg.
164 E3 Pulheim Germany
143 C3 Pulicat Lake inlet India
143 B3 Pulivendla India
143 B4 Puliyangudi India
158 N2 Pulkkila Fin.
194 C2 Pullman U.S.A.
158 P1 Pulozero Russia
206 B2 Púlpito, Punta pt Mex.
144 E1 Pulu China
137 G2 Pülümür Turkey
153 C5 Pulutan Indon.
145 G3 Puma Yumco l. China
210 B4 Puná, Isla i. Ecuador
145 G3 Punakha Bhutan
144 C2 Punch India
186 E4 Punchaw Canada
145 G3 Püncogling China
181 I1 Punda Maria S. Africa
144 B3 Pundri India
152 E3 P'ungsan N. Korea
179 D5 Púngué r. Moz.
178 C4 Punia Dem. Rep. Congo
215 B1 Punitaqui Chile
144 C3 Punjab state India
144 B3 Punjab prov. Pak.
144 D2 Punmah Glacier Pak.
172 G3 Punpun r. India
205 K5 Punta, Cerro de mt. Puerto Rico
215 D3 Punta Alta Arg.
212 B8 Punta Arenas Chile
215 F2 Punta del Este Uruguay
215 D4 Punta Delgada Arg.
206 G4 Punta Gorda Belize
206 I6 Punta Gorda Nicaragua
201 D7 Punta Gorda U.S.A.
215 D4 Punta Norte Arg.
206 H6 Puntarenas Costa Rica
134 C6 Puntland reg. Somalia
213 C2 Punto Fijo Venez.
202 D4 Punxsutawney U.S.A.
158 N2 Puokio Fin.
158 N3 Puolanka Fin.
140 E5 Pur Iran
133 I3 Pur r. Russia
213 A4 Puracé, Parque Nacional nat. park Col.
213 A4 Puracé, Volcán de vol. Col.
199 D5 Purcell U.S.A.
186 F4 Purcell Mountains Canada
215 C6 Purén Chile
195 G4 Purgatoire r. U.S.A.
145 F6 Puri India
164 C2 Purmerend Neth.
143 B2 Purna India
144 D5 Purna r. Maharashtra India
144 D6 Purna r. Maharashtra India
145 G4 Purnabhaba r. India
215 B4 Purranque Chile
206 D3 Puruándiro Mex.
145 F5 Puruliya India
210 F4 Purus r. Brazil
159 O3 Puruvesi l. Fin.
155 C4 Purwakarta Indon.
155 C4 Purwodadi Indon.
155 C4 Purwokerto Indon.
152 E2 Puryŏng N. Korea
144 D6 Pus r. India
143 C2 Pusad India
203 I2 Pushaw Lake U.S.A.
144 C4 Pushkar India
172 D3 Pushkin Russia
173 H5 Pushkino Russia
172 H2 Pushma Russia
Pusht-i-Rud reg. Afgh. see Zamīndāwar
169 N2 Pustoshka Russia
176 D4 Putao Myanmar
149 F5 Putian China
152 B2 Putian China
144 E5 Putla Mex.
165 K3 Putlitz Germany
171 L2 Putna r. Romania
203 H4 Putnam U.S.A.
203 G3 Putney U.S.A.
132 I3 Putorana, Plato plat. Russia
135 I6 Putrajaya Indon.
145 H3 Putrang La pass China
180 D4 Puttalam Sri Lanka
143 A5 Puttalam Lagoon Sri Lanka
164 G2 Putten Neth.
164 C3 Puttershoek Neth.
168 E3 Puttgarden Germany
210 D4 Putumayo r. Col.
136 C2 Pütürge Turkey
155 D2 Putussibau Indon.
172 G4 Putyatino Russia
173 F5 Putyvl' Ukr.
159 O3 Puumala Fin.
196 ☐ Pu'uwai U.S.A.
188 F1 Puvirnituq Canada
194 B2 Puyallup U.S.A.
148 E3 Puyang China
215 B4 Puyehue, Parque Nacional nat. park Chile
166 F5 Puylaurens France
128 A7 Puysegur Point N.Z.
179 C4 Pweto Dem. Rep. Congo
161 C5 Pwllheli U.K.
172 H4 Pyal'ma Russia
158 O2 Pyaozero, Ozero l. Russia
159 O3 Pyaozerskiy Russia
132 J2 Pyasina r. Russia
173 G6 Pyatigorsk Russia
138 B2 Pyatimarskoye Kazakh.
173 E5 P"yatykhatky Ukr.
145 H6 Pyè Myanmar
128 E4 Pye, Mount h. N.Z.
152 E5 Pyeongchang S. Korea
152 E5 Pyeongtaek S. Korea
201 C4 Pyeongtaek S. Korea
172 H3 Pyetrykaw Belarus
145 H5 Pyin-U-Lwin Myanmar
145 H6 Pyle U.K.
132 J3 Pyl'karamo Russia
171 I5 Pylos Greece
191 F4 Pymatuning Reservoir U.S.A.
152 C5 Pyŏkseong N. Korea
152 E5 P'yŏktong N. Korea
152 E3 P'yŏnggang N. Korea
152 C4 P'yŏngsong N. Korea
126 F3 P'yŏngyang N. Korea
191 D3 Pyramid Hill Australia
196 C2 Pyramid Lake U.S.A.
196 C2 Pyramid Point U.S.A.
196 C2 Pyramid Range mts U.S.A.
170 F2 Pyramids of Giza tourist site Egypt
166 E5 Pyrenees mts France/Spain
171 I6 Pyrgos Greece
173 E5 Pyryatyn Ukr.
168 G4 Pyrzyce Poland
172 H2 Pyshchug Russia

Sabarmati

144 C5 Sabarmati r. India
170 E4 Sabaudia Italy
141 E3 Sabbeh Iran
180 E5 Sabelo S. Africa
177 D2 Sabhā Libya
140 B6 Şabḩā' Saudi Arabia
144 D3 Sabi r. India
181 J2 Sabie Moz.
181 J2 Sabie r. Moz./S. Africa
181 I2 Sabie S. Africa
206 D2 Sabinas Mex.
207 D2 Sabinas Hidalgo Mex.
199 E6 Sabine Lake U.S.A.
137 L1 Sabirabad Azer.
153 B3 Sablayan Phil.
185 L5 Sable, Cape Canada
201 D7 Sable, Cape U.S.A.
185 M5 Sable Island Canada
189 I5 Sable Island National Park Reserve nat. park Canada
191 F2 Sables, River aux r. Canada
140 D4 Sablū'īyeh Iran
138 A4 Şabran Azer.
177 D1 Şabrātah Libya
129 C6 Sabrina Coast coastal area Antarctica
153 B1 Sabtang i. Phil.
167 C2 Sabugal Port.
190 B4 Sabula U.S.A.
142 B6 Şabyā Saudi Arabia
141 E2 Sabzevār Iran
171 M2 Sacalinul Mare, Insula i. Romania
171 K2 Săcele Romania
179 B5 Sachanga Angola
152 E6 Sacheon Gyeongsangnam-do S. Korea
152 E6 Sacheon Gyeongsangnam-do S. Korea
188 B3 Sachigo r. Canada
188 B3 Sachigo Lake Canada
144 C5 Sachin India
144 D2 Sach Pass India
165 K3 Sachsen land Germany
165 J3 Sachsen-Anhalt land Germany
165 H6 Sachsenheim Germany
184 F2 Sachs Harbour Canada
203 E3 Sackets Harbor U.S.A.
165 G4 Sackpfeife h. Germany
189 H4 Sackville Canada
203 H3 Saco ME U.S.A.
194 F1 Saco MT U.S.A.
153 B5 Sacol i. Phil.
196 B2 Sacramento U.S.A.
196 B2 Sacramento r. U.S.A.
195 F5 Sacramento Mountains U.S.A.
194 B3 Sacramento Valley U.S.A.
181 G6 Sada S. Africa
167 F1 Sádaba Spain
140 C4 Sa'dābād Iran
136 F4 Şadad Syria
145 G4 Sadakphu mt. India/Nepal
154 B4 Sadao Thai.
137 J5 Saddat al Hindīyah Iraq
181 I2 Saddleback pass S. Africa
154 C3 Sa Đec Vietnam
145 H3 Sadêng China
140 D4 Şādeqīyeh Iran
141 E5 Sadīj watercourse Iran
144 B3 Sadiqabad Pak.
144 C1 Sad Ishtrāgh mt. Afgh./Pak.
137 K5 Sa'dīyah, Hawr as imp. l. Iraq
140 D5 Sa'diyyat i. U.A.E.
140 E2 Şad Kharv Iran
167 B3 Sado r. Port.
151 F6 Sadoga-shima i. Japan
146 F3 Sado-shima i. Japan
167 H3 Sa Dragonera i. Spain
159 J4 Sæby Denmark
140 D4 Şafāshahr Iran
137 K6 Safayal Maqūf well Iraq
141 H2 Safēd Khir, Kōh-e mts Afgh.
141 F3 Safēd Kōh, Silsilah-ye mts Afgh.
159 K4 Säffle Sweden
197 H5 Safford U.S.A.
161 H5 Saffron Walden U.K.
176 B1 Safi Morocco
140 C2 Safīd r. Iran
140 D3 Safīd Ab Iran
141 F4 Safīd Ābeh Iran
136 F4 Şāfītā Syria
132 F3 Safonovo Arkhangel'skaya Oblast' Russia
158 P1 Safonovo Murmanskaya Oblast' Russia
172 E4 Safonovo Smolenskaya Oblast' Russia
136 D1 Safranbolu Turkey
137 K6 Safwān Iraq
145 F3 Saga China
151 B8 Saga Japan
138 E2 Saga Kostanayskaya Oblast' Kazakh.
138 F2 Saga Kostanayskaya Oblast' Kazakh.
151 F7 Sagamihara Japan
151 F7 Sagami-nada g. Japan
151 F7 Sagami-wan b. Japan
213 B3 Sagamoso r. Col.
139 I4 Sagankuduk China
154 A2 Saganthit Kyun i. Myanmar
143 A3 Sagar Karnataka India
143 B2 Sagar Karnataka India
144 D5 Sagar Madhya Pradesh India
173 H7 Sagarejo Georgia
145 G5 Sagar Island India
133 N2 Sagastyr Russia
140 D3 Sāghand Iran
141 F3 Sāghar Afgh.
143 B3 Sagileru r. India
191 F4 Saginaw U.S.A.
191 F4 Saginaw Bay U.S.A.
189 H2 Saglek Bay Canada
170 C3 Sagone, Golfe de b. Corsica France
167 B4 Sagres Port.
145 H5 Sagu Myanmar
195 F4 Saguache U.S.A.
205 H4 Sagua la Grande Cuba
197 G5 Saguaro National Park U.S.A.
189 F4 Saguenay r. Canada
167 F3 Sagunto Spain
144 C5 Sagwara India
138 C2 Sagyz Kazakh.
138 C2 Sagyz r. Kazakh.
213 B2 Sahagún Col.
167 D1 Sahagún Spain
137 K3 Sahand, Kūh-e mt. Iran
176 C2 Sahara des. Africa
144 D3 Saharanpur India
145 F4 Saharsa India
144 D3 Sahaswan India
140 C6 Sahbā', Wādī as watercourse Saudi Arabia
137 L1 Sahil Azer.
144 C3 Sahiwal Pak.
141 E3 Sahlābād Iran
137 K4 Şaḩneh Iran
137 J6 Şaḩrā al Ḩijārah reg. Iraq
206 B1 Sahuaripa Mex.
197 G6 Sahuarita U.S.A.
206 D3 Sahuayo Mex.
154 D2 Sa Huynh Vietnam
144 C5 Sahyadriparvat Range hills India
144 E4 Sai r. India
154 B4 Sai Buri Thai.
154 B4 Sai Buri, Mae Nam r. Thai.
Saïda Lebanon see Sidon
141 E5 Sa'īdābād Iran
154 B2 Sai Dao Tai, Khao mt. Thai.
141 F5 Sa'īdī Iran
145 G4 Saidpur Bangl.
144 C2 Saidu Pak.
Saigon Vietnam see Ho Chi Minh City
154 C3 Sai Gon, Sông r. Vietnam
Saigon, Sông r. Vietnam see Sai Gon, Sông
145 H5 Saiha India
148 D1 Saihan Tal China
148 A1 Saihan Toroi China
151 C8 Saijō Japan
151 B8 Saiki Japan
149 □ Sai Kung Hong Kong China
159 O3 Saimaa l. Fin.
136 F2 Saimbeyli Turkey
206 D3 Sain Alto Mex.
141 F4 Saindak Pak.
162 F5 St Abb's Head U.K.
161 B7 St Agnes U.K.
161 A8 St Agnes i. U.K.
189 I4 St Alban's Canada
161 G6 St Albans U.K.
203 G2 St Albans VT U.S.A.
202 C5 St Albans WV U.S.A.
St Alban's Head U.K. see St Aldhelm's Head
186 G4 St Albert Canada
161 E7 St Aldhelm's Head U.K.
164 B4 St-Amand-les-Eaux France
166 F3 St-Amand-Montrond France
166 G3 St-Amour France
203 J2 St Andrews Canada
162 F4 St Andrews U.K.
205 I5 St Ann's Bay Jamaica
163 F6 St Ann's Head U.K.
189 I3 St Anthony Canada
194 E3 St Anthony U.S.A.
126 E6 St Arnaud Australia
128 D5 St Arnaud Range mts N.Z.
189 I3 St-Augustin Canada
201 D6 St Augustine U.S.A.
161 C7 St Austell U.K.
166 E3 St-Avertin France
164 E5 St-Avold France
205 L5 St-Barthélemy terr. Caribbean Sea
160 D3 St Bees U.K.
160 D3 St Bees Head U.K.
161 B6 St Bride's Bay U.K.
166 C2 St-Brieuc France
191 H4 St Catharines Canada
201 D6 St Catherines Island U.S.A.
161 F7 St Catherine's Point U.K.
166 E4 St-Céré France
203 G2 St-Césaire Canada
166 G4 St-Chamond France
194 E3 St Charles ID U.S.A.
202 E5 St Charles MD U.S.A.
190 A4 St Charles MN U.S.A.
198 F4 St Charles MO U.S.A.
191 F4 St Clair U.S.A.
191 F4 St Clair Shores U.S.A.
166 G3 St-Claude France
161 C6 St Clears U.K.
198 E2 St Cloud U.S.A.
189 G4 St Croix r. Canada
190 A2 St Croix r. U.S.A.
205 L5 St Croix i. Virgin Is (U.S.A.)
190 A3 St Croix Falls U.S.A.
197 G6 St David U.S.A.
163 F6 St David's U.K.
161 B6 St David's Head U.K.
164 A6 St-Denis France
166 H2 St-Dié-des-Vosges France
166 G2 St-Dizier France
187 J5 Sainte Anne Canada
189 G3 Ste-Anne, Lac l. Canada
189 F4 Ste-Anne-de-Beaupré Canada
203 I1 Ste-Anne-de-Madawaska Canada
191 J2 Ste-Anne-du-Lac Canada
203 H1 Ste-Camille-de-Lellis Canada
166 G4 St-Égrève France
203 H1 Ste-Justine Canada
203 I1 St-Éleuthère Canada
186 B2 St Elias Mountains Canada
189 G3 Ste-Marguerite r. Canada
166 H5 Ste-Maxime France
166 D4 Saintes France
203 G2 Ste-Thérèse Canada
166 G4 St-Étienne France
203 F2 St Eugene Canada
203 G2 St-Eustache Canada
189 F4 St-Félicien Canada
163 F3 Saintfield U.K.
170 C3 St-Florent Corsica France
166 F3 St-Florent-sur-Cher France
203 I1 St Francis r. Canada/U.S.A.
198 C4 St Francis KS U.S.A.
203 I1 St Francis ME U.S.A.
199 F4 St Francis r. U.S.A.
189 J4 St Francis, Cape Canada
203 I1 St Froid Lake U.S.A.
166 E5 St-Gaudens France
203 H2 St-Gédéon Canada
127 H2 St George Australia
203 J2 St George Canada
201 D5 St George SC U.S.A.
197 F3 St George UT U.S.A.
125 F2 St George, Cape P.N.G.
194 A3 St George, Point U.S.A.
201 C6 St George Island U.S.A.
189 F4 St-Georges Canada
205 L6 St George's Grenada
189 I4 St George's Bay Canada
161 A6 St George's Channel Ireland/U.K.
124 F2 St George's Channel P.N.G.
168 D7 St Gotthard Pass pass Switz.
161 C6 St Govan's Head U.K.
190 E3 St Helen U.S.A.
174 D6 St Helena i. Atlantic Ocean
120 St Helena, Ascension and Tristan da Cunha terr. Atlantic Ocean
180 C6 St Helena Bay S. Africa
180 C6 St Helena Bay b. S. Africa
127 H8 St Helens Australia
161 E4 St Helens U.K.
194 B2 St Helens, Mount vol. U.S.A.
127 H8 St Helens Point Australia
166 C2 St Helier U.K.
164 D4 St-Hubert Belgium
188 F4 St-Hyacinthe Canada
190 E3 St Ignace U.S.A.
190 C1 St Ignace Island Canada
161 C6 St Ishmael U.K.
161 B7 St Ives England U.K.
161 G5 St Ives England U.K.
203 I1 St-Jacques Canada
190 E3 St James U.S.A.
186 C4 St James, Cape Canada
189 F4 St-Jean, Lac l. Canada
166 D4 St-Jean-d'Angély France
166 C3 St-Jean-de-Monts France
188 F4 St-Jean-sur-Richelieu Canada
188 F4 St-Jérôme Canada
194 C2 St Joe r. U.S.A.
189 G4 Saint John Canada
203 J2 St John r. Canada/U.S.A.
197 F1 St John U.S.A.
205 L5 St John i. Virgin Is (U.S.A.)
205 L5 St John's Antigua and Barbuda
189 J4 St John's Canada
197 H4 St Johns AZ U.S.A.
190 E4 St Johns MI U.S.A.
201 D6 St Johns r. U.S.A.
203 H2 St Johnsbury U.S.A.
160 E3 St John's Chapel U.K.
190 D4 St Joseph MI U.S.A.
198 E4 St Joseph MO U.S.A.
190 E5 St Joseph r. U.S.A.
188 B3 St Joseph, Lake Canada
189 F4 St-Joseph-de-Beauce Canada
191 F2 St Joseph Island Canada
199 D7 St Joseph Island U.S.A.
188 F4 St-Jovité Canada
166 E4 St-Junien France
161 B7 St Just U.K.
164 A5 St-Just-en-Chaussée France
161 B7 St Keverne U.K.
205 L5 St Kitts and Nevis country Caribbean Sea
St-Laurent, Golfe du g. Canada/U.S.A. see St Lawrence, Gulf of
211 H2 St-Laurent-du-Maroni Fr. Guiana
189 J4 St Lawrence Canada
189 G4 St Lawrence inlet Canada
189 H4 St Lawrence, Gulf of Canada/U.S.A.
184 B3 St Lawrence Island U.S.A.
191 J3 St Lawrence Islands National Park Canada
203 F2 St Lawrence Seaway sea chan. Canada/U.S.A.
189 G4 St-Léonard Canada
189 I3 St Lewis Canada
189 I3 St Lewis r. Canada
166 D2 St-Lô France
176 A3 St-Louis Senegal
190 E4 St Louis MI U.S.A.
198 F4 St Louis MO U.S.A.
190 A2 St Louis r. U.S.A.
205 L6 St Lucia country Caribbean Sea
181 J3 St Lucia, Lake S. Africa
181 J4 St Lucia Estuary S. Africa
162 □ St Magnus Bay U.K.
166 D3 St-Maixent-l'École France
166 C2 St-Malo France
166 C2 St-Malo, Golfe de g. France
181 G6 St Marks S. Africa
205 L5 St-Martin terr. Caribbean Sea
180 B6 St Martin, Cape S. Africa
187 J4 St Martin, Lake Canada
190 D3 St Martin Island U.S.A.
161 A8 St Martin's i. U.K.
145 H5 St Martin's Island Bangl.
126 C3 St Mary Peak Australia
127 H8 St Marys Australia
191 G4 St Mary's Canada
162 F2 St Mary's U.K.
161 A8 St Mary's i. U.K.
202 A4 St Marys OH U.S.A.
202 D4 St Marys PA U.S.A.
202 C5 St Marys WV U.S.A.
202 A4 St Marys r. U.S.A.
189 J4 St Mary's, Cape Canada
184 A3 St Matthew Island U.S.A.
124 E2 St Matthias Group is P.N.G.
188 F4 St-Maurice r. Canada
161 B7 St Mawes U.K.
166 D4 St-Médard-en-Jalles France
189 I3 St Michael's Bay Canada
166 C3 St-Nazaire France
161 G5 St Neots U.K.
166 H2 St-Nicolas-de-Port France
166 F1 St-Omer France
203 I1 St-Pamphile Canada
189 G4 St-Pascal Canada
187 G4 St Paul Canada
190 A3 St Paul MN U.S.A.
198 D3 St Paul NE U.S.A.
202 B6 St Paul VA U.S.A.
218 J7 St-Paul, Île i. Indian Ocean
193 H3 St Peter U.S.A.
166 C2 St Peter Port U.K.
172 D3 St Petersburg Russia (City Plan 107)
201 D7 St Petersburg U.S.A.
166 G5 St-Pierre mt. France
189 I4 St-Pierre N. America
188 F4 St-Pierre, Lac l. Canada
185 M5 St Pierre and Miquelon terr. N. America
166 D4 St-Pierre-d'Oléron France
166 F3 St-Pierre-le-Moûtier France
164 A4 St-Pol-sur-Ternoise France
166 F3 St-Pourçain-sur-Sioule France
203 H1 St-Prosper Canada
166 F2 St-Quentin France
166 H5 St-Raphaël France
203 F2 St Regis r. U.S.A.
203 F2 St Regis Falls U.S.A.
203 G2 St-Rémi Canada
203 H2 St-Sébastien Canada
189 G4 St-Siméon Canada
201 D6 St Simons Island U.S.A.
203 J2 St Stephen Canada
201 E5 St Stephen U.S.A.
203 H2 St-Théophile Canada
187 K4 St Theresa Point Canada
191 G4 St Thomas Canada
166 H5 St-Tropez France
187 J5 St Vincent U.S.A.
127 F9 St Vincent, Cape Australia
126 B5 St Vincent, Gulf Australia
205 L6 St Vincent and the Grenadines country Caribbean Sea
164 E4 St-Vith Belgium
187 H4 St Walburg Canada
191 G4 St Williams Canada
166 E4 St-Yrieix-la-Perche France
148 C1 Sain Us China
167 F1 Saioa mt. Spain
144 E3 Saipal mt. Nepal
147 G5 Saipan i. N. Mariana Is
149 □ Sai Pok Liu Hoi Hap Hong Kong China
151 F7 Saitama Japan
158 N2 Saittanulkki h. Fin.
210 E7 Sajama, Nevado mt. Bol.
140 B5 Sājir Saudi Arabia
180 D5 Sak watercourse S. Africa
154 B2 Sa Kaeo Thai.
151 D7 Sakai Japan
151 C7 Sakaide Japan
151 C7 Sakaiminato Japan
142 B3 Sakākā Saudi Arabia
141 G5 Saka Kalat Pak.
198 C2 Sakakawea, Lake U.S.A.
188 E3 Sakami Canada
188 F3 Sakami r. Canada
188 E3 Sakami Lake Canada
171 L4 Sakar mts Bulg.
Sakarya Turkey see Adapazarı
136 C1 Sakarya r. Turkey
150 F5 Sakata Japan
152 C3 Sakchu N. Korea
139 H2 Saken Seyfullin Kazakh.
154 B2 Sa Keo r. Thai.
176 C4 Sakété Benin
146 G2 Sakhalin i. Russia
146 G1 Sakhalinskiy Zaliv b. Russia
144 C3 Sakhi India
181 H3 Sakhile S. Africa
137 K1 Şäki Azer.
159 M5 Šakiai Lith.
144 A3 Sakir mt. Pak.
146 E4 Sakishima-shotō is Japan
154 C1 Sakon Nakhon Thai.
154 □ Sakra, P. Sing.
144 B4 Sakrand Pak.
180 D5 Sakrivier S. Africa
138 E3 Saksaul'skiy Kazakh.
151 B9 Sakura-jima vol. Japan
173 E6 Saky Crimea
159 M3 Säkylä Fin.
176 □ Sal i. Cape Verde
173 G6 Sal r. Russia
206 H5 Sal, Punta pt Hond.
159 M4 Sala Latvia
159 L4 Sala Sweden
188 F4 Salaberry-de-Valleyfield Canada
159 N4 Salacgrīva Latvia
170 F4 Sala Consilina Italy
197 E5 Salada, Laguna salt l. Mex.
215 E2 Saladillo Arg.
215 D2 Saladillo r. Arg.
215 E2 Salado r. Buenos Aires Arg.
215 C2 Salado r. La Pampa Arg.
215 D4 Salado r. Río Negro Arg.
215 E1 Salado r. Santa Fe Arg.
215 C3 Salado r. Arg.
207 E2 Salado r. Mex.
212 B3 Salado, Quebrada de r. Chile
176 B4 Salaga Ghana
180 F1 Salajwe Botswana
177 D3 Salal Chad
142 D6 Şalālah Oman
207 G5 Salamá Guat.
206 H5 Salamá Hond.
215 B1 Salamanca Chile
206 D3 Salamanca Mex.
167 D2 Salamanca Spain
202 D3 Salamanca U.S.A.
181 J3 Salamanga Moz.
140 B3 Salāmatābād Iran
213 B3 Salamina Col.
136 F4 Salamīyah Syria
190 E5 Salamonie r. U.S.A.
190 E5 Salamonie Lake U.S.A.
137 L5 Sāland Iran
145 F5 Salandi r. India
159 M4 Salantai Lith.
148 D1 Salaqi China
167 C1 Salas Spain
159 N4 Salaspils Latvia
154 C2 Salavan Laos
138 C1 Salavat Russia
147 F7 Salawati i. Indon.
144 B5 Salaya India
208 C5 Sala y Gómez, Isla i. S. Pacific Ocean
215 D3 Salazar Arg.
159 N5 Šalčininkai Lith.
161 D7 Salcombe U.K.
213 B4 Saldaña r. Col.
167 D1 Saldaña Spain
180 B6 Saldanha S. Africa
180 B6 Saldanha Bay S. Africa
215 E3 Saldungaray Arg.
159 M4 Saldus Latvia
127 G7 Sale Australia
140 C3 Şāleḩābād Hamadān Iran
137 K5 Şāleḩābād Īlām Iran
132 H3 Salekhard Russia
143 B4 Salem India
203 H3 Salem MA U.S.A.
199 F4 Salem MO U.S.A.
200 F4 Salem NJ U.S.A.
203 G3 Salem NY U.S.A.
202 C4 Salem OH U.S.A.
194 B2 Salem OR U.S.A.
200 D4 Salem VA U.S.A.
162 C4 Salen Scotland U.K.
162 C4 Salen Scotland U.K.
170 F4 Salerno Italy
170 F4 Salerno, Golfo di g. Italy
161 E4 Salford U.K.
211 K5 Salgado r. Brazil
169 I6 Salgótarján Hungary
211 K5 Salgueiro Brazil
153 C6 Salibabu i. Indon.
192 E4 Salida U.S.A.
166 D5 Salies-de-Béarn France
141 F4 Şāliḩān Afgh.
136 B2 Salihli Turkey
172 C4 Salihorsk Belarus
179 D5 Salima Malawi
179 D5 Salimo Moz.
198 D4 Salina KS U.S.A.
197 G2 Salina UT U.S.A.
170 F5 Salina, Isola i. Isole Lipari Italy
207 F4 Salina Cruz Mex.
214 D2 Salinas Brazil
210 B4 Salinas Ecuador
206 D3 Salinas Mex.
196 B3 Salinas r. U.S.A.
215 C2 Salinas, Pampa de las salt pan Arg.
195 F5 Salinas Peak U.S.A.
199 E5 Saline r. AR U.S.A.
198 C4 Saline r. KS U.S.A.
167 H3 Salines, Cap de ses c. Spain
196 D3 Saline Valley depr. U.S.A.
211 I4 Salinópolis Brazil
210 C6 Salinosó Lachay, Punta pt Peru
161 F6 Salisbury U.K.
203 F5 Salisbury MD U.S.A.
201 D5 Salisbury NC U.S.A.
161 E6 Salisbury Plain U.K.
211 J6 Salitre r. Brazil
215 C3 Salitroso, Gran Bajo salt flat Arg.
136 F5 Şalkhad Syria
143 D1 Salki r. India
158 O2 Salla Fin.
215 D3 Salliqueló Arg.
199 E5 Sallisaw U.S.A.
185 K3 Salluit Canada
145 E3 Sallyana Nepal
140 B2 Salmās Iran
172 D2 Salmi Russia
186 F5 Salmo Canada
194 D2 Salmon U.S.A.
194 D2 Salmon r. U.S.A.
186 F4 Salmon Arm Canada
203 F3 Salmon Reservoir U.S.A.
194 D2 Salmon River Mountains U.S.A.
164 E5 Salmtal Germany
159 M3 Salo Fin.
145 E4 Salon India
166 G5 Salon-de-Provence France
178 C4 Salonga Nord, Parc National de la nat. park Dem. Rep. Congo
178 C4 Salonga Sud, Parc National de la nat. park Dem. Rep. Congo
169 J7 Salonta Romania
176 A3 Saloum Delta tourist site Senegal
176 □ Sal Rei Cape Verde
215 D1 Salsacate Arg.
173 G6 Sal'sk Russia
170 C2 Salsomaggiore Terme Italy
180 E5 Salt watercourse S. Africa
197 G5 Salt r. AZ U.S.A.
190 B6 Salt r. MO U.S.A.
212 C2 Salta Arg.
160 F4 Saltaire U.K.
161 C7 Saltash U.K.
162 D5 Saltcoats U.K.
202 B5 Salt Creek r. U.S.A.
163 E5 Saltee Islands Ireland
158 K2 Saltfjellet-Svartisen Nasjonalpark nat. park Norway
199 B6 Salt Flat U.S.A.
202 C4 Salt Fork Lake U.S.A.
206 D2 Saltillo Mex.
194 E3 Salt Lake City U.S.A.
215 E2 Salto Arg.
214 C3 Salto Brazil
215 F1 Salto Uruguay
214 E2 Salto da Divisa Brazil
214 A4 Salto del Guairá Para.
212 E4 Salto Grande, Embalse de resr Uruguay
197 E5 Salton Sea salt l. U.S.A.
144 C2 Salt Range hills Pak.
187 G2 Salt River Canada
202 B5 Salt Rock U.S.A.
201 D5 Saluda SC U.S.A.
202 E6 Saluda VA U.S.A.
144 C4 Salumbar India
143 C2 Salur India
170 B2 Saluzzo Italy
215 D1 Salvador Arg.
214 E1 Salvador Brazil
199 F6 Salvador, Lake U.S.A.
206 D3 Salvatierra Mex.
197 G2 Salvation Creek r. U.S.A.
140 C5 Salwah Qatar
140 C5 Salwah, Dawḩat b. Qatar/Saudi Arabia
146 B4 Salween r. China/Myanmar
147 B5 Salween r. China/Myanmar
137 L2 Salyan Azer.
202 B6 Salyersville U.S.A.
180 B2 Salzbrunn Namibia
168 F7 Salzburg Austria
165 I2 Salzgitter Germany
165 I1 Salzhausen Germany
165 G3 Salzkotten Germany
165 J3 Salzmünde Germany
165 J2 Salzwedel Germany
144 B4 Sam India
149 B7 Sam, Nâm r. Laos/Vietnam
154 B2 Samae San, Laem c. Thai.
140 B4 Samāh well Saudi Arabia
210 F7 Samaipata Bol.
153 C5 Samal i. Phil.
153 B5 Samales Group is Phil.
143 C2 Samalkot India
136 E3 Samandağı Turkey
150 H3 Samani Japan
136 C6 Samannūd Egypt
153 C4 Samar i. Phil.
138 B1 Samara Russia
138 B1 Samara r. Russia
213 D3 Samariapo Venez.
155 E3 Samarinda Indon.
139 H2 Samarka Kazakh.
150 D2 Samarka Russia
Samarkand Uzbek. see Samarqand
139 F5 Samarqand Uzbek.
139 G5 Samarqand, Qullai mt. Tajik.
137 I4 Sāmarrā' Iraq
153 C4 Samar Sea g. Phil.
172 I4 Samarskaya Oblast' admin. div. Russia
139 J2 Samarskoye Kazakh.
137 L1 Şamaxı Azer.
178 C4 Samba Dem. Rep. Congo
155 E2 Sambaliung mts Indon.
143 D1 Sambalpur India
155 D3 Sambar, Tanjung pt Indon.
155 C2 Sambas Indon.
179 F5 Sambava Madag.
145 G4 Sambha India
144 D3 Sambhal India
144 C4 Sambhar Lake India
173 B5 Sambir Ukr.
211 J5 Sambito r. Brazil
215 F2 Samborombón, Bahía b. Arg.
164 B4 Sambre r. Belgium/France
213 A3 Sambú r. Panama
152 E5 Samcheok S. Korea
137 J3 Samdi Dag mt. Turkey
178 D4 Same Tanz.
Samīrum Iran see Īzad Khvāst
152 E3 Samjiyŏn N. Korea
137 K1 Şämkir Azer.
152 E6 Samnangjin S. Korea
Sam Neua Laos see Xam Nua
125 I3 Samoa country Pacific Ocean
216 H7 Samoa Basin sea feature Pacific Ocean
170 F2 Samobor Croatia
172 G2 Samoded Russia
171 J3 Samokov Bulg.
168 H6 Šamorín Slovakia
171 L6 Samos i. Greece
155 A2 Samosir i. Indon.
171 K4 Samothraki Greece
171 K4 Samothraki i. Greece
153 B3 Sampaloc Point Phil.
155 D3 Sampit Indon.
155 D3 Sampit, Teluk b. Indon.
179 C4 Sampwe Dem. Rep. Congo
154 B2 Sâmraông Cambodia
199 E6 Sam Rayburn Reservoir U.S.A.
145 E3 Samsang China
149 B6 Sam Sao, Phou mts Laos/Vietnam
154 C1 Sâm Sơn Vietnam
136 F1 Samsun Turkey
173 G7 Samt'redia Georgia
154 B3 Samui, Ko i. Thai.
173 I7 Samur r. Azer./Russia
154 B2 Samut Prakan Thai.
154 B2 Samut Sakhon Thai.
154 B2 Samut Songkhram Thai.
145 G3 Samyai China
176 B3 San Mali
154 B1 San, Phou mt. Laos
154 C2 San, Tônlé r. Cambodia
142 B6 Şan'ā' Yemen
129 D3 SANAE IV research stn Antarctica
177 D4 Sanaga r. Cameroon
213 A4 San Agustín Col.
153 C5 San Agustin, Cape Phil.
215 C1 San Agustín de Valle Fértil Arg.
140 B6 Sanām Saudi Arabia
217 N7 San Ambrosio, Isla i. S. Pacific Ocean
140 B3 Sanandaj Iran
196 B2 San Andreas U.S.A.
153 C3 San Andres Phil.
206 I5 San Andrés, Isla de i. Col.
195 F5 San Andres Mountains U.S.A.
207 F4 San Andrés Tuxtla Mex.
199 C6 San Angelo U.S.A.
206 G4 San Antonio Belize
215 B2 San Antonio Chile
153 B3 San Antonio Phil.
199 D6 San Antonio U.S.A.
196 B3 San Antonio r. U.S.A.
215 F3 San Antonio, Cabo c. Arg.
205 H4 San Antonio, Cabo c. Cuba
196 D4 San Antonio, Mount U.S.A.
212 C2 San Antonio de los Cobres Arg.
213 D2 San Antonio de Tamanaco Venez.
215 D4 San Antonio Oeste Arg.
196 B4 San Antonio Reservoir U.S.A.
196 B3 San Ardo U.S.A.
215 E3 San Augustín Arg.
144 D5 Sanawad India
207 D3 San Bartolo Mex.
170 E3 San Benedetto del Tronto Italy
204 B5 San Benedicto, Isla i. Mex.
199 D7 San Benito U.S.A.
196 B3 San Benito r. U.S.A.
196 B3 San Benito Mountain U.S.A.
196 D4 San Bernardino U.S.A.
195 C5 San Bernardino Mountains U.S.A.
215 B2 San Bernardo Chile
206 C2 San Bernardo Mex.
151 C7 Sanbe-san vol. Japan
206 C3 San Blas Nayarit Mex.
206 B2 San Blas Sinaloa Mex.
206 J6 San Blas, Archipiélago de is Panama
201 C6 San Blas, Cape U.S.A.
206 J6 San Blas, Serranía de mts Panama
210 E6 San Borja Bol.
203 H3 Sanbornville U.S.A.
206 D2 San Buenaventura Mex.
215 C2 San Carlos Arg.
215 B3 San Carlos Chile
206 D1 San Carlos Coahuila Mex.
207 E2 San Carlos Tamaulipas Mex.
206 H6 San Carlos Nicaragua
153 B4 San Carlos Negros Occidental Phil.
153 B3 San Carlos Pangasinan Phil.
215 F2 San Carlos Uruguay
197 G5 San Carlos U.S.A.
213 D4 San Carlos Amazonas Venez.
213 C2 San Carlos Cojedes Venez.
215 E1 San Carlos Centro Arg.
215 B4 San Carlos de Bariloche Arg.
215 E3 San Carlos de Bolívar Arg.
213 C2 San Carlos del Zulia Venez.
197 G5 San Carlos Lake U.S.A.
148 C2 Sancha Gansu China
148 D2 Sancha Shanxi China
149 C5 Sancha He r. China
139 I5 Sanchakou China
144 D5 Sanchi India
149 B6 San Chien Pau mt. Laos
144 B4 Sanchor India
148 D2 Sanchuan He r. China
172 H3 Sanchursk Russia
207 E3 San Ciro de Acosta Mex.
215 B2 San Clemente Chile
196 D5 San Clemente U.S.A.
196 C5 San Clemente Island U.S.A.
166 F3 Sancoins France
215 E1 San Cristóbal Arg.
San Cristobal i. Solomon Is see Makira
213 B3 San Cristóbal Venez.
210 □ San Cristóbal, Isla i. Galapagos Is Ecuador
207 F4 San Cristóbal de las Casas Mex.
197 F5 San Cristobal Wash watercourse U.S.A.
205 I4 Sancti Spíritus Cuba
150 D3 Sandagou Russia
162 C5 Sanda Island U.K.
155 E1 Sandakan Sabah Malaysia
159 I3 Sandane Norway
171 J4 Sandanski Bulg.
165 K2 Sandau (Elbe) Germany
162 F1 Sanday i. U.K.
162 F1 Sanday Sound sea chan. U.K.
161 E4 Sandbach U.K.
159 J4 Sandefjord Norway
129 E4 Sandercock Nunataks nunataks Antarctica
197 H4 Sanders U.S.A.
165 J3 Sandersleben Germany
199 C6 Sanderson U.S.A.
127 J1 Sandgate Australia
162 D6 Sandhead U.K.
210 E6 Sandia Peru
196 D5 San Diego U.S.A.
212 C8 San Diego, Cabo c. Arg.
136 C2 Sandıklı Turkey
144 E4 Sandila India
190 B2 Sand Island U.S.A.
190 E2 Sand Lake Canada
159 I4 Sandnes Norway
158 K2 Sandnessjøen Norway
179 C4 Sandoa Dem. Rep. Congo
169 J5 Sandomierz Poland
213 A4 Sandoná Col.
170 E2 San Donà di Piave Italy
Sandoway Myanmar see Thandwe
161 F7 Sandown U.K.
180 C7 Sandown Bay S. Africa
158 □ Sandoy i. Faroe Is
194 C1 Sandpoint U.S.A.
162 A4 Sandray i. U.K.
169 M7 Şandrul Mare, Vârful mt. Romania
159 K3 Sandsjö Sweden
186 C4 Sandspit Canada
199 D4 Sand Springs U.S.A.
196 C2 Sand Springs Salt Flat U.S.A.
190 A2 Sandstone U.S.A.
197 F5 Sand Tank Mountains U.S.A.
149 C5 Sandu Guizhou China
149 D5 Sandu Hunan China
191 F4 Sandusky MI U.S.A.
202 B4 Sandusky OH U.S.A.
202 B4 Sandusky Bay U.S.A.
180 C5 Sandveld mts S. Africa
180 B3 Sandverhaar Namibia
159 J4 Sandvika Norway
158 K3 Sandvika Sweden
159 L3 Sandviken Sweden
189 I3 Sandwich Bay Canada
162 □ Sandwick U.K.
145 G5 Sandwip Channel Bangl.
203 H2 Sandy r. U.S.A.
187 I3 Sandy Bay Canada
125 F4 Sandy Cape Qld Australia
127 F8 Sandy Cape Tas. Australia
202 B5 Sandy Hook U.S.A.
203 F4 Sandy Hook pt U.S.A.
Sandykachi Turkm. see Sandykgaçy
141 F2 Sandykgaçy Turkm.
138 E5 Sandykly Gumy des. Turkm.
188 B3 Sandy Lake Canada
188 B3 Sandy Lake l. Canada
203 E3 Sandy Pond U.S.A.
214 A4 San Estanislao Para.
153 B2 San Fabian Phil.
215 B2 San Felipe Chile
204 B2 San Felipe Baja California Mex.
206 C2 San Felipe Chihuahua Mex.
206 D3 San Felipe Guanajuato Mex.
213 C2 San Felipe Venez.
196 D5 San Felipe Creek watercourse U.S.A.
217 N7 San Félix, Isla i. S. Pacific Ocean
215 E2 San Fernando Arg.
215 B2 San Fernando Chile
207 E2 San Fernando Mex.
153 B2 San Fernando La Union Phil.
153 B3 San Fernando Pampanga Phil.
167 C4 San Fernando Spain
213 E2 San Fernando Trin. and Tob.
196 C4 San Fernando U.S.A.
213 D3 San Fernando de Apure Venez.
213 D3 San Fernando de Atabapo Venez.
201 D6 Sanford FL U.S.A.
203 H3 Sanford ME U.S.A.
201 E5 Sanford NC U.S.A.
190 E4 Sanford Lake U.S.A.
215 D1 San Francisco Arg.
206 I6 San Francisco Panama
196 A3 San Francisco U.S.A. (City Plan 113)
197 H5 San Francisco r. U.S.A.
212 C3 San Francisco, Paso de pass Arg.
196 A3 San Francisco Bay inlet U.S.A.
206 C2 San Francisco del Oro Mex.
206 D3 San Francisco del Rincón Mex.
205 J5 San Francisco de Macorís Dom. Rep.
212 C7 San Francisco de Paula, Cabo c. Arg.
207 E3 San Francisco el Alto Mex.
206 G5 San Francisco Gotera El Salvador
213 A4 San Gabriel Ecuador
206 A1 San Gabriel, Punta pt Mex.
196 C4 San Gabriel Mountains U.S.A.
144 C6 Sangamner India
190 C6 Sangamon r. U.S.A.
141 G3 Sangān Afgh.
141 F4 Sangān Iran
141 G3 Sangān, Kōh-e mt. Afgh.
Sangan, Koh-i- mt. Afgh. see Sangān, Kōh-e
133 N3 Sangar Russia
143 B2 Sangareddy India
170 C5 San Gavino Monreale Sardinia Italy
210 C4 Sangay, Parque Nacional nat. park Ecuador
141 E3 Sang Bast Iran
153 B5 Sangboy Islands Phil.
155 E4 Sangeang i. Indon.
148 B1 Sangejing China
196 C3 Sanger U.S.A.
165 J3 Sangerhausen Germany
148 E1 Sanggan He r. China
148 B3 Sanggarmai China
155 D2 Sanggau Indon.
152 B5 Sanggou Wan b. China
178 B3 Sangha r. Congo
144 B4 Sanghar Pak.
144 B3 Sanghar r. Pak.
177 D4 Sangha Trinational nat. park Africa
213 B3 San Gil Col.
170 G5 San Giovanni in Fiore Italy
170 F4 San Giovanni Rotondo Italy
153 C6 Sangir i. Indon.
147 E6 Sangir, Kepulauan is Indon.
152 E5 Sangju S. Korea
154 B2 Sângke, Stœ̆ng r. Cambodia
154 C2 Sângkôm Thmei Cambodia
155 E2 Sangkulirang Indon.
141 H2 Sanglēch Afgh.
143 A2 Sangli India
176 D4 Sangmélima Cameroon
144 D3 Sangnam India
145 H3 Sangngagqoiling China
152 E3 Sang-ni N. Korea
179 D6 Sango Zimbabwe
143 A2 Sangole India
196 D4 San Gorgonio Mountain U.S.A.
195 F4 Sangre de Cristo Range mts U.S.A.
213 E2 Sangre Grande Trin. and Tob.
144 C3 Sangrur India
145 F3 Sangsang China
186 G4 Sangudo Canada
211 G6 Sangue r. Brazil
140 E4 Sangū'īyeh Iran
181 J1 Sangutane r. Moz.
139 G5 Sangvor Tajik.
149 D4 Sangzhi China
206 A2 San Hipólito, Punta pt Mex.
136 C7 Sanhūr Egypt
207 G4 San Ignacio Belize
210 E6 San Ignacio Beni Bol.
210 F7 San Ignacio Santa Cruz Bol.
206 A2 San Ignacio Baja California Sur Mex.
206 D2 San Ignacio Durango Mex.
188 E2 Sanikiluaq Canada
153 B2 San Ildefonso, Cape Phil.
153 B2 San Ildefonso Peninsula Phil.
153 C4 San Isidro Phil.
S. A. Niyazova, imeni Turkm. see S. A. Nyýazow Adyndaky
153 B3 San Jacinto Phil.
196 D5 San Jacinto U.S.A.
196 D5 San Jacinto Peak U.S.A.
145 F5 Sanjai r. India

Segorbe

215 E1 San Javier Arg.
215 B2 San Javier Chile
144 B3 Sanjawi Pak.
179 D4 Sanje Tanz.
213 A3 San Jerónimo, Serranía de mts Col.
137 J3 Sanjī Iran
149 C5 Sanjiang China
152 B2 Sanjiangkou China
151 F6 Sanjō Japan
196 B3 San Joaquin U.S.A.
196 B3 San Joaquin r. U.S.A.
196 B3 San Joaquin Valley U.S.A.
215 E1 San Jorge Arg.
213 B2 San Jorge r. Col.
212 C7 San Jorge, Golfo de g. Arg.
206 H6 San José Costa Rica
153 B3 San Jose Nueva Ecija Phil.
153 B3 San Jose Occidental Mindoro Phil.
196 B3 San Jose U.S.A.
215 D4 San José, Golfo g. Arg.
206 B2 San José, Isla i. Mex.
215 C2 San José, Volcán vol. Chile
213 E2 San José de Amacuro Venez.
153 B4 San Jose de Buenavista Phil.
210 F7 San José de Chiquitos Bol.
206 B2 San José de Comondú Mex.
215 E1 San José de Feliciano Arg.
206 A2 San José de Gracia Baja California Sur Mex.
206 C2 San José de Gracia Sinaloa Mex.
213 D2 San José de Guanipa Venez.
215 C1 San José de Jáchal Arg.
206 B2 San José de la Brecha Mex.
215 D1 San José de la Dormida Arg.
215 B3 San José de la Mariquina Chile
205 H4 San José de las Lajas Cuba
206 B3 San José del Cabo Mex.
213 B4 San José del Guaviare Col.
215 F2 San José de Mayo Uruguay
213 C3 San José de Ocuné Col.
206 B1 San José de Primas Mex.
207 D2 San José de Raíces Mex.
215 C1 San Juan Arg.
215 C1 San Juan prov. Arg.
213 A3 San Juan r. Col.
206 D2 San Juan Mex.
206 H6 San Juan r. Nicaragua/Panama
153 C4 San Juan Phil.
205 K5 San Juan Puerto Rico
196 B4 San Juan r. CA U.S.A.
197 H3 San Juan r. UT U.S.A.
213 D3 San Juan Venez.
213 E2 San Juan r. Venez.
206 G5 San Juan, Punta pt El Salvador
212 E3 San Juan Bautista Para.
207 E4 San Juan Bautista Tuxtepec Mex.
206 H5 San Juancito Hond.
215 B4 San Juan dela Costa Chile
206 I6 San Juan del Norte Nicaragua
206 I6 San Juan del Norte, Bahía b. Nicaragua
213 C2 San Juan de los Cayos Venez.
213 D2 San Juan de los Morros Venez.
206 C2 San Juan del Río Durango Mex.
207 E3 San Juan del Río Querétaro Mex.
206 H6 San Juan del Sur Nicaragua
206 A2 San Juanico, Punta pt Mex.
197 F4 San Juan Mountains U.S.A.
144 D1 Sanju He watercourse China
215 E1 San Justo Arg.
143 A2 Sankeshwar India
143 D1 Sankh r. India
Sanko India see Sanku
164 F4 Sankt Augustin Germany
168 D7 Sankt Gallen Switz.
168 D7 Sankt Moritz Switz.
Sankt-Peterburg Russia see St Petersburg
168 G6 Sankt Pölten Austria
164 F5 Sankt Wendel Germany
144 D2 Sanku India
206 B3 San Lázaro, Sierra de mts Mex.
136 G3 Şanlıurfa Turkey
215 E2 San Lorenzo Arg.
210 F8 San Lorenzo Bol.
210 C3 San Lorenzo Ecuador
195 F6 San Lorenzo Mex.
167 E1 San Lorenzo mt. Spain
206 A1 San Lorenzo, Isla i. Mex.
210 C6 San Lorenzo, Isla i. Peru
212 B7 San Lorenzo, Monte mt. Arg./Chile
167 C4 Sanlúcar de Barrameda Spain
206 A2 San Lucas Mex.
206 B3 San Lucas, Cabo c. Mex.
215 C2 San Luis Arg.
215 C2 San Luis prov. Arg.
207 G4 San Luis Guat.
197 E5 San Luis AZ U.S.A.
197 G5 San Luis AZ U.S.A.
215 C2 San Luis, Sierra de mts Arg.
207 D3 San Luis de la Paz Mex.
196 B4 San Luis Obispo U.S.A.
196 B4 San Luis Obispo Bay U.S.A.
206 D3 San Luis Potosí Mex.
206 D3 San Luis Potosí state Mex.
196 B3 San Luis Reservoir U.S.A.
204 B2 San Luis Río Colorado Mex.
170 E6 San Marco, Capo c. Sicily Italy
207 G5 San Marcos Guat.
207 E4 San Marcos Mex.
199 D6 San Marcos U.S.A.
170 E3 San Marino country Europe
170 E3 San Marino San Marino
129 E2 San Martín research stn Antarctica
212 C3 San Martín Catamarca Arg.
215 C2 San Martín Mendoza Arg.
210 F6 San Martín r. Bol.
213 B4 San Martín Col.
212 B7 San Martín, Lago l. Arg./Chile
206 D3 San Martín de Bolaños Mex.
215 B4 San Martín de los Andes Arg.
196 A3 San Mateo U.S.A.
215 D4 San Matías, Golfo g. Arg.
213 D2 San Mauricio Venez.
149 F4 Sanmen China
149 F4 Sanmen Wan b. China
148 D3 Sanmenxia China
210 F6 San Miguel r. Bol.
213 B4 San Miguel r. Col.
206 G5 San Miguel El Salvador
206 J6 San Miguel Panama
197 G6 San Miguel AR U.S.A.
196 B4 San Miguel CA U.S.A.
197 H2 San Miguel r. U.S.A.
153 B3 San Miguel Bay Phil.
206 D3 San Miguel de Allende Mex.
215 E2 San Miguel del Monte Arg.
212 C3 San Miguel de Tucumán Arg.
196 B4 San Miguel Island U.S.A.
153 A5 San Miguel Islands Phil.
206 J6 San Miguelito Panama
207 E4 San Miguel Sola de Vega Mex.
149 E5 Sanming China
153 B3 San Narciso Phil.
170 F4 Sannicandro Garganico Italy
215 E2 San Nicolás de los Arroyos Arg.
196 C5 San Nicolas Island U.S.A.
181 F3 Sannieshof S. Africa
176 B4 Sanniquellie Liberia
169 K6 Sanok Poland
207 E3 San Pablo Mex.
153 B3 San Pablo Phil.
153 B3 San Pascual Phil.
215 E2 San Pedro Buenos Aires Arg.
212 D2 San Pedro Jujuy Arg.
207 H4 San Pedro Belize
210 F7 San Pedro Bol.
176 B4 San-Pédro Côte d'Ivoire
206 B3 San Pedro Mex.
197 G5 San Pedro watercourse U.S.A.
167 C3 San Pedro, Sierra de mts Spain
196 C5 San Pedro Channel U.S.A.
213 C3 San Pedro de Arimena Col.
206 D2 San Pedro de las Colonias Mex.
213 A4 San Pedro de Naya Col.
212 E2 San Pedro de Ycuamandyyú Para.
206 G5 San Pedro Sula Hond.
170 C5 San Pietro, Isola di i. Sardinia Italy
162 E5 Sanquhar U.K.
210 C3 Sanquianga, Parque Nacional nat. park Col.
204 A2 San Quintín, Cabo c. Mex.
215 C2 San Rafael Arg.
196 A3 San Rafael U.S.A.
197 G2 San Rafael r. U.S.A.
213 C2 San Rafael Venez.
197 G2 San Rafael Knob mt. U.S.A.
196 C4 San Rafael Mountains U.S.A.
210 F6 San Ramón Bol.
170 B3 Sanremo Italy
213 C1 San Román, Cabo c. Venez.
167 B1 San Roque Spain
199 D6 San Saba U.S.A.
215 E1 San Salvador Arg.
205 J4 San Salvador i. Bahamas
207 G5 San Salvador El Salvador
212 C2 San Salvador de Jujuy Arg.
167 F1 San Sebastián Spain
167 E2 San Sebastián de los Reyes Spain
170 E3 Sansepolcro Italy
170 F4 San Severo Italy
149 F5 Sansha China
149 D6 Sanshui China
170 G2 Sanski Most Bos. & Herz.
149 C5 Sansui China
210 E7 Santa Ana Bol.
207 G5 Santa Ana El Salvador
125 G3 Santa Ana i. Solomon Is
196 D5 Santa Ana U.S.A.
199 D6 Santa Anna U.S.A.
213 B3 Santa Bárbara Col.
206 G5 Santa Bárbara Hond.
206 C2 Santa Bárbara Mex.
196 C4 Santa Barbara U.S.A.
196 B4 Santa Barbara Channel U.S.A.
196 C5 Santa Barbara Island U.S.A.
212 C3 Santa Catalina Chile
206 I6 Santa Catalina Panama
196 D5 Santa Catalina, Gulf of U.S.A.
167 B1 Santa Cataliña de Armada Spain
196 C5 Santa Catalina Island U.S.A.
207 D2 Santa Catarina Mex.
210 E4 Santa Clara Col.
205 I4 Santa Clara Cuba
196 B3 Santa Clara CA U.S.A.
197 F3 Santa Clara UT U.S.A.
215 F2 Santa Clara de Olimar Uruguay
196 C4 Santa Clarita U.S.A.
170 F6 Santa Croce, Capo c. Sicily Italy
212 C8 Santa Cruz r. Arg.
210 F7 Santa Cruz Bol.
215 B2 Santa Cruz Chile
153 B2 Santa Cruz Ilocos Sur Phil.
153 B3 Santa Cruz Laguna Phil.
153 A3 Santa Cruz Zambales Phil.
196 A3 Santa Cruz U.S.A.
195 E5 Santa Cruz watercourse U.S.A.
210 □ Santa Cruz, Isla i. Galapagos Is Ecuador
207 G5 Santa Cruz Barillas Guat.
214 E2 Santa Cruz Cabrália Brazil
167 F3 Santa Cruz de Moya Spain
176 A2 Santa Cruz de Tenerife Canary Is
212 F3 Santa Cruz do Sul Brazil
196 C4 Santa Cruz Island U.S.A.
125 G3 Santa Cruz Islands Solomon Is
215 E1 Santa Elena Arg.
210 B4 Santa Elena, Bahía de b. Ecuador
206 H6 Santa Elena, Cabo c. Costa Rica
170 G5 Santa Eufemia, Golfo di g. Italy
215 E1 Santa Fe Arg.
215 E1 Santa Fe prov. Arg.
206 I6 Santa Fe Panama
195 F5 Santa Fe U.S.A.
214 B2 Santa Helena de Goiás Brazil
148 B4 Santai Sichuan China
139 J3 Santai Xinjiang Uygur Zizhiqu China
212 B8 Santa Inés, Isla i. Chile
215 C3 Santa Isabel Arg.
125 F2 Santa Isabel i. Solomon Is
207 G5 Santa Lucia Guat.
215 F2 Santa Lucía r. Uruguay
195 B4 Santa Lucia Range mts U.S.A.
214 A2 Santa Luisa, Serra de hills Brazil
176 □ Santa Luzia i. Cape Verde
206 B2 Santa Margarita, Isla i. Mex.
212 C3 Santa María Arg.
156 A7 Santa Maria i. Azores
211 G4 Santa Maria Amazonas Brazil
214 C1 Santa Maria Distrito Federal Brazil
212 F3 Santa Maria Rio Grande do Sul Brazil
215 F1 Santa Maria r. Brazil
176 □ Santa Maria Cape Verde
204 C2 Santa María r. Mex.
210 D4 Santa María Peru
196 B4 Santa Maria U.S.A.
181 J3 Santa Maria, Cabo de c. Moz.
167 C4 Santa Maria, Cabo de c. Port.
201 F7 Santa Maria, Cape Bahamas
215 B3 Santa María, Isla i. Chile
211 I5 Santa Maria das Barreiras Brazil
214 D1 Santa Maria da Vitória Brazil
213 D2 Santa María de Ipire Venez.
206 C2 Santa María del Oro Mex.
206 D3 Santa María del Río Mex.
171 H5 Santa Maria di Leuca, Capo c. Italy
125 G3 Santa Maria Island Vanuatu
213 B2 Santa Marta Col.
213 B2 Santa Marta, Sierra Nevada de mts Col.
196 C4 Santa Monica U.S.A.
196 C5 Santa Monica Bay U.S.A.
211 H4 Santana Amapá Brazil
211 J6 Santana Bahia Brazil
214 B2 Santana r. Brazil
215 G1 Santana da Boa Vista Brazil
215 F1 Santana do Livramento Brazil
167 E1 Santander Spain
213 A4 Santander de Quilichao Col.
197 G5 Santan Mountain h. U.S.A.
170 C5 Sant'Antioco Sardinia Italy
170 C5 Sant'Antioco, Isola di i. Sardinia Italy
167 G3 Sant Antoni de Portmany Spain
196 C4 Santa Paula U.S.A.
211 J4 Santa Quitéria Brazil
211 H4 Santarém Brazil
167 B3 Santarém Port.
206 D2 Santa Rita Mex.
213 C2 Santa Rita Venez.
214 B2 Santa Rita do Araguaia Brazil
196 B3 Santa Rita Park U.S.A.
215 D3 Santa Rosa La Pampa Arg.
215 C4 Santa Rosa Río Negro Arg.
212 F3 Santa Rosa Brazil
207 G4 Santa Rosa Mex.
196 A2 Santa Rosa CA U.S.A.
195 F5 Santa Rosa NM U.S.A.
206 H6 Santa Rosa, Parque Nacional nat. park Costa Rica
206 G5 Santa Rosa de Copán Hond.
215 D1 Santa Rosa del Río Primero Arg.
210 D5 Santa Rosa do Purus Brazil
196 B5 Santa Rosa Island U.S.A.
206 A2 Santa Rosalía Mex.
194 C3 Santa Rosa Range mts U.S.A.
197 G5 Santa Rosa Wash watercourse U.S.A.
207 G5 Santa Tecla El Salvador
215 G2 Santa Vitória do Palmar Brazil
196 D5 Santee U.S.A.
201 E5 Santee r. U.S.A.
167 G3 Sant Francesc de Formentera Spain
212 F3 Santiago Brazil
176 □ Santiago i. Cape Verde
215 B2 Santiago Chile
215 B2 Santiago admin. reg. Chile
205 J5 Santiago Dom. Rep.
206 B3 Santiago Mex.
206 I6 Santiago Panama
153 B2 Santiago Phil.
210 □ Santiago, Isla i. Galapagos Is Ecuador
206 C3 Santiago, Río Grande de r. Mex.
207 F4 Santiago Astata Mex.
167 B1 Santiago de Compostela Spain
205 I4 Santiago de Cuba Cuba
212 D3 Santiago del Estero Arg.
206 C3 Santiago Ixcuintla Mex.
206 C2 Santiago Papasquiaro Mex.
215 F2 Santiago Vázquez Uruguay
206 C2 Santiaguillo, Laguna de l. Mex.
187 M2 Santianna Point Canada
167 G3 Sant Joan de Labritja Spain
167 G2 Sant Jordi, Golf de g. Spain
214 E1 Santo Amaro Brazil
214 C4 Santo Amaro, Ilha de i. Brazil
214 E3 Santo Amaro de Campos Brazil
214 C3 Santo André Brazil
212 F3 Santo Ângelo Brazil
176 □ Santo Antão i. Cape Verde
214 D2 Santo Antônio r. Brazil
214 E1 Santo Antônio, Cabo c. Brazil
214 B3 Santo Antônio da Platina Brazil
214 E1 Santo Antônio de Jesus Brazil
214 A1 Santo Antônio de Leverger Brazil
210 E4 Santo Antônio do Içá Brazil
214 D3 Santo Antônio do Monte Brazil
211 G7 Santo Corazón Bol.
205 K5 Santo Domingo Dom. Rep.
207 G5 Santo Domingo Guat.
206 A1 Santo Domingo Baja California Mex.
206 B2 Santo Domingo Baja California Sur Mex.
206 D3 Santo Domingo San Luis Potosí Mex.
206 H5 Santo Domingo Nicaragua
213 C2 Santo Domingo r. Venez.
192 E4 Santo Domingo Pueblo U.S.A.
167 E1 Santoña Spain
152 D2 Santong He r. China
214 D1 Santo Onofre r. Brazil
171 K6 Santorini i. Greece
214 C3 Santos Brazil
214 D3 Santos Dumont Brazil
213 D3 Santos Luzardo, Parque Nacional nat. park Venez.
219 F7 Santos Plateau sea feature S. Atlantic Ocean
206 C1 Santo Tomás Mex.
206 H5 Santo Tomás Nicaragua
210 D6 Santo Tomás Peru
212 E3 Santo Tomé Arg.
197 F3 Sanup Plateau U.S.A.
212 B7 San Valentín, Cerro mt. Chile
206 G5 San Vicente El Salvador
153 B2 San Vicente Phil.
210 C6 San Vicente de Cañete Peru
213 B4 San Vicente del Caguán Col.
170 D3 San Vincenzo Italy
170 E5 San Vito, Capo c. Sicily Italy
149 C4 Sanxia Shuiku resr China
149 C7 Sanya China
148 C3 Sanyuan China
152 C2 Sanyuanpu China
141 F2 S. A. Nyýazow Adyndaky Turkm.
178 B4 Sanza Pombo Angola
214 C3 São Bernardo do Campo Brazil
212 E3 São Borja Brazil
214 C3 São Carlos Brazil
211 K6 São Cristóvão Brazil
214 C1 São Domingos Brazil
214 B2 São Domingos r. Brazil
211 H6 São Félix do Araguaia Brazil
211 H5 São Félix do Xingu Brazil
214 E3 São Fidélis Brazil
176 □ São Filipe Cape Verde
214 D1 São Francisco Brazil
211 K5 São Francisco r. Brazil
212 G3 São Francisco do Sul Brazil
215 F1 São Gabriel Brazil
213 D5 São Gabriel da Cachoeira Brazil
214 D3 São Gonçalo Brazil
214 D2 São Gotardo Brazil
214 E3 São João da Barra Brazil
214 C3 São João da Boa Vista Brazil
214 C1 São João d'Aliança Brazil
167 B2 São João da Madeira Port.
214 D1 São João do Paraíso Brazil
214 D3 São João Nepomuceno Brazil
214 C3 São Joaquim da Barra Brazil
156 A6 São Jorge i. Azores
213 D5 São José Brazil
214 E3 São José do Calçado Brazil
215 G2 São José do Norte Brazil
214 C3 São José do Rio Preto Brazil
214 D3 São José dos Campos Brazil
214 C4 São José dos Pinhais Brazil
214 D3 São Lourenço Brazil
214 A2 São Lourenço r. Brazil
214 A2 São Lourenço, Pantanal de marsh Brazil
215 G1 São Lourenço do Sul Brazil
211 J4 São Luís Brazil
214 C3 São Manuel Brazil
214 C2 São Marcos r. Brazil
211 J4 São Marcos, Baía de b. Brazil
214 E2 São Mateus Brazil
214 E2 São Mateus r. Brazil
156 A6 São Miguel i. Azores
214 C2 São Miguel r. Brazil
166 G3 Saône r. France
176 □ São Nicolau i. Cape Verde
214 C3 São Paulo Brazil (City Plan 116)
214 C3 São Paulo state Brazil
219 H5 São Pedro e São Paulo is N. Atlantic Ocean
211 J5 São Raimundo Nonato Brazil
214 D2 São Romão Brazil
211 K5 São Roque, Cabo de c. Brazil
214 D3 São Sebastião Brazil
214 D3 São Sebastião, Ilha do i. Brazil
214 C3 São Sebastião do Paraíso Brazil
215 G1 São Sepé Brazil
214 B2 São Simão Brazil
214 B2 São Simão, Barragem de resr Brazil
147 E6 Sao-Siu Indon.
São Tiago i. Cape Verde see Santiago
176 C4 São Tomé i. São Tomé and Príncipe
214 E3 São Tomé, Cabo de c. Brazil
176 C4 São Tomé and Príncipe country Africa
214 C3 São Vicente Brazil
176 □ São Vicente i. Cape Verde
167 B4 São Vicente, Cabo de c. Port.
136 C1 Sapanca Turkey
138 D4 Saparmyrat Türkmenbaşy Turkm.
124 C2 Saparua Indon.
136 C2 Şaphane Dağı mt. Turkey
206 J7 Sapo, Serranía del mts Panama
176 B4 Sapo National Park Liberia
150 G3 Sapporo Japan
170 F4 Sapri Italy
155 D4 Sapudi i. Indon.
199 D4 Sapulpa U.S.A.
141 E3 Sāqī Iran
140 B2 Saqqez Iran
137 K3 Sarā Iran
140 B2 Sarāb Iran
154 B2 Sara Buri Thai.
141 F2 Saragt Turkm.
210 C4 Saraguro Ecuador
171 H3 Sarajevo Bos. & Herz.
141 F2 Sarakhs Iran
138 D2 Saraktash Russia
138 C2 Saralzhin Kazakh.
145 H4 Saramati mt. India
139 H2 Saran' Kazakh.
155 D3 Saran, Gunung mt. Indon.
203 G2 Saranac r. U.S.A.
203 F2 Saranac Lake U.S.A.
171 I5 Sarandë Albania
215 F2 Sarandí del Yí Uruguay
215 F2 Sarandí Grande Uruguay
153 C5 Sarangani i. Phil.
153 C5 Sarangani Bay Phil.
153 C5 Sarangani Islands Phil.
153 C5 Sarangani Strait Phil.
172 H4 Saransk Russia
154 A1 Saraphi Thai.
132 G4 Sarapul Russia
213 C3 Sarare r. Venez.
201 D7 Sarasota U.S.A.
144 B5 Saraswati r. India
173 D6 Sarata Ukr.
194 F3 Saratoga U.S.A.
203 G3 Saratoga Springs U.S.A.
155 D2 Saratok Sarawak Malaysia
173 H5 Saratov Russia
173 H5 Saratovskaya Oblast' admin. div. Russia
172 I4 Saratovskoye Vodokhranilishche resr Russia
171 K5 Saratsina, Akrotirio pt Greece
141 F5 Sarāvān Iran
Saravan Laos see Salavan
154 A2 Sarawa r. Myanmar
155 D2 Sarawak state Malaysia
136 A1 Saray Turkey
136 B3 Sarayköy Turkey
136 D2 Sarayönü Turkey
139 F5 Sarazm tourist site Tajik.
139 G5 Sarband Tajik.
141 F5 Sarbāz Iran
141 F5 Sarbāz r. Iran
141 E3 Sar Bīsheh Iran
170 D2 Sarca r. Italy
137 L3 Sarcham-e Soflá Iran
144 E3 Sarda r. India/Nepal
145 E3 Sarda r. Nepal
144 C3 Sardarshahr India
140 B2 Sardasht Iran
Sardegna i. Sardinia Italy see Sardinia
213 B2 Sardinata Col.
170 C4 Sardinia i. Sardinia Italy
137 K3 Sardrūd Iran
140 C5 Sareb, Rās as pt U.A.E.
158 L2 Sareks nationalpark nat. park Sweden
158 L2 Sarektjåkkå mt. Sweden
140 B3 Sar-e Pol-e Żahāb Iran
141 G2 Sar-e Pul Sar-e Pul Afgh.
141 G3 Sar-e Pul Sar-e Pul Afgh.
139 H5 Sarez, Kŭli l. Tajik.
219 E4 Sargasso Sea Atlantic Ocean
144 C2 Sargodha Pak.
177 D4 Sarh Chad
140 D2 Sārī Iran
171 L7 Saria i. Greece
144 D2 Sarigh Jilganang Kol salt l. China
136 B2 Sarıgöl Turkey
137 I1 Sarıkamış Turkey
136 D3 Sarıkavak Turkey
144 D4 Sarila India
154 □ Sarimbun Reservoir Sing.
124 E4 Sarina Australia
136 E2 Sarıoğlan Turkey
Sar-i-Pul Afgh. see Sar-e Pul
137 I2 Sarısu Turkey
152 C4 Sariwŏn N. Korea
136 C2 Sarıyar Barajı resr Turkey
136 B1 Sarıyer Turkey
136 F2 Sarız Turkey
144 E4 Sarju r. India
139 I3 Sarkand Kazakh.
144 B4 Sarkari Tala India
136 C2 Şarkikaraağaç Turkey
136 F2 Şarkışla Turkey
173 C7 Şarköy Turkey
141 G4 Sarlath Range mts Afgh./Pak.
166 E4 Sarlat-la-Canéda France
138 C5 Şarlawuk Turkm.
147 F7 Sarmi Indon.
159 K3 Särna Sweden
137 K5 Sarneh Iran
170 C1 Sarnen Switz.
191 F4 Sarnia Canada
173 C5 Sarny Ukr.
141 H3 Sarōbī Afgh.
155 B3 Sarolangun Indon.
150 H2 Saroma-ko l. Japan
171 J6 Saronikos Kolpos g. Greece
173 C7 Saros Körfezi b. Turkey
144 C4 Sarotra India
172 G4 Sarov Russia
173 H5 Sarpa, Ozero l. Russia
173 H6 Sarpa, Ozero l. Russia
159 J4 Sarpsborg Norway
166 H2 Sarrebourg France
164 F5 Sarreguemines France
167 C1 Sarria Spain
167 F2 Sarrión Spain
164 C6 Sarry France
170 C4 Sartène Corsica France
140 C3 Sarud, Rūdkhāneh-ye r. Iran
141 G5 Saruna Pak.
137 L4 Sārūq Iran
137 J2 Şärur Azer.
137 K4 Sarvābād Iran
168 H7 Sárvár Hungary
140 D4 Sarvestān Iran
139 G4 Saryagash Kazakh.
139 G2 Saryarka plain Kazakh.
140 D4 Sar Yazd Iran
138 E3 Sarybasat Kazakh.
139 H4 Sary-Bulak Kyrg.
139 I4 Sary-Jaz r. Kyrg.
138 C3 Sarykamys Atyrauskaya Oblast' Kazakh.
139 F2 Sarykamys Karagandinskaya Oblast' Kazakh.
138 D4 Sarykamyshskoye Ozero salt l. Turkm./Uzbek.
139 G4 Sarykemer Kazakh.
139 H2 Sarykiyak Kazakh.
138 F1 Sarykol' Kazakh.
139 H5 Sarykol Range mts China/Tajik.
139 H3 Sarykomey Kazakh.
139 I3 Saryozek Kazakh.
138 B2 Saryozen r. Kazakh./Russia
139 H3 Saryshagan Kazakh.
139 F3 Sarysu watercourse Kazakh.
138 B3 Sarytash Kazakh.
139 H5 Sary-Tash Kyrg.
Sary Yazikskoye Vodokhranilishche resr Turkm. see Saryýazy Suw Howdany
141 F2 Saryýazy Suw Howdany resr Turkm.
139 H3 Saryyesik-Atyrau, Peski des. Kazakh.
139 I4 Saryzhaz Kazakh.
138 B4 Sarzha Kazakh.
197 G6 Sasabe U.S.A.
145 F4 Sasaram India
151 A8 Sasebo Japan
187 H4 Saskatchewan prov. Canada
187 I4 Saskatchewan r. Canada
187 H4 Saskatoon Canada
133 M2 Saskylakh Russia
206 H5 Saslaya mt. Nicaragua
206 H5 Saslaya, Parque Nacional nat. park Nicaragua
181 G3 Sasolburg S. Africa
172 G4 Sasovo Russia
203 F5 Sassafras U.S.A.
176 B4 Sassandra Côte d'Ivoire
170 C4 Sassari Sardinia Italy
165 G3 Sassenberg Germany
168 F3 Sassnitz Germany
139 J3 Sasykkol', Ozero l. Kazakh.
173 H6 Sasykoli Russia
176 A3 Satadougou Mali
151 B9 Sata-misaki c. Japan
144 C5 Satana India
143 A2 Satara India
181 I2 Satara S. Africa
173 G4 Satinka Russia
145 G5 Satkhira Bangl.
144 C3 Satluj r. Pak.
143 B2 Satmala Range hills India
144 E4 Satna India
139 F2 Satpayev Kazakh.
144 C5 Satpura Range mts India
151 B9 Satsuma-hantō pen. Japan
151 B9 Satsuma-Sendai Japan
154 B2 Sattahip Thai.
165 I5 Satteldorf Germany
144 D2 Satti India
169 K7 Satu Mare Romania
154 B4 Satun Thai.
215 E1 Sauce Arg.
206 D2 Sauceda Mex.
197 F5 Sauceda Mountains U.S.A.
206 C1 Saucillo Mex.
159 I4 Sauda Norway
139 G4 Saudakent Kazakh.
158 C2 Sauðárkrókur Iceland
142 B4 Saudi Arabia country Asia
165 F3 Sauerland reg. Germany
190 D4 Saugatuck U.S.A.
203 G3 Saugerties U.S.A.
198 E2 Sauk Center U.S.A.
190 C4 Sauk City U.S.A.
166 G3 Saulieu France
191 E2 Sault Sainte Marie Canada
190 E2 Sault Sainte Marie U.S.A.
139 G1 Saumalkol' Kazakh.
147 F7 Saumlakki Indon.
166 D3 Saumur France
209 G7 Saunders Island S. Sandwich Is
145 F4 Saura r. India
138 B3 Saura Kazakh.
179 C4 Saurimo Angola
144 D5 Sausar India
171 I2 Sava r. Europe
127 F8 Savage River Australia
125 I3 Savai'i i. Samoa
173 G5 Savala r. Russia
176 C4 Savalou Benin
190 B4 Savanna U.S.A.
201 D6 Savannah GA U.S.A.
201 B5 Savannah TN U.S.A.
201 D5 Savannah r. U.S.A.
201 E7 Savannah Sound Bahamas
154 C1 Savannakhét Laos
205 I5 Savanna-la-Mar Jamaica
188 B3 Savant Lake Canada
143 A3 Savanur India
158 M3 Sävar Sweden
171 L5 Savaştepe Turkey
176 C4 Savè Benin
179 D6 Save r. Moz.
140 C3 Sāveh Iran
158 O3 Saviaho Fin.
132 F3 Savinskiy Russia
170 C2 Savona Italy
159 O3 Savonlinna Fin.
158 O3 Savonranta Fin.
166 H4 Savoy reg. France
137 I1 Şavşat Turkey
159 K4 Sävsjö Sweden
158 O2 Savukoski Fin.
137 H3 Savur Turkey
Savu Sea Indon. see Sawu, Laut
144 D4 Sawai Madhopur India
154 A1 Sawankhalok Thai.
195 F4 Sawatch Range mts U.S.A.
162 A6 Sawel Mountain h. U.K.
154 A3 Sawi, Ao b. Thai.
127 J3 Sawtell Australia
190 B2 Sawtooth Mountains hills U.S.A.
147 E7 Sawu, Laut sea Indon.
161 G4 Saxilby U.K.
161 I5 Saxmundham U.K.
158 K2 Saxnäs Sweden
139 I3 Sayak Kazakh.
146 B1 Sayano-Shushenskoye Vodokhranilishche resr Russia
Sayat Turkm. see Saýat
138 E5 Saýat Turkm.
207 G4 Sayaxché Guat.
140 D4 Sāyen Iran
142 D6 Sayḫūt Yemen
138 A2 Saykyn Kazakh.
178 E2 Saylac Somalia
146 D2 Saynshand Mongolia
139 J3 Sayram Hu salt l. China
199 D5 Sayre OK U.S.A.
202 E4 Sayre PA U.S.A.
206 D4 Sayula Jalisco Mex.
207 F4 Sayula Veracruz Mex.
186 D4 Sayward Canada
138 B3 Sazdy Kazakh.
144 C2 Sazin Pak.
172 E3 Sazonovo Russia
176 B2 Sbaa Alg.
176 C1 Sbeitla Tunisia
160 D3 Scafell Pike h. U.K.
162 B4 Scalasaig U.K.
170 F5 Scalea Italy
162 □ Scalloway U.K.
163 C5 Scalp h. Ireland
162 B3 Scalpay i. Scotland U.K.
162 C3 Scalpay i. Scotland U.K.
127 H8 Scamander Australia
162 E2 Scapa Flow inlet U.K.
162 C4 Scarba i. U.K.
191 H4 Scarborough Canada
213 E2 Scarborough Trin. and Tob.
160 G3 Scarborough U.K.
153 A3 Scarborough Reef sea feature Phil.
162 A2 Scarp i. U.K.
165 I1 Schaale r. Germany
165 I1 Schaalsee l. Germany
164 C4 Schaerbeek Belgium
168 D7 Schaffhausen Switz.
165 J3 Schafstädt Germany
164 C2 Schagen Neth.
164 C2 Schagerbrug Neth.
180 B3 Schakalskuppe Namibia
141 F4 Schao watercourse Afgh./Iran
168 F6 Schärding Austria
164 B3 Scharendijke Neth.
165 H1 Scheeßel Germany
189 G3 Schefferville Canada
Schelde r. Belgium see Scheldt
164 C3 Scheldt r. Belgium
197 E2 Schell Creek Range mts U.S.A.
165 I2 Schellerten Germany
203 G3 Schenectady U.S.A.
165 H1 Schenefeld Germany
164 C2 Schermerhorn Neth.
162 D4 Schiehallion mt. U.K.
165 K6 Schierling Germany
164 E1 Schiermonnikoog Neth.
164 E1 Schiermonnikoog i. Neth.
164 E1 Schiermonnikoog, Nationaal Park nat. park Neth.
165 G1 Schiffdorf Germany
165 J1 Schilde r. Germany
164 D4 Schinnen Neth.
170 D2 Schio Italy
165 K3 Schkeuditz Germany
164 E4 Schleiden Germany
165 J4 Schleiz Germany
168 D3 Schleswig Germany
165 H1 Schleswig-Holstein land Germany
165 I4 Schleusingen Germany
165 H4 Schlitz Germany
165 G3 Schloß Holte-Stukenbrock Germany
165 H4 Schlüchtern Germany
165 I5 Schlüsselfeld Germany
165 I4 Schmalkalden Germany
165 G3 Schmallenberg Germany
165 K4 Schneeberg Germany
165 J3 Schneidlingen Germany
165 H1 Schneverdingen Germany
203 G3 Schodack Center U.S.A.
190 C3 Schofield U.S.A.
196 □1 Schofield Barracks military base U.S.A.
164 D2 Schokland tourist site Neth.
165 K1 Schönebeck Germany
165 J2 Schönebeck (Elbe) Germany
165 I2 Schöningen Germany
165 H5 Schöntal Germany
203 I2 Schoodic Lake U.S.A.
190 E4 Schoolcraft U.S.A.
164 C3 Schoonhoven Neth.
165 I5 Schopfloch Germany
165 I2 Schöppenstedt Germany
165 F1 Schortens Germany
127 H9 Schouten Island Australia
124 E2 Schouten Islands P.N.G.
190 D1 Schreiber Canada
203 G3 Schroon Lake U.S.A.
197 F5 Schuchuli U.S.A.
163 B6 Schull Ireland
187 J2 Schultz Lake Canada
196 C2 Schurz U.S.A.
164 F2 Schüttorf Germany
203 G3 Schuylerville U.S.A.
165 J5 Schwabach Germany
168 D6 Schwäbische Alb mts Germany
165 H5 Schwäbisch Hall Germany
168 E6 Schwabmünchen Germany
165 G2 Schwaförden Germany
165 H4 Schwalmstadt-Ziegenhain Germany
165 K5 Schwandorf Germany
155 D3 Schwaner, Pegunungan mts Indon.
165 G1 Schwanewede Germany
165 H2 Schwarmstedt Germany
165 L3 Schwarze Elster r. Germany
165 I1 Schwarzenbek Germany
165 K4 Schwarzenberg/Erzgebirge Germany
164 E4 Schwarzer Mann h. Germany
180 B2 Schwarzrand mts Namibia
Schwarzwald mts Germany see Black Forest
168 E7 Schwaz Austria
165 I5 Schwebheim Germany
168 G4 Schwedt/Oder Germany
165 G5 Schwegenheim Germany
164 E5 Schweich Germany
165 I4 Schweinfurt Germany
165 L3 Schweinitz Germany
165 K1 Schweinrich Germany
181 F3 Schweizer-Reneke S. Africa
164 F3 Schwelm Germany
168 D6 Schwenningen Germany
165 J1 Schwerin Germany
165 J1 Schweriner See l. Germany
165 G5 Schwetzingen Germany
168 D7 Schwyz Switz.
170 E6 Sciacca Sicily Italy
170 F6 Scicli Sicily Italy
161 A8 Scilly, Isles of U.K.
202 B5 Scioto r. U.S.A.
197 F2 Scipio U.S.A.
194 F1 Scobey U.S.A.
161 I5 Scole U.K.
127 I4 Scone Australia
162 E4 Scone U.K.
203 I1 Scopan Lake U.S.A.
185 P2 Scoresby Land reg. Greenland
219 G9 Scotia Ridge sea feature S. Atlantic Ocean
219 G9 Scotia Sea S. Atlantic Ocean
191 G4 Scotland Canada
162 D4 Scotland admin. div. U.K.
186 D4 Scott, Cape Canada
129 B5 Scott Base research stn Antarctica
181 I5 Scottburgh S. Africa
198 C4 Scott City U.S.A.
129 B5 Scott Coast coastal area Antarctica
202 D4 Scottdale U.S.A.
185 K2 Scott Inlet Canada
129 A6 Scott Island i. Antarctica
187 H3 Scott Lake Canada
129 E4 Scott Mountains mts Antarctica
198 C3 Scottsbluff U.S.A.
201 C5 Scottsboro U.S.A.
200 C4 Scottsburg U.S.A.
127 G8 Scottsdale Australia
195 E5 Scottsdale U.S.A.
196 A3 Scotts Valley U.S.A.
190 D4 Scottville U.S.A.
196 D3 Scottys Junction U.S.A.
162 C2 Scourie U.K.
162 □ Scousburgh U.K.
162 E2 Scrabster U.K.
203 F4 Scranton U.S.A.
162 B4 Scridain, Loch inlet U.K.
160 G4 Scunthorpe U.K.
161 H7 Seaford U.K.
203 F5 Seaford U.S.A.
191 G4 Seaforth Canada
153 A4 Seahorse Shoal sea feature Phil.
187 J3 Seal r. Canada
180 E7 Seal, Cape S. Africa
126 E5 Sea Lake Australia
203 I3 Seal Island U.S.A.
189 H3 Seal Lake Canada
180 F7 Seal Point S. Africa
197 E3 Seaman Range mts U.S.A.
160 G3 Seamer U.K.
197 E4 Searchlight U.S.A.
199 F5 Searcy U.S.A.
196 D4 Searles Lake U.S.A.
190 E4 Sears U.S.A.
203 I2 Searsport U.S.A.
196 B3 Seaside CA U.S.A.
194 B2 Seaside OR U.S.A.
162 E6 Seaton U.K.
194 B2 Seattle U.S.A.
186 B2 Seattle, Mount Canada/U.S.A.
203 F5 Seaville U.S.A.
203 H3 Sebago Lake U.S.A.
206 A1 Sebastián Vizcaíno, Bahía b. Mex.
203 I2 Sebasticook r. U.S.A.
155 E2 Sebatik i. Indon.
136 C1 Seben Turkey
171 J2 Sebeş Romania
155 C4 Sebesi i. Indon.
191 F4 Sebewaing U.S.A.
172 D3 Sebezh Russia
136 E3 Sebil Turkey
136 G1 Şebinkarahisar Turkey
203 I2 Seboeis Lake U.S.A.
203 I2 Seboomook U.S.A.
203 I2 Seboomook Lake U.S.A.
201 D7 Sebring U.S.A.
173 G5 Sebrovo Russia
210 B5 Sechura Peru
210 B5 Sechura, Bahía de b. Peru
165 H5 Seckach Germany
203 H2 Second Lake U.S.A.
176 □ Secos, Ilhéus is Cape Verde
128 A6 Secretary Island N.Z.
181 H3 Secunda S. Africa
143 B2 Secunderabad India
198 E4 Sedalia U.S.A.
143 B2 Sedam India
126 C5 Sedan Australia
166 G2 Sedan France
128 E4 Seddon N.Z.
128 C4 Seddonville N.Z.
203 I2 Sedgwick U.S.A.
176 A3 Sédhiou Senegal
168 G6 Sedlčany Czech Rep.
136 E6 Sedom Israel
197 G4 Sedona U.S.A.
170 B6 Sédrata Alg.
159 M5 Šeduva Lith.
165 I1 Seedorf Germany
163 D5 Seefin h. Ireland
165 J2 Seehausen Germany
165 J2 Seehausen (Altmark) Germany
179 B6 Seeheim Namibia
165 G5 Seeheim-Jugenheim Germany
180 E6 Seekoegat S. Africa
197 E5 Seeley U.S.A.
129 B4 Seelig, Mount mt. Antarctica
165 H2 Seelze Germany
Seemandhra state India see Andhra Pradesh
166 E2 Sées France
165 I3 Seesen Germany
165 I1 Seevetal Germany
181 G1 Sefare Botswana
171 L5 Seferihisar Turkey
141 G3 Sefid Kūh mts Afgh.
181 G1 Sefophe Botswana
159 J3 Segalstad Norway
153 A5 Segama r. Sabah Malaysia
155 B2 Segamat Malaysia
165 K2 Segeletz Germany
172 E2 Segezha Russia
139 F3 Segiz salt l. Kazakh.
139 F3 Segiz, Ozera lakes Kazakh.
167 F3 Segorbe Spain

South Downs National Park

171 K2 **Sibiu** Romania
155 A2 **Sibolga** Indon.
154 A5 **Siborongborong** Indon.
155 D2 **Sibu** Sarawak Malaysia
153 B5 **Sibuco** Phil.
153 B5 **Sibuguey** r. Phil.
153 B5 **Sibuguey Bay** Phil.
178 B3 **Sibut** C.A.R.
153 A5 **Sibutu** i. Phil.
153 A5 **Sibutu Passage** Phil.
153 B3 **Sibuyan** i. Phil.
153 B3 **Sibuyan Sea** Phil.
153 B2 **Sicapoo** mt. Phil.
154 A3 **Sichon** Thai.
149 B4 **Sichuan** prov. China
148 B4 **Sichuan Giant Panda Sanctuaries** tourist site China
149 B4 **Sichuan Pendi** basin China
166 G5 **Sicié, Cap** c. France
Sicilia i. Italy see **Sicily**
170 E6 **Sicilian Channel** Italy/Tunisia
170 E6 **Sicily** i. Italy
210 D6 **Sicuani** Peru
143 B2 **Siddipet** India
171 L7 **Sideros, Akrotirio** pt Greece
180 E6 **Sidesaviwa** S. Africa
144 C5 **Sidhpur** India
167 H5 **Sidi Aïssa** Alg.
167 G4 **Sidi Ali** Alg.
176 B1 **Sidi Bel Abbès** Alg.
170 C7 **Sidi Bouzid** Tunisia
170 D7 **Sidi El Hani, Sebkhet de** salt pan Tunisia
176 A2 **Sidi Ifni** Morocco
176 B1 **Sidi Kacem** Morocco
154 A5 **Sidikalang** Indon.
162 E4 **Sidlaw Hills** U.K.
129 B4 **Sidley, Mount** mt. Antarctica
161 D7 **Sidmouth** U.K.
186 E5 **Sidney** Canada
194 F2 **Sidney** MT U.S.A.
198 C3 **Sidney** NE U.S.A.
203 F3 **Sidney** NY U.S.A.
202 A4 **Sidney** OH U.S.A.
201 D5 **Sidney Lanier, Lake** U.S.A.
145 H5 **Sidoktaya** Myanmar
136 E5 **Sidon** Lebanon
172 G3 **Sidorovo** Russia
214 A3 **Sidrolândia** Brazil
181 I3 **Sidvokodvo** Swaziland
Sidzhak Uzbek. see **Sijjaq**
166 F5 **Sié, Col de** pass France
169 K4 **Siedlce** Poland
165 G4 **Siegen** Germany
154 B2 **Siĕm Réab** Cambodia
170 D3 **Siena** Italy
169 I5 **Sieradz** Poland
145 H3 **Si'erdingka** China
215 D4 **Sierra, Punta** pt Arg.
199 B6 **Sierra Blanca** U.S.A.
215 C4 **Sierra Colorada** Arg.
206 H5 **Sierra de Agalta, Parque Nacional** nat. park Hond.
215 D4 **Sierra Grande** Arg.
176 A4 **Sierra Leone** country Africa
219 H5 **Sierra Leone Basin** sea feature N. Atlantic Ocean
219 H5 **Sierra Leone Rise** sea feature N. Atlantic Ocean
196 C4 **Sierra Madre Mountains** U.S.A.
206 D2 **Sierra Mojada** Mex.
213 C2 **Sierra Nevada, Parque Nacional** nat. park Venez.
213 B2 **Sierra Nevada de Santa Marta, Parque Nacional** nat. park Col.
196 B2 **Sierraville** U.S.A.
197 G6 **Sierra Vista** U.S.A.
168 C7 **Sierre** Switz.
158 N3 **Sievi** Fin.
149 C6 **Sifang Ling** mts China
171 K6 **Sifnos** i. Greece
167 F5 **Sig** Alg.
185 M2 **Sigguup Nunaa** pen. Greenland
169 K7 **Sighetu Marmației** Romania
169 L7 **Sighișoara** Romania
143 C5 **Sigiriya** Sri Lanka
154 □ **Siglap** Sing.
155 A1 **Sigli** Indon.
158 C1 **Siglufjörður** Iceland
153 B4 **Sigma** Phil.
168 D6 **Sigmaringen** Germany
164 E4 **Signal de Botrange** h. Belgium
197 E5 **Signal Peak** U.S.A.
129 C2 **Signy** research stn Antarctica
164 C5 **Signy-l'Abbaye** France
190 A5 **Sigourney** U.S.A.
219 C4 **Sigsbee Deep** sea feature G. of Mexico
207 H5 **Siguatepeque** Hond.
167 E2 **Sigüenza** Spain
176 B3 **Siguiri** Guinea
159 N4 **Sigulda** Latvia
154 B3 **Sihanoukville** Cambodia
148 F3 **Sihong** China
144 E5 **Sihora** India
149 D6 **Sihui** China
158 N2 **Siikajoki** Fin.
158 N3 **Siilinjärvi** Fin.
137 H3 **Siirt** Turkey
139 G4 **Sijjaq** Uzbek.
155 B3 **Sijunjung** Indon.
186 E3 **Sikanni Chief** Canada
186 E3 **Sikanni Chief** r. Canada
144 C4 **Sikar** India
141 H3 **Sikaram** mt. Afgh.
176 B3 **Sikasso** Mali
139 K3 **Sikeshu** China
199 F4 **Sikeston** U.S.A.
146 F2 **Sikhote-Alin'** mts Russia
171 K6 **Sikinos** i. Greece
144 B5 **Sikka** India
145 G4 **Sikkim** state India
158 L2 **Siksjö** Sweden
152 B4 **Sikuaishi** China
155 E1 **Sikuati** Sabah Malaysia
167 C1 **Sil** r. Spain
153 C4 **Silago** Phil.
159 M5 **Šilal** Lith.
206 D3 **Silao** Mex.
153 B4 **Silay** Phil.
165 H1 **Silberberg** h. Germany
145 H4 **Silchar** India
136 B1 **Şile** Turkey
143 C2 **Sileru** r. India
139 H2 **Silety** Kazakh.
139 H1 **Silety** r. Kazakh.
139 H1 **Siletyteniz, Ozero** salt l. Kazakh.
170 C6 **Siliana** Tunisia
136 D3 **Silifke** Turkey
145 G3 **Siling Co** salt l. China
171 L2 **Silistra** Bulg.
136 B1 **Silivri** Turkey
159 K3 **Siljan** l. Sweden
159 J4 **Silkeborg** Denmark
159 N4 **Sillamäe** Estonia
144 C5 **Sillod** India
181 I3 **Silobela** S. Africa
145 G3 **Silong** China
199 E6 **Silsbee** U.S.A.
158 N2 **Siltaharju** Fin.
141 F5 **Sīlūp** r. Iran
159 M5 **Šilut** Lith.
137 H2 **Silvan** Turkey
144 C5 **Silvassa** India
190 B2 **Silver Bay** U.S.A.
195 E5 **Silver City** U.S.A.
190 C1 **Silver Islet** Canada
194 B3 **Silver Lake** U.S.A.
196 D4 **Silver Lake** l. CA U.S.A.
190 D2 **Silver Lake** l. MI U.S.A.
163 C5 **Silvermine Mountains** hills Ireland
196 D3 **Silver Peak Range** mts U.S.A.
202 E5 **Silver Spring** U.S.A.
196 C2 **Silver Springs** U.S.A.
126 D3 **Silverton** Australia
161 D7 **Silverton** U.K.
191 F3 **Silver Water** Canada
207 G4 **Silvituc** Mex.
153 B3 **Simara** i. Phil.
191 H2 **Simard, Lac** l. Canada
137 K5 **Şīmareh, Rūdkhāneh-ye** r. Iran
145 F4 **Simaria** India
136 B2 **Simav** Turkey
136 B2 **Simav Dağları** mts Turkey
178 C3 **Simba** Dem. Rep. Congo
191 G4 **Simcoe** Canada
191 H3 **Simcoe, Lake** Canada
143 D1 **Simdega** India
178 D2 **Simēn** mts Eth.
Simēn Mountains Eth. see **Simēn**
155 A2 **Simeulue** i. Indon.
173 E6 **Simferopol'** Crimea
145 E3 **Simikot** Nepal
213 B3 **Simití** Col.
196 C4 **Simi Valley** U.S.A.
195 F4 **Simla** U.S.A.
169 K7 **Şimleu Silvaniei** Romania
164 E4 **Simmerath** Germany
164 F5 **Simmern/Hunsrück** Germany
196 C4 **Simmler** U.S.A.
197 F4 **Simmons** U.S.A.
201 F7 **Simm's** Bahamas
158 N2 **Simojärvi** l. Fin.
206 D2 **Simon** Mex.
186 F4 **Simonette** r. Canada
187 I4 **Simonhouse** Canada
159 O3 **Simpele** Fin.
168 D7 **Simplon Pass** Switz.
124 D4 **Simpson Desert** Australia
190 D1 **Simpson Island** Canada
196 D2 **Simpson Park Mountains** U.S.A.
159 K5 **Simrishamn** Sweden
153 A5 **Simunul** i. Phil.
146 H2 **Simushir, Ostrov** i. Russia
143 A2 **Sina** r. India
177 F2 **Sīnā', Shibh Jazīrat** pen. Egypt
155 A2 **Sinabang** Indon.
154 A5 **Sinabung** vol. Indon.
164 C5 **Sinai, Mont** h. France
206 B2 **Sinaloa** state Mex.
170 D3 **Sinalunga** Italy
149 C5 **Sinan** China
152 C4 **Sinanju** N. Korea
145 H5 **Sinbyugyun** Myanmar
136 F2 **Sincan** Turkey
213 B2 **Sincé** Col.
213 B2 **Sincelejo** Col.
201 D5 **Sinclair, Lake** U.S.A.
186 E4 **Sinclair Mills** Canada
180 B2 **Sinclair Mine** Namibia
162 E2 **Sinclair's Bay** U.K.
144 D4 **Sind** r. India
153 B4 **Sindañgan** Phil.
155 C4 **Sindangbarang** Indon.
144 B4 **Sindari** India
168 D6 **Sindelfingen** Germany
143 B2 **Sindgi** India
144 B4 **Sindh** prov. Pak.
143 B3 **Sindhnur** India
136 B2 **Sındırgı** Turkey
144 D6 **Sindkhed** India
144 C5 **Sindkheda** India
152 C4 **Sin-do** i. China
172 I2 **Sindor** Russia
145 F5 **Sindri** India
144 B3 **Sind Sagar Doab** lowland Pak.
172 I3 **Sinegor'ye** Russia
171 L4 **Sinekçi** Turkey
167 B4 **Sines** Port.
167 B4 **Sines, Cabo de** c. Port.
158 N2 **Sinettä** Fin.
176 B4 **Sinfra** Côte d'Ivoire
177 F3 **Singa** Sudan
144 E3 **Singahi** India
144 D2 **Singa Pass** India
154 □ **Singapore** country Asia
154 B5 **Singapore** Sing. (City Plan **102**)
154 □ **Singapore, Strait of** Indon./Sing.
155 E4 **Singaraja** Indon.
154 B2 **Sing Buri** Thai.
191 G3 **Singhampton** Canada
178 D4 **Singida** Tanz.
155 C2 **Singkawang** Indon.
154 A5 **Singkil** Indon.
127 I4 **Singleton** Australia
152 D4 **Sin'gye** N. Korea
143 C5 **Sinharaja Forest Reserve** nature res. Sri Lanka
152 D3 **Sinhŭng** N. Korea
170 C4 **Siniscola** Sardinia Italy
138 E2 **Siniy-Shikhan** Russia
170 G3 **Sinj** Croatia
124 C2 **Sinjai** Indon.
137 H3 **Sinjār** Iraq
137 H3 **Sinjār, Jabal** mt. Iraq
177 F3 **Sinkat** Sudan
Sinkiang aut. reg. China see **Xinjiang Uygur Zizhiqu**
152 C4 **Sinmi-do** i. N. Korea
165 G4 **Sinn** Germany
211 H2 **Sinnamary** Fr. Guiana
171 M2 **Sinoie, Lacul** lag. Romania
173 E7 **Sinop** Turkey
Sinp'a N. Korea see **Kimjŏngsuk**
152 E3 **Sinp'o** N. Korea
152 D4 **Sinp'yŏng** N. Korea
152 D4 **Sinsang** N. Korea
165 G5 **Sinsheim** Germany
155 D2 **Sintang** Indon.
205 L5 **Sint Eustatius** i. West Indies
164 B3 **Sint-Laureins** Belgium
205 L5 **Sint Maarten** terr. West Indies
164 C3 **Sint-Niklaas** Belgium
199 D6 **Sinton** U.S.A.
164 D4 **Sint-Truiden** Belgium
213 A2 **Sinú** r. Col.
152 C3 **Sinŭiju** N. Korea
164 F4 **Sinzig** Germany
153 B5 **Siocon** Phil.
168 I7 **Siófok** Hungary
168 C7 **Sion** Switz.
163 D3 **Sion Mills** U.K.
198 D3 **Sioux Center** U.S.A.
198 D3 **Sioux City** U.S.A.
198 D3 **Sioux Falls** U.S.A.
188 B3 **Sioux Lookout** Canada
207 G5 **Sipacate** Guat.
153 B4 **Sipalay** Phil.
152 C2 **Siping** China
187 J3 **Sipiwesk** Canada
187 J3 **Sipiwesk Lake** Canada
144 C5 **Sipra** r. India
201 C5 **Sipsey** r. U.S.A.
155 A3 **Sipura** i. Indon.
206 H5 **Siquia** r. Nicaragua
153 B4 **Siquijor** Phil.
153 B4 **Siquijor** i. Phil.
144 B5 **Sir** r. Pak.
143 B3 **Sira** India
159 I4 **Sira** r. Norway
140 D5 **Şīr Abū Nu'āyr** i. U.A.E.
154 B2 **Si Racha** Thai.
Siracusa Sicily Italy see **Syracuse**
186 E4 **Sir Alexander, Mount** Canada
137 G1 **Şiran** Turkey
141 G5 **Siranda Lake** Pak.
140 D5 **Şīr Banī Yās** i. U.A.E.
137 L3 **Sīrdān** Iran
139 G4 **Sirdaryo** Uzbek.
124 D3 **Sir Edward Pellew Group** is Australia
190 A3 **Siren** U.S.A.
140 E5 **Sīrīk** Iran
154 B1 **Siri Kit, Khuan** Thai.
140 D4 **Sīrīz** Iran
186 D2 **Sir James MacBrien, Mount** Canada
140 D4 **Sīrjān** Iran
140 D4 **Sīrjān** salt flat Iran
126 B5 **Sir Joseph Banks Group** is Australia
144 E4 **Sirmour** India
137 I3 **Şırnak** Turkey
143 C2 **Sironcha** India
144 D4 **Sironj** India
143 B2 **Sirpur** India
196 C4 **Sirretta Peak** U.S.A.
140 D5 **Sīrrī, Jazīreh-ye** i. Iran
144 C3 **Sirsa** Haryana India
145 E4 **Sirsa** Uttar Pradesh India
186 F4 **Sir Sandford, Mount** Canada
143 A3 **Sirsi** Karnataka India
144 D3 **Sirsi** Uttar Pradesh India
143 B2 **Sirsilla** India
177 D1 **Sirte** Libya
177 D1 **Sirte, Gulf of** Libya
143 A2 **Sirur** India
137 L2 **Şirvan** Azer.
137 I2 **Şirvan** Turkey
159 N5 **Širvintos** Lith.
137 J4 **Sīrwān** r. Iraq
186 F4 **Sir Wilfrid Laurier, Mount** Canada
170 G2 **Sisak** Croatia
154 C2 **Sisaket** Thai.
207 G3 **Sisal** Mex.
180 E3 **Sishen** S. Africa
148 C2 **Sishilisu** China
137 K2 **Sisian** Armenia
190 C2 **Siskiwit Bay** U.S.A.
154 B2 **Sisŏphŏn** Cambodia
196 B4 **Sisquoc** r. U.S.A.
198 D2 **Sisseton** U.S.A.
203 J1 **Sisson Branch Reservoir** Canada
141 F4 **Sīstān** reg. Iran
127 F8 **Sisters Beach** Australia
141 E5 **Sīt** Iran
144 C5 **Sitamau** India
153 A5 **Sitangkai** Phil.
144 E4 **Sitapur** India
171 L7 **Siteia** Greece
181 I3 **Siteki** Swaziland
148 E1 **Site of Xanadu** tourist site China
171 J4 **Sithonias, Chersonisos** pen. Greece
214 C1 **Sítio d'Abadia** Brazil
214 D1 **Sítio do Mato** Brazil
186 B3 **Sitka** U.S.A.
144 B3 **Sitpur** Pak.
164 D4 **Sittard** Neth.
145 H4 **Sittaung** Myanmar
165 H1 **Sittensen** Germany
161 H6 **Sittingbourne** U.K.
145 H5 **Sittwe** Myanmar
149 □ **Siu A Chau** i. Hong Kong China
206 H5 **Siuna** Nicaragua
145 F5 **Siuri** India
143 B4 **Sivaganga** India
143 B4 **Sivakasi** India
140 D4 **Sivand** Iran
136 F2 **Sivas** Turkey
145 H4 **Sivasagar** India
136 B2 **Sivaslı** Turkey
137 G3 **Siverek** Turkey
137 G2 **Sivrice** Turkey
136 C2 **Sivrihisar** Turkey
181 H3 **Sivukile** S. Africa
177 E2 **Sīwah** Egypt
144 D3 **Siwalik Range** mts India/Nepal
145 F4 **Siwan** India
144 C4 **Siwana** India
166 G5 **Six-Fours-les-Plages** France
148 E3 **Sixian** China
190 E4 **Six Lakes** U.S.A.
163 D3 **Sixmilecross** U.K.
181 H2 **Siyabuswa** S. Africa
141 G2 **Sīyāh, Daryā-ye** r. Afgh.
141 F3 **Sīyāh Band, Kōh-e** mts Afgh.
141 G3 **Sīyāh Kōh** mts Afgh.
141 G4 **Sīyāh Sang, Kōtal-e** Afgh.
149 C5 **Siyang** Guizhou China
148 F3 **Siyang** Jiangsu China
138 A4 **Siyäzän** Azer.
148 C1 **Siyitang** China
140 D3 **Sīyunī** Iran
Sjælland i. Denmark see **Zealand**
171 I3 **Sjenica** Serbia
159 K5 **Sjöbo** Sweden
158 L1 **Sjøvegan** Norway
173 E6 **Skadovs'k** Ukr.
158 C3 **Skaftárós** r. mouth Iceland
158 C1 **Skagafjörður** inlet Iceland
159 J4 **Skagen** Denmark
159 J4 **Skagerrak** str. Denmark/Norway
194 B1 **Skagit** r. Canada/U.S.A.
186 B3 **Skagway** U.S.A.
158 N1 **Skaidi** Norway
158 L1 **Skaland** Norway
158 K2 **Skalmodal** Sweden
159 J4 **Skanderborg** Denmark
203 E3 **Skaneateles Lake** U.S.A.
190 C2 **Skanee** U.S.A.
171 K5 **Skantzoura** i. Greece
159 K4 **Skara** Sweden
159 M4 **Skärgårdshavets nationalpark** nat. park Fin.
159 J3 **Skarnes** Norway
169 J5 **Skarżysko-Kamienna** Poland
158 M2 **Skaulo** Sweden
169 I6 **Skawina** Poland
186 D3 **Skeena** r. Canada
186 D3 **Skeena Mountains** Canada
161 H4 **Skegness** U.K.
158 M2 **Skellefteå** Sweden
158 M2 **Skellefteälven** r. Sweden
158 M2 **Skelleftehamn** Sweden
160 E4 **Skelmersdale** U.K.
163 E4 **Skerries** Ireland
159 J4 **Ski** Norway
171 J5 **Skiathos** i. Greece
163 B6 **Skibbereen** Ireland
158 M1 **Skibotn** Norway
160 D3 **Skiddaw** h. U.K.
159 J4 **Skien** Norway
169 J5 **Skierniewice** Poland
176 C1 **Skikda** Alg.
160 G4 **Skipsea** U.K.
126 E6 **Skipton** Australia
160 E4 **Skipton** U.K.
160 G4 **Skirlaugh** U.K.
159 J4 **Skive** Denmark
158 C2 **Skjálfandafljót** r. Iceland
159 J5 **Skjern** Denmark
159 I3 **Skjolden** Norway
139 H5 **Skobeleva, Pik** mt. Kyrg.
158 I3 **Skodje** Norway
158 N1 **Skoganvarri** Norway
163 F6 **Skokholm Island** U.K.
190 D4 **Skokie** U.S.A.
138 E2 **Skol'** Kazakh.
161 B6 **Skomer Island** U.K.
171 J5 **Skopelos** i. Greece
172 F4 **Skopin** Russia
171 I4 **Skopje** Macedonia
173 F5 **Skorodnoye** Russia
159 K4 **Skövde** Sweden
203 I2 **Skowhegan** U.S.A.
159 M4 **Skrunda** Latvia
186 B2 **Skukum, Mount** Canada
181 I2 **Skukuza** S. Africa
196 D3 **Skull Peak** U.S.A.
190 B5 **Skunk** r. U.S.A.
159 M4 **Skuodas** Lith.
159 K5 **Skurup** Sweden
159 L3 **Skutskär** Sweden
Skuvvanvárri Norway see **Skoganvarri**
173 D5 **Skvyra** Ukr.
162 B3 **Skye** i. U.K.
171 K5 **Skyros** Greece
171 K5 **Skyros** i. Greece
159 J5 **Slagelse** Denmark
158 L2 **Slagnäs** Sweden
155 C4 **Slamet, Gunung** vol. Indon.
163 E4 **Slane** Ireland
163 E5 **Slaney** r. Ireland
172 D3 **Slantsy** Russia
173 G5 **Slashchevskaya** Russia
190 D1 **Slate Islands** Canada
170 G2 **Slatina** Croatia
171 K2 **Slatina** Romania
187 G2 **Slave** r. Canada
176 C4 **Slave Coast** Africa
186 G3 **Slave Lake** Canada
139 I1 **Slavgorod** Russia
169 N2 **Slavkovichi** Russia
Slavonia reg. Croatia see **Slavonija**
171 H2 **Slavonija** reg. Croatia
171 H2 **Slavonski Brod** Croatia
173 C5 **Slavuta** Ukr.
173 D5 **Slavutych** Ukr.
150 B3 **Slavyanka** Russia
173 F6 **Slavyansk-na-Kubani** Russia
172 D4 **Slawharad** Belarus
168 H3 **Sławno** Poland
161 G4 **Sleaford** U.K.
126 A5 **Sleaford Bay** Australia
163 A5 **Slea Head** Ireland
162 C3 **Sleat** pen. U.K.
162 C3 **Sleat, Sound of** sea chan. U.K.
188 E2 **Sleeper Islands** Canada
190 D3 **Sleeping Bear Dunes National Lakeshore** nature res. U.S.A.
190 D3 **Sleeping Bear Point** U.S.A.
173 H7 **Sleptsovskaya** Russia
129 C3 **Slessor Glacier** glacier Antarctica
199 F6 **Slidell** U.S.A.
163 A5 **Slievanea** h. Ireland
163 D3 **Slieve Anierin** h. Ireland
163 D5 **Slieveardagh Hills** Ireland
163 C4 **Slieve Aughty Mountains** hills Ireland
163 D3 **Slieve Beagh** h. Ireland/U.K.
163 C5 **Slieve Bernagh** hills Ireland
163 D4 **Slieve Bloom Mountains** hills Ireland
163 B5 **Slievecallan** h. Ireland
163 B3 **Slieve Car** h. Ireland
163 F3 **Slieve Donard** h. U.K.
163 B4 **Slieve Elva** h. Ireland
Slieve Gamph hills Ireland see **Ox Mountains**
163 C3 **Slieve League** h. Ireland
163 B5 **Slieve Mish Mountains** hills Ireland
163 B5 **Slieve Miskish Mountains** hills Ireland
163 A3 **Slievemore** h. Ireland
163 D4 **Slieve na Calliagh** h. Ireland
163 D5 **Slievenamon** h. Ireland
163 D2 **Slieve Snaght** h. Ireland
162 B3 **Sligachan** U.K.
163 C3 **Sligo** Ireland
163 C3 **Sligo Bay** Ireland
159 L4 **Slite** Sweden
171 L3 **Sliven** Bulg.
172 H2 **Sloboda** Russia
172 I2 **Slobodchikovo** Russia
171 L2 **Slobozia** Romania
186 F5 **Slocan** Canada
164 E1 **Slochteren** Neth.
172 C4 **Slonim** Belarus
164 C2 **Slootdorp** Neth.
164 D2 **Sloten** Neth.
164 D2 **Slotermeer** l. Neth.
161 G6 **Slough** U.K.
169 I6 **Slovakia** country Europe
170 F1 **Slovenia** country Europe
170 F1 **Slovenj Gradec** Slovenia
173 F5 **Slov"yans'k** Ukr.
154 C3 **S'Lung, B'Nom** mt. Vietnam
168 H3 **Słupsk** Poland
158 L2 **Slussfors** Sweden
172 C4 **Slutsk** Belarus
163 A4 **Slyne Head** Ireland
133 L4 **Slyudyanka** Russia
154 B3 **Smăch, Kaôh** i. Cambodia
203 I3 **Small Point** U.S.A.
189 H3 **Smallwood Reservoir** Canada
172 D4 **Smalyavichy** Belarus
169 M3 **Smarhon'** Belarus
180 E5 **Smartt Syndicate Dam** resr S. Africa
187 I4 **Smeaton** Canada
171 I2 **Smederevo** Serbia
171 I2 **Smederevska Palanka** Serbia
202 D4 **Smethport** U.S.A.
173 D5 **Smila** Ukr.
164 E2 **Smilde** Neth.
159 N4 **Smiltene** Latvia
139 G1 **Smirnovo** Kazakh.
186 G3 **Smith** Canada
196 C2 **Smith** U.S.A.
202 C6 **Smith** r. U.S.A.
184 C2 **Smith Bay** U.S.A.
186 D4 **Smithers** Canada
181 G5 **Smithfield** S. Africa
201 E5 **Smithfield** NC U.S.A.
194 E3 **Smithfield** UT U.S.A.
203 E5 **Smith Island** MD U.S.A.
203 F6 **Smith Island** VA U.S.A.
202 D6 **Smith Mountain Lake** U.S.A.
186 D3 **Smith River** Canada
191 I3 **Smiths Falls** Canada
185 K2 **Smith Sound** sea chan. Canada/Greenland
127 F8 **Smithton** Australia
196 C1 **Smoke Creek Desert** U.S.A.
186 F4 **Smoky** r. Canada
127 J3 **Smoky Cape** Australia
188 D3 **Smoky Falls** Canada
198 C4 **Smoky Hill** r. U.S.A.
198 D4 **Smoky Hills** U.S.A.
186 G4 **Smoky Lake** Canada
158 I3 **Smøla** i. Norway
138 B2 **Smolenka** Russia
172 E4 **Smolensk** Russia
172 E4 **Smolenskaya Oblast'** admin. div. Russia
139 K1 **Smolenskoye** Russia
171 K4 **Smolyan** Bulg.
150 C3 **Smolyaninovo** Russia
188 D4 **Smooth Rock Falls** Canada
188 C3 **Smoothrock Lake** Canada
187 H4 **Smoothstone Lake** Canada
158 N1 **Smørfjord** Norway
203 F5 **Smyrna** DE U.S.A.
201 C5 **Smyrna** GA U.S.A.
202 C4 **Smyrna** OH U.S.A.
203 I1 **Smyrna Mills** U.S.A.
158 D2 **Snæfell** mt. Iceland
160 C3 **Snaefell** h. U.K.
186 A2 **Snag (abandoned)** Canada
194 D3 **Snake** r. U.S.A.
197 E2 **Snake Range** mts U.S.A.
194 D3 **Snake River Plain** U.S.A.
Snare Lakes Canada see **Wekweètì**
125 G6 **Snares Islands** N.Z.
158 K2 **Snåsa** Norway
164 D1 **Sneek** Neth.
163 B6 **Sneem** Ireland
180 F6 **Sneeuberge** mts S. Africa
189 H3 **Snegamook Lake** Canada
161 H5 **Snettisham** U.K.
132 J3 **Snezhnogorsk** Russia
170 F2 **Snežnik** mt. Slovenia
169 J4 **Śniardwy, Jezioro** l. Poland
173 E6 **Snihurivka** Ukr.
162 B3 **Snizort, Loch** b. U.K.
194 B2 **Snohomish** U.S.A.
194 B2 **Snoqualmie Pass** U.S.A.
158 K2 **Snøtinden** mt. Norway
187 I2 **Snowbird Lake** Canada
161 C4 **Snowdon** mt. U.K.
161 D5 **Snowdonia National Park** U.K.
197 G4 **Snowflake** U.S.A.
203 F5 **Snow Hill** MD U.S.A.
201 E5 **Snow Hill** NC U.S.A.
187 I4 **Snow Lake** Canada
126 C4 **Snowtown** Australia
194 D3 **Snowville** U.S.A.
127 H6 **Snowy** r. Australia
127 H6 **Snowy Mountains** Australia
127 G9 **Snug** Australia
189 I3 **Snug Harbour** Nfld and Lab. Canada
191 G3 **Snug Harbour** Ont. Canada
154 C2 **Snuŏl** Cambodia
199 D5 **Snyder** OK U.S.A.
199 C5 **Snyder** TX U.S.A.
179 E5 **Soalala** Madag.
144 B2 **Soan** r. Pak.
152 D6 **Soan-gundo** is S. Korea
179 E5 **Soanierana-Ivongo** Madag.
213 B3 **Soatá** Col.
162 B3 **Soay** i. U.K.
152 D6 **Sobaek-sanmaek** mts S. Korea
177 F4 **Sobat** r. South Sudan
147 G7 **Sobger** r. Indon.
151 B8 **Sobo-san** mt. Japan
211 J6 **Sobradinho, Barragem de** resr Brazil
211 J4 **Sobral** Brazil
173 F7 **Sochi** Russia
123 I5 **Society Islands** Fr. Polynesia
214 C3 **Socorro** Brazil
213 B3 **Socorro** Col.
195 F5 **Socorro** U.S.A.
204 B5 **Socorro, Isla** i. Mex.
142 D7 **Socotra** i. Yemen
154 C3 **Soc Trăng** Vietnam
167 E3 **Socuéllamos** Spain
196 D4 **Soda Lake** U.S.A.
158 N2 **Sodankylä** Fin.
144 D2 **Soda Plains** China
194 E3 **Soda Springs** U.S.A.
159 L3 **Söderhamn** Sweden
159 L4 **Söderköping** Sweden
159 L4 **Södertälje** Sweden
177 E3 **Sodiri** Sudan
178 D3 **Sodo** Eth.
159 L3 **Södra Kvarken** str. Fin./Sweden
164 D3 **Soerendonk** Neth.
165 G3 **Soest** Germany
164 D2 **Soest** Neth.
127 H4 **Sofala** Australia
171 J3 **Sofia** Bulg.
Sofiya Bulg. see **Sofia**
158 O2 **Sofporog** Russia
171 L6 **Sofrana** i. Greece
151 G10 **Sōfu-gan** i. Japan
145 H3 **Sog** China
213 B3 **Sogamoso** Col.
137 G1 **Soğanlı Dağları** mts Turkey
164 F2 **Sögel** Germany
159 I4 **Søgne** Norway
159 I3 **Sognefjorden** inlet Norway
153 C4 **Sogod** Phil.
172 H2 **Sogra** Russia
148 A3 **Sogruma** China
136 C1 **Söğüt** Turkey
Sohâg Egypt see **Sūhāj**
144 D5 **Sohagpur** India
161 H5 **Soham** U.K.
125 F2 **Sohano** P.N.G.
143 C1 **Sohela** India
144 D3 **Sohna** India
152 E3 **Sŏho-ri** N. Korea
152 C6 **Sohŭksan** S. Korea
164 C4 **Soignes, Forêt de** for. Belgium
164 C4 **Soignies** Belgium
158 N3 **Soini** Fin.
166 F2 **Soissons** France
144 C4 **Sojat** India
153 B4 **Sojoton Point** Phil.
173 C5 **Sokal'** Ukr.
152 E4 **Sokcho** S. Korea
171 L6 **Söke** Turkey
173 G7 **Sokhumi** Georgia
176 C4 **Sokodé** Togo
149 □ **Soko Islands** Hong Kong China
172 G3 **Sokol** Russia
169 K4 **Sokółka** Poland
176 B3 **Sokolo** Mali
165 K4 **Sokolov** Czech Rep.
150 C3 **Sokolovka** Russia
169 K4 **Sokołow Podlaski** Poland
176 C3 **Sokoto** Nigeria
176 C3 **Sokoto** r. Nigeria
173 C5 **Sokyryany** Ukr.
144 D3 **Solan** India
128 A7 **Solander Island** N.Z.
143 A2 **Solapur** India
213 B2 **Soledad** Col.
196 B3 **Soledad** U.S.A.
213 E2 **Soledad** Venez.
207 E4 **Soledad de Doblado** Mex.
173 G6 **Solenoye** Russia
158 K2 **Solfjellsjøen** Norway
137 H2 **Solhan** Turkey
172 G3 **Soligalich** Russia
161 F5 **Solihull** U.K.
132 G4 **Solikamsk** Russia
138 C2 **Sol'-Iletsk** Russia
207 H4 **Solimón, Punta** pt Mex.
164 F3 **Solingen** Germany
180 A1 **Solitaire** Namibia
137 L1 **Şollar** Azer.
158 L3 **Sollefteå** Sweden
165 K3 **Söllichau** Germany
165 H3 **Solling** hills Germany
165 I3 **Sollstedt** Germany
165 G4 **Solms** Germany
172 F3 **Solnechnogorsk** Russia
155 B3 **Solok** Indon.
207 G5 **Sololá** Guat.
125 G2 **Solomon Islands** country Pacific Ocean
124 F2 **Solomon Sea** P.N.G./Solomon Is
139 K2 **Soloneshnoye** Russia
190 B2 **Solon Springs** U.S.A.
147 E7 **Solor, Kepulauan** is Indon.
168 C7 **Solothurn** Switz.
172 E1 **Solovetskiye Ostrova** is Russia
172 H3 **Solovetskoye** Russia
170 G3 **Šolta** i. Croatia
141 E2 **Solţānābād** Khorāsān-e Razavī Iran
141 E3 **Solţānābād** Khorāsān-e Razavī Iran
165 H2 **Soltau** Germany
172 D3 **Sol'tsy** Russia
203 E3 **Solvay** U.S.A.
159 K4 **Sölvesborg** Sweden
162 E6 **Solway Firth** est. U.K.
179 C5 **Solwezi** Zambia
151 G6 **Sōma** Japan
136 A2 **Soma** Turkey
164 B4 **Somain** France
178 E3 **Somalia** country Africa
218 H5 **Somali Basin** sea feature Indian Ocean
178 E3 **Somaliland** disp. terr. Somalia
179 C4 **Sombo** Angola
171 H2 **Sombor** Serbia
206 D3 **Sombrerete** Mex.
144 C4 **Somdari** India
159 M3 **Somero** Fin.
200 C4 **Somerset** KY U.S.A.
190 E4 **Somerset** MI U.S.A.
202 D5 **Somerset** PA U.S.A.
181 F6 **Somerset East** S. Africa
185 I2 **Somerset Island** Canada
203 I2 **Somerset Junction** U.S.A.
203 G3 **Somerset Reservoir** U.S.A.
180 C7 **Somerset West** S. Africa
203 H3 **Somersworth** U.S.A.
199 D6 **Somerville Reservoir** U.S.A.
140 B3 **Someydeh** Iran
159 K4 **Sommen** l. Sweden
165 J3 **Sömmerda** Germany
189 G3 **Sommet, Lac du** l. Canada
144 B5 **Somnath** India
190 C5 **Somonauk** U.S.A.
139 G5 **Somoniyon** Tajik.
206 H5 **Somotillo** Nicaragua
206 H5 **Somoto** Nicaragua
215 C4 **Somuncurá, Mesa Volcánica de** plat. Arg.
145 F4 **Son** r. India
206 I7 **Soná** Panama
139 G2 **Sonaly** Karagandinskaya Oblast' Kazakh.
139 G2 **Sonaly** Karagandinskaya Oblast' Kazakh.
145 F5 **Sonamukhi** India
145 G5 **Sonamura** India
144 D4 **Sonar** r. India
145 H4 **Sonari** India
152 F2 **Sŏnbong** N. Korea
152 C4 **Sŏnch'ŏn** N. Korea
172 E2 **Sondaly** Russia
159 J5 **Sønderborg** Denmark
165 I3 **Sondershausen** Germany
170 C1 **Sondrio** Italy
143 B2 **Sonepet** India
144 B5 **Songadh** India
148 E4 **Songbu** China
154 D2 **Sông Câu** Vietnam
179 D5 **Songea** Tanz.
152 D3 **Sŏnggan** N. Korea
152 D2 **Songhua Hu** resr China
152 C1 **Songhuajiang** China
150 B1 **Songhua Jiang** r. Heilongjiang/Jilin China
152 C1 **Songhua Jiang** r. Jilin China
152 E2 **Songjiang** Jilin China
148 F4 **Songjiang** Shanghai China
152 D2 **Songjianghe** China
149 C4 **Songkan** China
154 B4 **Songkhla** Thai.
139 H4 **Songköl** l. Kyrg.
148 F1 **Song Ling** mts China
152 C4 **Songnim** N. Korea
178 B4 **Songo** Angola
179 D5 **Songo** Moz.
148 B3 **Songpan** China
145 G4 **Songsak** India
148 D3 **Song Shan** mt. China
152 D3 **Songshu** China
149 C4 **Songtao** China
149 F5 **Songxi** China
148 D3 **Songxian** China
152 C1 **Songyuan** China
149 D4 **Songzi** China
154 D2 **Sơn Ha** Vietnam
154 D3 **Sơn Hai** Vietnam
144 D3 **Sonipat** India
158 N3 **Sonkajärvi** Fin.
149 B6 **Sơn La** Vietnam
141 G5 **Sonmiani** Pak.
141 G5 **Sonmiani Bay** Pak.
165 J4 **Sonneberg** Germany
214 D2 **Sono** r. Minas Gerais Brazil
211 I6 **Sono** r. Tocantins Brazil
197 F6 **Sonoita** Mex.
197 F6 **Sonoita** watercourse Mex.
197 G6 **Sonoita** U.S.A.
206 B1 **Sonora** r. Mex.
206 B2 **Sonora** state Mex.
196 B3 **Sonora** CA U.S.A.
199 C6 **Sonora** TX U.S.A.
140 B3 **Sonqor** Iran
143 G3 **Sonsogad** mt. India
213 B3 **Sonsón** Col.
207 G5 **Sonsonate** El Salvador
149 B6 **Sơn Tây** Vietnam
181 H5 **Sonwabile** S. Africa
215 F1 **Sopas** r. Uruguay
177 E4 **Sopo** watercourse South Sudan
171 K3 **Sopot** Bulg.
169 I3 **Sopot** Poland
168 H7 **Sopron** Hungary
139 H4 **Sopu-Korgon** Kyrg.
170 E4 **Sora** Italy
143 D2 **Sorada** India
159 L3 **Söråker** Sweden
188 F4 **Sorel** Canada
127 G9 **Sorell** Australia
127 G9 **Sorell Lake** Australia
136 E2 **Sorgun** Turkey
167 E2 **Soria** Spain
132 C2 **Sørkappøya** i. Svalbard
140 D3 **Sorkh, Daqq-e** salt flat Iran
Sorkh, Kavīr-e Daqq-e salt flat Iran see **Sorkh, Daqq-e**
140 D3 **Sorkh, Kūh-e** mts Iran
140 D3 **Sorkheh** Iran
158 K2 **Sørli** Norway
159 J5 **Sorø** Denmark
145 F5 **Soro** India
173 D5 **Soroca** Moldova
214 C3 **Sorocaba** Brazil
138 C1 **Sorochinsk** Russia
139 K1 **Sorokino** Russia
147 G6 **Sorol** atoll Micronesia
147 F7 **Sorong** Indon.
178 D3 **Soroti** Uganda
158 M1 **Sørøya** i. Norway
167 B3 **Sorraia** r. Port.
158 L1 **Sørreisa** Norway
126 F7 **Sorrento** Australia
170 F4 **Sorrento** Italy
179 B6 **Sorris Sorris** Namibia
158 L2 **Sorsele** Sweden
153 C3 **Sorsogon** Phil.
172 D2 **Sortavala** Russia
158 K1 **Sortland** Norway
172 I2 **Sortopolovskaya** Russia
172 I3 **Sorvizhi** Russia
181 H2 **Soshanguve** S. Africa
173 F4 **Sosna** r. Russia
215 C2 **Sosneado** mt. Arg.
172 J2 **Sosnogorsk** Russia
139 I2 **Sosnovka** Kazakh.
172 H2 **Sosnovka** Arkhangel'skaya Oblast' Russia
132 F3 **Sosnovka** Murmanskaya Oblast' Russia
172 G4 **Sosnovka** Tambovskaya Oblast' Russia
158 P2 **Sosnovyy** Russia
159 O4 **Sosnovyy Bor** Russia
169 I5 **Sosnowiec** Poland
173 F6 **Sosyka** r. Russia
213 A4 **Sotara, Volcán** vol. Col.
158 O2 **Sotkamo** Fin.
215 D1 **Soto** Arg.
207 E3 **Soto la Marina** Mex.
207 G3 **Sotuta** Mex.
178 B3 **Souanké** Congo
176 B4 **Soubré** Côte d'Ivoire
203 F4 **Souderton** U.S.A.
171 L4 **Soufli** Greece
166 E4 **Souillac** France
164 D5 **Souilly** France
176 C1 **Souk Ahras** Alg.
Sŏul S. Korea see **Seoul**
166 D5 **Soulom** France
Soûr Lebanon see **Tyre**
167 H4 **Sour el Ghozlane** Alg.
187 I5 **Souris** Man. Canada
189 H4 **Souris** P.E.I. Canada
187 I5 **Souris** r. Canada/U.S.A.
211 K5 **Sousa** Brazil
176 D1 **Sousse** Tunisia
166 D5 **Soustons** France
180 E4 **South Africa** country Africa
208 **South America**
191 G3 **Southampton** Canada
161 F7 **Southampton** U.K.
203 G4 **Southampton** U.S.A.
187 L2 **Southampton Island** Canada
202 E6 **South Anna** r. U.S.A.
161 F4 **South Anston** U.K.
189 H2 **South Aulatsivik Island** Canada
124 D5 **South Australia** state Australia
218 L7 **South Australian Basin** sea feature Indian Ocean
199 F5 **Southaven** U.S.A.
195 F5 **South Baldy** mt. U.S.A.
160 F3 **South Bank** U.K.
202 B4 **South Bass Island** U.S.A.
191 F3 **South Baymouth** Canada
190 D5 **South Bend** IN U.S.A.
194 B2 **South Bend** WA U.S.A.
201 E7 **South Bight** sea chan. Bahamas
202 D6 **South Boston** U.S.A.
128 D5 **Southbridge** N.Z.
203 G3 **Southbridge** U.S.A.
South Cape pt U.S.A. see **Ka Lae**
201 D5 **South Carolina** state U.S.A.
203 I2 **South China** U.S.A.
155 C1 **South China Sea** Pacific Ocean
198 C2 **South Dakota** state U.S.A.
203 G3 **South Deerfield** U.S.A.
161 G7 **South Downs** hills U.K.
161 G7 **South Downs National Park** nat. park U.K.

South East

181 F2 South East admin. dist. Botswana
127 G9 South East Cape Australia
127 H6 South East Forests National Park Australia
218 J7 Southeast Indian Ridge sea feature Indian Ocean
217 L10 Southeast Pacific Basin sea feature S. Pacific Ocean
187 I3 Southend Canada
162 C5 Southend U.K.
161 H6 Southend-on-Sea U.K.
190 A5 South English U.S.A.
180 E2 Southern admin. dist. Botswana
128 C5 Southern Alps mts N.Z.
124 B5 Southern Cross Australia
187 J3 Southern Indian Lake Canada
177 E4 Southern National Park South Sudan
216 E10 Southern Ocean
201 E5 Southern Pines U.S.A.
209 G7 Southern Thule S. Sandwich Is
162 D5 Southern Uplands hills U.K.
162 F4 South Esk r. U.K.
190 B6 South Fabius r. U.S.A.
216 G7 South Fiji Basin sea feature S. Pacific Ocean
195 F4 South Fork U.S.A.
190 E3 South Fox Island U.S.A.
129 C5 South Geomagnetic Pole Antarctica
212 □ South Georgia i. S. Atlantic Ocean
129 C1 South Georgia and the South Sandwich Islands terr. S. Atlantic Ocean
162 A3 South Harris pen. U.K.
145 G5 South Hatia Island Bangl.
190 D4 South Haven U.S.A.
187 J2 South Henik Lake Canada
203 G2 South Hero U.S.A.
202 D6 South Hill U.S.A.
216 E3 South Honshu Ridge sea feature N. Pacific Ocean
187 J3 South Indian Lake Canada
203 G4 Southington U.S.A.
128 C6 South Island N.Z.
178 D3 South Island National Park Kenya
153 A4 South Islet reef Phil.
143 D1 South Koel r. India
152 D5 South Korea country Asia
196 B2 South Lake Tahoe U.S.A.
179 D5 South Luangwa National Park Zambia
129 C6 South Magnetic Pole Antarctica
190 D3 South Manitou Island U.S.A.
201 D7 South Miami U.S.A.
161 H6 Southminster U.K.
187 I4 South Moose Lake Canada
202 E5 South Mountains hills U.S.A.
184 F3 South Nahanni r. Canada
162 □ South Nesting Bay U.K.
219 G10 South Orkney Islands S. Atlantic Ocean
173 G7 South Ossetia disp. terr. Georgia
125 H5 South Pacific Ocean
203 H2 South Paris U.S.A.
194 G3 South Platte r. U.S.A.
129 C4 South Pole Antarctica
191 G1 South Porcupine Canada
127 J1 Southport Australia
160 D4 Southport U.K.
203 H3 South Portland U.S.A.
191 H3 South River Canada
162 F2 South Ronaldsay i. U.K.
203 G3 South Royalton U.S.A.
181 I5 South Sand Bluff pt S. Africa
219 H9 South Sandwich Islands S. Atlantic Ocean
219 H9 South Sandwich Trench sea feature S. Atlantic Ocean
187 H4 South Saskatchewan r. Canada
187 J3 South Seal r. Canada
129 B2 South Shetland Islands is Antarctica
219 E10 South Shetland Trough sea feature S. Atlantic Ocean
160 F2 South Shields U.K.
190 A5 South Skunk r. U.S.A.
216 F6 South Solomon Trench sea feature Pacific Ocean
177 E4 South Sudan country Africa
128 E3 South Taranaki Bight b. N.Z.
218 N8 South Tasman Rise sea feature Southern Ocean
197 G2 South Tent mt. U.S.A.
145 E4 South Tons r. India
188 E3 South Twin Island Canada
160 E3 South Tyne r. U.K.
162 A3 South Uist i. U.K.
127 G9 South West Cape Australia
128 A7 South West Cape N.Z.
218 G7 Southwest Indian Ridge sea feature Indian Ocean
189 G4 Southwest Miramichi r. Canada
127 G9 South West National Park Australia
217 I8 Southwest Pacific Basin sea feature S. Pacific Ocean
South-West Peru Ridge sea feature S. Pacific Ocean see Nazca Ridge
127 J3 South West Rocks Australia
190 E5 South Whitley U.S.A.
203 H3 South Windham U.S.A.
161 I5 Southwold U.K.
181 H1 Soutpansberg mts S. Africa
170 G5 Soverato Italy
172 B4 Sovetsk Kaliningradskaya Oblast' Russia
172 I3 Sovetsk Kirovskaya Oblast' Russia
146 G2 Sovetskaya Gavan' Russia
132 H3 Sovetskiy Khanty-Mansiyskiy Avtonomnyy Okrug-Yugra Russia
172 D2 Sovetskiy Leningradskaya Oblast' Russia
172 I3 Sovetskiy Respublika Mariy El Russia
181 G3 Soweto S. Africa
137 L3 Şowma'eh Sarā Iran
139 G5 So'x Tajik.
207 F4 Soyaló Mex.
150 G2 Sōya-misaki c. Japan
152 D4 Soyang-ho l. S. Korea
139 G3 Sozak Kazakh.
169 O4 Sozh r. Belarus
171 L3 Sozopol Bulg.
164 D4 Spa Belgium
167 D2 Spain country Europe
161 G5 Spalding U.K.
161 D6 Span Head h. U.K.
191 F2 Spanish Canada
191 G2 Spanish r. Canada
197 G1 Spanish Fork U.S.A.
205 I5 Spanish Town Jamaica
196 C2 Sparks U.S.A.
Sparta Greece see Sparti
202 C6 Sparta NC U.S.A.
190 B4 Sparta WI U.S.A.
201 D5 Spartanburg U.S.A.
171 J6 Sparti Greece
170 G6 Spartivento, Capo c. Italy
186 G5 Sparwood Canada
172 E4 Spas-Demensk Russia
172 E2 Spasskaya Guba Russia
146 F2 Spassk-Dal'niy Russia
171 J7 Spatha, Akrotirio pt Greece
186 D3 Spatsizi Plateau Wilderness Provincial Park Canada
198 C2 Spearfish U.S.A.
199 C4 Spearman U.S.A.
203 F3 Speculator U.S.A.
198 E3 Spencer IA U.S.A.
194 D2 Spencer ID U.S.A.
202 C5 Spencer WV U.S.A.
126 B5 Spencer, Cape Australia
186 B3 Spencer, Cape U.S.A.
126 B5 Spencer Gulf est. Australia
186 E4 Spences Bridge Canada
160 F3 Spennymoor U.K.
179 B6 Sperrgebiet National Park Namibia
180 A3 Sperrgebiet National Park nat. park Namibia
163 D3 Sperrin Mountains hills U.K.
202 D5 Sperryville U.S.A.
165 H5 Spessart reg. Germany
171 J6 Spetses i. Greece
162 E3 Spey r. U.K.
165 G5 Speyer Germany
141 G4 Spezand Pak.
165 F1 Spiekeroog i. Germany
168 C7 Spiez Switz.
164 E1 Spijk Neth.
164 C3 Spijkenisse Neth.
170 E1 Spilimbergo Italy
161 H4 Spilsby U.K.
141 G4 Spīn Böldak Afgh.
144 B3 Spintangi Pak.
186 F3 Spirit River Canada
190 C3 Spirit River Flowage resr U.S.A.
187 H4 Spiritwood Canada
141 G3 Spirsang Pass Afgh.
169 J6 Spišská Nová Ves Slovakia
137 J1 Spitak Armenia
144 D3 Spiti r. India
132 C2 Spitsbergen i. Svalbard
168 F7 Spittal an der Drau Austria
170 G3 Split Croatia
187 J3 Split Lake Canada
187 J3 Split Lake l. Canada
194 C2 Spokane U.S.A.
170 E3 Spoleto Italy
154 C2 Spóng Cambodia
190 B3 Spooner U.S.A.
165 J1 Spornitz Germany
194 F2 Spotted Horse U.S.A.
191 F2 Spragge Canada
186 E4 Spranger, Mount Canada
147 D6 Spratly Islands S. China Sea
194 C2 Spray U.S.A.
168 G5 Spree r. Germany
164 D4 Sprimont Belgium
191 F3 Spring Bay Canada
180 B4 Springbok S. Africa
189 I4 Springdale Canada
199 E4 Springdale U.S.A.
165 H2 Springe Germany
195 F4 Springer U.S.A.
197 H4 Springerville U.S.A.
199 C4 Springfield CO U.S.A.
190 C6 Springfield IL U.S.A.
203 G3 Springfield MA U.S.A.
203 I2 Springfield ME U.S.A.
198 E2 Springfield MN U.S.A.
199 E4 Springfield MO U.S.A.
202 B5 Springfield OH U.S.A.
199 C4 Springfield OR U.S.A.
203 G3 Springfield VT U.S.A.
202 D5 Springfield WV U.S.A.
190 C6 Springfield, Lake U.S.A.
181 F5 Springfontein S. Africa
190 B4 Spring Green U.S.A.
190 B4 Spring Grove U.S.A.
189 H4 Springhill Canada
201 D6 Spring Hill U.S.A.
190 D4 Spring Lake U.S.A.
197 E3 Spring Mountains U.S.A.
128 D5 Springs Junction N.Z.
190 A4 Spring Valley U.S.A.
202 D3 Springville NY U.S.A.
197 G1 Springville UT U.S.A.
161 I5 Sprowston U.K.
186 G4 Spruce Grove Canada
202 D5 Spruce Knob-Seneca Rocks National Recreation Area park U.S.A.
194 D3 Spruce Mountain U.S.A.
160 H4 Spurn Head U.K.
186 E5 Spuzzum Canada
186 E5 Squamish Canada
203 H3 Squam Lake U.S.A.
203 I1 Square Lake U.S.A.
170 G5 Squillace, Golfo di g. Italy
Srbija country Europe see Serbia
154 B3 Srê Âmběl Cambodia
171 H2 Srebrenica Bos. & Herz.
171 L3 Sredets Bulg.
133 Q4 Sredinnyy Khrebet mts Russia
171 J3 Sredna Gora mts Bulg.
133 Q3 Srednekolymsk Russia
Sredne-Russkaya Vozvyshennost' hills Russia see Central Russian Upland
Sredne-Sibirskoye Ploskogor'ye plat. Russia see Central Siberian Plateau
158 O2 Sredneye Kuyto, Ozero l. Russia
154 C2 Srêpôk, Tônlé r. Cambodia
146 D1 Sretensk Russia
155 D2 Sri Aman Sarawak Malaysia
143 C3 Sriharikota Island India
143 B5 Sri Jayewardenepura Kotte Sri Lanka
143 D2 Srikakulam India
143 B3 Sri Kalahasti India
144 D3 Srikanta mt. India
218 C5 Sri Lanka country Asia
144 C2 Srinagar Jammu and Kashmir India
144 D3 Srinagar Uttarakhand India
Sri Pada mt. Sri Lanka see Adam's Peak
143 B4 Srirangam India
154 B1 Sri Thep tourist site Thai.
143 B4 Srivaikuntam India
143 A2 Srivardhan India
143 B4 Srivilliputtur India
139 K1 Srostki Russia
143 C2 Srungavarapukota India
165 H1 Stade Germany
164 B4 Staden Belgium
164 E2 Stadskanaal Neth.
165 H4 Stadtallendorf Germany
165 H2 Stadthagen Germany
165 J4 Stadtilm Germany
164 E3 Stadtlohn Germany
165 H3 Stadtoldendorf Germany
165 J4 Stadtroda Germany
162 B4 Staffa i. U.K.
165 J4 Staffelberg h. Germany
161 E5 Stafford U.K.
202 E5 Stafford U.S.A.
159 N4 Staicele Latvia
161 G6 Staines-upon-Thames U.K.
173 F5 Stakhanov Ukr.
161 E7 Stalbridge U.K.
161 I5 Stalham U.K.
Stalingrad Russia see Volgograd
169 K5 Stalowa Wola Poland
171 K3 Stamboliyski Bulg.
161 G5 Stamford U.K.
203 G4 Stamford CT U.S.A.
203 F3 Stamford NY U.S.A.
179 B6 Stampriet Namibia
158 K1 Stamsund Norway
198 E3 Stanberry U.S.A.
164 C3 Standdaarbuiten Neth.
181 H3 Standerton S. Africa
191 F4 Standish U.S.A.
200 C4 Stanford U.S.A.
Stanger S. Africa see KwaDukuza
201 E7 Staniard Creek Bahamas
165 L5 Staňkov Czech Rep.
127 F8 Stanley Australia
203 J1 Stanley Canada
149 □ Stanley Hong Kong China
212 E8 Stanley Falkland Is
160 F3 Stanley U.K.
194 D2 Stanley ID U.S.A.
198 C1 Stanley ND U.S.A.
190 B3 Stanley WI U.S.A.
127 F8 Stanley, Mount h. Australia
143 B4 Stanley Reservoir India
160 F2 Stannington U.K.
146 D1 Stanovoye Nagor'ye mts Russia
146 E1 Stanovoy Khrebet mts Russia
127 I2 Stanthorpe Australia
161 H5 Stanton U.K.
202 B6 Stanton KY U.S.A.
190 E4 Stanton MI U.S.A.
198 C3 Stapleton U.S.A.
169 J5 Starachowice Poland
Stara Planina mts Bulg./Serbia see Balkan Mountains
172 H4 Staraya Kulatka Russia
173 H5 Staraya Poltavka Russia
172 D3 Staraya Russa Russia
169 O2 Staraya Toropa Russia
172 I4 Staraya Tumba Russia
171 K3 Stara Zagora Bulg.
123 I4 Starbuck Island Kiribati
168 G4 Stargard Szczeciński Poland
172 E3 Staritsa Russia
201 D6 Starke U.S.A.
199 F5 Starkville U.S.A.
168 E7 Starnberger See l. Germany
139 J2 Staroaleyskoye Russia
173 F5 Starobil's'k Ukr.
169 P4 Starodub Russia
169 I4 Starogard Gdański Poland
173 C5 Starokostyantyniv Ukr.
173 F6 Starominskaya Russia
173 F6 Staroshcherbinovskaya Russia
138 D1 Starosubkhangulovo Russia
196 C1 Star Peak U.S.A.
161 D7 Start Point U.K.
169 N4 Staryya Darohi Belarus
138 D2 Staryy Karabutak Kazakh.
133 L2 Staryy Kayak Russia
173 F5 Staryy Oskol Russia
165 J3 Staßfurt Germany
202 E4 State College U.S.A.
201 D5 Statesboro U.S.A.
201 D5 Statesville U.S.A.
220 W1 Station Nord Greenland
165 L3 Stauchitz Germany
165 G4 Staufenberg Germany
202 D5 Staunton U.S.A.
159 I4 Stavanger Norway
161 F4 Staveley U.K.
165 K1 Stavenhagen Germany
173 G6 Stavropol' Russia
138 F1 Stavropolka Kazakh.
173 G6 Stavropol'skaya Vozvyshennost' hills Russia
173 G6 Stavropol'skiy Kray admin. div. Russia
126 E6 Stawell Australia
181 H4 Steadville S. Africa
196 C2 Steamboat U.S.A.
194 F3 Steamboat Springs U.S.A.
202 E4 Steelton U.S.A.
164 E2 Steenderen Neth.
181 I2 Steenkampsberge mts S. Africa
186 F3 Steen River Canada
194 C3 Steens Mountain U.S.A.
Steenstrup Gletscher glacier Greenland see Sermersuaq
164 A4 Steenvoorde France
164 E2 Steenwijk Neth.
184 H2 Stefansson Island Canada
165 I5 Steigerwald mts Germany
165 J5 Stein Germany
165 J4 Steinach Germany
187 J5 Steinbach Canada
165 G2 Steinfeld (Oldenburg) Germany
164 F2 Steinfurt Germany
179 B6 Steinhausen Namibia
165 H3 Steinheim Germany
165 H2 Steinhuder Meer l. Germany
158 J2 Steinkjer Norway
180 B4 Steinkopf S. Africa
197 H5 Steins (abandoned) U.S.A.
158 J2 Steinsdalen Norway
180 F3 Stella S. Africa
201 F7 Stella Maris Bahamas
180 C6 Stellenbosch S. Africa
170 C3 Stello, Monte mt. Corsica France
164 D5 Stenay France
165 J2 Stendal Germany
149 □ Stenhouse, Mount h. Hong Kong China
162 E4 Stenhousemuir U.K.
159 J4 Stenungsund Sweden
Stepanakert Azer. see Xankändi
173 H7 Step'anavan Armenia
187 J5 Stephen U.S.A.
126 D4 Stephens watercourse Australia
128 D4 Stephens, Cape N.Z.
126 D3 Stephens Creek Australia
190 D3 Stephenson U.S.A.
186 C3 Stephens Passage U.S.A.
189 I4 Stephenville Canada
199 D5 Stephenville U.S.A.
139 G1 Stepnogorsk Kazakh.
139 H4 Stepnoy Kyrg.
138 E1 Stepnoye Chelyabinskaya Oblast' Russia
173 H5 Stepnoye Saratovskaya Oblast' Russia
139 G1 Stepnyak Kazakh.
181 H4 Sterkfontein Dam resr S. Africa
181 G5 Sterkstroom S. Africa
138 C1 Sterlibashevo Russia
180 D5 Sterling S. Africa
194 G3 Sterling CO U.S.A.
190 C5 Sterling IL U.S.A.
198 C2 Sterling ND U.S.A.
197 G2 Sterling UT U.S.A.
199 C6 Sterling City U.S.A.
191 F4 Sterling Heights U.S.A.
138 C1 Sterlitamak Russia
165 J1 Sternberg Germany
186 G4 Stettler Canada
190 D2 Steuben U.S.A.
202 C4 Steubenville U.S.A.
161 G6 Stevenage U.K.
187 J4 Stevenson Lake Canada
190 C3 Stevens Point U.S.A.
184 D3 Stevens Village U.S.A.
186 D3 Stewart Canada
186 B2 Stewart r. Canada
186 B2 Stewart Crossing Canada
128 A7 Stewart Island N.Z.
125 G2 Stewart Islands Solomon Is
185 J3 Stewart Lake Canada
162 D5 Stewarton U.K.
190 A4 Stewartville U.S.A.
181 F5 Steynsburg S. Africa
168 G6 Steyr Austria
180 F6 Steytlerville S. Africa
164 D1 Stiens Neth.
186 C3 Stikine r. Canada/U.S.A.
186 C3 Stikine Plateau Canada
180 D7 Stilbaai S. Africa
190 A3 Stillwater MN U.S.A.
196 C2 Stillwater NV U.S.A.
199 D4 Stillwater OK U.S.A.
195 C4 Stillwater Range mts U.S.A.
161 G5 Stilton U.K.
171 J4 Štip Macedonia
126 C5 Stirling Australia
162 E4 Stirling U.K.
196 B2 Stirling City U.S.A.
126 B4 Stirling North Australia
158 J3 Stjørdalshalsen Norway
168 H6 Stockerau Austria
165 J4 Stockheim Germany
159 L4 Stockholm Sweden
203 I1 Stockholm U.S.A.
161 E4 Stockport U.K.
219 G6 Stocks Seamount sea feature S. Atlantic Ocean
196 B3 Stockton CA U.S.A.
198 D4 Stockton KS U.S.A.
197 F1 Stockton UT U.S.A.
190 B2 Stockton Island U.S.A.
199 E4 Stockton Lake U.S.A.
160 F3 Stockton-on-Tees U.K.
203 I2 Stockton Springs U.S.A.
159 L3 Stöde Sweden
154 C2 Stœng Trêng Cambodia
162 C2 Stoer, Point of U.K.
161 E4 Stoke-on-Trent U.K.
160 F3 Stokesley U.K.
127 E8 Stokes Point Australia
158 B3 Stokkseyri Iceland
158 K2 Stokkvågen Norway
158 K1 Stokmarknes Norway
171 G3 Stolac Bos. & Herz.
164 E4 Stolberg (Rheinland) Germany
139 K2 Stolboukha (abandoned) Kazakh.
173 C5 Stolin Belarus
165 K4 Stollberg Germany
165 H2 Stolzenau Germany
161 E5 Stone U.K.
191 I2 Stonecliffe Canada
203 F5 Stone Harbor U.S.A.
162 F4 Stonehaven U.K.
161 F6 Stonehenge tourist site U.K.
186 E3 Stone Mountain Provincial Park Canada
197 H3 Stoner U.S.A.
203 F4 Stone Ridge U.S.A.
187 J4 Stonewall Canada
202 C5 Stonewall Jackson Lake U.S.A.
191 F4 Stoney Point Canada
203 I2 Stonington U.S.A.
196 A2 Stonyford U.S.A.
203 E3 Stony Point U.S.A.
187 H3 Stony Rapids Canada
158 L2 Stora Lulevatten l. Sweden
158 L2 Stora Sjöfallets nationalpark nat. park Sweden
158 L2 Storavan l. Sweden
Store Bælt sea chan. Denmark see Great Belt
158 J3 Støren Norway
158 K2 Storforshei Norway
158 K2 Storjord Norway
184 H2 Storkerson Peninsula Canada
127 G9 Storm Bay Australia
181 G5 Stormberg S. Africa
181 G5 Stormberge mts S. Africa
198 E3 Storm Lake U.S.A.
162 B2 Stornoway U.K.
172 J2 Storozhevsk Russia
173 C5 Storozhynets' Ukr.
203 G4 Storrs U.S.A.
158 L2 Storseleby Sweden
158 K3 Storsjön l. Sweden
159 J3 Storskrymten mt. Norway
158 M1 Storslett Norway
164 D1 Stortemelk sea chan. Neth.
158 L2 Storuman Sweden
158 L2 Storuman l. Sweden
159 L3 Storvik Sweden
159 J4 Storvorde Denmark
159 L4 Storvreta Sweden
161 G5 Stotfold U.K.
190 C4 Stoughton U.S.A.
161 E7 Stour r. England U.K.
161 F5 Stour r. England U.K.
161 H6 Stour r. England U.K.
161 I6 Stour r. England U.K.
161 E5 Stourbridge U.K.
161 E5 Stourport-on-Severn U.K.
187 K4 Stout Lake Canada
172 C4 Stowbtsy Belarus
203 F4 Stowe U.S.A.
161 H5 Stowmarket U.K.
163 D3 Strabane U.K.
163 D4 Stradbally Ireland
161 I5 Stradbroke U.K.
170 C2 Stradella Italy
127 F9 Strahan Australia
197 G3 Straight Cliffs ridge U.S.A.
168 F6 Strakonice Czech Rep.
168 F3 Stralsund Germany
180 C7 Strand S. Africa
158 I3 Stranda Norway
201 E7 Strangers Cay i. Bahamas
163 F3 Strangford U.K.
163 F3 Strangford Lough inlet U.K.
162 C6 Stranraer U.K.
166 H2 Strasbourg France
202 D5 Strasburg U.S.A.
127 G6 Stratford Australia
191 G4 Stratford Canada
128 E3 Stratford N.Z.
199 C4 Stratford TX U.S.A.
190 B3 Stratford WI U.S.A.
161 F5 Stratford-upon-Avon U.K.
126 C5 Strathalbyn Australia
162 D5 Strathaven U.K.
162 G3 Strathbeg, Loch of l. U.K.
162 D3 Strathcarron val. U.K.
186 D5 Strathcona Provincial Park Canada
162 D3 Strathconon val. U.K.
162 D3 Strath Dearn val. U.K.
162 D2 Strath Fleet val. U.K.
186 G4 Strathmore Canada
186 E4 Strathnaver Canada
162 D2 Strathnaver val. U.K.
162 E2 Strath of Kildonan val. U.K.
191 G4 Strathroy Canada
162 E3 Strathspey val. U.K.
162 E2 Strathy U.K.
162 D2 Strathy Point U.K.
161 C7 Stratton U.K.
203 H2 Stratton U.S.A.
165 K6 Straubing Germany
158 B1 Straumnes pt Iceland
190 B4 Strawberry Point U.S.A.
197 G1 Strawberry Reservoir U.S.A.
124 D5 Streaky Bay Australia
124 D5 Streaky Bay b. Australia
190 C5 Streator U.S.A.
161 E6 Street U.K.
171 J2 Strehaia Romania
165 L3 Strehla Germany
133 Q3 Strelka Russia
159 N4 Strenči Latvia
165 K5 Stříbro Czech Rep.
162 F3 Strichen U.K.
215 D4 Stroeder Arg.
163 C4 Strokestown Ireland
162 E2 Stroma, Island of U.K.
170 F5 Stromboli, Isola i. Isole Lipari Italy
162 E2 Stromness U.K.
198 D3 Stromsburg U.S.A.
159 J4 Strömstad Sweden
158 K3 Strömsund Sweden
202 C4 Strongsville U.S.A.
162 F1 Stronsay i. U.K.
127 I4 Stroud Australia
161 E6 Stroud U.K.
127 I4 Stroud Road Australia
203 F4 Stroudsburg U.S.A.
159 J4 Struer Denmark
171 I4 Struga Macedonia
172 D3 Strugi-Krasnyye Russia
180 D7 Struis Bay S. Africa
165 I5 Strullendorf Germany
171 J4 Struma r. Bulg.
161 B5 Strumble Head U.K.
171 J4 Strumica Macedonia
171 K3 Stryama r. Bulg.
180 E4 Strydenburg S. Africa
171 J4 Strymonas r. Greece
159 I3 Stryn Norway
173 B5 Stryy Ukr.
126 D2 Strzelecki Creek watercourse Australia
126 D2 Strzelecki Desert des. Australia
127 H8 Strzelecki Peak h. Australia
201 D7 Stuart FL U.S.A.
202 C6 Stuart VA U.S.A.
186 E4 Stuart Lake Canada
202 D5 Stuarts Draft U.S.A.
127 H4 Stuart Town Australia
128 C6 Studholme Junction N.Z.
158 L3 Studsviken Sweden
199 C6 Study Butte U.S.A.
187 K4 Stull Lake Canada
172 F4 Stupino Russia
129 B6 Sturge Island i. Antarctica
190 D2 Sturgeon r. U.S.A.
187 J4 Sturgeon Bay b. Canada
190 D3 Sturgeon Bay U.S.A.
190 E3 Sturgeon Bay b. U.S.A.
190 D3 Sturgeon Bay Canal lake channel U.S.A.
191 H2 Sturgeon Falls Canada
188 B3 Sturgeon Lake Canada
200 C4 Sturgis KY U.S.A.
190 E5 Sturgis MI U.S.A.
198 C2 Sturgis SD U.S.A.
126 D2 Sturt, Mount h. Australia
126 B5 Sturt Bay Australia
124 C3 Sturt Creek watercourse Australia
126 D2 Sturt National Park Australia
126 D2 Sturt Stony Desert Australia
181 G6 Stutterheim S. Africa
168 D6 Stuttgart Germany
199 F5 Stuttgart U.S.A.
158 B2 Stykkishólmur Iceland
169 L5 Styr r. Ukr.
214 D2 Suaçuí Grande r. Brazil
177 F3 Suakin Sudan
149 F5 Su'ao Taiwan
206 B1 Suaqui Grande Mex.
213 B3 Suárez r. Col.
169 L3 Subačius Lith.
145 H4 Subansiri r. India
143 C1 Subarnapur India
145 F5 Subarnarekha r. India
137 G6 Şubayḩah Saudi Arabia
155 C2 Subi Besar i. Indon.
148 A1 Sub Nur l. China
171 H1 Subotica Serbia
169 M7 Suceava Romania
150 C3 Suchan r. Russia
163 C4 Suck r. Ireland
165 J1 Suckow Germany
210 E7 Sucre Bol.
213 B2 Sucre Col.
213 C3 Sucuaro Col.
214 B2 Sucuriú r. Brazil
125 G4 Sud, Grand Récif du reef New Caledonia
173 E6 Sudak Crimea
177 E3 Sudan country Africa
172 G3 Suday Russia
137 J6 Sudayr, Sha'īb watercourse Iraq
191 G2 Sudbury Canada
161 H5 Sudbury U.K.
177 E4 Sudd swamp South Sudan
165 J1 Sude r. Germany
168 H5 Sudety mts Czech Rep./Poland
203 F5 Sudlersville U.S.A.
172 G4 Sudogda Russia
136 D7 Sudr Egypt
158 □ Suðuroy i. Faroe Is
177 E4 Sue watercourse South Sudan
167 F3 Sueca Spain
177 F2 Suez Egypt
202 E6 Suffolk U.S.A.
140 B2 Sūfiān Iran
190 C4 Sugar r. U.S.A.
203 H2 Sugarloaf Mountain U.S.A.
127 J4 Sugarloaf Point Australia
153 C4 Sugbuhan Point Phil.
139 I5 Sugun China
155 E1 Sugut r. Sabah Malaysia
153 A5 Sugut, Tanjung pt Sabah Malaysia
148 B2 Suhait China
177 F2 Sūhāj Egypt
142 E5 Şuḩār Oman
146 C1 Sühbaatar Mongolia
165 I4 Suhl Germany
165 I2 Suhlendorf Germany
136 C2 Şuhut Turkey
144 B3 Sui Pak.
150 B1 Suibin China
149 F4 Suichang China
149 E5 Suichuan China
148 D2 Suide China
152 F1 Suifenhe China
144 B4 Suigam India
146 E2 Suihua China
149 B4 Suijiang China
149 D5 Suining Hunan China
148 E3 Suining Jiangsu China
149 B4 Suining Sichuan China
148 E3 Suiping China
164 C5 Suippes France
163 D5 Suir r. Ireland
148 E3 Suixi China
148 E3 Suixian China
149 C5 Suiyang Guizhou China
148 E3 Suiyang Henan China
148 F1 Suizhong China
148 D4 Suizhou China
148 C1 Suj China
144 C4 Sujangarh India
144 B4 Sujawal Pak.
155 C4 Sukabumi Indon.
155 C3 Sukadana Indon.
151 G6 Sukagawa Japan
153 A5 Sukau Sabah Malaysia
152 C4 Sukchŏn N. Korea
150 C1 Sukhanovka Russia
172 E4 Sukhinichi Russia
172 H2 Sukhona r. Russia
154 A1 Sukhothai Thai.
172 E2 Sukkozero Russia
144 B4 Sukkur Pak.
143 C2 Sukma India
144 C4 Sukri r. India
172 F3 Sukromny Russia
151 C8 Sukumo Japan
159 I3 Sula i. Norway
147 E7 Sula, Kepulauan is Indon.
144 B3 Sulaiman Range mts Pak.
173 H7 Sulak r. Russia
140 C4 Sūlār Iran
162 B1 Sula Sgeir i. U.K.
Sulawesi i. Indon. see Celebes
137 J4 Sulaymān Beg Iraq
162 D1 Sule Skerry i. U.K.
162 D1 Sule Stack i. U.K.
136 F3 Süleymanlı Turkey
176 A4 Sulima Sierra Leone
165 G2 Sulingen Germany
158 L2 Sulitjelma Norway
159 O3 Sulkava Fin.
210 B4 Sullana Peru
198 F4 Sullivan U.S.A.
187 G4 Sullivan Lake Canada
203 I1 Sully Canada
170 E3 Sulmona Italy
199 E6 Sulphur U.S.A.
199 E5 Sulphur Springs U.S.A.
191 F2 Sultan Canada
141 F4 Sultan, Koh-i- mts Pak.
136 C2 Sultan Dağları mts Turkey
136 D2 Sultanhanı Turkey
145 E4 Sultanpur India
153 B5 Sulu Archipelago is Phil.
139 H5 Suluke China
139 G5 Sülüktü Kyrg.
136 F2 Sulusaray Turkey
153 A4 Sulu Sea Phil.
138 F3 Sulutobe Kazakh.
165 J5 Sulzbach-Rosenberg Germany
129 B5 Sulzberger Bay b. Antarctica
141 E6 Sumāil Oman
212 D3 Sumampa Arg.
213 B4 Sumapaz, Parque Nacional nat. park Col.
137 J5 Sūmār Iran
Sumatera i. Indon. see Sumatra
155 B3 Sumatra i. Indon.
168 F6 Šumava mts Czech Rep.
137 I3 Sumayl/Sêmêl Iraq
147 E7 Sumba i. Indon.
147 D7 Sumba, Selat sea chan. Indon.
138 C5 Sumbar r. Turkm.
155 E4 Sumbawa i. Indon.
155 E4 Sumbawabesar Indon.
179 D4 Sumbawanga Tanz.
179 B5 Sumbe Angola
162 □ Sumburgh U.K.
162 □ Sumburgh Head U.K.
144 D2 Sumdo China
155 D4 Sumenep Indon.
151 F9 Sumisu-jima i. Japan
188 C3 Summer Beaver Canada
189 J4 Summerford Canada
190 D3 Summer Island U.S.A.
162 C2 Summer Isles U.K.
189 H4 Summerside Canada
202 C5 Summersville U.S.A.
202 C5 Summersville Lake U.S.A.
186 E4 Summit Lake Canada
190 E5 Summit Lake l. U.S.A.
196 D2 Summit Mountain U.S.A.
144 D2 Sumnal China/India
128 D5 Sumner N.Z.
190 A4 Sumner U.S.A.
128 D5 Sumner, Lake N.Z.
186 C3 Sumner Strait U.S.A.
151 F6 Sumon-dake mt. Japan
151 D7 Sumoto Japan
168 H6 Šumperk Czech Rep.
138 A4 Sumqayıt Azer.
137 L1 Sumqayıtçay r. Azer.
144 B4 Sumrahu Pak.
201 D5 Sumter U.S.A.
173 E5 Sumy Ukr.
194 D2 Sun r. U.S.A.
172 I3 Suna Russia
150 G3 Sunagawa Japan
145 G4 Sunamganj Bangl.
152 C4 Sunan N. Korea
162 C4 Sunart, Loch inlet U.K.
140 D6 Şunaynah Oman
137 J4 Sunbula Kūh mts Iran
194 E1 Sunburst U.S.A.
126 F6 Sunbury Australia
202 B4 Sunbury OH U.S.A.
202 E4 Sunbury PA U.S.A.
215 E1 Sunchales Arg.
152 D6 Suncheon S. Korea
152 C4 Sunch'ŏn N. Korea
181 G2 Sun City S. Africa
203 H3 Suncook U.S.A.
155 C4 Sunda, Selat str. Indon.
194 F2 Sundance U.S.A.
145 G5 Sundarbans coastal area Bangl./India
145 G5 Sundarbans National Park Bangl./India
143 D1 Sundargarh India
144 D3 Sundarnagar India
218 L4 Sunda Shelf sea feature Indian Ocean
160 F3 Sunderland U.K.
165 G3 Sundern (Sauerland) Germany
136 C2 Sündiken Dağları mts Turkey
191 H3 Sundridge Canada
159 L3 Sundsvall Sweden
132 C3 Sundsvall commune Sweden
Sundukli, Peski des. Turkm. see Sandykly Gumy
181 I4 Sundumbili S. Africa
144 D4 Sunel India
154 B5 Sungaikabung Indon.
155 C3 Sungailiat Indon.
155 B3 Sungaipenuh Indon.
155 B1 Sungai Petani Malaysia
Sungei Petani Malaysia see Sungai Petani
154 □ Sungei Seletar Reservoir Sing.
136 E1 Sungurlu Turkey
139 H3 Sunkar, Gora mt. Kazakh.
145 F4 Sun Kosi r. Nepal
159 I3 Sunndal Norway
158 J3 Sunndalsøra Norway
159 K4 Sunne Sweden
194 C2 Sunnyside U.S.A.
196 A3 Sunnyvale U.S.A.
190 C4 Sun Prairie U.S.A.
196 □1 Sunset Beach U.S.A.
197 G4 Sunset Crater National Monument nat. park U.S.A.
133 M3 Suntar Russia
141 F5 Suntsar Pak.
194 D3 Sun Valley U.S.A.
152 C5 Sunwi-do i. N. Korea
176 B4 Sunyani Ghana
158 O2 Suolijärvet l. Fin.
190 C1 Suomi Canada
158 O2 Suomussalmi Fin.
151 B8 Suō-nada b. Japan
Suonan China see Dongxiang
158 N3 Suonenjoki Fin.
154 C3 Suŏng Cambodia
149 B7 Suong r. Laos
172 E2 Suoyarvi Russia
143 A3 Supa India
197 F3 Supai U.S.A.
213 E3 Supamo r. Venez.
145 F4 Supaul India
197 G5 Superior AZ U.S.A.
198 D3 Superior NE U.S.A.
190 A2 Superior WI U.S.A.
207 F4 Superior, Laguna lag. Mex.
190 C2 Superior, Lake Canada/U.S.A.
154 B2 Suphan Buri Thai.
137 I2 Süphan Dağı mt. Turkey
172 E4 Suponevo Russia
152 C3 Supung N. Korea
137 K6 Sūq ash Shuyūkh Iraq
148 F3 Suqian China
Suquṭrá i. Yemen see Socotra
142 E5 Şūr Oman
196 B3 Sur, Point U.S.A.
215 F3 Sur, Punta pt Arg.
172 H4 Sura Russia
172 H4 Sura r. Russia
137 L1 Şuraabad Azer.
141 G4 Surab Pak.
155 D4 Surabaya Indon.
141 E5 Sūrak Iran
155 D4 Surakarta Indon.
127 H1 Surat Australia
144 C5 Surat India
144 C3 Suratgarh India
154 A3 Surat Thani Thai.
172 E4 Surazh Russia
137 J4 Surdash Iraq
171 J3 Surdulica Serbia
164 E5 Sûre r. Lux.
144 B5 Surendranagar India
206 I6 Suretka Costa Rica
196 B4 Surf U.S.A.
132 I3 Surgut Russia
143 B2 Suriapet India
153 C4 Surigao Phil.
153 C4 Surigao Strait Phil.
154 B2 Surin Thai.
211 G3 Suriname country S. America
139 F5 Surkhandar'ya r. Uzbek.
145 E3 Surkhet Nepal
139 G5 Surkhob r. Tajik.
140 D4 Sūrmaq Iran
137 H1 Sürmene Turkey
173 G5 Surovikino Russia
140 A6 Surrah, Nafūd as des. Saudi Arabia
202 E6 Surry U.S.A.
172 H4 Sursk Russia
Surt Libya see Sirte
Surt, Khalīj g. Libya see Sirte, Gulf of
158 B3 Surtsey i. Iceland
141 E5 Sūrū Iran
136 G3 Suruç Turkey
151 F7 Suruga-wan b. Japan
155 B3 Surulangun Indon.
153 C5 Surup Phil.
164 F2 Surwold Germany
137 K2 Şuşa Azer.
151 B7 Susa Japan
151 C8 Susaki Japan
140 C4 Sūsangerd Iran
172 G3 Susanino Russia
196 B1 Susanville U.S.A.
136 G1 Suşehri Turkey
154 A4 Suso Thai.
149 E4 Susong China
203 E4 Susquehanna r. U.S.A.
202 D4 Susquehanna, West Branch r. U.S.A.
189 G4 Sussex Canada
203 F4 Sussex U.S.A.
153 A5 Susul Sabah Malaysia
133 P3 Susuman Russia
136 B2 Susurluk Turkey
144 D2 Sutak India
196 C2 Sutcliffe U.S.A.
180 D6 Sutherland S. Africa
198 C3 Sutherland U.S.A.
Sutlej r. Pak. see Satluj

Techiman

176 B4 **Techiman** Ghana
212 B6 **Tecka** Arg.
164 F2 **Tecklenburger Land** *reg.* Germany
207 E3 **Tecolutla** Mex.
206 D4 **Tecomán** Mex.
196 D4 **Tecopa** U.S.A.
206 B1 **Tecoripa** Mex.
206 D4 **Técpan** Mex.
169 M7 **Tecuci** Romania
191 F5 **Tecumseh** U.S.A.
Tedzhen Turkm. *see* **Tejen**
Tedzhen *r.* Turkm. *see* **Tejen**
141 F2 **Tedzhenstroy** Turkm.
197 H3 **Teec Nos Pos** U.S.A.
135 H1 **Teeli** Russia
160 F3 **Tees** *r.* U.K.
160 E3 **Teesdale** *val.* U.K.
210 E4 **Tefé** *r.* Brazil
136 B3 **Tefenni** Turkey
155 C4 **Tegal** Indon.
165 L2 **Tegel** *airport* Germany
Tegid, Llyn *l.* U.K. *see* **Bala Lake**
206 H5 **Tegucigalpa** Hond.
176 C3 **Teguidda-n-Tessoumt** Niger
196 C4 **Tehachapi** U.S.A.
195 C5 **Tehachapi Mountains** U.S.A.
196 C4 **Tehachapi Pass** U.S.A.
187 J2 **Tehek Lake** Canada
Teheran Iran *see* **Tehrān**
176 B4 **Téhini** Côte d'Ivoire
140 C3 **Tehrān** Iran
(City Plan **106**)
207 E4 **Tehuacán** Mex.
207 F5 **Tehuantepec, Gulf of** Mex.
207 F4 **Tehuantepec, Istmo de** *isth.* Mex.
217 M5 **Tehuantepec Ridge** *sea feature* N. Pacific Ocean
207 E4 **Tehuitzingo** Mex.
161 C5 **Teifi** *r.* U.K.
161 D7 **Teign** *r.* U.K.
161 D7 **Teignmouth** U.K.
Te Ika-a-Māui N.Z. *see* **North Island**
214 E2 **Teixeira de Freitas** Brazil
138 E5 **Tejen** Turkm.
141 F2 **Tejen** *r.* Turkm.
167 B3 **Tejo** *r.* Port.
alt. **Tajo (Spain),**
conv. **Tagus**
196 C4 **Tejon Pass** U.S.A.
206 D4 **Tejupan, Punta** *pt* Mex.
128 D1 **Te Kao** N.Z.
128 C5 **Tekapo, Lake** N.Z.
145 F4 **Tekari** India
207 G3 **Tekax** Mex.
139 H1 **Teke, Ozero** *salt l.* Kazakh.
138 E2 **Tekeli** *Aktyubinskaya Oblast'* Kazakh.
139 I3 **Tekeli** *Almatinskaya Oblast'* Kazakh.
139 J4 **Tekes** China
139 J4 **Tekes** Kazakh.
139 J3 **Tekes He** *r.* China
178 D2 **Tekeze** *resr* Eth.
178 D2 **Tekezē Wenz** *r.* Eritrea/Eth.
144 E1 **Tekiliktag** *mt.* China
136 A1 **Tekirdağ** Turkey
143 D2 **Tekkali** India
137 H2 **Tekman** Turkey
145 H5 **Teknaf** Bangl.
190 E4 **Tekonsha** U.S.A.
128 E3 **Te Kuiti** N.Z.
143 C2 **Tel** *r.* India
206 H5 **Tela** Hond.
143 B3 **Telangana** *state* India
173 H7 **Telavi** Georgia
136 E5 **Tel Aviv-Yafo** Israel
168 G6 **Telč** Czech Rep.
207 G3 **Telchac Puerto** Mex.
186 C3 **Telegraph Creek** Canada
214 B4 **Telêmaco Borba** Brazil
215 D3 **Telén** Arg.
155 E2 **Telen** *r.* Indon.
171 K2 **Teleorman** *r.* Romania
196 D3 **Telescope Peak** U.S.A.
211 G5 **Teles Pires** *r.* Brazil
161 E5 **Telford** U.K.
165 F3 **Telgte** Germany
136 E5 **Tel Hazor** *tourist site* Israel
206 H5 **Telica** Nicaragua
176 A3 **Télimélé** Guinea
186 D4 **Telkwa** Canada
184 B3 **Teller** U.S.A.
164 D4 **Tellin** Belgium
137 K6 **Telloh** Iraq
207 E4 **Teloloapán** Mex.
215 C4 **Telsen** Arg.
159 M5 **Telšiai** Lith.
165 L2 **Teltow** Germany
Teluk Anson Malaysia *see* **Teluk Intan**
155 A2 **Telukdalam** Indon.
155 B2 **Teluk Intan** Malaysia
191 H2 **Temagami** Canada
191 G2 **Temagami Lake** Canada
155 D4 **Temanggung** Indon.
207 G3 **Temax** Mex.
181 H2 **Temba** S. Africa
133 K3 **Tembenchi** *r.* Russia
155 B3 **Tembilahan** Indon.
181 H3 **Tembisa** S. Africa
178 B4 **Tembo Aluma** Angola
161 E5 **Teme** *r.* U.K.
196 D5 **Temecula** U.S.A.
136 D2 **Temelli** Turkey
155 B2 **Temerluh** Malaysia
137 L5 **Temīleh** Iran
138 D2 **Temir** *Aktyubinskaya Oblast'* Kazakh.
139 G4 **Temir** *Yuzhnyy Kazakhstan* Kazakh.
139 G4 **Temirlan** Kazakh.
139 H2 **Temirtau** Kazakh.
191 H2 **Témiscaming** Canada
191 H2 **Témiscamingue, Lac** *l.* Canada
189 G4 **Témiscouata, Lac** *l.* Canada
127 F8 **Temma** Australia
158 N2 **Temmes** Fin.
172 G4 **Temnikov** Russia
127 G5 **Temora** Australia
206 C1 **Temósachic** Mex.
197 G5 **Tempe** U.S.A.
165 L2 **Tempelhof** *airport* Germany
170 C4 **Tempio Pausania** *Sardinia* Italy
190 E3 **Temple** *MI* U.S.A.
199 D6 **Temple** *TX* U.S.A.
161 C5 **Temple Bar** U.K.
163 D5 **Templemore** Ireland
153 A4 **Templer Bank** *sea feature* Phil.
160 E3 **Temple Sowerby** U.K.
165 L1 **Templin** Germany
207 E3 **Tempoal** Mex.
173 F6 **Temryuk** Russia
215 B3 **Temuco** Chile
128 C6 **Temuka** N.Z.
210 C4 **Tena** Ecuador
196 D1 **Tenabo, Mount** U.S.A.
143 C2 **Tenali** India
207 E4 **Tenancingo** Mex.
154 A2 **Tenasserim** Myanmar
154 A2 **Tenasserim** *r.* Myanmar
161 E5 **Tenbury Wells** U.K.
161 C6 **Tenby** U.K.
191 F2 **Tenby Bay** Canada
178 E2 **Tendaho** Eth.
166 H4 **Tende** France
135 H6 **Ten Degree Channel** India
150 G5 **Tendō** Japan
137 I2 **Tendürek Dağı** *mt.* Turkey
176 B3 **Ténenkou** Mali
176 D3 **Ténéré** *reg.* Niger
176 D3 **Ténéré, Erg du** *des.* Niger
176 D2 **Ténéré du Tafassâsset** *des.* Niger
176 A2 **Tenerife** *i.* Canary Is
167 G4 **Ténès** Alg.
155 E4 **Tengah, Kepulauan** *is* Indon.
138 C4 **Tenge** Kazakh.
154 □ **Tengeh Reservoir** Sing.
148 B2 **Tengger Shamo** *des.* China
154 B4 **Tenggul** *i.* Malaysia
139 G2 **Tengiz, Ozero** *salt l.* Kazakh.
176 B3 **Tengréla** Côte d'Ivoire
149 D6 **Tengxian** China
148 E3 **Tengzhou** China
138 F1 **Teniz, Ozero** *l.* Kazakh.
179 C5 **Tenke** Dem. Rep. Congo
133 P2 **Tenkeli** Russia
176 B3 **Tenkodogo** Burkina Faso
124 D3 **Tennant Creek** Australia
201 C5 **Tennessee** *r.* U.S.A.
202 B6 **Tennessee** *state* U.S.A.
195 F4 **Tennessee Pass** U.S.A.
158 L1 **Tennevoll** Norway
215 B2 **Teno** *r.* Chile
158 O1 **Tenojoki** *r.* Fin./Norway
207 G4 **Tenosique** Mex.
194 F2 **Ten Sleep** U.S.A.
124 C2 **Tenteno** Indon.
161 H6 **Tenterden** U.K.
127 J2 **Tenterfield** Australia
201 D7 **Ten Thousand Islands** U.S.A.
167 C3 **Tentudia** *mt.* Spain
214 B3 **Teodoro Sampaio** Brazil
214 E2 **Teófilo Otoni** Brazil
207 F4 **Teopisca** Mex.
207 E4 **Teotihuacán** *tourist site* Mex.
195 E6 **Tepache** Mex.
128 D1 **Te Paki** N.Z.
206 D4 **Tepalcatepec** Mex.
206 D3 **Tepatitlán** Mex.
137 H3 **Tepe** Turkey
137 I3 **Tepe Gawra** *tourist site* Iraq
206 C2 **Tepehuanes** Mex.
207 E4 **Tepeji** Mex.
171 I4 **Tepelenë** Albania
207 E4 **Tepelmeme de Morelos** Mex.
165 K5 **Tepelská vrchovina** *hills* Czech Rep.
213 E4 **Tepequem, Serra** *mts* Brazil
206 C3 **Tepic** Mex.
128 C5 **Te Pirita** N.Z.
168 F5 **Teplice** Czech Rep.
172 J2 **Teplogorka** Russia
172 F4 **Teploye** Russia
128 F2 **Te Puke** N.Z.
137 J4 **Teq Teq** Iraq
207 F4 **Tequisistlán** Mex.
207 E3 **Tequisquiapán** Mex.
167 H1 **Ter** *r.* Spain
123 I3 **Teraina** *i.* Kiribati
144 D2 **Teram Kangri** *mt.* China
170 E3 **Teramo** Italy
126 E7 **Terang** Australia
164 F2 **Ter Apel** Neth.
173 F4 **Terbuny** Russia
137 H2 **Tercan** Turkey
156 A6 **Terceira** *i.* Azores
169 L6 **Terebovlya** Ukr.
173 H7 **Terek** Russia
173 H7 **Terek** *r.* Russia
139 G2 **Terekty** *Karagandinskaya Oblast'* Kazakh.
139 K2 **Terekty** *Vostochnyy Kazakhstan* Kazakh.
172 I4 **Teren'ga** Russia
214 A3 **Terenos** Brazil
138 F3 **Terenozek** Kazakh.
138 D2 **Terensay** Russia
213 C2 **Terepaima, Parque Nacional** *nat. park* Venez.
172 H4 **Tereshka** *r.* Russia
211 J5 **Teresina** Brazil
214 D3 **Teresópolis** Brazil
164 B5 **Tergnier** France
139 F2 **Terisakkan** *r.* Kazakh.
212 D3 **Termas de Río Hondo** Arg.
136 F1 **Terme** Turkey
Termez Uzbek. *see* **Termiz**
170 E6 **Termini Imerese** *Sicily* Italy
207 G4 **Términos, Laguna de** *lag.* Mex.
177 D3 **Termit and Tin Toumma National Nature and Cultural Reserve** Niger
139 F5 **Termiz** Uzbek.
170 F4 **Termoli** Italy
161 E5 **Tern** *r.* U.K.
147 E6 **Ternate** Indon.
164 B3 **Terneuzen** Neth.
150 E2 **Terney** Russia
170 E3 **Terni** Italy
173 C5 **Ternopil'** Ukr.
126 C4 **Terowie** Australia
146 G2 **Terpeniya, Mys** *c.* Russia
146 G2 **Terpeniya, Zaliv** *g.* Russia
186 D4 **Terrace** Canada
190 D1 **Terrace Bay** Canada
180 E2 **Terra Firma** S. Africa
158 K2 **Terråk** Norway
170 C5 **Terralba** *Sardinia* Italy
189 J4 **Terra Nova National Park** Canada
199 F6 **Terrebonne Bay** U.S.A.
200 C4 **Terre Haute** U.S.A.
189 J4 **Terrenceville** Canada
194 F2 **Terry** U.S.A.
173 G5 **Tersa** *r.* Russia
164 D1 **Terschelling** *i.* Neth.
139 I4 **Terskey Ala-Too** *mts* Kyrg.
170 C5 **Tertenia** *Sardinia* Italy
167 F2 **Teruel** Spain
158 N2 **Tervola** Fin.
170 G2 **Tešanj** Bos. & Herz.
178 D2 **Teseney** Eritrea
172 G4 **Tesha** *r.* Russia
184 C2 **Teshekpuk Lake** U.S.A.
150 I3 **Teshikaga** Japan
150 G2 **Teshio** Japan
150 H3 **Teshio-dake** *mt.* Japan
150 G2 **Teshio-gawa** *r.* Japan
206 B2 **Tesia** Mex.
186 C2 **Teslin** Canada
186 C2 **Teslin** *r.* Canada
186 C2 **Teslin Lake** Canada
214 B1 **Tesouras** *r.* Brazil
214 B2 **Tesouro** Brazil
176 C3 **Tessaoua** Niger
161 F6 **Test** *r.* U.K.
170 C6 **Testour** Tunisia
212 B2 **Tetas, Punta** *pt* Chile
179 D5 **Tete** Moz.
128 F3 **Te Teko** N.Z.
169 O5 **Teteriv** *r.* Ukr.
165 K1 **Teterow** Germany
169 N6 **Tetiyiv** Ukr.
160 G4 **Tetney** U.K.
194 E2 **Teton** *r.* U.S.A.
194 E3 **Teton Range** *mts* U.S.A.
176 B1 **Tétouan** Morocco
171 I3 **Tetovo** Macedonia
172 I4 **Tetyushi** Russia
212 D2 **Teuco** *r.* Arg.
180 B1 **Teufelsbach** Namibia
165 G1 **Teufelsmoor** *reg.* Germany
128 F3 **Te Urewera National Park** N.Z.
150 G2 **Teuri-tō** *i.* Japan
165 G2 **Teutoburger Wald** *hills* Germany
159 M3 **Teuva** Fin.
Tevere *r.* Italy *see* **Tiber**
Teverya Israel *see* **Tiberias**
162 F5 **Teviot** *r.* U.K.
162 F5 **Teviotdale** *val.* U.K.
128 A7 **Te Waewae Bay** N.Z.
Te Waipounamu N.Z. *see* **South Island**
181 G1 **Tewane** Botswana
125 F4 **Tewantin** Australia
128 E4 **Te Wharau** N.Z.
161 E6 **Tewkesbury** U.K.
148 B3 **Têwo** China
186 E5 **Texada Island** Canada
199 E5 **Texarkana** U.S.A.
127 I2 **Texas** Australia
199 D6 **Texas** *state* U.S.A.
199 E6 **Texas City** U.S.A.
207 E4 **Texcoco** Mex.
164 C1 **Texel** *i.* Neth.
199 C4 **Texhoma** U.S.A.
199 D5 **Texoma, Lake** U.S.A.
181 G4 **Teyateyaneng** Lesotho
172 G3 **Teykovo** Russia
172 G3 **Teza** *r.* Russia
207 E4 **Teziutlán** Mex.
145 H4 **Tezpur** India
145 I4 **Tezu** India
187 J2 **Tha-anne** *r.* Canada
181 H4 **Thabana-Ntlenyana** *mt.* Lesotho
181 G4 **Thaba Nchu** S. Africa
181 G4 **Thaba Putsoa** *mt.* Lesotho
181 H4 **Thaba-Tseka** Lesotho
181 G2 **Thabazimbi** S. Africa
154 B1 **Tha Bo** Laos
181 G3 **Thabong** S. Africa
140 B5 **Thādiq** Saudi Arabia
154 A2 **Thagyettaw** Myanmar
149 C6 **Thai Binh** Vietnam
154 A1 **Thailand** *country* Asia
154 B3 **Thailand, Gulf of** Asia
154 A3 **Thai Muang** Thai.
149 B6 **Thai Nguyên** Vietnam
140 C5 **Thaj** Saudi Arabia
154 C1 **Thakhèk** Laos
144 E5 **Thakurtola** India
165 I4 **Thal** Germany
144 B2 **Thal** Pak.
170 C7 **Thala** Tunisia
154 A3 **Thalang** Thai.
143 A4 **Thalassery** India
144 B3 **Thal Desert** Pak.
165 J3 **Thale** Germany
154 B1 **Tha Li** Thai.
127 H2 **Thallon** Australia
141 G4 **Thalo** Pak.
181 F2 **Thamaga** Botswana
140 B5 **Thāmām, 'Irq ath** *des.* Saudi Arabia
142 C7 **Thamar, Jabal** *mt.* Yemen
142 D6 **Thamarīt** Oman
161 G5 **Thame** *r.* U.K.
128 E2 **Thames** N.Z.
161 H6 **Thames** *est.* U.K.
161 G6 **Thames** *r.* U.K.
191 G4 **Thamesville** Canada
144 B5 **Than** India
154 A2 **Thanbyuzayat** Myanmar
144 C5 **Thandla** India
147 B5 **Thandwe** Myanmar
143 A2 **Thane** India
Thăng Binh Vietnam *see* **Ha Lam**
154 C1 **Thanh Hoa** Vietnam
143 B4 **Thanjavur** India
154 B1 **Tha Pla** Thai.
154 A3 **Thap Put** Thai.
154 A3 **Thap Sakae** Thai.
144 B4 **Tharad** India
144 B4 **Thar Desert** India/Pak.
126 E1 **Thargomindah** Australia
137 I5 **Tharthār, Buḩayrat ath** *l.* Iraq
137 I4 **Tharthār, Wādī ath** *r.* Iraq
171 K4 **Thasos** *i.* Greece
197 H5 **Thatcher** U.S.A.
149 C6 **Thât Khê** Vietnam
147 B5 **Thaton** Myanmar
144 A4 **Thatta** Pak.
145 H4 **Thaungdut** Myanmar
154 A1 **Thaungyin** *r.* Myanmar/Thai.
154 C1 **Tha Uthen** Thai.
147 B5 **Thayetmyo** Myanmar
128 F2 **The Aldermen Islands** N.Z.
197 F5 **Theba** U.S.A.
205 I3 **The Bahamas** *country* Caribbean Sea
201 E7 **The Bluff** Bahamas
160 E2 **The Cheviot** *h.* U.K.
126 C5 **The Coorong** *inlet* Australia
194 B2 **The Dalles** U.S.A.
198 C3 **Thedford** U.S.A.
162 □ **The Faither** *stack* U.K.
161 G5 **The Fens** *reg.* U.K.
203 I2 **The Forks** U.S.A.
176 A3 **The Gambia** *country* Africa
126 E6 **The Grampians** *mts* Australia
142 D4 **The Gulf** Asia
164 C2 **The Hague** Neth.
128 C6 **The Hunters Hills** N.Z.
154 A3 **Theinkun** Myanmar
128 A6 **The Key** N.Z.
187 H2 **Thekulthili Lake** Canada
187 I2 **Thelon** *r.* Canada
187 I2 **Thelon Game Sanctuary** *nature res.* Canada
165 I4 **Themar** Germany
180 F6 **Thembalesizwe** S. Africa
181 H3 **Thembalihle** S. Africa
162 C2 **The Minch** *sea chan.* U.K.
161 F7 **The Needles** *stack* U.K.
167 H4 **Thenia** Alg.
167 H5 **Theniet El Had** Alg.
210 F5 **Theodore Roosevelt** *r.* Brazil
197 G5 **Theodore Roosevelt Dam** U.S.A.
197 G5 **Theodore Roosevelt Lake** U.S.A.
198 C2 **Theodore Roosevelt National Park** U.S.A.
163 B5 **The Paps** *h.* Ireland
187 I4 **The Pas** Canada
127 H6 **The Pilot** *mt.* Australia
164 A5 **Thérain** *r.* France
203 F2 **Theresa** U.S.A.
171 J4 **Thermaïkos Kolpos** *g.* Greece
196 B2 **Thermalito** U.S.A.
194 E3 **Thermopolis** U.S.A.
127 G5 **The Rock** Australia
164 A4 **Thérouanne** France
126 E3 **The Salt Lake** *salt l.* Australia
184 F2 **Thesiger Bay** Canada
163 A6 **The Skelligs** *is* Ireland
161 F7 **The Solent** *str.* U.K.
191 F2 **Thessalon** Canada
171 J4 **Thessaloniki** Greece
162 B3 **The Storr** *h.* U.K.
161 H5 **Thet** *r.* U.K.
153 A4 **The Teeth** *mt.* Phil.
161 H5 **Thetford** U.K.
189 F4 **Thetford Mines** Canada
162 D4 **The Trossachs** *hills* U.K.
126 A2 **The Twins** Australia
154 C1 **Theun** *r.* Laos
181 G4 **Theunissen** S. Africa
161 H5 **The Wash** *b.* U.K.
161 H6 **The Weald** *reg.* U.K.
199 F6 **Thibodaux** U.S.A.
187 J3 **Thicket Portage** Canada
198 D1 **Thief River Falls** U.S.A.
129 C4 **Thiel Mountains** *mts* Antarctica
166 F4 **Thiers** France
176 A3 **Thiès** Senegal
178 D4 **Thika** Kenya
Thiladhunmathee Atoll Maldives *see* **Thiladhunmathi**
143 A5 **Thiladhunmathi** Maldives
145 G4 **Thimphu** Bhutan
166 H2 **Thionville** France
Thira *i.* Greece *see* **Santorini**
171 K6 **Thirasia** *i.* Greece
160 F3 **Thirsk** U.K.
143 B4 **Thiruvananthapuram** India
159 J4 **Thisted** Denmark
126 B5 **Thistle Island** Australia
171 J5 **Thiva** Greece
187 J2 **Thlewiaza** *r.* Canada
187 H2 **Thoa** *r.* Canada
154 B3 **Thô Chu, Đao** *i.* Vietnam
181 I1 **Thohoyandou** S. Africa
164 C3 **Tholen** Neth.
164 F5 **Tholey** Germany
202 D5 **Thomas** U.S.A.
201 C5 **Thomaston** *GA* U.S.A.
203 I2 **Thomaston** *ME* U.S.A.
203 J2 **Thomaston Corner** Canada
163 D5 **Thomastown** Ireland
201 D6 **Thomasville** U.S.A.
164 E4 **Thommen** Belgium
187 J3 **Thompson** Canada
186 E4 **Thompson** *r.* Canada
190 D3 **Thompson** *MI* U.S.A.
203 F4 **Thompson** *PA* U.S.A.
198 E3 **Thompson** *r.* U.S.A.
194 D2 **Thompson Falls** U.S.A.
201 D5 **Thomson** U.S.A.
168 C7 **Thonon-les-Bains** France
Thoothukudi India *see* **Tuticorin**
195 E5 **Thoreau** U.S.A.
127 F2 **Thorlindah, Lake** *salt flat* Australia
164 D3 **Thorn** Neth.
160 F3 **Thornaby-on-Tees** U.K.
190 E4 **Thornapple** *r.* U.S.A.
161 E6 **Thornbury** U.K.
191 H2 **Thorne** Canada
160 G4 **Thorne** U.K.
196 C2 **Thorne** U.S.A.
186 C3 **Thorne Bay** U.S.A.
190 D5 **Thorntown** U.S.A.
190 B3 **Thorp** U.S.A.
129 D4 **Thorshavnheiane** *reg.* Antarctica
181 G4 **Thota-ea-Moli** Lesotho
166 D3 **Thouars** France
203 E2 **Thousand Islands** Canada
197 G2 **Thousand Lake Mountain** U.S.A.
196 C4 **Thousand Oaks** U.S.A.
171 L4 **Thrace** *reg.* Europe
171 K4 **Thrakiko Pelagos** *sea* Greece
194 E2 **Three Forks** U.S.A.
Three Gorges Reservoir *resr* China *see* **Sanxia Shuiku**
186 G4 **Three Hills** Canada
127 F8 **Three Hummock Island** Australia
128 D1 **Three Kings Islands** N.Z.
190 C3 **Three Lakes** U.S.A.
190 D5 **Three Oaks** U.S.A.
154 A2 **Three Pagodas Pass** Myanmar/Thai.
176 B4 **Three Points, Cape** Ghana
190 E5 **Three Rivers** *MI* U.S.A.
199 D6 **Three Rivers** *TX* U.S.A.
194 B2 **Three Sisters** *mt.* U.S.A.
143 B4 **Thrissur** India
199 D5 **Throckmorton** U.S.A.
Thu, Cu Lao *i.* Vietnam *see* **Phu Quy, Đao**
154 C1 **Thuân An** Vietnam
154 D1 **Thu Bôn, Sông** *r.* Vietnam
187 G2 **Thubun Lakes** Canada
154 C3 **Thu Dâu Môt** Vietnam
154 C3 **Thu Đuc** Vietnam
164 C4 **Thuin** Belgium
Thule Greenland *see* **Qaanaaq**
185 L2 **Thule Air Base** Greenland
179 C6 **Thuli** Zimbabwe
168 C7 **Thun** Switz.
190 C1 **Thunder Bay** Canada
190 C1 **Thunder Bay** *b.* Canada
191 F3 **Thunder Bay** *b.* U.S.A.
165 H5 **Thüngen** Germany
154 A3 **Thung Song** Thai.
154 A4 **Thung Wa** Thai.
165 I4 **Thüringen** *land* Germany
165 J3 **Thüringer Becken** *reg.* Germany
165 I4 **Thüringer Wald** *mts* Germany
163 D5 **Thurles** Ireland
202 E5 **Thurmont** U.S.A.
168 F7 **Thurn, Pass** Austria
203 F2 **Thurso** Canada
162 E2 **Thurso** U.K.
162 E2 **Thurso** *r.* U.K.
129 A3 **Thurston Island** *i.* Antarctica
165 H2 **Thüster Berg** *h.* Germany
160 E3 **Thwaite** U.K.
159 J4 **Thyborøn** Denmark
148 A1 **Tiancang** China
148 F3 **Tianchang** China
149 C6 **Tiandeng** China
149 C6 **Tiandong** China
149 C5 **Tian'e** China
211 J4 **Tianguá** Brazil
148 E2 **Tianjin** China
148 E2 **Tianjin** *mun.* China
146 B3 **Tianjun** China
149 C5 **Tianlin** China
149 D4 **Tianmen** China
149 F4 **Tianmu Shan** *mts* China
152 E2 **Tianqiaoling** China
149 B4 **Tianquan** China
152 C3 **Tianshifu** China
148 B3 **Tianshui** China
144 D2 **Tianshuihai** China
149 F4 **Tiantai** China
148 E1 **Tiantaiyong** China
149 C6 **Tianyang** China
148 B2 **Tianzhu** *Gansu* China
149 C5 **Tianzhu** *Guizhou* China
176 C1 **Tiaret** Alg.
176 B4 **Tiassalé** Côte d'Ivoire
214 B4 **Tibagi** *r.* Brazil
137 I5 **Tibal, Wādī** *watercourse* Iraq
177 D4 **Tibati** Cameroon
170 E3 **Tiber** *r.* Italy
136 E5 **Tiberias** Israel
Tiberias, Lake Israel *see* **Galilee, Sea of**
194 E1 **Tiber Reservoir** U.S.A.
177 D2 **Tibesti** *mts* Chad
Tibet *aut. reg.* China *see* **Xizang Zizhiqu**
135 G3 **Tibet, Plateau of** China
177 D2 **Tībīstī, Sarīr** *des.* Libya
126 E2 **Tibooburra** Australia
145 E3 **Tibrikot** Nepal
159 K4 **Tibro** Sweden
206 A1 **Tiburón, Isla** *i.* Mex.
153 B3 **Ticao** *i.* Phil.
161 H6 **Ticehurst** U.K.
191 I3 **Tichborne** Canada
176 B3 **Tîchît** Mauritania
176 A2 **Tichla** W. Sahara
168 D7 **Ticino** *r.* Switz.
203 G3 **Ticonderoga** U.S.A.
207 G3 **Ticul** Mex.
159 K4 **Tidaholm** Sweden
145 H5 **Tiddim** Myanmar
176 C2 **Tidikelt, Plaine du** *plain* Alg.
176 A3 **Tidjikja** Mauritania
139 K3 **Tiechanggou** China
Tiefa China *see* **Diaobingshan**
164 D3 **Tiel** Neth.
150 A1 **Tieli** China
152 B2 **Tieling** China
144 D2 **Tielongtan** China
164 B4 **Tielt** Belgium
176 B4 **Tiémé** Côte d'Ivoire
164 C4 **Tienen** Belgium
135 F2 **Tien Shan** *mts* China/Kyrg.
Tientsin China *see* **Tianjin**
159 L3 **Tierp** Sweden
195 F4 **Tierra Amarilla** U.S.A.
207 E4 **Tierra Blanca** Mex.
207 E4 **Tierra Colorada** Mex.
212 C8 **Tierra del Fuego, Isla Grande de** *i.* Arg./Chile
167 D2 **Tiétar** *r.* Spain
167 D2 **Tiétar, Valle del** *val.* Spain
214 C3 **Tietê** Brazil
214 B3 **Tietê** *r.* Brazil
202 B4 **Tiffin** U.S.A.
Tiflis Georgia *see* **Tbilisi**
201 D6 **Tifton** U.S.A.
138 B3 **Tigen** Kazakh.
171 K3 **Tigheciului, Dealurile** *hills* Moldova
Tighina Moldova *see* **Bender**
139 J2 **Tigiretskiy Khrebet** *mts* Kazakh./Russia
145 F5 **Tigiria** India
177 D4 **Tignère** Cameroon
189 H4 **Tignish** Canada
210 C4 **Tigre** *r.* Ecuador/Peru
213 E2 **Tigre** *r.* Venez.
137 K5 **Tigris** *r.* Asia
alt. **Dicle (Turkey),**
alt. **Dijlah, Nahr (Iraq/Syria)**
136 D7 **Tīh, Jabal at** *plat.* Egypt
142 B6 **Tihāmat 'Asīr** *reg.* Saudi Arabia
204 A2 **Tijuana** Mex.
214 C2 **Tijuco** *r.* Brazil
207 G4 **Tikal** *tourist site* Guat.
207 G4 **Tikal, Parque Nacional** *nat. park* Guat.
144 D4 **Tikamgarh** India
173 G6 **Tikhoretsk** Russia
172 E3 **Tikhvin** Russia
172 E3 **Tikhvinskaya Gryada** *ridge* Russia
217 K7 **Tiki Basin** *sea feature* Pacific Ocean
128 F3 **Tikokino** N.Z.
125 G3 **Tikopia** *i.* Solomon Is
137 I4 **Tikrīt** Iraq
158 P2 **Tikshozero, Ozero** *l.* Russia
133 N2 **Tiksi** Russia
145 E3 **Tila** *r.* Nepal
145 F4 **Tilaiya Reservoir** India
140 B2 **Tīlakūh** Iran
140 D2 **Tilavar** Iran
127 F1 **Tilbooroo** Australia
164 D3 **Tilburg** Neth.
161 H6 **Tilbury** U.K.
212 C2 **Tilcara** Arg.
126 D2 **Tilcha (abandoned)** Australia
139 G2 **Tilekey** Kazakh.
145 H5 **Tilin** Myanmar
176 C3 **Tillabéri** Niger
194 B2 **Tillamook** U.S.A.
162 E4 **Tillicoultry** U.K.
191 G4 **Tillsonburg** Canada
162 F3 **Tillyfourie** U.K.
171 L6 **Tilos** *i.* Greece
126 F3 **Tilpa** Australia
173 F5 **Tim** Russia
154 □ **Timah, Bukit** Sing.
172 J1 **Timanskiy Kryazh** *ridge* Russia
137 I2 **Timar** Turkey
128 C6 **Timaru** N.Z.
173 F6 **Timashëvsk** Russia
176 B3 **Timbedgha** Mauritania
124 D3 **Timber Creek** Australia
196 D3 **Timber Mountain** U.S.A.
202 D5 **Timberville** U.S.A.
126 E7 **Timboon** Australia
176 B3 **Timbuktu** Mali
176 B3 **Timétrine** *reg.* Mali
176 C2 **Timimoun** Alg.
173 C7 **Timiou Prodromou, Akrotirio** *pt* Greece
139 F1 **Timiryazev** Kazakh.
138 F1 **Timiryazevo** Kazakh.
171 I2 **Timişoara** Romania
191 G1 **Timmins** Canada
172 F3 **Timokhino** Russia
211 J5 **Timon** Brazil
147 E7 **Timor** *i.* Indon.
Timor-Leste *country* Asia *see* **East Timor**
124 C3 **Timor Sea** Australia/Indon.
172 H3 **Timoshino** Russia
215 D2 **Timote** Arg.
159 L3 **Timrå** Sweden
201 C5 **Tims Ford Lake** U.S.A.
144 D5 **Timurni Muafi** India
213 C2 **Tinaco** Venez.
143 B3 **Tindivanam** India
176 B2 **Tindouf** Alg.
154 C5 **Tinggi** *i.* Malaysia
127 I2 **Tingha** Australia
149 E5 **Ting Jiang** *r.* China
145 F3 **Tingri** China
159 K4 **Tingsryd** Sweden
215 B2 **Tinguiririca, Volcán** *vol.* Chile
158 J3 **Tingvoll** Norway
162 E1 **Tingwall** U.K.
214 E1 **Tinharé, Ilha de** *i.* Brazil
154 C1 **Tinh Gia** Vietnam
147 G5 **Tinian** *i.* N. Mariana Is
212 C3 **Tinogasta** Arg.
171 K6 **Tinos** *i.* Greece
164 B5 **Tinqueux** France
176 C2 **Tinrhert, Hamada de** Alg.
145 H4 **Tinsukia** India
161 C7 **Tintagel** U.K.
126 D5 **Tintinara** Australia
162 E5 **Tinto** *h.* U.K.
202 E4 **Tioga** *r.* U.S.A.
155 B2 **Tioman** *i.* Malaysia
154 C2 **Ti On, Nui** *mt.* Vietnam
191 F1 **Tionaga** Canada
202 D4 **Tionesta Lake** U.S.A.
203 E3 **Tioughnioga** *r.* U.S.A.
167 H4 **Tipasa** Alg.
206 H5 **Tipitapa** Nicaragua
190 D5 **Tippecanoe** *r.* U.S.A.
190 E5 **Tippecanoe Lake** U.S.A.
163 C5 **Tipperary** Ireland
145 F4 **Tiptala Bhanjyang** *pass* Nepal
190 B5 **Tipton** *IA* U.S.A.
190 D5 **Tipton** *IN* U.S.A.
197 E4 **Tipton, Mount** U.S.A.
190 E1 **Tip Top Hill** Canada
161 H6 **Tiptree** U.K.
213 C4 **Tiquié** *r.* Brazil
207 G5 **Tiquisate** Guat.
211 I4 **Tiracambu, Serra do** *hills* Brazil
141 H3 **Tīrah, Kōtal-e** Afgh.
171 H4 **Tirana** Albania
Tiranë Albania *see* **Tirana**
170 D1 **Tirano** Italy
173 D6 **Tiraspol** Moldova
144 D3 **Tira Sujanpur** India
180 B3 **Tiraz Mountains** Namibia
136 A2 **Tire** Turkey
162 B4 **Tiree** *i.* U.K.
144 B1 **Tirich Mir** *mt.* Pak.
143 B2 **Tirna** *r.* India
143 A3 **Tirthahalli** India
145 F5 **Tirtol** India
143 B4 **Tiruchchendur** India
143 B4 **Tiruchchirappalli** India
143 B4 **Tiruchengodu** India
143 B4 **Tirunelveli** India
143 B3 **Tirupati** India
143 B3 **Tiruppattur** India
143 B4 **Tiruppur** India
143 B4 **Tirutturaippundi** India
143 B3 **Tiruvannamalai** India
143 B4 **Tisaiyanvilai** India
187 I4 **Tisdale** Canada
143 C5 **Tissamaharama** Sri Lanka
167 G5 **Tissemsilt** Alg.
145 G4 **Tista** *r.* India
129 C4 **Titan Dome** *ice feature* Antarctica
133 N2 **Tit-Ary** Russia
210 E7 **Titicaca, Lake** Bol./Peru
143 C1 **Titlagarh** India
191 E4 **Tittabawassee** *r.* U.S.A.
171 K2 **Titu** Romania
201 D6 **Titusville** *FL* U.S.A.
202 D4 **Titusville** *PA* U.S.A.
191 G3 **Tiverton** Canada
161 D7 **Tiverton** U.K.
170 E4 **Tivoli** Italy
207 G3 **Tixkokob** Mex.
207 E4 **Tixtla** Mex.
206 D3 **Tizapán el Alto** Mex.
207 G3 **Tizimín** Mex.
167 I4 **Tizi Ouzou** Alg.
213 D2 **Tiznados** *r.* Venez.
139 I5 **Tiznap He** *r.* China
176 B2 **Tiznit** Morocco
206 D2 **Tizoc** Mex.
181 I2 **Tjaneni** Swaziland
158 L2 **Tjappsåive** Sweden
164 D2 **Tjeukemeer** *l.* Neth.
159 I4 **Tjorhom** Norway
207 E4 **Tlacolula** Mex.
207 F4 **Tlacotalpán** Mex.
206 D2 **Tlahualilo** Mex.
207 E4 **Tlalnepantla** Mex.
207 E4 **Tlapa** Mex.
206 D3 **Tlaquepaque** Mex.
207 E4 **Tlaxcala** Mex.
207 E4 **Tlaxcala** *state* Mex.
207 E4 **Tlaxiaco** Mex.
176 B1 **Tlemcen** Alg.
180 E4 **Tlhakalatlou** S. Africa
181 H4 **Tlholong** S. Africa
181 F2 **Tlokweng** Botswana
154 C3 **Tnaôt, Prêk** *l.* Cambodia
186 D3 **Toad River** Canada
179 E5 **Toamasina** Madag.
154 □ **Toa Payoh** Sing.
215 D3 **Toay** Arg.
151 E7 **Toba** Japan
154 A5 **Toba, Danau** *l.* Indon.
144 A3 **Toba and Kakar Ranges** *mts* Pak.
210 F1 **Tobago** *i.* Trin. and Tob.
Tobar an Choire Ireland *see* **Tobercurry**
147 E6 **Tobelo** Indon.
163 C3 **Tobercurry** Ireland
191 G3 **Tobermory** Canada
162 B4 **Tobermory** U.K.
153 B4 **Tobias Fornier** Phil.
196 D1 **Tobin, Mount** U.S.A.
187 I4 **Tobin Lake** Canada
203 J1 **Tobique** *r.* Canada
150 F5 **Tobi-shima** *i.* Japan
155 C3 **Toboali** Indon.
138 E1 **Tobyl** Kazakh.
132 H4 **Tobyl** *r.* Kazakh./Russia
211 I5 **Tocantinópolis** Brazil
211 I4 **Tocantins** *r.* Brazil
214 C1 **Tocantinzinha** *r.* Brazil
201 D5 **Toccoa** U.S.A.
144 B2 **Tochi** *r.* Pak.
159 J4 **Töcksfors** Sweden
212 B2 **Tocopilla** Chile
127 F5 **Tocumwal** Australia
213 C2 **Tocuyo** *r.* Venez.
170 E3 **Todi** Italy
168 D7 **Todi** *mt.* Switz.
139 J3 **Todog** China
150 H5 **Todoga-saki** *pt* Japan
150 G4 **Todohokke** Japan
210 E7 **Todos Santos** Bol.
206 B3 **Todos Santos** Mex.
196 D6 **Todos Santos, Bahía de** *b.* Mex.
186 G4 **Tofield** Canada
186 D5 **Tofino** Canada
162 □ **Toft** U.K.
190 B2 **Tofte** U.S.A.
125 I3 **Tofua** *i.* Tonga
147 E7 **Togian, Kepulauan** *is* Indon.
176 C4 **Togo** *country* Africa
190 A2 **Togo** U.S.A.
148 D1 **Togrog Ul** China
148 D1 **Togtoh** China
145 H2 **Togton He** *r.* China
138 E3 **Togyz** Kazakh.
197 H4 **Tohatchi** U.S.A.
158 N3 **Toholampi** Fin.
148 B1 **Tohom** China
145 G3 **Toiba** China
159 M3 **Toijala** Fin.
151 B9 **Toi-misaki** *pt* Japan
159 N3 **Toivakka** Fin.
196 D2 **Toiyabe Range** *mts* U.S.A.
139 G5 **Tojikobod** Tajik.
138 C1 **Tok** *r.* Russia
184 D3 **Tok** U.S.A.
151 F6 **Tōkamachi** Japan
128 B7 **Tokanui** N.Z.
177 F3 **Tokar** Sudan
146 E4 **Tokara-rettō** *is* Japan
136 F1 **Tokat** Turkey
152 D4 **Tŏkch'ŏn** N. Korea
125 I2 **Tokelau** *terr.* Pacific Ocean
173 E6 **Tokmak** Ukr.
139 H4 **Tokmok** Kyrg.
128 G3 **Tokomaru Bay** N.Z.
128 E3 **Tokoroa** N.Z.
181 H3 **Tokoza** S. Africa
132 J5 **Toksun** China
139 H4 **Toktogul** Kyrg.
139 H4 **Toktogul Suu Saktagychy** *resr* Kyrg.
139 J3 **Tokty** Kazakh.
151 D7 **Tokushima** Japan
151 F7 **Tōkyō** Japan
(City Plan **104**)
151 F7 **Tōkyō-wan** *b.* Japan
128 G3 **Tolaga Bay** N.Z.
179 E6 **Tôlañaro** Madag.
138 C1 **Tolbazy** Russia
206 I6 **Tolé** Panama
207 E3 **Toleant** *tourist site* Mex.
139 H4 **Tole Bi** Kazakh.
214 B4 **Toledo** Brazil
167 D3 **Toledo** Spain
190 A5 **Toledo** *IA* U.S.A.
202 B4 **Toledo** *OH* U.S.A.
167 D3 **Toledo, Montes de** *mts* Spain
199 E6 **Toledo Bend Reservoir** U.S.A.
215 B3 **Tolhuaca, Parque Nacional** *nat. park* Chile
139 J3 **Toli** China
179 E6 **Toliara** Madag.
213 B3 **Tolima, Nevado del** *vol.* Col.
147 E6 **Tolitoli** Indon.
132 J3 **Tol'ka** Russia
165 L1 **Tollensesee** *l.* Germany
172 D3 **Tolmachevo** Russia
170 E1 **Tolmezzo** Italy
149 □ **Tolo Channel** *Hong Kong* China
149 □ **Tolo Harbour** *b. Hong Kong* China
167 E1 **Tolosa** Spain
191 F3 **Tolsmaville** Canada
162 B2 **Tolsta Head** U.K.
213 B2 **Tolú** Col.
207 E4 **Toluca** Mex.
172 I4 **Tol'yatti** Russia
138 E2 **Tolybay** *Aktyubinskaya Oblast'* Kazakh.
138 E2 **Tolybay** *Aktyubinskaya Oblast'* Kazakh.
190 B4 **Tomah** U.S.A.
190 C3 **Tomahawk** U.S.A.
150 G3 **Tomakomai** Japan
150 G2 **Tomamae** Japan
125 H3 **Tomanivi** *mt.* Fiji
213 E5 **Tomar** Brazil
167 B3 **Tomar** Port.
136 E2 **Tomarza** Turkey
215 F1 **Tomás Gomensoro** Uruguay
169 K5 **Tomaszów Lubelski** Poland
169 J5 **Tomaszów Mazowiecki** Poland
162 E3 **Tomatin** U.K.
206 C4 **Tomatlán** Mex.
201 B6 **Tombigbee** *r.* U.S.A.
178 B4 **Tomboco** Angola
214 D3 **Tombos** Brazil
Tombouctou Mali *see* **Timbuktu**
197 G6 **Tombstone** U.S.A.
179 B5 **Tombua** Angola
181 H1 **Tom Burke** S. Africa
138 F4 **Tomdibuloq** Uzbek.
215 B3 **Tomé** Chile
181 K1 **Tome** Moz.
159 K5 **Tomelilla** Sweden
167 E3 **Tomelloso** Spain
139 F4 **Tomenaryk** Kazakh.
139 H2 **Tomengi Kayrakty** Kazakh.
191 H2 **Tomiko** Canada
127 H4 **Tomingley** Australia
147 E7 **Tomini, Teluk** *g.* Indon.
176 B3 **Tominian** Mali
162 E3 **Tomintoul** U.K.
170 G3 **Tomislavgrad** Bos. & Herz.
158 K2 **Tømmerneset** Norway
133 N4 **Tommot** Russia
213 D4 **Tomo** Col.
213 C3 **Tomo** *r.* Col.
148 D1 **Tomortei** China
133 O3 **Tompo** Russia
124 B4 **Tom Price** Australia
146 A1 **Tomsk** Russia
159 K4 **Tomtabacken** *h.* Sweden
133 P3 **Tomtor** Russia
150 H3 **Tomuraushi-yama** *mt.* Japan
173 G6 **Tomuzlovka** *r.* Russia
207 F4 **Tonalá** Mex.
197 G3 **Tonalea** U.S.A.
210 E4 **Tonantins** Brazil
194 C1 **Tonasket** U.S.A.
140 D5 **Tonb-e Bozorg, Jazīreh-ye** *i.* Iran
161 H6 **Tonbridge** U.K.

Uchte

147 E6 **Tondano** Indon.
159 J5 **Tønder** Denmark
161 E6 **Tone** *r.* U.K.
140 C2 **Tonekābon** Iran
125 I4 **Tonga** *country* Pacific Ocean
126 F6 **Tongala** Australia
149 F5 **Tong'an** China
128 E3 **Tongariro National Park** N.Z.
125 I4 **Tongatapu Group** *is* Tonga
216 H7 **Tonga Trench** *sea feature* S. Pacific Ocean
148 D3 **Tongbai** China
148 D3 **Tongbai Shan** *mts* China
148 E4 **Tongcheng** *Anhui* China
149 D4 **Tongcheng** *Hubei* China
152 D4 **T'ongch'ŏn** N. Korea
148 C3 **Tongchuan** China
149 C5 **Tongdao** China
148 A3 **Tongde** China
164 D4 **Tongeren** Belgium
149 E4 **Tonggu** China
149 D7 **Tonggu Zui** *pt* China
149 B5 **Tonghai** China
150 A2 **Tonghe** China
152 C3 **Tonghua** *Jilin* China
152 C3 **Tonghua** *Jilin* China
148 C4 **Tongjiang** China
152 B2 **Tongjiangkou** China
152 D4 **Tongjosŏn-man** *b.* N. Korea
149 C6 **Tongking, Gulf of** China/Vietnam
149 C4 **Tongliang** China
152 B2 **Tongliao** China
148 E4 **Tongling** China
149 F4 **Tonglu** China
149 B4 **Tongnan** China
126 E3 **Tongo** Australia
126 E3 **Tongo Lake** *salt flat* Australia
153 B5 **Tongquil** *i.* Phil.
149 C5 **Tongren** *Guizhou* China
148 A3 **Tongren** *Qinghai* China
149 E4 **Tongshan** *Hubei* China
Tongshan *Jiangsu* China *see* **Xuzhou**
Tongtian He *r.* China *see* **Yangtze**
162 D2 **Tongue** U.K.
194 F2 **Tongue** *r.* U.S.A.
201 E7 **Tongue of the Ocean** *sea chan.* Bahamas
148 B3 **Tongwei** China
148 B2 **Tongxin** China
148 E4 **Tongyang** China
152 E6 **Tongyeong** S. Korea
152 B1 **Tongyu** China
152 B3 **Tongyuanpu** China
148 E2 **Tongzhou** *Beijing* China
148 F3 **Tongzhou** *Jiangsu* China
149 C4 **Tongzi** China
190 C5 **Tonica** U.S.A.
206 B1 **Tónichi** Mex.
144 C4 **Tonk** India
149 B6 **Tonkin** *reg.* Vietnam
172 H3 **Tonkino** Russia
Tônlé Sab, Bœng *l.* Cambodia *see* **Tonle Sap**
154 B2 **Tonle Sap** *l.* Cambodia
150 G5 **Tōno** Japan
196 D2 **Tonopah** U.S.A.
213 E2 **Tonoro** *r.* Venez.
206 I7 **Tonosí** Panama
179 C6 **Tonota** Botswana
144 D3 **Tons** *r.* India
159 J4 **Tønsberg** Norway
159 I4 **Tonstad** Norway
197 G5 **Tonto National Monument** *nat. park* U.S.A.
145 H5 **Tonzang** Myanmar
127 H2 **Toobeah** Australia
194 D3 **Tooele** U.S.A.
127 J1 **Toogoolawah** Australia
126 E5 **Tooleybuc** Australia
126 A4 **Tooligie** Australia
127 H6 **Tooma** *r.* Australia
127 G7 **Toora** Australia
127 H3 **Tooraweenah** Australia
180 F6 **Toorberg** *mt.* S. Africa
127 I1 **Toowoomba** Australia
197 G6 **Topawa** U.S.A.
196 C2 **Topaz** U.S.A.
139 J1 **Topchikha** Russia
198 E4 **Topeka** U.S.A.
206 C2 **Topia** Mex.
186 D4 **Topley Landing** Canada
165 K2 **Töplitz** Germany
215 B2 **Topocalma, Punta** *pt* Chile
197 E4 **Topock** U.S.A.
168 I6 **Topoľčany** Slovakia
138 B3 **Topoli** Kazakh.
206 B2 **Topolobampo** Mex.
171 L3 **Topolovgrad** Bulg.
158 P2 **Topozero, Ozero** *l.* Russia
194 B2 **Toppenish** U.S.A.
203 J2 **Topsfield** U.S.A.
197 F3 **Toquerville** U.S.A.
171 L5 **Torbalı** Turkey
141 E3 **Torbat-e Ḩeydarīyeh** Iran
141 F3 **Torbat-e Jām** Iran
172 G4 **Torbeyevo** Russia
190 E3 **Torch Lake** U.S.A.
167 D2 **Tordesillas** Spain
158 M2 **Töre** Sweden
167 H1 **Torelló** Spain
164 D2 **Torenberg** *h.* Neth.
165 K3 **Torgau** Germany
139 H2 **Torgay** *Akmolinskaya Oblast'* Kazakh.
138 E2 **Torgay** *Kostanayskaya Oblast'* Kazakh.
173 H5 **Torgun** *r.* Russia
164 B3 **Torhout** Belgium
178 D3 **Torī** Eth.
Torino Italy *see* **Turin**
151 G9 **Tori-shima** *i.* Japan
177 F4 **Torit** South Sudan
214 B2 **Torixoréu** Brazil
137 K3 **Torkamānchāy** Iran
Torkestān, Band-e *mts* Afgh. *see* **Turkistān, Silsilah-ye Band-e**
172 G3 **Tor'kovskoye Vodokhranilishche** *resr* Russia
167 D2 **Tormes** *r.* Spain
158 M2 **Torneälven** *r.* Fin./Sweden
158 L1 **Torneträsk** Sweden
158 L1 **Torneträsk** *l.* Sweden
189 H2 **Torngat Mountains** Canada
189 H2 **Torngat Mountains National Park** *nat. park* Canada
158 N2 **Tornio** Fin.
215 D3 **Tornquist** Arg.
167 D2 **Toro** Spain
206 D2 **Toro, Pico del** *mt.* Mex.
146 F1 **Torom** *r.* Russia
127 I4 **Toronto** Australia
191 H4 **Toronto** Canada (City Plan **113**)
196 D5 **Toro Peak** U.S.A.
172 D3 **Toropets** Russia
178 D3 **Tororo** Uganda
Toros Dağları *mts* Turkey *see* **Taurus Mountains**
162 F3 **Torphins** U.K.
161 D7 **Torquay** U.K.
196 C5 **Torrance** U.S.A.
167 B3 **Torrão** Port.
167 C2 **Torre** *mt.* Port.
167 G2 **Torreblanca** Spain
167 D1 **Torrecerredo** *mt.* Spain
170 F4 **Torre del Greco** Italy
167 D1 **Torrelavega** Spain
167 D4 **Torremolinos** Spain
126 B3 **Torrens, Lake** *imp. l.* Australia
167 F3 **Torrent** Spain
206 D2 **Torreón** Mex.
206 B1 **Torres** Mex.
125 G3 **Torres Islands** Vanuatu
167 B3 **Torres Novas** Port.
124 E2 **Torres Strait** Australia
167 B3 **Torres Vedras** Port.
167 F4 **Torrevieja** Spain
197 G2 **Torrey** U.S.A.
161 C7 **Torridge** *r.* U.K.
162 C3 **Torridon, Loch** *b.* U.K.
167 D3 **Torrijos** Spain
127 I2 **Torrington** Australia
203 G4 **Torrington** *CT* U.S.A.
194 F3 **Torrington** *WY* U.S.A.
167 H1 **Torroella de Montgrí** Spain
159 K3 **Torsby** Sweden
158 □ **Tórshavn** Faroe Is
139 G4 **Tortkol'** Kazakh.
138 E4 **To'rtko'l** Uzbek.
139 H2 **Tortkuduk** Kazakh.
170 C5 **Tortolì** *Sardinia* Italy
170 C2 **Tortona** Italy
167 G2 **Tortosa** Spain
206 I6 **Tortuguero, Parque Nacional** *nat. park* Costa Rica
137 H1 **Tortum** Turkey
139 I4 **Toru-Aygyr** Kyrg.
140 D3 **Ţorūd** Iran
137 G1 **Torul** Turkey
169 I4 **Toruń** Poland
163 C2 **Tory Island** Ireland
163 C2 **Tory Sound** *sea chan.* Ireland
172 E3 **Torzhok** Russia
151 C8 **Tosa** Japan
151 C8 **Tosashimizu** Japan
158 K2 **Tosbotn** Norway
180 E2 **Tosca** S. Africa
170 C3 **Toscano, Arcipelago** *is* Italy
150 G4 **Tōshima-yama** *mt.* Japan
139 G4 **Toshkent** Uzbek.
172 D3 **Tosno** Russia
212 D3 **Tostado** Arg.
165 H1 **Tostedt** Germany
151 B8 **Tosu** Japan
136 E1 **Tosya** Turkey
172 G3 **Tot'ma** Russia
207 E4 **Totolapan** Mex.
138 C1 **Totskoye** Russia
161 F7 **Totton** U.K.
151 D7 **Tottori** Japan
176 B4 **Touba** Côte d'Ivoire
176 A3 **Touba** Senegal
176 B1 **Toubkal, Jebel** *mt.* Morocco
148 B2 **Toudaohu** China
176 B3 **Tougan** Burkina Faso
176 C1 **Touggourt** Alg.
176 A3 **Tougué** Guinea
166 G2 **Toul** France
166 G5 **Toulon** France
166 E5 **Toulouse** France
176 B4 **Toumodi** Côte d'Ivoire
176 B2 **Tounassine, Hamada** *des.* Alg.
Toungoo Myanmar *see* **Taung-ngu**
149 D5 **Toupai** China
154 B1 **Tourakom** Laos
164 B4 **Tourcoing** France
164 B4 **Tournai** Belgium
166 G4 **Tournon-sur-Rhône** France
166 G3 **Tournus** France
211 K5 **Touros** Brazil
166 E3 **Tours** France
180 D6 **Touwsrivier** S. Africa
165 K4 **Toužim** Czech Rep.
213 C2 **Tovar** Venez.
161 F5 **Tove** *r.* U.K.
137 J1 **Tovuz** Azer.
150 G4 **Towada** Japan
150 G5 **Towada-Hachimantai Kokuritsu-kōen** *nat. park* Japan
150 G4 **Towada-ko** *l.* Japan
128 E1 **Towai** N.Z.
203 E4 **Towanda** U.S.A.
197 H3 **Towaoc** U.S.A.
161 G5 **Towcester** U.K.
163 C6 **Tower** Ireland
190 A2 **Tower** U.S.A.
187 I5 **Towner** U.S.A.
196 D3 **Townes Pass** U.S.A.
194 E2 **Townsend** U.S.A.
127 H6 **Townsend, Mount** Australia
124 E3 **Townsville** Australia
147 E7 **Towori, Teluk** *b.* Indon.
202 E5 **Towson** U.S.A.
139 I4 **Toxkan He** *r.* China
150 G3 **Tōya-ko** *l.* Japan
151 E6 **Toyama** Japan
151 E6 **Toyama-wan** *b.* Japan
151 E7 **Toyohashi** Japan
151 E7 **Toyokawa** Japan
151 D7 **Toyonaka** Japan
151 D7 **Toyooka** Japan
151 E7 **Toyota** Japan
139 G4 **To'ytepa** Uzbek.
176 C1 **Tozeur** Tunisia
173 G7 **T'q'ibuli** Georgia
173 G7 **T'q'varcheli** Georgia
164 F5 **Traben** Germany
Trâblous Lebanon *see* **Tripoli**
171 J4 **Trabotivište** Macedonia
137 G1 **Trabzon** Turkey
203 J2 **Tracy** Canada
196 B3 **Tracy** *CA* U.S.A.
198 E2 **Tracy** *MN* U.S.A.
190 A4 **Traer** U.S.A.
167 C4 **Trafalgar, Cabo** *c.* Spain
215 B3 **Traiguén** Chile
186 F5 **Trail** Canada
159 N5 **Trakai** Lith.
172 I2 **Trakt** Russia
163 B5 **Tralee** Ireland
163 B5 **Tralee Bay** Ireland
213 E3 **Tramán Tepuí** *mt.* Venez.
163 D5 **Tramore** Ireland
159 K4 **Tranås** Sweden
212 C3 **Trancas** Arg.
159 K4 **Tranemo** Sweden
162 F5 **Tranent** U.K.
154 A4 **Trang** Thai.
147 F7 **Trangan** *i.* Indon.
149 B6 **Trang An** *tourist site* Vietnam
127 G4 **Trangie** Australia
215 F1 **Tranqueras** Uruguay
129 B5 **Transantarctic Mountains** *mts* Antarctica
187 G4 **Trans Canada Highway** Canada
187 J5 **Transcona** Canada
169 N7 **Transnistria** *disp. terr.* Moldova
171 J2 **Transylvanian Alps** *mts* Romania
170 E5 **Trapani** *Sicily* Italy
127 G7 **Traralgon** Australia
145 G4 **Trashigang** Bhutan
170 E3 **Trasimeno, Lago** *l.* Italy
167 E3 **Trasvase, Canal de** Spain
154 B2 **Trat** Thai.
144 B3 **Tratani** *r.* Pak.
168 F7 **Traunsee** *l.* Austria
168 F7 **Traunstein** Germany
126 E4 **Travellers Lake** *imp. l.* Australia
128 D5 **Travers, Mount** N.Z.
209 G7 **Traversay Islands** S. Sandwich Is
190 E3 **Traverse City** U.S.A.
154 C3 **Tra Vinh** Vietnam
199 D6 **Travis, Lake** U.S.A.
170 G2 **Travnik** Bos. & Herz.
170 F1 **Trbovlje** Slovenia
125 F2 **Treasury Islands** Solomon Is
165 L2 **Trebbin** Germany
168 G6 **Třebíč** Czech Rep.
171 H3 **Trebinje** Bos. & Herz.
169 J6 **Trebišov** Slovakia
170 F2 **Trebnje** Slovenia
165 G5 **Trebur** Germany
165 I3 **Treffurt** Germany
190 B3 **Trego** U.S.A.
162 D4 **Treig, Loch** *l.* U.K.
215 F2 **Treinta y Tres** Uruguay
212 C6 **Trelew** Arg.
159 K5 **Trelleborg** Sweden
164 C4 **Trélon** France
161 C5 **Tremadog Bay** U.K.
188 F4 **Tremblant, Mont** *h.* Canada
170 F3 **Tremiti, Isole** *is* Italy
194 D3 **Tremonton** U.S.A.
167 G1 **Tremp** Spain
190 B3 **Trempealeau** *r.* U.S.A.
161 B7 **Trenance** U.K.
168 I6 **Trenčín** Slovakia
165 H3 **Trendelburg** Germany
215 D2 **Trenque Lauquén** Arg.
160 G4 **Trent** *r.* U.K.
170 D1 **Trento** Italy
191 I3 **Trenton** Canada
198 E3 **Trenton** *MO* U.S.A.
203 F4 **Trenton** *NJ* U.S.A.
161 D6 **Treorchy** U.K.
189 J4 **Trepassey** Canada
215 F2 **Tres Árboles** Uruguay
215 E3 **Tres Arroyos** Arg.
161 A8 **Tresco** *i.* U.K.
214 D3 **Três Corações** Brazil
213 B4 **Tres Esquinas** Col.
162 B4 **Treshnish Isles** U.K.
214 B3 **Três Irmãos, Represa** *resr* Brazil
214 B3 **Três Lagoas** Brazil
212 B7 **Tres Lagos** Arg.
215 D3 **Tres Lomas** Arg.
214 D2 **Três Marias, Represa** *resr* Brazil
215 B4 **Tres Picos** *mt.* Arg.
207 F5 **Tres Picos** Mex.
215 E3 **Tres Picos, Cerro** *mt.* Arg.
195 F4 **Tres Piedras** U.S.A.
214 D3 **Três Pontas** Brazil
212 C7 **Tres Puntas, Cabo** *c.* Arg.
214 D3 **Três Rios** Brazil
207 E4 **Tres Valles** Mex.
207 F4 **Tres Zapotes** *tourist site* Mex.
159 J3 **Tretten** Norway
165 I6 **Treuchtlingen** Germany
165 K2 **Treuenbrietzen** Germany
159 J4 **Treungen** Norway
170 C2 **Treviglio** Italy
170 E2 **Treviso** Italy
161 B7 **Trevose Head** U.K.
127 G9 **Triabunna** Australia
171 L6 **Tria Nisia** *i.* Greece
171 M6 **Trianta** Greece
144 B2 **Tribal Areas** *admin. div.* Pak.
171 H5 **Tricase** Italy
Trichur India *see* **Thrissur**
164 A5 **Tricot** France
127 F4 **Trida** Australia
164 E5 **Trier** Germany
170 E2 **Trieste** Italy
170 E1 **Triglav** *mt.* Slovenia
171 I5 **Trikala** Greece
136 D4 **Trikomon** Cyprus
147 F7 **Trikora, Puncak** *mt.* Indon.
163 E4 **Trim** Ireland
143 C4 **Trincomalee** Sri Lanka
214 C2 **Trindade** Brazil
219 H7 **Trindade, Ilha da** *i.* S. Atlantic Ocean
210 F6 **Trinidad** Bol.
213 C3 **Trinidad** Col.
205 I4 **Trinidad** Cuba
210 F1 **Trinidad** *i.* Trin. and Tob.
215 F2 **Trinidad** Uruguay
195 F4 **Trinidad** U.S.A.
213 E2 **Trinidad and Tobago** *country* Caribbean Sea
189 J4 **Trinity Bay** Canada
184 C4 **Trinity Islands** U.S.A.
196 C1 **Trinity Range** *mts* U.S.A.
201 C5 **Trion** U.S.A.
165 J1 **Tripkau** Germany
171 J6 **Tripoli** Greece
136 E4 **Tripoli** Lebanon
177 D1 **Tripoli** Libya
177 D1 **Tripolitania** *reg.* Libya
143 B4 **Tripunittura** India
145 G5 **Tripura** *state* India
219 I8 **Tristan da Cunha** *i.* S. Atlantic Ocean
144 D3 **Trisul** *mt.* India
145 F4 **Trisul Dam** Nepal
165 I1 **Trittau** Germany
164 E5 **Trittenheim** Germany
Trivandrum India *see* **Thiruvananthapuram**
170 F4 **Trivento** Italy
168 H6 **Trnava** Slovakia
124 F2 **Trobriand Islands** P.N.G.
158 K2 **Trofors** Norway
170 G3 **Trogir** Croatia
170 F4 **Troia** Italy
164 F4 **Troisdorf** Germany
164 D4 **Trois-Ponts** Belgium
189 F4 **Trois-Rivières** Canada
138 E1 **Troitsk** Russia
139 K1 **Troitskoye** *Altayskiy Kray* Russia
138 C1 **Troitskoye** *Orenburgskaya Oblast'* Russia
138 D1 **Troitskoye** *Respublika Bashkortostan* Russia
173 H6 **Troitskoye** *Respublika Kalmykiya-Khalm'g-Tangch* Russia
129 D3 **Troll** *research stn* Antarctica
159 K4 **Trollhättan** Sweden
211 G3 **Trombetas** *r.* Brazil
175 I6 **Tromelin, Île** *i.* Indian Ocean
215 B3 **Tromen, Volcán** *vol.* Arg.
181 F5 **Trompsburg** S. Africa
158 L1 **Tromsø** Norway
196 D4 **Trona** U.S.A.
215 B4 **Tronador, Monte** *mt.* Arg.
158 J3 **Trondheim** Norway
158 J3 **Trondheimsfjorden** *sea chan.* Norway
145 G4 **Trongsa Chhu** *r.* Bhutan
136 D4 **Troödos** Cyprus
162 D5 **Troon** U.K.
214 D1 **Tropeiros, Serra dos** *hills* Brazil
197 F3 **Tropic** U.S.A.
163 E2 **Trostan** *h.* U.K.
162 F3 **Troup Head** U.K.
186 E2 **Trout** *r.* Canada
191 H3 **Trout Creek** Canada
197 F2 **Trout Creek** U.S.A.
186 G3 **Trout Lake** *Alta* Canada
186 E2 **Trout Lake** *N.W.T.* Canada
186 E2 **Trout Lake** *l. N.W.T.* Canada
188 B3 **Trout Lake** *l. Ont.* Canada
190 E2 **Trout Lake** U.S.A.
190 C2 **Trout Lake** *l.* U.S.A.
194 E2 **Trout Peak** U.S.A.
202 E4 **Trout Run** U.S.A.
161 E6 **Trowbridge** U.K.
127 F8 **Trowutta** Australia
171 L5 **Troy** *tourist site* Turkey
201 C6 **Troy** *AL* U.S.A.
194 D2 **Troy** *MT* U.S.A.
203 G3 **Troy** *NH* U.S.A.
203 G3 **Troy** *NY* U.S.A.
202 A4 **Troy** *OH* U.S.A.
202 E4 **Troy** *PA* U.S.A.
171 K3 **Troyan** Bulg.
166 G2 **Troyes** France
196 D4 **Troy Lake** U.S.A.
197 E2 **Troy Peak** U.S.A.
171 I3 **Trstenik** Serbia
173 E4 **Trubchevsk** Russia
167 C1 **Truchas** Spain
172 E3 **Trud** Russia
150 C3 **Trudovoye** Russia
206 H5 **Trujillo** Hond.
210 C5 **Trujillo** Peru
167 D3 **Trujillo** Spain
213 C2 **Trujillo** Venez.
164 F5 **Trulben** Germany
203 G4 **Trumbull** U.S.A.
197 F3 **Trumbull, Mount** U.S.A.
155 A2 **Trumon** Indon.
127 G4 **Trundle** Australia
154 C2 **Trưng Hiêp** Vietnam
149 C6 **Trưng Khanh** China
189 H4 **Truro** Canada
161 B7 **Truro** U.K.
163 C3 **Truskmore** *h.* Ireland
186 E3 **Trutch** Canada
195 F5 **Truth or Consequences** U.S.A.
168 G5 **Trutnov** Czech Rep.
Truva *tourist site* Turkey *see* **Troy**
171 K7 **Trypiti, Akrotirio** *pt* Greece
159 K3 **Trysil** Norway
168 G3 **Trzebiatów** Poland
146 A2 **Tsagaannuur** Mongolia
173 H6 **Tsagan Aman** Russia
173 H6 **Tsagan Nur** Russia
173 G7 **Tsageri** Georgia
137 J1 **Ts'alk'a** Georgia
179 E5 **Tsaratanana, Massif du** *mts* Madag.
171 L3 **Tsarevo** Bulg.
180 B2 **Tsaris Mountains** Namibia
173 H5 **Tsatsa** Russia
180 A3 **Tsaukaib** Namibia
178 D4 **Tsavo East National Park** Kenya
173 G6 **Tselina** Russia
179 B6 **Tses** Namibia
179 C6 **Tsetseng** Botswana
146 C2 **Tsetserleg** *Arhangay* Mongolia
146 B2 **Tsetserleg** *Hövsgöl* Mongolia
179 C6 **Tshabong** Botswana
179 C6 **Tshane** Botswana
178 B4 **Tshela** Dem. Rep. Congo
178 C4 **Tshibala** Dem. Rep. Congo
178 C4 **Tshikapa** Dem. Rep. Congo
178 C4 **Tshikapa** *r.* Dem. Rep. Congo
181 G3 **Tshing** S. Africa
181 I1 **Tshipise** S. Africa
179 C4 **Tshitanzu** Dem. Rep. Congo
178 C4 **Tshofa** Dem. Rep. Congo
181 I2 **Tshokwane** S. Africa
178 C4 **Tshuapa** *r.* Dem. Rep. Congo
Tshwane S. Africa *see* **Pretoria**
173 G6 **Tsimlyansk** Russia
173 G6 **Tsimlyanskoye Vodokhranilishche** *resr* Russia
179 E6 **Tsimmanampesotse, Parc National de** Madag.
180 E3 **Tsineng** S. Africa
Tsingtao China *see* **Qingdao**
149 □ **Tsing Yi** *i. Hong Kong* China
179 E6 **Tsiombe** Madag.
179 E5 **Tsiroanomandidy** Madag.
186 D4 **Tsitsutl Peak** Canada
172 H4 **Tsivil'sk** Russia
173 G7 **Tskhinvali** Georgia
172 G4 **Tsna** *r.* Russia
148 B1 **Tsogttsetsiy** Mongolia
144 D2 **Tsokar Chumo** *l.* India
181 H5 **Tsolo** S. Africa
181 G6 **Tsomo** S. Africa
173 G7 **Ts'q'alt'ubo** Georgia
151 E7 **Tsu** Japan
151 G6 **Tsuchiura** Japan
149 □ **Tsuen Wan** *Hong Kong* China
150 G4 **Tsugarū-kaikyō** *str.* Japan
179 B5 **Tsumeb** Namibia
179 B6 **Tsumis Park** Namibia
179 C5 **Tsumkwe** Namibia
145 G4 **Tsunthang** India
151 E7 **Tsuruga** Japan
151 D8 **Tsurugi-san** *mt.* Japan
150 F5 **Tsuruoka** Japan
151 A7 **Tsushima** Japan
151 A7 **Tsushima** *is* Japan
151 D7 **Tsuyama** Japan
180 D1 **Tswaane** Botswana
181 F4 **Tswaraganang** S. Africa
181 F3 **Tswelelang** S. Africa
169 L4 **Tsyelyakhany** Belarus
158 P1 **Tsypnavolok** Russia
173 E6 **Tsyurupyns'k** Ukr.
147 F7 **Tual** Indon.
163 C4 **Tuam** Ireland
128 D4 **Tuamarina** N.Z.
Tuamotu, Archipel des *is* Fr. Polynesia *see* **Tuamotu Islands**
123 J5 **Tuamotu Islands** Fr. Polynesia
149 B6 **Tuân Giao** Vietnam
154 A5 **Tuangku** *i.* Indon.
173 F6 **Tuapse** Russia
154 □ **Tuas** Sing.
128 A7 **Tuatapere** N.Z.
162 B2 **Tuath, Loch a'** *b.* U.K.
197 G3 **Tuba City** U.S.A.
155 D4 **Tuban** Indon.
212 G3 **Tubarão** Brazil
153 A4 **Tubbataha Reefs** Phil.
Tubbercurry Ireland *see* **Tobercurry**
168 D6 **Tübingen** Germany
176 A4 **Tubmanburg** Liberia
153 B4 **Tubod** Phil.
177 E1 **Tubruq** Libya
217 J7 **Tubuai** *i.* Fr. Polynesia
123 I6 **Tubuai Islands** Fr. Polynesia
211 K6 **Tucano** Brazil
215 B3 **Tucapel, Punta** *pt* Chile
211 G7 **Tucavaca** Bol.
165 K1 **Tüchen** Germany
165 K2 **Tuchheim** Germany
186 D2 **Tuchitua** Canada
203 F5 **Tuckerton** U.S.A.
197 G5 **Tucson** U.S.A.
197 G5 **Tucson Mountains** U.S.A.
213 B2 **Tucuco** *r.* Venez.
195 G5 **Tucumcari** U.S.A.
213 E2 **Tucupita** Venez.
211 I4 **Tucuruí** Brazil
211 I4 **Tucuruí, Represa de** *resr* Brazil
137 L5 **Tū Dār** Iran
167 F1 **Tudela** Spain
167 C2 **Tuela** *r.* Port.
149 □ **Tuen Mun** *Hong Kong* China
145 H4 **Tuensang** India
140 C5 **Ţufayḩ** Saudi Arabia
217 J2 **Tufts Abyssal Plain** *sea feature* N. Pacific Ocean
153 C4 **Tugnug Point** Phil.
153 B2 **Tuguegarao** Phil.
133 O4 **Tugur** Russia
139 K3 **Tugyl** Kazakh.
148 F2 **Tuhai He** *r.* China
154 A5 **Tuhemberua** Indon.
167 B1 **Tui** Spain
206 J6 **Tuira** *r.* Panama
138 D1 **Tukan** Russia
147 E7 **Tukangbesi, Kepulauan** *is* Indon.
188 E2 **Tukarak Island** Canada
139 H5 **Tŭkhtamish** Tajik.
128 F3 **Tukituki** *r.* N.Z.
184 E3 **Tuktoyaktuk** Canada
159 M4 **Tukums** Latvia
141 G3 **Tukzār** Afgh.
207 E3 **Tula** Mex.
172 F4 **Tula** Russia
145 H1 **Tulagt Ar Gol** *r.* China
207 E3 **Tulancingo** Mex.
196 C3 **Tulare** U.S.A.
196 C4 **Tulare Lake Bed** U.S.A.
195 F5 **Tularosa** U.S.A.
143 C2 **Tulasi** *mt.* India
180 C6 **Tulbagh** S. Africa
210 C3 **Tulcán** Ecuador
171 M2 **Tulcea** Romania
173 D5 **Tul'chyn** Ukr.
196 C3 **Tule** *r.* U.S.A.
140 D3 **Tuleh** Iran
145 G4 **Tule La** *pass* Bhutan
187 I2 **Tulemalu Lake** Canada
199 C5 **Tulia** U.S.A.
186 D2 **Tulita** Canada
136 E5 **Ţūlkarm** West Bank
163 C5 **Tulla** Ireland
127 F8 **Tullah** Australia
201 C5 **Tullahoma** U.S.A.
127 G4 **Tullamore** Australia
163 D4 **Tullamore** Ireland
166 E4 **Tulle** France
158 K3 **Tulleråsen** Sweden
127 G4 **Tullibigeal** Australia
199 E6 **Tullos** U.S.A.
163 E5 **Tullow** Ireland
124 E3 **Tully** Australia
163 D3 **Tully** U.K.
203 E3 **Tully** U.S.A.
172 D2 **Tulos** Russia
199 D4 **Tulsa** U.S.A.
172 F4 **Tul'skaya Oblast'** *admin. div.* Russia
213 A3 **Tuluá** Col.
184 B3 **Tuluksak** U.S.A.
207 H3 **Tulum** *tourist site* Mex.
215 C1 **Tulum, Valle de** *val.* Arg.
146 C1 **Tulun** Russia
155 D4 **Tulungagung** Indon.
145 H4 **Tulung La** *pass* China
153 A4 **Tuluran** *i.* Phil.
213 A4 **Tumaco** Col.
181 G3 **Tumahole** S. Africa
173 I6 **Tumak** Russia
143 B3 **Tumakuru** India
159 L4 **Tumba** Sweden
178 B4 **Tumba, Lac** *l.* Dem. Rep. Congo
155 D3 **Tumbangsamba** Indon.
210 B4 **Tumbes** Peru
186 E3 **Tumbler Ridge** Canada
126 B5 **Tumby Bay** Australia
148 B2 **Tumen** *Gansu* China
152 E2 **Tumen** *Jilin* China
152 E2 **Tumen** *r.* China/N. Korea
210 F2 **Tumereng** Guyana
153 A5 **Tumindao** *i.* Phil.
Tumkur India *see* **Tumakuru**
145 G3 **Tum La** *pass* China
162 E4 **Tummel, Loch** *l.* U.K.
146 G2 **Tumnin** *r.* Russia
141 F5 **Tump** Pak.
154 B4 **Tumpat** Malaysia
176 B3 **Tumu** Ghana
211 G3 **Tumucumaque, Parque Indígena do** *nat. park* Brazil
211 G3 **Tumucumaque, Serra** *hills* Brazil
127 H5 **Tumut** Australia
127 H5 **Tumut** *r.* Australia
139 J4 **Tumxuk** China
137 G2 **Tunceli** Turkey
149 D7 **Tunchang** China
127 J4 **Tuncurry** Australia
141 F3 **Tundī** *imp. l.* Afgh.
144 D4 **Tundla** India
179 D5 **Tunduru** Tanz.
171 L3 **Tundzha** *r.* Bulg.
143 B3 **Tungabhadra** *r.* India
143 A3 **Tungabhadra Reservoir** India
145 H3 **Tunga La** China/India
153 B5 **Tungawan** Phil.
149 □ **Tung Chung Wan** *b. Hong Kong* China
158 C2 **Tungnaá** *r.* Iceland
186 D2 **Tungsten (abandoned)** Canada
172 E1 **Tunguda** Russia
149 □ **Tung Wan** *b. Hong Kong* China
143 C2 **Tuni** India
176 D1 **Tunis** Tunisia
170 D6 **Tunis, Golfe de** *g.* Tunisia
176 C1 **Tunisia** *country* Africa
213 B3 **Tunja** Col.
148 D2 **Tunliu** China
158 K2 **Tunnsjøen** *l.* Norway
161 I5 **Tunstall** U.K.
158 O2 **Tuntsa** Fin.
158 O2 **Tuntsayoki** *r.* Fin./Russia
189 G2 **Tunulic** *r.* Canada
189 H2 **Tunungayualok Island** Canada
215 C2 **Tunuyán** Arg.
215 C2 **Tunuyán** *r.* Arg.
148 E3 **Tuo He** *r.* China
148 F2 **Tuoji Dao** *i.* China
154 C3 **Tuŏl Khpós** Cambodia
196 B3 **Tuolumne** U.S.A.
192 B4 **Tuolumne** *r.* U.S.A.
196 C3 **Tuolumne Meadows** U.S.A.
149 B5 **Tuoniang Jiang** *r.* China
Tuotuo He *r.* China *see* **Togton He**
139 I4 **Tüp** Kyrg.
214 B3 **Tupã** Brazil
214 C2 **Tupaciguara** Brazil
137 K3 **Tūp Āghāj** Iran
212 F3 **Tupanciretã** Brazil
213 C3 **Tuparro** *r.* Col.
199 F5 **Tupelo** U.S.A.
210 E8 **Tupiza** Bol.
138 B3 **Tupkaragan, Mys** *pt* Kazakh.
203 F2 **Tupper Lake** U.S.A.
203 F2 **Tupper Lake** *l.* U.S.A.
215 C2 **Tupungato** Arg.
215 C2 **Tupungato, Cerro** *mt.* Arg./Chile
137 J7 **Tuqayyid** *well* Iraq
152 A1 **Tuquan** China
213 A4 **Túquerres** Col.
145 G4 **Tura** India
133 L3 **Tura** Russia
142 B5 **Turabah** Saudi Arabia
213 D3 **Turagua, Serranía** *mt.* Venez.
128 E4 **Turakina** N.Z.
140 E3 **Turan** Iran
146 F1 **Turana, Khrebet** *mts* Russia
128 E3 **Turangi** N.Z.
140 E2 **Turan Lowland** Asia
139 G4 **Turar Ryskulov** Kazakh.
136 G6 **Ţurayf** Saudi Arabia
140 C5 **Ţurayf** *well* Saudi Arabia
159 N4 **Turba** Estonia
213 B2 **Turbaco** Col.
141 F5 **Turbat** Pak.
213 A2 **Turbo** Col.
169 K7 **Turda** Romania
140 C3 **Türeh** Iran
Turfan China *see* **Turpan**
138 E3 **Turgay** *r.* Kazakh.
138 E2 **Turgayskaya Dolina** *val.* Kazakh.
138 E2 **Turgayskaya Stolovaya Strana** *reg.* Kazakh.
136 C2 **Turgut** Turkey
136 A2 **Turgutlu** Turkey
136 F1 **Turhal** Turkey
159 N4 **Türi** Estonia
167 F3 **Turia** *r.* Spain
213 D2 **Turiamo** Venez.
170 B2 **Turin** Italy
150 B2 **Turiy Rog** Russia
173 C5 **Turiys'k** Ukr.
178 D3 **Turkana, Lake** *salt l.* Eth./Kenya
171 L4 **Türkeli Adası** *i.* Turkey
139 G5 **Turkestan Range** *mts* Asia
136 E2 **Turkey** *country* Asia
190 B4 **Turkey** *r.* U.S.A.
173 G5 **Turki** Russia
Turkish Republic of Northern Cyprus *disp. terr.* Asia *see* **Northern Cyprus**
139 G4 **Turkistan** Kazakh.
141 F3 **Turkistān, Silsilah-ye Band-e** *mts* Afgh.
138 E5 **Türkmenabat** Turkm.
Turkmenabat Turkm. *see* **Türkmenabat**
138 C5 **Türkmen Aýlagy** *b.* Turkm.
Turkmenbashi Turkm. *see* **Türkmenbaşy**
138 C4 **Türkmenbaşy** Turkm.
138 C5 **Türkmenbaşy Aýlagy** *b.* Turkm.
136 C2 **Türkmen Dağı** *mt.* Turkey
138 E5 **Türkmengala** Turkm.
Turkmengala Turkm. *see* **Türkmengala**
138 C5 **Turkmenistan** *country* Asia
Turkmenskiy Zaliv *b.* Turkm. *see* **Türkmen Aýlagy**
136 F3 **Türkoğlu** Turkey
205 J4 **Turks and Caicos Islands** *terr.* Caribbean Sea
205 J4 **Turks Islands** Turks and Caicos Is
159 M3 **Turku** Fin.
178 D3 **Turkwel** *watercourse* Kenya
196 B3 **Turlock** U.S.A.
196 B3 **Turlock Lake** U.S.A.
128 F4 **Turnagain, Cape** N.Z.
162 D5 **Turnberry** U.K.
197 G5 **Turnbull, Mount** U.S.A.
207 H4 **Turneffe Islands** *atoll* Belize
191 F3 **Turner** U.S.A.
164 C3 **Turnhout** Belgium
187 H3 **Turnor Lake** Canada
171 K3 **Turnu Măgurele** Romania
127 H4 **Turon** *r.* Australia
172 G3 **Turovets** Russia
146 A2 **Turpan** China
146 A2 **Turpan Pendi** *depr.* China
205 I4 **Turquino, Pico** *mt.* Cuba
162 F3 **Turriff** U.K.
137 J5 **Tursāq** Iraq
Turtkul' Uzbek. *see* **To'rtko'l**
190 B2 **Turtle Flambeau Flowage** *resr* U.S.A.
187 H4 **Turtleford** Canada
190 A3 **Turtle Lake** U.S.A.
139 H4 **Turugart Pass** China/Kyrg.
214 B2 **Turvo** *r. São Paulo* Brazil
214 C3 **Turvo** *r. São Paulo* Brazil
138 D3 **Turysh** Kazakh.
197 F4 **Tusayan** U.S.A.
201 C5 **Tuscaloosa** U.S.A.
202 C4 **Tuscarawas** *r.* U.S.A.
202 E4 **Tuscarora Mountains** *hills* U.S.A.
190 C6 **Tuscola** *IL* U.S.A.
199 D5 **Tuscola** *TX* U.S.A.
201 C5 **Tuskegee** U.S.A.
202 D4 **Tussey Mountains** *hills* U.S.A.
137 I2 **Tutak** Turkey
172 F3 **Tutayev** Russia
143 B4 **Tuticorin** India
198 D4 **Tuttle Creek Reservoir** U.S.A.
168 D7 **Tuttlingen** Germany
185 P2 **Tuttut Nunaat** *reg.* Greenland
125 I3 **Tutuila** *i.* Pacific Ocean
179 C6 **Tutume** Botswana
207 E4 **Tututepec** Mex.
152 D3 **Tuun-bong** *mt.* N. Korea
158 O3 **Tuupovaara** Fin.
158 O3 **Tuusniemi** Fin.
125 H2 **Tuvalu** *country* Pacific Ocean
140 B5 **Tuwayq, Jabal** *hills* Saudi Arabia
206 D4 **Tuxpan** *Jalisco* Mex.
207 E3 **Tuxpan** *Veracruz* Mex.
207 F4 **Tuxtla Gutiérrez** Mex.
213 D2 **Tuy** *r.* Venez.
154 C2 **Tuy Đức** Vietnam
149 B6 **Tuyên Quang** Vietnam
154 D2 **Tuy Hoa** Vietnam
140 C3 **Tūyserkān** Iran
Tŭytepa Uzbek. *see* **To'ytepa**
139 I4 **Tuyyk** Kazakh.
136 D2 **Tuz, Lake** *salt l.* Turkey
Tuz Gölü *salt l.* Turkey *see* **Tuz, Lake**
197 F4 **Tuzigoot National Monument** *nat. park* U.S.A.
137 J4 **Tuz Khurmātū** Iraq
171 H2 **Tuzla** Bos. & Herz.
137 H2 **Tuzla** *r.* Turkey
173 F6 **Tuzlov** *r.* Russia
159 J4 **Tvedestrand** Norway
172 E3 **Tver'** Russia
172 E3 **Tverskaya Oblast'** *admin. div.* Russia
191 I3 **Tweed** Canada
162 F5 **Tweed** *r.* U.K.
127 J2 **Tweed Heads** Australia
186 D4 **Tweedsmuir Provincial Park** Canada
180 C6 **Tweefontein** S. Africa
180 C2 **Twee Rivier** Namibia
164 E2 **Twente** *reg.* Neth.
196 D4 **Twentynine Palms** U.S.A.
189 J4 **Twillingate** Canada
194 D2 **Twin Bridges** U.S.A.
199 C6 **Twin Buttes Reservoir** U.S.A.
189 H3 **Twin Falls** Canada
194 D3 **Twin Falls** U.S.A.
186 F3 **Twin Lakes** Canada
203 H2 **Twin Mountain** U.S.A.
202 C6 **Twin Oaks** U.S.A.
196 B2 **Twin Peak** U.S.A.
165 G2 **Twistringen** Germany
128 C6 **Twizel** N.Z.
127 H6 **Twofold Bay** Australia
197 G4 **Two Guns** U.S.A.
190 B2 **Two Harbors** U.S.A.
187 G4 **Two Hills** Canada
194 D1 **Two Medicine** *r.* U.S.A.
190 D3 **Two Rivers** U.S.A.
145 H5 **Tyao** *r.* India/Myanmar
158 J3 **Tydal** Norway
Tyddewi U.K. *see* **St David's**
202 D5 **Tygart Lake** U.S.A.
202 D5 **Tygart Valley** U.S.A.
146 E1 **Tygda** Russia
199 E5 **Tyler** U.S.A.
199 F6 **Tylertown** U.S.A.
146 E1 **Tynda** Russia
186 A2 **Tyndall Glacier** U.S.A.
162 F4 **Tyne** *r.* U.K.
160 F2 **Tynemouth** U.K.
159 J3 **Tynset** Norway
136 E5 **Tyre** Lebanon
129 B3 **Tyree, Mount** *mt.* Antarctica
158 N2 **Tyrnävä** Fin.
171 J5 **Tyrnavos** Greece
202 D4 **Tyrone** U.S.A.
126 E5 **Tyrrell** *r.* Australia
126 E5 **Tyrrell, Lake** *dry lake* Australia
187 H2 **Tyrrell Lake** Canada
170 D4 **Tyrrhenian Sea** France/Italy
133 P3 **Tyubelyakh** Russia
132 I4 **Tyukalinsk** Russia
138 B3 **Tyulen'i, Ostrova** *is* Kazakh.
138 D1 **Tyul'gan** Russia
132 H4 **Tyumen'** Russia
139 J1 **Tyumentsevo** Russia
133 M3 **Tyung** *r.* Russia
138 F1 **Tyuntyugur** Kazakh.
161 C6 **Tywi** *r.* U.K.
161 C5 **Tywyn** U.K.
181 I1 **Tzaneen** S. Africa
171 K6 **Tzia** *i.* Greece

U

179 C5 **Uamanda** Angola
213 E4 **Uatatás** *r.* Brazil
211 K5 **Uauá** Brazil
213 C4 **Uaupés** *r.* Brazil
207 G4 **Uaxactún** Guat.
140 B4 **U'aywij** *well* Saudi Arabia
137 I7 **U'aywij, Wādī al** *watercourse* Saudi Arabia
214 D3 **Ubá** Brazil
138 F1 **Ubagan** *r.* Kazakh.
214 D2 **Ubaí** Brazil
214 E1 **Ubaitaba** Brazil
178 B3 **Ubangi** *r.* C.A.R./Dem. Rep. Congo
213 B3 **Ubaté** Col.
137 I5 **Ubayyiḍ, Wādī al** *watercourse* Iraq/Saudi Arabia
151 B8 **Ube** Japan
167 E3 **Úbeda** Spain
214 C2 **Uberaba** Brazil
211 G7 **Uberaba, Lagoa** *l.* Bol./Brazil
214 C2 **Uberlândia** Brazil
154 □ **Ubin, Pulau** *i.* Sing.
167 D1 **Ubiña, Peña** *mt.* Spain
154 B1 **Ubolratna, Ang Kep Nam** Thai.
181 J3 **Ubombo** S. Africa
Ubonrat, Angkep Nam *resr* Thai. *see* **Ubolratna, Ang Kep Nam**
154 C2 **Ubon Ratchathani** Thai.
165 G5 **Ubstadt-Weiher** Germany
178 C4 **Ubundu** Dem. Rep. Congo
138 E5 **Üçajy** Turkm.
137 K1 **Ucar** Azer.
210 D5 **Ucayali** *r.* Peru
144 B3 **Uch** Pak.
Uch-Adzhi Turkm. *see* **Üçajy**
138 D1 **Uchaly** Russia
140 C2 **Ūchān** Iran
150 G3 **Uchiura-wan** *b.* Japan
Uchkuduk Uzbek. *see* **Uchquduq**
138 E4 **Uchquduq** Uzbek.
Uchsay Uzbek. *see* **Uchsoy**
138 D4 **Uchsoy** Uzbek.
165 G2 **Uchte** Germany

Uchte

165 J2 **Uchte** *r.* Germany
146 F1 **Uchur** *r.* Russia
161 H7 **Uckfield** U.K.
186 D5 **Ucluelet** Canada
197 H3 **Ucolo** U.S.A.
194 F2 **Ucross** U.S.A.
148 C2 **Ud** China
133 O4 **Uda** *r.* Russia
173 H6 **Udachnoye** Russia
133 M3 **Udachnyy** Russia
143 B4 **Udagamandalam** India
144 C4 **Udaipur** *Rajasthan* India
145 G5 **Udaipur** *Tripura* India
145 E5 **Udanti** *r.* India/Myanmar
143 B3 **Udayagiri** India
159 J4 **Uddevalla** Sweden
162 D5 **Uddingston** U.K.
158 L2 **Uddjaure** *l.* Sweden
164 D3 **Uden** Neth.
143 B2 **Udgir** India
172 H2 **Udimskiy** Russia
170 E1 **Udine** Italy
189 I2 **Udjuktok Bay** Canada
172 E3 **Udomlya** Russia
154 B1 **Udon Thani** Thai.
146 F1 **Udskaya Guba** *b.* Russia
143 B4 **Udumalaippettai** India
143 A3 **Udupi** India
146 F1 **Udyl', Ozero** *l.* Russia
168 G4 **Ueckermünde** Germany
151 F6 **Ueda** Japan
124 C2 **Uekuli** Indon.
178 C3 **Uele** *r.* Dem. Rep. Congo
184 B3 **Uelen** Russia
165 I2 **Uelzen** Germany
178 C3 **Uere** *r.* Dem. Rep. Congo
165 H1 **Uetersen** Germany
165 H5 **Uettingen** Germany
165 I2 **Uetze** Germany
132 G4 **Ufa** Russia
165 I5 **Uffenheim** Germany
179 B6 **Ugab** *watercourse* Namibia
178 D4 **Ugalla** *r.* Tanz.
178 D3 **Uganda** *country* Africa
181 H5 **Ugie** S. Africa
146 G2 **Uglegorsk** Russia
150 C3 **Uglekamensk** Russia
172 F3 **Uglich** Russia
170 F2 **Ugljan** *i.* Croatia
172 E3 **Uglovka** Russia
150 C3 **Uglovoye** Russia
139 J2 **Uglovskoye** Russia
133 P3 **Ugol'noye** Russia
133 S3 **Ugol'nyye Kopi** Russia
172 E4 **Ugra** Russia
139 H4 **Ügüt** Kyrg.
168 H6 **Uherské Hradiště** Czech Rep.
202 C4 **Uhrichsville** U.S.A.
162 B3 **Uig** U.K.
178 B4 **Uíge** Angola
152 D5 **Uijeongbu** S. Korea
152 C3 **Ŭiju** N. Korea
158 O3 **Uimaharju** Fin.
197 F3 **Uinkaret Plateau** U.S.A.
194 E3 **Uinta Mountains** U.S.A.
152 E5 **Uiseong** S. Korea
179 B6 **Uis Mine** Namibia
163 D4 **Uisneach** *h.* Ireland
181 F6 **Uitenhage** S. Africa
164 C2 **Uithoorn** Neth.
164 E1 **Uithuizen** Neth.
189 H2 **Uivak, Cape** Canada
151 D7 **Uji** Japan
151 A9 **Uji-guntō** *is* Japan
144 C5 **Ujjain** India
Ujung Pandang Indon. *see* **Makassar**
181 H4 **uKhahlamba-Drakensberg Park** *nat. park* S. Africa
137 I5 **Ukhaydir** *tourist site* Iraq
145 H4 **Ukhrul** India
172 J2 **Ukhta** Russia
172 J2 **Ukhta** *r.* Russia
127 J2 **Uki** Australia
196 A2 **Ukiah** *CA* U.S.A.
194 C2 **Ukiah** *OR* U.S.A.
185 J3 **Ukkusiksalik National Park** Canada
185 M2 **Ukkusissat** Greenland
159 N5 **Ukmerg** Lith.
173 D5 **Ukraine** *country* Europe
139 J2 **Ukrainka (abandoned)** Kazakh.
172 I2 **Uktym** Russia
151 A8 **Uku-jima** *i.* Japan
180 D1 **Ukwi** Botswana
180 D1 **Ukwi Pan** *salt pan* Botswana
Ulaanbaatar Mongolia *see* **Ulan Bator**
148 D1 **Ulaanbadrah** Mongolia
146 B2 **Ulaangom** Mongolia
127 H4 **Ulan** Australia
148 C2 **Ulan** China
146 C2 **Ulan Bator** Mongolia
139 G3 **Ulanbel'** Kazakh.
148 C1 **Ulan Buh Shamo** *des.* China
173 H6 **Ulan Erge** Russia
146 E2 **Ulanhot** China
148 D1 **Ulan Hua** China
173 H6 **Ulan-Khol** Russia
148 D1 **Ulan Qab** China
148 C1 **Ulansuhai Nur** *l.* China
148 A1 **Ulan Tohoi** China
146 C1 **Ulan-Ude** Russia
145 G2 **Ulan Ul Hu** *l.* China
136 F2 **Ulaş** Turkey
125 G2 **Ulawa Island** Solomon Is
141 E4 **Ulāy, Kūh-e** *h.* Iran
139 J2 **Ul'bi** Kazakh.
159 J4 **Ulefoss** Norway
126 E2 **Ulenia, Lake** *salt flat* Australia
159 N4 **Ülenurme** Estonia
139 F2 **Ul'gili** Kazakh.
143 A2 **Ulhasnagar** India
146 D2 **Uliastai** China
146 B2 **Uliastay** Mongolia
164 C3 **Ulicoten** Neth.
158 P1 **Ulita** *r.* Russia
147 F6 **Ulithi** *atoll* Micronesia
152 E5 **Uljin** S. Korea
139 I4 **Ul'ken Aksu** Kazakh.
139 J2 **Ul'ken Boken** Kazakh.
139 K2 **Ul'ken Naryn** Kazakh.
139 H4 **Ul'ken Sulutor** Kazakh.
127 I5 **Ulladulla** Australia
162 C3 **Ullapool** U.K.
158 M3 **Ullava** Fin.
152 F5 **Ulleung-do** *i.* S. Korea
160 E3 **Ullswater** *l.* U.K.
168 D6 **Ulm** Germany
127 J2 **Ulmarra** Australia
164 E4 **Ulmen** Germany
159 K4 **Ulricehamn** Sweden
164 E1 **Ulrum** Neth.
152 E6 **Ulsan** S. Korea
158 J3 **Ulsberg** Norway
163 D3 **Ulster Canal** Ireland/U.K.
126 E5 **Ultima** Australia
207 G5 **Ulúa** *r.* Hond.
136 B1 **Ulubat Gölü** *l.* Turkey
136 C2 **Uluborlu** Turkey
136 B1 **Uludağ** *mt.* Turkey
139 H5 **Ulugqat** China
154 B5 **Ulu Kali, Gunung** *mt.* Malaysia
184 G2 **Ulukhaktok** Canada
136 E3 **Ulukışla** Turkey
181 I4 **Ulundi** S. Africa
146 A2 **Ulungur Hu** *l.* China
154 □ **Ulu Pandan** Sing.
124 D4 **Uluṟu** *h.* Australia
136 D1 **Ulus** Turkey
162 B4 **Ulva** *i.* U.K.
164 C3 **Ulvenhout** Neth.
160 D3 **Ulverston** U.K.
127 G8 **Ulverstone** Australia
159 K3 **Ulvsjön** Sweden
Ul'yanovo Uzbek. *see* **Dashtobod**
172 I4 **Ul'yanovsk** Russia
172 H4 **Ul'yanovskaya Oblast'** *admin. div.* Russia
199 C4 **Ulysses** U.S.A.
139 F2 **Ulytau** Kazakh.
139 F3 **Ulytau, Gory** *mts* Kazakh.
207 G3 **Umán** Mex.
173 D5 **Uman'** Ukr.
141 G4 **Umarao** Pak.
144 E5 **Umaria** India
144 D6 **Umarkhed** India
143 C2 **Umarkot** India
144 B4 **Umarkot** Pak.
194 C2 **Umatilla** U.S.A.
132 E3 **Umba** Russia
203 H2 **Umbagog Lake** U.S.A.
124 E2 **Umboi** *i.* P.N.G.
158 M3 **Umeå** Sweden
158 L2 **Umeälven** *r.* Sweden
137 K7 **Umgharah** Kuwait
181 I4 **uMhlanga** S. Africa
185 N3 **Umiiviip Kangertiva** *inlet* Greenland
184 H3 **Umingmaktok** Canada
188 E2 **Umiujaq** Canada
181 I5 **Umkomaas** S. Africa
181 I4 **Umlazi** S. Africa
137 J6 **Umma** *tourist site* Iraq
140 D5 **Umm al Qaywayn** U.A.E.
140 C5 **Umm Bāb** Qatar
177 E3 **Umm Keddada** Sudan
137 K6 **Umm Qaşr** Iraq
177 F3 **Umm Ruwaba** Sudan
177 E1 **Umm Sa'ad** Libya
140 C5 **Umm Sa'id** Qatar
140 C5 **Umm Şalāl Muḩammad** Qatar
194 A3 **Umpqua** *r.* U.S.A.
179 B5 **Umpulo** Angola
144 D5 **Umred** India
144 C5 **Umreth** India
181 I5 **Umtentweni** S. Africa
176 C4 **Umuahia** Nigeria
214 B3 **Umuarama** Brazil
181 H5 **Umzimkulu** S. Africa
181 I5 **Umzinto** S. Africa
170 G2 **Una** *r.* Bos. & Herz./Croatia
214 E1 **Una** Brazil
136 F6 **'Unāb, Wādī al** *watercourse* Jordan
214 C2 **Unaí** Brazil
184 B3 **Unalakleet** U.S.A.
162 C2 **Unapool** U.K.
213 D2 **Unare** *r.* Venez.
136 E6 **'Unayzah** Jordan
142 B4 **'Unayzah** Saudi Arabia
137 G5 **'Unayzah, Jabal** *h.* Iraq
195 E4 **Uncompahgre Plateau** U.S.A.
181 H4 **Underberg** S. Africa
126 D5 **Underbool** Australia
198 C2 **Underwood** U.S.A.
172 E4 **Unecha** Russia
127 G4 **Ungarie** Australia
126 B5 **Ungarra** Australia
188 F1 **Ungava, Péninsule d'** *pen.* Canada
189 G2 **Ungava Bay** Canada
173 C6 **Ungheni** Moldova
138 E5 **Unguz, Solonchakovyye Vpadiny** *salt flat* Turkm.
138 D4 **Üngüz Angyrsyndaky Garagum** *des.* Turkm.
172 I3 **Uni** Russia
214 B4 **União da Vitória** Brazil
213 B4 **Unilla** *r.* Col.
210 F4 **Unini** *r.* Brazil
214 A4 **Unión** Para.
203 I2 **Union** *ME* U.S.A.
201 D5 **Union** *SC* U.S.A.
202 C6 **Union** *WV* U.S.A.
197 F4 **Union, Mount** U.S.A.
190 E5 **Union City** *OH* U.S.A.
202 D4 **Union City** *PA* U.S.A.
201 B4 **Union City** *TN* U.S.A.
180 E6 **Uniondale** S. Africa
201 C5 **Union Springs** U.S.A.
202 D5 **Uniontown** U.S.A.
191 F4 **Unionville** U.S.A.
140 D6 **United Arab Emirates** *country* Asia
132 E3 **United Kingdom** *country* Europe
192 D4 **United States of America** *country* N. America
187 H4 **Unity** Canada
203 I2 **Unity** *ME* U.S.A.
194 C2 **Unity** *OR* U.S.A.
144 C5 **Unjha** India
165 F3 **Unna** Germany
144 E4 **Unnao** India
152 C4 **Ŭnp'a** N. Korea
152 C3 **Unsan** N. Korea
152 D4 **Ŭnsan** N. Korea
162 □ **Unst** *i.* U.K.
165 J3 **Unstrut** *r.* Germany
145 G2 **Unuli Horog** China
151 F6 **Uonuma** Japan
143 D1 **Upar Ghat** *reg.* India
213 E2 **Upata** Venez.
179 C4 **Upemba, Lac** *l.* Dem. Rep. Congo
179 C4 **Upemba, Parc National de l'** *nat. park* Dem. Rep. Congo
153 C5 **Upi** Phil.
213 B3 **Upía** *r.* Col.
180 D4 **Upington** S. Africa
144 B5 **Upleta** India
158 O2 **Upoloksha** Russia
Upolu *i.* Samoa *see* **'Upolu**
125 I3 **'Upolu** *i.* Samoa
194 B3 **Upper Alkali Lake** U.S.A.
202 B4 **Upper Arlington** U.S.A.
186 F4 **Upper Arrow Lake** Canada
128 E4 **Upper Hutt** N.Z.
190 B4 **Upper Iowa** *r.* U.S.A.
203 J1 **Upper Kent** Canada
194 B3 **Upper Klamath Lake** U.S.A.
196 A2 **Upper Lake** U.S.A.
186 D2 **Upper Liard** Canada
163 D3 **Upper Lough Erne** *l.* U.K.
202 E5 **Upper Marlboro** U.S.A.
154 □ **Upper Peirce Reservoir** Sing.
189 I4 **Upper Salmon Reservoir** Canada
202 B4 **Upper Sandusky** U.S.A.
203 F2 **Upper Saranac Lake** U.S.A.
128 D4 **Upper Takaka** N.Z.
159 L4 **Uppsala** Sweden
188 B4 **Upsala** Canada
203 H2 **Upton** U.S.A.
137 K7 **'Uqlat al 'Udhaybah** *well* Iraq
137 K6 **Ur** *tourist site* Iraq
213 A2 **Urabá, Golfo de** *b.* Col.
140 E4 **Ūrāf** Iran
150 H3 **Urakawa** Japan
127 G4 **Ural** *h.* Australia
138 B3 **Ural** *r.* Kazakh./Russia
127 I3 **Uralla** Australia
132 G4 **Ural Mountains** Russia
138 B2 **Ural'sk** Kazakh.
Ural'skiy Khrebet *mts* Russia *see* **Ural Mountains**
178 D4 **Urambo** Tanz.
127 G5 **Urana** Australia
127 G5 **Urana, Lake** Australia
214 D1 **Urandi** Brazil
187 H3 **Uranium City** Canada
127 G5 **Uranquinty** Australia
213 E4 **Uraricoera** Brazil
213 E4 **Uraricoera** *r. Roraima* Brazil
213 E4 **Uraricoera** *r.* Brazil
213 E3 **Uraucaima, Serra** *mt.* Brazil
197 H2 **Uravan (abandoned)** U.S.A.
140 B5 **'Urayq ad Duḩūl** *des.* Saudi Arabia
173 F5 **Urazovo** Russia
190 C5 **Urbana** *IL* U.S.A.
202 B4 **Urbana** *OH* U.S.A.
127 J2 **Urbenville** Australia
170 E3 **Urbino** Italy
210 D6 **Urcos** Peru
172 I2 **Urdoma** Russia
160 F3 **Ure** *r.* U.K.
172 H3 **Uren'** Russia
132 I3 **Urengoy** Russia
125 G3 **Uréparapara** *i.* Vanuatu
172 H4 **Urga** *r.* Russia
138 E4 **Urganch** Uzbek.
Urgench Uzbek. *see* **Urganch**
141 H3 **Urgūn-e Kalān** Afgh.
136 E2 **Ürgüp** Turkey
139 F5 **Urgut** Uzbek.
158 N1 **Urho Kekkosen kansallispuisto** *nat. park* Fin.
213 B2 **Uribia** Col.
126 E2 **Urisino** Australia
159 M3 **Urjala** Fin.
164 D2 **Urk** Neth.
173 H7 **Urkarakh** Russia
171 L5 **Urla** Turkey
163 D5 **Urlingford** Ireland
139 G5 **Urmetan** Tajik.
140 B2 **Urmia** Iran
140 B2 **Urmia, Lake** *salt l.* Iran
149 □ **Urmston Road** *sea chan. Hong Kong* China
Uroševac Kosovo *see* **Ferizaj**
145 F3 **Urru Co** *salt l.* China
207 E3 **Ursulo Galván** Mex.
Urt Mongolia *see* **Gurvantes**
206 B2 **Uruáchic** Mex.
214 C1 **Uruaçu** Brazil
206 D4 **Uruapan** Mex.
210 D6 **Urubamba** *r.* Peru
211 G4 **Urucará** Brazil
211 J5 **Uruçuí** Brazil
214 D2 **Urucuia** *r.* Brazil
211 J5 **Uruçuí Preto** *r.* Brazil
211 G4 **Urucurituba** Brazil
212 E3 **Uruguaiana** Brazil
212 E4 **Uruguay** *r.* Arg./Uruguay
215 F2 **Uruguay** *country* S. America
146 A2 **Ürümqi** China
127 J3 **Urunga** Australia
173 G6 **Urup** *r.* Russia
146 H2 **Urup, Ostrov** *i.* Russia
173 H7 **Urus-Martan** Russia
173 G5 **Uryupinsk** Russia
139 J3 **Urzhar** Kazakh.
172 I3 **Urzhum** Russia
171 L2 **Urziceni** Romania
151 B8 **Usa** Japan
172 I4 **Usa** *r.* Russia
136 B2 **Uşak** Turkey
179 B6 **Usakos** Namibia
129 B6 **Usarp Mountains** *mts* Antarctica
212 E8 **Usborne, Mount** *h.* Falkland Is
132 I1 **Ushakova, Ostrov** *i.* Russia
139 J2 **Ushanovo** Kazakh.
139 J3 **Usharal** *Almatinskaya Oblast'* Kazakh.
139 G4 **Usharal** *Zhambylskaya Oblast'* Kazakh.
151 B8 **Ushibuka** Japan
139 I3 **Ushtobe** Kazakh.
212 C8 **Ushuaia** Arg.
165 G4 **Usingen** Germany
132 G3 **Usinsk** Russia
161 E6 **Usk** U.K.
161 E6 **Usk** *r.* U.K.
145 E4 **Uska** India
172 C4 **Uskhodni** Belarus
165 H3 **Uslar** Germany
173 F4 **Usman'** Russia
159 M4 **Usmas ezers** *l.* Latvia
172 I2 **Usogorsk** Russia
146 C1 **Usol'ye-Sibirskoye** Russia
139 I1 **Uspenka** Kazakh.
139 H2 **Uspenskoye** Kazakh.
166 F4 **Ussel** France
150 D1 **Ussuri** *r.* China/Russia
146 F2 **Ussuriysk** Russia
172 H3 **Usta** *r.* Russia
133 L4 **Ust'-Barguzin** Russia
173 G5 **Ust'-Buzulukskaya** Russia
139 J1 **Ust'-Charyshskaya Pristan'** Russia
173 G6 **Ust'-Donetskiy** Russia
170 E5 **Ustica, Isola di** *i. Sicily* Italy
146 C1 **Ust'-Ilimsk** Russia
146 C1 **Ust'-Ilimskoye Vodokhranilishche** *resr* Russia
132 G3 **Ust'-Ilych** Russia
168 G5 **Ústí nad Labem** Czech Rep.
168 H3 **Ustka** Poland
139 J1 **Ust'-Kalmanka** Russia
133 R4 **Ust'-Kamchatsk** Russia
139 J2 **Ust'-Kamenogorsk** Kazakh.
139 K2 **Ust'-Kan** Russia
139 K2 **Ust'-Koksa** Russia
146 C1 **Ust'-Kut** Russia
133 O2 **Ust'-Kuyga** Russia
173 F6 **Ust'-Labinsk** Russia
159 O4 **Ust'-Luga** Russia
133 O3 **Ust'-Maya** Russia
132 G3 **Ust'-Nem** Russia
133 P3 **Ust'-Nera** Russia
172 I2 **Ust'-Ocheya** Russia
133 M2 **Ust'-Olenek** Russia
133 P3 **Ust'-Omchug** Russia
146 C1 **Ust'-Ordynskiy** Russia
132 J3 **Ust'-Port** Russia
172 G2 **Ust'-Shonosha** Russia
132 K2 **Ust'-Tareya** Russia
132 G3 **Ust'-Tsil'ma** Russia
172 H2 **Ust'-Ura** Russia
138 E1 **Ust'-Uyskoye** Kazakh.
172 G2 **Ust'-Vayen'ga** Russia
172 H2 **Ust'-Vyyskaya** Russia
172 G2 **Ust'ya** *r.* Russia
172 F3 **Ust'ye** Russia
172 F3 **Ust'ye** *r.* Russia
138 C3 **Ustyurt Plateau** Kazakh./Uzbek.
172 F3 **Ustyuzhna** Russia
151 B8 **Usuki** Japan
206 G5 **Usulután** El Salvador
207 G4 **Usumacinta** *r.* Guat./Mex.
172 D4 **Usvyaty** Russia
197 G2 **Utah** *state* U.S.A.
197 G1 **Utah Lake** U.S.A.
158 N2 **Utajärvi** Fin.
140 C5 **Utayyiq** Saudi Arabia
159 N5 **Utena** Lith.
133 S3 **Utesiki** Russia
154 B2 **Uthai Thani** Thai.
141 G5 **Uthal** Pak.
154 A2 **U Thong** Thai.
181 I4 **uThukela** *r.* S. Africa
154 C2 **Uthumphon Phisai** Thai.
203 F3 **Utica** U.S.A.
167 F3 **Utiel** Spain
186 F3 **Utikuma Lake** Canada
206 H4 **Utila** Hond.
181 F3 **Utlwanang** S. Africa
145 E4 **Utraula** India
164 D2 **Utrecht** Neth.
181 I3 **Utrecht** S. Africa
167 D4 **Utrera** Spain
158 N1 **Utsjoki** Fin.
151 F6 **Utsunomiya** Japan
173 H6 **Utta** Russia
154 B1 **Uttaradit** Thai.
144 D3 **Uttarakhand** *state* India
144 D4 **Uttar Pradesh** *state* India
161 F5 **Uttoxeter** U.K.
125 G3 **Utupua** *i.* Solomon Is
210 E8 **Uturunco, Cerro** *mt.* Bol.
185 L2 **Uummannaq (abandoned)** Greenland
185 M2 **Uummannaq Fjord** *inlet* Greenland
185 P2 **Uunartoq Qeqertoq** *i.* Greenland
158 N3 **Uurainen** Fin.
159 M3 **Uusikaupunki** Fin.
213 C4 **Uva** *r.* Col.
199 D6 **Uvalde** U.S.A.
173 G5 **Uvarovo** Russia
138 E1 **Uvel'ka** *r.* Russia
178 D4 **Uvinza** Tanz.
181 I5 **Uvongo** S. Africa
146 B1 **Uvs Nuur** *salt l.* Mongolia
151 C8 **Uwajima** Japan
177 E2 **Uweinat, Jebel** *mt.* Sudan
161 G6 **Uxbridge** U.K.
148 C2 **Uxin Ju** China
207 G3 **Uxmal** *tourist site* Mex.
138 E1 **Uy** *r.* Russia
138 E3 **Uyaly** Kazakh.
146 B1 **Uyar** Russia
Üydzin Mongolia *see* **Manlay**
176 C4 **Uyo** Nigeria
212 C2 **Uyuni** Bol.
210 E8 **Uyuni, Salar de** *salt flat* Bol.
172 H4 **Uza** *r.* Russia
137 J4 **'Uẓaym, Nahr al** *r.* Iraq
138 E4 **Uzbekistan** *country* Asia
166 G4 **Uzès** France
173 B5 **Uzhhorod** Ukr.
171 H3 **Užice** Serbia
172 F4 **Uzlovaya** Russia
172 G3 **Uzola** *r.* Russia
136 C3 **Üzümlü** Turkey
139 G5 **Uzun** Uzbek.
139 K3 **Uzunbulak** China
137 K3 **Ūzūn Darreh** *r.* Iran
173 C7 **Uzunköprü** Turkey
173 D5 **Uzyn** Ukr.
139 I4 **Uzynagash** Kazakh.
138 E3 **Uzynkair** Kazakh.
138 F1 **Uzynkol'** Kazakh.

V

159 N3 **Vaajakoski** Fin.
180 H3 **Vaal** *r.* S. Africa
158 N2 **Vaala** Fin.
180 F4 **Vaalbos National Park** S. Africa
181 H3 **Vaal Dam** S. Africa
181 H2 **Vaalwater** S. Africa
158 M3 **Vaasa** Fin.
Vabkent Uzbek. *see* **Vobkent**
169 I7 **Vác** Hungary
212 F3 **Vacaria** Brazil
214 A3 **Vacaria** *r. Mato Grosso do Sul* Brazil
214 D2 **Vacaria** *r. Minas Gerais* Brazil
214 A3 **Vacaria, Serra** *hills* Brazil
196 B2 **Vacaville** U.S.A.
172 G4 **Vad** *r.* Russia
144 C6 **Vada** India
143 A4 **Vadakara** India
159 I4 **Vadla** Norway
144 C5 **Vadodara** India
158 O1 **Vadsø** Norway
168 D7 **Vaduz** Liechtenstein
158 K2 **Værøy** *i.* Norway
172 G2 **Vaga** *r.* Russia
159 J3 **Vågåmo** Norway
170 F2 **Vaganski Vrh** *mt.* Croatia
158 □ **Vágar** *i.* Faroe Is
137 J1 **Vagharshapat** Armenia
158 L2 **Vägsele** Sweden
158 □ **Vágur** Faroe Is
158 M3 **Vähäkyrö** Fin.
140 E4 **Vahhābī** Iran
125 H2 **Vaiaku** Tuvalu
159 N4 **Vaida** Estonia
143 B4 **Vaigai** *r.* India
197 G5 **Vail** U.S.A.
164 B5 **Vailly-sur-Aisne** France
125 H2 **Vaitupu** *i.* Tuvalu
139 H5 **Vakhan** Tajik.
139 G5 **Vakhsh** Tajik.
143 C5 **Valachchenai** Sri Lanka
191 J2 **Val-Barrette** Canada
159 L3 **Valbo** Sweden
215 C4 **Valcheta** Arg.
170 D2 **Valdagno** Italy
172 E3 **Valday** Russia
172 E3 **Valdayskaya Vozvyshennost'** *hills* Russia
167 D3 **Valdecañas, Embalse de** *resr* Spain
159 M4 **Valdemārpils** Latvia
159 L4 **Valdemarsvik** Sweden
167 E3 **Valdepeñas** Spain
166 E2 **Val-de-Reuil** France
215 D4 **Valdés, Península** *pen.* Arg.
191 J3 **Val-des-Bois** Canada
184 D3 **Valdez** U.S.A.
215 B3 **Valdivia** Chile
191 I1 **Val-d'Or** Canada
201 D6 **Valdosta** U.S.A.
159 J3 **Valdres** *val.* Norway
137 I1 **Vale** Georgia
194 C2 **Vale** U.S.A.
186 F4 **Valemount** Canada
214 E1 **Valença** Brazil
166 G4 **Valence** France
167 F3 **Valencia** Spain
167 F3 **Valencia** *reg.* Spain
213 D2 **Valencia** Venez.
167 G3 **Valencia, Golfo de** *g.* Spain
167 C3 **Valencia de Alcántara** Spain
167 D1 **Valencia de Don Juan** Spain
163 A6 **Valencia Island** Ireland
166 F1 **Valenciennes** France
150 D3 **Valentin** Russia
197 F4 **Valentine** *AR* U.S.A.
198 C3 **Valentine** *NE* U.S.A.
199 B6 **Valentine** *TX* U.S.A.
153 B3 **Valenzuela** Phil.
159 J3 **Våler** Norway
213 C2 **Valera** Venez.
139 G1 **Valikhanov** Kazakh.
171 H2 **Valjevo** Serbia
159 N4 **Valka** Latvia
159 N3 **Valkeakoski** Fin.
164 D3 **Valkenswaard** Neth.
173 E5 **Valky** Ukr.
129 D4 **Valkyrie Dome** *ice feature* Antarctica
207 G3 **Valladolid** Mex.
167 D2 **Valladolid** Spain
159 I4 **Valle** Norway
213 D2 **Valle de la Pascua** Venez.
206 D3 **Valle de Santiago** Mex.
213 B2 **Valledupar** Col.
215 C1 **Valle Fértil, Sierra de** *mts* Arg.
210 F7 **Valle Grande** Bol.
207 E2 **Valle Hermoso** Mex.
196 A2 **Vallejo** U.S.A.
207 E4 **Valle Nacional** Mex.
195 F5 **Valles Caldera National Preserve** *res.* U.S.A.
170 F7 **Valletta** Malta
161 C4 **Valley** U.K.
198 D2 **Valley City** U.S.A.
194 B3 **Valley Falls** U.S.A.
202 C5 **Valley Head** U.S.A.
186 F3 **Valleyview** Canada
167 G2 **Valls** Spain
187 H5 **Val Marie** Canada
159 N4 **Valmiera** Latvia
167 E1 **Valnera** *mt.* Spain
172 C4 **Valozhyn** Belarus
188 E4 **Val-Paradis** Canada
214 B3 **Valparaíso** Brazil
215 B2 **Valparaíso** Chile
215 B2 **Valparaíso** *admin. reg.* Chile
206 D3 **Valparaíso** Mex.
190 D5 **Valparaiso** U.S.A.
166 G4 **Valréas** France
147 F7 **Vals, Tanjung** *c.* Indon.
144 C5 **Valsad** India
180 F3 **Valspan** S. Africa
158 O3 **Valtimo** Fin.
173 G6 **Valuyevka** Russia
173 F5 **Valuyki** Russia
167 C4 **Valverde del Camino** Spain
154 C3 **Vam Co Tây** *r.* Vietnam
159 M3 **Vammala** Fin.
143 C2 **Vamsadhara** *r.* India
137 I2 **Van** Turkey
137 I2 **Van, Lake** *salt l.* Turkey
137 J1 **Vanadzor** Armenia
199 E5 **Van Buren** *AR* U.S.A.
203 J1 **Van Buren** *ME* U.S.A.
154 D2 **Vân Canh** Vietnam
203 J2 **Vanceboro** U.S.A.
202 B5 **Vanceburg** U.S.A.
186 E5 **Vancouver** Canada
194 B2 **Vancouver** U.S.A.
186 A2 **Vancouver, Mount** Canada/U.S.A.
186 D5 **Vancouver Island** Canada
200 B4 **Vandalia** *IL* U.S.A.
202 A5 **Vandalia** *OH* U.S.A.
181 G3 **Vanderbijlpark** S. Africa
190 E3 **Vanderbilt** U.S.A.
202 D4 **Vandergrift** U.S.A.
186 E4 **Vanderhoof** Canada
180 F5 **Vanderkloof Dam** *resr* S. Africa
124 D3 **Vanderlin Island** Australia
197 H4 **Vanderwagen** U.S.A.
124 D3 **Van Diemen Gulf** Australia
159 N4 **Vändra** Estonia
159 K4 **Vänern** *l.* Sweden
159 K4 **Vänersborg** Sweden
202 E3 **Van Etten** U.S.A.
179 E6 **Vangaindrano** Madag.
154 D2 **Van Gia** Vietnam
Van Gölü *salt l.* Turkey *see* **Van, Lake**
199 B6 **Van Horn** U.S.A.
191 J3 **Vanier** Canada
125 G3 **Vanikoro Islands** Solomon Is
124 E2 **Vanimo** P.N.G.
146 G2 **Vanino** Russia
143 B3 **Vanivilasa Sagara** *resr* India
143 B3 **Vaniyambadi** India
139 G5 **Vanj** Tajik.
139 G5 **Vanj, Qatorkŭhi** *mts* Tajik.
133 U3 **Vankarem** Russia
203 F2 **Vankleek Hill** Canada
Vanna *i.* Norway *see* **Vannøya**
158 L3 **Vännäs** Sweden
166 C3 **Vannes** France
158 L1 **Vannøya** *i.* Norway
147 F7 **Van Rees, Pegunungan** *mts* Indon.
180 C5 **Vanrhynsdorp** S. Africa
159 K3 **Vansbro** Sweden
159 N3 **Vantaa** Fin.
125 G3 **Vanua Lava** *i.* Vanuatu
125 H3 **Vanua Levu** *i.* Fiji
125 G3 **Vanuatu** *country* Pacific Ocean
202 A4 **Van Wert** U.S.A.
180 D5 **Van Wyksvlei** S. Africa
180 D5 **Van Wyksvlei Dam** *l.* S. Africa
149 B6 **Văn Yên** Vietnam
180 E3 **Van Zylsrus** S. Africa
143 A3 **Varada** *r.* India
159 N4 **Varakļāni** Latvia
140 C3 **Varāmīn** Iran
145 E4 **Varanasi** India
158 O1 **Varangerfjorden** *sea chan.* Norway
158 O1 **Varangerhalvøya** *pen.* Norway
170 G1 **Varaždin** Croatia
159 K4 **Varberg** Sweden
143 B2 **Vardannapet** India
171 J4 **Vardar** *r.* Macedonia
159 J5 **Varde** Denmark
140 B1 **Vardenis** Armenia
158 O1 **Vardø** Norway
165 G1 **Varel** Germany
215 C2 **Varela** Arg.
159 N5 **Varna** Lith.
170 C2 **Varese** Italy
150 C2 **Varfolomeyevka** Russia
159 K4 **Vårgårda** Sweden
214 D3 **Varginha** Brazil
164 D3 **Varik** Neth.
158 N3 **Varkaus** Fin.
171 L3 **Varna** Bulg.
138 E1 **Varna** Russia
159 K4 **Värnamo** Sweden
159 K3 **Värnäs** Sweden
172 H3 **Varnavino** Russia
136 D4 **Varosia (abandoned)** Cyprus
158 N3 **Varpaisjärvi** Fin.
168 I7 **Várpalota** Hungary
137 H2 **Varto** Turkey
145 E4 **Varuna** *r.* India
202 D3 **Varysburg** U.S.A.
140 D3 **Varzaneh** Iran
214 D2 **Várzea da Palma** Brazil
214 A1 **Várzea Grande** Brazil
172 H2 **Vashka** *r.* Russia
172 H2 **Vasil'yevo** Russia
159 N4 **Vasknarva** Estonia
169 M7 **Vaslui** Romania
191 F4 **Vassar** U.S.A.
159 L4 **Västerås** Sweden
159 K3 **Västerdalälven** *r.* Sweden
158 L2 **Västerfjäll** Sweden
159 L4 **Västerhaninge** Sweden
158 L3 **Västernorrland** *county* Sweden
159 L4 **Västervik** Sweden
170 F3 **Vasto** Italy
173 D5 **Vasyl'kiv** Ukr.
166 E3 **Vatan** France
162 A4 **Vatersay** *i.* U.K.
143 A2 **Vathar** India
171 L6 **Vathy** Greece
170 E4 **Vatican City** Europe
158 C2 **Vatnajökull** *ice cap* Iceland
158 C2 **Vatnajökulsþjóðgarður** *nat. park* Iceland
169 L7 **Vatra Dornei** Romania
159 K4 **Vättern** *l.* Sweden
195 F5 **Vaughn** U.S.A.
164 B4 **Vaulx** *tourist site* Belgium
213 C4 **Vaupés** *r.* Col.
166 G5 **Vauvert** France
125 I3 **Vava'u Group** *is* Tonga
Vava'u Group *is* Tonga *see* **Vava'u Group**
176 B4 **Vavoua** Côte d'Ivoire
143 C4 **Vavuniya** Sri Lanka
172 C4 **Vawkavysk** Belarus
159 K4 **Växjö** Sweden
154 B3 **Vay, Đao** *i.* Vietnam
143 B3 **Vayalpad** India
133 S3 **Vayegi** Russia
172 H1 **Vazhgort** Russia
179 E5 **Vazobe** *mt.* Madag.
154 B2 **Véal Vêng** Cambodia
165 G2 **Vechta** Germany
164 E2 **Vechte** *r.* Germany
165 H3 **Veckerhagen (Reinhardshagen)** Germany
143 B4 **Vedaranniyam** India
159 K4 **Veddige** Sweden
171 K3 **Vedea** *r.* Romania
173 H7 **Vedeno** Russia
137 J2 **Vedi** Armenia
215 E2 **Vedia** Arg.
172 E2 **Vedlozero** Russia
190 D5 **Veedersburg** U.S.A.
164 E1 **Veendam** Neth.
164 D2 **Veenendaal** Neth.
158 J2 **Vega** *i.* Norway
199 C5 **Vega** U.S.A.
187 G4 **Vegreville** Canada
144 C3 **Vehari** Pak.
159 N3 **Vehkalahti** Fin.
144 B3 **Vehowa** *r.* Pak.
144 B4 **Veirwaro** Pak.
165 H5 **Veitshöchheim** Germany
167 D4 **Vejer de la Frontera** Spain
159 J5 **Vejle** Denmark
213 B1 **Vela, Cabo de la** *c.* Col.
164 F3 **Velbert** Germany
171 J3 **Velbŭzhdki Prokhod** *pass* Macedonia
180 C6 **Velddrif** S. Africa
170 F2 **Velebit** *mts* Croatia
164 E3 **Velen** Germany
170 F1 **Velenje** Slovenia
171 I4 **Veles** Macedonia
213 B3 **Vélez** Col.
167 D4 **Vélez-Málaga** Spain
167 E4 **Vélez-Rubio** Spain
214 D2 **Velhas** *r.* Brazil
173 H6 **Velichayevskoye** Russia
170 G2 **Velika Gorica** Croatia
171 I2 **Velika Plana** Serbia
172 I3 **Velikaya** Russia
133 S3 **Velikaya** *r.* Russia
172 D3 **Velikaya** *r.* Russia
172 E2 **Velikaya Guba** Russia
150 E2 **Velikaya Kema** Russia
171 L3 **Veliki Preslav** Bulg.
172 D3 **Velikiye Luki** Russia
172 D3 **Velikiy Novgorod** Russia
172 H2 **Velikiy Ustyug** Russia
143 B3 **Velikonda Range** *hills* India
169 P2 **Velikooktyabr'skiy** Russia
171 K3 **Veliko Tarnovo** Bulg.
172 F3 **Velikoye** Russia
172 G4 **Velikoye, Ozero** *l. Ryazanskaya Oblast'* Russia
172 F3 **Velikoye, Ozero** *l. Tverskaya Oblast'* Russia
170 F2 **Veli Lošinj** Croatia
176 A3 **Vélingara** Senegal
169 O3 **Velizh** Russia
168 H7 **Veľký Meder** Slovakia
125 F2 **Vella Lavella** *i.* Solomon Is
143 B4 **Vellar** *r.* India
165 H5 **Vellberg** Germany
165 H3 **Vellmar** Germany
143 B3 **Vellore** India
165 I2 **Velpke** Germany
172 G2 **Vel'sk** Russia
165 L2 **Velten** Germany
164 D2 **Veluwe** *reg.* Neth.
164 E2 **Veluwezoom, Nationaal Park** *nat. park* Neth.
187 I5 **Velva** U.S.A.
219 J8 **Vema Seamount** *sea feature* S. Atlantic Ocean
218 I5 **Vema Trench** *sea feature* Indian Ocean
143 B4 **Vembanad Lake** India
162 D4 **Venachar, Loch** *l.* U.K.
215 E2 **Venado Tuerto** Arg.
170 F4 **Venafro** Italy
213 E3 **Venamo** *r.* Guyana/Venez.
213 E3 **Venamo, Cerro** *mt.* Venez.
166 E3 **Vendôme** France
172 F4 **Venev** Russia
Venezia Italy *see* **Venice**
213 C3 **Venezuela** *country* S. America
213 C2 **Venezuela, Golfo de** *g.* Venez.
219 E4 **Venezuelan Basin** *sea feature* S. Atlantic Ocean
143 A3 **Vengurla** India
170 E2 **Venice** Italy
201 D7 **Venice** U.S.A.
170 E2 **Venice, Gulf of** Europe
166 G4 **Vénissieux** France
143 B3 **Venkatagiri** India
143 C2 **Venkatapuram** India
164 E3 **Venlo** Neth.
159 I4 **Vennesla** Norway
164 D3 **Venray** Neth.
159 M4 **Venta** *r.* Latvia/Lith.
159 M4 **Venta** Lith.
215 D3 **Ventana, Sierra de la** *hills* Arg.
181 G4 **Ventersburg** S. Africa
181 G3 **Ventersdorp** S. Africa
181 F5 **Venterstad** S. Africa
161 F7 **Ventnor** U.K.
166 G4 **Ventoux, Mont** *mt.* France
159 M4 **Ventspils** Latvia
213 D3 **Ventuari** *r.* Venez.
196 C4 **Ventucopa** U.S.A.
196 C4 **Ventura** U.S.A.
126 F7 **Venus Bay** Australia
206 D2 **Venustiano Carranza** Mex.
206 D2 **Venustiano Carranza, Presa** *resr* Mex.
212 D3 **Vera** Arg.
167 F4 **Vera** Spain
207 E4 **Veracruz** Mex.
207 E3 **Veracruz** *state* Mex.
144 B5 **Veraval** India
170 C2 **Verbania** Italy
170 C2 **Vercelli** Italy
158 J3 **Verdalsøra** Norway
215 D4 **Verde** *r.* Arg.
214 C2 **Verde** *r. Goiás* Brazil
214 C2 **Verde** *r. Goiás/Minas Gerais* Brazil
214 B2 **Verde** *r. Mato Grosso do Sul* Brazil
214 B2 **Verde** *r. Minas Gerais* Brazil
192 E6 **Verde** *r.* Mex.
212 E2 **Verde** *r.* Para.
197 G4 **Verde** *r.* U.S.A.
215 D3 **Verde, Península** *pen.* Arg.
214 D1 **Verde Grande** *r.* Brazil
153 B3 **Verde Island Passage** Phil.
165 H2 **Verden (Aller)** Germany
199 E4 **Verdigris** *r.* U.S.A.
166 H5 **Verdon** *r.* France
166 G2 **Verdun** France
181 G3 **Vereeniging** S. Africa
215 G2 **Vergara** Uruguay
203 G2 **Vergennes** U.S.A.
167 C2 **Verín** Spain
173 F6 **Verkhnebakanskiy** Russia
169 P3 **Verkhnedneprovskiy** Russia
132 J3 **Verkhneimbatsk** Russia
158 O1 **Verkhnetulomskiy** Russia
138 D1 **Verkhneural'sk** Russia
133 N3 **Verkhnevilyuysk** Russia
172 D1 **Verkhneye Kuyto, Ozero** *l.* Russia
138 D1 **Verkhniy Avzyan** Russia
173 H5 **Verkhniy Baskunchak** Russia
173 I5 **Verkhniy Kushum** Russia
158 P2 **Verkhnyaya Pirenga, Ozero** *l.* Russia
172 H2 **Verkhnyaya Toyma** Russia
172 G2 **Verkhovazh'ye** Russia
172 F4 **Verkhov'ye** Russia
173 C5 **Verkhovyna** Ukr.
133 O3 **Verkhoyansk** Russia
133 N3 **Verkhoyanskiy Khrebet** *mts* Russia
139 J2 **Verkhuba** Kazakh.
164 B5 **Vermand** France
214 B1 **Vermelho** *r.* Brazil
187 G4 **Vermilion** Canada
190 C5 **Vermilion** *r.* U.S.A.
197 F3 **Vermilion Cliffs** U.S.A.
190 A2 **Vermilion Lake** U.S.A.
190 A2 **Vermilion Range** *hills* U.S.A.
198 D3 **Vermillion** U.S.A.
187 K5 **Vermillion Bay** Canada
203 G3 **Vermont** *state* U.S.A.
129 E2 **Vernadsky** *research stn* Antarctica
194 E3 **Vernal** U.S.A.
191 G2 **Verner** Canada
180 D5 **Verneuk Pan** *salt pan* S. Africa
186 F4 **Vernon** Canada
197 H4 **Vernon** *AR* U.S.A.
203 G4 **Vernon** *CT* U.S.A.
199 D5 **Vernon** *TX* U.S.A.
197 F1 **Vernon** *UT* U.S.A.
201 D7 **Vero Beach** U.S.A.
171 J4 **Veroia** Greece
170 D2 **Verona** Italy
215 F2 **Verónica** Arg.
126 B4 **Verran** Australia
166 F2 **Versailles** France
165 G2 **Versmold** Germany
166 D3 **Vertou** France
181 I4 **Verulam** S. Africa
164 D4 **Verviers** Belgium
166 F2 **Vervins** France
164 C5 **Verzy** France
170 C3 **Vescovato** *Corsica* France
132 G4 **Veselaya, Gora** *mt.* Russia
173 E6 **Vesele** Ukr.
173 G6 **Veselovskoye Vodokhranilishche** *resr* Russia
139 J2 **Veseloyarsk** Russia
138 F1 **Veselyy Podol** Kazakh.
150 D3 **Veselyy Yar** Russia
173 G5 **Veshenskaya** Russia
164 B5 **Vesle** *r.* France
166 H3 **Vesoul** France
164 D3 **Vessem** Neth.
158 K1 **Vesterålen** *is* Norway
158 K1 **Vesterålsfjorden** *sea chan.* Norway
159 J4 **Vestfjorddalen** *val.* Norway
158 K2 **Vestfjorden** *sea chan.* Norway
158 □ **Vestmanna** Faroe Is
158 B3 **Vestmannaeyjar** Iceland

W

Zadonsk

203 E4 **Wysox** U.S.A.
169 J4 **Wyszków** Poland
161 F5 **Wythall** U.K.
202 C6 **Wytheville** U.S.A.
203 I2 **Wytopitlock** U.S.A.

X

178 F2 **Xaafuun** Somalia
138 A4 **Xaçmaz** Azer.
180 E1 **Xade** Botswana
145 H3 **Xagquka** China
144 D1 **Xaidulla** China
154 B1 **Xaignabouli** Laos
145 G3 **Xainza** China
179 D6 **Xai-Xai** Moz.
207 G3 **Xal, Cerro de** *h.* Mex.
207 E4 **Xalapa** Mex.
138 D4 **Xalqobod** Uzbek.
137 L1 **Xaltan Aşırımı** Azer.
148 C1 **Xamba** China
146 B4 **Xamgyi'nyilha** China
147 C4 **Xam Nua** Laos
154 B1 **Xan** *r.* Laos
Xan, Xê *r.* Vietnam *see* **Pe Cô, Krông**
148 E1 **Xanadu, Site of** *tourist site* China
179 C6 **Xanagas** Botswana
148 B1 **Xangd** China
148 D1 **Xangdin Hural** China
Xangdoring China *see* **Xungba**
179 B5 **Xangongo** Angola
137 K2 **Xankändi** Azer.
171 K4 **Xanthi** Greece
210 E6 **Xapuri** Brazil
137 L2 **Xaraba Şăhăr Sayı** *sea feature* Azer.
137 L2 **Xärä Zirä Adası** *is* Azer.
145 F3 **Xarba La** *pass* China
148 F1 **Xar Moron** *r.* China
167 F3 **Xàtiva** Spain
179 C6 **Xau, Lake** Botswana
211 I6 **Xavantes, Serra dos** *hills* Brazil
139 J4 **Xayar** China
139 I5 **Xekargol** China
154 C2 **Xékong** Laos
202 B5 **Xenia** U.S.A.
152 F1 **Xiachengzi** China
149 D6 **Xiachuan Dao** *i.* China
148 B3 **Xiahe** China
148 E2 **Xiajin** China
149 F5 **Xiamen** China
148 C3 **Xi'an** China
149 C4 **Xianfeng** China
148 D3 **Xiangcheng** *Henan* China
148 E3 **Xiangcheng** *Henan* China
Xianggang *Hong Kong* China *see* **Hong Kong**
Xianggang *aut. reg.* China *see* **Hong Kong**
149 F4 **Xiangshan** China
149 D5 **Xiangtan** China
149 D5 **Xiangxiang** China
148 D3 **Xiangyang** China
149 D4 **Xiangyin** China
149 F4 **Xianju** China
149 E4 **Xianning** China
149 D4 **Xiantao** China
149 E5 **Xianxia Ling** *mts* China
148 E2 **Xianxian** China
148 C3 **Xianyang** China
149 F5 **Xianyou** China
149 F4 **Xianyuan** China
148 D4 **Xiaochang** China
149 C6 **Xiaodong** China
149 D4 **Xiaogan** China
146 E1 **Xiao Hinggan Ling** *mts* China
148 B4 **Xiaojin** China
145 H2 **Xiaonanchuan** China
149 F4 **Xiaoshan** China
149 E5 **Xiaotao** China
148 E2 **Xiaowutai Shan** *mt.* China
148 E3 **Xiaoxian** China
149 B4 **Xiaoxiang Ling** *mts* China
Xiaoxita China *see* **Yiling**
149 G4 **Xiaoyang Shan** *is* China
148 D2 **Xiaoyi** China
149 F5 **Xiapu** China
152 A2 **Xiawa** China
148 D3 **Xiayukou** China
149 B5 **Xichang** China
148 B4 **Xichong** China
149 B6 **Xichou** China
148 D3 **Xichuan** China
149 B4 **Xide** China
213 D4 **Xié** *r.* Brazil
154 C1 **Xiêng Lam** Vietnam
149 C6 **Xieyang Dao** *i.* China
148 E3 **Xifei He** *r.* China
Xifeng *Gansu* China *see* **Qingyang**
149 C5 **Xifeng** *Guizhou* China
152 C2 **Xifeng** *Liaoning* China
148 C2 **Xi Ganqu** *r.* China
135 G4 **Xigazê** China
148 C3 **Xihan Shui** *r.* China
148 B3 **Xihe** China
152 A3 **Xi He** *r.* China
148 B3 **Xiji** China
149 D6 **Xi Jiang** *r.* China
145 G2 **Xijir** China
145 G2 **Xijir Ulan Hu** *salt l.* China
148 B2 **Xijishui** China
148 D1 **Xil** China
152 B2 **Xiliao He** *r.* China
149 B5 **Xilin** China
148 B2 **Xilin Gol** China
148 E1 **Xilinhot** China
148 A1 **Ximiao** China
148 C2 **Xin** China
181 J2 **Xinavane** Moz.
152 C3 **Xinbin** China
148 D1 **Xin Bulag** China
148 E3 **Xincai** China
149 F4 **Xinchang** China
149 C5 **Xincheng** *Guangxi Zhuangzu Zizhiqu* China
148 C2 **Xincheng** *Shaanxi* China
148 A2 **Xinchengzi** China
149 D6 **Xindu** *Guangxi Zhuangzu Zizhiqu* China
148 B4 **Xindu** *Sichuan* China
149 E5 **Xinfeng** *Guangdong* China
149 E5 **Xinfeng** *Jiangxi* China
149 E6 **Xinfengjiang Shuiku** *resr* China
149 D5 **Xing'an** China
149 E5 **Xingan** China
152 A4 **Xingang** China
Xingba China *see* **Lhünzê**
148 F1 **Xingcheng** China
149 E5 **Xingguo** China
135 H3 **Xinghai** China
148 D1 **Xinghe** China
148 F3 **Xinghua** China
149 F5 **Xinghua Wan** *b.* China
150 C2 **Xingkai** China
Xingkai Hu *l.* China/Russia *see* **Khanka, Lake**
149 E5 **Xingning** *Guangdong* China
149 D5 **Xingning** *Hunan* China
149 D4 **Xingou** China
148 C3 **Xingping** China
149 B5 **Xingren** China
148 A3 **Xingsagoinba** China
148 D4 **Xingshan** China
148 E2 **Xingtai** China
211 H4 **Xingu** *r.* Brazil
211 H6 **Xingu, Parque Indígena do** *res.* Brazil
149 B4 **Xingwen** China
148 D2 **Xingxian** China
148 D3 **Xingyang** China
149 C6 **Xingye** China
149 B5 **Xingyi** China
149 E4 **Xingzi** China
139 J4 **Xinhe** China
148 E1 **Xin Hot** China
149 D5 **Xinhua** China
148 B2 **Xinhuacun** China
149 C5 **Xinhuang** China
149 D6 **Xinhui** *Guangdong* China
148 F1 **Xinhui** *Nei Mongol Zizhiqu* China
148 A2 **Xining** China
148 E2 **Xinji** China
149 E4 **Xinjian** China
148 D3 **Xinjiang** China
145 D1 **Xinjiang Uygur Zizhiqu** China
145 E1 **Xinjiang Uygur Zizhiqu** *aut. reg.* China
148 C2 **Xinjie** *Nei Mongol Zizhiqu* China
149 B6 **Xinjie** *Yunnan* China
149 B4 **Xinjin** China
152 B1 **Xinkai He** *r.* China
148 D2 **Xinkou** China
152 B3 **Xinmin** China
149 D5 **Xinning** China
149 A5 **Xinping** China
149 E5 **Xinquan** China
149 D5 **Xinshao** China
148 E3 **Xintai** China
149 D5 **Xintian** China
148 E4 **Xinxian** China
148 D3 **Xinxiang** China
149 D6 **Xinxing** China
148 E3 **Xinyang** China
148 D3 **Xinye** China
149 D6 **Xinyi** *Guangdong* China
148 F3 **Xinyi** *Jiangsu* China
148 F3 **Xinyi He** *r.* China
149 C7 **Xinying** China
149 F6 **Xinying** Taiwan
149 E5 **Xinyu** China
139 J4 **Xinyuan** China
148 D2 **Xinzhou** China
149 F5 **Xinzhu** Taiwan
167 C1 **Xinzo de Limia** Spain
152 B3 **Xiongyue** China
148 D3 **Xiping** *Henan* China
148 E3 **Xiping** *Henan* China
148 A3 **Xiqing Shan** *mts* China
211 J6 **Xique-Xique** Brazil
148 C1 **Xishanzui** China
149 C4 **Xishui** *Guizhou* China
149 E4 **Xishui** *Hubei* China
149 F4 **Xiuning** China
149 C4 **Xiushan** China
149 E4 **Xiushui** China
149 E4 **Xiu Shui** *r.* China
149 C5 **Xiuwen** China
148 D3 **Xiuwu** China
152 B3 **Xiuyan** China
149 D6 **Xiuying** China
138 E4 **Xiva** Uzbek.
145 F3 **Xixabangma Feng** *mt.* China
148 D3 **Xixia** *Henan* China
148 C2 **Xixia** *Ningxia Huizu Zizhiqu* China
148 E3 **Xixian** *Henan* China
148 D2 **Xixian** *Shanxi* China
148 C3 **Xixiang** China
Xixón Spain *see* **Gijón/Xixón**
149 F5 **Xiyang Dao** *i.* China
149 B5 **Xiyang Jiang** *r.* China
149 F6 **Xiyuping Yu** *i.* Taiwan
145 G3 **Xizang Zizhiqu** *aut. reg.* China
152 A4 **Xizhong Dao** *i.* China
138 D4 **Xo'jayli** Uzbek.
145 H3 **Xoka** China
Xom An Lôc Vietnam *see* **An Lôc**
139 H4 **Xonobod** Uzbek.
139 G4 **Xovos** Uzbek.
148 F4 **Xuancheng** China
149 C4 **Xuan'en** China
148 C4 **Xuanhan** China
148 B2 **Xuanhe** China
148 E1 **Xuanhua** China
154 C3 **Xuân Lôc** Vietnam
149 B5 **Xuanwei** China
Xuanzhou China *see* **Xuancheng**
148 D3 **Xuchang** China
138 A4 **Xudat** Azer.
178 E3 **Xuddur** Somalia
149 C5 **Xuefeng Shan** *mts* China
149 F5 **Xue Shan** *mt.* Taiwan
145 H2 **Xugui** China
145 E2 **Xungba** China
145 F3 **Xungru** China
148 C3 **Xun He** *r.* China
149 D6 **Xun Jiang** *r.* China
149 E5 **Xunwu** China
148 E3 **Xunxian** China
148 C3 **Xunyang** China
148 C3 **Xunyi** China
149 D5 **Xupu** China
167 F3 **Xúquer, Riu** *r.* Spain
145 F3 **Xuru Co** *l.* China
148 E2 **Xushui** China
149 D6 **Xuwen** China
148 F3 **Xuyi** China
149 B4 **Xuyong** China
148 E3 **Xuzhou** China

Y

149 B4 **Ya'an** China
126 E5 **Yaapeet** Australia
176 C4 **Yabassi** Cameroon
178 D3 **Yabēlo** Eth.
146 C1 **Yablonovyy Khrebet** *mts* Russia
148 B2 **Yabrai** China
148 B2 **Yabrai Shan** *mts* China
136 F5 **Yabrūd** Syria
152 E1 **Yabuli** China
213 C2 **Yacambú, Parque Nacional** *nat. park* Venez.
149 C7 **Yacheng** China
149 C5 **Yachi He** *r.* China
210 E6 **Yacuma** *r.* Bol.
143 B2 **Yadgir** India
193 J4 **Yadkin** *r.* U.S.A.
172 H4 **Yadrin** Russia
177 D1 **Yafran** Libya
148 B1 **Yagan** China
219 E9 **Yaghan Basin** *sea feature* S. Atlantic Ocean
150 G2 **Yagishiri-tō** *i.* Japan
138 C5 **Yagman** Turkm.
177 D3 **Yagoua** Cameroon
145 E3 **Yagra** China
145 H2 **Yagradagzê Feng** *mt.* China
215 F1 **Yaguarí** *r.* Uruguay
207 E4 **Yagul and Mitla, Prehistoric Caves of** *tourist site* Mex.
154 B4 **Yaha** Thai.
136 D2 **Yahşihan** Turkey
136 E2 **Yahyalı** Turkey
141 H4 **Yaḥyá Wēnē Ghar** Afgh.
151 F6 **Yaita** Japan
151 F7 **Yaizu** Japan
149 A4 **Yajiang** China
136 F3 **Yakacık** Turkey
141 G4 **Yakhchāl** Afgh.
194 B2 **Yakima** U.S.A.
194 B2 **Yakima** *r.* U.S.A.
140 D3 **Yakinish** Iran
Yakkabag Uzbek. *see* **Yakkabog'**
139 F5 **Yakkabog'** Uzbek.
141 F4 **Yakmach** Pak.
176 B3 **Yako** Burkina Faso
186 B3 **Yakobi Island** U.S.A.
150 C2 **Yakovlevka** Russia
150 G3 **Yakumo** Japan
151 B9 **Yaku-shima** *i.* Japan
186 B3 **Yakutat** U.S.A.
186 B3 **Yakutat Bay** U.S.A.
133 N3 **Yakutsk** Russia
173 E6 **Yakymivka** Ukr.
154 B4 **Yala** Thai.
191 F4 **Yale** U.S.A.
207 G3 **Yalkubul, Punta** *pt* Mex.
127 G7 **Yallourn** Australia
149 A5 **Yalong Jiang** *r.* China
136 B1 **Yalova** Turkey
173 E6 **Yalta** Crimea
173 F6 **Yalta** Ukr.
152 C3 **Yalu Jiang** *r.* China/N. Korea
152 C4 **Yalujiang Kou** *r. mouth* N. Korea
136 C2 **Yalvaç** Turkey
150 G5 **Yamada** Japan
150 G5 **Yamagata** Japan
151 B9 **Yamagawa** Japan
151 B7 **Yamaguchi** Japan
Yamal, Poluostrov *pen.* Russia *see* **Yamal Peninsula**
132 H2 **Yamal Peninsula** Russia
127 J2 **Yamba** Australia
127 E7 **Yambacoona** Australia
187 G2 **Yamba Lake** Canada
213 C4 **Yambi, Mesa de** *hills* Col.
177 E4 **Yambio** South Sudan
171 L3 **Yambol** Bulg.
132 I3 **Yamburg** Russia
148 A2 **Yamenzhuang** China
151 G6 **Yamizo-san** *mt.* Japan
159 O4 **Yamm** Russia
176 B4 **Yamoussoukro** Côte d'Ivoire
194 E3 **Yampa** *r.* U.S.A.
173 D5 **Yampil'** Ukr.
144 E4 **Yamuna** *r.* India
144 D3 **Yamunanagar** India
139 I2 **Yamyshevo** Kazakh.
145 G3 **Yamzho Yumco** *l.* China
133 O3 **Yana** *r.* Russia
126 D6 **Yanac** Australia
143 C2 **Yanam** India
148 C2 **Yan'an** China
210 D6 **Yanaoca** Peru
142 A5 **Yanbu' al Baḩr** Saudi Arabia
148 F3 **Yancheng** China
124 B5 **Yanchep** Australia
148 C2 **Yanchi** China
148 D2 **Yanchuan** China
127 G5 **Yanco** Australia
126 D3 **Yanco Glen** Australia
127 F3 **Yanda** *watercourse* Australia
126 D3 **Yandama Creek** *watercourse* Australia
176 B3 **Yanfolila** Mali
145 H3 **Ya'ngamdo** China
145 G3 **Yangbajain** China
148 D3 **Yangcheng** China
149 D6 **Yangchun** China
148 E2 **Yangcun** China
152 D4 **Yangdok** N. Korea
152 E5 **Yangdong** *tourist site* South Korea
148 D1 **Yanggao** China
148 E2 **Yanggu** China
148 E1 **Yang He** *r.* China
Yangiabad Uzbek. *see* **Yangiobod**
Yangikishlak Uzbek. *see* **Yangiqishloq**
Yangi-Nishan Uzbek. *see* **Yangi Nishon**
138 F5 **Yangi Nishon** Uzbek.
139 G4 **Yangiobod** Uzbek.
139 F4 **Yangiqishloq** Uzbek.
Yangirabad Uzbek. *see* **Yangirabot**
138 F4 **Yangirabot** Uzbek.
139 G4 **Yangiyo'l** Uzbek.
Yangiyul' Uzbek. *see* **Yangiyo'l**
149 D6 **Yangjiang** China
Yangôn Myanmar *see* **Rangoon**
148 D4 **Yangping** China
148 D2 **Yangquan** China
149 D5 **Yangshan** China
149 D5 **Yangshuo** China
154 D2 **Yang Sin, Chư** *mt.* Vietnam
149 E4 **Yangtze** *r.* China
alt. **Chang Jiang,**
alt. **Jinsha Jiang,**
alt. **Tongtian He,**
alt. **Zhi Qu,**
long **Yangtze Kiang**
178 E2 **Yangudi Rassa National Park** Eth.
149 D6 **Yangxi** China
148 C3 **Yangxian** China
152 E5 **Yangyang** S. Korea
148 E1 **Yangyuan** China
148 F3 **Yangzhou** China
149 C4 **Yanhe** China
148 D2 **Yan He** *r.* China
145 E2 **Yanhuqu** China
126 A4 **Yaninee, Lake** *salt flat* Australia
152 E2 **Yanji** China
149 B4 **Yanjin** China
176 C4 **Yankari National Park** Nigeria
198 D3 **Yankton** U.S.A.
149 D5 **Yanling** China
133 O2 **Yano-Indigirskaya Nizmennost'** *lowland* Russia
213 D3 **Yanomami, Parque Indígena** *nat. park* Brazil
143 C4 **Yan Oya** *r.* Sri Lanka
148 E1 **Yanqing** China
148 E2 **Yanshan** *Hebei* China
149 E4 **Yanshan** *Jiangxi* China
149 B6 **Yanshan** *Yunnan* China
148 E1 **Yan Shan** *mts* China
145 H2 **Yanshiping** China
152 E1 **Yanshou** China
133 O2 **Yanskiy Zaliv** *g.* Russia
127 F2 **Yantabulla** Australia
152 A5 **Yantai** China
126 E2 **Yantara Lake** *salt flat* Australia
169 I3 **Yantarnyy** Russia
152 D2 **Yantongshan** China
149 A5 **Yanyuan** China
148 E3 **Yanzhou** China
176 D4 **Yaoundé** Cameroon
Yaoxian China *see* **Yaozhou**
154 A3 **Yao Yai, Ko** *i.* Thai.
148 C3 **Yaozhou** China
147 F6 **Yap** *i.* Micronesia
213 D4 **Yapacana, Cerro** *mt.* Venez.
147 F7 **Yapen** *i.* Indon.
147 F7 **Yapen, Selat** *sea chan.* Indon.
216 E5 **Yap Trench** *sea feature* N. Pacific Ocean
206 B1 **Yaqui** *r.* Mex.
213 C2 **Yaracuy** *r.* Venez.
124 E4 **Yaraka** Australia
172 H3 **Yaransk** Russia
126 A4 **Yardea** Australia
136 C3 **Yardımcı Burnu** *pt* Turkey
137 L2 **Yardımlı** Azer.
161 I5 **Yare** *r.* U.K.
172 J2 **Yarega** Russia
125 G2 **Yaren** Nauru
172 I2 **Yarensk** Russia
213 B4 **Yari** *r.* Col.
151 E6 **Yariga-take** *mt.* Japan
213 C2 **Yaritagua** Venez.
139 I5 **Yarkant He** *r.* China
191 I3 **Yarker** Canada
144 C1 **Yarkhun** *r.* Pak.
189 G5 **Yarmouth** Canada
161 F7 **Yarmouth** U.K.
203 H4 **Yarmouth Port** U.S.A.
197 F4 **Yarnell** U.S.A.
172 F3 **Yaroslavl'** Russia
172 F3 **Yaroslavskaya Oblast'** *admin. div.* Russia
150 C2 **Yaroslavskiy** Russia
126 F6 **Yarra** *r.* Australia
127 G7 **Yarram** Australia
127 I1 **Yarraman** Australia
145 H3 **Yartö Tra La** *pass* China
132 J3 **Yartsevo** *Krasnoyarskiy Kray* Russia
172 E4 **Yartsevo** *Smolenskaya Oblast'* Russia
213 B3 **Yarumal** Col.
145 F5 **Yasai** *r.* India
125 H3 **Yasawa Group** *is* Fiji
173 F6 **Yasenskaya** Russia
173 G6 **Yashalta** Russia
139 H5 **Yashilkŭl** *l.* Tajik.
173 H6 **Yashkul'** Russia
138 D2 **Yasnyy** Russia
154 C2 **Yasothon** Thai.
127 H5 **Yass** Australia
127 H5 **Yass** *r.* Australia
140 C4 **Yāsūj** Iran
210 C4 **Yasuní, Parque Nacional** *nat. park* Ecuador
136 B3 **Yatağan** Turkey
125 G4 **Yaté** New Caledonia
199 E4 **Yates Center** U.S.A.
187 J2 **Yathkyed Lake** Canada
151 F7 **Yatsuga-take** *vol.* Japan
151 B8 **Yatsushiro** Japan
161 E6 **Yatton** U.K.
149 □ **Yau Tong** *b. Hong Kong* China
210 D5 **Yavarí** *r.* Brazil/Peru
206 B2 **Yávaros** Mex.
144 D5 **Yavatmal** India
137 H2 **Yavi** Turkey
213 D3 **Yaví, Cerro** *mt.* Venez.
173 B5 **Yavoriv** Ukr.
151 C8 **Yawatahama** Japan
145 E1 **Yawatongguz He** *r.* China
145 H5 **Yaw Chaung** *r.* Myanmar
207 G4 **Yaxchilan** *tourist site* Guat.
140 D4 **Yazd** Iran
141 F3 **Yazdān** Iran
136 G2 **Yazıhan** Turkey
199 F5 **Yazoo** *r.* U.S.A.
199 F5 **Yazoo City** U.S.A.
159 J5 **Yding Skovhøj** *h.* Denmark
171 J6 **Ydra** *i.* Greece
154 A2 **Ye** Myanmar
126 F6 **Yea** Australia
161 D7 **Yealmpton** U.K.
139 I5 **Yecheng** China
206 B1 **Yécora** Mex.
201 D7 **Yeehaw Junction** U.S.A.
126 A5 **Yeelanna** Australia
172 F4 **Yefremov** Russia
137 J2 **Yeghegnadzor** Armenia
139 I2 **Yegindybulak** Kazakh.
139 G2 **Yegindykol'** Kazakh.
173 G6 **Yegorlyk** *r.* Russia
173 G6 **Yegorlykskaya** Russia
150 E2 **Yegorova, Mys** *pt* Russia
172 F4 **Yegor'yevsk** Russia
177 F4 **Yei** South Sudan
148 E4 **Yeji** China
132 H4 **Yekaterinburg** Russia
139 H2 **Yekibastuz** Kazakh.
173 G5 **Yelan'** Russia
173 G5 **Yelan'** *r.* Russia
127 I2 **Yelarbon** Australia
138 E5 **Yelbarsli** Turkm.
173 F4 **Yelets** Russia
176 A3 **Yélimané** Mali
162 □ **Yell** *i.* U.K.
143 C2 **Yellandu** India
143 A3 **Yellapur** India
148 E2 **Yellow** *r.* China
190 B3 **Yellow** *r.* U.S.A.
202 D4 **Yellow Creek** U.S.A.
184 G3 **Yellowknife** Canada
127 G4 **Yellow Mountain** *h.* Australia
152 B6 **Yellow Sea** Pacific Ocean
194 F2 **Yellowstone** *r.* U.S.A.
194 E2 **Yellowstone Lake** U.S.A.
194 E2 **Yellowstone National Park** U.S.A.
194 E2 **Yellowtail Reservoir** U.S.A.
162 □ **Yell Sound** *str.* U.K.
Yeloten Turkm. *see* **Ýolöten**
173 D5 **Yel'sk** Belarus
139 J3 **Yel'tay** Kazakh.
185 J1 **Yelverton Bay** Canada
139 J3 **Yemel'** *r.* Kazakh.
178 C7 **Yemen** *country* Asia
172 G2 **Yemetsk** Russia
172 G2 **Yemtsa** Russia
172 I2 **Yemva** Russia
158 O2 **Yena** Russia
176 C4 **Yenagoa** Nigeria
173 F5 **Yenakiyeve** Ukr.
145 H5 **Yenangyat** Myanmar
145 H5 **Yenangyaung** Myanmar
145 H6 **Yenanma** Myanmar
149 B6 **Yên Bai** Vietnam
139 I2 **Yenbek** Kazakh.
149 B6 **Yên Châu** Vietnam
127 G5 **Yenda** Australia
176 B4 **Yendi** Ghana
178 B4 **Yénéganou** Congo
137 K3 **Yengejeh** Iran
139 I5 **Yengisar** China
136 D1 **Yeniçağa** Turkey
171 L5 **Yenice** *Çanakkale* Turkey
136 E3 **Yenice** *Mersin* Turkey
136 D2 **Yeniceoba** Turkey
136 B1 **Yenişehir** Turkey
132 K4 **Yenisey** *r.* Russia
132 K4 **Yeniseysk** Russia
132 K4 **Yeniseyskaya Ravnina** *ridge* Russia
132 I2 **Yeniseyskiy Zaliv** *inlet* Russia
149 B6 **Yên Minh** Vietnam
173 H6 **Yenotayevka** Russia
152 D5 **Yeoju** S. Korea
144 C5 **Yeola** India
152 D6 **Yeongam** S. Korea
152 E6 **Yeongcheon** S. Korea
152 E5 **Yeongdeok** S. Korea
152 D6 **Yeonggwang** S. Korea
152 E5 **Yeongju** S. Korea
152 D6 **Yeongsan-gang** *r.* S. Korea
152 D6 **Yeongsanpo** S. Korea
152 E5 **Yeongwol** S. Korea
152 D6 **Yeosu** S. Korea
Yeotmal India *see* **Yavatmal**
127 H4 **Yeoval** Australia
161 E7 **Yeovil** U.K.
206 B1 **Yepachi** Mex.
124 F4 **Yeppoon** Australia
138 D5 **Yerbent** Turkm.
133 L3 **Yerbogachen** Russia
137 J1 **Yerevan** Armenia
139 H2 **Yereymentau** Kazakh.
139 H2 **Yereymentau, Gory** *hills* Kazakh.
173 H6 **Yergeni** *hills* Russia
196 C2 **Yerington** U.S.A.
136 E2 **Yerköy** Turkey
143 A2 **Yerla** *r.* India
220 A1 **Yermak Plateau** *sea feature* Arctic Ocean
206 C2 **Yermo** Mex.
196 D4 **Yermo** U.S.A.
173 I5 **Yershov** Russia
139 H1 **Yertis** Kazakh.
Yertis *r.* Kazakh./Russia *see* **Irtysh**
172 G2 **Yertsevo** Russia
Yerushalayim Israel/West Bank *see* **Jerusalem**
173 H5 **Yeruslan** *r.* Russia
152 D5 **Yesan** S. Korea
138 B2 **Yesbol** Kazakh.
139 I4 **Yesik** Kazakh.
138 F2 **Yesil'** Kazakh.
139 F1 **Yesil'** *r.* Russia
136 E2 **Yeşilhisar** Turkey
136 F1 **Yeşilırmak** *r.* Turkey
136 B3 **Yeşilova** Turkey
138 C3 **Yeskene** Kazakh.
139 H4 **Yespe** Kazakh.
173 G6 **Yessentuki** Russia
133 L3 **Yessey** Russia
161 C7 **Yes Tor** *h.* U.K.
127 I2 **Yetman** Australia
146 B4 **Ye-U** Myanmar
166 C3 **Yeu, Île d'** *i.* France
137 K1 **Yevlax** Azer.
173 E6 **Yevpatoriya** Crimea
148 D3 **Yexian** China
173 F6 **Yeya** *r.* Russia
145 E1 **Yeyik** China
173 F6 **Yeysk** Russia
172 H1 **Yezhuga** *r.* Russia
172 D4 **Yezyaryshcha** Belarus
215 F2 **Yí** *r.* Uruguay
149 B4 **Yibin** China
145 F2 **Yibug Caka** *salt l.* China
149 D4 **Yichang** China
148 D4 **Yicheng** *Hubei* China
148 D3 **Yicheng** *Shanxi* China
148 D3 **Yichuan** China
146 E2 **Yichun** *Heilongjiang* China
149 E5 **Yichun** *Jiangxi* China
149 E4 **Yifeng** China
148 D3 **Yi He** *r. Henan* China
148 D3 **Yi He** *r. Shandong* China
149 E5 **Yihuang** China
148 C3 **Yijun** China
150 A1 **Yilan** China
171 L4 **Yıldız Dağları** *mts* Turkey
136 F2 **Yıldızeli** Turkey
149 B5 **Yiliang** *Yunnan* China
149 B5 **Yiliang** *Yunnan* China
149 D4 **Yiling** China
149 B6 **Yilong Hu** *l.* China
149 B5 **Yimen** China
152 E1 **Yimianpo** China
148 F3 **Yinan** China
148 C2 **Yinchuan** China
152 C2 **Yingchengzi** China
149 D5 **Yingde** China
149 C7 **Yinggehai** China
148 E3 **Ying He** *r.* China
152 B3 **Yingkou** China
148 B2 **Yingpanshui** China
149 E4 **Yingshan** *Hubei* China
148 C4 **Yingshan** *Sichuan* China
148 E3 **Yingshang** China
149 E4 **Yingtan** China
148 D2 **Yingxian** China
139 J4 **Yining** China
149 C5 **Yinjiang** China
145 H5 **Yinmabin** Myanmar
152 C1 **Yinma He** *r.* China
148 C1 **Yin Shan** *mts* China
145 H3 **Yi'ong Zangbo** *r.* China
149 A5 **Yipinglang** China
178 D3 **Yirga Alem** Eth.
148 F2 **Yi Shan** *mt.* China
148 F3 **Yishui** China
154 □ **Yishun** Sing.
152 C2 **Yitong** China
152 C1 **Yitong He** *r.* China
146 B2 **Yiwu** China
152 A3 **Yiwulü Shan** *mts* China
149 E4 **Yixian** *Anhui* China
152 A3 **Yixian** *Liaoning* China
148 F4 **Yixing** China
149 D4 **Yiyang** *Hunan* China
149 E4 **Yiyang** *Jiangxi* China
149 D5 **Yizhang** China
149 C5 **Yizhou** China
159 M3 **Yläne** Fin.
158 M3 **Ylihärmä** Fin.
158 N2 **Yli-Ii** Fin.
158 N2 **Yli-Kärppä** Fin.
158 N2 **Ylikiiminki** Fin.
158 O2 **Yli-Kitka** *l.* Fin.
158 M3 **Ylistaro** Fin.
158 M2 **Ylitornio** Fin.
158 N2 **Ylivieska** Fin.
159 M3 **Ylöjärvi** Fin.
139 G2 **Yntaly** Kazakh.
199 D6 **Yoakum** U.S.A.
150 G3 **Yobetsu-dake** *vol.* Japan
155 D4 **Yogyakarta** Indon.
186 F4 **Yoho National Park** Canada
177 D4 **Yokadouma** Cameroon
151 E7 **Yokkaichi** Japan
177 D4 **Yoko** Cameroon
151 F7 **Yokohama** Japan
151 F7 **Yokosuka** Japan
150 G5 **Yokote** Japan
150 G4 **Yokotsu-dake** *mt.* Japan
177 D4 **Yola** Nigeria
138 E5 **Ýolöten** Turkm.
207 E4 **Yoloxóchitl** Mex.
154 B2 **Yom, Mae Nam** *r.* Thai.
176 B4 **Yomou** Guinea
152 D5 **Yŏnan** N. Korea
151 G6 **Yonezawa** Japan
126 C4 **Yongala** Australia
149 E5 **Yong'an** China
148 A2 **Yongchang** China
148 E3 **Yongcheng** China
149 F5 **Yongchun** China
148 B2 **Yongdeng** China
149 E5 **Yongding** China
148 E2 **Yongdinghe Ganqu** *r.* China
149 E5 **Yongfeng** China
149 C5 **Yongfu** China
145 H3 **Yonggyap La** *pass* India
152 D4 **Yŏnghŭng** N. Korea
152 D4 **Yŏnghŭng-man** *b.* N. Korea
152 D2 **Yongji** China
149 F4 **Yongjia** China
148 B3 **Yongjing** China
148 D2 **Yongjin Qu** *r.* China
149 F4 **Yongkang** China
152 C3 **Yongling** China
148 E2 **Yongnian** China
149 C6 **Yongning** China
149 A5 **Yongren** China
149 C4 **Yongshun** China
149 F5 **Yongtai** China
149 E5 **Yongxin** China
149 D5 **Yongxing** China
149 E4 **Yongxiu** China
149 D5 **Yongzhou** China
152 D3 **Yŏnhwa-san** *mt.* N. Korea
203 G4 **Yonkers** U.S.A.
166 F2 **Yonne** *r.* France
213 B3 **Yopal** Col.
139 I5 **Yopurga** China
124 B5 **York** Australia
160 F4 **York** U.K.
198 D3 **York** *NE* U.S.A.
202 E5 **York** *PA* U.S.A.
201 D5 **York** *SC* U.S.A.
124 E3 **York, Cape** Australia
160 F3 **York, Vale of** *val.* U.K.
126 B5 **Yorke Peninsula** Australia
126 B5 **Yorketown** Australia
160 E3 **Yorkshire Dales National Park** U.K.
160 G4 **Yorkshire Wolds** *hills* U.K.
187 I4 **Yorkton** Canada
202 E6 **Yorktown** U.S.A.
206 H5 **Yoro** Hond.
176 B3 **Yorosso** Mali
196 C3 **Yosemite National Park** U.S.A.
196 C3 **Yosemite Village** U.S.A.
151 C8 **Yoshino-gawa** *r.* Japan
151 D7 **Yoshino-Kumano Kokuritsu-kōen** *nat. park* Japan
172 H3 **Yoshkar-Ola** Russia
136 E7 **Yotvata** Israel
163 D6 **Youghal** Ireland
202 D5 **Youghiogheny River Lake** U.S.A.
149 C6 **You Jiang** *r.* China
127 H5 **Young** Australia
215 F2 **Young** Uruguay
126 B3 **Younghusband, Lake** *salt flat* Australia
126 C5 **Younghusband Peninsula** Australia
129 B6 **Young Island** *i.* Antarctica
202 C4 **Youngstown** U.S.A.
149 D4 **You Shui** *r.* China
176 B3 **Youvarou** Mali
149 F5 **Youxi** China
149 D5 **Youxian** China
149 C4 **Youyang** China
150 B1 **Youyi** China
148 D2 **Youyu** China
139 G5 **Yovon** Tajik.
127 F1 **Yowah** *watercourse* Australia
136 E2 **Yozgat** Turkey
214 A3 **Ypané** *r.* Para.
214 A3 **Ypé-Jhú** Para.
Ypres Belgium *see* **Ieper**
194 B3 **Yreka** U.S.A.
138 E2 **Yrgyz** Kazakh.
138 E2 **Yrgyz** *r.* Kazakh.
Yr Wyddfa *mt.* U.K. *see* **Snowdon**
164 A4 **Yser** *r.* France
164 D3 **Ysselsteyn** Neth.
159 K5 **Ystad** Sweden
161 D5 **Ystwyth** *r.* U.K.
Ysyk-Köl Kyrg. *see* **Balykchy**
139 I4 **Ysyk-Köl** *salt l.* Kyrg.
162 F3 **Ythan** *r.* U.K.
133 O3 **Ytyk-Kyuyel'** Russia
154 A1 **Yuam, Nam Mae** *r.* Myanmar/Thai.
148 D4 **Yuan'an** China
149 C5 **Yuanbao Shan** *mt.* China
149 D4 **Yuanjiang** *Hunan* China
149 A6 **Yuanjiang** *Yunnan* China
149 D4 **Yuan Jiang** *r. Hunan* China
149 B6 **Yuan Jiang** *r. Yunnan* China
149 F5 **Yuanli** Taiwan
149 D4 **Yuanling** China
149 A5 **Yuanmou** China
148 D2 **Yuanping** China
148 D3 **Yuanqu** China
196 B2 **Yuba** *r.* U.S.A.
196 B2 **Yuba City** U.S.A.
150 G3 **Yūbari** Japan
149 C4 **Yubei** China
207 G4 **Yucatán** *pen.* Mex.
207 G3 **Yucatán** *state* Mex.
204 G4 **Yucatan Channel** Cuba/Mex.
197 E4 **Yucca** U.S.A.
196 D3 **Yucca Lake** U.S.A.
196 D4 **Yucca Valley** U.S.A.
148 E2 **Yucheng** China
133 O4 **Yudoma** *r.* Russia
149 E5 **Yudu** China
149 C4 **Yuechi** China
124 D4 **Yuendumu** Australia
149 □ **Yuen Long** *Hong Kong* China
149 F4 **Yueqing** China
149 E4 **Yuexi** *Anhui* China
149 B4 **Yuexi** *Sichuan* China
149 D4 **Yueyang** China
149 E4 **Yugan** China
132 H3 **Yugorsk** Russia
172 J2 **Yugydtydor** Russia
149 F4 **Yuhuan** China
148 E2 **Yuhuang Ding** *mt.* China
149 E4 **Yujiang** China
149 D6 **Yu Jiang** *r.* China
133 Q3 **Yukagirskoye Ploskogor'ye** *plat.* Russia
136 E2 **Yukarısarıkaya** Turkey
178 B4 **Yuki** Dem. Rep. Congo
186 B2 **Yukon** *admin. div.* Canada
184 C3 **Yukon** *r.* Canada/U.S.A.
137 J3 **Yüksekova** Turkey
138 D1 **Yuldybayevo** Russia
201 D6 **Yulee** U.S.A.
149 F6 **Yuli** Taiwan
149 D6 **Yulin** *Guangxi Zhuangzu Zizhiqu* China
149 C7 **Yulin** *Hainan* China
148 C2 **Yulin** *Shaanxi* China
197 E5 **Yuma** U.S.A.
197 E5 **Yuma Desert** U.S.A.
213 A4 **Yumbo** Col.
139 J3 **Yumin** China
136 E3 **Yumurtalık** Turkey
136 C2 **Yunak** Turkey
149 D6 **Yunan** China
148 E3 **Yuncheng** *Shandong* China
148 D3 **Yuncheng** *Shanxi* China
149 D6 **Yunfu** China
149 B5 **Yungui Gaoyuan** *plat.* China
149 F4 **Yunhe** China
149 D6 **Yunkai Dashan** *mts* China
148 D4 **Yunmeng** China
149 A5 **Yunnan** *prov.* China
148 D4 **Yun Shui** *r.* China
126 C4 **Yunta** Australia
149 D6 **Yunwu Shan** *mts* China
148 D3 **Yunxi** China
148 D3 **Yunxian** China
149 E6 **Yunxiao** China
148 C4 **Yunyang** *Chongqing* China
148 D3 **Yunyang** *Henan* China
149 C5 **Yuping** China
149 F4 **Yuqian** China
148 E1 **Yuqiao Shuiku** *resr* China
149 C5 **Yuqing** China
127 J2 **Yuraygir National Park** Australia
146 A1 **Yurga** Russia
150 G5 **Yurihonjō** Japan
210 C5 **Yurimaguas** Peru
213 E3 **Yuruán** *r.* Venez.
213 E3 **Yuruari** *r.* Venez.
213 C2 **Yurubí, Parque Nacional** *nat. park* Venez.
144 E1 **Yurungkax He** *r.* China
172 I3 **Yur'ya** Russia
172 G3 **Yur'yevets** Russia
172 F3 **Yur'yev-Pol'skiy** Russia
206 H5 **Yuscarán** Hond.
149 F4 **Yushan** China
149 F6 **Yu Shan** *mt.* Taiwan
148 D2 **Yushe** China
172 E1 **Yushkozero** Russia
152 D1 **Yushu** *Jilin* China
146 B3 **Yushu** *Qinghai* China
172 I3 **Yushut** *r.* Russia
173 H6 **Yusta** Russia
137 H1 **Yusufeli** Turkey
148 E3 **Yutai** China
145 E1 **Yutian** China
148 C2 **Yuwang** China
149 B5 **Yuxi** China
148 E2 **Yuxian** *Hebei* China
148 D2 **Yuxian** *Shanxi* China
149 F4 **Yuyao** China
150 G5 **Yuzawa** Japan
172 G3 **Yuzha** Russia
146 D1 **Yuzhno-Muyskiy Khrebet** *mts* Russia
146 G2 **Yuzhno-Sakhalinsk** Russia
173 H6 **Yuzhno-Sukhokumsk** Russia
173 D6 **Yuzhnoukrayins'k** Ukr.
138 E1 **Yuzhnoural'sk** Russia
173 G6 **Yuzhnyy** Russia
132 G2 **Yuzhnyy, Ostrov** *i.* Russia
139 G4 **Yuzhnyy Kazakhstan** *admin. div.* Kazakh.
138 D1 **Yuzhnyy Ural** *mts* Russia
148 B3 **Yuzhong** China
148 D3 **Yuzhou** China
Yuzkuduk Uzbek. *see* **Yuzquduq**
138 E4 **Yuzquduq** Uzbek.
168 C7 **Yverdon-les-Bains** Switz.
166 E2 **Yvetot** France
154 A1 **Ywathit** Myanmar
Ylanly Turkm. *see* **Gurbansoltan Eje**

Z

Zaamin Uzbek. *see* **Zomin**
164 C2 **Zaandam** Neth.
137 I3 **Zāb al Kabīr, Nahr az** *r.* Iraq
137 I4 **Zāb aş Şaghīr, Nahr az** *r.* Iraq
146 D2 **Zabaykal'sk** Russia
140 B2 **Zab-e Kuchek** *r.* Iran
142 B7 **Zabīd** Yemen
Zābolī *Sīstān va Balūchestān* Iran *see* **Mehrestān**
141 F5 **Zābolī** *Sīstān va Balūchestān* Iran
138 B3 **Zaburun'ye** Kazakh.
207 G5 **Zacapa** Guat.
206 D4 **Zacapu** Mex.
206 D3 **Zacatecas** Mex.
206 D3 **Zacatecas** *state* Mex.
207 E4 **Zacatlán** Mex.
138 B2 **Zachagansk** Kazakh.
171 I6 **Zacharo** Greece
170 F2 **Zadar** Croatia
154 A3 **Zadetkale Kyun** *i.* Myanmar
154 A3 **Zadetkyi Kyun** *i.* Myanmar
145 H2 **Zadoi** China
173 F4 **Zadonsk** Russia

Ẕafarābād

137 K4 **Ẕafarābād** Iran
167 C3 **Zafra** Spain
140 E3 **Zaghdeh** *well* Iran
137 L5 **Zāgheh** Iran
170 D6 **Zaghouan** Tunisia
170 F2 **Zagreb** Croatia
Zagros, Kūhhā-ye *mts* Iran *see* **Zagros Mountains**
140 B3 **Zagros Mountains** Iran
145 G3 **Za'gya Zangbo** *r.* China
141 F4 **Zāhedān** Iran
136 E5 **Zahlé** Lebanon
138 E5 **Zāhmet** Turkm.
141 G4 **Zahri Nur Gama** Pak.
Zair Uzbek. *see* **Zoir**
Zaire *country* Africa *see* **Congo, Democratic Republic of the**
171 J3 **Zaječar** Serbia
Zakhmet Turkm. *see* **Zāhmet**
137 I3 **Zākhū/Zaxo** Iraq
177 D3 **Zakouma, Parc National de** *nat. park* Chad
171 I6 **Zakynthos** Greece
171 I6 **Zakynthos** *i.* Greece
168 H7 **Zalaegerszeg** Hungary
168 H7 **Zalai-domsag** *hills* Hungary
167 D3 **Zalamea de la Serena** Spain
169 K7 **Zalău** Romania
172 F3 **Zales'ye** Russia
177 E3 **Zalingei** Sudan
169 L6 **Zalishchyky** Ukr.
172 D3 **Zaluch'ye** Russia
136 E2 **Zamanti** *r.* Turkey
153 B3 **Zambales Mountains** Phil.
179 C5 **Zambeze** *r.* Africa *alt.* **Zambezi (Angola)**
179 D5 **Zambezi** *r.* Angola *alt.* **Zambeze**
179 C5 **Zambezi** Zambia
179 C5 **Zambia** *country* Africa
153 B5 **Zamboanga** Phil.
153 B5 **Zamboanga Peninsula** Phil.
141 F4 **Zamīndāwar** *reg.* Afgh.
210 C4 **Zamora** Ecuador
167 D2 **Zamora** Spain
206 D4 **Zamora de Hidalgo** Mex.
169 K5 **Zamość** Poland
148 A3 **Zamtang** China
213 C2 **Zamuro, Punta** *pt* Venez.
213 E3 **Zamuro, Sierra del** *mts* Venez.
144 D3 **Zanda** China
181 K2 **Zandamela** Moz.
164 C3 **Zandvliet** Belgium
202 C5 **Zanesville** U.S.A.
139 I5 **Zangguy** China
144 D2 **Zangla** India
140 C2 **Zanjān** Iran
137 K3 **Zanjān Rūd** *r.* Iran
144 D2 **Zanskar** *r.* India
144 D2 **Zanskar Mountains** India
Zante *i.* Greece *see* **Zakynthos**
178 D4 **Zanzibar** Tanz.
178 D4 **Zanzibar Island** Tanz.
149 D4 **Zaoshi** China
176 C2 **Zaouatallaz** Alg.
148 D3 **Zaoyang** China
146 B1 **Zaozernyy** Russia
137 I3 **Zap** *r.* Turkey
172 E3 **Zapadnaya Dvina** Russia
172 D4 **Zapadnaya Dvina** *r.* Russia *alt.* **Daugava (Latvia),** *alt.* **Zakhodnyaya Dzvina,** *conv.* **Western Dvina**
171 J4 **Zapadni Rodopi** *mts* Bulg.
Zapadno-Sibirskaya Ravnina *plain* Russia *see* **West Siberian Plain**
139 H4 **Zapadnyy Alamedin, Pik** *mt.* Kyrg.
138 C3 **Zapadnyy Chink Ustyurta** *esc.* Kazakh.
138 C3 **Zapadnyy Chink Ustyurta** *esc.* Kazakh.
138 C4 **Zapadnyy Chink Ustyurta** *esc.* Kazakh.
138 B2 **Zapadnyy Kazakhstan** *admin. div.* Kazakh.
158 P1 **Zapadnyy Kil'din** Russia
135 G1 **Zapadnyy Sayan** *reg.* Russia
215 B3 **Zapala** Arg.
199 D7 **Zapata** U.S.A.
213 B3 **Zapatoca** Col.
213 B2 **Zapatoza, Ciénaga de** *l.* Col.
158 O1 **Zapolyarnyy** Russia
173 E6 **Zaporizhzhya** Ukr.
144 E2 **Zapug** China
137 K1 **Zaqatala** Azer.
145 H2 **Zaqên** China
145 H2 **Za Qu** *r.* China
136 F2 **Zara** Turkey
137 J2 **Zarābād** Iran
Zarafshan Uzbek. *see* **Zarafshon**
139 G5 **Zarafshon** Tajik.
138 F4 **Zarafshon** Uzbek.
138 F5 **Zarafshon** *r.* Uzbek.
139 F5 **Zarafshon, Qatorkŭhi** *mts* Tajik.
213 B3 **Zaragoza** Col.
195 F6 **Zaragoza** *Chihuahua* Mex.
206 D1 **Zaragoza** *Coahuila* Mex.
167 F2 **Zaragoza** Spain
141 H3 **Zaṟah Sharan** Afgh.
140 E4 **Zarand** Iran
136 E6 **Zaranikh Protected Area** *nature res.* Egypt
141 F4 **Zaranj** Afgh.
159 N5 **Zarasai** Lith.
215 E2 **Zárate** Arg.
213 D2 **Zaraza** Venez.
Zarbdar Uzbek. *see* **Zarbdor**
139 G4 **Zarbdor** Uzbek.
137 K1 **Zārdab** Azer.
158 O2 **Zarechensk** Russia
137 L4 **Zāreh** Iran
186 C3 **Zarembo Island** U.S.A.
141 H3 **Zarghūn Shahr** Afgh.
144 A3 **Zargun** *mt.* Pak.
176 C3 **Zaria** Nigeria
173 C5 **Zarichne** Ukr.
140 B2 **Zarīneh Rūd** *r.* Iran
141 F3 **Zarmardān** Afgh.
137 K5 **Zarneh** Iran
171 K2 **Zărnești** Romania
140 D4 **Zarqān** Iran
140 D3 **Zarrīn** Iran
150 B3 **Zarubino** Russia
168 G5 **Żary** Poland
138 D2 **Zarya Oktyabrya** Kazakh.
213 A3 **Zarzal** Col.
177 D1 **Zarzis** Tunisia
158 O2 **Zasheyek** Russia
Zaskar *r.* India *see* **Zanskar**
Zaskar Range India *see* **Zanskar Mountains**
172 C4 **Zaslawye** Belarus
181 G5 **Zastron** S. Africa
165 K2 **Zauche** *reg.* Germany
Zaunguzskiye Karakumy *des.* Turkm. *see* **Üngüz Angyrsyndaky Garagum**
179 D6 **Zavala** Moz.
140 D3 **Zavāreh** Iran
171 H2 **Zavidovići** Bos. & Herz.
146 E1 **Zavitinsk** Russia
139 K1 **Zavodskoye** Russia
139 J1 **Zav'yalovo** Russia
148 A2 **Zawa** China
169 I5 **Zawiercie** Poland
141 H3 **Zayd Ābād** Afgh.
139 K3 **Zaysan** Kazakh.
139 J2 **Zaysan, Lake** Kazakh.
Zayü China *see* **Zhigang**
168 G6 **Žďár nad Sázavou** Czech Rep.
173 C5 **Zdolbuniv** Ukr.
159 J5 **Zealand** *i.* Denmark
181 H2 **Zebediela** S. Africa
164 B3 **Zedelgem** Belgium
164 B3 **Zeebrugge** Belgium
127 F8 **Zeehan** Australia
181 G2 **Zeerust** S. Africa
164 B3 **Zeeuwsch-Vlaanderen** *reg.* Neth.
136 E5 **Ẕefat** Israel
165 L2 **Zehdenick** Germany
124 D4 **Zeil, Mount** Australia
Zeila Somalia *see* **Saylac**
165 I4 **Zeil am Main** Germany
164 D2 **Zeist** Neth.
165 K3 **Zeitz** Germany
148 A3 **Zêkog** China
139 H1 **Zelenaya Roshcha** Kazakh.
158 P2 **Zelenoborskiy** Russia
172 I4 **Zelenodol'sk** Russia
159 O3 **Zelenogorsk** Russia
172 F3 **Zelenograd** Russia
172 B4 **Zelenogradsk** Russia
173 G6 **Zelenokumsk** Russia
172 H3 **Zelentsovo** Russia
139 G2 **Zelenyy Gay** Kazakh.
168 F7 **Zell am See** Austria
165 H5 **Zellingen** Germany
164 B3 **Zelzate** Belgium
148 A3 **Zêmdasam** China
172 G4 **Zemetchino** Russia
178 C3 **Zémio** C.A.R.
167 G5 **Zemmora** Alg.
207 E4 **Zempoala, Pirámides de** *tourist site* Mex.
207 F4 **Zempoaltépetl, Nudo de** *mt.* Mex.
149 D6 **Zengcheng** China
152 E2 **Zengfeng Shan** *mt.* China
196 A1 **Zenia** U.S.A.
171 G2 **Zenica** Bos. & Herz.
161 B7 **Zennor** U.K.
196 C2 **Zephyr Cove** U.S.A.
139 I5 **Zepu** China
141 F4 **Zerah, Gowd-e** *depr.* Afgh.
Zeravshan *r.* Uzbek. *see* **Zarafshon**
165 K3 **Zerbst/Anhalt** Germany
Zereh, Lake *plain* Afgh. *see* **Zerah, Gowd-e**
139 G1 **Zerendy** Kazakh.
164 E5 **Zerf** Germany
165 I1 **Zernien** Germany
165 K2 **Zernitz** Germany
173 G6 **Zernograd** Russia
173 G7 **Zest'aponi** Georgia
Zêtang China *see* **Nêdong**
165 F1 **Zetel** Germany
165 J4 **Zeulenroda** Germany
165 H1 **Zeven** Germany
164 E3 **Zevenaar** Neth.
146 E1 **Zeya** Russia
146 E1 **Zeya** *r.* Russia
140 D4 **Zeydābād** Iran
141 E2 **Zeydar** Iran
141 E4 **Zeynalābād** Iran
146 E1 **Zeyskoye Vodokhranilishche** *resr* Russia
167 C3 **Zêzere** *r.* Port.
169 I5 **Zgierz** Poland
172 C4 **Zhabinka** Belarus
139 F2 **Zhaksy** Kazakh.
139 G2 **Zhaksy-Kon** *watercourse* Kazakh.
138 E3 **Zhaksykylysh** Kazakh.
138 E3 **Zhaksykylysh, Ozero** *salt l.* Kazakh.
138 F3 **Zhalagash** Kazakh.
139 J2 **Zhalgyztobe** Kazakh.
138 B2 **Zhalpaktal** Kazakh.
139 G2 **Zhaltyr** *Akmolinskaya Oblast'* Kazakh.
139 I2 **Zhaltyr** *Pavlodarskaya Oblast'* Kazakh.
138 B3 **Zhaltyr, Ozero** *l.* Kazakh.
138 E2 **Zhamanakkol', Ozero** *salt l.* Kazakh.
138 C3 **Zhamansor** Kazakh.
139 G3 **Zhambyl** Kazakh.
139 G3 **Zhambylskaya Oblast'** *admin. div.* Kazakh.
139 J3 **Zhameuka** Kazakh.
139 G3 **Zhanabas (abandoned)** Kazakh.
138 B2 **Zhanakala** Kazakh.
138 B2 **Zhanakazan** Kazakh.
138 E3 **Zhanakentkala** *tourist site* Kazakh.
139 F4 **Zhanakorgan** Kazakh.
138 E3 **Zhanakurylys** Kazakh.
138 F3 **Zhanala** *tourist site* Kazakh.
139 H3 **Zhanaortalyk** Kazakh.
138 C4 **Zhanaozen** Kazakh.
139 I4 **Zhanatalan** Kazakh.
139 G4 **Zhanatas** Kazakh.
138 E3 **Zhanay** Kazakh.
138 B3 **Zhanbay** Kazakh.
148 E1 **Zhangbei** China
152 E1 **Zhangguangcai Ling** *mts* China
152 B2 **Zhanggutai** China
148 E2 **Zhang He** *r.* China
149 F5 **Zhanghua** Taiwan
149 D4 **Zhangjiajie** China
148 E1 **Zhangjiakou** China
148 B3 **Zhangla** China
149 E5 **Zhangping** China
149 E5 **Zhangpu** China
152 B2 **Zhangqiang** China
149 E4 **Zhangshu** China
148 E2 **Zhangwei Xinhe** *r.* China
152 B2 **Zhangwu** China
148 B3 **Zhangxian** China
148 A2 **Zhangye** China
149 E5 **Zhangzhou** China
148 D2 **Zhangzi** China
152 B4 **Zhangzi Dao** *i.* China
148 F2 **Zhanhua** China
138 A2 **Zhanibek** Kazakh.
149 D6 **Zhanjiang** China
139 I3 **Zhansugirov** Kazakh.
138 C3 **Zhanterek** Kazakh.
149 B5 **Zhanyi** China
149 E6 **Zhao'an** China
149 B4 **Zhaojue** China
149 D5 **Zhaoping** China
149 D6 **Zhaoqing** China
139 J4 **Zhaosu** China
152 B2 **Zhaosutai He** *r.* China
149 B5 **Zhaotong** China
148 E2 **Zhaoxian** China
152 C1 **Zhaoyuan** China
149 D6 **Zhapo** China
139 J3 **Zharbulak** Kazakh.
145 F3 **Zhari Namco** *salt l.* China
138 D3 **Zharkamys** Kazakh.
139 J3 **Zharkent** Kazakh.
172 E4 **Zharkovskiy** Russia
138 C4 **Zharma** *Mangystauskaya Oblast'* Kazakh.
139 J2 **Zharma** *Vostochnyy Kazakhstan* Kazakh.
139 J3 **Zharsuat (abandoned)** Kazakh.
139 J2 **Zharyk** Kazakh.
173 D5 **Zhashkiv** Ukr.
148 C3 **Zhashui** China
Zhaslyk Uzbek. *see* **Jasliq**
145 F2 **Zhaxi Co** *salt l.* China
144 D2 **Zhaxigang** China
139 G2 **Zhayrem** Kazakh.
Zhayyk *r.* Kazakh./Russia *see* **Ural**
148 E3 **Zhecheng** China
149 F4 **Zhejiang** *prov.* China
139 H2 **Zhekezhal** Kazakh.
132 H2 **Zhelaniya, Mys** *c.* Russia
139 H1 **Zhelezinka** Kazakh.
173 E4 **Zheleznogorsk** Russia
139 H3 **Zheltorangy** Kazakh.
138 C3 **Zhem** *r.* Kazakh.
148 C3 **Zhen'an** China
148 C3 **Zhenba** China
149 C4 **Zheng'an** China
148 E2 **Zhengding** China
149 F5 **Zhenghe** China
148 C3 **Zhengning** China
148 E3 **Zhengyang** China
148 D3 **Zhengzhou** China
149 F4 **Zhenhai** China
148 F3 **Zhenjiang** China
148 B3 **Zhenjiangguan** China
149 B5 **Zhenning** China
148 D3 **Zhenping** China
149 B5 **Zhenxiong** China
148 C3 **Zhenyuan** *Gansu* China
149 C5 **Zhenyuan** *Guizhou* China
173 G5 **Zherdevka** Russia
149 F5 **Zherong** China
172 I2 **Zheshart** Russia
138 C4 **Zhetybay** Kazakh.
138 E2 **Zhetykol', Ozero** *l.* Russia
135 F2 **Zhetysuskiy Alatau** *mts* China/Kazakh.
149 D4 **Zhexi Shuiku** *resr* China
139 F2 **Zhezdy** Kazakh.
139 F3 **Zhezkazgan** *Karagandinskaya Oblast'* Kazakh.
139 F3 **Zhezkazgan** *Karagandinskaya Oblast'* Kazakh.
149 D4 **Zhicheng** China
148 C2 **Zhidan** China
145 H2 **Zhidoi** China
146 B4 **Zhigang** China
133 N3 **Zhigansk** Russia
145 G3 **Zhigung** China
149 D4 **Zhijiang** *Hubei* China
149 C5 **Zhijiang** *Hunan* China
149 B5 **Zhijin** China
Zhi Qu *r.* China *see* **Yangtze**
173 H5 **Zhirnovsk** Russia
138 E1 **Zhitikara** Kazakh.
173 H5 **Zhitkur** Russia
137 K4 **Zhīvār** Iran
172 D4 **Zhlobin** Belarus
173 D5 **Zhmerynka** Ukr.
144 B3 **Zhob** Pak.
144 B3 **Zhob** *r.* Pak.
133 Q2 **Zhokhova, Ostrov** *i.* Russia
139 J2 **Zholnuskau** Kazakh.
139 G2 **Zholymbet** Kazakh.
145 F3 **Zhongba** China
148 B4 **Zhongjiang** China
148 B2 **Zhongning** China
129 E5 **Zhongshan** *research stn* Antarctica
149 D6 **Zhongshan** *Guangdong* China
149 D5 **Zhongshan** *Guangxi Zhuangzu Zizhiqu* China
Zhongshan *Guizhou* China *see* **Liupanshui**
148 D3 **Zhongtiao Shan** *mts* China
148 B2 **Zhongwei** China
149 C4 **Zhongxian** China
149 E5 **Zhongxin** China
149 F6 **Zhongyang Shanmo** *mts* Taiwan
Zhongyicun China *see* **Gucheng**
149 D7 **Zhongyuan** China
138 F3 **Zhosaly** Kazakh.
148 E3 **Zhoucheng** China
148 C4 **Zhou He** *r.* China
148 B2 **Zhoujiajing** China
148 E3 **Zhoukou** China
149 F5 **Zhouning** China
149 G4 **Zhoushan** China
173 E5 **Zhovti Vody** Ukr.
152 B4 **Zhuanghe** China
148 B3 **Zhuanglang** China
139 G3 **Zhuantobe** Kazakh.
148 F3 **Zhucheng** China
152 C1 **Zhuchengzi** China
149 F5 **Zhudong** Taiwan
148 B3 **Zhugqu** China
149 D6 **Zhuhai** China
149 F4 **Zhuji** China
148 F4 **Zhujing** China
172 E4 **Zhukovka** Russia
148 E2 **Zhulong He** *r.* China
148 E3 **Zhumadian** China
138 B3 **Zhumysker** Kazakh.
149 C4 **Zhuo He** *r.* China
148 E1 **Zhuolu** China
148 E2 **Zhuozhou** China
148 D1 **Zhuozi** China
139 G2 **Zhuravlevka** Kazakh.
138 D2 **Zhuryn** Kazakh.
139 H3 **Zhusandala, Step'** *plain* Kazakh.
148 D3 **Zhushan** China
148 C3 **Zhuxi** China
149 D5 **Zhuzhou** *Hunan* China
149 D5 **Zhuzhou** *Hunan* China
173 C5 **Zhydachiv** Ukr.
138 C2 **Zhympity** Kazakh.
138 B3 **Zhyngyldy** Kazakh.
173 C4 **Zhytkavichy** Belarus
173 D5 **Zhytomyr** Ukr.
169 I6 **Žiar nad Hronom** Slovakia
137 I3 **Zībār** Iraq
148 F2 **Zibo** China
148 C2 **Zichang** China
168 G5 **Zielona Góra** Poland
165 H3 **Zierenberg** Germany
165 K2 **Ziesar** Germany
136 C6 **Ziftá** Egypt
137 L1 **Zığ** Azer.
145 H5 **Zigaing** Myanmar
145 G2 **Zigê Tangco** *l.* China
149 B4 **Zigong** China
176 A3 **Ziguinchor** Senegal
159 N4 **Žīguri** Latvia
148 F2 **Zi He** *r.* China
206 D4 **Zihuatanejo** Mex.
149 E6 **Zijin** China
164 E2 **Zijpenberg** *h.* Neth.
136 E5 **Zikhron Ya'aqov** Israel
138 D1 **Zilair** Russia
136 E1 **Zile** Turkey
169 I6 **Žilina** Slovakia
146 C1 **Zima** Russia
207 E3 **Zimapán** Mex.
207 E4 **Zimatlán** Mex.
179 C5 **Zimba** Zambia
179 C5 **Zimbabwe** *country* Africa
140 B3 **Zīmkān, Rūdkhāneh-ye** *r.* Iran
176 A4 **Zimmi** Sierra Leone
171 K3 **Zimnicea** Romania
173 G6 **Zimovniki** Russia
136 E4 **Zimrīn** Syria
141 F3 **Zindah Jān** Afgh.
176 C3 **Zinder** Niger
176 B3 **Ziniaré** Burkina Faso
197 F3 **Zion National Park** U.S.A.
188 B3 **Zionz Lake** Canada
213 B3 **Zipaquirá** Col.
145 H2 **Ziqudukou** China
165 I5 **Zirndorf** Germany
145 H4 **Ziro** India
149 D4 **Zi Shui** *r.* China
168 H6 **Zistersdorf** Austria
207 D4 **Zitácuaro** Mex.
168 G5 **Zittau** Germany
137 J3 **Zīveh** Iran
149 E5 **Zixi** China
148 E2 **Ziya He** *r.* China
138 D2 **Ziyanchurino** Russia
148 C3 **Ziyang** *Shaanxi* China
149 B4 **Ziyang** *Sichuan* China
149 D5 **Ziyuan** China
149 C5 **Ziyun** China
149 B4 **Zizhong** China
171 K3 **Zlatitsa** Bulg.
168 H6 **Zlín** Czech Rep.
173 D4 **Zlynka** Russia
139 J2 **Zmeinogorsk** Russia
173 F5 **Zmiyiv** Ukr.
139 I2 **Znamenka** Kazakh.
139 I1 **Znamenka** *Altayskiy Kray* Russia
172 E4 **Znamenka** *Orlovskaya Oblast'* Russia
138 D1 **Znamenskiy** Russia
173 E5 **Znam"yanka** Ukr.
168 H6 **Znojmo** Czech Rep.
180 D6 **Zoar** S. Africa
137 K4 **Zobeyrī** Iran
164 C2 **Zoetermeer** Neth.
137 J4 **Zohāb** Iran
148 B3 **Zoigê** China
138 D4 **Zoir** Uzbek.
144 C2 **Zoji La** *pass* India
181 G6 **Zola** S. Africa
164 D3 **Zolder** Belgium
173 E5 **Zolochiv** *Kharkivs'ka Oblast'* Ukr.
173 C5 **Zolochiv** *L'vivs'ka Oblast'* Ukr.
173 E5 **Zolotonosha** Ukr.
139 G1 **Zolotorunnoye** Kazakh.
173 F4 **Zolotukhino** Russia
179 D5 **Zomba** Malawi
139 G5 **Zomin** Uzbek.
136 C1 **Zonguldak** Turkey
145 G3 **Zongxoi** China
149 E4 **Zongyang** China
170 C4 **Zonza** *Corsica* France
165 K3 **Zörbig** Germany
176 B3 **Zorgho** Burkina Faso
139 H5 **Zorkŭl** *l.* Afgh./Tajik.
176 B4 **Zorzor** Liberia
164 B4 **Zottegem** Belgium
177 D2 **Zouar** Chad
148 E3 **Zoucheng** China
176 A2 **Zouérat** Mauritania
148 E2 **Zouping** China
149 D4 **Zoushi** China
171 I2 **Zrenjanin** Serbia
165 L4 **Zschopau** Germany
165 K3 **Zschornewitz** Germany
213 D2 **Zuata** *r.* Venez.
140 A4 **Zubālah, Birkat** *waterhole* Saudi Arabia
215 D3 **Zubillaga** Arg.
172 G4 **Zubova Polyana** Russia
176 B4 **Zuénoula** Côte d'Ivoire
168 D7 **Zug** Switz.
173 G7 **Zugdidi** Georgia
168 D7 **Zuger See** *l.* Switz.
168 E7 **Zugspitze** *mt.* Austria/Germany
Zuider Zee *l.* Neth. *see* **IJsselmeer**
164 E1 **Zuidhorn** Neth.
164 C2 **Zuid-Kennemerland, Nationaal Park** *nat. park* Neth.
167 D3 **Zújar** *r.* Spain
213 B2 **Zulia** *r.* Col.
164 E4 **Zülpich** Germany
179 D5 **Zumbo** Moz.
190 A3 **Zumbro** *r.* U.S.A.
190 A3 **Zumbrota** U.S.A.
207 E4 **Zumpango** Mex.
176 C4 **Zungeru** Nigeria
148 F1 **Zunhua** China
197 H4 **Zuni** U.S.A.
197 H4 **Zuni Mountains** U.S.A.
149 C5 **Zunyi** *Guizhou* China
149 C5 **Zunyi** *Guizhou* China
149 C6 **Zuo Jiang** *r.* China/Vietnam
148 D2 **Zuoquan** China
148 D2 **Zuoyun** China
137 K5 **Zurbāṭīyah** Iraq
168 D7 **Zürich** Switz.
141 H3 **Zurmat** *reg.* Afgh.
164 E2 **Zutphen** Neth.
177 D1 **Zuwārah** Libya
172 I3 **Zuyevka** Russia
159 N4 **Zvejniekciems** Latvia
172 I4 **Zvenigovo** Russia
173 D5 **Zvenyhorodka** Ukr.
138 F1 **Zverinogolovskoye** Russia
179 D6 **Zvishavane** Zimbabwe
169 I6 **Zvolen** Slovakia
171 H2 **Zvornik** Bos. & Herz.
176 B4 **Zwedru** Liberia
164 E2 **Zweeloo** Neth.
164 F5 **Zweibrücken** Germany
181 G6 **Zwelitsha** S. Africa
165 L3 **Zwethau** Germany
168 G6 **Zwettl** Austria
165 K4 **Zwickau** Germany
165 K3 **Zwochau** Germany
164 E2 **Zwolle** Neth.
165 K4 **Zwönitz** Germany
133 Q3 **Zyryanka** Russia
139 K2 **Zyryanovsk** Kazakh.

ACKNOWLEDGEMENTS

Maps, design and origination by Collins Bartholomew Ltd HarperCollins Publishers, Glasgow

Earthquake data: United States Geological Survey (USGS) National Earthquakes Information Center, Denver, USA

Köppen classification map: Kottek, M., J. Grieser, C. Beck, B. Rudolf, and F. Rubel, 2006: World Map of the Köppen-Geigerclimate classification updated. Meteorol. Z., 15, 259–263. http://koeppen-geiger.vu-wien.ac.at Climate Change 2007: Impacts, Adaptation and Vulnerability, summary for Policymakers, Intergovernmental Panel on Climate Change

Climate: Tracks of tropical storms from National Oceanic and Atmospheric Administration (NOAA) National Hurricane Centre

IPCC, 2013: Summary for Policymakers. In: Climate Change 2013: The Physical Science Basis. Contribution of Working Group I to the Fifth Assessment Report of the Intergovernmental Panel on Climate Change [Stocker, T.F., D. Qin, G.-K. Plattner, M. Tignor, S.K. Allen, J. Boschung, A. Nauels, Y. Xia, V. Bex and P.M. Midgley (eds.)]. Cambridge University Press, Cambridge, United Kingdom and New York, NY, USA, in press.

Scripps Institution of Oceanography/NOAA Earth Systems Research Laboratory

Population statistics: United Nations Department of Economic and Social Affairs (UN DESA) World Population Prospects http://esa.un.org/wpp/

Population map: International Food Policy Research Institute (IFPRI); and World Resources Institute (WRI). 2000 Gridded Population of the World (GPW), Version 3. Palisades, NY: CIESIN, Columbia University. Available at http://sedac.ciesin.columbia.edu/plue/gpw

Bathymetric data: The GEBCO Digital Atlas published by the British Oceanographic Data Centre on behalf of IOC and IHO, 1994

Communications Statistics: International Telecommunication Union (ITU), ICT statistics http://www.itu.int/en/ITU-D/Statistics/Pages/stat/default.aspx and Groupe Speciale Mobile Association (GSMA) Intelligence https://gsmaintelligence.com/

Pages 129 and 220 Sea ice extents data: National Snow and Ice Data Center (NSIDC), University of Colorado, USA

IMAGE CREDITS

Cover

The Norwegian fjords viewed from space: © J Marshall – Tribaleye Images/Alamy

Pages 4–17

Blue Marble: Next Generation. NASA's Earth Observatory

Pages 18–19

Landsat Image Mosaic of Antarctica (LIMA) Project and Blue Marble: Next Generation. NASA's Earth Observatory

Pages 20–21

NASA images courtesy Jeff Schmaltz, LANCE/EOSDIS MODIS Rapid Response Team at NASA GSFC. NASA VIIRS image by Jesse Allen, using data from the Suomi National Polar-orbiting Partnership.

Pages 22–23

NASA Earth Observatory image by Jesse Allen, using Landsat data from the U.S. Geological Survey.

Pages 24–25

NASA Earth Observatory image by Jesse Allen, using VIIRS Day-Night Band data from the Suomi National Polar-orbiting Partnership.

Pages 26–27

USGS/European Space Agency/Science Photo Library

Pages 28–29

NASA Earth Observatory image by Michael Taylor and Adam Voiland, using Landsat data from the U.S. Geological Survey.

Pages 30–31

NASA Earth Observatory image created by Jesse Allen and Robert Simmon, using Advanced Land Imager data from the NASA EO-1 team.

Pages 32–33

Jeff Schmaltz MODIS Land Rapid Response Team, NASA GSFC

Pages 34–35

NASA Earth Observatory image by Jesse Allen, using Landsat data from the U.S. Geological Survey.

Pages 90–91

Nepal earthquake: © ZUMA Press, Inc./Alamy

Bárðarbunga: © Marisa Estivill/Shutterstock

Pages 92–93

Cyclone Pam: NASA images courtesy Jeff Schmaltz, LANCE/EOSDIS MODIS Rapid Response Team at NASA GSFC. NASA VIIRS image by Jesse Allen, using data from the Suomi National Polar-orbiting Partnership.

Pages 94–95

Pedersen Glacier: NSIDC/Louis H. Pedersen (top);

NSIDC/Bruce F. Molina (bottom)

Pages 96–97

Shanghai, China: TonyV3112/Shutterstock.com

Pages 100–101

Lake Eyre, Caspian Sea, Madagascar: MODIS/NASA

Mississippi: ASTER/NASA

Mt Everest: © Vadim Petrakov/Shutterstock

ARCTIC OCEAN
220

184–185

186–187

NORTH AMERICA
182–183

188–189

194–195

198–199

192–193

200–201

190–191

203

202–205

196–197

204–205

206–207

ATLANTIC OCEAN
219

196

206

210–211

213

210

PACIFIC OCEAN
216–217

SOUTH AMERICA
208–209

214

212

OCEANIA
122–123

215

212

158

158

162

162

163

160–161

166

167

176–177

AFR
174–

176